Pro VB 2008 and the .NET 3.5 Platform

Andrew Troelsen

Apress®

Pro VB 2008 and the .NET 3.5 Platform

ISBN-13 (pbk): 978-1-59059-822-1

ISBN-10 (pbk): 1-59059-822-9

ISBN-13 (electronic): 978-1-4302-0200-4

ISBN-10 (electronic): 1-4302-0200-9

Printed and bound in the United States of America 9 8 7 6 5 4 3 2 1

Lead Editor: Ewan Buckingham
Technical Reviewer: Andy Olsen
Editorial Board: Clay Andres, Steve Anglin, Ewan Buckingham, Tony Campbell, Gary Cornell, Jonathan Gennick, Matthew Moodie, Joseph Ottinger, Jeffrey Pepper, Frank Pohlmann, Ben Renow-Clarke, Dominic Shakeshaft, Matt Wade, Tom Welsh
Production Director and Project Manager: Grace Wong
Senior Copy Editor: Ami Knox
Copy Editor: Nicole Flores
Associate Production Director: Kari Brooks-Copony
Production Editor: Laura Esterman
Compositor: Dina Quan
Artist: April Milne
Proofreaders: April Eddy, Linda Seifert, Liz Welch
Indexer: Broccoli Information Management
Cover Designer: Kurt Krames
Manufacturing Director: Tom Debolski

Distributed to the book trade worldwide by Springer-Verlag New York, Inc., 233 Spring Street, 6th Floor, New York, NY 10013. Phone 1-800-SPRINGER, fax 201-348-4505, e-mail `orders-ny@springer-sbm.com`, or visit `http://www.springeronline.com`.

For information on translations, please contact Apress directly at 2855 Telegraph Avenue, Suite 600, Berkeley, CA 94705. Phone 510-549-5930, fax 510-549-5939, e-mail `info@apress.com`, or visit `http://www.apress.com`.

Apress and friends of ED books may be purchased in bulk for academic, corporate, or promotional use. eBook versions and licenses are also available for most titles. For more information, reference our Special Bulk Sales–eBook Licensing web page at `http://www.apress.com/info/bulksales`.

The source code for this book is available to readers at `http://www.apress.com` in the Source Code section. You may need to answer questions pertaining to this book in order to successfully download the code.

To my Grandmother, Maxine.
Hey Lady! I honestly don't think I've ever met a stronger woman.
You are a rock, Gerta.
Love ya.

Contents at a Glance

PART 4 ■■■ Programming with .NET Assemblies

PART 5 ■■■ Introducing the .NET Base Class Libraries

PART 6 ■■■ Desktop Applications with Windows Forms

PART 7 ■■■ Desktop Applications with WPF

PART 8 ■■■ Building Web Applications with ASP.NET

Contents

PART 3 ■■■ Advanced VB Programming Constructs

PART 6 ■ ■ ■ Desktop Applications with Windows Forms

About the Author

ANDREW TROELSEN is a Microsoft MVP (Visual C#) and a partner, trainer, and consultant with Intertech Training (`http://www.Intertech.com`), a .NET and J2EE developer education center. He is the author of numerous books, including *Developer's Workshop to COM and ATL 3.0* (Wordware Publishing, 2000), *COM and .NET Interoperability* (Apress, 2002), *Visual Basic .NET and the .NET Platform: An Advanced Guide* (Apress, 2001), and the award-winning *C# and the .NET Platform* (Apress, 2003). Andrew has also authored numerous articles on .NET for MSDN, DevX, and *MacTech*, and is frequently a speaker at various .NET conferences and user groups.

Andrew lives in Minneapolis, Minnesota, with his wife, Amanda. He spends his free time waiting for the Wild to win the Stanley Cup, but has given up all hope of the Vikings winning a Super Bowl and feels quite strongly that the Timberwolves will never get back to the playoffs until current management is replaced.

About the Technical Reviewer

ANDY OLSEN is a freelance developer and consultant based in the UK. Andy has been working with .NET since its Beta 1 days and has coauthored and reviewed several books for Apress, covering C#, Visual Basic, ASP.NET, and other topics. Andy is a keen football and rugby fan and enjoys running and skiing (badly). Andy lives by the seaside in Swansea with his wife, Jayne, and children, Emily and Thomas, who have just discovered the thrills of surfing and look much cooler than he ever will!

Acknowledgments

This book is the result of the hard work of many people, of which I am only one. First of all, I'd like to extend a major thank you to my primary technical editor, Andy Olsen. You did a fantastic job of finding typos, omissions, and other issues, which I would have never found without you (as always, any remaining technical issues are my responsibility alone). Next, huge thanks to all of the folks at Apress. Each of you has done an awesome job polishing my initial Word documents into a readable text. Last and certainly not least, thanks and love to Mandy for her support during the process of writing yet another technical book.

Introduction and Welcome

The initial release of the .NET platform (circa 2001) caused quite a stir within the Visual Basic programming community. One the one hand, many die-hard VB6 developers were up in arms at the major differences between VB6 and Visual Basic .NET (VB .NET). Individuals in this group were a bit stunned to see that VB .NET was not in fact "VB7" (i.e., the same syntax and programming constructs as VB6 with some new features thrown in for good measure), but something altogether different.

The truth of the matter is that VB .NET had little to do with VB6, and might best be regarded as a new language in the BASIC family. This cold hard fact caused some individuals to recoil to such a degree that they coined terms such as "VB .NOT" or "Visual Fred" to express their displeasure. In fact, there are even websites (`http://vb.mvps.org/vfred/Trust.asp`) and petitions dedicated to criticizing Microsoft's decision to abandon VB6 in favor of this new creature known as *VB .NET*.

Beyond the major syntactical changes introduced with VB .NET, several VB6-isms were nowhere to be found under the .NET platform, which only added to the confusion. The core .NET programming models for data access, form development, and website construction are entirely different from their COM-based counterparts.

As time has progressed, and the .NET platform has become a mainstream programming model, it seems that even the most die-hard VB6 developer has come to see the writing on the wall: VB6 is quickly becoming a legacy programming tool. Even Microsoft itself has made it clear that support for VB6 will be phased out over time. For better or for worse, the hand of change has been forced upon us.

Note With the release of .NET 2.0 (circa 2005), VB .NET was renamed to "Visual Basic 2005." As of .NET 3.5, Microsoft's BASIC language has been renamed yet again, this time to "Visual Basic 2008" (yes, the VB rename-game is maddening). Throughout this text, when you see the term Visual Basic, VB, or Visual Basic 2008, do know I am referring to the BASIC language that we find within the .NET platform. When I am referring to the COM-centric BASIC language, I'll use the terms Visual Basic 6.0 or simply VB6.

On the other end of the spectrum, there were many VB6 developers who were excited by the myriad new language features and openly embraced the necessary learning curve. Members of this group were ready to dive into the details of object-oriented programming (OOP), multithreaded application development, and the wealth of functionality found within the .NET base class libraries. These individuals quickly realized that in many (if not a majority of) cases, existing VB6 code could remain VB6 code, while new development could take place using the .NET platform and the latest iteration of the Visual Basic language.

Strangely enough, there is also a *third* group of individuals, formed with the release of Visual Basic .NET. Given that VB .NET was in fact a brand new OOP language, many developers who would have never considered learning a BASIC-centric language (typically C++, Java, and C# programmers) were now much more open to the idea of exploring a language devoid of semicolons and curly brackets.

In any case, regardless of which group you identify with, I do welcome you to this book. The overall approach I will be taking is to treat VB 2008 as a unique member of the BASIC family. As you read over the many chapters that follow, you will be exposed to the syntax and semantics of

VB 2008. Here you will find a thorough grounding in OOP, coverage of all of the new VB 2008 language features (such as object initialization syntax, anonymous types, extension methods, and Language Integrated Query [LINQ]), and guidance for working within the Visual Studio 2008 integrated development environment.

As well, this text will dive into each of the major .NET code libraries you will make use of as you build .NET applications. You will be exposed to each of the .NET desktop programming frameworks (Windows Forms and Windows Presentation Foundation), database programming with ADO.NET, web development with ASP.NET, as well as a number of other critical .NET topics such as assembly configuration, Windows Communication Foundation, Windows Workflow Foundation, and file IO operations.

We're a Team, You and I

Technology authors write for a demanding group of people (I should know—I'm one of them). You know that building software solutions using any platform is extremely detailed and is very specific to your department, company, client base, and subject matter. Perhaps you work in the electronic publishing industry, develop systems for the state or local government, or work at NASA or a branch of the military. Speaking for myself, I have developed children's educational software, various n-tier systems, and numerous projects within the medical and legal industries. The chances are almost 100 percent that the code you write at your place of employment has little to do with the code I write at mine (unless we happened to work together previously!).

Therefore, in this book, I have deliberately chosen to avoid creating examples that tie the example code to a specific industry or vein of programming. Given this, I choose to explain VB 2008, OOP, the CLR, and the .NET 3.5 base class libraries using industry-agnostic examples. Rather than having every blessed example fill a grid with data, calculate payroll, or whatnot, I'll stick to subject matter we can all relate to: automobiles (with some geometric structures and employees thrown in for good measure). And that's where you come in.

My job is to explain the VB 2008 programming language and the core aspects of the .NET platform the best I possibly can. To this end, I will do everything I can to equip you with the tools and strategies you need to continue your studies at this book's conclusion.

Your job is to take this information and apply it to your specific programming assignments. I obviously understand that your projects most likely don't revolve around automobiles with pet names, but that's what applied knowledge is all about! Rest assured, once you understand the concepts presented within this text, you will be in a perfect position to build .NET solutions that map to your own unique programming environment.

Who Should Read This Book?

I do not expect that you have any current experience with BASIC-centric languages or the Microsoft .NET platform (however, if this is the case, all the better). I am assuming that you are either a professional software engineer or a student of computer science. Given this, please know that this book may not be a tight fit for individuals who are brand-new to software development, as we will be exploring many lower-level/advanced topics and will not be spending all of our time binding data to grids (at least not until Chapter 22) or examining every single option of the Visual Studio 2008 menu system.

While this book will dive into some more advanced topics, this is not to say the material covered here is impractical! This book focuses on the details you must understand to be a proficient Visual Basic 2008 developer. While some of this information can be challenging (for example, understanding the role of delegates and lambda expressions), I hope you'll find the text is written in a friendly and approachable vibe.

My assumption is that you are the sort of developer who wishes to understand the inner workings of VB 2008, and are not content with authoring code by simply "dragging and dropping." While this book will most certainly examine how Visual Studio 2008 can be used to reduce the amount of code you must author by hand, I'll typically only illustrate the use of integrated wizards once you have seen how to author the code yourself. This will make it easy for you to modify the IDE-generated code to your liking.

An Overview of This Book

Pro VB 2008 and the .NET 3.5 Platform is logically divided into eight distinct parts, each of which contains some number of chapters that are focused on a given technology set and/or specific task. To set the stage, here is a part-by-part and chapter-by-chapter breakdown of the book you are holding in your hands.

Part 1: Introducing Visual Basic 2008 and the .NET Platform

The purpose of Part 1 is to acclimate you to the core aspects of the .NET platform, the .NET type system, and various development tools used during the construction of .NET applications. Along the way, you will also check out some basic details of the VB 2008 programming language.

Chapter 1: The Philosophy of .NET

This first chapter functions as the backbone for the remainder of the text. We begin by examining the world of traditional Windows development and uncovering the shortcomings with the previous state of affairs. The primary goal of this chapter, however, is to acquaint you with a number of .NET building blocks, such as the common language runtime (CLR), Common Type System (CTS), Common Language Specification (CLS), and base class libraries. Also, you will take an initial look at the VB 2008 programming language and the .NET assembly format, and you'll examine the platform-independent nature of the .NET platform and the role of the Common Language Infrastructure (CLI).

Chapter 2: Building Visual Basic 2008 Applications

The goal of this chapter is to introduce you to the process of compiling VB 2008 source code files using various tools and techniques. First, you will learn how to make use of the command-line compiler (`vbc.exe`) and VB 2008 response files. Over the remainder of the chapter, you will examine numerous IDEs, including SharpDevelop, Visual Basic 2008 Express, and (of course) Visual Studio 2008. As well, you will be exposed to a number of open source tools that many .NET developers have in their back pocket.

Part 2: Core VB Programming Constructs

This part explores the core aspects of the VB 2008 programming language such as intrinsic data types, decision and iteration constructs, constructing (and overloading) methods, as well as manipulating arrays, strings, enumerations, and modules. Next, you will dive into the details of object-oriented programming (OOP) as seen through the eyes of VB. As well, you will learn about the role of structured exception handling and how the CLR handles memory management details.

Chapter 3: VB 2008 Programming Constructs, Part I

This chapter begins by examining the role of the VB 2008 module type and the related topic of an executable's entry point—the `Main()` method. You will also come to understand the intrinsic data types of VB 2008 (and their CTS equivalents), implicit and explicit casting operations, iteration and decision constructs, and the construction of valid code statements.

Chapter 4: VB 2008 Programming Constructs, Part II

Here you will complete your examination of basic coding constructs. The major thrust of this chapter is to dive into the details of building subroutines and functions using the syntax of VB 2008. Along the way, you will get to know the roles of the `ByVal`, `ByRef`, and `ParamArray` keywords and understand the topic of method overloading. This chapter also examines how to build and manipulate arrays, enums, and structures, and the underlying classes that lurk in the background (`System.Array`, `System.Enum`, and `System.ValueType`).

Chapter 5: Designing Encapsulated Class Types

This chapter will dive into the first "pillar of OOP," encapsulation services. Not only will you learn the basics of class construction (constructors, shared members, and property syntax), but you will also investigate several auxiliary class design techniques such as the role of the `Partial` keyword and XML code documentation syntax.

Chapter 6: Understanding Inheritance and Polymorphism

The role of Chapter 6 is to examine the details of how VB 2008 accounts for the remaining "pillars" of OOP: inheritance and polymorphism. Here you will learn how to build families of related classes using inheritance, virtual methods, abstract methods (and classes!), as well as various casting operations. This chapter will also explain the role of the ultimate base class in the .NET libraries: `System.Object`.

Chapter 7: Understanding Structured Exception Handling

The point of this chapter is to discuss how to handle runtime anomalies in your code base through the use of structured exception handling. Not only will you learn about the VB 2008 keywords that allow you to handle such problems (`Try`, `Catch`, `Throw`, and `Finally`), but you will also come to understand the distinction between application-level and system-level exceptions. In addition, this chapter examines various tools within Visual Studio 2008 that allow you to debug the exceptions that have escaped your view.

Chapter 8: Understanding Object Lifetime

This chapter examines how the CLR manages memory using the .NET garbage collector. Here you will come to understand the role of application roots, object generations, and the `System.GC` type. Once you understand the basics, the remainder of this chapter covers the topics of building "disposable objects" (via the `IDisposable` interface) and how to interact with the finalization process (via the `System.Object.Finalize()` method).

Part 3: Advanced VB Programming Constructs

This part furthers your understanding of OOP using VB 2008. Here you will learn the role of interface types, delegates, and events, and several advanced topics such as operator overloading and generics. As well, this section dives into the details of the new .NET 3.5 language features, including your first look at LINQ.

Chapter 9: Working with Interface Types

The material in this chapter builds upon your understanding of object-based development by covering the topic of interface-based programming. Here you will learn how to define types that support multiple behaviors, how to discover these behaviors at runtime, and how to selectively hide particular behaviors from an object level. To showcase the usefulness of interface types, you will learn how interfaces can be used to build a custom event architecture.

Chapter 10: Collections, Generics, and Nullable Data Types

This chapter begins by examining the collection types of the `System.Collections` namespace, which has been part of the .NET platform since its initial release. However, since the release of .NET 2.0, the VB programming language offers support for *generics*. As you will see, generic programming greatly enhances application performance and type safety. Not only will you explore various generic types within the `System.Collections.Generic` namespace, but you will also learn how to build your own generic methods and types (with and without constraints).

Chapter 11: Delegates, Events, and Lambdas

The purpose of Chapter 11 is to demystify the delegate type. Simply put, a .NET delegate is an object that "points" to other methods in your application. Using this pattern, you are able to build systems that allow multiple objects to engage in a two-way conversation. After you have examined the use of .NET delegates, you will then be introduced to the VB 2008 `Event`, `RaiseEvent`, `Handles`, and `Custom` keywords, which are used to simplify the manipulation of programming with delegates in the raw. Finally, you will come to understand the role of *lambda expressions* and the VB 2008 lambda operator.

Chapter 12: Operator Overloading and Custom Conversion Routines

This chapter deepens your understanding of the VB 2008 programming language by introducing a number of advanced programming techniques. Here, you will find a detailed examination of value types and reference types. Next, you will learn how to overload operators and create custom conversion routines (both implicit and explicit). We wrap up by contrasting the use of `CType()`, `DirectCast()`, and `TryCast()` for explicit casting operations.

Chapter 13: VB 2008–Specific Language Features

With the release of .NET 3.5, the VB language has been enhanced to support a great number of new programming constructs, many of which are used to enable the LINQ API (which you will begin to examine in Chapter 14). Here, you will learn the role of implicit typing of local variables, extension methods, anonymous types, and object initialization syntax.

Chapter 14: An Introduction to LINQ

This chapter will begin your examination of LINQ, which could easily be considered the most intriguing aspect of .NET 3.5. As you will see in this chapter, LINQ allows you to build strongly typed *query expressions*, which can be applied to a number of LINQ targets to manipulate "data" in the broadest sense of the word. Here, you will learn about LINQ to Objects, which allows you to apply LINQ expressions to containers of data (arrays, collections, custom types). This information will serve you well when we examine how to apply LINQ expressions to relational databases (via LINQ to ADO) and XML documents (à la LINQ to XML) later in Chapter 24.

Part 4: Programming with .NET Assemblies

Part 4 dives into the details of the .NET assembly format. Not only will you learn how to deploy and configure .NET code libraries, but you will also understand the internal composition of a .NET binary image. This section of the text also explains the role of .NET attributes and the construction of multithreaded applications as well as accessing legacy COM applications using interop assemblies.

Chapter 15: Introducing .NET Assemblies

From a very high level, *assembly* is the term used to describe a managed `*.dll` or `*.exe` file. However, the true story of .NET assemblies is far richer than that. Here you will learn the distinction between single-file and multifile assemblies, and how to build and deploy each entity. You'll examine how private and shared assemblies may be configured using XML-based `*.config` files and publisher policy assemblies. You will also investigate the role of the .NET Framework configuration utility.

Chapter 16: Type Reflection, Late Binding, and Attribute-Based Programming

Chapter 16 continues our examination of .NET assemblies by checking out the process of runtime type discovery via the `System.Reflection` namespace. Using these types, you are able to build applications that can read an assembly's metadata on the fly. You will learn how to dynamically activate and manipulate types at runtime using late binding. The final topic of this chapter explores the role of .NET attributes (both standard and custom). To illustrate the usefulness of each of these topics, the chapter concludes with the construction of an extendable Windows Forms application.

Chapter 17: Processes, AppDomains, and Object Contexts

Now that you have a solid understanding of assemblies, this chapter dives deeper into the composition of a loaded .NET executable. The goal of this chapter is to illustrate the relationship between processes, application domains, and contextual boundaries. These topics provide the proper foundation for the topic of the following chapter, where we examine the construction of multithreaded applications.

Chapter 18: Building Multithreaded Applications

This chapter examines how to build multithreaded applications and illustrates a number of techniques you can use to author thread-safe code. The chapter opens by revisiting the .NET delegate type in order to understand a delegate's intrinsic support for asynchronous method invocations. Next, you will investigate the types within the `System.Threading` namespace. You will look at numerous types (`Thread`, `ThreadStart`, etc.) that allow you to easily create additional threads of execution. We wrap up by examining the `BackgroundWorker` type, which greatly simplifies the creation of threads from within a desktop user interface.

Chapter 19: .NET Interoperability Assemblies

The last chapter in this part will examine a unique type of .NET assembly termed an *interop assembly*. These binary images are used to allow .NET applications to make use of classic COM types. Once you dive into the details of how .NET applications can consume COM servers, you will then learn the functional opposite: COM applications consuming .NET objects. Once you have completed this chapter, you will have a solid understanding of the interoperability layer.

Part 5: Introducing the .NET Base Class Libraries

By this point in the text, you have a very solid handle of the VB 2008 language and the details of the .NET type system and assembly format. Part 5 leverages your newfound knowledge by exploring a number of commonly used services found within the base class libraries, including file IO and database access using ADO.NET. This part also covers the construction of distributed applications using Windows Communication Foundation (WCF) and workflow-enabled applications that make use of the Windows Workflow Foundation (WF) API.

Chapter 20: File and Directory Manipulation

As you can gather from its name, the `System.IO` namespace allows you to interact with a machine's file and directory structure. Over the course of this chapter, you will learn how to programmatically create (and destroy) a directory system as well as move data into and out of various streams (file based, string based, memory based, etc.).

Chapter 21: Introducing Object Serialization

This chapter examines the object serialization services of the .NET platform. Simply put, serialization allows you to persist the state of an object (or a set of related objects) into a stream for later use. Deserialization (as you might expect) is the process of plucking an object from the stream into memory for consumption by your application. Once you understand the basics, you will then learn how to customize the serialization process via the `ISerializable` interface and a number of .NET attributes.

Chapter 22: ADO.NET Part I: The Connected Layer

In this first of two database-centric chapters, you will learn about the ADO.NET programming API. Specifically, this chapter will introduce the role of .NET data providers and how to communicate with a relational database using the *connected layer* of ADO.NET, represented by connection objects, command objects, transaction objects, and data reader objects. Be aware that this chapter will also walk you through the creation of a custom database and a data access library that will be used throughout the remainder of this text.

Chapter 23: ADO.NET Part II: The Disconnected Layer

This chapter continues your study of database manipulation by examining the *disconnected layer* of ADO.NET. Here, you will learn the role of the `DataSet` type, data adapter objects, and numerous tools of Visual Studio 2008 that can greatly simplify the creation of data-driven applications. Along the way, you will learn how to bind `DataTable` objects to user interface elements, such as the `GridView` type of the Windows Forms API.

Chapter 24: Programming with the LINQ APIs

Chapter 14 introduced you to the LINQ programming model, specifically LINQ to Objects. Here, you will deepen your understanding of Language Integrated Query by examining how to apply LINQ queries to relational databases, `DataSet` objects, and XML documents. Along the way, you will learn the role of data context objects, the `sqlmetal.exe` utility, and various LINQ-specific aspects of Visual Studio 2008.

Chapter 25: Introducing Windows Communication Foundation

.NET 3.0 introduced a brand-new API, WCF, that allows you to build distributed applications, regardless of their underlying plumbing, in a symmetrical manner. This chapter will expose you to the construction of WCF services, hosts, and clients. As you will see, WCF services are extremely flexible, in that clients and hosts can leverage XML-based configuration files to declaratively specify addresses, bindings, and contracts.

Chapter 26: Introducing Windows Workflow Foundation

In addition to WCF, .NET 3.0 also introduced an API, WF, that allows you to define, execute, and monitor *workflows* to model complex business processes. Here, you will learn the overall purpose of Windows Workflow Foundation, as well as the role of activities, workflow designers, the workflow runtime engine, and the creation of workflow-enabled code libraries.

Part 6: Desktop Applications with Windows Forms

This section of the text examines how to build graphical desktop applications using the Windows Forms API. As you may know, Windows Forms is the original desktop GUI framework that has been part of the .NET base class libraries since version 1.0. While it is true that .NET 3.0 shipped a new GUI framework (Windows Presentation Foundation), Windows Forms is still a key part of .NET development and will most likely be your UI toolkit of choice for many traditional business applications.

Chapter 27: Introducing Windows Forms

This chapter begins your examination of the `System.Windows.Forms` namespace. Here you will learn the details of building traditional desktop GUI applications that support menu systems, toolbars, and status bars. As you would hope, various design-time aspects of Visual Studio 2008 will be examined.

Chapter 28: Rendering Graphical Data with GDI+

This chapter covers how to dynamically render graphical data in the Windows Forms environment. In addition to discussing how to manipulate fonts, colors, geometric images, and image files, this chapter examines hit testing and GUI-based drag-and-drop techniques. You will learn about the Windows Forms resource format, which allows you to embed graphics image files, string data, and other aspects of a desktop application into the executable itself.

Chapter 29: Programming with Windows Forms Controls

This final Windows Forms chapter will examine numerous GUI widgets that ship with the .NET Framework 3.5. Not only will you learn how to program against various Windows Forms controls, but you will also learn about dialog box development and Form inheritance. As well, this chapter examines how to build custom Windows Forms controls that integrate into the IDE.

Part 7: Desktop Applications with WPF

This section of the text focuses on a brand-new desktop programming model named Windows Presentation Foundation (WPF). As you will see, WPF is a "supercharged" UI toolkit that allows you to build highly interactive and media-rich desktop programs. Here you will understand the role of

WPF, the use of an XML-based grammar named XAML, and several WPF features such as animation, graphical rendering, and data binding.

Chapter 30: Introducing Windows Presentation Foundation and XAML

.NET 3.0 introduced a brand-new GUI toolkit termed *WPF*. Essentially, WPF allows you to build extremely interactive and media-rich front ends for desktop applications (and indirectly, web applications). Unlike Windows Forms, this supercharged UI framework integrates a number of key services (2D and 3D graphics, animations, rich documents, etc.) into a single unified object model. In this chapter, you will begin your examination of WPF and the Extendable Application Markup Language (XAML). Here, you will learn how to build WPF programs XAML-free, using nothing but XAML, and a combination of each. We wrap up by building a custom XAML viewer, which will be used during the remainder of the WPF-centric chapters.

Chapter 31: Programming with WPF Controls

In this chapter, you will learn how to work with the WPF control content model as well as a number of related control-centric topics such as dependency properties and routed events. As you would hope, this chapter provides coverage of working with a number of WPF controls; however, more interestingly, this chapter will explain the use of layout managers, control commands, and the WPF data binding model.

Chapter 32: WPF 2D Graphical Rendering, Resources, and Themes

The final chapter of this part will wrap up your examination of WPF by examining three seemingly independent topics. However, as you will see, WPF's graphical rendering services typically require you to define custom resources. Using these resources, you are able to generate custom WPF animations, and using graphics, resources, and animations, you are able to build custom themes for a WPF application. To pull all of these topics together, this chapter wraps up by illustrating how to apply custom graphical themes at runtime.

Part 8: Building Web Applications with ASP.NET

The final part of this text is devoted to the construction of web applications using ASP.NET. As you will see, ASP.NET was intentionally designed to model the creation of desktop user interfaces by layering on top of standard HTTP request/response an event-driven, object-oriented framework.

Chapter 33: Building ASP.NET Web Pages

This chapter begins your study of web technologies supported under the .NET platform using ASP.NET. As you will see, server-side scripting code is now replaced with "real" object-oriented languages (such as VB 2008, C#, and the like). This chapter will introduce you to key ASP.NET topics such as working with (or without) code-behind files, the ASP.NET 3.5 directory structure, and the role of the `web.config` file.

Chapter 34: ASP.NET Web Controls, Themes, and Master Pages

This chapter will dive into the details of the ASP.NET web controls. Once you understand the basic functionality of these web widgets, you will then build a simple but illustrative website making use of various .NET 3.5 features (master pages, `*.sitemap` files, themes, and skins). As well, this chapter will examine the use of the validator controls and the enhanced data binding engine.

Chapter 35: ASP.NET State Management Techniques

This chapter extends your current understanding of ASP.NET by examining various ways to handle state management under .NET. Like classic ASP, ASP.NET allows you to easily create cookies, as well as application-level and session-level variables. Once you have looked at the numerous ways to handle state with ASP.NET, you will then come to learn the role of the `System.HttpApplication` base class (lurking within the `Global.asax` file). We wrap up with an examination of the ASP.NET profile management API.

Obtaining This Book's Source Code

All of the code examples contained within this book (minus small code snippets here and there) are available for free and immediate download from the Source Code area of the Apress website. Simply navigate to `http://www.apress.com`, select the Source Code/Download link, and look up this title by name. Once you are on the "homepage" for *Pro VB 2008 and the .NET 3.5 Platform*, you may download a self-extracting `*.zip` file. After you unzip the contents, you will find that the code has been logically divided by chapter.

Do be aware that Source Code notes like the following in the chapters are your cue that the example under discussion may be loaded into Visual Studio 2008 for further examination and modification:

Source Code This is a source code note referring you to a specific directory!

To do so, simply open the `*.sln` file found in the correct subdirectory. If you are not making use of Visual Studio 2008 (see Chapter 2 for additional IDEs), you can manually load the provided source code files into your development tool of choice.

Obtaining Updates for This Book

As you read through this text, you may find an occasional grammatical or code error (although I sure hope not). If this is the case, my apologies. Being human, I am sure that a glitch or two may be present, despite my best efforts. If this is the case, you can obtain the current errata list from the Apress website (located once again on the "homepage" for this book) as well as information on how to notify me of any errors you might find.

Contacting Me

If you have any questions regarding this book's source code, are in need of clarification for a given example, or simply wish to offer your thoughts regarding the .NET platform, feel free to drop me a line at the following e-mail address (to ensure your messages don't end up in my junk mail folder, please include "VB TE" in the Subject line somewhere): `atroelsen@intertech.com`.

Please understand that I will do my best to get back to you in a timely fashion; however, like yourself, I get busy from time to time. If I don't respond within a week or two, do know I am not trying to be a jerk or don't care to talk to you. I'm just busy (or, if I'm lucky, on vacation somewhere).

So, then! Thanks for buying this text (or at least looking at it in the bookstore while you try to decide if you will buy it). I hope you enjoy reading this book and putting your newfound knowledge to good use.

PART 1

Introducing Visual Basic 2008 and the .NET Platform

CHAPTER 1

The Philosophy of .NET

Every few years or so, the modern-day programmer must be willing to perform a self-inflicted knowledge transplant to stay current with the new technologies of the day. The languages (C++, Visual Basic 6.0, Java), frameworks (OWL, MFC, ATL, STL), architectures (COM, CORBA, EJB), and APIs (including .NET's Windows Forms and GDI+ libraries) that were touted as the silver bullets of software development eventually become overshadowed by something better or at the very least something new. Regardless of the frustration you can feel when upgrading your internal knowledge base, it is frankly unavoidable. To this end, this book will examine the details of Microsoft's current offering within the landscape of software engineering: the .NET platform and the latest version of the Visual Basic programming language.

The point of this chapter is to lay the conceptual groundwork for the remainder of the book. It begins with a high-level discussion of a number of .NET-related topics such as assemblies, the common intermediate language (CIL), and just-in-time (JIT) compilation. In addition to previewing some key features of the Visual Basic 2008 programming language, you will also come to understand the relationship between various aspects of the .NET Framework, such as the common language runtime (CLR), the Common Type System (CTS), and the Common Language Specification (CLS).

This chapter also provides you with an overview of the functionality supplied by the .NET base class libraries, sometimes abbreviated as the BCL or alternatively as the FCL (being the Framework class libraries). Finally, this chapter investigates the language-agnostic and platform-independent nature of the .NET platform (yes it's true! .NET is not confined to the Windows family of operating systems). As you would hope, a majority of these topics are explored in much more detail throughout the remainder of this text.

Understanding the Previous State of Affairs

Before examining the specifics of the .NET universe, it's helpful to consider some of the issues that motivated the genesis of Microsoft's current platform. To get in the proper mind-set, let's begin this chapter with a brief and painless history lesson to remember our roots and understand the limitations of the previous state of affairs. After completing this quick tour of life as we knew it, we turn our attention to the numerous benefits provided by Visual Basic 2008 and the .NET platform.

Life As a C/Win32 API Programmer

Traditionally speaking, developing software for the Windows family of operating systems involved using the C programming language in conjunction with the Windows application programming interface (API) and the Windows Software Development Kit (SDK). While it is true that numerous applications have been successfully created using this time-honored approach, few of us would disagree that building applications using the raw API/SDK is a complex undertaking.

The first obvious problem is that C is a very terse language. C developers are forced to contend with manual memory management, complex pointer arithmetic, and ugly syntactical constructs. Furthermore, given that C is a procedural language, it lacks the benefits provided by the object-oriented approach. When you combine the thousands of global functions and data types defined by the Windows API to an already formidable language, it is little wonder that there are so many buggy applications floating around today.

Life As a C++/MFC Programmer

One vast improvement over raw C/API development is the use of the C++ programming language. In many ways, C++ can be thought of as an object-oriented *layer* on top of C. Thus, even though C++ programmers benefit from the famed "pillars of OOP" (encapsulation, inheritance, and polymorphism), they are still at the mercy of the painful aspects of the C language (e.g., manual memory management, complex pointer arithmetic, and ugly syntactical constructs).

Despite its complexity, many C++ frameworks exist today. For example, the Microsoft Foundation Classes (MFC) provides the developer with a set of C++ classes that simplifies the construction of Windows applications. The main role of MFC is to wrap a "sane subset" of the raw Windows API behind a number of classes and numerous code-generation tools (aka *wizards*). Regardless of the helpful assistance offered by the MFC framework (as well as many other C++-based toolkits), the fact of the matter is that C++ programming remains a difficult and error-prone experience, given its historical roots in C.

Life As a Visual Basic 6.0 Programmer

Due to a heartfelt desire to enjoy a simpler lifestyle, many programmers avoided the world of C(++)-based frameworks altogether in favor of kinder, gentler languages such as Visual Basic 6.0 (VB6). VB6 is popular due to its ability to build sophisticated graphical user interfaces (GUIs), code libraries (e.g., ActiveX servers), and data access logic with minimal fuss and bother. Much more than MFC, VB6 hides the complexities of the raw Windows API from view using a number of integrated programming wizards, intrinsic data types, classes, and VB6-specific functions.

The major limitation of VB6 (which has been rectified given the advent of the .NET platform) is that it is not a fully object-oriented language; rather, it is "object aware." For example, VB6 does not allow the programmer to establish "is-a" relationships between types (i.e., no classical inheritance) and has no intrinsic support for parameterized class construction. Moreover, VB6 doesn't provide the ability to build multithreaded applications unless you are willing to drop down to low-level Windows API calls (which is complex at best and dangerous at worst).

Life As a Java/J2EE Programmer

Enter Java. Java is an object-oriented programming language that has its syntactic roots in C++. As many of you are aware, Java's strengths are far greater than its support for platform independence. Java (as a language) cleans up many unsavory syntactical aspects of C++. Java (as a platform) provides programmers with a large number of predefined "packages" that contain various type definitions. Using these types, Java programmers are able to build "100% Pure Java" applications complete with database connectivity, messaging support, web-enabled front ends, and a rich desktop user interface (UI).

Although Java is a very elegant language, one potential problem is that using Java typically means that you must use Java front-to-back during the development cycle. In effect, Java offers little hope of language integration, as this goes against the grain of Java's primary goal (a single programming language for every need). In reality, however, there are millions of lines of existing code out there in the world that would ideally like to commingle with newer Java code. Sadly, Java makes this task problematic.

Pure Java is often not appropriate for many graphically or numerically intensive applications (in these cases, you may find Java's execution speed leaves something to be desired). A better approach for such programs would be to use a lower-level language (such as C++) where appropriate. Again, while Java does provide a limited ability to access non-Java APIs, there is little support for true cross-language integration.

Life As a COM Programmer

The Component Object Model (COM) was Microsoft's first attempt at a unified component framework. COM is an architecture that says in effect, "If you build your classes in accordance with the rules of COM, you end up with a block of reusable binary code."

The beauty of a binary COM server is that it can be accessed in a language-independent manner. Thus, VB6 programmers can build COM classes that can be used by C++ programs. Delphi programmers can use COM classes built using C, and so forth. However, as you may be aware, COM's language independence is somewhat limited. For example, there is no way to derive a new COM class using an existing COM class (as COM has no support for classical inheritance).

Another benefit of COM is its location-transparent nature. Using constructs such as application identifiers (AppIDs), stubs, proxies, and the COM runtime environment, programmers can avoid the need to work with raw sockets, manual remote procedure calls, and other low-level details. For example, consider the following VB6 COM client code:

```
' The MyCOMClass type could be written in
' any COM-aware language, and may be located anywhere
' on the network (including your local machine).
Dim myObj As MyCOMClass
Set myObj = New MyCOMClass    ' Location resolved using AppID.
myObj.DoSomeWork
```

Although COM can be considered a very successful object model, it is extremely complex under the hood. To help simplify the development of COM binaries, numerous COM-aware frameworks have come into existence (most notably VB6). However, framework support alone is not enough to hide the complexity of COM. Even when you choose a relatively simply COM-aware language such as VB6, you are still forced to contend with fragile registration entries and numerous deployment-related issues (collectively termed *DLL hell*).

Life As a Windows DNA Programmer

To further complicate matters, there is a little thing called the Internet. Over the last several years, Microsoft has been adding more Internet-aware features into its family of operating systems and products. Sadly, building a web application using COM-based Windows Distributed interNet Applications Architecture (DNA) is also quite complex.

Some of this complexity is due to the simple fact that Windows DNA requires the use of numerous technologies and languages (ASP, HTML, XML, JavaScript, VBScript, COM(+), as well as a data access API such as ADO). One problem is that many of these technologies are completely unrelated from a syntactic point of view. For example, JavaScript has a syntax much like C, while VBScript is a subset of VB6. The COM servers that are created to run under the COM+ runtime have an entirely different look and feel from the ASP pages that invoke them. The result is a highly confused mishmash of technologies.

Furthermore, and perhaps more important, each language and/or technology has its own type system (that may look nothing like another's type system). Beyond the fact that each API ships with its own collection of prefabricated code, even basic data types cannot always be treated identically. A `BSTR` in C++ is not quite the same as a `String` in VB6, both of which have very little to do with a `char*` in C.

The .NET Solution

So much for the brief history lesson. The bottom line is that life as a Windows programmer has been less than perfect. The .NET Framework is a rather radical and brute-force approach to streamlining the application development process. The solution proposed by .NET is "Change everything" (sorry, you can't blame the messenger for the message). As you will see during the remainder of this book, the .NET Framework is a completely new model for building systems on the Windows family of operating systems, as well as on numerous non-Microsoft operating systems such as Mac OS X and various Unix/Linux distributions. To set the stage, here is a quick rundown of some core features provided courtesy of .NET:

- *Comprehensive interoperability with existing code*: This is (of course) a good thing. ActiveX components can commingle (i.e., interop) with newer .NET applications and vice versa. Also, Platform Invocation Services (PInvoke) allows you to call C-based libraries (including the underlying API of the operating system) from .NET code.
- *Integration among .NET programming languages*: .NET supports cross-language inheritance, cross-language error handling, and cross-language debugging of code.
- *A common runtime engine shared by all .NET-aware languages*: One aspect of this engine is a well-defined type system that each .NET-aware language "understands."
- *A comprehensive base class library*: This library provides shelter from the complexities of raw Windows API calls and offers a consistent object model used by all .NET-aware languages.
- *No more COM plumbing*: Legacy COM interfaces (such as `IUnknown` and `IDispatch`), COM type libraries, and the COM-centric `Variant` data type have no place in a native .NET binary.
- *A truly simplified deployment model*: Under .NET, there is no need to register a binary unit into the system registry. Furthermore, .NET allows multiple versions of the same `*.dll` to exist in harmony on a single machine.

As you can most likely gather from the previous bullet points, the .NET platform has nothing to do with COM (beyond the fact that both frameworks originated from Microsoft). In fact, the only way .NET and COM types can interact with each other is using the interoperability layer.

■ **Note** Coverage of the .NET interoperability layer can be found in Chapter 19.

Introducing the Building Blocks of the .NET Platform (the CLR, CTS, and CLS)

Now that you know some of the benefits provided by .NET, let's preview three key (and interrelated) entities that make it all possible: the CLR, CTS, and CLS. From a programmer's point of view, .NET can be understood as a new runtime environment and a comprehensive base class library. The runtime layer is properly referred to as the *common language runtime*, or CLR. The primary role of the CLR is to locate, load, and manage .NET types on your behalf. The CLR also takes care of a number of low-level details such as memory management, loading external libraries, and performing security checks.

Another building block of the .NET platform is the *Common Type System*, or CTS. The CTS specification fully describes the underlying type system and programming constructs supported by the runtime, specifies how these entities can interact with each other, and details how they are represented in the .NET metadata format (more information on metadata later in this chapter).

Understand that a given .NET-aware language might not support each and every feature defined by the CTS. The *Common Language Specification* (CLS) is a related specification that defines a subset of common types and programming constructs that all .NET programming languages can agree on. Thus, if you build .NET types that only expose CLS-compliant features, you can rest assured that all .NET-aware languages can consume them. Conversely, if you make use of a data type or programming construct that is outside of the bounds of the CLS, you cannot guarantee that every .NET programming language can interact with your .NET code library.

The Role of the Base Class Libraries

In addition to the CLR and CTS/CLS specifications, the .NET platform provides a base class library that is available to all .NET programming languages. Not only does this base class library encapsulate various primitives such as threads, file input/output (I/O), graphical rendering, and interaction with various external hardware devices, but it also provides support for a number of services required by most real-world applications.

For example, the base class libraries define types that facilitate database access, XML document manipulation, programmatic security, and the construction of web-enabled (as well as traditional desktop and console-based) front ends. From a high level, you can visualize the relationship between the CLR, CTS, CLS, and the base class library, as shown in Figure 1-1.

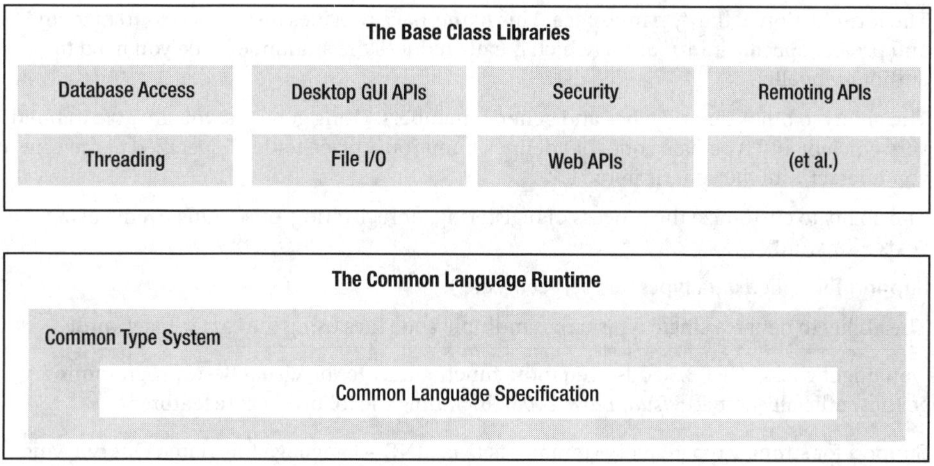

Figure 1-1. *The CLR, CTS, CLS, and base class library relationship*

What Visual Basic 2008 Brings to the Table

Because .NET is such a radical departure from previous Microsoft technologies, it should be clear that legacy COM-based languages such as VB6 are unable to directly integrate with the .NET platform. Given this fact, Microsoft introduced a brand-new programming language, Visual Basic .NET (VB .NET), with the release of .NET 1.0. As developers quickly learned, although VB .NET had a similar look and feel to VB6, it introduced such a large number of new keywords and constructs that many programmers (including myself) eventually regarded VB .NET as a new member of the BASIC family rather than "Visual Basic 7.0."

For example, unlike VB6, VB .NET provided developers with a full-blown object-oriented language that is just as powerful as languages such as C++, Java, or C#. For example, using VB .NET, developers are able to build multithreaded desktop applications, websites, and XML web services; define custom class construction subroutines; overload members; and define callback functions (via delegates). In a nutshell, here are some of the core features provided courtesy of VB .NET:

- Full support for classical inheritance and classical polymorphism.
- Strongly typed keywords to define classes, structures, enumerations, delegates, and interfaces. Given these new keywords, VB .NET code is always contained within a `*.vb` file (in contrast to the VB6-centric `*.cls`, `*.bas`, and `*.frm` files).
- Full support for interface-based programming techniques.
- Full support for attribute-based programming. This brand of development allows you to annotate types and their members to further qualify their behavior (more details in Chapter 16).

With the release of .NET 2.0, the VB .NET programming language was referred to as *Visual Basic 2005* (VB 2005). While VB 2005 is fully backward-compatible with VB .NET, it added numerous new additional bells and whistles, most notability the following:

- The ability to redefine how intrinsic operators of the language (such as the + symbol) can be interpreted by your custom classes or structures. Formally speaking, this feature is termed *operator overloading*.
- The introduction of the `My` namespace. This namespace provides instant access to machine- and project-specific information (which greatly reduces the amount of code you need to author manually).
- The ability to build generic types and generic members. Using generics, you are able to build very efficient and type-safe code that defines numerous "placeholders" specified at the time you interact with the generic item.
- The ability to customize the process of registering, unregistering, or sending events using the `Custom` keyword.
- Support for signed data types (`SByte`, `ULong`, etc.).
- The ability to define a single type across multiple code files using the `Partial` keyword.

As you might guess, .NET 3.5 adds even more functionality to the Visual Basic programming language (now officially named *Visual Basic 2008*), including the following core features:

- Support for strongly typed query statements (à la LINQ—Language Integrated Query), which can interact with a variety of data stores (databases, XML documents, collection objects)
- Support for *anonymous types*, which allow you quickly model the "shape" of a type rather than its behavior
- The ability to extend the functionality of a compiled type using *extension methods*
- Support for *lambda expressions*, which greatly simplify how we can work with .NET delegate types
- A new *object initialization syntax*, which allows you to set property values at the time of object creation

Perhaps the most important point to understand about Visual Basic 2008 is that it can only produce code that can execute within the .NET runtime (therefore, you could never use VB 2008 to build a native ActiveX COM server). Officially speaking, the term used to describe the code targeting the .NET runtime is *managed code*. The binary unit that contains the managed code is termed an *assembly* (more details on assemblies in just a bit). Conversely, code that cannot be directly hosted by the .NET runtime is termed *unmanaged code*.

Additional .NET-Aware Programming Languages

Understand that Visual Basic 2008 is not the only language that can be used to build .NET applications. When the .NET platform was first revealed to the general public during the 2000 Microsoft Professional Developers Conference (PDC), several vendors announced they were busy building .NET-aware versions of their respective compilers.

At the time of this writing, dozens of different languages have undergone .NET enlightenment. In addition to the five languages that ship with Visual Studio 2008 (Visual Basic 2008, C#, J#, C++/CLI, and JScript .NET), there are .NET compilers for Smalltalk, COBOL, and Pascal (to name a few). Although this book focuses (almost) exclusively on Visual Basic 2008, be aware of the following website (please note that this URL is subject to change):

```
http://www.dotnetlanguages.net
```

Once you have navigated to this page, click the Resources link located on the page's topmost menu system. Here you will find a list of numerous .NET programming languages and related links where you are able to download various compilers (see Figure 1-2).

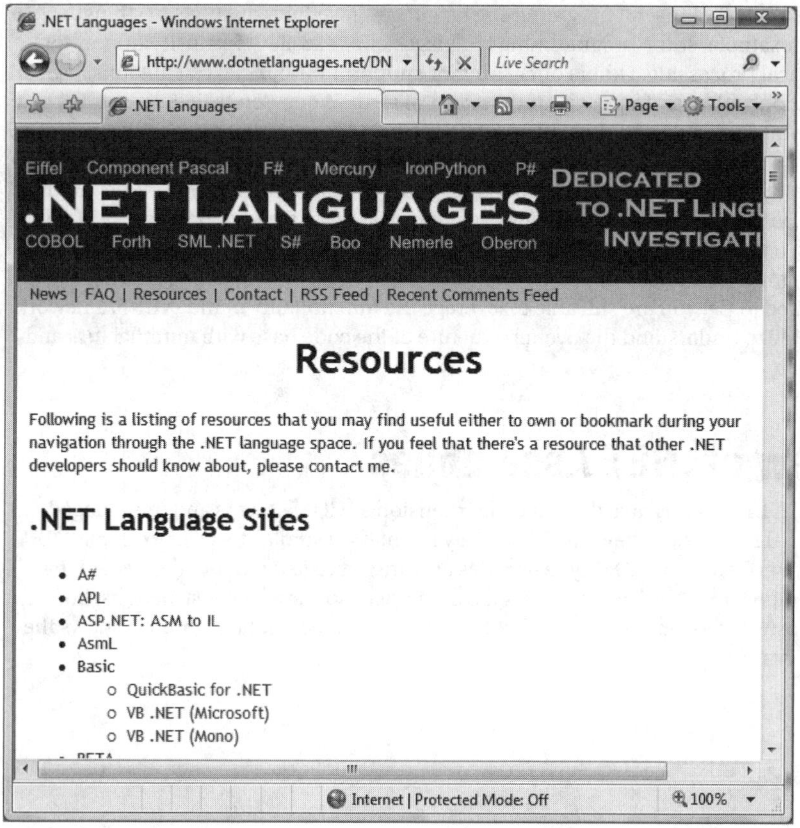

Figure 1-2. *.NET Languages is one of many sites documenting known .NET programming languages.*

While I assume you are primarily interested in building .NET programs using the syntax of VB 2008, I encourage you to visit this site, as you are sure to find many .NET languages worth investigating at your leisure (LISP .NET, anyone?).

Life in a Multilanguage World

As developers first come to understand the language-agnostic nature of .NET, numerous questions arise. The most prevalent of these questions would have to be, "If all .NET languages compile down to "managed code," why do we need more than one compiler?" There are a number of ways to answer this question. First, we programmers are a *very* particular lot when it comes to our choice of programming language (myself included). Some prefer languages full of semicolons and curly brackets, with as few keywords as possible (such as C#, C++, and J#). Others enjoy a language that offers more "human-readable" syntax (such as Visual Basic 2008). Still others may want to leverage their mainframe skills while moving to the .NET platform (via COBOL .NET).

Now, be honest. If Microsoft were to build a single "official" .NET language that was derived from the C family of languages, can you really say all programmers would be happy with this choice? Or, if the only "official" .NET language was based on Fortran syntax, imagine all the folks out there who would ignore .NET altogether. Because the .NET runtime couldn't care less which language was used to build an assembly, .NET programmers can stay true to their syntactic preferences, and share the compiled code among teammates, departments, and external organizations (regardless of which .NET language others choose to use).

Another excellent byproduct of integrating various .NET languages into a single unified software solution is the simple fact that all programming languages have their own sets of strengths and weaknesses. For example, some programming languages offer excellent intrinsic support for advanced mathematical processing. Others offer superior support for financial calculations, logical calculations, interaction with mainframe computers, and so forth. When you take the strengths of a particular programming language and then incorporate the benefits provided by the .NET platform, everybody wins.

Of course, in reality the chances are quite good that you will spend much of your time building software using your .NET language of choice. However, once you learn the syntax of one .NET language, it is very easy to master another. This is also quite beneficial, especially to the consultants of the world. If your language of choice happens to be Visual Basic 2008, but you are placed at a client site that has committed to C#, you are still able to leverage the functionality of the .NET Framework, and you should be able to understand the overall structure of the code base with minimal fuss and bother. Enough said.

An Overview of .NET Assemblies

Despite the fact that .NET binaries take the same file extension as COM servers and unmanaged Windows binaries (`*.dll` or `*.exe`), they have absolutely no internal similarities. For example, .NET assemblies are not described using COM type libraries and are not registered into the system registry. Perhaps most important, .NET binaries do not contain platform-specific instructions, but rather platform-agnostic *intermediate language* (IL) as well as type metadata. Figure 1-3 shows the big picture of the story thus far.

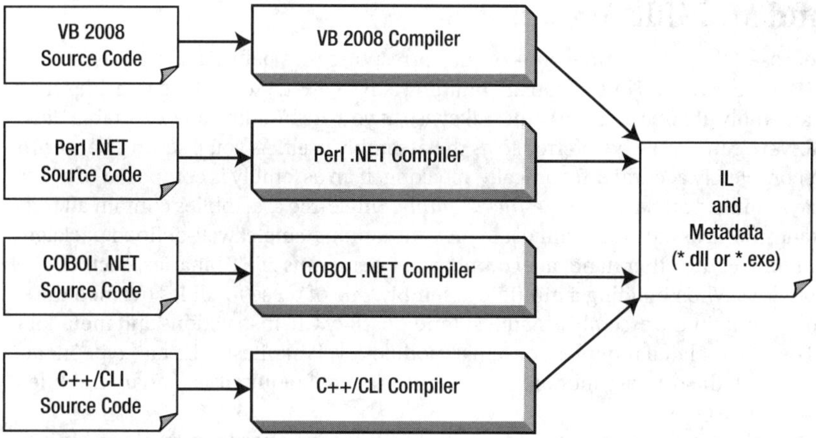

Figure 1-3. *All .NET-aware compilers emit IL instructions and metadata.*

■ **Note** There is one point to be made regarding the abbreviation "IL." During the development of .NET, the official term for IL was Microsoft intermediate language (MSIL). However, with the final release of .NET 1.0, the term was changed to common intermediate language (CIL). Thus, as you read the .NET literature, understand that IL, MSIL, and CIL are all describing the same exact entity. In keeping with the current terminology, I will use the abbreviation CIL throughout this text.

When a `*.dll` or `*.exe` has been created using a .NET-aware compiler, the resulting module is bundled into an *assembly*. You will examine numerous details of .NET assemblies in Chapter 15. However, to facilitate the discussion of the .NET runtime environment, you do need to understand some basic properties of this new file format.

As mentioned, an assembly contains CIL code, which is conceptually similar to Java bytecode in that it is not compiled to platform-specific instructions until absolutely necessary. Typically, "absolutely necessary" is the point at which a block of CIL instructions (such as a method implementation) is referenced for use by the .NET runtime.

In addition to CIL instructions, assemblies also contain *metadata* that describes in vivid detail the characteristics of every "type" living within the binary. For example, if you have a class named `SportsCar`, the type metadata describes details such as `SportsCar`'s base class, which interfaces are implemented by `SportsCar` (if any), as well as a full description of each member supported by the `SportsCar` type.

.NET metadata is a dramatic improvement to COM type metadata. As you may already know, COM binaries are typically described using an associated type library (which is little more than a binary version of Interface Definition Language [IDL] code). The problems with COM type information are that it is not guaranteed to be present and the fact that IDL code has no way to document the externally referenced servers that are required for the correct operation of the current COM server. In contrast, .NET metadata is always present and is automatically generated by a given .NET-aware compiler.

Finally, in addition to CIL and type metadata, assemblies themselves are also described using metadata, which is officially termed a *manifest*. The manifest contains information about the current version of the assembly, culture information (used for localizing string and image resources), and a list of all externally referenced assemblies that are required for proper execution. You'll examine various tools that can be used to investigate an assembly's types, metadata, and manifest information over the course of the next few chapters.

Single-File and Multifile Assemblies

In a great number of cases, there is a simple one-to-one correspondence between a .NET assembly and the binary file (`*.dll` or `*.exe`). Thus, if you are building a .NET `*.dll`, it is safe to consider that the binary and the assembly are one and the same. Likewise, if you are building an executable desktop application, the `*.exe` can simply be referred to as the assembly itself. As you'll see in Chapter 15, however, this is not completely accurate. Technically speaking, if an assembly is composed of a single `*.dll` or `*.exe` module, you have a *single-file assembly*. Single-file assemblies contain all the necessary CIL, metadata, and associated manifest in an autonomous, single, well-defined package.

Multifile assemblies, on the other hand, are composed of numerous .NET binaries, each of which is termed a *module*. When building a multifile assembly, one of these modules (termed the *primary module*) must contain the assembly manifest (and possibly CIL instructions and metadata for various types). The other related modules contain a module-level manifest, CIL, and type metadata. As you might suspect, the primary module documents the set of required secondary modules within the assembly manifest.

So, why would you choose to create a multifile assembly? When you partition an assembly into discrete modules, you end up with a more flexible deployment option. For example, if a user is referencing a remote assembly that needs to be downloaded onto his or her machine, the runtime will only download the required modules. Therefore, you are free to construct your assembly in such a way that less frequently required types (such as a type named `HardDriveReformatter`) are kept in a separate stand-alone module.

In contrast, if all your types were placed in a single-file assembly, the end user may end up downloading a large chunk of data that is not really needed (which is obviously a waste of time). Thus, as you can see, an assembly is really a *logical grouping* of one or more related modules that are intended to be initially deployed and versioned as a single unit.

The Role of the Common Intermediate Language

Now that you have a better feel for .NET assemblies, let's examine the role of the common intermediate language (CIL) in a bit more detail. CIL is a language that sits above any particular platform-specific instruction set. Regardless of which .NET-aware language you choose, the associated compiler emits CIL instructions. For example, the following Visual Basic 2008 code models a trivial calculator. Don't concern yourself with the exact syntax for now, but do notice the format of the `Add()` function in the `Calc` class:

```
' Calc.vb
Imports System

Namespace CalculatorExample
  ' Defines the program's entry point.
  Module Program
    Sub Main()
      Dim ans As Integer
      Dim c As New Calc()
      ans = c.Add(10, 84)

      Console.WriteLine("10 + 84 is {0}.", ans)
      Console.ReadLine()
    End Sub
  End Module

  ' The VB 2008 calculator.
  Class Calc
    Public Function Add(ByVal x As Integer, ByVal y As Integer) As Integer
```

```
      Return x + y
    End Function
  End Class
End Namespace
```

Once the VB 2008 compiler (`vbc.exe`) compiles this source code file, you end up with a single-file executable assembly that contains a manifest, CIL instructions, and metadata describing each aspect of the `Calc` and `Program` types.

Note Chapter 2 examines the details of compiling code using the VB compiler.

If you were to open this assembly using the `ildasm.exe` utility (examined a little later in this chapter), you would find that the `Add()` method is represented using CIL such as the following:

```
.method public instance int32 Add(int32 x, int32 y) cil managed
{
  // Code size 9 (0x9)
  .maxstack  2
  .locals init ([0] int32 Add)
  IL_0000:  nop
  IL_0001:  ldarg.1
  IL_0002:  ldarg.2
  IL_0003:  add.ovf
  IL_0004:  stloc.0
  IL_0005:  br.s IL_0007
  IL_0007:  ldloc.0
  IL_0008:  ret
}  // end of method Calc::Add
```

Don't worry if you are unable to make heads or tails of the resulting CIL code for this method. In reality, a vast majority of .NET developers could care less about the details of the CIL programming language. Simply understand that the Visual Basic 2008 compiler translates your code statements into terms of CIL.

Now, recall that this is true of all .NET-aware compilers. To illustrate, assume you created this same application using C#, rather than VB 2008 (again, don't sweat the syntax, but do note the similarities in the code bases):

```
// Calc.cs
using System;

namespace CalculatorExample
{
  // Defines the program's entry point.
  public class Program
  {
    static void Main()
    {
      Calc c = new Calc();
      int ans = c.Add(10, 84);
      Console.WriteLine("10 + 84 is {0}.", ans);
      Console.ReadLine();
    }
  }
```

```
  // The C# calculator.
  public class Calc
  {
    public int Add(int x, int y)
    { return x + y; }
  }
}
```

If you examine the CIL for the Add() method, you find similar instructions (slightly tweaked by the C# compiler):

```
.method public hidebysig instance int32 Add(int32 x, int32 y) cil managed
{
  // Code size  8 (0x8)
  .maxstack  2
  .locals init ([0] int32 CS$1$0000)
  IL_0000:  ldarg.1
  IL_0001:  ldarg.2
  IL_0002:  add
  IL_0003:  stloc.0
  IL_0004:  br.s       IL_0006
  IL_0006:  ldloc.0
  IL_0007:  ret
} // end of method Calc::Add
```

Source Code The Calc.vb and Calc.cs code files are included under the Chapter 1 subdirectory.

Benefits of CIL

At this point, you might be wondering exactly what is gained by compiling source code into CIL rather than directly to a specific instruction set. One benefit is language integration. As you have already seen, each .NET-aware compiler produces nearly identical CIL instructions. Therefore, all languages are resolved to a well-defined binary arena that makes use of the same identical type system.

Furthermore, given that CIL is platform-agnostic, the .NET Framework itself is platform-agnostic, providing the same benefits Java developers have grown accustomed to (i.e., a single code base running on numerous operating systems). In fact, .NET distributions already exist for many non-Windows operating systems (more details at the conclusion of this chapter). In contrast to the J2EE platform, however, .NET allows you to build applications using your language of choice.

Compiling CIL to Platform-Specific Instructions

Due to the fact that assemblies contain CIL instructions, rather than platform-specific instructions, CIL code must be compiled on the fly before use. The entity that compiles CIL code into meaningful CPU instructions is termed a *just-in-time (JIT) compiler*, which sometimes goes by the friendly name of *Jitter*. The .NET runtime environment leverages a JIT compiler for each CPU targeting the runtime, each optimized for the underlying platform.

For example, if you are building a .NET application that is to be deployed to a handheld device (such as a Pocket PC or .NET-enabled cell phone), the corresponding Jitter is well equipped to run within a low-memory environment. On the other hand, if you are deploying your assembly to a back-end server machine (where memory is seldom an issue), the Jitter will be optimized to function in a high-memory environment. In this way, developers can write a single body of code that can be efficiently JIT-compiled and executed on machines with different architectures.

Furthermore, as a given Jitter compiles CIL instructions into corresponding machine code, it will cache the results in memory in a manner suited to the target operating system. In this way, if a call is made to a method named `PrintDocument()`, the CIL instructions are compiled into platform-specific instructions on the first invocation and retained in memory for later use. Therefore, the next time `PrintDocument()` is called, there is no need to recompile the CIL.

The Role of .NET Type Metadata

In addition to CIL instructions, a .NET assembly contains full, complete, and accurate metadata, which describes each and every type (class, structure, enumeration, and so forth) defined in the binary, as well as the members of each type (properties, functions, events, and so on). Thankfully, it is always the job of the compiler (not the programmer) to define the latest and greatest type metadata. Because .NET metadata is so wickedly meticulous, assemblies are completely self-describing entities—so much so, in fact, that .NET binaries have no need to be registered into the system registry.

To illustrate the format of .NET type metadata, let's take a look at the metadata that has been generated for the `Add()` method of the VB `Calc` class you examined previously (the metadata generated for the C# version of the `Add()` method is similar):

```
TypeDef #2 (02000003)
-------------------------------------------------------
  TypDefName: CalculatorExample.Calc  (02000003)
  Flags     : [Public] [AutoLayout] [Class]
  [AnsiClass] [BeforeFieldInit]  (00100001)
  Extends   : 01000001 [TypeRef] System.Object
  Method #1 (06000003)
-------------------------------------------------------
  MethodName: Add (06000003)
  Flags     : [Public] [HideBySig] [ReuseSlot]  (00000086)
  RVA       : 0x00002090
  ImplFlags : [IL] [Managed]  (00000000)
  CallCnvntn: [DEFAULT]
  hasThis
  ReturnType: I4
    2 Arguments
    Argument #1:  I4
    Argument #2:  I4
    2 Parameters
    (1) ParamToken : (08000001) Name : x flags: [none] (00000000)
    (2) ParamToken : (08000002) Name : y flags: [none] (00000000)
```

Despite what you may be thinking, metadata is a very useful entity (rather than an academic detail) consumed by numerous aspects of the .NET runtime environment, as well as by various development tools. For example, the IntelliSense feature provided by Visual Studio 2008 is made possible by reading an assembly's metadata at design time. Metadata is also used by various object-browsing utilities, debugging tools, and the Visual Basic 2008 compiler itself. To be sure, metadata is the backbone of numerous .NET technologies including Windows Communication Foundation, reflection services, late binding facilities, XML web services/the .NET remoting layer, and the object serialization process. Chapter 16 will formalize the role of .NET metadata.

The Role of the Assembly Manifest

Last but not least, remember that a .NET assembly also contains metadata that describes the assembly itself (technically termed a *manifest*). Among other details, the manifest documents all external assemblies required by the current assembly to function correctly, the assembly's version number, copyright information, and so forth. Like type metadata, it is always the job of the compiler to generate the assembly's manifest. Here are some relevant details of the manifest generated when compiling the `Calc.vb` code file seen earlier in this chapter (assume we instructed the compiler to name our assembly `Calc.exe`):

```
.assembly extern mscorlib
{
  .publickeytoken = (B7 7A 5C 56 19 34 E0 89 )
  .ver 2:0:0:0
}
...
.assembly Calc
{
...
  .ver 0:0:0:0
}
.module Calc.exe
.imagebase 0x00400000
.subsystem 0x00000003
.file alignment 512
.corflags 0x00000001
```

In a nutshell, this manifest documents the list of external assemblies required by `Calc.exe` (via the `.assembly extern` directives) as well as various characteristics of the assembly itself (version number, module name, etc.). Chapter 15 will examine the usefulness of manifest data in much more detail.

Understanding the Common Type System

A given assembly may contain any number of distinct "types." In the world of .NET, "type" is simply a general term used to refer to a member from the set {class, interface, structure, enumeration, delegate}. When you build solutions using a .NET-aware language, you will most likely interact with each of these types. For example, your assembly may define a single class that implements some number of interfaces. Perhaps one of the interface methods takes an enumeration as an input parameter and returns a structure to the caller.

Recall that the Common Type System (CTS) is a formal specification that documents how types must be defined in order to be hosted by the CLR. Typically, the only individuals who are deeply concerned with the inner workings of the CTS are those building tools and/or compilers that target the .NET platform. It is important, however, for all .NET programmers to learn about how to work with the five types defined by the CTS in their language of choice. Here is a brief overview.

CTS Class Types

Every .NET-aware language supports, at the very least, the notion of a *class type*, which is the cornerstone of object-oriented programming (OOP). A class may be composed of any number of members (such as properties, methods, and events) and data points (field data, otherwise known as *member variables*). In Visual Basic 2008, classes are declared using the `Class` keyword:

```
' A class type.
Public Class Calc
  Public Function Add(ByVal x As Integer, ByVal y As Integer) As Integer
    Return x + y
  End Function
End Class
```

If you have a background in VB6 class development, be aware that class types are no longer defined within a `*.cls` file, given the fact that we now have a specific keyword for defining class types (recall that all VB code is now contained within `*.vb` files). Chapters 5 and 6 will examine the details of building class types with Visual Basic 2008.

CTS Interface Types

An *interface* is nothing more than a named collection of member definitions that may be supported (i.e., implemented) by a given class or structure. Unlike COM, .NET interfaces do *not* derive a common base interface such as `IUnknown`. In VB 2008, interface types are defined using the `Interface` keyword, for example:

```
' Classes or structures that implement this interface
' know how to render themselves.
Public Interface IDraw
  Sub Draw()
End Interface
```

On their own, interfaces are of little use. However, when a class or structure implements a given interface in its unique way, you are able to request access to the supplied functionality using an interface reference in a "polymorphic manner." Interface-based programming will be fully explored in Chapter 9.

CTS Structure Types

The concept of a *structure* is also formalized under the CTS. In a nutshell, a structure can be thought of as a lightweight alternative to class types, which have value-based semantics (see Chapter 12 for full details). Typically, structures are best suited for modeling numerical, geometric, or mathematical data types and are created in VB 2008 using the `Structure` keyword:

```
' A structure type.
Public Structure Point
  Public xPos As Integer
  Public yPos As Integer

  Public Sub New(ByVal x As Integer, ByVal y As Integer)
    xPos = x
    yPos = y
  End Sub

  Public Sub Display()
    Console.WriteLine("({0}, {1}", xPos, yPos)
  End Sub
End Structure
```

CTS Enumeration Types

Enumerations are a handy programming construct that allows you to group name/value pairs. For example, assume you are creating a video game application that allows the player to select one of three character categories (Wizard, Fighter, or Thief). Rather than keeping track of arbitrary numerical values to represent each possibility, you could build a custom enumeration using the VB 2008 Enum keyword:

```
' An enumeration type.
Public Enum CharacterType
  Wizard = 100
  Fighter = 200
  Thief = 300
End Enum
```

The CTS demands that enumerated types derive from a common base class, System.Enum. As you will see in Chapter 4, this base class defines a number of interesting members that allow you to extract, manipulate, and transform the underlying name/value pairs programmatically.

CTS Delegate Types

Delegates are perhaps the most complex .NET type; however, they are very important as they are used to form the foundation of the .NET event architecture. To be sure, anytime you wish to handle the click of a button, intercept mouse activity, or process postbacks to a web server, delegates will be used in the background. Simply put, a delegate is used to store method addresses that can be invoked at a later time. In Visual Basic 2008, delegates are declared using the Delegate keyword:

```
' This delegate type can "point to" any method
' returning an integer and taking two integers as input.
Public Delegate Function BinaryOp(ByVal x As Integer, _
  ByVal y As Integer) As Integer
```

Chapters 11 and 18 will examine the details of .NET delegate types, including numerous related details such as multicasting (i.e., forwarding a request to multiple recipients) and asynchronous (i.e., nonblocking) method invocations.

■ **Note** VB 2008 provides numerous keywords (see Chapter 11) that remove the need to manually define delegate types. However, you are able to define delegates directly when you wish to build more intricate and powerful solutions.

CTS Type Members

Now that you have previewed each of the types formalized by the CTS, realize that most types can contain any number of *members*. Formally speaking, a *type member* is constrained by the set {constructor, finalizer, shared constructor, nested type, operator, method, property, indexer, field, read-only field, constant, event}.

The CTS defines various "adornments" that may be associated with a given member. For example, each member has a given visibility level marked with a specific VB 2008 keyword (e.g., Public, Private, Protected, etc.). Some members may be declared as "abstract" to enforce a polymorphic behavior on derived types as well as "virtual" to define a canned (but overridable) implementation. Also, most members may be configured as shared (bound at the class level) or instance (bound at the object level). The construction of type members is examined over the course of the next several chapters.

Note As described in Chapter 10, VB 2008 supports the construction of generic types and generic members.

Intrinsic CTS Data Types

The final aspect of the CTS to be aware of for the time being is that it establishes a well-defined set of fundamental data types. Although a given language typically has a unique keyword used to declare an intrinsic CTS data type, all language keywords ultimately resolve to the same type defined in an assembly named `mscorlib.dll`. Consider Table 1-1, which documents how key CTS data types are expressed in various .NET languages.

Table 1-1. *The Intrinsic CTS Data Types*

CTS Data Type	VB 2008 Keyword	C# Keyword	C++/CLI Keyword
`System.Byte`	`Byte`	`byte`	`unsigned char`
`System.SByte`	`SByte`	`sbyte`	`signed char`
`System.Int16`	`Short`	`short`	`short`
`System.Int32`	`Integer`	`int`	`int or long`
`System.Int64`	`Long`	`long`	`__int64`
`System.UInt16`	`UShort`	`ushort`	`unsigned short`
`System.UInt32`	`UInteger`	`uint`	`unsigned int or unsigned long`
`System.UInt64`	`ULong`	`ulong`	`unsigned __int64`
`System.Single`	`Single`	`float`	`float`
`System.Double`	`Double`	`double`	`double`
`System.Object`	`Object`	`object`	`Object^`
`System.Char`	`Char`	`char`	`wchar_t`
`System.String`	`String`	`string`	`String^`
`System.Decimal`	`Decimal`	`decimal`	`Decimal`
`System.Boolean`	`Boolean`	`bool`	`bool`

Note VB keywords for signed data types (`SByte`, `UShort`, `UInteger`, and `ULong`) are supported only in .NET 2.0 or higher.

Understanding the Common Language Specification

As you are aware, different languages express the same programming constructs in unique, language-specific terms. For example, in VB 2008 you typically denote string concatenation using the ampersand operator (&), while in C# you always make use of the plus sign (+). Even when two distinct languages express the same programmatic idiom (e.g., a method with no return value), the chances are very good that the syntax will appear quite different on the surface:

```
' A VB 2008 subroutine.
Public Sub MyMethod()
  ' Some interesting code...
End Sub

// A C# method with no return value.
public void MyMethod()
{
  // Some interesting code...
}
```

As you have already seen, these minor syntactic variations are inconsequential in the eyes of the .NET runtime, given that the respective compilers (vbc.exe or csc.exe, in this case) emit a similar set of CIL instructions. However, languages can also differ with regard to their overall level of functionality. For example, a .NET language may or may not have a keyword to represent unsigned data, and may or may not support pointer types. Given these possible variations, it would be ideal to have a baseline to which all .NET-aware languages are expected to conform.

The Common Language Specification (CLS) is a set of rules that describe in vivid detail the minimal and complete set of features a given .NET-aware compiler must support to produce code that can be hosted by the CLR, while at the same time be accessed in a uniform manner by all languages that target the .NET platform. In many ways, the CLS can be viewed as a *subset* of the full functionality defined by the CTS.

The CLS is ultimately a set of rules that compiler builders must conform to, if they intend their products to function seamlessly within the .NET universe. Each rule is assigned a simple name (e.g., "CLS Rule 6") and describes how this rule affects those who build the compilers as well as those who (in some way) interact with them. The crème de la crème of the CLS is the mighty Rule 1:

- *Rule 1*: CLS rules apply only to those parts of a type that are exposed outside the defining assembly.

Given this rule, you can (correctly) infer that the remaining rules of the CLS do not apply to the logic used to build the inner workings of a .NET type. The only aspects of a type that must conform to the CLS are the member definitions themselves (i.e., naming conventions, parameters, and return types). The implementation logic for a member may use any number of non-CLS techniques, as the outside world won't know the difference.

To illustrate, the following Add() method is not CLS-compliant, as the parameters and return values make use of unsigned data (which is not a requirement of the CLS):

```
Public Class Calc
  ' Exposed unsigned data is not CLS compliant!
  Public Function Add(ByVal x As ULong, ByVal y As ULong) As ULong
    Return x + y
  End Function
End Class
```

However, if you were to simply make use of unsigned data internally as follows:

```
Public Class Calc
  Public Function Add(ByVal x As Integer, ByVal y As Integer) As Integer
    ' As this ULong variable is only used internally,
    ' we are still CLS compliant.
    Dim temp As ULong = 0
    ...
```

```
    Return x + y
  End Function
End Class
```

you would have still conformed to the rules of the CLS, and could rest assured that all .NET languages are able to invoke the `Add()` method.

Of course, in addition to Rule 1, the CLS defines numerous other rules. For example, the CLS describes how a given language must internally represent text strings, how enumerations should be represented internally (the base type used for storage), how to define shared members, and so forth. Luckily, you don't have to commit these rules to memory to be a proficient .NET developer. Again, by and large, an intimate understanding of the CTS and CLS specifications is only of interest to tool/compiler builders.

Ensuring CLS Compliance

As you will see over the course of this book, VB 2008 does define a few programming constructs that are *not* CLS-compliant. The good news, however, is that you can instruct the VB 2008 compiler to check your code for CLS compliance using a single .NET attribute:

```
' Tell the compiler to check for CLS compliance.
<Assembly: System.CLSCompliant(True)>
```

Chapter 16 dives into the details of attribute-based programming. Until then, simply understand that the `<CLSCompliant()>` attribute will instruct the VB 2008 compiler to check each and every line of code against the rules of the CLS. If any CLS violations are discovered, you receive a compiler error and a description of the offending code.

Understanding the Common Language Runtime

In addition to the CTS and CLS specifications, the next TLA (three-letter abbreviation) to contend with at the moment is the CLR. Programmatically speaking, the term *runtime* can be understood as a collection of external services that are required to execute a given compiled unit of code. For example, when developers make use of the Microsoft Foundation Classes (MFC) to create a new application, they are aware that their program requires the MFC runtime library (e.g., `mfc42.dll`). Other popular languages also have a corresponding runtime. VB6 programmers are also tied to a runtime module or two (e.g., `msvbvm60.dll`). Java developers are tied to the Java Virtual Machine (JVM) and so forth.

The .NET platform offers yet another runtime system. The key difference between the .NET runtime and the various other runtimes I just mentioned is the fact that the .NET runtime provides a single well-defined runtime layer that is shared by *all* languages and platforms that are .NET-aware.

The crux of the CLR is physically represented by a library named `mscoree.dll` (aka the Common Object Runtime Execution Engine). When an assembly is referenced for use, `mscoree.dll` is loaded automatically, which in turn loads the required assembly into memory. The runtime engine is responsible for a number of tasks. First and foremost, it is the entity in charge of resolving the location of an assembly and finding the requested type within the binary by reading the contained metadata. The CLR then lays out the type in memory, compiles the associated CIL into platform-specific instructions, performs any necessary security checks, and then executes the code in question.

In addition to loading your custom assemblies and creating your custom types, the CLR will also interact with the types contained within the .NET base class libraries when required. Although the entire base class library has been broken into a number of discrete assemblies, the key assembly is `mscorlib.dll`. `mscorlib.dll` contains a large number of core types that encapsulate a wide variety of common programming tasks as well as the core data types used by all .NET languages. When you build .NET solutions, you automatically have access to this particular assembly.

Figure 1-4 illustrates the workflow that takes place between your source code (which is making use of base class library types), a given .NET compiler, and the .NET execution engine.

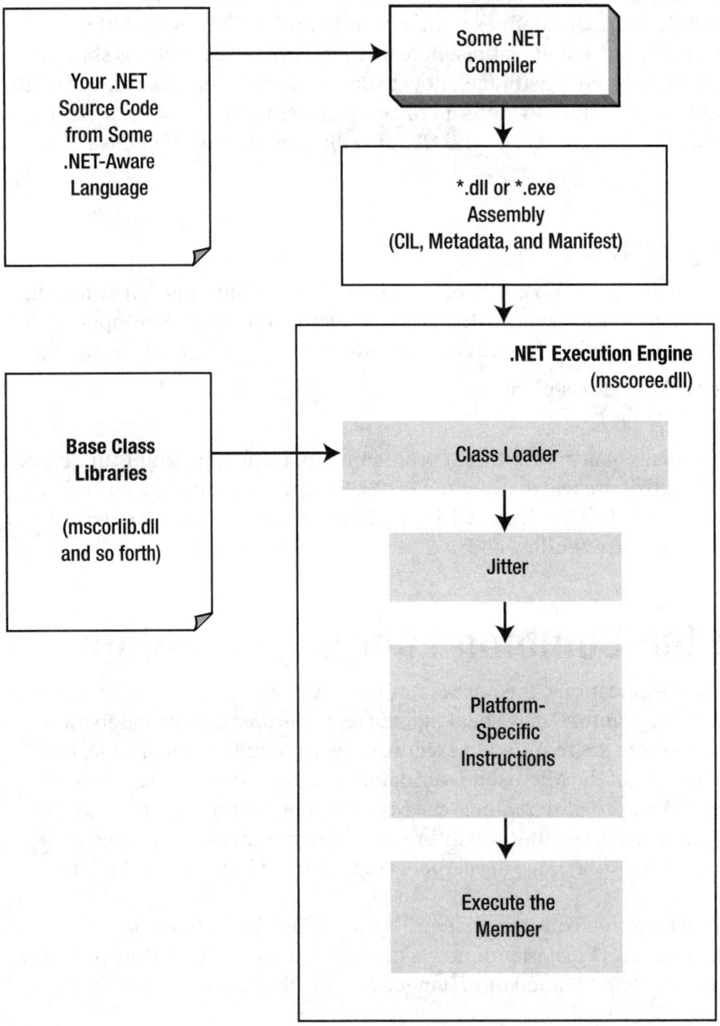

Figure 1-4. `mscoree.dll` *in action*

The Assembly/Namespace/Type Distinction

Each of us understands the importance of code libraries. The point of libraries found within VB6, J2EE, or MFC is to give developers a well-defined set of existing code to leverage in their applications. However, the VB 2008 language does not come with a language-specific code library. Rather, VB 2008 developers leverage the language-neutral .NET libraries. To keep all the types within the base class libraries well organized, the .NET platform makes extensive use of the *namespace* concept.

Simply put, a namespace is a grouping of related types contained in an assembly. For example, the `System.IO` namespace contains file I/O–related types, the `System.Data` namespace defines core database access types, the `System.Windows.Forms` namespace defines GUI elements, and so on. It is very important to point out that a single assembly (such as `mscorlib.dll`) can contain any number of namespaces, each of which can contain any number of types (classes, interfaces, structures, enumerations, or delegates).

To clarify, Figure 1-5 shows a screen shot of the Visual Studio 2008 Object Brower utility (you'll learn more about this tool in Chapter 2). This tool allows you to examine the assemblies referenced by your current solution, the namespaces within a particular assembly, the types within a given namespace, and the members of a specific type. Note that `mscorlib.dll` contains many different namespaces, each with its own semantically related types.

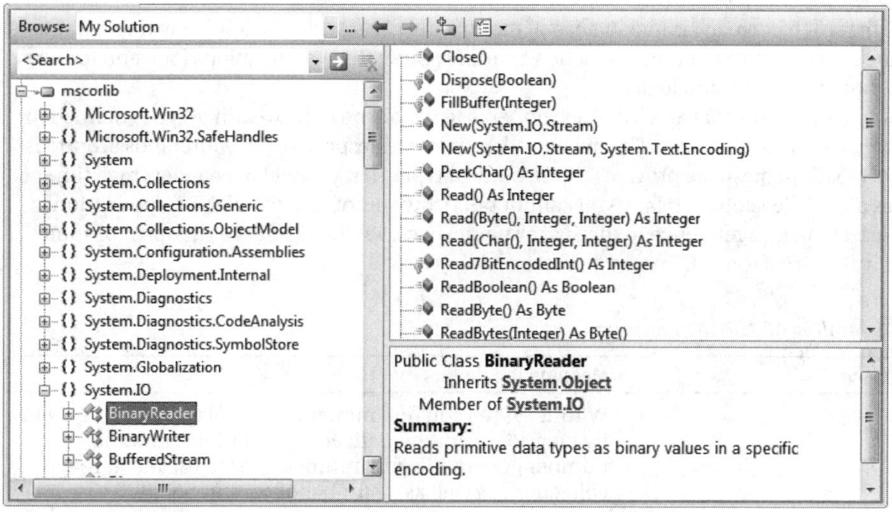

Figure 1-5. *A single assembly can have any number of namespaces.*

The key difference between this approach and a language-specific library such as the Java API is that any language targeting the .NET runtime makes use of the *same* namespaces and *same* types. For example, the following three programs all illustrate the ubiquitous "Hello World" application, written in VB 2008, C#, and C++/CLI:

```
' Hello world in VB 2008
Imports System

Public Module MyApp
  Sub Main()
    Console.WriteLine("Hi from VB 2008")
  End Sub
End Module

// Hello world in C#
using System;

public class MyApp
{
  static void Main()
  {
```

```
    Console.WriteLine("Hi from C#");
  }
}

// Hello world in C++/CLI
#include "stdafx.h"
using namespace System;

int main(array<System::String ^> ^args)
{
  Console::WriteLine(L"Hi from C++/CLI");
  return 0;
}
```

Notice that each language is making use of the Console class, which is defined within a namespace named System. Beyond minor syntactic variations, these three applications look and feel very much alike, both physically and logically.

Clearly, your primary goal as a .NET developer is to get to know the wealth of types defined in the (numerous) .NET namespaces. The most fundamental namespace to get your hands around is named System. This namespace provides a core body of types that you will need to leverage time and again as a .NET developer. In fact, you cannot build any sort of functional .NET application without at least making a reference to the System namespace. Table 1-2 offers a rundown of some (but certainly not all) of the .NET namespaces.

Table 1-2. *A Sampling of .NET Namespaces*

.NET Namespace	Meaning in Life
System	Within System you find numerous useful types dealing with intrinsic data, mathematical computations, random number generation, environment variables, and garbage collection, as well as a number of commonly used exceptions and attributes.
System.Collections System.Collections.Generic	These namespaces define a number of stock container types, as well as base types and interfaces that allow you to build customized collections.
System.Data System.Data.Odbc System.Data.OracleClient System.Data.OleDb System.Data.SqlClient	These namespaces are used for interacting with relational databases using ADO.NET.
System.IO System.IO.Compression System.IO.Ports	These namespaces define numerous types used to work with file I/O, compression of data, and port manipulation.
System.Reflection System.Reflection.Emit	These namespaces define types that support runtime type discovery as well as dynamic creation of types.
System.Runtime.InteropServices	This namespace provides facilities to allow .NET types to interact with "unmanaged code" (e.g., C-based DLLs and COM servers) and vice versa.
System.Drawing System.Windows.Forms	These namespaces define types used to build desktop applications using .NET's original UI toolkit (Windows Forms).

.NET Namespace	Meaning in Life
System.Windows System.Windows.Controls System.Windows.Shapes	The System.Windows namespace is the root for several new namespaces (introduced with .NET 3.0) that represent the Windows Presentation Foundation UI toolkit.
System.Linq System.Xml.Linq System.Data.Linq	These namespaces define types used when programming against the LINQ API.
System.Web	This is one of many namespaces that allow you to build ASP.NET web applications and XML web services.
System.ServiceModel	This is one of many namespaces used to build distributed applications using the (.NET 3.0–centric) Windows Communication Foundation API.
System.Workflow.Runtime System.Workflow.Activities	These are two of many namespaces that define types used to build "workflow-enabled" applications using the .NET 3.0 Windows Workflow Foundation API.
System.Threading	This namespace defines numerous types to build multithreaded applications.
System.Security	Security is an integrated aspect of the .NET universe. In the security-centric namespaces, you find numerous types dealing with permissions, cryptography, and so on.
System.Xml	The XML-centric namespaces contain numerous types used to interact with XML data.

■Note Chapter 2 will illustrate the use of the .NET Framework 3.5 SDK documentation, which provides details regarding every namespace and type found within the base class libraries.

Accessing a Namespace Programmatically

It is worth reiterating that a namespace is nothing more than a convenient way for us mere humans to logically understand and organize related types. Consider again the System namespace. From your perspective, you can assume that System.Console represents a class named Console that is contained within a namespace called System. However, in the eyes of the .NET runtime, this is not so. The runtime engine only sees a single entity named System.Console.

In Visual Basic 2008, the Imports keyword simplifies the process of referencing types defined in a particular namespace. Here is how it works. Let's say you are interested in building a traditional desktop application. The main window renders a bar chart based on some information obtained from a back-end database and displays your company logo. While learning the types each namespace contains takes study and experimentation, here are some possible candidates to reference in your program:

```
' Here are all the namespaces used to build this application.
Imports System                    ' General base class library types.
Imports System.Drawing            ' Graphical rendering types.
Imports System.Windows.Forms      ' GUI widget types.
Imports System.Data               ' General data-centric types.
Imports System.Data.SqlClient     ' MS SQL Server data access types.
```

Once you have specified some number of namespaces (and set a reference to the assemblies that define them, which is explained in Chapter 2), you are free to create instances of the types they contain. For example, if you are interested in creating an instance of the `Bitmap` class (defined in the `System.Drawing` namespace), you can write the following:

```
' Explicitly list the namespaces used by this file.
Imports System
Imports System.Drawing

Public Class Program
  Public Sub DisplayLogo()
    ' Create a 20 x 20 pixel bitmap.
    Dim companyLogo As New Bitmap(20, 20)
    ...
  End Sub
End Class
```

Because your application is importing `System.Drawing`, the compiler is able to resolve the `Bitmap` class as a member of this namespace. If you did not specify the `System.Drawing` namespace, you would be issued a compiler error. However, you are free to declare variables using a fully qualified name as well:

```
' Not listing System.Drawing namespace!
Imports System

Public Class Program
  Public Sub DisplayLogo()
    ' Create a 20 x 20 pixel bitmap.
    Dim companyLogo As New System.Drawing.Bitmap(20, 20)
    ...
  End Sub
End Class
```

While defining a type using the fully qualified name provides greater readability, I think you'd agree that the VB 2008 `Imports` keyword reduces keystrokes. In this text, I will avoid the use of fully qualified names (unless there is a definite ambiguity to be resolved) and opt for the simplified approach of the `Imports` keyword.

However, always remember that this technique is simply a shorthand notation for specifying a type's fully qualified name, and each approach results in the exact same underlying CIL (given the fact that CIL code always makes use of fully qualified names) and has no effect on performance or the size of the generated assembly.

Referencing External Assemblies

In addition to specifying a namespace via the VB 2008 `Imports` keyword, you also need to tell the VB 2008 compiler the name of the assembly containing the actual CIL definition for the referenced type. As mentioned, many core .NET namespaces live within `mscorlib.dll`. However, the `System.Drawing.Bitmap` type is contained within a separate assembly named `System.Drawing.dll`. A vast majority of the .NET Framework assemblies are located under a specific directory termed the *global assembly cache* (GAC). On a Windows machine, this can be located under C:\Windows\assembly, as shown in Figure 1-6.

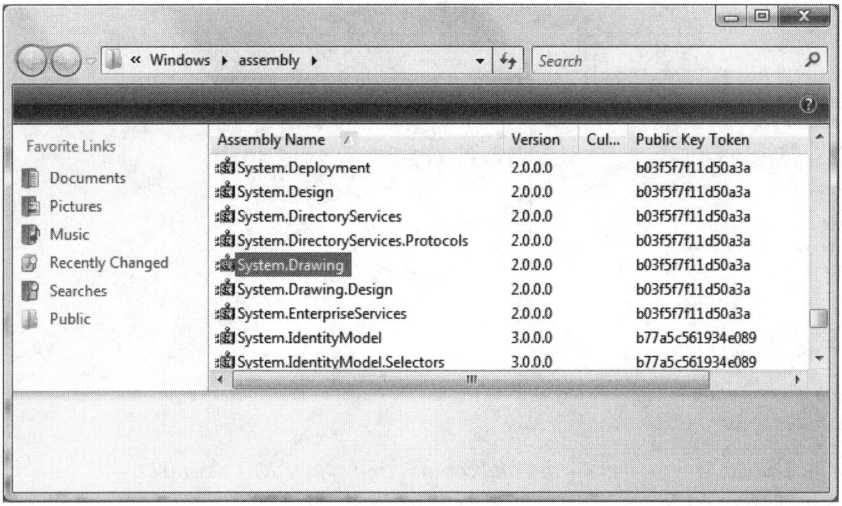

Figure 1-6. *The base class libraries reside in the GAC.*

Depending on the development tool you are using to build your .NET applications, you will have various ways to inform the compiler which assemblies you wish to include during the compilation cycle. You'll examine how to do so in the next chapter, so I'll hold off on the details for now.

Using ildasm.exe

If you are beginning to feel a tad overwhelmed at the thought of gaining mastery over every namespace in the .NET platform, just remember that what makes a namespace unique is that it contains types that are somehow *semantically related*. Therefore, if you have no need for a user interface beyond a simple console application, you can forget all about the `System.Windows` and `System.Web` namespaces (among others). If you are building a painting application, the database namespaces are most likely of little concern. Like any new set of prefabricated code, you learn as you go. (Sorry, there is no shortcut to "magically" know all the assemblies, namespaces, and types at your disposal; then again, that is why you are reading this book!)

The Intermediate Language Disassembler utility (`ildasm.exe`) allows you to load up any .NET assembly and investigate its contents, including the associated manifest, CIL code, and type metadata. By default, `ildasm.exe` should be installed under C:\Program Files\Microsoft SDKs\Windows\V6.0A\Bin (if you cannot find `ildasm.exe` in this location, simply search your machine for an application named "ildasm.exe").

Note If you have installed Visual Studio 2008, you can also load `ildasm.exe` by opening a Visual Studio 2008 Command Prompt (see Chapter 2 for details) and typing the name of the tool (`ildasm`) and pressing the return key.

Once you loaded this tool, proceed to the File ➤ Open menu command and navigate to an assembly you wish to explore. By way of illustration, Figure 1-7 shows the `Calc.exe` assembly built by compiling the `Calc.vb` code file seen earlier in this chapter. As you can see, `ildasm.exe` presents the structure of an assembly using a familiar tree-view format.

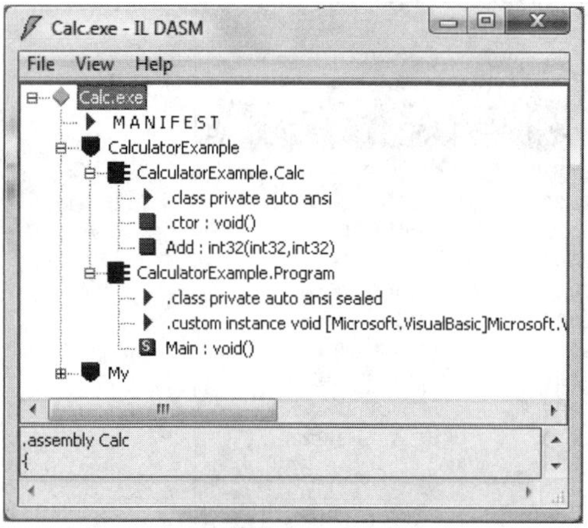

Figure 1-7. `ildasm.exe` *allows you to view the internal composition of any .NET assembly.*

Viewing CIL Code

In addition to showing the namespaces, types, and members contained in a given assembly, `ildasm.exe` also allows you to view the CIL instructions for a given member. For example, if you were to double-click the `Main()` method of the `Program` type, a separate window would display the underlying CIL (see Figure 1-8).

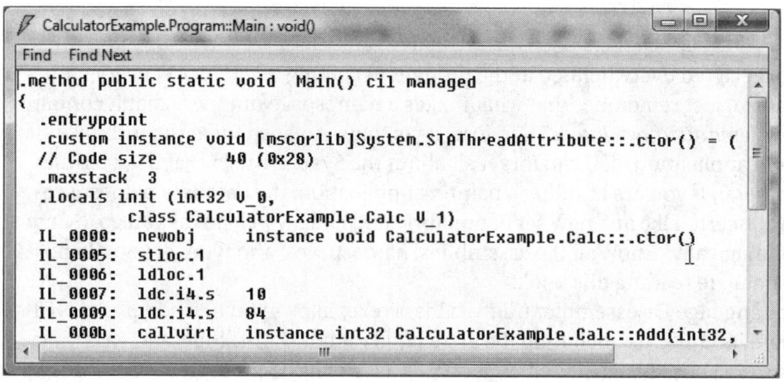

Figure 1-8. *Viewing the underlying CIL via* `ildasm.exe`

Viewing Type Metadata

If you wish to view the type metadata for the currently loaded assembly, press Ctrl+M. Figure 1-9 shows the metadata for the `Calc.Add()` method.

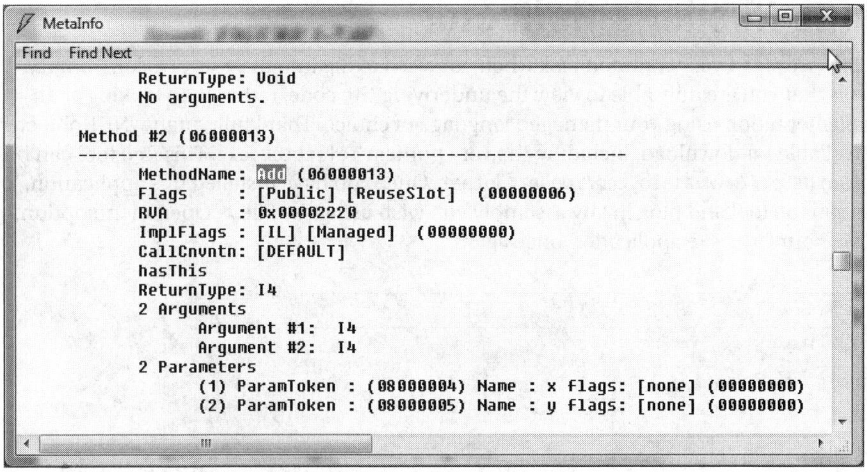

Figure 1-9. *Viewing type metadata via* `ildasm.exe`

Viewing Assembly Metadata (aka the Manifest)

Finally, if you are interested in viewing the contents of the assembly's manifest, simply double-click the MANIFEST icon in the main `ildasm.exe` window (see Figure 1-10).

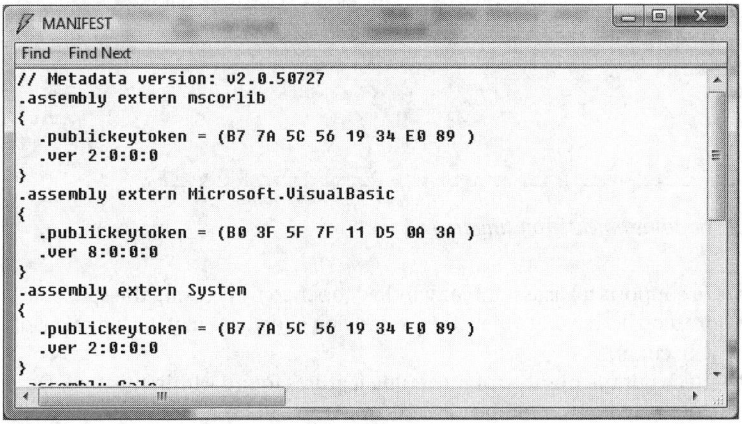

Figure 1-10. *Viewing manifest data via* `ildasm.exe`

To be sure, `ildasm.exe` has more options than shown here, and I will illustrate additional features of the tool where appropriate in the text. As you read through this book, I strongly encourage you to open your assemblies using `ildasm.exe` to see how your VB 2008 code is represented in terms of platform-agnostic CIL code. Although you do *not* need to become an expert in CIL code to be a proficient VB 2008 programmer, understanding some basics of CIL will only strengthen your programming muscle.

Using Lutz Roeder's Reflector

While using `ildasm.exe` is a very common task when you wish to dig into the guts of a .NET binary, the one gotcha is that you are only able to view the underlying CIL code, rather than looking at an assembly's implementation using your managed language of choice. Thankfully, many .NET object browsers are available for download, including the very popular `reflector.exe`. This free tool can be downloaded from `http://www.aisto.com/roeder/dotnet`. Once you have installed this application, you are able to run the tool and plug in any assembly you wish using the File ➤ Open menu option. Figure 1-11 shows our `Calc.exe` application once again.

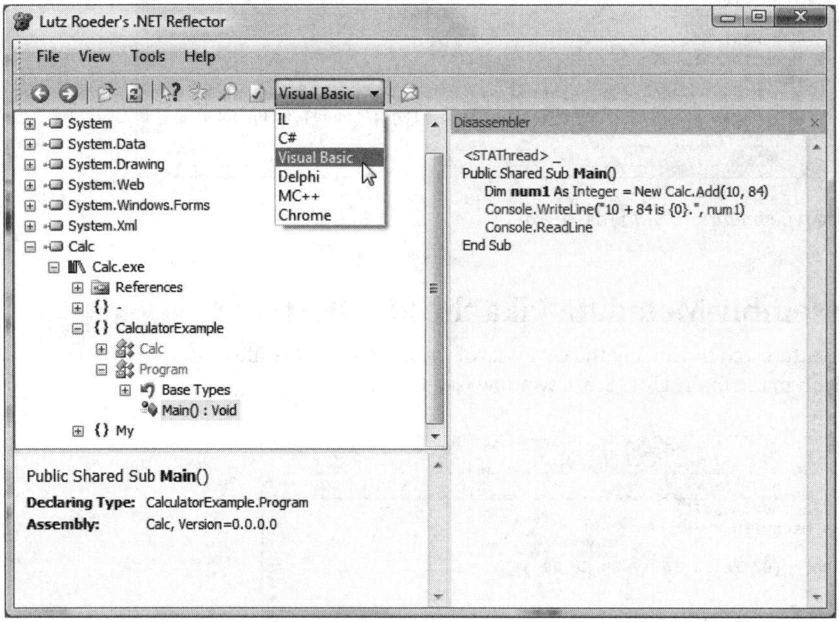

Figure 1-11. *Reflector is a very popular object browsing tool.*

Notice that `reflector.exe` supports a Disassembler window (opened by pressing the spacebar) as well as a drop-down list box that allows you to view the underlying code base in your language of choice (including, of course, CIL code).

I'll leave it up to you to check out the number of intriguing features found within this tool. Do be aware that over the course of the remainder of the book, I'll make use of both `ildasm.exe` as well as `reflector.exe` to illustrate various concepts.

Deploying the .NET Runtime

It should come as no surprise that .NET assemblies can be executed only on a machine that has the .NET Framework installed. For an individual who builds .NET software, this should never be an issue, as your development machine will be properly configured at the time you install the freely available .NET Framework 3.5 SDK (as well as commercial .NET development environments such as Visual Studio 2008).

However, if you deploy an assembly to a computer that does not have .NET installed, it will fail to run. For this reason, Microsoft provides a setup package named `dotNetFx35setup.exe` that can be freely shipped and installed along with your .NET software. This installation program can be downloaded from Microsoft from its .NET download area (`http://msdn.microsoft.com/netframework`). Once `dotNetFx35setup.exe` is installed, the target machine will now contain the .NET base class libraries, .NET runtime (`mscoree.dll`), and additional .NET infrastructure (such as the GAC).

Note The Vista operating system is preconfigured with all of the necessary .NET runtime infrastructure. However, if you are deploying your application to other versions of the Windows operating system, you will want to ensure the target machine has the .NET runtime environment installed and configured.

The Platform-Independent Nature of .NET

To close this chapter, allow me to briefly comment on the platform-independent nature of the .NET platform. To the surprise of most developers, .NET assemblies can be developed and executed on non-Microsoft operating systems (Mac OS X, numerous Linux distributions, and Solaris, to name a few). To understand how this is possible, you need to come to terms with yet another abbreviation in the .NET universe: CLI (Common Language Infrastructure).

When Microsoft released the .NET platform, it also crafted a set of formal documents that described the syntax and semantics of the C# and CIL languages, the .NET assembly format, core .NET namespaces, and the mechanics of a hypothetical .NET runtime engine (known as the Virtual Execution System, or VES). Better yet, these documents have been submitted to ECMA International as official international standards (`http://www.ecma-international.org`). The specifications of interest are

- *ECMA-334*: The C# Language Specification
- *ECMA-335*: The Common Language Infrastructure (CLI)

Note Microsoft has not defined a formal specification regarding the Visual Basic 2008 programming language. The good news, however, is that the major open source .NET distributions ship with a compatible BASIC compiler.

The importance of these documents becomes clear when you understand that they enable third parties to build distributions of the .NET platform for any number of operating systems and/or processors. ECMA-335 is perhaps the more "meaty" of the two specifications, so much so that is has been broken into six partitions, as shown in Table 1-3.

Table 1-3. *Partitions of the CLI*

Partitions of ECMA-335	Meaning in Life
Partition I: Concepts and Architecture	Describes the overall architecture of the CLI, including the rules of the CTS and CLS, and the mechanics of the .NET runtime engine
Partition II: Definitions and Semantics	Describes the details of .NET metadata
Partition III: Instruction Set	Describes the syntax and semantics of CIL code
Partition IV: Profiles and Libraries	Gives a high-level overview of the minimal and complete class libraries that must be supported by a .NET distribution

Continued

Table 1-3. *Continued*

Partitions of ECMA-335	Meaning in Life
Partition V: Debug Exchange Format	Defines details of .NET debugging symbols
Partition VI: Annexes	Provides a collection of "odds and ends" details such as class library design guidelines and the implementation details of a CIL compiler

Be aware that Partition IV (Profiles and Libraries) defines only a *minimal* set of namespaces that represent the core services expected by a CLI distribution (collections, console I/O, file I/O, threading, reflection, network access, core security needs, XML manipulation, and so forth). The CLI does *not* define namespaces that facilitate web development (ASP.NET), database access (ADO.NET), or desktop GUI application development (via Windows Forms or Windows Presentation Foundation).

The good news, however, is that the mainstream .NET distributions extend the CLI libraries with Microsoft-compatible equivalents of ASP.NET, ADO.NET, and Windows Forms (among other APIs) in order to provide full-featured, production-level development platforms. To date, there are two major implementations of the CLI (beyond Microsoft's Windows-specific offering). Although this text focuses on the creation of .NET applications using Microsoft's .NET distribution, Table 1-4 provides information regarding the Mono and Portable.NET projects.

Table 1-4. *Open Source .NET Distributions*

Distribution	Meaning in Life
`http://www.mono-project.com`	The Mono project is an open source distribution of the CLI that targets various Linux distributions (e.g., SuSE, Fedora, and so on) as well as Windows and Mac OS X.
`http://www.dotgnu.org`	Portable.NET is another open source distribution of the CLI that runs on numerous operating systems. Portable.NET aims to target as many operating systems as possible (Win32, AIX, BeOS, Mac OS X, Solaris, all major Linux distributions, and so on).

Both Mono and Portable.NET provide an ECMA-compliant C# compiler, .NET runtime engine, code samples, and documentation, as well as numerous development tools that are functionally equivalent to the tools that ship with Microsoft's .NET Framework 3.5 SDK. Furthermore, Mono and Portable.NET collectively ship with a Visual Basic, Java, and C compiler.

Note If you wish to learn more about Mono or Portable.NET, check out *Cross-Platform .NET Development: Using Mono, Portable.NET, and Microsoft .NET* by M. J. Easton and Jason King (Apress, 2004).

Summary

The point of this chapter was to lay out the conceptual framework necessary for the remainder of this book. I began by examining a number of limitations and complexities found within the technologies prior to .NET, and followed up with an overview of how .NET and Visual Basic 2008 attempt to streamline the current state of affairs.

.NET basically boils down to a runtime execution engine (`mscoree.dll`) and base class library (`mscorlib.dll` and associates). The common language runtime (CLR) is able to host any .NET binary (aka assembly) that abides by the rules of managed code. As you have seen, assemblies contain CIL instructions (in addition to type metadata and the assembly manifest) that are compiled to platform-specific instructions using a just-in-time (JIT) compiler. In addition, you explored the role of the Common Language Specification (CLS) and Common Type System (CTS).

This was followed by an examination of the `ildasm.exe` and `reflector.exe` object browsing utilities, as well as coverage of how to configure a machine to host .NET applications using `dotNetFx35setup.exe`. I wrapped up by briefly addressing the platform-independent nature of the .NET platform using alternative open source .NET distributions such as Mono or Portable.NET.

CHAPTER 2

Building Visual Basic 2008 Applications

As a VB 2008 programmer, you may choose among numerous tools to build your .NET applications. This approach is quite different from the world of VB6, where we had only a single IDE to contend with: Microsoft Visual Basic 6.0. That being said, the point of this chapter is to provide a tour of various .NET development options, including, of course, Visual Studio 2008. The chapter opens, however, with an examination of working with the VB 2008 command-line compiler, `vbc.exe`, and the simplest of all text editors, Notepad (`notepad.exe`).

While you could work through this entire text using nothing other than `vbc.exe` and a simple text editor, I'd bet you are also interested in working with feature-rich integrated development environments (IDEs). To this end, you will be introduced to an open source IDE named SharpDevelop. This IDE rivals the functionality of many commercial .NET development environments (and it's free!). After briefly examining the Visual Basic 2008 Express IDE, you will turn your attention to Visual Studio 2008. This chapter wraps up with a brief discussion regarding the role of the `Microsoft.VisualBasic.dll` assembly and a survey of additional .NET development tools you may wish to investigate at your leisure.

Note Over the course of this chapter, you will see a number of VB programming constructs we have not formally examined. If you are unfamiliar with the syntax, don't fret. Chapter 3 will formally begin your examination of the VB language.

The Role of the .NET Framework 3.5 SDK

One common misconception regarding .NET development is the belief that programmers must purchase a copy of Visual Studio in order to build their VB applications. The truth of the matter is that you are able to build any sort of .NET program using the freely downloadable .NET Framework 3.5 Software Development Kit (SDK). This SDK provides you with numerous managed compilers, command-line utilities, white papers, sample code, the .NET base class libraries, and a complete documentation system.

Note The .NET Framework 3.5 SDK (`dotNetFx35setup.exe`) can be obtained from the .NET download website (`http://msdn.microsoft.com/netframework`).

If you are indeed going to be using Visual Studio 2008 or Visual Basic 2008 Express, you have no need to manually install the .NET Framework 3.5 SDK. When you install either of these products, the SDK is installed automatically, thereby giving you everything you need out of the box. However, if you are *not* going to be using a Microsoft IDE as you work through this text, be sure to install the SDK before proceeding.

The Visual Studio 2008 Command Prompt

When you install the .NET Framework 3.5 SDK, Visual Studio 2008, or Visual Basic 2008 Express, you will end up with a number of new directories on your local hard drive, each of which contains various .NET development tools. Many of these tools are driven from the command prompt, so if you wish to use these utilities from any Windows command window, you will need to register these paths with the operating system.

While you could update your PATH variable manually to do so (which we will not bother to do here), you can save yourself some time by simply making use of the Visual Studio 2008 Command Prompt that is accessible from the Start ➤ Programs ➤ Microsoft Visual Studio 2008 ➤ Visual Studio Tools folder (see Figure 2-1).

Figure 2-1. *The Visual Studio 2008 command prompt*

The benefit of using this particular command prompt is that it has been preconfigured to provide access to each of the .NET development tools without the need to modify your PATH variable settings. Assuming you have installed a .NET development environment, type the following command and press the Enter key:

```
vbc -?
```

If all is well, you should see a list of command-line arguments of the VB command-line compiler (where vbc stands for the *Visual Basic compiler*).

The VB 2008 Command-Line Compiler (vbc.exe)

There are a number of techniques you may use to compile VB 2008 source code. In addition to Visual Studio 2008 (as well as various third-party .NET IDEs), you are able to create .NET assemblies using the VB 2008 command-line compiler, vbc.exe. While it is true that you may never decide to build a large-scale application using the command-line compiler, it is important to understand the basics of how to compile your *.vb files by hand. I can think of a few reasons you should get a grip on the process:

- The most obvious reason is the simple fact that you might not have a copy of Visual Studio 2008.
- You may be in a university setting where you are prohibited from using code generation tools/IDEs in the classroom.

- You plan to make use of automated .NET build tools such as MSBuild or NAnt.
- You want to deepen your understanding of VB 2008. When you use graphical IDEs to build applications, you are ultimately instructing `vbc.exe` how to manipulate your VB 2008 input files. In this light, it's edifying to see what takes place behind the scenes.

Another nice by-product of working with `vbc.exe` in the raw is that you become that much more comfortable manipulating other command-line tools included with the .NET Framework 3.5 SDK. As you will see throughout this book, a number of important utilities are accessible only from the command line.

Building VB 2008 Applications Using vbc.exe

To illustrate how to build a .NET application IDE-free, we will build a simple single-file assembly named `TestApp.exe` using the VB 2008 command-line compiler and Notepad. First, you need some source code. Open Notepad and enter the following:

```
' A simple VB 2008 application.
Imports System

Module TestApp
  Sub Main()
    Console.WriteLine("Testing! 1, 2, 3")
  End Sub
End Module
```

Once you have finished, save the file in a convenient location (e.g., C:\VbcExample) as `TestApp.vb`. Now, let's get to know the core options of the VB 2008 compiler. The first point of interest is to understand how to specify the name and type of assembly to create (e.g., a console application named `MyShell.exe`, a code library named `MathLib.dll`, a Windows Forms application named `MyWinApp.exe`, etc.). Each possibility is represented by a specific flag passed into `vbc.exe` as a command-line parameter (see Table 2-1).

Table 2-1. *Output-centric Options of the VB 2008 Compiler*

Option	Meaning in Life
`/out`	This option is used to specify the name of the assembly to be created. By default, the assembly name is the same as the name of the initial input `*.vb` file.
`/target:exe`	This option builds an executable console application. This is the default target, and thus may be omitted when building console applications.
`/target:library`	This option builds a single-file `*.dll` assembly.
`/target:module`	This option builds a *module*. Modules are elements of multifile assemblies (fully described in Chapter 15).
`/target:winexe`	This option builds an executable Windows application. Although you are free to build Windows-based applications using the `/target:exe` flag, the `/target:winexe` flag prevents a console window from appearing in the background.

To compile `TestApp.vb` into a console application named `TestApp.exe`, open a Visual Studio 2008 command prompt and change to the directory containing your `*.vb` source code file using the `cd` command:

```
cd c:\VbcExample
```

Next, enter the following command set (note that command-line flags must come before the name of the input files, not after):

```
vbc /target:exe TestApp.vb
```

Here I did not explicitly specify an `/out` flag, therefore the executable will be named `TestApp.exe`, given the name of the initial input file. However, if you wish to specify a unique name for your assembly, you could enter the following command:

```
vbc /target:exe /out:MyFirstApp.exe TestApp.vb
```

Also be aware that most of the VB 2008 compiler flags support an abbreviated version, such as `/t` rather than `/target` (you can view all abbreviations by entering `vbc /?` at the command prompt). For example, you can save yourself a few keystrokes by specifying the following:

```
vbc /t:exe TestApp.vb
```

Furthermore, given that the `/t:exe` flag is the default output used by the VB 2008 compiler, you could also compile `TestApp.vb` simply by typing the following:

```
vbc TestApp.vb
```

`TestApp.exe` can now be run from the command line by typing the name of the executable and pressing the Enter key. If all is well, you should see the message "Testing! 1, 2, 3" print out to the command window (see Figure 2-2).

Figure 2-2. `TestApp.exe` *in action*

Referencing External Assemblies Using vbc.exe

Next up, let's examine how to compile an application that makes use of types defined in an external .NET assembly. Speaking of which, just in case you are wondering how the VB 2008 compiler understood your reference to the `System.Console` type, recall from Chapter 1 that `mscorlib.dll` (the assembly that contains the `System.Console` type) is automatically referenced during the compilation process.

To illustrate the process of referencing additional external assemblies, let's update the `TestApp.exe` application to display a Windows Forms message box. Open your `TestApp.vb` file and modify it as follows:

```
' A simple VB 2008 application.
Imports System

' Add this!
Imports System.Windows.Forms

Module TestApp
  Sub Main()
    Console.WriteLine("Testing! 1, 2, 3")
```

```
    ' Add this!
    MessageBox.Show("Hello!")
  End Sub
End Module
```

Notice the reference to the `System.Windows.Forms` namespace via the VB 2008 `Imports` keyword (introduced in Chapter 1). Recall that when you explicitly list the namespaces used within a given `*.vb` file, you avoid the need to make use of fully qualified names (which can lead to hand cramps).

At the command line, you must inform `vbc.exe` which assembly contains the imported namespaces. Given that you have made use of the `MessageBox` class, you must specify the `System.Windows.Forms.dll` assembly using the `/reference` flag (which can be abbreviated to `/r`):

```
vbc /r:System.Windows.Forms.dll TestApp.vb
```

If you now rerun your application, you should see what appears in Figure 2-3 in addition to the console output.

Figure 2-3. *Your first Windows Forms application*

Compiling Multiple Source Files Using vbc.exe

The current incarnation of the `TestApp.exe` application was created using a single `*.vb` source code file. While it is perfectly permissible to have all of your .NET types defined in a single `*.vb` file, most projects are composed of multiple `*.vb` files to keep your code base a bit more flexible. Assume you have authored an additional class (again, using Notepad) contained in a new file named `HelloMsg.vb`:

```
' The HelloMessage class
Imports System
Imports System.Windows.Forms

Class HelloMessage
  Sub Speak()
    MessageBox.Show("Hello Again")
  End Sub
End Class
```

Assuming you have saved this new file in the same location as your first file (e.g., C:\VbcExample), update your `TestApp` class to make use of this new type, and comment out the previous Windows Forms logic. Here is the complete update:

```
' A simple VB 2008 application.
Imports System
```

```
' Don't need this anymore.
' Imports System.Windows.Forms

Module TestApp
  Sub Main()
    Console.WriteLine("Testing! 1, 2, 3")

    ' Don't need this anymore either.
    ' MessageBox.Show("Hello!")

    ' Exercise the HelloMessage class!
    Dim hello As New HelloMessage()
    hello.Speak()
  End Sub
End Module
```

You can compile your VB 2008 files by listing each input file explicitly:

```
vbc /r:System.Windows.Forms.dll TestApp.vb HelloMsg.vb
```

As an alternative, the VB 2008 compiler allows you to make use of the wildcard character (*) to inform vbc.exe to include all *.vb files contained in the project directory as part of the current build:

```
vbc /r:System.Windows.Forms.dll *.vb
```

When you run the program again, the output is identical. The only difference between the two applications is the fact that the current logic has been split among multiple files.

Referencing Multiple External Assemblies Using vbc.exe

On a related note, what if you need to reference numerous external assemblies using vbc.exe? Simply list each assembly using a comma-delimited list. You don't need to specify multiple external assemblies for the current example, but some sample usage follows:

```
vbc /r:System.Windows.Forms.dll,System.Drawing.dll *.vb
```

Working with vbc.exe Response Files

As you might guess, if you were to build a complex VB 2008 application at the command prompt, your life would be full of pain as you type in the flags that specify numerous referenced assemblies and *.vb code files. To help lessen your typing burden, the VB 2008 compiler honors the use of *response files*.

VB 2008 response files contain all the instructions to be used during the compilation of your current build. By convention, these files end in an *.rsp (response) extension. Assume that you have created a response file named TestApp.rsp that contains the following arguments (as you can see, comments are denoted with the # character):

```
# This is the response file
# for the TestApp.exe app
# of Chapter 2.

# External assembly references.
/r:System.Windows.Forms.dll
```

```
# Output and files to compile (using wildcard syntax).
/t:exe /out:TestApp.exe *.vb
```

Now, assuming this file is saved in the same directory as the VB 2008 source code files to be compiled, you are able to build your entire application as follows (note the use of the @ symbol):

```
vbc @TestApp.rsp
```

If the need should arise, you are also able to specify multiple *.rsp files as input (e.g., vbc @FirstFile.rsp @SecondFile.rsp @ThirdFile.rsp). If you take this approach, do be aware that the compiler processes the command options as they are encountered! Therefore, command-line arguments in a later *.rsp file can override options in a previous response file.

Also note that flags listed explicitly on the command line before a response file will be overridden by the specified *.rsp file. Thus, if you were to enter

```
vbc /out:MyCoolApp.exe @TestApp.rsp
```

the name of the assembly would still be TestApp.exe (rather than MyCoolApp.exe), given the /out:TestApp.exe flag listed in the TestApp.rsp response file. However, if you list flags after a response file, the flag will override settings in the response file. Thus, in the following command set, your assembly is indeed named MyCoolApp.exe.

```
vbc @TestApp.rsp /out:MyCoolApp.exe
```

Note The /reference flag is cumulative. Regardless of where you specify external assemblies (before, after, or within a response file), the end result is a summation of each reference assembly.

The Default Response File (vbc.rsp)

The final point to be made regarding response files is that the VB 2008 compiler has an associated default response file (vbc.rsp), which is located in the same directory as vbc.exe itself (e.g., C:\Windows\Microsoft.NET\Framework\v3.5). If you were to open this file using Notepad, you would find that numerous .NET assemblies have already been specified using the /r: flag. As you would expect, you will come to understand the role of many of these .NET libraries over the course of the text. However, to set the stage, here is a look within vbc.rsp:

```
# This file contains command-line options that the VB
# command-line compiler (VBC) will process as part
# of every compilation, unless the "/noconfig" option
# is specified.

# Reference the common Framework libraries
/r:Accessibility.dll
/r:Microsoft.Vsa.dll
/r:System.Configuration.dll
/r:System.Configuration.Install.dll
/r:System.Data.dll
/r:System.Data.OracleClient.dll
/r:System.Deployment.dll
/r:System.Design.dll
/r:System.DirectoryServices.dll
/r:System.dll
/r:System.Drawing.Design.dll
/r:System.Drawing.dll
```

```
/r:System.EnterpriseServices.dll
/r:System.Management.dll
/r:System.Messaging.dll
/r:System.Runtime.Remoting.dll
/r:System.Runtime.Serialization.Formatters.Soap.dll
/r:System.Security.dll
/r:System.ServiceProcess.dll
/r:System.Transactions.dll
/r:System.Web.dll
/r:System.Web.Mobile.dll
/r:System.Web.RegularExpressions.dll
/r:System.Web.Services.dll
/r:System.Windows.Forms.Dll
/r:System.XML.dll

/r:System.Workflow.Activities.dll
/r:System.Workflow.ComponentModel.dll
/r:System.Workflow.Runtime.dll
/r:System.Runtime.Serialization.dll
/r:System.ServiceModel.dll

/r:System.Core.dll
/r:System.Xml.Linq.dll
/r:System.Data.Linq.dll
/r:System.Data.DataSetExtensions.dll
/r:System.Web.Extensions.dll
/r:System.Web.Extensions.Design.dll
/r:System.ServiceModel.Web.dll

# Import System and Microsoft.VisualBasic
/imports:System
/imports:Microsoft.VisualBasic
/imports:System.Linq
/imports:System.Xml.Linq

/optioninfer+
```

■ **Note** Understand that the default response file is only referenced when working with the command-line compiler. The Visual Basic 2008 Express and Visual Studio 2008 IDEs do not automatically set references to these libraries.

When you are building your VB 2008 programs using `vbc.exe`, this file will be automatically referenced, even when you supply a custom `*.rsp` file. Given the presence of the default response file, the current `TestApp.exe` application could be successfully compiled using the following command set (as `System.Windows.Forms.dll` is referenced within `vbc.rsp`):

```
vbc /out:TestApp.exe *.vb
```

In the event that you wish to disable the automatic reading of `vbc.rsp`, you can specify the `/noconfig` option:

```
vbc @TestApp.rsp /noconfig
```

Obviously, the VB 2008 command-line compiler has many other options that can be used to control how the resulting .NET assembly is to be generated. At this point, however, you should have a handle on the basics. If you wish to learn more details regarding the functionality of `vbc.exe`, search the .NET Framework 3.5 documentation for the term "vbc.exe".

Source Code The VbcExample project is included under the Chapter 2 subdirectory.

Building .NET Applications Using SharpDevelop

While Notepad is fine for creating simple .NET programs, it offers nothing in the way of developer productivity. It would be ideal to author `*.vb` files using an editor that supports (at a minimum) keyword coloring and integration with the VB compiler. Furthermore, we would hope to build our VB programs using a tool that supports rich IntelliSense capabilities, designers for building graphical user interfaces, project templates, and database manipulation tools. As luck would have it, numerous such tools do exist, many of which are completely free of charge.

To address such needs, allow me to introduce the next .NET development option: SharpDevelop (also known as *#develop*). SharpDevelop is an open source and feature-rich IDE that you can use to build .NET assemblies using VB or C# as well as using CIL and a Python-inspired .NET language named Boo. Beyond the fact that this IDE is completely free, it is interesting to note that it was written entirely in C# (and could have just as easily been written in Visual Basic). In fact, you have the choice to download and compile the `*.cs` files manually or run a setup program to install SharpDevelop on your development machine. Both distributions can be obtained from `http://www.sharpdevelop.com` (at the time of this writing, the current version is 2.2; however, be sure to download the latest and greatest).

SharpDevelop provides numerous productivity enhancements and in many cases is as feature rich as Visual Studio 2008 Standard Edition. Here is a partial hit list of some of the major benefits:

- IntelliSense, code completion, and code snippet capabilities
- An Add Reference dialog box to reference external assemblies, including assemblies deployed to the global assembly cache (GAC)
- A visual Windows Forms designer
- Integrated object browsing and code definition utilities
- Visual database designer utilities
- A VB to C# (and vice versa) code conversion utility
- Integration with the NUnit (a .NET unit testing utility) and NAnt (a .NET build utility)
- Integration with the .NET Framework 3.5 SDK documentation

Impressive for a free IDE, is it not? Although this chapter doesn't cover each of these points in detail, let's walk through a few items of interest.

Building a Simple Test Project

Once you have installed SharpDevelop, the File ➤ New ➤ Solution menu option allows you to pick which type of project you wish to generate (and in which .NET language). For example, assume you have created a VB Windows Application named MySDWinApp (see Figure 2-4).

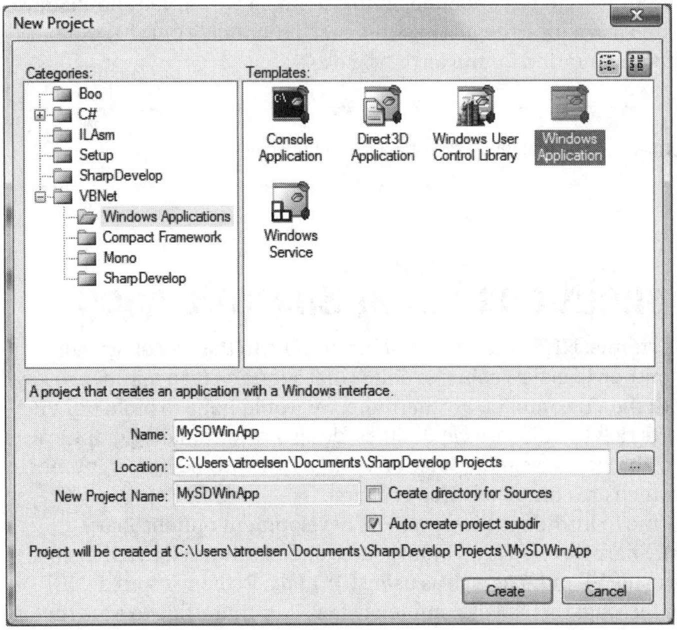

Figure 2-4. *The SharpDevelop New Project dialog box*

Like Visual Studio, you have a GUI designer, toolbox (to drag and drop controls onto the designer), and a Properties window to set up the look and feel of each UI item. Figure 2-5 illustrates configuring a button type using the IDE (by default, the IDE will show the source code of the current form; select the Design tab at the bottom of the main window to activate the designer).

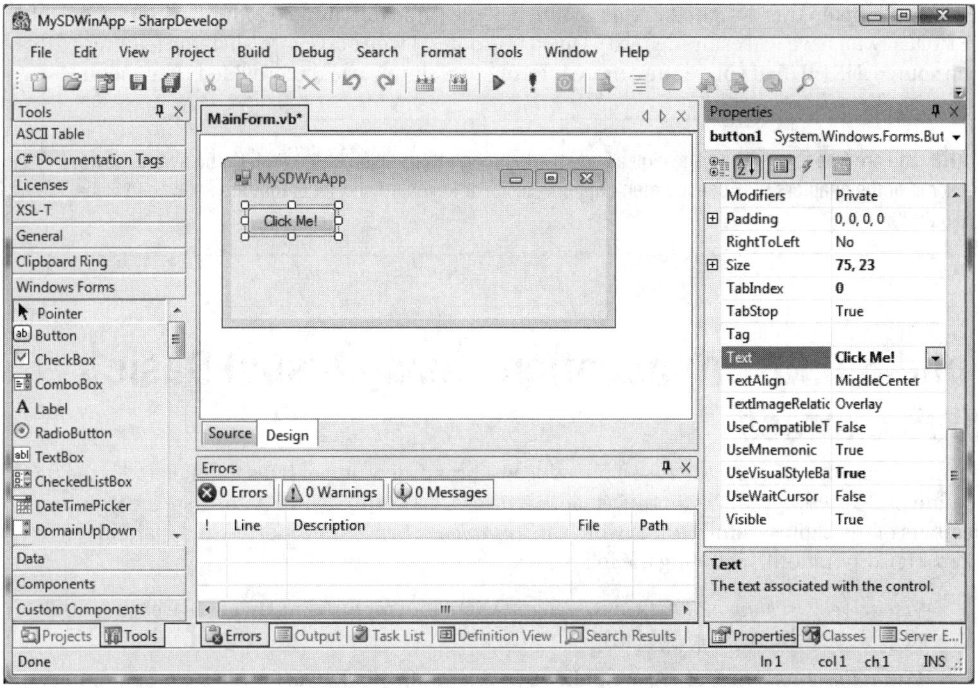

Figure 2-5. *Graphically designing a Windows Forms application with SharpDevelop*

If you were to click the Source button mounted to the bottom of the form's designer, you would find the expected IntelliSense, code completion, and integrated help features (see Figure 2-6).

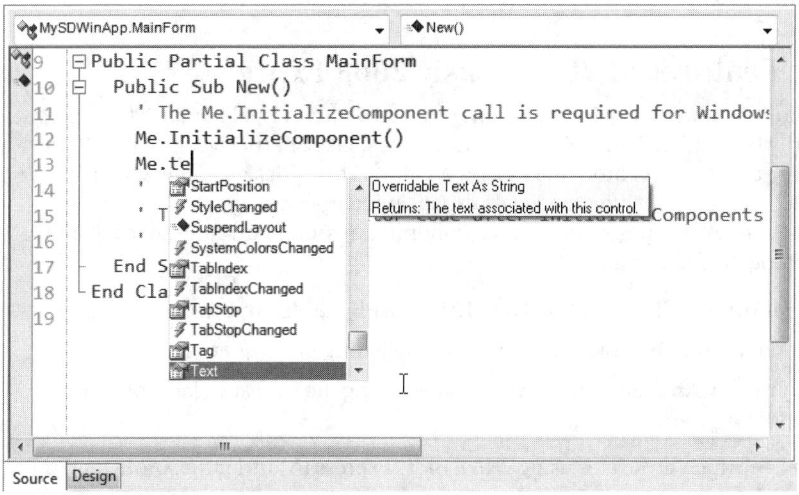

Figure 2-6. *SharpDevelop supports numerous code-generation utilities.*

SharpDevelop was designed to mimic much of the same functionality found within Microsoft's .NET IDEs (which we will examine next). Given this point, I won't dive into all of the features of this open source .NET IDE. If you require more information, simply use the provided Help menu.

■ **Note** You are free to use SharpDevelop as you work through this edition of the text. Do be aware, however, that some of the chapters may specify menu options, tools, or keyboard shortcuts that are specific to Visual Studio 2008.

Building .NET Applications Using Visual Basic 2008 Express

During the summer of 2004, Microsoft introduced a brand-new line of IDEs that fall under the designation of "Express" products (`http://msdn.microsoft.com/express`). To date, there are various members of the Express family (all of which are *completely free* and supported and maintained by Microsoft Corporation), including the following:

- *Visual Web Developer 2008 Express*: A lightweight tool for building dynamic websites and XML web services using ASP.NET
- *Visual Basic 2008 Express*: A streamlined programming tool ideal for novice programmers who want to learn how to build applications using the user-friendly syntax of Visual Basic
- *Visual C# 2008 Express and Visual C++ 2008 Express*: Targeted IDEs for students and enthusiasts who wish to learn the fundamentals of computer science in their syntax of choice
- *SQL Server 2005 Express*: An entry-level database management system geared toward hobbyists, enthusiasts, and student developers

Some Unique Features of Visual Basic 2008 Express

By and large, the Express products are slimmed-down versions of their Visual Studio 2008 counterparts and are primarily targeted at .NET hobbyists and students. Like SharpDevelop, Visual Basic 2008 Express provides various object browsing tools, a Windows Forms designer, the Add References dialog box, IntelliSense capabilities, and code expansion templates.

However, Visual Basic 2008 Express offers a few (important) features currently not available in SharpDevelop, including the following:

- Rich support for Windows Presentation Foundation (WPF) XAML applications
- IntelliSense for new VB 2008 syntactical constructs including LINQ query statements
- The ability to program Xbox 360 and PC video games using the freely available Microsoft XNA Game Studio

Consider Figure 2-7, which illustrates using Visual Basic Express to author the XAML markup for a WPF project.

Because the look and feel of Visual Basic 2008 Express is so similar to that of Visual Studio 2008 (and, to some degree, SharpDevelop), I do not provide a walk-through of this particular IDE here. However, do remember that this tool is completely free to use and will provide you with all the features you need to work through the remainder of this text.

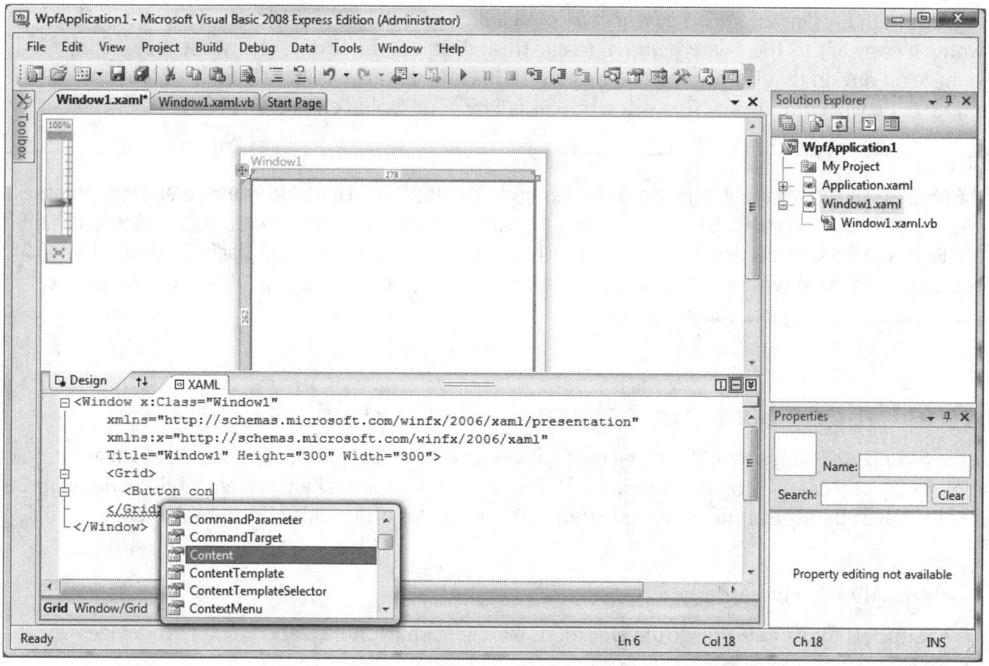

Figure 2-7. *Visual Basic 2008 Express has integrated support for .NET 3.0 and .NET 3.5 APIs.*

■ **Note** You are free to use Visual Basic Express as you work through this edition of the text. Again, do be aware, however, that some of the chapters may call out menu options, tools, or keyboard shortcuts that are specific to Visual Studio 2008.

Building .NET Applications Using Visual Studio 2008

If you are a professional .NET software engineer, the chances are extremely good that your employer has purchased Microsoft's premier IDE, Visual Studio 2008, for your development endeavors (`http://msdn.microsoft.com/vstudio`). This tool is far and away the most feature-rich and enterprise-ready IDE examined in this chapter. Of course, this power comes at a price, which will vary based on the version of Visual Studio 2008 you purchase. As you might suspect, each version supplies a unique set of features.

■ **Note** There are a staggering number of members within the Visual Studio 2008 family. My assumption during the remainder of this text is that you have chosen to make use of Visual Studio 2008 Professional as your IDE.

Although I will assume you have a copy of Visual Studio 2008 Professional, understand that owning a copy of this IDE is *not required* to use this edition of the text. In the worst case, I may examine an option that is not provided by your IDE. However, rest assured that all of this book's sample code will compile just fine when processed by your tool of choice.

Note Once you download the source code for this book from the Source Code/Downloads area of the Apress website (`http://www.apress.com`), you may load the current example into Visual Studio 2008 (or Visual Basic 2008 Express) by double-clicking the example's `*.sln` file. If you are not using Visual Studio 2008/Visual Basic 2008 Express, you will need to manually insert the provided `*.vb` files into your IDE's project workspace.

Some Unique Features of Visual Studio 2008

Visual Studio 2008 ships with the expected GUI designers, code snippet support, database manipulation tools, object and project browsing utilities, and an integrated help system. Unlike many of the IDEs we have already examined, Visual Studio 2008 provides numerous additions. Here is a partial list:

- Visual XML editors/designers
- Support for mobile device development (such as Smartphones and Pocket PC devices)
- Support for Microsoft Office development
- Designer support for Windows Workflow Foundation (WF) projects
- Integrated support for code refactoring
- Visual class design utilities
- The Object Test Bench window, which allows you to create objects and invoke their members directly within the IDE

To be completely honest, Visual Studio 2008 provides so many features that it would take an entire book (a rather large book at that) to fully describe every aspect of the IDE. *This is not that book.* However, I do want to point out some of the major features in the pages that follow. As you progress through the text, you'll learn more about the Visual Studio 2008 IDE where appropriate.

Targeting the .NET Framework Using the New Project Dialog Box

To examine some of the basic features of Visual Studio 2008, create a new VB Console Application (named Vs2008Example) using the File ➤ New ➤ Project menu item. As you can see in Figure 2-8, Visual Studio 2008 now (*finally*) supports the ability to select which version of the .NET Framework you wish to build against (2.0, 3.0, or 3.5) using the drop-down list box on the upper right of the New Project dialog box. For each project in this text, you can simply leave the default selection of .NET Framework 3.5.

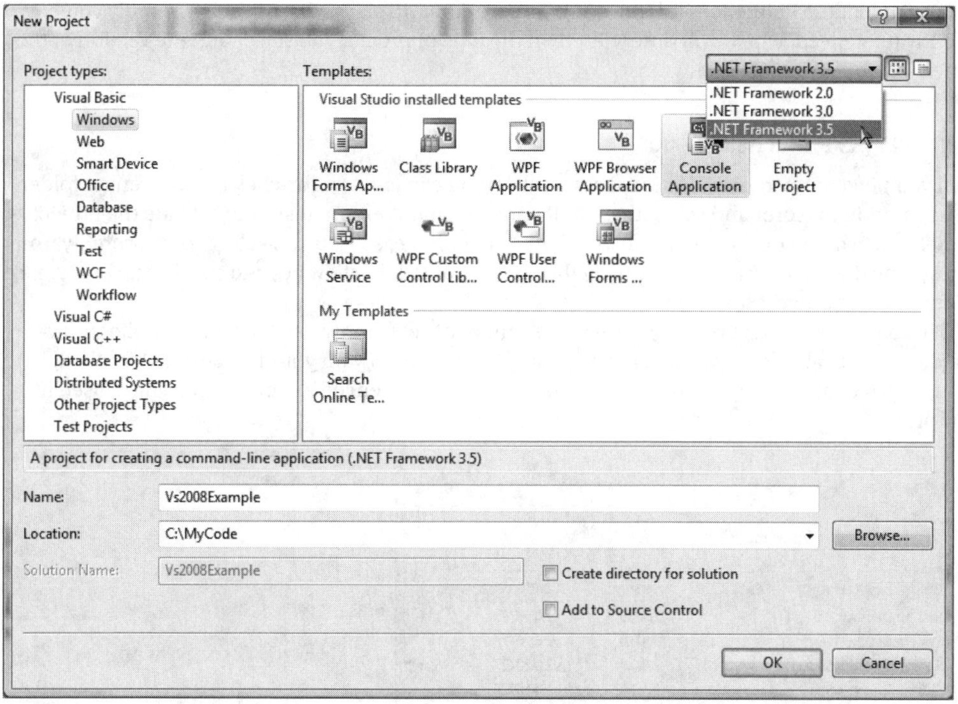

Figure 2-8. *Visual Studio 2008 now allows you to target a particular version of the .NET Framework.*

Using the Solution Explorer Utility

The Solution Explorer utility (accessible from the View menu) allows you to view the set of all content files and referenced assemblies that comprise the current project. By default, Solution Explorer will not show you the set of referenced assemblies used by your project or the output directories used by Visual Studio 2008 (such as \bin\Debug). To view *all* aspects of your project, you must click the Show All Files button of the Solution Explorer toolbar (see Figure 2-9).

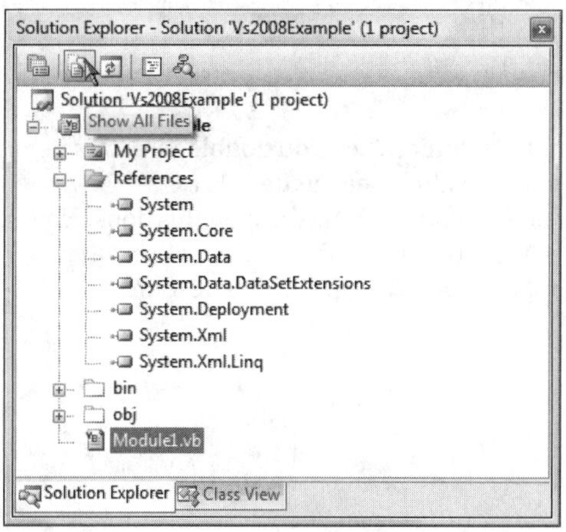

Figure 2-9. *The Solution Explorer utility*

Notice that the References folder of Solution Explorer displays a list of each assembly you have currently referenced, which will differ based on the type of project you select and the version of the Framework you are compiling against.

Referencing External Assemblies

When you need to reference additional assemblies, you can either right-click the References folder within Solution Explorer and select the Add Reference menu option or simply activate the Project ➤ Add Reference menu option of Visual Studio 2008. In either case, you can select your assembly from the resulting dialog box (this is essentially the way Visual Studio allows you to specify the `/reference` option of the command-line compiler).

The .NET tab (see Figure 2-10) displays a number of commonly used .NET assemblies; however, the Browse tab allows you to navigate to any .NET assembly on your hard drive. As well, the very useful Recent tab keeps a running tally of frequently referenced assemblies you have used in other projects.

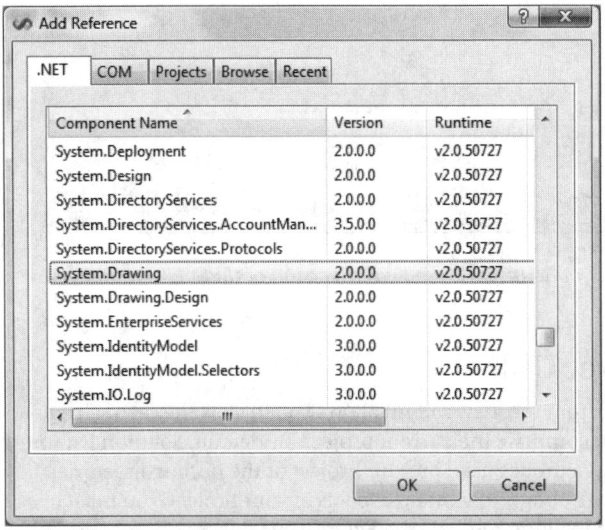

Figure 2-10. *The Add Reference dialog box*

Viewing Project Properties

Finally, notice an icon named My Project within Solution Explorer. When you double-click this item, you are presented with a sophisticated project configuration editor (see Figure 2-11).

You will see various aspects of the My Project window as you progress through this book. However, if you take some time to poke around, you will see that you can establish various security settings, strongly name your assembly, deploy your application, insert application resources, and configure pre- and postbuild events.

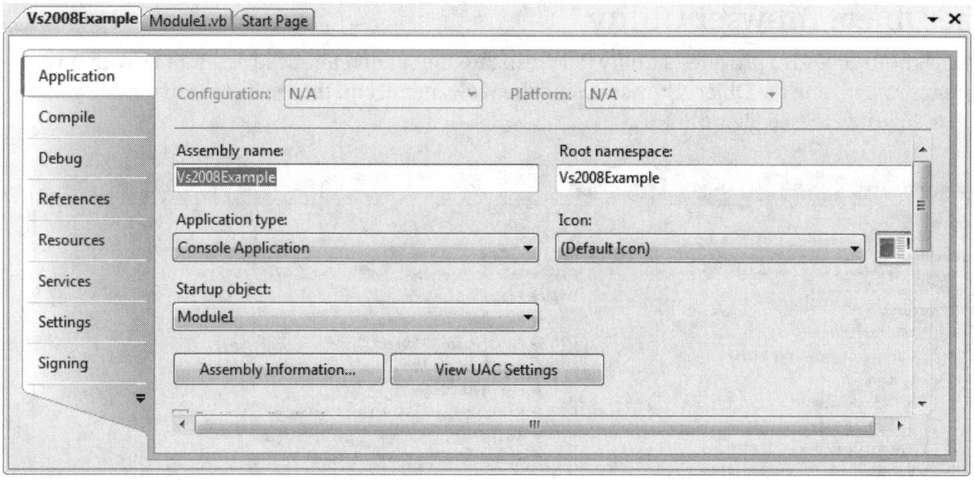

Figure 2-11. *The My Project window*

The Class View Utility

The next tool to examine is the Class View utility, which you can open from the View menu. The purpose of this utility is to show all of the types in your current project from a more object-oriented perspective (rather than a file-based view of Solution Explorer). The top pane displays the set of namespaces and their types, while the bottom pane displays the currently selected type's members (see Figure 2-12).

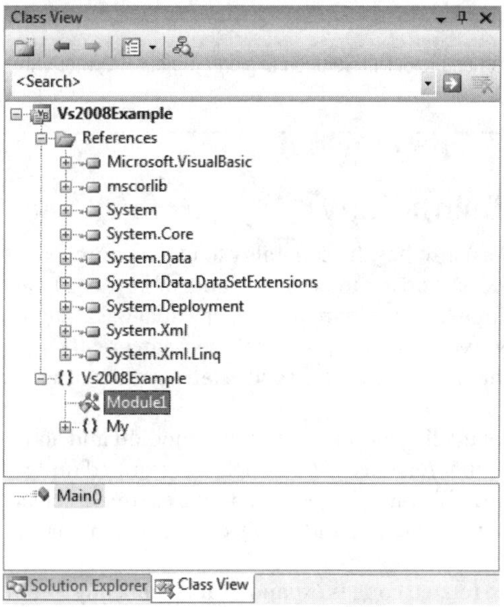

Figure 2-12. *The Class View utility*

The Object Browser Utility

Visual Studio 2008 also provides a utility to investigate the set of referenced assemblies within your current project. Activate Object Browser using the View menu, and then select the assembly you wish to investigate (see Figure 2-13).

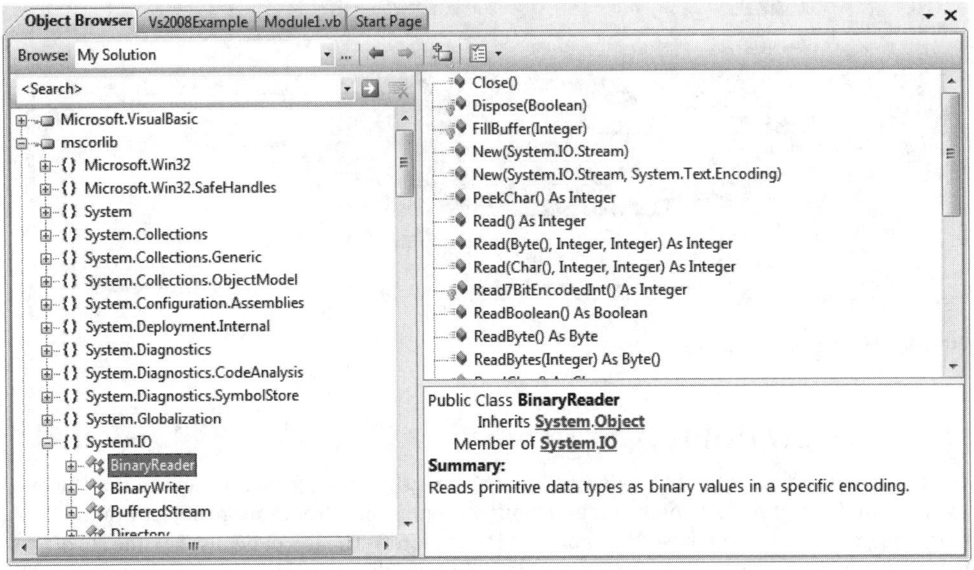

Figure 2-13. *The Object Browser utility*

Note If you double-click an assembly icon from the References folder of Solution Explorer, Object Browser will open automatically with the selected assembly highlighted.

Visual Studio 2008 Code Snippet Technology

Visual Studio 2008 (as well as Visual Basic 2008 Express) also has the capability to insert complex blocks of VB 2008 code using menu selections, context-sensitive mouse clicks, and/or keyboard shortcuts using *code snippets*. Simply put, a code snippet is a predefined block of Visual Basic 2008 code that will expand within the active code file. As you would guess, code snippets can greatly help increase productivity given that the tool will generate the necessary code statements (rather than us!).

To see this functionality firsthand, right-click a blank line within your `Main()` method and activate the Insert Snippet menu. From here, you will see that related code snippets are grouped under a specific category (Code Patterns, Data, Windows Forms Application, etc.). For this example, select the fundamentals ➤ math category and then activate the Calculate a Monthly Payment on a Loan snippet (see Figure 2-14).

Once you select a given snippet, you will find the related code is expanded automatically (press the Esc key to dismiss the pop-up menu). Many predefined code snippets identify specific "placeholders" for custom content. For example, once you activate the Calculate a Monthly Payment on a Loan snippet, you will find three regions are highlighted within the code window. Using the Tab key, you are able to cycle through each selection to modify the code as you see fit (see Figure 2-15).

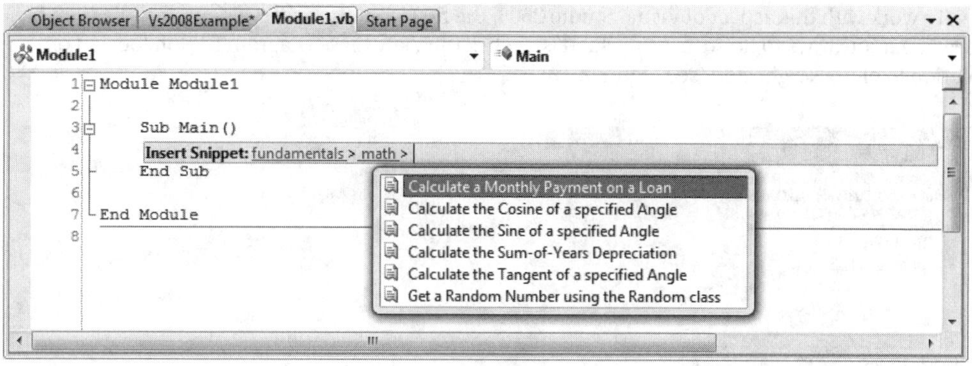

Figure 2-14. *Inserting VB 2008 code snippets*

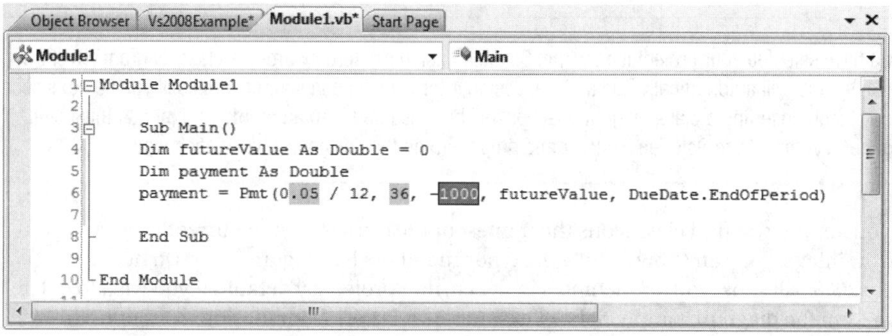

Figure 2-15. *The inserted snippet*

As you can see, Visual Studio 2008 defines a good number of code snippets. To be sure, the best way to learn about each possibility is simply through experimentation. Under the hood, each code snippet is defined within an XML document (taking a `*.snippet` extension by default) located under the C:\Program Files\Microsoft Visual Studio 9.0\VB\Snippets\1033 directory. In fact, given that each snippet is simply an XML description of the code to be inserted within the IDE, it is very simple to build custom code snippets.

■ **Note** Details of how to build custom snippets can be found in my article "Investigating Code Snippet Technology" at `http://msdn.microsoft.com`. While the article illustrates building C# code snippets, you can very easily build VB 2008 snippets by authoring VB 2008 code (rather than C# code) within the snippet's CDATA section.

The Visual Class Designer

Visual Studio 2008 gives us the ability to design classes visually (but this capability is not included in Visual Basic 2008 Express). The Class Designer utility allows you to view and modify the relationships of the types (classes, interfaces, structures, enumerations, and delegates) in your project. Using this tool, you are able to visually add (or remove) members to (or from) a type and have your modifications reflected in the corresponding `*.vb` file. As well, as you modify a given VB 2008 file, changes are reflected in the class diagram.

To work with this aspect of Visual Studio 2008, the first step is to insert a new class diagram file. There are many ways to do so, one of which is to click the View Class Diagram button located on Solution Explorer's right side (see Figure 2-16).

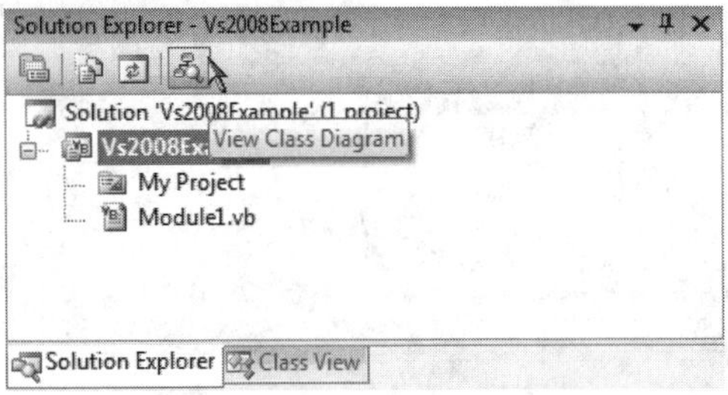

Figure 2-16. *Inserting a class diagram file*

Note If you have selected your project icon within Solution Explorer before inserting a class diagram (as shown in Figure 2-16), the IDE will automatically add a visual designer for each type in your code files. If you do not select the project icon before inserting a class diagram file, you will be presented with an empty designer. At this point, you can drag the `*.vb` files from Solution Explorer and drop them on the designer to view each type.

Once you do, you will find class icons that represent the classes in your current project. If you click the arrow image, you can show or hide the type's members (see Figure 2-17). Do note that Visual Studio 2008 will show you *all* members in the current project by default. If you wish to delete a given item from the diagram, simply right-click and select Delete from the context menu (this will *not* delete the related code file).

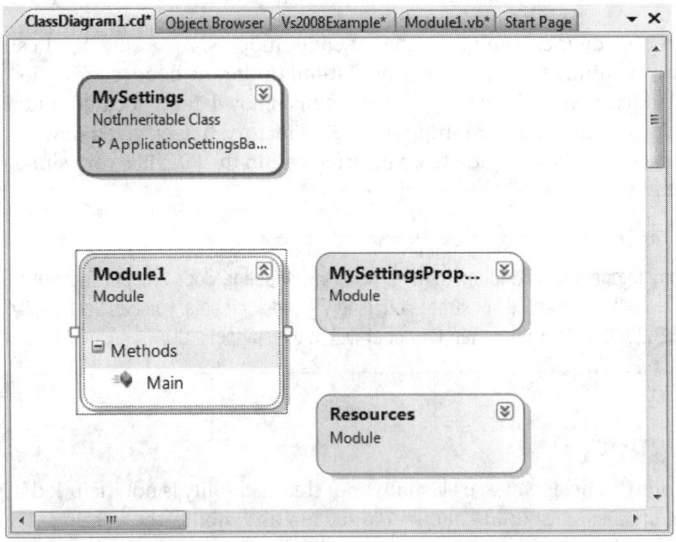

Figure 2-17. *The Class Diagram viewer*

This utility works in conjunction with two other aspects of Visual Studio 2008: the Class Details window (activated using the View ➤ Other Windows menu) and the Class Designer Toolbox (activated using the View ➤ Toolbox menu item). The Class Details window not only shows you the details of the currently selected item in the diagram, but also allows you to modify existing members and insert new members on the fly (see Figure 2-18).

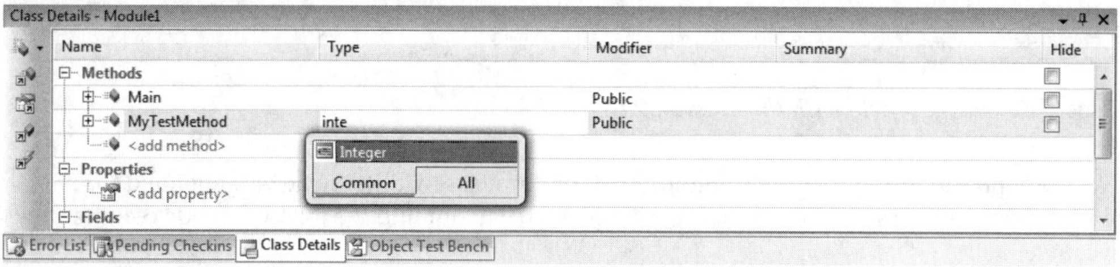

Figure 2-18. *The Class Details window*

The Class Designer Toolbox (see Figure 2-19) allows you to insert new types into your project (and create relationships between these types) visually. (Be aware that you must have a class diagram as the active window to view this toolbox.) As you do so, the IDE automatically creates new VB 2008 type definitions in the background.

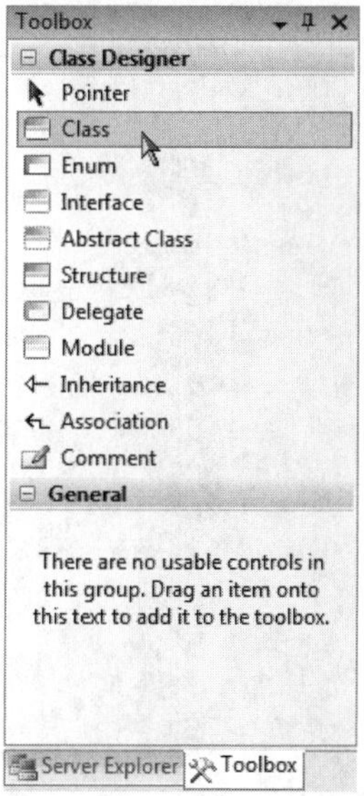

Figure 2-19. *The Class Designer Toolbox*

By way of example, drag a new class from the Class Designer Toolbox onto your Class Designer. Name this class `Car` in the resulting dialog box. Now, using the Class Details window, add a public `String` field named `petName` (see Figure 2-20).

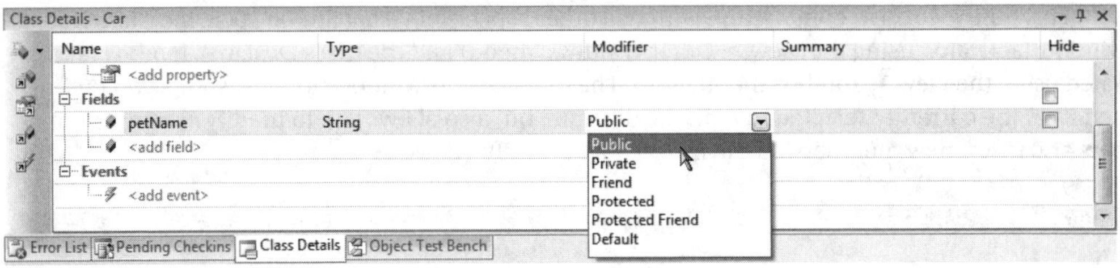

Figure 2-20. *Adding a field with the Class Details window*

If you now look at the VB 2008 definition of the Car class (within the newly generated Car.vb file), you will see it has been updated accordingly (you will not find the following code comments, of course):

```
Public Class Car
  ' Public data is typically a bad idea,
  ' however it will simplify this example.
  Public petName As String
End Class
```

Now, add another new class to the designer named SportsCar. Next, select the Inheritance icon from the Class Designer Toolbox and click the SportsCar icon. Next, move the mouse cursor on top of the Car class icon and click the mouse again. If you performed these steps correctly, you have just derived the SportsCar class from Car (see Figure 2-21).

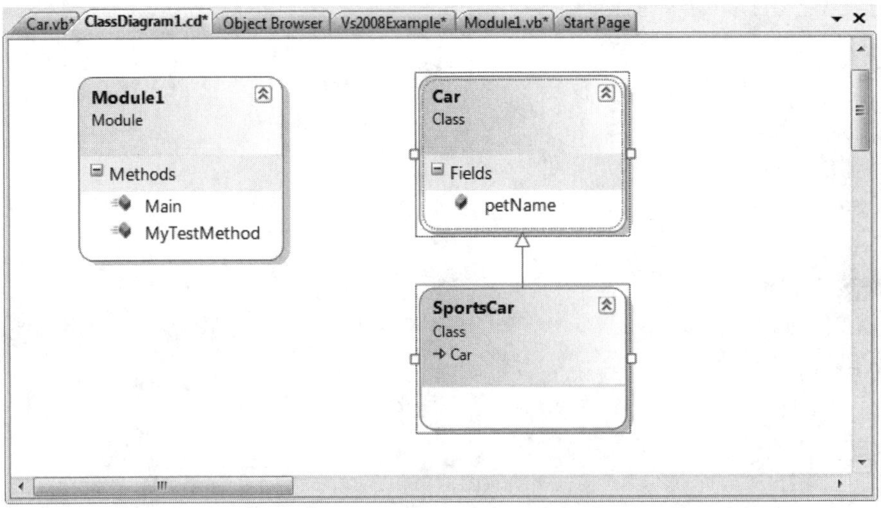

Figure 2-21. *Visually deriving from an existing class*

To complete this example, update the generated SportsCar class with a public method named PrintPetName() as follows (don't concern yourself with the syntax at this point; you'll dig into the details of class design beginning in the next chapter):

```
Public Class SportsCar
  Inherits Car
  Public Function PrintPetName() As String
    petName = "Fred"
    Return String.Format("Name of this car is: {0}", petName)
  End Sub
End Class
```

The Object Test Bench

Another nice visual tool provided by Visual Studio 2008 is Object Test Bench (OTB). This aspect of the IDE allows you to quickly create an instance of a class and invoke its members without the need to compile and run the entire application. This can be extremely helpful when you wish to test a specific method, but would rather not step through dozens of lines of code to do so. This is also extremely useful when you are building a .NET class library (`*.dll`) and wish to quickly test your members without creating a separate testing application.

To work with the OTB, right-click the type you wish to create using the Class Designer. For example, right-click the `SportsCar` type, and from the resulting context menu select Create Instance ➤ SportsCar(). This will display a dialog box that allows you to name your temporary object variable (and supply any constructor arguments if required). Once the process is complete, you will find your object hosted within the IDE. Right-click the object icon and invoke the `PrintPetName()` method (see Figure 2-22).

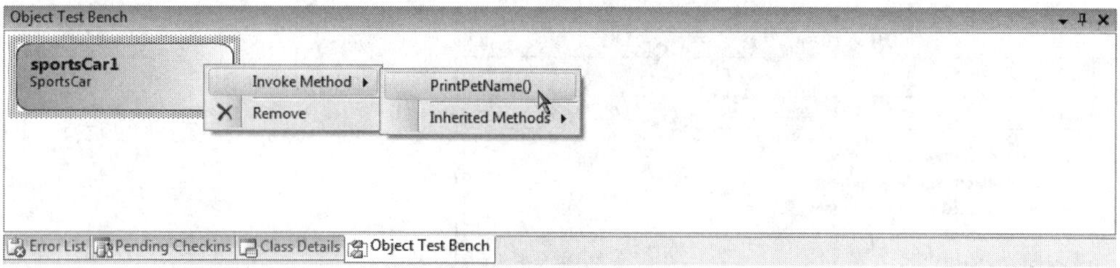

Figure 2-22. *The Visual Studio 2008 Object Test Bench*

Once you do, the OTB will show you the function return value, which is a `String` set to the value "Name of this car is: Fred". Notice in Figure 2-23, you can elect to save this new `String` object on the OTB as well, after which you can invoke various members of the `String` type.

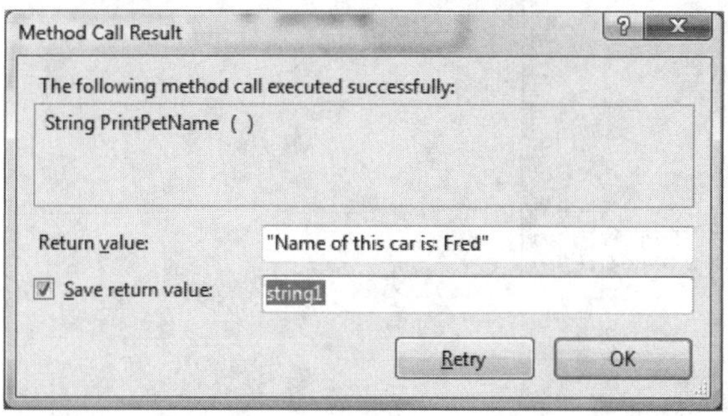

Figure 2-23. *Viewing our function return value*

The Integrated Help System

The final aspect of Visual Studio 2008 you must be comfortable with from the outset is the fully integrated help system. The .NET Framework 3.5 SDK documentation (aka the MSDN Library) is extremely good, very readable, and full of useful information. Given the huge number of predefined .NET types (which number well into the thousands), you must be willing to roll up your sleeves and dig into the provided documentation. If you resist, you are doomed to a long, frustrating, and painful existence as a .NET developer.

Visual Studio 2008 provides the Dynamic Help window (accessed via the Help ➤ Dynamic Help menu selection), which changes its contents (dynamically!) based on what item (window, menu, source code keyword, etc.) is currently selected. For example, if you place the cursor on the `Console` class, the Dynamic Help window displays a set of links regarding the `System.Console` type.

■ **Note** Another handy shortcut is the F1 key of Visual Studio 2008. Simply locate your mouse cursor inside a keyword, type, or method and press the F1 key. The IDE will automatically take you to the correct help page.

You should also be aware of a very important subdirectory of the .NET Framework 3.5 SDK documentation. First, activate the Help ➤ Contents menu option of the documentation. Under the .NET Development ➤ .NET Framework SDK ➤ .NET Framework ➤ .NET Framework Class Library Reference node of the documentation, you will find complete documentation of each and every namespace in the .NET base class libraries (see Figure 2-24).

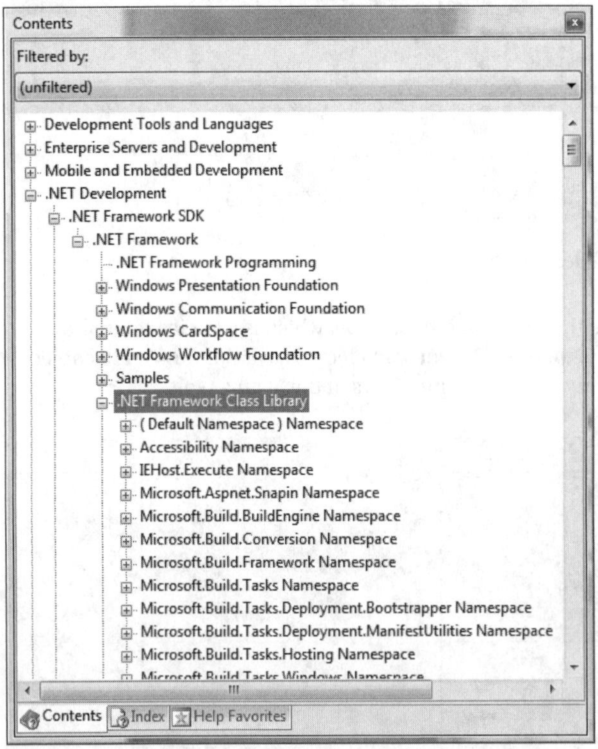

Figure 2-24. *The .NET base class library reference*

Each node defines the set of types in a given namespace, the members of a given type, and the parameters of a given member. Furthermore, when you view the help page for a given type, you will be told the name of the assembly and namespace that contains the type in question (located at the top of said page). As you read through the remainder of this book, I assume that you will dive into this very, very critical node to read up on additional details of the entity under examination.

■ **Note** I'd like to stress again the importance of working with the supplied .NET Framework 3.5 documentation. When you are learning a brand-new framework and programming language, you will need to roll up your sleeves and dig into the details. No book, regardless of its size, can cover every detail of building applications with Visual Basic 2008 or the .NET platform. Thus, if you encounter a type or member that you would like more information about as you work through this text, be sure to leverage your help system!

The Role of the Visual Basic 6.0 Compatibility Assembly

As you will most certainly come to realize over the course of this book, Visual Basic 2008 is such a major overhaul of VB6 that it is often best to simply regard VB 2008 as a brand-new language in the BASIC family, rather than as "Visual Basic 7.0." To this end, many familiar VB6 functions, enumerations, user-defined types, and intrinsic objects are nowhere to be found directly within the .NET base class libraries.

While this is technically true, every Visual Basic 2008 project created with Visual Studio 2008 (as well as Visual Basic 2008 Express Edition) automatically references a particular .NET assembly named `Microsoft.VisualBasic.dll`, which defines types that provide the same functionality of the legacy VB6 constructs. Like any assembly, `Microsoft.VisualBasic.dll` is composed of numerous namespaces that group together likeminded types (see Figure 2-25).

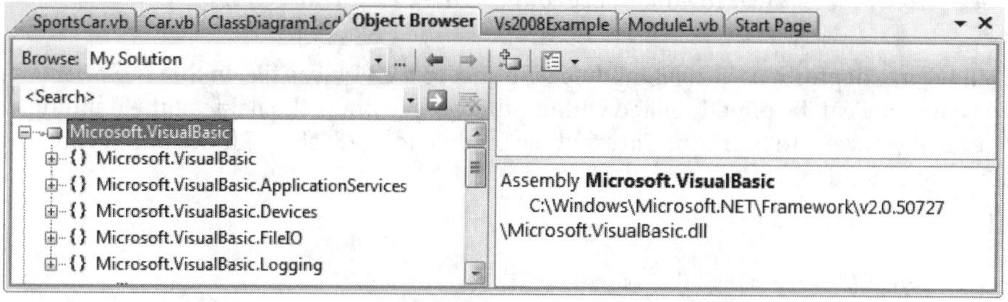

Figure 2-25. *The* `Microsoft.VisualBasic.dll` *VB6 compatibility assembly*

Furthermore, each of these namespaces are automatically available to each `*.vb` file in your project. Given this point, you do not need to explicitly add a set of `Imports` statements to gain access to their types. Thus, if you wished to do so, you could still make use of various VB6-isms, such as the `MsgBox()` call to display a simple message box:

```
' The Microsoft.VisualBasic namespaces
' are automatically referenced by a
' Visual Studio 2008 VB project.
Module Module1
  Sub Main()
```

```
    MsgBox("Hello, old friend...")
  End Sub
End Module
```

Notice how it appears that you are calling a global method named `MsgBox()` directly within `Main()`. In reality, the `MsgBox()` method is a member of a VB 2008 module named `Interaction` that is defined within the `Microsoft.VisualBasic` namespace (see Figure 2-26).

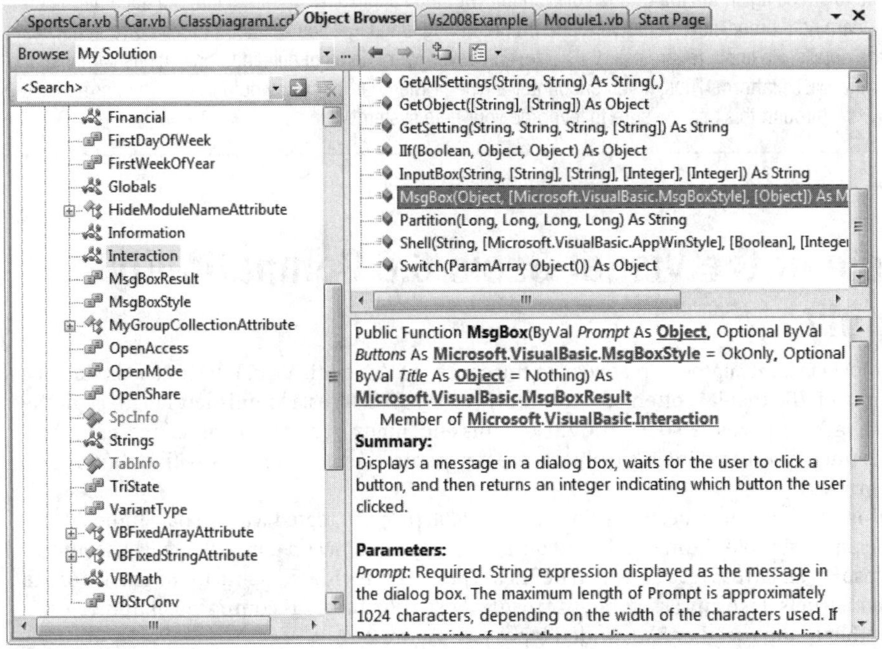

Figure 2-26. *The* `Microsoft.VisualBasic` *namespace contains the* `Interaction` *type.*

As you will see in Chapter 3, a VB 2008 module is similar to a VB6 `*.bas` file, in that members defined within a module can be directly called without the need to prefix the name of the defining module. However, if you were to prefix the `Interaction` module to the `MsgBox()` function, the program would function identically:

```
Module Module1
  Sub Main()
    Interaction.MsgBox("Everything old is new again!")
  End Sub
End Module
```

Now although it may feel a bit reassuring to know that the functionality of VB6 can still be simulated within new Visual Basic 2008 projects, I recommend that you *avoid* using these types where possible. First of all, the writing seems to be on the wall regarding the lifetime of VB6, in that Microsoft itself plans to phase out support for VB6 over time, and given this, you cannot guarantee that this compatibility assembly will be supported in the future.

As well, the base class libraries provide numerous managed types that offer much more functionality than the (soon-to-be) legacy VB6 programming language. Given these points, this text will not make use of the VB6 compatibility layer. Rather, you will focus on learning the .NET base class libraries and how to interact with these types using the syntax of Visual Basic 2008.

A Partial Catalog of Additional .NET Development Tools

To conclude this chapter, I would like to point out a number of .NET development tools that complement the functionality provided by your IDE of choice. Many of the tools mentioned here are open source, and all of them are free of charge. While I don't have the space to cover the details of these utilities, Table 2-2 lists a number of the tools I have found to be extremely helpful as well as URLs you can visit to find more information about them.

Table 2-2. *Select .NET Development Tools*

Tool	Meaning in Life	URL
FxCop	This is a must-have for any .NET developer interested in .NET best practices. FxCop will test any .NET assembly against the official Microsoft .NET best-practice coding guidelines.	`http://blogs.msdn.com/fxcop/`
Lutz Roeder's Reflector	This advanced .NET decompiler/object browser allows you to view the .NET implementation of any .NET type using a variety of languages.	`http://www.aisto.com/roeder/dotnet`
NAnt	NAnt is the .NET equivalent of Ant, the popular Java automated build tool. NAnt allows you to define and execute detailed build scripts using an XML-based syntax.	`http://sourceforge.net/projects/nant`
NDoc	NDoc is a tool that will generate code documentation files for commented VB code (or a compiled .NET assembly) in a variety of popular formats (MSDN's `*.chm`, XML, HTML, Javadoc, and LaTeX).	`http://sourceforge.net/projects/ndoc`
NUnit	NUnit is the .NET equivalent of the Java-centric JUnit unit testing tool. Using NUnit, you are able to facilitate the testing of your managed code.	`http://www.nunit.org`

Summary

So as you can see, you have many new toys at your disposal! The point of this chapter was to provide you with a tour of the major programming tools a VB 2008 programmer may leverage during the development process. You began the journey by learning how to generate .NET assemblies using nothing other than the free VB 2008 compiler and Notepad.

You also examined three feature-rich IDEs, starting with the open source SharpDevelop, followed by Microsoft's Visual Basic 2008 Express and Visual Studio 2008. While this chapter only scratched the surface of each tool's functionality, you should be in a good position to explore your chosen IDE at your leisure. The chapter wrapped up by describing the role of `Microsoft.VisualBasic.dll` and mentioned a number of open source .NET development tools that extend the functionality of your IDE of choice.

PART 2

Core VB Programming Constructs

CHAPTER 3

VB 2008 Programming Constructs, Part I

This chapter begins your formal investigation of the Visual Basic 2008 programming language. Do be aware this chapter and the next will present a number of bite-sized stand-alone topics you must be comfortable with as you explore the .NET Framework. Unlike the remaining chapters in this text, there is no overriding theme in the next two chapters beyond examining the core syntactical features of VB 2008.

This being said, the first order of business is to understand the role of the `Module` keyword as well as the format of a program's entry point: the `Main()` method. Next, you will investigate the intrinsic VB 2008 data types (and their equivalent types in the `System` namespace) as well as various data type conversion routines. We wrap up by examining the set of operators, iteration constructs, and decision constructs used to build valid code statements.

The Role of the Module Type

Visual Basic 2008 supports a specific programming construct termed a *module*, which is declared with the `Module` keyword. For example, when you create a Console Application project using Visual Studio 2008, you automatically receive a `*.vb` file that contains the following code:

```
Module Module1
  Sub Main()
  End Sub
End Module
```

Under the hood, the `Module` keyword defines a class type, with a few notable exceptions. First and foremost, any public function, subroutine, property, or member variable defined within the scope of a module is exposed as a "shared member" that is directly accessible throughout an application. Simply put, *shared members* allow you to simulate a global scope within your application that is roughly analogous to the functionality provided by a VB6 `*.bas` file (full details on shared members can be found in Chapter 5).

Given that members in a module are directly accessible, you are not required to prefix the module's name when accessing its contents. To illustrate working with modules, create a new Console Application project (named FunWithModules) and update your initial code file as follows:

```
Module Module1
  Sub Main()
    ' Show banner.
    DisplayBanner()
```

```
    ' Get user's name and say howdy.
    GreetUser()
  End Sub

  Sub DisplayBanner()
    ' Get the current color of the console text.
    Dim currColor As ConsoleColor = Console.ForegroundColor

    ' Set text color to yellow.
    Console.ForegroundColor = ConsoleColor.Yellow
    Console.WriteLine("******* Welcome to FunWithModules *******")
    Console.WriteLine("This simple program illustrates the role")
    Console.WriteLine("of the Module type.")
    Console.WriteLine("*****************************************")

    ' Reset to previous color of your console text.
    Console.ForegroundColor = currColor
    Console.WriteLine()
  End Sub

  Sub GreetUser()
    Dim userName As String
    Console.Write("Please enter your name: ")
    userName = Console.ReadLine()
    Console.WriteLine("Hello there {0}. Nice to meet ya.", userName)
  End Sub
End Module
```

Figure 3-1 shows one possible output.

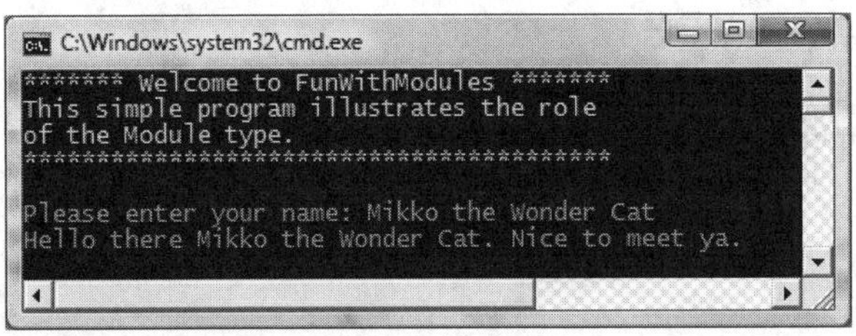

Figure 3-1. *Modules at work*

Projects with Multiple Modules

In our current example, notice that the `Main()` method is able to directly call the `DisplayBanner()` and `GreetUser()` methods. Because these methods are defined within the same module as `Main()`, we are not required to prefix the name of our module (`Module1`) to the member name. However, if you wish to do so, you could retrofit `Main()` as follows:

```
Sub Main()
  ' Show banner.
  Module1.DisplayBanner()
  ' Get user's name and say howdy.
  Module1.GreetUser()
End Sub
```

In the current example, this is a completely optional bit of syntax (there is no difference in terms of performance or the size of the compiled assembly). However, assume you were to define a new module (MyModule) in your project (within the same *.vb file, for example), which defines an identically formed GreetUser() method:

```
Module MyModule
  Public Sub GreetUser()
    Console.WriteLine("Hello user...")
  End Sub
End Module
```

If you wish to call MyModule.GreetUser() from within the Main() method, you would now need to *explicitly* prefix the module's name. If you do not specify the name of the module, the Main() method automatically calls the Module1.GreetUser() method, as it is in the same module scope as Main():

```
Sub Main()
  ' Show banner.
  DisplayBanner()

  ' Call the GreetUser() method in MyModule.
  MyModule.GreetUser()
End Sub
```

Again, do understand that when a single project defines multiple modules, you are not required to prefix the module name unless the methods are ambiguous. Thus, if your current project were to define yet another module named MyMathModule:

```
Module MyMathModule
  Function Add(ByVal x As Integer, ByVal y As Integer) As Integer
    Return x + y
  End Function

  Function Subtract(ByVal x As Integer, ByVal y As Integer) As Integer
    Return x - y
  End Function
End Module
```

you could directly invoke the Add() and Subtract() functions anywhere within your application (or optionally prefix the module's name):

```
Sub Main()
...
  ' Add some numbers.
  Console.WriteLine("10 + 10 is {0}.", Add(10, 10))

  ' Subtract some numbers
  ' (module prefix optional).
  Console.WriteLine("10 - 10 is {0}.", MyMathModule.Subtract(10, 10))
End Sub
```

Note If you are new to the syntax of BASIC languages, rest assured that Chapter 4 will cover the details of building functions and subroutines.

Modules Are Not Creatable

Another trait of the module type is that it cannot be directly created using the VB 2008 New keyword (any attempt to do so will result in a compiler error). Therefore, the following code is illegal:

```
' Nope! Error, can't allocated modules!
Dim m as New Module1()
```

Rather, a module simply exposes shared members.

■Note If you already have a background in object-oriented programming, be aware that module types cannot be used to build class hierarchies as they are implicitly sealed. Furthermore, unlike "normal" classes, modules cannot implement interfaces.

Renaming Your Initial Module

By default, Visual Studio 2008 names the initial module type of a Console Application using the rather nondescript Module1. If you were to change the name of the module defining your Main() method to a more fitting name (Program, for example), the compiler will generate an error such as the following:

```
'Sub Main' was not found in 'FunWithModules.Module1'.
```

In order to inform Visual Studio 2008 of the new module name, you are required to reset the "startup object" using the Application tab of the My Project dialog box, as you see in Figure 3-2. Once you do so, you will be able to compile your application without error.

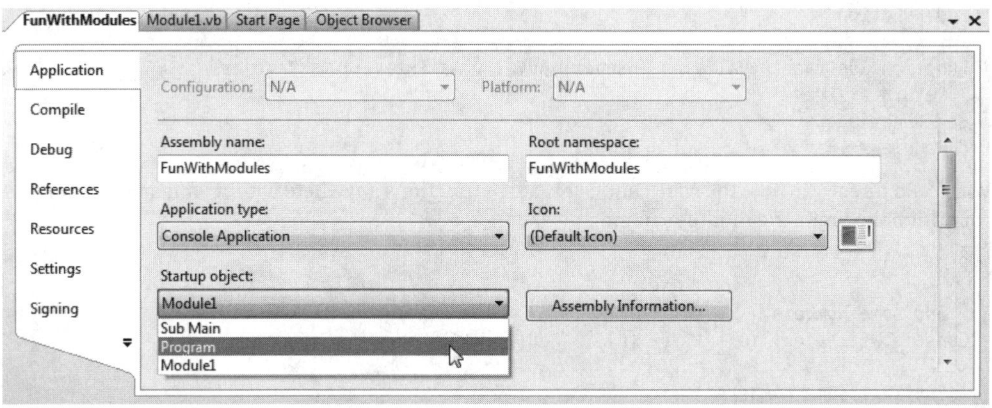

Figure 3-2. *Resetting the module name*

■Note As a shortcut, you can also rename your initial module by changing the name of the defining file using the Solution Explorer window of Visual Studio. This will automatically "reset" the startup object.

Members of Modules

To wrap up our investigation of module types, do know that modules can have additional members beyond subroutines and functions. If you wish to define field data (as well as other members, such as properties or events), you are free to do so. For example, assume you wish to update `MyModule` to contain a single piece of public string data. Note that the `GreetUser()` method will now print out this value when invoked:

```
Module MyModule
  Public UserName As String

  Sub GreetUser()
    Console.WriteLine("Hello, {0}.", UserName)
  End Sub
End Module
```

Like any module member, the `UserName` field can be directly accessed by any part of your application. For example:

```
Sub Main()
...
  ' Set user's name and call second form of GreetUser().
  UserName = "Fred"
  MyModule.GreetUser()
...
End Sub
```

Source Code The FunWithModules project is located under the Chapter 3 subdirectory.

The Role of the Main Method

Every VB 2008 executable application (such as a console program, Windows service, or a desktop GUI application) must contain a type defining a `Main()` method, which represents the entry point of the application. As you have just seen, the `Main()` method is typically placed within a module type, which as you recall implicitly defines `Main()` as a shared method.

Strictly speaking, however, `Main()` can also be defined within the scope of a class type or structure type as well. If you do define your `Main()` method within either of these types, you must explicitly make use of the `Shared` keyword. To illustrate, create a new Console Application named FunWithMain. Delete the code within the initial `*.vb` file and replace it with the following:

```
Class Program
  ' Unlike Modules, members in a class are not
  ' automatically shared. Thus, we must declare Main()
  ' with the Shared keyword.
  Shared Sub Main()
  End Sub
End Class
```

If you attempt to compile your program, you will again receive a compiler error informing you that the `Main()` method cannot be located. Using the Application tab of the My Project dialog box, you can now specify `Program` as the startup object of the program (as previously shown in Figure 3-2).

Processing Command-Line Arguments Using System.Environment

One common task Main() will undertake is to process any incoming command-line arguments. For example, consider the VB command-line compiler, vbc.exe (see Chapter 2). As you recall, we specified various options (such as /target, /out, and so forth) when compiling our code files. The vbc.exe compiler processed these input flags in order to compile the output assembly. When you wish to build a Main() method that can process incoming command-line arguments for your custom applications, you have a few possible ways to do so.

Your first approach is to make use of the shared GetCommandLineArgs() method defined by the System.Environment type. This method returns you an array of String objects. The first item in the array is simply the name of the executable program, while any remaining items in the array represent the command-line arguments themselves. To illustrate, update your current Main() method as follows:

```
Class Program
  Shared Sub Main()
    Console.WriteLine("***** Fun with Main() *****")
    ' Get command-line args.
    Dim args As String() = Environment.GetCommandLineArgs()
    Dim s As String
    For Each s In args
      Console.WriteLine("Arg: {0}", s)
    Next
  End Sub
End Class
```

Assuming you have built your application, if you were to now run your application at the command prompt, you can feed in your arguments in an identical manner as you did when working with vbc.exe (see Figure 3-3).

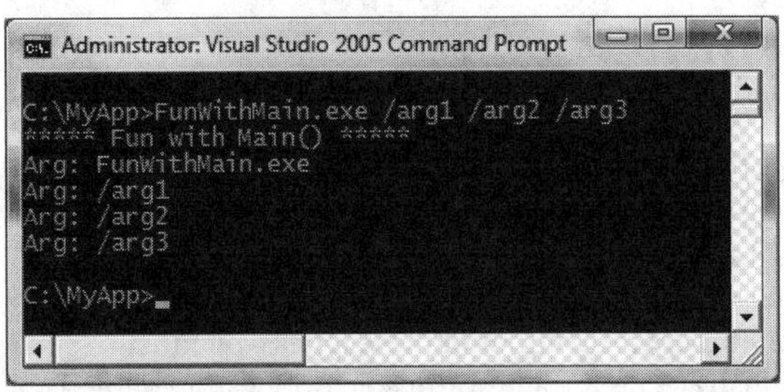

Figure 3-3. *Processing command-line arguments*

Of course, it is up to you to determine which command-line arguments your program will respond to and how they must be formatted (such as with a - or / prefix). Here we simply passed in a series of options that were printed to the command prompt. Assume, however, you were creating a new video game and programmed your application to process an option named -godmode. If the user starts your application with the flag, you know the user is in fact a *cheater*, and you can take an appropriate course of action.

Processing Command-Line Arguments with Main()

If you would rather not make use of the System.Environment type to process command-line arguments, you can define your Main() method to take an incoming array of strings. To illustrate, update your code base as follows:

```
Shared Sub Main(ByVal args As String())
  Console.WriteLine("***** Fun with Main() *****")
  ' Get command-line args.
  Dim s As String
  For Each s In args
    Console.WriteLine("Arg: {0}", s)
  Next
End Sub
```

When you take this approach, the first item in the incoming array is indeed the first command-line argument (rather than the name of the executable). If you were to run your application once again, you would find each command-line option is printed to the console.

Main() As a Function (Not a Subroutine)

It is also possible to define Main() as a function returning an Integer, rather than a subroutine (which never has a return value). This approach to building a Main() method has its roots in C-based languages, where returning the value 0 typically indicates the program has terminated without error. You will seldom (if ever) need to build your Main() method in this manner; however, for the sake of completion, here is one example:

```
Shared Function Main(ByVal args As String()) As Integer
  Console.WriteLine("***** Fun with Main() *****")
  Dim s As String
  For Each s In args
    Console.WriteLine("Arg: {0}", s)
  Next
  ' Return a value to the OS.
  Return 0
End Function
```

Regardless of how you define your Main() method, the purpose remains the same: interact with the types that carry out the functionality of your application. Once the final statement within the Main() method has executed, Main() exits and your application terminates.

Specifying Command-Line Arguments Using Visual Studio 2008

Finally, let me point out that Visual Studio 2008 does allow you to specify incoming command-line arguments, which can be very helpful when testing and debugging your application. Rather than having to run your application at a command line to feed in arguments manually, you can explicitly specify arguments using the Debug tab of the My Project dialog box, shown in Figure 3-4 (note the Command line arguments text area).

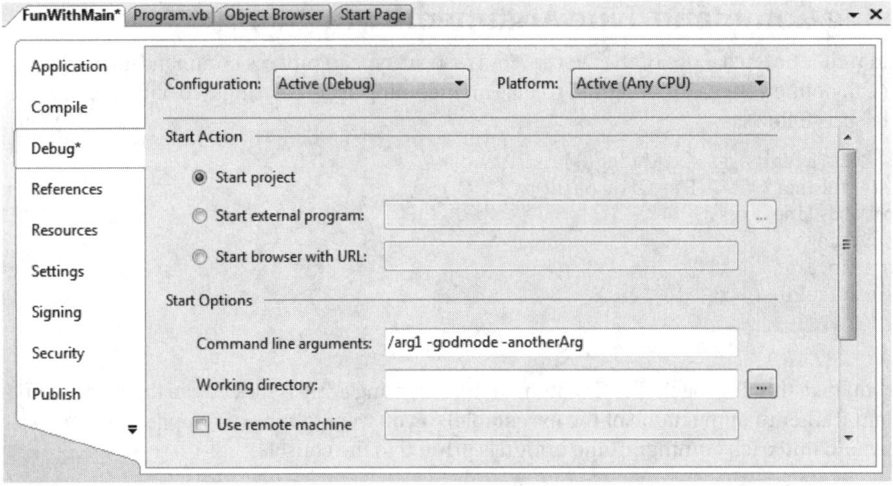

Figure 3-4. *Simulating command-line arguments*

When you compile and run your application under Debug mode, the specified arguments are passed to your `Main()` method automatically. Do know that when you compile and run a Release build of your application (which can be established using the Compile tab of the My Project dialog box), this is no longer the case.

An Interesting Aside: Some Additional Members of the System.Environment Class

The `Environment` type exposes a number of extremely helpful methods beyond `GetCommandLineArgs()`. Specifically, this class allows you to obtain a number of details regarding the operating system currently hosting your .NET application using various shared members. To illustrate the usefulness of `System.Environment`, update your `Main()` method with the following logic:

```
Shared Function Main(ByVal args As String()) As Integer
...
  ' OS running this app?
  Console.WriteLine("Current OS: {0}", Environment.OSVersion)

  ' List the drives on this machine.
  Dim drives As String() = Environment.GetLogicalDrives()
  Dim d As String
  For Each d In drives
    Console.WriteLine("You have a drive named {0}.", d)
  Next

  ' Which version of the .NET platform is running this app?
  Console.WriteLine("Executing version of .NET: {0}", _
    Environment.Version)
  Return 0
End Function
```

Figure 3-5 shows a possible test run.

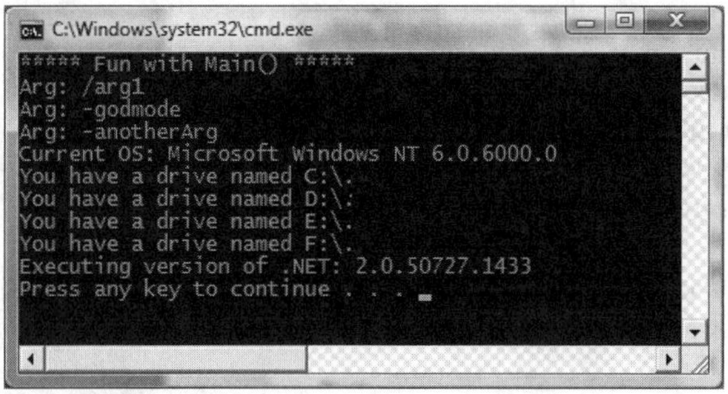

Figure 3-5. *Displaying system environment variables*

The `Environment` type defines members other than those seen in the previous example. Table 3-1 documents some additional properties of interest; however, be sure to check out the .NET Framework 3.5 SDK documentation for full details.

Table 3-1. *Select Properties of* `System.Environment`

Property	Meaning in Life
`CurrentDirectory`	Gets the full path to the current application
`MachineName`	Gets the name of the current machine
`NewLine`	Gets the newline symbol for the current environment
`ProcessorCount`	Returns the number of processors on the current machine
`SystemDirectory`	Returns the full path to the system directory
`UserName`	Returns the name of the user who started this application

■ **Source Code** The FunWithMain project is located under the Chapter 3 subdirectory.

The System.Console Class

Almost all of the example applications created over the course of the initial chapters of this text make extensive use of the `System.Console` class. While it is true that a console user interface (sometimes called a *CUI*) is not as enticing as a graphical user interface (GUI) or web-based front end, restricting the early examples to console programs will allow us to keep focused on the syntax of Visual Basic and the core aspects of the .NET platform, rather than dealing with the complexities of building GUIs.

As its name implies, the `Console` class encapsulates input, output, and error stream manipulations for console-based applications. Table 3-2 lists some (but definitely not all) of the members of interest.

Table 3-2. *Select Members of* `System.Console`

Member	Meaning in Life
`Beep()`	This method forces the console to emit a beep of a specified frequency and duration.
`BackgroundColor` `ForegroundColor`	These properties set the background/foreground colors for the current output. They may be assigned any member of the `ConsoleColor` enumeration.
`BufferHeight` `BufferWidth`	These properties control the height/width of the console's buffer area.
`Title`	This property sets the title of the current console.

`WindowHeight`
`WindowWidth`
`WindowTop`
`WindowLeft`
	These properties control the dimensions of the console in relation to the established buffer.

`Clear()`	This method clears the established buffer and console display area.

Basic Input and Output with the Console Class

In addition to the members in Table 3-2, the `Console` type defines a set of methods to capture input and output, all of which are shared and are therefore called by prefixing the name of the class (`Console`) to the method name. As you have seen, `WriteLine()` pumps a text string (including a carriage return) to the output stream. The `Write()` method pumps text to the output stream without a carriage return. `ReadLine()` allows you to receive information from the input stream up until the carriage return, while `Read()` is used to capture a single character from the input stream.

To illustrate basic I/O using the `Console` class, create a new Console Application named BasicConsoleIO and update your `Main()` method with logic that prompts the user for some bits of information and echoes each item to the standard output stream.

```
Sub Main()
  Console.WriteLine("***** Fun with Console IO *****")
  ' Echo some information to the console.
  Console.Write("Enter your name: ")
  Dim s As String = Console.ReadLine()
  Console.WriteLine("Hello, {0}", s)

  Console.Write("Enter your age: ")
  s = Console.ReadLine()
  Console.WriteLine("You are {0} years old", s)
End Sub
```

Formatting Console Output

During these first few chapters, you have certainly noticed numerous occurrences of the tokens `{0}`, `{1}`, and the like embedded within a string literal. The .NET platform introduces a new style of string formatting, which can be used by any .NET programming language. Simply put, when you are defining a string literal that contains segments of data whose value is not known until runtime, you are able to specify a placeholder within the literal using this curly-bracket syntax. At runtime, the value(s) passed into `Console.WriteLine()` are substituted for each placeholder. To illustrate, update your current `Main()` method as follows:

```
Sub Main()
...
  ' Specify string placeholders and values to use at
  ' runtime.
  Dim theInt As Integer = 90
  Dim theDouble As Double = 9.99
  Dim theBool As Boolean = True
  Console.WriteLine("Value of theInt: {0}", theInt)
  Console.WriteLine("theDouble is {0} and theBool is {1}.", _
    theDouble, theBool)
End Sub
```

The first parameter to `WriteLine()` represents a string literal that contains optional placeholders designated by `{0}`, `{1}`, `{2}`, and so forth. Be very aware that the first ordinal number of a curly-bracket placeholder always begins with 0. The remaining parameters to `WriteLine()` are simply the values to be inserted into the respective placeholders (in this case, an `Integer`, a `Double`, and a `Boolean`).

■ **Note** If you have a fewer number of uniquely numbered curly-bracket placeholders than fill arguments, you will receive a `FormatException` exception at runtime.

It is also permissible for a given placeholder to repeat within a given string. For example, if you are a Beatles fan and want to build the string `"9, Number 9, Number 9"`, you would write:

```
' John says...
Console.WriteLine("{0}, Number {0}, Number {0}", 9)
```

Also know that it is possible to position each placeholder in any location within a string literal, and you need not follow an increasing sequence. For example, consider the following code snippet:

```
' Prints: 20, 10, 30.
Console.WriteLine("{1}, {0}, {2}", 10, 20, 30)
```

.NET String Formatting Flags

If you require more elaborate formatting, each placeholder can optionally contain various format characters. Each format character can be typed in either uppercase or lowercase with little or no consequence. Table 3-3 shows your core formatting options.

Table 3-3. *.NET String Format Characters*

String Format Character	Meaning in Life
`C` or `c`	Used to format currency. By default, the flag will prefix the local cultural symbol (a dollar sign [$] for U.S. English).
`D` or `d`	Used to format decimal numbers. This flag may also specify the minimum number of digits used to pad the value.
`E` or `e`	Used for exponential notation.
`F` or `f`	Used for fixed-point formatting.
`G` or `g`	Stands for *general*. This character can be used to format a number to fixed or exponential format.

Continued

Table 3-3. *Continued*

String Format Character	Meaning in Life
N or n	Used for basic numerical formatting (with commas).
X or x	Used for hexadecimal formatting. If you use an uppercase "X", your hex format will also contain uppercase characters.

These format characters are suffixed to a given placeholder value using the colon token (e.g., {0:C}, {1:d}, {2:X}, and so on). Now, update the Main() method with the following logic:

```
' Now make use of some format tags.
Sub Main()
...
  Console.WriteLine("C format: {0:C}", 99989.987)
  Console.WriteLine("D9 format: {0:D9}", 99999)
  Console.WriteLine("E format: {0:E}", 99999.76543)
  Console.WriteLine("F3 format: {0:F3}", 99999.9999)
  Console.WriteLine("N format: {0:N}", 99999)
  Console.WriteLine("X format: {0:X}", 99999)
  Console.WriteLine("x format: {0:x}", 99999)
End Sub
```

Here we are defining numerous string literals, each of which has a segment not known until runtime. At runtime, the format character will be used internally by the Console type to print out the entire string in the desired format.

Formatting Strings Using String.Format()

Be aware that the use of the .NET string formatting characters are not limited to console programs! These same flags can be used when calling the shared String.Format() method. This can be helpful when you need to build a string containing numerical values in memory for use in any application type (Windows Forms, ASP.NET, XML web services, and so on). To illustrate, update Main() with the following final code:

```
' Now make use of some format tags.
Sub Main()
...
  ' Use the shared String.Format() method to build a new string.
  Dim formatStr As String
  formatStr = _
    String.Format("Don't you wish you had {0:C} in your account?", 99989.987)
  Console.WriteLine(formatStr)
End Sub
```

Figure 3-6 shows the output for the formatting logic used by the current application.

■ **Source Code** The BasicConsoleIO project is located under the Chapter 3 subdirectory.

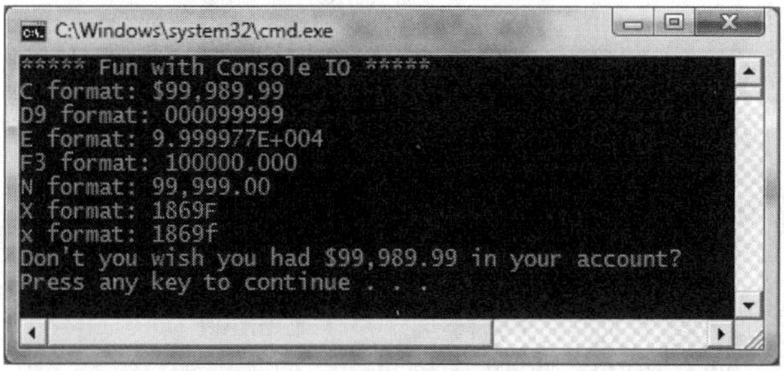

Figure 3-6. *The* `System.Console` *type in action*

System Data Types and VB Shorthand Notation

Like any programming language, VB defines an intrinsic set of data types, which are used to represent local variables, member variables, return values, and input parameters. Although many of the VB data types are named identically to data types found under VB6, be aware that there is *not* a direct mapping (especially in terms of a data type's maximum and minimum range).

■ **Note** The `UInteger`, `ULong`, and `SByte` data types are *not* CLS compliant (see Chapters 1 and 16 for details on CLS compliance). Therefore, if you expose these data types from an assembly, you cannot guarantee that every .NET programming language will be able to process this data.

The most significant change from VB6 is that the data type keywords of Visual Basic 2008 are actually shorthand notations for full-blown types in the `System` namespace. Table 3-4 documents the data types of VB 2008 (with the size of storage allocation), the `System` data type equivalents, and the range of each type.

Table 3-4. *The Intrinsic Data Types of VB 2008*

VB Keyword	CLS Compliant?	System Type	Range	Meaning in Life
`Boolean`	Yes	`System.Boolean`	`True` or `False`	Represents truth or falsity
`SByte`	No	`System.SByte`	–128 to 127	Signed 8-bit number
`Byte`	Yes	`System.Byte`	0 to 255	Unsigned 8-bit number
`Short`	Yes	`System.Int16`	–32,768 to 32,767	Signed 16-bit number
`UShort`	No	`System.UInt16`	0 to 65,535	Unsigned 16-bit number
`Integer`	Yes	`System.Int32`	–2,147,483,648 to 2,147,483,647	Signed 32-bit number
`UInteger`	No	`System.UInt32`	0 to 4,294,967,295	Unsigned 32-bit number
`Long`	Yes	`System.Int64`	–9,223,372,036,854,775,808 to 9,223,372,036,854,775,807	Signed 64-bit number

Continued

Table 3-4. *Continued*

VB Keyword	CLS Compliant?	System Type	Range	Meaning in Life
`ULong`	No	`System.UInt64`	0 to 18,446,744,073,709,551,615	Unsigned 64-bit number
`Char`	Yes	`System.Char`	U+0000 to U+ffff	A single 16-bit Unicode character
`Single`	Yes	`System.Single`	$\pm 1.5 \times 10^{45}$ to $\pm 3.4 \times 10^{38}$	32-bit floating-point number
`Double`	Yes	`System.Double`	$\pm 5.0 \times 10^{324}$ to $\pm 1.7 \times 10^{308}$	64-bit floating-point number
`Decimal`	Yes	`System.Decimal`	$\pm 1.0 \times 10e^{28}$ to $\pm 7.9 \times 10e^{28}$	A 96-bit signed number
`String`	Yes	`System.String`	Limited by system memory	Represents a set of Unicode characters
`Date`	Yes	`System.DateTime`	January 1, 0001 to December 31, 9999	Represents a time/date value
`Object`	Yes	`System.Object`	Any type can be stored in an object variable	The base class of all types in the .NET universe

Each of the numerical types (`Short`, `Integer`, and so forth) as well as the `Date` type map to a corresponding *structure* in the `System` namespace. In a nutshell, structures are "value types" allocated on the stack. On the other hand, `String` and `Object` are "reference types," meaning the variable is allocated on the managed heap. You will examine full details of value and reference types in Chapter 12; however, for the time being, simply understand that value types can be allocated into memory quickly and have a very fixed and predictable lifetime.

Variable Declaration and Initialization

When you are declaring a data type as a local variable (e.g., a variable within a member scope), you do so using the `Dim` and `As` keywords. By way of a few examples:

```
Sub MyMethod()
  ' Local variables are declared as follows:
  ' Dim variableName As dataType
  Dim age As Integer
  Dim firstName As String
  Dim isUserOnline As Boolean
End Sub
```

One helpful syntactic change that has occurred with the release of the .NET platform is the ability to declare a sequence of variables on a single line of code. VB6 also supported this ability, but the semantics were a bit nonintuitive and a source of subtle bugs. For example, under VB6, if you do not explicitly set the data types of each variable, the unqualified variables were set to the VB6 `Variant` data type:

```
' In this line of VB6 code, varOne
' is implicitly defined as a Variant!
Dim varOne, varTwo As Integer
```

This behavior is more than a bit annoying, given that the only way you are able to define multiple variables of the same type under VB6 is to write the following slightly redundant code:

```
Dim varOne As Integer, varTwo As Integer
```

or worse yet, on multiple lines of code:

```
Dim varOne As Integer
Dim varTwo As Integer
```

Although these approaches are still valid using VB 2008, when you declare multiple variables on a single line, they *all* are defined in terms of the specified data type. Thus, in the following VB 2008 code, you have created two variables of type `Integer`:

```
Sub MyOtherMethod()
  ' In this line of VB 2008 code, varOne
  ' and varTwo are both of type Integer!
  Dim varOne, varTwo As Integer
End Sub
```

On a final note, VB 2008 now supports the ability to assign a value to a variable directly at the point of declaration. To understand the significance of this new bit of syntax, consider the fact that under VB6, you were forced to write the following:

```
' VB6 code.
Dim i As Integer
i = 99
```

VB 2008 allows you to streamline variable assignment using the following notation:

```
Sub MyMethod()
  ' Local data can be initialized at the time of declaration:
  ' Dim variableName As dataType = initialValue
  Dim age As Integer = 36
  Dim firstName As String = "Sid"
  Dim isUserOnline As Boolean = True
End Sub
```

Default Values of Data Types

All VB 2008 data types have a default value that will automatically be assigned to the variable. The default values are very predictable, and can be summarized as follows:

- `Boolean` variables are set to `False`.
- Numeric data is set to `0` (or `0.0` in the case of floating-point data types).
- `Char` variables are set to a single empty character.
- `Date` types are set to `1/1/0001 12:00:00 AM`.
- Uninitialized object references (including `String` types) are set to `Nothing`.

Given these rules, ponder the following code, which illustrates the default values assigned to members in a `Module` (the same defaults would be applied to members of a `Class` as well):

```
' Fields of a class or module receive automatic default assignments.
Module Program
  Public myInt As Integer      ' Set to 0.
  Public myString As String    ' Set to Nothing.
  Public myBool As Boolean     ' Set to False.
  Public myObj As Object       ' Set to Nothing.
End Module
```

In Visual Basic 2008, the same rules of default values hold true for local variables defined within a given scope. Given this, the following method would return the value 0, as each local Integer has been automatically assigned the value 0:

```
Function Add() As Integer
  Dim a, b As Integer
  Return a + b  ' Returns zero.
End Function
```

The Data Type Class Hierarchy

It is very interesting to note that even the primitive .NET data types are arranged in a "class hierarchy." If you are new to the world of inheritance, you will discover the full details in Chapter 6. Until then, just understand that types at the top of a class hierarchy provide some default behaviors that are granted to the derived types. The relationship between these core system types can be depicted as shown in Figure 3-7.

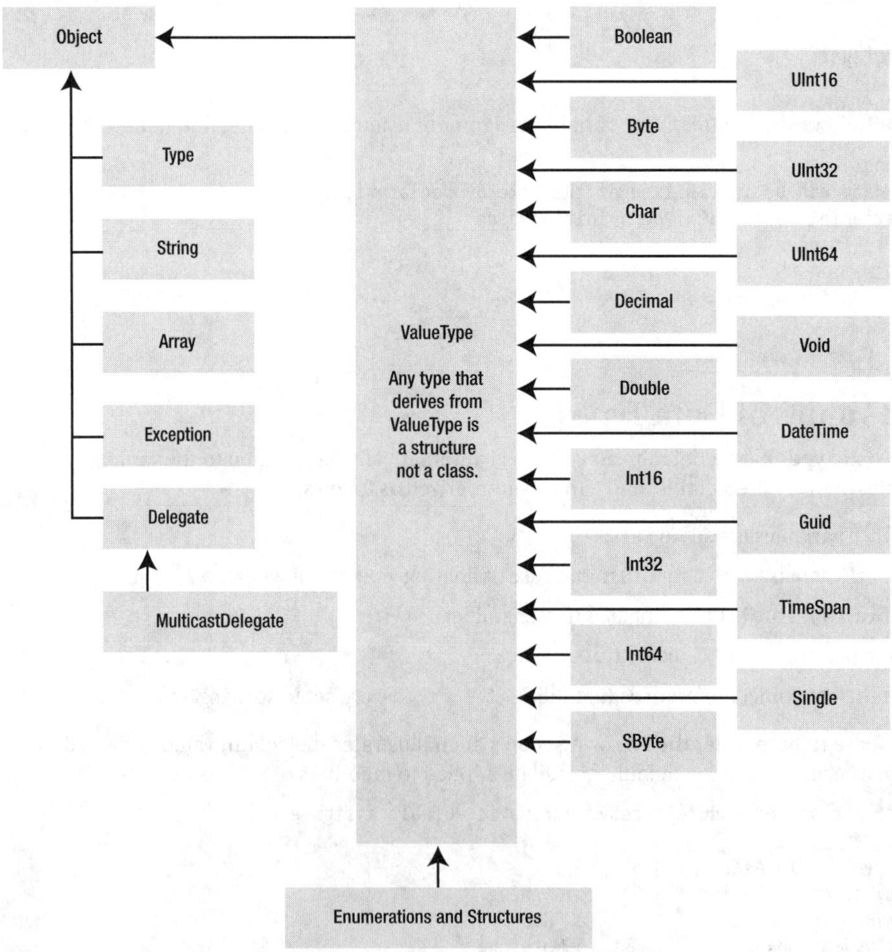

Figure 3-7. *The class hierarchy of* System *types*

Notice that each of these types ultimately derives from `System.Object`, which defines a set of methods (`ToString()`, `Equals()`, `GetHashCode()`, and so forth) common to all types in the .NET base class libraries (these methods are fully detailed in Chapter 6).

Also note that numerical data types derive from a class named `System.ValueType`. Descendants of `ValueType` are automatically allocated on the stack and therefore have a very predictable lifetime and are quite efficient. On the other hand, types that do not have `System.ValueType` in their inheritance chain (such as `System.Type`, `System.String`, `System.Array`, `System.Exception`, and `System.Delegate`) are not allocated on the stack, but on the garbage-collected heap.

Without getting too hung up on the details of `System.Object` and `System.ValueType` for the time being (again, more details in Chapter 12), simply know that because a VB 2008 keyword (such as `Integer`) is shorthand notation for the corresponding system type (in this case, `System.Int32`), the following is perfectly legal syntax, given that `System.Int32` (the VB 2008 `Integer`) eventually derives from `System.Object`, and therefore can invoke any of its public members:

```
Sub Main()
  ' A VB 2008 Integer is really a shorthand for System.Int32,
  ' which inherits the following members from System.Object.
  Console.WriteLine(12.GetHashCode())    ' Prints the type's hash code value.
  Console.WriteLine(12.Equals(23))       ' Prints False
  Console.WriteLine(12.ToString())       ' Returns the string value "12"
  Console.WriteLine(12.GetType())        ' Prints System.Int32
End Sub
```

Intrinsic Data Types and the New Keyword

All intrinsic data types support what is known as a *default constructor* (see Chapter 5). In a nutshell, this feature allows you to create a variable using the `New` keyword, which automatically sets the variable to its default value. Although it is more cumbersome to use the `New` keyword when creating a basic data type variable, the following is syntactically well-formed VB 2008 code:

```
' When you create a basic data type with New,
' it is automatically set to its default value.
Dim b1 As New Boolean()   ' b1 automatically set to False.
```

On a related note, you could also declare an intrinsic data type variable using the full type name through either of these approaches:

```
' These statements are also functionally identical.
Dim b2 As System.Boolean = New System.Boolean()
Dim b3 As System.Boolean
```

Of course, the chances that you will define a simple `Boolean` using the full type name or the `New` keyword in your code is slim to none. It is important, however, to always remember that the VB 2008 keywords for simple data types are little more than a shorthand notation for real types in the `System` namespace.

Experimenting with Numerical Data Types

To experiment with the intrinsic VB 2008 data types, create a new Console Application named BasicDataTypes. First of all, understand that the numerical types of .NET support `MaxValue` and `MinValue` properties that provide information regarding the range a given type can store. For example:

```
Sub Main()
  Console.WriteLine("***** Fun with Data Types *****")
  Console.WriteLine("Max of Integer: {0}", Integer.MaxValue)
```

```
  Console.WriteLine("Min of Integer: {0}", Integer.MinValue)
  Console.WriteLine("Max of Double: {0}", Double.MaxValue)
  Console.WriteLine("Min of Double: {0}", Double.MinValue)
End Sub
```

In addition to the MinValue/MaxValue properties, a given numerical system type may define additional useful members. For example, the System.Double type allows you to obtain the values for epsilon and infinity (which may be of interest to those of you with a mathematical flare):

```
Console.WriteLine("Double.Epsilon: {0}", Double.Epsilon)
Console.WriteLine("Double.PositiveInfinity: {0}", _
  Double.PositiveInfinity)
Console.WriteLine("Double.NegativeInfinity: {0}", _
 Double.NegativeInfinity)
```

Members of System.Boolean

Next, consider the System.Boolean data type. The only valid assignment a VB 2008 Boolean can take is from the set {True | False}. Given this point, it should be clear that System.Boolean does not support a MinValue/MaxValue property set, but rather TrueString/FalseString (which yields the string "True" or "False", respectively):

```
Console.WriteLine("Boolean.FalseString: {0}", Boolean.FalseString)
Console.WriteLine("Boolean.TrueString: {0}", Boolean.TrueString)
```

Members of System.Char

VB 2008 textual data is represented by the intrinsic String and Char keywords, which are simple shorthand notations for System.String and System.Char, both of which are Unicode under the hood. As you most certainly already know, a string is a contiguous set of characters (e.g., "Hello"). The Char data type can represent a single slot in a String type (e.g., "H").

By default, when you define textual data within double quotes, the VB 2008 compiler assumes you are defining a full-blown String type. However, to build a single character string literal that should be typed as a Char, place the character between double quotes and tack on a single "c" after the closing quote. Doing so ensures that the double-quoted text literal is indeed represented as a System.Char, rather than a System.String:

```
Dim myChar As Char = "a"c
```

Note When you enable Option Strict (described in the section "Understanding Option Strict" later in this chapter) for your project, the VB 2008 compiler demands that you tack on the c suffix to a Char data type when assigning a value.

The System.Char type provides you with a great deal of functionality beyond the ability to hold a single point of character data. Using the shared methods of System.Char, you are able to determine whether a given character is numerical, alphabetical, a point of punctuation, or whatnot. To illustrate, update Main() with the following statements:

```
' Fun with System.Char.
Dim myChar As Char = "a"c
Console.WriteLine("Char.IsDigit('a'): {0}", Char.IsDigit(myChar))
Console.WriteLine("Char.IsLetter('a'): {0}", Char.IsLetter(myChar))
```

```
Console.WriteLine("Char.IsWhiteSpace('Hello There', 5): {0}", _
  Char.IsWhiteSpace("Hello There", 5))
Console.WriteLine("Char.IsWhiteSpace('Hello There', 6): {0}", _
  Char.IsWhiteSpace("Hello There", 6))
Console.WriteLine("Char.IsPunctuation('?'): {0}", _
  Char.IsPunctuation("?"c))
```

As illustrated in the previous code snippet, the members of System.Char have two calling conventions: a single character or a string with a numerical index that specifies the position of the character to test.

Parsing Values from String Data

The .NET data types provide the ability to generate a variable of their underlying type given a textual equivalent (e.g., parsing). This technique can be extremely helpful when you wish to convert a bit of user input data (such as a selection from a GUI-based drop-down list box) into a numerical value. Consider the following parsing logic:

```
' Fun with parsing.
Dim b As Boolean = Boolean.Parse("True")
Console.WriteLine("Value of myBool: {0}", b)

Dim d As Double = Double.Parse("99.884")
Console.WriteLine("Value of myDbl: {0}", d)

Dim i As Integer = Integer.Parse("8")
Console.WriteLine("Value of myInt: {0}", i)

Dim c As Char = Char.Parse("w")
Console.WriteLine("Value of myChar: {0}", c)
```

■ **Source Code** The BasicDataTypes project is located under the Chapter 3 subdirectory.

Understanding the System.String Type

As mentioned, String is a native data type in VB 2008. Like all intrinsic types, the VB 2008 String keyword actually is a shorthand notation for a true type in the .NET base class library, which in this case is System.String. Therefore, you are able to declare a String variable using either of these notations:

```
' These two string declarations are functionally equivalent.
Dim firstName As String
Dim lastName As System.String
```

System.String provides a number of methods you would expect from such a utility class, including methods that return the number of characters in the string, find substrings within the current string, convert to and from uppercase/lowercase, and so forth. Table 3-5 lists some (but by no means all) of the interesting members.

Table 3-5. *Select Members of* `System.String`

Member of `String` Class	Meaning in Life
`Chars`	This property returns a specific character within the current string.
`Length`	This property returns the length of a string.
`Compare()`	This method compares two strings.
`Contains()`	This method determines whether a string contains a specific substring.
`Equals()`	This method tests whether two string objects contain identical character data.
`Format()`	This method formats a string using other primitives (i.e., numerical data, other strings) and the `{0}` notation examined earlier in this chapter.
`Insert()`	This method inserts a string within a given string.
`PadLeft()` `PadRight()`	These methods are used to pad a string with some character.
`Remove()` `Replace()`	These methods are used to receive a copy of a string, with modifications (characters removed or replaced).
`Split()`	This method returns a `String` array containing the substrings in this instance that are delimited by elements of a specified `Char` or `String` array.
`Trim()`	This method removes all occurrences of a set of specified characters from the beginning and end of the current string.
`ToUpper()` `ToLower()`	These methods create a copy of the current string in uppercase or lowercase format.

Basic String Manipulation

Working with the members of `System.String` is as you would expect. Simply create a `String` variable and make use of the provided functionality via the dot operator. Do be aware that a few of the members of `System.String` are shared members and are therefore called at the class (rather than the object) level. Assume you have created a new Console Application named FunWithStrings and updated `Main()` as follows:

```
Module Program
  Sub Main()
    Console.WriteLine("***** Fun with Strings *****")
    Dim firstName As String = "June"
    Console.WriteLine("Value of firstName: {0}", firstName)
    Console.WriteLine("firstName has {0} characters.", firstName.Length)
    Console.WriteLine("firstName in uppercase: {0}", firstName.ToUpper())
    Console.WriteLine("firstName in lowercase: {0}", firstName.ToLower())

    Dim myValue As Integer = 3456787
    Console.WriteLine("Hex vaule of myValue is: {0:X}", myValue)
    Console.WriteLine("Currency value of myValue is: {0:C}", myValue)
  End Sub
End Module
```

Notice how the `ToUpper()` and `ToLower()` methods (as well as the `Length` property) have not been implemented as shared members and are therefore called directly from a `String` object.

String Concatenation (and the "Newline" Constant)

String variables can be connected together to build a larger `String` via the VB 2008 ampersand operator (&). As you may know, this technique is formally termed *string concatenation*:

```
Module Program
  Sub Main()
    Console.WriteLine("***** Fun with Strings *****")
...
    Dim s1 As String = "Programming the "
    Dim s2 As String = "PsychoDrill (PTP)"
    Dim s3 As String = s1 & s2
    Console.WriteLine(s3)
  End Sub
End Module
```

Note VB 2008 also allows you to concatenate `String` objects using the plus sign (+). However, given that the + symbol can be applied to numerous data types, there is a possibility that your `String` object cannot be "added" to one of the operands. Therefore use of the ampersand (&) is the recommend approach.

You may be interested to know that the VB 2008 & symbol is processed by the compiler to emit a call to the shared `String.Concat()` method. In fact, if you were to compile the previous code and open the assembly within `ildasm.exe` (see Chapter 1), you would find CIL code similar to what is shown in Figure 3-8.

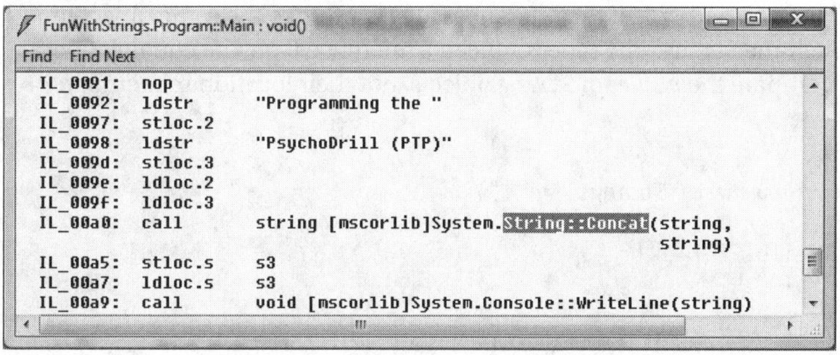

Figure 3-8. *The VB 2008 & operator results in a call to* `String.Concat()`.

Given this, it is possible to perform string concatenation by calling `String.Concat()` directly (although you really have not gained anything by doing so, in fact you have incurred additional keystrokes!):

```
Module Program
  Sub Main()
    Console.WriteLine("***** Fun with Strings *****")
...
    Dim s1 As String = "Programming the "
    Dim s2 As String = "PsychoDrill (PTP)"
    Dim s3 As String = String.Concat(s1, s2)
    Console.WriteLine(s3)
  End Sub
End Module
```

On a related note, do know that the VB6-style string constants (such as `vbLf`, `vbCrLf`, and `vbCr`) are still exposed through the `Microsoft.VisualBasic.dll` assembly (see Chapter 2). Therefore, if you wish to concatenate a string that contains various newline characters (for display purposes), you may do so as follows:

```
Module Program
  Sub Main()
    Console.WriteLine("***** Fun with Strings *****")
...
    Dim s1 As String = "Programming the "
    Dim s2 As String = "PsychoDrill (PTP)"
    Dim s3 As String = String.Concat(s1, s2)
    s3 &= vbLf & "was a great industrial project."
    Console.WriteLine(s3)
  End Sub
End Module
```

■ Note If you have a background in C-based languages, understand that the `vbLf` constant is functionally equivalent to the newline escape character (`\n`).

Strings and Equality

As fully explained in Chapter 12, a *reference type* is an object allocated on the garbage-collected managed heap. By default, when you perform a test for equality on reference types (via the VB 2008 = and <> operators), you will be returned `True` if the references are pointing to the same object in memory. However, even though the `String` data type is indeed a reference type, the equality operators have been redefined to compare the *values* of `String` objects, not their location in memory:

```
Module Program
  Sub Main()
    Console.WriteLine("***** Fun with Strings *****")
...
    Dim strA As String = "Hello!"
    Dim strB As String = "Yo!"
    ' False!
    Console.WriteLine("strA = strB?: {0}", strA = strB)
    strB = "HELLO!"

    ' False!
    Console.WriteLine("strA = strB?: {0}", strA = strB)
    strB = "Hello!"

    ' True!
    Console.WriteLine("strA = strB?: {0}", strA = strB)
  End Sub
End Module
```

Notice that the VB 2008 equality operators perform a case-sensitive, character-by-character equality test. Therefore, `"Hello!"` is not equal to `"HELLO!"`, which is different from `"hello!"`.

Strings Are Immutable

One of the interesting aspects of System.String is that once you assign a String object with its initial value, the character data *cannot be changed.* At first glance, this might seem like a flat-out lie, given that we are always reassigning strings to new values and due to the fact that the System.String type defines a number of methods that appear to modify the character data in one way or another (uppercase, lowercase, etc.). However, if you look closer at what is happening behind the scenes, you will notice the methods of the String type are in fact returning you a brand-new String object in a modified format:

```
Module Program
  Sub Main()
    Console.WriteLine("***** Fun with Strings *****")
...
    ' Set initial string value.
    Dim initialString As String = "This is my string."
    Console.WriteLine("Initial value: {0}", initialString)

    ' Uppercase the initialString?
    Dim upperString As String = initialString.ToUpper()
    Console.WriteLine("Upper case copy: {0}", upperString)

    ' initialString is in the same format!
    Console.WriteLine("Initial value: {0}", initialString)
  End Sub
End Module
```

If you examine the relevant output in Figure 3-9, you can verify that the original String object (initialString) is not uppercased when calling ToUpper(), rather you are returned a copy of the string in a modified format.

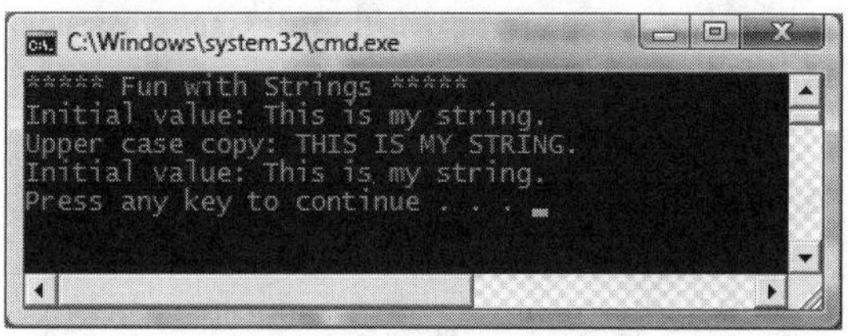

Figure 3-9. *Strings are immutable!*

The same law of immutability holds true when you use the VB 2008 assignment operator. To illustrate, comment out any existing code within Main() (to decrease the amount of generated CIL code) and add the following code statements:

```
Module Program
  Sub Main()
    Dim strObjA As String = "String A reporting."
    strObjA = "This is a new string"
  End Sub
End Module
```

Now, compile your application and load the assembly into ildasm.exe (again, see Chapter 1). If you were to double-click the Main() method, you would find the CIL code shown in Figure 3-10.

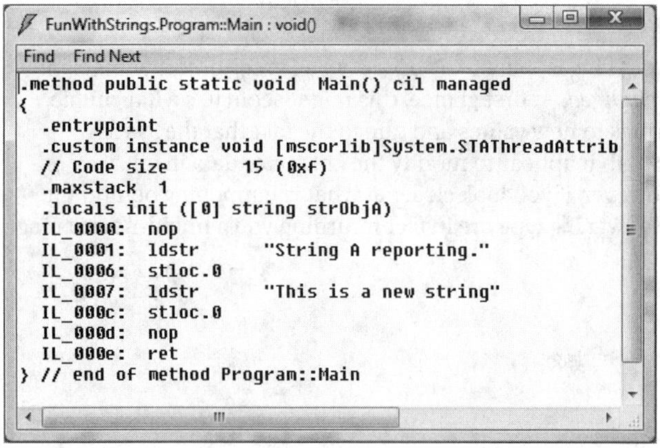

Figure 3-10. *Assigning a value to a* `String` *object results in a new* `String` *object.*

Although I don't imagine you are too interested in the low-level details of the CIL, do note that the `Main()` method makes numerous calls to the `ldstr` (load string) opcode. Simply put, the `ldstr` opcode of CIL creates a new `String` object. The previous `String` object that contained the value `"String A reporting."` is no longer being used by the program, and will eventually be garbage collected.

So, what exactly are we to gather from this insight? In a nutshell, the `String` type can be inefficient and result in bloated code if misused. If you need to represent basic character data such as a US Social Security number, first or last names, or simple string literals used within your application, the `String` data type is the perfect choice.

However, if you are building an application that makes heavy use of textual data (such as a word processing program), it would be a very bad idea to represent the word processing data using `String` types, as you will most certainly (and often indirectly) end up making unnecessary copies of string data. So what is a programmer to do? Glad you asked.

The System.Text.StringBuilder Type

Given that the `String` type can be quite inefficient when used with reckless abandon, the .NET base class libraries provide the `System.Text` namespace. Within this (relatively small) namespace lives a class named `StringBuilder`. Like the `System.String` class, `StringBuilder` defines methods that allow you to replace or format segments and so forth.

What is unique about `StringBuilder` is that when you call members of `StringBuilder`, you are directly modifying the object's internal character data, not obtaining a copy of the data in a modified format (and it is thus more efficient). When you create an instance of `StringBuilder`, you will supply the object's initial startup values via one of many *constructors*. Chapter 5 dives into the details of class constructors; however, if you are new to the topic, simply understand that constructors allow you to create an object with an initial state when you apply the `New` keyword. Consider the following usage of `StringBuilder`:

```
Imports System.Text  ' StringBuilder lives here!

Module Program
  Sub Main()
  ...
    ' Use the StringBuilder.
    Dim sb As New StringBuilder("**** Fantastic Games ****")
    sb.Append(vbLf)
```

```
    sb.AppendLine("Half Life 2")
    sb.AppendLine("Beyond Good and Evil")
    sb.AppendLine("Deus Ex 1 and 2")
    sb.Append("System Shock")
    sb.Replace("2", "Deus Ex: Invisible War")
    Console.WriteLine(sb)
    Console.WriteLine("sb has {0} chars.", sb.Length)
  End Sub
End Module
```

Here we see constructed a `StringBuilder` set to the initial value `"**** Fantastic Games ****"`. As you can see, we are appending to the internal buffer and are able to replace (or remove) characters at will. By default, a `StringBuilder` is only able to hold a string of 16 characters or less; however, this initial value can be changed via a constructor argument. While the buffer will expand automatically when needed, this might not be particularly efficient if you know the buffer will need to be quite large, so a more efficient approach is to create the buffer with a bigger size from the outset:

```
' Make a StringBuilder with an initial size of 256.
Dim sb As New StringBuilder("**** Fantastic Games ****", 256)
```

Again, if you append more characters than the specified limit, the `StringBuilder` object will copy its data into a new instance and grow the buffer by the specified limit.

■ **Source Code** The FunWithStrings project is located under the Chapter 3 subdirectory.

Narrowing (Explicit) and Widening (Implicit) Data Type Conversions

Now that you understand how to interact with intrinsic data types, let's examine the related topic of *data type conversion*. Assume you have a new Console Application (named TypeConversions) that defines the following module:

```
Module Program
  Sub Main()
    Console.WriteLine("***** The Amazing Addition Program *****")
    Dim a As Short = 9
    Dim b As Short = 10
    Console.WriteLine("a + b = {0}", Add(a, b))
  End Sub

  Function Add(ByVal x As Integer, ByVal y As Integer) As Integer
    Return x + y
  End Function
End Module
```

Notice that the `Add()` method expects to be sent two `Integer` parameters. However, note that the `Main()` method is in fact sending in two `Short` variables. While this might seem like a complete and total mismatch of data types, the program compiles and executes without error, returning the expected result of 19.

The reason that the compiler treats this code as syntactically sound is due to the fact that there is no possibility for loss of data. Given that the maximum value of a `Short` (32,767) is well within the range of an `Integer` (2,147,483,647), the compiler automatically *widens* each `Short` to an `Integer` by copying the `Short` into an `Integer`. Technically speaking, *widening* is the term used to define a safe "upward cast" that does not result in a loss of data. Table 3-6 illustrates which data types can be safely widened to specific data types.

Table 3-6. *Safe Widening Conversions*

VB 2008 Type	Safely Widens to . . .
Byte	SByte, UInteger, Integer, ULong, Long, Single, Double, Decimal
SByte	SByte, Integer, Long, Single, Double, Decimal
Short	Integer, Long, Single, Double, Decimal
SByte	UInteger, Integer, ULong, Long, Single, Double, Decimal
Char	SByte, UInteger, Integer, ULong, Long, Single, Double, Decimal
Integer	Long, Double, Decimal
UInteger	Long, Double, Decimal
Long	Decimal
ULong	Decimal
Single	Double

Although this automatic widening worked in our favor for the previous example, other times this "automatic type conversion" can be the source of subtle and difficult-to-debug runtime errors. For example, assume that you have modified the values assigned to the a and b variables within Main() to values that (when added together) overflow the maximum value of a Short. Furthermore, assume you are storing the return value of the Add() method within a new local Short variable, rather than directly printing the result to the console:

```
Module Program
  Sub Main()
    Console.WriteLine("***** The Amazing Addition Program *****")
    Dim a As Short = 30000
    Dim b As Short = 30000
    Dim answer As Short = Add(a, b)
    Console.WriteLine("a + b = {0}", answer)
  End Sub

  Function Add(ByVal x As Integer, ByVal y As Integer) As Integer
    Return x + y
  End Function
End Module
```

In this case, although your application compiles just fine, when you run the application you will find the CLR throws a runtime error, specifically a System.OverflowException, as shown in Figure 3-11.

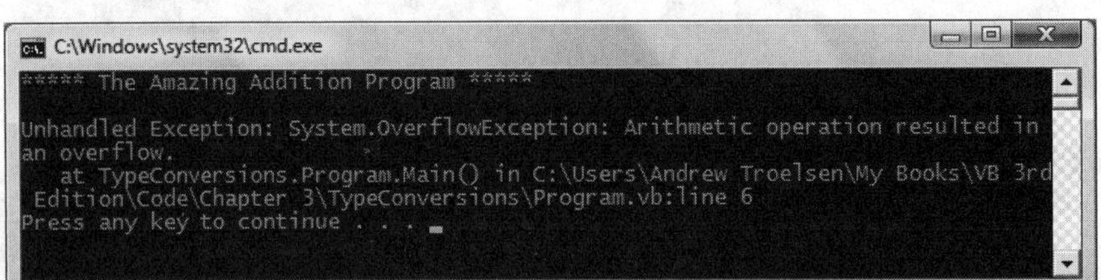

Figure 3-11. *Oops! The value returned from* Add() *was greater than the maximum value of a* Short!

The problem is that although the `Add()` method can return an `Integer` with the value `60,000` (as this fits within the range of an `Integer`), the value cannot be stored in a `Short` (as it overflows the bounds of this data type). In this case, the CLR attempts to apply a *narrowing operation*, which results in a runtime error. As you can guess, narrowing is the logical opposite of widening, in that a larger value is stored within a smaller variable. Not all narrowing conversions result in a `System.OverflowException`, of course. For example, consider the following code:

```
' This narrowing conversion is a-OK.
Dim myByte As Byte
Dim myInt As Integer = 200
myByte = myInt
Console.WriteLine("Value of myByte: {0}", myByte)
```

Here, the value contained within the `Integer` variable `myInt` is safely within the range of a `Byte`, therefore the narrowing operation does not result in a runtime error. Although it is true that many narrowing conversions are safe and nondramatic in nature, you may agree that it would be ideal to trap narrowing conversions at *compile time* rather than *runtime*. Thankfully, there is such a way, using the VB 2008 `Option Strict` directive.

Understanding Option Strict

`Option Strict` ensures compile-time (rather than runtime) notification of any narrowing conversion so it can be corrected in a timely fashion. If we are able to identify these narrowing conversions upfront, we can take a corrective course of action and decrease the possibility of nasty runtime errors.

A Visual Basic 2008 project, as well as specific `*.vb` files within a given project, can elect to enable or disable implicit narrowing via the `Option Strict` directive. When turning this option `On`, you are informing the compiler to check for such possibilities during the compilation process. Thus, if you were to add the following to the very top of your current file:

```
' Option directives must be the very first code statements in a *.vb file!
Option Strict On
```

you would now find a compile-time error for each implicit narrowing conversion, as shown in Figure 3-12.

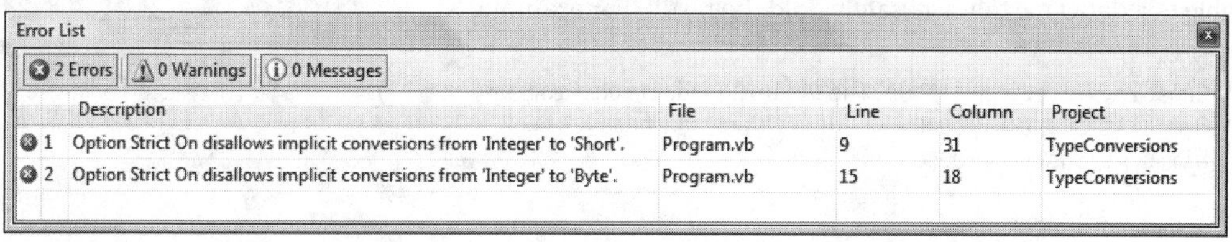

Figure 3-12. `Option Strict` *disables automatic narrowing of data.*

Here, we have enabled `Option Strict` on a single file within our project. This approach can be useful when you wish to selectively allow narrowing conversions within specific `*.vb` files. However, if you wish to enable `Option Strict` for each and every file in your project, you can do so using the Compile tab of the My Project dialog box, as shown in Figure 3-13.

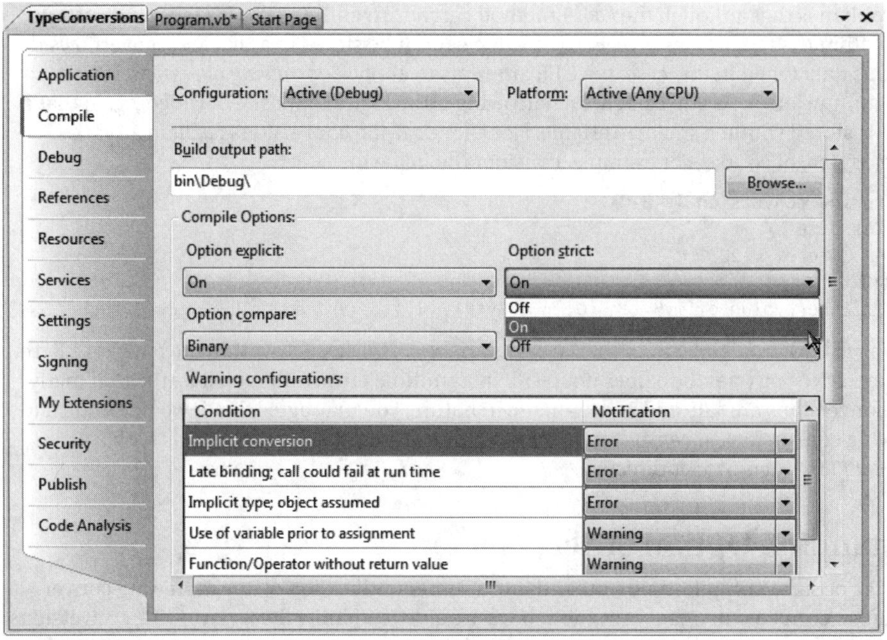

Figure 3-13. *Enabling* `Option Strict` *on the project level*

Note Under Visual Studio 2008, `Option Strict` is disabled for new Visual Basic 2008 projects. I would recommend, however, that you always enable this setting for each application you are creating, given that it is far better to resolve problems at compile time than runtime!

Now that we have some compile-time checking, we are able to resolve the error using one of two approaches. The most direct (and often more favorable) choice is to simply redefine the variable to a data type that will safely hold the result. For example:

```
Sub Main()
  Console.WriteLine("***** The Amazing Addition Program *****")
  Dim a As Short = 30000
  Dim b As Short = 30000

  ' Can no longer use:
  ' Dim answer As Short = Add(a, b)

  Dim answer As Integer = Add(a, b)
  Console.WriteLine("a + b = {0}", answer)
...
End Sub
```

Another approach is to make use of an explicit Visual Basic 2008 type conversion function, such as `CByte()` for this example:

```
Sub Main()
...
  Dim myByte As Byte
  Dim myInt As Integer = 200
```

```
  ' This will no longer work:
  ' myByte = myInt

  myByte = CByte(myInt)
  Console.WriteLine("Value of myByte: {0}", myByte)
End Sub
```

Explicit Conversion Functions

Visual Basic 2008 provides a number of conversion functions in addition to CByte() that enable you to explicitly allow a narrowing cast when Option Strict is enabled. Table 3-7 documents the core VB 2008 conversion functions.

Table 3-7. *VB 2008 Conversion Functions*

Conversion Function	Meaning in Life
CBool	Copies a Boolean expression (such as the number 0) into a Boolean value
CByte	Copies an expression into a Byte
CChar	Copies the first character of a string into a Char
CDate	Copies a string containing a data expression into a Date
CDbl	Copies a numeric expression double precision
CDec	Copies a numeric expression of the Decimal type
CInt	Copies a numeric expression into an Integer by rounding
CLng	Copies a numeric expression into a long integer by rounding
CObj	Copies any item into an Object
CSByte	Copies a numeric expression into an SByte by rounding
CShort	Copies a numeric expression into a Short by rounding
CSng	Copies a numeric expression into a Single
CStr	Returns a new string representation of the expression
CUInt	Copies a numeric expression into a UInteger by rounding
CULng	Copies a numeric expression into a ULong by rounding
CUShort	Copies a numeric expression into a UShort by rounding

Visual Basic 2008 also supports the CType function. CType takes two arguments, the first is the "thing you have," while the second is the "thing you want." For example, the following conversions are functionally equivalent:

```
Sub Main()
...
  Dim myByte As Byte
  Dim myInt As Integer = 200
  myByte = CByte(myInt)
  myByte = CType(myInt, Byte)
  Console.WriteLine("Value of myByte: {0}", myByte)
End Sub
```

One benefit of the CType function is that it handles all the conversions of the (primarily VB6-centric) conversion functions shown in Table 3-7. Furthermore, as you will see later in this text,

CType allows you to convert between base and derived classes, as well as objects and their implemented interfaces.

■ **Note** As you will see in Chapter 12, VB 2008 provides alternatives to CType—DirectCast and TryCast. However, they can be used only if the arguments are related by inheritance or interface implementation.

The Role of System.Convert

To wrap up the topic of data type conversions, I'd like to point out the fact that the System namespace defines a class named Convert that can also be used to widen or narrow a data assignment:

```
Sub Main()
...
  Dim myByte As Byte
  Dim myInt As Integer = 200
  myByte = CByte(myInt)
  myByte = CType(myInt, Byte)
  myByte = Convert.ToByte(myInt)
  Console.WriteLine("Value of myByte: {0}", myByte)
End Sub
```

One benefit of using System.Convert is that it provides a language-neutral manner to convert between data types. However, given that Visual Basic 2008 provides numerous built-in conversion functions (CBool, CByte, and the like), using the Convert type to do your data type conversions is usually nothing more than a matter of personal preference.

■ **Source Code** The TypeConversions project is located under the Chapter 3 subdirectory.

Building Visual Basic 2008 Code Statements

As a software developer, you are no doubt aware that a *statement* is simply a line of code that can be processed by the compiler (without error, of course). For example, you have already seen how to craft a local variable declaration statement over the course of this chapter:

```
' VB 2008 variable declaration statements.
Dim i As Integer = 10
Dim j As System.Int32 = 20
Dim k As New Integer()
```

On a related note, you have also previewed the correct syntax to declare a Function using the syntax of VB 2008:

```
Function Add(ByVal x As Integer, ByVal y As Integer) As Integer
  Return x + y
End Function
```

While it is true that when you are comfortable with the syntax of your language of choice, you tend to intuitively know what constitutes a valid statement, there are two idioms of VB 2008 code statements that deserve special mention to the uninitiated.

The Statement Continuation Character

White space (meaning blank lines of code) are ignored by the VB 2008 compiler unless you attempt to define a single code statement over multiple lines of code. This is quite different from C-based languages, where white space never matters, given that languages in the C family explicitly mark the end of a statement with a semicolon and scope with curly brackets.

In this light, the following two C# functions are functionally identical (although the second version is hardly readable and very bad style!):

```
// C# Add() method take one.
public int Add(int x, int y)
{ return x + y; }

// C# Add() method take two.
public int Add(
int x, int y) { return x
   +
 y;      }
```

Under Visual Basic 2008, if you wish to define a statement or member over multiple lines of code, you must split each line using the underbar (_) token, formally termed the *statement continuation character*. Furthermore, there *must* be a blank space on each side of the statement continuation character. Thus the following:

```
' VB 2008 Add() method take one.
Function Add(ByVal x As Integer, _
  ByVal y As Integer) As Integer
    Return x + y
End Function

' VB 2008 Add() method take two.
Function Add(ByVal x As Integer, _
  ByVal y As Integer) _
  As Integer
    Return x + y
End Function

' VB 2008 Add() method take three.
Function Add(ByVal x As Integer, _
  ByVal y As Integer) _
  As Integer
    Return x + y
End _
Function
```

Of course, you would never use the statement continuation character as shown in the last iteration of the `Add()` method, as the code is less than readable. In the real world, this feature is most helpful when defining or calling a member that takes a great number of arguments, to space them out in such a way that you can view them within your editor of choice (rather than scrolling the horizontal scrollbar to see the full list of arguments!).

Defining Multiple Statements on a Single Line

Sometimes it is convenient to define multiple code statements on a single line of code within the editor. For example, assume you have a set of local variables that need to be assigned to initial values. While you could assign a value to each variable on discrete lines of code:

```
Sub MyMethod()
  Dim s As String
  Dim i As Integer
  s = "Fred"
  i = 10
End Sub
```

you can compact the scope of this subroutine using the colon character:

```
Sub MyMethod()
  Dim s As String
  Dim i As Integer
  s = "Fred" : i = 10
End Sub
```

Understand that misuse of the colon can easily result in hard-to-read code. As well, when combined with the statement continuation character, you can end up with nasty statements such as the following:

```
Sub MyMethod()
  Dim s As String : Dim i As Integer
  s = "Fred" _
  : i = 10
End Sub
```

To be sure, defining multiple statements on a single line using the colon character should be used sparingly. For the most part, this language feature is most useful when you need to make simple assignments to multiple variables.

VB 2008 Flow-Control Constructs

Now that you can define a single simple code statement, let's examine the flow-control keywords that allow you to alter the flow of your program and several keywords that allow you to build complex code statements using the `And`, `Or`, and `Not` operators.

Like other programming languages, VB 2008 defines several ways to make runtime decisions regarding how your application should function. In a nutshell, we are offered the following flow-control constructs:

- The `If/Then/Else` statement
- The `Select/Case` statement

The If/Then/Else Statement

First up, you have your good friend, the `If/Then/Else` statement. In the simplest form, the `If` construct does not have a corresponding `Else`. Within the `If` statement, you will construct an expression that can resolve to a Boolean value. For example:

```
Sub Main()
  Dim userDone As Boolean

  ' Gather user input to assign
  ' Boolean value...

  If userDone = True Then
    Console.WriteLine("Thanks for running this app")
```

```
  End If
End Sub
```

A slightly more complex `If` statement can involve any number of `Else` statements to account for a range of values set to the expression being tested against:

```
Sub Main()
  Dim userOption As String

  ' Read user option from command line.
  userOption = Console.ReadLine()

  If userOption = "GodMode" Then
    Console.WriteLine("You will never die...cheater!")
  ElseIf userOption = "FullLife" Then
    Console.WriteLine("At the end, heh?")
  ElseIf userOption = "AllAmmo" Then
    Console.WriteLine("Now we can rock and roll!")
  Else
    Console.WriteLine("Unknown option...")
  End If
End Sub
```

Note that any secondary "else" condition is marked with the `ElseIf` keyword, while the final condition is simply `Else`.

Building Complex Conditional Expressions

The expression tested against within a flow-control construct need not be a simple comparison. If required, you are able to leverage the VB 2008 equality/relational operators listed in Table 3-8.

Table 3-8. *VB 2008 Relational and Equality Operators*

VB 2008 Equality/Relational Operator	Example Usage	Meaning in Life
=	`If age = 30 Then`	Returns `True` only if the two expressions are the same
<>	`If "Foo" <> myStr Then`	Returns `True` only if the two expressions are different

<
>
<=
>=
	`If bonus < 2000 Then`
	`If bonus > 2000 Then`
	`If bonus <= 2000 Then`
	`If bonus >= 2000 Then`
		Returns `True` if the first expression is less than, greater than, less than or equal to, or greater than or equal to expression B, respectively

■ **Note** Unlike C-based languages, the VB 2008 = token is used to denote both assignment and equality semantics (therefore VB 2008 does not supply a == operator).

In addition, you may build a complex expression to test within a flow-control construct using the code conditional operators (also known as the logical operators) listed in Table 3-9. This table outlines the most common conditional operators of the language.

Table 3-9. *VB 2008 Conditional Operators*

VB 2008 Conditional Operator	Example	Meaning in Life
And	If age = 30 And name = "Fred" Then	Conditional AND operator, where both conditions must be True for the condition to be True
AndAlso	If age = 30 AndAlso name = "Fred" Then	Conditional AND operator that supports *short-circuiting*, meaning if the first expression is False, the second expression is not evaluated
Or	If age = 30 Or name = "Fred" Then	Conditional OR operator
OrElse	If age = 30 OrElse name = "Fred" Then	Conditional OR operator that supports *short-circuiting*, meaning if either expression is True, True is returned
Not	If Not myBool Then	Conditional NOT operator

As I am assuming you have prior experience in BASIC or C-based languages, I won't belabor the use of these operators. If you require additional details beyond the following code snippet, I will assume you will consult the .NET Framework 3.5 SDK documentation. However, here is a simple example:

```
Sub Main()
  Dim userOption As String
  Dim userAge As Integer

  ' Read user option from command line.
  userOption = Console.ReadLine()
  userAge = Integer.Parse(Console.ReadLine())

If userOption = "AdultMode" And userAge >= 21 Then
    Console.WriteLine("We call this Hot Coffee Mode...")
  ElseIf userOption = "AllAmmo" Then
    Console.WriteLine("Now we can rock and roll!")
  Else
    Console.WriteLine("Unknown option...")
  End If
End Sub
```

The Select/Case Statement

The other selection construct offered by VB 2008 is the Select statement. This can be a more compact alternative to the If/Then/Else statement when you wish to handle program flow based on a known set of choices. For example, the following Main() method prompts the user for one of three known values. If the user enters an unknown value, you can account for this using the Case Else statement:

```
Sub Main()
  ' Prompt user with choices.
  Console.WriteLine("Welcome to the world of .NET")
  Console.WriteLine("1 = C#  2 = C++/CLI 3 = VB 2008")
  Console.Write("Please select your implementation language: ")
```

```
  ' Get choice.
  Dim s As String = Console.ReadLine()
  Dim n As Integer = Integer.Parse(s)

  ' Based on input, act accordingly...
  Select Case n
    Case Is = 1
      Console.WriteLine("C# is all about managed code.")
    Case Is = 2
      Console.WriteLine("Maintaining a legacy system, are we?")
    Case Is = 3
      Console.WriteLine("VB 2008: Full OO capabilities...")
    Case Else
      Console.WriteLine("Well...good luck with that!")
  End Select
End Sub
```

VB 2008 Iteration Constructs

All programming languages provide ways to repeat blocks of code until a terminating condition has been met. Regardless of which language you are coming from, the VB 2008 iteration statements should cause no raised eyebrows and require little explanation. In a nutshell, VB 2008 provides the following iteration constructs:

- For/Next loop
- For Each loop
- Do/While loop
- Do/Until loop
- With loop

Let's quickly examine each looping construct in turn. Here, I will only concentrate on the core features of each construct. I'll assume that you will consult the .NET Framework 3.5 SDK documentation if you require further details.

For/Next Loop

When you need to iterate over a block of code statements a fixed number of times, the For statement is the looping construct of champions. In essence, you are able to specify how many times a block of code repeats itself:

```
Sub Main()
  ' Prints out the numbers 5 - 25, inclusive.
  Dim i As Integer
  For i = 5 To 25
    Console.WriteLine("Number is: {0}", i)
  Next
End Sub
```

One nice improvement to the For looping construct is we are now able declare the counter variable directly within the For statement itself (rather than in a separate code statement). Therefore, the previous code sample could be slightly streamlined as the following:

```
Sub Main()
  ' A slightly simplified For loop.
  For i As Integer = 5 To 25
    Console.WriteLine("Number is: {0}", i)
  Next
End Sub
```

The For loop can also make use of the Step keyword to offset the value of the counter. For example, if you wish to increment the counter variable by five with each iteration, you would do so with the following:

```
Sub Main()
  ' Increment i by 5 with each pass.
  For i As Integer = 5 To 25 Step 5
    Console.WriteLine("Number is: {0}", i)
  Next
End Sub
```

For/Each Loop

The For/Each construct is a variation of the standard For loop, where you are able to iterate over the contents of an array without the need to explicitly monitor the container's upper limit (as in the case of a traditional For/Next loop). Assume you have defined an array of String objects and wish to print each item to the command window (VB 2008 array syntax will be fully examined in the next chapter). In the following code snippet, note that the For Each statement can define the type of item iterated over directly within the statement:

```
Sub Main()
  Dim myStrings() As String = _
    {"Fun", "with", "VB 2008"}

  For Each str As String In myStrings
    Console.WriteLine(str)
  Next
End Sub
```

or on discrete lines of code:

```
Sub Main()
  Dim myStrings() As String = _
    {"Fun", "with", "VB 2008"}

  Dim item As String
  For Each item In myStrings
    Console.WriteLine(item)
  Next
End Sub
```

In these examples, our iterator was explicitly defined as a String data type, given that our array is full of strings as well. However, if you wish to iterate over an array of Integers (or any other type), you would simply define the counter in the terms of the items in the array. For example:

```
Sub Main()
  ' Looping over an array of Integers.
  Dim myInts() As Integer = _
  {10, 20, 30, 40}
```

```
  For Each int As Integer In myInts
    Console.WriteLine(int)
  Next
End Sub
```

■ **Note** The `For Each` construct can iterate over any object that supports the correct infrastructure. I'll hold off on the details until Chapter 9, as this aspect of the `For Each` loop entails an understanding of interface-based programming and the system-supplied `IEnumerator` and `IEnumerable` interfaces.

Do/While and Do/Until Looping Constructs

You have already seen that the `For/Next` statement is typically used when you have some foreknowledge of the number of iterations you want to perform. The `Do` statements, on the other hand, are useful for those times when you are uncertain how long it might take for a terminating condition to be met (such as when gathering user input).

`Do/While` and `Do/Until` are (in many ways) interchangeable. `Do/While` keeps looping *while* the terminating condition is true. On the other hand, `Do/Until` keeps looping *until* the terminating condition is true. For example:

```
' Keep looping until X is not equal to an empty string.
Do
  ' Some code statements to loop over.
Loop Until X <> ""

' Keep looping as long as X is equal to an empty string.
Do
  ' Some code statements to loop over.
Loop While X = ""
```

Note that in these last two examples, the test for the terminating condition was placed at the end of the `Loop` keyword. Using this syntax, you can rest assured that the code within the loop will be executed at least once (given that the test to exit the loop occurs after the first iteration). If you prefer to allow for the possibility that the code within the loop may never be executed, move the `Until` or `While` clause to the beginning of the loop:

```
' Keep looping until X is not equal to an empty string.
Do Until X <> ""
  ' Some code to loop over.
Loop

' Keep looping as long as X is not equal to an empty string.
Do While X = ""
  ' Some code to loop over.
Loop
```

Finally, understand that VB 2008 still supports the raw `While` loop. However, the `Wend` keyword has been replaced with a more fitting `End While`:

```
Dim j As Integer
While j < 20
  Console.Write(j & ", ")
  j += 1
End While
```

The With Construct

To wrap this chapter up, allow me to say that the VB6 `With` construct is still supported under VB 2008. In a nutshell, the `With` keyword allows you to invoke members of a type within a predefined scope. Do know that the `With` keyword is nothing more than a typing time saver.

For example, the `System.Collections` namespace has a type named `ArrayList`, which like any type has a number of members. You are free to manipulate the `ArrayList` on a statement-by-statement basis as follows:

```
Sub Main()
  Dim myStuff As New ArrayList()
  myStuff.Add(100)
  myStuff.Add("Hello")
  Console.WriteLine("Size is: {0}", myStuff.Count)
End Sub
```

or use the VB 2008 `With` keyword:

```
Sub Main()
  Dim myStuff As New ArrayList()
  With myStuff
    .Add(100)
    .Add("Hello")
    Console.WriteLine("Size is: {0}", .Count)
  End With
End Sub
```

■ **Note** As you will see in Chapter 13, the `With` keyword (as of .NET 3.5) can also be used to build anonymous data types.

Summary

Recall that the goal of this chapter was to expose you to numerous core aspects of the VB 2008 programming language. Here, we examined the constructs that will be commonplace in any application you may be interested in building. After examining the `Module` type, you learned that every VB 2008 executable program must have a type defining a `Main()` method, which serves as the program's entry point. Within the scope of `Main()`, you typically create any number of objects that work together to breathe life into your application.

Next, we explored the details of the built-in data types of VB 2008, and you came to understand that each data type keyword (e.g., `Integer`) is really a shorthand notation for a full-blown type in the `System` namespace (`System.Int32` in this case). Given this, each VB 2008 data type has a number of built-in members. Along the same vein, you also learned about the role of *widening* and *narrowing* as well as the role of `Option Strict`.

We wrapped up by checking out the various iteration and decision constructs supported by VB 2008. Now that you have some of the basic nuts-and-bolts in your mind, the next chapter completes our examination of core language features. After that point, you will be well prepared to examine the object-oriented features of Visual Basic 2008.

CHAPTER 4

VB 2008 Programming Constructs, Part II

This chapter picks up where the previous chapter left off and completes your investigation of the core aspects of the Visual Basic 2008 programming language. We begin by examining various details regarding the construction of VB 2008 subroutines and functions, exploring the `Optional`, `ByRef`, `ByVal`, and `ParamArray` keywords along the way.

Once you examine the topic of *method overloading*, the next task is to investigate the details behind manipulating array types using the syntax of VB 2008 and get to know the functionality contained within the related `System.Array` class type. We wrap things up with a discussion regarding the construction of enumeration and structure types. Once you have completed this chapter, you will be well prepared for the next chapter where we begin to dive into the world of object-oriented development.

Defining Subroutines and Functions

To begin this chapter, let's examine the details of defining subroutines and functions. As you know, a method exists to perform a unit of work. Methods may or may not take parameters and may or may not return values. Visual Basic has long distinguished between a *subroutine* and a *function*. While you can collectively refer to each syntactic variation as a *method*, the distinction is that subroutines do not return a value once the method has completed, whereas functions do.

When you define a subroutine, simply use the `Sub` keyword and list any necessary arguments. If you wish to define a function, use the `Function` keyword (with any necessary arguments) and establish the return value via the `As` keyword. To illustrate, create a new Console Application project named FunWithMethods, and rename your initial module type to `Program`.

Insert a new module into your current project named `HelperFunctions.vb` via the Project ➤ Add Module menu option of Visual Studio 2008. Update the `HelperFunctions` module as follows:

```
Module HelperFunctions
  ' Subroutines have no return value.
  Sub PrintMessage(ByVal msg As String)
    Console.WriteLine(msg)
  End Sub

  ' Functions have a return value.
  Function Add(ByVal x As Integer, ByVal y As Integer) As Integer
    ' Return sum using VB6 style syntax.
    Add = x + y
  End Function
End Module
```

As seen here, Visual Basic 2008 supports the VB6-style function return syntax, where a function's return value is denoted by assigning the function name to the resulting output. However, since the release of the .NET platform, we were supplied with a `Return` keyword for an identical purpose. Thus, the `Add()` method could be implemented like so:

```
' Much cleaner!
Function Add(ByVal x As Integer, ByVal y As Integer) As Integer
  Return x + y
End Function
```

The final introductory note regarding functions is that it is possible to forgo specifying an explicit return value for a function if (and only if) `Option Strict` is not enabled. If you do not specify a return value for a function, `System.Object` is assumed. As you will learn later in Chapter 6, `System.Object` is the parent class for all types in the .NET base class libraries, and therefore everything (even numerical data) can be represented as an `Object`:

```
' This will not compile if Option Strict is on!
Function Test()  ' As Object assumed.
  Return 5
End Function
```

As you will see throughout the remainder of this book, subroutines and functions can be defined and implemented within the scope of modules, classes, and structures (and prototyped within interface types). While the definition of a method in VB 2008 is quite straightforward, there are a handful of keywords that you can use to control how arguments are passed to the method in question, and these are listed in Table 4-1.

Table 4-1. *Visual Basic 2008 Parameter Modifier*

Parameter Modifier Keyword	Meaning in Life
`ByVal`	The method is passed a copy of the original data. This is the default parameter-passing behavior.
`ByRef`	The method is passed a reference to the original data in memory.
`Optional`	This marks an argument that does not need to be specified by the caller.
`ParamArray`	This defines an argument that may be passed a variable number of arguments of the same type.

Let's walk through the role of each keyword in turn.

The ByVal Parameter Modifier

Under Visual Basic 2008, all parameters are passed *by value* by default. When an argument is marked with the `ByVal` keyword, the method receives a copy of the original data declared elsewhere. Given that this is indeed a local copy, the method is free to change the parameter's value; however, the caller will *not* see the change. For example, if our `Add()` function were to reassign the values of the incoming `Integer` data types as follows:

```
Function Add(ByVal x As Integer, ByVal y As Integer) As Integer
  Dim answer As Integer = x + y
  ' Try to set the params to a new value for the caller.
  x = 22 : y = 30
  Return answer
End Function
```

the caller (the `Main()` method in this case) would be totally unaware of this attempted reassignment, given that a *copy* of the data was modified, not the caller's original data. This can be verified by printing out the input values after the call to `Add()`:

```
Sub Main()
  Console.WriteLine("***** Fun with Methods *****")
  ' Pass two Integers by value.
  Dim x, y As Integer
  x = 10 : y = 20
  Console.WriteLine("{0} + {1} = {2}", x, y, Add(x, y))

  ' X is still 10 and y is still 20.
  Console.WriteLine("After call x = {0} and y = {1}", x, y)
End Sub
```

It is also worth pointing out that the `ByVal` keyword is technically optional, given that this is the default setting for all parameters:

```
' These args are implicitly ByVal.
Function Add(x As Integer, y As Integer) As Integer
End Function
```

However, if you do not specify `ByVal` or `ByRef` for a given parameter, Visual Studio 2008 will automatically add the `ByVal` modifier when you hit the Enter key.

Note If you have a background VB6 or earlier, be aware that this default setting for parameters is the exact opposite behavior as we had in the past! Before the release of the .NET platform, VB passed parameters by reference by default.

The ByRef Parameter Modifier

Some methods need to be created in such a way that the caller should be able to realize any reassignments that have taken place within the method scope. For example, you might have a method that needs to change incoming character data, assign an incoming parameter to a new object in memory, or simply modify the value of a numerical argument. For this very reason, VB 2008 supplies the `ByRef` keyword. Consider the following update to the `PrintMessage()` method:

```
Sub PrintMessage(ByRef msg As String)
  Console.WriteLine("Your message is: {0}", msg)

  ' Caller will see this change, as "msg" is passed ByRef.
  msg = "Thank you for calling this method"
End Sub
```

If we were to update Main() as follows:

```
Sub Main()
  Console.WriteLine("***** Fun with Methods *****")
...
  Dim msg As String = "Hello from Main!"
  PrintMessage(msg)
  Console.WriteLine("After call msg = {0}", msg)
End Sub
```

and you were to compile and run the current project, you would find the output shown in Figure 4-1.

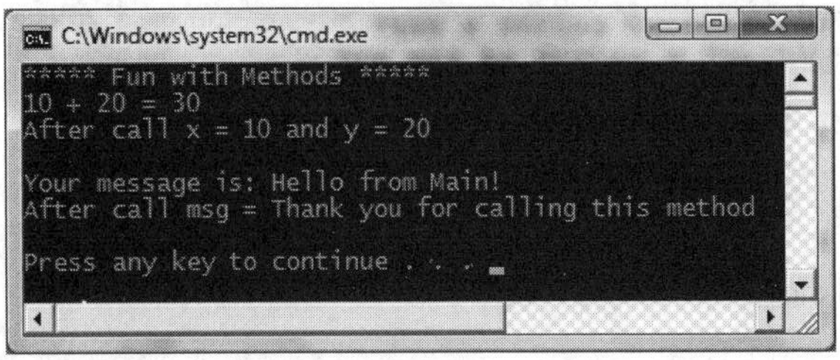

Figure 4-1. ByRef *parameters can be changed by the called method.*

There is one additional parameter-passing-centric language feature of VB 2008, which is a carryover from earlier versions of the language. If you are calling a method prototyped to take a parameter ByRef, you can force the runtime to pass in a copy of the data (thereby treating it as if it were defined with the ByVal keyword). To do so, when you call the method, wrap the ByRef argument within an extra set of parentheses. For example, if you were to update the call to PrintMessage() like so:

```
Sub Main()
  Console.WriteLine("***** Fun with Methods *****")
...
  ' This String is now passed by value,
  ' even though the parameter was marked ByRef.
  Dim msg As String = "Hello from Main!"
  PrintMessage((msg))
  Console.WriteLine("After call msg = {0}", msg)
End Sub
```

you would find that the string reassignment is not "remembered" as indicated in Figure 4-2.

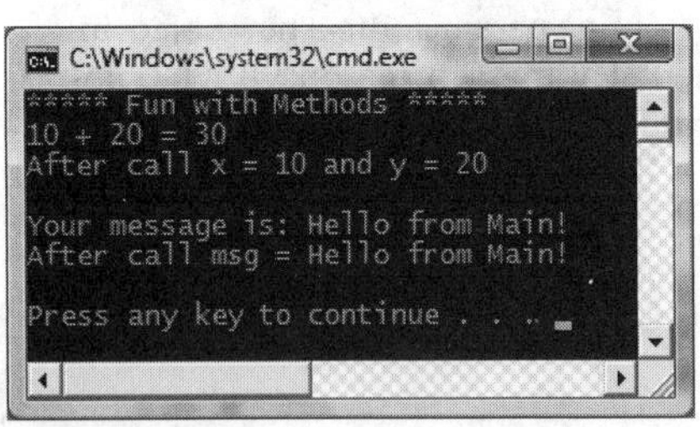

Figure 4-2. ByRef *parameters can be passed by value by wrapping the argument within parentheses.*

■ **Note** The `ByRef` and `ByVal` keywords will be revisited in Chapter 12. As you will see, the behaviors of these keywords change just a bit depending on whether the incoming parameter is a "value type" (a structure) or "reference type" (a class).

Defining Optional Arguments

VB has long supported the use of optional arguments. Simply put, this language feature allows you to define a set of parameters that are not required to be supplied by the caller. If the caller chooses not to pass these optional elements, the argument will be assigned to a specified default value. As you would hope, this feature is also part of VB 2008 with one important distinction—all optional parameters must now be set to an *explicit* default value. In contrast, under Visual Basic 6.0, optional arguments were assigned to their default values automatically.

Assume we have defined a new subroutine named `PrintFormattedMessage()` within the `HelperFunctions` module, which takes three optional arguments that are used to control how the incoming `String` is to be printed to the console:

```
Sub PrintFormattedMessage(ByVal msg As String, _
  Optional ByVal upperCase As Boolean = False, _
  Optional ByVal timesToRepeat As Integer = 0, _
  Optional ByVal textColor As ConsoleColor = ConsoleColor.Green)
    ' Store current console foreground color.
    Dim fGroundColor As ConsoleColor = Console.ForegroundColor
    ' Set console foreground color.
    Console.ForegroundColor = textColor
    ' Print message in correct case x number of times.
    For i As Integer = 0 To timesToRepeat
      Console.WriteLine(msg)
    Next
    ' Reset current console foreground color.
    Console.ForegroundColor = fGroundColor
End Sub
```

Given this definition, we are now able to call `PrintFormattedMessage()` in a variety of ways. First, if we wish to accept all defaults, we can simply supply the mandatory `String` argument as follows:

```
' Accept all defaults for the optional args.
PrintFormattedMessage("Call One")
```

If we would rather provide custom values for each optional argument, we can do so explicitly as follows:

```
' Provide each optional argument.
PrintFormattedMessage("Call Two", True, 5, ConsoleColor.Yellow)
```

Furthermore, when you are calling a method that has some number of optional arguments, you may be interested in providing only a subset of specific values, given that some of the default values fit the bill. To do so, your first approach is to skip over the optional arguments for which you wish to accept the defaults using a blank parameter:

```
' Print this message in current case, one time, in gray.
PrintFormattedMessage("Call Three", , , ConsoleColor.Gray)
```

While skipping over optional arguments is syntactically valid, it does not necessarily lend itself to readable (or easily maintainable) code. A more elegant manner in which to skip over select optional arguments is using *named arguments*:

```
' Same as previously shown, but cleaner!
PrintFormattedMessage("Call Four", textColor:=ConsoleColor.Gray)
```

As you can see, an argument is named by using the := operator. The left side is the name of the parameter itself, while the right side is the value to pass this argument. Using this approach, the unnamed optional arguments will still be assigned to their predefined default.

A Brief Word Regarding Named Parameters

As an interesting side note, given that VB 2008 supports named arguments, it is possible to call a method and pass in each argument in any order you so choose. This behavior is possible for any method, not simply for methods that define optional parameters. For example, the `Add()` method could be legally called like so:

```
' Pass x and y values out of order.
Add(y:=10, x:=90)
```

Of course, if you overuse this language feature, you not only incur additional keystrokes, but your code can also be much harder on the eyes. By and large, you should limit your use of named arguments to the invocation of methods that define optional arguments.

Working with ParamArrays

In addition to optional parameters, Visual Basic 2008 supports the use of *parameter arrays*. To understand the role of the `ParamArray` keyword, you must (as the name implies) understand how to manipulate VB 2008 arrays. If you don't feel particularly comfortable with VB 2008 arrays yet, you may wish to return to this section once you have finished this chapter, as we will formally examine the `System.Array` class in bit later in this chapter in the section "Array Manipulation in VB 2008."

In a nutshell, the `ParamArray` keyword allows you to pass a method a variable number of parameters (of the same type) as a *single logical parameter*. As well, arguments marked with the `ParamArray` keyword can be processed if the caller sends in a strongly typed array or a comma-delimited list of items. Yes, this can be confusing. To clear things up, assume you wish to create a function named `CalculateAverage()`. Given the nature of this method, you would like to allow the caller to pass in any number of arguments and return the calculated average.

If you were to prototype this method to take an array of `Integers`, this would force the caller to first define the array, and then fill the array, and finally pass it into the method. However, if you define `CalculateAverage()` to take a `ParamArray` of `Integer` data types, the caller can simply pass a comma-delimited list of `Integers`. The .NET runtime will automatically package the set of `Integers` into an array of type `Integer` behind the scenes:

```
Function CalculateAverage(ByVal ParamArray itemsToAvg() As Integer) As Double
  Dim itemCount As Integer = UBound(itemsToAvg)
  Dim result As Integer
  For i As Integer = 0 To itemCount
    result += itemsToAvg(i)
  Next
  Return result / itemCount
End Function
```

As mentioned, when calling this method, you may send in an explicitly defined array of `Integers`, or alternatively, implicitly specify an array of `Integers` as a comma-delimited list. For example:

```
Sub Main()
  ...
  ' ParamArray data can be sent as a caller-supplied array
  ' or a comma-delimited list of arguments.
  Console.WriteLine(CalculateAverage(10, 11, 12, 44))

  Dim data() As Integer = {22, 33, 44, 55}
  Console.WriteLine(CalculateAverage(data))
End Sub
```

As you might guess, this technique is nothing more than a convenience for the caller, given that the array is created by the CLR as necessary. By the time the arguments are within the scope of the method being called, you are able to treat it as a full-blown .NET array that contains all the function of the `System.Array` base class library type.

■ **Note** To avoid any ambiguity, VB 2008 demands a method only support a single `ParamArray` argument, which must be the final argument in the parameter list.

Method Calling Conventions

The next aspect of building VB 2008 methods to be aware of is that *all* methods (subroutines and functions) are now called by wrapping arguments in parentheses (even if the method in question takes no arguments whatsoever). In stark contrast, VB6 supported some rather ridiculous calling conventions that forced you to call subs using a different syntax than functions. In general, under VB6, subs do not require parentheses, while functions do. However, the following variations do occur:

```
' VB6 function calling insanity.
Dim i as Integer
i = MyFunction(myArg)     ' Use () to capture return value.
MyFunction myArg          ' Forgo () if you don't care about return value.
Call MyFunction(myArg)    ' Same as previous line.
MyFunction(myArg)         ' Pass myArg by value.

' VB6 Subroutine calling insanity.
MySub myArg              ' Subs don't take ()...
Call MySub (myArg)       ' ...unless you use the Call keyword...
MySub (myArg)            ' ...or you want to pass by value.
```

VB 2008 stops the madness once and for all by stating that all functions and all subs must be called using parentheses. Thus, if a sub or function does not require arguments, parentheses are still used:

```
' VB 2008 simplicity.
Dim i as Integer
i = AFuncWithNoArgs()                      ' Use ()
ASubWithNoArgs()                           ' Use ()
ASubWithArgs(89, 44, "Ahhh. Better")       ' Use ()

Dim IAmPassedByValue as Boolean
SomeMethod((IAmPassedByValue))             ' Use ()
```

Methods Containing Static Local Variables

In VB 2008 (as well as earlier versions of the language), the `Static` keyword is used to define a point of data that is in memory as long as the application is running, but is visible only within the function in which it was declared. Assume you have added the following subroutine to your `HelperFunctions` module:

```
Sub PrintLocalCounter()
  ' Note the Static keyword.
  Static Dim localCounter As Integer

  localCounter += 1
  Console.Write("{0} ", localCounter)
End Sub
```

As you would expect, the first time this function is called, the static data is allocated and initialized to its default value (zero in the case of an `Integer`). However, because the local variable has been defined with the `Static` keyword, its previous value is retained across each method invocation. Therefore, if you invoke `PrintLocalCounter()` a handful of times within your `Main()` method as follows:

```
Sub Main()
...
  For i As Integer = 0 To 10
    PrintLocalCounter()
  Next
End Sub
```

you would see the printout to the console shown in Figure 4-3.

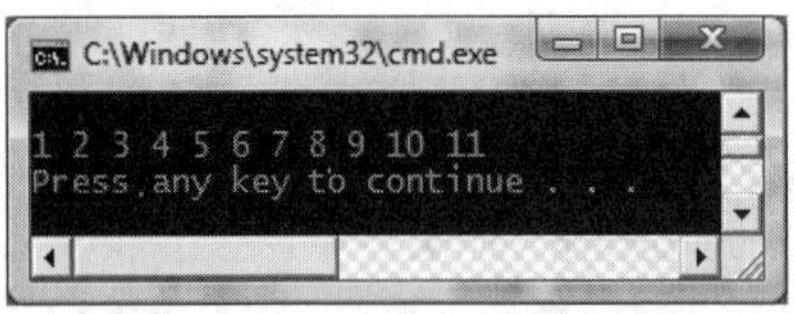

Figure 4-3. *Static local variables retain their value between calls.*

Of course, if a local variable is not defined with the `Static` keyword:

```
Sub PrintLocalCounter()
  Dim localCounter As Integer
  localCounter += 1
  Console.Write("{0} ", localCounter)
End Sub
```

you would see "1" printed out 11 times, as the `Integer` is re-created between calls.

Note Unlike VB6, VB 2008 no longer allows you to apply the `Static` keyword on the method level (in order to treat all local variables as `Static`). If you require the same behavior from a VB 2008 application, you need to explicitly define each data point using the `Static` keyword.

Source Code The FunWithMethods project is located under the Chapter 4 subdirectory.

Understanding Member Overloading

Like other modern object-oriented languages, VB 2008 allows a method to be *overloaded*. Simply put, when you define a set of identically named members that differ by the number (or type) of parameters, the member in question is said to be overloaded.

To understand why overloading is so useful, consider life as a VB6 developer. Assume you are using VB6 to build a set of methods that return the sum of various incoming types (`Integers`, `Doubles`, and so on). Given that VB6 does not support method overloading, we would be required to define a unique set of methods that essentially do the same thing (return the sum of the arguments):

```
' VB6 code.
Function AddInts(ByVal x As Integer, ByVal y As Integer) As Integer
  AddInts = x + y
End Function

Function AddDoubles(ByVal x As Double, ByVal y As Double) As Double
  AddDoubles = x + y
End Function

Function AddLongs(ByVal x As Long, ByVal y As Long) As Long
  AddLongs = x + y
End Function
```

Not only can code such as this become tough to maintain, but the object user must now be painfully aware of the name of each method. Using overloading, we are able to allow the caller to call a single method named `Add()`. Again, the key is to ensure that each version of the method has a distinct set of arguments (members differing only by return type are *not* unique enough). To check this out firsthand, create a new Console Application project named MethodOverloading. Consider the following module definition:

```
' VB 2008 code.
Module MathUtils
  Function Add(ByVal x As Integer, ByVal y As Integer) As Integer
    Return x + y
  End Function

  Function Add(ByVal x As Double, ByVal y As Double) As Double
    Return x + y
  End Function

  Function Add(ByVal x As Long, ByVal y As Long) As Long
    Return x + y
  End Function
End Module
```

The caller can now simply invoke `Add()` with the required arguments, and the compiler is happy to comply, given the fact that the compiler is able to resolve the correct implementation to invoke given the provided arguments:

```
Sub Main()
  Console.WriteLine("***** Fun with Method Overloading *****")
  ' Calls Integer version of Add()
  Console.WriteLine(Add(10, 10))
  ' Calls Long version of Add()
  Console.WriteLine(Add(900000000000, 900000000000))
  ' Calls Double version of Add()
  Console.WriteLine(Add(4.3, 4.4))
End Sub
```

The Overloads Keyword

Also know that VB 2008 provides the `Overloads` keyword, which can be used when you want to explicitly mark a member as overloaded. Using this keyword, however, is completely optional (be aware that if one method *is* marked as `Overloads`, all other versions of that overloaded method must also be marked as `Overloads`). The compiler assumes you are overloading if it finds identically named methods with varying arguments. Also be aware that the `Overloads` keyword can only be used if the method has been defined within a class or structure (but not a module). Here is some example usage:

```
' The Overloads keyword is optional and can only be used within
' a class or structure without compiler warnings.
Class MathUtilsClass
  Overloads Function Add(ByVal x As Integer, ByVal y As Integer) As Integer
    Return x + y
  End Function
  Overloads Function Add(ByVal x As Double, ByVal y As Double) As Double
    Return x + y
  End Function
  Overloads Function Add(ByVal x As Long, ByVal y As Long) As Long
    Return x + y
  End Function
End Class
```

Details of Method Overloading

When you are overloading a method, the VB 2008 parameter modifiers come into play to define valid forms of overloading. First of all, if the only point of differentiation between two methods is the `ByVal`/`ByRef` parameter modifier, it is *not unique* enough to be overloaded:

```
' Compiler error! Methods can't differ only by
' ByRef/ByVal
Sub TestSub(ByVal a As Integer)
End Sub
Sub TestSub(ByRef a As Integer)
End Sub
```

Also, if a method is overloaded by nothing more than an argument marked with the `Optional` keyword, you will once again receive a compiler error. Consider the following:

```
Sub TestSub(ByVal a As Integer)
End Sub
Sub TestSub(ByVal a As Integer, Optional ByVal b As Integer = 0)
End Sub
```

The reason the compiler refuses to allow this overload is due to the fact that it cannot disambiguate the following code:

```
Sub Main()
...
  ' Are you calling the one-arg version,
  ' or the two-arg version and omitting the second parameter?
  TestSub(1)
End Sub
```

Source Code The MethodOverloading project is located under the Chapter 4 subdirectory.

That wraps up our examination of building methods using the syntax of VB 2008. Next up, let's check out how to build and manipulate arrays, enumerations, and structures. Once we complete these topics, you will be well prepared to dive into object-oriented development beginning with Chapter 5.

Array Manipulation in VB 2008

As I would guess you are already aware, an *array* is a set of items, accessed using a numerical index. More specifically, an array is a set of contiguous items of the same type (an array of `Integers`, an array of `Strings`, an array of `SportsCars`, and so on). Declaring an array with Visual Basic 2008 is quite straightforward. To illustrate the basics, create a new Console Application project named FunWithArrays that contains the following helper method named `SimpleArrays()`, invoked from within `Main()`:

```
Module Program
  Sub Main()
    Console.WriteLine("***** Fun with Arrays *****")
    SimpleArrays()
  End Sub

  Sub SimpleArrays()
    Console.WriteLine("=> Simple Array Creation.")
    ' An array of 11 Strings.
    Dim myStrings(10) As String

    ' An array of 3 Integers.
    Dim myInts(2) As Integer

    ' An array of 5 Objects.
    Dim myObjs(4) As Object
  End Sub
End Module
```

Look closely at the previous code comments. When declaring a VB 2008 array, the number used in the array declaration represents the *upper bound* of the array, not the *maximum number* of elements. Thus, unlike C-based languages, when you write `Dim myInts(2) As Integer`, you end up with *three* elements (0 through 2, inclusive).

Once you have defined an array, you are then able to fill the elements index by index as shown in the updated `SimpleArrays()` method:

```
Sub SimpleArrays()
  ' Create and fill an array of three Integers.
  Dim myInts(2) As Integer
  myInts(0) = 100
  myInts(1) = 200
  myInts(2) = 300

  ' Now print each value.
  For Each i As Integer In myInts
    Console.WriteLine(i)
  Next
End Sub
```

Do be aware that if you declare an array, but do not explicitly fill each index, each item will be set to the default value of the data type (e.g., an array of `Booleans` will be set to `False`, an array of

Integers will be set to zero, and so forth). Given this, the following code will first print out the value zero three times, followed by the character data Cerebus, Jaka, and Astoria:

```
Sub SimpleArrays()
  ' An array of unassigned numerical data.
  Dim myInts(2) As Integer
  For Each i As Integer In myInts
    Console.WriteLine(i)
  Next

  ' String array with assigned data.
  Dim myStrs(2) As String
  myStrs(0) = "Cerebus"
  myStrs(1) = "Jaka"
  myStrs(2) = "Astoria"
  For Each s As String In myStrs
    Console.WriteLine(s)
  Next
End Sub
```

VB 2008 Array Initialization Syntax

In addition to filling an array using an item-by-item approach, you are also able to fill the items of an array using the VB 2008 member initialization syntax. To do so, specify each array item within the scope of curly brackets ({}). This syntax can be helpful when you are creating an array of a known size and wish to quickly specify the initial values. For example, the values of the `myInts` array could be established as follows:

```
Sub SimpleArrays()
  ' An array of 3 Integers.
  Dim myInts() As Integer = {100, 200, 300}
  For Each i As Integer In myInts
    Console.WriteLine(i)
  Next
...
End Sub
```

Notice that when you make use of this "curly bracket array" syntax, you do not specify the size of the array, given that this will be inferred by the number of items within the scope of the curly brackets. Thus, the following statement results in a compiler error:

```
' OOPS! Don't specify upper bound when using
' curly bracket array initialization syntax!
Dim badArrayDeclaration(2) As Integer = {100, 200, 300}
```

Defining an Array of Objects

As mentioned, when you define an array, you do so by specifying the type of item that can be within the array variable. While this seems quite straightforward, there is one notable twist. As you will come to understand in Chapter 6, `System.Object` is the ultimate base class to each and every type (including fundamental data types) in the .NET type system. Given this fact, if you were to define an array of `Objects`, the subitems could be anything at all. Consider the following `ArrayOfObjects()` method (which again can be invoked from `Main()` for testing):

```
Sub ArrayOfObjects()
  Console.WriteLine("=> Array of Objects.")
  ' An array of Objects can be anything at all.
  Dim myObjects(3) As Object
  myObjects(0) = 10
  myObjects(1) = False
  myObjects(2) = New DateTime(1969, 3, 24)
  myObjects(3) = "Form & Void"

  For Each obj As Object In myObjects
    ' Print the type and value for each item in array.
    Console.WriteLine("Type: {0}, Value: {1}", obj.GetType(), obj)
  Next
End Sub
```

Here, as we are iterating over the contents of `myObjects`, we print out the underlying type of each item using the `GetType()` method of `System.Object` as well as the value of the current item. Without going into too much detail regarding `System.Object.GetType()` at this point in the text, simply understand that this method can be used to obtain the fully qualified name of the item (Chapter 16 fully examines the topic of type information and reflection services). Figure 4-4 shows the output of the previous snippet.

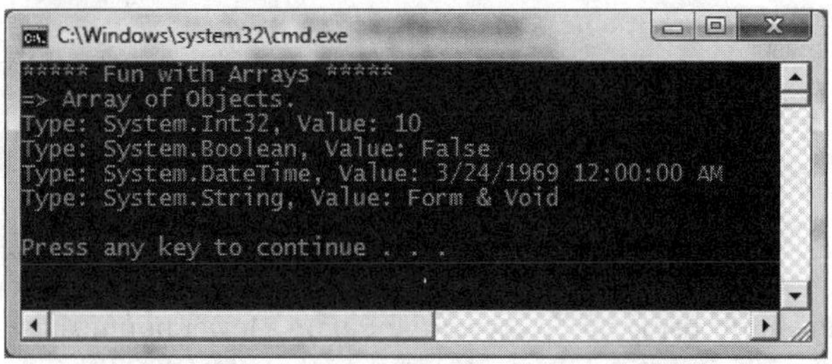

Figure 4-4. *Arrays of type* `Object` *can hold anything at all.*

Defining the Lower Bound of an Array

Visual Basic 6.0 allows developers to build an array with an arbitrary lower bound using the `To` keyword. To determine the upper and lower bounds of an array, we were provided with the `LBound()` and `UBound()` helper functions:

```
' VB6 code!
Dim myNumbers(5 To 7) As Integer
myNumbers(5) = 10
myNumbers(6) = 10
myNumbers(7) = 10
Dim i As Integer
For i = LBound(myNumbers) To UBound(myNumbers)
  MsgBox i
Next i
```

Although the `To` keyword can still be used under VB 2008, the lower bound of an array is *always* zero in order to keep VB 2008 in step with the rules of the Common Type System (CTS). Given this point, the `To` keyword is more or less optional under the .NET platform:

```
' Under VB 2008, the To keyword does not bring much to the table.
Dim myNumbers(0 To 5) as Integer
Dim moreNumbers(5) as Integer
```

For new VB 2008 projects, the fact should pose no problems; however, if you are building an application that needs to communicate with a legacy VB6 COM application that sends or receives arrays with arbitrary lower bounds, this can be an issue. For example, assume you are building a new .NET application that is making use of an ActiveX `*.dll` that contains a COM object that returns an array with a lower bound of 5. Given all .NET arrays have a lower bound of zero, how would you be able to process this array back within the .NET program?

Under the .NET platform, the only way to create (or represent) an array with a lower bound other than zero is to use the shared `CreateInstance()` method of `System.Array`. We will examine the role of `System.Array` in just a moment; however, ponder the following method, which does indeed build an array with a lower bound of 5 and an upper bound of 7:

```
Sub ArrayLowerBounds()
  Console.WriteLine("=> Using Array.CreateInstance().")
  ' An array representing the length of each dimension.
  Dim myLengths() As Integer = {3}
  ' An array representing the lower bound of each dimension.
  Dim myBounds() As Integer = {5}

  ' Call Array.CreateInstance() specifying
  ' the type of array, length and bounds.
  Dim mySpecialArray As Array = _
    Array.CreateInstance(GetType(Integer), myLengths, myBounds)
  Console.WriteLine("Lower Bound: {0}", LBound(mySpecialArray))
  Console.WriteLine("Upper Bound: {0}", UBound(mySpecialArray))
  Console.WriteLine()
End Sub
```

While this code is more verbose than simply using the `To` keyword to set up a lower bound, it is not as complex as it might look. We begin by declaring two arrays of `Integers` that represent the length and lower bounds of each dimension of the array we are interested in building. The reason we have to represent the length and lower bound as an array of `Integers` (rather than two simple numbers) is due to the fact that `Array.CreateInstance()` can create single or multidimensional arrays. Here, we are creating an array of a single dimension, given that the `myLengths` and `myBounds` variables contain a single item. If you were to invoke this method from within `Main()`, you would find the output shown in Figure 4-5.

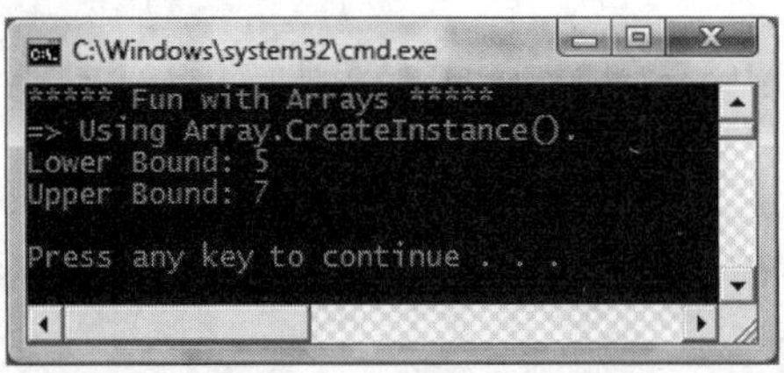

Figure 4-5. *The* `Array.CreateInstance()` *method allows you to build arrays with arbitrary lower bounds.*

The Redim/Preserve Syntax

VB 2008 allows you to dynamically reestablish the upper bound of a previous allocated array using the `Redim/Preserve` syntax. For example, assume you created an array of 10 `Integers` somewhere within your program. At a later time, you realize that this array needs to grow by 5 items (to hold a maximum of 16 `Integers`). To do so, you are able to author the following code:

```
Sub RedimPreserve()
  Console.WriteLine("=> Redim / Preserve keywords.")
  ' Make an array with ten slots.
  Dim myValues(9) As Integer
  For i As Integer = 0 To 9
    myValues(i) = i
  Next
  For i As Integer = 0 To UBound(myValues)
    Console.Write("{0} ", myValues(i))
  Next

  ' ReDim the array with extra slots.
  ReDim Preserve myValues(15)
  For i As Integer = 9 To UBound(myValues)
    myValues(i) = i
  Next
  For i As Integer = 0 To UBound(myValues)
    Console.Write("{0} ", myValues(i))
  Next
  Console.WriteLine()
End Sub
```

Now, be very aware that the `ReDim/Preserve` syntax generates quite a bit of CIL code behind the scenes, as a new array will be created followed by a member-by-member transfer of the items from the old array into the new array (load your assembly into `ildasm.exe` to check out the code firsthand).

Simply put, overuse of the `ReDim/Preserve` syntax can be inefficient. When you wish to use a container whose contents can dynamically grow (or shrink) on demand, you will always prefer using members from the `System.Collections` or `System.Collections.Generic` namespaces (see Chapter 10).

Note This `System.Array` class provides the language-neutral `Resize()` method, which serves a similar function as VB 2008's `ReDim/Preserve` syntax.

Working with Multidimensional Arrays

In addition to the single-dimensional arrays you have seen thus far, VB 2008 also supports the creation of multidimensional arrays. To declare and fill a multidimensional array, proceed as follows:

```
Sub MultiDimArray()
  Console.WriteLine("=> Multidimensional arrays.")
  Dim myMatrix(6, 6) As Integer  ' Makes a 7x7 array
  ' Populate array.
  Dim k As Integer, j As Integer
  For k = 0 To 6
    For j = 0 To 6
      myMatrix(k, j) = k * j
```

```
    Next j
  Next k

  ' Show array.
  For k = 0 To 6
    For j = 0 To 6
      Console.Write(myMatrix(k, j) & "  ")
    Next j
      Console.WriteLine()
  Next k
  Console.WriteLine()
End Sub
```

So, at this point you should (hopefully) feel comfortable with the process of defining, filling, and examining the contents of a VB 2008 array type. To complete the picture, let's now examine the role of the `System.Array` class.

The System.Array Class

The most striking difference between VB6 and VB 2008 .NET arrays is the fact that every array you create gathers much of its functionality from the `System.Array` class. Using these common members, we are able to operate on an array using a consistent object model. In fact, in most cases you are able to simply use the members of `System.Array` rather than the VB6-style array functions (`LBound()`, `UBound()`, and so on). Table 4-2 gives a rundown of some of the more interesting members (be sure to check the .NET Framework 3.5 SDK for full details).

Table 4-2. *Select Members of* `System.Array`

Member of Array Class	Meaning in Life
`Clear()`	This shared method sets a range of elements in the array to default values (`0` for value items, `False` for `Booleans`, `Nothing` for object references).
`CopyTo()`	This method copies elements from the source array into the destination array.
`GetEnumerator()`	This method returns the `IEnumerator` interface for a given array. Chapter 9 will examine the `IEnumerator` interface, but for the time being, keep in mind that this interface is required by the `For Each` construct.
`Length`	This property returns the number of items within the array.
`Rank`	This property returns the number of dimensions of the current array.
`Reverse()`	This shared method reverses the contents of a one-dimensional array.
`Sort()`	This shared method sorts a one-dimensional array of intrinsic types. If the elements in the array implement the `IComparable` interface, you can also sort your custom types (see Chapter 9).

Notice that many members of `System.Array` are defined as shared members and are therefore called at the class level (for example, the `Array.Sort()` or `Array.Reverse()` methods). Methods such as these are passed in the array you wish to process. Other members of `System.Array` (such as the `GetUpperBound()` method or `Length` property) are bound at the object level, and thus you are able to invoke the member directly on the array.

■ **Note** Chapter 5 will provide detailed coverage of "shared" members and the `Shared` keyword of VB 2008.

Let's see some of these members in action. The following helper method makes use of the shared Reverse() and Clear() methods to pump out information about an array of string types to the console:

```
Sub SystemArrayFunctionality()
  Console.WriteLine("=> Working with System.Array.")
  ' Initialize items at startup.
  Dim gothicBands() As String = _
    {"Tones on Tail", "Bauhaus", "Sisters of Mercy"}

  ' Print out names in declared order.
  Console.WriteLine(" -> Here is the array:")
  For i As Integer = 0 To gothicBands.GetUpperBound(0)
    ' Print a name
    Console.Write(gothicBands(i) & " ")
  Next
  Console.WriteLine()
  Console.WriteLine()

  ' Reverse them...
  Array.Reverse(gothicBands)
  Console.WriteLine(" -> The reversed array")
  ' ... and print them.
  For i As Integer = 0 To gothicBands.GetUpperBound(0)
    ' Print a name
    Console.Write(gothicBands(i) & " ")
  Next
  Console.WriteLine()
  Console.WriteLine()

  ' Clear out all but the final member.
  Console.WriteLine(" -> Cleared out all but one...")
  Array.Clear(gothicBands, 1, 2)
  For i As Integer = 0 To gothicBands.GetUpperBound(0)
    ' Print a name
    Console.Write(gothicBands(i) & " ")
  Next
  Console.WriteLine()
End Sub
```

If you invoke this method from within Main(), the output will be as shown in Figure 4-6.

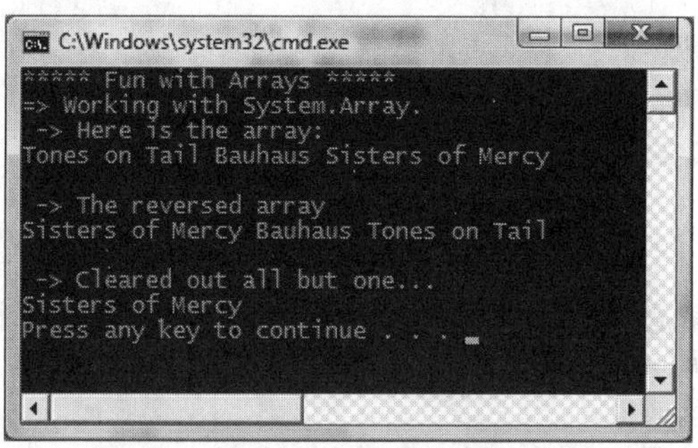

Figure 4-6. *The* System.Array *class provides functionality to all .NET arrays.*

■ **Source Code** The FunWithArrays project is located under the Chapter 4 subdirectory.

Understanding VB 2008 Enumerations

Recall from Chapter 1 that the .NET type system is composed of classes, structures, enumerations, interfaces, and delegates (also recall that a module is nothing more than a specialized class type in disguise). To begin our exploration of these types, let's check out the role of *enumerations* using a new Console Application project named FunWithEnums.

When building a system, it is often convenient to create a set of symbolic names that map to known numerical values. For example, if you are creating a payroll system, you may want to refer to the type of employees using constants such as vice president, manager, contractor, and "grunt." Like other languages, VB 2008 supports the notion of custom enumerations for this very reason. For example, here is an enumeration named EmpType:

```
' A custom enumeration.
Enum EmpType
  Manager       ' = 0
  Grunt         ' = 1
  Contractor    ' = 2
  VicePresident ' = 3
End Enum
```

The EmpType enumeration defines four named constants, corresponding to discrete numerical values. By default, the first element is set to the value zero (0), followed by an *n+1* progression. You are free to change the initial value as you see fit. For example, if it made sense to number the members of EmpType as 102 through 105, you could do so as follows:

```
' Begin with 102.
Enum EmpType
  Manager = 102
  Grunt         ' = 103
  Contractor    ' = 104
  VicePresident ' = 105
End Enum
```

Enumerations do not necessarily need to follow a sequential ordering. If (for some reason or another) it makes sense to establish your EmpType as shown here, the compiler continues to be happy:

```
' Elements of an enumeration need not be sequential!
Enum EmpType
  Manager = 10
  Grunt = 1
  Contractor = 100
  VicePresident = 9
End Enum
```

Finally, be aware that if required, the values assigned to a given enumeration name can repeat. Thus, if it made sense, you could author EmpType as follows:

```
' Values of an enumeration can repeat!
Enum EmpType
  Manager = 10
  Grunt = 10
```

```
  Contractor = 100
  VicePresident = 100
End Enum
```

Controlling the Underlying Storage for an Enum

By default, the storage type used to hold the values of an enumeration is a `System.Int32` (the VB 2008 `Integer`); however, you are free to change this to your liking. VB 2008 enumerations can be defined in a similar manner for any of the core numerical types (`Byte`, `Short`, `Integer`, or `Long`). For example, if you want to set the underlying storage value of `EmpType` to be a `Byte` rather than an `Integer`, you can write the following:

```
' This time, EmpType maps to an underlying Byte.
Enum EmpType As Byte
  Manager = 10
  Grunt = 1
  Contractor = 100
  VicePresident = 9
End Enum
```

Changing the underlying type of an enumeration can be helpful if you are building a .NET application that will be deployed to a low-memory device, such as a .NET-enabled cell phone or PDA, and need to conserve memory wherever possible. Of course, if you do establish your enumeration to use a `Byte` as storage, each value must be within its range!

Declaring and Using Enums

Once you have established the range and storage type of your enumeration, you can use them in as strongly typed data in your programs. Because enumerations are nothing more than a user-defined type, you are able to use them as function return values, method parameters, local variables, and so forth. Assume you have a method named `AskForBonus()`, taking an `EmpType` variable as the sole parameter. Based on the value of the incoming parameter, you will print out a fitting response to the pay bonus request:

```
Module Program
  ' Enums as parameters.
  Sub AskForBonus(ByVal e As EmpType)
    Select Case (e)
      Case EmpType.Contractor
        Console.WriteLine("You already get enough cash...")
      Case EmpType.Grunt
        Console.WriteLine("You have got to be kidding...")
      Case EmpType.Manager
        Console.WriteLine("How about stock options instead?")
      Case EmpType.VicePresident
        Console.WriteLine("VERY GOOD, Sir!")
    End Select
  End Sub

  Sub Main()
    Console.WriteLine("**** Fun with Enums *****")
     ' Make a contractor type.
     Dim emp as EmpType = EmpType.Contractor
    AskForBonus(emp)
  End Sub
End Module
```

Notice that when you are assigning a value to an Enum variable, you must scope the Enum name (EmpType) to the value (e.g., Grunt). Because enumerations are a fixed set of name/value pairs, it is illegal to set an Enum variable to a value that is not defined directly by the enumerated type. However, it is permissible to set the value of an enumeration variable to the associated numerical value, although doing so results in a far less robust code base:

```
Sub Main()
  Console.WriteLine("**** Fun with Enums *****")
  Dim emp as EmpType
  ' Error! SalesManager is not in the EmpType enum!
  emp = EmpType.SalesManager

  ' Error! Forgot to scope Grunt to EmpType!
  emp= Grunt

  ' OK, but not preferred. Use of enum's name is
  ' always recommended.
  emp= 9
End Sub
```

■ **Note** If Option Strict is enabled, it will always be a compiler error to assign a numerical value to an enumeration (as shown in the previous code example).

The System.Enum Type (and a Lesson in Resolving Keyword Name Clashes)

The interesting thing about .NET enumerations is that they gain functionality from the System.Enum class type. This class defines a number of methods that allow you to interrogate and transform a given enumeration. Before seeing some of this functionality firsthand, you have one VB-ism to be aware of.

As you know, VB is a case-insensitive language. Therefore, in the eyes of the VB compiler, Enum, enum, and ENUM all refer to the intrinsic Enum keyword. While the case insensitivity of VB can be helpful (given that the Visual Studio 2008 IDE transforms keywords, type names and member names to the correct case), there is a problem.

Specifically, if you attempt to access the shared members of Enum directly using the dot operator, you will be issued a compiler error. The problem is that the compiler assumes "Enum" refers to the VB 2008 keyword, *not* the System.Enum type!

Assume you have updated your Main() method with the following call to Enum.GetUnderlyingType(). As the name implies, this method returns the data type used to store the values of the enumerated type (System.Byte in the case of the current EmpType declaration):

```
' Print out the data type used to store the values?
Sub Main()
  Console.WriteLine("**** Fun with Enums *****")
  Dim emp As EmpType
  emp = EmpType.Contractor
  AskForBonus(emp)

  ' Compiler error!
  Console.WriteLine("EmpType uses a {0} for storage", _
    Enum.GetUnderlyingType(emp.GetType()))
End Sub
```

To resolve this name clash, you have a few choices. First, you could explicitly specify the fully qualified name (System.Enum) everywhere in your code base when you wish to invoke members of this type:

```
Sub Main()
  Console.WriteLine("**** Fun with Enums *****")
  Dim emp As EmpType
  emp = EmpType.Contractor
  AskForBonus(emp)

  ' Use fully qualified name.
  Console.WriteLine("EmpType uses a {0} for storage", _
    System.Enum.GetUnderlyingType(emp.GetType()))
End Sub
```

While this fits the bill, it can be cumbersome to use fully qualified names. To help lessen your typing burden, you can make use of a variation of the VB 2008 Imports statement that allows you to define a simple alias that maps to a fully qualified name:

```
Imports DotNetEnum = System.Enum
...
Module Program
  Sub Main()
    Console.WriteLine("**** Fun with Enums *****")
    Dim emp As EmpType
    emp = EmpType.Contractor
    AskForBonus(emp)

    ' Use alias to reference System.Enum's functionality.
    Console.WriteLine("EmpType uses a {0} for storage", _
      DotNetEnum.GetUnderlyingType(emp.GetType()))
  End Sub
...
End Module
```

In this case, you defined an alias to System.Enum, called DotNetEnum. In your code, you can make use of this moniker whenever you want to make use of the members of the Enum type. At compile time, however, all occurrences of DotNetEnum are replaced with System.Enum.

The final manner to resolve this name clash is to wrap the Enum token within square brackets. This informs the compiler that you are referring to the System.Enum *type*, not the VB Enum *keyword*:

```
Sub Main()
  Console.WriteLine("**** Fun with Enums *****")
  Dim emp As EmpType
  emp = EmpType.Contractor
  AskForBonus(emp)
  ' Wrap token in square brackets.
  Console.WriteLine("EmpType uses a {0} for storage", _
    [Enum].GetUnderlyingType(emp.GetType()))
End Sub
```

Be aware that there are a few other instances in VB where you find similar name clashes. For example, as you will see later in Chapter 16, VB supplies a keyword named Assembly, which can clash with the Assembly class in the System.Reflection namespace. Again, you can wrap Assembly in brackets ([Assembly]) to inform the VB compiler you are referring to the System.Reflection. Assembly type, rather than the Assembly keyword.

Dynamically Discovering an Enum's Name/Value Pairs

Beyond the `Enum.GetUnderlyingType()` method, all VB 2008 enumerations support a method named `ToString()`, which returns the string name of the current enumeration's value. For example:

```
Sub Main()
  Console.WriteLine("**** Fun with Enums *****")
  Dim emp As EmpType
  emp = EmpType.Contractor

  ' Prints out "emp is a Contractor".
  Console.WriteLine("emp is a {0}.", emp.ToString())
End Sub
```

If you are interested in discovering the numeric value of a given enumeration variable, rather than its name, you can simply using the VB `CInt()` conversion function. For example:

```
Sub Main()
  Console.WriteLine("**** Fun with Enums *****")
  Dim emp As EmpType
  emp = EmpType.Contractor

  ' Prints out "Contractor = 100".
  Console.WriteLine("{0} = {1}", emp.ToString(), CInt(emp))
End Sub
```

■ **Note** The shared `Enum.Format()` method provides a finer level of formatting options by specifying a desired format flag. Consult the .NET Framework 3.5 SDK documentation for full details of the `System.Enum.Format()` method.

`System.Enum` also defines another shared method named `GetValues()`. This method returns an instance of `System.Array`. Each item in the array corresponds to a member of the specified enumeration. Consider the following method, which will print out each name/value pair within any enumeration you pass in as a parameter:

```
' This method will print out the details of any enum.
Sub EvaluateEnum(ByVal e As [Enum])
  Console.WriteLine("=> Information about {0}", e.GetType().Name)

  Console.WriteLine("Underlying storage type: {0}", _
    [Enum].GetUnderlyingType(e.GetType()))

  ' Get all name/value pairs for incoming parameter.
  Dim enumData As Array = [Enum].GetValues(e.GetType())
  Console.WriteLine("This enum has {0} members.", enumData.Length)

  ' Now show the string name and associated value.
  For i As Integer = 0 To enumData.Length - 1
    Console.WriteLine("Name: {0}, Value: {1}", _
      enumData.GetValue(i).ToString(), CInt(enumData.GetValue(i)))
  Next
  Console.WriteLine()
End Sub
```

The ability to dynamically obtain the name/value pairs of an enumeration can be very helpful when building graphical user interfaces. For example, you could fill a `ListBox` control with string name of a custom enumeration. To test our new method, we simply display the data to the console.

To test this new method, update your `Main()` method to create variables of several enumeration types declared in the `System` namespace (as well as an `EmpType` enumeration for good measure). For example:

```
Sub Main()
  Console.WriteLine("**** Fun with Enums *****")
  Dim e2 As EmpType

  ' These two enumerations are defined in the System namesapce.
  Dim day As DayOfWeek
  Dim cc As ConsoleColor

  EvaluateEnum(e2)
  EvaluateEnum(day)
  EvaluateEnum(cc)
End Sub
```

The output is shown in Figure 4-7.

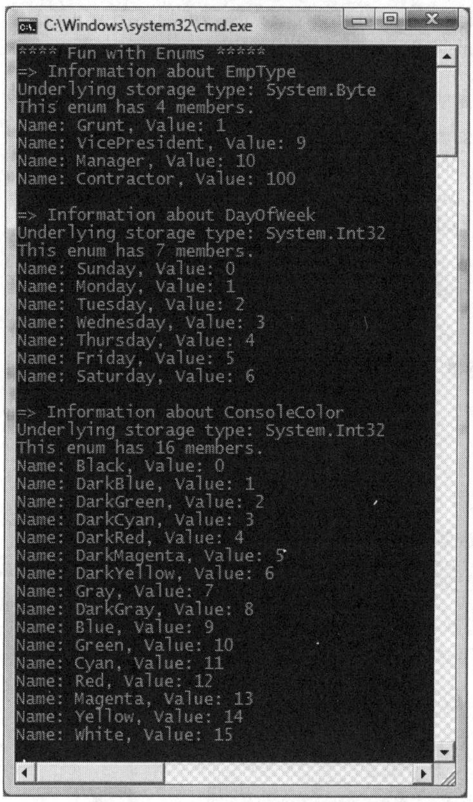

Figure 4-7. *Dynamically discovering name/value pairs of enumeration types.*

As you will see over the course of this text, enumerations are used extensively throughout the .NET base class libraries. For example, ADO.NET makes use of numerous enumerations to represent the state of a database connection (opened, closed, etc.), the state of a row in a `DataTable` (changed, new, detached, etc.), and so forth. Therefore, when you make use of any enumeration, always remember that you are able to interact with the name/value pairs using the members of `System.Enum`.

■ **Source Code** The FunWithEnums project is located under the Chapter 4 subdirectory.

Introducing the VB 2008 Structure Type

Now that you understand the role of enumeration types, let's conclude this chapter by introducing the use of .NET *structures*. Structure types are well suited for modeling mathematical, geometrical, and other "atomic" entities in your application. A structure (like an enumeration) is a user-defined type; however, structures are not simply a collection of name/value pairs. Rather, structures are types that can contain any number of fields and members that operate on these fields.

For example, structures can define constructors, can implement interfaces, and can contain any number of properties, methods, events, and overloaded operators. (If some of these terms are unfamiliar at this point, don't fret. All of these topics are fully examined in later chapters.)

■ **Note** If you have a background in OOP, you can think of a structure as a "lightweight class type," given that structures provide a way to define a type that supports encapsulation but cannot be used to build a hierarchy of related types (as structures are implicitly *sealed*, which means you cannot derive a structure from another structure). When you need to build a family of related types through inheritance, you will need to make use of class types.

To check out the basics of structure types, create a new Console Application project named FunWithStructures. To define a structure in VB 2008, you use the `Structure` keyword (and the required `End Structure` scope marker). For example:

```
Structure Point
End Structure
```

If you were to attempt to compile your project as it currently stands, you might be surprised to find a compiler error informing you that structures must contain at least one member variable (or an event, which we have not examined yet). Unlike a class or module, structures *cannot* be composed simply solely of functions and subroutines.

Here is a somewhat interesting `Point` structure that defines two member variables of type `Integer` and a set of methods to interact with said data:

```
Structure Point
  Public X, Y As Integer

  Sub Display()
    Console.WriteLine("X = {0}, Y = {1}", X, Y)
  End Sub

  Sub Increment()
    X += 1 : Y += 1
```

```
    End Sub
    Sub Decrement()
      X -= 1 : Y -= 1
    End Sub

    ' Recall that the "x" format flag displays the
    ' data in hex format.
    Function PointAsHexString() As String
      Return String.Format("X = {0:x}, Y = {1:x}", X, Y)
    End Function
  End Structure
```

Here, we have defined our two Integer fields (X and Y) using the Public keyword, which is an access control modifier (full details on access control modifiers appear in the next chapter). Declaring data with the Public keyword ensures the caller has direct access to the data from a given Point variable.

Notice, however, that the three subroutines and the PointAsHexString() function have not been declared with an access modifier keyword. By default, any method of a structure (or class) is automatically assumed to be Public unless you say otherwise.

■ Note It is typically considered bad style to define data publically. Rather, you will want to define *private* data that can be accessed and changed using *public* properties. These details will be examined in Chapter 5.

Here is a Main() method that takes our Point type out for a test drive. Figure 4-8 shows the program's output.

```
Sub Main()
  Console.WriteLine("***** A First Look at Structures *****")
  ' Create an initial Point.
  Dim myPoint As New Point()
  myPoint.X = 349
  myPoint.Y = 76
  myPoint.Display()

  ' Adjust the X and Y values.
  myPoint.Increment()
  myPoint.Display()
  Console.WriteLine("Point in hex: {0}", myPoint.PointAsHexString())
End Sub
```

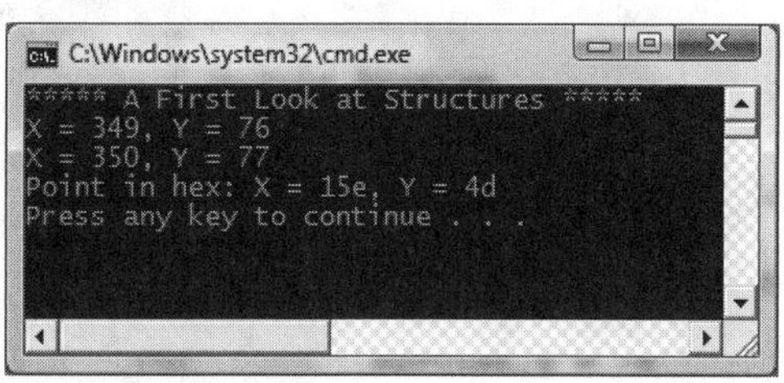

Figure 4-8. *Our* Point *structure in action*

Unlike arrays, strings, or enumerations, VB 2008 structures do not have an identically named class representation in the .NET library (that is, there is no `System.Structure` class), but are implicitly derived from `System.ValueType`.

Simply put, the role of `System.ValueType` is to ensure that the derived type (e.g., any structure) is allocated on the *stack* rather than the garbage-collected *heap*. Given this, the lifetime of a structure is very predictable. When a structure variable falls out of the defining scope, it is removed from memory immediately.

We will revisit `Structure` types (and `System.ValueType`) and learn about numerous additional details in Chapter 12 when we drill into the distinction between value types and reference types. Until that point, just understand that a `Structure` allows you to define types that have a fixed and predictable lifetime.

■ **Source Code** The FunWithStructures project is located under the Chapter 4 subdirectory.

Summary

This chapter began with an examination of several VB 2008 keywords that allow you to build custom subroutines and functions. Recall that by default, parameters are passed by value (via the `ByVal` keyword); however, you may pass a parameter by reference if you mark it with `ByRef`. You also learned about the role of optional parameters and how to define and invoke methods taking parameter arrays.

Once we investigated the topic of method overloading, the remainder of this chapter examined several details regarding how arrays, enumerations, and structures are defined in Visual Basic 2008 and represented within the .NET base class libraries. Here, you were only introduced to the concept of structure types, and will revisit this topic in Chapter 12.

With this, our initial investigation of the Visual Basic 2008 programming language is complete! In the next chapter, we will begin to dig into the details of object-oriented development and the role of class types.

CHAPTER 5

Designing Encapsulated Class Types

In the previous two chapters, you investigated a number of core syntactical constructs that are commonplace to any VB application you may be developing. Here, you will begin your examination of the object-oriented capabilities of VB 2008. Unlike Visual Basic 6.0, VB 2008 is a full-blown object-oriented programming language that has complete support for the famed "pillars of OOP" (encapsulation, inheritance, and polymorphism) and is therefore just as powerful as other OO languages such as Java, C++, or C#.

The first order of business is to examine the process of building well-defined class types that define any number of *constructors*. Once you understand the basics of defining classes and allocating objects, the remainder of this chapter will examine the role of *encapsulation*. Along the way you will understand how to define class properties as well as the role of shared fields and members, read-only fields, and constant data. We wrap up by examining the VB 2008 XML code documentation syntax. The final pillars of OOP (inheritance and polymorphism) will be detailed in Chapter 6.

Introducing the VB 2008 Class Type

As far as the .NET platform is concerned, the most fundamental programming construct is the *class type*. Formally, a class is a user-defined type that is composed of field data (often called *member variables*) and members that operate on this data (such as constructors, properties, subroutines, functions, and so forth). Collectively, the set of field data represents the "state" of a class instance (otherwise known as an *object*). The power of object-oriented languages such as Visual Basic 2008 is that by grouping data and related functionality in a class definition, you are able to model your software after entities in the real world.

To get the ball rolling, create a new VB 2008 Console Application named SimpleClassExample. Next, insert a new class file (named `Car.vb`) into your project using the Project ➤ Add New Item menu selection, choose the Class icon from the resulting dialog box as shown in Figure 5-1, and click the Add button.

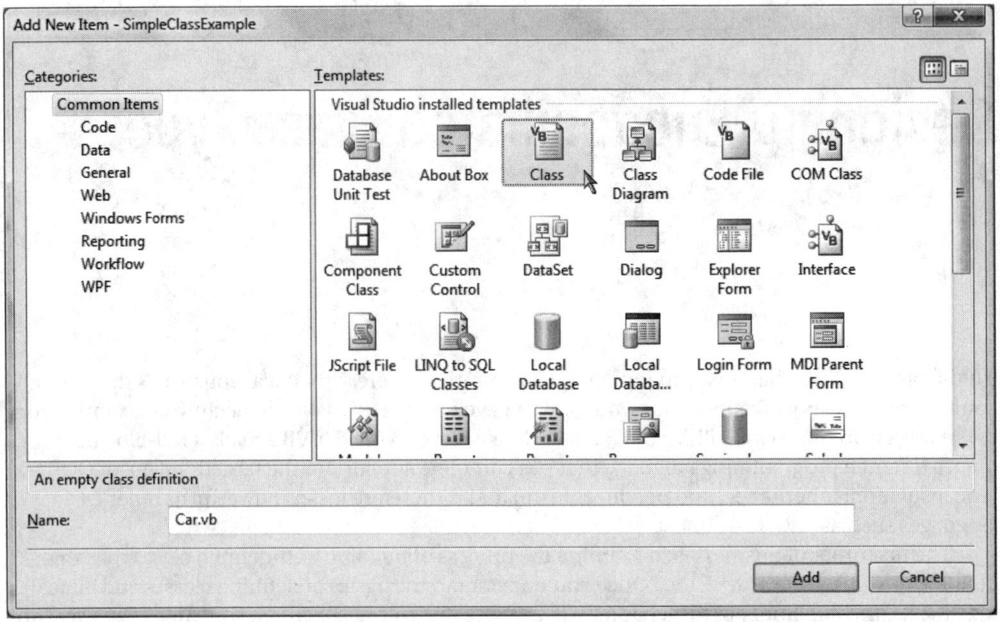

Figure 5-1. *Inserting a new* `Class` *type*

A class is defined in VB 2008 using the `Class` keyword. Like other constructs in the language, the scope of a class is terminated using the `End` keyword (`End Class` to be specific):

```
Public Class Car
End Class
```

Once you have defined a class type, you will need to consider the set of member variables that will be used to represent its state. For example, you may decide that cars have an `Integer` data type to represent the current speed and a `String` data type to represent the car's friendly pet name. Given these initial design notes, update your `Car` class as follows:

```
Public Class Car
  ' The "state" of a Car.
  Public petName As String
  Public currSpeed As Integer
End Class
```

Notice that these member variables are declared using the `Public` access modifier. Public members of a class are directly accessible once an *object* of this type has been created. As you may already know, the term "object" is used to represent an instance of a given class type created in memory using the `New` keyword.

■ **Note** Field data of a class should seldom (if ever) be defined as `Public`. To preserve the integrity of your state data, it is a far better design to define data as `Private` and allow controlled access to the data via type properties (as shown later in this chapter). However, to keep this first example as simple as possible, `Public` data fits the bill.

After you have defined the set of member variables that represent the state of a `Car` object, the next design step is to establish the members that model its behavior. For this example, the `Car` class will define one subroutine named `SpeedUp()` and another named `PrintState()`:

```
Public Class Car
  ' The "state" of the Car.
  Public petName As String
  Public currSpeed As Integer

  ' The functionality of the Car.
  Public Sub PrintState()
    Console.WriteLine("{0} is going {1} MPH.", _
      petName, currSpeed)
  End Sub
  Public Sub SpeedUp(ByVal delta As Integer)
    currSpeed += delta
  End Sub
End Class
```

As you can see, PrintState() is more or less a diagnostic method that will simply dump the current state of a given Car object to the command window. SpeedUp() will increase the speed of a Car object by the amount specified by the incoming Integer parameter. Now, update your module's Main() method with the following code:

```
' If you rename your module, don't forget to reset the startup object
' using the My Project dialog box (see Chapter 3).
Module Program
  Sub Main()
    Console.WriteLine("***** Fun with Class Types *****")
    ' Allocate and configure a Car object.
    Dim myCar As New Car()
    myCar.petName = "Sven"
    myCar.currSpeed = 10

    ' Speed up the car a few times and print out the
    ' new state.
    For i As Integer = 0 To 10
      myCar.SpeedUp(5)
      myCar.PrintState()
    Next
  End Sub
End Module
```

Once you run your program, you will see that the Car object (myCar) maintains its current state throughout the life of the sample application, as shown in Figure 5-2.

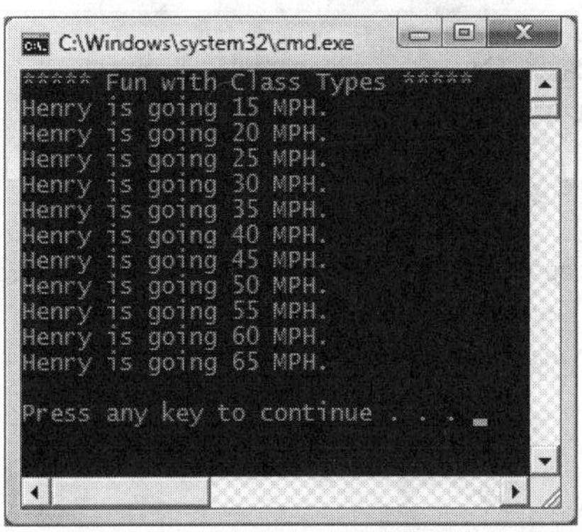

Figure 5-2. *Taking the* Car *for a test drive (pun intended)*

Creating Objects with the New Keyword

As shown in the previous code example, objects must be allocated into memory using the New keyword. If you do not make use of the New keyword and attempt to make use of your variable in a subsequent statement, you will receive a compiler warning. Even worse, if you execute code that makes use of an unallocated class variable, you will receive a runtime error (specifically, an exception of type NullReferenceException, which is the .NET equivalent of the dreaded VB6 runtime error 91 "Object variable or With block variable not set"):

```
Sub Main()
  ' Compiler warning / Runtime error!
  ' Forgot to use "New"!
  Dim myCar As Car
  myCar.petName = "Fred"
End Sub
```

To correctly create a class type variable, you may define and allocate a Car object on a single line of code as follows:

```
Sub Main()
  Dim myCar As New Car()
  myCar.petName = "Fred"
End Sub
```

As an alternative, you can allocate an object using the assignment operator in conjunction with the New keyword. This syntax is provided to offer consistency within the language, given that this approach mimics the initialization of simple data types (such as an Integer). For example:

```
Sub Main()
  ' An alternative manner to allocate an object.
  Dim myInt as Integer = 10
  Dim myCar As Car = New Car()
End Sub
```

Finally, if you wish to define a class variable and allocate an object on separate lines of code, you may do so as follows:

```
Sub Main()
  Dim myCar as Car
  myCar = New Car()
  myCar.petName = "Fred"
End Sub
```

■ **Note** Under the .NET platform, the Set keyword has been deprecated. Thus, you no longer allocate objects using the VB6 Set keyword (if you do so, Visual Studio 2008 will delete Set from the code statement when you hit the Enter key).

Here, the first code statement simply declares a reference to a yet-to-be-determined Car object. It is not until you assign a reference to an object via the New keyword that this reference points to a valid class instance. Without "new-ing" the reference, class variables are automatically assigned the value Nothing, as verified with the following If statement:

```
Sub Main()
  Dim ref As Car
  ' The following condition is true!
  If ref Is Nothing Then
```

```
    Console.WriteLine("ref is not initialized!")
  End If
End Sub
```

Note The VB `Nothing` keyword is a special value that can be assigned to object reference variables to indicate the variable does not point to an actual object in memory.

So at this point we have a trivial class type that defines a few fields and some basic methods. To enhance the functionality of the current `Car` type, we need to understand the role of class *constructors*.

Understanding Class Constructors

Given that objects have state (represented by the values of an object's member variables), the object user will typically want to assign relevant values to the object's field data before use. Currently, the `Car` type demands that the `petName` and `currSpeed` fields be assigned on a field-by-field basis. For the current example, this is not too problematic, given that we have only two fields. However, it is not uncommon for a class to have a good number of fields to contend with. As you might imagine, it would be undesirable to author 15 initialization statements to set 15 points of data. Even using the `With` construct, we are at a disadvantage. By way of illustration:

```
Sub Main()
  Dim o As New SomeClass()
  With o
    .Field1 = 10
    .Field2 = True
    .Field3 = New AnotherClass()
    .Field4 = 9.99
    ...
    .Field15 = "Gad, this is nasty!"
End Sub
```

Before the release of the .NET platform, VB class designers handled the `Initialize` event to establish default values of an object's field data. Within the handler for the `Initialize` event, you were able to perform any necessary startup logic, to ensure the object came to life in a proper state. Thus, if you were to define a `Car` type in Visual Basic 6.0, and wish to assume that all car objects begin life named "Clunker" moving at 10 MPH, you might define the VB6 `Car.cls` file as shown in Figure 5-3.

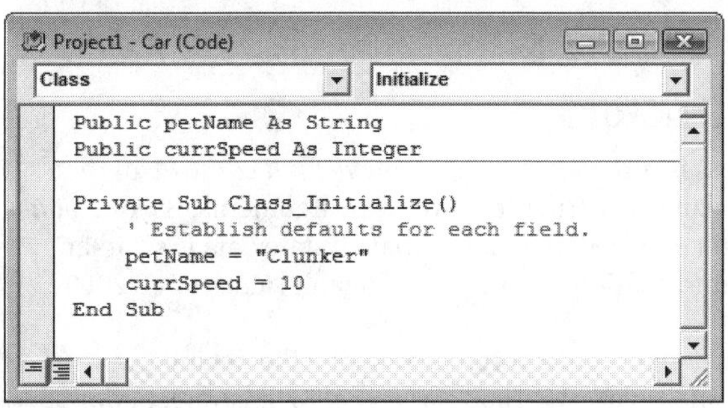

Figure 5-3. *A VB6* `Car` *class*

The problem with this approach is that the Initialize event handler does not allow the object user to supply initialization parameters. Without this possibility, the object user is still required to establish the state of the object on a member-by-member basis:

```
' VB6 would require something like so.
Dim vb6Car As Car
Set vb6Car = New Car  ' Initialize event fired!
With vb6Car
  .currSpeed = 90
  .petName = "Chucky"
End With
```

To help the object user along and reduce the number of "hits" required to establish the state of the object, many VB6 developers created an ad hoc construction subroutine, often named Create(). For example, assume we have added the following method to the VB6 Car.cls file:

```
Public Sub Create(ByVal pn As String, ByVal cs As Integer)
  petName = pn
  currSpeed = cs
End Sub
```

Although this technique does indeed reduce the number of hits to construct the object, it is now the responsibility *of the caller* to invoke the custom Create() method. If this step is forgotten, the object's state data is assigned to the values established within the Initialize event handler. In any case, here is an example of invoking our ad hoc VB6 Create() method:

```
' A slightly better VB6 solution.
Dim vb6Car As Car
Set vb6Car = New Car         ' Initialize fired! Default values established.
Vb6Car.Create "Zippy", 90    ' Supply custom values.
```

In an ideal world, the object user could specify startup values at the time of creation. In essence, you would *like* to be able to write the following VB6 code:

```
' ILLEGAL VB6 code!!!
Dim vb6Car As New Car("Zippy", 90)
```

While illegal in VB6, using VB 2008 you are able to do this very thing by defining any number of class constructors. Simply put, a constructor is a subroutine of a class that is called *by the CLR at runtime* when you create an object using the New keyword.

■ **Note** The VB6 class Initialize (and Terminate) events are no longer available under VB 2008. However, the default constructor (examined next) is the functional equivalent of Initialize. On a related note, Chapter 8 examines the garbage collection process and the logical replacement of the VB6 Terminate event.

The Role of the Default Constructor

First of all, understand that every VB 2008 class is provided with a freebie *default constructor* that you may redefine if need be. By definition, default constructors never take arguments. Beyond allocating the new object into memory, the default constructor ensures that all state data is set to an appropriate default value (see Chapter 3 for information regarding the default values of VB 2008 data types).

If you are not satisfied with these default assignments, you may redefine the default constructor by defining a Public subroutine named New() on any VB 2008 class type. To illustrate, update your VB 2008 Car class as follows:

```
Public Class Car
  ' The "state" of the Car.
  Public petName As String
  Public currSpeed As Integer

  ' A custom default constructor.
  Public Sub New()
    petName = "Chuck"
    currSpeed = 10
  End Sub
...
End Class
```

In this case, we are forcing all Car objects to begin life named Chuck moving down the road at 10 MPH. With this, you are able to create a Car object set to these default values as follows:

```
Sub Main()
  ' Invoking the default constructor.
  Dim chuck As New Car()
  ' Prints "Chuck is going 10 MPH."
  chuck.PrintState()
End Sub
```

Strictly speaking, the VB 2008 compiler allows you to omit the empty parentheses when invoking the default constructor. This is purely a typing time saver and has no effect on performance or code size. Given this point, we could allocate a Car type using the default constructor as follows:

```
Sub Main()
  ' Note lack of () on constructor call.
  Dim chuck As New Car
End Sub
```

Defining Custom Constructors

Typically, classes define additional constructors beyond the default. In doing so, you provide the object user with a simple and consistent way to initialize the state of an object directly at the time of creation. Given this fact, VB 2008 developers have no need to author VB6-style ad hoc creations methods (such as a Create() method) to allow the caller to set the object's state data. Ponder the following update to the Car class, which now supports a total of three class constructors:

```
Public Class Car
...
  ' A custom default constructor.
  Public Sub New()
    petName = "Chuck"
    currSpeed = 10
  End Sub

  ' Here, currSpeed will receive the
  ' default value of an Integer (zero).
  Public Sub New(ByVal pn As String)
    petName = pn
  End Sub

  Public Sub New(ByVal pn As String, ByVal cs As Integer)
    petName = pn
    currSpeed = cs
```

```
  End Sub
End Class
```

Keep in mind that what makes one constructor different from another (in the eyes of the VB 2008 compiler) is the number of and type of constructor arguments. Recall from Chapter 4, when you define a method of the same name that differs by the number or type of arguments, you have *overloaded* the method. Thus, the Car type has *overloaded* the constructor to provide a number of ways to create the object at the time of declaration. In any case, you are now able to create Car objects using any of the public constructors. For example:

```
Sub Main()
  ' Make a Car called Chuck going 10 MPH.
  Dim chuck As New Car()
  chuck.PrintState()

  ' Make a Car called Mary going 0 MPH.
  Dim mary As New Car("Mary")
  mary.PrintState()

  ' Make a Car called Daisy going 75 MPH.
  Dim daisy As New Car("Daisy", 75)
  daisy.PrintState()
End Sub
```

Notice that the variable named mary will automatically have the currSpeed variable set to 0 regardless of the fact that we did not specify a current speed via a constructor parameter. Again, this due to the fact that fields of a class always receive a safe default value that will be used unless a constructor says otherwise.

The Default Constructor Revisited

As you have just learned, all classes are endowed with a free default constructor. Thus, if you insert a new class into your current project named Motorcycle, defined like so:

```
Public Class Motorcycle
  Public Sub PopAWheely()
    Console.WriteLine("Yeeeeeee Haaaaaeewww!")
  End Sub
End Class
```

you are able to create an instance of the Motorcycle type via the default constructor out of the box:

```
Sub Main()
  Dim mc As New Motorcycle()
  mc.PopAWheely()
End Sub
```

However, as soon as you define a custom constructor, the default constructor is *silently removed* from the class and is no longer available! Think of it this way: if you do not define a custom constructor, the VB 2008 compiler grants you a default in order to allow the object user to create an instance of your type with field data set to their default values. However, when you define one or more custom constructors, the compiler assumes you have taken matters into your own hands.

Therefore, if you wish to allow the object user to create an instance of your type with the default constructor, as well as your custom constructor, you must *explicitly* redefine the default. To this end, understand that in a vast majority of cases, the implementation of the default constructor of a class is intentionally empty of code statements, as all you require is the ability to create an object with default values:

```
Public Class Motorcycle
  Public driverIntensity As Integer

  Public Sub PopAWheely()
    For i As Integer = 0 To driverIntensity
      Console.WriteLine("Yeeeeeee Haaaaaeewww!")
    Next
  End Sub

  ' Put back the default constructor.
  ' Remember, fields of a class automatically
  ' are set to a default value, so driverIntensity
  ' is set to zero on our behalf.
  Public Sub New()
  End Sub

  ' Our custom constructor.
  Public Sub New(ByVal intensity As Integer)
    driverIntensity = intensity
  End Sub
End Class
```

The Role of the Me Keyword

Like earlier additions of Visual Basic, VB 2008 supplies a Me keyword that provides access to the current class instance. One possible use of the Me keyword is to resolve name clashes, which can arise when an incoming parameter is named identically to a data field of the type. Of course, ideally you would simply adopt a naming convention that does not result in such ambiguity; however, to illustrate this use of the Me keyword, update your Motorcycle class with a new public String field (named name) to represent the driver's name. Next, add a new subroutine named SetDriverName() implemented as follows:

```
Public Class Motorcycle
  Public driverIntensity As Integer
  Public name As String

  Public Sub SetDriverName(ByVal name As String)
    name = name
  End Sub
...
End Class
```

Although this code will compile just fine, if you update Main() to call SetDriverName() and then print out the value of the name field, you may be surprised to find that the value of the name field is an empty string!

```
' Make a Motorcycle named Tiny?
Dim c As New Motorcycle(5)
c.SetDriverName("Tiny")
c.PopAWheely()
Console.WriteLine("Rider name is {0}", c.name) ' Prints an empty name value!
```

The problem is that the implementation of SetDriverName() is assigning the incoming parameter *back to itself* given that the compiler assumes name is referring to the variable currently in the method scope rather than the name field at the class scope. To inform the compiler that you wish to set the current object's name data field to the incoming name parameter, simply use Me:

```
Public Sub SetDriverName(ByVal name As String)
  Me.name = name
End Sub
```

Do understand that if there is no name clash, you are not required to make use of the `Me` keyword when a class wishes to access its own data or members. For example, if we rename the `String` data member from `name` to `driverName`, the use of `Me` is optional as there is no longer a name clash between the field and parameter:

```
Public Class Motorcycle
  Public driverIntensity As Integer
  Public driverName As String

  Public Sub SetDriverName(ByVal name As String)
    ' These two lines are functionally identical.
    driverName = name
    Me.driverName = name
  End Sub
...
End Class
```

Even though there is little to be gained when using `Me` in unambiguous situations, you may still find this keyword useful when implementing members, as IDEs such as Visual Studio 2008 and SharpDevelop will enable IntelliSense when `Me` is specified. This can be very helpful when you have forgotten the name of a class item and want to quickly recall the definition. Consider Figure 5-4.

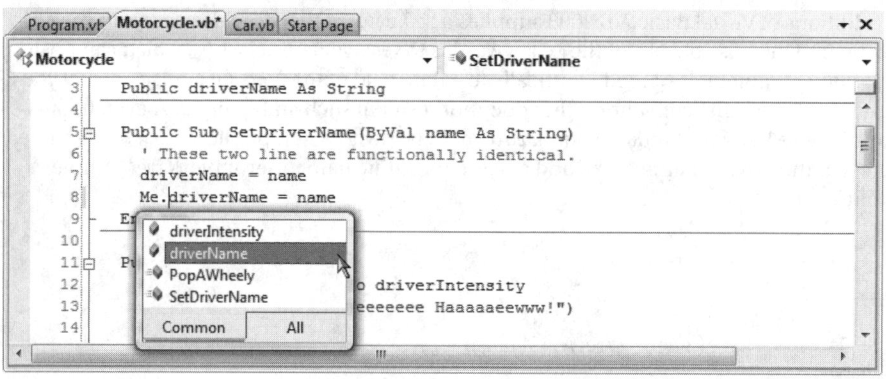

Figure 5-4. *The IntelliSense of* `Me`

■ **Note** It is a compiler error to use the `Me` keyword within the implementation of a `Shared` member (explained shortly). As you will see, shared methods operate on the class (not object) level, and therefore at the class level, there is no current object (thus no `Me`)!

Chaining Constructor Calls Using Me

Another use of the `Me` keyword is to design a class using a technique termed *constructor chaining.* This OOP programming idiom is helpful when you have a class that defines multiple constructors. Given the fact that constructors often validate the incoming arguments to enforce various business rules, it can be quite common to find redundant validation logic within a class's constructor set. Consider the following updated Motorcycle class:

```
Public Class Motorcycle
  Public driverIntensity As Integer
  Public driverName As String
...
  ' Redundant constructor logic below!
  Public Sub New()
  End Sub

  Public Sub New(ByVal intensity As Integer)
    If intensity > 10 Then
      intensity = 10
    End If
    driverIntensity = intensity
  End Sub

  Public Sub New(ByVal intensity As Integer, ByVal name As String)
    If intensity > 10 Then
      intensity = 10
    End If
    driverIntensity = intensity
    driverName = name
  End Sub
End Class
```

Here (perhaps in an attempt to ensure the safety of the rider), each constructor is ensuring that the intensity level is never greater than 10. While this is all well and good, we do have redundant code statements in two constructors. This is less than ideal, as we are now required to update code in multiple locations if our rules change (for example, if the intensity should not be greater than 5).

One way to improve the current situation is to define a helper method in the Motorcycle class that will validate the incoming argument(s). If we were to do so, each constructor could make a call to this method before making the field assignment(s). While this approach does allow us to isolate the code we need to update when the business rules change, we are now dealing with the following redundancy:

```
Public Class Motorcycle
  Public driverIntensity As Integer
  Public driverName As String
...
  ' Constructors.
  Public Sub New()
  End Sub

  Public Sub New(ByVal intensity As Integer)
    ValidateIntensity(intensity)
    driverIntensity = intensity
  End Sub

  Public Sub New(ByVal intensity As Integer, ByVal name As String)
    ValidateIntensity(intensity)
    driverIntensity = intensity
    driverName = name
  End Sub
```

```
  Sub ValidateIntensity(ByRef intensity As Integer)
    If intensity > 10 Then
      intensity = 10
    End If
  End Sub
End Class
```

Under VB 2008, a cleaner approach is to designate the constructor that takes the *greatest number of arguments* as the "master constructor" and have its implementation perform the required validation logic. The remaining constructors can make use of the Me keyword to forward the incoming arguments to the master constructor and provide any additional parameters as necessary. In this way, we only need to worry about maintaining validation logic for a single constructor for the entire class, while the remaining constructors are basically empty. Here is the final iteration of the Motorcycle class (with one additional constructor for the sake of illustration):

```
Public Class Motorcycle
  Public driverIntensity As Integer
  Public driverName As String
...
  ' Constructors.
  Public Sub New()
  End Sub

  Public Sub New(ByVal intensity As Integer)
    Me.New(intensity, "")
  End Sub

  Public Sub New(ByVal name As String)
    Me.New(5, name)
  End Sub

  ' This is the "master" constructor that does all the real work.
  Public Sub New(ByVal intensity As Integer, ByVal name As String)
    If intensity > 10 Then
      intensity = 10
    End If
    driverIntensity = intensity
    driverName = name
  End Sub
End Class
```

Note When a constructor forwards parameters to the master constructor using Me.New(), it must do so on the very first line within the constructor body. If you fail to do so, you will receive a compiler error.

Understand that using the Me keyword to chain constructor calls is never mandatory. However, when you make use of this technique, you do tend to end up with a more maintainable and concise class definition. Again, using this technique you can simplify your programming tasks, as the real work is delegated to a single constructor (typically the constructor that has the most parameters), while the other constructors simply "pass the buck."

Observing Constructor Flow

On a final note, do know that once a constructor passes arguments to the designated master constructor (and that constructor has processed the data), the constructor invoked originally by the object user will finish executing any remaining code statements. To clarify, update each of the constructors of the Motorcycle class with a fitting call to Console.WriteLine():

```
Public Class Motorcycle
...
  ' Constructors.
  Public Sub New()
    Console.WriteLine("In default c-tor")
  End Sub

  Public Sub New(ByVal intensity As Integer)
    Me.New(intensity, "")
    Console.WriteLine("In c-tor taking an Integer")
  End Sub

  Public Sub New(ByVal name As String)
    Me.New(5, name)
    Console.WriteLine("In c-tor taking a String")
  End Sub

  Public Sub New(ByVal intensity As Integer, ByVal name As String)
    Console.WriteLine("In master c-tor")
    If intensity > 10 Then
      intensity = 10
    End If
    driverIntensity = intensity
    driverName = name
  End Sub
End Class
```

Now, ensure your Main() method exercises a Motorcycle object as follows:

```
Sub Main()
...
  ' Make a Motorcycle.
  Dim c As New Motorcycle(5)
  c.SetDriverName("Tiny")
  c.PopAWheely()
  Console.WriteLine("Rider name is {0}", c.name)
End Sub
```

With this, ponder the output in Figure 5-5.

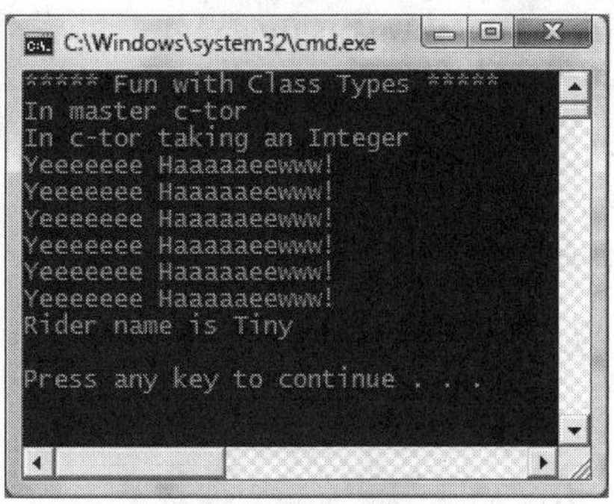

Figure 5-5. *Constructor chaining at work*

As you can see, the flow of constructor logic is as follows:

- We create our object and initialize it by invoking the constructor requiring a single Integer.
- This constructor forwards the supplied data to the master constructor and provides any additional startup arguments not specified by the caller.
- The master constructor assigns the incoming data to the object's field data.
- Control is returned to the constructor originally called, and any remaining code statements in that constructor are executed.

Great! At this point you are able to define a class with field data and various members that can be initialized using any number of constructors. Next up, let's formalize the role of the Shared keyword.

■ **Source Code** The SimpleClassExample project is included under the Chapter 5 subdirectory.

Understanding the Shared Keyword

A VB 2008 class (or structure) may define any number of *shared members* via the Shared keyword. When you do so, the member in question must be invoked directly from the class level, rather than from an object variable. To illustrate the distinction, consider our good friend System.Console. As you have seen, you do not invoke the WriteLine() method from the object level:

```
' Error! Can't create Console objects!
Dim c As New Console()
c.WriteLine("I can't be printed...")
```

but instead simply prefix the type name to the shared WriteLine() member:

```
' Correct! WriteLine() is a Shared method.
Console.WriteLine("Thanks...")
```

Simply put, Shared members are items that are deemed (by the type designer) to be so commonplace that there is no need to create an instance of the type when invoking the member.

Defining Shared Methods (and Fields)

Assume you have a new Console Application project named SharedMethods and have inserted a class named Teenager that defines a Shared function named Complain(). This method returns a random string, obtained in part by calling a helper function named GetRandomNumber():

```
Public Class Teenager
  Public Shared r As New Random()

  Public Shared Function GetRandomNumber(ByVal upperLimit As Short) As Integer
    Return r.Next(upperLimit)
  End Function

  Public Shared Function Complain() As String
    Dim messages As String() = _
      {"Do I have to?", "He started it!", "I'm too tired...", _
        "I hate school!", "You are sooo wrong."}
```

```
    Return messages(GetRandomNumber(5))
  End Function
End Class
```

Notice that the System.Random member variable (named simply r) and the GetRandomNumber() helper method have also been declared as Shared members of the Teenager class, given the rule that Shared members can operate only on other Shared members.

Note Allow me to repeat myself. Shared members can operate only on Shared data and call Shared methods of the defining class. If you attempt to make use of non-Shared data or call a non-Shared method within a Shared member, you'll receive a compiler error.

Like any Shared member, to call Complain(), prefix the name of the defining class:

```
Sub Main()
  Console.WriteLine("***** Shared Methods *****")
  For i As Integer = 0 To 5
    Console.WriteLine(Teenager.Complain())
  Next
End Sub
```

As stated, shared members are bound at the *class* not *object* level. However, a strange VB-ism exists that allows us to invoke the shared Complain() method as follows:

```
Sub Main()
  Console.WriteLine("***** Shared Methods *****")

  ' VB-ism!
  Dim bob As New Teenager()
  For i As Integer = 0 To 5
    Console.WriteLine(bob.Complain())
  Next
End Sub
```

Although the previous code will result in invoking the Complain() method, you will also receive a compiler warning:

```
Access of shared member, constant member, enum member or nested
type through an instance; qualifying expression will not be evaluated.
```

Basically, this warning is informing us that Complain() is not to be invoked from a Teenager object named bob. How then is Complain() invoked? Under the covers, the VB 2008 compiler simply substitutes a correct call to Teenager.Complain() in the CIL code, which can be verified using ildasm.exe (see Chapter 1):

```
.method public static void  Main() cil managed
{
...
  IL_002c: call string SharedMethods.Teenager::Complain()
...
} // end of method Program::Main
```

As you might agree, the VB-ism is confusing at best. If you wish to inform the VB 2008 compiler to emit an error (rather than a warning) when invoking a shared member from an object variable, you can do so by double-clicking the My Project icon in the Solution Explorer, selecting the Compile tab, and setting the Instance variable accesses shared member condition to Error (see Figure 5-6).

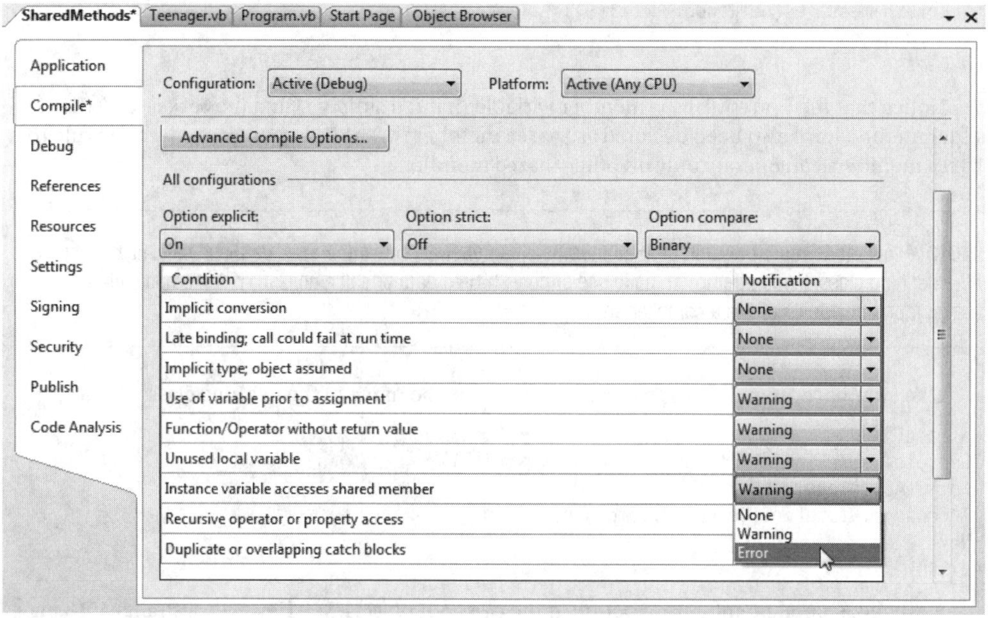

Figure 5-6. *Configuring compiler errors when using an object to call shared members*

By doing so, we would now receive a compile-time error when writing code such as

```
Sub Main()
  Dim bob as New Teenager()
  For i As Integer = 0 To 5
    ' Now a compile-time error.
    Console.WriteLine(bob.Complain())
  Next
End Sub
```

■ **Source Code** The SharedMethods project is located under the Chapter 5 subdirectory.

Defining Shared Data

In addition to Shared methods, a type may also define Shared field data (such as the Random member variable seen in the previous Teenager class). Understand that when a class defines non-Shared data (properly referred to as *instance data*), each object of this type maintains an independent copy of the field. For example, assume a class that models a savings account is defined in a new Console Application project named SharedData:

```
' This class has a single piece of non-Shared data.
Public Class SavingsAccount
  Public currBalance As Double

  Public Sub New(ByVal balance As Double)
    currBalance = balance
  End Sub
End Class
```

When you create SavingsAccount objects, memory for the currBalance field is allocated for each class instance. Shared data, on the other hand, is allocated once and shared among all objects of the same type. To illustrate the usefulness of Shared data, assume you add a piece of Shared data named currInterestRate to the SavingsAccount class:

```
Public Class SavingsAccount
  Public currBalance As Double

  ' A Shared point of data.
  Public Shared currInterestRate As Double = 0.04

  Public Sub New(ByVal balance As Double)
    currBalance = balance
  End Sub
End Class
```

If you were to create three instances of SavingsAccount as follows:

```
Sub Main()
  Console.WriteLine("***** Fun with Shared Data *****")
  Dim s1 As New SavingsAccount(50)
  Dim s2 As New SavingsAccount(100)
  Dim s3 As New SavingsAccount(10000.75)
End Sub
```

the in-memory data allocation would look something like Figure 5-7.

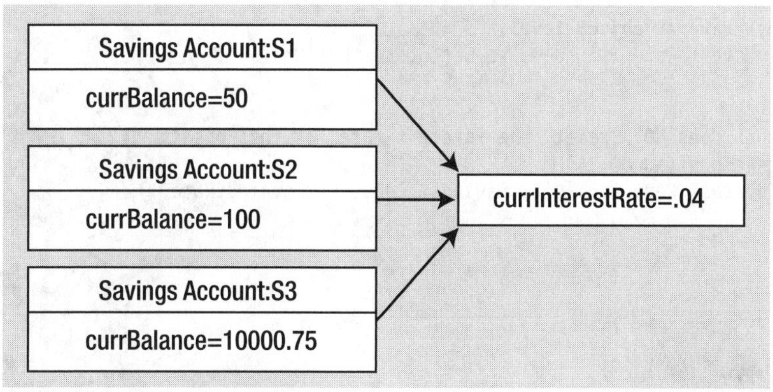

Figure 5-7. *Shared data is allocated once and shared among all instances of the class.*

Let's update the SavingsAccount class to define two Shared methods to get and set the interest rate value (named SetInterestRate() and GetInterestRate()) as well as two instance-level members (named SetInterestRateObj() and GetInterestRateObj()) that operate on the same shared data:

```
Public Class SavingsAccount
  Public currBalance As Double
  Public Shared currInterestRate As Double = 0.04

  Public Sub New(ByVal balance As Double)
    currBalance = balance
  End Sub
```

```
  ' Shared members to get/set interest rate.
  Public Shared Sub SetInterestRate(ByVal newRate As Double)
    currInterestRate = newRate
  End Sub
  Public Shared Function GetInterestRate() As Double
    Return currInterestRate
  End Function

  ' Instance members to get/set interest rate.
  Public Sub SetInterestRateObj(ByVal newRate As Double)
    currInterestRate = newRate
  End Sub
  Public Function GetInterestRateObj() As Double
    Return currInterestRate
  End Function
End Class
```

As stated, Shared methods can operate only on Shared data. However, a non-Shared method can make use of both Shared and non-Shared data. This should make sense, given that Shared data is available to all instances of the type. Now, observe the following usage and the output in Figure 5-8:

```
Sub Main()
  Console.WriteLine("***** Fun with Shared Data *****")
  Dim s1 As New SavingsAccount(50)
  Dim s2 As New SavingsAccount(100)

  ' Get and Set interest rate at object level.
  Console.WriteLine("Interest Rate is: {0}", s1.GetInterestRateObj())
  s2.SetInterestRateObj(0.08)

  ' Make new object; this does NOT "reset" the interest rate for this object.
  Dim s3 As New SavingsAccount(10000.75)
  Console.WriteLine("Interest Rate is: {0}", SavingsAccount.GetInterestRate())
  Console.ReadLine()
End Sub
```

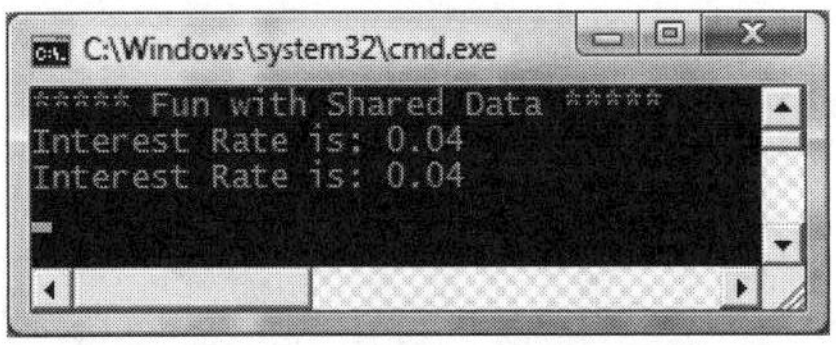

Figure 5-8. *Shared data is allocated only once.*

As you can see, when you create new instances of the SavingsAccount class, the value of the Shared data is not reset when we create new objects, as the CLR will allocate the data into memory exactly one time for the current application. After that point, all objects of type SavingsAccount operate on the same value. Thus, if one object were to change the interest rate, all other objects would report the same value:

```
Sub Main()
...
  SavingsAccount.SetInterestRate(0.09)
  ' All three lines print out "Interest Rate is: 0.09"
```

```
    Console.WriteLine("Interest Rate is: {0}", s1.GetInterestRateObj())
    Console.WriteLine("Interest Rate is: {0}", s2.GetInterestRateObj())
    Console.WriteLine("Interest Rate is: {0}", SavingsAccount.GetInterestRate())
    Console.ReadLine()
  End Sub
```

Defining Shared Constructors

As you have learned earlier in this chapter, constructors are used to set the value of an object's data at the time of construction. Thus, if you were to assign a value to a piece of Shared data within an instance-level constructor, you would be saddened to find that the shared data item is reset each time you create a new object! For example, assume you have updated the SavingsAccount class as follows:

```
Class SavingsAccount
  Public currBalance As Double
  Public Shared currInterestRate As Double

  Public Sub New(ByVal balance As Double)
    currBalance = balance
    currInterestRate = 0.04
  End Sub
...
End Class
```

If you execute the previous Main() method, notice how the currInterestRate variable is reset each time you create a new SavingsAccount object (see Figure 5-9).

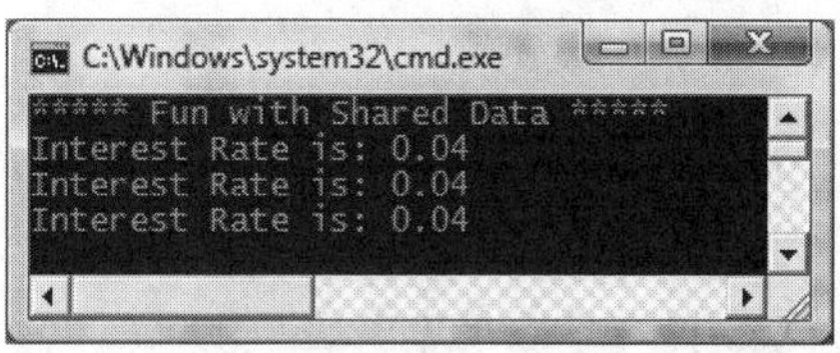

Figure 5-9. *Assigning* Shared *data in a constructor "resets" the value.*

While you are always free to establish the initial value of Shared data using member initialization syntax, what if the value for your Shared data needed to be obtained from a database or external file? To perform such tasks requires a method scope (such as a constructor) to execute the code statements. However, if we were to write this code in an instance-level constructor, we could execute the same code (and therefore reset the shared data) every time we create a new object. For this very reason, VB 2008 allows you to define a Shared constructor:

```
Class SavingsAccount
  Public currBalance As Double
  Public Shared currInterestRate As Double

  ' A shared constructor.
  Shared Sub New()
    Console.WriteLine("In Shared ctor!")
    currInterestRate = 0.04
  End Sub
...
End Class
```

Simply put, a *shared constructor* is a special constructor that is an ideal place to initialize the values of shared data when the value is not known at compile time (e.g., you need to read in the value from an external file, database, etc.). Here are a few points of interest regarding Shared constructors:

- A given class (or structure) may define only a single Shared constructor.
- A Shared constructor does not take an access modifier and cannot take any parameters (which should make sense, given that we never directly call it).
- A Shared constructor executes exactly one time, regardless of how many objects of the type are created.
- The runtime invokes the Shared constructor when it creates an instance of the class or before accessing the first Shared member invoked by the caller.
- The Shared constructor executes before any instance-level constructors.

Given this modification, when you create new SavingsAccount objects, the value of the Shared data is preserved, and the output is identical to Figure 5-8 (shown previously).

■ **Source Code** The SharedData project is located under the Chapter 5 subdirectory.

At this point in the chapter, you (hopefully) feel comfortable defining simple class types containing constructors, fields, and shared members. Now that you have the basics of class design under your belt, we can formally investigate the three pillars of object-oriented programming.

Defining the Pillars of OOP

All object-oriented languages must contend with three core principals, often called the "pillars of object-oriented programming (OOP)":

- *Encapsulation*: How does this language hide an object's internal implementation details and preserve data integrity?
- *Inheritance*: How does this language promote code reuse between related classes?
- *Polymorphism*: How does this language let you treat related objects in a similar way?

As you are may be aware, VB6 did not support each pillar of object technology. Specifically, VB6 lacked inheritance (and therefore lacked true polymorphism). VB 2008, on the other hand, supports each aspect of OOP, and is on par with any other modern-day OO language (C#, Java, C++, Delphi, etc.). Before digging into the syntactic details of each pillar, it is important that you understand the basic role of each. Here is an overview of each pillar, which will be examined in full detail over the remainder of this chapter and the next.

The Role of Encapsulation

The first pillar of OOP is called *encapsulation*. This trait boils down to the language's ability to hide unnecessary implementation details from the object user. For example, assume you are using a class named DatabaseReader, which has two primary methods: Open() and Close():

```
' This object encapsulates the details of opening and closing a database.
Dim dbReader As New DatabaseReader()
dbReader.Open("C:\MyCars.mdf")

' Do something with data file...

dbReader.Close()
```

The fictitious DatabaseReader class encapsulates the inner details of locating, loading, manipulating, and closing the data file. Object users love encapsulation, as this pillar of OOP keeps programming tasks simpler. There is no need to worry about the numerous lines of code that are working behind the scenes to carry out the work of the DatabaseReader class. All you do is create an instance and send the appropriate messages (e.g., "Open the file named MyCars.mdf located on my C drive").

Closely related to the notion of encapsulating programming logic is the idea of data hiding. Ideally, an object's state data should be specified as Private (or possibly Protected, which will be fully explained in Chapter 6). In this way, the outside world must ask politely in order to change or obtain the underlying value. This is a good thing, as publicly declared data points can easily become corrupted (hopefully by accident rather than intent!). You will formally examine this aspect of encapsulation in just a bit.

The Role of Inheritance

The next pillar of OOP, *inheritance*, boils down to the language's ability to allow you to build *new* class definitions based on *existing* class definitions. In essence, inheritance allows you to extend the behavior of a *base* (or *parent*) class by inheriting its functionality into the derived *subclass* (also called a *child class*). Figure 5-10 shows a simple example.

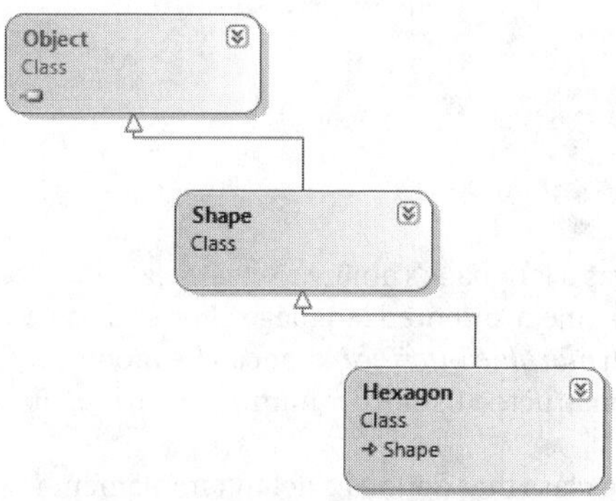

Figure 5-10. *The "is-a" relationship*

You can read the diagram in Figure 5-10 as "A Hexagon is-a Shape that is-an Object." When you have classes related by inheritance, you establish "is-a" relationships between types. The "is-a" relationship is often termed *classical inheritance*. Under the .NET platform, System.Object is always the topmost base class in any class hierarchy, which defines some bare-bones functionality fully described in the next chapter. The Shape class extends Object. You can assume that Shape defines some number of members that are common to all descendents. The Hexagon class extends Shape, and inherits the functionality and state defined by Shape and Object, as well as defines additional hexagon-related details of its own (whatever those may be).

There is another form of code reuse in the world of OOP: the containment/delegation model (also known as the *"has-a" relationship* or *aggregation*). This form of reuse (used exclusively by VB6) is *not* used to establish parent/child relationships. Rather, the "has-a" relationship allows one class instance to contain an instance of another class and expose its functionality (if required) to the object user indirectly.

For example, assume you are again modeling an automobile. You might want to express the idea that a car "has-a" radio. It would be illogical to attempt to derive the Car class from a Radio, or vice versa (a Car "is-a" Radio? I think not!). Rather, you have two independent classes working together, where the Car class creates and exposes the Radio's functionality:

```
Public Class Radio
  Public Sub PowerUp(ByVal turnOn As Boolean)
    Console.WriteLine("Radio on: {0}", turnOn)
  End Sub
End Class

Public Class Car
  ' Car "has-a" Radio
  Private myRadio As New Radio()

  Public Sub TurnOnRadio(ByVal onOff As Boolean)
    ' Delegate call to inner object.
    myRadio.PowerUp(onOff)
  End Sub
End Class
```

Notice that the object user has no clue that the Car class is making use of an inner object.

```
Sub Main()
  ' Call is forwarded to Radio internally.
  Dim viper as New Car()
  viper.TurnOnRadio(False)
End Sub
```

The Role of Polymorphism

The final pillar of OOP is *polymorphism*. This trait captures a language's ability to treat related objects in a similar manner. Specifically, this tenant of an object-oriented language allows a base class to define a set of members (formally termed the *polymorphic interface*) that can be modified by each descendant. A class's polymorphic interface is constructed using any number of *virtual* or *abstract* members (see Chapter 6 for full details).

In a nutshell, a *virtual member* is a member in a base class that defines a default implementation that may be changed (or more formally speaking, *overridden*) by a derived class. In contrast, an *abstract method* is a member in a base class that does *not* provide a default implementation, but does provide a signature. When a class derives from a base class defining an abstract method, it *must* be overridden by a derived type. In either case, when derived types override the members defined by a base class, they are essentially redefining how they respond to the same request.

To preview polymorphism, let's provide some details behind the shapes hierarchy shown in Figure 5-10. Assume that the Shape class has defined a virtual subroutine named Draw() that takes no parameters. Given the fact that every shape needs to render itself in a unique manner, subclasses (such as Hexagon and Circle) are free to override this method to their own liking (see Figure 5-11).

Once a polymorphic interface has been designed, you can begin to make various assumptions in your code. For example, given that Hexagon and Circle derive from a common parent (Shape), an array of Shape types could contain anything deriving from this base class. Furthermore, given that Shape defines a polymorphic interface to all derived types (the Draw() method in this example), we know each member in the Shape array has this functionality.

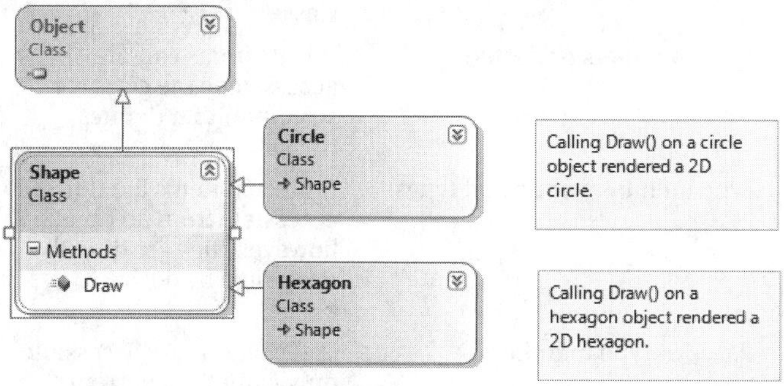

Figure 5-11. *Classical polymorphism*

Consider the following Main() method, which instructs an array of Shape-derived types to render themselves using the Draw() method:

```
Module Program
  Sub Main()
    Dim myShapes(2) As Shape
    myShapes(0) = New Hexagon()
    myShapes(1) = New Circle()
    myShapes(2) = New Hexagon()

    For Each s As Shape In myShapes
      s.Draw()
    Next
    Console.ReadLine()
  End Sub
End Module
```

This wraps up our brisk overview of the pillars of OOP. Now that you have the theory in your mind, the remainder of this chapter explores further details of how encapsulation is handled under Visual Basic 2008. The next chapter will tackle the details of inheritance and polymorphism.

Visual Basic 2008 Access Modifiers

When working with encapsulation, you must always take into account which aspects of a type are visible to various parts of your application. Specifically, types (classes, interfaces, structures, enumerations, delegates) and their members (properties, subroutines, functions, constructors, fields, and so forth) can be defined using a specific keyword to control how "visible" the item is to other parts of your application. Although VB 2008 defines numerous keywords to control access, they differ on where they can be successfully applied (type or member). Table 5-1 documents the role of each access modifier and where they may be applied.

Table 5-1. *Visual Basic Access Modifiers*

Visual Basic 2008 Access Modifier	May Be Applied To	Meaning in Life
`Public`	Types or type members	Public items have no access restrictions. A public item can be accessed from an object as well as any derived class.
`Private`	Type members or nested types	Private items can only be accessed by the class (or structure) that defines the item.
`Protected`	Type members or nested types	Protected items are not accessible from an object; however, they are directly accessible by derived classes.
`Friend`	Types or type members	`Friend` items are accessible only within the current assembly. Therefore, if you define a set of `Friend`-level types within a .NET class library, other assemblies are not able to make use of them.
`Protected Friend`	Type members or nested types	When the `Protected` and `Friend` members are combined on an item, the item is accessible within the defining assembly, the defining class, and by derived classes.

In this chapter, we are primarily concerned with the `Public` and `Private` keywords. Later chapters will examine the role of the `Friend` and `Protected Friend` modifiers (useful when you build .NET code libraries) and the `Protected` modifier (useful when you are creating class hierarchies).

Access Modifiers and Nested Types

Notice that the `Private`, `Protected`, and `Protected Friend` access modifiers can be applied to a "nested type." Chapter 6 will examine nesting in detail. What you need to know at this point, however, is that a nested type is a type declared directly within the scope of `Class` or `Structure`. By way of example, here is a private enumeration (named `CarColor`) nested within a public class (named `SportsCar`):

```
Public Class SportsCar
  ' OK!  Nested types can be marked Private.
  Private Enum CarColor
    Red
    Green
    Blue
  End Enum
End Class
```

Here, it is permissible to apply the `Private` access modifier on the nested type. However, nonnested types (such as the `SportsCar`) can only be defined with the `Public` or `Friend` modifiers. Therefore, the following `Class` is illegal:

```
' Error! Nonnested types cannot be marked Private!
Private Class Radio
End Class
```

The Default Access Modifiers

By default, a type's set of properties, subroutines, and functions are implicitly `Public`. Furthermore, `Friend` is the default access modifier for any VB type declaration.

```
' A friend class with a public default constructor.
Class Radio
  Sub New()
  End Sub
End Class
```

If you wish to be very clear in your intentions, you are free to explicitly mark members and types with the `Friend` and `Public` keywords; however, the end result is identical in terms of performance and the size of the output assembly:

```
' Functionally identical to the previous class definition.
Friend Class Radio
  Public Sub New()
  End Sub
End Class
```

Access Modifiers and Field Data

Fields of a `Class` or `Structure` *must* be defined with an access modifier. Unlike constructors, properties, subroutines, or functions, there is not a "default" access level for field data. Consider the following illegal update to the `Radio` class:

```
Public Class Radio
  ' Error! Must define access modifer
  ' for field data!
  favoriteStation as Double

  Public Sub New()
  End Sub
End Class
```

To rectify the situation, simply define the type with your access modifier of choice:

```
Public Class Radio
  Private favoriteStation as Double

  Public Sub New()
  End Sub
End Class
```

■ **Note** It is possible to define a data field of a `Class` or `Structure` using the `Dim` keyword (although it is considered bad style). If you do so, the variable behaves as if it were declared with the `Private` access modifier.

The First Pillar: VB 2008's Encapsulation Services

The concept of encapsulation revolves around the notion that an object's internal data should not be directly accessible to the user of the object. Rather, if the caller wants to view or modify the state of an object, the user does so indirectly using *accessor* (i.e., *getter*) and *mutator* (i.e., *setter*) methods. In VB 2008, encapsulation is enforced at the syntactic level using the `Public`, `Private`, `Friend`, and `Protected` keywords. To illustrate the need for encapsulation services, assume you have created the following class definition:

```
' A class with a single field.
Public Class Book
  Public numberOfPages As Integer
End Class
```

The problem with public field data is that the items have no ability to intrinsically "understand" whether the current value to which they are assigned is valid with regard to the current business rules of the system. As you know, the upper range of a VB 2008 `Integer` is quite large (2,147,483,647). Therefore, the compiler allows the following assignment:

```
' Hmmm. That is one heck of a mini-novel!
Sub Main()
  Dim miniNovel As New Book()
  miniNovel.numberOfPages = 30000000
End Sub
```

Although you have not overflowed the boundaries of an `Integer` data type, it should be clear that a mini-novel with a page count of 30,000,000 pages is a bit unreasonable. As you can see, public fields do not provide a way to trap logical upper (or lower) limits. If your current system has a business rule that states a book must be between 1 and 1,000 pages, you are at a loss to enforce this programmatically. Because of this, public fields typically have no place in a production-level class definition.

Encapsulation provides a way to preserve the integrity of an object's state data. Rather than defining public fields (which can easily foster data corruption), you should get in the habit of defining *private data*, which is indirectly manipulated using one of two main techniques:

- Define a pair of accessor (get) and mutator (set) methods.
- Define a property.

Additionally, VB 2008 supports the special keywords `ReadOnly` and `WriteOnly`, which also deliver a level of data protection (more details later in this chapter). Whichever technique you choose, the point is that a well-encapsulated class should hide the details of how it operates from the prying eyes of the outside world. This is often termed *black box programming*. The beauty of this approach is that an object is free to change how a given method is implemented under the hood. It does this without breaking any existing code making use of it, provided that the signature of the method remains constant.

Encapsulation Using Traditional Accessors and Mutators

Over the remaining pages in this chapter, we will be building a fairly complete class that models a general employee. To get the ball rolling, create a new Console Application named EmployeeApp and insert a new `Class` (named `Employee`) using the Project ➤ Add Class menu item. Update the `Employee` class with the following fields, subroutines, and constructors:

```
Public Class Employee
  ' Field data.
  Private empName As String
```

```
  Private empID As Integer
  Private currPay As Single

  ' Constructors
  Public Sub New()
  End Sub
  Public Sub New(ByVal name As String, ByVal id As Integer, ByVal pay As Single)
    empName = name
    empID = id
    currPay = pay
  End Sub

  ' Methods.
  Public Sub GiveBonus(ByVal amount As Single)
    currPay += amount
  End Sub
  Public Sub DisplayStats()
    Console.WriteLine("Name: {0}", empName)
    Console.WriteLine("ID: {0}", empID)
    Console.WriteLine("Pay: {0}", currPay)
  End Sub
End Class
```

Notice that the fields of the Employee class are currently defined using the Private access keyword. Given this, the empName, empID, and currPay fields are not directly accessible to the outside world. For example, if we create an Employee object and try to access its fields, we get a compiler error:

```
Sub Main()
  ' Error! Cannot directly access Private members
  ' from an object!
  Dim emp As New Employee()
  emp.empName = "Marv"
End Sub
```

If you want the outside world to interact with your private string representing a worker's full name, tradition dictates defining an accessor (get method) and mutator (set method). For example, to encapsulate the empName field, you could add the following Public methods to the existing Employee class type:

```
' Traditional accessor and mutator for a point of private data.
Public Class Employee
  ' Field data.
  Private empName As String
...
  ' Accessor (get method).
  Public Function GetName() As String
    Return empName
  End Function

  ' Mutator (set method).
  Public Sub SetName(ByVal name As String)
    ' Remove any illegal characters (!,@,#,$,%),
    ' check maximum length or case before making assignment.
    empName = name
  End Sub
End Class
```

This technique requires two uniquely named methods to operate on a single data point. To illustrate, update your `Main()` method as follows:

```
Sub Main()
  Console.WriteLine("***** Fun with Encapsulation *****")
  Dim emp As New Employee("Marvin", 456, 30000)
  emp.GiveBonus(1000)
  emp.DisplayStats()

  ' Use the get/set methods to interact with the object's name.
  emp.SetName("Marv")
  Console.WriteLine("Employee is named: {0}", emp.GetName())
  Console.ReadLine()
End Sub
```

Encapsulation Using Properties

Although you can encapsulate a piece of field data using traditional get and set methods, .NET languages prefer to enforce data protection using *properties* that are defined via the `Property` keyword. Visual Basic 6.0 programmers have long used properties to simulate direct access to field data; however, the syntax to do so has been modified under the .NET platform.

First of all, understand that properties always map to "real" accessor and mutator methods in terms of CIL code. Therefore, as a class designer, you are still able to perform any internal logic necessary before making the value assignment (e.g., uppercase the value, scrub the value for illegal characters, check the bounds of a numerical value, and so on). Here is the updated `Employee` class, now enforcing encapsulation of each field using property syntax rather than get and set methods:

```
Public Class Employee
  ' Field data.
  Private empName As String
  Private empID As Integer
  Private currPay As Single

  ' Properties.
  Public Property Name() As String
    Get
      Return empName
    End Get
    Set(ByVal value As String)
      empName = value
    End Set
  End Property

  Public Property ID() As Integer
    Get
      Return empID
    End Get
    Set(ByVal value As Integer)
      empID = value
    End Set
  End Property

  Public Property Pay() As Single
    Get
      Return currPay
    End Get
```

```
    Set(ByVal value As Single)
      currPay = value
    End Set
  End Property
...
End Class
```

Unlike VB6, a property is not represented by independent Get, Let, or Set members. Rather, a VB 2008 property is composed by defining a Get scope (accessor) and Set scope (mutator) directly within the property scope itself. Once we have these properties in place, it appears to object users that they are getting and setting a public point of data; however, the correct Get and Set block is called behind the scenes:

```
Sub Main()
  Console.WriteLine("***** Fun with Encapsulation *****")
  Dim emp As New Employee("Marvin", 456, 30000)
  emp.GiveBonus(1000)
  emp.DisplayStats()

  ' Set and Get the Name property.
  emp.Name = "Marv"
  Console.WriteLine("Employee is named: {0}", emp.Name)
  Console.ReadLine()
End Sub
```

Properties (as opposed to accessors and mutators) also make your types easier to manipulate, in that properties are able to respond to the intrinsic operators of VB 2008. To illustrate, assume that the Employee class type has an internal private member variable representing the age of the employee. Here is our update:

```
Public Class Employee
...
  Private empAge As Integer
...
  Public Property Age() As Integer
    Get
      Return empAge
    End Get
    Set(ByVal value As Integer)
      empAge = value
    End Set
  End Property

  ' Constructors.
  Public Sub New()
  End Sub
  Public Sub New(ByVal name As String, ByVal age As Integer, _
    ByVal id As Integer, ByVal pay As Single)
    empName = name
    empAge = age
    empID = id
    currPay = pay
  End Sub

...
  Sub DisplayStats()
    Console.WriteLine("Name: {0}", empName)
    Console.WriteLine("Age: {0}", empAge)
```

```
    Console.WriteLine("ID: {0}", empID)
    Console.WriteLine("Pay: {0}", currPay)
  End Sub
End Class
```

Now assume you have created an Employee object named joe. On his birthday, you wish to increment the age by one. Using traditional accessor and mutator methods, you would need to write code such as the following:

```
Dim joe As New Employee()
joe.SetAge(joe.GetAge() + 1)
```

However, if you encapsulate empAge using property syntax, you are able to simply write

```
Dim joe As New Employee()
joe.Age = joe.Age + 1
```

Internal Representation of Properties

Many programmers (especially those who program with a C-based language such as C++ or Java) tend to design traditional accessor and mutator methods using "get_" and "set_" prefixes (e.g., get_Name() and set_Name()). This naming convention itself is not problematic as far as VB 2008 is concerned. However, it is important to understand that under the hood, a property is represented in CIL code using these same prefixes. For example, if you open up the EmployeeApp.exe assembly using ildasm.exe, you see that each property is mapped to hidden get_XXX()/set_XXX() methods called internally by the CLR (see Figure 5-12).

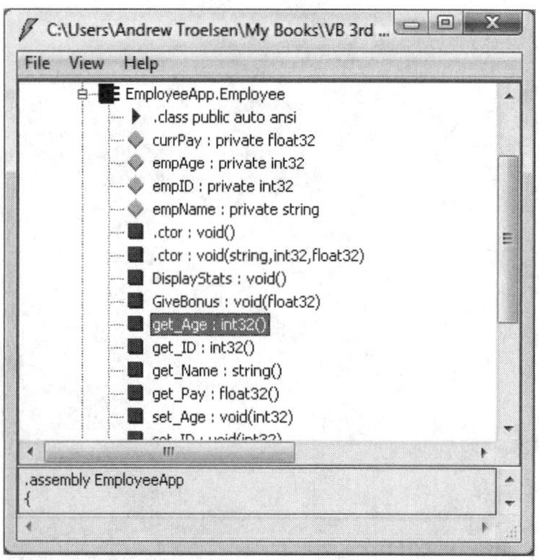

Figure 5-12. *A property is represented by get/set methods internally.*

Assume the Employee class now has a private member variable named empSSN to represent an individual's Social Security number, which is manipulated by a property named SocialSecurityNumber:

```
' Add support for a new field representing the employee's SSN.
Public Class Employee
...
  Private empSSN As String
```

```
...
  Public Property SocialSecurityNumber() As String
    Get
      Return empSSN
    End Get
    Set(ByVal value As String)
      empSSN = value
    End Set
  End Property
  ' Constructors.
  Public Sub New()
  End Sub
  Public Sub New(ByVal name As String, ByVal age As Integer, _
    ByVal id As Integer, ByVal pay As Single, _
    ByVal ssn As String)
    empName = name
    empAge = age
    empID = id
    currPay = pay
    empSSN = ssn
  End Sub
...
  Sub DisplayStats()
    Console.WriteLine("Name: {0}", empName)
    Console.WriteLine("Age: {0}", empAge)
    Console.WriteLine("SSN: {0}", empSSN)
    Console.WriteLine("ID: {0}", empID)
    Console.WriteLine("Pay: {0}", currPay)
  End Sub
End Class
```

If you were to also define two methods named get_SocialSecurityNumber() and set_SocialSecurityNumber(), you would be issued compile-time errors:

```
' Remember, a property really maps to a get_/set_ pair.
Public Class Employee
...
  Public Function get_SocialSecurityNumber() As String
    Return empSSN
  End Function
  Public Sub set_SocialSecurityNumber(ByVal val As String)
    empSSN = val
  End Sub
End Class
```

Note The .NET base class libraries always favor type properties over traditional accessor and mutator methods. Therefore, if you wish to build custom types that integrate well with the .NET platform, avoid defining traditional get and set methods.

Controlling Visibility Levels of Property Get/Set Statements

Prior to .NET 2.0, the visibility of get and set logic was solely controlled by the access modifier of the property declaration:

```
' The get and set logic is both public,
' given the declaration of the property.
Public Property SocialSecurityNumber() As String
  Get
    Return empSSN
  End Get
  Set(ByVal value As String)
    empSSN = value
  End Set
End Property
```

In some cases, it would be helpful to specify unique accessibility levels for get and set logic. To do so, simply prefix an accessibility keyword to the appropriate `Get` or `Set` keyword (the unqualified scope takes the visibility of the property's declaration):

```
' Object users can only get the value, however
' the Employee class and derived types can set the value.
Public Property SocialSecurityNumber() As String
  Get
    Return empSSN
  End Get
  Protected Set(ByVal value As String)
    empSSN = value
  End Set
End Property
```

In this case, the set logic of `SocialSecurityNumber` can only be called by the current class and derived classes and therefore cannot be called from external code.

Read-Only and Write-Only Properties

When creating class types, you may wish to configure a *read-only property*. To do so, simply build a property using the `ReadOnly` keyword and omit the `Set` block. Likewise, if you wish to have a *write-only property*, build a property using the `WriteOnly` keyword and omit the `Get` block. For example, here is how the `SocialSecurityNumber` property could be retrofitted as read-only:

```
Public Class Employee
...
  ' Now as a read-only property.
  Public ReadOnly Property SocialSecurityNumber() As String
    Get
      Return empSSN
    End Get
  End Property
End Class
```

Given this adjustment, the only manner in which an employee's Social Security number can be set is through a constructor argument.

Shared Properties

VB 2008 also supports shared properties. Recall from earlier in this chapter that shared members are accessed at the class level, not via an instance (object) of that class. For example, assume that the `Employee` type defines a shared point of data to represent the name of the organization employing these workers. You may encapsulate a shared property as follows:

```
' Shared properties must operate on shared data!
Public Class Employee
...
  Private Shared companyName As String
...
  Public Shared Property Company() As String
    Get
      Return companyName
    End Get
    Set(ByVal value As String)
      companyName = value
    End Set
  End Property
End Class
```

Shared properties are manipulated in the same manner as shared methods, as seen here:

```
' Interact with the Shared property.
Sub Main()
  Employee.Company = "Intertech Training"
  Console.WriteLine("These folks work at {0}", Employee.Company)
End Sub
```

Finally, recall that classes can support shared constructors. Thus, if you wanted to ensure that the name of the shared companyName field was always assigned to "Intertech Training", you would write the following:

```
' Shared constructors are used to initialize shared data.
Public Class Employee
  Private Shared companyName As String
    ....
  Shared Sub New()
    companyName = "Intertech Training"
  End Sub
End Class
```

Using this approach, there is no need to explicitly set the companyName value:

```
' Set to Intertech Training via Shared constructor.
Sub Main()
  Console.WriteLine("These folks work at {0}", Employee.Company)
End Sub
```

To wrap up the examination of encapsulation using VB 2008 properties, understand that these syntactic entities are used for the same purpose as a classical accessor/mutator pair. The benefit of properties is that the users of your objects are able to manipulate the internal data point using a single named item.

Understanding Constant Data

Now that you can create fields that can be modified using properties, allow me to illustrate how to define data that can never change after the initial assignment. VB 2008 offers the Const keyword to define constant data. As you might guess, this can be helpful when you are defining a set of known values for use in your applications that are logically connected to a given class or structure.

Turning away from the Employee example for a moment, assume you are building a utility class named MyMathClass that needs to define a value for the value PI (which we will assume to be 3.14).

Given that we would not want to allow other developers to change this value in code, PI could be modeled with the following constant:

```
Public Class MyMathClass
  Public Const PI As Double = 3.14
End Class

Module Program
  Sub Main()
    Console.WriteLine("The value of PI is: {0}", MyMathClass.PI)
  End Sub
End Module
```

Because PI has been defined as constant, it would be a compile-time error to attempt to modify this value within our code base:

```
Module Program
  Sub Main()
    Console.WriteLine("The value of PI is: {0}", MyMathClass.PI)

    ' Error! Can't change a constant!
    MyMathClass.PI = 3.1444
  End Sub
End Module
```

Notice that we are referencing the constant data defined by the MyMathClass class using a class name prefix. This is due to the fact that constant fields of a class or structure are implicitly *shared*. As mentioned early in this chapter, VB 2008 does allow you to access shared members via an object (provided you have not altered your compiler error settings!). Thus, you could write the following code to access the value of PI:

```
Module Program
  Sub Main()
    Dim m As New MyMathClass()
    Console.WriteLine("The value of PI is: {0}", m.PI)
  End Sub
End Module
```

As well, it is permissible to define a local piece of constant data within the body of a method or property. By way of example:

```
Module Program
  Sub Main()
    Console.WriteLine("The value of PI is: {0}", MyMathClass.PI)

    ' A local constant data point.
    Const fixedStr As String = "Fixed String Data"
    Console.WriteLine(fixedStr)

    ' Error!
    fixedStr = "This will not work!"
  End Sub
End Module
```

Regardless of where you define a constant piece of data, the one point to always remember is that the initial value assigned to the constant must be specified at the time you define the constant. Thus, if you were to modify your MyMathClass in such a way that the value of PI is assigned in a class constructor as follows:

```
Public Class MyMathClass
  Public Const PI As Double
  Public Sub New()
  ' Nope! Compiler error!
    PI = 3.14
  End Sub
End Class
```

you would receive a compile-time error. The reason for this restriction has to do with the fact the value of constant data must be known *at compile time*. Constructors, as you know, are invoked at *runtime*.

Understanding Read-Only Fields

Closely related to constant data is the notion of *read-only field data*. Like a constant, a read-only field cannot be changed after the initial assignment. However, unlike a constant, the value assigned to a read-only field can be determined at runtime, and therefore can legally be assigned within the scope of a constructor (but nowhere else).

This can be very helpful when you don't know the value of a field until runtime (perhaps because you need to read an external file to obtain the value), but wish to ensure that the value will not change after that point. For the sake of illustration, assume the following update to MyMathClass:

```
Public Class MyMathClass
  ' Now as a read only field.
  Public ReadOnly PI As Double

  Public Sub New()
    ' This is now OK.
    PI = 3.14
  End Sub
End Class
```

Again, any attempt to make assignments to a field marked ReadOnly outside the scope of a constructor results in a compiler error:

```
Module Program
  Sub Main()
    Dim m As New MyMathClass()
    ' Error.
    m.PI = 9
  End Sub
End Module
```

Shared Read-Only Fields

Unlike a constant field, read-only fields are not implicitly shared. Thus, if you wish to expose PI from the class level, you must explicitly make use of the Shared keyword when you declare it. If you know the value of a shared read-only field at compile time, the initial assignment has a very similar effect to that of a constant:

```
Public Class MyMathClass
  Public Shared ReadOnly PI As Double = 3.14
End Class
```

```
Module Program
  Sub Main()
    Console.WriteLine("The value of PI is {0}", MyMathClass.PI)
  End Sub
End Module
```

However, if the value of a shared read-only field is not known until runtime, you must make use of a shared constructor as described earlier in this chapter:

```
Public Class MyMathClass
  Public Shared ReadOnly PI As Double
  Shared Sub New()
    PI = 3.14
  End Sub
End Class

Module Program
  Sub Main()
    Console.WriteLine("The value of PI is {0}", MyMathClass.PI)
  End Sub
End Module
```

Now that we have examined the role of constant data and read-only fields, we can return to the `Employee` example and put the wraps on this chapter.

Source Code The ConstData project can be found under the Chapter 5 subdirectory.

Understanding Partial Type Definitions

Classes and structures can be declared using a modifier named `Partial` that allows you to define a type across multiple `*.vb` files. Earlier versions of the VB programming language (specifically, before the release of .NET 2.0) required all code for a given type be defined within a single `*.vb` file. Given the fact that a production-level VB 2008 class may be hundreds of lines of code (or more), this can end up being a mighty lengthy file indeed.

In these cases, it might be useful to partition a type's implementation across numerous `*.vb` files in order to separate code that is in some way more important for other details. For example, using the `Partial` class modifier, you could place all of the `Employee` constructors, fields, and properties into a new file named `Employee.Internals.vb`:

```
Partial Public Class Employee
  ' Private fields.
  ...
  ' Constructors.
  ...
  ' Properties.
  ...
End Class
```

while the public methods are defined within the initial `Employee.vb`:

```
Partial Public Class Employee
  ' Public methods.
  Public Sub GiveBonus(ByVal amount As Single)
    currPay += amount
  End Sub
```

```
  Public Sub DisplayStats()
    Console.WriteLine("Name: {0}", empName)
    Console.WriteLine("Age: {0}", empAge)
    Console.WriteLine("SSN: {0}", empSSN)
    Console.WriteLine("ID: {0}", empID)
    Console.WriteLine("Pay: {0}", currPay)
  End Sub
End Class
```

■ **Note** Strictly speaking, a partial class can be defined over any number of VB code files, and only one aspect of the partial class needs to be marked with the `Partial` keyword. As long as each aspect of the partial class is defined in the same namespace, the compiler will assume they are related.

The idea in this example is that the `Employee.Internals.vb` file contains the "infrastructure" of the class, whereas the `Employee.vb` file contains useful public operations. Of course, once these files are compiled by the VB 2008 compiler, the end result is a single unified type. To this end, the `Partial` modifier is purely a design-time construct.

■ **Note** As you will see during our examination of Windows Forms, Windows Presentation Foundation and ASP.NET, Visual Studio 2008 makes use of the `Partial` keyword to partition code generated by the IDE's designer tools. Using this approach, you can keep focused on your current solution and be blissfully unaware of the designer-generated code.

Documenting VB 2008 Source Code via XML

To wrap this chapter up, the final task is to examine VB 2008–specific comment tokens that yield XML-based code documentation. If you have worked with the Java programming language, you may be familiar with the `javadoc` utility. Using `javadoc`, you are able to turn Java source code into a corresponding HTML representation. The VB 2008 documentation model is slightly different, in that the "code comments to XML" conversion process is the job of the VB 2008 compiler (via the `/doc` option) rather than a stand-alone utility.

So, why use XML to document our type definitions rather than HTML tokens? The main reason is that XML is a very "enabling technology." We can apply any number of XML transformations to the underlying XML to display the code documentation in a variety of formats (MSDN format, HTML, Microsoft Word documents, etc.).

When you wish to document your VB 2008 types in XML, your first step is to make use of the triple tick (`'''`) code comment notations. Once a documentation comment has been declared, you are free to use any well-formed XML elements, including the recommended set shown in Table 5-2.

Table 5-2. *Recommended Code Comment XML Elements*

Predefined XML Documentation Element	Meaning in Life
`<c>`	Indicates that the following text should be displayed in a specific "code font"
`<code>`	Indicates multiple lines should be marked as code

Continued

Table 5-2. *Continued*

Predefined XML Documentation Element	Meaning in Life
<example>	Mocks up a code example for the item you are describing
<exception>	Documents which exceptions a given class may throw
<list>	Inserts a list or table into the documentation file
<param>	Describes a given parameter
<paramref>	Associates a given XML tag with a specific parameter
<permission>	Documents the security constraints for a given member
<remarks>	Builds a description for a given member
<returns>	Documents the return value of the member
<see>	Cross-references related items in the document
<seealso>	Builds an "also see" section within a description
<summary>	Documents the "executive summary" for a given member
<value>	Documents a given property

If you are making use of the new VB 2008 XML code comment notation, do be aware the Visual Studio 2008 IDE will generate documentation skeletons on your behalf. For example, if you right-click the `Employee` class definition and select the Insert Comment menu option, as shown in Figure 5-13, the IDE will autocomplete the initial set of XML elements.

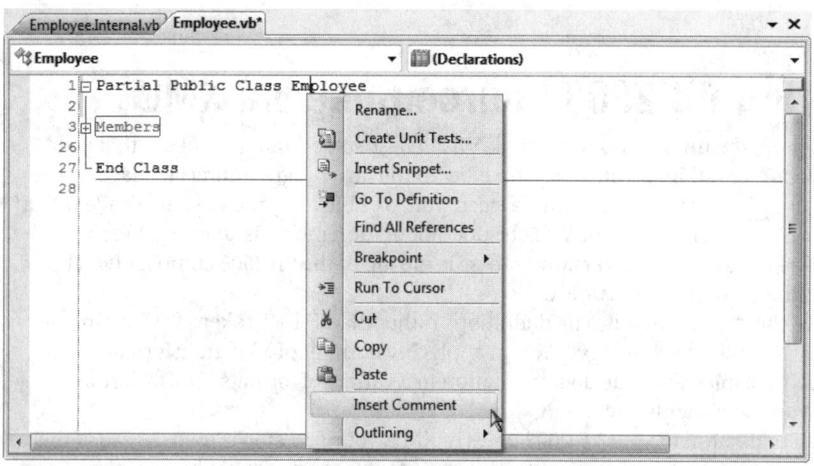

Figure 5-13. *Inserting an XML comment via Visual Studio 2008*

Simply fill in the blanks with your custom content:

```
''' <summary>
''' This is the employee class.
''' </summary>
''' <remarks></remarks>
Partial Public Class Employee
...
End Class
```

By way of another example, right-click your custom five-argument constructor and insert a code comment. This time the comment builder utility has been kind enough to add `<param>` elements:

```
''' <summary>
'''
''' </summary>
''' <param name="name"></param>
''' <param name="age"></param>
''' <param name="id"></param>
''' <param name="pay"></param>
''' <param name="ssn"></param>
''' <remarks></remarks>
Sub New(ByVal name As String, ByVal age As Integer, _
  ByVal id As Integer, ByVal pay As Single, _
  ByVal ssn As String)
...
End Sub
```

Once you have documented your code with XML comments, you will need to generate a corresponding `*.xml` file. If you are building your VB 2008 programs using the command-line compiler (`vbc.exe`), the `/doc` flag is used to generate a specified `*.xml` file based on your XML code comments:

```
vbc /doc:XmlCarDoc.xml *.vb
```

Visual Studio 2008 projects allow you to specify the name of an XML documentation file using the Generate XML documentation file check box option found on the Build tab of the Properties window (see Figure 5-14).

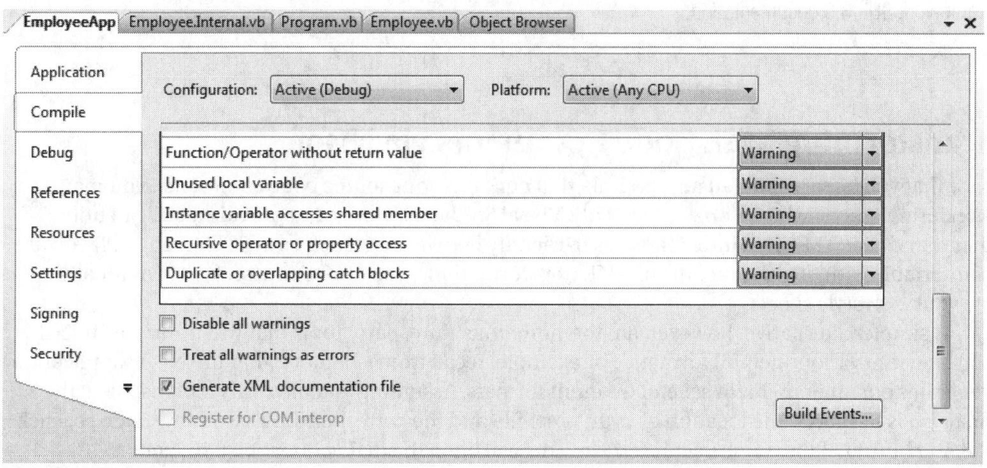

Figure 5-14. *Generating an XML code comment file via Visual Studio 2008*

Once you have enabled this behavior, the compiler will place the generated `*.xml` file within your project's `\bin\Debug` folder. You can verify this for yourself by clicking the Show All Files button on Solution Explorer, generating the result in Figure 5-15.

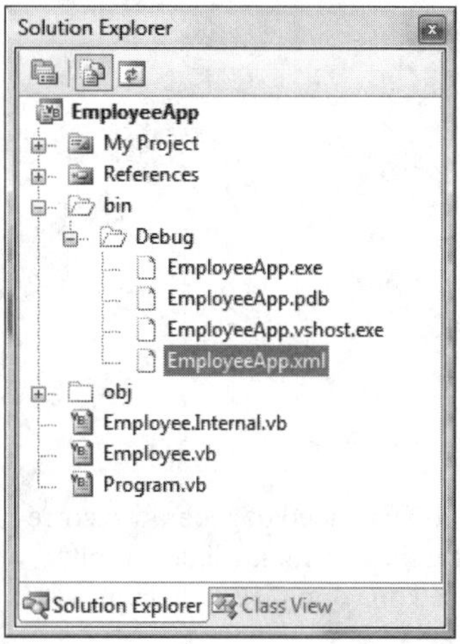

Figure 5-15. *Locating the generated XML documentation file*

■ **Note** There are many other elements and notations that may appear in VB 2008 XML code comments. If you are interested in more details, look up the topic "Documenting Your Code with XML (Visual Basic)" within the .NET Framework SDK 3.5 documentation.

Transforming XML Code Comments via NDoc

Now that you have generated an `*.xml` file that contains your source code comments, you may be wondering exactly what to do with it. Sadly, Visual Studio 2008 does not provide a built-in utility that transforms XML data into a more user-friendly help format (such as an HTML page). If you are comfortable with the ins and outs of XML transformations, you are, of course, free to manually create your own style sheets.

A simpler alternative, however, are the numerous third-party tools that will translate an XML code file into various helpful formats. For example, recall from Chapter 2 that the NDoc application generates documentation in several different formats. Assuming you have this tool installed, the first step is to specify the location of your `*.xml` file and the corresponding assembly. To do so, click the Add button of the NDoc user interface. This will open the dialog box shown in Figure 5-16.

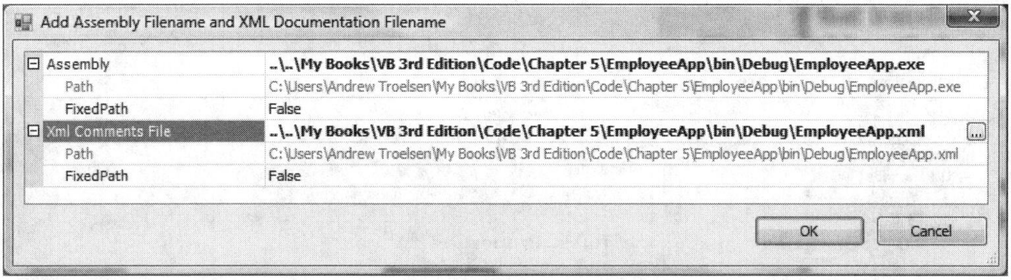

Figure 5-16. *Specifying the XML file and corresponding assembly*

At this point, you can select for output location (via the `OutputDirectory` property) and document type (via the Documentation Type drop-down list). For this example, let's pick an MSDN-CHM format, which will generate documentation that looks and feels like the .NET Framework documentation (see Figure 5-17).

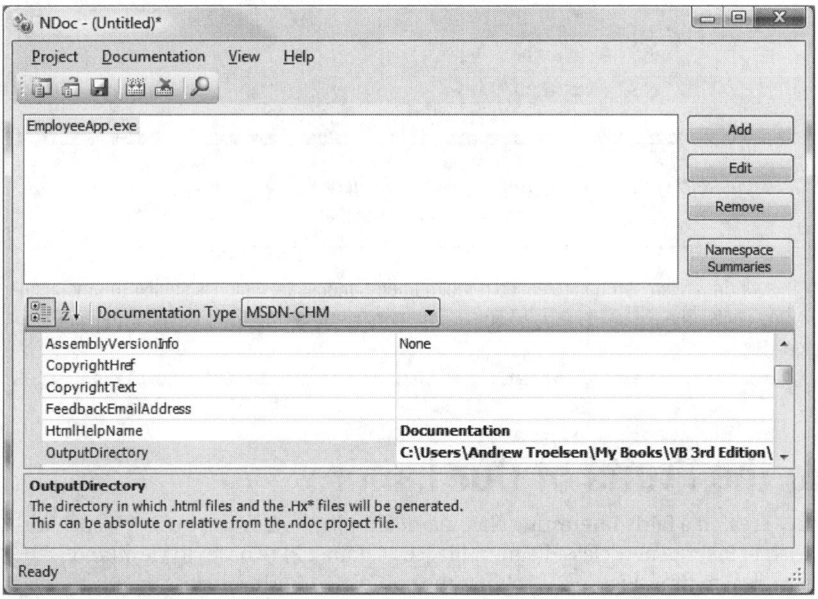

Figure 5-17. *Specifying the output directory and documentation format*

Obviously, we could establish other settings using NDoc; however, once you select the Documentation ➤ Build menu option, NDoc will generate a full help system for your application. Figure 5-18 shows the end result.

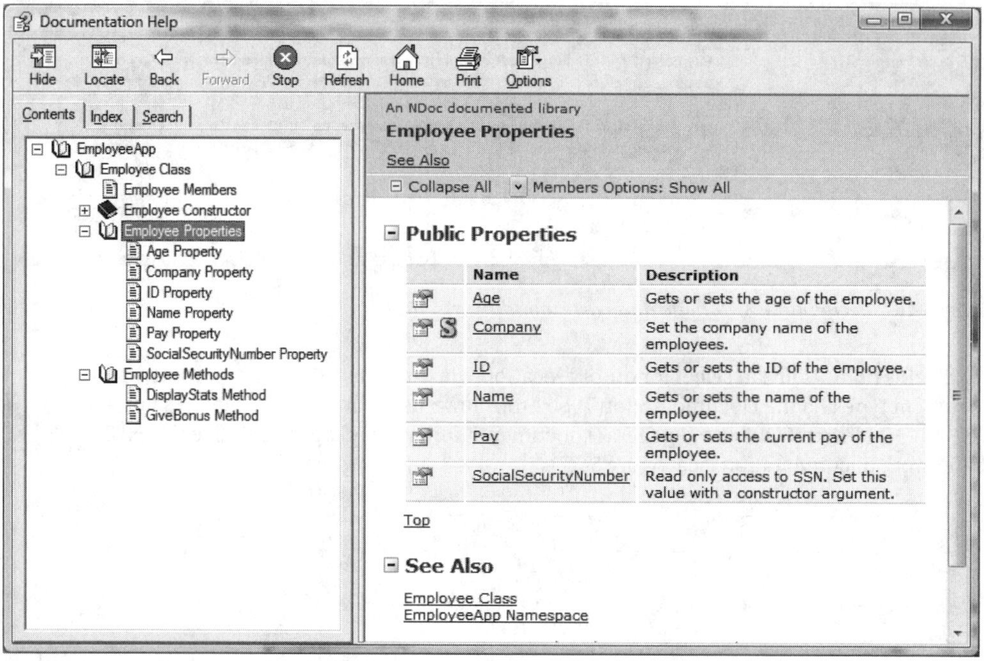

Figure 5-18. *Our MSDN-style help system for the EmployeeApp project*

■ **Note** At the time of this writing, Microsoft has released a tool named Sandcastle, which is similar in functionality to the open source NDoc utility. Check out `http://blogs.msdn.com/sandcastle` for more information (this URL is subject to change).

Visualizing the Fruits of Our Labor

At this point, you have created a fairly interesting class named `Employee`. If you are using Visual Studio 2008, you may wish to insert a new class diagram file (see Chapter 2) in order to view (and maintain) your class at design time. Figure 5-19 shows the completed `Employee` class type.

As you will see in the next chapter, this `Employee` class will function as a base class for a family of derived class types (`WageEmployee`, `SalesEmployee`, and `Manager`).

■ **Source Code** The EmployeeApp project can be found under the Chapter 5 subdirectory.

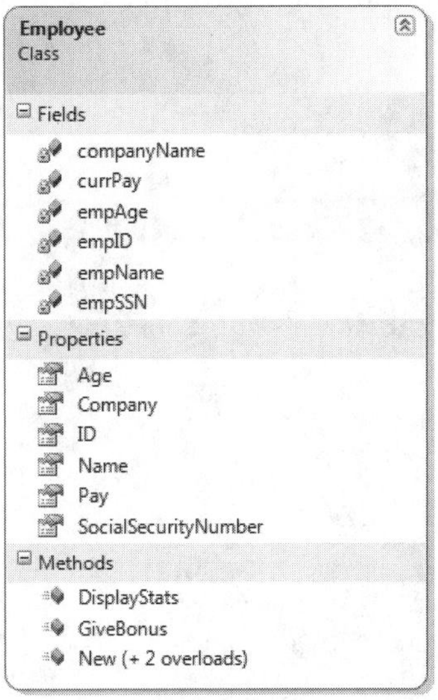

Figure 5-19. *The completed* `Employee` *class*

Summary

The point of this chapter was to introduce you to the role of the VB 2008 class type. As you have seen, classes can take any number of *constructors* that enable the object user to establish the state of the object upon creation. This chapter also illustrated several class design techniques (and related keywords). Recall that the `Me` keyword can be used to obtain access to the current object, the `Shared` keyword allows you to define members that are bound at the class (not object) level, and the `Const` keyword allows you to define a point of data that can never change after the initial assignment.

The bulk of this chapter dug into the details of the first pillar of OOP: encapsulation. Here you learned about the access modifiers of Visual Basic 2008 and the role of type properties, partial classes, and XML code documentation. Now that you have a firm handle on defining a single class type, the next chapter will deepen your understanding of object-oriented programming by examining the details of inheritance and polymorphism.

CHAPTER 6

■ ■ ■

Understanding Inheritance and Polymorphism

The previous chapter examined the first pillar of OOP: encapsulation. At that time, you learned how to build a single well-defined class type with constructors and various members (fields, properties, constants, read-only fields, etc.). This chapter will focus on the remaining two pillars of OOP: inheritance and polymorphism.

First, you will learn how to build families of related classes using *inheritance*. As you will see, this form of code reuse allows you to define common functionality in a parent class that can be leveraged (and possibly altered) by child classes. Along the way, you will learn how to establish a *polymorphic interface* into the class hierarchies using virtual and abstract members. We wrap up by examining the role of the ultimate parent class in the .NET base class libraries: `System.Object`.

The Basic Mechanics of Inheritance

Recall from the previous chapter that *inheritance* is an aspect of OOP that facilitates code reuse. Specifically speaking, code reuse comes in two flavors: classical inheritance (the "is-a" relationship) and the containment/delegation model (the "has-a" relationship). Let's begin by examining classical inheritance (the "is-a" model).

When you establish "is-a" relationships between classes, you are building a dependency between two or more class types. The basic idea behind classical inheritance is that new classes may extend (and possibly change) the functionality of existing classes. To begin, create a new Console Application project named BasicInheritance. Now assume you have designed a simple class named `Car` that models some basic details of an automobile:

```
' A simple Car class.
Public Class Car
  Public ReadOnly MaxSpeed As Integer
  Private currSpeed As Integer

  Public Sub New(ByVal max As Integer)
    MaxSpeed = max
  End Sub
  Public Sub New()
    MaxSpeed = 55
  End Sub

  Public Property Speed() As Integer
    Get
      Return currSpeed
    End Get
```

```
    Set(ByVal value As Integer)
      currSpeed = value
      If currSpeed > MaxSpeed Then
        currSpeed = MaxSpeed
      End If
    End Set
  End Property
End Class
```

Notice that the Car class is making use of encapsulation services to control access to the private currSpeed field using a public property named Speed. At this point you can exercise your Car type as follows:

```
Module Program
  Sub Main()
    Console.WriteLine("***** Basic Inheritance *****")
    ' Make a Car object.
    Dim myCar As New Car(80)
    myCar.Speed = 50
    Console.WriteLine("My car is going {0} MPH", _
      myCar.Speed)
    Console.ReadLine()
  End Sub
End Module
```

The Inherits Keyword

Now assume you wish to build a new class named MiniVan. Like a basic Car, you wish to define the MiniVan class to support a maximum speed, current speed, and a property named Speed to allow the object user to modify the object's state. However, unlike a basic automobile, the MiniVan might have unique traits (such as a sliding door or seating for 10). Clearly, the Car and MiniVan classes are related, in fact we can say that a MiniVan "*is-a*" Car. The "is-a" relationship (formally termed *classical inheritance*) allows you to build new class definitions that extend the functionality of an existing class.

The existing class that will serve as the basis for the new class is termed a *base* or *parent* class. The role of a base class is to define all the common members for the classes that extend it. The "extending" classes are formally termed *derived* or *child* classes. In VB 2008, we make use of the Inherits keyword to establish an "is-a" relationship between classes:

```
' MiniVan derives from Car.
Public Class MiniVan
  Inherits Car
  ' Here, we can now define members that are unique to
  ' the MiniVan type.
End Class
```

So, what have we gained by building our MiniVan by deriving from the Car base class? Simply put, the MiniVan class automatically gains the functionality of each and every member in the parent class declared as Public or Protected.

Note Unlike other members (fields, subroutines, functions, etc.), constructors are never inherited by child classes, regardless of their access modifier.

Given the relation between these two class types, we could now make use of the MiniVan type like so:

```
Module Program
  Sub Main()
...
    ' Now create a MiniVan object.
    Dim myVan As New MiniVan()
    myVan.Speed = 10
    Console.WriteLine("My van is going {0} MPH", _
      myVan.Speed)
    Console.ReadLine()
  End Sub
End Module
```

Notice that although we have not added any members to the MiniVan type, we have direct access to the public Speed property (thus we have reused code). Recall, however, that encapsulation is preserved, therefore the following code results in a compiler error:

```
Module Program
  Sub Main()
...
    Dim myVan As New MiniVan()
    myVan.Speed = 10
    Console.WriteLine("My van is going {0} MPH", _
      myVan.Speed)

    ' Error! Cannot access private data of the parent from an object!
    myVan.currSpeed = 10
    Console.ReadLine()
  End Sub
End Module
```

As well, if the MiniVan defined its own set of members, these members would not be able to access any private member of the Car base class either:

```
Public Class MiniVan
  Inherits Car

  Public Sub TestMethod()
    ' OK! Can use public Car members
    ' within derived type.
    Speed = 10

    ' Error! Cannot access private Car
    ' members within derived type.
    currSpeed = 10
  End Sub
End Class
```

Regarding Multiple Base Classes

Speaking of base classes, it is important to keep in mind that the .NET platform demands that a given class have exactly *one* direct base class. It is not possible to create a class type that derives from two or more base classes (this technique is known as *multiple inheritance*, or simply *MI*):

```
' Illegal! The .NET platform does not allow
' multiple inheritance for classes!
Public Class WontWork
  Inherits BaseClassOne
  Inherits BaseClassTwo
End Class
```

As you will see in Chapter 9, VB 2008 does allow a given type to implement any number of *interfaces*. In this way, a VB 2008 class can exhibit a number of behaviors while avoiding the complexities associated with MI. On a related note, it is permissible for a single interface to derive from multiple interfaces (again, see Chapter 9).

The NotInheritable Keyword

VB 2008 supplies another keyword, named `NotInheritable`, that *prevents* inheritance from occurring. When you mark a class as `NotInheritable`, the compiler will not allow you to derive from this type. For example, assume you have decided that it makes no sense to further extend the `MiniVan` class:

```
' This class cannot be extended!
Public NotInheritable Class MiniVan
  Inherits Car
End Class
```

If you (or a teammate) were to attempt to derive from this class, you would receive a compile-time error:

```
' Error! Cannot extend
' a class marked NotInheritable!
Public Class BetterMiniVan
  Inherits MiniVan
End Class
```

Formally speaking, the `MiniVan` class has now been *sealed*. Most often, sealing a class makes the best sense when you are designing a utility class. For example, the `System` namespace defines numerous sealed classes (`System.Console`, `System.Math`, `System.Environment`, `System.String`, etc.). You can verify this for yourself by opening up the Visual Studio 2008 Object Browser (via the View menu) and selecting the `System.Console` type defined within `mscorlib.dll`. Notice in Figure 6-1 the use of the `NotInheritable` keyword.

Thus, just like the `MiniVan`, if you attempted to build a new class that extends `System.Console`, you will receive a compile-time error:

```
' Another error! Cannot extend
' a class marked NotInheritable!
Public Class MyConsole
  Inherits Console
End Class
```

■ **Note** In Chapter 4, you were introduced to the structure type. Structures are always implicitly sealed. Therefore, you can never derive one structure from another structure, a class from a structure, or a structure from a class.

As you would guess, there are many more details to inheritance that you will come to know during the remainder of this chapter. For now, simply keep in mind that the `Inherits` keyword allows you to establish base/derived class relationships, while the `NotInheritable` keyword prevents inheritance from occurring.

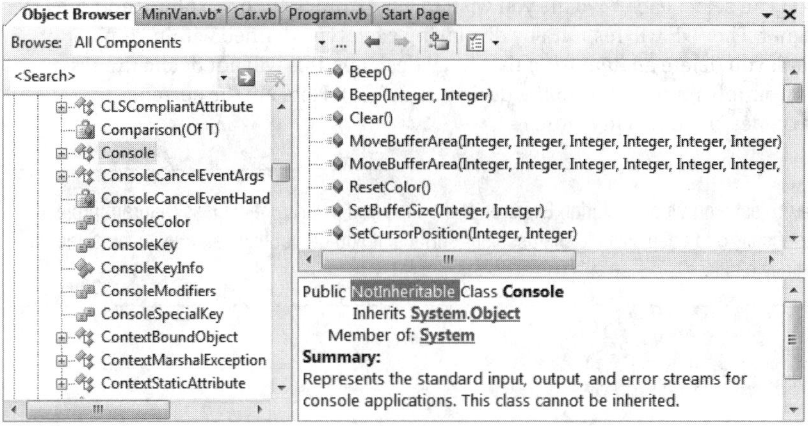

Figure 6-1. *The base class libraries define numerous sealed types.*

Revising Visual Studio 2008 Class Diagrams

Back in Chapter 2, I mentioned that Visual Studio 2008 now allows you to establish base/derived class relationships visually at design time. To leverage this aspect of the IDE, your first step is to include a new class diagram file into your current project. To do so, access the Project ➤ Add New Item menu option and select the Class Diagram icon (in Figure 6-2, I renamed the file from `ClassDiagram1.cd` to `Cars.cd`).

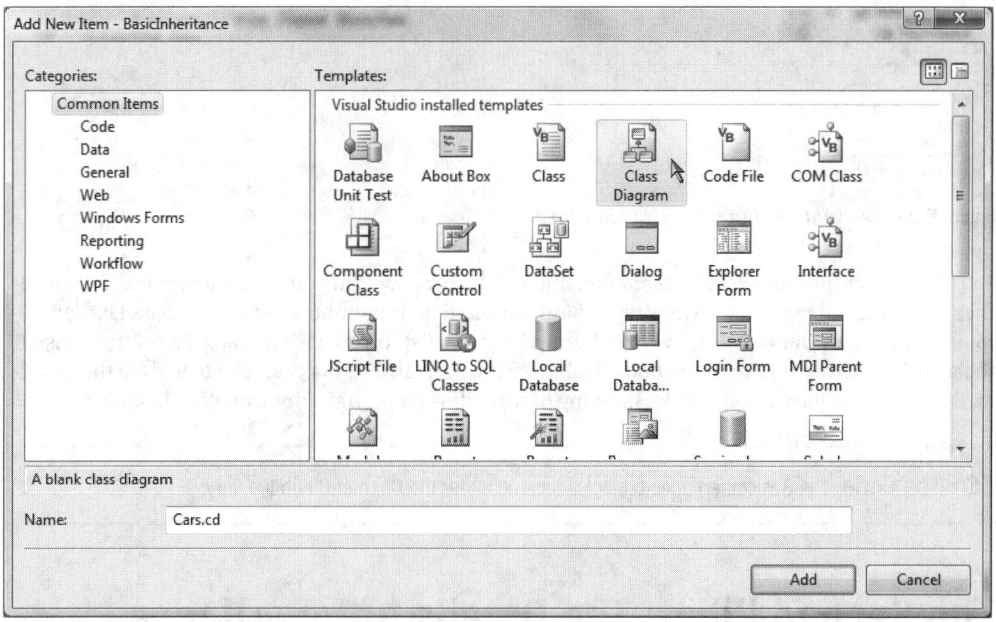

Figure 6-2. *Inserting a new class diagram*

At this point, you can select each *.vb file you wish to view from Solution Explorer and drag it onto the visual designer. The IDE will respond by displaying each type defined within your code files. Also realize that if you delete an item from the visual designer, this will not delete the associated source code (you simply remove it from the designer surface). Here are the current Car, MiniVan, and Program types, as shown in Figure 6-3.

Note If you select a project icon within Solution Explorer at the time you insert a new Class Diagram project type, the IDE will automatically add each class to the designer surface. If you do not have a project icon selected, the designer will be initially blank.

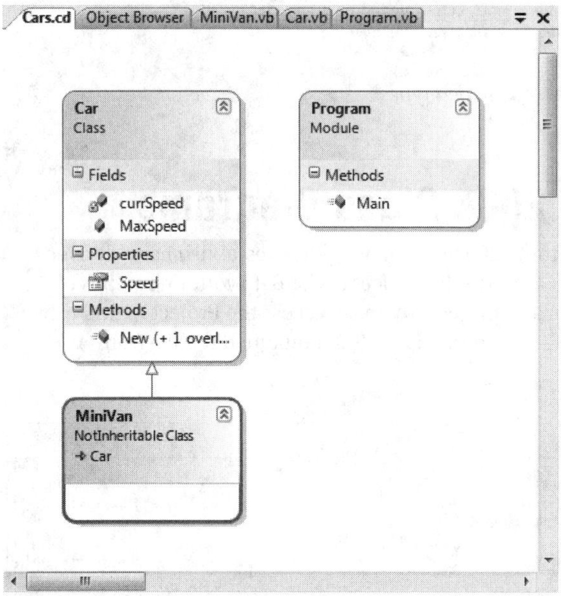

Figure 6-3. *The visual designer of Visual Studio 2008*

Beyond simply displaying the relationships of the types within your current application, recall that you can also create brand-new types (and populate their members) using the Class Designer toolbox and Class Details window (see Chapter 2 for details). If you wish to make use of these visual tools during the remainder of the book, feel free. However, always make sure you analyze the generated code so you have a solid understanding of what these tools have done on your behalf.

Source Code The BasicInheritance project is located under the Chapter 6 subdirectory.

The Second Pillar: The Details of Inheritance

Now that you have seen the basics of inheritance, let's create a more complex example and get to know the numerous details of building class hierarchies. To do so, we will be reusing the Employee class we designed in Chapter 5. To begin, create a brand-new Console Application named Employees. Next, activate the Project ➤ Add Existing Item menu option and navigate to the location of your `Employee.vb` and `Employee.Internals.vb` files. Select each of them (via a Ctrl-click) and click the OK button. Visual Studio 2008 responds by copying each file into the current project. Once you have done so, compile your current application just to ensure you are up and running.

Our goal is to create a family of classes that model various types of employees in a company. Assume that you wish to leverage the functionality of the `Employee` class to create two new classes (`SalesPerson` and `Manager`). The class hierarchy we will be building initially looks something like what you see in Figure 6-4.

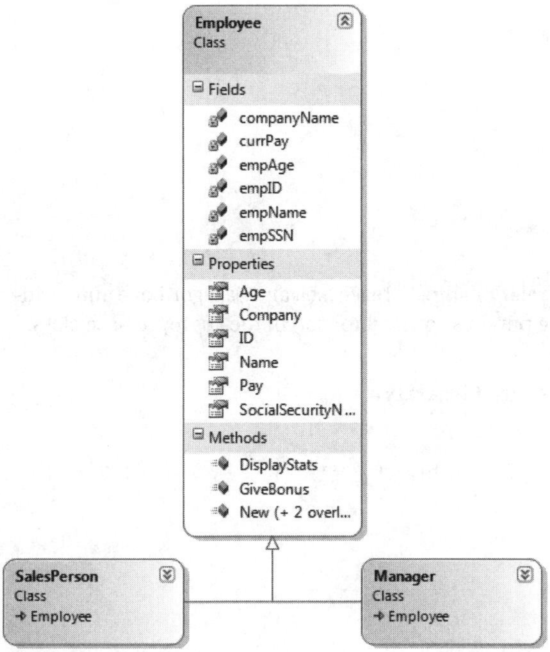

Figure 6-4. *The initial Employees project hierarchy*

As illustrated in Figure 6-4, you can see that a `SalesPerson` "is-a" `Employee` (as is the `Manager` type). Remember that under the classical inheritance model, base classes (such as `Employee`) are used to define general characteristics that are common to all descendants. Subclasses (such as `SalesPerson` and `Manager`) extend this general functionality while adding more specific behaviors.

For our example, we will assume that the `Manager` class extends `Employee` by recording the number of stock options, while the `SalesPerson` class maintains the number of sales made. Insert a new class file (`Manager.vb`) that defines the `Manager` type as follows:

```
' Managers need to know their number of stock options.
Public Class Manager
  Inherits Employee

  Private numberOfOptions As Integer
  Public Property StockOptions() As Integer
    Get
      Return numberOfOptions
    End Get
```

```
    Set(ByVal value As Integer)
      numberOfOptions = value
    End Set
  End Property
End Class
```

Next, add another new class file (SalesPerson.vb) that defines the SalesPerson type:

```
' Salespeople need to know their number of sales.
Public Class SalesPerson
  Inherits Employee

  Private numberOfSales As Integer
  Public Property SalesNumber() As Integer
    Get
      Return numberOfSales
    End Get
    Set(ByVal value As Integer)
      numberOfSales = value
    End Set
  End Property
End Class
```

Now that you have established an "is-a" relationship, SalesPerson and Manager have automatically inherited all public members (minus the parent's constructor set) of the Employee base class. To illustrate:

```
' Create a subclass and access base class functionality.
Module Program
  Sub Main()
    Console.WriteLine("***** The Employee Class Hierarchy *****")
    Console.WriteLine()

    ' Make a salesperson.
    Dim danny As New SalesPerson()
    With danny
      .Age = 29
      .ID = 100
      .SalesNumber = 50
      .Name = "Dan McCabe"
    End With
  End Sub
End Module
```

Controlling Base Class Creation with MyBase

Currently, SalesPerson and Manager can only be created using the freebie default constructor (see Chapter 5). With this in mind, assume you have added a new six-argument constructor to the Manager type, which is invoked as follows:

```
Sub Main()
...
  ' Assume we now have the following constructor for the Manager.
  ' (name, age, ID, pay, SSN, number of stock options).
  Dim chucky As New Manager("Chucky", 45, 101, 30000, "222-22-2222", 90)
End Sub
```

If you look at the argument list, you can clearly see that most of these parameters should be stored in the member variables defined by the Employee base class. To do so, you might implement this custom constructor in the Manager class as follows:

```
' New constructor for the Manager class.
Public Sub New(ByVal fullName As String, ByVal empAge As Integer, _
  ByVal empID As Integer, ByVal currPay As Single, _
  ByVal ssn As String, ByVal numbOfOpts As Integer)
  ' This field is defined by the Manager class.
  numberOfOptions = numbOfOpts

  ' Assign incoming parameters using the
  ' inherited properties of the parent class.
  ID = empID
  Age = empAge
  Name = fullName
  Pay = currPay

  ' OOPS! This would be a compiler error,
  ' as the SSN property is read-only!
  SocialSecurityNumber = ssn
End Sub
```

The first issue with this approach is that we defined the SocialSecurityNumber property in the parent as read-only, therefore we are unable to assign the incoming String parameter to this field.

The second issue is that we have indirectly created a rather inefficient constructor, given the fact that under VB 2008, unless you say otherwise, the default constructor of a base class is called automatically before the logic of the custom Manager constructor is executed. After this point, the current implementation accesses numerous public properties of the Employee base class to establish its state. Thus, you have really made seven hits (five inherited properties and two constructor calls) during the creation of a Manager object!

To help optimize the initialization of derived objects, you will do well to implement your subclass constructors to explicitly call an appropriate custom base class constructor, rather than the default. In this way, you are able to reduce the number of calls to inherited initialization members (which saves processing time). Let's retrofit the custom constructor to do this very thing using the MyBase keyword:

```
' This time, use the VB 2008 "MyBase" keyword to call a custom
' constructor on the base class.
Public Sub New(ByVal fullName As String, ByVal empAge As Integer, _
  ByVal empID As Integer, ByVal currPay As Single, _
  ByVal ssn As String, ByVal numbOfOpts As Integer)

  ' Pass these arguments to the parent's constructor.
  MyBase.New(fullName, empAge, empID, currPay, ssn)

  ' This belongs with us!
  numberOfOptions = numbOfOpts
End Sub
```

Here, the first statement within your custom constructor is making use of the MyBase keyword. In this situation, you are explicitly calling the five-argument constructor defined by Employee and saving yourself unnecessary calls during the creation of the child class. The custom SalesPerson constructor looks almost identical:

```
' As a general rule, all subclasses should explicitly call an appropriate
' base class constructor.
Public Sub New(ByVal fullName As String, ByVal empAge As Integer, _
  ByVal empID As Integer, ByVal currPay As Single, _
  ByVal ssn As String, ByVal numbOfSales As Integer)

  ' Pass these arguments to the parent's constructor.
  MyBase.New(fullName, empAge, empID, currPay, ssn)

  ' This belongs with us!
  numberOfSales = numbOfSales
End Sub
```

Also be aware that you may use the `MyBase` keyword anytime a subclass wishes to access a public or protected member defined by a parent class. Use of this keyword is not limited to constructor logic. You will see examples using `MyBase` in this manner during our examination of polymorphism later in this chapter.

■Note When using `MyBase` to call a parent's constructor, the `MyBase.New()` statement must be the very first executable code statement within the constructor body. If this is not the case, you will receive a compiler error.

Finally, recall that once you add a custom constructor to a class definition, the default constructor is silently removed. Therefore, be sure to redefine the default constructor for the `SalesPerson` and `Manager` types:

```
' Be sure to add back a default constructor for
' the Manager and SalesPerson types.
Public Sub New()
End Sub
```

Keeping Family Secrets: The Protected Keyword

As you already know, public items are directly accessible from anywhere, while private items cannot be accessed from any object beyond the class that has defined it. Recall from Chapter 5 that VB 2008 takes the lead of many other modern object languages and provides an additional keyword to define member accessibility: `Protected`.

When a base class defines members, it establishes a set of items that can be accessed directly by any descendant. If you wish to allow the `SalesPerson` and `Manager` child classes to directly access the data sector defined by `Employee`, you can update the original `Employee` class definition as follows:

```
' Protected state data.
Partial Public Class Employee
  ' Derived classes can directly access this information.
  Protected empName As String
  Protected empID As Integer
  Protected currPay As Single
  Protected empAge As Integer
  Protected empSSN As String
  Protected Shared companyName As String
...
End Class
```

The benefit of defining protected members in a base class is that derived types no longer have to access the data using public methods or properties. The possible downfall, of course, is that when a derived type has direct access to its parent's internal data, it is very possible to accidentally bypass existing business rules found within public properties. When you define protected members, you are creating a level of trust between the parent and child class, as the compiler will not catch any violation of your type's business rules.

Finally, understand that as far as the object user is concerned, protected data is regarded as private (as the user is "outside" of the family). Therefore, the following is illegal:

```
Sub Main()
  ' Error! Can't access protected data from object instance.
  Dim emp As New Employee()
  emp.empSSN = "111-11-1111"
End Sub
```

Note Although `Protected` field data can break encapsulation, it is quite safe (and useful) to define `Protected` methods and properties. When building class hierarchies, it is very common to define a set of methods/properties that are only for use by the defining class and derived types.

Adding a Sealed Class

Recall that a *sealed* class cannot be extended by other classes. As mentioned, this technique is most often used when you are designing a utility class. However, when building class hierarchies, you might find that a certain branch in the inheritance chain should be "capped off," as it makes no sense to further extend the linage. For example, assume you have added yet another class to your program (`PTSalesPerson`) that extends the existing `SalesPerson` type (where `PTSalesPerson` is a class representing a *part-time* salesperson). Figure 6-5 shows the current update.

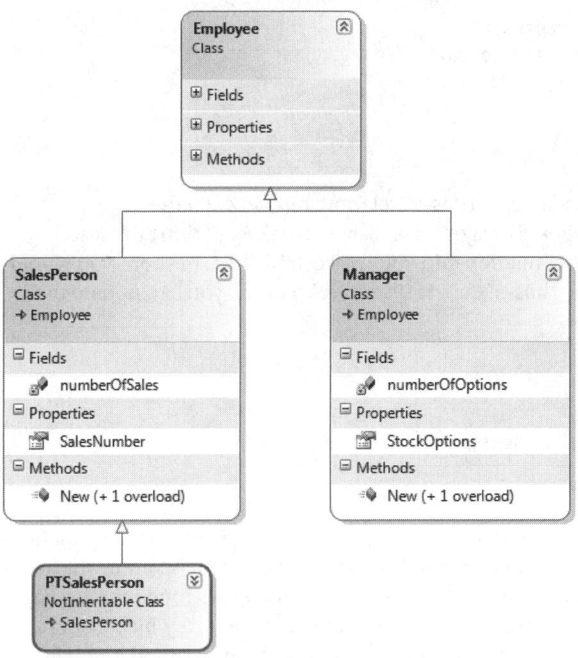

Figure 6-5. *The* `PTSalesPerson` *class*

For the sake of argument, let's say that you wish to ensure that no other developer is able to subclass from PTSalesPerson. (After all, how much more part-time can you get than "part-time"?) To prevent others from extending a class, make use of the VB 2008 NotInheritable keyword:

```
Public NotInheritable Class PTSalesPerson
  Inherits SalesPerson

  Public Sub New(ByVal fullName As String, ByVal empAge As Integer, _
    ByVal empID As Integer, ByVal currPay As Single, _
    ByVal ssn As String, ByVal numbOfSales As Integer)
    ' Pass these arguments to the parent's constructor.
    MyBase.New(fullName, empAge, empID, currPay, ssn, numbOfSales)
  End Sub
    ' Assume other members here...
End Class
```

Given that sealed classes cannot be extended, you may wonder if it is possible to reuse the code within a class marked NotInheritable. If you wish to build a new class that leverages the functionality of a sealed class, your only option is to forego classical inheritance and make use of the containment/delegation model (aka the "has-a" relationship).

Programming for Containment/Delegation

As noted a bit earlier in this chapter, code reuse comes in two flavors. We have just explored the classical "is-a" relationship. To conclude the exploration of the second pillar of OOP, let's examine the "has-a" relationship (also known as the containment/delegation *model* or *aggregation*). Assume you have created a new class that models an employee benefits package:

```
' This type will function as a contained class.
Public Class BenefitPackage
  ' Assume we have other members that represent
  ' 401K plans, dental/health benefits, and so on.
  Public Function ComputePayDeduction() As Double
    Return 125.0
  End Function
End Class
```

Obviously, it would be rather odd to establish an "is-a" relationship between the BenefitPackage class and the employee types. (Manager "is-a" BenefitPackage? I don't think so.) However, it should be clear that some sort of relationship could be established. In short, you would like to express the idea that each employee "has-a" BenefitPackage. To do so, you can update the Employee class definition as follows:

```
' Employees now have benefits.
Partial Public Class Employee
  ' Contain a BenefitPackage object.
  Protected empBenefits As New BenefitPackage()
...
End Class
```

At this point, you have successfully contained another object. However, to expose the functionality of the contained object to the outside world requires delegation. *Delegation* is simply the act of adding members to the containing class that make use of the contained object's functionality. For example, we could update the Employee class to expose the contained empBenefits object using a custom property as well as make use of its functionality internally using a new method named GetBenefitCost():

```
Partial Public Class Employee
  ' Contain a BenefitPackage object.
  Protected empBenefits As New BenefitPackage()

  ' Expose certain benefit behaviors of object.
  Public Function GetBenefitCost() As Double
    Return empBenefits.ComputePayDeduction()
  End Function

  ' Expose object through a custom property.
  Public Property Benefits() As BenefitPackage
    Get
      Return empBenefits
    End Get
    Set(ByVal value As BenefitPackage)
      empBenefits = value
    End Set
  End Property
...
End Class
```

In the following updated `Main()` method, notice how we can interact with the internal `BenefitsPackage` object within the `Employee` object:

```
Module Program
  Sub Main()
...
    Dim chucky As New Manager("Chucky", 45, 101, 30000, "222-22-2222", 90)
    Dim cost As Double = chucky.GetBenefitCost()
    Console.ReadLine()
  End Sub
End Module
```

Nested Type Definitions

Before examining the final pillar of OOP (polymorphism), let's explore a programming technique termed *nesting types* (briefly mentioned in the Chapter 5). In VB 2008, it is possible to define a type (enum, class, interface, struct, or delegate) directly within the scope of a class or structure. When you have done so, the nested (or "inner") type is considered a member of the nesting (or "outer") class, and in the eyes of the runtime can be manipulated like any other member (fields, properties, methods, events, etc.). The syntax used to nest a type is quite straightforward:

```
Public Class OuterClass
  ' A public nested type can be used by anybody.
  Public Class PublicInnerClass
  End Class

  ' A private nested type can only be used by members
  ' of the containing class.
  Private Class PrivateInnerClass
  End Class
End Class
```

Although the syntax is clean, understanding why you might do this is not readily apparent. To understand this technique, ponder the following traits of nesting a type:

- Nesting types is similar to aggregation ("has-a"), except that you have complete control over the access level of the inner type instead of a contained object.
- Because a nested type is a member of the containing class, it can access private shared members of the containing class.
- Oftentimes, a nested type is only useful as a helper for the outer class, and is not intended for use by the outside world.

When a type nests another class type, it can create member variables of the type, just as it would for any point of data. However, if you wish to make use of a nested type from outside of the containing type, you must qualify it by the scope of the nesting type. Consider the following code:

```
Sub Main()
  ' Create and use the public inner Class. OK!
  Dim inner As New OuterClass.PublicInnerClass()

  ' Compiler error! Cannot access the private class.
  Dim inner2 As New OuterClass.PrivateInnerClass()
End Sub
```

To make use of this concept within our employees example, assume we have now nested the `BenefitPackage` directly within the `Employee` class type:

```
Partial Public Class Employee

  Public Class BenefitPackage
    ' Assume we have other members that represent
    ' 401K plans, dental/health benefits, and so on.
    Public Function ComputePayDeduction() As Double
      Return 125.0
    End Function
  End Class
...
End Class
```

The nesting process can be as "deep" as you require. For example, assume we wish to create an enumeration named `BenefitPackageLevel`, which documents the various benefit levels an employee may choose. To programmatically enforce the tight connection between `Employee`, `BenefitPackage`, and `BenefitPackageLevel`, we could nest the enumeration as follows:

```
' Employee nests BenefitPackage.
Partial Public Class Employee

  ' BenefitPackage nests BenefitPackageLevel.
  Public Class BenefitPackage

      Public Enum BenefitPackageLevel
        Standard
        Gold
        Platinum
      End Enum

      Public Function ComputePayDeduction() As Double
        Return 125.0
    End Function
  End Class
...
End Class
```

Because of the nesting relationships, note how we are required to make use of this enumeration:

```
Sub Main()
...
  ' Define my benefit level.
  Dim myBenefitLevel As Employee.BenefitPackage.BenefitPackageLevel = _
    Employee.BenefitPackage.BenefitPackageLevel.Platinum
  Console.ReadLine()
End Sub
```

At this point you have been exposed to a number of keywords (and concepts) that allow you to build hierarchies of related types via inheritance. If the overall process is not quite crystal clear, don't sweat it. You will be building a number of additional hierarchies over the remainder of this text. Next up, let's examine the final pillar of OOP: polymorphism.

The Third Pillar: VB 2008's Polymorphic Support

Recall that the `Employee` base class defined a method named `GiveBonus()`, which was originally implemented as follows:

```
Partial Public Class Employee
  Public Sub GiveBonus(ByVal amount As Single)
    currPay += amount
  End Sub
...
End Class
```

Because this method has been defined with the `Public` keyword, you can now give bonuses to salespeople and managers (as well as part-time salespeople):

```
Module Program
  Sub Main()
    Console.WriteLine("***** The Employee Class Hierarchy *****")
    Console.WriteLine()
    ' Give each employee a bonus.
    Dim chucky As New Manager("Chucky", 50, 92, 100000, "333-23-2322", 9000)
    chucky.GiveBonus(300)
    chucky.DisplayStats()
    Console.WriteLine()

    Dim fran As New SalesPerson("Fran", 43, 93, 3000, "932-32-3232", 31)
    fran.GiveBonus(200)
    fran.DisplayStats()
    Console.ReadLine()
  End Sub
End Module
```

The problem with the current design is that the inherited `GiveBonus()` method operates identically for all subclasses. Ideally, the bonus of a salesperson or part-time salesperson should take into account the number of sales. Perhaps managers should gain additional stock options in conjunction with a monetary bump in salary. Given this, you are suddenly faced with an interesting question: "How can related types respond differently to the same request?" Glad you asked!

The Overridable and Overrides Keywords

Polymorphism provides a way for a subclass to define its own version of a method (or property, for that matter) defined by its base class, using the process termed *method overriding*. To retrofit your current design, you need to understand the meaning of the VB 2008 `Overridable` and `Overrides` keywords. If a base class wishes to define a method that *may be* (but does not have to be) overridden by a subclass, it must mark the method with the `Overridable` keyword in the base class:

```
Partial Public Class Employee
  ' This method may now be "overridden" by derived classes.
  Public Overridable Sub GiveBonus(ByVal amount As Single)
    currPay += amount
  End Sub
...
End Class
```

■ **Note** Methods or properties that have been marked with the `Overridable` keyword are termed *virtual members*.

When a subclass wishes to redefine a virtual member, it does so using the `Overrides` keyword. For example, the `SalesPerson` and `Manager` could override `GiveBonus()` as follows (assume that `PTSalesPerson` will not override `GiveBonus()` and therefore simply inherit the version defined by `SalesPerson`):

```
Public Class SalesPerson
  Inherits Employee
...
  ' A salesperson's bonus is influenced by the number of sales.
  Public Overrides Sub GiveBonus(ByVal amount As Single)
    Dim salesBonus As Integer = 0
    If numberOfSales >= 0 AndAlso numberOfSales <= 100 Then
      salesBonus = 10
    Else
      If numberOfSales >= 101 AndAlso numberOfSales <= 200 Then
        salesBonus = 15
      Else
        salesBonus = 20
      End If
    End If
      MyBase.GiveBonus(amount * salesBonus)
    End Sub
End Class

Public Class Manager
  Inherits Employee
...
  Public Overrides Sub GiveBonus(ByVal amount As Single)
    MyBase.GiveBonus(amount)
    Dim r As New Random()
    numberOfOptions += r.Next(500)
  End Sub
End Class
```

Notice how each overriding method is free to leverage the default behavior of the parent implementation using the `MyBase` keyword. In this way, you have no need to completely reimplement the logic behind `GiveBonus()`, but can reuse (and possibly extend) the default behavior of the parent class.

Also assume that `Employee.DisplayStats()` has been declared virtual, and has been overridden by each subclass to account for displaying the number of sales (for salespeople) and current stock options (for managers). For example, consider the `Manager`'s version of `DisplayStats()`:

```
Public Overrides Sub DisplayStats()
  MyBase.DisplayStats()
  Console.WriteLine("Number of Stock Options: {0}", numberOfOptions)
End Sub
```

The `SalesPerson`'s version of `DisplayStats()` is very similar:

```
Public Overrides Sub DisplayStats()
  MyBase.DisplayStats()
  Console.WriteLine("Number of Sales: {0}", numberOfSales)
End Sub
```

Now that each subclass can interpret what these virtual methods means to itself, each object behaves as a more independent (but related) entity:

```
Module Program
  Sub Main()
    Console.WriteLine("***** The Employee Class Hierarchy *****")
    Console.WriteLine()
    ' A better bonus system!
    Dim chucky As New Manager("Chucky", 50, 92, 100000, "333-23-2322", 9000)
    chucky.GiveBonus(300)
    chucky.DisplayStats()
    Console.WriteLine()

    Dim fran As New SalesPerson("Fran", 43, 93, 3000, "932-32-3232", 31)
    fran.GiveBonus(200)
    fran.DisplayStats()
    Console.ReadLine()
  End Sub
End Module
```

Figure 6-6 shows the output of our application thus far.

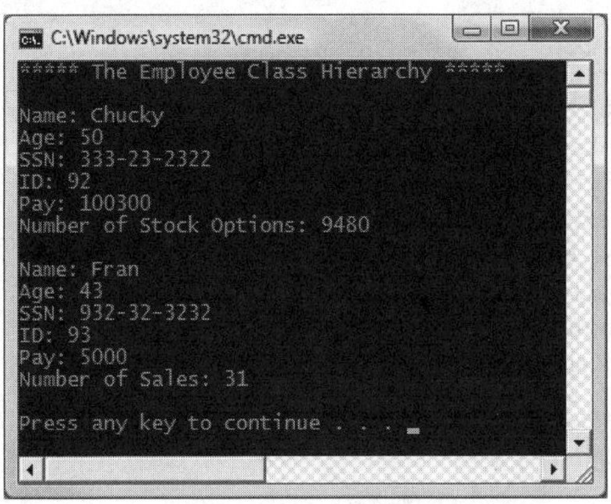

Figure 6-6. *Output of the current Employees application*

Overriding with Visual Studio 2008

As you may have already noticed, when you are overriding a member, you must recall the type of each and every parameter—not to mention the method name and parameter passing conventions (ByRef, ParamArray, etc.). Visual Studio 2008 has a very helpful feature that you can make use of when overriding a virtual member. If you type the word "Overrides" within the scope of a class type, IntelliSense will automatically display a list of all the overridable members defined in your parent classes, as you see in Figure 6-7.

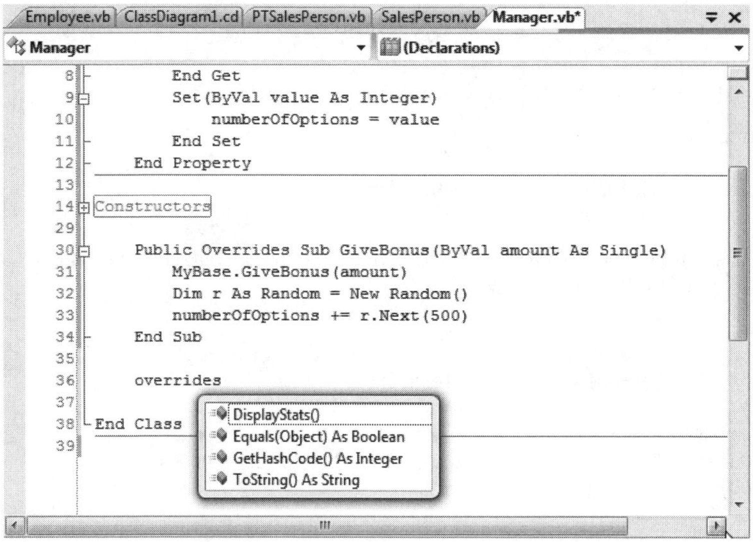

Figure 6-7. *Quickly viewing virtual members à la Visual Studio 2008*

When you select a member and hit the Enter key, the IDE responds by automatically filling in the method stub on your behalf. Note that you also receive a code statement that calls your parent's version of the virtual member (you are free to delete this line if it is not required):

```
Public Overrides Sub DisplayStats()
  MyBase.DisplayStats()
End Sub
```

The NotOverridable Keyword

Recall that the NotInheritable keyword can be applied to a class type to prevent other types from extending its behavior via inheritance. As you may remember, we sealed PTSalesPerson as we assumed it made no sense for other developers to extend this line of inheritance any further.

On a related note, sometimes you may not wish to seal an entire class, but simply want to prevent derived types from overriding particular virtual members. For example, assume we do not want part-time salespeople to obtain customized bonuses. To prevent the PTSalesPerson class from overriding the virtual GiveBonus(), we could effectively seal this method in the SalesPerson class with the NotOverridable keyword:

```
' SalesPerson has sealed the GiveBonus() method!
Public Class SalesPerson
  Inherits Employee
```

```
...
  Public NotOverridable Overrides Sub GiveBonus(ByVal amount As Single)
    ...
  End Sub
End Class
```

Here, SalesPerson has indeed overridden the virtual GiveBonus() method defined in the Employee class; however, it has explicitly marked it as NotOverridable. Thus, if we attempted to override this method in the derived PTSalesPerson class:

```
Public Class PTSalesPerson
    Inherits SalesPerson
...
  ' No custom bonus for you! Error!
  Public Overrides Sub GiveBonus(ByVal amount As Single)
    ' Rats. Can't change this method any further.
  End Sub
End Class
```

we receive compile-time errors.

Understanding Abstract Classes and the MustInherit Keyword

Currently, the Employee base class has been designed to supply protected member variables for its descendents, as well as supply two virtual methods (GiveBonus() and DisplayStats()) that may be overridden by a given descendent. While this is all well and good, there is a rather odd byproduct of the current design: you can directly create instances of the Employee base class:

```
' What exactly does this mean?
Dim X As New Employee()
```

In this example, the only real purpose of the Employee base class is to define common members for all subclasses. In all likelihood, you did not intend anyone to create a direct instance of this class, reason being that the Employee type itself is too general of a concept. For example, if I were to walk up to you and say, "I'm an employee!" I would bet your very first question to me would be, "What *kind* of employee are you?" (a consultant, trainer, admin assistant, copy editor, White House aide, etc.).

Given that many base classes tend to be rather nebulous entities, a far better design for our example is to prevent the ability to directly create a new Employee object in code. In VB 2008, you can enforce this programmatically by using the MustInherit keyword. Formally speaking, classes marked with the MustInherit keyword are termed *abstract base classes*:

```
' Update the Employee class as abstract
' to prevent direct instantiation.
Partial Public MustInherit Class Employee
...
End Class
```

With this, if you now attempt to create an instance of the Employee class, you are issued a compile-time error:

```
' Error! Cannot create an abstract class!
Dim X As New Employee()
```

Excellent! At this point you have constructed a fairly interesting employee hierarchy. We will add a bit more functionality to this application later in this chapter when examining VB 2008 casting rules. Until then, Figure 6-8 illustrates the core design of our current types.

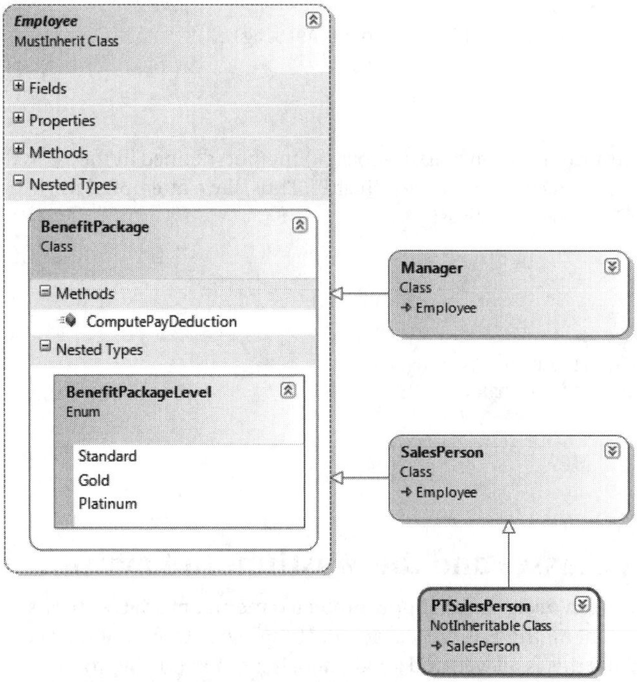

Figure 6-8. *The current* `Employees` *project hierarchy*

Source Code The Employees project is included under the Chapter 6 subdirectory.

Building a Polymorphic Interface with MustOverride

When a class has been defined as an abstract base class (via the `MustInherit` keyword), it may define any number of *abstract members*. Abstract members can be used whenever you wish to define a member that does *not* supply a default implementation. By doing so, you enforce a *polymorphic interface* on each descendant, leaving them to contend with the task of providing the details behind your abstract methods or properties.

Simply put, an abstract base class's polymorphic interface simply refers to its set of virtual (`Overridable`) and abstract (`MustOverride`) methods. This is much more interesting than first meets the eye, as this trait of OOP allows us to build very extendable and flexible software applications. To illustrate, we will be implementing (and slightly modifying) the shapes hierarchy briefly examined in Chapter 5 during our overview of the pillars of OOP. To begin, create a new Console Application project named Shapes, which will eventually contain a set of three interrelated classes (`Shape`, `Hexagon`, and `Circle`).

In Figure 6-9, notice that the `Hexagon` and `Circle` types will be designed to extend the `Shape` base class. Like any base class, `Shape` defines a number of members (a `PetName` property and `Draw()` method in this case) that are common to all descendants.

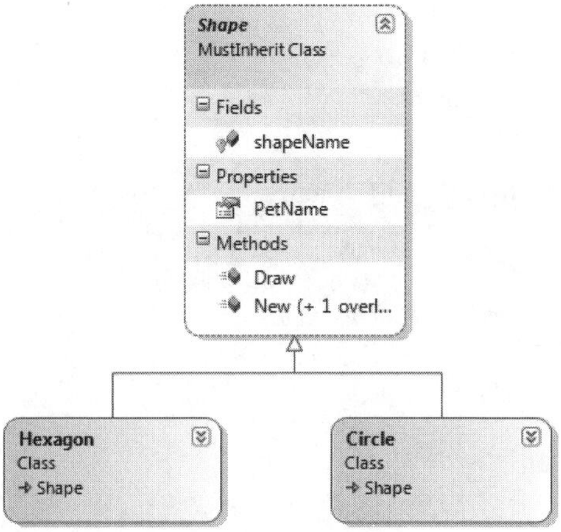

Figure 6-9. *The shapes hierarchy*

Much like the employee hierarchy, you should be able to tell that you don't want to allow the object user to create an instance of Shape directly, as it is too abstract of a concept. Again, to prevent the direct creation of the Shape type, you can define it as a MustInherit class. As well, given that we wish the derived types to respond uniquely to the Draw() method, let's mark it as Overridable and define a default implementation:

```
' The abstract base class of the hierarchy.
Public MustInherit Class Shape
  Protected shapeName As String

  Public Sub New()
    shapeName = "NoName"
  End Sub
  Public Sub New(ByVal s As String)
    shapeName = s
  End Sub

  Public Overridable Sub Draw()
    Console.WriteLine("Inside Shape.Draw()")
  End Sub

  Public Property PetName() As String
    Get
      Return shapeName
    End Get
    Set(ByVal value As String)
      shapeName = value
    End Set
  End Property
End Class
```

Notice that the virtual Draw() method provides a default implementation that simply prints out a message that informs us we are calling the Draw() method within the Shape base class. Now recall that when a method is marked with the Overridable keyword, the method provides a default implementation that all derived types automatically inherit. If a child class so chooses, it *may* override the method but does not *have* to. Given this, consider the following implementation of the Circle and Hexagon types:

```
'Circle DOES NOT override Draw().
Public Class Circle
  Inherits Shape

  Public Sub New()
  End Sub
  Public Sub New(ByVal name As String)
    MyBase.New(name)
  End Sub
End Class

' Hexagon DOES override Draw().
Public Class Hexagon
  Inherits Shape

  Public Sub New()
  End Sub
  Public Sub New(ByVal name As String)
    MyBase.New(name)
  End Sub

  Public Overrides Sub Draw()
    Console.WriteLine("Drawing {0} the Hexagon", shapeName)
  End Sub
End Class
```

The usefulness of abstract methods becomes crystal clear when you once again remember that subclasses are never required to override virtual methods (as in the case of `Circle`). Therefore, if you create an instance of the `Hexagon` and `Circle` types, you'd find that the `Hexagon` understands how to draw itself correctly (or at lease print out a fitting message to the console). The `Circle`, however, is more than a bit confused (see Figure 6-10 for output):

```
Sub Main()
  Console.WriteLine("***** Fun with Polymorphism *****")
  Console.WriteLine()
  Dim hex As New Hexagon("Beth")
  hex.Draw()

  Dim cir As New Circle("Cindy")
  ' Calls base class implementation!
  cir.Draw()
  Console.ReadLine()
End Sub
```

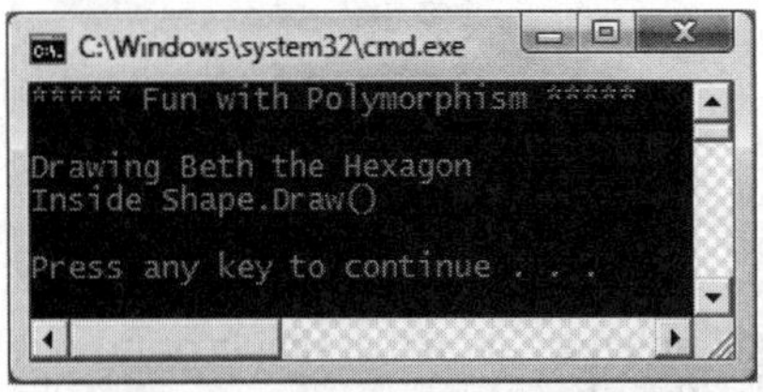

Figure 6-10. *Hmm . . . something is not quite right.*

Clearly, this is not a very intelligent design for the current hierarchy. To force each child class to override the Draw() method, you can define Draw() as an abstract method of the Shape class, which by definition means you provide no default implementation whatsoever. To mark a method as abstract in VB 2008, you use the MustOverride keyword and define your member *without* an End construct:

```
' Force all child classes to define how to be rendered.
Public MustInherit Class Shape
...
  Public MustOverride Sub Draw()
...
End Class
```

Note MustOverride methods can only be defined in MustInherit classes. If you attempt to do otherwise, you will be issued a compiler error.

Methods marked with MustOverride are pure protocol. They simply define the name, return value (if any), and argument set (if any). Here, the abstract Shape class informs the derived types "I have a subroutine named Draw() that takes no arguments. If you derive from me, you figure out the details."

Given this, we are now obligated to override the Draw() method in the Circle class. If you do not, Circle is also assumed to be a noncreatable abstract type that must be adorned with the MustInherit keyword (which is obviously not very useful in this example). Here is the code update:

```
' If we did not implement the MustOverride Draw() method, Circle would also be
' considered abstract, and would have to be marked MustInherit!
Public Class Circle
  Inherits Shape

  Public Sub New()
  End Sub
  Public Sub New(ByVal name As String)
    MyBase.New(name)
  End Sub

  Public Overrides Sub Draw()
    Console.WriteLine("Drawing {0} the Circle", shapeName)
  End Sub
End Class
```

The short answer is that we can now make the assumption that anything deriving from Shape does indeed have a unique version of the Draw() method. To illustrate the full story of polymorphism, consider the following code:

```
Module Program
  Sub Main()
    Console.WriteLine("***** Fun with Polymorphism *****")
    Console.WriteLine()

    ' Make an array of Shape compatible objects.
    Dim myShapes() As Shape = {New Hexagon(), New Circle(), _
      New Hexagon("Mick"), New Circle("Beth"), _
      New Hexagon("Linda")}
```

```
    ' Loop over each item and interact with the
    ' polymorphic interface.
    For Each s As Shape In myShapes
      s.Draw()
    Next
    Console.ReadLine()
  End Sub
End Module
```

Figure 6-11 shows the output.

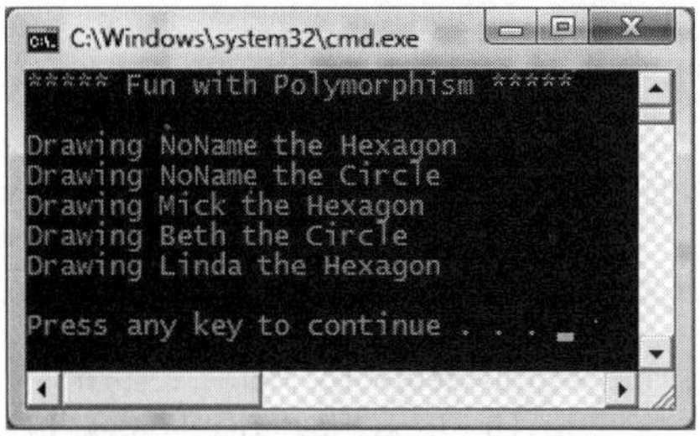

Figure 6-11. *Polymorphism in action*

This Main() method illustrates polymorphism at its finest. Although it is not possible to *directly* create an instance of an abstract base class (the Shape), you are able to freely store references to any subclass with an abstract base variable. Therefore, when you are creating an array of Shapes, the array can hold any object deriving from the Shape base class (if you attempt to place Shape-incompatible objects into the array, you receive a compiler error).

Given that all items in the myShapes array do indeed derive from Shape, we know they all support the same polymorphic interface (or said more plainly, they all have a Draw() method). As you iterate over the array of Shape references, it is at runtime that the underlying type is determined. At this point, the correct version of the Draw() method is invoked.

This technique also makes it very simple to safely extend the current hierarchy. For example, assume we derived five more classes from the abstract Shape base class (Triangle, Square, etc.). Due to the polymorphic interface, the code within our For loop would not have to change in the slightest as the compiler enforces that only Shape-compatible types are placed within the myShapes array.

Understanding Member Shadowing

VB 2008 provides a facility that is the logical opposite of method overriding termed *shadowing*. Formally speaking, if a derived class defines a member that is identical to a member defined in a base class, the derived class has *shadowed* the parent's version.

For the sake of illustration, assume you receive a class named ThreeDCircle from a coworker (or classmate) that defines a subroutine named Draw() taking no arguments:

```
Public Class ThreeDCircle
  Public Sub Draw()
    Console.WriteLine("Drawing a 3D Circle")
  End Sub
End Class
```

You figure that a ThreeDCircle "is-a" Circle, so you derive from your existing Circle type:

```
Public Class ThreeDCircle
  Inherits Circle
  Public Sub Draw()
    Console.WriteLine("Drawing a 3D Circle")
  End Sub
End Class
```

Once you do so, you find the warning you see in Figure 6-12 shown in Visual Studio 2008.

Figure 6-12. *Oops! We just shadowed a member in our parent class.*

To address this issue, you have two options. You could simply update the parent's version of Draw() using the Overrides keyword (as suggested by the compiler). With this approach, the ThreeDCircle type is able to extend the parent's default behavior as required.

As an alternative, you can include the Shadows keyword to the offending Draw() member of the ThreeDCircle type. Doing so explicitly states that the derived type's implementation is intentionally designed to hide the parent's version (again, in the real world, this can be helpful if external .NET software somehow conflicts with your current software).

```
' This class extends Circle and hides the inherited Draw() method.
Public Class ThreeDCircle
  Inherits Circle

  ' Hide any Draw() implementation above me.
  Public Shadows Sub Draw()
    Console.WriteLine("Drawing a 3D Circle")
  End Sub
End Class
```

Finally, be aware that it is still possible to trigger the base class implementation of a shadowed member using an explicit cast (described in the next section). For example:

```
Module Program
  Sub Main()
 ...
    ' Fun with shadowing.
    Dim o As New ThreeDCircle()
    o.Draw()
    CType(o, Circle).Draw()
    Console.ReadLine()
  End Sub
End Module
```

The need for member shadowing is the greatest when you are subclassing from a class you (or your team) did not create yourselves (for example, if you purchase a third-party .NET software package). If extending this third-party class introduces a name clash with your new subclass, you can use the Shadows keyword to resolve the ambiguity.

Source Code The Shapes project can be found under the Chapter 6 subdirectory.

Understanding Base Class/Derived Class Casting Rules

Now that you can build a family of related class types, you need to learn the laws of VB 2008 casting operations. To do so, let's return to the Employees hierarchy created earlier in this chapter. Under the .NET platform, the ultimate base class in the system is System.Object. Therefore, everything "is-a" Object and can be treated as such. Given this fact, it is legal to store an instance of any type within an object variable:

```
' A Manager "is-a" System.Object.
Dim frank As Object = _
  New Manager("Frank Zappa", 9, 3000, 40000, "111-11-1111", 5)
```

In the Employees system, Manager, SalesPerson, and PTSalesPerson types all extend Employee, so we can store any of these objects in a valid base class reference. Therefore, the following statements are also legal:

```
' A Manager "is-a" Employee too.
Dim moonUnit As Employee = New Manager("MoonUnit Zappa", 2, 3001, _
    20000, "101-11-1321", 1)

' A PTSalesPerson "is-a" SalesPerson.
Dim jill As SalesPerson = New PTSalesPerson("Jill", 834, 3002, _
    100000, "111-12-1119", 90)
```

The first law of casting between class types is that when two classes are related by classical inheritance (the "is-a" relationship), it is always safe to store a derived object within a base class reference. Formally, this is called an *implicit cast*, as "it just works" given the laws of inheritance. This leads to some powerful programming constructs. For example, assume you have defined a new method within your current module:

```
Sub FireThisPerson(ByVal emp As Employee)
  ' Remove employee from company database...

  ' Get key and pencil sharpener from fired employee...
End Sub
```

Because this method takes a single parameter of type Employee, you can effectively pass any descendent from the Employee class into this method directly, given the "is-a" relationship. For example:

```
' Streamline the staff.
FireThisPerson(moonUnit)    ' "moonUnit" was declared as an Employee.
FireThisPerson(jill)        ' "jill" was declared as a PTSalesPerson.
```

The following code compiles given that an implicit cast occurs when passing in these derived types (moonUnit and jill) into a method prototyped to take a base class type (Employee) parameter. However, what if you also wanted to fire "Frank Zappa" (the frank object currently stored in a generic System.Object reference)? If you pass the frank object directly into FireThisPerson() as follows:

```
' This will only work if Option Strict is Off!
Dim frank As Object = _
  New Manager("Frank Zappa", 9, 3000, 40000, "111-11-1111", 5)

' Remember!  FireThisPerson() is expecting an Employee-derived
' type here.
FireThisPerson(frank)
```

you will find the code will *only* work if `Option Strict` is disabled. However, if you were to enable this option for your project (which is always a good idea), you are issued a compiler error. The reason is you cannot automatically treat a `System.Object` as a derived `Employee` directly, given that `Object` "is-not-a" `Employee`. As you can see, however, the object reference is pointing to an `Employee`-compatible object. You can satisfy the compiler by performing an explicit cast.

This is the second law of casting: you must explicitly downcast using the VB 2008 `CType()` function. `CType()` takes two parameters. The first parameter is the object you currently have access to. The second parameter is the name of the type you want to have access to. The value returned from `CType()` is the result of the downward cast. Thus, the previous problem can be avoided as follows:

```
' OK even with Option Strict enabled.
FireThisPerson(CType(frank, Manager))
```

As you will see in Chapter 9, `CType()` is also the safe way of obtaining an interface reference from a type. Furthermore, `CType()` may operate safely on numerical types, but don't forget you have a number of related conversion functions at your disposal (`CInt()` and so on). Finally, be aware that if you attempt to cast an object into an incompatible type, you receive an invalid cast exception at runtime. Chapter 7 examines the details of structured exception handling.

■ **Note** In Chapter 12, you will examine two additional manners in which you can perform explicit casts using the `DirectCast` and `TryCast` keywords of VB 2008.

Determining the "Type of" Employee

Given that the `FireThisPerson()` method has been designed to take any possible type derived from `Employee`, one question on your mind may be how this method can determine which derived type was sent into the method. On a related note, given that the incoming parameter is of type `Employee`, how can you gain access to the specialized members of the `SalesPerson` and `Manager` types?

The VB 2008 language provides the `TypeOf/Is` statement to determine whether a given base class reference is actually referring to a derived type. Consider the following implementation of the `FireThisPerson()` method:

```
Public Sub FireThisPerson(ByVal emp As Employee)

  If TypeOf emp Is SalesPerson Then
    Console.WriteLine("Lost a sales person named {0}", emp.Name)
    Console.WriteLine("{0} made {1} sale(s)...", emp.Name, _
      CType(emp, SalesPerson).SalesNumber)
    Console.WriteLine()
  End If

  If TypeOf emp Is Manager Then
    Console.WriteLine("Lost a suit named {0}", emp.Name)
    Console.WriteLine("{0} had {1} stock options...", emp.Name, _
      CType(emp, Manager).StockOptions)
```

```
    Console.WriteLine()
  End If
End Sub
```

Here you are performing a runtime check to determine what the incoming base class reference is actually pointing to in memory. Once you determine whether you received a SalesPerson or Manager type, you are able to perform an explicit cast via CType() to gain access to the specialized members of the class.

The Master Parent Class: System.Object

To wrap up this chapter, I'd like to examine the details of the master parent class in the .NET platform: Object. As you were reading the previous section, you may have noticed that the base classes in our hierarchies (Car, Employee, and Shape) never explicitly marked their parent classes using the Inherits keyword. For example:

```
' Who is the parent of Car?
Public Class Car
...
End Class
```

In the .NET universe, every type ultimately derives from a common base class named System.Object. The Object class defines a set of common members for every type in the framework. In fact, when you do build a class that does not explicitly define its parent, the compiler automatically derives your type from Object. If you want to be very clear in your intentions, you are free to define classes that derive from Object as follows:

```
' Here we are explicitly deriving from System.Object.
Class Car
  Inherits System.Object
End Class
```

Like any class, System.Object defines a set of members. In the following formal VB definition, note that some of these items are declared Overridable, which specifies that a given member may be overridden by a subclass, while others are marked with Shared (and are therefore called at the class level):

```
' The topmost class in the .NET world: System.Object
Public Class Object
  Public Overridable Function Equals(ByVal obj As Object) As Boolean
  Public Shared Function Equals(ByVal objA As Object, _
    ByVal objB As Object) As Boolean
  Public Shared Function ReferenceEquals(ByVal objA As Object, _
    ByVal objB As Object) As Boolean

  Public Overridable Function GetHashCode() As Integer
  Public Function GetType() As Type
  Public Overridable Function ToString() As String

  Protected Overridable Sub Fianlize()
  Protected Function MemberwiseClone() As Object
End Class
```

Table 6-1 offers a rundown of the functionality provided by each method.

Table 6-1. *Core Members of* `System.Object`

Instance Method of Object Class	Meaning in Life
`Equals()`	By default, this method returns `True` only if the items being compared refer to the exact same item in memory. Thus, `Equals()` is used to compare object references, not the state of the object. Typically, this method is overridden to return `True` only if the objects being compared have the same internal state values (that is, value-based semantics). Be aware that if you override `Equals()`, you should also override `GetHashCode()`.
`GetHashCode()`	Returns an `Integer` that identifies an object based on its current state.
`GetType()`	This method returns a `Type` object that fully describes the object you are currently referencing. In short, this is a Runtime Type Identification (RTTI) method available to all objects (discussed in greater detail in Chapter 16).
`ToString()`	This method returns a string representation of this object, using the `<namespace>.<type name>` format (termed the *fully qualified name*). This method is typically overridden by a subclass to return a tokenized string of name/value pairs that represent the object's internal state, rather than its fully qualified name.
`Finalize()`	For the time being, you can understand this method (when overridden) is called to free any allocated resources before the object is destroyed. I talk more about the CLR garbage collection services in Chapter 8.
`MemberwiseClone()`	This method exists to return a member-by-member copy of the current object. This method cannot be overridden or accessed by the outside world from an object instance. If you need to allow the outside world to obtain deep copies of a given type, implement the `ICloneable` interface, which you do in Chapter 9.

To illustrate some of the default behavior provided by the `Object` base class, create a new Console Application named ObjectOverrides. Add an empty class definition for a type named `Person` (shown in the following code snippet). Finally, update your `Main()` subroutine to interact with the inherited members of `System.Object`.

```
' Remember! Person extends Object!
Public Class Person
End Class

Module Program
  Sub Main()
    Console.WriteLine("***** Fun with System.Object *****")
    Dim p1 As New Person()

    ' Use inherited members of System.Object.
    Console.WriteLine("ToString: {0}", p1.ToString())
    Console.WriteLine("Hash code: {0}", p1.GetHashCode())
    Console.WriteLine("Type: {0}", p1.GetType())

    ' Make some other references to hc.
    Dim p2 As Person = p1
    Dim o As Object = p2
```

```
    ' Are the references pointing to the same object in memory?
    If o.Equals(p1) AndAlso p2.Equals(o) Then
      Console.WriteLine("Same instance!")
    End If
    Console.ReadLine()
  End Sub
End Module
```

Figure 6-13 shows the output.

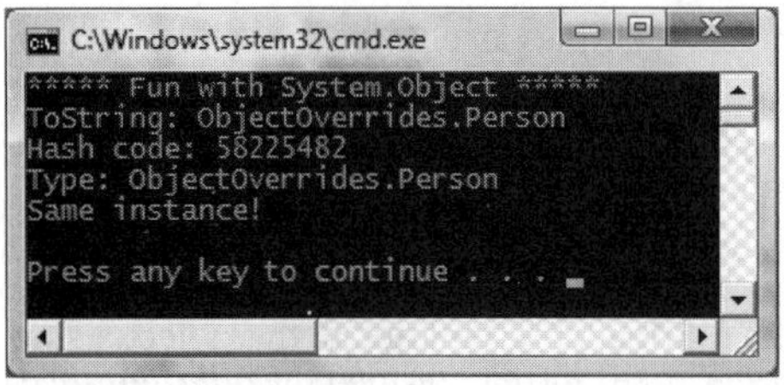

Figure 6-13. *Invoking the inherited members of* `System.Object`

First, notice how the default implementation of `ToString()` returns the fully qualified name of the current type (`ObjectOverrides.Person`). As you will see later during our examination of building custom namespaces (Chapter 15), every VB project defines a *default namespace*, which is the same name of the project itself. Here, we created a project named ObjectOverrides; thus the `Person` type (as well as the initial module) have both been placed within the `ObjectOverrides` namespace.

The default behavior of `Equals()` is to test whether two variables are pointing to the same object in memory. Here, you create a new `Person` object and store it in the `p1` variable. At this point, a new `Person` object is placed on the managed heap. `p2` is also of type `Person`. However, you are not creating a *new* instance, but rather assigning this variable to reference the same object as `p1`. Therefore, `p1` and `p2` are both pointing to the same object in memory, as is the variable `o` (of type `Object`, which was thrown in for good measure). Given that `p1`, `p2`, and `o` all point to the same memory location, the equality test succeeds.

Although the canned behavior of `System.Object` can fit the bill in a number of cases, it is quite common for your custom types to override some of these inherited methods. To illustrate, update the `Person` class to support some state data representing an individual's first name, last name, and age, each of which can be set by a custom constructor:

```
' Remember! Person extends Object.
Class Person
  ' Public only for simplicity. Properties and Private data
  ' would obviously be perferred.
  Public fName As String
  Public lName As String
  Public personAge As Byte

  Public Sub New(ByVal firstName As String, ByVal lastName As String, _
    ByVal age As Byte)
    fName = firstName
    lName = lastName
    personAge = age
  End Sub
  Public Sub New()
  End Sub
End Class
```

Now, let's make use of this new functionality by overriding various members of Object.

Overriding System.Object.ToString()

Many classes (and structures) that you create can benefit from overriding ToString() in order to return a string textual representation of the type's state. This can be quite helpful for purposes of debugging (among other reasons). How you choose to construct this string is a matter of personal choice; however, a recommended approach is to separate each name/value pair with semicolons and wrap the entire string within square brackets (many types in the .NET base class libraries follow this approach). Consider the following overridden ToString() for our Person class:

```
Public Overrides Function ToString() As String
  Dim myState As String
  myState = String.Format("[First Name: {0}; Last Name: {1}; Age: {2}]", _
    fName, lName, personAge)
  Return myState
End Function
```

This implementation of ToString() is quite straightforward, given that the Person class only has three pieces of state data. However, always remember that a proper ToString() override should also account for any data defined up the chain of inheritance. When you override ToString() for a class extending a custom base class, the first order of business is to obtain the ToString() value from your parent using MyBase. Once you have obtained your parent's string data, you can append the derived class's custom information.

Overriding System.Object.Equals()

Let's also override the behavior of Object.Equals() to work with *value-based semantics*. Recall that by default, Equals() returns True only if the two objects being compared reference the same object instance in memory. For the Person class, it may be helpful to implement Equals() to return True if the two variables being compared contain the same state values (e.g., first name, last name, and age).

First of all, notice that the incoming argument of the Equals() method is a generic System.Object. Given this, our first order of business is to ensure the caller has indeed passed in a Person type, and as an extra safeguard, to make sure the incoming parameter is not an unallocated object.

Once we have established the caller has passed us an allocated Person, one approach to implement Equals() is to perform a field-by-field comparison against the data of the incoming object to the data of the current object:

```
Public Overrides Function Equals(ByVal obj As Object) As Boolean
   If TypeOf obj Is Person AndAlso obj IsNot Nothing Then
     Dim temp As Person = CType(obj, Person)
     If temp.fName = Me.fName AndAlso _
       temp.lName = Me.fName AndAlso _
       temp.personAge = Me.personAge Then
       Return True
     Else
       Return False
     End If
     Return False
  End If
End Function
```

Here, you are examining the values of the incoming object against the values of our internal values (note the use of the Me keyword). If the name and age of each are identical, you have two objects with the exact same state data and therefore return True. Any other possibility results in returning False.

While this approach does indeed work, you can certainly imagine how labor intensive it would be to implement a custom Equals() method for nontrivial types that may contain dozens of data fields. One common shortcut is to leverage your own implementation of ToString(). If a class has a prim-and-proper implementation of ToString() that accounts for all field data up the chain of inheritance, you can simply perform a comparison of the object's string data:

```
Public Overrides Function Equals(ByVal obj As Object) As Boolean
  ' No need to cast "obj" to a Person anymore,
  ' as everything has a ToString() method.
  Return obj.ToString = Me.ToString()
End Function
```

Overriding System.Object.GetHashCode()

When a class overrides the Equals() method, you should also override the default implementation of GetHashCode(). Simply put, a *hash code* is a numerical value that represents an object as a particular state. For example, if you create two string objects that hold the value Hello, you would obtain the same hash code. However, if one of the string objects were in all lowercase (hello), you would obtain different hash codes.

By default, System.Object.GetHashCode() uses your object's current location in memory to yield the hash value. However, if you are building a custom type that you intend to store in a Hashtable type (within the System.Collections namespace), you should always override this member, as the Hashtable will be internally invoking Equals() and GetHashCode() to retrieve the correct object.

Although we are not going to place our Person into a System.Collections.Hashtable, for completion, let's override GetHashCode(). There are many algorithms that can be used to create a hash code, some fancy, others not so fancy. Most of the time, you are able to generate a hash code value by leveraging the System.String's GetHashCode() implementation.

Given that the String class already has a solid hash code algorithm that is using the character data of the String to compute a hash value, if you can identify a piece of field data on your class that should be unique for all instances (such as the Social Security number), simply call GetHashCode() on that point of field data. If this is not the case, but you have overridden ToString(), call GetHashCode() on your own string representation:

```
' Return a hash code based on the person's ToString() value.
Public Overrides Function GetHashCode() As Integer
  Return Me.ToString().GetHashCode()
End Function
```

Testing Our Modified Person Class

Now that we have overridden the Overridable members of Object, update Main() to test your updates (see Figure 6-14 for output).

```
Module Program
  Sub Main()
    Console.WriteLine("***** Fun with System.Object *****")
    Console.WriteLine()

    ' NOTE: We want these to be identical to test
    ' the Equals() and GetHashCode() methods.
```

```
    Dim p1 As New Person("Homer", "Simpson", 50)
    Dim p2 As New Person("Homer", "Simpson", 50)

    ' Get stringified version of objects.
    Console.WriteLine("p1.ToString() = {0}", p1.ToString())
    Console.WriteLine("p2.ToString() = {0}", p2.ToString())

    ' Test Overridden Equals()
    Console.WriteLine("p1 = p2?: {0}", p1.Equals(p2))

    ' Test hash codes.
    Console.WriteLine("Same hash codes?: {0}", _
      p1.GetHashCode() = p2.GetHashCode())
    Console.WriteLine()

    ' Change age of p2 and test again.
    p2.personAge = 45
    Console.WriteLine("p1.ToString() = {0}", p1.ToString())
    Console.WriteLine("p2.ToString() = {0}", p2.ToString())
    Console.WriteLine("p1 = p2?: {0}", p1.Equals(p2))
    Console.WriteLine("Same hash codes?: {0}", _
      p1.GetHashCode() = p2.GetHashCode())
    Console.ReadLine()
  End Sub
End Module
```

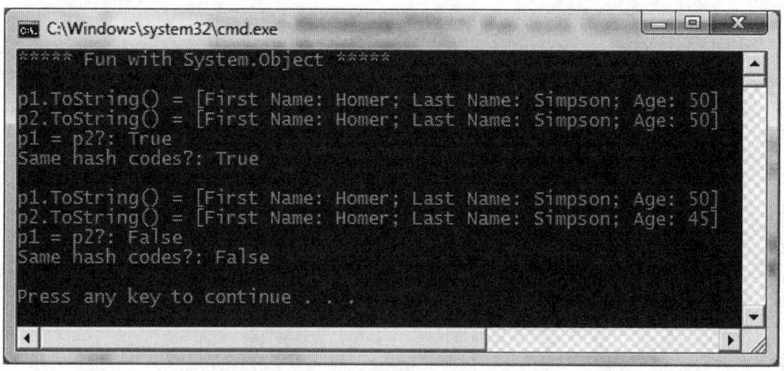

Figure 6-14. *Our customized* Person *type*

The Shared Members of System.Object

In addition to the instance-level members you have just examined, System.Object does define two (very helpful) shared members that also test for value-based or reference-based equality. Consider the following code:

```
Sub SharedMembersOfObject()
  ' Shared members of System.Object.
  Dim p3 As New Person("Sally", "Jones", 4)
  Dim p4 As New Person("Sally", "Jones", 4)
  Console.WriteLine("P3 and P4 have same state: {0}", Object.Equals(p3, p4))
  Console.WriteLine("P3 and P4 are pointing to same object: {0}", _
    Object.ReferenceEquals(p3, p4))
End Sub
```

Here, you are able to simply send in two objects (of any type) and allow the `System.Object` class to determine the details automatically.

■ **Source Code** The ObjectOverrides project is located under the Chapter 6 subdirectory.

Summary

This chapter explored the role and details of inheritance and polymorphism. Over these pages you were introduced to numerous new keywords to support each of these techniques. For example, recall that the `Inherits` keyword is used to establish the parent class of a given type. Parent types are able to define any number of virtual (`Overridable`) and/or abstract (`MustOverride`) members to establish a polymorphic interface. Derived types override such members using the `Overrides` keyword.

In addition to building numerous class hierarchies, this chapter also examined how to explicitly cast between base and derived types using the `CType()` operator, and wrapped up by diving into the details of the cosmic parent class in the .NET base class libraries: `System.Object`.

CHAPTER 7

Understanding Structured Exception Handling

The point of this chapter is to understand how to handle runtime anomalies in your VB code base through the use of *structured exception handling* (SEH). Not only will you learn about the keywords that allow you to handle such matters (`Try`, `Catch`, `Throw`, `Finally`), but you will also come to understand the distinction between application-level and system-level exceptions. This discussion will also serve as a lead-in to the topic of building custom exceptions, as well as how to leverage the exception-centric debugging tools of Visual Studio 2008.

Ode to Errors, Bugs, and Exceptions

Despite what our (sometimes inflated) egos may tell us, no programmer is perfect. Writing software is a complex undertaking, and given this complexity, it is quite common for even the best software to ship with various *problems*. Sometimes the problem is caused by "bad code" (such as overflowing the bounds of an array). Other times, a problem is caused by bogus user input that has not been accounted for in the application's code base (e.g., a phone number field assigned "Chucky"). Now, regardless of the cause of said problem, the end result is that your application does not work as expected. To help frame the upcoming discussion of structured exception handling, allow me to provide definitions for three commonly used anomaly-centric terms:

- *Bugs*: This is, simply put, an error on the part of the programmer. For example, assume you are programming with unmanaged C++. If you make calls on a `NULL` pointer or fail to delete allocated memory (resulting in a memory leak), you have a bug.
- *User errors*: Unlike bugs, user errors are typically caused by the individual running your application, rather than by those who created it. For example, an end user who enters a malformed string into a text box could very well generate an error *if* you fail to handle this faulty input in your code base.
- *Exceptions*: Exceptions are typically regarded as runtime anomalies that are difficult, if not impossible, to account for while programming your application. Possible exceptions include attempting to connect to a database that no longer exists, opening a corrupted file, or contacting a machine that is currently offline. In each of these cases, the programmer (and end user) has little control over these "exceptional" circumstances.

Given the previous definitions, it should be clear that .NET structured *exception* handling is a technique well suited to deal with runtime *exceptions*. However, as for the bugs and user errors that have escaped your view, the CLR will often generate a corresponding exception that identifies the problem at hand. For example, the .NET base class libraries define numerous exceptions such as

FormatException, IndexOutOfRangeException, FileNotFoundException, ArgumentOutOfRangeException, and so forth.

Before we get too far ahead of ourselves, let's formalize the role of structured exception handling and check out how it differs from traditional error handling techniques.

■ **Note** To make the code examples used in this book as clean as possible, I will not catch every possible exception that may be thrown by a given method in the base class libraries. In your production-level projects, you should, of course, make liberal use of the techniques presented in this chapter.

The Role of .NET Exception Handling

Prior to .NET, error handling under the Windows operating system was a confused mishmash of techniques. Many programmers rolled their own error handling logic within the context of a given application. For example, a development team may define a set of numerical constants that represent known error conditions and make use of them as function return values.

This approach is less than ideal, given the fact that raw numerical values are not self-describing and offer little detail regarding how to deal with the problem at hand. Even worse, those who call such functions are not obligated to capture any returned error code, and therefore they may be completely unaware that an error occurred until it is too late. Ideally, you would like to wrap the name, message, and other helpful information regarding this error condition into a single, well-defined package (which is exactly what happens under structured exception handling).

In addition to a developer's ad hoc techniques, the Windows API defines hundreds of predefined error codes. Also, many COM developers have made use of a small set of standard COM interfaces (e.g., ISupportErrorInfo, IErrorInfo, ICreateErrorInfo) and COM objects (such as the VB6 Err object) to return meaningful error information to a COM client.

The obvious problem with these previous techniques is the tremendous lack of symmetry. Each approach is more or less tailored to a given technology, a given language, and perhaps even a given project. In order to put an end to this madness, the .NET platform provides a standard technique to send and trap runtime errors: structured exception handling.

■ **Note** Be aware that SEH is not unique to the .NET platform. Java and unmanaged C++ also provide support for structured exception handling.

The beauty of this approach is that developers now have a unified approach to error handling, which is common to all languages targeting the .NET universe. Therefore, the way in which a VB programmer handles errors is syntactically similar (and semantically identical) to that of a C# programmer. As an added bonus, the syntax used to throw and catch exceptions across assemblies and machine boundaries is identical. Therefore, the way you handle runtime exceptions is identical, regardless of whether the error was thrown from a local machine or a remote machine located thousands of miles away.

Another bonus of .NET exceptions is the fact that rather than receiving a raw numerical value that identifies the problem at hand, exceptions are objects that contain a human-readable description of the problem, as well as a detailed snapshot of the call stack that triggered the exception in the first place. Last but not least, exceptions cannot be ignored (unlike simple return values as described previously). If an exception is unhandled by your code base, the .NET application will fail.

The Atoms of .NET Exception Handling

Programming with structured exception handling involves the use of four interrelated entities:

- A class that represents the exception itself
- A member (property, subroutine, or function) that *throws* an instance of the exception class to the caller under the appropriate conditions
- A block of code on the caller's side that invokes the exception-prone member
- A block of code on the caller's side that will process (or *catch*) the exception should it occur

The VB programming language offers four keywords (Try, Catch, Throw, and Finally) that allow you to throw and handle exceptions. The type that represents the problem at hand is a class derived from System.Exception (or a descendant thereof). Given this fact, let's check out the role of this exception-centric base class.

The System.Exception Base Class

All user- and system-defined exceptions ultimately derive from the System.Exception base class (which in turn derives from System.Object). Notice that some of these members are declared with the Overridable keyword and may thus be overridden by derived types:

```
' Member prototypes of select members.
Public Class Exception
  Implements ISerializable, _Exception

  ' Methods
  Public Overridable Function GetBaseException() As Exception
...
  ' Properties
  Public Overridable ReadOnly Property Data As IDictionary
  Public Overridable Property HelpLink As String
  Protected Property HResult As Integer
  Public ReadOnly Property InnerException As Exception
  Public Overridable ReadOnly Property Message As String
  Public Overridable Property Source As String
  Public Overridable ReadOnly Property StackTrace As String
  Public ReadOnly Property TargetSite As MethodBase
End Class
```

As you can see, many of the properties defined by System.Exception are read-only in nature. This is due to the simple fact that derived types will typically supply default values for each property (for example, the default message of the IndexOutOfRangeException type is "Index was outside the bounds of the array").

Note The Implements keyword shown in the previous code allows a class or structure to support interface types. Although we have yet to examining interfaces (see Chapter 9), simply understand that the _Exception interface allows a .NET exception to be processed by an unmanaged code base (such as a COM application), while the ISerializable interface allows an exception object to be persisted across boundaries (such as a machine boundary).

Table 7-1 describes the details of some (but not all) of the members of System.Exception.

Table 7-1. *Core Members of the* System.Exception *Type*

System.Exception Property	Meaning in Life
Data	This property retrieves a collection of key/value pairs (represented by an object implementing IDictionary) that provides additional, user-defined information about the exception. By default, this collection is empty.
HelpLink	This property returns a URI to a help file describing the error in full detail.
InnerException	This read-only property can be used to obtain information about the previous exception(s) that caused the current exception to occur. The previous exception(s) are recorded by passing them into the constructor of the most current exception.
Message	This read-only property returns the textual description of a given error. The error message itself is set as a constructor parameter.
Source	This property returns the name of the entity that threw the exception.
StackTrace	This read-only property contains a string that identifies the sequence of calls that triggered the exception. As you might guess, this property is very useful during debugging.
TargetSite	This read-only property returns a MethodBase type, which describes numerous details about the method that threw the exception (ToString() will identify the method by name).

The Simplest Possible Example

To illustrate the usefulness of structured exception handling, we need to create a type that may throw an exception under the correct circumstances. Assume we have created a new Console Application project (named SimpleException) that defines two class types (Car and Radio) associated using the "has-a" relationship. The Radio type defines a single method that turns the radio's power on or off:

```
Public Class Radio
  Public Sub TurnOn(ByVal state As Boolean)
    If state = True Then
      Console.WriteLine("Jamming...")
    Else
      Console.WriteLine("Quiet time...")
    End If
  End Sub
End Class
```

In addition to leveraging the Radio type, the Car type is defined in such a way that if the user accelerates a Car object beyond a predefined maximum speed (specified using a constant member variable), its engine explodes, rendering the Car unusable (captured by a Boolean member variable named carIsDead). Beyond these points, the Car type has a few member variables to represent the current speed and a user-supplied "pet name" as well as various constructors. Here is the complete definition (with code annotations):

```
Public Class Car
  ' Constant for maximum speed.
  Public Const maxSpeed As Integer = 100
```

```
  ' Internal state data.
  Private currSpeed As Integer
  Private petName As String

  ' Is the car still operational?
  Private carIsDead As Boolean

  ' A car has a radio.
  Private theMusicBox As New Radio()

  ' Constructors.
  Public Sub New()
  End Sub
  Public Sub New(ByVal name As String, ByVal currSp As Integer)
    currSpeed = currSp
    petName = name
  End Sub

  Public Sub CrankTunes(ByVal state As Boolean)
    theMusicBox.TurnOn(state)
  End Sub

  ' See if Car has overheated.
  Public Sub Accelerate(ByVal delta As Integer)
    If carIsDead Then
      Console.WriteLine("{0} is out of order...", petName)
    Else
      currSpeed += delta
      If currSpeed > maxSpeed Then
        Console.WriteLine("{0} has overheated!", petName)
        currSpeed = 0
        carIsDead = True
      Else
        Console.WriteLine("=> CurrSpeed = {0}", currSpeed)
      End If
    End If
  End Sub
End Class
```

Now, if we were to implement a `Main()` method that forces a `Car` object to exceed the predefined maximum speed (represented by the `maxSpeed` constant) as shown here:

```
Module Program
  Sub Main()
    Console.WriteLine("***** Simple Exception Example *****")
    Console.WriteLine("=> Creating a car and stepping on it!")
    Dim myCar As New Car("Zippy", 20)
    myCar.CrankTunes(True)

    For i As Integer = 0 To 10
      myCar.Accelerate(10)
    Next
    Console.ReadLine()
  End Sub
End Module
```

we would see the output displayed in Figure 7-1.

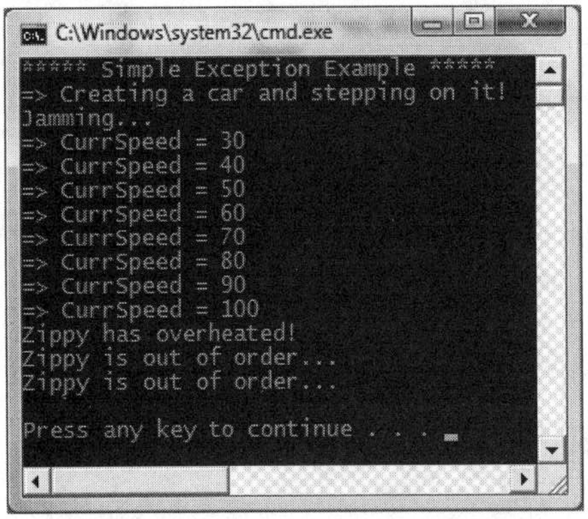

Figure 7-1. *The initial* Car *type in action*

Throwing a Simple Exception

Now that we have a functional Car type, I'll illustrate the simplest way to throw an exception. The current implementation of Accelerate() displays an error message if the caller attempts to speed up the Car beyond its upper limit. To retrofit this method to throw an exception if the user attempts to speed up the automobile after it has met its maker, you want to create and configure a new instance of the System.Exception class, setting the value of the read-only Message property via the class constructor. When you wish to send the error object back to the caller, make use of the VB 2008 Throw keyword. Here is the relevant code update to the Accelerate() method (the remainder of the Car class has been unchanged):

```
' See if Car has overheated.
Public Sub Accelerate(ByVal delta As Integer)
  If carIsDead Then
    Console.WriteLine("{0} is out of order...", petName)
  Else
    currSpeed += delta
    If currSpeed >= maxSpeed Then
      carIsDead = True
      currSpeed = 0
      ' Throw new exception! This car is toast!
      Throw New Exception(String.Format("{0} has overheated!", petName))
    Else
      Console.WriteLine("=> CurrSpeed = {0}", currSpeed)
    End If
  End If
End Sub
```

Before examining how a caller would catch this exception, a few points of interest. First of all, when you are throwing an exception, it is always up to you to decide exactly what constitutes the error in question, and when it should be thrown. Here, you are making the assumption that if the program attempts to increase the speed of a car that has expired, a System.Exception type should be thrown to indicate the Accelerate() method cannot continue (which may or may not be a valid assumption).

Alternatively, you could implement Accelerate() to recover automatically without needing to throw an exception in the first place. By and large, exceptions should be thrown only when a more terminal condition has been met (for example, not finding a necessary file, failing to connect to a database, and whatnot). Deciding exactly what constitutes throwing an exception is a design issue you must always contend with. For the purpose of illustrating the role of structured exception handling, assume that asking a doomed automobile to increase its speed justifies a cause to throw an exception.

Catching Exceptions

Because the `Accelerate()` method now throws an exception, the caller needs to be ready to handle the exception should it occur. When you are invoking a method that may throw an exception, you make use of a `Try/Catch` block. Once you have caught the exception type, you are able to invoke the members of the `System.Exception` type to extract the details of the problem.

What you do with this data is largely up to you. You may wish to log this information to a report file, write the data to the Windows event log, e-mail a system administrator, or display the basic details of the problem to the end user in a message box. Here, you will simply dump the contents of the error to the console window:

```
Module Program
  Sub Main()
    Console.WriteLine("***** Simple Exception Example *****")
    Console.WriteLine("=> Creating a car and stepping on it!")
    Dim myCar As New Car("Zippy", 20)
    myCar.CrankTunes(True)

    ' Try/Catch logic.
    Try
      For i As Integer = 0 To 10
        myCar.Accelerate(10)
      Next
    Catch ex As Exception
      Console.WriteLine("*** Error! ***")
      Console.WriteLine("Method: {0}", ex.TargetSite)
      Console.WriteLine("Message: {0}", ex.Message)
      Console.WriteLine("Source: {0}", ex.Source)
    End Try

    ' The error has been handled, processing continues with the next statement.
    Console.WriteLine("***** Out of exception logic *****")
    Console.ReadLine()
  End Sub
End Module
```

In essence, a `Try` block is a group of statements that *may* throw an exception during execution. If an exception is detected, the flow of program execution is sent to the appropriate `Catch` block (as you will see in just a bit, it is possible to define multiple `Catch` blocks for a single `Try`). On the other hand, if the code within a `Try` block does not trigger an exception, the `Catch` block is skipped entirely, and all is right with the world. Figure 7-2 shows a test run of this program.

As you can see, once an exception has been handled, the application is free to continue on from the point after the `Catch` block. In some circumstances, a given exception may be critical enough to warrant the termination of the application. However, in a good number of cases, the logic within the exception handler will ensure the application will be able to continue on its merry way (although it may be slightly less functional, such as the case of not being able to connect to a remote data source).

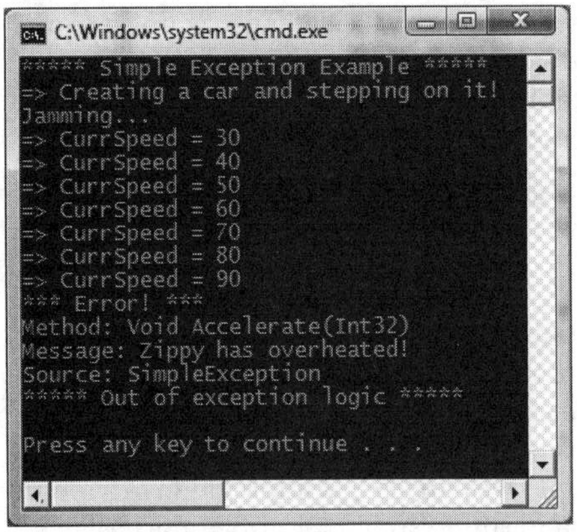

Figure 7-2. *Dealing with the error using structured exception handling*

Configuring the State of an Exception

Currently, the `System.Exception` object configured within the `Accelerate()` method simply establishes a value exposed by the `Message` property (via a constructor parameter). As shown previously in Table 7-1, however, the `Exception` class also supplies a number of additional members (`TargetSite`, `StackTrace`, `HelpLink`, and `Data`) that can be useful in further qualifying the nature of the problem. To spruce up our current example, let's examine further details of these members on a case-by-case basis.

The TargetSite Property

The `System.Exception.TargetSite` property allows you to determine various details about the method that threw a given exception. As shown in the previous `Main()` method, printing the value of `TargetSite` will display the return value, name, and parameters of the method that threw the exception. However, `TargetSite` does not simply return a vanilla-flavored string, but a strongly typed `System.Reflection.MethodBase` object. This type can be used to gather numerous details regarding the offending method as well as the class that defines the offending method. To illustrate, assume the previous `Catch` logic has been updated as follows:

```
Module Program
  Sub Main()
...
    Try
      For i As Integer = 0 To 10
        myCar.Accelerate(10)
      Next
    Catch ex As Exception
      Console.WriteLine("*** Error! ***")
      Console.WriteLine("Member name: {0}", ex.TargetSite)
      Console.WriteLine("Class defining member: {0}", _
        ex.TargetSite.DeclaringType)
      Console.WriteLine("Member type: {0}", ex.TargetSite.MemberType)
      Console.WriteLine("Message: {0}", ex.Message)
      Console.WriteLine("Source: {0}", ex.Source)
```

```
    End Try
    ...
  End Sub
End Module
```

This time, you make use of the `MethodBase.DeclaringType` property to determine the fully qualified name of the class that threw the error (`SimpleException.Car` in this case) as well as the `MemberType` property of the `MethodBase` object to identify the type of member (such as a property versus a method) where this exception originated. Figure 7-3 shows the updated output.

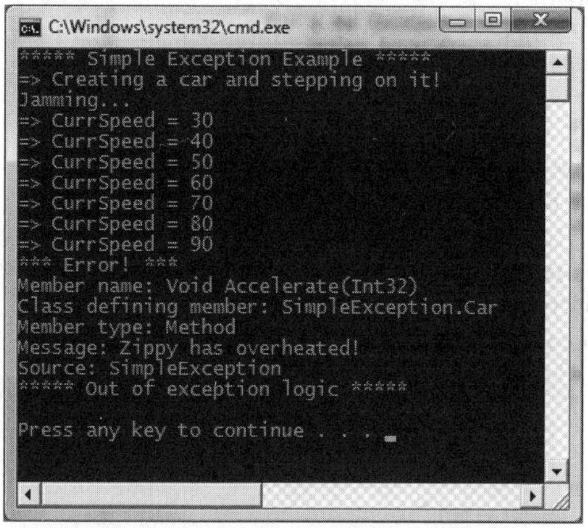

Figure 7-3. *Obtaining aspects of the target site*

■ **Note** As you may agree, this type of low-level error detail would be of little help to an end user. However, this same information is very often dumped to an external error log, which makes diagnosing errors much easier for programmers and support staff.

The StackTrace Property

The `System.Exception.StackTrace` property allows you to identify the series of calls that resulted in the exception. Be aware that you never set the value of `StackTrace`, as it is established automatically at the time the exception is created. To illustrate, assume you have updated your `Catch` logic with the following additional statement:

```
Try
  For i As Integer = 0 To 10
    myCar.Accelerate(10)
  Next
Catch ex As Exception
...
  Console.WriteLine("Stack: {0}", ex.StackTrace)
End Try
```

If you were to run the program, you would find the following stack trace is printed to the console (your line numbers and application path may differ, of course):

```
Stack: at SimpleException.Car.Accelerate(Int32 delta)
in C:\Ch_07 Code\SimpleException\Car.vb:line 36
at SimpleException.Program.Main() in C:\SimpleException\Program.vb:line 9
```

The string returned from StackTrace documents the sequence of calls that resulted in the throwing of this exception. Notice how the bottommost line number of this string identifies the first call in the sequence, while the topmost line number identifies the exact location of the offending member. Again, this information can be quite helpful during the debugging of a given application, as you are able to "follow the flow" of the error's origin.

The HelpLink Property

While the TargetSite and StackTrace properties allow programmers to gain an understanding of a given exception, this information is of little use to the end user. As you have already seen, the System.Exception.Message property can be used to obtain human-readable information that may be displayed to the current user. In addition, the HelpLink property can be set to point the user to a specific URL or standard Windows help file that contains more detailed information.

By default, the value managed by the HelpLink property is an empty string. If you wish to fill this property with an interesting value, you will need to do so before throwing the System.Exception type. Here are the relevant updates to the Car.Accelerate() method:

```
' See if Car has overheated.
Public Sub Accelerate(ByVal delta As Integer)
  If carIsDead Then
    Console.WriteLine("{0} is out of order...", petName)
  Else
    currSpeed += delta
    If currSpeed >= maxSpeed Then
      carIsDead = True
      currSpeed = 0

      ' We need to call the HelpLink property, thus we need to
      ' create a local variable before throwing the Exception object.
      Dim ex As New Exception(String.Format("{0} has overheated!", petName))
      ex.HelpLink = "http://www.CarsRUs.com"
      Throw ex
    Else
      Console.WriteLine("=> CurrSpeed = {0}", currSpeed)
    End If
  End If
End Sub
```

The Catch logic could now be updated to print out this help link information as follows:

```
Catch ex As Exception
...
  Console.WriteLine("Help Link: {0}", ex.HelpLink)
End Try
```

The Data Property

The Data property of System.Exception allows you to fill an exception object with any additional relevant bits of information (such as a time stamp or what have you). The Data property returns an object implementing an interface named IDictionary, defined in the System.Collections namespace. Chapter 9 examines the role of interface-based programming, while the System.Collections namespace is detailed in Chapter 10. For the time being, just understand that dictionary collections allow you to create a set of values that are retrieved using a specific key value. Observe the next relevant update to the Car.Accelerate() method:

```
' See if Car has overheated.
Public Sub Accelerate(ByVal delta As Integer)
  If carIsDead Then
    Console.WriteLine("{0} is out of order...", petName)
  Else
    currSpeed += delta
    If currSpeed >= maxSpeed Then
      carIsDead = True
      currSpeed = 0

      Dim ex As New Exception(String.Format("{0} has overheated!", petName))
      ex.HelpLink = "http://www.CarsRUs.com"

      ' Stuff in custom data regarding the error.
      ex.Data.Add("TimeStamp", _
        String.Format("The car exploded at {0}", DateTime.Now))
      ex.Data.Add("Cause", "You have a lead foot.")
        Throw ex
    Else
      Console.WriteLine("=> CurrSpeed = {0}", currSpeed)
    End If
  End If
End Sub
```

Next, we need to update the Catch logic to test that the value returned from the Data property is not Nothing (the default setting). After this point, we make use of the Key and Value properties of the DictionaryEntry type to print the custom user data to the console:

```
Catch ex As Exception
...
  ' By default, the data field is empty, so check for Nothing.
  Console.WriteLine("-> Custom Data:")
  If (ex.Data IsNot Nothing) Then
    For Each de As DictionaryEntry In ex.Data
      Console.WriteLine("-> {0} : {1}", de.Key, de.Value)
    Next
  End If
End Try
```

With this, we would now find the update shown in Figure 7-4.

Cool! At this point you hopefully have a better idea how to throw and catch exception objects to account for runtime errors. Next, let's examine the process of building strongly typed custom exception objects.

Source Code The SimpleException project is included under the Chapter 7 subdirectory.

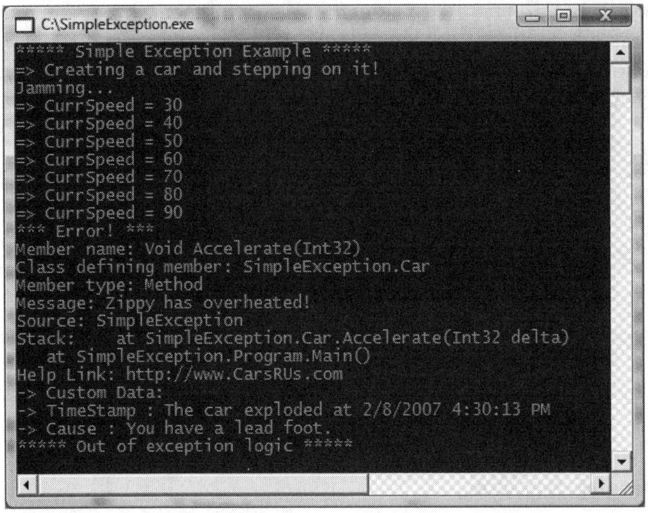

Figure 7-4. *Obtaining custom data*

System-Level Exceptions (System.SystemException)

The .NET base class libraries define many classes derived from `System.Exception`. For example, the `System` namespace defines core exception classes such as `ArgumentOutOfRangeException`, `IndexOutOfRangeException`, `StackOverflowException`, and so forth. Other namespaces define exceptions that reflect the behavior of that namespace (e.g., `System.Drawing.Printing` defines printing exceptions, `System.IO` defines I/O-based exceptions, `System.Data` defines database-centric exceptions, and so forth).

Exceptions that are thrown by the CLR are (appropriately) called *system exceptions*. These exceptions are typically regarded as nonrecoverable, fatal errors. System exceptions derive directly from a base class named `System.SystemException`, which in turn derives from `System.Exception` (which derives from `System.Object`):

```
Public Class SystemException
  Inherits Exception
  ' Various constructors...
End Class
```

Given that the `System.SystemException` type does not add any additional functionality beyond a set of constructors (which you can view for yourself using the Visual Studio 2008 object browser), you might wonder why `SystemException` exists in the first place.

Simply put, when an exception type derives from `System.SystemException`, you are able to determine that the .NET runtime is the entity that has thrown the exception, rather than the code base of the executing application. For example, the `NullReferenceException` class extends `SystemException`. You can verify this quite simply using the VB 2008 `TypeOf`/`Is` construct:

```
' True!
Dim nullRefEx As New NullReferenceException()
Console.WriteLine("NullReferenceException is-a SystemException? : {0}", _
  TypeOf nullRefEx Is SystemException)
```

Application-Level Exceptions (System.ApplicationException)

Given that all .NET exceptions are class types, you are free to create your own application-specific exceptions. However, due to the fact that the System.SystemException base class represents exceptions thrown from the CLR, you may naturally assume that you should derive your custom exceptions from the System.Exception type. While you could do so, best practice dictates that you instead derive from the System.ApplicationException type:

```
Public Class ApplicationException
  Inherits Exception
  ' Various constructors...
End Class
```

Like SystemException, ApplicationException does not define any additional members beyond a set of constructors. Functionally, the only purpose of System.ApplicationException is to identify the source of the (nonfatal) error. When you handle an exception deriving from System.ApplicationException, you can assume the exception was raised by the code base of the executing application, rather than by the .NET base class libraries.

Building Custom Exceptions, Take One

While you can always throw instances of System.Exception to signal a runtime error (as shown in our first example), it is sometimes advantageous to build a *strongly typed exception* that represents the unique details of your current problem. For example, assume you wish to build a custom exception (named CarIsDeadException) to represent the error of speeding up a car beyond its threshold and causing it to explode. The first step is to derive a new class from System.ApplicationException (by convention, all exception classes end with the "Exception" suffix; in fact, this is a .NET best practice).

Create a new Console Application project named CustomException, and copy the previous Car and Radio definitions into your new project using the Project ➤ Add Existing Item menu option. Next, add the following new class definition:

```
' This custom exception describes the details of the car-is-dead condition.
Public Class CarIsDeadException
  Inherits ApplicationException
End Class
```

Like any class, you are free to include any number of custom members that can be called within the Catch block of the calling logic. You are also free to override any virtual members defined by your parent classes. For example, we could implement CarIsDeadException by overriding the virtual Message property:

```
Public Class CarIsDeadException
  Inherits ApplicationException

  ' Default error message.
  Private messageDetails As String = "Car Error"

  ' Constructors.
  Public Sub New()
  End Sub
  Public Sub New(ByVal msg As String)
    messageDetails = msg
  End Sub
```

```
  ' Override the Exception.Message property.
  Public Overrides ReadOnly Property Message() As String
    Get
      Return String.Format("Car Error Message: {0}", messageDetails)
    End Get
  End Property
End Class
```

Here, the `CarIsDeadException` type maintains a private data member (`messageDetails`) that represents data regarding the current exception, which can be set to a unique message using a custom constructor. Throwing this error from the `Accelerate()` is straightforward. Simply create, configure, and throw a `CarIsDeadException` object rather than a `System.Exception`:

```
' Throw the custom CarIsDeadException.
Public Sub Accelerate(ByVal delta As Integer)
...
  Dim ex As New CarIsDeadException(String.Format("{0} has overheated!", petName))
...
End Sub
```

To catch this incoming exception explicitly, your `Catch` scope can now be updated to catch a specific `CarIsDeadException` type (however, given that `CarIsDeadException` "is-a" `System.Exception`, it is still permissible to catch a `System.Exception` as well):

```
Sub Main()
...
  Catch ex As CarIsDeadException
    ' Process incoming exception.
  End Try
...
End Sub
```

So, now that you understand the basic process of building a custom exception, you may wonder when you are required to do so. Typically, you only need to create custom exceptions when the error is tightly bound to the class issuing the error (for example, a custom `File` class that throws a number of file-related errors, a `Car` class that throws a number of car-related errors, and so forth). In doing so, you provide the caller with the ability to handle numerous exceptions on an error-by-error (and strongly typed) basis.

Building Custom Exceptions, Take Two

The current `CarIsDeadException` type has overridden the `System.Exception.Message` property in order to configure a custom error message. However, we can simplify our programming tasks if we set the parent's `Message` property via an incoming constructor parameter. By doing so, we have no need to write anything other than the following:

```
Public Class CarIsDeadException
  Inherits ApplicationException

  Public Sub New()
  End Sub
  Public Sub New(ByVal msg As String)
    MyBase.New(msg)
  End Sub
End Class
```

Notice that this time you have *not* defined a string variable to represent the message, and have *not* overridden the Message property. Rather, you are simply passing the parameter to your base class constructor. With this design, a custom exception class is little more than a uniquely named class deriving from System.ApplicationException, devoid of any member variables (or base class overrides).

Don't be surprised if most (if not all) of your custom exception classes follow this simple pattern. Many times, the role of a custom exception is not necessarily to provide additional functionality beyond what is inherited from the base classes, but to provide a strongly named type that clearly identifies the nature of the error.

Building Custom Exceptions, Take Three

If you wish to build a truly prim-and-proper custom exception class, you would want to make sure your type adheres to the following .NET best practices. Specifically, this requires that your custom exception

- Derives from Exception/ApplicationException
- Is marked with the <System.Serializable()> attribute
- Defines a default constructor
- Defines a constructor that sets the inherited Message property
- Defines a constructor to handle setting any "inner exceptions"
- Defines a constructor to handle the serialization of your type

Now, based on your current background with .NET, you may have no idea regarding the role of attributes or object serialization, which is just fine. I'll address these topics later in the text (in Chapters 16 and 21, respectively). However, to finalize our examination of building custom exceptions, here is the final iteration of CarIsDeadException (note we are importing the System.Runtime.Serialization namespace, to gain access to the SerializationInfo and StreamingContext classes):

```
Imports System.Runtime.Serialization

<Serializable()> _
Public Class CarIsDeadException
  Inherits ApplicationException
  Public Sub New()
  End Sub
  Public Sub New(ByVal message As String)
    MyBase.New(message)
  End Sub
  Public Sub New(ByVal message As String, ByVal inner As System.Exception)
    MyBase.New(message, inner)
  End Sub
  Protected Sub New(ByVal info As SerializationInfo, _
    ByVal context As StreamingContext)
    MyBase.New(info, context)
  End Sub
End Class
```

Building Custom Exceptions à la Visual Studio

As you might agree, building a prim-and-proper custom exception requires a good deal of repeat code; in fact all that typically changes is the name of the exception class itself (the remaining code is little more than necessary plumbing). Thankfully, Visual Studio provides a code snippet that will autogenerate an exception type on your behalf. Simply type **except** within a VB code file and press the Tab key. As an alternative, you can right-click within a VB code file and select the Insert Snippet menu option. From here, navigate to the Define an Exception Class code snippet (see Figure 7-5).

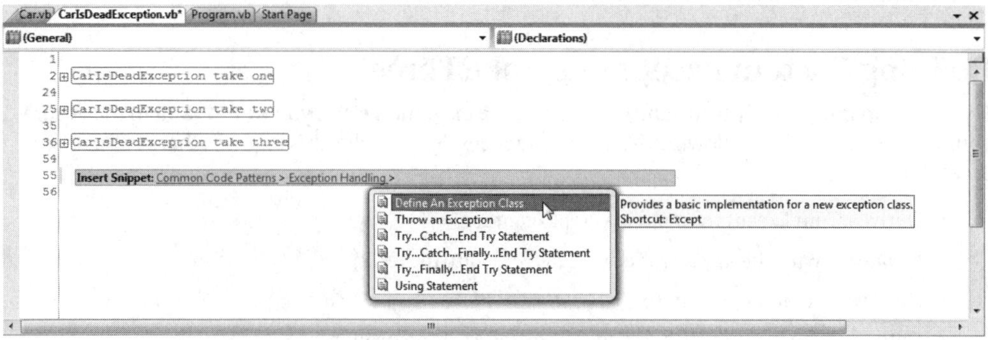

Figure 7-5. *Activating the Custom Exception code snippet*

So, at this point, you are able to build custom strongly typed exceptions that represent the application-specific errors your program may generate. Next up, we need to examine the process of handling multiple exceptions that may result from a single `Try` scope.

Processing Multiple Exceptions

In its simplest form, a `Try` block has a single `Catch` block. In reality, you often run into a situation where the statements within a `Try` block could trigger *numerous* possible exceptions. For example, assume the car's `Accelerate()` method also throws the predefined `ArgumentOutOfRangeException` if you pass an invalid parameter (which we will assume is any value less than zero):

```
Public Sub Accelerate(ByVal delta As Integer)
  If delta < 0 Then
    Throw New ArgumentOutOfRangeException()
  End If
...
End Sub
```

The `Catch` logic could now specifically respond to each type of exception:

```
Module Program
  Sub Main()
    Console.WriteLine("***** Creating a car and stepping on it *****")
    Dim myCar As New Car("Zippy", 20)
    myCar.CrankTunes(True)

    Try
      For i As Integer = 0 To 10
        myCar.Accelerate(10)
      Next
```

```
    Catch ex As ArgumentOutOfRangeException
      ' Process bad arguments.
    Catch ex As CarIsDeadException
      ' Process CarIsDeadException.
    End Try
...
  End Sub
End Module
```

When you are authoring multiple Catch blocks, you must be aware that when an exception is thrown, it will be processed by the first available catch. To illustrate exactly what the "first available" catch means, assume you retrofitted the previous logic with an additional Catch scope that attempts to handle all exceptions beyond CarIsDeadException and ArgumentOutOfRangeException by catching a general System.Exception as follows:

```
' This code will generate warnings!
Module Program
  Sub Main()
    Console.WriteLine("***** Creating a car and stepping on it *****")
    Dim myCar As New Car("Zippy", 20)
    myCar.CrankTunes(True)

    Try
      For i As Integer = 0 To 10
        myCar.Accelerate(10)
      Next
    Catch ex As Exception
      ' Try to catch all other exceptions here?
    Catch ex As ArgumentOutOfRangeException
      ' Process bad arguments.
    Catch ex As CarIsDeadException
      ' Process CarIsDeadException.
    End Try
...
  End Sub
End Module
```

This exception handling logic generates several warnings. The problem is due to the fact that the first Catch block can handle System.Exception and anything derived from it (given the "is-a" relationship), including the CarIsDeadException and ArgumentOutOfRangeException types. Therefore, the final two Catch blocks are unreachable!

The rule of thumb to keep in mind is to make sure your Catch blocks are structured such that the very first Catch is the most specific exception (i.e., the most derived type in an exception type inheritance chain), leaving the final Catch for the most general (i.e., the base class of a given exception inheritance chain, in this case System.Exception).

Thus, if you wish to define a Catch statement that will handle any errors beyond CarIsDeadException and ArgumentOutOfRangeException, you would write the following:

```
' This code compiles without warning.
Module Program
  Sub Main()
    Console.WriteLine("***** Creating a car and stepping on it *****")
    Dim myCar As New Car("Zippy", 20)
    myCar.CrankTunes(True)

    Try
      For i As Integer = 0 To 10
```

```
        myCar.Accelerate(10)
      Next
    Catch ex As ArgumentOutOfRangeException
      ' Process bad arguments.
    Catch ex As CarIsDeadException
      ' Process CarIsDeadException.
    Catch ex As Exception
      ' Try to catch all other exceptions here? OK!
    End Try
...
  End Sub
End Module
```

Generalized Catch Statements

VB 2008 also supports a catch-all `Catch` scope (pardon the redundancy) that does not explicitly receive the exception object thrown by a given member:

```
' A generic catch.
Module Program
  Sub Main()
    Console.WriteLine("***** Creating a car and stepping on it *****")
    Dim myCar As New Car("Zippy", 20)
    myCar.CrankTunes(True)

    Try
      For i As Integer = 0 To 10
        myCar.Accelerate(10)
      Next
    Catch
      Console.WriteLine("Oops!  Something bad happened...")
    End Try
  End Sub
End Module
```

Obviously, this is not the most informative way to handle exceptions, given that you have no way to obtain meaningful data about the error that occurred (such as the method name, call stack, or custom message). Nevertheless, VB 2008 does allow for such a construct, which can be helpful when you wish to handle all errors in a very generalized fashion.

Rethrowing Exceptions

Be aware that it is permissible for logic in a `Try` block to *rethrow* an exception up the call stack to the previous caller. To do so, simply make use of the `Throw` keyword within a `Catch` block. This passes the exception up the chain of calling logic, which can be helpful if your `Catch` block is only able to partially handle the error at hand:

```
' Passing the buck!
Module Program
  Sub Main()
    Console.WriteLine("***** Creating a car and stepping on it *****")
    Dim myCar As New Car("Zippy", 20)
    myCar.CrankTunes(True)

    Try
      For i As Integer = 0 To 10
```

```
        myCar.Accelerate(10)
      Next
    Catch ex As ArgumentOutOfRangeException
      ' Process bad arguments.
    Catch ex As CarIsDeadException
      ' Do any partial processing of this error and pass the buck.
      ' Here, we are rethrowing the incoming CarIsDeadException object.
      ' However, you are also free to throw a different exception if need be.
     Throw ex
    Catch ex As Exception
      ' Try to catch all other exceptions here? OK!
    End Try
...
  End Sub
End Module
```

In this example code, the ultimate receiver of CarIsDeadException is the CLR, given that it is the Main() method rethrowing the exception. Given this point, your end user is presented with a system-supplied error dialog box. Typically, you would only rethrow a partially handled exception to a caller that has the ability to handle the incoming exception more gracefully.

Inner Exceptions

As you may suspect, it is entirely possible to trigger an exception at the time you are handling another exception. For example, assume that you are handling a CarIsDeadException within a particular Catch scope, and during the process you attempt to record the stack trace to a file on your C drive named carErrors.txt. Although we have not yet examined the topic of file I/O, assume you have imported the System.IO namespace (via the Imports keyword) and authored the following code:

```
Catch ex As CarIsDeadException
  ' Attempt to open a file named carErrors.txt on the C drive.
  Dim fs As FileStream = File.Open("C:\carErrors.txt", FileMode.Open)
...
End Try
```

Now, if the specified file is not located on your C drive, the call to File.Open() results in a FileNotFoundException! Later in this text, you will learn all about the System.IO namespace where you will discover how to programmatically determine whether a file exists on the hard drive before attempting to open the file in the first place (thereby avoiding the exception altogether). However, to keep focused on the topic of exceptions, assume the exception has indeed been raised.

When you encounter an exception while processing another exception, best practice states that you should record the new exception object as an "inner exception" within a new object of the same type as the initial exception (that was a mouthful). The reason we need to allocate a new object of the exception being handled is that the only way to document an inner exception is via a constructor parameter. Consider the following code:

```
Module Program
  Sub Main()
...
    Try
      For i As Integer = 0 To 10
        myCar.Accelerate(10)
      Next
    Catch ex As ArgumentOutOfRangeException
        ' process any bad arguments here.
```

```
    Catch ex As CarIsDeadException
      Try
        ' Attempt to open a file named carErrors.txt on the C drive.
        Dim fs As FileStream = File.Open("C:\carErrors.txt", FileMode.Open)
        ' Now process the CarIsDeadException.
      Catch ex2 As Exception
       ' Throw an exception that records the new exception,
       ' as well as the message of the first exception.
        Throw New CarIsDeadException(ex.Message, ex2)
      End Try
...
    Catch ex As Exception
      ' Try to catch all other exceptions here? OK!
    End Try
...
  End Sub
End Module
```

Notice in this case, we have passed in the FileNotFoundException object as the second parameter to the CarIsDeadException constructor. Once we have configured this new object, we throw it up the call stack to the next caller, which in this case would be the Main() method.

Given that there is no "next caller" beyond the CLR after Main() to catch the exception, we would be again presented with an error dialog box. Much like the act of rethrowing an exception, recording inner exceptions is usually only useful when the caller has the ability to gracefully catch the exception in the first place. If this is the case, the caller's Catch logic can make use of the InnerException property to extract the details of the inner exception object.

The Finally Block

A Try/Catch scope may also define an optional Finally block. The motivation behind a Finally block is to ensure that a set of code statements will *always* execute, exception (of any type) or not. To illustrate, assume you wish to always power down the car's radio before exiting Main(), regardless of any handled exception:

```
Module Program
  Sub Main()
    Console.WriteLine("***** Creating a car and stepping on it *****")
    Dim myCar As New Car("Zippy", 20)
    myCar.CrankTunes(True)

    Try
      ' Speed up logic
    Catch ex As ArgumentOutOfRangeException
      ' Process arg out of range.
    Catch ex As CarIsDeadException
      ' Process car is dead.
    Catch ex As Exception
      ' Try to catch all other exceptions here.
    Finally
      ' This will always execute, error or not.
      myCar.CrankTunes(False)
    End Try
    ' The error has been handled, processing continues with the next statement.
    Console.WriteLine("***** Out of exception logic *****")
    Console.ReadLine()
```

```
  End Sub
End Module
```

If you did not include a `Finally` block, the radio would not be turned off if an exception is encountered (which may or may not be problematic). In a more real-world scenario, when you need to dispose of objects, close a file, detach from a database (or whatever), a `Finally` block ensures a location for proper cleanup.

■ Note It is also possible to create a `Try/Final` block that has no `Catch` scopes whatsoever. This is commonly used when working with "disposable" objects, as examined in Chapter 8.

Who Is Throwing What?

Given that a method in the .NET Framework could throw any number of exceptions (under various circumstances), a logical question would be "How do I know which exceptions may be thrown by a given base class library method?" The ultimate answer is simple: consult the .NET Framework 3.5 SDK documentation. Each method in the help system documents the exceptions a given member may throw.

For example, if you wish to see the exceptions the `Console.ReadLine()` method could throw, click the `ReadLine()` method and press the F1 key. This will open up the correct help page for the method in question. From here, simply consult the Exceptions table (see Figure 7-6).

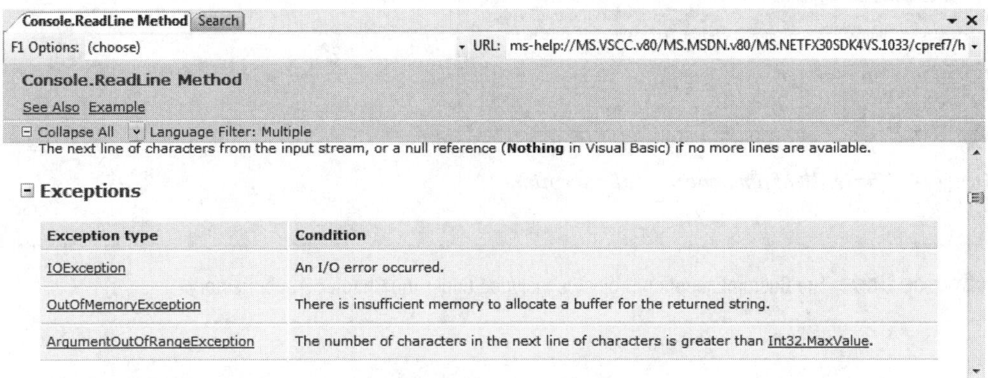

Figure 7-6. *Identifying the exceptions thrown from a given method*

Do understand that if a given member throws multiple exceptions, you are not literally required to catch each object within a separate `Catch` block. In many cases, you can handle all possible errors thrown from a set scope by catching a single `System.Exception`:

```
Sub Main()
  Try
    ' This one catch will handle all exceptions
    ' thrown from the Open() method.
    File.Open("IDontExist.txt", FileMode.Open)
  Catch ex As Exception
    Console.WriteLine(ex.Message)
  End Try
End Sub
```

However, if you do wish to handle specific exceptions uniquely, just make use of multiple `Catch` blocks as shown throughout this chapter. Using this approach, you can take unique courses of action based on the type of exception object, and therefore have a finer grain of control.

The Result of Unhandled Exceptions

At this point, you might be wondering what would happen if you do not handle an exception thrown your direction. Assume that the logic in `Main()` increases the speed of the `Car` object beyond the maximum speed, without the benefit of `Try/Catch` logic. The result of ignoring an exception would be highly obstructive to the end user of your application, as an "unhandled exception" dialog box is displayed (see Figure 7-7).

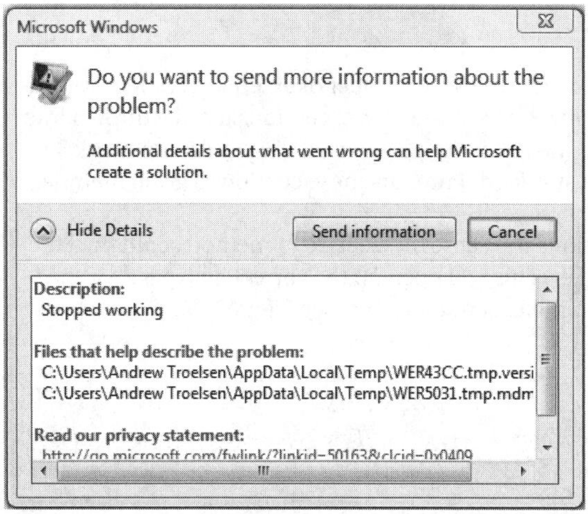

Figure 7-7. *The result of not dealing with exceptions*

■ **Source Code** The CustomException project is included under the Chapter 7 subdirectory.

Debugging Unhandled Exceptions Using Visual Studio 2008

As you would hope, Visual Studio 2008 provides a number of tools that help you debug exceptions. Again, assume you have increased the speed of a `Car` object beyond the maximum and are not making use of structured exception handling. If you were to start a debugging session (using the Debug ➤ Start Debugging menu selection), Visual Studio automatically breaks at the time the uncaught exception is thrown. Better yet, you are presented with a window (see Figure 7-8) displaying the value of the `Message` property.

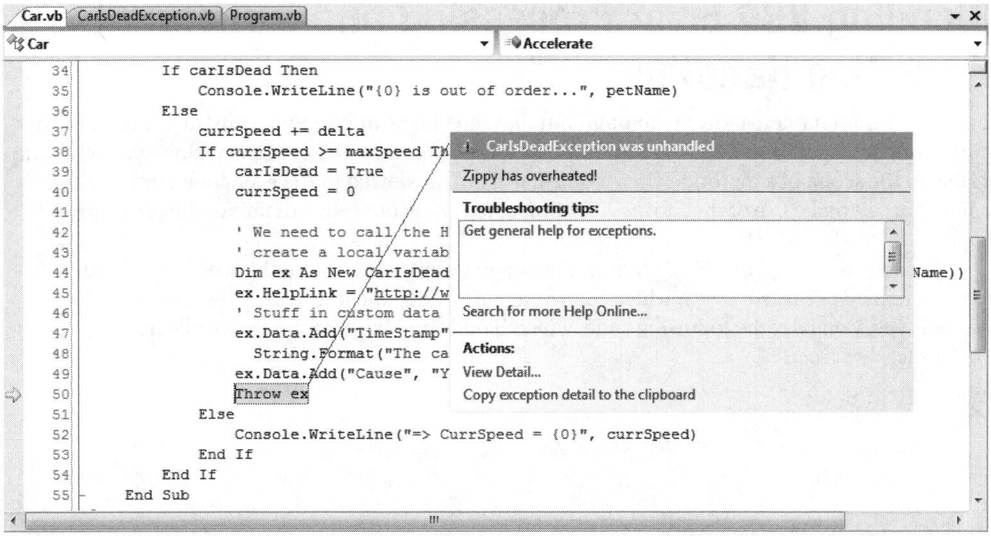

Figure 7-8. *Debugging unhandled custom exceptions with Visual Studio 2008*

If you click the View Detail link, you will find the details regarding the state of the object (see Figure 7-9).

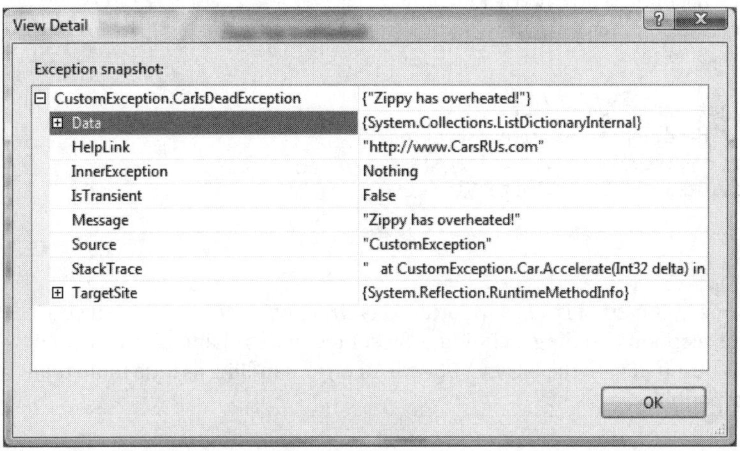

Figure 7-9. *Viewing the details of an exception with Visual Studio 2008*

Note If you fail to handle an exception thrown by a method in the .NET base class libraries, the Visual Studio 2008 debugger breaks at the statement that called the offending method.

Blending VB6 Error Processing and Structured Exception Handling

To wrap up this chapter, allow me to point out that the VB6 error handling constructs are still supported under Visual Basic 2008. As you may know, the `On Error Goto` construct allows you to define a label in the scope of a method, where control will be transferred in the event of an error. At this point, you can make use of the intrinsic `Err` object to scrape out select details of the problem at hand.

Since the release of the .NET platform, the VB `Err` object has been enhanced with a new method named `GetException()`, which returns a reference to the underlying `System.Exception` derived type. Consider the following code, which blends both approaches to handle the `CarIsDeadException`:

```
Module Program
  Sub Main()
    Console.WriteLine("***** VB6 Style Error Handling *****")
    On Error GoTo OOPS

    Dim myCar As New Car("Sven", 80)
    For i As Integer = 0 To 10
      myCar.Accelerate(10)
    Next

OOPS:
    ' Use Err object.
    Console.WriteLine("=> Handling error with Err object.")
    Console.WriteLine(Err.Description)
    Console.WriteLine(Err.Source)

    ' Use Err object to get exception object.
    Console.WriteLine("=> Handling error with exception.")
    Console.WriteLine(Err.GetException().StackTrace)
    Console.WriteLine(Err.GetException().TargetSite)
    Console.ReadLine()
  End Sub
End Module
```

Although the `On Error GoTo` construct is still supported, it is *strongly recommended* that you make use of the structured exception handling techniques presented in this chapter. As you build new VB 2008 programs, it is best to regard the legacy VB6 style of error handling as little more than a vehicle for backward compatibility.

■ **Source Code** The Vb6StyleErrorHandling project is included under the Chapter 7 subdirectory.

Summary

In this chapter, you examined the role of structured exception handling. When a method needs to send an error object to the caller, it will create, configure, and throw a class derived from `System.Exception` via the VB 2008 `Throw` keyword. The caller is able to handle any possible incoming exceptions using the VB 2008 `Try`/`Catch` keywords. As you have also seen, you can optionally define a `Finally` scope to ensure a place to perform any cleanup (error or not).

When you are defining your own custom exception types, you ultimately create a class type deriving from `System.ApplicationException`, which denotes an exception thrown from the currently executing application. In contrast, error objects deriving from `System.SystemException` represent critical (and fatal) errors thrown by the CLR.

This chapter also illustrated various tools within Visual Studio 2008 that can be used to debug exceptions as they occur. Last but not least, I pointed out that the legacy VB6 style of error handling (`On Error`) is still supported for purposes of backward compatibility. As mentioned, it is best to let go of this VB6-centric approach to handle errors and instead make liberal use of structure exception handling techniques.

CHAPTER 8

Understanding Object Lifetime

At this point in the text, you have learned a good deal about how to define classes. In this chapter, you will come to understand how the CLR is managing allocated objects via *garbage collection*. VB 2008 programmers never directly deallocate a managed object from memory and, unlike classic COM, we are no longer required to interact with finicky interface reference counting logic (which as you may know occurred behind the scenes in VB6). Rather, .NET objects are allocated onto a region of memory termed the *managed heap*, where they will be automatically destroyed by the garbage collector at "some time in the future."

Once you have examined the core details of the garbage collection process, you will learn how to programmatically interact with the garbage collector using the `System.GC` class type. Next you examine how the virtual `System.Object.Finalize()` method and `System.IDisposable` interface can be used to build types that release internal *unmanaged resources* (such as file handles) in a timely manner. By the time you have completed this chapter, you will have a solid understanding of how .NET objects are managed by the CLR.

Classes, Objects, and References

To frame the topics examined in this chapter, it is important to further clarify the distinction between classes, objects, and references. Recall that a class is nothing more than a blueprint that describes how an instance of this type will look and feel in memory. Classes, of course, are defined within a code file (which takes a `*.vb` extension by convention). Create a new Console Application project named SimpleGC and define a simple `Car` class:

```
' Car.vb
Public Class Car
  Private currSpeed As Integer
  Private petName As String

  Public Sub New()
  End Sub
  Public Sub New(ByVal name As String, ByVal speed As Integer)
    petName = name
    currSpeed = speed
  End Sub

  Public Overrides Function ToString() As String
    Return String.Format("{0} is going {1} MPH", petName, currSpeed)
  End Function
End Class
```

Once a class is defined, you can create any number of objects using the VB 2008 `New` keyword. Understand, however, that the `New` keyword returns a *reference* to the object on the heap, not the actual object itself. This reference variable is stored on the stack for further use in your application. When you wish to invoke members on the object, apply the VB 2008 dot operator on the stored reference:

```
Module Program
  Sub Main()
    ' Create a new Car object on
    ' the managed heap. We are
    ' returned a reference to this
    ' object that we store in the
    ' 'refToMyCar' local variable.
    Dim refToMyCar As New Car("Zippy", 50)

    ' The VB 2008 dot operator (.) is used
    ' to invoke members on the object
    ' using our reference variable.
    Console.WriteLine(refToMyCar.ToString())
    Console.ReadLine()
  End Sub
End Module
```

Figure 8-1 illustrates the class, object, and reference relationship.

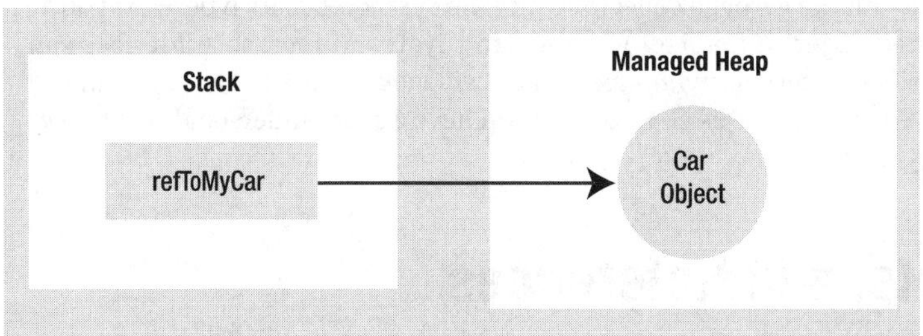

Figure 8-1. *References to objects on the managed heap*

The Basics of Object Lifetime

When you are building your VB 2008 applications, you are correct to assume that the managed heap will take care of itself without your direct intervention. In fact, the golden rule of .NET memory management is simple:

Rule Allocate an object onto the managed heap using the `New` keyword and forget about it.

Once you create an object, the garbage collector will destroy it when it is no longer needed. The next obvious question, of course, is, "How does the garbage collector determine when an object is no longer needed?" The short (i.e., incomplete) answer is that the garbage collector removes an object from the heap when it is *unreachable* by any part of your code base. Assume you have a method that allocates a local `Car` object:

```
Sub MakeACar()
  ' If myCar is the only reference to the Car object,
  ' it may be destroyed when the method returns.
  Dim myCar As New Car()
End Sub
```

Notice that the Car reference (myCar) has been declared within the MakeACar() method and has not been passed outside of the defining scope. Thus, once this method call completes, the myCar reference is no longer reachable, and the associated Car object is now a *candidate* for garbage collection. Understand, however, that you cannot guarantee that this object will be reclaimed from memory immediately after MakeACar() has completed. All you can assume at this point is that when the CLR performs the next garbage collection, the object referenced by myCar could be safely destroyed.

As you will most certainly discover, programming in a garbage-collected environment will greatly simplify your application development. By allowing the garbage collector to be in charge of destroying objects, the burden of memory management has been taken from your shoulders and placed onto those of the CLR.

■ **Note** If you happen to have a background in COM development, do know that .NET objects do not maintain an internal reference counter, and therefore managed objects do not expose methods such as AddRef() or Release().

The CIL of New

Before we examine the exact rules that determine when an object is removed from the managed heap, let's check out the role of the New keyword a bit more closely. First, understand that the managed heap is more than just a random chunk of memory accessed by the CLR. The .NET garbage collector is quite a tidy housekeeper of the heap, given that it will compact empty blocks of memory (when necessary) to optimize the process of locating allocated objects. To aid in this endeavor, the managed heap maintains a pointer (commonly referred to as the *next object pointer* or *new object pointer*) that identifies exactly where the next object will be located.

To better understand the dirty details of exactly how objects are allocated on the heap requires us to examine a bit of CIL code. When the VB 2008 compiler encounters the New keyword, it will emit a CIL newobj instruction into the assembly. If you were to compile the current example code and investigate the resulting assembly using ildasm.exe (see Chapter 1), you would find CIL statements similar to the following within the MakeACar() method:

```
.method public static void MakeACar() cil managed
{
  // Code size 9 (0x9)
  .maxstack  1
  .locals init ([0] class SimpleGC.Car myCar)
  IL_0000:  nop
  IL_0001:  newobj instance void SimpleGC.Car::.ctor()
  IL_0006:  stloc.0
  IL_0007:  nop
  IL_0008:  ret
} // end of method Program::MakeACar
```

The newobj instruction informs the CLR to perform the following core tasks:

- Calculate the total amount of memory required for the object to be allocated (including the necessary memory required by the type's member variables and the type's base classes).
- Examine the managed heap to ensure that there is indeed enough room to host the object to be allocated. If this is the case, the type's constructor is called, and the caller is ultimately returned a reference to the new object in memory, whose address just happens to be identical to the last position of the next object pointer.
- Finally, before returning the reference to the caller, advance the next object pointer to point to the next available slot on the managed heap.

The basic process is illustrated in Figure 8-2.

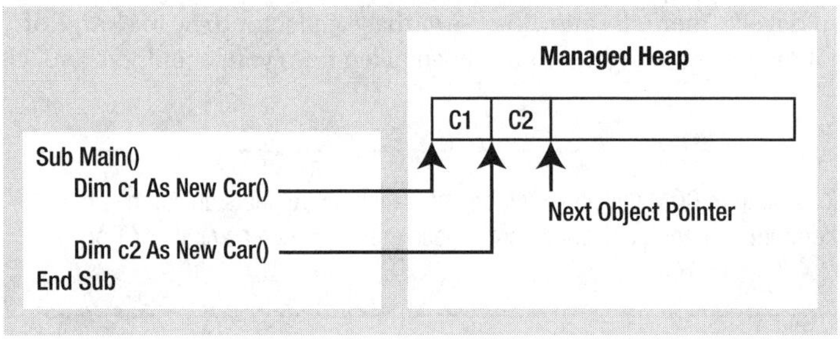

Figure 8-2. *The details of allocating objects onto the managed heap*

As you are busy allocating objects in your application, the space on the managed heap may eventually become full. When processing the newobj instruction, if the CLR determines that the managed heap does not have sufficient memory to allocate the requested type, it will perform a garbage collection in an attempt to free up memory. Thus, the next rule of garbage collection is also quite simple:

■ **Rule** If the managed heap does not have sufficient memory to allocate a requested object, a garbage collection will occur.

When a collection does take place, the garbage collector temporarily suspends all active *threads* within the current process to ensure that the application does not access the heap during the collection process. We will examine the topic of threads in Chapter 18; however, for the time being, simply regard a thread as a path of execution within a running executable. Once the garbage collection cycle has completed, the suspended threads are permitted to carry on their work. Thankfully, the .NET garbage collector is highly optimized; you will seldom (if ever) notice this brief interruption in your application.

Setting Object References to Nothing

Those who have created COM objects using Visual Basic 6.0 were well aware that it was always preferable to set their references to Nothing when they were finished using them. Under the covers, the reference count of the COM object was decremented by one, and may be removed from memory if the object's reference count equaled zero.

Of course, .NET objects do *not* make use of the COM reference counting scheme. Given this fact, you might wonder what the end result is of assigning object references to Nothing under Visual Basic 2008. For example, assume the previous MakeACar() subroutine has now been updated as follows:

```
Sub MakeACar()
  Dim myCar As New Car()
  myCar = Nothing
End Sub
```

When you assign references to Nothing, the compiler will generate CIL code that ensures the reference (myCar in this example) no longer points to any object. If you were once again to make use of ildasm.exe to view the CIL code of the modified MakeACar(), you would find the ldnull opcode:

```
.method public static void  MakeACar() cil managed
{
  // Code size 11 (0xb)
  .maxstack  1
  .locals init ([0] class SimpleGC.Car myCar)
  IL_0000:  nop
  IL_0001:  newobj instance void SimpleGC.Car::.ctor()
  IL_0006:  stloc.0
  IL_0007:  ldnull
  IL_0008:  stloc.0
  IL_0009:  nop
  IL_000a:  ret
} // end of method Program::MakeACar
```

What you must understand, however, is that assigning a reference to Nothing does not in any way force the garbage collector to fire up at that exact moment and remove the object from the heap. The only thing you have accomplished is explicitly clipping the connection between the reference and the object it previously pointed to.

Note Although setting a reference to Nothing does not guarantee that your object will be destroyed immediately, do get in the habit of assigning references to Nothing when you are done using them. This will ensure the garbage collector can clean up objects in the timeliest of manners.

The Role of Application Roots

Now, back to the topic of how the garbage collector determines when an object is "no longer needed." To understand the details, you need to be aware of the notion of *application roots*. Simply put, a *root* is a storage location containing a reference to an object on the heap. Strictly speaking, a root can fall into any of the following categories:

- References to global objects (while not allowed in VB 2008, CIL code does permit allocation of global objects)
- References to currently used shared objects/shared fields
- References to local objects within a given method
- References to object parameters passed into a method
- References to objects waiting to be *finalized* (described later in this chapter)
- Any CPU register that references a local object

During a garbage collection process, the runtime will investigate objects on the managed heap to determine whether they are still reachable (aka *rooted*) by the application. To do so, the CLR will build an *object graph*, which represents each reachable object on the heap. Object graphs will be explained in greater detail during our discussion of object serialization (in Chapter 21). For now, just understand that object graphs are used to document all reachable objects. As well, be aware that the garbage collector will never graph the same object twice, thus avoiding the nasty circular reference count that could be found in classic COM programming.

Assume the managed heap contains a set of objects named A, B, C, D, E, F, and G. During a garbage collection, these objects (as well as any internal object references they may contain) are examined for active roots. Once the graph has been constructed, unreachable objects (which we will assume are objects C and F) are marked as garbage. Figure 8-3 diagrams a possible object graph for the scenario just described (you can read the directional arrows using the phrase *depends on* or *requires*, for example, "E depends on G and indirectly B," "A depends on nothing," and so on).

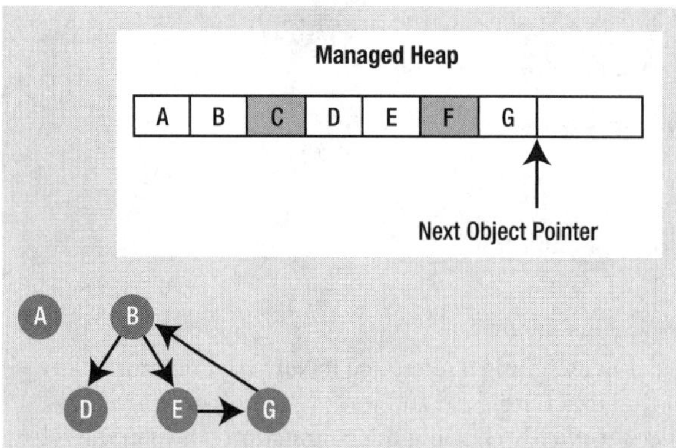

Figure 8-3. *Object graphs are constructed to determine which objects are reachable by application roots.*

Once an object has been marked for termination (C and F in this case—as they are not accounted for in the object graph), they are swept from memory. At this point, the remaining space on the heap is compacted, which in turn will cause the CLR to modify the set of active application roots to refer to the correct memory location (this is done automatically and transparently). Last but not least, the next object pointer is readjusted to point to the next available slot. Figure 8-4 illustrates the resulting readjustment.

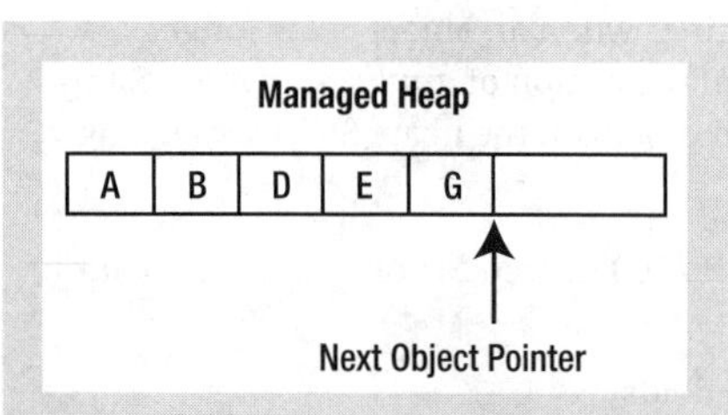

Figure 8-4. *A clean and compacted heap*

■ **Note** Strictly speaking, the garbage collector makes use of two distinct heaps, one of which is specifically used to store very large objects. This heap is less frequently consulted during the collection cycle, given possible performance penalties involved with relocating large objects. Regardless of this fact, it is safe to consider the "managed heap" as a single region of memory.

Understanding Object Generations

When the CLR is attempting to locate unreachable objects, is does *not* literally examine each and every object placed on the managed heap in order to free up unused memory. Obviously, doing so would involve considerable time, especially in larger (i.e., real-world) applications.

To help optimize the process, each object on the heap is assigned to a specific "generation." The idea behind generations is simple: the longer an object has existed on the heap, the more likely it is to stay there. For example, the object representing the main window of a Windows Forms application will be in memory until the program terminates. Conversely, objects that have been recently placed on the heap are likely to be unreachable rather quickly (such as an object created within a local method scope). Given these assumptions, each object on the heap belongs to one of the following generations:

- *Generation 0*: Identifies a newly allocated object that has never been marked for collection
- *Generation 1*: Identifies an object that has survived a garbage collection (i.e., it was marked for collection, but was not removed due to the fact that the sufficient heap space was acquired)
- *Generation 2*: Identifies an object that has survived more than one sweep of the garbage collector

The garbage collector will investigate all generation 0 objects first. If marking and sweeping these objects results in the required amount of free memory, any surviving objects are promoted to generation 1. To illustrate how an object's generation affects the collection process, ponder Figure 8-5, which diagrams how a set of surviving generation 0 objects (A, B, and E) are promoted once the required memory has been reclaimed.

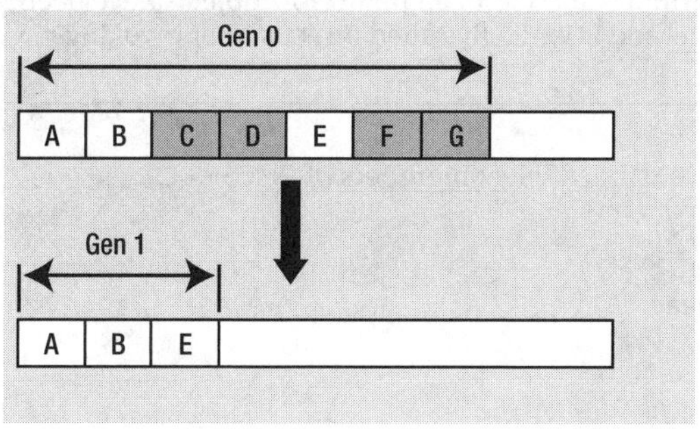

Figure 8-5. *Generation 0 objects that survive a garbage collection are promoted to generation 1.*

If all generation 0 objects have been evaluated, but additional memory is still required, generation 1 objects are then investigated for their "reachability" and collected accordingly. Surviving generation 1 objects are then promoted to generation 2. If the garbage collector *still* requires additional memory, generation 2 objects are then evaluated for their reachability. At this point, if a generation 2 object survives a garbage collection, it remains a generation 2 object given the predefined upper limit of object generations. (As of .NET 3.5, that is. Future versions of the platform may increase this upper generational limit.)

The bottom line is that by assigning a generational value to objects on the heap, newer objects (such as local variables) will be removed quickly, while older objects (such as a program's main Form) are not "bothered" as often.

The System.GC Type

The base class libraries provide a class type named `System.GC` that allows you to programmatically interact with the garbage collector using a set of shared members. Now, do be very aware that you will seldom (if ever) need to make use of this type directly in your code. Typically speaking, the only time you will make use of the members of `System.GC` is when you are creating types that make use of *unmanaged resources*. Table 8-1 provides a rundown of some of the more interesting members (consult the .NET Framework 3.5 SDK documentation for complete details).

Table 8-1. *Select Members of the* `System.GC` *Type*

System.GC Member	Meaning in Life
`Collect()`	Forces the GC to perform a garbage collection.
`CollectionCount()`	Returns a numerical value representing how many times a given generation has been swept.
`GetGeneration()`	Returns the generation to which an object currently belongs.
`GetTotalMemory()`	Returns the estimated amount of memory (in bytes) currently allocated on the managed heap. The Boolean parameter specifies whether the call should wait for garbage collection to occur before returning.
`MaxGeneration`	Returns the maximum of generations supported on the target system. Under Microsoft's .NET 3.5, there are three possible generations (0, 1, and 2).
`SuppressFinalize()`	Sets a flag indicating that the specified object should not have its `Finalize()` method called.
`WaitForPendingFinalizers()`	Suspends the current thread until all finalizable objects have been finalized. This method is typically called directly after invoking `GC.Collect()`.

Ponder the following `Main()` method, which illustrates select members of `System.GC`:

```
Sub Main()
  Console.WriteLine("***** Fun with System.GC *****")
  ' Print out estimated number of bytes on heap.
  Console.WriteLine("Estimated bytes on heap: {0}", _
    GC.GetTotalMemory(False))

  ' MaxGeneration is zero based, so add 1 for display purposes.
  Console.WriteLine("This OS has {0} object generations.", _
    (GC.MaxGeneration + 1))

  Dim refToMyCar As New Car("Zippy", 100)
  Console.WriteLine(refToMyCar.ToString())
```

```
    ' Print out generation of refToMyCar object.
    Console.WriteLine("Generation of refToMyCar is: {0}", _
      GC.GetGeneration(refToMyCar))
    Console.ReadLine()
  End Sub
```

Forcing a Garbage Collection

Again, the whole purpose of the .NET garbage collector is to manage memory on our behalf. However, under some very rare (and I do mean *very rare*) circumstances, it may be beneficial to programmatically force a garbage collection using `GC.Collect()`. Specifically:

- Your application is about to enter into a block of code that you do not wish to be interrupted by a possible garbage collection.
- Your application has just finished allocating an extremely large number of objects and you wish to clean up as much of the acquired memory as possible.

If you determine it may be beneficial to have the garbage collector check for unreachable objects, you could explicitly trigger a garbage collection, as follows:

```
Sub Main()
...
  ' Force a garbage collection and wait for
  ' each object to be finalized.
  GC.Collect()
  GC.WaitForPendingFinalizers()
...
End Sub
```

When you manually force a garbage collection, you should always make a call to `GC.WaitForPendingFinalizers()`. With this approach, you can rest assured that all *finalizable objects* (described in detail later in this chapter) have had a chance to perform any necessary cleanup before your program continues forward. Under the hood, `GC.WaitForPendingFinalizers()` will suspend the calling thread during the collection process. This is a good thing, as it ensures your code does not invoke methods on an object currently being destroyed!

The `GC.Collect()` method can also be supplied a numerical value that identifies the oldest generation on which a garbage collection will be performed. For example, if you wished to instruct the CLR to only investigate generation 0 objects, you would write the following:

```
Sub Main()
...
  ' Only investigate generation 0 objects.
  GC.Collect(0)
  GC.WaitForPendingFinalizers()
...
End Sub
```

Like any garbage collection, calling `GC.Collect()` will promote surviving generations. To illustrate, assume that our `Main()` method has been updated as follows:

```
Sub Main()
  Console.WriteLine("***** Fun with System.GC *****")

  ' Print out estimated number of bytes on heap.
  Console.WriteLine("Estimated bytes on heap: {0}", _
    GC.GetTotalMemory(False))
```

```
  ' MaxGeneration is zero based.
  Console.WriteLine("This OS has {0} object generations.", _
    (GC.MaxGeneration + 1))

  Dim refToMyCar As New Car("Zippy", 100)
  Console.WriteLine(refToMyCar.ToString())

  ' Print out generation of refToMyCar.
  Console.WriteLine("Generation of refToMyCar is: {0}", _
    GC.GetGeneration(refToMyCar))

  ' Make a ton of objects for testing purposes.
  Dim tonsOfObjects(5000) As Object
  For i As Integer = 0 To UBound(tonsOfObjects)
    tonsOfObjects(i) = New Object()
  Next

  ' Collect only gen 0 objects.
  GC.Collect(0)
  GC.WaitForPendingFinalizers()

  ' Print out generation of refToMyCar.
  Console.WriteLine("Generation of refToMyCar is: {0}", _
    GC.GetGeneration(refToMyCar))

  ' See if tonsOfObjects(4000) is still alive.
  If (tonsOfObjects(4000) IsNot Nothing)
    Console.WriteLine("Generation of tonsOfObjects(4000) is: {0}", _
      GC.GetGeneration(tonsOfObjects(4000)))
  Else
    Console.WriteLine("tonsOfObjects(4000) is no longer alive.")
  End If

  ' Print out how many times a generation has been swept.
  Console.WriteLine("Gen 0 has been swept {0} times", _
    GC.CollectionCount(0))
  Console.WriteLine("Gen 1 has been swept {0} times", _
    GC.CollectionCount(1))
  Console.WriteLine("Gen 2 has been swept {0} times", _
    GC.CollectionCount(2))
  Console.ReadLine()
End Sub
```

Here, we have purposely created a very large array of `System.Objects` for testing purposes. As you can see from the output shown in Figure 8-6, even though this `Main()` method only made one explicit request for a garbage collection, the CLR performed a number of them in the background, as object 4000 has survived a series of garbage collections.

At this point in the chapter, I hope you feel more comfortable regarding the details of object lifetime. The remainder of this chapter examines the garbage collection process a bit further by addressing how you can build *finalizable objects* as well as *disposable objects*. Be very aware that the following techniques will only be useful if you are building managed classes that maintain internal unmanaged resources.

■ **Source Code** The SimpleGC project is included under the Chapter 8 subdirectory.

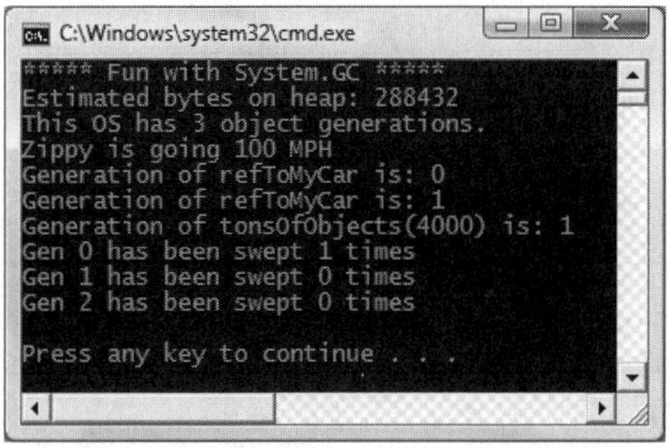

Figure 8-6. *Interacting with the CLR garbage collector via* `System.GC`

Building Finalizable Objects

In Chapter 6, you learned that the supreme base class of .NET, `System.Object`, defines a virtual method named `Finalize()`. The default implementation of this method does nothing whatsoever; however, do note this method has been marked as `Overridable`:

```
' System.Object
Public Class Object
  ...
  Protected Overridable Sub Finalize()
  End Sub
End Class
```

When you override `Finalize()` for your custom classes, you establish a specific location to perform any necessary cleanup logic for your type. Given that this member is defined as protected, it is not possible to directly call an object's `Finalize()` method. Rather, the *garbage collector* will call an object's `Finalize()` method (if supported) before removing the object from memory.

Of course, a call to `Finalize()` will (eventually) occur during a "natural" garbage collection or possibly when you programmatically force a collection via `GC.Collect()`. In addition, a type's finalizer method will automatically be called when the *application domain* hosting your application is unloaded from memory.

Based on your current background in .NET, you may know that application domains (or simply AppDomains) are used to host an executable assembly and any necessary external code libraries. If you are not familiar with this .NET concept, you will be by the time you've finished Chapter 17. The short answer is that when your AppDomain is unloaded from memory, the CLR automatically invokes finalizers for every finalizable object created during its lifetime.

Now, despite what your developer instincts may tell you, a *vast majority* of your classes will not require any explicit cleanup logic. The reason is simple: if your types are simply making use of other managed objects, everything will eventually be garbage collected. The only time you would need to design a class that can clean up after itself is when you are making use of *unmanaged resources* (such as raw OS file handles, raw unmanaged database connections, or other unmanaged resources).

As you may know, unmanaged resources are obtained by directly calling into the API of the operating system using PInvoke (Platform Invocation Services) or due to some very elaborate COM interoperability scenarios. We will examine interoperability in Chapter 19; however, consider the next rule of garbage collection:

■ **Rule** The only reason to override `Finalize()` is if your VB 2008 class is making use of unmanaged resources via PInvoke or complex COM interoperability tasks (typically via the `System.Runtime.InteropServices.Marshal` type).

■ **Note** As you will see in Chapter 12, it is illegal to override `Finalize()` on structure types. This makes perfect sense given that structures are value types, which are never allocated on the heap to begin with, and therefore are not garbage collected!

Overriding System.Object.Finalize()

In the rare case that you do build a VB 2008 class that makes use of unmanaged resources, you will obviously wish to ensure that the underlying memory is released in a predictable manner. Assume you have created a new Console Application named SimpleFinalize and inserted a class named `MyResourceWrapper` that makes use of an unmanaged resource (whatever that may be) and you wish to override `Finalize()`.

Perhaps because the act of overriding `Finalize()` is considered a rather rare task, the Visual Studio 2008 IDE does not display `Finalize()` as an `Overridable` method when you type the `Overrides` keyword, as you see in Figure 8-7.

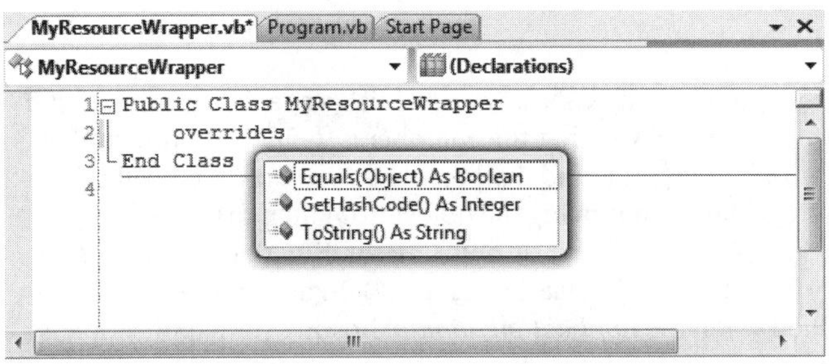

Figure 8-7. *Although not displayed, it is still legal to override* `Finalize()`*!*

Given this, you are required to manually type the definition of `Finalize()` within the code editor. Here is a custom finalizer for the `MyResourceWrapper` class that will issue a system beep when invoked. Obviously, this is only for instructional purposes. A real-world finalizer would do nothing more than free any unmanaged resources and would *not* interact with the members of other managed objects, as you cannot assume they are still alive at the point the garbage collector invokes your `Finalize()` method:

```
Public Class MyResourceWrapper
  ' Override System.Object.Finalize()
  Protected Overrides Sub Finalize()
    ' Clean up any unmanaged resources here!

    ' Beep when destroyed (testing purposes only!)
    Console.Beep()
  End Sub
End Class
```

While the previous implementation of Finalize() is syntactically correct, best practices state that a proper finalization routine should explicitly call the Finalize() method of its base class after your custom finalization logic, to ensure that any unmanaged resources up the chain of inheritance are cleaned up as well. Furthermore, to make a Finalize() method as robust as possible, you should wrap your code statements within a Try/Finally construct, as this will ensure that the finalization occurs even in the event of a runtime exception (see previous chapter). Given these notes, here is a prim-and-proper Finalize() method:

```
Public Class MyResourceWrapper
  ' Override System.Object.Finalize()
  Protected Overrides Sub Finalize()
    Try
      ' Clean up any unmanaged resources here!

      ' Beep when destroyed (testing purposes only!)
      Console.Beep()
    Finally
      MyBase.Finalize()
    End Try
  End Sub
End Class
```

If you were to now test the MyResourceWrapper type, you would find that a system beep occurs when the application terminates, given that the CLR will automatically invoke finalizers upon AppDomain shutdown:

```
Sub Main()
  Console.WriteLine("***** Fun with Finalizers *****")
  Console.WriteLine("Hit the return key to shut down this app")
  Console.WriteLine("and force the GC to invoke Finalize()")
  Console.WriteLine("for finalizable objects created in this AppDomain.")
  Console.ReadLine()
  Dim rw As New MyResourceWrapper()
End Sub
```

Source Code The SimpleFinalize project is included under the Chapter 8 subdirectory.

Detailing the Finalization Process

Not to beat a dead horse, but always remember that the role of the Finalize() method is to ensure that a .NET object can clean up *unmanaged resources* when garbage collected. Thus, if you are building a type that does not make use of unmanaged entities (by far the most common case), finalization is of little use. In fact, if at all possible, you should design your types to avoid supporting a Finalize() method for the very simple reason that *finalization takes time.*

When you allocate an object onto the managed heap, the runtime automatically determines whether your object has a custom Finalize() method. If so, the object is marked as *finalizable,* and a pointer to this object is stored on an internal queue named the *finalization queue.* The finalization queue is a table maintained by the garbage collector that points to each and every object that must be finalized before it is removed from the heap.

When the garbage collector determines it is time to free an object from memory, it examines each entry on the finalization queue, and copies the object off the heap to yet another managed structure termed the *finalization reachable* table (often abbreviated as freachable, and pronounced "eff-reachable"). At this point, a separate thread is spawned to invoke the Finalize() method for each object on the freachable table *at the next garbage collection*. Given this, it will take at the very least *two* garbage collections to truly finalize an object.

The bottom line is that while finalization of an object does ensure an object can clean up unmanaged resources, it is still nondeterministic in nature (i.e., you don't actually know exactly when it will happen, because it depends on when the garbage collector decides to run), and due to the extra behind-the-curtains processing, considerably slower.

Building Disposable Objects

Given that so many unmanaged resources are "precious items" that should be cleaned up ASAP, allow me to introduce you to another possible technique used to handle an object's cleanup. As an alternative to overriding `Finalize()`, your class could implement the `IDisposable` interface (defined in the `System` namespace), which defines a single method named `Dispose()`:

```
Public Interface IDisposable
  Sub Dispose()
End Interface
```

If you are new to interface-based programming, Chapter 9 will take you through the details. In a nutshell, an interface is a collection of abstract members a class or structure may support. When you do support the `IDisposable` interface, the assumption is that when the *object user* is finished using the object, the object user manually calls `Dispose()` before allowing the object reference to drop out of scope. In this way, your objects can perform any necessary cleanup of unmanaged resources without incurring the hit of being placed on the finalization queue and without waiting for the garbage collector to trigger the class's finalization logic.

■ **Note** Structures and class types can both implement `IDisposable` (unlike overriding `Finalize()`, which is reserved for class types), as the object user (not the garbage collector) invokes the `Dispose()` method.

Create a new Console Application named SimpleDispose. Here is an updated `MyResourceWrapper` class that now implements `IDisposable`, rather than overriding `System.Object.Finalize()`:

```
' Implementing IDisposable.
Public Class MyResourceWrapper
  Implements IDisposable

  ' The object user should call this method
  ' when they have finished with the object.
  Public Sub Dispose() Implements IDisposable.Dispose
    ' Clean up unmanaged resources here.
    ' Dispose other contained disposable objects.
    ' Just for tracing purposes.
    Console.WriteLine("In Dispose method")
  End Sub
End Class
```

■ **Note** Visual Studio 2008 will autocomplete interface implementation as soon as you hit the Enter key after typing in the name of the interface you are implementing. In fact, when implementing `IDisposable`, the IDE injects a good number of code statements, which will become more understandable once you complete this chapter. For the time being, delete (or ignore) the autogenerated code and keep focused on the implementation shown here.

Notice that a Dispose() method is not only responsible for releasing the type's unmanaged resources, but also should call Dispose() on any other contained disposable methods. Unlike Finalize(), it is perfectly safe to communicate with other managed objects within a Dispose() method. The reason is simple: the garbage collector has no clue about the IDisposable interface and will never call Dispose(). Therefore, when the object user calls this method, the object is still living a productive life on the managed heap and has access to all other heap-allocated objects. The calling logic is straightforward:

```
Sub Main
  Console.WriteLine("***** Fun with Dispose *****")
  Dim rw As New MyResourceWrapper()
  rw.Dispose()
  Console.ReadLine()
End Sub
```

Of course, before you attempt to call Dispose() on an object, you will want to ensure the type supports the IDisposable interface. While you will typically know which objects implement IDisposable by consulting the .NET Framework 3.5 SDK documentation, a programmatic check can be accomplished using the TypeOf/Is syntax discussed in Chapter 6:

```
Sub Main()
  Console.WriteLine("***** Fun with Dispose *****")
  Dim rw As New MyResourceWrapper()
  If (TypeOf rw Is IDisposable) Then
    rw.Dispose()
  End If
  Console.ReadLine()
End Sub
```

This example exposes yet another rule of working with .NET memory management:

■ **Rule** Always call Dispose() on any object you directly create if the object implements IDisposable. The assumption you should make is that if the class designer chose to support the Dispose() method, the type has some cleanup to perform.

The VB Using Keyword

When you are handling a managed object that implements IDisposable, it will be quite common to make use of structured exception handling (see Chapter 7) to ensure the type's Dispose() method is called in the event of a runtime exception:

```
Module Program
  Sub Main()
    Console.WriteLine("***** Fun with Dispose *****")
    Dim rw As New MyResourceWrapper()
    Try
      ' Call members of rw.
    Finally
      rw.Dispose()
    End Try
    Console.ReadLine()
  End Sub
End Module
```

While this is a fine example of defensive programming, the truth of the matter is that few developers are thrilled by the prospects of wrapping each and every disposable type within a Try/Finally block just to ensure the Dispose() method is called. To achieve the same result in a much less obtrusive manner, VB 2008 supports a special bit of syntax that looks like this:

```
Module Program
  Sub Main()
    Console.WriteLine("***** Fun with Dispose *****")

    Using rw As New MyResourceWrapper()
      ' Use the object, Dispose() automatically called!
    End Using

    Console.ReadLine()
  End Sub
End Module
```

Notice that the Using keyword allows you to establish a scope within a given method. Within this scope, you are free to call any methods of the type, and once the scope has ended, the type's Dispose() method is called *automatically*. As you might agree, this can certainly simplify your coding efforts. Also be aware that a single scope defined with the Using keyword can define multiple objects, each of which is denoted using a comma-delimited list. For example:

```
Module Program
  Sub Main()
    Console.WriteLine("***** Fun with Dispose *****")
    Using rw As New MyResourceWrapper(), _
          rw2 As New MyResourceWrapper(), _
          myCar As New Car()
      ' Use the objects, Dispose() automatically called!
    End Using
  Console.ReadLine()
  End Sub
End Module
```

■ **Note** If you attempt to "use" an object that does not implement IDisposable, you will receive a coding error.

If you were to look at the CIL code behind this Main() method using ildasm.exe, you would find the Using construct informs the compiler to wrap your code within Try/Finally logic, with the expected call to Dispose() in the Finally scope. In this light, the new VB 2008 Using keyword is simply a shortcut for wrapping disposable objects within exception handling logic.

■ **Source Code** The SimpleDispose project is included under the Chapter 8 subdirectory.

Building Finalizable and Disposable Types

At this point, we have seen two different approaches to construct a class that cleans up internal unmanaged resources. On the one hand, we could override System.Object.Finalize(). Using this technique, we have the peace of mind that comes with knowing the object cleans itself up when garbage collected (whenever that may be) without the need for user interaction. On the other hand, we could implement IDisposable to provide a way for the object user to clean up the object as soon as it is finished. However, if the caller forgets to call Dispose(), the unmanaged resources may be held in memory indefinitely.

As you might suspect, it is possible to blend both techniques into a single class definition. By doing so, you gain the best of both models. If the object user *does* remember to call Dispose(), you can inform the garbage collector to bypass the finalization process by calling GC.SuppressFinalize(). If the object user *forgets* to call Dispose(), the object will eventually be finalized. The good news is that the object's internal unmanaged resources will be freed one way or another in the most optimal manner. Here is the next iteration of MyResourceWrapper, which is now finalizable and disposable, defined in a Console Application named FinalizableDisposableClass:

```
' A sophisticated resource wrapper.
Public Class MyResourceWrapper
  Implements IDisposable

  ' The object user should call this method
  ' when they have finished with the object.
  Public Sub Dispose() Implements IDisposable.Dispose
    ' Clean up unmanaged resources here.
    ' Dispose other contained disposable objects.

     ' No need to finalize if user called Dispose(),
     ' so suppress finalization.
     GC.SuppressFinalize(Me)
  End Sub

  ' The garbage collector will call this method if the
  ' object user forgets to call Dispose().
  Protected Overrides Sub Finalize()
    Try
      ' Clean up any internal unmanaged resources.
      ' Do **not** call Dispose() on any managed objects.
    Finally
      MyBase.Finalize()
    End Try
  End Sub
End Class
```

Notice that this Dispose() method has been updated to call GC.SuppressFinalize(), which informs the CLR that it is no longer necessary to call the finalizer when this object is garbage collected, given that the unmanaged resources have already been freed via the Dispose() logic.

A Formalized Disposal Pattern

The current implementation of MyResourceWrapper does work fairly well; however, we are left with a few minor drawbacks. First, the Finalize() and Dispose() method each have to clean up the same unmanaged resources. This of course results in duplicate code, which can easily become a nightmare to maintain. Ideally, you would define a private helper function that is called by either method. Next, you would like to make sure that the Finalize() method does not attempt to dispose of any managed objects, while the Dispose() method should do so. Finally, you would also like to make sure that the object user can safely call Dispose() multiple times without error. Currently, our Dispose() method has no such safeguards.

To address these design issues, Microsoft has defined a formal, prim-and-proper disposal pattern that strikes a balance between robustness, maintainability, and performance. Here is the final (and annotated) version of MyResourceWrapper, which makes use of this official pattern (and is very similar to the autogenerated code injected by the IDE when implementing the IDisposable interface using Visual Studio 2008):

```
Public Class MyResourceWrapper
  Implements IDisposable

  ' Used to determine if Dispose()
  ' has already been called.
  Private disposed As Boolean = False

  Public Sub Dispose() Implements IDisposable.Dispose
    ' Call our helper method.
    ' Specifying True signifies that
    ' the object user triggered the cleanup.
    CleanUp(True)
    GC.SuppressFinalize(Me)
  End Sub

  Private Sub CleanUp(ByVal disposing As Boolean)
    ' Be sure we have not already been disposed!
    If Not Me.disposed Then
      If disposing Then
        ' Dispose managed resources.
      End If
      ' Clean up unmanaged resources here.
    End If
    disposed = True
  End Sub

  Protected Overrides Sub Finalize()
    ' Call our helper method.
    ' Specifying False signifies that
    ' the GC triggered the cleanup.
    CleanUp(False)
  End Sub
End Class
```

Notice that MyResourceWrapper now defines a private helper method named CleanUp(). When specifying True as an argument, we are signifying that the object user has initiated the cleanup, therefore we should clean up all managed *and* unmanaged resources. However, when the garbage collector initiates the cleanup, we specify False when calling CleanUp() to ensure that internal disposable objects are *not* disposed (as we can't assume they are still in memory!). Last but not least, our Boolean member variable (disposed) is set to True before exiting CleanUp() to ensure that Dispose() can be called numerous times without error.

Source Code The FinalizableDisposableClass project is included under the Chapter 8 subdirectory.

That wraps up our investigation of how the CLR is managing your objects via garbage collection. While there are additional advanced details regarding the collection process I have not examined here (such as weak references and object resurrection), you are certainly in a perfect position for further exploration on your own terms if you so choose.

Summary

The point of this chapter was to demystify the garbage collection process. As you have seen, the garbage collector will only run when it is unable to acquire the necessary memory from the managed heap (or when a given AppDomain unloads from memory). When a garbage collection does occur, you can rest assured that Microsoft's collection algorithm has been optimized by the use of object generations, secondary threads for the purpose of object finalization, and a managed heap dedicated to host large objects.

This chapter also illustrated how to programmatically interact with the garbage collector using the `System.GC` class type. As mentioned, the only time when you will really need to do so is when you are building finalizable or disposable class types. Recall that finalizable types are classes that have overridden the virtual `System.Object.Finalize()` method to clean up unmanaged resources (at some time in the future). Disposable objects, on the other hand, are classes (or structures) that implement the `IDisposable` interface. Using this technique, you expose a public method to the object user that can be called to perform internal cleanup ASAP. Finally, you learned about an official "disposal" pattern that blends both approaches.

PART 3

Advanced VB Programming Constructs

CHAPTER 9

Working with Interface Types

This chapter builds on your current understanding of object-oriented development by examining the topic of interface-based programming. Here you learn how to define and implement interfaces, and come to understand the benefits of building classes and structures that support "multiple behaviors."

Once you understand how to build and implement custom interfaces, the remainder of this chapter is spent examining a number of interfaces defined within the .NET base class libraries. As you will see, your custom types are free to implement these predefined interfaces to support a number of advanced behaviors such as object cloning, object enumeration, and object sorting.

We wrap up by examining how interface types can be used to create a custom event architecture. Using interfaces, it is possible to equip a set of objects to communicate in a bidirectional manner. While it is true that the "official" event architecture of the .NET platform is not founded on interface-based programming, understanding how to use interfaces in this manner can be helpful when you need to enable callback functionality between programming frameworks.

Understanding Interface Types

To begin this chapter, allow me to provide a formal definition of the interface type. An *interface* is nothing more than a named set of *abstract members*. Recall from Chapter 6 that abstract members (defined using the `MustOverride` keyword) are pure protocol, in that they do not provide a default implementation. The specific members defined by an interface depend on the exact behavior it is modeling. Yes, it's true. An interface expresses a *behavior* that a given class or structure may choose to implement.

As you might guess, the .NET base class libraries ship with hundreds of predefined interface types that are implemented by various classes and structures. For example, as you will see in Chapter 22, ADO.NET ships with multiple data providers that allow you to communicate with a particular database management system. Thus, unlike COM-based ADO, under ADO.NET we have numerous connection objects we may choose between (`SqlConnection`, `OracleConnection`, `OdbcConnection`, etc.).

Regardless of the fact that each connection object has a unique name, are defined within different namespaces, and (in some cases) are bundled within different assemblies, they all implement a common interface named `IDbConnection`:

```
' The IDbConnection interface defines a common
' set of members supported by all connection objects.
Public Interface IDbConnection
  Inherits IDisposable

  ' Methods.
  Function BeginTransaction() As IDbTransaction
  Function BeginTransaction(ByVal il As IsolationLevel) As IDbTransaction
```

```
  Sub ChangeDatabase(ByVal databaseName As String)
  Sub Close()
  Function CreateCommand() As IDbCommand
  Sub Open()

  ' Properties.
  Property ConnectionString() As String
  ReadOnly Property ConnectionTimeout() As Integer
  ReadOnly Property Database() As String
  ReadOnly Property State() As ConnectionState
End Interface
```

Note By convention, .NET interface types are prefixed with a capital letter "I." When you are creating your own custom interfaces, it is considered a best practice to do the same.

Don't sweat the details of what these members actually do at this point. Simply understand that the IDbConnection interface defines a set of members that are common to all ADO.NET connection objects. Given this, you are guaranteed that each and every connection object supports members such as Open(), Close(), CreateCommand(), and so forth. Furthermore, given that interface members are always abstract, each connection object is free to implement these methods in its own unique manner.

Another example: the System.Windows.Forms namespace defines a class named Control, which is a base class to a number of UI widgets (DataGrid, Label, StatusBar, TreeView, etc.). The Control class implements an interface named IDropTarget, which defines drag-and-drop functionality:

```
Public Interface IDropTarget
  ' Methods.
  Sub OnDragDrop(ByVal e As DragEventArgs)
  Sub OnDragEnter(ByVal e As DragEventArgs)
  Sub OnDragLeave(ByVal e As EventArgs)
  Sub OnDragOver(ByVal e As DragEventArgs)
End Interface
```

Based on this interface, we can now correctly assume that any class that extends System.Windows.Forms.Control supports four subroutines named OnDragDrop(), OnDragEnter(), OnDragLeave(), and OnDragOver().

As we work through the remainder of this text, you will be exposed to dozens of interfaces that ship with the .NET base class libraries. As well, you will discover that you are free to implement these standard interfaces on your own custom classes and structures to define types that integrate tightly within the framework.

Contrasting Interface Types to Abstract Base Classes

Given your work in Chapter 6, the interface type may seem functionally equivalent to abstract base classes. Recall that when a class is marked as abstract (via the MustInherit keyword), it *may* define any number of abstract members (via the MustOverride keyword) to define a polymorphic interface to all derived types. However, when a class type does define a set of abstract members, it is also free to define any number of constructors, field data, nonabstract members (with implementation), and so on.

The polymorphic interface established by a parent class suffers from one major limitation in that *only derived types* support virtual members of the abstract parent. However, in larger systems, it is very common to develop multiple class hierarchies that have no common parent beyond System.Object. Given that abstract members in an abstract base class *only* apply to derived types, we have no way to configure types in different hierarchies to support the same polymorphic interface.

As you would guess, interface types come to the rescue. When you define an interface, they can be implemented by any type, in any hierarchy, within any namespaces. Given this, interfaces are *highly* polymorphic. By way of a simple example, consider a standard .NET interface named ICloneable. This interface defines a single method named Clone():

```
Public Interface ICloneable
  Function Clone() As Object
End Interface
```

If you were to examine the .NET Framework 3.5 SDK documentation, you would find that a large number of seemingly unrelated types (System.Array, System.Data.SqlClient.SqlConnection, System.OperatingSystem, System.String, etc.) all implement this interface type. Although these types have no common parent (other than System.Object), we can treat them polymorphically via the ICloneable interface type.

Another limitation of abstract base classes is that *each and every derived type* must contend with the set of abstract members and provide an implementation. In fact, the only way that a type can "ignore" abstract members is if the derived class is also defined as abstract (aka MustInherit). To see the problem, recall the shapes hierarchy we defined in Chapter 6. Assume we wish to define an abstract method in the Shape base class named GetNumberOfPoints(), which allows the derived type to return the number of points required to render the shape:

```
Public MustInherit Class Shape
...
  ' An abstract method in an abstract class.
  Public MustOverride Function GetNumberOfPoints() As Byte
End Class
```

Clearly, the only type that has any points in the first place is Hexagon. However, with this update, *every* derived type (Circle, Hexagon, and ThreeDCircle) must now provide a concrete implementation of this function even if it makes no sense to do so.

Again, the interface type provides a solution. If we were to define an interface that represents the behavior of "having points," we could simply plug it into the Hexagon type, leaving Circle and ThreeDCircle untouched.

Defining Custom Interfaces

Now that you better understand the overall role of interface types, let's see an example of defining custom interfaces. To begin, create a brand-new Console Application project named CustomInterface. Using the Project ➤ Add Existing Item menu option, insert the MyShapes.vb file you created back in Chapter 6 during the Shapes example. Finally, insert a new interface into your project named IPointy using the Project ➤ Add New Item menu option, as shown in Figure 9-1.

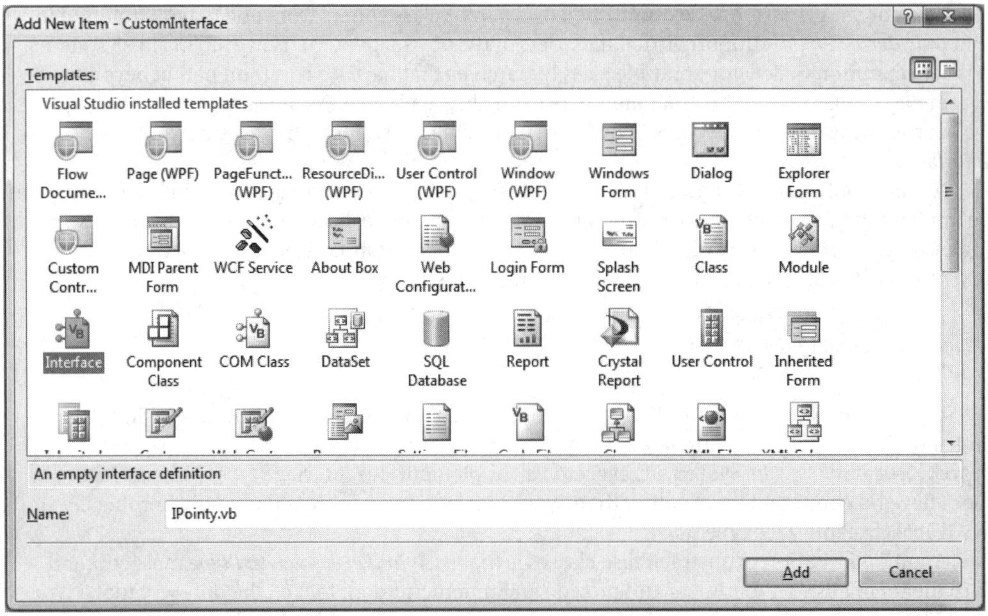

Figure 9-1. *Interfaces, like classes, can be defined in any* `*.vb` *file.*

An interface is defined using the `Interface` keyword. Unlike .NET class types, interfaces never specify a base class (not even `System.Object`) and contain members that are always implicitly `Public` and abstract (`MustOverride`). Our custom `IPointy` interface will model the behavior of "having points." Therefore, we could define a single function as follows:

```
' This interface defines the behavior of "having points."
Public Interface IPointy
  ' Implicitly public and abstract.
  Function GetNumberOfPoints() As Byte
End Interface
```

Notice that when you define a member within an interface, you do *not* close the member with the expected `End Sub`, `End Function`, or `End Property` syntax. Interfaces are pure protocol, and therefore never define an implementation (that is up to the supporting class or structure). Therefore, the following version of `IPointy` would result in compiler errors:

```
' Ack! Compiler errors abound!
Public Interface IPointy
  ' Error! Interfaces can't define field data!
  Public myInt as Integer

  ' Error! Interfaces can't provide implementation!
  Function GetNumberOfPoints() As Byte
    Return 0
  End Function
End Interface
```

.NET interface types are also able to define any number of properties. For example, you could define the `IPointy` interface to use a read-only property rather than a function:

```
' The pointy behavior as a read-only property.
Public Interface IPointy
  ReadOnly Property Points() As Byte
End Interface
```

Interface types are quite useless on their own, as they are nothing more than a named collection of abstract members. Given this, you cannot allocate interface types as you would a class or structure:

```
Module Program
  Sub Main()
    ' It is a compiler error to directly create
    ' interface types!
    Dim i As New IPointy()
  End Sub
End Module
```

Interfaces do not bring much to the table until they are implemented by a class or structure. As suggested, the `IPointy` behavior might be useful in the shapes hierarchy developed in Chapter 6. The idea is simple: some classes in the shapes hierarchy have points (such as the `Hexagon`), while others (such as the `Circle` and `ThreeDCircle`) do not.

Implementing an Interface

When a class (or structure) chooses to extend its functionality by supporting interface types, it does so using the `Implements` keyword. To illustrate, insert a brand-new class into your project named `Triangle` that extends the abstract `Shape` base class and implements the `IPointy` interface. If you are using Visual Studio 2008 or Visual Basic 2008 Express, you will find that the integrated IntelliSense will automatically define skeleton code for each member defined by the interface (as well as any `MustOverride` methods in the parent class) as soon as you press the Enter key at the end of an `Implements` clause. Given this, our `Triangle` initially appears like so:

```
Public Class Triangle
  Inherits Shape
  Implements IPointy

  Public Overrides Sub Draw()
  End Sub

  Public ReadOnly Property Points() As Byte Implements IPointy.Points
    Get
    End Get
  End Property
End Class
```

Notice that the `Implements` keyword is used *twice*. First, the class definition is updated to list each interface supported by the type. Second, the `Implements` keyword is used to "attach" the interface member to a member on the class itself. At first glance, this can appear to be quite redundant; however, as you will see later in this chapter, this approach can be quite helpful when you need to resolve name clashes that can occur when a type implements multiple interfaces.

Recall that when a class or structure implements an interface, it is now under obligation to provide a fitting implementation for each member. Given that the `IPointy` interface defines a single read-only property, this is not too much of a burden. However, if you are implementing an interface that defines ten members, the implementing type is now responsible for fleshing out the details of the ten abstract entities.

To complete the Triangle class, we will simply return the correct number of points (3), provide a fitting implementation of the abstract Draw() method defined by the Shape parent class, and define a set of constructors:

```
Public Class Triangle
  Inherits Shape
  Implements IPointy

  Public Sub New()
  End Sub
  Public Sub New(ByVal name As String)
    MyBase.New(name)
  End Sub

  Public Overrides Sub Draw()
    Console.WriteLine("Drawing {0} the Triangle", shapeName)
  End Sub

  Public ReadOnly Property Points() As Byte Implements IPointy.Points
    Get
      Return 3
    End Get
  End Property
End Class
```

Updating the Hexagon Class

Given that the Hexagon class also has some number of points, let's update the class definition to now support the IPointy interface as well. This time, our read-only Points property returns the expected value of 6.

```
' The Hexagon now supports the IPointy interface
Public Class Hexagon
  Inherits Shape
  Implements IPointy
...
  Public ReadOnly Property Points() As Byte Implements IPointy.Points
    Get
      Return 6
    End Get
  End Property
End Class
```

Each class now returns its number of points to the caller when asked to do so. To sum up the story so far, the Visual Studio 2008 class diagram shown in Figure 9-2 illustrates IPointy-compatible classes using the popular "lollipop" notation.

Again notice that Circle and ThreeDCircle do not support the IPointy interface, and therefore do not have a Points property. In contrast, if we defined Points as an abstract member in the Shapes base class, we would be forced to do so (which, again, really makes no sense for these "nonpointy" classes).

■ Note It is possible to implement an interface on a class or structure using the visual designer of Visual Studio 2008. To do so, select the interface you wish to have implemented on the designer, and with the mouse button held down, drag the mouse cursor on top of the supporting class.

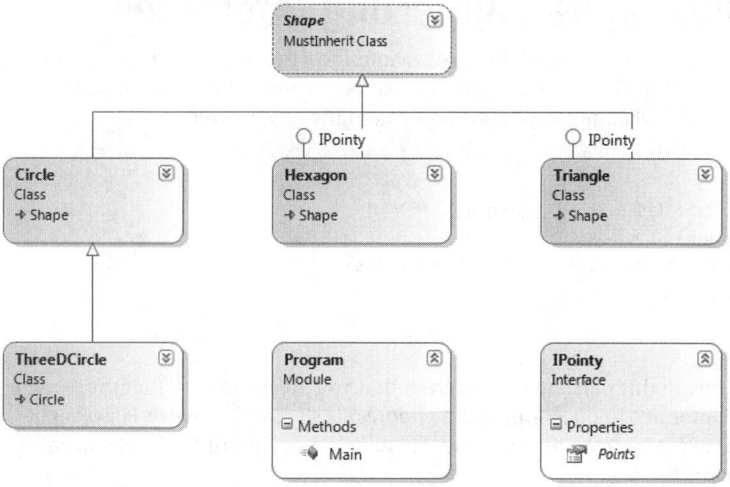

Figure 9-2. *The shapes hierarchy, now with interfaces*

Types Supporting Multiple Interfaces

As far as the .NET platform is concerned, a class can only have one direct base class. However, a class or structure can implement any number of interfaces, each of which defines some number of members that models a particular behavior. When you wish to show support for numerous interfaces on a single type, you may either list each interface using a comma-delimited list or specify each interface with a discrete `Implements` statement.

We have no need to do so at this point; however, if we did wish to update the `Hexagon` to support `System.ICloneable` as well as `IPointy`, either of the following class definitions would do:

```
' Multiple interfaces via a comma-delimited list.
Public Class Hexagon
  Inherits Shape
  Implements IPointy, ICloneable
...
End Class
```

or

```
' Multiple interfaces via multiple Implements statements
Public Class Hexagon
  Inherits Shape
  Implements IPointy
  Implements ICloneable
...
End Class
```

As you can see, interface types are quite helpful given that VB (and .NET-aware languages in general) only support single inheritance; the interface-based protocol allows a given type to support numerous behaviors, while avoiding the issues that arise when deriving from extending multiple-base classes.

Interacting with Types Supporting Interfaces

Now that you have a set of classes that support the IPointy interface, the next question is how you interact with the new functionality. The most straightforward way to interact with functionality supplied by a given interface is to invoke the members directly from the object level:

```
Module Program
  Sub Main()
    Console.WriteLine("***** Fun with Interfaces *****")
    Dim hex As New Hexagon()
    Console.WriteLine("Number of Points: {0}", hex.Points)
    Console.ReadLine()
  End Sub
End Module
```

This approach works fine in this particular case, given that you are well aware that the Hexagon type has implemented the interface in question, and therefore has a Points property. However, if you attempted to invoke the Points property on a type that did not implement IPointy, you will receive a compile-time error:

```
Module Program
  Sub Main()
...
    ' Compiler error! Circle does not implement IPointy!
    Dim c As New Circle()
    Console.WriteLine("Number of Points: {0}", c.Points)
    Console.ReadLine()
  End Sub
End Module
```

Other times, however, you will not be able to determine at compile time which interfaces are supported by a given type. For example, assume you have an array containing 50 Shape-compatible types, only some of which support IPointy. Again, if you attempt to invoke the Points property on a type that has not implemented IPointy, you receive a runtime error. This brings up a very important question: how can we determine at runtime which interfaces are supported by a given type?

Obtaining Interface References Using CType()

The first way you can determine at runtime whether a type supports a specific interface is to perform an explicit cast via CType(). If the type does not support the requested interface, you receive an InvalidCastException. On the other hand, if the type does support the interface, you are returned a reference to the implemented interface. Using this variable, you are able to call any member defined by the interface itself. Because explicit casting is not evaluated until runtime, you will most certainly want to make use of structured exception handling to account for the possibility of an invalid cast:

```
Module Program
  Sub Main()
...
  ' Recall, Circle does not support IPointy!
  Dim c As New Circle()
  Dim itfPointy As IPointy

  ' Try to get IPointy from Circle.
  Try
    itfPointy = CType(c, IPointy)
```

```
      Console.WriteLine("Number of Points: {0}", itfPointy.Points)
    Catch ex As Exception
      Console.WriteLine("{0} does not implement IPointy!", c)
    End Try
      Console.ReadLine()
    End Sub
End Module
```

Although we could make use of Try/Catch logic to determine whether a given type supports an interface, it would be ideal to determine which interfaces are supported before invoking the interface members prior to casting in the first place. If we were able to do so, we would have no need to account for a possible InvalidCastException object being thrown at runtime when performing the explicit cast.

Note As you will see in Chapter 12, Visual Basic provides two additional keywords, TryCast and DirectCast, which can be used to test for interface support (as well as to test whether a type extends a given parent class).

Obtaining Interface References Using TypeOf/Is

A more type-safe manner to determine whether a given type supports an interface is to make use of the TypeOf/Is construct, which was first introduced in Chapter 6. Recall that this construct can be used to test whether a given object derives from a particular base class. This same syntax can be used to determine whether an object implements a given interface. If the object in question is not compatible with the specified interface, you are returned the value False. Consider the following runtime tests:

```
Module Program
  Sub Main()
    Console.WriteLine("***** Fun with Interfaces *****")
    Dim hex As New Hexagon()
    Dim c As New Circle()
...
    ' See which objects support IPointy.
    Console.WriteLine("Circle implements IPointy?: {0}", TypeOf c Is IPointy)
    Console.WriteLine("Hexagon implements IPointy?: {0}", TypeOf hex Is IPointy)
    Console.ReadLine()
  End Sub
End Module
```

Now assume we have defined an array of Shape-compatible types, only some of which implement IPointy. Notice how simple it is to dynamically determine which members of the array support IPointy. If the object is compatible with the interface in question, you can safely call the members without needing to make use of Try/Catch logic, given that you would never fall into the scope of the If block when the evaluation returns False. Consider the following retrofitted Main() method:

```
Module Program
  Sub Main()
    Console.WriteLine("***** Fun with Interfaces *****")
    ' Make an array of Shape-compatible types.
    Dim myShapes() As Shape = {New Hexagon("Fred"), New Circle("Angie"), _
      New ThreeDCircle(), New Triangle("Adam")}
```

```
    ' Now figure out which ones support IPointy.
    Dim itfPointy As IPointy
    For Each s As Shape In myShapes
      If TypeOf s Is IPointy Then
        itfPointy = CType(s, IPointy)
        Console.WriteLine("{0} has {1} points.", _
          s.PetName, itfPointy.Points)
      Else
        Console.WriteLine("{0} does not implement IPointy!", s)
      End If
    Next
    Console.ReadLine()
  End Sub
End Module
```

The output can be seen in Figure 9-3.

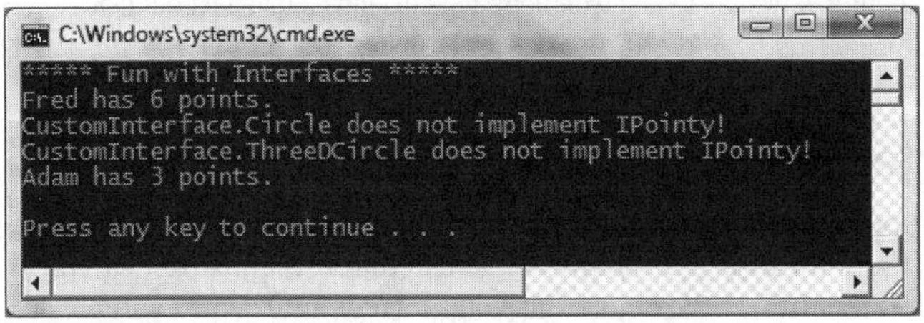

Figure 9-3. *Who supports* `IPointy`*?*

Interfaces As Member Parameters

Given that interfaces are valid .NET types, you may construct methods that take interfaces as parameters. To illustrate, assume you have defined another interface named `IDraw3D` that supports a single subroutine named `Draw3D()`:

```
' Models the ability to render a type in stunning 3D.
Public Interface IDraw3D
  Sub Draw3D()
End Interface
```

Next, assume that two of your shapes (`Circle` and `Hexagon`) have been configured to support this new behavior:

```
' Circle supports IDraw3D.
Public Class Circle
  Inherits Shape
  Implements IDraw3D
...
  Public Sub Draw3D() Implements IDraw3D.Draw3D
    Console.WriteLine("Drawing circle in 3D!")
  End Sub
End Class

' Hexagon supports IPointy and IDraw3D.
Public Class Hexagon
  Inherits Shape
  Implements IPointy, IDraw3D
```

```
...
  Public Sub Draw3D() Implements IDraw3D.Draw3D
    Console.WriteLine("Drawing Hexagon in 3D!")
  End Sub
End Class
```

Figure 9-4 presents the updated Visual Studio 2008 class diagram.

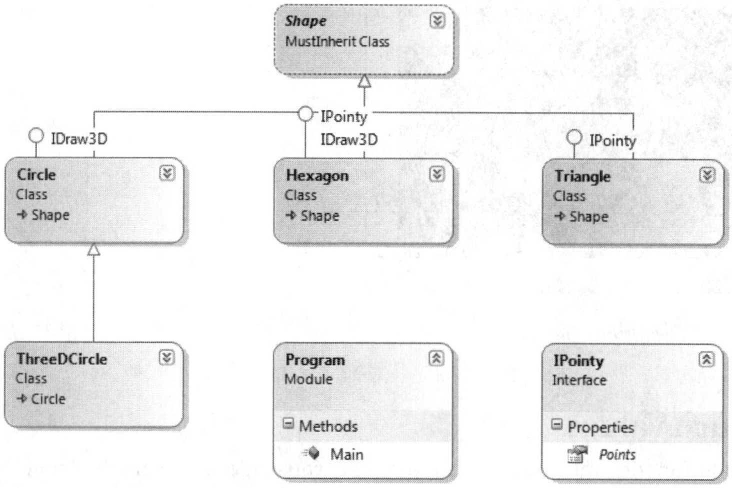

Figure 9-4. *The updated shapes hierarchy*

If you now define a new method within your module taking an IDraw3D interface as a parameter, you are able to effectively send in *any* object implementing IDraw3D. Furthermore, because interfaces are strongly typed entities, if you attempt to pass into this method an object that does not support IDraw3D, you will receive a compile-time error. Consider the following method, defined within your initial module type:

```
' This method can receive anything implementing IDraw3D.
Sub DrawIn3D(ByVal itf3d As IDraw3D)
  Console.WriteLine("-> Drawing IDraw3D compatible type")
  itf3d.Draw3D()
End Sub
```

If we were to now call this method while cycling through the array of Shapes, only the IDraw3D-compatible types are sent into our new subroutine (see Figure 9-5 for output).

```
Sub Main()
...
  Dim itfPointy As IPointy
  For Each s As Shape In myShapes
    If TypeOf s Is IPointy Then
      itfPointy = CType(s, IPointy)
      Console.WriteLine("{0} has {1} points.", s.PetName, itfPointy.Points)
    Else
      Console.WriteLine("{0} does not implement IPointy!", s)
    End If
    ' Is this item IDraw3D aware?
    If TypeOf s Is IDraw3D Then
```

```
      DrawIn3D(CType(s, IDraw3D))
    End If
  Next
  Console.ReadLine()
End Sub
```

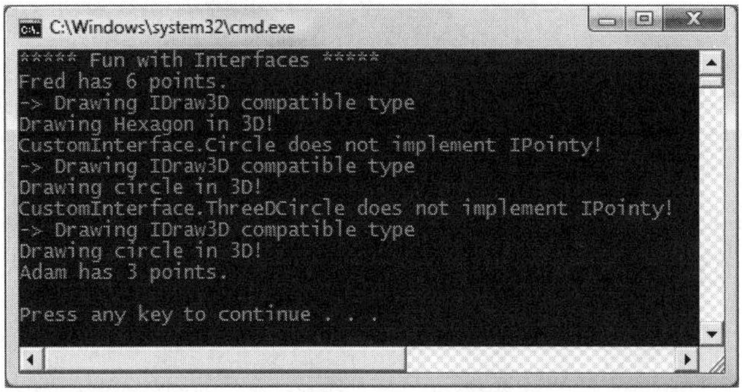

Figure 9-5. *Rendering the* `IDraw3D`*-compatible types*

Interfaces As Return Values

Interfaces can also be used as function return values. For example, you could write a method that takes any `System.Object`, checks for `IPointy` compatibility, and returns a reference to the extracted interface (if it exists):

```
' This method tests for IPointy compatibility and,
' if able, returns an interface reference.
Function ExtractPointyness(ByVal o As Object) As IPointy
  If TypeOf o Is IPointy Then
    Return CType(o, IPointy)
  Else
    Return Nothing
  End If
End Function
```

We could interact with this method as follows:

```
Sub Main()
...
  ' Can we extract IPointy from an Array of Integers?
  Dim myInts() As Integer = {10, 20, 30}
  Dim i As IPointy = ExtractPointyness(myInts)

  ' Nope!
  If i Is Nothing Then
    Console.WriteLine("Sorry, this object was not IPointy compatible")
  End If
  Console.ReadLine()
End Sub
```

Notice here we are making an array of `Integers`, which obviously does *not* implement `IPointy`. Therefore, when we run this test, we find the message "Sorry, this object was not IPointy compatible" prints to the output window.

Arrays of Interface Types

The true power of interfaces comes through loud and clear when you recall that the same interface can be implemented by numerous classes (or structures), even if they are not defined within the same class hierarchy and do not share a common base class beyond `System.Object`. This can yield some very powerful programming constructs.

For example, assume that you have developed a brand-new class hierarchy modeling kitchen utensils and another modeling gardening equipment. Although these hierarchies are completely unrelated from a classical inheritance point of view, you can treat them polymorphically using a common interface. Consider Figure 9-6, which illustrates the basic idea (if you really wanted to take this even further, you could perhaps create a base class named `Utensil` from which the `Knife` and `Fork` type derive).

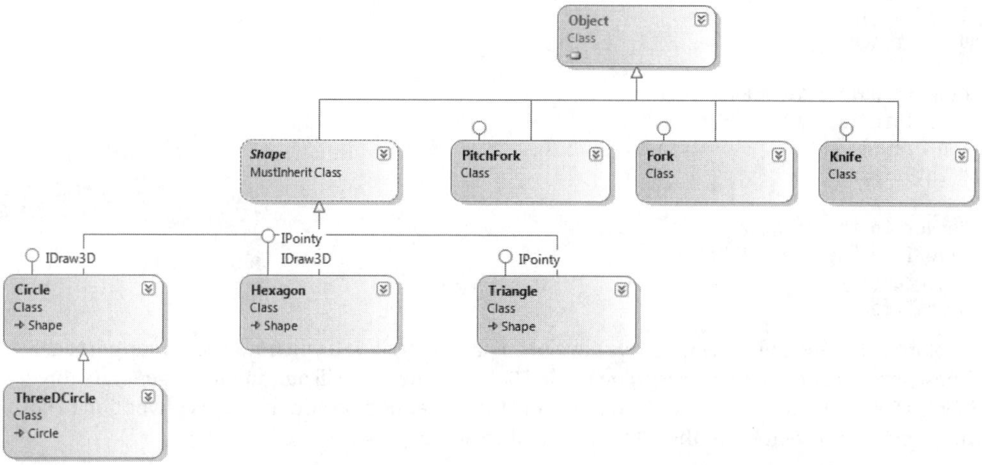

Figure 9-6. *Recall that interfaces can be "plugged in" to any type in any part of a class hierarchy.*

If you did create the `PitchFork`, `Fork`, and `Knife` types, you could now define an array of `IPointy`-compatible objects. Given that each object in the array supports the same interface, you are able to iterate through the array and treat each object as an `IPointy`-compatible object, regardless of the overall diversity of the class hierarchies:

```
Sub Main()
...
  ' This array can only contain objects that
  ' implement the IPointy interface.
  Dim pointyThings() As IPointy = {New Hexagon(), New Knife(), _
    New Triangle(), New Fork(), New PitchFork()}

  For Each p As IPointy In pointyThings
    Console.WriteLine("Object has {0} points.", p.Points)
  Next
End Sub
```

Source Code The CustomInterface project is located under the Chapter 9 subdirectory.

Resolving Name Clashes with the Implements Keyword

As you have seen earlier in this chapter, a single class or structure can implement any number of interfaces. Given this, there is always a possibility that you may implement interfaces that contain identically named members, and therefore have a name clash to contend with. To illustrate various manners in which you can resolve this issue, create a brand-new Console Application named (not surprisingly) InterfaceNameClash.

Now design three custom interfaces that represent various locations to which an implementing type could render its output:

```
' Draw image to a Form.
Public Interface IDrawToForm
  Sub Draw()
End Interface

' Draw to buffer in memory.
Public Interface IDrawToMemory
  Sub Draw()
End Interface

' Render to the printer
Public Interface IDrawToPrinter
  Sub Draw()
End Interface
```

Notice that each of these methods have been named `Draw()`. If you now wish to support each of these interfaces on a single class type named `Octagon`, the IDE will automatically generate three different `Public` members on the class, following the rather nondescript naming convention of suffixing a numerical value after the interface member name:

```
' To resolve name clashes,
' the IDE will autogenerate unique names where necessary.
Public Class Octagon
  Implements IDrawToForm, IDrawToMemory, IDrawToPrinter

  Public Sub Draw() Implements IDrawToForm.Draw
  End Sub

  Public Sub Draw1() Implements IDrawToMemory.Draw
  End Sub

  Public Sub Draw2() Implements IDrawToPrinter.Draw
  End Sub
End Class
```

Although the generated method names (`Draw1()`, `Draw2()` etc.) leave something to be desired, it should be clear that the coding logic used to render image data to a window, a region of memory, or a piece of paper is quite different. Therefore, the most straightforward manner to clean up the `Octagon` type is to simply rename the autogenerated class members to a more fitting title and provide a simple implementation of each:

```
Public Class Octagon
  Implements IDrawToForm, IDrawToMemory, IDrawToPrinter
```

```
  Public Sub Draw() Implements IDrawToForm.Draw
    Console.WriteLine("Drawing to the screen")
  End Sub

  Public Sub RenderToMemory() Implements IDrawToMemory.Draw
    Console.WriteLine("Drawing to off screen memory")
  End Sub

  Public Sub Print() Implements IDrawToPrinter.Draw
    Console.WriteLine("Printing to printer")
  End Sub
End Class
```

Notice that the name of the method defined on the class does not necessarily need to match the name of the interface method, given the fact that it is the `Implements` keyword at the end of the method signature that binds an interface member to a supporting class member. Thus, if we were to create an instance of `Octagon`, we would find the members shown in Figure 9-7 exposed through IntelliSense.

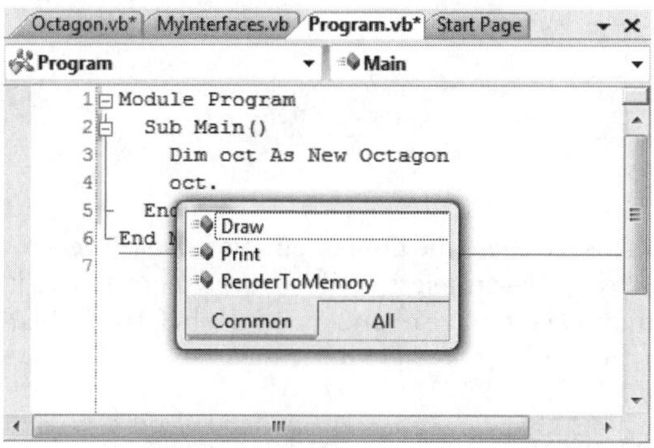

Figure 9-7. *Invoking interface members from the object level*

However, if the caller obtains an interface reference using an explicit cast, only the specific interface methods are exposed. Consider the following code, which obtains a specific interface reference using an explicit cast (which is not technically required for this particular example):

```
Module Program
  Sub Main()
    Console.WriteLine("***** Fun with Interface Name Clashes *****")
    Dim o As New Octagon

    ' Call IDrawToMemory.Draw()
    Dim iMem As IDrawToMemory
    iMem = CType(o, IDrawToMemory)
    iMem.Draw()

    ' Call IDrawToPrinter.Draw()
    Dim iPrint As IDrawToPrinter
    iPrint = CType(o, IDrawToPrinter)
    iPrint.Draw()

    ' Call IDrawToForm.Draw()
    Dim iForm As IDrawToForm
```

```
    iForm = CType(o, IDrawToForm)
    iForm.Draw()
    Console.ReadLine()
  End Sub
End Module
```

Defining a Common Implementation with the Implements Keyword

Given the fact that the Implements keyword allows you to explicitly bind an interface member to a class (or structure) member, it is permissible to define a single member that implements the members of multiple interfaces (provided each interface member has an identical signature). By way of example:

```
Public Class Line
  Implements IDrawToForm, IDrawToMemory, IDrawToPrinter

  ' This single class method defines an implementation for
  ' each interface method.
  Public Sub Draw() Implements IDrawToForm.Draw, _
    IDrawToMemory.Draw, IDrawToPrinter.Draw
    ' Common rendering logic...
  End Sub
End Class
```

Of course, in this example, it really makes no sense to share the implementation of each version of Draw() given the semantics of the interface types. Nevertheless, under some circumstances it can be the case that a shared implementation of multiple interface members fits the bill. Using this approach, you are able to simplify the overall class design.

Hiding Interface Methods from the Object Level Using the Implements Keyword

The final aspect of the Implements keyword to be aware of is that it is possible to bind an interface member to a *private* class member:

```
' Notice each class method has been defined as Private
' and has been given a very nondescript name.
Public Class BlackAndWhiteBitmap
  Implements IDrawToForm, IDrawToMemory, IDrawToPrinter

  Private Sub X() Implements IDrawToForm.Draw
    ' Insert interesting code...
  End Sub

  Private Sub Y() Implements IDrawToMemory.Draw
    ' Insert interesting code...
  End Sub

  Private Sub Z() Implements IDrawToPrinter.Draw
    ' Insert interesting code...
  End Sub
End Class
```

When you map an interface member to a `Private` type member, it is now illegal to call the interface member from the object level. Thus, if we were to create an instance of `BlackAndWhiteBitmap`, we would only see the inherited members of our good friend `System.Object`, as shown in Figure 9-8.

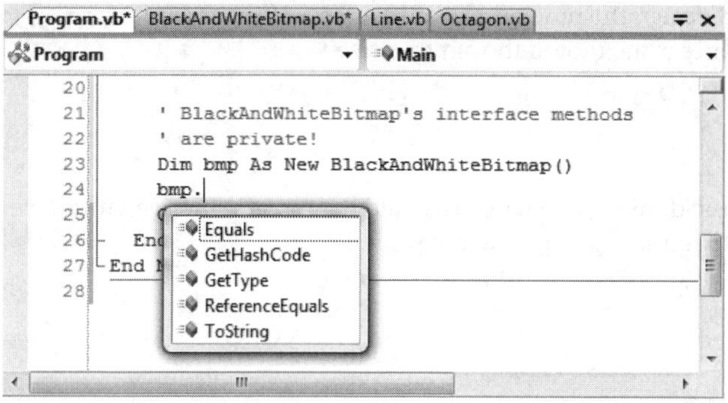

Figure 9-8. *Explicitly implemented interface members are not visible from the object level.*

When you hide interface members from the implementing type, the only possible way to call these members is by extracting out the interface using an explicit cast:

```
Dim bmp As New BlackAndWhiteBitmap()
Dim i As IDrawToForm
i = CType(bmp, IDrawToForm)
i.Draw()
```

Notice that the actual methods that implement the interface members (`X()`, `Y()`, and `Z()`) are never exposed in any manner. Like any other `Private` member, the only part of your system that can directly call these members is the type that defines them (`BlackAndWhiteBitmap` in this case).

So, when would you choose to explicitly implement an interface member? Truth be told, this class design technique is never mandatory. However, by doing so you can hide some more "advanced" members from the object level. In this way, when the object user applies the dot operator, that user will only see a subset of the type's overall functionality. However, those who require the more advanced behaviors can extract out the desired interface via an explicit cast.

This design pattern is found in numerous places within the .NET base class libraries. For example, if you examine the formal definition of the `System.Int32` type (e.g., the VB `Integer`), you will find that `Int32` implements a large number of interfaces (`IComparable`, `IConvertable`, `IFormatable`, etc.). The members of these interfaces have been implemented by *private* members of the class and are therefore only available via an explicit cast. In this way, the "simple" data types such as `Integer` have the necessary infrastructure to work within the framework; however, they are not directly exposed from an instance of the type.

Source Code The InterfaceNameClash project is located under the Chapter 9 subdirectory.

Designing Interface Hierarchies

Before we turn our attention to working with various predefined interfaces that ship with the .NET base class libraries, it is worth pointing out that interfaces can be arranged into an interface hierarchy. Like a class hierarchy, when an interface extends an existing interface, it inherits the abstract members defined by the parent interface(s). Of course, unlike class inheritance, derived interfaces never inherit true implementation. Rather, a derived interface simply extends its own definition with additional abstract members.

Interface hierarchies can be useful when you wish to extend the functionality of an existing interface without breaking existing code bases. To illustrate, create a new Console Application named InterfaceHierarchy. Now, let's redesign the previous set of interfaces (from the Interface-NameClash example) such that `IDrawable` is the root of the family tree:

```
Public Interface IDrawable
  Sub Draw()
End Interface
```

Given that `IDrawable` defines a basic drawing behavior, we could now create a derived interface that extends this type with the ability to render its output to the printer:

```
Public Interface IPrintable
  Inherits IDrawable
  Sub Print()
End Interface
```

And just for good measure, we could define a final interface named `IRenderToMemory`, which extends `IPrintable`:

```
Public Interface IRenderToMemory
  Inherits IPrintable
  Sub Render()
End Interface
```

Given our design, if a type were to implement `IRenderToMemory`, we would now be required to implement each and every member defined up the chain of inheritance (specifically, the `Render()`, `Print()`, and `Draw()` subroutines). On the other hand, if a type were to only implement `IPrintable`, we would only need to contend with `Print()` and `Draw()`. For example:

```
Public Class SuperShape
  Implements IRenderToMemory
  Public Sub Draw() Implements IDrawable.Draw
    Console.WriteLine("Drawing...")
  End Sub

  Public Sub Print() Implements IPrintable.Print
    Console.WriteLine("Printing...")
  End Sub

  Public Sub Render() Implements IRenderToMemory.Render
    Console.WriteLine("Rendering...")
  End Sub
End Class
```

Now, when we make use of the `SuperShape`, we are able to invoke each method at the object level (as they are all `Public`) as well as extract out a reference to each supported interface explicitly via casting:

```
Module Program
  Sub Main()
    Console.WriteLine("***** The SuperShape *****")

    ' Call from object level.
    Dim myShape As New SuperShape()
    myShape.Draw()
```

```
    ' Get IPrintable explicitly.
    ' (and IDrawable implicitly!)
    Dim iPrint As IPrintable
    iPrint = CType(myShape, IPrintable)
    iPrint.Draw()
    iPrint.Print()
  End Sub
End Module
```

At this point, you hopefully feel more comfortable with the process of defining and implementing custom interfaces using the syntax of Visual Basic. To be honest, interface-based programming can take awhile to get comfortable with, so if you are in fact still scratching your head just a bit, this is a perfectly normal reaction. Do be aware, however, that interfaces are a fundamental aspect of the .NET Framework. Regardless of the type of application you are developing (web-based, desktop GUIs, etc.), working with interfaces will be part of the process. To summarize the story thus far, remember that interfaces can be extremely useful when

- You have a single hierarchy where only a subset of the derived types support a common behavior.
- You need to model a common behavior that is found across multiple hierarchies.

Next up, let's check out the role of several predefined interfaces found within the .NET base class libraries.

■Source Code The InterfaceHierarchy project is located under the Chapter 9 subdirectory.

Building Enumerable Types (IEnumerable and IEnumerator)

The `System.Collections` namespace defines two interfaces named `IEnumerable` and `IEnumerator`. When you build a type that supports these behaviors, you are able to iterate over any contained subitems using the `For Each` construct of Visual Basic.

■Note In Chapter 10, you will learn more about the collection namespaces of .NET, including the generic collection classes and generic versions of `IEnumerable`/`IEnumerator`.

Assume you have developed a new Console Application project named CustomEnumerator and added a class named `Garage` that contains a set of individual `Car` types (see the CustomException example of Chapter 7) stored within a `System.Array`:

```
' Garage contains a set of Car objects.
Public Class Garage
  Private myCars() As Car = New Car(3) {}

  Public Sub New()
    myCars(0) = New Car("Fred", 40)
    myCars(1) = New Car("Zippy", 60)
    myCars(2) = New Car("Mabel", 0)
```

```
    myCars(3) = New Car("Max", 80)
  End Sub
End Class
```

Ideally, it would be convenient to iterate over the Garage object's subitems using the For Each construct. Assuming your Car class now supports two properties (Name and Speed) that encapsulate the petName and currSpeed member variables, the following logic would be ideal:

```
' This seems reasonable...
Module Program
  Sub Main()
  Console.WriteLine("***** Info about my Cars *****")
    Dim myCars As New Garage()
    ' Hand over each car in the collection?
    For Each c As Car In myCars
      Console.WriteLine("{0} is going {1} MPH", _
        c.Name, c.Speed)
    Next
    Console.ReadLine()
  End Sub
End Module
```

Sadly, the compiler informs you that the Garage class is not a "collection type." Specifically, collection types support a method named GetEnumerator(), which is formalized by the System.Collections.IEnumerable interface:

```
' This interface informs the caller
' that the object's subitems can be enumerated.
Public Interface IEnumerable
  Function GetEnumerator() As IEnumerator
End Interface
```

As you can see, the GetEnumerator() method returns a reference to yet another interface named System.Collections.IEnumerator. This interface provides the infrastructure to allow the caller to traverse the internal objects contained by the IEnumerable-compatible container:

```
Public Interface IEnumerator
  ' Advance to the next object in collection.
  Function MoveNext() As Boolean

  ' Reset to first object in collection.
  Sub Reset()

  ' Pluck out current object pointed to.
  ReadOnly Property Current() As Object
End Interface
```

If you wish to update the Garage type to support these interfaces, you could take the long road and implement each method manually. While you are certainly free to provide customized versions of GetEnumerator(), MoveNext(), Current, and Reset(), there is a simpler way. As the System.Array type (as well as many other collection types) already implements IEnumerable and IEnumerator, you can simply forward the request to the System.Array as follows:

```
Public Class Garage
  Implements System.Collections.IEnumerable

  Private myCars() As Car = New Car(3) {}
```

```
  Public Sub New()
    myCars(0) = New Car("Fred", 40)
    myCars(1) = New Car("Zippy", 60)
    myCars(2) = New Car("Mabel", 0)
    myCars(3) = New Car("Max", 80)
  End Sub

  Public Function GetEnumerator() As System.Collections.IEnumerator _
    Implements System.Collections.IEnumerable.GetEnumerator
    Return myCars.GetEnumerator()
  End Function
End Class
```

Once you have updated your Garage type, you can now safely use the type within the For Each construct. Furthermore, given that the GetEnumerator() method has been defined publicly, the object user could also interact with the IEnumerator type:

```
Sub Main()
  Console.WriteLine("***** Info about my Cars *****")
  Dim myCars As New Garage()

  ' Iterate over subobjects.
  For Each c As Car In myCars
    Console.WriteLine("{0} is going {1} MPH", _
      c.Name, c.Speed)
  Next

  ' Get IEnumerable directly.
  Dim iEnum As IEnumerator
  iEnum = myCars.GetEnumerator()
  iEnum.Reset()
  iEnum.MoveNext()

  Dim firstCar As Car = CType(iEnum.Current, Car)
  Console.WriteLine("First car in collection is: {0}", firstCar.Name)
  Console.ReadLine()
End Sub
```

Given that the only part of your system that is typically interested in manipulating the IEnumerator interface directly is indeed the For Each construct, you may wish to define GetEnumerator() as Private, to hide this member from the object level:

```
Private Function GetEnumerator() As System.Collections.IEnumerator _
  Implements System.Collections.IEnumerable.GetEnumerator
    Return myCars.GetEnumerator()
End Function
```

Source Code The CustomEnumerator project is located under the Chapter 9 subdirectory.

Building Cloneable Objects (ICloneable)

As you may recall from Chapter 6, System.Object defines a member named MemberwiseClone(). This method is used to obtain a *shallow copy* of the current object. Object users do not call this method directly (as it is protected); however, a given object may call this method itself during the *cloning* process. Simply put, a shallow copy produces a copy of an object where each point of field data is copied verbatim. To illustrate, assume you have a class named `Point` defined within a new Console Application project named CloneablePoint:

```
' A class named Point.
Public Class Point
  ' Public for easy access, feel free to add properties
  ' to wrap private data if you choose.
  Public xPos, yPos As Integer

  Public Sub New()
  End Sub
  Public Sub New(ByVal x As Integer, ByVal y As Integer)
    xPos = x : yPos = y
  End Sub

  Public Overrides Function ToString() As String
    Return String.Format("X = {0} ; Y = {1}", xPos, yPos)
  End Function
End Class
```

As fully described in Chapter 12, when you assign one reference type to another, you are simply redirecting which object the reference is pointing to in memory. To clarify, the following assignment operation results in two references to the same `Point` instance; modifications using either reference affect the same object on the heap. Therefore, each of the following calls to `Console.WriteLine()` prints the string "`X = 0 ; Y = 50`":

```
Sub Main()
  Console.WriteLine("***** Fun with ICloneable *****")
  ' Two references to same object!
  Dim p1 As New Point(50, 50)
  Dim p2 As Point = p1
  p2.xPos = 0

  ' Both print out X = 0 ; Y = 50.
  Console.WriteLine(p1)
  Console.WriteLine(p2)
  Console.ReadLine()
End Sub
```

When you wish to equip your custom types to support the ability to return an identical copy of itself (often called a *deep copy*) to the caller, you may implement the standard `ICloneable` interface. As shown at the beginning of this chapter, this type defines a single method named `Clone()`:

```
Public Interface ICloneable
  Function Clone() As Object
End Interface
```

■ **Note** The usefulness of the `ICloneable` interface is currently under debate within the .NET community. The problem has to do with the fact that the official specification does not explicitly say that objects implementing this interface must return a *deep copy* of the object (e.g., internal reference types of an object result in brand-new objects with identical state). Thus, it is technically possible that objects implementing `ICloneable` actually return a *shallow copy* of the interface (e.g., internal references point to the same object on the heap), which clearly generates a good deal of confusion. In our example, I am assuming we are implementing `Clone()` to return a full, deep copy of the object.

Obviously, the implementation of the Clone() method varies between objects. However, the basic functionality tends to be the same: copy the values of the current object's member variables into a new instance, and return it to the user. To illustrate, ponder the following update to the Point class:

```
' The Point now supports "clone-ability."
Public Class Point
  Implements ICloneable
...
  Public Function Clone() As Object Implements System.ICloneable.Clone
    Return New Point(xPos, yPos)
  End Function
End Class
```

In this way, you can create exact stand-alone copies of the Point type, as illustrated by the following code:

```
Module Program
  Sub Main()
    Console.WriteLine("***** Fun with ICloneable *****")
    Dim p1 As New Point(50, 50)

    ' If Option Strict is enabled, you must
    ' perform an explicit cast, as Clone()
    ' returns a System.Object.
    Dim p2 As Point = CType(p1.Clone(), Point)
    p2.xPos = 0

    ' Prints X = 50 ; Y = 50
    Console.WriteLine(p1)

    ' Prints X = 0 ; Y = 50
    Console.WriteLine(p2)
    Console.ReadLine()
  End Sub
End Module
```

While the current implementation of Point fits the bill, you can streamline things just a bit. Because the Point type does not contain reference type variables, you could simplify the implementation of the Clone() method as follows:

```
Public Function Clone() As Object Implements System.ICloneable.Clone
  ' Copy each field of the Point member by member.
  Return Me.MemberwiseClone()
End Function
```

Be aware, however, that if the Point did contain any reference type member variables, MemberwiseClone() will copy the references to those objects (aka a *shallow copy*). If you wish to support a true deep copy, you will need to create a new instance of any reference type variables during the cloning process. Let's see an example.

A More Elaborate Cloning Example

Now assume the Point class contains a reference type member variable of type PointDescription. This class maintains a point's friendly name as well as an identification number expressed as a System.Guid (if you don't come from a COM background, know that a globally unique identifier [GUID] is a statistically unique 128-bit number). Here is the implementation:

```
Public Class PointDescription
  Public petName As String
  Public pointID As Guid

  Public Sub New()
    Me.petName = "No-name"
    Me.pointID = Guid.NewGuid()
  End Sub
End Class
```

The initial updates to the `Point` class itself included modifying `ToString()` to account for these new bits of state data, as well as defining and initializing the `PointDescription` reference type. To allow the outside world to establish a string moniker for the `Point`, you also update the arguments passed into the overloaded constructor:

```
Public Class Point
  Implements ICloneable
  Public xPos, yPos As Integer

  ' Point "has-a" PointDescription.
  Public desc As New PointDescription()

  Public Sub New()
  End Sub
  Sub New(ByVal x As Integer, ByVal y As Integer)
    xPos = x : yPos = y
  End Sub
   Public Sub New(ByVal x As Integer, ByVal y As Integer, ByVal name As String)
    xPos = x : yPos = y
    desc.petName = name
  End Sub

  Public Overrides Function ToString() As String
    Return String.Format("X = {0} ; Y = {1} ; Name = {2} : ID = {3}", _
      xPos, yPos, desc.petName, desc.pointID)
  End Function

  Public Function Clone() As Object Implements System.ICloneable.Clone
    Return Me.MemberwiseClone()
  End Function
End Class
```

Notice that you did not yet update your `Clone()` method. Therefore, when the object user asks for a clone using the current implementation, a shallow (member-by-member) copy is achieved. To illustrate, assume you have updated `Main()` as follows:

```
Module Program
  Sub Main()
    Console.WriteLine("***** Fun with ICloneable *****")
    Dim p1 As New Point(50, 50, "Brad")
    Dim p2 As Point = CType(p1.Clone(), Point)

    Console.WriteLine("Before modification:")
    Console.WriteLine("p1: {0} ", p1)
    Console.WriteLine("p2: {0} ", p2)
```

```
    p2.desc.petName = "This is my second point"
    p2.xPos = 9
    Console.WriteLine("Changed p2.desc.petName and p2.x")

    Console.WriteLine("After modification:")
    Console.WriteLine("p1: {0} ", p1)
    Console.WriteLine("p2: {0} ", p2)
    Console.ReadLine()
  End Sub
End Module
```

Now, observe the output in Figure 9-9.

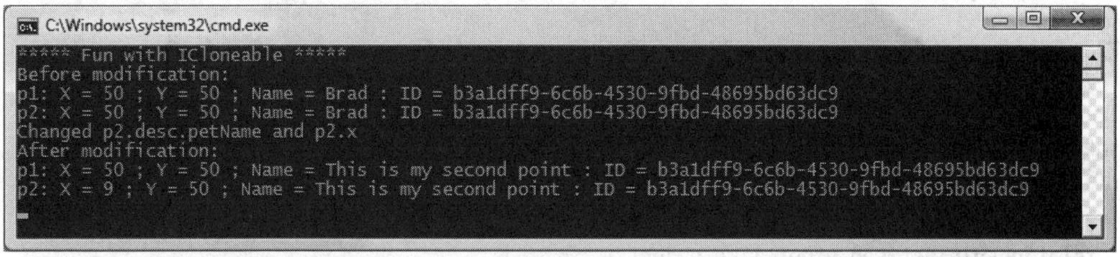

Figure 9-9. *Oops! We just copied the* `PointDescription` *reference!*

The problem with the current application is that the internal reference of the `PointDescription` type was *shallow-copied*. Thus, any changes to that object using the `p1` or `p2` objects modify the same object in memory.

In order for your `Clone()` method to make a complete deep copy of the internal reference types, you need to configure the object returned by `MemberwiseClone()` to account for the current point's name (the `System.Guid` type is in fact a structure, so the numerical data is indeed copied). Here is one possible implementation of the `Point`'s `Clone()` method:

```
' This version of Clone() returns a deep copy.
Public Function Clone() As Object Implements System.ICloneable.Clone
  Dim newPoint As Point = CType(Me.MemberwiseClone(), Point)

  Dim currentDesc As New PointDescription()
  currentDesc.petName = Me.desc.petName
  currentDesc.pointID = Me.desc.pointID

  newPoint.desc = currentDesc
  Return newPoint
End Function
```

If you rerun the application once again, you see that the `Point` returned from `Clone()` does copy its internal reference type member variables (see Figure 9-10).

To summarize the cloning process, if you have a class or structure that contains nothing but value types, implement your `Clone()` method using `MemberwiseClone()`. However, if you have a custom type that maintains other reference types, you need to establish a new object that takes into account the state of each member variable.

Source Code The CloneablePoint project is located under the Chapter 9 subdirectory.

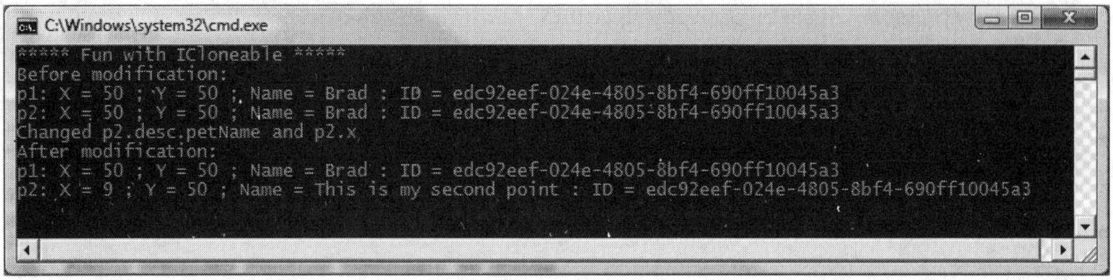

Figure 9-10. *Much better! We now copied the* `PointDescription` *object!*

Building Comparable Objects (IComparable)

The `System.IComparable` interface specifies a behavior that allows an object to be sorted based on some specified key. Here is the formal definition (you'll see the role of the `Integer` return value of the `CompareTo()` method in just a bit):

```
' This interface allows an object to specify its
' relationship between other like objects.
Public Interface IComparable
  Function CompareTo(ByVal obj As Object) As Integer
End Interface
```

Create a new Console Application project named ComparableCar. Let's assume you have updated the `Car` class (see Chapter 7) to maintain a numerical identifier (represented by a simple integer named `carID`) that can be set via a constructor parameter and manipulated using a new property named `ID`. Here are the relevant updates to the `Car` type:

```
Public Class Car
...
  Private carID As Integer
  Public Property ID() As Integer
    Get
      Return carID
    End Get
    Set(ByVal value As Integer)
      carID = value
    End Set
  End Property

  Public Sub New(ByVal name As String, _
    ByVal currSp As Integer, ByVal id As Integer)
    currSpeed = currSp
    petName = name
    carID = id
  End Sub
...
End Class
```

As well, assume this `Car` type has defined new properties (`Name` and `Speed`) to get and set the existing `currSpeed` and `petName` fields. Given this, object users might create an array of `Car` objects as follows:

```
Module Program
  Sub Main()
    Console.WriteLine("***** Fun with IComparable *****")
    ' Make an array of Car objects.
    Dim myAutos(4) As Car
    myAutos(0) = New Car("Rusty", 80, 1)
    myAutos(1) = New Car("Mary", 40, 234)
    myAutos(2) = New Car("Viper", 40, 34)
    myAutos(3) = New Car("Mel", 40, 4)
    myAutos(4) = New Car("Chucky", 40, 5)

    ' Print the name and ID of each car.
    For Each c As Car In myAutos
      Console.WriteLine("Car {0} is named {1}.", c.ID, c.Name)
    Next
    Console.ReadLine()
  End Sub
End Module
```

As you may recall from Chapter 4, the System.Array class defines a shared method named Sort(). When you invoke this method on an array of intrinsic types (Integer, Short, String, etc.), you are able to sort the items in the array in numerical/alphabetic order as these intrinsic data types implement IComparable. However, what if you were to send an array of Car types into the Sort() method as follows?

```
' Sort my cars?
Array.Sort(myAutos)
```

If you run this test, you would find that an exception is thrown by the runtime. When you build custom types, you can implement IComparable to allow arrays of your types to be sorted. When you flesh out the details of CompareTo(), it will be up to you to decide what the baseline of the ordering operation will be. For the Car type, the internal carID seems to be the most logical candidate. Assume Car implements IComparable and implements CompareTo() as follows:

```
' The iteration of the Car can be ordered
' based on the carID.
Public Function CompareTo(ByVal obj As Object) As Integer _
  Implements System.IComparable.CompareTo
  Dim temp As Car = CType(obj, Car)
  If Me.carID > temp.carID Then
    Return 1
  End If
  If Me.carID < temp.carID Then
    Return -1
  Else
    Return 0
  End If
End Function
```

Note If you wish to build a more bulletproof implementation of CompareTo(), you would do well to perform a runtime check to ensure the incoming Object parameter is comparable with the object being compared to (a Car in our example).

As you can see, the logic behind CompareTo() is to test the incoming type against the current instance based on a specific field you want to sort upon (carID in our example). The return value of CompareTo() is used to discover whether this type is less than, greater than, or equal to the object it is being compared with (see Table 9-1).

Table 9-1. CompareTo() *Return Values*

CompareTo() **Return Value**	**Meaning in Life**
Any number less than zero	The current object comes before the parameter object in the sort order.
Zero	The current object instance is equal to the specified object.
Any number greater than zero	This instance comes after the specified object in the sort order.

Now that your Car type understands how to compare itself to like objects, you can write the following user code:

```
Module Program
  Sub Main()
    Console.WriteLine("***** Fun with IComparable *****")

    ' Make an array of Car objects.
    Dim myAutos(4) As Car
    myAutos(0) = New Car("Rusty", 80, 1)
    myAutos(1) = New Car("Mary", 40, 234)
    myAutos(2) = New Car("Viper", 40, 34)
    myAutos(3) = New Car("Mel", 40, 4)
    myAutos(4) = New Car("Chucky", 40, 5)

    Console.WriteLine("-> Before Sorting:")
    For Each c As Car In myAutos
      Console.WriteLine("Car {0} is named {1}.", c.ID, c.Name)
    Next
    Console.WriteLine()

    ' Sort my cars!
    Array.Sort(myAutos)
    Console.WriteLine("-> After Sorting:")
    For Each c As Car In myAutos
      Console.WriteLine("Car {0} is named {1}.", c.ID, c.Name)
    Next
    Console.ReadLine()
  End Sub
End Module
```

Figure 9-11 illustrates a test run.

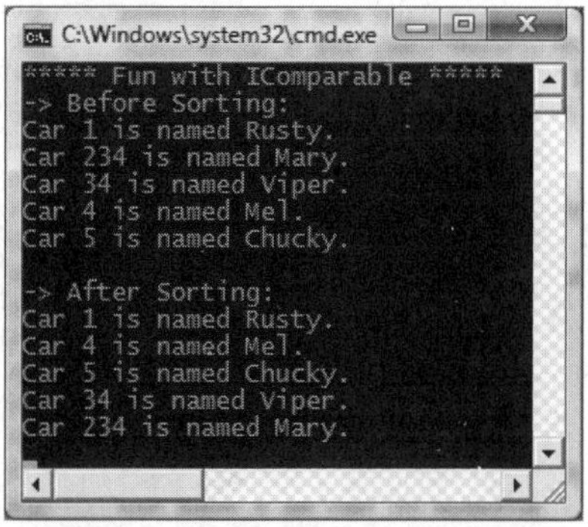

Figure 9-11. *Sorting Cars by ID via* `IComparable`

Specifying Multiple Sort Orders (IComparer)

In this version of the `Car` type, you made use of the car's ID to function as the baseline of the sort order. Another design might have used the pet name of the car as the basis of the sorting algorithm (to list cars alphabetically). Now, what if you wanted to build a `Car` that could be sorted by ID *as well as* by pet name? If this is the behavior you are interested in, you need to make friends with another standard interface named `IComparer`, defined within the `System.Collections` namespace as follows:

```
' A general way to compare two objects.
Public Interface IComparer
  Function Compare(ByVal x As Object, ByVal y As Object) As Integer
End Interface
```

Unlike the `IComparable` interface, `IComparer` is typically *not* implemented on the type you are trying to sort (i.e., the `Car`). Rather, you implement this interface on any number of helper classes, one for each sort order (pet name, car ID, etc.). Currently, the `Car` type already knows how to compare itself against other cars based on the internal car ID. Therefore, to allow the object user to sort an array of `Car` types by pet name will require an additional helper class that implements `IComparer`. Here's the code:

```
' This helper class is used to sort an array of Cars by pet name.
Public Class PetNameComparer
  Implements IComparer

  Public Function Compare(ByVal x As Object, ByVal y As Object) _
    As Integer Implements System.Collections.IComparer.Compare
    Dim c1 As Car = CType(x, Car)
    Dim c2 As Car = CType(y, Car)
    Return String.Compare(c1.Name, c2.Name)
  End Function
End Class
```

The object user code is able to make use of this helper class. `System.Array` has a number of overloaded `Sort()` methods, one that just happens to take an object implementing `IComparer` (see Figure 9-12 for output):

```
Module Program
  Sub Main()
...
    ' Now sort by pet name.
    Array.Sort(myAutos, New PetNameComparer())
```

```
    Console.WriteLine("-> Ordering by pet name:")
    For Each c As Car In myAutos
      Console.WriteLine("{0} has the ID of {1}.", c.Name, c.ID)
    Next
  Console.ReadLine()
  End Sub
End Module
```

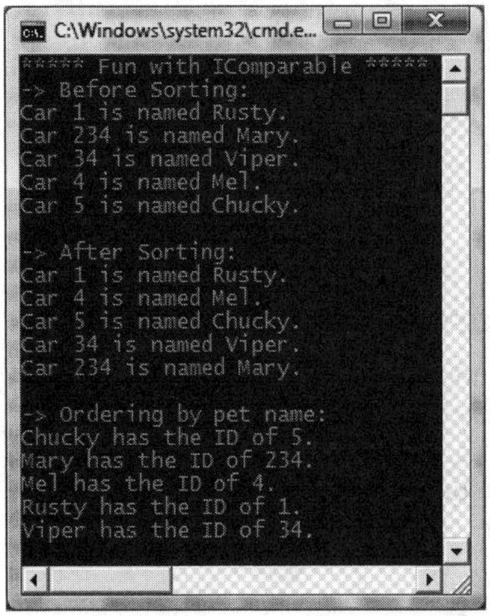

Figure 9-12. *Sorting* Cars *via* IComparable

Custom Properties, Custom Sort Types

When building custom types that can be sorted in a variety of manners (numerically, alphabetically, etc.), it is a common coding practice to define the related IComparer helper class *directly within* the type being sorted. As you may recall from Chapter 6, when you define a class within the scope of another related class, you have *nested* a class. While it is not mandatory to nest the IComparer helper classes within the type being sorted, doing so can simplify coding for those using your comparable objects.

Assume the Car class has indeed defined PetNameComparer within its scope, and added a shared read-only property named SortByPetName that returns an instance of an object implementing the IComparer interface (PetNameComparer, in this case):

```
' We now support a custom property to return
' the correct IComparer interface.
Public Class Car
  Implements IComparable
...
  ' Assume PetNameComparer has been nested within the Car type.

  ' Property to return the pet name comparer.
  Public Shared ReadOnly Property SortByPetName() As IComparer
    Get
      Return New PetNameComparer()
    End Get
  End Property
End Class
```

The object user code can now sort by pet name using a strongly associated property, rather than just "having to know" to use the stand-alone PetNameComparer class type:

```
' Sorting by pet name made a bit cleaner.
Array.Sort(myAutos, Car.SortByPetName)
```

Source Code The ComparableCar project is located under the Chapter 9 subdirectory.

So, at this point, you not only understand how to define and implement interface types, but also have a better idea regarding a few useful interfaces defined in the .NET base class libraries. To be sure, interfaces will be found within every major .NET namespace. As you would expect, some interfaces are more immediately useful than others, so be sure to consult the .NET Framework 3.5 SDK documentation for full details regarding the interfaces you encounter throughout the remainder of this text. To wrap up this chapter, let's examine how interfaces can be used to build a custom event architecture.

Using Interfaces As a Callback Mechanism

As illustrated throughout this chapter, interfaces can be used to define a behavior that may be supported by various types in your system. Beyond using interfaces to establish polymorphism across hierarchies, interfaces may also be used as a *callback mechanism*. This technique enables objects to engage in a two-way conversation using an agreed-upon set of members.

To illustrate the use of callback interfaces, let's retrofit the now familiar Car type (as defined in Chapter 7) in such a way that it is able to inform the caller when the engine is about to explode (when the current speed is 10 miles below the maximum speed) and has exploded (when the current speed is at or above the maximum speed). The ability to send and receive these events will be facilitated with a custom interface named IEngineEvents defined within a new Console Application named EventInterface.

```
' The callback interface.
Public Interface IEngineEvents
  Sub AboutToBlow(msg As String)
  Sub Exploded(msg As String)
End Interface
```

In order to keep an application's code base as flexible and reusable as possible, callback interfaces are not typically implemented directly by the object interested in receiving the events, but rather by a helper object called a *sink object*.

Assume we have created a class named CarEventSink that implements IEngineEvents by printing the incoming messages to the console. As well, our sink object will also maintain a string used as a textual identifier. As you will see, it is possible to register multiple sink objects for a given event source; therefore, it will prove helpful to identify a sink by name. This being said, consider the following implementation:

```
' Car event sink.
Public Class CarEventSink
  Implements IEngineEvents
  Private name As String

  Public Sub New(ByVal sinkName As String)
    name = sinkName
  End Sub
```

```
  Public Sub AboutToBlow(ByVal msg As String) _
    Implements IEngineEvents.AboutToBlow
    Console.WriteLine("{0} reporting: {1}", name, msg)
  End Sub
  Public Sub Exploded(ByVal msg As String) _
    Implements IEngineEvents.Exploded
    Console.WriteLine("{0} reporting: {1}", name, msg)
  End Sub
End Class
```

Now that you have a sink object that implements the event interface, your next task is to pass a reference to this sink into the Car type. The Car holds onto this object and makes calls back on the sink when appropriate.

In order to allow the Car to receive the caller-supplied sink reference, we will need to add a public helper member to the Car type that we will call Connect(). Likewise, to allow the caller to detach from the event source, we will define another helper method on the Car type named Disconnect().

Finally, to enable the caller to register multiple sink objects (for the purposes of multicasting), the Car now maintains a System.Collections.ArrayList to represent each outstanding connection. Here are the relevant updates to the Car type:

```
' This iteration of the Car type maintains a list of
' objects implementing the IEngineEvents interface.
Public Class Car
  ' The set of connected clients.
  Private clientSinks As New ArrayList()

  ' The client calls these methods to connect
  ' to, or detach from, the event notification.
  Public Sub Connect(ByVal sink As IEngineEvents)
    clientSinks.Add(sink)
  End Sub

  Public Sub Disconnect(ByVal sink As IEngineEvents)
    clientSinks.Remove(sink)
  End Sub
...
End Class
```

To actually send the events, let's update the Car.Accelerate() method to iterate over the list of sinks maintained by the ArrayList and send the correct notification when appropriate. Here is the updated member in question:

```
' The Accelerate method now fires event notifications to the caller,
' rather than throwing a custom exception.
Public Sub Accelerate(ByVal delta As Integer)
  ' If the car is doomed, send out event to
  ' each connected client.
  If carIsDead Then
    For Each i As IEngineEvents In clientSinks
      i.Exploded("Sorry!  This car is toast!")
    Next
  Else
    currSpeed += delta
    ' Send out "about to blow" event?
    If (maxSpeed - currSpeed) = 10 Then
      For Each i As IEngineEvents In clientSinks
```

```
          i.AboutToBlow("Careful! About to blow!")
        Next
      End If
      ' Is the car doomed?
      If currSpeed >= maxSpeed Then
        carIsDead = True
      Else
        ' We are OK, just print out speed.
        Console.WriteLine("=> CurrSpeed = {0}", currSpeed)
      End If
    End If
  End Sub
```

To complete the example, here is a Main() method making use of a callback interface to listen to the Car events:

```
' Make a car and listen to the events.
Module Program
  Sub Main()
    Console.WriteLine("***** Interfaces as event enablers *****")
    Dim myCar As New Car("SlugBug", 10)

    ' Make sink object.
    Dim sink As New CarEventSink("MySink")

    ' Register the sink with the Car.
    myCar.Connect(sink)

    ' Speed up (this will trigger the event notifications).
    For i As Integer = 0 To 5
      myCar.Accelerate(20)
    Next

    ' Detach from event source.
    myCar.Disconnect(sink)
    Console.ReadLine()
  End Sub
End Module
```

Figure 9-13 shows the end result of this interface-based event protocol.

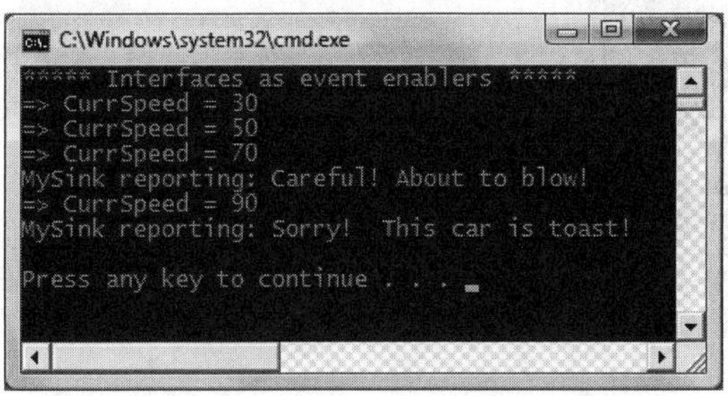

Figure 9-13. *Interfaces as event protocols*

Notice that we call Disconnect() before exiting Main(), although this is not actually necessary for the example to function as intended. However, the Disconnect() method can be very helpful in that it allows the caller to selectively detach from an event source at will. Assume that the application now wishes to register two sink objects, dynamically remove a particular sink during the flow of execution, and continue processing the program at large:

```
Module Program
  Sub Main()
    Console.WriteLine("***** Interfaces as event enablers *****")
    Dim myCar As New Car("SlugBug", 10)

    ' Make sink object.
    Console.WriteLine("***** Creating Sinks! *****")
    Dim sink As New CarEventSink("First Sink")
    Dim otherSink As New CarEventSink("Second Sink")

    ' Pass both sinks to car.
    myCar.Connect(sink)
    myCar.Connect(otherSink)

    ' Speed up (this will trigger the events).
    For i As Integer = 0 To 5
      myCar.Accelerate(20)
    Next

    ' Detach from first sink.
    myCar.Disconnect(sink)

    ' Speed up again (only otherSink will be called).
    For i As Integer = 0 To 5
      myCar.Accelerate(20)
    Next

    ' Detach from other sink.
    myCar.Disconnect(otherSink)
    Console.ReadLine()
  End Sub
End Module
```

Figure 9-14 shows the update.

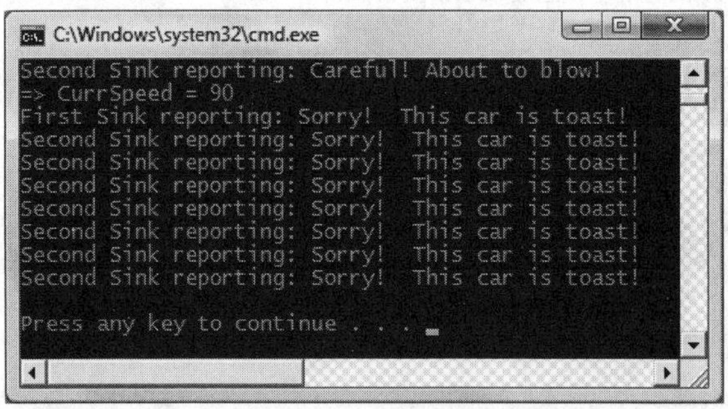

Figure 9-14. *Working with multiple sinks*

Again, remember that event interfaces can be helpful in that they can be used under any language (VB, C#, C++, etc.) or platform (COM, .NET, or Java EE) that supports interface-based programming. However, as you may be suspecting, the .NET platform defines an "official" event protocol that is not dependent on the construction of interfaces. To understand .NET's intrinsic event architecture, you must understand the role of the delegate type, which will be addressed in Chapter 11.

■ **Source Code** The EventInterface project is located under the Chapter 9 subdirectory.

Summary

An interface can be defined as a named collection of *abstract members*. Because an interface does not provide any implementation details, it is common to regard an interface as a behavior that may be supported by a given type. When two or more classes implement the same interface, you are able to treat each type the same way (via interface-based polymorphism) even if the types are defined in different class hierarchies.

VB 2008 provides the `Interface` keyword to allow you to define a new interface. As you have seen, a type can support as many interfaces as necessary using the `Implements` keyword. Furthermore, it is permissible to build interfaces that derive from multiple base interfaces.

In addition to building your custom interfaces, the .NET libraries define a number of framework-supplied interfaces. As you have seen, you are free to build custom types that implement these predefined interfaces to gain a number of desirable traits such as cloning, sorting, and enumerating.

Finally, we examined how an interface type can be used to create a custom event architecture. While it is true that the official event system of the .NET platform does not demand the use of interfaces, this approach can be helpful when you need to have objects communicate in a bidirectional manner.

CHAPTER 10

Collections, Generics, and Nullable Data Types

Since the release of .NET 2.0, the VB programming language was enhanced to support a specific feature of the Common Type System termed *generics*. Simply put, generics provide a way for programmers to define "placeholders" (formally termed *type parameters*) for members (subroutines, functions, fields, properties, etc.) and type definitions (classes, structures, interfaces, and delegates), which are specified at the time of invoking the generic member or creating an instance of the generic type.

While it's true that you could build an entire .NET 3.5 application without ever directly using a generic item in your code, you gain several benefits by doing so. Given this, the chapter opens by qualifying the need for generic types by examining the limitations of working with the nongeneric types of `System.Collections`. Once you understand the problems generics attempt to solve, you will then learn how to make use of existing generic types defined within the `System.Collections.Generic` namespace.

Next, you will get to know the role of the `System.Nullable(Of T)` generic type and come to understand a language feature termed *nullable data types*. As you will see, this generic type allows you to define numerical data that can be set to the value `Nothing` (which can be particularly helpful when working with relational databases). As well, you will be exposed to a new .NET 3.5 notation used to define nullable data types via the VB ? operator.

After you've seen generic support within the base class libraries, the remainder of this chapter examines how you can build your own generic members, classes, structures, interfaces, and delegates (and when you might wish to do so).

The Nongeneric Types of System.Collections

The most primitive of all containers in the .NET universe would have to be our good friend `System.Array`. As you have already seen in Chapter 4, this class provides a number of services (e.g., reversing, sorting, clearing, and enumerating) that allow you to process a set of data points of the same underlying type (e.g., an array of `Integers`, an array of `Bitmaps`, or what have you).

While basic arrays will always be a useful programming construct, the simple `Array` class has a number of limitations: most notably it does not dynamically resize itself as you add or clear items. When needing to contain data in a more flexible container, .NET programmers historically made use of the types within the `System.Collections` namespace, which has been part of the .NET base class libraries since the initial release of the platform (version 1.0).

Although the `System.Collections` namespace is still supported under .NET 3.5 (and will be supported for some time to come), these days it is preferable to make use of *generic* container classes within the `System.Collections.Generic` namespace. As you progress through this chapter, you will come to see the benefits generic containers provide; however, before diving into the topic too far, we will begin with an overview of the legacy `System.Collections` namespace. There are several reasons to do so:

- A large body of existing .NET code makes use of `System.Collections`, therefore understanding this namespace will help you maintain and update existing code bases.
- By and large, the generic types of `System.Collections.Generic` have been designed to mimic their nongeneric counterparts. Therefore, the more you know about `System.Collections`, the more you know about `System.Collections.Generic`.
- When you understand the limitations of the nongeneric types of `System.Collections`, the usefulness of `System.Collections.Generic` is much more obvious.

This all being said, without further ado, let's begin to examine the interface types found within `System.Collections`.

The Interfaces of the System.Collections Namespace

The `System.Collections` namespace defines a number of interfaces that a majority of the collection classes implement to provide access to their contents. Table 10-1 gives a breakdown of the core interfaces.

Table 10-1. *Key Interfaces of* `System.Collections`

Interface	Meaning in Life
`ICollection`	Defines general characteristics (e.g., size, enumeration, thread safety) for all nongeneric collection types.
`IComparer`	Allows two objects to be compared.
`IDictionary`	Allows a nongeneric collection object to represent its contents using name/value pairs.
`IDictionaryEnumerator`	Enumerates the contents of a type supporting `IDictionary`.
`IEnumerable`	Returns the `IEnumerator` interface for a given collection.
`IEnumerator`	Enables `For Each` style iteration of items in a collection.
`IList`	Provides behavior to add, remove, and index items in a list of objects. Also, this interface defines members to determine whether the implementing collection type is read-only and/or a fixed-size container.

Many of these interfaces are related by an interface hierarchy, while others are stand-alone types. Figure 10-1 illustrates the relationship between each type (recall that it is permissible for a single interface to derive from multiple interfaces).

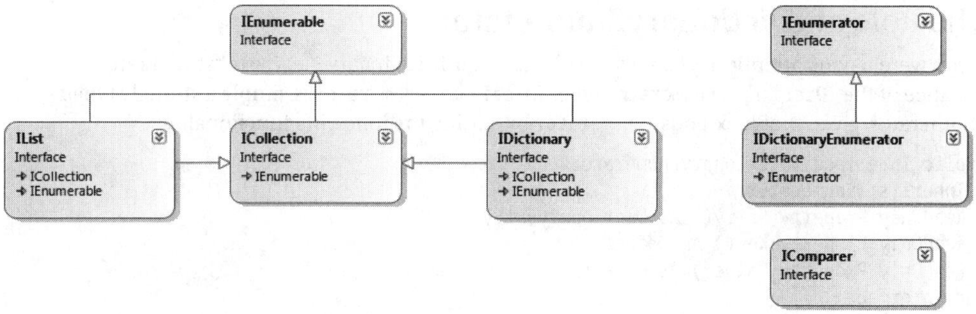

Figure 10-1. *The relationship of the key interfaces of* `System.Collections`

The Role of ICollection

The `ICollection` interface is the most primitive interface of the `System.Collections` namespace in that it defines a behavior supported by a collection type. In a nutshell, this interface provides a small set of members that allow you to determine (a) the number of items in the container, (b) the thread safety of the container, as well as (c) the ability to copy the contents into a `System.Array` type. Formally, `ICollection` is defined as follows (note that `ICollection` extends `IEnumerable`):

```
Public Interface ICollection
  Inherits IEnumerable
  Sub CopyTo(ByVal array As Array, ByVal index As Integer)
  ReadOnly Property Count() As Integer
  ReadOnly Property IsSynchronized() As Boolean
  ReadOnly Property SyncRoot() As Object
End Interface
```

The Role of IDictionary

As you may already be aware, a *dictionary* is simply a collection that maintains a set of name/value pairs. For example, you could build a custom type that implements `IDictionary` such that you can store `Car` objects (the values) that may be retrieved by ID or pet name (e.g., names). Given this functionality, you can see that the `IDictionary` interface defines a `Keys` and `Values` property as well as `Add()`, `Remove()`, and `Contains()` methods. The individual items may be obtained by the *type indexer*, which as you will see a bit later in this chapter allows you to retrieve subitems using an arraylike syntax. Here is the formal definition:

```
Public Interface IDictionary
  Inherits ICollection, IEnumerable
  Sub Add(ByVal key As Object, ByVal value As Object)
  Sub Clear()
  Function Contains(ByVal key As Object) As Boolean
  Function GetEnumerator() As IDictionaryEnumerator
  Sub Remove(ByVal key As Object)
  ReadOnly Property IsFixedSize() As Boolean
  ReadOnly Property IsReadOnly() As Boolean
  Property Item(ByVal key As Object) As Object
  ReadOnly Property Keys() As ICollection
  ReadOnly Property Values() As ICollection
End Interface
```

The Role of IDictionaryEnumerator

If you were paying attention, you may have noted that `IDictionary.GetEnumerator()` returns an instance of the `IDictionaryEnumerator` type. `IDictionaryEnumerator` is simply a strongly typed enumerator, given that it extends `IEnumerator` by adding the following functionality:

```
Public Interface IDictionaryEnumerator
  Inherits IEnumerator
  ReadOnly Property Entry() As DictionaryEntry
  ReadOnly Property Key() As Object
  ReadOnly Property Value() As Object
End Interface
```

Notice how `IDictionaryEnumerator` allows you to enumerate over items in the dictionary via the `Entry` property, which returns a `System.Collections.DictionaryEntry` class type. In addition, you are also able to traverse the name/value pairs using the `Key`/`Value` properties.

The Role of IList

The final key interface of `System.Collections` is `IList`, which provides the ability to insert, remove, and index items into (or out of) an indexed container:

```
Public Interface IList
  Inherits ICollection, IEnumerable
  Function Add(ByVal value As Object) As Integer
  Sub Clear()
  Function Contains(ByVal value As Object) As Boolean
  Function IndexOf(ByVal value As Object) As Integer
  Sub Insert(ByVal index As Integer, ByVal value As Object)
  Sub Remove(ByVal value As Object)
  Sub RemoveAt(ByVal index As Integer)
  ReadOnly Property IsFixedSize() As Boolean
  ReadOnly Property IsReadOnly() As Boolean
  Property Item(ByVal index As Integer) As Object
End Interface
```

The Class Types of System.Collections

As I hope you understand by this point in the chapter, interfaces by themselves are not very useful until they are implemented by a given class or structure. Table 10-2 provides a rundown of the core classes in the `System.Collections` namespace and the key interfaces they support.

Table 10-2. *Classes of* `System.Collections`

Class	Meaning in Life	Key Implemented Interfaces

`ArrayList`	Represents a dynamically sized array of objects.	`IList`
		`ICollection`
		`IEnumerable`
		`ICloneable`

`Hashtable`	Represents a collection of objects identified by a numerical key. Custom types stored in a `Hashtable` should always override `System.Object.GetHashCode()`.	`IDictionary`
		`ICollection`
		`IEnumerable`
		`ICloneable`

Class	Meaning in Life	Key Implemented Interfaces

`Queue`	Represents a standard first-in, first-out (FIFO) queue.	`ICollection`
		`ICloneable`
		`IEnumerable`

`SortedList`	Like a dictionary; however, the elements can also be accessed by ordinal position (e.g., index).	`IDictionary`
		`ICollection`
		`IEnumerable`
		`ICloneable`

`Stack`	Represents a last-in, first-out (LIFO) queue and provides push and pop (and peek) functionality.	`ICollection`
		`ICloneable`
		`IEnumerable`

In addition to these key types, `System.Collections` defines some minor players (at least in terms of their day-to-day usefulness) such as `BitArray`, `CaseInsensitiveComparer`, and `CaseInsensitiveHashCodeProvider`. Furthermore, this namespace also defines a small set of abstract base classes (`CollectionBase`, `ReadOnlyCollectionBase`, and `DictionaryBase`) that can be used to build strongly typed containers.

As you begin to experiment with the `System.Collections` types, you will find they all tend to share common functionality (that's the point of interface-based programming). Thus, rather than listing out the members of each and every collection class, the next task of this chapter is to illustrate how to interact with three common collection types: `ArrayList`, `Queue`, and `Stack`. Once you understand the functionality of these types, gaining an understanding of the remaining collection classes (such as the `Hashtable`) should naturally follow, especially since each of the types is fully documented within the .NET Framework 3.5 documentation.

Working with the ArrayList Type

To illustrate working with these collection types, create a new Console Application project named CollectionTypes, and insert the current iteration of the `Car` type. The `ArrayList` type is bound to be your most frequently used type in the `System.Collections` namespace in that it allows you to dynamically resize the contents at your whim. To illustrate the basics of this type, ponder the following method, which leverages the `ArrayList` to manipulate a set of simple `Car` objects:

```
Sub ArrayListTest()
  ' Make ArrayList and add a range of Cars.
  Dim carArList As New ArrayList()
  carArList.AddRange(New Car() {New Car("Fred", 90, 10), _
    New Car("Mary", 100, 50), New Car("MB", 190, 11)})
  Console.WriteLine("Items in carArList: {0}", carArList.Count)

  ' Iterate over contents using For/Each.
  For Each c As Car In carArList
    Console.WriteLine("Car pet name: {0}", c.Name)
  Next

  ' Insert new car.
  Console.WriteLine("->Inserting new Car.")
  carArList.Insert(2, New Car("TheNewCar", 0, 12))
  Console.WriteLine("Items in carArList: {0}", carArList.Count)
```

```
    ' Get the subobjects as an array.
    Dim arrayOfCars As Object() = carArList.ToArray()
    Dim i As Integer = 0

    ' Now iterate over array using While loop/Length property.
    While i < arrayOfCars.Length
      Console.WriteLine("Car pet name: {0}", CType(arrayOfCars(i), Car).Name)
      i = i + 1
    End While
  End Sub
```

Here you are making use of the AddRange() method to populate your ArrayList with a set of Car objects (as you can tell, this is basically a shorthand notation for calling Add() *n* number of times). Once you print out the number of items in the collection (as well as enumerate over each item to obtain the pet name), you invoke Insert(), which allows you to plug a new item into the ArrayList at a specified index. Finally, notice the call to the ToArray() method, which returns an array of type System.Object based on the contents of the original ArrayList.

Working with the Queue Type

Queues are containers that ensure items are accessed using a first-in, first-out manner. Sadly, we humans are subject to queues all day long: lines at the bank, lines at the movie theater, and lines at the morning coffeehouse. When you are modeling a scenario in which items are handled on a first-come, first-served basis, System.Collections.Queue is your type of choice. In addition to the functionality provided by the supported interfaces, Queue defines the key members shown in Table 10-3.

Table 10-3. *Select Members of the* Queue *Type*

Member	Meaning in Life
Dequeue()	Removes and returns the object at the beginning of the Queue
Enqueue()	Adds an object to the end of the Queue
Peek()	Returns the object at the beginning of the Queue without removing it

To illustrate these methods, we will leverage our automobile theme once again and build a Queue object that simulates a line of cars waiting to enter a car wash. First, assume the following shared helper method to your module type:

```
Public Sub WashCar(ByVal c As Car)
  Console.WriteLine("Cleaning {0}", c.Name)
End Sub
```

Now, consider the addition method, which calls WashCar():

```
Sub QueueTest()
  ' Make a Q with three items.
  Dim carWashQ As New Queue()
  carWashQ.Enqueue(New Car("FirstCar", 0, 1))
  carWashQ.Enqueue(New Car("SecondCar", 0, 2))
  carWashQ.Enqueue(New Car("ThirdCar", 0, 3))

  ' Peek at first car in Q.
  Console.WriteLine("First in Q is {0}", _
    CType(carWashQ.Peek(), Car).Name)
```

```
  ' Remove each item from Q.
  WashCar(CType(carWashQ.Dequeue(), Car))
  WashCar(CType(carWashQ.Dequeue(), Car))
  WashCar(CType(carWashQ.Dequeue(), Car))

  ' Try to de-Q again?
  Try
    WashCar(CType(carWashQ.Dequeue(), Car))
  Catch ex As Exception
    Console.WriteLine("Error!! {0}", ex.Message)
  End Try
End Sub
```

Here, you insert three items into the Queue object via its Enqueue() method. The call to Peek() allows you to view (but not remove) the first item currently in the Queue, which in this case is the car named FirstCar. Finally, the call to Dequeue() removes the item from the line and sends it into the WashCar() helper method for processing. Do note that if you attempt to remove items from an empty queue, a runtime exception is thrown.

Working with the Stack Type

The System.Collections.Stack type represents a collection that maintains items using a last-in, first-out manner. As you would expect, Stack defines members named Push() and Pop() (to place items onto or remove items from the stack). The following StackTest() method creates a Stack object containing a handful of String objects:

```
Sub StackTest()
  Dim stringStack As New Stack()
  stringStack.Push("One")
  stringStack.Push("Two")
  stringStack.Push("Three")

  ' Now look at the top item, pop it, and look again.
  Console.WriteLine("Top item is: {0}", stringStack.Peek())
  Console.WriteLine("Popped off {0}", stringStack.Pop())
  Console.WriteLine("Top item is: {0}", stringStack.Peek())
  Console.WriteLine("Popped off {0}", stringStack.Pop())
  Console.WriteLine("Top item is: {0}", stringStack.Peek())
  Console.WriteLine("Popped off {0}", stringStack.Pop())

  Try
    Console.WriteLine("Top item is: {0}", stringStack.Peek())
    Console.WriteLine("Popped off {0}", stringStack.Pop())
  Catch ex As Exception
    Console.WriteLine("Error!! {0}", ex.Message)
  End Try
End Sub
```

Here, you build a Stack that contains three String objects, named according to their order of insertion. As you peek into the stack, you will always see the item at the very top, and therefore the first call to Peek() reveals the third string. After a series of Pop() and Peek() calls, the stack is eventually empty, at which time additional Peek()/Pop() calls raise a system exception.

■ **Source Code** The CollectionTypes project can be found under the Chapter 10 subdirectory.

System.Collections.Specialized Namespace

In addition to the types defined within the `System.Collections` namespace, you should also be aware that the `System.dll` assembly provides the `System.Collections.Specialized` namespace, which defines another set of types that are more (pardon the redundancy) specialized. For example, the `StringDictionary` and `ListDictionary` types each provide a stylized implementation of the `IDictionary` interface. Table 10-4 documents the key class types.

Table 10-4. *Types of the* `System.Collections.Specialized` *Namespace*

Member	Meaning in Life
`BitVector32`	Represents a simple structure that stores `Boolean` values and small integers in 32 bits of memory.
`CollectionsUtil`	Creates collections that ignore the case in strings.
`HybridDictionary`	Implements `IDictionary` by using a `ListDictionary` while the collection is small, and then switching to a `Hashtable` when the collection gets large.
`ListDictionary`	Implements `IDictionary` using a singly linked list. Recommended for collections that typically contain ten items or fewer.
`NameValueCollection`	Represents a sorted collection of associated `String` keys and `String` values that can be accessed either with the key or with the index.
`StringCollection`	Represents a collection of `Strings`.
`StringDictionary`	Implements a hash table with the keys and values strongly typed to be `Strings` rather than `Objects`.
`StringEnumerator`	Supports a simple iteration over a `StringCollection`.

So, at this point in the chapter you have seen how to make use of various collection classes using the `System.Collections`/`System.Collections.Specialized` namespaces. Now, here is the rub: .NET applications built using .NET 2.0 or higher typically should never make use of them.

Again, while it is important to understand the use of these legacy containers for maintaining existing code, new .NET applications should prefer the use of *generic collections*. To understand why this is the case, we need to investigate the limitations of the nongeneric collection classes, beginning with the topic of boxing and unboxing.

Understanding Boxing and Unboxing Operations

The .NET platform defines two major categories that a data type could belong to, specifically *value types* and *reference types*. Value types were briefly mentioned in Chapter 4, during our examination of the VB `Structure` type. Specifically speaking, structures (and enumerations) are termed value types, and are automatically allocated into a region of memory named the *stack*. Stack-based data is not monitored by the .NET garbage collector (see Chapter 8) and has a very predictable lifetime, lasting as long as the defining scope:

```
Public Sub SomeFunction()
  ' Assume we have a structure named MyStruct.
  Dim s As New MyStruct()
End Sub  ' s is destroyed once this method returns.
```

In contrast, a reference type (which would be any class or delegate) is allocated on a region of memory named the *managed heap*, which as you learned in Chapter 8 is maintained by the CLR garbage collector. When you create an instance of a reference type, you cannot know for sure when the object will be destroyed:

```
Public Sub SomeFunction()
  ' Assume we have a Class named MyCustomClass.
  Dim c As New MyCustomClass()
End Sub  ' c will be garbage collected at some time in the future.
```

■ **Note** Chapter 12 will dive deeper into the differences between value types and reference types. For the purpose of this chapter, simply understand that value types are allocated on the stack, while reference types are allocated on the managed heap.

Now, given the fact that the .NET platform supports two broad categories of data types, you may occasionally need to represent a variable of one category as a variable of the other category. The .NET platform provides a very simple mechanism, known as *boxing*, to convert a value type to a reference type. Assume that you have created a variable of type `Short` (which is in fact a structure of type `System.Int16`):

```
' Make a short value type.
Dim s As Short = 25
```

If, during the course of your application, you wish to represent this value type as a reference type, you would box the value as follows:

```
' Box the value into an object reference.
Dim objShort As Object = s
```

Boxing can be formally defined as the process of assigning a value type to a `System.Object` variable. When you do so, the CLR allocates a new object on the heap and copies the value type's value (in this case `25`) into that instance. What is returned to you is a reference to the newly allocated object. Using this technique, .NET developers have no need to make use of a set of wrapper classes used to temporarily treat stack data as heap-allocated objects.

The opposite operation is also permitted through *unboxing*. Unboxing is the process of converting the value held in the object back into a corresponding value type on the stack. The unboxing operation begins by verifying that the receiving data type is equivalent to the boxed type, and if so, it copies the value back into a local stack-based variable. For example, the following unboxing operation works successfully, given that the underlying type of the `objShort` is indeed a `Short`:

```
' Unbox the reference back into a corresponding short.
Dim anotherShort As Short = CType(objShort, Short)
```

■ **Note** If you do not have `Option Strict` enabled, you are not required to explicitly cast via `CType()` to perform an unboxing operation. However, given that enabling `Option Strict` is always a good idea, use of `CType()` is necessary.

Some Practical (Un)Boxing Examples

So, you may be wondering when you would really need to manually box (or unbox) a data type. The previous examples were purely illustrative in nature, as there was no good reason to box (and then unbox) the `Short` variable. The truth of the matter is that you will seldom—if ever—need to manually box data types. Much of the time, the VB compiler automatically boxes variables when appropriate. For example, if you pass a value type into a method requiring an `Object` parameter, boxing occurs behind the curtains. Consider the following Console Application project named Boxing:

```
Module Program
  Sub Main()
    ' Make a value type.
    Dim s As Short = 25

    ' Because "s" is passed into a
    ' method prototyped to take an Object,
    ' it is boxed automatically.
    UseThisObject(s)
    Console.ReadLine()
  End Sub

  Sub UseThisObject(ByVal o As Object)
    Console.WriteLine("Value of o is: {0}", o)
  End Sub
End Module
```

Automatic boxing also occurs when working with the types of the .NET base class libraries. For example, recall that the `System.Collections` namespace defines a class type named `ArrayList`. Like most collection types, `ArrayList` provides members that allow you to insert, obtain, and remove items. Consider the following member prototypes:

```
Public Class ArrayList
  Implements IList, ICollection, IEnumerable, ICloneable
...
  Public Overrideable Function Add(ByVal value As Object) As Integer
  Public Overrideable Sub Insert(ByVal index As Integer, ByVal value As Object)
  Public Overrideable Sub Remove(ByVal value As Object)
End Class
```

As you can see, these members operate on generic `System.Object` types. Given that everything ultimately derives from this common base class, the following code is perfectly legal:

```
Sub Main()
...
  Dim myData As New ArrayList()
  myData.Add(88)
  myData.Add(3.33)
  myData.Add(False)
  Console.ReadLine()
End Sub
```

However, given your understanding of value types and reference types, you might wonder exactly what was placed into the `ArrayList` type. (References? Copies of references? Copies of structures?) Just like with the previous `UseThisObject()` method, it should be clear that each of these value types were indeed boxed before being placed into the `ArrayList` type. To retrieve an item from the `ArrayList` type, you are required to unbox accordingly:

```
Sub Main()
...
  Dim myData As New ArrayList()
  myData.Add(88)
  myData.Add(3.33)
  myData.Add(False)
```

```
    ' Unbox first item from ArrayList.
    Dim firstItem As Integer = CType(myData(0), Integer)
    Console.WriteLine("First item is {0}", firstItem)
    Console.ReadLine()
End Sub
```

Unboxing Custom Value Types

When you pass custom structures or enumerations into a method prototyped to take a `System.Object`, a boxing operation also occurs. However, once the incoming parameter has been received by the called method, you will not be able to access any members of the structure (or enum) until you unbox the type. Assume you've defined the following simple `MyPoint` structure:

```
' Structures are value types!
Structure MyPoint
  Public x, y As Integer
End Structure
```

Now say you want to send a `MyPoint` variable into a new method named `UseBoxedMyPoint()`:

```
Sub Main()
...
  Dim p As MyPoint
  p.x = 10
  p.y = 20
  UseBoxedMyPoint(p)
  Console.ReadLine()
End Sub
```

If you attempt to access the field data of `MyPoint`, you will receive a compiler error (assuming `Option Strict` is enabled), as the method assumes you are operating on a strongly typed `System.Object`:

```
Sub UseBoxedMyPoint(ByVal o As Object)
  ' Error! System.Object does not have
  ' member variables named "x" or "y".
  Console.WriteLine("{0}, {1}", o.x, o.y)
End Sub
```

To access the field data of `MyPoint`, you must first unbox the parameter:

```
Sub UseBoxedMyPoint(ByVal o As Object)
  If TypeOf o Is MyPoint Then
    Dim p As MyPoint = CType(o, MyPoint)
    Console.WriteLine("{0}, {1}", p.x, p.y)
  End If
End Sub
```

Source Code The Boxing project is included under the Chapter 10 subdirectory.

The Problem with (Un)Boxing Operations

Although boxing and unboxing are very convenient from a programmer's point of view, this approach to stack/heap memory transfer comes with the baggage of performance issues.

To understand the performance issues, consider the steps that must occur to box and unbox a simple Integer:

1. A new Object must be allocated on the managed heap.
2. The value of the stack-based data must be transferred into that memory location.
3. When unboxed, the value stored on the heap-based object must be transferred back to the stack using an explicit cast (via CType).
4. The now unused Object on the heap will (eventually) be garbage collected.

Although occasional boxing or unboxing operations won't cause a major bottleneck in terms of performance, you could certainly feel the impact if an ArrayList contained thousands of Integers (or any structure for that matter) that are manipulated by your program on a somewhat regular basis. This would result in numerous objects on the heap that must be managed by the garbage collector, which can be yet another possible performance penalty.

In an ideal world, the VB compiler would be able to store sets of value types in a container that did not require boxing in the first place. If this were the case, we not only gain a higher degree of type safety (as this would remove the need for explicit casting), but also build more performance-driven code. As you would guess, .NET generics are the solution to each of these issues.

Type Safety and Strongly Typed Collections

Another issue we have in a generic-less world has to do with the construction of strongly typed collections. Again, recall that a majority of the class types within the System.Collections namespace have been constructed to contain System.Object types, which resolves to anything at all. In some cases, this is the exact behavior you require given the extreme flexibility:

```
Sub Main()
  ' The ArrayList can hold any item whatsoever.
  Dim myStuff As New ArrayList()
  myStuff.Add(10)
  myStuff.Add(New ArrayList())
  myStuff.Add(True)
  myStuff.Add("Some text data")
  Console.ReadLine()
End Sub
```

While this loose typing can be helpful in some circumstances, it's often advantageous to build a *strongly typed* collection. Prior to .NET version 2.0, this was most often achieved by leveraging the container classes of System.Collections to build a new class that only operates on a specific type of data. To illustrate, create a new Console Application project named StronglyTypedCollections. Now, assume you wish to create a custom collection that can only contain objects of type Person, defined as follows:

```
Public Class Person
  ' Made Public for simplicity.
  Public currAge As Integer
  Public fName As String
  Public lName As String

  ' Constructors.
  Public Sub New()
  End Sub
  Public Sub New(ByVal firstName As String, ByVal lastName As String, _
    ByVal age As Integer)
```

```
    currAge = age
    fName = firstName
    lName = lastName
  End Sub

  Public Overrides Function ToString() As String
    Return String.Format("{0}, {1} is {2} years old.", _
      lName, fName, currAge)
  End Function
End Class
```

To build a custom collection that can only hold Person objects, you could define a System.Collections.ArrayList member variable within a class named PeopleCollection and configure all members to operate on strongly typed Person objects, rather than on System.Objects. For example:

```
Public Class PeopleCollection
  Implements IEnumerable
  Private arPeople As New ArrayList()

  Public Function GetPerson(ByVal pos As Integer) As Person
    Return CType(arPeople(pos), Person)
  End Function

  Public Sub AddPerson(ByVal p As Person)
    arPeople.Add(p)
  End Sub

  Public Sub ClearPeople()
    arPeople.Clear()
  End Sub

  Public ReadOnly Property Count() As Integer
    Get
      Return arPeople.Count
    End Get
  End Property

  ' The "indexer" of this custom collection.
  Default Public Property Item(ByVal p As Integer) As Person
    Get
      Return CType(arPeople(p), Person)
    End Get
    Set(ByVal value As Person)
      arPeople.Insert(p, value)
    End Set
  End Property

  Public Function GetEnumerator() As IEnumerator _
    Implements IEnumerable.GetEnumerator
    Return arPeople.GetEnumerator()
  End Function
End Class
```

Notice that our PeopleCollection has implemented IEnumerable, so we can pluck out the subobjects using a For Each iteration construct (see Chapter 9). As well, notice that the members of PeopleCollection have been prototyped to receive and return Person objects. Last but not least, note that we have defined a property named Item, which has been marked with the Default keyword:

```
' The "indexer" of this custom collection.
Default Public Property Item(ByVal p As Integer) As Person
  Get
    Return CType(arPeople(p), Person)
  End Get
  Set(ByVal value As Person)
    arPeople.Insert(p, value)
  End Set
End Property
```

It is very common for custom collections (generic or nongeneric) to support a default property named Item. Formally speaking, these special methods are termed *type indexers* and are used to get and set subobjects using an arraylike syntax (shown in the following code example). In any case, with these types defined, you are now assured of type safety, given that the VB compiler will be able to determine any attempt to insert an object of an incompatible type:

```
Sub Main()
  Console.WriteLine("***** Strongly Typed Collections *****")
  Console.WriteLine()

  ' Add some people.
  Dim myPeople As New PeopleCollection()
  myPeople.AddPerson(New Person("Homer", "Simpson", 40))
  myPeople.AddPerson(New Person("Marge", "Simpson", 38))
  myPeople.AddPerson(New Person("Lisa", "Simpson", 9))
  myPeople.AddPerson(New Person("Bart", "Simpson", 7))
  myPeople.AddPerson(New Person("Maggie", "Simpson", 2))

  ' This would be a compile-time error!
  ' myPeople.AddPerson(New Car())

  ' Get Person objects using For Each.
  For Each p As Person In myPeople
    Console.WriteLine(p)
  Next

  ' Get/Set new Person object using type indexer.
  myPeople(5) = New Person("Waylon", "Smithers", 47)
  Console.WriteLine("Person #5 is {0}", myPeople(5))

  Console.ReadLine()
End Sub
```

While custom collections do ensure type safety, this approach leaves you in a position where you must create a (almost identical) custom collection for each type you wish to contain. Thus, if you need a custom collection that will be able to operate only on Car-comparable objects, you need to build a very similar class, which typically only differs by the type of subobject they contain (People or Car objects in this example):

```
Public Class CarCollection
  Implements IEnumerable
  Private arCars As New ArrayList()

  Public Function GetCar(ByVal pos As Integer) As Car
    Return CType(arCars(pos), Car)
  End Function
```

```
  Public Sub AddCar(ByVal c As Car)
    arCars.Add(c)
  End Sub

  Public Sub ClearCars()
    arCars.Clear()
  End Sub

  Public ReadOnly Property Count() As Integer
    Get
      Return arCars.Count
    End Get
  End Property

  Public Function GetEnumerator() As IEnumerator _
    Implements IEnumerable.GetEnumerator
    Return arCars.GetEnumerator()
  End Function

  Default Public Property Item(ByVal c As Integer) As Car
    Get
      Return CType(arCars(c), Car)
    End Get
    Set(ByVal value As Car)
      arCars.Insert(c, value)
    End Set
  End Property
End Class
```

As you may know from firsthand experience, the process of creating multiple strongly typed collections to account for various types is not only labor intensive, but also a nightmare to maintain.

Generic collections allow us to delay the specification of the contained type until the time of creation. Don't fret about the syntactic details just yet, however. Consider the following code, which makes use of the generic `List(Of T)` class to create two type-safe container objects (be aware that `System.Collections.Generic` is imported automatically into all VB projects):

```
Module Program
  Sub Main()
    ' Use the generic List type to hold only people.
    Dim morePeople As New List(Of Person)
    morePeople.Add(New Person())

    ' Use the generic List type to hold only cars.
    Dim moreCars As New List(Of Car)
    moreCars.Add(New Car())

    ' Compile-time error! Can't add Person objects to List(Of Car)!
    moreCars.Add(New Person())
    Console.ReadLine()
  End Sub
End Module
```

Boxing Issues and Strongly Typed Collections

Strongly typed collections are found throughout the .NET base class libraries and are very useful programming constructs. However, these custom containers do little to solve the issue of boxing/unboxing penalties. Even if you were to create a custom collection named `IntegerCollection` that was constructed to operate only on `Integer` data types, you must allocate a reference type to hold the numerical data (`System.Array`, `System.Collections.ArrayList`, etc.). Again, given that the nongeneric types operate on `System.Objects`, we incur boxing and unboxing penalties:

```
Public Class IntegerCollection
  Implements IEnumerable
  Private arInts As New ArrayList()

  Public Function GetInt(ByVal pos As Integer) As Integer
    ' Unboxing!
    Return CType(arInts(pos), Integer)
  End Function

  Public Sub AddInt(ByVal i As Integer)
    ' Boxing!
    arInts.Add(i)
  End Sub
...
End Class
```

Regardless of which type you may choose to hold the integers (`System.Array`, `System.Collections.ArrayList`, etc.), you cannot escape the boxing dilemma using nongeneric types. As you might guess, generics come to the rescue again. The following code leverages the `List(Of T)` class to create a container of `Integers` that does *not* incur any boxing or unboxing penalties when inserting or obtaining the value type:

```
Module Program
  Sub Main()
    ' No boxing!
    Dim myInts As New List(Of Integer)
    myInts.Add(10)

    ' No unboxing!
    Console.WriteLine("Int value is: {0}", myInts(0))
  End Sub
End Module
```

To summarize the story thus far, generics address the following issues:

- Performance issues incurred with boxing and unboxing
- Type-safety issues found with loosely typed collections
- Code maintenance issues incurred with the construction of strongly typed collections

So now that you have a better feel for the problems generics attempt to solve, you're ready to dig into the details. To begin, allow me to formally introduce the `System.Collections.Generic` namespace.

■ **Source Code** The StronglyTypedCollections project is located under the Chapter 10 subdirectory.

The System.Collections.Generic Namespace

Generic types are found sprinkled throughout the .NET base class libraries; however, the `System.Collections.Generic` namespace is chock full of them (as its name implies). Like its nongeneric counterpart (`System.Collections`), the `System.Collections.Generic` namespace contains numerous class and interface types that allow you to contain subitems in a variety of containers. Not surprisingly, the generic interfaces mimic the corresponding nongeneric types in the `System.Collections` namespace:

- `ICollection(Of T)`
- `IComparer(Of T)`
- `IDictionary(Of K, V)`
- `IEnumerable(Of T)`
- `IEnumerator(Of T)`
- `IList(Of T)`

■ Note By convention, generic types specify their placeholders using uppercase letters. Although any letter (or word) will do, typically `T` is used to represent types, `K` (or `TKey`) is used for keys, and `V` (or `TValue`) is used for values.

The `System.Collections.Generic` namespace (in addition to the related `System.Collections.ObjectModel` namespace) also defines a number of classes that implement many of these key interfaces. Table 10-5 describes the core class types of this namespace and any corresponding type in the `System.Collections` namespace.

Table 10-5. *Classes of* `System.Collections.Generic/System.Collections.ObjectModel`

Generic Type	Nongeneric Counterpart Class in Generic Type System.Collections	Meaning in Life
`Collection(Of T)`	`CollectionBase`	The basis for a generic collection
`Comparer(Of T)`	`Comparer`	Type that compares two generic objects for equality
`Dictionary(Of K, V)`	`Hashtable`	A generic collection of name/value pairs
`List(Of T)`	`ArrayList`	A dynamically resizable list of items
`Queue(Of T)`	`Queue`	A generic implementation of a FIFO list
`SortedDictionary(Of K, V)`	`SortedList`	A generic implementation of a sorted set of name/value pairs
`Stack(Of T)`	`Stack`	A generic implementation of a LIFO list
`LinkedList(Of T)`	N/A	A generic implementation of a doubly linked list
`ReadOnlyCollection(Of T)`	`ReadOnlyCollectionBase`	A generic implementation of a set of read-only items

The `System.Collections.Generic` namespace also defines a number of "helper" classes and structures that work in conjunction with a specific container. For example, the `LinkedListNode(Of T)` type represents a node within a generic `LinkedList(Of T)`, the `KeyNotFoundException` exception is raised when attempting to grab an item from a container using a nonexistent key, and so forth.

Rather than examining how to use every member shown in Table 10-5, I'll focus on the use of the `List(Of T)` class to illustrate the process of working with generics. If you require details regarding other members of the `System.Collections.Generic` namespace, consult the .NET Framework 3.5 SDK documentation.

Examining the List(Of T) Type

Like nongeneric types, generic types are created via the `New` keyword and any necessary constructor arguments. In addition, you are required to specify the type(s) to be substituted for the type parameter(s) defined by the generic type. For example, `System.Collections.Generic.List(Of T)` requires you to specify a single type parameter that describes the type of item the `List(Of T)` will operate upon. Therefore, if you wish to create three `List(Of T)` objects to contain integers and `Person` and `Car` objects, you would make use of the VB `Of` keyword as follows:

```
Module Program
  Sub Main()
    ' A list of Integers.
    Dim myInts As New List(Of Integer)

    ' A list of Person objects.
    Dim myPeople As New List(Of Person)

    ' A list of Cars.
    Dim myCars As New List(Of Car)
  End Sub
End Module
```

At this point, you might wonder what exactly becomes of the specified placeholder value. If you were to make use of the Visual Studio 2008 Object Browser, you would find that the placeholder `T` is used throughout the definition of the `List(Of T)` type, as you see in Figure 10-2.

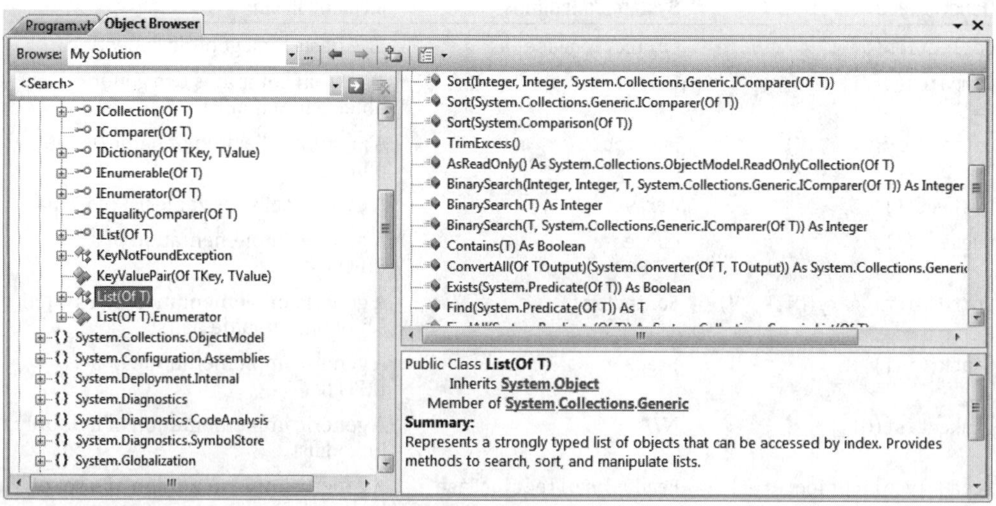

Figure 10-2. *A generic type parameter is used as a placeholder throughout a type definition.*

Thus, when you create a List(Of T) specifying Car types, Car is substituted for T throughout the List type. Likewise, if you were to build a List(Of T) of type Integers, T is of type Integer. Of course, when you create a generic List(Of T), the compiler does not literally create a brand-new implementation of the List(Of T) type. Rather, it will address only the members of the generic type you actually invoke. For example, if you were to author the following Main() method, which invokes the Add() and Count members of the List(Of T) type:

```
Module Program
  Sub Main()
    ' A list of Cars.
    Dim myCars As New List(Of Car)
    myCars.Add(New Car())
    Console.WriteLine("myCars contains {0} items", _
      myCars.Count)
    Console.ReadLine()
  End Sub
End Module
```

you would find the VB compiler generates the following (slightly edited and annotated) CIL code (which can be verified using ildasm.exe):

```
.method public static void  Main() cil managed
{
...
  // Create the List(Of T) type where "T" is of type Car.
  .locals init ([0]  class
   [mscorlib]System.Collections.Generic.List`1
  <class SimpleGenerics.Car> myCars)
  IL_0001:  newobj instance void class
   [mscorlib]System.Collections.Generic.List`1
  <class SimpleGenerics.Car>::.ctor()
...
  // Create a Car and add it into the List of
  // Cars via the Add() method.
  IL_0008:  newobj     instance void SimpleGenerics.Car::.ctor()
  IL_000d:  callvirt   instance void class
   [mscorlib]System.Collections.Generic.List`1
  <class SimpleGenerics.Car>::Add(!0)
...
  // Call the ReadOnly Count property.
  IL_0019: callvirt instance int32 class
  [mscorlib]System.Collections.Generic.List`1
  <class SimpleGenerics.Car>::get_Count()
...
}
```

Notice that in terms of CIL code, a type parameter is specified using angled brackets. Thus, the Visual Basic List(Of T) syntax translates into List`1<T> in terms of CIL. Also notice the type parameters of the List(Of T) constructor, Add() method, and Count property have all been set to be of type Car.

Now assume you have created a List(Of T) object where you specify T to be of type Integer:

```
Module Program
  Sub Main()
...
    ' A list of Integers.
    Dim myInts As New List(Of Integer)
```

```
    ' No boxing!
    myInts.Add(50)

    ' No unboxing!
    Dim val As Integer = myInts.Count
    Console.WriteLine("myInts contains {0} items", myInts.Count)
    Console.ReadLine()
  End Sub
End Module
```

This time, the compiler generates CIL code wherein each occurrence of T is now of type int32 (the internal representation of the VB Integer type):

```
.method public static void  Main() cil managed
{
...
  // Make a List of Integers.
  .locals init ([0] class  [mscorlib]
  System.Collections.Generic.List`1<int32> MyInts)
  IL_0001:  newobj  instance void class
  [mscorlib]System.Collections.Generic.List`1<int32>::.ctor()

  // Add the value "50" to the List.
  IL_0008:  ldc.i4.s   50
  IL_000a:  callvirt   instance void class
  [mscorlib]System.Collections.Generic.List`1<int32>::Add(!0)
...
  // Call the ReadOnly Count property.
  IL_0016:  callvirt  instance int32 class
  [mscorlib]System.Collections.Generic.List`1<int32>::get_Count()
...
}
```

The most telling aspect of this CIL code snippet is the fact that we have not incurred any boxing or unboxing penalties when inserting or obtaining the numerical data from the List(Of T) type! This is in stark contrast to inserting numerical data (or any structure) within the nongeneric System.Collections.ArrayList.

■ **Source Code** The SimpleGenerics project is located under the Chapter 10 subdirectory.

So, at this point you've looked at the process of working with the generic List(Of T) type. Again, do understand that the remaining types of System.Collections.Generic would be manipulated in a similar manner. Next up, let's turn our attention to the use of another useful generic type named Nullable(Of T), which is a member of the System namespace.

Understanding Nullable Data Types and the System.Nullable(Of T) Generic Type

Another very interesting generic class is System.Nullable(Of T), which allows you to define *nullable data types*. As you know, CLR data types have a fixed range of possible values. For example, the System.Boolean data type can be assigned a value from the set {True, False}. However, since the release of .NET 2.0, it became possible to create nullable data types. Simply put, a nullable type can represent all the values of its underlying type, plus an empty (aka *undefined*) value. Thus, if we declare a nullable Boolean, it could be assigned a value from the set {True, False, Nothing}.

To define a nullable variable type, simply create a new Nullable(Of T) object and specify the type parameter. Be aware, however, that the specified type must be a *value type*! If you attempt to create a nullable reference type (including Strings, which as you recall are classes and therefore belong to the reference type category), you are issued a compile-time error. For example:

```
Sub Main()
  ' Define some local nullable types.
  Dim nullableInt As New Nullable(Of Integer)()
  Dim nullableDouble As New Nullable(Of Double)()
  Dim nullableBool As New Nullable(Of Boolean)()

  ' Error! Strings are reference types!
  Dim s As New Nullable(Of String)()
End Sub
```

Like any type, System.Nullable(Of T) provides a set of members that all nullable types can make use of. For example, you are able to programmatically discover whether the nullable variable indeed has been assigned an undefined Nothing value using the HasValue property. The assigned value of a nullable object may be obtained via the Value property.

Working with Nullable Types

Nullable data types can be particularly useful when you are interacting with databases, given that columns in a database table may be intentionally empty (e.g., undefined). To illustrate, assume the following class (defined in a new Console Application project named NullableData) that simulates the process of accessing a database containing a table of two columns that may be undefined. Note that the GetIntFromDatabase() method is returning the value of Nothing via the nullable Integer member variable, while GetBoolFromDatabase() is returning the value True via the nullable Boolean member:

```
Class DatabaseReader
  ' Nullable data fields.
  Public numericValue As Nullable(Of Integer) = Nothing
  Public boolValue As Nullable(Of Boolean) = True

  ' Note the nullable return type.
  Public Function GetIntFromDatabase() As Nullable(Of Integer)
    Return numericValue
  End Function

  ' Note the nullable return type.
  Public Function GetBoolFromDatabase() As Nullable(Of Boolean)
    Return boolValue
  End Function
End Class
```

Now, assume the following Main() method, which invokes each member of the DatabaseReader class, and discovers the assigned values using the HasValue and Value members:

```
Module Program
  Sub Main()
    Console.WriteLine("***** Fun with Nullable Data *****" & vbLf)

    Dim dr As New DatabaseReader()
```

```
    ' Get integer from "database".
    Dim i As Nullable(Of Integer) = dr.GetIntFromDatabase()
    If (i.HasValue) Then
      Console.WriteLine("Value of 'i' is: {0}", i.Value)
    Else
      Console.WriteLine("Value of 'i' is undefined.")
    End If

    ' Get boolean from "database".
    Dim b As Nullable(Of Boolean) = dr.GetBoolFromDatabase()
    If (b.HasValue) Then
      Console.WriteLine("Value of 'b' is: {0}", b.Value)
    Else
      Console.WriteLine("Value of 'b' is undefined.")
    End If
    Console.ReadLine()
  End Sub
End Module
```

The Visual Basic 2008 Nullable Operator (?)

The current version of VB shipping with .NET 3.5 provides a specific operator that simplifies the construction of nullable data types. Rather than manually creating a new `System.Nullable(Of T)` variable in your code, you can do so indirectly using the new ? operator. When processed by the compiler, the ? operator is translated into a `Nullable(Of T)` in terms of CIL code. Given this point, using ? is always optional, as you could use the `Nullable(Of T)` type. However, it is a great shorthand notation. Consider the following reworking of the previous `DatabaseReader` class:

```
Class DatabaseReader
  ' Note the use of the ? operator in the class
  ' definition.
  Public numericValue As Integer?
  Public boolValue As Boolean? = True

  ' Note the nullable operator.
  Public Function GetIntFromDatabase() As Integer?
    Return numericValue
  End Function

  ' Note the nullable operator.
  Public Function GetBoolFromDatabase() As Boolean?
    Return boolValue
  End Function
End Class
```

We could also update the previous logic in `Main()` to use the nullable operator as shown in the following code snippet. Notice that you are still able to access all of the members of `System.Nullable(Of T)`, as `Integer?` is just a simplified way of defining a `Nullable(Of Integer)` variable:

```
Sub Main()
...
  Dim i As Integer? = dr.GetIntFromDatabase()
...
  Dim b As Boolean? = dr.GetBoolFromDatabase()
...
End Sub
```

Cool! At this point, you hopefully understand how to interact with generic types that lurk within the .NET base class libraries. During the remainder of this chapter, you'll examine how to create your own generic methods, types, and collections (and why you might want to do so). First up, let's check out how to build a custom generic method.

Source Code The NullableData project is located under the Chapter 10 subdirectory.

Creating Generic Methods

As you learned back in Chapter 4, methods can be `overloaded`. Recall that this language feature allows you to define multiple versions of the same method, provided each variation differs by the number (or type) of parameters. For example, assume you wish to build a method that can swap two `Integer`s. To do so, simply pass in each argument by reference and flip the values around with the help of a local `Integer` variable:

```
Module NonGenericMethods
  Public Function Swap(ByRef a As Integer, _
    ByRef b As Integer) As Integer
    Dim temp As Integer
    temp = a
    a = b
    b = temp
  End Function
End Module
```

With this, we could now call our `Swap()` method like so:

```
Module Program
  Sub Main()
    ' Call the nongeneric Swap() methods.
    Dim a, b As Integer
    a = 10
    b = 40
    Console.WriteLine("Before swap: a={0}, b={1}", a, b)
    Swap(a, b)
    Console.WriteLine("After swap: a={0}, b={1}", a, b)
    Console.ReadLine()
  End Sub
End Module
```

Although this `Swap()` method works as expected, assume you now wish to build a method that can swap two `Double`s. This would require you to build a second version of `Swap()` that now operates on floating-point data:

```
Public Function Swap(ByRef a As Double, _
  ByRef b As Double) As Double
  Dim temp As Double
  temp = a
  a = b
  b = temp
End Function
```

As you would expect, if you require other swap routines to operate on `String`s, `Boolean`s, `SportsCar`s, and whatnot, you would need to build new versions of the `Swap()` function. Clearly, this would be a pain to maintain over the long run, not to mention the fact that each version of Swap() is doing more or less the same thing.

Before the use of generics, one way to avoid this redundancy was to create a single Swap() method that operates on Object data types. Because everything in .NET can be represented as a System.Object, this approach would allow us to have a single version of Swap(); however, we are once again incurring boxing and unboxing penalties when operating on value types (in addition to a lack of type safety, etc.).

To simplify our coding (and avoid undesirable boxing/unboxing operations), we could author a generic Swap() method. Consider the following generic Swap() method (which I'll assume you defined within your initial module) that can swap any two data types of type T (remember, the name you give to a type parameter is entirely up to you):

```
' This generic method can swap any two items of type "T".
Public Function Swap(Of T)(ByRef a As T, ByRef b As T) As T
  Console.WriteLine("T is a {0}.", GetType(T))
  Dim temp As T
  temp = a
  a = b
  b = temp
End Function
```

Notice how a generic method is defined by specifying the type parameter after the method name but before the parameter list. Here, you're stating that the Swap() method can operate on any two parameters of type T. Just to spice things up a bit, you're printing out the type name of the supplied placeholder to the console using the VB GetType() operator. Now ponder the following Main() method, which swaps Integers and Strings:

```
Sub Main()
  Console.WriteLine("***** Fun with Generic Methods *****" & vbLf)

  ' Swap two Integers.
  Dim a, b As Integer
  a = 10 : b = 40

  Console.WriteLine("Before swap: a={0}, b={1}", a, b)
  Swap(Of Integer)(a, b)
  Console.WriteLine("After swap: a={0}, b={1}", a, b)
  Console.WriteLine()

  ' Swap two Strings.
  Dim s1, s2 As String
  s1 = "Generics" : s2 = "Rock"

  Console.WriteLine("Before swap: s1={0}, s2={1}", s1, s2)
  Swap(Of String)(s1, s2)
  Console.WriteLine("After swap: s1={0}, s2={1}", s1, s2)
  Console.ReadLine()
End Sub
```

The output of this program can be seen in Figure 10-3.

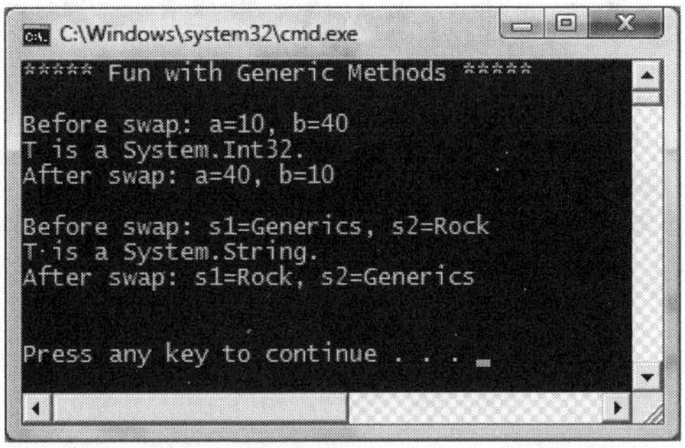

Figure 10-3. *Our generic swap method in action*

Omission of Type Parameters

When you invoke generic methods such as Swap(Of T), you can optionally omit the type parameter if (and only if) the generic method requires arguments, as the compiler can infer the type parameter based on the member parameters. For example, you could swap two System.Boolean instances as follows:

```
' Compiler will infer System.Boolean.
Dim b1, b2 As Boolean
b1 = True
b2 = False
Console.WriteLine("Before swap: b1={0}, b2={1}", b1, b2)
Swap(b1, b2)
Console.WriteLine("After swap: b1={0}, b2={1}", b1, b2)
```

However, if you have another generic method named DisplayBaseClass(Of T) that does not take any incoming parameters, as follows:

```
Sub DisplayBaseClass(Of T)()
  Console.WriteLine("Base class of {0} is: {1}.", _
    GetType(T), GetType(T).BaseType)
End Sub
```

you are required to supply the type parameter upon invocation:

```
Sub Main()
...
  ' Must specify "T" when a generic
  ' method takes no parameters.
  DisplayBaseClass(Of Boolean)()
  DisplayBaseClass(Of String)()
  DisplayBaseClass(Of Integer)()
End Sub
```

■ **Source Code** The GenericSwapMethod project is located under the Chapter 10 subdirectory.

Creating Generic Structures (or Classes)

Now that you understand how to define and invoke generic methods, let's turn our attention to the construction of a generic structure (the process of building a generic class is identical). Assume you have built a flexible Point structure that supports a single type parameter representing the underlying storage for the (*x*, *y*) coordinates. The caller would then be able to create Point(Of T) types as follows:

```
' Point using Integer.
Dim intPt As New Point(Of Integer)(100, 100)

' Point using Double.
Dim dblPt As New Point(Of Double)(5.6, 3.23)
```

Here is the complete definition of Point(Of T), with analysis to follow:

```
Public Structure Point(Of T)
  Private xPos, yPos As T

  Public Sub New(ByVal x As T, ByVal y As T)
    xPos = x : yPos = y
  End Sub

  Public Property X() As T
    Get
      Return xPos
    End Get
    Set(ByVal value As T)
      xPos = value
    End Set
  End Property
  Public Property Y() As T
    Get
      Return xPos
    End Get
    Set(ByVal value As T)
      yPos = value
    End Set
  End Property

  Public Overrides Function ToString() As String
    Return String.Format("({0}, {1})", xPos, yPos)
  End Function
End Structure
```

Notice that our Point structure has been defined to operate internally with type T, just like the previous generic Swap() method. Given that the caller must specify T at the time of creating a Point object, we are free to use T throughout the definition, as we have here for field data, property definitions, and member arguments.

Assuming this new example has implemented the Swap(Of T) method from the previous example, we can now create, manipulate, and swap instances of the Point(Of T) type like so:

```
Sub Main()
  Console.WriteLine("***** Fun with Custom Generic Types *****")
  Console.WriteLine()

  ' Make a Point using Integers.
  Dim intPt As New Point(Of Integer)(100, 100)
```

```
    Console.WriteLine("intPt.ToString()={0}", intPt.ToString())
    Console.WriteLine()

    ' Point using Double.
    Dim dblPt As New Point(Of Double)(5.6, 3.23)
    Console.WriteLine("dblPt.ToString()={0}", dblPt.ToString())
    Console.WriteLine()

    ' Swap two Points.
    Dim p1 As New Point(Of Integer)(10, 43)
    Dim p2 As New Point(Of Integer)(6, 987)
    Console.WriteLine("Before swap: {0} , {1}", p1, p2)

    ' Here we are swapping two points of type Integer.
    Swap(Of Point(Of Integer))(p1, p2)
    Console.WriteLine("After swap: {0} , {1}", p1, p2)
    Console.ReadLine()
  End Sub
```

Notice when we swap our two `Point` types, we are explicitly specifying the type parameters for the `Point`'s `T` as well as the `Swap()` method's `T`. While this approach makes our code very explicit, type inference allows us to simply call `Swap()` as follows:

```
' The compiler is able to infer we are using Points
' of type Integer.
Swap(p1, p2)
```

In either case, Figure 10-4 shows the output.

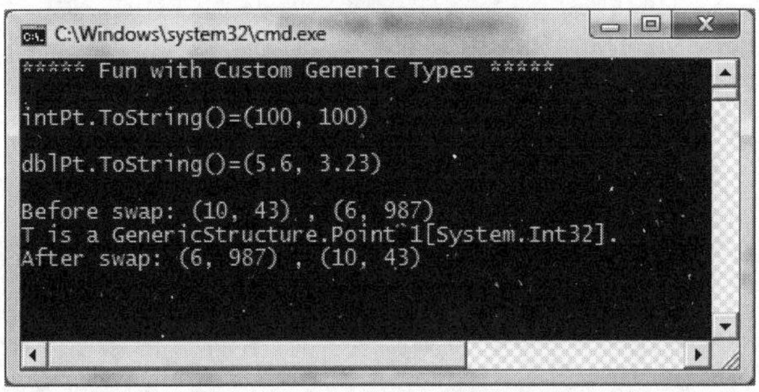

Figure 10-4. *Working with our generic structure*

Source Code The GenericStructure project is located under the Chapter 10 subdirectory.

Creating a Custom Generic Collection

As you have seen, the `System.Collections.Generic` namespace provides numerous types that allow you to create type-safe and efficient containers. Given the set of available choices, the chances are quite good that you will *not* need to build custom generic collection types. Nevertheless, to illustrate how you could build a stylized generic container, the next task is to build a generic collection class named `CarCollection(Of T)`, and then examine what (if any) benefits we have gained.

Like the nongeneric CarCollection created earlier in this chapter, this iteration will leverage an existing collection type to hold the subitems (a List(Of T) in this case). As well, you will support For Each iteration by implementing the generic IEnumerable(Of T) interface. Do note that IEnumerable(Of T) extends the nongeneric IEnumerable interface; therefore, the compiler expects you to implement *two* versions of the GetEnumerator() method. Here is the definition of our type:

```
Public Class CarCollection(Of T)
  Implements IEnumerable(Of T)

  Private myCars As New List(Of T)

  ' Generic default property.
  Default Public Property Item(ByVal index As Integer) As T
    Get
      Return myCars(index)
    End Get
    Set(ByVal value As T)
      myCars.Add(value)
    End Set
  End Property

  Public Sub ClearCars()
    myCars.Clear()
  End Sub

  Public Function CarCount() As Integer
    Return myCars.Count()
  End Function

  Public Function GetEnumeratorGeneric() As IEnumerator(Of T) _
    Implements IEnumerable(Of T).GetEnumerator
    Return myCars.GetEnumerator()
  End Function

  Public Function GetEnumerator() As IEnumerator _
    Implements IEnumerable.GetEnumerator
    Return myCars.GetEnumerator()
  End Function
End Class
```

You could now make use of CarCollection(Of T) as follows:

```
Module Program
  Sub Main()
    Console.WriteLine("***** Custom Generic Collection *****")
    Console.WriteLine()

    ' Make a collection of Cars.
    Dim myCars As New CarCollection(Of Car)()
    myCars(0) = New Car("Rusty", 20)
    myCars(1) = New Car("Zippy", 90)

    For Each c As Car In myCars
      Console.WriteLine("PetName: {0}, Speed: {1}", _
      c.PetName, c.Speed)
    Next
    Console.ReadLine()
```

```
  End Sub
End Module
```

Here you are creating a CarCollection(Of T) type that contains only Car types. Again, you could achieve a similar end result if you make use of the List(Of T) type directly. The only real benefit at this point is the fact that you are free to define uniquely named methods to the CarCollection that delegate the request to the internal List(Of T). For example, notice that we have defined two members that clearly express we are operating on the Car type (ClearCars() and CarCount()).

While this benefit may be quite negligible, another possible benefit of building a custom generic container is that you gain the ability to author custom code statements that should execute during the scope of your methods. For example, the Add() method of List(Of T) simply inserts the new item into the internally maintained list. However, if you needed to ensure that when a type was added to the List(of T) you wrote data out to an event log, fired out a custom event, or what have you, a custom container is the most straightforward way to do so.

Just How Useful Are Custom Generic Collection Classes?

Currently, the CarCollection(Of T) class does not buy you much beyond uniquely named public methods. Furthermore, given that T (or any type parameter) by default can be used to specify anything at all, a user could create an instance of CarCollection(Of T) and specify a completely unrelated type parameter, such as an Integer:

```
' Huh? This is syntactically correct, but confusing at best!
Dim myInts As New CarCollection(Of Integer)()
myInts(0) = 4
myInts(1) = 44
```

Given that generic types can hold any sort of data, you are correct to wonder why you would bother to make a custom generic class in the first place (as you could simply use a List(Of T) and specify a Car as the type parameter). Again, as things now stand, there is little benefit of the CarCollection(Of T) class beyond uniquely named methods.

To illustrate another form of generics abuse, assume that you have now created two new classes (SportsCar and MiniVan) that derive from the Car type:

```
Public Class SportsCar
  Inherits Car
  Public Sub New(ByVal p As String, ByVal s As Integer)
    MyBase.New(p, s)
  End Sub
  ' Assume additional SportsCar methods.
End Class

Public Class MiniVan
  Inherits Car
  Public Sub New(ByVal p As String, ByVal s As Integer)
    MyBase.New(p, s)
  End Sub
  ' Assume additional MiniVan methods.
End Class
```

Given the laws of inheritance, it's permissible to add a MiniVan or SportsCar type directly into a CarCollection(Of T) created with a type parameter of Car:

```
' CarCollection(Of Car) can hold any type deriving from Car.
Dim otherCars As New CarCollection(Of Car)()
otherCars(0) = New MiniVan("Mel", 10)
otherCars(1) = New SportsCar("Suzy", 30)
```

Although this is syntactically correct, what if you wished to update CarCollection(Of T) with a new Public method named PrintPetName()? This seems simple enough—just access the correct object in the List(Of T) and invoke the PetName property:

```
' Error! System.Object does not have a
' property named PetName.
Public Sub PrintPetName(ByVal pos As Integer)
  Console.WriteLine(myCars(pos).PetName)
End Sub
```

However, this will not compile, given that the true identity of T is not yet known, and you cannot say for certain whether the item in the List(Of T) type has a PetName property. When a type parameter is not constrained in any way (as is the case here), the generic type is said to be *unbound*. By design, unbound type parameters are assumed to have only the members of System.Object (which clearly does not provide a PetName property).

You may try to trick the compiler by casting the item returned from the List(Of T)'s indexer method into a strongly typed Car and invoking PetName from the returned object:

```
' Error! System.Object does not have a
' property named PetName.
Public Sub PrintPetName(ByVal pos As Integer)
  Console.WriteLine(CType(myCars(pos), Car).PetName)
End Sub
```

This again does not compile, given that the compiler does not yet know the value of the type parameter (Of T) and cannot guarantee the cast would be legal. Given the current issues with our CarCollection(Of T) class, when exactly would you need to bother to create a custom generic collection class?

Constraining Type Parameters

For the most part, the only time it will be beneficial to build a custom generic class is when you need to add specialized code that must execute (such as writing to an error log within a custom method) or when you need to *constrain type parameters*. When you constrain a type parameter, you are able to get very specific regarding what a type parameter must look like, and by doing so, you can build *extremely* type-safe containers. As of .NET 3.5, generics may be constrained in the ways listed in Table 10-6.

Table 10-6. *Possible Constraints for Generic Type Parameters*

Generic Constraint	Meaning in Life
Of T As Structure	The type parameter (Of T) must be a value type (e.g., structures).
Of T As Class	The type parameter (Of T) must be a reference type (e.g., classes).
Of T As New	The type parameter (Of T) must have a default constructor. This is very helpful if your generic type must create an instance of the type parameter, as you cannot assume the format of custom constructors. Note that this constraint must be listed last on a multiconstrained type.
Of T As *NameOfBaseClass*	The type parameter (Of T) must be derived from the class specified by *NameOfBaseClass*.
Of T As *NameOfInterface*	The type parameter (Of T) must implement the interface specified by *NameOfInterface*.

When you wish to apply constraints on a type parameter, simply make use of the As keyword. Furthermore, a single type parameter may be assigned multiple constraints by grouping them within curly brackets. By way of a few concrete examples, consider the following constraints of a generic class named MyGenericClass:

```
' Contained items must have a default constructor.
Public Class MyGenericClass(Of T As New)
End Class

' Contained items must implement ICloneable
' and support a default constructor.
Public Class MyGenericClass(Of T As {ICloneable, New})
End Class

' MyGenericClass derives from SomeBaseClass
' and implements ISomeInterface,
' while the contained items must be structures.
Public Class MyGenericClass(Of T As Structure)
  Inherits SomeBaseClass
  Implements ISomeInterface
End Class
```

On a related note, if you are building a generic type that specifies multiple type parameters, you can specify a unique set of constraints for each:

```
' (Of K) must have a default constructor, while (Of T) must
' implement the generic IComparable interface.
Public Class MyGenericClass(Of K As New, T As IComparable(Of T))
End Class
```

For the current example, if you wish to update CarCollection(Of T) to ensure that only Car-derived types can be placed within it, you could write the following:

```
Public Class CarCollection(Of T As Car)
  Implements IEnumerable(Of T)

  Private myCars As New List(Of T)()

  ' This is now A-OK, as the compiler knows "T" must derive from Car.
  Public Sub PrintPetName(ByVal pos As Integer)
    Console.WriteLine(myCars(pos).PetName)
  End Sub
  ...
End Class
```

Notice that once you constrain CarCollection(Of T) such that it can contain only Car-derived types, the implementation of PrintPetName() is straightforward, given that the compiler now assumes (Of T) is a Car-derived type. Furthermore, if the specified type parameter is not Car-compatible, you are issued a compiler error:

```
' Now a compile-time error!
Dim myInts As New CarCollection(Of Integer)()
myInts(0) = 4
myInts(1) = 44
```

Now be aware that even though our CarCollection(Of T) type can only contain Car-related objects, we still have not gained too much by way of functionality by creating this custom generic class, as we could simply say the following:

```
Dim cars As New List(Of Car)
```

However, anytime you need to build extremely type-safe containers (that perform custom bits of functionality beyond a standard generic container, such as List(Of T)), type parameters fit the bill.

Finally, be aware that type parameters of generic methods can also be constrained. For example, if you wish to ensure that only value types are passed into the Swap() method created previously in this chapter, update the code accordingly:

```
' Type "T" must be a structure.
Public Function Swap(Of T As Structure) _
  (ByRef a As T, ByRef b As T) As T
    ...
End Function
```

Understand of course, that if you were to constrain the Swap() method in this manner, you would no longer be able to swap String objects (as they are reference types).

The Lack of Operator Constraints

When you are creating generic methods, it may come as a surprise to you that it's a compiler error to apply any VB 2008 operators (+, -, *, etc.) on the type parameters. As an example, I am sure you could imagine the usefulness of a class that can add or subtract generic types:

```
' Compiler error! Cannot apply
' operators to type parameters!
Public Class BasicMath(Of T)
  Public Function Add(ByVal a As T, _
    ByVal b As T) As T
    Return a + b  ' Error!
  End Function

  Public Function Subtract(ByVal a As T, _
    ByVal b As T) As T
    Return a - b   ' Error!
  End Function
End Class
```

Sadly, the preceding BasicMath(Of T) class will not compile, as the compiler cannot guarantee that T has overloaded the + and - operators (see Chapter 12 for details of operator overloading). While this may seem like a major restriction, you need to remember that generics *are* generic.

Of course, the Integer type can work just fine with the binary operators of VB. However, for the sake of argument, if (Of T) were a custom class or structure type, the compiler cannot assume it has overloaded the +, -, *, and / operators. Ideally, VB would allow a generic type to be constrained by supported operators, for example:

```
' Illustrative code only!
' This is not legal VB code!
Public Class BasicMath(Of T As Operator +, -)
    Public Function Add(ByVal a As T, _
     ByVal b As T) As T
       Return a + b
    End Function
    Public Function Subtract(ByVal a As T, _
     ByVal b As T) As T
       Return a - b
    End Function
End Class
```

Alas, operator constraints are not supported on .NET 3.5 generics.

■ **Source Code** The CustomGenericCollection project is located under the Chapter 10 subdirectory.

Creating Generic Interfaces

As you saw earlier in the chapter during the examination of the `System.Collections.Generic` namespace, generic interfaces are also permissible (e.g., `IEnumerable(Of T)`). You are, of course, free to define your own generic interfaces (with or without constraints) should the need arise (which it most likely will *not* for a majority of your projects). Assume you wish to define an interface that can perform binary operations on a generic type parameter:

```
Public Interface IBasicMath(Of T)
  Function Add(ByVal a As T, ByVal b As T) As T
  Function Subtract(ByVal a As T, ByVal b As T) As T
  Function Multiply(ByVal a As T, ByVal b As T) As T
  Function Divide(ByVal a As T, ByVal b As T) As T
End Interface
```

Of course, interfaces are more or less useless until they are implemented by a class or structure. When you implement a generic interface, the supporting type specifies the placeholder type:

```
Public Class BasicMath
  Implements IBasicMath(Of Integer)

  Public Function Add(ByVal a As Integer, ByVal b As Integer) _
    As Integer Implements IBasicMath(Of Integer).Add
    Return a + b
  End Function

  Public Function Divide(ByVal a As Integer, ByVal b As Integer) _
    As Integer Implements IBasicMath(Of Integer).Divide
    Return CInt(a / b)
  End Function

  Public Function Multiply(ByVal a As Integer, ByVal b As Integer) _
    As Integer Implements IBasicMath(Of Integer).Multiply
    Return a * b
  End Function

  Public Function Subtract(ByVal a As Integer, ByVal b As Integer) _
    As Integer Implements IBasicMath(Of Integer).Subtract
    Return a - b
  End Function
End Class
```

At this point, you make use of `BasicMath` as you would expect:

```
Module Program
  Sub Main()
    Console.WriteLine("***** Generic Interfaces *****")
    Dim m As New BasicMath()
    Console.WriteLine("1 + 1 = {0}", m.Add(1, 1))
    Console.ReadLine()
  End Sub
End Module
```

If you would rather create a BasicMath class that operates on floating-point numbers, you could specify the type parameter like so:

```
Public Class BasicMath
  Implements IBasicMath(Of Double)

  Public Function Add(ByVal a As Double, ByVal b As Double) _
    As Double Implements IBasicMath(Of Double).Add
    Return a + b
  End Function
...
End Class
```

■ **Source Code** The GenericInterface project is located under the Chapter 10 subdirectory.

Creating Generic Delegates

Last but not least, Visual Basic does allow you to define generic *delegate types*, which we have not yet formally examined at this point in the text. Chapter 11 will dive headlong into the details of the .NET delegate type, so you may wish to return to this part of the chapter at a later time if you are new to the topic.

■ **Note** Allow me to reiterate, the next chapter will examine the details of the .NET delegate type. You may safely skip this section if you are unfamiliar with the use of .NET delegates.

By way of illustration, assume you wish to define a delegate that can call any subroutine taking a single argument. If the argument in question may differ, you could model this using a type parameter. To illustrate, ponder the following code:

```
' This generic delegate can point to any method
' taking a single argument (specified at the time
' of creation).
Public Delegate Sub MyGenericDelegate(Of T)(ByVal arg As T)

Module Program
  Sub Main()
    Console.WriteLine("***** Fun with generic delegates *****")
    Console.WriteLine()

    ' Make instance of delegate pointing to method taking an
    ' integer.
    Dim d As New MyGenericDelegate(Of Integer) _
     (AddressOf IntegerTarget)

    ' Invoke what the delegate is pointing to.
    d(100)

    ' Now pointing to a method taking a String.
    Dim d2 As New MyGenericDelegate(Of String)(AddressOf StringTarget)
```

```
    ' Invoke what the delegate is pointing to.
    d2("Cool!")
    Console.ReadLine()
  End Sub

  Public Sub IntegerTarget(ByVal arg As Integer)
    Console.WriteLine("You passed me a {0} with the value of {1}", _
      arg.GetType().Name, arg)
  End Sub

  Public Sub StringTarget(ByVal arg As String)
    Console.WriteLine("You passed me a {0} with the value of {1}", _
      arg.GetType().Name, arg)
  End Sub
End Module
```

Notice that MyGenericDelegate(Of T) defines a single type parameter that represents the argument to pass to the delegate target. When creating an instance of this type, you are required to specify the value of the type parameter as well as the name of the method the delegate will invoke. Thus, if you specified the String type, you send a String object to the target method:

```
' Create an instance of MyGenericDelegate(Of T)
' with String as the type parameter.
Dim d2 As New MyGenericDelegate(Of String)(AddressOf StringTarget)
d2("Cool!")
```

Given the format of the MyGenericDelegate delegate type, the StringTarget() method must now take a single String as a parameter:

```
Public Sub StringTarget(ByVal arg As String)
  Console.WriteLine("You passed me a {0} with the value of {1}", _
    arg.GetType().Name, arg)
End Sub
```

Simulating Generic Delegates Using System.Object

Generic delegates offer a more flexible way to specify the method to be invoked in a type-safe manner. If you were programming an application before the release of .NET 2.0, you could achieve a similar end result using a generic System.Object:

```
Public Delegate Sub MyDelegate(ByVal arg As Object)
```

Although this allows you to send any type of data to a delegate target (as everything can be represented as an Object), you do so without type safety and with possible boxing penalties. For instance, assume you have created two instances of MyDelegate, both of which point to the same method, MyTarget. Note the boxing/unboxing penalties as well as the inherent lack of type safety:

```
Module NonGenericDelegateTest
  Sub TestMethod()
    ' Register target with "traditional" delegate syntax.
    Dim d As New MyDelegate(AddressOf MyTarget)
    d("More string data")

    ' Register target using method group conversion.
    Dim d2 As New MyDelegate(AddressOf MyTarget)
    d2(9)    ' Boxing penalty!
  End Sub
```

```
  ' Due to a lack of type safety, we must
  ' determine the underlying type before casting.
  Sub MyTarget(ByVal arg As Object)
    If TypeOf arg Is Integer
      Dim i As Integer = CType(arg, Integer)  ' Unboxing penalty!
      Console.WriteLine("++arg is: {0}", ++i)
    End If
    If TypeOf arg Is string
      Dim s As String = CType(arg, String)
      Console.WriteLine("arg in uppercase is: {0}", s.ToUpper())
    End If
  End Sub
End Module
```

When you send out a value type to the target site, the value is (of course) boxed and unboxed once received by the target method. As well, given that the incoming parameter could be anything at all, you must dynamically check the underlying type before casting. Using generic delegates, you can still obtain the desired flexibility without the "issues."

Source Code The GenericDelegate project is located under the Chapter 10 directory.

Summary

Generics are a major language feature of VB that have been available since the release of .NET 2.0. To be sure, any new .NET application development should make liberal use of the generic containers and avoid the use of the (legacy) `System.Collections` namespace. As you have seen, a generic item allows you to specify "placeholders" (i.e., type parameters) that are supplied at the time of creation (or invocation, in the case of generic methods). Essentially, generics provide a solution to the boxing/unboxing performance issues and numerous type-safety issues that plagued .NET 1.1 development.

While you will most often simply make use of the generic types provided in the .NET base class libraries, you are also able to create your own generic types. When you do so, you have the option of specifying any number of constraints (via the `As` clause) to increase the level of type safety and ensure that you are performing operations on types of a "known quantity."

CHAPTER 11

Delegates, Events, and Lambdas

Up to this point in the text, most of the applications you have developed added various bits of code to `Main()`, which, in some way or another, sent requests to a given object. In Chapter 9, you briefly examined how the interface type can be used to build objects that can "talk back" to the entity that created it. While callback interfaces can be used to configure objects that engage in two-way conversations, the .NET delegate type is the preferred manner to define and respond to callbacks under the .NET platform.

Essentially, the .NET delegate type is a type-safe object that "points to" other method(s) that can be invoked at a later time. As you will see, .NET delegates are quite sophisticated in that they have built-in support for multicasting and asynchronous (e.g., nonblocking) invocations.

Once you learn how to create and manipulate delegate types, you then investigate a set of VB 2008 keywords (`Event`, `Handles`, `RaiseEvent`, etc.) that simplify the process of working with delegate types in the raw. As well, this chapter examines the ability to build *custom events* in order to intercept the process of registering with, detaching from, and sending an event notification.

I wrap up this chapter by investigating a new VB 2008 language feature termed *lambda expressions*. Using the new lambda statement (`Function`), it is now possible to directly specify a block of parameters and an evaluating code statement wherever a strongly typed delegate is required. As you will see, this new language feature allows you to build very compact and concise Visual Basic code.

Note You will be happy to know that the event-centric techniques shown in this chapter are found all throughout the .NET platform. In fact, when you are handling Windows Forms, Windows Presentation Foundation (WPF), or ASP.NET events, you will be using the exact same syntax.

Understanding the .NET Delegate Type

Before formally defining .NET delegates, let's gain a bit of historical perspective regarding the Windows platform. Since its inception many years ago, the Win32 API made use of C-style function pointers to support callback functionality. Using these function pointers, programmers were able to configure one function in the program to invoke (e.g., *call back to*) another function in the application. As you would imagine, this approach allowed applications to handle events from various UI elements, intercept messages in a distributed system, and numerous other techniques. Although BASIC-style languages have historically avoided the complexity of working with function pointers (thankfully), the callback construct is burned deep into the fabric of the Windows API.

One of the problems found with C-style callback functions is that they represent little more than a raw address in memory, which offers little by way of type safety or object orientation. Ideally, callback functions could be configured to include additional type-safe information such as the number of (and types of) parameters and the return type (if any) of the method being "pointed to." Alas, this is not always the case in traditional C-style callback functions, and, as you may suspect, can therefore be a frequent source of bugs, hard crashes, and other runtime disasters.

Nevertheless, callbacks are useful entities in that they can be used to build event architectures. In the .NET Framework, callbacks are still possible, and their functionality is accomplished in a much safer and more object-oriented manner using *delegates*. In essence, a delegate is a type-safe object that points to another method (or possibly multiple methods) in the application, which can be invoked at a later time. Specifically speaking, a delegate type maintains three important pieces of information:

- The *address* of the method on which it will make calls
- The *argument types* (if any) required by this method
- The *return type* (if any) returned from this method

Once a delegate has been defined and provided the necessary information, you may dynamically invoke the method(s) it points to at runtime. As you will see, every delegate in the .NET Framework (including your custom delegates) is automatically endowed with the ability to call their methods *synchronously* (using the calling thread) or *asynchronously* (on a secondary thread in a nonblocking manner). This fact greatly simplifies programming tasks, given that we can call a method on a secondary thread of execution without manually creating and managing a `Thread` object. This chapter will focus on the synchronous aspect of the delegate type. We will examine the asynchronous behavior of delegate types during our investigation of the `System.Threading` namespace in Chapter 18.

Defining a Delegate Type in VB 2008

When you want to create a delegate in VB 2008, you make use of the `Delegate` keyword. The name of your delegate can be whatever you desire. However, you must define the delegate to match the signature of the method it will point to. For example, assume you wish to build a delegate named `BinaryOp` that can point to any function that returns an `Integer` and takes two `Integers` (passed by value) as input parameters:

```
' This delegate can point to any function,
' taking two Integers and returning an
' Integer.
Public Delegate Function BinaryOp(ByVal x as Integer, _
  ByVal y as Integer) As Integer
```

When the VB 2008 compiler processes a delegate type, it automatically generates a sealed class deriving from `System.MulticastDelegate`. This class (in conjunction with its base class, `System.Delegate`) provides the necessary infrastructure for the delegate to hold onto the list of methods to be invoked at a later time. For example, if you examine the `BinaryOp` delegate using `ildasm.exe`, you would find the autogenerated class type depicted in Figure 11-1.

As you can see, the generated `BinaryOp` class defines three public methods. `Invoke()` is perhaps the core method, as it is used to invoke each method maintained by the delegate type in a synchronous manner, meaning the caller must wait for the call to complete before continuing on its way. Strangely enough, the synchronous `Invoke()` method is typically not directly called in code. As you will see in just a bit, `Invoke()` is called behind the scenes when you make use of the appropriate VB 2008 syntax.

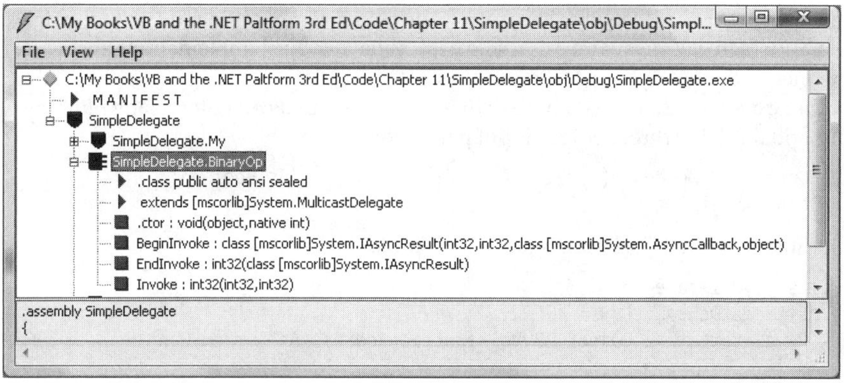

Figure 11-1. *The* `BinaryOp` *delegate under the hood*

`BeginInvoke()` and `EndInvoke()` provide the ability to call the method pointed to by the delegate asynchronously on a second thread of execution. If you have a background in multithreading, you are aware that one of the most common reasons developers create secondary threads of execution is to invoke methods that require a good deal of time to complete. Although the .NET base class libraries provide an entire namespace devoted to multithreaded programming (`System.Threading`), delegates provide this functionality out of the box (again, see Chapter 18 for details regarding asynchronous delegates).

Investigating the Autogenerated Class Type

So, how exactly does the compiler know how to define the `Invoke()`, `BeginInvoke()`, and `EndInvoke()` methods? To understand the process, here is the crux of the generated `BinaryOp` class type, shown in dazzling pseudo-code:

```
' This is only pseudo-code!
NotInheritable Class BinaryOp
  Inherits System.MulticastDelegate

  ' Compiler-generated constructor.
  Public Sub New(ByVal target As Object, ByVal functionAddress As System.UInt32)
  End Sub

  ' Used for synchronous calls.
  Public Function Invoke(ByVal x As Integer, ByVal y As Integer) As Integer
  End Sub

  ' Used for asynchronous calls on a second thread.
  Public Function BeginInvoke(ByVal x As Integer, ByVal y As Integer, _
    ByVal cb As AsyncCallback, ByVal state As Object) As IAsyncResult
  End Function
  Public Function EndInvoke(ByVal result As IAsyncResult) As Integer
  End Function
End Class
```

First, notice that the parameters and return value defined for the `Invoke()` method exactly match the definition of the `BinaryOp` delegate. The initial parameters to `BeginInvoke()` members (two `Integers` in our case) are also based on the `BinaryOp` delegate; however, `BeginInvoke()` will always provide two final parameters (of type `AsyncCallback` and `Object`) that are used to facilitate asynchronous method invocations. Finally, the return value of EndInvoke() is identical to the original delegate declaration and will always take as a sole parameter an object implementing the IAsyncResult interface.

Let's see another example. Assume you have defined a delegate that can point to any function returning a String and receiving three Boolean input parameters:

```
Public Delegate Function MyDelegate(ByVal a As Boolean, ByVal b As Boolean, _
  ByVal c As Boolean) As String
```

This time, the autogenerated class breaks down as follows:

```
NotInheritable Class MyDelegate
Inherits System.MulticastDelegate
  Public Sub New(ByVal target As Object, ByVal functionAddress As System.UInt32)
  End Sub

  Public Function Invoke(ByVal a As Boolean, ByVal b As Boolean, _
    ByVal c As Boolean) As String
  End Function

  Public Function BeginInvoke(ByVal a As Boolean, ByVal b As Boolean, _
    ByVal c As Boolean, ByVal cb As AsyncCallback, _
    ByVal state As Object) As IAsyncResult
  End Function
  Public Function EndInvoke(ByVal result As IAsyncResult) As String
  End Function
End Class
```

Delegates can also "point to" methods that contain any number of ByRef parameters. For example, assume the following delegate type definition:

```
Public Delegate Function MyOtherDelegate(ByRef a As Boolean, _
  ByRef b As Boolean, ByVal c As Integer) As String
```

The signatures of the Invoke() and BeginInvoke() methods look as you would expect; however, check out the EndInvoke() method, which now includes the set of all ByRef arguments defined by the delegate type:

```
NotInheritable Class MyOtherDelegate
  Inherits System.MulticastDelegate
  Public Sub New(ByVal target As Object, ByVal functionAddress As System.UInt32)
  End Sub

  Public Function Invoke(ByRef a As Boolean, ByRef b As Boolean, _
    ByVal c As Integer) As String
  End Function

  Public Function BeginInvoke(ByRef a As Boolean, ByRef b As Boolean, _
    ByVal c As Integer, ByVal cb As AsyncCallback, _
    ByVal state As Object) As IAsyncResult
  End Function
  Public Function EndInvoke(ByRef a As Boolean, ByRef b As Boolean, _
    ByVal result As IAsyncResult) As String
  End Function

End Class
```

To summarize the story thus far, a VB 2008 delegate type definition (using the Delegate keyword) results in a compiler-generated sealed class containing three key methods (as well as an internally called constructor) whose parameter and return types are based on the delegate's declaration. Again, the good news is that the VB 2008 compiler is the entity in charge of defining the actual delegate definition on our behalf.

Note The previous examples demonstrated how to build a VB delegate that points to functions, not subroutines. If you wish to build a delegate that can point to a subroutine (meaning a method with no return value), simply use the `Sub` keyword. Furthermore, delegates do not need to point to methods that take parameters. Thus, if you wish to build a delegate type that can point to subroutines taking no arguments whatsoever, you could author the following: `Public Delegate Sub SomeDelegate()`.

The System.MulticastDelegate and System.Delegate Base Classes

So, when you build a type using the VB 2008 `Delegate` keyword, you indirectly declare a class type that derives from `System.MulticastDelegate`. This class provides descendents with access to a list that contains the addresses of the methods maintained by the delegate type, as well as several additional methods to interact with the invocation list. `MulticastDelegate` obtains additional functionality from its parent class, `System.Delegate`.

Now, do understand that you will never derive directly from these base classes (in fact, it is a compiler error to do so). However, all delegate types inherit the members documented in Table 11-1 (consult the .NET Framework 3.5 documentation for full details).

Table 11-1. *Select Members of* `System.MultcastDelegate/System.Delegate`

Inherited Member	Meaning in Life
`Method`	This property returns a `System.Reflection.MethodInfo` type that represents details of the method that is maintained by the delegate.
`Target`	If the method to be called is defined at the object level (rather than a shared method), `Target` returns a `System.Object` that represents the object on which the delegate will invoke the specified method. If the value returned from `Target` equals `Nothing`, the method to be called is a shared member.
`Combine()`	This shared method adds a method to the list maintained by the delegate.
`GetInvocationList()`	This method returns an array of `System.Delegate` objects, each representing a particular method maintained by the delegate's invocation list.
`Remove()` `RemoveAll()`	These shared methods remove a method (or all methods) from the invocation list.

The Simplest Possible Delegate Example

Delegates tend to cause a great deal of confusion when encountered for the first time (even for those who do have experience with C-style callback functions). Thus, to get the ball rolling, let's take a look at a very simple Console Application project (named SimpleDelegate) that makes use of our `BinaryOp` delegate type. Here is the complete code (defined within a single `*.vb` file), with analysis to follow:

```
' Our delegate type can point to any method
' taking two Integers and returning an Integer.
Public Delegate Function BinaryOp(ByVal x As Integer, _
  ByVal y As Integer) As Integer

' This class defines the methods that will be "pointed to" by the delegate.
Public Class SimpleMath
  Public Shared Function Add(ByVal x As Integer, ByVal y As Integer) As Integer
    Return x + y
  End Function
  Public Shared Function Subtract(ByVal x As Integer, _
    ByVal y As Integer) As Integer
    Return x - y
  End Function
End Class

Module Program
  Sub Main()
    Console.WriteLine("***** Simple Delegate Example *****" & VbLf)

    ' Make a delegate object and add a method to the invocation
    ' list using the AddressOf keyword.
    Dim b As BinaryOp = New BinaryOp(AddressOf SimpleMath.Add)

    ' Invoke the method "pointed to."
    Console.WriteLine("10 + 10 is {0}", b(10, 10))
    Console.ReadLine()
  End Sub
End Module
```

Again notice the format of the BinaryOp delegate, which can point to any function taking two Integers and returning an Integer. Given this, we have created a class named SimpleMath, which defines two shared methods that (surprise, surprise) match the pattern defined by the BinaryOp delegate. When you want to insert the target method to a given delegate, simply pass in the address of the method to the delegate's constructor using the VB 2008 AddressOf keyword:

```
' Make a delegate object and add a method to the invocation
' list using the AddressOf keyword.
Dim b As BinaryOp = New BinaryOp(AddressOf SimpleMath.Add)
```

At this point, you are able to invoke the member pointed to using syntax that looks like a direct method invocation (note that b is the name of our BinaryOp variable):

```
' Invoke() is really called here!
Console.WriteLine("10 + 10 is {0}", b(10, 10))
```

Under the hood, the runtime actually calls the compiler-generated Invoke() method. You can verify this fact for yourself if you open your assembly in ildasm.exe and investigate the CIL code within the Main() method. In this light, if you wish to call the Invoke() method directly, you are free to do so; however, the end result is identical:

```
' Call Invoke() directly.
Console.WriteLine("10 + 10 is {0}", b.Invoke(10, 10))
```

Recall that .NET delegates are intrinsically *type safe*. Therefore, if you attempt to pass a delegate object the address of a method that does not "match the pattern," you receive a coding error. To illustrate, assume the SimpleMath class now defines an additional shared method named SquareNumber() as follows:

```
Public Class SimpleMath
...
  Public Shared Function SquareNumber(ByVal a As Integer) As Integer
    Return a * a
  End Function
End Class
```

Given that the BinaryOp delegate can *only* point to methods that take two Integers and return an Integer, the following code is illegal and will not compile, as SquareNumber() does not match the pattern demanded by the BinaryOp delegate:

```
' Error! Method does not match delegate pattern!
Dim b As New BinaryOp(AddressOf SimpleMath.SquareNumber)
```

Interacting with a Delegate Object

Let's spice up the current example by defining a helper function within our module named DisplayDelegateInfo(). This method will print out names of the methods maintained by the incoming delegate object as well as the name of the class defining the method pointed to. To do so, we will iterate over the System.Delegate array returned by GetInvocationList(), invoking each object's Target and Method properties:

```
Sub DisplayDelegateInfo(ByVal delObj As System.Delegate)
  For Each d As System.Delegate In delObj.GetInvocationList()
    Console.WriteLine("Method Name: {0}", d.Method)
    Console.WriteLine("Type Name: {0}", d.Target)
  Next
End Sub
```

Assuming you have updated your Main() method to actually call this new helper method by passing in your BinaryOp object:

```
Sub Main()
...
  Dim b As BinaryOp = New BinaryOp(AddressOf SimpleMath.Add)
  Console.WriteLine("10 + 10 is {0}", b(10, 10))

  ' Display details about "b"
  DisplayDelegateInfo(b)
...
End Sub
```

you would find the output shown in Figure 11-2.

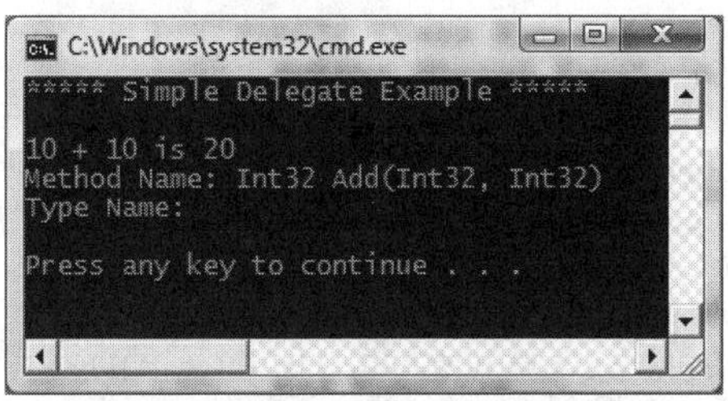

Figure 11-2. *Investigation of our* BinaryOp *delegate variable*

Notice that the name of the type (SimpleMath) is currently not displayed by the Target property. The reason has to do with the fact that our BinaryOp delegate is pointing to shared methods and therefore there is no object to reference! However, if we update the Add() and Subtract() methods to be instance-level members (simply by deleting the Shared keywords), we could now create an instance of the SimpleMath type and specify the methods to invoke as follows:

```
Sub Main()
  Console.WriteLine("***** Simple Delegate Example *****" & VbLf)

  ' Make a new SimpleMath object.
  Dim myMath As New SimpleMath()

  ' Use this object to specify the address of the Add method.
  Dim b As BinaryOp = New BinaryOp(AddressOf myMath.Add)

  ' Invoke the method "pointed to" as before.
  Console.WriteLine("10 + 10 is {0}", b(10, 10))
  DisplayDelegateInfo(b)
  Console.ReadLine()
End Sub
```

In this case, we would find the output shown in Figure 11-3. Notice the type name is the fully qualified name, of the SimpleMath class.

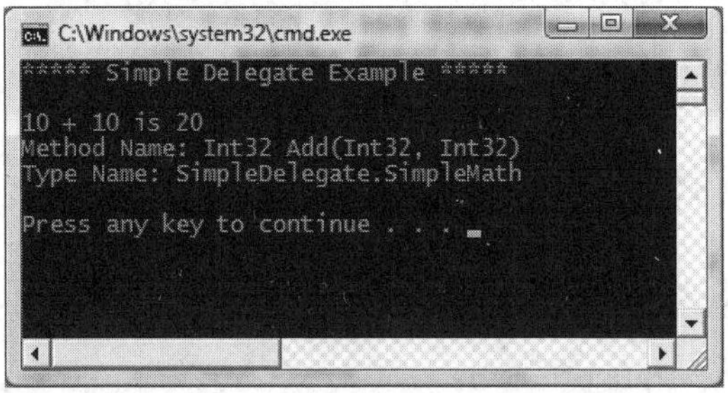

Figure 11-3. *"Pointing to" instance-level methods*

Source Code The SimpleDelegate project is located under the Chapter 11 subdirectory.

Retrofitting the Car Type with Delegates

Clearly, the previous SimpleDelegate example was intended to be purely illustrative in nature, given that there would be no compelling reason to build a delegate simply to add or subtract two numbers. Hopefully, however, this example demystifies the basic process of working with delegate types.

To provide a more realistic use of delegate types, let's retrofit our Car class to send the "Exploded" and "AboutToBlow" notifications using .NET delegates rather than a custom event interface as we did in Chapter 9. Beyond no longer implementing IEngineEvents, here are the steps we will take:

- Define a custom delegate type named CarDelegateHandler.
- Declare member variables of this delegate type in the Car class to represent each event notification.
- Create helper functions on the Car that allow the caller to specify the methods to add to the delegate member variable's invocation lists.
- Update the Accelerate() method to invoke the delegate's invocation list under the correct circumstances.

First, consider the following updates to the Car class, which address the first three points:

```
Public Class Car
  ' Our delegate type is nested in the Car type.
  Public Delegate Sub CarDelegateHandler(ByVal msg As String)

  ' Because delegates are simply classes, we can create
  ' member variables of delegate types.
  Private almostDeadList As CarDelegateHandler
  Private explodedList As CarDelegateHandler

  ' To allow the caller to pass us a delegate object.
  Public Sub OnAboutToBlow(ByVal clientMethod As CarDelegateHandler)
    almostDeadList = clientMethod
  End Sub
  Public Sub OnExploded(ByVal clientMethod As CarDelegateHandler)
    explodedList = clientMethod
  End Sub
...
End Class
```

Notice in this example that we define the delegate type directly within the scope of the Car class. From a design point of view, it is quite natural to define a delegate within the scope of the type it naturally works with, given that it illustrates a tight association between the two types (although this is certainly not mandatory). Furthermore, given that the compiler transforms a delegate into a full class definition, what we have actually done is indirectly created a nested class.

Next, note that we declare two member variables (one to represent each possible notification) and two helper functions (OnAboutToBlow() and OnExploded()) that allow the client to add a method to the delegate's invocation list. In concept, these methods are similar to the Connect() and Disconnect() methods we created during the EventInterface example of Chapter 9. Of course, in this case, the incoming parameter is a client-allocated delegate object rather than a sink implementing a specific event interface.

At this point, we need to update the Accelerate() method to invoke each delegate, rather than iterate over an ArrayList of client-supplied sinks:

```
Public Sub Accelerate(ByVal delta As Integer)
  If carIsDead Then
    ' If the car is doomed, send out the "Exploded" notification.
    If explodedList IsNot Nothing Then
      explodedList("Sorry, this car is dead...")
    End If
  Else
    currSpeed += delta
    ' Are we almost doomed? If so, send out "AboutToBlow" notification.
    If 10 = maxSpeed - currSpeed AndAlso almostDeadList IsNot Nothing Then
      almostDeadList("Careful buddy!  Gonna blow!")
    End If
```

```
    If currSpeed >= maxSpeed Then
      carIsDead = True
    Else
      Console.WriteLine("->CurrSpeed = {0}", currSpeed)
    End If
  End If
End Sub
```

Notice that before we invoke the methods maintained by the almostDeadList and explodedList member variables, we are checking them against the value Nothing. The reason is that it will be the job of the caller to allocate these objects when calling the OnAboutToBlow() and OnExploded() helper methods. If the caller does not call these methods (given that it may not wish to hear about these events), and we attempt to invoke the delegate's invocation list, we will trigger a NullReferenceException and bomb at runtime (which would obviously be a bad thing!).

Now that we have the delegate infrastructure in place within the Car class, observe the updates to the Program module:

```
Module Program
  Sub Main()
    Console.WriteLine("***** Delegates as event enablers *****")
    Dim c1 As New Car("SlugBug", 10)

    ' Pass the address of the methods that will be maintained
    ' by the delegate member variables of the Car type.
    c1.OnAboutToBlow(AddressOf CarAboutToBlow)
    c1.OnExploded(AddressOf CarExploded)

    Console.WriteLine("***** Speeding up *****")
    For i As Integer = 0 To 5
      c1.Accelerate(20)
    Next
    Console.ReadLine()
  End Sub

  ' These are called by the Car object.
  Public Sub CarAboutToBlow(ByVal msg As String)
    Console.WriteLine(msg)
  End Sub
  Public Sub CarExploded(ByVal msg As String)
    Console.WriteLine(msg)
  End Sub
End Module
```

Notice that in this code example, we are not directly allocating an instance of the Car.CarDelegateHandler delegate objects. This is because as a shortcut, when we make use of the VB 2008 AddressOf keyword, the compiler will automatically generate a new instance of the related delegate type. This can be verified using ildasm.exe (which I will leave as an exercise to the interested reader).

While the fact that the AddressOf keyword automatically generates the delegate objects in the background is quite helpful, there will be times when you will prefer to allocate the delegate object manually for later use in your application. You will see a practical reason to do so in the next section; however, to illustrate the process, consider the following iteration of Main():

```
Module Program
  Sub Main()
    Console.WriteLine("***** Delegates as event enablers *****")
    Dim c1 As New Car("SlugBug", 10)
```

```
    ' Manually create the delegate objects.
    Dim aboutToBlowDel As New Car.CarDelegateHandler(AddressOf CarAboutToBlow)
    Dim explodedDel As New Car.CarDelegateHandler(AddressOf CarExploded)

    ' Now pass in delegate objects.
    c1.OnAboutToBlow(aboutToBlowDel)
    c1.OnExploded(explodedDel)
...
  End Sub

  Public Sub CarAboutToBlow(ByVal msg As String)
    Console.WriteLine(msg)
  End Sub
  Public Sub CarExploded(ByVal msg As String)
    Console.WriteLine(msg)
  End Sub
End Module
```

The only major point to be made here is that because the CarDelegateHandler delegate is nested within the Car class, we must allocate objects of this type using its full name (e.g., Car.CarDelegateHandler). Finally, like any delegate constructor, we pass in the name of the method to add to the invocation list.

Enabling Multicasting

Recall that .NET delegates have the intrinsic ability to *multicast*. In other words, a delegate object can maintain a list of methods to call (provided they match the pattern defined by the delegate), rather than a single method. When you wish to add multiple methods to a delegate object, you will need to call System.Delegate.Combine(). To enable multicasting on the Car type, we could update the OnAboutToBlow() and OnExploded() methods as follows:

```
Class Car
...
  ' Now with multicasting!
  Public Sub OnAboutToBlow(ByVal clientMethod As CarDelegateHandler)
    almostDeadList = System.Delegate.Combine(almostDeadList, clientMethod)
  End Sub

  Public Sub OnExploded(ByVal clientMethod As CarDelegateHandler)
    explodedList = System.Delegate.Combine(explodedList, clientMethod)
  End Sub
...
End Class
```

Be aware that the previous code will only compile if Option Strict is not enabled in your project. Since it is always good practice to in fact enable Option Strict, here would be a more type-safe (and compiler-acceptable) implementation of these methods using explicit casting:

```
' Now with type-safe multicasting!
Public Sub OnAboutToBlow(ByVal clientMethod As CarDelegateHandler)
  almostDeadList = CType(System.Delegate.Combine(almostDeadList, _
    clientMethod), CarDelegateHandler)
End Sub
Public Sub OnExploded(ByVal clientMethod As CarDelegateHandler)
  explodedList = CType(System.Delegate.Combine(explodedList, _
    clientMethod), CarDelegateHandler)
End Sub
```

In either case, the first argument to pass into Combine() is the delegate object that is maintaining the current invocation list, while the second argument is the new delegate object you wish to add to the list. At this point, the caller can now register multiple targets as follows:

```
Module Program
  Sub Main()
    Console.WriteLine("***** Delegates as event enablers *****")
    Dim c1 As New Car("SlugBug", 10)

    ' Register multiple event handlers!
    c1.OnAboutToBlow(AddressOf CarAboutToBlow)
    c1.OnAboutToBlow(AddressOf CarIsAlmostDoomed)
    c1.OnExploded(AddressOf CarExploded)
...
  End Sub

  ' This time, two methods are called
  ' when the AboutToBlow notification fires.
  Public Sub CarAboutToBlow(ByVal msg As String)
    Console.WriteLine(msg)
  End Sub

  Public Sub CarIsAlmostDoomed(ByVal msg As String)
    Console.WriteLine("Critical Message from Car: {0}", msg)
  End Sub

  Public Sub CarExploded(ByVal msg As String)
    Console.WriteLine(msg)
  End Sub
End Module
```

Removing a Target from a Delegate's Invocation List

The Delegate class also defines a shared Remove() method that allows a caller to dynamically remove a member from the invocation list. If you wish to allow the caller the option to detach from the event notifications, you could add the following additional helper methods to the Car type:

```
Class Car
...
  ' To remove a target from the list.
  Public Sub RemoveAboutToBlow(ByVal clientMethod As CarDelegateHandler)
    almostDeadList = CType(System.Delegate.Remove(almostDeadList, _
      clientMethod), CarDelegateHandler)
  End Sub

  Public Sub RemoveExploded(ByVal clientMethod As CarDelegateHandler)
    explodedList = CType(System.Delegate.Remove(explodedList, _
      clientMethod), CarDelegateHandler)
  End Sub
...
End Class
```

With this update, we could stop receiving the Exploded notification by updating Main() as follows:

```
Sub Main()
  Console.WriteLine("***** Delegates as event enablers *****")
  Dim c1 As New Car("SlugBug", 10)

  ' Register multiple event handlers!
  c1.OnAboutToBlow(AddressOf CarAboutToBlow)
  c1.OnAboutToBlow(AddressOf CarIsAlmostDoomed)
  c1.OnExploded(AddressOf CarExploded)

  Console.WriteLine("***** Speeding up *****")
  For i As Integer = 0 To 5
    c1.Accelerate(20)
  Next

  ' Remove CarExploded from invocation list.
  c1.RemoveExploded(AddressOf CarExploded)

  ' This will not fire the Exploded event.
  For i As Integer = 0 To 5
    c1.Accelerate(20)
  Next
  Console.ReadLine()
End Sub
```

The final output of our current Console Application can be seen in Figure 11-4.

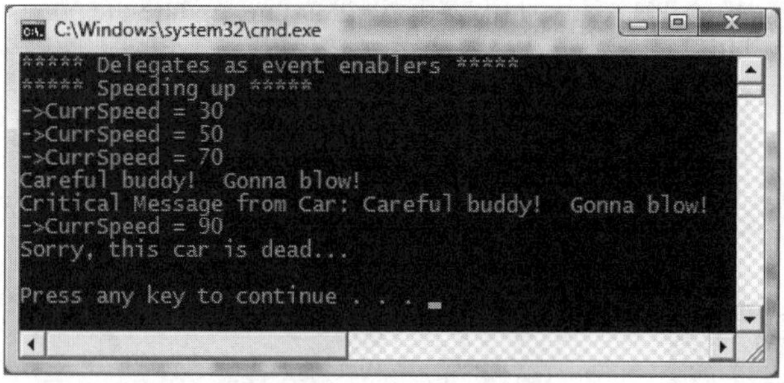

Figure 11-4. *The* `Car` *type, now with delegates*

■ Source Code The CarDelegate project is located under the Chapter 11 subdirectory.

Understanding (and Using) Events

Delegates are fairly interesting constructs in that they enable objects in memory to engage in a two-way conversation in a type-safe and object-oriented manner. As you may agree, however, working with delegates in the raw does entail a good amount of boilerplate code (defining the delegate, declaring any necessary member variables, and creating custom registration/unregistration methods).

Because the ability for one object to call back to another object is such a helpful construct, VB 2008 provides a small set of keywords to lessen the burden of using delegates in the raw. For example, when the compiler processes the Event keyword, you are automatically provided with registration and unregistration methods that allow the caller to hook into an event notification. Better yet, using the Event keyword removes the need to define delegate objects in the first place. In this light, the Event keyword is little more than syntactic sugar, which can be used to save you some typing time.

To illustrate these new event-centric keywords, let's reconfigure the Car class to make use of events, rather than raw delegates. First, you need to define the events themselves using the Event keyword. Notice here we are defining two events with regards to the set of parameters passed into the registered handler:

```
Public Class Car
...
  ' This car can send these events.
  Public Event Exploded(ByVal msg As String)
  Public Event AboutToBlow(ByVal msg As String)
...
End Class
```

Firing an Event Using the RaiseEvent Keyword

Firing an event is as simple as specifying the event by name (with any specified parameters) using the RaiseEvent keyword. One benefit of using this VB keyword is that we are no longer required to test for Nothing before firing the event itself, as this is done implicitly. To illustrate, update the previous implementation of Accelerate() to send each event accordingly:

```
Public Sub Accelerate(ByVal delta As Integer)
  If carIsDead Then
    ' If the car is doomed, raise Exploded event.
    RaiseEvent Exploded("Sorry, this car is dead...")
  Else
    currSpeed += delta
    ' Are we almost doomed? If so, send out AboutToBlow event.
    If 10 = maxSpeed - currSpeed Then
      RaiseEvent AboutToBlow("Careful buddy!  Gonna blow!")
    End If
    If currSpeed >= maxSpeed Then
      carIsDead = True
    Else
      Console.WriteLine("->CurrSpeed = {0}", currSpeed)
    End If
  End If
End Sub
```

With this, you have configured the car to send two custom events (under the correct conditions). You will see the usage of this new automobile in just a moment, but first, let's dig a bit deeper into the Event keyword.

Events Under the Hood

A VB 2008 event actually encapsulates a good deal of information. Each time you declare an event with the Event keyword, the compiler generates the following information within the defining class:

- A new hidden, nested delegate is created automatically and added to your class. The name of this delegate is always EventName+EventHandler. For example, if you have an event named Exploded, the autogenerated delegate is named ExplodedEventHandler.
- Two hidden public functions, one having an "add_" prefix, the other having a "remove_" prefix, are automatically added to your class. These are used internally to call Delegate.Combine() and Delegate.Remove(), in order to add and remove methods to/from the list maintained by the delegate.
- A new hidden member variable is added to your class that represents a new instance of the autogenerated delegate type (see the first bullet item).

As you can see, the Event keyword is indeed a time-saver, as it instructs the compiler to author the same sort of code you created manually when using the delegate type directly!

If you were to compile the CarEvent example and load the assembly into ildasm.exe, you could check out the CIL instructions behind the compiler-generated add_AboutToBlow(). Notice it calls Delegate.Combine() on your behalf. Also notice that the parameter passed to add_AboutToBlow() is an instance of the autogenerated AboutToBlowEventHandler delegate:

```
.method public specialname instance void
  add_AboutToBlow(class CarEvent.Car/AboutToBlowEventHandler obj)
  cil managed synchronized
{
...
  IL_0008:  call class [mscorlib]System.Delegate
    [mscorlib]System.Delegate::Combine(class [mscorlib]System.Delegate,
    class [mscorlib]System.Delegate)
...
} // end of method Car::add_AboutToBlow
```

Furthermore, remove_AboutToBlow() makes the call to Delegate.Remove() automatically, passing in the incoming AboutToBlowEventHandler delegate:

```
.method public specialname instance void
  remove_AboutToBlow(class CarEvent.Car/AboutToBlowEventHandler obj)
  cil managed synchronized
{
...
  IL_0008:  call class [mscorlib]System.Delegate
    [mscorlib]System.Delegate::Remove(class [mscorlib]System.Delegate,
    class [mscorlib]System.Delegate)
...
} // end of method Car::remove_AboutToBlow
```

The CIL instructions for the event declaration itself (which appears in ildasm.exe as an inverted green triangle icon) makes use of the .addon and .removeon CIL tokens to connect the correct add_XXX() and remove_XXX() methods:

```
.event CarEvents.Car/EngineHandler AboutToBlow
{
  .addon
  instance void CarEvents.Car::add_AboutToBlow(class
    CarEvents.Car/AboutToBlowEventHandler)
  .removeon
   instance void CarEvents.Car::remove_AboutToBlow(class
    CarEvents.Car/AboutToBlowEventHandler)
} // end of event Car::AboutToBlow
```

Perhaps most importantly, if you were to check out the CIL behind this iteration of the Accelerate() method, you would find that the delegate is invoked on your behalf. Here is a partial snapshot of the CIL that invokes the invocation list maintained by the ExplodedEventHandler delegate:

```
.method public instance
  void Accelerate(int32 delta) cil managed
{
...
  IL_001d:  callvirt
    instance void CarEvents.Car/ExplodedEventHandler::Invoke(string)
...
}
```

As you can see, the VB 2008 Event keyword is quite helpful, given that it builds and manipulates raw delegates on your behalf. As you saw earlier in this chapter, however, you are able to directly manipulate delegates if you so choose.

Hooking into Incoming Events Using WithEvents and Handles

Now that you understand how to build a class that can send events, the next big question is how you can configure an object to receive these events. Assume you have now created an instance of the Car class and want to listen to the events it is capable of sending.

The first step is to declare a member variable for which you wish to process incoming events using the WithEvents keyword. Next, you will associate an event to a particular event handler using the Handles keyword. For example:

```
Module Program
  ' Declare member variables "WithEvents" to
  ' capture the events.
  Private WithEvents c As New Car("NightRider", 50)

  Sub Main()
    Console.WriteLine("***** Fun with Events *****")
    Dim i As Integer
    For i = 0 To 5
      c.Accelerate(10)
    Next
  End Sub

  ' Event Handlers.
  Public Sub MyExplodedHandler(ByVal s As String) _
    Handles c.Exploded
    Console.WriteLine(s)
  End Sub
  Public Sub MyAboutToDieHandler(ByVal s As String) _
    Handles c.AboutToBlow
    Console.WriteLine(s)
  End Sub
End Module
```

In many ways, things look more or less like traditional VB6 event logic. The only new spin is the fact that the Handles keyword is now used to connect the handler to an object's event.

■Note As you may know, VB6 demanded that event handlers always be named using very strict naming conventions (*NameOfTheObject_NameOfTheEvent*) that could easily break as you renamed the objects in your code base. With the VB 2008 `Handles` keyword, however, the name of your event handlers can be anything you choose.

Multicasting Using the Handles Keyword

Another extremely useful aspect of the `Handles` statement is the fact that you are able to configure multiple methods to process the same event. For example, if you update your module as follows:

```
Module Program
...
  Public Sub MyExplodedHandler(ByVal s As String) _
    Handles c.Exploded
    Console.WriteLine(s)
  End Sub

  ' Both of these handlers will be called when AboutToBlow is fired.
  Public Sub MyAboutToDieHandler(ByVal s As String) _
    Handles c.AboutToBlow
    Console.WriteLine(s)
  End Sub

  Public Sub MyAboutToDieHandler2(ByVal s As String) _
    Handles c.AboutToBlow
    Console.WriteLine(s)
  End Sub
End Module
```

you would see the incoming `String` object sent by the `AboutToBlow` event print out twice, as we have handled this event using two different event handlers.

Defining a Single Handler for Multiple Events

The `Handles` keyword also allows you to define a single handler to (pardon the redundancy) handle multiple events, provided that the events are passing in the same set of arguments. This should make sense, as the VB 2008 `Event` keyword is simply a shorthand notation for working with type-safe delegates. In our example, given that the `Exploded` and `AboutToBlow` events are both passing a single string by value, we could intercept each event using the following handler:

```
Module Program
  Private WithEvents c As New Car("NightRider", 50)

  Sub Main()
    Console.WriteLine("***** Fun with Events *****")
    Dim i As Integer
    For i = 0 To 5
      c.Accelerate(10)
    Next
  End Sub
```

```
  ' A single handler for each event.
  Public Sub MyExplodedHandler(ByVal s As String) _
    Handles c.Exploded, c.AboutToBlow
    Console.WriteLine(s)
  End Sub
End Module
```

Source Code The CarEvent project is located under the Chapter 11 subdirectory.

Dynamically Hooking into Incoming Events with AddHandler/RemoveHandler

Currently, we have been hooking into an event by explicitly declaring the variable using the WithEvents keyword. When you do so, you make a few assumptions in your code:

- The variable is *not* a local variable inside of a method, but a member variable of the defining type (Module, Class, or Structure).
- You wish to be informed of the event throughout the lifetime of your application.

Given these points, it is not possible to declare a local variable using the WithEvents keyword:

```
Sub Main()
  ' Error! Local variables cannot be
  ' declared "with events."
  Dim WithEvents myCar As New Car()
End Sub
```

However, you do have an alternative approach that may be used to hook into an event. It is possible to declare a local object (as well as a member variable of a type) without using the WithEvents keyword, and dynamically rig together an event handler at runtime.

To do so, you ultimately need to call the correct autogenerated add_XXX() method to ensure that your method is added to the list of function pointers maintained by the Car's internal delegate (remember, the Event keyword expands to produce—among other things—a delegate type). Of course, you do not call add_XXX() directly, but rather use the AddHandler statement.

As well, if you wish to dynamically remove an event handler from the underlying delegate's invocation list, you can indirectly call the compiler-generated remove_XXX() method using the RemoveHandler statement.

In a nutshell, AddHandler/RemoveHandler allows us to gain "delegate-like" functionality without directly defining the delegate types themselves. Consider the following reworked Main() method:

```
Module Program
  Sub Main()
    Console.WriteLine("***** Fun with AddHandler/RemoveHandler *****")

    ' Note lack of WithEvents keyword.
    Dim c As New Car("NightRider", 50)

    ' Dynamically hook into event using AddHandler.
    AddHandler c.Exploded, AddressOf CarEventHandler
    AddHandler c.AboutToBlow, AddressOf CarEventHandler
```

```
    For i As Integer = 0 To 5
      c.Accelerate(10)
    Next
    Console.ReadLine()
  End Sub

  ' Event Handler for both events
  ' (note lack of Handles keyword).
  Public Sub CarEventHandler(ByVal s As String)
    Console.WriteLine(s)
  End Sub
End Module
```

As you can see, the AddHandler statement requires the name of the event you want to listen to and the address of the method that will be invoked when the event is sent. Here, you also routed each event to a single handler (which is of course not required). As well, if you wish to enable multicasting, simple use the AddHandler statement multiple times and specify unique targets:

```
' Multicasting!
AddHandler c.Exploded, AddressOf MyExplodedHandler
AddHandler c.Exploded, AddressOf MySecondExplodedHandler
```

RemoveHandler works in the same manner. If you wish to stop receiving events from a particular object, you may do so using the following syntax:

```
' Dynamically unhook a handler using RemoveHandler.
RemoveHandler c. Exploded, AddressOf MySecondExplodedHandler
```

At this point, you may wonder when (or if) you would ever need to make use of the AddHandler and RemoveHandler statements, given that VB 2008 supports the WithEvents syntax. Again, understand that this approach is very powerful as you have the ability to detach from an event source at will.

When you make use of the WithEvent keyword, you will continuously receive events from the source object until the object dies (which typically means until the client application is terminated). Using the RemoveHandler statements, you can simply tell the object "Stop sending me this event," even though the object may be alive and well in memory.

■ **Source Code** The DynamicCarEvents project is located under the Chapter 11 subdirectory.

Defining a "Prim-and-Proper" Event

Truth be told, there is one final enhancement we could make to our example that mirrors Microsoft's recommended event pattern. As you begin to explore the events sent by a given type in the base class libraries, you will find that the target method's first parameter is a System.Object, while the second parameter is a type deriving from System.EventArgs.

The System.Object argument represents a reference to the object that sent the event (such as the Car), while the second parameter represents any relevant information regarding the event at hand. The System.EventArgs base class represents an event that is not sending any custom information:

```
Public Class EventArgs
  Public Shared ReadOnly Empty As EventArgs
```

```
  Shared Sub New()
  End Sub
  Public Sub New()
  End Sub

End Class
```

Our current examples have specified the parameters they send directly within the definition of the event itself:

```
Public Class Car
...
  ' Notice we are specifying the event arguments directly.
  Public Event Exploded(ByVal msg As String)
  Public Event AboutToBlow(ByVal msg As String)
...
End Class
```

As you have learned, the compiler will take these arguments to define a proper delegate behind the scenes. While this approach is very straightforward, if you do wish to follow the recommended design pattern, the Exploded and AboutToBlow events should be retrofitted to send a System.Object and System.EventArgs descendent.

Although you can pass an instance of EventArgs directly, you lose the ability to pass in custom information to the registered event handler. Thus, when you wish to pass along custom data, you should build a suitable class deriving from EventArgs. For our example, assume we have a class named CarEventArgs, which maintains a read-only String representing the message sent to the receiver:

```
Public Class CarEventArgs
  Inherits EventArgs

  Public ReadOnly msgData As String

  Public Sub New(ByVal msg As String)
    msgData = msg
  End Sub
End Class
```

With this, we would now update the events sent from the Car type like so:

```
Public Class Car
...
  ' These events follow Microsoft design guidelines.
  Public Event Exploded(ByVal sender As Object, ByVal e As CarEventArgs)
  Public Event AboutToBlow(ByVal sender As Object, ByVal e As CarEventArgs)
...
End Class
```

When firing our events from within the Accelerate() method, we would now need to supply a reference to the current Car (via the Me keyword) and an instance of our CarEventArgs type:

```
Public Sub Accelerate(ByVal delta As Integer)
  If carIsDead Then
    ' If the car is doomed, send out the Exploded notification.
    RaiseEvent Exploded(Me, New CarEventArgs("This car is doomed..."))
  Else
    currSpeed += delta
    ' Are we almost doomed? If so, send out AboutToBlow notification.
    If 10 = maxSpeed - currSpeed Then
```

```
      RaiseEvent AboutToBlow(Me, New CarEventArgs("Slow down!"))
    End If
    If currSpeed >= maxSpeed Then
      carIsDead = True
    Else
      Console.WriteLine("->CurrSpeed = {0}", currSpeed)
    End If
  End If
End Sub
```

On the caller's side, all we would need to do is update our event handlers to receive the incoming parameters and obtain the message via our read-only field. For example:

```
' Assume this event was handled using AddHandler.
Public Sub AboutToBlowHandler(ByVal sender As Object, ByVal e As CarEventArgs)
  Console.WriteLine("{0} says: {1}", sender, e.msgData)
End Sub
```

If the receiver wishes to interact with the object that sent the event, we can explicitly cast the System.Object. Thus, if we wish to power down the radio when the Car object is about to meet its maker, we could author an event handler looking something like the following:

```
' Assume this event was handled using AddHandler.
Public Sub ExplodedHandler(ByVal sender As Object, ByVal e As CarEventArgs)
  If TypeOf sender Is Car Then
    Dim c As Car = CType(sender, Car)
    c.CrankTunes(False)
  End If
  Console.WriteLine("Critical message from {0}: {1}", sender, e.msgData)
End Sub
```

Source Code The PrimAndProperEvent project is located under the Chapter 11 subdirectory.

Defining Strongly Typed Events

As I am sure you have figured out by now (given that I have mentioned it numerous times), the VB 2008 Event keyword automatically creates a delegate behind the scenes. However, if you have already defined a delegate type, you are able to associate it to an event using an As clause. By doing so, you inform the VB 2008 compiler to make use of your delegate-specific type, rather than generating a delegate class on the fly. For example:

```
Public Class Car
...
  ' Define the delegate used for these events
  Public Delegate Sub CarDelegate(ByVal sender As Object, ByVal e As CarEventArgs)

  ' Now associate the delegate to the event.
  Public Event Exploded As CarDelegate
  Public Event AboutToBlow As CarDelegate
...
End Class
```

While many of your event declarations may not require such strong typing, the benefit of doing so is you are able to create a set of events that all operate on the same underlying delegate, and therefore "point to" methods of the same signature (e.g., any required parameters and a possible return value). As well, defining strongly typed events is necessary when you wish to customize the event registration process.

Customizing the Event Registration Process

Although a vast majority of your applications will simply make use of the Event, Handles, and RaiseEvent keywords, the Custom keyword allows you to author additional code that will execute when a caller interacts with an event or when the event is raised in your code, thereby providing a way to customize the event process.

The first question probably on your mind is what exactly is meant by "customizing the event process." Simply put, using the Custom keyword, you are able to author code that will execute when the caller registers with an event via AddHandler or detaches from an event via RemoveHandler, or when your code base sends the event via RaiseEvent. Custom events also have a very important restriction:

- The event must be defined in terms of a specific delegate.

In many cases, the delegate you associate to the event will be a standard type that ships with the base class libraries named System.EventHandler (although as you will see, you can make use of any delegate, including custom delegates you have created yourself). The System.EventHandler delegate can point to any subroutine that takes a System.Object as the first parameter and a System.EventArgs as the second. Given this requirement, here is a skeleton of what a custom event looks like using VB 2008 syntax:

```
Public Custom Event MyEvent As RelatedDelegate
  ' Triggered when caller uses AddHandler.
  AddHandler(ByVal value As RelatedDelegate)
  End AddHandler

  ' Triggered when caller uses RemoveHandler.
  RemoveHandler(ByVal value As RelatedDelegate)
  End RemoveHandler

  ' Triggered when RaiseEvent is called.
  RaiseEvent(Parameters required by RelatedDelegate)
  End RaiseEvent
End Event
```

As you can see, a custom event is defined in terms of the associated delegate via the As keyword. Next, notice that within the scope of the custom event we have three subscopes that allow us to author code to execute when the AddHandler, RemoveHandler, or RaiseEvent statements are used.

Defining a Custom Event

To illustrate, assume a simple Car type that defines a custom event named EngineStart, defined in terms of the standard System.EventHandler delegate. The Car defines a member variable of type ArrayList that will be used to hold onto each of the incoming delegate objects passed by the caller (very much like our interface-based approach created in Chapter 9).

Furthermore, when the Car fires the EngineStart event (from a method named Start()), our customization of RaiseEvent will iterate over each connection to invoke the client-side event handler. Ponder the following class definition:

```
Public Class Car
  ' This ArrayList will hold onto the delegates
  ' sent from the caller.
  Private arConnections As New ArrayList()

  ' This event has been customized!
  Public Custom Event EngineStart As System.EventHandler
    AddHandler(ByVal value As EventHandler)
      Console.WriteLine("Added connection")
      arConnections.Add(value)
    End AddHandler

    RemoveHandler(ByVal value As System.EventHandler)
      Console.WriteLine("Removed connection")
      arConnections.Remove(value)
    End RemoveHandler

    RaiseEvent(ByVal sender As Object, ByVal e As System.EventArgs)
      For Each h As EventHandler In arConnections
        Console.WriteLine("Raising event")
        h(sender, e)
      Next
    End RaiseEvent
  End Event

  Public Sub Start()
    RaiseEvent EngineStart(Me, New EventArgs())
  End Sub
End Class
```

Beyond adding (and removing) System.EventHandler delegates to the ArrayList member variable, the other point of interest to note is that the implementation of Start() must now raise the EngineStart event by passing a System.Object (representing the sender of the event) and a new System.EventArgs, given the use of the System.EventHandler delegate (that was a mouthful!). Also recall that we are indirectly calling Invoke() on each System.EventHandler delegate to invoke the target in a synchronous manner:

```
' We could also call Invoke() directly
' like so: h.Invoke(sender, e)
h(sender, e)
```

On the caller's side, we could now proceed as expected using AddHandler and RemoveHandler:

```
Module Program
  Sub Main()
    Console.WriteLine("***** Fun with Custom Events *****")
    Dim c As New Car()

    ' Dynamically hook into event.
    AddHandler c.EngineStart, AddressOf EngineStartHandler
    c.Start()

    ' Just to trigger our custom logic.
    RemoveHandler c.EngineStart, AddressOf EngineStartHandler

    ' Just to test we are no longer sending event.
    c.Start()
```

```
    Console.ReadLine()
  End Sub

  ' Our handler must match this signature given that
  ' EngineStart has been prototyped using the System.EventHandler delegate.
  Public Sub EngineStartHandler(ByVal sender As Object, ByVal e As EventArgs)
    Console.WriteLine("Car has started")
  End Sub
End Module
```

The output can be seen in Figure 11-5. While not entirely fascinating, we are able to verify that our custom code statements are executing whenever AddHandler, RemoveHandler, or RaiseEvent is used in our code base.

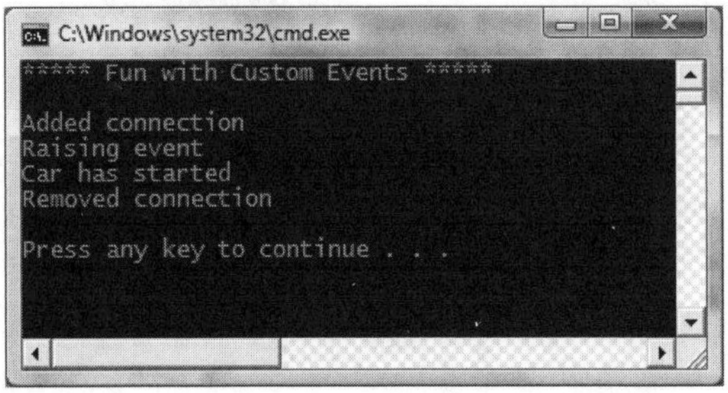

Figure 11-5. *Interacting with a custom event*

Note If the caller invokes an event on a member variable declared using the WithEvents modifier, the custom AddHandler and RemoveHandler scope is (obviously) not executed.

Source Code The CustomEvent project is located under the Chapter 11 subdirectory.

Custom Events Using Custom Delegates

Currently, our custom event has been defined in terms of a standard delegate named System.EventHandler. However, we can make use of any delegate that meets our requirements, including our own custom delegate. Here would be a retrofitted Car type that is now making use of a custom delegate named CarDelegate (which takes our CarEventArgs as a second parameter):

```
Public Class Car
  ' The custom delegate.
  Public Delegate Sub CarDelegate(ByVal sender As Object, _
    ByVal args As CarEventArgs)
  Private arConnections As New ArrayList()

  ' Now using CarDelegate.
  Public Custom Event EngineStart As CarDelegate
    AddHandler(ByVal value As CarDelegate)
      Console.WriteLine("Added connection")
```

```
      arConnections.Add(value)
    End AddHandler

    RemoveHandler(ByVal value As CarDelegate)
      Console.WriteLine("Removed connection")
      arConnections.Remove(value)
    End RemoveHandler

    RaiseEvent(ByVal sender As Object, ByVal e As CarEventArgs)
      For Each h As CarDelegate In arConnections
        Console.WriteLine("Raising event")
        h.Invoke(sender, e)
      Next
    End RaiseEvent
  End Event

  Public Sub Start()
    RaiseEvent EngineStart(Me, New CarEventArgs("Enjoy the ride"))
  End Sub
End Class
```

The caller's code would now be modified to make sure that the event handlers take a `CarEventArgs` as the second parameter, rather than the `System.EventArgs` type required by the `System.EventHandler` delegate:

```
Module Program
...
  Public Sub EngineStartHandler(ByVal sender As Object, ByVal e As CarEventArgs)
    Console.WriteLine("Message from {0}: {1}", sender, e.msgData)
  End Sub
End Module
```

The output can be seen in Figure 11-6.

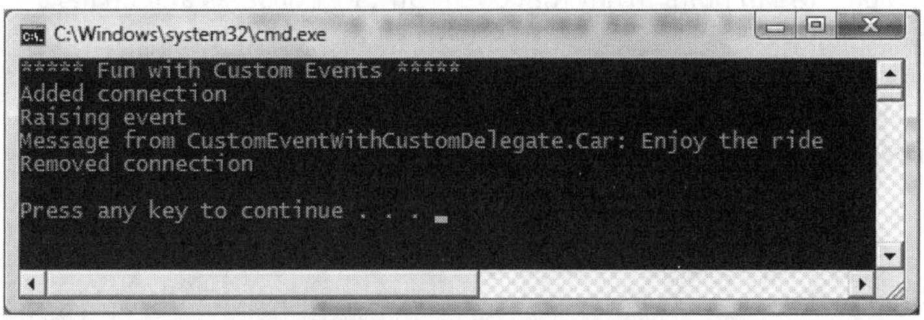

Figure 11-6. *Interacting with a custom event, take two*

So, now that you have seen the process of building a custom event, you might be wondering when you might need to do so. While the simple answer is "whenever you want to customize the event process," a very common use of this technique is when you wish to fire out events in a nonblocking manner using secondary threads of execution.

However, at this point in the text, I have yet to dive into the details of the `System.Threading` namespace or the asynchronous nature of the delegate type (see Chapter 18 for details). In any case, just understand that the `Custom` keyword allows you to author custom code statements that will execute during the handling and sending of events.

Source Code The CustomEventWithCustomDelegate project is located under the Chapter 11 subdirectory.

Visual Basic Lambda Expressions

To conclude our look at the .NET event architecture, we will close with an examination of *lambda expressions.* With the release of .NET 3.5, the Visual Basic programming language has been provided with yet another way to simplify the way we work with delegate types using *lambdas.* In a nutshell, a lambda expression allows us to inline function parameters and a code statement to evaluate said arguments using a very concise syntax via the `Function` statement.

If you are thinking this sounds very similar in concept to what a .NET delegate is designed to do, you are correct! In fact, the `Function` statement is little more than a way to reduce the amount of code you would normally need to author by hand when working with a delegate type.

Note Like VB, the latest edition of C# also supports the construction of lambda expressions using the C# lambda operator (=>). Unfortunately, as of .NET 3.5, VB's support for lambda expressions is less expressive than that of C#. However, by and large, the VB `Function` statement can be seen as the rough equivalent of C#'s => operator.

To begin our examination of lambda expressions, create a new Console Application project named SimpleLambdaExpressions. Now, consider the `FindAll()` method of the generic `List(Of T)` type. As the name suggests, this method allows you to obtain from a `List(Of T)` a subset of the contained items. To do so, the `FindAll()` method requires a delegate object, which "points to" the method that will be used to evaluate each contained object.

Specifically speaking, the `FindAll()` method is expecting a generic delegate parameter of type `System.Predicate(Of T)`. This delegate can point to any function returning a `Boolean` and taking a specified `T` as the only input parameter.

To see how to work with `FindAll()` using traditional delegate syntax, add a method (named `TraditionalDelegateSyntax()`) within your initial module type that interacts with the `System.Predicate(Of T)` type to discover the even numbers in a `List(Of T)` of `Integers`:

```
Module Program
  Sub Main()
    Console.WriteLine("***** Fun with Lambdas *****")
    TraditionalDelegateSyntax()

    Console.ReadLine()
  End Sub

  Sub TraditionalDelegateSyntax()
    Dim list As New List(Of Integer)()
    list.AddRange(New Integer() {20, 1, 4, 8, 9, 44})

    ' Create a Predicate(Of T) object for use by
    ' the List(Of T).FindAll() method.
    Dim callback As New Predicate(Of Integer)(AddressOf IsEvenNumber)

    ' Call FindAll() passing the delegate object.
    Dim evenNumbers As List(Of Integer) = list.FindAll(callback)
```

```
    ' Print out the result set.
    Console.WriteLine("Here are the even numbers:")
    For Each evenNumber As Integer In evenNumbers
      Console.WriteLine(evenNumber)
    Next
  End Sub

  ' Target for the Predicate(Of T) delegate.
  Function IsEvenNumber(ByVal i As Integer) As Boolean
    ' Is it an even number?
    Return (i Mod 2) = 0
  End Function
End Module
```

Here, we have a method (`IsEvenNumber()`) that is in charge of testing the incoming `Integer` parameter to see whether it is even or odd via the VB modulo operator, `Mod`. If you execute your application, you will find the numbers 20, 4, 8, and 44 print out to the console.

While this traditional approach to working with delegates works as expected, the `IsEvenNumber()` method, however, is only invoked under very limited circumstances, specifically, when we call `FindAll()`, which leaves us with the baggage of a full method definition.

Lambda expressions can be used to simplify our call to `FindAll()`. When we make use of this new syntax, there is no trace of the underlying delegate (however, the compiler still guarantees type safety) or stand-alone delegate target method whatsoever. The end result is a more compact body of code.

Consider the following new method in our initial module, which performs the same duties as the previous `TraditionalDelegateSyntax()` method, using lambda syntax:

```
Sub LambdaExpressionSyntax()
  Dim list As New List(Of Integer)()
  list.AddRange(New Integer() {20, 1, 4, 8, 9, 44})

  ' Call FindAll() using a VB lambda.
  Dim evenNumbers As List(Of Integer) = list.FindAll(Function(i)(i Mod 2) = 0)

  ' Print out the result set.
  Console.WriteLine("Here are the even numbers:")
  For Each evenNumber As Integer In evenNumbers
    Console.WriteLine(evenNumber)
  Next
End Sub
```

In this case, notice the rather strange statement of code passed into the `FindAll()` method, which is in fact a VB lambda expression. Notice that in this iteration of the example, there is no trace whatsoever of the `Predicate(Of T)` delegate. Also note that we have not authored a separate method in our module to test for odd or even numbers. All we have specified is the lambda expression: `Function(i)(i Mod 2) = 0`.

Before we break this syntax down, at this level simply understand that lambda expressions can be used anywhere you would have used a strongly typed delegate (typically with far fewer keystrokes). Under the hood, the compiler translates our lambda expression into traditional delegate syntax, making use of the `Predicate(Of T)` delegate type (which can be verified using `ildasm.exe` or `reflector.exe`) and generates a hidden method within the defining type to process any incoming parameters.

Dissecting a Lambda Expression

A VB lambda expression is written using the `Function` statement, followed by a set of parameter names wrapped in parentheses, followed by a single code statement that will process these arguments. From a very high level, a lambda expression can be understood as follows:

```
Function(ArgumentsToProcess) StatementToProcessThem
```

■ **Note** The arguments of a lambda expression must always be wrapped in parentheses. Furthermore, the statement that processes the parameters must provide a return value that is identical to the underlying delegate. Said another way, the `Function` statement literally represents a VB *function*, not a VB *subroutine*. This is perhaps the biggest limitation of VB lambda syntax (in contrast, a C# lambda expression does not need to return a value).

Within our `LambdaExpressionSyntax()` method, things break down like so:

```
' "i" is our parameter list.
' "(i Mod 2) = 0" is our statement to process "i".
Dim evenNumbers As List(Of Integer) = list.FindAll(Function(i)(i Mod 2) = 0)
```

The parameters of a lambda expression can be explicitly or implicitly typed. Currently, the underlying data type representing the `i` parameter (an `Integer`) is determined implicitly. The compiler is able to figure out that `i` is an `Integer` based on the context of the overall lambda expression and the underlying delegate. However, it is also possible to explicitly define the type of each parameter in the expression by making use of an `As` clause:

```
' Now, explicitly state what the parameter type.
Dim evenNumbers As List(Of Integer) = _
  list.FindAll(Function(i As Integer) (i Mod 2) = 0)
```

Assuming your `Main()` method has been updated to call both helper methods, you should not be too surprised to find that the output of each method is identical (see Figure 11-7). The major difference is that the `Function` statement allows us to simplify our coding efforts by allowing the compiler to generate the necessary delegate grunge at compile time.

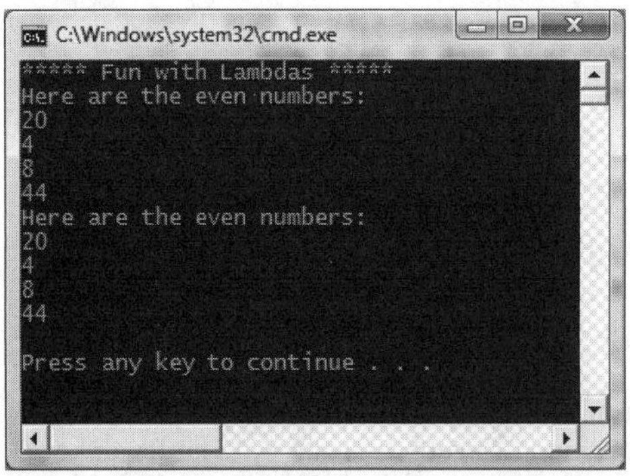

Figure 11-7. *The output of your first lambda expression*

■ **Source Code** The SimpleLambdaExpressions project can be found under the Chapter 11 subdirectory.

Lambda Expressions with Multiple Parameters

Your first lambda expression processed a single incoming parameter. This is not a requirement, however, as the evaluation statement of a lambda expression may process multiple arguments. To illustrate, create a new Console Application project named LambdaExpressionsMultipleParams. Assume the following simplified incarnation of the BinaryOp example, seen at the beginning of this chapter:

```
Public Delegate Function BinaryOp(ByVal x As Integer, _
  ByVal y As Integer) As Integer

Module Program
  Sub Main()
    Console.WriteLine("***** Lambdas with Multiple Params! *****")

    ' Register w/ delegate as a lambda expression.
    Dim b As New BinaryOp(Function(x, y) x + y)

    ' This will execute the lambda expression.
    Console.WriteLine(b(10, 10))

    Console.ReadLine()
  End Sub
End Module
```

Recall that the BinaryOp delegate is expecting to "point to" a method taking two Integer parameters as input and a single Integer as output. However, rather than having to manually define a separate method to perform the parameter processing (as we did in the SimpleDelegate example), we can use a proper lambda expression.

Again, the VB compiler will translate a lambda expression into a "normal" method that will be pointed to by the underlying delegate object. By way of a simple test, here is an update to the Program module that makes a call to the DisplayDelegateInfo() method also used within the SimpleDelegate example:

```
Module Program
  Sub Main()
    Console.WriteLine("***** Lambdas with Multiple Params! *****")

    ' Register w/ delegate as a lambda expression.
    Dim b As New BinaryOp(Function(x, y) x + y)

    ' What method is b pointing to?
    DisplayDelegateInfo(b)

    Console.WriteLine(b(10, 10))
    Console.ReadLine()
  End Sub

  Sub DisplayDelegateInfo(ByVal delObj As System.Delegate)
    For Each d As System.Delegate In delObj.GetInvocationList()
      Console.WriteLine("Method Name: {0}", d.Method)
      Console.WriteLine("Type Name: {0}", d.Target)
    Next
  End Sub
End Module
```

If you were to execute this code example, you would be able to view the name of the autogenerated method stored within the delegate object (see Figure 11-8; your name will most likely differ). Also note that the value of the Target property is empty, as the compiler implicitly generated a shared method, due to the fact that our lambda expression was in fact created in a module type (which you recall only contains shared members).

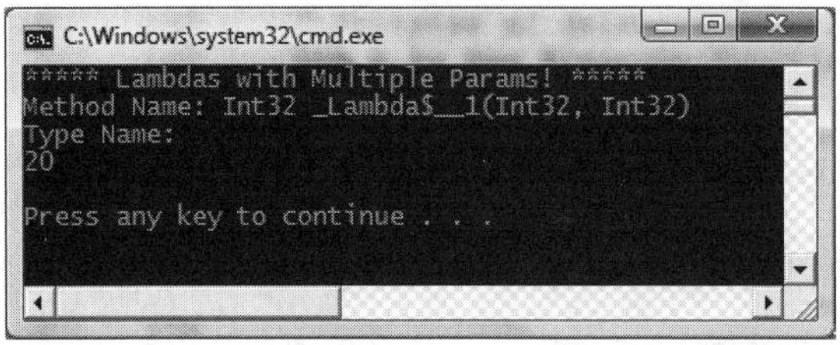

Figure 11-8. *Lambda expressions result in a compiler-generated method*

Essentially, the lambda expression

```
Function(x, y) x + y
```

has been represented internally as follows (again, the name of the method is determined by the compiler, and not directly visible in our VB code):

```
Shared Function _Lambda$__1(ByVal x as Integer, ByVal y As Integer) As Integer
  Return x + y
End Function
```

Notice that the parameters do indeed become Integer data types (based on the definition of BinaryOp), and the evaluation statement (x+y) is placed within the scope of the compiler-generated function.

Evaluating Lambda Parameters Using Custom Methods

The code statement that will evaluate incoming arguments can in fact specify a shared method of a given class or structure, as well as an instance-level member of type instance. Assume once again the SimpleMath class used within the SimpleDelegate example (note that both methods have been defined using the Shared keyword):

```
Public Class SimpleMath
  Public Shared Function Add(ByVal x As Integer, ByVal y As Integer) As Integer
    Return x + y
  End Function

  Public Shared Function Subtract(ByVal x As Integer, _
    ByVal y As Integer) As Integer
    Return x - y
  End Function
End Class
```

Our lambda expression could now be authored as follows:

```
Dim b As New BinaryOp(Function(x, y) SimpleMath.Add(x, y))
```

If the Add() and Subtract() methods were *not* shared, we could use a SimpleMath object reference within our lambda code statement:

```
Dim m as New SimpleMath()
Dim b As New BinaryOp(Function(x, y) m.Add(x, y))
```

The one critical point to always remember when authoring a lambda expression using Visual Basic is that the code statement evaluating the incoming parameters *must* have a return value. This should not be too hard to remember, as the keyword for a lambda expression is in fact `Function` (not `Sub`!).

Lambda Expressions with Zero Parameters

Last but not least, if you are creating a lambda expression to interact with a delegate taking no parameters at all, you may do so by supplying a pair of empty parentheses rather than a stack of parameters. Consider, for example, the following VB code:

```
' Note this delegate returns a String, but takes no arguments.
Public Delegate Function GetTime() As String

Module Test
  Sub LambdaNoArgsTest()
    Console.WriteLine("***** Lambdas with No Params! *****")

    ' No parameters to pass "function" here.
    Dim t As New GetTime(Function() DateTime.Now.ToString())
    Console.WriteLine(t)

    Console.ReadLine()
  End Sub
End Module
```

So hopefully at this point you can see the overall role of lambda expressions and understand how they provide a more concise manner to work with delegate objects. Although the new lambda statement (`Function`) might take a bit to get used to, always remember a lambda expression can be broken down to the following simple equation:

```
Function(ArgumentsToProcess) StatementToProcessThem
```

While most of your VB projects may not make great use of lambda expressions, it is worth pointing out that the LINQ programming model also makes substantial use of lambda expressions in the background to help simplify your coding efforts. You will examine LINQ (and how LINQ uses lambda expressions) beginning in Chapter 14.

Source Code The LambdaExpressionsMultipleParams project can be found under the Chapter 11 subdirectory.

Summary

Over the course of this chapter, you have seen numerous approaches that can be used to "connect" two objects in order to enable a two-way conversation (interface types, delegates, and the VB 2008 event architecture). Recall that the `Delegate` keyword is used to indirectly construct a class derived from `System.MulticastDelegate`. As you have seen, a delegate instance is simply an object that maintains a list of methods to call when told to do so (most often using the `Invoke()` method).

Next, we examined the `Event`, `RaiseEvent`, and `WithEvents` keywords. Although they have been retrofitted under the hood to work with .NET delegates, they look and feel much the same as the legacy event-centric keywords of VB6. As you have seen, VB now supports the `Handles` statement, which is used to syntactically associate an event to a given method (as well as enable multicasting).

You also examined the process of hooking into (and detaching from) an event dynamically using the `AddHandler` and `RemoveHandler` statements. This is a very useful feature of the Visual Basic language, given that you now have a type-safe way to dynamically intercept events on the fly. You also learned about the new `Custom` keyword, which allows you to control how events are handled and sent by a given type.

We wrapped up by examining the use of lambda expressions, which are a new VB language feature introduced with .NET 3.5. As you have seen, the `Function` statement can be used to inline a single-statement function used to evaluate incoming parameters. In a nutshell, this new syntax provides a simplified manner in which we can register the target method of a .NET delegate object.

CHAPTER 12

Operator Overloading and Custom Conversion Routines

This chapter will examine some somewhat more advanced topics regarding the Visual Basic programming language. The first topic, *operator overloading*, is a technique that allows you to build custom classes and structures that can respond uniquely to the intrinsic VB operators (+, -, >, etc.). While this technique is never mandatory, when used correctly, you are able to build custom types that behave like the fundamental CLR data types (`System.Int32`, `System.String`, and so forth).

Custom conversion routines, the second topic, allow you to define how your types (most often structures) can respond to casting operations (via `CType()`). However, before examining the details of building custom conversion routines (and understanding why you might wish to do so), this chapter will dive into a number of important details regarding the distinction between .NET reference types (e.g., classes) and value types (e.g., structures). This will provide a proper context for the understanding of custom conversions.

Finally, we'll examine two additional casting operators (`DirectCast` and `TryCast`) that often are used in place of `CType` calls. As you will see, the `DirectCast` and `TryCast` operators offer a more type-safe way to covert between data types than the legacy `CType`.

Understanding Operator Overloading

Visual Basic, like any programming language, has a canned set of tokens that are used to perform basic operations on intrinsic data types. For example, you know that the + operator can be applied to two `Integer`s in order to yield a larger `Integer` (assuming the numbers are both positive!):

```
' The + operator applied to Integers.
Dim a As Integer = 100
Dim b As Ingeter = 240
Dim c As Integer = a + b  ' c is now 340
```

Again, this is no major newsflash, but have you ever stopped and noticed how the same + operator can be applied to most intrinsic VB data types? For example, consider this code, which concatenates `String` types using the same operator (rather than the expected `&`):

```
' The + operator applied to Strings.
Dim s1 As String = "Hello"
Dim s2 As String = " world!"
Dim s3 As String = s1 + s2  ' s3 is now "Hello world!"
```

In essence, the + operator functions in unique ways based on the supplied data types (`Strings` or `Integers` in this case). When the + operator is applied to numerical types, the result is the summation of the operands. However, when the + operator is applied to `String` objects, the result is string concatenation.

Since the release of .NET 2.0, the VB language was provided with the capability to create custom classes and structures that also respond uniquely to the same set of basic tokens (such as the + operator). As you will see over the next several pages, if you use this language feature correctly, your custom classes and structures can be used in a more intuitive manner.

Before examining our first operator overloading example, be aware that although VB defines many operators, only a subset can be redefined for your custom types. Table 12-1 lists the possibilities.

Table 12-1. *Valid Overloadable Operators*

VB Operator	Overloadability
+, -, Not, IsTrue, IsFalse	The unary operators (including the unary versions of + and -) can be overloaded.
+, -, *, /, \, &, ^, Mod, And, Or, Xor, Like	The binary operators of VB of can be overloaded.
=, <>, <, >, <=, >=, <<, >>	The comparison operators of VB (which are technically also binary operators) can be overloaded. VB will demand that "like" operators (i.e., < and >, <= and >=, = and <>) are overloaded together to keep the defining type consistent.
CType	The CType operator can be overloaded to implement a custom conversion routine.

The Case for Operator Overloading

Strictly speaking, any class or structure can redefine how it will respond to the intrinsic operators seen in Table 12-1. However, just because a type *could* overload an operator does not mean it necessarily makes sense to do so. By and large, this particular VB programming feature is best suited for types that are modeling numerical, geometrical, or other forms of atomic data (time, dates, etc.).

To understand the usefulness of this feature, create a new Console Application project named OverloadedOps, and rename your initial VB file to Program.vb. Now, assume the following MyPoint structure, which supports an overridden version of ToString() and a custom constructor that will set two private points of numerical data:

```
Public Structure MyPoint
  Private x As Integer, y As Integer

  Public Sub New(ByVal xPos As Integer, ByVal yPos As Integer)
    x = xPos
    y = yPos
  End Sub

  Public Overrides Function ToString() As String
    Return String.Format("[{0}, {1}]", Me.x, Me.y)
  End Function
End Structure
```

Now, logically speaking, it makes sense to add MyPoints together to yield a new MyPoint that is based on the result of adding the x and y values of MyPoint objects. On a related note, it may be helpful to subtract one MyPoint from another (by subtracting the x and y values of MyPoint objects).

In languages that do not support operator overloading (including earlier versions of Visual Basic), the only way to do so would be to define custom methods on the class/structure in question. For example, we could update MyPoint with two new functions, Add() and Subtract(), implemented as follows:

```
' Adding two MyPoint objects to yield a new MyPoint.
Public Shared Function Add(ByVal p1 As MyPoint, ByVal p2 As MyPoint) As MyPoint
  Return New MyPoint(p1.x + p2.x, p1.y + p2.y)
End Function

' Subtracting two MyPoint objects to yield a new MyPoint.
Public Shared Function Subtract(ByVal p1 As MyPoint, ByVal p2 As MyPoint) As MyPoint
  Return New MyPoint(p1.x - p2.x, p1.y - p2.y)
End Function
```

■ Note The `Add()` and `Subtract()` functions do not need to be defined as shared members; however, this more closely approximates what takes place with operator overloading.

With this in place, we could now "'add" or "subtract" `MyPoint` variables as follows:

```
Module Program
  Sub Main()
    Console.WriteLine("***** Fun with Operator Overloading *****" & vbLf)
    AddSubtractMyPointsWithMethodCalls()
    Console.ReadLine()
  End Sub

  Sub AddSubtractMyPointsWithMethodCalls()
    Dim p As New MyPoint(10, 10)
    Dim p2 As New MyPoint(20, 30)

    ' Add two MyPoints using Add() method.
    Dim newPoint = MyPoint.Add(p, p2)
    Console.WriteLine("p + p2 = {0}", newPoint)

    ' Subtract two MyPoints using Subtract() method.
    Console.WriteLine("p - p2 = {0}", MyPoint.Subtract(p, p2))
  End Sub
End Module
```

Based on the values sent into the constructors of each `MyPoint` variable, we could find the output shown in Figure 12-1.

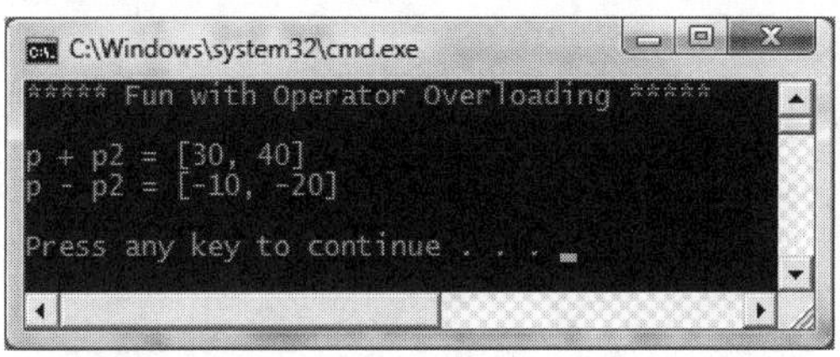

Figure 12-1. *Adding/Subtracting* `MyPoint` *data with traditional method calls*

While these methods fit the bill, it would be much cleaner for programmers who are using the `MyPoint` data type if they could simply apply the more natural + or - symbol, rather than having to make calls to shared members. For example, you would like to be able to author the following code:

```
' Adding and subtracting two MyPoints?
Sub AddSubtractMyPointsWithOperators()
  Dim p As New MyPoint(10, 10)
  Dim p2 As New MyPoint(20, 30)

  ' Add two MyPoints?
  Dim newPoint As MyPoint = p + p2
  Console.WriteLine("p + p2 = {0}", newPoint)

  ' Subtract two MyPoints?
  Console.WriteLine("p - p2 = {0}", p - p2)
End Sub
```

If you do attempt to author the previous code, you will find the coding errors shown in Figure 12-2.

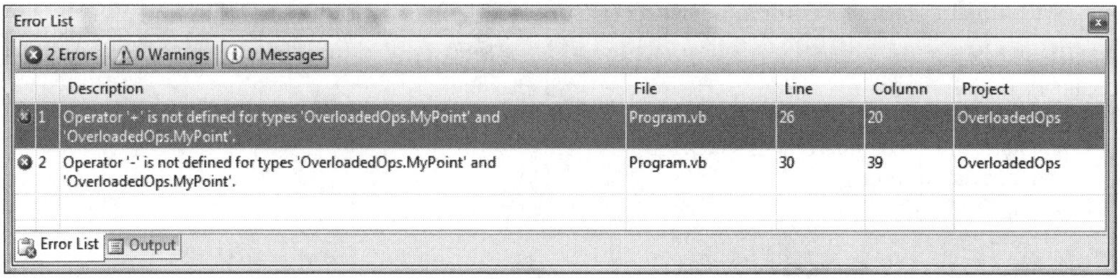

Figure 12-2. *Intrinsic operators cannot be applied directly to custom types.*

As you can see, it is not permissible to apply intrinsic operators to custom types by default. How then can we configure `MyPoint` to respond to the + and - operators?

Overloading Binary Operators

To allow a custom type to respond uniquely to intrinsic operators, VB provides the `Operator` keyword, which you can *only* use in conjunction with the `Shared` keyword. When you are overloading a binary operator (such as + or -), you will typically pass in two arguments that are the same type as the defining class (a `MyPoint` in this example), as illustrated in the following code update:

```
' A more intelligent MyPoint type.
Public Structure MyPoint
...
  ' Overloaded operator +.
  Public Shared Operator +(ByVal p1 As MyPoint, ByVal p2 As MyPoint) As MyPoint
    Return New MyPoint(p1.x + p2.x, p1.y + p2.y)
  End Operator

  ' Overloaded operator -.
  Public Shared Operator -(ByVal p1 As MyPoint, ByVal p2 As MyPoint) As MyPoint
    Return New MyPoint(p1.x - p2.x, p1.y - p2.y)
  End Operator
End Structure
```

Like the previous `Add()` method, the logic behind `Operator +` is simply to return a brand new `MyPoint` based on the summation of the fields of the incoming `MyPoint` parameters. In a similar manner, `Operator -` is implemented identically to the previous `Subtract()` method. The only major difference is the use of the `Operator` keyword, rather than the expected `Function` keyword.

With these operators in place, the previous `AddSubtractMyPointsWithOperators()` method compiles without error. Thus, when you author code such as `p + p2`, under the hood, you can envision the following hidden call to the shared operator + method.

```
Sub AddSubtractMyPointsWithOperators()
  Dim p As New MyPoint(10, 10)
  Dim p2 As New MyPoint(20, 30)

  ' Really calls: MyPoint.Operator+(p, p2)
  Dim newPoint As MyPoint = p + p2
  Console.WriteLine("p + p2 = {0}", newPoint)

  ' Really calls: MyPoint.Operator-(p, p2)
  Console.WriteLine("p - p2 = {0}", p - p2)
End Sub
```

If you were to call `AddSubtractMyPointsWithOperators()` from within `Main()`, you would find the same identical output as shown in Figure 12-1, when we were adding/subtracting `MyPoints` using traditional function syntax.

Overloading Equality Operators

As you may recall from Chapter 6, `System.Object.Equals()` can be overridden to perform value-based (rather than referenced-based) comparisons between objects. If you choose to override `Equals()` (and the often-related `System.Object.GetHashCode()` method), it is trivial to overload the VB equality operators (= and <>). To illustrate, here is the updated `MyPoint` structure:

```
' This incarnation of MyPoint also overloads the = and <> operators.
Public Structure MyPoint
...
  ' Overridden methods of System.Object.
  Public Overrides Function Equals(ByVal o As Object) As Boolean
    If TypeOf o Is MyPoint Then
      If Me.ToString() = o.ToString() Then
        Return True
      End If
    End If
    Return False
  End Function
  Public Overrides Function GetHashCode() As Integer
    Return Me.ToString().GetHashCode()
  End Function

  ' Now let's overload the = and <> operators.
  Public Shared Operator =(ByVal p1 As MyPoint, ByVal p2 As MyPoint) As Boolean
    Return p1.Equals(p2)
  End Operator
  Public Shared Operator <>(ByVal p1 As MyPoint, ByVal p2 As MyPoint) As Boolean
    Return Not p1.Equals(p2)
  End Operator
End Structure
```

Notice how the implementation of operator = and operator <> simply makes a call to the overridden `Equals()` method to get the bulk of the work done. Given this, you can now exercise your `MyPoint` class as follows:

```
' Make use of the overloaded equality operators.
Sub TestMyPointsForEquality()
  Dim ptOne As New MyPoint(10, 2)
  Dim ptTwo As New MyPoint(10, 44)

  Console.WriteLine("ptOne = ptTwo : {0}", ptOne = ptTwo)   ' False!
  Console.WriteLine("ptOne <> ptTwo : {0}", ptOne <> ptTwo) ' True!
End Sub
```

As you may agree, it is quite intuitive to compare two objects using the well-known = and <> operators rather than making a call to `Object.Equals()`. If you do overload the equality operators for a given class, keep in mind that VB demands that if you override the = operator, you *must* also override the <> operator (if you forget, the compiler will let you know).

Overloading Comparison Operators

In Chapter 9, you learned how to implement the `IComparable` interface in order to compare the relative relationship between two like objects. Additionally, you may also overload the comparison operators (<, >, <=, and >=) for the same class or structure. Like the equality operators, VB demands that if you overload <, you must also overload >. The same holds true for the <= and >= operators. If the `MyPoint` type overloaded these comparison operators, you could now compare `MyPoints` as follows:

```
' Using the overloaded comparison operators.
Sub TestMyPointsForGreaterLessThan()
  Dim ptOne As New MyPoint(5, 2)
  Dim ptTwo As New MyPoint(5, 44)

  Console.WriteLine("ptOne > ptTwo : {0}", ptOne > ptTwo)   ' False!
  Console.WriteLine("ptOne < ptTwo : {0}", ptOne < ptTwo)   ' False!
  Console.WriteLine("ptOne >= ptTwo : {0}", ptOne >= ptTwo) ' True!
  Console.WriteLine("ptOne <= ptTwo : {0}", ptOne <= ptTwo) ' True!
End Sub
```

Assuming you have implemented the `IComparable` interface, overloading the comparison operators is trivial. Here is the updated class definition:

```
' MyPoint is also comparable using the comparison operators.
Public Structure MyPoint
  Implements IComparable
...
  Public Function CompareTo(ByVal obj As Object) As Integer _
    Implements IComparable.CompareTo
    If TypeOf obj Is MyPoint Then
      Dim p As MyPoint = CType(obj, MyPoint)
      If Me.x > p.x AndAlso Me.y > p.y Then
        Return 1
      End If
      If Me.x < p.x AndAlso Me.y < p.y Then
        Return -1
      Else
        Return 0
      End If
    Else
      Throw New ArgumentException()
    End If
  End Function
```

```
  ' The overloaded comparison ops.
  Public Shared Operator <(ByVal p1 As MyPoint, ByVal p2 As MyPoint) As Boolean
    Return (p1.CompareTo(p2) < 0)
  End Operator
  Public Shared Operator >(ByVal p1 As MyPoint, ByVal p2 As MyPoint) As Boolean
    Return (p1.CompareTo(p2) > 0)
  End Operator
  Public Shared Operator <=(ByVal p1 As MyPoint, ByVal p2 As MyPoint) As Boolean
    Return (p1.CompareTo(p2) <= 0)
  End Operator
  Public Shared Operator >=(ByVal p1 As MyPoint, ByVal p2 As MyPoint) As Boolean
    Return (p1.CompareTo(p2) >= 0)
  End Operator
End Structure
```

Final Thoughts Regarding Operator Overloading

As you have seen, VB provides the capability to build types that can respond uniquely to various intrinsic, well-known operators. Now, before you go and retrofit all your classes to support such behavior, you must be sure that the operator(s) you are about to overload make some sort of logical sense in the world at large.

For example, let's say you overloaded the multiplication operator for the `Engine` class. What exactly would it mean to multiply two `Engine` objects? Not much. Remember, overloading operators is generally only useful when you're building utility types. Strings, points, rectangles, fractions, and hexagons make good candidates for operator overloading. People, managers, cars, database connections, and dialog boxes do not. As a rule of thumb, if an overloaded operator makes it *harder* for the user to understand a type's functionality, don't do it. Use this feature wisely.

■ **Source Code** The OverloadedOps project is located under the Chapter 12 subdirectory.

The Details of Value Types and Reference Types

Before we examine the related topic of custom conversion routines, our next task is to dive into the details regarding .NET *value types* and *reference types*. By doing so, you will have a much better foundation for understanding the usefulness of redefining how your custom types can respond to conversion routines.

Like any programming language, VB defines a number of keywords that represent basic data types such as whole numbers, character data, floating-point numbers, and Boolean values. Each of these intrinsic types are fixed entities in the Common Type System, meaning that when you create an integer variable (which is captured using the `Integer` keyword in VB), all .NET-aware languages understand the fixed nature of this type, and all agree on the range it is capable of handling.

Specifically speaking, a .NET data type may be *value-based* or *reference-based*. Value-based types, which include all numerical data types (`Integer`, `Double`, etc.), as well as enumerations and structures, are allocated *on the stack*. Given this fact, value types can be quickly removed from memory once they fall out of the defining scope:

```
' Integers are value types!
Public Sub SomeMethod()
  Dim i As Integer = 0
  Console.WriteLine("Value of i is: {0}", i)
End Sub  ' i is popped off the stack here!
```

When you assign one value type to another, a member-by-member copy is achieved by default. In terms of numerical or Boolean data types, the only "member" to copy is the value of the variable itself:

```
' Assigning two intrinsic value types results in
' two independent variables on the stack.
Public Sub SomeOtherMethod()
  Dim i As Integer = 99
  Dim k As Integer = i

  ' After the following assignment, "i" is still 99.
  k = 8732
End Sub
```

While the previous example is no major newsflash, understand that .NET structures and enumerations are also value types. Structures, as you may recall from Chapter 4, provide a way to achieve the bare-bones benefits of object orientation (i.e., encapsulation) while having the efficiency of stack-allocated data. Like a class, structures can take constructors (provided they have arguments) and define any number of members (properties, fields, subroutines, etc.).

All structures are implicitly derived from a class named `System.ValueType`. Functionally, the only purpose of `System.ValueType` is to override the virtual methods defined by `System.Object` to honor value-based, versus reference-based, semantics. In fact, the instance methods defined by `System.ValueType` are identical to those of `System.Object`, as you can see from the following method prototypes:

```
' Structures and enumerations extend System.ValueType.
Public MustInherit Class ValueType
  Inherits Object
  Public Overrides Function Equals(ByVal obj As Object) As Boolean
  Public Overrides Function GetHashCode() As Integer
  Public Overrides Function ToString() As String
End Class
```

To illustrate the differences between value types and reference types, create a new Console Application project (named ValAndRef), change the name of your existing VB file to `Program.vb`, and include the previous `MyPoint.vb` into your new project using the Project ➤ Add Existing Item menu option. Finally, to simplify our coding efforts, change the access modifier of each `Integer` member variable from `Private` to `Public`:

```
' Structures are value types!
Public Structure MyPoint
  Implements IComparable

  Public x As Integer, y As Integer
  ...
End Structure
```

To allocate an instance of a structure type, you may make use of the `New` keyword, which may seem counterintuitive given that we typically think `New` always implies heap allocation. This is part of the smoke and mirrors maintained by the CLR. As programmers, we can assume everything can be treated as an object. However, when the runtime encounters a type derived from `System.ValueType`, stack allocation is achieved:

```
Sub CreateValueTypes()
  ' Allocated on the stack!
  Dim p As New MyPoint()
End Sub
```

As an alternative, structures can be allocated without using the `New` keyword:

```
Sub CreateValueTypes()
  ' Allocated on the stack!
  Dim p As New MyPoint()

  ' Note lack of New keyword.
  Dim p1 As MyPoint
  p1.x = 100
  p1.y = 100
End Sub
```

In either case, the `MyPoint` variables are allocated on the stack and will be removed from memory as soon as the defining scope (the `CreateValueTypes()` method in this case) exits.

Value Types, References Types, and the Assignment Operator

Now, consider the following new method that makes use of our `MyPoint` structure (see Figure 12-3 for output):

```
Sub ValueTypesRefTypesAndAssignment()
  Console.WriteLine("***** Value Types and the Assignment Operator *****")
  Console.WriteLine("-> Creating p1")
  Dim p1 As New MyPoint(100, 100)

  Console.WriteLine("-> Assigning p2 to p1")
  Dim p2 As MyPoint = p1

  ' Here is p1.
  Console.WriteLine("p1.x = {0}", p1.x)
  Console.WriteLine("p1.y = {0}", p1.y)

  ' Here is p2.
  Console.WriteLine("p2.x = {0}", p2.x)
  Console.WriteLine("p2.y = {0}", p2.y)

  ' Change p2.x. This will NOT change p1.x.
  Console.WriteLine("-> Changing p2.x to 900")
  p2.x = 900

  ' Print again.
  Console.WriteLine("-> Here are the X values again...")
  Console.WriteLine("p1.x = {0}", p1.x)
  Console.WriteLine("p2.x = {0}", p2.x)
  Console.ReadLine()
End Sub
```

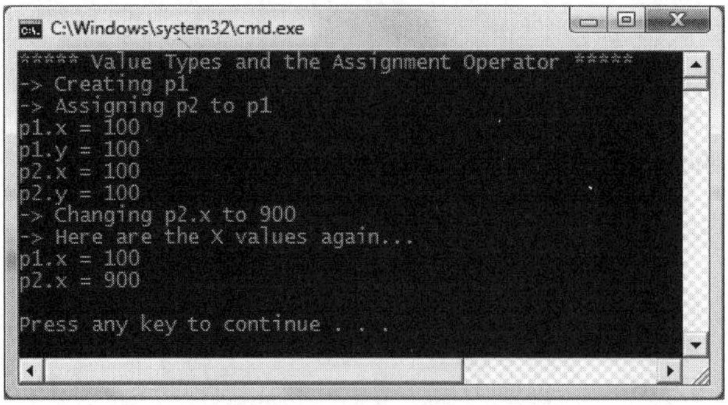

Figure 12-3. *Assigning one value type to another results in a bitwise copy of the field data.*

Here you have created a variable of type `MyPoint` (named `p1`) that is then assigned to another `MyPoint` (`p2`). Because `MyPoint` is a value type, you have two copies of the `MyPoint` type on the stack, each of which can be independently manipulated. Therefore, when you change the value of `p2.x`, the value of `p1.x` is unaffected.

In stark contrast, reference types (classes) are allocated on the managed heap. These objects stay in memory until the .NET garbage collector destroys them. By default, assignment of reference types results in a new reference to the *same* object on the heap. To illustrate, let's change the definition of the `MyPoint` type from a VB structure to a VB class:

```
' Classes are always reference types.
Public Class MyPoint
  ...
End Class ' Now a class!
```

If you were to run the test program once again, you would notice a change in behavior (see Figure 12-4).

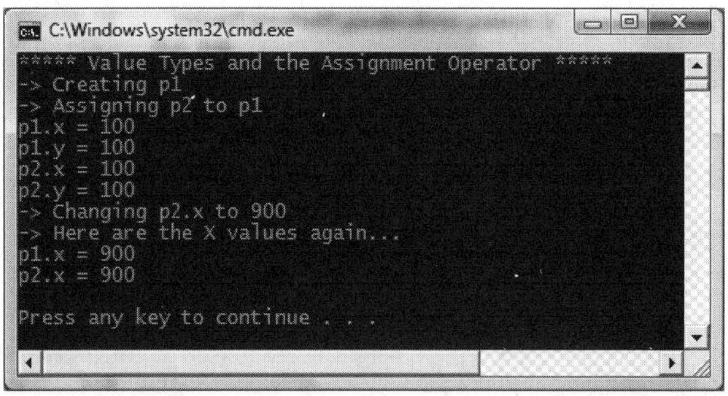

Figure 12-4. *Assigning one reference type to another results in redirecting the reference.*

In this case, you have two references pointing to the same object on the managed heap. Therefore, when you change the value of `x` using the `p2` reference, `p1.x` reports the same value.

Source Code The ValAndRef project is located under the Chapter 12 subdirectory.

Value Types Containing Reference Types

Now that you have a better feeling for the differences between value types and reference types, let's examine a more complex example; create a new Console Application project named ValType-ContainingRefType and change your initial VB file to `Program.vb`. Assume you have the following reference (i.e., a class) type that maintains an informational `String` that can be set using a custom constructor:

```
Public Class ShapeInfo
  Public infoString As String

  Public Sub New(ByVal info As String)
    infoString = info
  End Sub
End Class
```

Now assume that you want to contain a variable of this class type within a value (i.e., a structure) type named `MyRectangle`. To allow the outside world to set the value of the inner `ShapeInfo`, you also provide a custom constructor (as explained in just a bit, the default constructor of a structure is reserved and cannot be redefined):

```
Public Structure MyRectangle
  ' The MyRectangle structure contains a reference type member.
  Public rectInfo As ShapeInfo

  Public top, left, bottom, right As Integer

  Public Sub New(ByVal info As String)
    rectInfo = New ShapeInfo(info)
    top = 10
    left = 10
    bottom = 10
    right = 100
  End Sub
End Structure
```

At this point, you have contained a reference type within a value type. The million-dollar question now becomes, what happens if you assign one `MyRectangle` variable to another? Given what you already know about value types, you would be correct in assuming that the `Integer` field data (which are indeed structures) should be independent entities for each `MyRectangle` variable. But what about the internal reference type? Will the object's state be fully copied, or will the *reference* to that object be copied? Consider the following `Main()` method and check out Figure 12-5 for the answer.

```
Sub Main()
  ' Create the first MyRectangle.
  Console.WriteLine("-> Creating r1")
  Dim r1 As New MyRectangle("This is my first rect")

  ' Now assign a new MyRectangle to r1.
  Console.WriteLine("-> Assigning r2 to r1")
  Dim r2 As MyRectangle
  r2 = r1

  ' Change values of r2.
  Console.WriteLine("-> Changing all values of r2")
  r2.rectInfo.infoString = "This is new info!"
  r2.bottom = 4444
```

```
    ' Print values
    Console.WriteLine("-> Values after change:")
    Console.WriteLine("-> r1.rectInfo.infoString: {0}", r1.rectInfo.infoString)
    Console.WriteLine("-> r2.rectInfo.infoString: {0}", r2.rectInfo.infoString)
    Console.WriteLine("-> r1.bottom: {0}", r1.bottom)
    Console.WriteLine("-> r2.bottom: {0}", r2.bottom)
    Console.ReadLine()
End Sub
```

When you run this program, you will find that when you change the value of the informational string using the `r2` reference, the `r1` reference displays the same value.

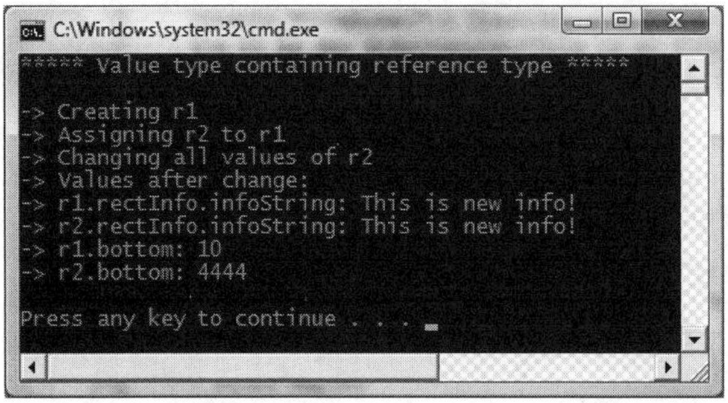

Figure 12-5. `r1` *and* `r2` *are both pointing to the same* `ShapeInfo` *object!*

By default, when a value type contains other reference types, assignment results in a copy *of the references*. In this way, you have two independent structures, each of which contains a reference pointing to the same object in memory (i.e., a *shallow copy*). When you want to perform a *deep copy*, where the state of internal references is fully copied into a new object, you need to implement the `ICloneable` interface (as you did in Chapter 9).

Source Code The ValTypeContainingRefType project is located under the Chapter 12 subdirectory.

Passing Reference Types by Value

Reference types can obviously be passed as parameters to functions and subroutines, using the `ByRef` keyword. However, passing a reference type by reference is quite different from passing it by value. To understand the distinction, assume you have a simple `Person` class, defined as follows, in a new Console Application project named RefTypeValTypeParams:

```
Public Class Person
  Public fullName As String
  Public age As Integer

  Public Sub New(ByVal n As String, ByVal a As Integer)
    fullName = n
    age = a
  End Sub
  Public Sub New()
  End Sub
```

```
  Public Overrides Function ToString() As String
    Return String.Format("Name: {0}, Age: {1}", fullName, age)
  End Function
End Class
```

Now, what if you create a method in your initial module that allows the caller to send in the Person type by value (note the ByVal keyword):

```
Sub SendAPersonByValue(ByVal p As Person)
  ' Change the age of "p"?
  p.age = 99

  ' Will the caller see this reassignment?
  p = New Person("Nikki", 999)
End Sub
```

Notice how the SendAPersonByValue() method attempts to reassign the incoming Person reference to a new Person object as well as change some state data. Now let's test this method using the following Main() method:

```
Sub Main()
  ' Passing ref types by value.
  Console.WriteLine("***** Passing Person object by value *****" & vbLf)
  Dim fred As New Person("Fred", 12)
  Console.WriteLine("Before by value call, Person is:")
  Console.WriteLine(fred)

  SendAPersonByValue(fred)
  Console.WriteLine("After by value call, Person is:")
  Console.WriteLine(fred)
  Console.ReadLine()
End Sub
```

Figure 12-6 shows the output of this code.

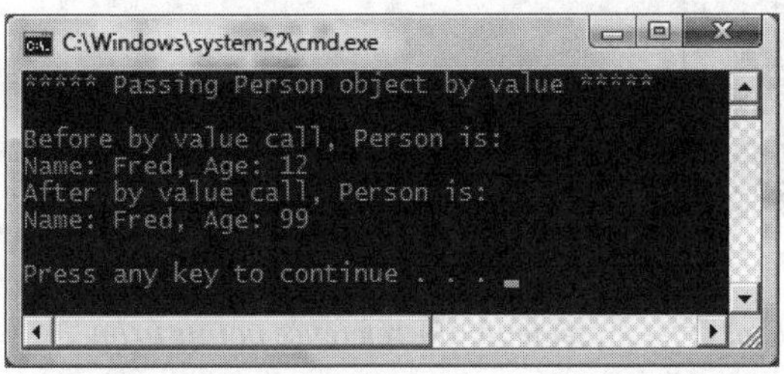

Figure 12-6. *Passing reference types by value "locks" which object the reference points to.*

As you can see, the value of age has been modified! This behavior seems to fly in the face of what it means to pass a parameter "by value." Given that you were able to change the state of the incoming Person, what was copied? The answer: a copy of the *reference* to the caller's object. Therefore, as the SendAPersonByValue() method is pointing to the same object as the caller, it is possible to alter the object's state data. What is *not* possible is to reassign what the reference is pointing to.

Passing Reference Types by Reference

Now assume you have a `SendAPersonByReference()` method, which passes a reference type by reference (note the `ByRef` parameter modifier):

```
Sub SendAPersonByReference(ByRef p As Person)
  ' Change some data of "p".
  p.age = 555

  ' "p" is now pointing to a new object on the heap!
  p = New Person("Nikki", 999)
End Sub
```

As you might expect, this allows complete flexibility of how the callee is able to manipulate the incoming parameter. Not only can the callee change the state of the object, but if it so chooses, it may also reassign the reference to a new `Person` object. Now ponder the following usage:

```
Sub Main()
  ' Assume previous code has been commented out...

  ' Passing ref types by ref.
  Console.WriteLine("***** Passing Person object by reference *****")
  Dim mel As New Person("Mel", 23)
  Console.WriteLine("Before by ref call, Person is:")
  Console.WriteLine(mel)
  SendAPersonByReference(mel)
  Console.WriteLine("After by ref call, Person is:")
  Console.WriteLine(mel)
  Console.ReadLine()
End Sub
```

As you can see from Figure 12-7, the `mel` object now points to a new object named `Nikki`.

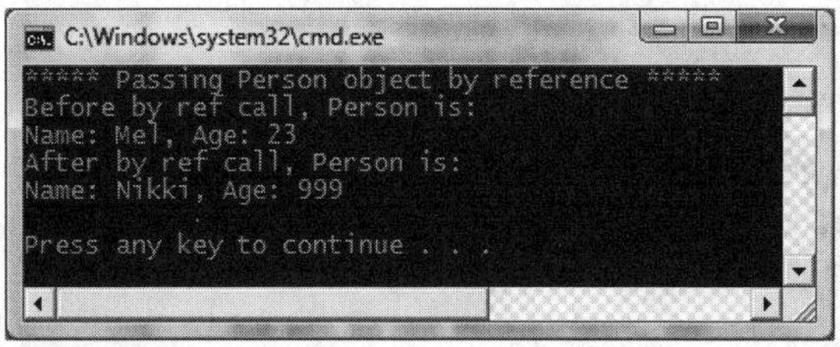

Figure 12-7. *Passing reference types by reference allows you to reset what the reference points to on the heap.*

The golden rule to keep in mind when passing reference types by reference is as follows:

- If a reference type is passed by reference, the callee may change the values of the object's state data as well as the object it is referencing.

Value and Reference Types: Final Details

To wrap up this topic, ponder the information in Table 12-2, which summarizes the core distinctions between value types and reference types.

Table 12-2. *Value Types and Reference Types Side by Side*

Intriguing Question	Value Type	Reference Type
Where is this type allocated?	Allocated on the stack.	Allocated on the managed heap.
How is a variable represented?	Value type variables are local copies.	Reference type variables are pointing to the memory occupied by the allocated instance.
What is the base type?	Must derive from `System.ValueType`.	Can derive from any other type (except `System.ValueType`), as long as that type is not "sealed" (see Chapter 6).
Can this type function as a base to other types?	No. Value types are always sealed and cannot be extended.	Yes. If the type is not sealed, it may function as a base to other types.
What is the default parameter passing behavior?	Variables are passed by value (i.e., a copy of the variable is passed into the called function).	Variables are passed by reference (i.e., the address of the variable is passed into the called function).
Can this type override `System.Object.Finalize()`?	No. Value types are never placed onto the heap and therefore do not need to be finalized.	Yes (see Chapter 8).
Can I define constructors for this type?	Yes, but the default constructor is reserved (i.e., your custom constructors must all have arguments).	But of course!
When do variables of this type die?	When they fall out of the defining scope.	When the managed heap is garbage collected.

Despite their differences, value types and reference types both have the ability to implement interfaces and may support any number of fields, methods, overloaded operators, constants, properties, and events.

■ Source Code The RefTypeValTypeParams project is located under the Chapter 12 subdirectory.

Now that we have examined the details of value types and reference types, we can move to the topic of custom type conversion routines. To set the stage for the discussion to follow, let's quickly review the notion of explicit and implicit conversions between numerical data and related class types.

Recall: Numerical Conversions

In terms of the intrinsic numerical types (`Byte`, `Integer`, `Double`, etc.), an *explicit conversion* (or *narrowing conversion*) is required when you attempt to store a larger value in a smaller container, as this may result in a loss of data. Basically, this is your way to tell the compiler, "Leave me alone, I know what I am trying to do." Conversely, an *implicit conversion* (or *widening conversion*) happens automatically when you attempt to place a smaller type in a destination type that will not result in a loss of data:

```
Sub Main()
  Dim a As Integer = 123
  Dim b As Long = a                       ' Implicit conversion from Integer to Long
  Dim c As Integer = CType(b, Integer)    ' Explicit conversion from Long to Integer
End Sub
```

Recall: Conversions Among Related Class Types

As shown in Chapter 6, class types may be related by classical inheritance (the "is-a" relationship). In this case, the VB conversion process allows you to cast up and down the class hierarchy. For example, a derived class can always be implicitly cast into a given base type. However, if you wish to store a base class type in a derived variable, you must perform an explicit cast:

```
' Two related class types.
Public Class Base
End Class

Public Class Derived
  Inherits Base
End Class

Module Program
  Sub Main()
    ' Implicit cast between derived to base.
    Dim myBaseType As Base
    myBaseType = New Derived()

    ' Must explicitly cast to store base reference
    ' in derived type.
    Dim myDerivedType As Derived = CType(myBaseType, Derived)
  End Sub
End Module
```

This explicit cast works due to the fact that the Base and Derived classes are related by classical inheritance. However, what if you have two class types in *different hierarchies* that require conversions? Given that they are not related by classical inheritance, explicit casting offers no help.

On a related note, consider value types. Assume you have two .NET structures named Square and Rectangle. Given that structures cannot leverage classic inheritance, you have no natural way to cast between these seemingly related types (assuming it made sense to do so).

While you could build helper methods in the structures (such as Rectangle.ToSquare()), VB allows you to build custom conversion routines that allow your types to respond to the CType() operator. Therefore, if you configured the Square structure correctly, you would be able to use the following syntax to explicitly convert between these structure types:

```
' Convert a Rectangle structure to a Square structure.
Dim rect As Rectangle
rect.Width = 3
rect.Height = 10
Dim sq As Square = CType(rect, Square)
```

Creating Custom Conversion Routines

VB provides two keywords, Widening and Narrowing, that can be used when redefining how your class or structure responds to the CType() operator. The difference between these conversion routines can be summarized as follows:

- Narrowing conversions do not always succeed at runtime, and may result in loss of data. If `Option Strict` is enabled, `CType` must be used for all narrowing conversions.
- Widening conversions always succeed at runtime and never incur data loss.

To illustrate, assume a new Console Application named CustomConversions, containing the following structure definitions:

```
Public Structure Rectangle
  ' Public for ease of use;
  ' however, feel free to encapsulate with properties.
  Public Width As Integer, Height As Integer

  Public Sub Draw()
    Console.WriteLine("Drawing a rect.")
  End Sub
  Public Overloads Overrides Function ToString() As String
    Return String.Format("[Width = {0}; Height = {1}]", Width, Height)
  End Function
End Structure

Public Structure Square
  Public Length As Integer

  Public Sub Draw()
    Console.WriteLine("Drawing a square.")
  End Sub
  Public Overloads Overrides Function ToString() As String
    Return String.Format("[Length = {0}]", Length)
  End Function

  ' Rectangles can be explicitly converted
  ' into Squares.
  Public Shared Narrowing Operator CType(ByVal r As Rectangle) As Square
    Dim s As Square
    s.Length = r.Width
    Return s
  End Operator
End Structure
```

Notice that this iteration of the `Square` type defines a custom narrowing conversion operation. Like the process of overloading an operator, conversion routines make use of the VB `Operator` keyword (in conjunction with the `Narrowing` or `Widening` keyword) and must be defined as a shared member. The incoming parameter is the entity you are converting *from*, while the return value is the entity you are converting *to*:

```
Public Shared Narrowing Operator CType(ByVal r As Rectangle) As Square
  ...
End Operator
```

In any case, the assumption is that a square (being a geometric pattern in which all sides are of equal length) can be obtained from the width of a rectangle. Thus, you are free to convert a `Rectangle` into a `Square` as follows:

```
Module Program
  Sub Main()
    Console.WriteLine("***** Fun with Custom Conversions *****")
    Console.WriteLine()
```

```
    ' Create a 10 * 5 Rectangle.
    Dim rect As Rectangle
    rect.Width = 10
    rect.Height = 5
    Console.WriteLine("rect = {0}", rect)

    ' Convert Rectangle to a 10 * 10 Square.
    Dim sq As Square = CType(rect, Square)
    Console.WriteLine("sq = {0}", sq)
    Console.ReadLine()
  End Sub
End Module
```

While it may not be all that helpful to convert a Rectangle into a Square within the same scope, assume you have a function that has been prototyped to take Square types.

```
' This method requires a Square type.
Sub DrawSquare(ByVal sq As Square)
  sq.Draw()
End Sub
```

Using your explicit conversion operation, you can safely pass in Rectangle types for processing:

```
Sub Main()
  Console.WriteLine("***** Fun with Custom Conversions *****" & vbLf)

  ' Create a 10 * 5 Rectangle.
  Dim rect As Rectangle
  rect.Width = 10
  rect.Height = 5
  Console.WriteLine("rect = {0}", rect)

  ' This is all right, as the Square has
  ' a custom narrowing CType() implementation.
  DrawSquare(CType(rect, Square))
End Sub
```

Additional Explicit Conversions for the Square Type

Now that you can explicitly convert Rectangles into Squares, let's examine a few additional explicit conversions. Given that a square is symmetrical on each side, it might be helpful to provide an explicit conversion routine that allows the caller to cast from an Integer type into a Square (which, of course, will have a side length equal to the incoming Integer). Likewise, what if you were to update Square such that the caller can cast *from* a Square into an Integer? Here is the calling logic:

```
Sub Main()
...
  ' Converting an Integer to a Square.
  Dim sq2 As Square = CType(90, Square)
  Console.WriteLine("sq2 = {0}", sq2)

  ' Converting a Square to an Integer.
  Dim side As Integer = CType(sq2, Integer)
  Console.WriteLine("Side length of sq2 = {0}", side)
End Sub
```

and here is the update to the Square type:

```
Structure Square
...
  Public Shared Narrowing Operator CType(ByVal sideLength As Integer) As Square
    Dim newSq As Square
    newSq.Length = sideLength
    Return newSq
  End Operator

  Public Shared Narrowing Operator CType(ByVal s As Square) As Integer
    Return s.Length
  End Operator
End Structure
```

Wild, huh? To be honest, converting from a Square into an Integer may not be the most intuitive (or useful) operation. However, this does point out a very important fact regarding custom conversion routines: the compiler does not care what you convert to or from, as long as you have written syntactically correct code. Thus, as with overloading operators, just because you can create an explicit cast operation for a given type does not mean you should. Typically, this technique will be most helpful when you're creating .NET structure types, given that they are unable to participate in classical inheritance (where casting comes for free).

Defining Implicit Conversion Routines

Thus far, you have created various custom *explicit* (i.e., *narrowing*) conversion operations. However, what about the following *implicit* (i.e., *widening*) conversion?

```
Sub Main()
...
  ' Attempt to make an implicit cast?
  Dim s3 As Square
  s3.Length = 83
  Dim rect2 As Rectangle = s3
...
End Sub
```

As you might expect, this code will not compile, given that you have not provided an implicit conversion routine for the Rectangle type. Now here is the catch: it is illegal to define explicit and implicit conversion functions on the same type, if they do not differ by their return type or parameter set. This might seem like a limitation; however, the second catch is that when a type defines an *implicit* conversion routine, it is legal for the caller to make use of the *explicit* cast syntax!

Confused? To clear things up, let's add an implicit conversion routine to the Rectangle structure using the VB Widening keyword (note that the following code assumes the width of the resulting Rectangle is computed by multiplying the side of the Square by 2):

```
Public Structure Rectangle
...
  Public Shared Widening Operator CType(ByVal s As Square) As Rectangle
    Dim r As Rectangle
    r.Height = s.Length

    ' Assume the length of the new Rectangle with
    ' (Length x 2)
    r.Width = s.Length * 2
    Return r
  End Operator
End Structure
```

With this update, you are now able to convert between types as follows:

```
Sub Main()
...
  ' Implicit cast OK!
  Dim s3 As Square
  s3.Length = 83
  Dim rect2 As Rectangle = s3
  Console.WriteLine("rect2 = {0}", rect2)
  DrawSquare(s3)

  ' Explicit cast syntax still OK!
  Dim s4 As Square
  s4.Length = 3
  Dim rect3 As Rectangle = CType(s4, Rectangle)
  Console.WriteLine("rect3 = {0}", rect3)
...
End Sub
```

Again, be aware that it is permissible to define explicit and implicit conversion routines for the same type as long as their signatures differ. Thus, you could update the Square as follows:

```
Public Structure Square
...
  ' Can call as:
  ' Dim sq2 As Square = CType(90, Square)
  ' or as:
  ' Dim sq2 As Square = 90
  Public Shared Widening Operator CType(ByVal sideLength As Integer) As Square
    Dim newSq As Square
    newSq.Length = sideLength
    Return newSq
  End Operator

  ' Must call as:
  ' Dim side As Integer = CType(mySquare, Square)
  Public Shared Narrowing Operator CType(ByVal s As Square) As Integer
    return s.Length
  End Operator
End Structure
```

■ **Source Code** The CustomConversions project is located under the Chapter 12 subdirectory.

The VB DirectCast Keyword

To wrap things up for this chapter, allow me to comment on two keywords that can be used as alternatives to CType(). As you know by this point in the text, CType() can be used to explicitly convert an expression to a specified data type, object, structure, class, or interface.

Also recall that when you use CType(), the CLR will throw a runtime exception if the arguments are incompatible. To illustrate, assume you have two class types and a single interface related as follows:

```
Public Interface ITurboBoost
  Sub TurboCharge(ByVal onOff As Boolean)
End Interface

Public Class Car
End Class

Public Class SportsCar
  Inherits Car
  Implements ITurboBoost
  Public Sub TurboCharge(ByVal onOff As Boolean) _
    Implements ITurboBoost.TurboCharge
  End Sub
End Class
```

Now observe the following CType() statements, all of which compile, and some of which cause a runtime exception (an InvalidCastException to be exact):

```
Sub Main()
  Console.WriteLine("***** Fun with CType / DirectCast / TryCast ******")
  Console.WriteLine()

  ' This CType() throws an exception,
  ' as Car does not implement ITurboBoost.
  Dim myCar As New Car()
  Dim iTB As ITurboBoost
  iTB = CType(myCar, ITurboBoost)

  ' This CType() is A-OK, as SportsCar does
  ' implement ITurboBoost.
  Dim myViper As New SportsCar()
  iTB = CType(myViper, ITurboBoost)

  ' CType() can also be used to narrow or widen
  ' between primitive types.
  Dim i As Integer = 200
  Dim b As Byte = CType(i, Byte)
End Sub
```

While using CType() to convert between types is always permissible, VB also provides an alternative keyword named DirectCast(). Syntactically, DirectCast() looks identical to CType(). Under the hood, however, DirectCast() offers better performance when converting to or from reference types. The reason is that DirectCast(), unlike CType(), does not make use of the Visual Basic runtime helper routines for conversion. However, remember that DirectCast can only be used if the arguments are related by the "is-a" relationship or interface implementation (and could therefore never be used to convert between structures [and thus numerical types]). Consider the following update to the previous Main() method:

```
Sub Main()
  Console.WriteLine("***** Fun with CType / DirectCast / TryCast ******" & vbLf)

  Dim myCar As New Car()
  Dim iTB As ITurboBoost
  iTB = DirectCast(myCar, ITurboBoost)

  Dim myViper As New SportsCar()
  iTB = DirectCast(myViper, ITurboBoost)
```

```
  ' Compiler error! Integer and Byte
  ' are not related to inheritance/interface
  ' implementation!
  Dim i As Integer = 200
  Dim b As Byte = DirectCast(i, Byte)
End Sub
```

Note that the first two DirectCast() calls are syntactically identical to using CType(). The final call to DirectCast() is a compile-time error, however. While it is true that DirectCast() can result in greater performance for large-scale applications, this is not to say the CType() is obsolete. In fact, in most applications, these two calls can be used interchangeably with little or no noticeable effect. However, when you wish to squeeze out every drop of performance from a VB application, DirectCast() is one part of the puzzle.

The VB TryCast Keyword

On a final note, VB also offers one final manner to perform runtime type conversions using TryCast(). Again, syntactically, TryCast() looks identical to CType(). The difference is that TryCast() returns Nothing if the arguments are not related by inheritance or interface implementation, rather than throwing a runtime exception. Thus, rather than wrapping a call to CType() or DirectCast() within Try/Catch logic, you can simply test the returned reference within a conditional statement.

This being said, here is the final iteration of our Main() method, which makes use of structured exception handling/conditional tests for Nothing as required by each of the conversion operators.

```
Sub Main()
  Console.WriteLine("***** Fun with CType / DirectCast / TryCast ******")
  Console.WriteLine()

  Dim myCar As New Car()
  Dim iTB As ITurboBoost

  ' CType() throws
  ' exceptions if the types are not compatible.
  Try
    iTB = CType(myCar, ITurboBoost)
  Catch ex As InvalidCastException
    Console.WriteLine(ex.Message)
    Console.WriteLine()
  End Try

  ' Like CType(), DirectCast() throws
  ' exceptions if the types are not compatible.
  Dim myViper As New SportsCar()
  Try
    iTB = DirectCast(myViper, ITurboBoost)
  Catch ex As Exception
    Console.WriteLine(ex.Message)
    Console.WriteLine()
  End Try

  ' TryCast() returns Nothing if the types are not
  ' compatible.
  Dim c As Car = TryCast(myViper, Car)
  If c Is Nothing Then
    Console.WriteLine("Sorry, types are not compatable...")
  Else
```

```
    Console.WriteLine(c.ToString())
  End If
End Sub
```

Source Code The Casting project is located under the Chapter 12 subdirectory.

Summary

This chapter has illustrated a number of more advanced aspects of the Visual Basic programming language. We began by looking at how it is possible to build custom types that respond to the built-in VB operators using the `Operator` keyword. As shown, this technique can simplify how others interact with your types, as they behave (more or less) identically to other native data types.

The next topic of this chapter was a detailed examination of the value type/reference type distinction, which served as a lead-in to the topic of custom conversion routines. Recall that this allows you to redefine how custom types (most often structures) respond to the `CType` operator. We wrapped up by examining two new conversion keywords (`DirectCast` and `TryCast`) that can be used in place of traditional calls to `CType()`.

CHAPTER 13

VB 2008–Specific Language Features

VB 2008, the current release of Microsoft's BASIC-centric .NET programming language, introduces a large number of new syntactic constructs, one of which (the use of lambda expressions via the `Function` statement) you have already explored in Chapter 11. This chapter will complete your investigation of the core language features offered by VB 2008. Specifically, you will examine implicit data typing, extension methods, object initializers, and the role of anonymous types.

While many of these new language features can be used directly out of the box to help build robust and highly functional .NET software, it is also worth pointing out that many of these new constructs are most helpful when interacting with the LINQ technology set, which we'll begin to examine in Chapter 14. Given this fact, don't be too concerned if the usefulness of some of these new constructs is not immediately obvious. Once you understand the role of LINQ, the role of many of these new features will become clear.

Understanding Implicit Data Typing

The first new language feature we will examine is *implicit data typing*. To illustrate, begin by creating a new Console Application named ImplicitDataTypes. As you have learned since the very beginning of this text, local variables (such as variables declared in a method scope) are declared in a very predictable, which is to say *explicit*, manner using the `As` clause:

```
Public Sub ExplicitTyping()
  ' Local variables are declared as follows:
  ' Dim variableName As dataType = initialValue
  Dim myInt As Integer = 0
  Dim myBool As Boolean = True
  Dim myString As String = "Time, marches on..."
End Sub
```

VB 2008 now provides a new compiler option setting (`Option Infer`), which is enabled by default for any new VB 2008 project created with Visual Studio 2008. You can view this default setting (`On`) within the Compile tab of the My Project editor (see Figure 13-1). On a related note, if you ever needed to enable this setting at the level of the command-line compiler (`vbc.exe`, discussed in Chapter 2), you can do so using the new `/optioninfer` command-line argument.

Note Older VB projects that are upgraded into Visual Studio 2008 will have `Option Infer` set to `Off` by default. You must manually set this option to `On` if you wish to enable this behavior for upgraded projects.

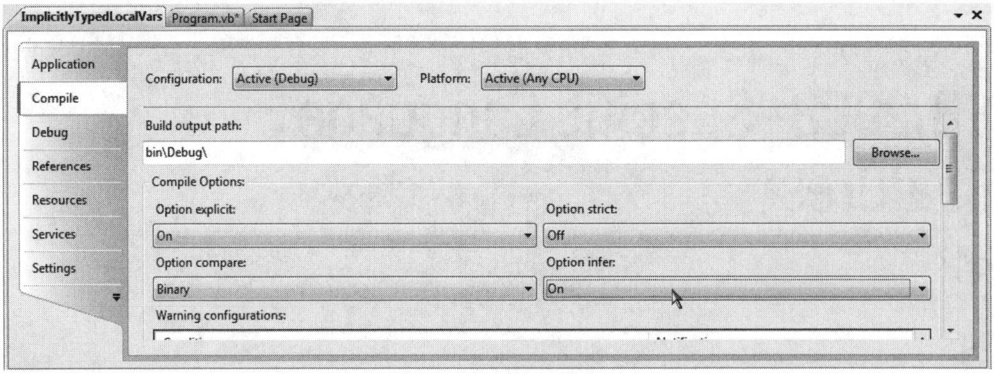

Figure 13-1. *VB 2008 projects enable* `Option Infer` *by default.*

When `Option Infer` is set to `On`, use of an `As` clause for local variables is optional (however, as explained in just a bit, the value assigned to `Option Strict` can complicate matters). The compiler will automatically (pardon the redundancy) infer the underlying data type based on the value used to initialize the data point. For example, the previous code example could now be reworked into a new method named `ImplicitTyping()` as follows (notice the absence of any `As` clauses):

```
Public Sub ImplicitTyping()
  ' Implicitly typed local variables.
  Dim myInt = 0
  Dim myBool = True
  Dim myString = "Time, marches on..."
End Sub
```

Here, the compiler is able to infer that `myInt` is in fact a `System.Int32`, `myBool` is a `System.Boolean`, and `myString` is indeed of type `System.String`, given the initially assigned value. You can verify this by printing out the type name via reflection:

```
Public Sub ImplicitTyping()
  ' Implicitly typed local variables.
  Dim myInt = 0
  Dim myBool = True
  Dim myString = "Time, marches on..."

  ' Print out the underlying type.
  Console.WriteLine("myInt is a: {0}", myInt.GetType().Name)
  Console.WriteLine("myBool is a: {0}", myBool.GetType().Name)
  Console.WriteLine("myString is a: {0}", myString.GetType().Name)
End Sub
```

■ Note If you do not provide an initial value assignment to an implicitly typed local variable, the underlying data type is assumed to be `System.Object`. However, this is only possible if `Option Strict` is disabled. More information on the interplay of `Option Strict` and implicit typing a bit later in this chapter in the section "Late Binding vs. Implicit Typing."

Be aware that you can use this implicit typing for any type in the base class libraries, including arrays, generics, or custom types. For example, we could update `ImplicitTyping()` with the following additional code statements:

```
Public Sub ImplicitTyping()
...
  ' Assume we have classes of type SportsCar
  ' and MiniVan somewhere in the project.
  Dim evenNumbers = New Integer() {2, 4, 6, 8}
  Dim myMinivans = New List(Of MiniVan)()
  Dim myCar = New SportsCar()

  Console.WriteLine("evenNumbers is a: {0}", evenNumbers.GetType().Name)
  Console.WriteLine("myMinivans is a: {0}", myMinivans.GetType().Name)
  Console.WriteLine("myCar is a: {0}", myCar.GetType().Name)
End Sub
```

In any case, if you were to now call your `ImplicitTyping()` method from within `Main()`:

```
Sub Main()
  Console.WriteLine("***** Fun with Impliict Typing *****")
  Console.WriteLine()
  ImplicitTyping()
  Console.ReadLine()
End Sub
```

you'll find the output shown in Figure 13-2.

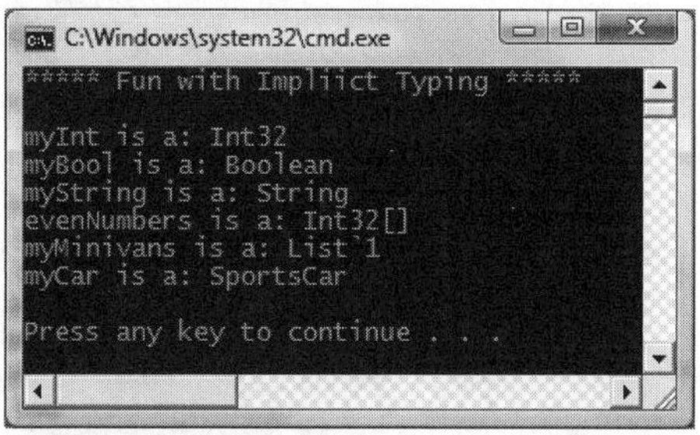

Figure 13-2. *Viewing the inferred data type via reflection*

Note A generic type is represented in CIL code using a forward single tick (`) to mark the number of type parameters. Therefore, given that the generic `List(Of T)` type has one type parameter, `myMinivans` is realized as ``List`1`` via reflection services.

The Visual Studio 2008 IDE offers a more direct way to quickly view the underlying type-of-type via IntelliSense. Simply place your mouse cursor over an implicitly typed local variable to examine the inferred data type (see Figure 13-3).

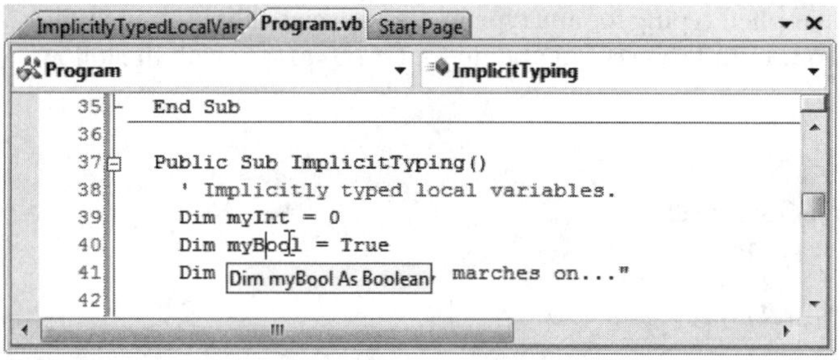

Figure 13-3. *Viewing the inferred data type via Visual Studio 2008 IntelliSense*

Implicit Typing Within Iteration Constructs

It is also possible to make use of implicit typing within a `For Each` looping construct. As you would expect, the compiler will correctly imply the correct type of type:

```
Public Sub ImplicitTypingInForEach()
  Dim evenNumbers() = New Integer() {2, 4, 6, 8}

  ' Use implicit typing in a standard For Each loop.
  ' Here, "item" is really a System.Int32.
  For Each item In evenNumbers
    Console.WriteLine("Item value: {0}", item)
  Next
End Sub
```

Understand, however, that a `For Each` loop can make use of a strongly typed iterator when processing an implicitly defined local variable. Thus, the following update to the previous code is also syntactically correct:

```
' Here, explicitly define the iterator type.
For Each item As Integer In evenNumbers
  Console.WriteLine("Item value: {0}", item)
Next
```

Implicitly Typed Data Is Strongly Typed Data

It is very important to understand that, unlike loosely typed data (such as the VB6 `Variant`), implicit typing does *not* imply loose typing. Once you have assigned an initial value to an implicitly typed variable, you can only assign values within the type's range. For example, if you were to attempt to assign `myBool` to a new `SportsCar` reference, you will receive a compile-time error:

```
' Error! Once initial assignment is made,
' implicit data is strongly typed!
Dim myBool = True
myBool = New SportsCar()
```

Disabling Option Infer

Recall that by default, all new VB 2008 projects have `Option Infer` enabled. Like other `Option` directives, you can change the default settings on a file-by-file basis. By way of a simple test, assume you have added the following code statement at the very top of your current `*.vb` file:

```
' Disable automatic type inference for the current file.
Option Infer Off
```

If you were to run your program once again, the output will be identical to what was shown in Figure 13-2. However, if you were to hover your mouse cursor over any of the implicitly typed local variables, you might be surprised to see they are now implicitly defined to be a `System.Object` (see Figure 13-4)!

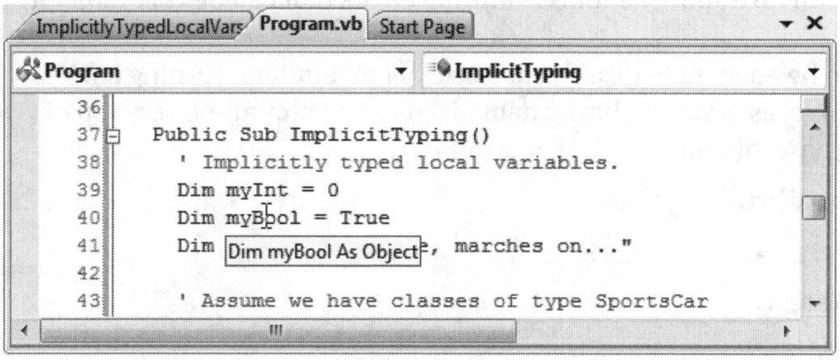

Figure 13-4. *Disabling* `Option Infer` *results in late binding!*

When you disable `Option Infer`, you are essentially *enabling* late binding. Thus, any local variable that is not declared using an `As` clause will be assigned to the underlying type of `System.Object`. To clarify:

```
' If Option Infer is On,
' myInt is of type System.Int32.
Dim myInt = 10

' If Option Infer is Off,
' myInt is of type System.Object.
Dim myInt = 10
```

To be sure, the inclusion of `Option Infer` can be a bit confusing, given that it appears to behave so closely to traditional VB late binding. To clarify matters, let's dive a bit deeper into the interplay of `Option Infer` and `Option Strict`.

Late Binding vs. Implicit Typing

Implicit typing of variables may appear to be "old news" to those of you who have used an earlier version of the Visual Basic language. For example, VB6 would allow us to author very similar looking code (again, notice the omission of any qualifying `As` clause):

```
' VB6 code follows!
Public Sub MyVb6Sub()
  Dim myInt
  myInt = 0

  Dim myBool
  myBool = True

  Dim myString
  myString = "Time, marches on..."
End Sub
```

The previous VB6 code is *not* making use of implicit typing, but rather *late binding*. Here, `myInt`, `myBool`, and `myString` are all assumed to be of type `Object` (the COM-based VB6 `Object`, not the .NET `System.Object`). Using late binding, the underlying type-of-type (`Integer`, `Boolean`, `String`) is not known until runtime.

Typically, use of late binding in any version of VB is not recommended, unless you are absolutely required to do so (and even then, it is safer to make use of the `System.Reflection` types), as this can hurt performance. Even worse, if you attempt to assign a variable declared via late binding to an incompatible value, you will no doubt encounter runtime errors that can be very difficult to diagnose.

The `Option Strict` setting can be enabled to disable this style of late binding. Turning back to the current Visual Basic 2008 example, assume you have enabled `Option Strict` at the very top of your code file, while still *disabling* type inference:

```
' Do not allow VB6-style late binding.
Option Strict On

' Do not allow VB 2008 type inference.
Option Infer Off
```

With this configuration of options, you would find a series of errors (see Figure 13-5). Specifically, each variable you declared without an `As` clause is in error, as enabling `Option Strict` demands explicit data typing.

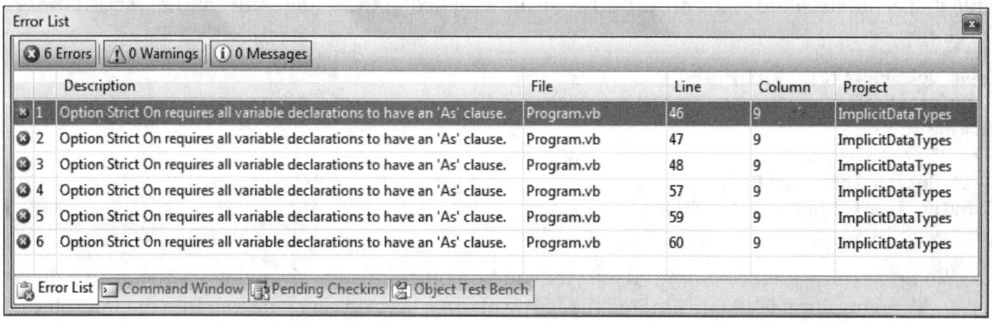

Figure 13-5. `Option Strict` *demands strong, explicit typing.*

However, if you were to enable type inference *and* `Option Strict` as follows:

```
' Do not allow VB6-style late binding.
Option Strict On

' Recall, this is the default setting.
Option Infer On
```

you would no longer find any compile-time errors, and end up with the same strong typing as illustrated by the Visual Studio 2008 IntelliSense (seen previously in Figure 13-4). Table 13-1 documents the end result of combining the `Option Strict` and `Option Infer` compiler options.

Note During the remainder of our examination of implicit typing, the assumption will be that `Option Strict` is enabled (which is always a good idea for every VB project you may be building).

Table 13-1. *Result of* `Option Strict`/`Option Infer` *Settings*

`Option Strict` **Setting**	`Option Infer` **Setting**	**Combination Results in Strongly Typed Data?**	**Combination Results in Coding Error?**
On	On	Yes	No
On	Off	Yes	Yes, if your data is declared without using an `As` clause
Off	Off	No	No
Off	On	Yes	No

Maximizing Type Safety

As if the interaction between `Option Strict` and `Option Infer` weren't enough to muddy the waters, you should also be very aware that the VB 2008 compiler can be tweaked in a number of ways that will alter how and when coding errors are reported. If you were to open up the My Project editor and click the Compile tab, you'll notice a series of "warning conditions" (such as Unused local variable, Implicit conversion, etc.), many of which are initially configured to generate warnings.

If you wish to build a VB 2008 project and force the compiler to keep your code as type safe as possible, I would suggest enabling `Option Strict` for all projects (as mentioned previously in this text) and check the Treat all warnings as errors check box (see Figure 13-6).

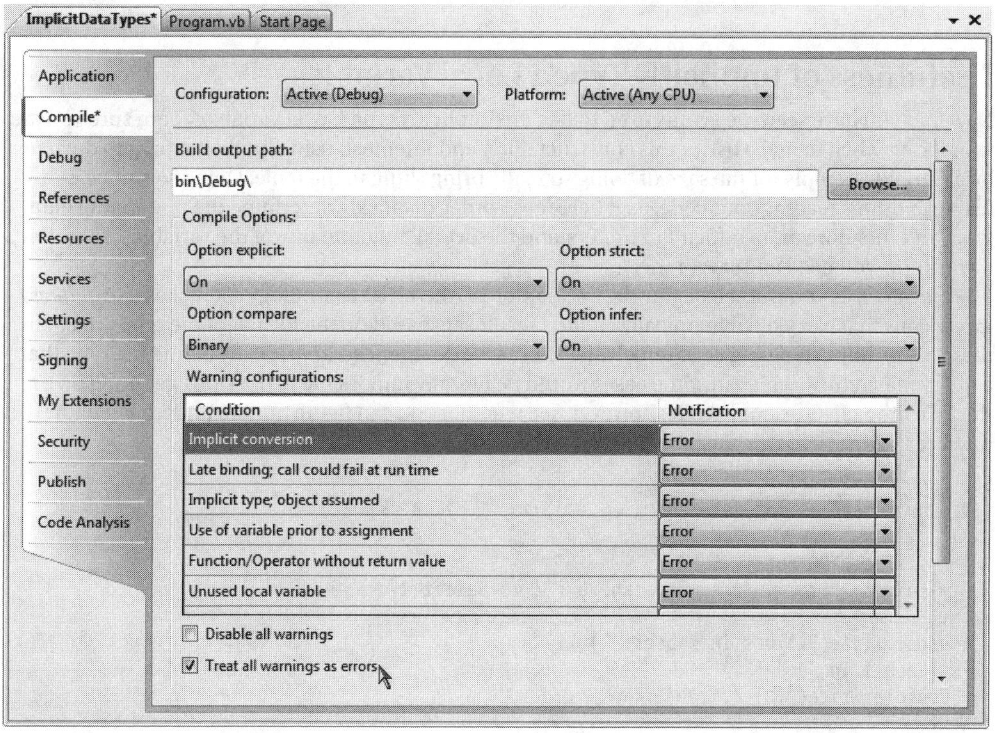

Figure 13-6. *Treating warnings as errors*

When you configure your projects in this way, you can rest assured that the compiler is doing everything it can to ensure you write type-safe, robust code.

Restrictions on Implicitly Typed Variables

There are, of course, restrictions regarding the use of implicit typing. First and foremost, implicit typing requires you to assign a value to the variable at their time of declaration (again, assuming `Option Strict` is enabled). The restriction makes the act of defining an implicitly typed variable look and feel like the process of defining a constant data point (via `Const`):

```
' Error! Must assign a value!
Dim myData

' Error! Must assign value at time of declaration!
Dim myInt
myInt = 0
```

It is permissible, however, to assign the value of an implicitly typed local variable to the value of other variables, implicitly typed or not:

```
' OK!
Dim myInt = 0
Dim anotherInt = myInt
Dim myString As String = "Wake up!"
Dim myData = myString
```

Usefulness of Implicitly Typed Local Variables

Now that you have seen the syntax used to declare implicitly typed local variables, I am sure you are wondering when to make use of this construct. First and foremost, using implicit typing to declare local variables simply for the sake of doing so really brings little to the table. Doing so can be confusing to others reading your code, as it becomes harder to quickly determine the underlying data type (and therefore more difficult to understand the overall functionality of the variable). Therefore, if you know you need an `Integer`, declare an `Integer`!

However, as you will see beginning in Chapter 14, the LINQ technology set makes use of *query expressions* that can yield dynamically created result sets based on the format of the query itself. In these cases, implicit typing is extremely helpful, as we do not need to explicitly define the type that a query may return, which in some cases would be literally impossible to do. Don't get hung up on the following LINQ example code; however, see whether you can figure out the underlying data type of `subset`:

```
Sub QueryOverInts()
  Dim numbers() As Integer = {10, 20, 30, 40, 1, 2, 3, 8}

  ' A simple LINQ query.
  Dim subset = From i In numbers Where i < 10 Select i

  Console.Write("Values in subset: ")
  For Each i In subset
    Console.Write("{0} ", i)
  Next
  Console.WriteLine()
```

```
  ' Hmmm...what type is subset?
  Console.WriteLine("subset is a: {0}", subset.GetType().Name)
  Console.WriteLine("Namespace of subset is: {0}", subset.GetType().Namespace)
End Sub
```

I'll let the interested reader verify the type-of-type of `subset` by executing the preceding code (and it is not an array of integers!). In any case, it should be clear that implicit typing does have its place within the LINQ technology set. In fact, it could be argued that the *only* time one would make use of implicit typing is when defining data returned from a LINQ query.

Source Code The ImplicitlyDataTypes project can be found under the Chapter 13 subdirectory.

Understanding Extension Methods

The next VB 2008 language feature we will examine is the use of *extension methods*. As you know, once a type is defined and compiled into a .NET assembly, its definition is, more or less, final. The only way to add new members, update members, or remove members is to recode and recompile the code base into an updated assembly (or take more drastic measures, such as using the `System.Reflection.Emit` namespace to dynamically reshape a compiled type in memory).

Under VB 2008, it is now possible to define extension methods. In a nutshell, extension methods allow existing compiled types (specifically, classes, structures, or interface implementations) as well as types currently being compiled (such as types in a project that contains extension methods) to gain new functionality without needing to directly update the type being extended.

As suggested, this technique can be quite helpful when you need to inject new functionality into types for which you do not have an existing code base. It can also be quite helpful when you need to force a type to support a set of members (in the interest of polymorphism), but cannot modify the original type declaration. Using extension methods, you can add functionality to precompiled types while providing the illusion these methods were there all along.

Note Understand that extension methods do not literally change the code in a compiled assembly! This technique only adds members to a type within the context of the application using the extension methods.

When you define extension methods, the first restriction is that they must be defined within a *module* (see Chapter 3) and cannot be defined within classes or structures. The second point is that all extension methods are marked as such by using the `<Extension()>` attribute defined within the `System.Runtime.CompilerServices` namespace. The third, and perhaps most subtle, point is that the first parameter of an extension method marks *the type of entity being extended*. Finally, every extension method can be called either from the correct instance in memory or directly via the defining module! Sound strange? Let's look at a full example to clarify matters.

Defining Extension Methods

Create a new Console Application named ExtensionMethods. Now, assume you are authoring a module named `MyExtensions` that defines two extension methods. The first method allows any `Object` in the .NET base class libraries to have a brand-new method named `DisplayDefiningAssembly()` that makes use of types in the `System.Reflection` namespace to display the assembly of the specified type.

The second extension method, named ReverseDigits(), allows any Integer to obtain a new version of itself where the value is reversed digit by digit. For example, if an Integer with the value 1234 called ReverseDigits(), the integer returned is set to the value 4321. Consider the following module implementation:

```
Imports System.Reflection
Imports System.Runtime.CompilerServices

Module MyExtensions

  ' This method allows any object to display the assembly
  ' it is defined in.
  <Extension()> _
  Public Sub DisplayDefiningAssembly(ByVal obj As Object)
    Console.WriteLine("{0} lives here: {1}", obj.GetType().Name, _
      obj.GetType().Assembly)
  End Sub

  ' This method allows any integer to reverse its digits.
  ' For example, 56 would return 65.
  <Extension()> _
  Public Function ReverseDigits(ByVal i As Integer) As Integer
    ' Translate integer into a string, and then
    ' get all the characters.
    Dim digits() As Char = i.ToString().ToCharArray()

    ' Now reverse items in the array.
    Array.Reverse(digits)

    ' Put back into string.
    Dim newDigits As String = New String(digits)

    ' Finally, return the modified string back as an integer.
    Return Integer.Parse(newDigits)
  End Function

End Module
```

Again, note how each extension method has been qualified with the <Extension()> attribute. Also remember that the very first parameter of an extension method represents the type of item being extended (Object in the case of DisplayDefiningAssembly() and Integer in the case of the ReverseDigits() method).

Overloading Extension Methods

Like a "normal" method, extension methods can of course have multiple parameters, and therefore can in fact be overloaded. For example, consider the following overloaded version of DisplayDefiningAssembly(), which allows the caller to specify that several "extra details" be displayed for the type:

```
' This version takes a Boolean argument when calling the method.
<Extension()> _
Public Sub DisplayDefiningAssembly(ByVal obj As Object, _
  ByVal showDetails As Boolean)
  Console.WriteLine("Defining Assembly: {0}", obj.GetType().Assembly)
```

```
  If showDetails Then
    Console.WriteLine("Name of type: {0}", obj.GetType().Name)
    Console.WriteLine("Parent of type: {0}", obj.GetType().BaseType)
    Console.WriteLine("Is generic?: {0}", obj.GetType().IsGenericType)
  End If
End Sub
```

At this point, we have two versions of `DisplayDefiningAssembly()`. If you wish to simplify the current example, you could of course make use of the `Optional` parameter modifier of VB, and end up with a single method named `DisplayDefiningAssembly()` looking like so:

```
' This version takes a optional Boolean argument when calling the method.
<Extension()> _
Public Sub DisplayDefiningAssembly(ByVal obj As Object, _
  Optional ByVal showDetails As Boolean = False)
...
End Sub
```

Invoking Extension Methods on an Instance Level

Now that we have these extension methods, look at how all `Objects` (which of course means every type in the .NET Framework) have a new method named `DisplayDefiningAssembly()`, while `Integers` (and only `Integers`) have methods named `ReverseDigits()`:

```
Sub Main()
  Console.WriteLine("***** Fun with Extension Methods *****" & vbLf)

  ' The Integer has assumed a new identity!
  Dim myInt As Integer = 12345678
  myInt.DisplayDefiningAssembly()

  ' So has the DataSet!
  Dim d = New System.Data.DataSet()
  d.DisplayDefiningAssembly()

  ' And the SoundPlayer (show details).
  Dim sp As New System.Media.SoundPlayer()
  sp.DisplayDefiningAssembly(True)

  ' Use new Integer functionality.
  Console.WriteLine(vbLf & "Value of myInt: {0}", myInt)
  Console.WriteLine("Reversed digits of myInt: {0}", myInt.ReverseDigits())

  Console.ReadLine()
End Sub
```

Figure 13-7 shows the output.

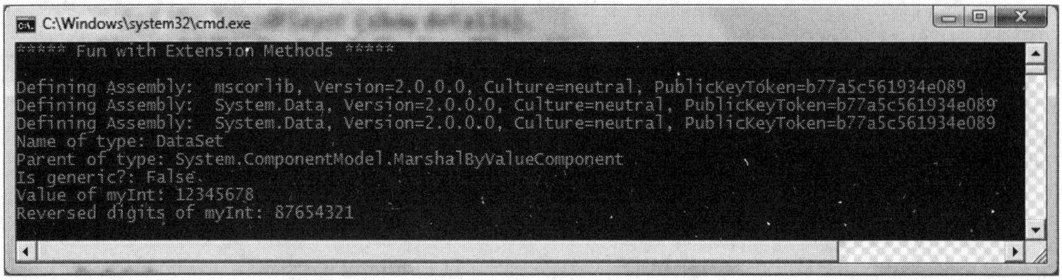

Figure 13-7. *Extension methods in action*

Invoking Extension Methods on the Defining Module

As you have seen, the first parameter of an extension method defines the type item the method is applicable to. If we peek at what is happening behind the scenes (as verified by a tool such as ildasm.exe), we will find that the compiler simply calls the "normal" shared method in the module, passing in the variable calling the method as a parameter. Consider the following valid VB code, which approximates the code substitution that took place:

```
Sub Main()
  Console.WriteLine("***** Fun with Extension Methods *****" & vbLf)

  ' The Integer has assumed a new identity!
  Dim myInt As Integer = 12345678
  MyExtensions.DisplayDefiningAssembly(myInt)

  ' So has the DataSet!
  Dim d = New System.Data.DataSet()
  MyExtensions.DisplayDefiningAssembly(d)

  ' And the SoundPlayer (with details).
  Dim sp As New System.Media.SoundPlayer()
  MyExtensions.DisplayDefiningAssembly(sp, True)

  ' Use new integer functionality.
  Console.WriteLine("Value of myInt: {0}", myInt)
  Console.WriteLine("Reversed digits of myInt: {0}", _
                    MyExtensions.ReverseDigits(myInt))
  Console.ReadLine()
End Sub
```

When you run your program, the output is identical to Figure 13-7. Given that calling an extension method from an object (thereby making it seem that the method is in fact an instance-level method) is just some smoke-and-mirrors effect provided by the compiler, you are always free to call extension methods as normal shared methods using the expected VB syntax (as just shown).

The Scope of an Extension Method

As just explained, extension methods are essentially shared methods that can be invoked from a variable of the extended type. Given this flavor of syntactic sugar, it is really important to point out that unlike a "normal" method, extension methods do not have direct access to the members of the type they are extending; said another way, *extending* is not *inheriting*. Consider the following simple Car type:

```
Public Class Car
  Public Speed As Integer
  Public Function SpeedUp() As Integer
    Speed += 1
    Return Speed
  End Function
End Class
```

If you were to build an extension method for the `Car` type named `SlowDown()`, you do not have direct access to the members of `Car` within the scope of the extension method, as we are not performing an act of classical inheritance. Therefore, the following would result in a compiler error:

```
Module CarExtensions
  <Extension()> _
  Public Function SlowDown(ByVal c As Car) As Integer
    ' Error! This method is not in a type deriving from Car!
    Speed -= 1
    Return Speed
  End Function
End Module
```

The problem here is that the `SlowDown()` extension method is attempting to access the `Speed` field of the `Car` type; however, because `SlowDown()` is a member of the `CarExtensions` module, `Speed` does not exist in this context! What is permissible, however, is to make use of the incoming parameter to access all public members (and *only* the public members) of the type being extending. Thus, the following code compiles as expected:

```
Module CarExtensions
  <Extension()> _
  Public Function SlowDown(ByVal c As Car) As Integer
    c.Speed -= 1
    Return c.Speed
  End Function
End Module
```

At this point, you could create a `Car` object and invoke the `SpeedUp()` and `SlowDown()` methods as follows:

```
Sub UseCar()
  Dim c As New Car()
  c.Speed = 10
  Console.WriteLine("Speed: {0}", c.SpeedUp())
  Console.WriteLine("Speed: {0}", c.SlowDown())
End Sub
```

Importing Types That Define Extension Methods

When you partition a set of modules containing extension methods in a unique namespace, other namespaces in that assembly will make use of the standard VB `Imports` keyword to import not only the modules themselves, but also each of the supported extension methods. This is important to remember, because if you do not explicitly import the correct namespace, the extension methods are not available for that VB code file.

In effect, although it can appear on the surface that extension methods are global in nature, they are in fact limited to the namespace that defines them or the namespaces that import them. Thus, if we wrap the definitions of our modules (`MyExtensions` and `CarExtensions`) into a namespace named `MyExtensionMethods` as follows:

```
Namespace MyExtensionMethods
  Module MyExtensions
    ...
  End Module

  Module CarExtensions
    ...
  End Module
End Namespace
```

other namespaces in the project would need to explicitly import the `MyExtensionMethods` namespace to gain the extension methods defined by these types. Therefore, the following is a compiler error:

```
' Here is our only imports directive.
Imports System

Namespace MyNewApp

  Class JustATest
    Sub SomeMethod()
      ' Error! Need to import ExtensionMethods.MyExtensionMethods
      ' namespace to extend integer with ReverseDigits()!
      Dim i As Integer = 0
      i.ReverseDigits()
    End Sub
  End Class

End Namespace
```

Identifying Extension Methods Using Visual Studio 2008

Given the fact that extension methods are not literally defined on the type being extended, it is certainly possible to become confused when examining an existing code base. For example, assume you have imported a namespace that defined some number of extension methods authored by a teammate. As you are authoring your code, you might create a variable of the extended type, apply the dot operator, and find dozens of new methods that are not members of the original class definition!

Thankfully, Visual Studio's Object Browser marks all extension methods with a unique "downward arrow" icon (see Figure 13-8).

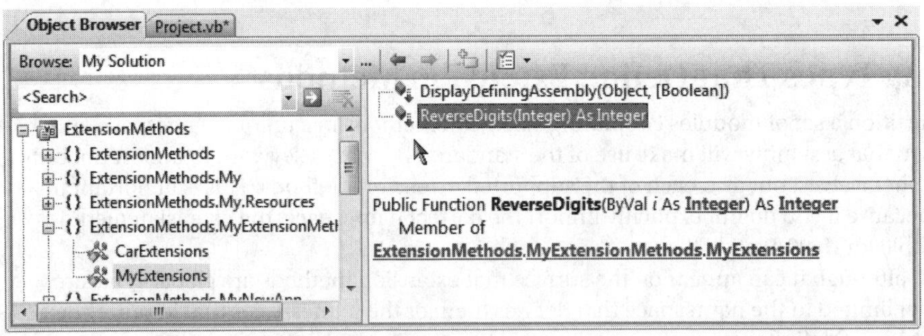

Figure 13-8. *Object Browser displays extension methods using a downward arrow icon.*

Any method marked with this visual icon is a friendly reminder that the method is defined outside of the original class definition via an extension method. Also be aware that this same icon is shown via the IDE's IntelliSense within the code window, making it easy to identify an extension method while authoring code.

Source Code The ExtensionMethods project can be found under the Chapter 13 subdirectory.

Building and Using Extension Libraries

The previous example extended the functionality of various types (such as the `Integer` type) for use by a specific console program. However, I am sure you could imagine the usefulness of building a .NET code library that defines numerous extensions that can be referenced by multiple applications. As luck would have it, doing so is very straightforward.

To illustrate, create a new Class Library project (named MyExtensionsLibrary). Next, rename your initial VB code file to `MyExtensions.vb`, import the `System.Runtime.CompilerServices` namespace, and copy the `MyExtensions` module definition in your new file, making sure the module is declared with the `Public` modifier.

Note If you wish to export extension methods from a .NET code library, the defining module must be declared with the `Public` keyword.

```
Imports System.Runtime.CompilerServices

Public Module MyExtensions
...
  ' Same code as previous example.
End Module
```

At this point, you can compile your library and reference the `MyExtensionsLibrary.dll` assembly within new .NET projects. When you do so, the new functionality provided to `System.Object` and `Integer` can be used by any application that references the library.

To test this out, add a new Console Application project named MyExtensionsLibraryClient. Next, add a reference to the `MyExtensionsLibrary.dll` assembly. Within the initial code file, specify that you are using the `MyExtensionsLibrary` namespace, and author some simple code that invokes these new methods on a local integer:

```
' Import our custom namespace.
Imports MyExtensionsLibrary

Module Program

  Sub Main()
    Console.WriteLine("***** Using Library with Extensions *****")
    ' This time, these extension methods
    ' have been defined within an external
    ' .NET class library.
    Dim myInt As Integer = 987
    myInt.DisplayDefiningAssembly()
    Console.WriteLine("{0} is reversed to {1}", _
```

```
      myInt, myInt.ReverseDigits())
    Console.ReadLine()
  End Sub

End Module
```

Microsoft recommends placing types that have extension methods in a dedicated *.dll assembly (within a dedicated namespace). The reason is simply to reduce cluttering of your programming environment. By way of example, if you were to author a core library for your company that every application was expected to make use of, and if the root namespace of that library defined 30 extension methods, the end result is that all applications would now find these methods pop up in IntelliSense (even if they are not required).

■ **Source Code** The MyExtensionsLibrary and MyExtensionsLibraryClient projects can be found under the Chapter 13 subdirectory.

Extending Interface Types via Extension Methods

At this point, you have seen how to extend classes (and, indirectly, structures that follow the same syntax) with new functionality via extension methods. To wrap up our investigation of VB 2008 extension methods, allow me to point out that it is possible to extend an *interface type* with new methods; however, the semantics of such an action are sure to be a bit different from what you might expect.

Create a new Console Application named InterfaceExtensions and define a simple interface type (IBasicMath) that contains a single method named Add(). Next, implement this interface on a class type (MyCalc) in a fitting manner. For example:

```
' Define a normal CLR interface in VB.
Interface IBasicMath
  Function Add(ByVal x As Integer, ByVal y As Integer) As Integer
End Interface

' Implementation of IBasicMath.
Class MyCalc
  Implements IBasicMath
  Public Function Add(ByVal x As Integer, _
    ByVal y As Integer) As Integer Implements IBasicMath.Add
    Return x + y
  End Function
End Class
```

Now, assume you do not have access to the code definition of IBasicMath, but wish to add a new member (such as a subtraction method) to expand its behavior. You might attempt to author the following extension class to do so:

```
Module MathExtensions
  ' Extend IBasicMath with subtraction method?
  <Extension()> _
  Public Subtract(ByVal itf As IBasicMath, _
    ByVal x As Integer, ByVal y As Integer) As Integer
End Module
```

However, this will result in coding errors. When you extend an interface with new members, you must *also supply an implementation* of these members! This seems to fly in the face of the very nature of interface types, as interfaces do not provide implementations, only definitions. Nevertheless, we are required to define our MathExtensions module as follows:

```
Module MathExtensions
  ' Extend IBasicMath with this method and this
  ' implementation.
  <Extension()> _
  Public Function Subtract(ByVal itf As IBasicMath, _
    ByVal x As Integer, ByVal y As Integer) As Integer
    Return x - y
  End Function
End Module
```

At this point, you might assume you could create a variable of type IBasicMath and directly invoke Subtract(). Again, if this were possible (which it is not), this would destroy the nature of .NET interface types. In reality, what we have actually said here is "Any class in my project implementing IBasicMath now has a Subtract() method, implemented in this manner." As before, all the basic rules apply, therefore the namespace defining MyCalc must have access to the namespace defining MathExtensions. Consider the following Main() method:

```
Sub Main()
  Console.WriteLine("***** Extending an interface *****")

  ' Call IBasicMath members from MyCalc object.
  Dim c As New MyCalc()
  Console.WriteLine("1 + 2 = {0}", c.Add(1, 2))
  Console.WriteLine("1 - 2 = {0}", c.Subtract(1, 2))
  Console.ReadLine()
End Sub
```

That wraps up our examination of VB 2008 extension methods. Remember that this particular language feature can be very useful whenever you wish to extend the functionality of a type, even if you do not have access to the original source code, for the purposes of polymorphism. And, much like implicitly typed local variables, extension methods are a key element of working with the LINQ API. As you will see in the next chapter, numerous existing types in the base class libraries have been extended with new functionality (via extension methods) to allow them to integrate with the LINQ programming model.

Source Code The InterfaceExtension project can be found under the Chapter 13 subdirectory.

Understanding Object Initializer Syntax

VB 2008 offers a new way to hydrate the state of a new class or structure variable termed *object initializer syntax*. Using this technique, it is possible to create a new type variable and assign a slew of properties and/or public fields in a few lines of code. Syntactically, an object initializer consists of a comma-delimited list of specified values, enclosed by the { and } tokens, preceded with the With keyword. Each member in the initialization list maps to the name of a public field or public property of the object being initialized.

To see this new syntax in action, create a new Console Application named ObjectInitializers. Now, consider the various geometric types created over the course of this text (Point, Rectangle, Hexagon, etc.). For example, recall our simple Point type used throughout this text:

```
Public Class Point
  Private xPos As Integer, yPos As Integer

  Public Sub New(ByVal x As Integer, ByVal y As Integer)
    xPos = x
    yPos = y
  End Sub
  Public Sub New()
  End Sub

  Public Property X() As Integer
    Get
      Return xPos
    End Get
    Set (ByVal value As Integer)
      xPos = value
    End Set
  End Property
  Public Property Y() As Integer
    Get
      Return yPos
    End Get
    Set (ByVal value As Integer)
      yPos = value
    End Set
  End Property

  Public Overrides Function ToString() As String
    Return String.Format("[{0}, {1}]", xPos, yPos)
  End Function
End Class
```

Under VB 2008, we could now make Points using any of the following approaches:

```
Sub Main()
  Console.WriteLine("***** Fun with Object Init Syntax *****")
  ' Make a Point by setting each property manually...
  Dim firstPoint As New Point()
  firstPoint.X = 10
  firstPoint.Y = 10
  Console.WriteLine(firstPoint.ToString())

  ' ...or make a Point via a custom constructor...
  Dim anotherPoint As New Point(20, 20)
  Console.WriteLine(anotherPoint.ToString())

  ' ...or make a Point type using the new object init syntax.
  Dim finalPoint As New Point With { .X = 30, .Y = 30 }
  Console.WriteLine(finalPoint.ToString())

  Console.ReadLine()
End Sub
```

The final Point variable is not making use of a custom type constructor (as one might do traditionally), but are rather setting values to the public X and Y properties. Behind the scenes, the type's default constructor is invoked, followed by setting the values to the specified properties. To this end, finalPoint is just shorthand notation for the syntax used to create the firstPoint variable (going property by property).

Now recall that this same syntax can be used to set public fields of a type, which Point currently does not support. However, for the sake of argument, assume that the xPos and yPos member variables have been declared publicly. We could now set values to these fields as follows:

```
Dim p As New Point With {.xPos = 2, .yPos = 3}
```

Given that Point now has four public members, the following syntax is also legal. However, try to figure out the actual final values of xPos and yPos:

```
Dim p As New Point With {.xPos = 2, .yPos = 3, .X = 900}
```

As you might guess, xPos is set to 900, while yPos is the value 3. From this, you can correctly infer that object initialization is performed in a left-to-right manner. To clarify, the previous initialization of p using standard object constructor syntax would appear as follows:

```
Dim p As New Point()
p.xPos = 2
p.yPos = 3
p.X = 900
```

Calling Custom Constructors with Initialization Syntax

The previous examples initialized Point types by implicitly calling the default constructor on the type:

```
' Here, the default constructor is called implicitly.
Dim finalPoint As New Point With { .X = 30, .Y = 30 }
```

If you wish to be very clear about this, it is permissible to explicitly call the default constructor as follows:

```
' Here, the default constructor is called explicitly.
Dim finalPoint As New Point() With { .X = 30, .Y = 30 }
```

Do be aware that when you are constructing a type using the new initialization syntax, you are able to invoke *any* constructor defined by the class or structure. Our Point type currently defines a two-argument constructor to set the (*x*, *y*) position. Therefore, the following Point declaration results in an X value of 100 and a Y value of 100, regardless of the fact that our constructor arguments specified the values 10 and 16:

```
' Calling a custom constructor.
Dim pt As New Point(10, 16) With { .X = 100, .Y = 100 }
```

Given the current definition of our Point type, calling the custom constructor while using initialization syntax is not terribly useful (and more than a bit verbose). However, if our Point type provides a new constructor that allows the caller to establish a color (via a custom enumeration named PointColor), the combination of custom constructors and object initialization syntax becomes clear. Assume we have updated Point as follows:

```
Public Enum PointColor
  LightBlue
  BloodRed
  Gold
End Enum
```

```
Public Class Point
  Public xPos, yPos As Integer
  Private c as PointColor

  Public Sub New(ByVal color As PointColor)
    xPos = 0
    yPos = 0
    c = color
  End Sub
  Public Sub New()
  End Sub

  Public Sub New(ByVal x As Integer, ByVal y As Integer)
    xPos = x
    yPos = y
    c = PointColor.Gold
  End Sub
  ...
  Public Overrides Function ToString() As String
    Return String.Format("[{0}, {1}, {2}]", xPos, yPos, c)
  End Function
End Class
```

With this new constructor, we can now create a golden point (positioned at 90, 20) as follows:

```
' Calling a more interesting custom constructor with init syntax.
Dim goldPoint As New Point(PointColor.Gold) With { .X = 90, .Y = 20 }
Console.WriteLine("Value of Point is: {0}", goldPoint)
```

Initializing Contained Types

Recall from Chapter 6 that the "has-a" relationship allows us to compose new types by defining member variables of existing types. For example, assume we now have a `Rectangle` class, which makes use of the `Point` type to represent its upper-left/bottom-right coordinates:

```
Public Class Rectangle
  Private m_topLeft As New Point()
  Private m_bottomRight As New Point()

  Public Property TopLeft() As Point
    Get
      Return m_topLeft
    End Get
    Set (ByVal value As Point)
      m_topLeft = value
    End Set
  End Property
  Public Property BottomRight() As Point
    Get
      Return m_bottomRight
    End Get
    Set (ByVal value As Point)
      m_bottomRight = value
    End Set
  End Property
```

```
  Public Overrides Function ToString() As String
    Return String.Format("[TopLeft: {0}, {1}, BottomRight: {2}, {3}]", _
      m_topLeft.X, m_topLeft.Y, m_bottomRight.X, m_bottomRight.Y)
  End Function
End Class
```

Using object initialization syntax, we could create a new Rectangle type and set the inner Points as follows:

```
' Create and initialize a Rectangle.
Dim myRect As New Rectangle() With _
{ _
  .TopLeft = New Point() With { .X = 10, .Y = 10 }, _
  .BottomRight = New Point() With { .X = 200, .Y = 200} _
}
```

Again, the benefit of this new syntax is that it basically decreases the number of keystrokes (assuming there is not a suitable constructor). Here is the traditional approach to establishing a similar Rectangle:

```
' Old-school approach.
Dim r As New Rectangle()
Dim p1 As New Point()
p1.X = 10
p1.Y = 10
r.TopLeft = p1
Dim p2 As New Point()
p2.X = 200
p2.Y = 200
r.BottomRight = p2
```

■ **Source Code** The ObjectInitializers project can be found under the Chapter 13 subdirectory.

Understanding Anonymous Types

As an OO programmer, you know the benefits of defining classes to represent the state and functionality of a given programming entity. To be sure, whenever you need to define a class that is intended to be reused across projects and provides numerous bits of functionality through a set of methods, events, properties, and custom constructors, creating a new VB class is common practice and often mandatory.

However, there are other times in programming when you would like to define a class simply to model a set of encapsulated (and somehow related) data points without any associated methods, events, or other custom functionality. Furthermore, what if this type is only used internally to your current application and it's not intended to be reused? If you need such a "temporary" type, earlier versions of VB would require you to nevertheless build a new class definition by hand:

```
Class SomeClass
  ' Define a set of private member variables...

  ' Make a property for each member variable...

  ' Override ToString() to account for each member variable...
```

```
  ' Override GetHashCode() and Equals() to work with value-based equality...
End Class
```

While building such a class is not rocket science, it can be rather labor intensive if you are attempting to encapsulate more than a handful of members. As of VB 2008, we are now provided with a massive shortcut for this very situation termed *anonymous types*.

When you define an anonymous type, you do so by making use of implicit typing, in conjunction with the object initialization syntax you have just examined. To illustrate, create a new Console Application named AnonymousTypes. Now, update `Main()` with the following anonymous class, which models a simple car type:

```
Sub Main()
  Console.WriteLine("***** Fun with Anonymous Types *****")

  ' Make an anonymous type representing a car.
  Dim myCar = New With { .Color = "Bright Pink", _
                         .Make = "Saab", .CurrentSpeed = 55 }

  ' Now show the color and make.
  Console.WriteLine("My car is a {0} {1}.", myCar.Color, myCar.Make)
  Console.ReadLine()
End Sub
```

Again note that the `myCar` variable must be implicitly typed, which makes good sense, as we are not modeling the concept of an automobile using a strongly typed class definition. At compile time, the VB compiler will autogenerate a uniquely named class on our behalf. Given the fact that this class name is not directly visible from our VB code base, the use of implicit typing is in this case mandatory.

Also notice that we have to specify (using object initialization syntax) the set of properties that model the data we are attempting to encapsulate. Once defined, these values can then be obtained using standard VB property invocation syntax.

The Internal Representation of Anonymous Types

All anonymous types are automatically derived from `System.Object`, and therefore support each of the members provided by this base class (see Chapter 6). Given this, we could invoke `ToString()`, `GetHashCode()`, `Equals()`, or `GetType()` on the implicitly typed `myCar` object. Assume your initial module defines the following new method:

```
Sub ReflectOverAnonymousType(ByVal obj As Object)
  Console.WriteLine("obj is an instance of: {0}", obj.GetType().Name)
  Console.WriteLine("Base class of {0} is {1}", _
    obj.GetType().Name, _
    obj.GetType().BaseType)
  Console.WriteLine("obj.ToString() = {0}", obj.ToString())
  Console.WriteLine("obj.GetHashCode() = {0}", obj.GetHashCode())
  Console.WriteLine()
End Sub
```

Now assume we invoke this method from `Main()`, passing in the `myCar` object as the parameter:

```
Sub Main()
  Console.WriteLine("***** Fun with Anonymous Types *****")

  ' Make an anonymous type representing a car.
  Dim myCar = New With {.Color = "Bright Pink", .Make = "Saab", .CurrentSpeed = 55}
```

```
    ' Now show the color and make.
    Console.WriteLine("My car is a {0} {1}.", myCar.Color, myCar.Make)

    ' Reflect over what the compiler generated.
    ReflectOverAnonymousType(myCar)
    Console.ReadLine()
  End Sub
```

Check out the output shown in Figure 13-9.

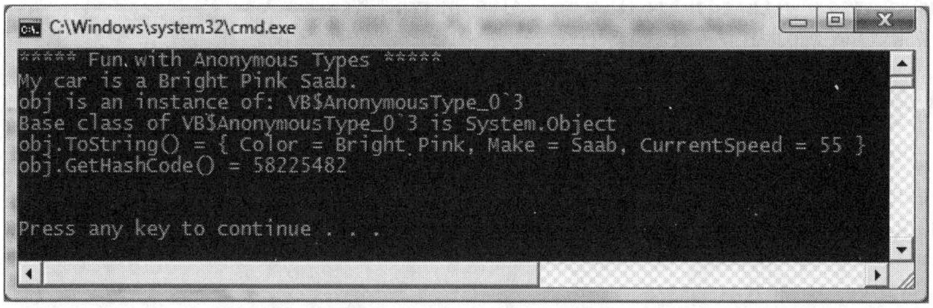

Figure 13-9. *Anonymous types are represented by a compiler-generated class type.*

First of all, notice that in this example, the `myCar` object is of type `VB$AnonymousType_0`3` (your name may differ). Remember that the assigned type name is completely determined by the compiler and is not directly accessible in your VB code base.

Perhaps most important, notice that each name/value pair defined using the object initialization syntax is mapped to an identically named property (which can be verified using tools such as `reflector.exe` or `ildasm.exe`). Because a VB anonymous type yields read/write properties for each item defined within the initialization list, you are free to change the state of your object after creation using standard property syntax:

```
' Make an anonymous type representing a car.
Dim myCar = New With {.Color = "Bright Pink", .Make = "Saab", .CurrentSpeed = 55}

' Now change the color.
myCar.Color = "Black"
```

Note As you might guess, anonymous type syntax is also supported in the C# programming language. One major difference between C# and VB anonymous types is that the C# compiler generates *read-only properties*. Thus, the previous attempt to change the value of `Color` to `"Black"` would be a C# compiler error!

The Implementation of ToString() and GetHashCode()

All anonymous types automatically derive from `System.Object` and are provided with an overridden version of `Equals()`, `GetHashCode()`, and `ToString()`. The `ToString()` implementation simply builds a string from each name/value pair (as shown in Figure 13-9).

The `GetHashCode()` implementation computes a hash value based on the value of each member variable of the anonymous type. Using this implementation of `GetHashCode()`, two anonymous types will yield the same hash value if (and only if) they have the same set of properties that have been assigned the same values. Given this implementation, anonymous types are well suited to be contained within a `Hashtable` container.

The Semantics of Equality for Anonymous Types

While the implementation of the overridden ToString() and GetHashCode() methods is fairly straightforward, you may be wondering how the Equals() method has been implemented. For example, if we were to define two "anonymous cars" variables that specify the same name/value pairs, would these two variables be considered equal or not? To see the results firsthand, update your initial module with the following new method:

```
Sub EqualityTest()

  ' Make 2 anonymous classes with identical name/value pairs.
  Dim firstCar = New With {.Color = "Bright Pink", _
                           .Make = "Saab", .CurrentSpeed = 55}
  Dim secondCar = New With {.Color = "Bright Pink",
                            .Make = "Saab", .CurrentSpeed = 55}

  ' Are they considered equal when using Equals()?
  If (firstCar.Equals(secondCar)) Then
    Console.WriteLine("Same anonymous object!")
  Else
    Console.WriteLine("Not the same anonymous object!")
  End If

  ' Are these objects the same underlying type?
  If (firstCar.GetType().Name = secondCar.GetType().Name) Then
    Console.WriteLine("We are both the same type!")
  Else
    Console.WriteLine("We are different types!")
  End If

  ' Show all the details.
  Console.WriteLine()
  ReflectOverAnonymousType(firstCar)
  ReflectOverAnonymousType(secondCar)
End Sub
```

Notice that each of our anonymous types have purposely been defined using identical property names with identical values. Also notice that we are testing for equality using the inherited Equals() method, rather than the expected VB equality operator (=). The reason is simple: anonymous types are not provided with custom overloaded operators! Therefore, when testing for equality, you *must* use Equals(). The following code would be a compilation error:

```
' Error!! No overloaded = operator for anonymous types!
If (firstCar = secondCar) Then
  Console.WriteLine("Same anonymous object!")
Else
  Console.WriteLine("Not the same anonymous object!")
End If
```

Assuming you have called this method from within Main(), Figure 13-10 shows the output.

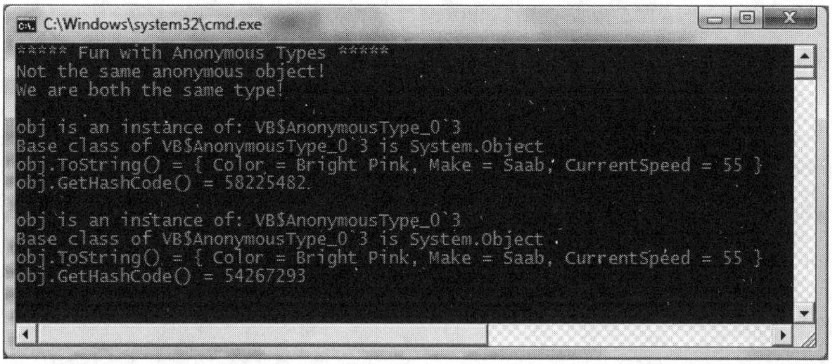

Figure 13-10. *The equality of anonymous types*

When you run this test code, you will see that the first conditional test where you are calling `Equals()` returns `False`, and therefore the message "Not the same anonymous object!" prints out to the screen. This is because the compiler-generated `Equals()` method makes use of *reference-based semantics* when testing for equality (e.g., checking the address of each object being compared).

In our final conditional test (where we are examining the underlying type name), we find that the anonymous types are instances of the same compiler-generated class type (in this example, `VB$AnonymousType_0`3`), due to the fact that `firstCar` and `secondCar` have the same properties (`Color`, `Make`, and `CurrentSpeed`).

This illustrates an important but subtle point: the compiler will only generate a new class definition when an anonymous type contains *unique* property names of the anonymous type. Thus, if you were to declare identical anonymous types (again, meaning the same property names) within the same assembly, the compiler only generates a single anonymous type definition.

Anonymous Types Containing Anonymous Types

It is possible to create an anonymous type that is composed of additional anonymous types. For example, assume you wish to model a purchase order that consists of a timestamp, a price point, and the automobile purchased. Here is a new (slightly more sophisticated) anonymous type representing such an entity:

```
Sub CompositeAnonymousType()
  ' Make an anonymous type that is composed of another.
  Dim purchaseItem = New With { _
    .TimeBought = DateTime.Now, _
    .ItemBought = New With {.Color = "Red", .Make = "Saab", .CurrentSpeed = 55}, _
    .Price = 34.0}
  ReflectOverAnonymousType(purchaseItem)
End Sub
```

At this point, you should understand the syntax used to define anonymous types, but you may still be wondering exactly where (and when) to make use of this new language feature. To be blunt, anonymous type declarations should be used sparingly, typically only when making use of the LINQ technology set (see Chapter 14). You would never want to abandon the use of strongly typed classes/structures simply for the sake of doing so, given anonymous types' numerous limitations, which include the following:

- You don't control the name of the anonymous type.
- Anonymous types always extend `System.Object`.
- Anonymous types cannot support events, custom methods, custom operators, or custom overrides.
- Anonymous types are always implicitly sealed.
- Anonymous types are always created using the default constructor.

However, when programming with the LINQ technology set, you will find that in many cases this syntax can be very helpful when you wish to quickly model the overall *shape* of an entity rather than its functionality.

Source Code The AnonymousTypes project can be found under the Chapter 13 subdirectory.

Summary

This chapter walked you through each of the core updates seen within Visual Basic 2008, beginning with the notion of implicitly typed local variables and the role of the `Option Infer` compiler setting. While the vast majority of your local variables will not need to be declared implicitly, doing so can greatly simplify your interactions with the LINQ family of technologies, as you will see in the next chapter.

This chapter also described the role of extension methods (which allow you to add new functionality to a compiled type) and the syntax of object initialization (which can be used to assign property values at the time of construction). The chapter wrapped up by examining the use of anonymous types. This language feature allows you to define the "shape" of a type rather than its functionality. This can be very helpful when you need to model a type for limited usage within a program, given that a majority of the workload is offloaded to the compiler.

Now that you have seen the core new language features brought forth with .NET 3.5, you are in a solid position to examine one of the biggest platform updates, Language Integrated Query (LINQ), beginning in the next chapter.

CHAPTER 14

■ ■ ■

An Introduction to LINQ

The previous chapter introduced you to numerous VB 2008 programming constructs. As you have seen, features such as implicitly typed local variables, anonymous types, object initialization syntax, extension methods, as well as lambda expressions (examined in Chapter 11) allow us to build very functional VB code. Recall that while many of these features can be used directly as is, their benefits are much more apparent when used within the context of the Language Integrated Query (LINQ) technology set.

This chapter will introduce you to the LINQ programming model and its role in the .NET platform. Here, you will come to learn the role of *query operators* and *query expressions*, which allow you to define statements that will interrogate a data source to yield the requested result set. Along the way, you will build numerous LINQ examples that interact with data contained within arrays as well as various collection types (both generic and nongeneric) and understand the assemblies and types that enable LINQ.

■ **Note** Chapter 24 will examine additional LINQ-centric APIs that allow you to interact with relational databases and XML documents. In that chapter, you will also learn about several new VB 2008 coding constructs that allow you to work with XML-based data.

Understanding the Role of LINQ

As software developers, it is hard to deny that the vast majority of our programming time is spent obtaining and manipulating *data*. When speaking of "data," it is very easy to immediately envision information contained within relational databases. However, another popular location in which data exists is within XML documents (`*.config` files, locally persisted `DataSets`, in-memory data returned from XML web services, etc.).

Data can be found in numerous places beyond these two common homes for information. For instance, say you have a generic `List(Of T)` type containing 300 integers, and you want to obtain a subset that meets a given criterion (e.g., only the odd or even members in the container, only prime numbers, only nonrepeating numbers greater than 50, etc.). Or perhaps you are making use of the reflection APIs and need to obtain only metadata descriptions for each class within an array of `Types` deriving from a particular parent class. Indeed, data is everywhere.

Prior to .NET 3.5, interacting with a particular flavor of data required programmers to make use of diverse APIs. Consider, for example, Table 14-1, which illustrates several common APIs used to access various types of data.

Table 14-1. *Ways to Manipulate Various Types of Data*

The Data We Want	How to Obtain It
Relational data	`System.Data`, `System.Data.SqlClient`, etc.
XML document data	`System.Xml`
Metadata tables	The `System.Reflection` namespace
Collections of objects	`System.Array` and the `System.Collections`/`System.Collections.Generic` namespaces

Of course, nothing is wrong with these approaches to data manipulation. In fact, when programming with .NET 3.5/VB 2008, you can (and will) certainly make direct use of ADO.NET, the XML namespaces, reflection services, and the various collection types. However, the basic problem is that each of these APIs is an island unto itself, which offers very little in the way of integration. True, it is possible (for example) to save an ADO.NET `DataSet` as XML, and then manipulate it via the `System.Xml` namespaces, but nonetheless, data manipulation remains rather *asymmetrical.*

The LINQ API is an attempt to provide a consistent, *symmetrical* manner in which programmers can obtain and manipulate "data" in the broad sense of the term. Using LINQ, we are able to create directly within the VB programming language entities called *query expressions*. These query expressions are based on numerous *query operators* that have been intentionally designed to look and feel very similar (but not quite identical) to a SQL expression.

The twist, however, is that a query expression can be used to interact with numerous types of data—even data that has nothing to do with a relational database. Specifically, LINQ allows query expressions to manipulate any object that implements the `IEnumerable(Of T)` interface (directly or indirectly via extension methods), relational databases, `DataSets`, or XML documents in a consistent manner.

■ **Note** Strictly speaking, "LINQ" is the term used to describe this overall approach to data access. LINQ to Objects is LINQ over objects implementing `IEnumerable(Of T)`, LINQ to SQL is LINQ over relational data, LINQ to DataSet is a superset of LINQ to SQL, and LINQ to XML is LINQ over XML documents. In the future, you are sure to find other APIs that have been injected with LINQ functionality (in fact, there are already other LINQ-centric projects under development at Microsoft).

LINQ Expressions Are Strongly Typed and Extendable

It is also very important to point out that a LINQ query expression (unlike a traditional SQL statement) is *strongly typed*. Therefore, the VB compiler will keep us honest and make sure that these expressions are syntactically well formed. On a related note, query expressions have metadata representation within the assembly that makes use of them. Tools such as Visual Studio 2008 can use this metadata for useful features such as IntelliSense, autocompletion, and so forth.

Also, before we dig into the details of LINQ, one final point is that LINQ is designed to be an extendable technology. While this initial release of LINQ is targeted for relational databases/ `DataSets`, XML documents, and objects implementing `IEnumerable(Of T)`, third parties can incorporate new query operators (or redefine existing operators) using extension methods (see Chapter 13) to account for additional forms of data.

Note Before you continue reading over this chapter, I wholeheartedly recommend that you first feel comfortable with the material presented in Chapter 13 (which covers numerous VB 2008–specific constructs). As you will see, LINQ programming makes use of several of the new VB features to simplify coding tasks.

The Core LINQ Assemblies

As mentioned in Chapter 2, the New Project dialog box of Visual Studio 2008 now has the option of selecting which version of the .NET platform you wish to compile against, using the drop-down list box mounted on the upper-right corner. When you opt to compile against the .NET Framework 3.5, each of the project templates will automatically reference the key LINQ assemblies. For example, if you were to create a new .NET 3.5 Console Application, you would find the assemblies shown in Figure 14-1 visible within Solution Explorer (provided you have clicked the Show All Files button).

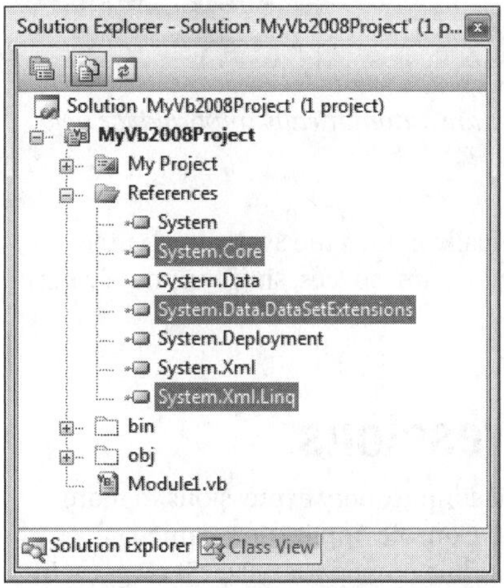

Figure 14-1. *.NET 3.5 project types automatically reference key LINQ assemblies.*

Table 14-2 documents the role of the core LINQ-specific assemblies.

Table 14-2. *Core LINQ-centric Assemblies*

Assembly	Meaning in Life
`System.Core.dll`	Defines the types that represent the core LINQ API. This is the one assembly you must have access to.
`System.Data.Linq.dll`	Provides functionality for using LINQ with relational databases (LINQ to SQL).
`System.Data.DataSetExtensions.dll`	Defines a handful of types to integrate ADO.NET types into the LINQ programming paradigm (LINQ to DataSet).
`System.Xml.Linq.dll`	Provides functionality for using LINQ with XML document data (LINQ to XML).

When you wish to do any sort of LINQ programming, you will at the very least need to import the `System.Linq` namespace (defined within `System.Core.dll`), which is automatically accounted for in new projects via the Imported namespaces settings of the References tab of the My Project editor (see Figure 14-2).

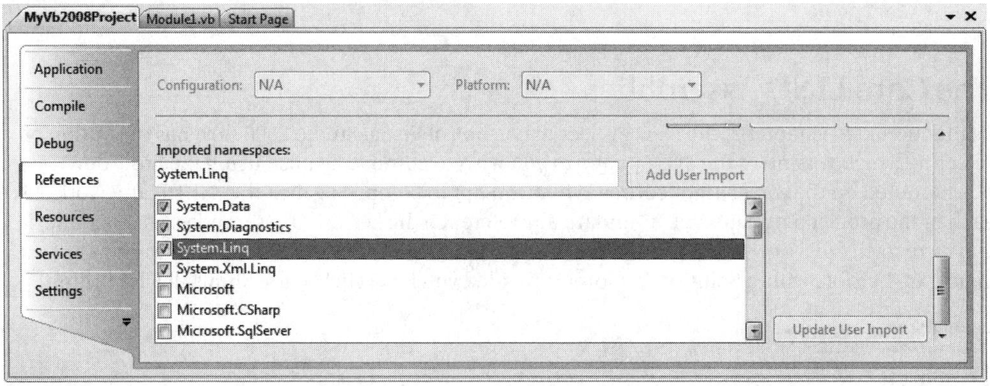

Figure 14-2. *The* `System.Linq` *and* `System.Xml.Linq` *namespaces are automatically imported for new VB 2008 projects.*

Also notice in Figure 14-2 that new project files automatically import the `System.Xml.Linq` namespace. If you wish to make use of additional LINQ-specific namespaces, simply update your code files with new `Import` statements.

A First Look at LINQ Query Expressions

To begin examining the LINQ programming model, let's build simple query expressions to manipulate data contained within various arrays. Create a .NET 3.5 Console Application named LinqOverArray, and define a new method within the initial module named `QueryOverStrings()`. In this method, create a `String` array containing six or so items of your liking (here, I listed out a batch of video games I am currently attempting to finish).

```
Sub QueryOverStrings()
  ' Assume we have an array of strings.
  Dim currentVideoGames As String() = {"Morrowind", "BioShock", _
    "Half Life 2: Episode 1", "The Darkness", _
    "Daxter", "System Shock 2"}
  Console.WriteLine()
End Sub
```

Now, update `Main()` to invoke `QueryOverStrings()`:

```
Sub Main()
  Console.WriteLine("***** Fun with LINQ *****")
  QueryOverStrings()
  Console.ReadLine()
End Sub
```

When you have any array of data, it is very common to extract a subset of items based on a given requirement. Maybe you want to obtain only the items with names that contain a number (e.g., System Shock 2 and Half Life 2: Episode 1), have more than some number of characters, or don't have embedded spaces (e.g., Morrowind). While you could certainly perform such tasks using members of the System.Array type and a bit of elbow grease, LINQ query expressions can greatly simplify the process.

Going on the assumption that we wish to obtain a subset from the array that contains items with names consisting of more than six characters, we could build the following query expression:

```
Sub QueryOverStrings()
  ' Assume we have an array of strings.
  ' some of which have more than 6 letters.
  Dim currentVideoGames As String() = {"Morrowind", "BioShock", _
    "Half Life 2: Episode 1", "The Darkness", _
    "Daxter", "System Shock 2"}

  ' Build a LINQ query.
  Dim subset As IEnumerable(Of String) = From g In currentVideoGames _
      Where g.Length > 6 Order By g Select g

  ' Print out the results.
  For Each s As String In subset
    Console.WriteLine("Item: {0}", s)
  Next
  Console.WriteLine()
End Sub
```

Notice that the query expression created here makes use of the From, In, Where, Order By, and Select LINQ query operators. We will dig into the formalities of query expression syntax in just a bit, but even now you should be able to parse this statement as "Give me the items inside of currentVideoGames that have more than six characters, ordered alphabetically." Here, each item that matches the search criteria has been given the name "g" (as in "game"); however, any valid VB variable name would do:

```
Dim subset As IEnumerable(Of String) = From game In currentVideoGames _
  Where game.Length > 6 Order By game Select game
```

Notice that the "result set" variable, subset, is represented by an object that implements the generic version of IEnumerable(Of T), where T is of type System.String (after all, we are querying an array of strings). Once we obtain the result set, we then simply print out each item using a standard For Each construct.

Before we see the results of our query, assume the initial module now defines an additional helper method named ReflectOverQueryResults() that will print out various details of the LINQ result set (note the parameter is a System.Object, to account for multiple types of LINQ result sets):

```
Sub ReflectOverQueryResults(ByVal resultSet As Object)
  Console.WriteLine("***** Info about your query *****")
  Console.WriteLine("resultSet is of type: {0}", resultSet.GetType().Name)
  Console.WriteLine("resultSet location: {0}", resultSet.GetType().Assembly)
  Console.WriteLine()
End Sub
```

Assuming you have called this method within QueryOverStrings() before printing out the obtained subset, if you run the application, you will see the subset is represented in terms of metadata as <SelectIterator>d__d`2 (see Figure 14-3).

This generic type is a low-level, hidden member of the System.Linq namespace, so much so you cannot view it with the Visual Studio object browser! However, if you are interested, you could use a tool such as reflector.exe to determine that SelectIterator is in fact a nested type within the System.Linq.Enumerable class type.

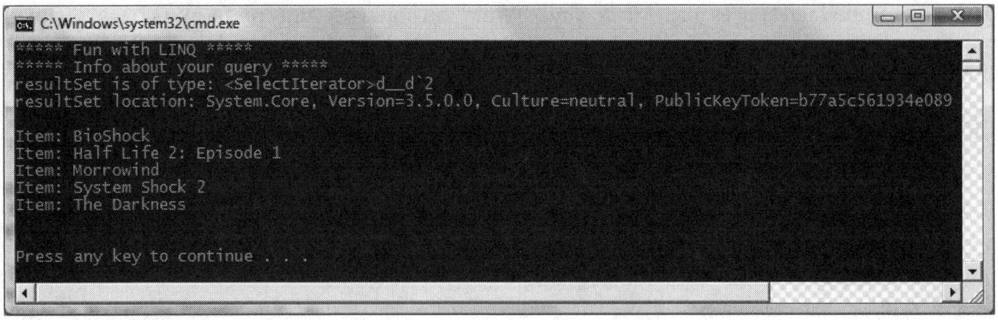

Figure 14-3. *The result of our LINQ query*

LINQ and Implicitly Typed Local Variables

While the current sample program makes it relatively easy to determine that the result set is enumerable as a `String` collection, I would guess that it is *not* clear that `subset` is really of type `SelectIterator`. Given the fact that LINQ result sets can be represented using a good number of types in various LINQ-centric namespaces, it would be tedious to define the proper type to hold a result set, because in many cases the underlying type may not be obvious or directly accessible from your code base (and as you will see, in some cases the type is generated at compile time).

Given the fact that the exact underlying type of a LINQ query is certainly not obvious, the current example has represented the query result as a local `IEnumerable(Of T)` variable. Given that `IEnumerable(Of T)` extends the nongeneric `IEnumerable` interface, it would also be permissible to capture the result of a LINQ query as follows:

```
Dim subset As System.Collections.IEnumerable = _
  From game In currentVideoGames _
  Where game.Length > 6 Order By game Select game
```

While this is syntactically correct, implicit typing cleans things up considerably when working with LINQ queries. Consider a new method in our module that extracts out any number less than 10 from an array of integers.

```
Sub QueryOverInts()
  Dim numbers() As Integer = {10, 20, 30, 40, 1, 2, 3, 8}

  ' Only print items less than 10.
  ' (note use of implicit typing)
  Dim subset = From i In numbers Where i < 10 Select i

  ' More implicit typing.
  For Each i In subset
    Console.WriteLine("Item: {0}", i)
  Next
  ReflectOverQueryResults(subset)
End Sub
```

Recall that implicitly typed local variables should not be confused with the legacy COM `Variant` or loosely typed variable declaration found in many scripting languages. The underlying type is determined by the compiler based on the result of the initial assignment. After that point, it is a compiler error to attempt to change the "type of type." Furthermore, given the fact that in many cases the underlying type is the result of a dynamically generated anonymous type, it is commonplace to use implicit typing whenever you wish to capture a LINQ result set.

LINQ and Extension Methods

In the previous chapter you learned that *extension methods* make it possible to add new functionality to a previously compiled type within the scope of a given project. Although the current example does not have you author any extension methods directly, you are in fact using them seamlessly in the background. LINQ query expressions can be used to iterate over data containers that implement the generic IEnumerable(Of T) interface. However, the .NET System.Array class type (used to represent our array of strings and array of integers) does *not* implement this behavior:

```
' The System.Array type does not seem to implement the correct
' infrastructure for query expressions!
Public MustInherit Class Array
  Implements ICloneable, IList, ICollection, IEnumerable
  ...
End Class
```

While System.Array does not directly implement the IEnumerable(Of T) interface, it indirectly gains the required functionality of this type (as well as many other LINQ-centric members) via the shared System.Linq.Enumerable class type.

This type defined a good number of generic extension methods (such as Aggregate(Of T)(), First(Of T)(), Max(Of T)(), etc.), which System.Array (and other types) acquire in the background. Thus, if you apply the dot operator on the numbers local variable, you will find a good number of members *not* found within the formal definition of System.Array (see Figure 14-4; recall from Chapter 13 that the "downward arrow" icon denotes an extension method).

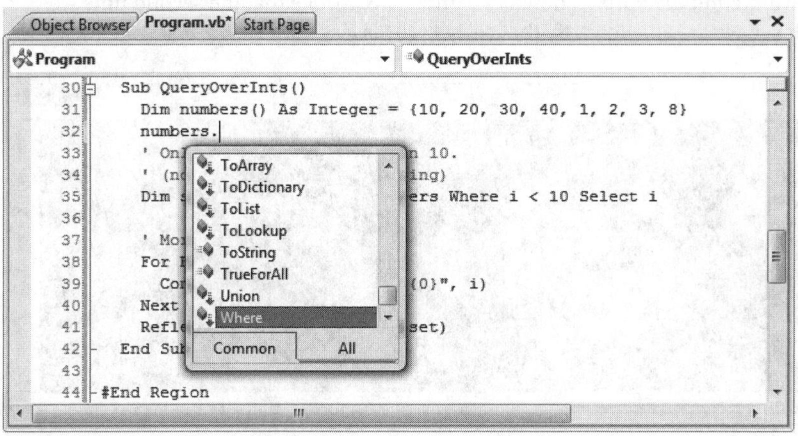

Figure 14-4. *The* System.Array *type has been extended with members of* System.Linq.Enumerable.

The Role of Deferred Execution

Another important point regarding LINQ query expressions is that they are not actually evaluated until you iterate over their contents. Formally speaking, this is termed *deferred execution.* The benefit of this approach is that you are able to apply the same LINQ query multiple times to the same container, and rest assured you are obtaining the latest and greatest results. Consider the following update to the QueryOverInts() method:

```
Sub QueryOverInts()
  Dim numbers() As Integer = {10, 20, 30, 40, 1, 2, 3, 8}

  ' Only print items less than 10.
  ' (note use of implicit typing)
  Dim subset = From i In numbers Where i < 10 Select i

  ' LINQ statment evaluated here!
  For Each i In subset
    Console.WriteLine("{0} < 10", i)
  Next

  ' Change some data in the array.
  numbers(0) = 4
  Console.WriteLine()

  ' Evaluate again.
  For Each i In subset
    Console.WriteLine("{0} < 10", i)
  Next
  ReflectOverQueryResults(subset)
End Sub
```

Notice that we are forming a single query; however, we are iterating over the result set two times (once after we have changed the first element in the array). If you were to execute the program yet again, you would find the output shown in Figure 14-5. Notice that the second time we iterate over the result set, we are able to verify that `numbers(0)` is less than 10.

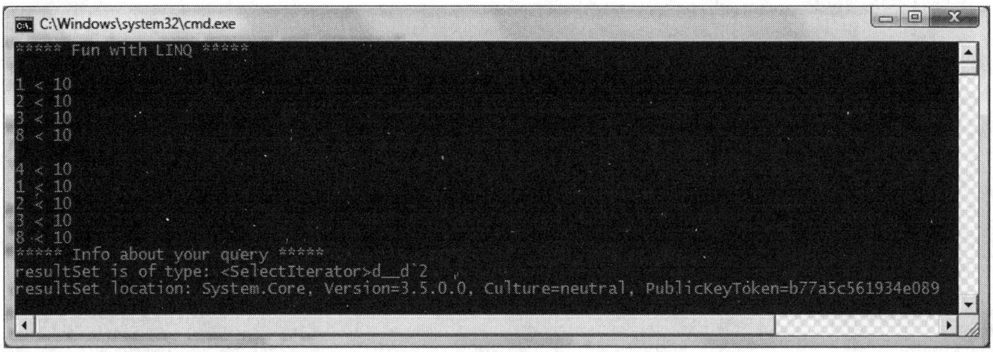

Figure 14-5. *LINQ expressions are executed when evaluated.*

One very useful aspect of Visual Studio 2008 is that if you set a breakpoint before the evaluation of a LINQ query, you are able to view the contents during a debugging session. Simply locate your mouse cursor above the LINQ result set variable (`subset` in Figure 14-6). When you do, you will be given the option of evaluating the query at that time by expanding the Results View option.

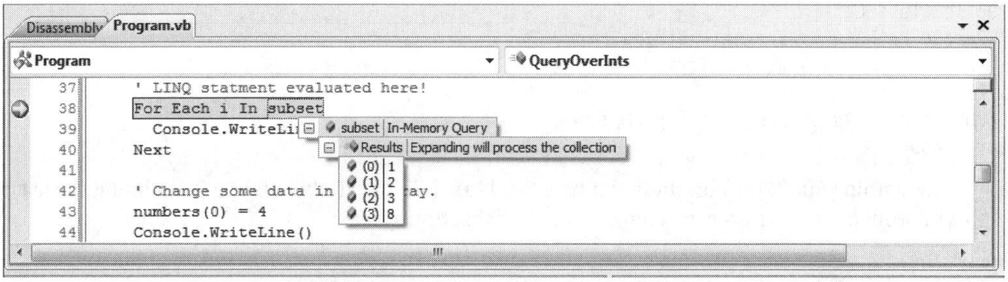

Figure 14-6. *Debugging LINQ expressions*

The Role of Immediate Execution

When you wish to evaluate a LINQ expression from outside the confines of `For Each` logic, you are able to call any number of extension methods defined by the `Enumerable` type to do so. `Enumerable` defines a number of extension methods such as `ToArray()`, `ToDictionary()`, and `ToList()`, which allow you to capture a LINQ query result set in a strongly typed container. Once you have done so, the container is no longer "connected" to the LINQ expression, and may be independently manipulated:

```
Sub ImmediateExecution()
  Dim numbers() As Integer = { 10, 20, 30, 40, 1, 2, 3, 8 }

  ' Get data RIGHT NOW as Integer().
  Dim subsetAsIntArray() As Integer = _
    (From i in numbers Where i < 10 Select i).ToArray()

  ' Get data RIGHT NOW as List(Of Integer).
  Dim subsetAsListOfInts As List(Of Integer) = _
    (From i In numbers Where i < 10 Select i).ToList()
End Sub
```

Notice that the entire LINQ expression is wrapped within parentheses to capture the correct underlying type (whatever that may be) in order to call the extension methods of `Enumerable`.

Source Code The LinqOverArray project can be found under the Chapter 14 subdirectory.

LINQ and Generic Collections

Beyond pulling results from a simple array of data, LINQ query expressions can also manipulate data within members of the `System.Collections.Generic` namespace, such as the `List(Of T)` type. Create a new .NET 3.5 Console Application project named LinqOverCustomObjects, and define a basic `Car` type that maintains a current speed, color, make, and pet name (here, public fields are used to easily set the fields—feel free to make use of properties and class constructors if you wish):

```
Public Class Car
  Public PetName As String = String.Empty
  Public Color As String = String.Empty
  Public Speed As Integer
  Public Make As String = String.Empty
End Class
```

Now, within your Main() method, define a local List(Of T) variable of type Car, and fill the list with a handful of new Car objects, using object initialization syntax:

```
Sub Main()
  Console.WriteLine("***** More fun with LINQ Expressions *****")

  ' Make a List of Car objects.
  Dim myCars As New List(Of Car)()
  myCars.Add(New Car With { .PetName = "Henry", .Color = "Silver", _
                           .Speed = 100, .Make = "BMW"})
  myCars.Add(New Car With { .PetName = "Daisy", .Color = "Tan", _
                           .Speed = 90, .Make = "BMW"})
  myCars.Add(New Car With { .PetName = "Mary", .Color = "Black", _
                           .Speed = 55, .Make = "VW"})
  myCars.Add(New Car With { .PetName = "Clunker", .Color = "Rust", _
                           .Speed = 5, .Make = "Yugo"})
  myCars.Add(New Car With { .PetName = "Melvin", .Color = "White", _
                           .Speed = 43, .Make = "Ford"})
End Sub
```

Applying a LINQ Expression

Our goal is to build a query expression to select only the items within the myCars list, where the speed is greater than 55. Once we get the subset, we will print out the name of each Car object. Assume you have the following helper method (taking a List(Of Car) parameter), which is called from within Main():

```
Sub GetFastCars(ByVal myCars As List(Of Car))
  ' Create a query expression.
  Dim fastCars = From c In myCars Where c.Speed > 55 Select c

  For Each car in fastCars
    Console.WriteLine("{0} is going too fast!", car.PetName)
  Next
End Sub
```

Notice that our query expression is only grabbing items from the List(Of T) where the Speed property is greater than 55. If we run the application, we will find that "Henry" and "Daisy" are the only two items that match the search criteria.

If we want to build a more complex query, we might wish to only find the BMWs that have a Speed value above 90. To do so, simply build a compound Boolean statement using the VB And operator:

```
Sub GetFastBMWs(ByVal myCars As List(Of Car))
  ' Find all items where Speed is greater than 90
  ' and Make is BMW.
  Dim fastCars = From c In myCars Where _
    c.Speed > 90 And c.Make = "BMW" Select c
  For Each car In fastCars
```

```
    Console.WriteLine("{0} is going too fast!", car.PetName)
  Next
End Sub
```

In this case, the only pet name printed out is "Henry".

Source Code The LinqOverCustomObjects project can be found under the Chapter 14 subdirectory.

LINQ and Nongeneric Collections

Recall that the query operators of LINQ are designed to work with any type implementing `IEnumerable(Of T)` (either directly or via extension methods). Given that `System.Array` has been provided with such necessary infrastructure, it may surprise you that the legacy (nongeneric) containers within `System.Collections` have *not*. Thankfully, it is still possible to iterate over data contained within nongeneric collections using the generic `Enumerable.OfType(Of T)()` method.

Note If you disable `Option Strict`, you would indeed be able to apply LINQ queries against the `ArrayList` type. However, you do so at the cost of late binding performance penalties.

The `OfType(Of T)()` method is one of the few members of `Enumerable` that does not extend generic types. When calling this member off a nongeneric container implementing the `IEnumerable` interface (such as the `ArrayList`), simply specify the type of item within the container to extract a compatible `IEnumerable(Of T)` object. Assume we have a new Console Application named LinqOverArrayList that defines the following `Main()` method (note that we are making use of the previously defined `Car` type, and the initial module has been renamed to `Program`).

```
Option Strict On

Module Program
  Sub Main()
    Console.WriteLine("***** LINQ over ArrayList *****")

    ' Remember, technically ArrayList is not LINQ compatible.
    Dim myCars As New ArrayList()
    myCars.Add(New Car With {.PetName = "Henry", .Color = "Silver", _
                             .Speed = 100, .Make = "BMW"})
    myCars.Add(New Car With {.PetName = "Daisy", .Color = "Tan", _
                             .Speed = 90, .Make = "BMW"})
    myCars.Add(New Car With {.PetName = "Mary", .Color = "Black", _
                             .Speed = 55, .Make = "VW"})
    myCars.Add(New Car With {.PetName = "Clunker", .Color = "Rust", _
                             .Speed = 5, .Make = "Yugo"})
    myCars.Add(New Car With {.PetName = "Melvin", .Color = "White", _
                             .Speed = 43, .Make = "Ford"})

    ' Transform ArrayList into an IEnumerable(Of T)-compatible type.
    ' Could also use implicit typing here.
    Dim myCarsEnum As IEnumerable(Of Car) = myCars.OfType(Of Car)()
```

```
    ' Create a query expression.
    Dim fastCars = From c In myCarsEnum Where c.Speed > 55 Select c
    For Each car In fastCars
      Console.WriteLine("{0} is going too fast!", car.PetName)
    Next
  End Sub
End Module
```

Filtering Data Using OfType(Of T)()

As you know, nongeneric types are capable of containing any combination of items, as the members of these containers (again, such as the ArrayList) are prototyped to receive System.Objects. For example, assume an ArrayList contains a variety of items, only a subset of which are numerical. If we want to obtain a subset that contains only numerical data, we can do so using OfType(Of T)(), since it filters out each element whose type is different from the given type during the iterations:

```
Sub ExtractNumericalData()
  ' Extract the integers from the ArrayList.
  Dim myStuff As New ArrayList()
  myStuff.AddRange(New Object() {10, 400, 8, False, New Car(), "string data"})
  Dim myInts As IEnumerable(Of Integer) = myStuff.OfType(Of Integer)()

  ' Print out 10, 400, and 8.
  For Each i As Integer In myInts
    Console.WriteLine("Int value: {0}", i)
  Next
End Sub
```

Source Code The LinqOverArrayList project can be found under the Chapter 14 subdirectory.

Now that you have seen how to use simple LINQ expressions to manipulate data contained within various arrays and collections, let's dig in a bit deeper to see what is happening behind the scenes. After this point, we'll drill into more details of the query operators themselves.

The Internal Representation of LINQ Query Operators

So at this point you have been briefly introduced to the process of building query expressions using various VB query operators (such as From, In, Where, Order By, and Select). When processed, the VB compiler actually translates these tokens into calls on various methods of the System.Linq.Enumerable type (and possibly other types, based on the format of your LINQ query).

As it turns out, a great many of the methods of Enumerable have been prototyped to take *delegates* as arguments. In particular, many methods require a generic delegate of type Func, defined within the System namespace of System.Core.dll. For example, consider the following members of Enumerable that extend the IEnumerable(Of T) interface. Notice how each version of the generic Where(Of T) method takes a Func delegate as an argument:

```
' Overloaded versions of the Enumerable.Where(Of T)() method.
' Note the second parameter is of type System.Func.
<Extension()> _
```

```
Public Shared Function Where(Of TSource)(ByVal source As IEnumerable(Of TSource), _
  ByVal predicate As Func(Of TSource, Boolean)) As IEnumerable(Of TSource)

<Extension()> _
Public Shared Function Where(Of TSource)(ByVal source As IEnumerable(Of TSource), _
  ByVal predicate As Func(Of TSource, Integer, Boolean)) As IEnumerable(Of TSource)
```

The Func delegate (as the name implies) represents a pattern for a given *func*tion with a set of arguments and a return value. If you were to examine this type using the Visual Studio 2008 object browser, you'd notice that the Func delegate can take between zero and four input arguments (here typed T1, T2, T3, and T4 and named arg1, arg2, arg3, and arg4), and a return type denoted by TResult:

```
' The various formats of the generic System.Func delegate.
Public Delegate Function Func(Of T1, T2, T3, T4, TResult)(ByVal arg1 As T1, _
  ByVal arg2 As T2, ByVal arg3 As T3, ByVal arg4 As T4) As TResult

Public Delegate Function Func(Of T1, T2, T3, TResult)(ByVal arg1 As T1, _
  ByVal arg2 As T2, ByVal arg3 As T3) As TResult

Public Delegate Function Func(Of T1, T2, TResult)(ByVal arg1 As T1, _
  ByVal arg2 As T2) As TResult

Public Delegate Function Func(Of T, TResult)(ByVal arg As T) As TResult

Public Delegate Function Func(Of TResult)() As TResult
```

Given that many members of System.Linq.Enumerable demand a delegate as input, when invoking them, we can either manually create a new delegate type and author the necessary target methods, make use of a proper lambda expression, or simply use LINQ query operators, which hide the low-level details from view. Regardless of which approach you take, the end result is identical.

While it is true that making use of VB LINQ query operators is far and away the simplest way to build a LINQ query expression, let's walk through each of these possible approaches just so you can see the connection between the VB LINQ query operators, the Func delegate the underlying Enumerable type.

Building Query Expressions with Query Operators (Revisited)

To begin, create a new Console Application named LinqUsingEnumerable. The initial module will define a series of methods (each of which is called within the Main() method) to illustrate the various manners in which we can build LINQ query expressions. The first method, QueryStringArrayWithOperators(), offers the most straightforward way to build a query expression and is identical to the code seen in the previous LinqOverArray example:

```
Sub QueryStringArrayWithOperators()
  Console.WriteLine("***** Using LINQ Query Operators *****")

  Dim currentVideoGames As String() = {"Morrowind", "BioShock", _
    "Half Life 2: Episode 1", "The Darkness", _
    "Daxter", "System Shock 2"}

  ' Build a LINQ query with VB LINQ operators.
  Dim subset = From g In currentVideoGames _
    Where g.Length > 6 Order By g Select g
```

```
    For Each s As String In subset
      Console.WriteLine("Item: {0}", s)
    Next
    Console.WriteLine()
  End Sub
```

The obvious benefit of using VB LINQ query operators to build query expressions is the fact that the Func delegates and calls on the Enumerable type are out of sight and out of mind, as it is the job of the VB compiler to perform this translation. To be sure, building LINQ expressions using various query operators (From, In, Where, Order By, etc.) is the most common and most straightforward approach.

Building Query Expressions Using the Enumerable Type and Lambdas

Keep in mind that the LINQ query operators used here are simply shorthand versions for calling various extension methods defined by the Enumerable type. Consider the following QueryStringsWithEnumerableAndLambdas() method, which is processing the local string array now making direct use of the Enumerable extension methods and various lambda expressions:

```
Sub QueryStringsWithEnumerableAndLambdas()
  Console.WriteLine("***** Using Enumerable / Lambda Expressions *****")

  Dim currentVideoGames() As String = {"Morrowind", "BioShock", _
    "Half Life 2: Episode 1", "The Darkness", _
    "Daxter", "System Shock 2"}

  ' Build a query expression using extension methods
  ' granted to the Array via the Enumerable type.
  Dim subset = currentVideoGames.Where(Function(game) game.Length > 6). _
    OrderBy(Function(game) game).Select(Function(game) game)

  ' Print out the results.
  For Each game In subset
    Console.WriteLine("Item: {0}", game)
  Next
  Console.WriteLine()
End Sub
```

Here, we are calling the generic Where(Of T)() method off the string array object, granted to the Array type as an extension method defined by Enumerable. The Enumerable.Where(Of T)() method makes use of the System.Func(Of T, TResult) delegate type. The first type parameter of this delegate represents the IEnumerable(Of T)-compatible data to process (an array of strings in this case), while the second type parameter represents the method that will process said data.

Given that we have opted for a lambda expression (rather than directly creating an instance of Func or crafting an anonymous method), we are specifying that the "game" parameter is processed by the statement game.Length > 6, which results in a Boolean return type.

The return value of the Where(Of T)() method has implicitly typed, but under the covers we are operating on an OrderedEnumerable type. From this resulting object, we call the generic OrderBy(Of T, K)() method, which also requires a Func(Of T, TResult) delegate parameter. Finally, from the result of the specified lambda expression, we select each element, using once again a Func(Of T, TResult) under the covers.

It is also worth remembering that extension methods are unique in that they can be called as instance-level members upon the type they are extending (System.Array in this case) *or* as shared members using the type they were defined within. Given this, we could also author our query expression as follows:

```
Dim subset = Enumerable.Where(currentVideoGames, _
  Function(game) game.Length > 6). _
  OrderBy(Function(game) game).Select(Function(game) game)
```

As you may agree, building a LINQ query expression using the methods of the `Enumerable` type directly is much more verbose than making use of the VB LINQ query operators. As well, given that the methods of `Enumerable` require delegates as parameters, you will typically need to author lambda expressions to allow the input data to be processed by the underlying delegate target.

Building Query Expressions Using the Enumerable Type and Raw Delegates

Finally, if we want to build a query expression using the *really verbose approach*, we could avoid the use of lambda syntax and directly create delegate targets for each `Func` type. Here is the final iteration of our query expression, modeled within a new class type named `VeryComplexQueryExpression`:

```
Class VeryComplexQueryExpression
  Public Shared Sub QueryStringsWithRawDelegates()
    Console.WriteLine("***** Using Raw Delegates *****")

    Dim currentVideoGames As String() = {"Morrowind", "BioShock", _
                                         "Half Life 2: Episode 1", "The Darkness", _
                                         "Daxter", "System Shock 2"}

    ' Build the necessary Func delegates.
    Dim searchFilter As New Func(Of String, Boolean)(AddressOf Filter)
    Dim itemToProcess As New Func(Of String, String)(AddressOf ProcessItem)

    ' Pass the delegates into the methods of Enumerable.
    Dim subset = currentVideoGames.Where(searchFilter). _
      OrderBy(itemToProcess).Select(itemToProcess)

    ' Print out the results.
    For Each game In subset
      Console.WriteLine("Item: {0}", game)
    Next
    Console.WriteLine()
  End Sub

  ' Delegate targets.
  Public Shared Function Filter(ByVal str As String) As Boolean
    Return str.Length > 6
  End Function
  Public Shared Function ProcessItem(ByVal str As String) As String
    Return str
  End Function

End Class
```

We can test this iteration of our string processing logic by calling this method within `Main()` method as follows:

```
VeryComplexQueryExpression.QueryStringsWithRawDelegates()
```

If you were to now run the application to test each possible approach, it should not be too surprising that the output is identical regardless of the path taken (see Figure 14-7).

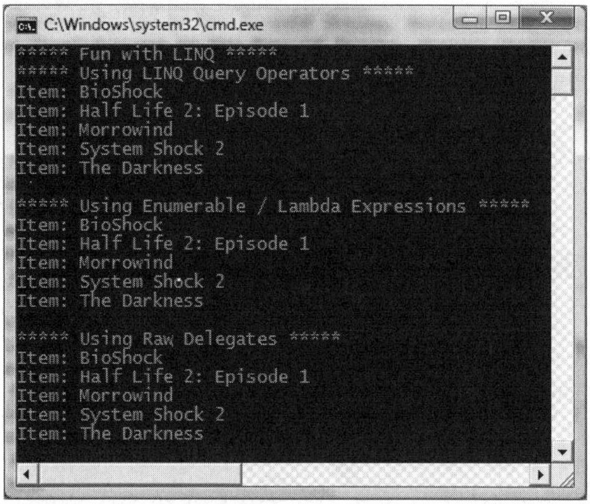

Figure 14-7. *Three approaches to a LINQ query*

Keep the following points in mind regarding how LINQ query expressions are represented under the covers:

- Query expressions are created using various VB LINQ query operators.
- Query operators are simply shorthand notations for invoking extension methods defined by the `System.Linq.Enumerable` type.
- Many methods of `Enumerable` require delegates (`Func` in particular) as parameters.
- Under VB 2008, methods requiring a delegate parameter can instead be passed a lambda expression.
- Lambda expressions are shorthand notations for allocating a raw delegate and manually building a delegate target method.

Whew! That might have been a bit deeper under the hood than you wish to have gone, but I hope this discussion has helped you understand what the user-friendly VB query operators are actually doing behind the scenes. Let's now turn our attention to the operators themselves.

■ Source Code The LinqOverArrayUsingEnumerable project can be found under the Chapter 14 subdirectory.

Investigating the VB LINQ Query Operators

VB defines a good number of query operators out of the box. Table 14-3 documents some of the more commonly used query operators.

Table 14-3. *Various LINQ Query Operators*

Query Operator	Meaning in Life
`From` `In`	Define the backbone for any LINQ expression, which allows you to extract a subset of data from a fitting container.
`Where`	Defines a restriction for which items to extract from a container.
`Select`	Selects a sequence from the container.

`Join`
`On`
`Equals`
`Into`
	Perform joins based on specified key. Remember, these "joins" do not need to have anything to do with data in a relational database.

`Order By`
`Ascending`
`Descending`
	Allow the resulting subset to be ordered in ascending or descending order.

`Group By`	Yield a subset with data grouped by a specified value.

■ Note The .NET Framework 3.5 SDK documentation provides full details regarding each of the VB LINQ operators. Look up the topic "LINQ General Programming Guide" for more information.

In addition to the partial list of operators shown in Table 14-3, the `Enumerable` type provides a set of methods that do not have a direct VB query operator shorthand notation, but are instead exposed as extension methods. These generic methods can be called to transform a result set in various manners (`Reverse()`, `ToArray()`, `ToList()`, etc.). Some are used to extract singletons from a result set, others perform various set operations (`Distinct()`, `Union()`, `Intersect()`, etc.), and still others aggregate results (`Count()`, `Sum()`, `Min()`, `Max()`, etc.).

Obtaining Counts Using Enumerable

Using these query operators (and auxiliary members of the `System.Linq.Enumerable` type), you are able to build very expressive query expressions in a strongly typed manner. To invoke the `Enumerable` extension methods, you typically wrap the LINQ expression within parentheses to cast the result to an `IEnumerable(Of T)`-compatible object to invoke the `Enumerable` extension method.

You have already done so during our examination of immediate execution; however, here is another example that allows you to discover the number of items returned by a LINQ query:

```
Sub GetCount()
  Dim currentVideoGames() As String = {"Morrowind", "BioShock", _
    "Half Life 2: Episode 1", "The Darkness", _
    "Daxter", "System Shock 2"}

  ' Get count from the query.
  Dim numb As Integer = (From g in currentVideoGames _
              Where g.Length > 6 _
              Order By g _
              Select g).Count()

  ' numb is the value 5.
  Console.WriteLine("{0} items honor the LINQ query.", numb)
End Sub
```

Building a New Test Project

To begin digging into more intricate LINQ queries, create a new Console Application named FunWithLinqExpressions. Next, define a trivial Car type, this time sporting a custom ToString() implementation to quickly view the object's state:

```
Public Class Car
  Public PetName As String = String.Empty
  Public Color As String = String.Empty
  Public Speed As Integer
  Public Make As String = String.Empty

  Public Overrides Function ToString() As String
    Return String.Format("Make={0}, Color={1}, Speed={2}, PetName={3}", _
      Make, Color, Speed, PetName)
  End Function
End Class
```

Now populate an array with the following Car objects within your Main() method (of course, this could be a generic List(Of T) or an ArrayList if you wish):

```
Sub Main()
  Console.WriteLine("***** Fun with Query Expressions *****")

  ' This array will be the basis of our testing...
  Dim myCars As Car() = {New Car With _
    {.PetName = "Henry", .Color = "Silver", _
     .Speed = 100, .Make = "BMW"}, _
  New Car With {.PetName = "Daisy", .Color = "Tan", .Speed = 90, .Make = "BMW"}, _
  New Car With {.PetName = "Mary", .Color = "Black", .Speed = 55, .Make = "VW"}, _
  New Car With {.PetName = "Clunker", _
               .Color = "Rust", .Speed = 5, .Make = "Yugo"}, _
  New Car With {.PetName = "Hank", .Color = "Tan", .Speed = 0, .Make = "Ford"}, _
  New Car With {.PetName = "Sven", .Color = "White", .Speed = 90, .Make = "Ford"}, _
  New Car With {.PetName = "Mary", .Color = "Black", .Speed = 55, .Make = "VW"}, _
  New Car With {.PetName = "Zippy", .Color = "Yellow", .Speed = 55, .Make = "VW"}, _
  New Car With {.PetName = "Melvin", .Color = "White", _
               .Speed = 43, .Make = "Ford"}}

  ' We will call various methods here!
  Console.ReadLine()
End Sub
```

Basic Selection Syntax

Because LINQ query expressions are validated at compile time, you need to remember that the ordering of these operators is critical. Thankfully Visual Basic's IntelliSense is very helpful in this regard, as the IDE will show you valid options as you type your LINQ query (see Figure 14-8).

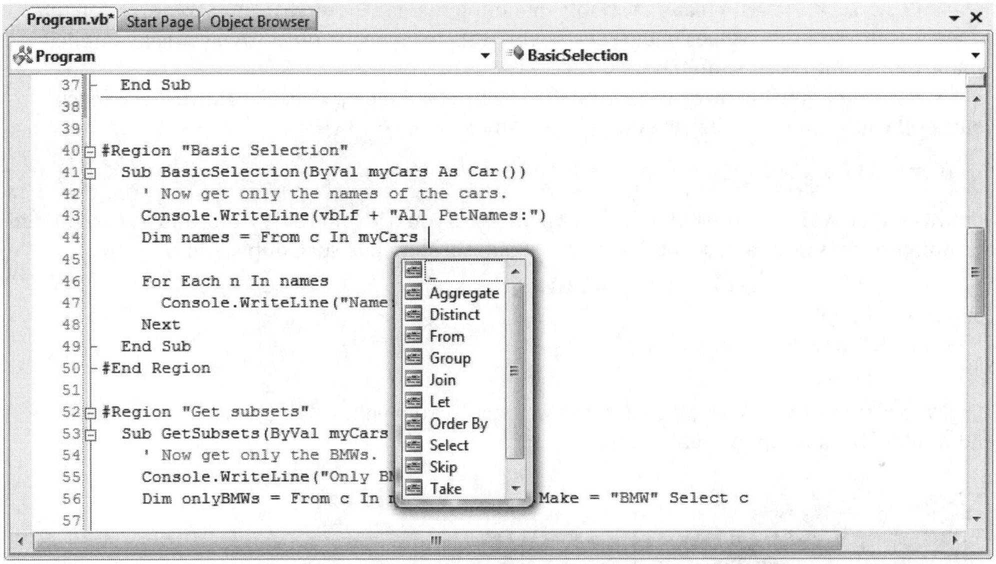

Figure 14-8. *VB's LINQ IntelliSense*

In the simplest terms, every LINQ query expression is built using the `From`, `In`, and `Select` operators:

```
Dim result = From item In container Select item
```

In this case, our query expression is doing nothing more than selecting every item in the container (similar to a `Select *` SQL statement). Consider the following method:

```
Sub BasicSelections(ByVal myCars As Car())
  ' Get all cars. Similar to Select * in SQL.
  Console.WriteLine(vbLf & "All Cars:")
  Dim allCars = From c In myCars Select c

  For Each c In allCars
    Console.WriteLine("Car: {0}", c)
  Next
End Sub
```

Again, this query expression is not entirely useful, given that our subset is identical to that of the data in the incoming parameter. If we wish, we could use this incoming parameter to extract only the `PetName` values of each car using the following selection syntax:

```
Sub BasicSelections(ByVal myCars As Car())
...
  ' Get only the pet names.
  Console.WriteLine(vbLf & "All PetNames:")
  Dim allNames = From c In myCars Select c.PetName

  For Each n In allNames
    Console.WriteLine("Pet Name: {0}", n)
  Next
End Sub
```

In this case, `allNames` is really a variable that implements `IEnumerable(Of String)`, given that we are selecting only the values of the `PetName` property for each `Car` object. Again, using implicit typing, our coding task is simplified.

Now consider the following task. What if you'd like to obtain and display the makes of each vehicle? If you author the following query expression:

```
Dim makes = From c in myCars Select c.Make
```

you will end up with a number of redundant listings, as you will find BMW, Ford, and VW accounted for multiple times. You can use the `Distinct` operator to eliminate such duplication:

```
Dim makes = From c in myCars Select c.Make Distinct
For Each m In makes
  Console.WriteLine("Make: {0}", m)
Next
```

Now, assuming you have called `BasicSelections()` from within `Main()`, Figure 14-9 shows the end result of running our current program.

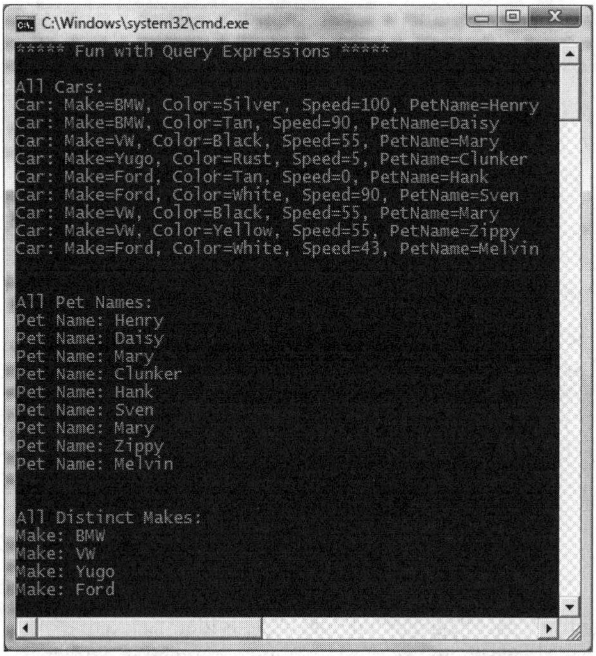

Figure 14-9. *Selecting basic data from the* `Car` *array parameter*

Obtaining Subsets of Data

To obtain a specific subset from a container, you can make use of the `Where` operator. When doing so, the general template now becomes as follows:

```
Dim result = From item In container Where Boolean expression Select item
```

Notice that the `Where` operator expects an expression that resolves to a Boolean. For example, to extract from the `Car()` parameter only the items that have `BMW` as the value assigned to the `Make` field, you could author the following code within a new method named `GetSubsets()`:

```
Sub GetSubsets(ByVal myCars As Car())
  ' Now get only the BMWs.
  Console.WriteLine("Only BMWs:")
  Dim onlyBMWs = From c In myCars Where c.Make = "BMW" Select c

  For Each n In onlyBMWs
    Console.WriteLine("Name: {0}", n)
  Next
End Sub
```

As seen earlier in this chapter, when you are building a `Where` clause, it is permissible to make use of any valid VB operators to build complex expressions. For example, consider the following query that only extracts out the BMWs going at least 100 mph:

```
' Get BMWs going at least 100 mph.
Dim onlyFastBMWs = From c In myCars _
                   where c.Make = "BMW" And c.Speed >= 100 _
                   Select c

For Each c As Car in onlyFastBMWs
  Console.WriteLine("{0} is going {1} MPH", c.PetName, c.Speed)
Next
```

Projecting New Data Types

It is also possible to *project* new forms of data from an existing data source. Let's assume that you wish to take the incoming `Car()` parameter and obtain a result set that accounts only for the make and color of each vehicle. To do so, you can define a `Select` statement that dynamically yields new types via VB 2008 *anonymous types*. Recall from Chapter 13 that the compiler defines a property for each specified name, and also is kind enough to override `ToString()`, `GetHashCode()`, and `Equals()`:

```
Sub GetProjection(ByVal myCars As Car())
  ' Now get structured data that only accounts for the
  ' Make and Color of each item.
  Console.WriteLine(vbLf & "Makes and Color:")

  Dim makesColors = From c In myCars Select New With {c.Make, c.Color}

  For Each n In makesColors
    Console.WriteLine("Name: {0}", n)
  Next
End Sub
```

Figure 14-10 shows the output of each of these new queries.

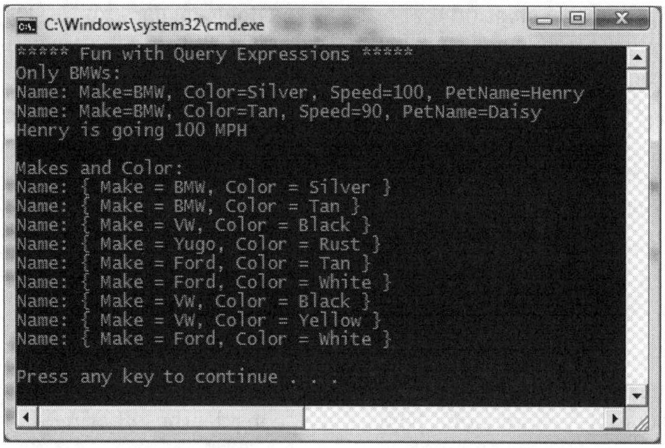

Figure 14-10. *Enumerating over subsets*

Reversing Result Sets

You can reverse the items within a result set quite simply using the generic `Reverse()` method of the `Enumerable` type. For example, the following method selects all items from the incoming `Car()` parameter in reverse (be aware that as of .NET 3.5, there is no "reverse" operator in the Visual Basic language, so you must explicitly call the `Reverse()` method):

```
Sub ReversedSelection(ByVal myCars As Car())
  ' Get everything in reverse.
  Console.WriteLine("All cars in reverse:")

  Dim subset = (From c In myCars Select c).Reverse()

  For Each c As Car in subset
    Console.WriteLine("{0} is going {1} MPH", c.PetName, c.Speed)
  Next
End Sub
```

Sorting Expressions

As you have seen over this chapter's initial examples, a query expression can take an `Order By` operator to sort items in the subset by a specific value. By default, the order will be ascending; thus, ordering by a string would be alphabetical, ordering by numerical data would be lowest to highest, and so forth. If you wish to view the results in a descending order, simply include the `Descending` operator. Ponder the following method:

```
Sub OrderedResults(ByVal myCars As Car())
  ' Order all the cars by PetName.
  Dim subset = From c In myCars Order By c.PetName Select c

  Console.WriteLine("Ordered by PetName:")
  For Each c As Car in subset
    Console.WriteLine("Car {0}", c)
  Next
```

```
  ' Now find the cars that are going faster than 55 mph,
  ' and order by descending PetName
  subset = From c In myCars _
    Where c.Speed > 55 Order By c.PetName Descending Select c

  Console.WriteLine(vbLf & _
    "Cars going faster than 55, ordered by descending PetName:")
  For Each c As Car in subset
    Console.WriteLine("Car {0}", c)
  Next
End Sub
```

Although ascending order is the default, you are able to make your intentions very clear by making use of the Ascending operator:

```
Dim subset = From c In myCars _
  Order By c.PetName Ascending Select c
```

Given these examples, you can now understand the format of a basic sorting query expression as follows:

```
Dim result = From item In container Order By value _
  Ascending/Descending Select item
```

Finding Differences

The last LINQ query we will examine for the time being involves obtaining a result set that determines the differences between two IEnumerable(Of T) compatible containers. Consider the following method, which makes use of the Enumerable.Except() method to yield (in this example) a Yugo:

```
Sub GetDiff()
  ' Two lists of strings.
  Dim myCars As String() = {"Yugo", "Aztec", "BMW"}
  Dim yourCars As String() = {"BMW", "Saab", "Aztec"}

  ' Find the differences.
  Dim carDiff = (From c In myCars Select c) _
    .Except(From c2 In yourCars Select c2)

  Console.WriteLine(vbLf & "Here is what you don't have, but I do:")
  For Each s As String In carDiff
    ' Prints Yugo.
    Console.WriteLine(s)
  Next
End Sub
```

These examples should give you enough knowledge to feel comfortable with the process of building LINQ query expressions. Chapter 24 will explore the related topics of LINQ to ADO (which is a catch-all term describing LINQ to SQL and LINQ to DataSet) and LINQ to XML later in the text. However, before wrapping up the current chapter, let's examine the topic of LINQ queries as method return values.

Source Code The FunWithLinqExpressions project can be found under the Chapter 14 subdirectory.

LINQ Queries: An Island unto Themselves?

You may have notice that each of the LINQ queries shown over the course of this chapter were all defined within the scope of a method. Moreover, to simplify our programming, the variable used to hold the result set was stored in an implicitly typed local variable (in fact, in the case of projections, this is mandatory). This being said, recall from Chapter 13 that implicitly typed local variables *cannot* be used to define parameters, return values, or fields of a class type.

Given this point, you may wonder exactly how you could return a query result to an external caller. The answer is it depends. If you have a result set consisting of strongly typed data (such as an array of strings, a `List(Of T)` of `Cars`, or whatnot), you could abandon the use of implicit typing and using a proper `IEnumerable(Of T)` or `IEnumerable`-compatible object. Consider the following example for a new .NET 3.5 Console Application named LinqRetValues:

```
Module Program
  Sub Main()
    Console.WriteLine("***** LINQ Transformations *****" & vbLf)
    Dim subset As IEnumerable(Of String) = GetStringSubset()
    For Each item As String In subset
      Console.WriteLine(item)
    Next
    Console.ReadLine()
  End Sub

  Function GetStringSubset() As IEnumerable(Of String)
    Dim currentVideoGames() As String = {"Morrowind", "BioShock", _
      "Half Life 2: Episode 1", "The Darkness", _
      "Daxter", "System Shock 2"}

    ' Note subset is an IEnumerable(OfString) compatible object.
    Dim subset As IEnumerable(Of String) = _
      From g In currentVideoGames Where g.Length > 6 Order By g Select g
    Return subset
  End Function
End Module
```

This example works as expected, only because the return value of the `GetStringSubset()` and the LINQ query within this method have been strongly typed. If you used implicit typing to define the `subset` variable within `Main()`, it would be permissible to return the value *only* if the method is still prototyped to return `IEnumerable(Of String)` (and if the implicitly typed local variable is in fact compatible with the specified return type).

However, always remember that when you have a LINQ query that makes use of a projection, you have no way of knowing the underlying data type, as this is determined at compile time. In these cases, implicit typing is mandatory. Given that return values cannot be implicitly typed, how can we return the `makesColors` object (from the earlier example) to an external caller?

Transforming Query Results to Array Types

When you wish to return projected data to a caller, one approach is to transform the query result into a standard CLR `Array` object using the `ToArray()` extension method. For example:

```
' Return value as an Array.
Public Function GetProjectedSubset() As Array
  ' This array will be the basis of our testing...
  Dim myCars As Car() = {New Car With _
    {.PetName = "Henry", .Color = "Silver", _
     .Speed = 100, .Make = "BMW"}, _
```

```
    New Car With {.PetName = "Daisy", .Color = "Tan", .Speed = 90, .Make = "BMW"}, _
    New Car With {.PetName = "Zippy", .Color = "Yellow", .Speed = 55, .Make = "VW"}}

  Dim makesColors = From c In myCars Select New With {c.Make, c.Color}

  ' Map set of anonymous objects to an Array object.
  ' Here were are relying on type inference of the generic
  ' type parameter, as we don't know the type of type!
  Return makesColors.ToArray()
End Function
```

We could invoke and process the data from `Main()` as follows:

```
Dim objs As Array = GetProjectedSubset()
For Each o As Object in objs
  Console.WriteLine(o)   ' Calls ToString() on each anonymous object.
Next
```

Note that we have to use a literal `System.Array` object and cannot make use of the VB array declaration syntax, given that we don't know the underlying type of type! Also note that we are not specifying the type parameter to the generic `ToArray()` method, as we (once again) don't know the underlying data type until compile time (which is too late for our purposes).

The obvious problem is that we lose any strong typing, as each item in the `Array` object is assumed to be of type `Object`. Nevertheless, when you need to return a LINQ result set that is the result of a projection operation, transforming the data into an `Array` type (or another suitable container via other members of the `Enumerable` type) is mandatory.

■ **Source Code** The LinqRetValues project can be found under the Chapter 14 subdirectory.

Summary

LINQ is a set of related technologies that attempts to provide a single, symmetrical manner to interact with diverse forms of data. As explained over the course of this chapter, LINQ can interact with any type implementing the `IEnumerable(Of T)` interface, including simple arrays as well as generic and nongeneric collections of data.

As you have seen over the course of this chapter, working with LINQ technologies is accomplished using several new VB 2008 language features. For example, given the fact that LINQ query expressions can return any number of result sets, it is common to make use of implicit typing to represent the underlying data type. As well, lambda expressions, object initialization syntax, and anonymous types can all be used to build very functional and compact LINQ queries.

More importantly, you have seen how the VB LINQ query operators are simply shorthand notations for making calls on shared members of the `System.Linq.Enumerable` type. As shown, most members of `Enumerable` operate on `Func` delegate types, which can take literal method addresses, anonymous methods, or lambda expressions as input to evaluate the query.

PART 4

Programming with .NET Assemblies

CHAPTER 15

Introducing .NET Assemblies

Each of the applications developed in this book's first 14 chapters were along the lines of traditional stand-alone applications, given that almost all of your custom programming logic was contained within a single executable file (`*.exe`). However, one major aspect of the .NET platform is the notion of *binary reuse*, where applications make use of the types contained within various external assemblies (aka code libraries). The point of this chapter is to examine the core details of creating, deploying, and configuring .NET assemblies.

Once you examine the .NET assembly format and understand how to define your own custom namespaces, you'll then learn the distinction between single-file and multifile assemblies, as well as private and shared assemblies. Next, you'll examine exactly how the .NET runtime resolves the location of an assembly and come to understand the role of the global assembly cache (GAC), application configuration files (`*.config` files), publisher policy assemblies, and the role of the `System.Configuration` namespace.

The Role of .NET Assemblies

.NET applications are constructed by piecing together any number of *assemblies*. Simply put, an assembly is a versioned, self-describing binary file hosted by the CLR. Now, despite the fact that .NET assemblies have exactly the same file extensions (`*.exe` or `*.dll`) as previous Windows binaries (including legacy COM servers), they have very little in common under the hood. Thus, to set the stage for the information to come, let's ponder some of the benefits provided by the assembly format.

Assemblies Promote Code Reuse

As you have been building your console applications over the previous chapters, it may have seemed that all of the applications' functionality was contained within the executable assembly you were constructing. In reality, your applications were leveraging numerous types contained within the always accessible .NET code library, `mscorlib.dll` (recall that the VB 2008 compiler references `mscorlib.dll` automatically), as well as `System.Windows.Forms.dll`, which was required for the occasional call to `MessageBox.Show()`.

As you may know, a code library (also termed a class library) is a `*.dll` that contains types intended to be used by external applications. When you are creating executable assemblies, you will no doubt be leveraging numerous system-supplied and custom code libraries as you create the application at hand. Do be aware, however, that a code library need not take a `*.dll` file extension. It is perfectly possible for an executable assembly to make use of types defined within an external executable file. In this light, a referenced `*.exe` can also be considered a code library; however, this is much less common than a traditional `*.dll`.

Regardless of how a code library is packaged, the .NET platform allows you to reuse types in a language-independent manner. For example, you could create a code library in VB 2008 and reuse that library in any other .NET programming language. It is possible to not only use types between languages, but derive from them as well. A base class defined in VB 2008 could be extended by a class authored in C#. Interfaces defined in Pascal .NET can be implemented by structures defined in VB 2008, and so forth. The point is that when you begin to break apart a single monolithic executable into numerous .NET assemblies, you achieve a language-neutral form of code reuse.

Assemblies Establish a Type Boundary

In Chapter 1, you were introduced to the topic of .NET namespaces, which were defined as a collection of semantically related types (for example, the `System.IO` namespace contains file I/O types, the `System.Windows.Forms` namespace defines Windows Forms GUI types, and so forth). Recall that a type's fully qualified name is composed by prefixing the type's namespace (e.g., `System`) to its name (e.g., `Console`). Strictly speaking, however, the assembly in which a type resides further establishes a type's identity. For example, if you have two uniquely named assemblies (say, `MyCars.dll` and `YourCars.dll`) that both define a namespace (`CarLibrary`) containing a class named `SportsCar`, they are considered unique types in the .NET universe.

Assemblies Are Versionable Units

.NET assemblies are assigned a four-part numerical version number of the form *major.minor.build.revision* (if you do not provide a version number explicitly, your assembly is automatically assigned a version of 0.0.0.0). This number, in conjunction with an optional *public key value*, allows multiple versions of the same assembly to coexist in harmony on a single machine. Formally speaking, assemblies that provide public key information are termed *strongly named*. As you will see in this chapter, using a strong name, the CLR is able to ensure that the correct version of an assembly is loaded on behalf of the calling client.

Assemblies Are Self-Describing

Assemblies are regarded as *self-describing* in part because they record every external assembly they must have access to in order to function correctly. Thus, if your assembly requires `System.Windows.Forms.dll` and `System.Drawing.dll`, they will be documented in the assembly's *manifest*. Recall from Chapter 1 that a manifest is a blob of metadata that describes the assembly itself (name, version, external assemblies, etc.).

In addition to manifest data, an assembly contains metadata that describes the composition (member names, implemented interfaces, base classes, constructors, and so forth) of every contained type. Given that an assembly is documented in such vivid detail, the CLR does not consult the Windows system registry to resolve its location (quite the radical departure from Microsoft's legacy COM programming model). As you will discover during this chapter, the CLR makes use of an entirely new scheme to resolve the location of external code libraries.

Assemblies Are Configurable

Assemblies can be deployed as *private* or *shared*. Private assemblies reside in the same directory (or possibly a subdirectory) as the client application making use of them. Shared assemblies, on the other hand, are libraries intended to be consumed by numerous applications on a single machine and are deployed to a specific directory termed the *global assembly cache*, or GAC.

Regardless of how you deploy your assemblies, you are free to author XML-based configuration files. Using these configuration files, the CLR can be instructed to "probe" for assemblies under a specific location, load a specific version of a referenced assembly for a particular client, or consult an arbitrary directory on your local machine, your network location, or a web-based URL. You'll learn a good deal more about XML configuration files throughout this chapter.

Understanding the Format of a .NET Assembly

Now that you've learned about several benefits provided by the .NET assembly, let's shift gears and get a better idea of how an assembly is composed under the hood. Structurally speaking, a .NET assembly (`*.dll` or `*.exe`) consists of the following elements:

- A Win32 file header
- A CLR file header
- CIL code
- Type metadata
- An assembly manifest
- Optional embedded resources

While the first two elements (the Win32 and CLR headers) are blocks of data that you can typically ignore, they do deserve some brief consideration. This being said, an overview of each element follows.

The Win32 File Header

The Win32 file header establishes the fact that the assembly can be loaded and manipulated by the Windows family of operating systems. This header data also identifies the kind of application (console-based, GUI-based, or `*.dll` code library) to be hosted by the Windows operating system. If you open a .NET assembly using the `dumpbin.exe` command-line utility (using a Visual Studio 2008 command prompt) and specify the `/headers` flag, you can view an assembly's Win32 header information. Figure 15-1 shows (partial) Win32 header information for the `CarLibrary.dll` assembly you will build a bit later in this chapter.

The CLR File Header

The CLR header is a block of data that all .NET files must support (and do support, courtesy of the VB 2008 compiler) in order to be hosted by the CLR. In a nutshell, this header defines numerous flags that enable the runtime to understand the layout of the managed file. For example, flags exist that identify the location of the metadata and resources within the file, the version of the runtime the assembly was built against, the value of the (optional) public key, and so forth. If you supply the `/clrheader` flag to `dumpbin.exe`, you are presented with the internal CLR header information for a given .NET assembly, as shown in Figure 15-2.

CLR header data is represented by an unmanaged C-style structure (`IMAGE_COR20_HEADER`). Again, as a .NET developer, you will not need to concern yourself with the gory details of Win32 or CLR header information (unless perhaps you are building a compiler for a new .NET programming language!). Just understand that every .NET assembly contains this data, which is used behind the scenes by the .NET runtime and Windows operating system.

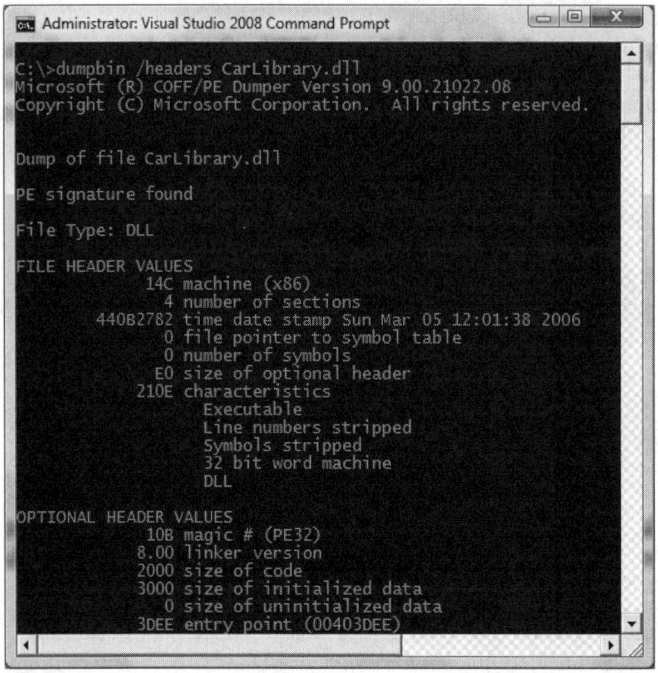

Figure 15-1. *An assembly's Win32 file header information*

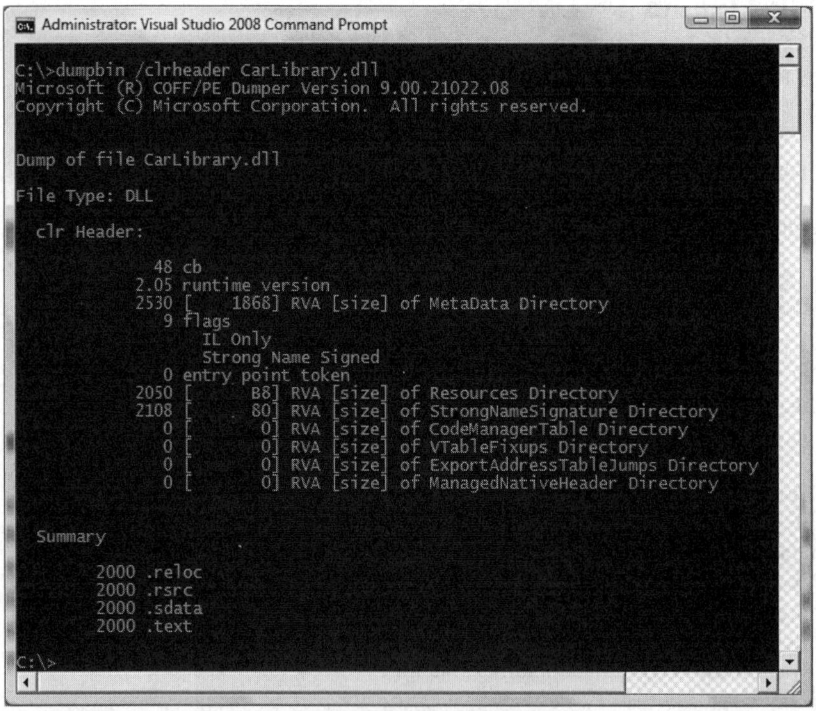

Figure 15-2. *An assembly's CLR file header information*

CIL Code, Type Metadata, and the Assembly Manifest

At its core, an assembly contains CIL code, which as you recall is a platform- and CPU-agnostic intermediate language. At runtime, the internal CIL is compiled on the fly (using a just-in-time [JIT] compiler) to platform- and CPU-specific instructions. Given this architecture, .NET assemblies can indeed execute on a variety of architectures, devices, and operating systems. Thankfully, it is always the job of the VB 2008 compiler to generate CIL code based on your VB 2008 code base.

An assembly also contains metadata that completely describes the format of the contained types as well as the format of external types referenced by this assembly. The .NET runtime uses this metadata to resolve the location of types (and their members) within the binary and lay out types in memory. You'll check out the details of the .NET metadata format in Chapter 16 during our examination of reflection services.

An assembly must also contain an associated *manifest* (also referred to as *assembly metadata*). The manifest documents each module within the assembly, establishes the version of the assembly, and also documents any external assemblies referenced by the current assembly (unlike legacy COM type libraries, which did not provide a way to document external dependencies). As you will see over the course of this chapter, the CLR makes extensive use of an assembly's manifest during the process of locating external assembly references.

Note Needless to say by this point in the book, when you wish to view an assembly's CIL code, type metadata, or manifest, `ildasm.exe` is the tool of choice. I will assume you will make extensive use of `ildasm.exe` or `reflector.exe` as you work through the code examples in this chapter (see Chapter 1).

Optional Assembly Resources

Finally, a .NET assembly may contain any number of embedded resources such as application icons, image files, sound clips, or string tables. In fact, the .NET platform supports satellite assemblies that contain nothing but localized resources. This can be useful if you wish to partition your resources based on a specific culture (English, German, etc.) for the purposes of building international software. The topic of building satellite assemblies is outside the scope of this text; however, you will learn how to embed application resources into an assembly using Windows Forms (Chapter 28) and Windows Presentation Foundation (Chapter 32).

Single-File and Multifile Assemblies

Technically speaking, an assembly can be composed of multiple modules. A module is really nothing more than a generic term for a valid .NET binary file. In most situations, an assembly is in fact composed of a single module. In this case, there is a one-to-one correspondence between the (logical) assembly and the underlying (physical) binary (hence the term single-file assembly).

Single-file assemblies contain all of the necessary elements (header information, CIL code, type metadata, manifest, and required resources) in a single `*.exe` or `*.dll` package. Figure 15-3 illustrates the composition of a single-file assembly.

A multifile assembly, on the other hand, is a set of .NET `*.dll`s that are deployed and versioned as a single logic unit. Formally speaking, one of these `*.dll`s is termed the `primary module` and contains the assembly-level manifest (as well as any necessary CIL code, metadata, header information, and optional resources). The manifest of the primary module records each of the related `*.dll` files it is dependent upon.

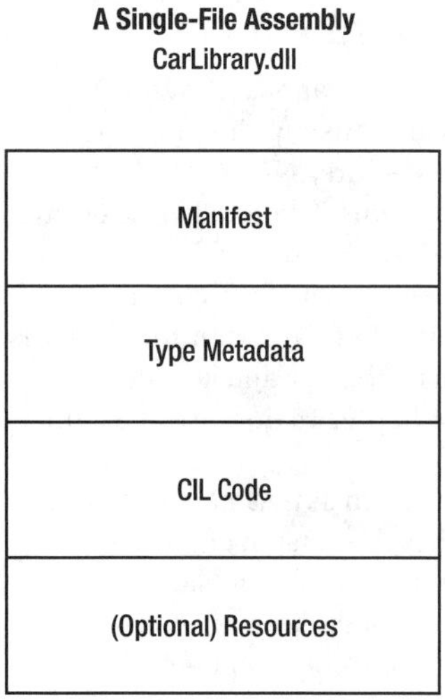

Figure 15-3. *A single-file assembly*

As a naming convention, the secondary modules in a multifile assembly take a `*.netmodule` file extension; however, this is not a requirement of the CLR. Secondary `*.netmodules` also contain CIL code and type metadata, as well as a module-level manifest, which simply records the externally required assemblies of that specific module.

The major benefit of constructing multifile assemblies is that they provide a very efficient way to download content. For example, assume you have a machine that is referencing a remote multifile assembly composed of three modules, where the primary module is installed on the client. If the client requires a type within a secondary remote `*.netmodule`, the CLR will download the binary to the local machine on demand to a specific location termed the *download cache*. If each `*.netmodule` is 1MB, I'm sure you can see the benefit.

Another benefit of multifile assemblies is that they enable modules to be authored using multiple .NET programming languages (which is very helpful in larger corporations, where individual departments tend to favor a specific .NET language). Once each of the individual modules has been compiled, the modules can be logically "connected" into a logical assembly using tools such as the command line compiler (`vbc.exe`).

In any case, do understand that the modules that compose a multifile assembly are *not* literally linked together into a single (larger) file. Rather, multifile assemblies are only logically related by information contained in the primary module's manifest. Figure 15-4 illustrates a multifile assembly composed of three modules, each authored using a unique .NET programming language.

At this point, you (hopefully) have a better understanding about the internal composition of a .NET binary file. With this necessary preamble out of the way, we are ready to dig into the details of building and configuring a variety of code libraries, beginning with the topic of defining custom namespaces.

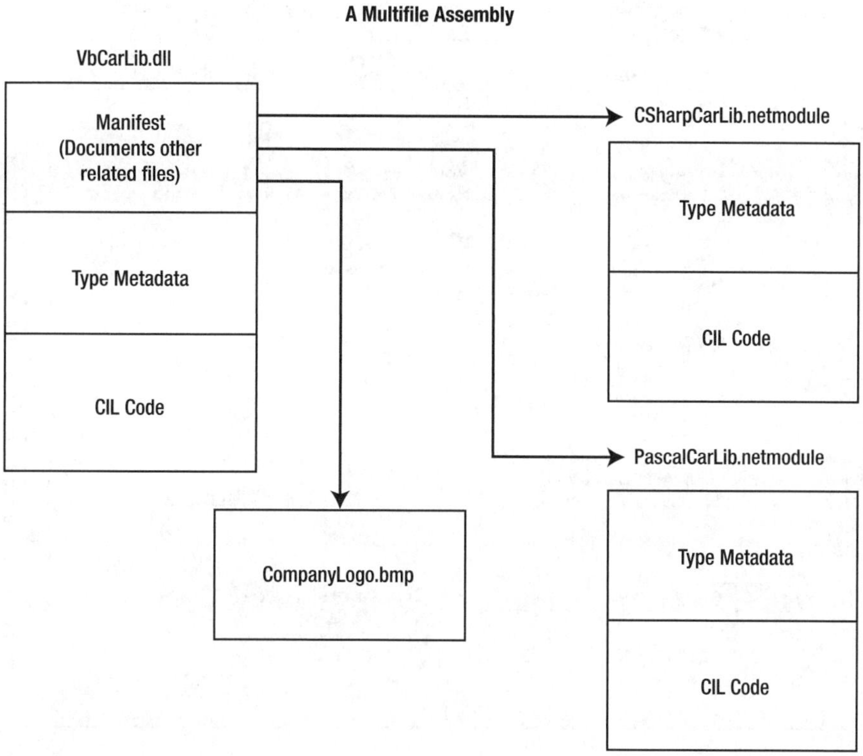

Figure 15-4. *The primary module records secondary modules in the assembly manifest.*

Constructing Custom .NET Namespaces

During the previous 14 chapters, as you created your stand-alone `*.exe` assemblies, Visual Basic 2008 was secretly grouping each one of your types within a *default namespace* (also known as the *root namespace*). By default, when you create a new VB 2008 Visual Studio 2008 project, your custom types are wrapped within a namespace that takes the identical name of the project itself. As you would expect, it is possible to change the name of this root namespace as well as define any number of additional namespaces via the VB 2008 `Namespace` keyword.

When you begin to build .NET `*.dll` assemblies, it is very important that you take time to organize your types into namespaces that make sense for the code library at hand, given that other developers will reference these libraries and need to know the set of `Import` statements required to make use of your types. To illustrate the ins-and-outs of namespace definitions, create a new Class Library project named MyCodeLibrary using Visual Studio 2008, as shown in Figure 15-5.

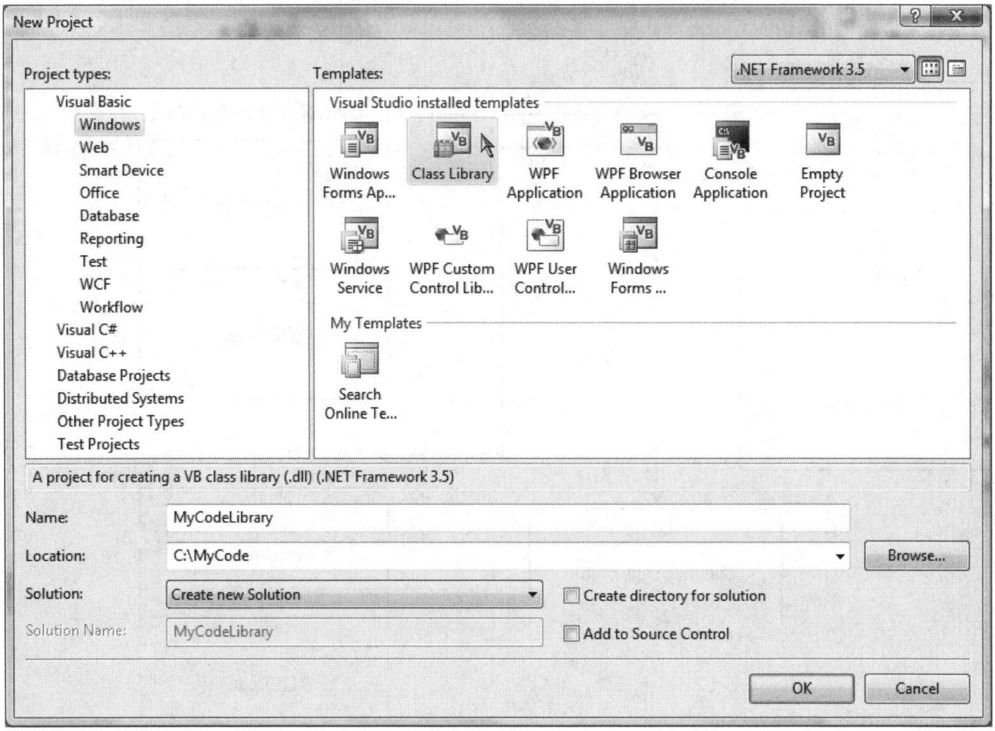

Figure 15-5. *Creating a VB 2008 Class Library project*

Observing the Root Namespace

Notice that when you create a Class Library project, you receive little more than an empty class definition for a type named `Class1`. Your goal when building a `*.dll` assembly is to populate the binary with any number of classes, interfaces, enumerations, structures, and delegates for the task at hand. Given this, it is important to point out that all of the skills you have developed during the previous chapters apply directly to a Class Library project. The only noticeable difference between a `*.dll` and `*.exe` assembly is how the image is loaded from disk.

In any case, double-click the My Project icon within Solution Explorer. Notice that the Application tab contains a text area that defines the root namespace, which as mentioned is by default named identically to the project you have just created, as you see in Figure 15-6.

You are always free to rename your root namespace as you see fit. Recall that a namespace does not need to be defined within an identically named assembly. Consider again our good friend `mscorlib.dll`. This core .NET assembly does not define a namespace named `mscorlib`. Rather the `mscorlib.dll` assembly defines a good number of unique namespaces (`System.IO`, `System`, `System.Threading`, `System.Collections`, etc.). This brings up another very important point: a single assembly can contain any number of uniquely named namespaces. In fact, it is also possible to have a single namespace defined across multiple assemblies. For example, the `System.IO` namespace is partially defined in `mscorlib.dll` as well as `System.dll`.

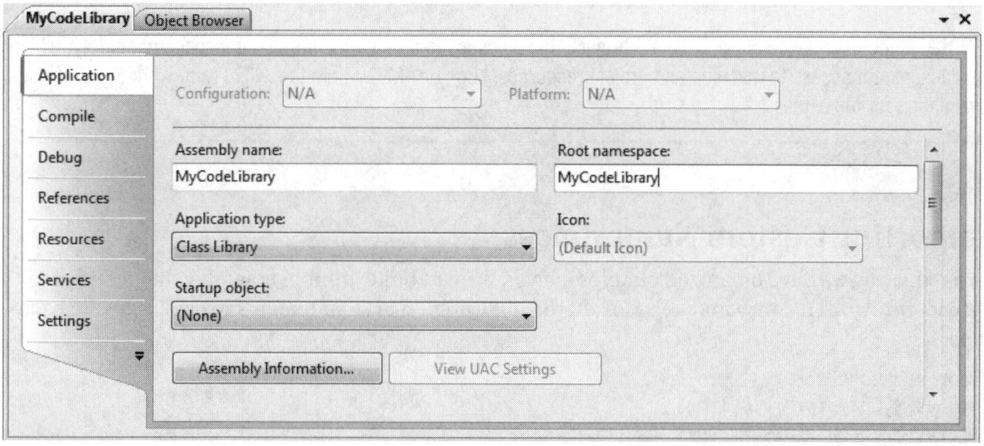

Figure 15-6. *The root namespace*

Defining Namespaces Beyond the Root

To illustrate the role of the VB 2008 Namespace keyword, update your initial *.vb file with the following code:

```
' This type is in the root namespace,
' which is (by default) the same name
' as the initial project.
Public Class SomeClass
End Class

' This namespace is nested within the
' root. Therefore the fully qualified
' name of this class is MyCodeLibrary.MyTypes.SomeClass
Namespace MyTypes
  Public Class SomeClass
  End Class

  ' It is possible to nest namespaces within other
  ' namespaces to gain a greater level of structure.
  ' Thus, the fully qualified name of this enum is:
  ' MyCodeLibrary.MyTypes.MyEnums.TestEnum
  Namespace MyEnums
    Public Enum TestEnum
      TestValue
    End Enum
  End Namespace
End Namespace
```

Notice that the Namespace keyword allows us to create customized namespaces that are nested within the root. To see the impact of this firsthand, open the Visual Studio 2008 Object Browser (via the View menu) and expand the tree view representing your project. As you can see, your single assembly defines three custom namespaces named MyCodeLibrary, MyCodeLibrary.MyTypes, and MyCodeLibrary.MyTypes.MyEnums (the additional "My" namespaces are autogenerated as a convenience for VB 2008 programmers).

■ **Note** Since the release of .NET 2.0, VB projects have access to an autogenerated namespace named `My`, which provides instant access to machine and project resources. Look up "My" within the .NET Framework 3.5 SDK documentation for full details.

Importing Custom Namespaces

Given the way we have organized our types, if you were to build another assembly that referenced `MyCodeLibrary.dll`, you would need to add the following `Imports` statements to gain access to each type:

```
Imports MyCodeLibrary
Imports MyCodeLibrary.MyTypes
Imports MyCodeLibrary.MyTypes.MyEnums
```

Also be aware that when you are building an assembly that contains multiple namespaces (such as `MyCodeLibrary.dll`), you may need to make use of the `Imports` keyword on a file-by-file basis where necessary. To illustrate, insert a new `Class` file into your current project (via the Project Add Class menu). Now, attempt to update the new `Class` with the following method:

```
Public Class Class2
  Public Sub MySub()
    Dim e As TestEnum
  End Sub
End Class
```

If you were to compile your assembly, you might be surprised to find a compiler error that states the `TestEnum` is not defined, regardless of the fact that this type is defined within a `*.vb` file in the same project! The reason, of course, is due to the fact that the `Class2` class type is defined within the root namespace, while `TestEnum` is within `MyCodeLibrary.MyTypes.MyEnums`. Therefore, this new `*.vb` file must import the defining namespace before we can compile the file successfully:

```
Imports MyCodeLibrary.MyTypes.MyEnums

Public Class Class2
  Public Sub MySub()
    Dim e As TestEnum
  End Sub
End Class
```

■ **Note** The References tab of the My Project namespace allows you to select any number of namespaces that should be automatically imported into each `*.vb` file within your current project. If a namespace is selected in this manner, you are not required to explicitly import the namespace using the `Imports` keyword.

Building Type Aliases Using the Imports Keyword

Before we build our first official code library, there is one final aspect of the `Imports` keyword I'd like to point out. In our current example, you may have noticed that we have two classes named `SomeClass`, one defined within `MyCodeLibrary` and the other within `MyCodeLibrary.MyTypes`. Surprisingly, if you wish to make use of the `SomeClass` defined within `MyCodeLibrary`, you are not required to add any additional Imports statements. Given that Class2 is defined within the MyCodeLibrary namespace, the compiler assumes you are requesting the SomeClass within the shared namespace scope:

```
Imports MyCodeLibrary.MyTypes.MyEnums

Public Class Class2
  Public Sub MySub()
    Dim e As TestEnum
    ' This is really MyCodeLibrary.SomeClass
    Dim s As New SomeClass()
  End Sub
End Class
```

However, for the sake of argument, what if you wished to make use of the SomeClass defined within MyCodeLibrary.MyTypes? You might think that you would simply add an Imports statement for MyCodeLibrary.MyTypes, as follows:

```
Imports MyCodeLibrary.MyTypes.MyEnums
Imports MyCodeLibrary.MyTypes

Public Class Class2
  Public Sub MySub()
    Dim e As TestEnum
      ' This is STILL MyCodeLibrary.SomeClass
    Dim s As New SomeClass()
  End Sub
End Class
```

However, s is still of type MyCodeLibrary.SomeClass (this can be verified using ildasm.exe)! To inform the compiler you explicitly wish to have the SomeClass defined within MyCodeLibrary.MyTypes, you can either use fully qualified names:

```
Imports MyCodeLibrary.MyTypes.MyEnums

Public Class Class2
  Public Sub MySub()
    Dim e As TestEnum
    Dim s As New MyCodeLibrary.MyTypes.SomeClass()
  End Sub
End Class
```

or make use of a specialized form of the Imports statement shown here:

```
Imports MyCodeLibrary.MyTypes.MyEnums

' A type alias!
Imports TypeIWant = MyCodeLibrary.MyTypes.SomeClass

Public Class Class2
  Public Sub MySub()
    Dim e As TestEnum
    ' "s" is now of type MyCodeLibrary.MyTypes.SomeClass
    Dim s As New TypeIWant()
    MsgBox(s.GetType().FullName)
  End Sub
End Class
```

This format of the `Imports` keyword is used to build a *type alias*. Simply put, this allows you to define a symbolic token (in this case `TypeIWant`) that is replaced at compile time with the assigned fully qualified name (`MyCodeLibrary.MyTypes.SomeClass`) of a type.

Source Code The MyCodeLibrary project is located under the Chapter 15 subdirectory.

Building and Consuming a Single-File Assembly

Now that you better understand the nature of defining and using custom .NET namespaces, our next task is to create a single-file `*.dll` assembly (named `CarLibrary`) that contains a small set of public types. To build a code library using Visual Studio 2008, simply select the Class Library project workspace (again, see Figure 15-5 earlier).

The design of your automobile library begins with an abstract base class named `Car` that defines a number of protected data members exposed through custom properties. This class has a single abstract method named `TurboBoost()`, which makes use of a custom enumeration (`EngineState`) representing the current condition of the car's engine. As all of these types will be in the root namespace (which would be `CarLibrary` based on our choice of project name), we have no need to make use of the VB 2008 `Namespace` keyword:

```
' Represents the state of the engine.
Public Enum EngineState
  engineAlive
  engineDead
End Enum

' The abstract base class in the hierarchy.
Public MustInherit Class Car
  Protected name As String
  Protected speed As Short
  Protected max_speed As Short
  Protected egnState As EngineState = EngineState.engineAlive

  Public MustOverride Sub TurboBoost()

  Public Sub New()
  End Sub
  Public Sub New(ByVal carName As String, ByVal max As Short, ByVal curr As Short)
    name = carName
    max_speed = max
    speed = curr
  End Sub

  Public Property PetName() As String
    Get
      Return name
    End Get
    Set(ByVal value As String)
      name = value
    End Set
  End Property
```

```
  Public Property CurrSpeed() As Short
    Get
      Return speed
    End Get
    Set(ByVal value As Short)
      speed = value
    End Set
  End Property

  Public ReadOnly Property MaxSpeed() As Short
    Get
      Return max_speed
    End Get
  End Property

  Public ReadOnly Property EngineState() As EngineState
    Get
      Return egnState
    End Get
  End Property
End Class
```

Now assume that you have two direct descendents of the Car type named MiniVan and SportsCar, both defined in a new file named DerivedCars.vb. Each overrides the abstract TurboBoost() method in an appropriate manner.

```
Imports System.Windows.Forms

Public Class SportsCar
  Inherits Car

  Public Sub New()
  End Sub
  Public Sub New(ByVal carName As String, ByVal max As Short, ByVal curr As Short)
    MyBase.New(carName, max, curr)
  End Sub

  Public Overrides Sub TurboBoost()
    MessageBox.Show("Ramming speed!", "Faster is better...")
  End Sub
End Class

Public Class MiniVan
  Inherits Car

  Public Sub New()
  End Sub
  Public Sub New(ByVal carName As String, ByVal max As Short, ByVal curr As Short)
    MyBase.New(carName, max, curr)
  End Sub

  ' Minivans have poor turbo capabilities!
  Public Overrides Sub TurboBoost()
    egnState = EngineState.engineDead
    MessageBox.Show("Time to call AAA", "Your car is dead")
  End Sub
End Class
```

Notice how each subclass implements `TurboBoost()` using the `MessageBox` class, which is defined in the `System.Windows.Forms.dll` assembly. For your assembly to make use of the types defined within this external assembly, the CarLibrary project must set a reference to this binary via the Add Reference dialog box (see Figure 15-7), which you can access through the Visual Studio 2008 Project ➤ Add Reference menu selection.

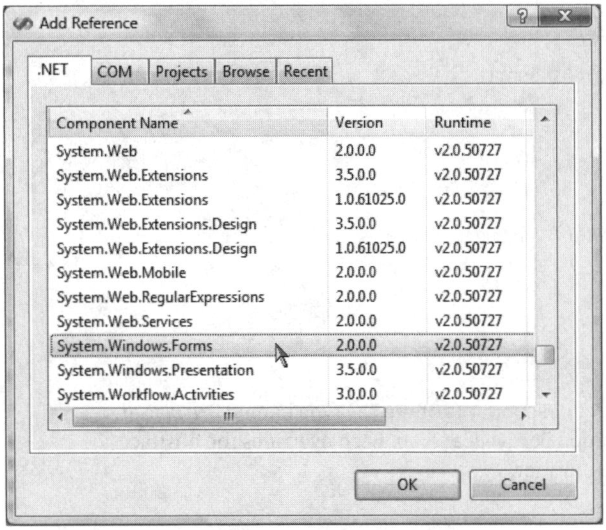

Figure 15-7. *Referencing external .NET assemblies begins here.*

It is *really* important to understand that the assemblies displayed in the .NET tab of the Add Reference dialog box do not represent each and every assembly on your machine. The Add Reference dialog box will *not* display your custom assemblies, and it does *not* display all assemblies located in the GAC. Rather, this dialog box simply presents a list of common assemblies that Visual Studio 2008 is preprogrammed to display. When you are building applications that require the use of an assembly not listed within the Add Reference dialog box, you need to click the Browse tab to manually navigate to the `*.dll` or `*.exe` in question.

Note Although it is technically possible to have your custom assemblies appear in the Add Reference dialog box's list by deploying a copy to `C:\Program Files\Microsoft Visual Studio 9.0\Common7\IDE\PublicAssemblies`, there is little benefit in doing so. As well, the Recent tab keeps a running list of previously referenced assemblies.

Exploring the Manifest

Before making use of `CarLibrary.dll` from a client application, let's check out how the code library is composed under the hood. Assuming you have compiled this project, load `CarLibrary.dll` into `ildasm.exe` (see Figure 15-8).

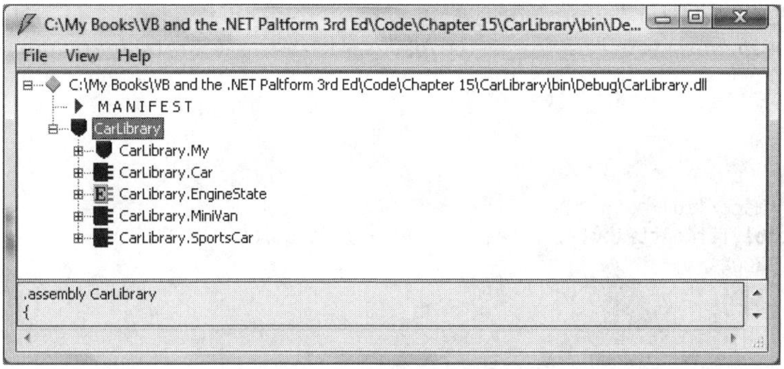

Figure 15-8. `CarLibrary.dll` *loaded into* `ildasm.exe`

Now, open the manifest of `CarLibrary.dll` by double-clicking the MANIFEST icon. The first code block encountered in a manifest is used to specify all external assemblies that are required by the current assembly to function correctly. As you recall, `CarLibrary.dll` made use of types within `mscorlib.dll` and `System.Windows.Forms.dll`, both of which are listed in the manifest using the `.assembly extern` token. As well, given that all VB 2008 applications created with Visual Studio 2008 automatically reference the VB 6.0 backward-compatibility assembly, you will also find references to `System.dll` and `Microsoft.VisualBasic` assemblies:

```
.assembly extern mscorlib
{
  .publickeytoken = (B7 7A 5C 56 19 34 E0 89 )
  .ver 2:0:0:0
}
.assembly extern Microsoft.VisualBasic
{
  .publickeytoken = (B0 3F 5F 7F 11 D5 0A 3A )
  .ver 8:0:0:0
}
.assembly extern System
{
  .publickeytoken = (B7 7A 5C 56 19 34 E0 89 )
  .ver 2:0:0:0
}
.assembly extern System.Windows.Forms
{
  .publickeytoken = (B7 7A 5C 56 19 34 E0 89 )
  .ver 2:0:0:0
}
```

Here, each `.assembly extern` block is qualified by the `.publickeytoken` and `.ver` directives. The `.publickeytoken` instruction is present only if the assembly has been configured with a `strong name` (more details later in this chapter). The `.ver` token marks (of course) the numerical version identifier.

After cataloging each of the external references, you will find a number of `.custom` tokens that identify assembly-level attributes. If you examine the `AssemblyInfo.vb` file created by Visual Studio 2008, you will find these attributes represent basic characteristics about the assembly such as company name, trademark, and so forth (all of which are currently empty). By default, `AssemblyInfo.vb` is hidden from view. To see this file, you must click the Show All Files button in Solution Explorer and expand the plus node under the My Project icon. Chapter 16 examines attributes in detail, so don't sweat the details at this point. Do be aware, however, that the attributes defined in AssemblyInfo.vb update the manifest with various .custom tokens, such as <AssemblyTitle()>, for example:

```
.assembly CarLibrary
{
...
  .custom instance void [mscorlib]
  System.Reflection.AssemblyTitleAttribute::.ctor(string) = ( 01 00 00 00 00 )
   .hash algorithm 0x00008004
  .ver 1:0:0:0
}
.module CarLibrary.dll
```

Finally, you can also see that the .assembly token is used to mark the friendly name of your assembly (CarLibrary), while the .module token specifies the name of the module itself (CarLibrary.dll). The .ver token defines the version number assigned to this assembly, as specified by the <AssemblyVersion()> attribute within AssemblyInfo.vb.

Exploring the CIL

Recall that an assembly does not contain platform-specific instructions; rather, it contains platform-agnostic CIL. When the .NET runtime loads an assembly into memory, the underlying CIL is compiled (using the JIT compiler) into instructions that can be understood by the target platform. If you double-click the TurboBoost() method of the SportsCar class, ildasm.exe will open a new window showing the CIL instructions, looking something like the following:

```
.method public hidebysig virtual instance void
  TurboBoost() cil managed
{
  // Code size       17 (0x11)
  .maxstack  2
  IL_0000:  ldstr      "Ramming speed!"
  IL_0005:  ldstr      "Faster is better..."
  IL_000a:  call       valuetype [System.Windows.Forms]
     System.Windows.Forms.DialogResult [System.Windows.Forms]
     System.Windows.Forms.MessageBox::Show(string, string)
  IL_000f:  pop
  IL_0010:  ret
}  // end of method SportsCar::TurboBoost
```

Notice that the .method tag is used to identify a method defined by the SportsCar type. Member variables defined by a type are marked with the .field tag. Recall that the Car class defined a set of protected data, such as speed. If you double-click the speed item on the Car class within ildasm.exe, you would find the following:

```
.field family int16 speed
```

Properties are marked with the .property tag. Here is the CIL describing the public CurrSpeed property (note that the read/write nature of a property is marked by .get and .set tags):

```
.property instance int16 CurrSpeed()
{
  .get instance int16 CarLibrary.Car::get_CurrSpeed()
  .set instance void CarLibrary.Car::set_CurrSpeed(int16)
}  // end of property Car::CurrSpeed
```

Exploring the Type Metadata

Finally, if you now press Ctrl+M, `ildasm.exe` displays the metadata for each type within the assembly, as you see in Figure 15-9.

Figure 15-9. *Type metadata for the types within* `CarLibrary.dll`

Now that you have looked inside the `CarLibrary.dll` assembly, you can build some client applications.

■ **Source Code** The CarLibrary project is located under the Chapter 15 subdirectory.

Building a VB 2008 Client Application

Because each of the `CarLibrary` types has been declared using the `Public` keyword, other assemblies are able to make use of them. Recall that you may also define types using the VB 2008 `Friend` keyword. Friend types can be used only by the assembly in which they are defined. External clients can neither see nor create friend types.

■ **Note** .NET provides a way to specify "friend assemblies" that allow `Friend` types to be consumed by specific assemblies. Look up the `InternalsVisibleToAttribute` class in the .NET Framework 3.5 SDK documentation for details.

To consume these types, create a new VB 2008 Console Application project (Vb2008CarClient). Once you have done so, set a reference to `CarLibrary.dll` using the Browse tab of the Add Reference dialog box (if you compiled `CarLibrary.dll` using Visual Studio 2008, your assembly is located under the \bin\Debug subdirectory of the CarLibrary project folder). Once you click the OK button and build your initial project, Visual Studio 2008 responds by placing a copy of `CarLibrary.dll` into the \bin\Debug folder of the Vb2008CarClient project folder, as shown in Figure 15-10.

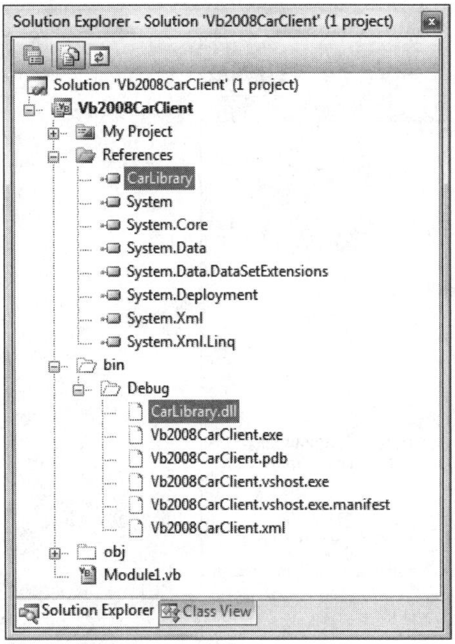

Figure 15-10. *Visual Studio 2008 copies private assemblies to the client's directory.*

Technically speaking, assemblies that are located within the same folder as the client application making use of them are termed *private assemblies*. We will drill into the details of private assemblies in just a bit; however, at this point you can build your client application to make use of the external types. Update your initial VB 2008 file like so:

```
' Import the CarLibrary namespace
' defined in the CarLibrary.dll assembly.
Imports CarLibrary

Module Program
  Sub Main()
    Console.WriteLine("***** Visual Basic 2008 Client *****")
    Dim myMiniVan As New MiniVan()
    myMiniVan.TurboBoost()

    Dim mySportsCar As New SportsCar()
    mySportsCar.TurboBoost()
    Console.ReadLine()
  End Sub
End Module
```

This code looks just like the other applications developed thus far. The only point of interest is that the VB 2008 client application is now making use of types defined within a separate custom assembly. Go ahead and run your program. As you would expect, the execution of this program results in the display of various message boxes.

Source Code The Vb2008CarClient project is located under the Chapter 15 subdirectory.

Building a C# Client Application

To illustrate the language-agnostic attitude of the .NET platform, let's create another Console Application project (CSharpCarClient), this time using the C# programming language (see Figure 15-11).

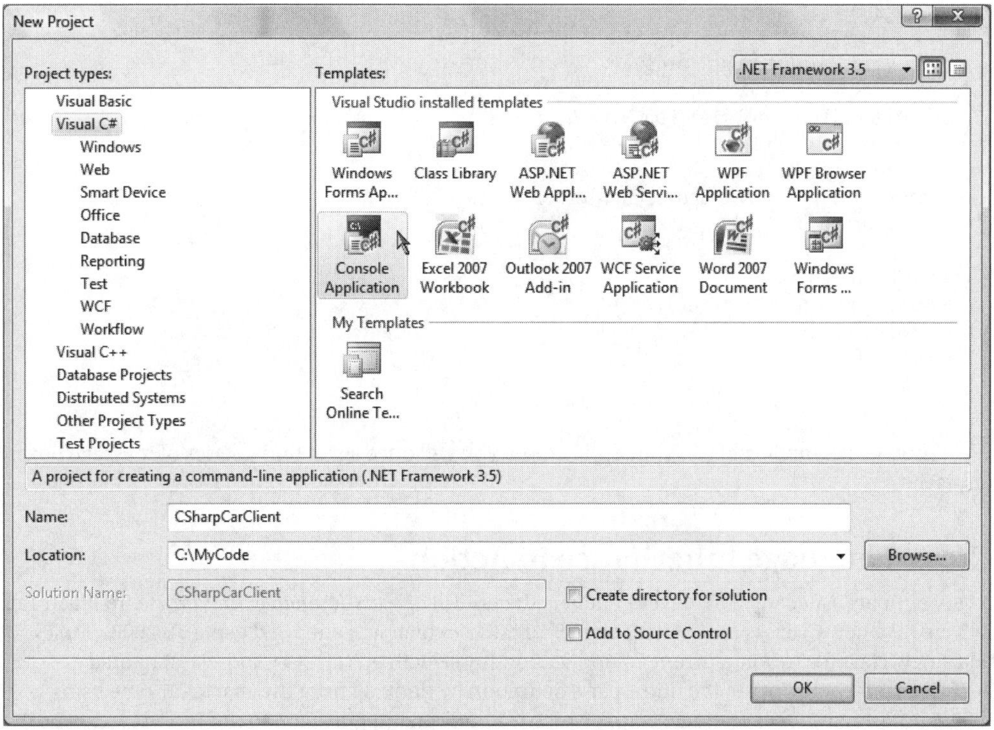

Figure 15-11. *Creating a C# Console Application project*

Once you have created the project, set a reference to `CarLibrary.dll` using the Add Reference dialog box. Like VB 2008, C# requires you to list each namespace used within the current file. However, C# offers the `using` keyword rather than the VB 2008 `Imports` keyword. Given this, add the following `using` statement within the `Class1.cs` code file (be aware, C# is a *case-sensitive* programming language!):

```
using System;
using System.Collections.Generic;
using System.Linq;
using System.Text;

using CarLibrary;

namespace CSharpCarClient
{
  class Program
```

```
  {
    static void Main(string[] args)
    {
    }
  }
}
```

Notice that the Main() method is defined within a C# class type (rather than the VB 2008–specific module type). In any case, to exercise the MiniVan and SportsCar types using the syntax of C#, update your Main() method like so:

```
class Program
{
  static void Main(string[] args)
  {
    Console.WriteLine("***** Fun with C# *****");

    // Make a sports car.
    SportsCar viper = new SportsCar("Viper", 240, 40);
    viper.TurboBoost();

    // Make a minivan.
    MiniVan mv = new MiniVan();
    mv.TurboBoost();
    Console.ReadLine();
  }
}
```

When you compile and run your application, you will once again find a series of message boxes displayed.

Cross-Language Inheritance in Action

A very enticing aspect of .NET development is the notion of *cross-language inheritance*. To illustrate, let's create a new C# class that derives from SportsCar (which was authored using VB 2008). First, add a new class file to your current C# application (by selecting Project ➤ Add Class) named PerformanceCar.cs. Update the initial class definition by deriving from the SportsCar type using the C# inheritance token (a single colon, which is functionally equivalent to the Inherits keyword). Furthermore, override the abstract TurboBoost() method using the override keyword:

```
using System;
using System.Collections.Generic;
using System.Text;

using CarLibrary;

namespace CSharpCarClient
{
  public class PerformanceCar : SportsCar
  {
    // This C# type is deriving from the VB 2008 SportsCar.
    public override void TurboBoost()
    {
      Console.WriteLine("Zero to 60 in a cool 4.8 seconds...");
    }
  }
}
```

To test this new class type, update the Main() method as follows:

```
static void Main(string[] args)
{
  Console.WriteLine("***** Fun with C# *****");

  // Make a sports car.
  SportsCar viper = new SportsCar("Viper", 240, 40);
  viper.TurboBoost();

  // Make a minivan.
  MiniVan mv = new MiniVan();
  mv.TurboBoost();

  PerformanceCar dreamCar = new PerformanceCar();
  // Inherited property.
  dreamCar.PetName = "Hank";
  dreamCar.TurboBoost();
  Console.ReadLine();
}
```

Notice that the dreamCar object is able to invoke any public member (such as the PetName property) found up the chain of inheritance, regardless of the fact that the base class has been defined in a completely different language and is defined in a completely different code library.

Source Code The CSharpCarClient project is located under the Chapter 15 subdirectory.

Building and Consuming a Multifile Assembly

Now that you have constructed and consumed a single-file assembly, let's examine the process of building a multifile assembly. Recall that a multifile assembly is simply a collection of related modules (which has nothing to do with the Visual Basic 2008 Module keyword!) that are deployed and versioned as a single logical unit. At the time of this writing, Visual Studio 2008 does not support a VB 2008 multifile assembly project template. Therefore, you will need to make use of the command-line compiler (vbc.exe) if you wish to build such a beast (see Chapter 2 for details of the command-line compiler).

To illustrate the process, you will build a multifile assembly named AirVehicles. The primary module (airvehicles.dll) will contain a single class type named Helicopter. The related manifest (also contained in airvehicles.dll) catalogs an additional *.netmodule file named ufo.netmodule, which contains another class type named (of course) Ufo. Although both class types are physically contained in separate binaries, you will group them into a single namespace named AirVehicles. Finally, both classes are created using VB 2008 (although you could certainly mix and match languages if you desire).

To begin, open a simple text editor (such as Notepad) and create the following Ufo class definition saved to a file named ufo.vb:

```
' This type will be placed
' within a *.netmodule binary,
' and is thus part of a multifile
' Assembly.
Namespace AirVehicles
  Public Class Ufo
```

```
    Public Sub AbductHuman()
      Console.WriteLine("Resistance is futile")
    End Sub
  End Class
End Namespace
```

To compile this class into a .NET module, switch back to the Visual Studio 2008 command prompt, navigate to the folder containing `ufo.vb`, and issue the following command to the VB 2008 compiler (the `module` option of the `/target` flag instructs `vbc.exe` to produce a `*.netmodule` as opposed to a `*.dll` or an `*.exe` file):

```
vbc.exe /t:module ufo.vb
```

If you now look in the folder that contains the `ufo.vb` file, you should see a new file named `ufo.netmodule` (take a peek). Next, create a new file named `helicopter.vb` that contains the following class definition:

```
' This type will be in the
' primary module of the multifile
' assembly, therefore this assembly
' will contain the assembly manifest.
Namespace AirVehicles
  Public Class Helicopter
    Public Sub TakeOff()
      Console.WriteLine("Helicopter taking off!")
    End Sub
  End Class
End Namespace
```

Given that `airvehicles.dll` is the intended name of the primary module of this multifile assembly, you will need to compile `helicopter.vb` using the `/t:library` and `/out:` options. To enlist the `ufo.netmodule` binary into the assembly manifest, you must also specify the `/addmodule` flag. The following command does the trick:

```
vbc /t:library /addmodule:ufo.netmodule /out:airvehicles.dll helicopter.vb
```

At this point, your directory should contain the primary `airvehicles.dll` module as well as the secondary `ufo.netmodule` binary.

Exploring the ufo.netmodule File

Now, using `ildasm.exe`, open `ufo.netmodule`. As you can see, `*.netmodules` contain a `module-level manifest`; however, its sole purpose is to list each external assembly referenced by the code base. Given that the `Ufo` class did little more than make a call to `Console.WriteLine()`, you find the following relevant code (in addition to a few other details, omitted here):

```
.assembly extern mscorlib
{
  .publickeytoken = (B7 7A 5C 56 19 34 E0 89 )
  .ver 2:0:0:0
}
.assembly extern Microsoft.VisualBasic
{
  .publickeytoken = (B0 3F 5F 7F 11 D5 0A 3A )
  .ver 8:0:0:0
}
.module ufo.netmodule
```

Exploring the airvehicles.dll File

Next, using ildasm.exe, open the primary airvehicles.dll module and investigate the assembly-level manifest. Notice that the .file token documents the associated modules in the multifile assembly (ufo.netmodule in this case). The .class extern tokens are used to document the names of the external types referenced for use from the secondary module (ufo):

```
.assembly extern mscorlib
{
  .publickeytoken = (B7 7A 5C 56 19 34 E0 89 )
  .ver 2:0:0:0
}

.assembly airvehicles
{
...
  .hash algorithm 0x00008004
  .ver 0:0:0:0
}

.file ufo.netmodule
...
.class extern public AirVehicles.Ufo
{
  .file ufo.netmodule
  .class 0x02000002
}
.module airvehicles.dll
```

Again, realize that the only entity that links together airvehicles.dll and ufo.netmodule is the assembly manifest. These two binary files have not been merged into a single, larger *.dll.

Consuming a Multifile Assembly

The consumers of a multifile assembly couldn't care less that the assembly they are referencing is composed of numerous modules. To keep things simple, let's create a new Visual Basic client application at the command line. Create a new file named Client.vb with the following Module definition. When you are done, save it in the same location as your multifile assembly.

```
Imports AirVehicles

Module Program
  Sub Main()
    Dim h As New Helicopter()
    h.TakeOff()

    ' This will load the *.netmodule on demand.
    Dim u As New Ufo()
    u.AbductHuman()
  End Sub
End Module
```

To compile this executable assembly at the command line, you will make use of the Visual Basic .NET command-line compiler, vbc.exe, with the following command set:

```
vbc /r:airvehicles.dll Client.vb
```

Notice that when you are referencing a multifile assembly, the compiler needs to be supplied only with the name of the primary module (the `*.netmodules` are loaded on demand when used by the client's code base). In and of themselves, `*.netmodules` do not have an individual version number and cannot be directly loaded by the CLR. Individual `*.netmodules` can be loaded only by the primary module (e.g., the file that contains the assembly manifest).

■ **Note** Visual Studio 2008 also allows you to reference a multifile assembly. Simply use the Add References dialog box and select the primary module. Any related `*.netmodules` are copied during the process.

At this point, you should feel comfortable with the process of building both single-file and multifile assemblies. To be completely honest, chances are that 99.99 percent of your assemblies will be single-file entities. Nevertheless, multifile assemblies can prove helpful when you wish to break a large physical binary into more modular units (and they are quite useful for remote download scenarios). Next up, let's formalize the concept of a private assembly.

■ **Source Code** The MultifileAssembly project is included under the Chapter 15 subdirectory.

Understanding Private Assemblies

Technically speaking, the assemblies you've created thus far in this chapter have been deployed as private assemblies. Private assemblies are required to be located within the same directory as the client application (termed the *application directory*) or a subdirectory thereof. Recall that when you set a reference to `CarLibrary.dll` while building the `Vb2008CarClient.exe` and `CSharpCarClient.exe` applications, Visual Studio 2008 responded by placing a copy of `CarLibrary.dll` within the client's application directory.

When a client program uses the types defined within this external assembly, the CLR simply loads the local copy of `CarLibrary.dll`. Because the .NET runtime does not consult the system registry when searching for referenced assemblies, you can relocate the `Vb2008CarClient.exe` (or `CSharpCarClient.exe`) and `CarLibrary.dll` assemblies to a location on your machine and run the application (this is often termed *Xcopy deployment*).

Uninstalling (or replicating) an application that makes exclusive use of private assemblies is a no-brainer: simply delete (or copy) the application folder. Unlike with COM applications, you do not need to worry about dozens of orphaned registry settings. More important, you do not need to worry that the removal of private assemblies will break any other applications on the machine.

The Identity of a Private Assembly

The full identity of a private assembly consists of the friendly name and numerical version, both of which are recorded in the assembly manifest. The friendly name simply is the name of the module that contains the assembly's manifest minus the file extension. For example, if you examine the manifest of the `CarLibrary.dll` assembly, you find the following:

```
.assembly CarLibrary
{
...
  .ver 1:0:0:0
}
```

Given the isolated nature of a private assembly, it should make sense that the CLR does not bother to make use of the version number when resolving its location. The assumption is that private assemblies do not need to have any elaborate version checking, as the client application is the only entity that "knows" of its existence. Given this, it is (very) possible for a single machine to have multiple copies of the same private assembly in various application directories.

Understanding the Probing Process

The .NET runtime resolves the location of a private assembly using a technique termed *probing*, which is much less invasive than it sounds. Probing is the process of mapping an external assembly request to the location of the requested binary file. Strictly speaking, a request to load an assembly may be either *implicit* or *explicit*. An implicit load request occurs when the CLR consults the manifest in order to resolve the location of an assembly defined using the `.assembly extern` tokens:

```
.assembly extern CarLibrary
{...}
```

An explicit load request occurs programmatically using the `Load()` or `LoadFrom()` method of the `System.Reflection.Assembly` class type, typically for the purposes of late binding and dynamic invocation of type members. You'll examine these topics further in Chapter 16, but for now you can see an example of an explicit load request in the following code (which assumes you have imported the `System.Reflection` namespace to gain access to the `Assembly` class):

```
' An explicit load request.
Dim asm As Assembly = Assembly.Load("CarLibrary")
```

In either case, the CLR extracts the friendly name of the assembly and begins probing the client's application directory for a file named `CarLibrary.dll`. If this file cannot be located, an attempt is made to locate an executable assembly based on the same friendly name (`CarLibrary.exe`). If neither of these files can be located in the application directory, the runtime gives up and throws a `FileNotFoundException` object at runtime.

■ Note Technically speaking, if a copy of the requested assembly cannot be found within the client's application directory, the CLR will also attempt to locate a client subdirectory with the exact same name as the assembly's friendly name (e.g., C:\MyClient\CarLibrary). If the requested assembly resides within this subdirectory, the CLR will load the assembly into memory.

Configuring Private Assemblies

While it is possible to deploy a .NET application by simply copying all required assemblies to a single folder on the user's hard drive, you will most likely wish to define a number of subdirectories to group related content. For example, assume you have an application directory named C:\MyApp that contains `Vb2008CarClient.exe`. Under this folder might be a subfolder named MyLibraries that contains `CarLibrary.dll`.

Regardless of the intended relationship between these two directories, the CLR will *not* probe the MyLibraries subdirectory unless you supply a configuration file. Configuration files contain various XML elements that allow you to influence the probing process. Configuration files must have the same name as the launching application and take a `*.config` file extension, and they must be deployed in the client's application directory. Thus, if you wish to create a configuration file for `Vb2008CarClient.exe`, it must be named `Vb2008CarClient.exe.config`.

To illustrate the process, create a new directory on your C drive named MyApp using Windows Explorer. Next, copy `Vb2008CarClient.exe` and `CarLibrary.dll` to this new folder, and run the program by double-clicking the executable. Your program should run successfully at this point (remember, assemblies are not registered!). Next, create a new subdirectory under C:\MyApp named MyLibraries, as shown in Figure 15-12, and place a copy of `CarLibrary.dll` into this location.

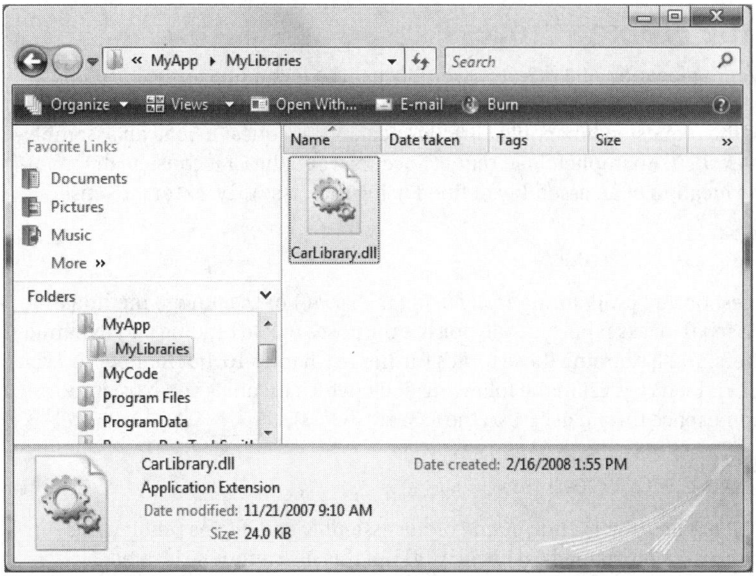

Figure 15-12. `CarLibrary.dll` *now resides under the MyLibraries subdirectory.*

Try to run your client program again. Because the CLR could not locate CarLibrary directly within the application directory, you are presented with a rather nasty unhandled `FileNotFoundException` object.

To rectify the situation, create a new configuration file named `Vb2008CarClient.exe.config` and save it in the *same* folder containing the `Vb2008CarClient.exe` application, which in this example would be C:\MyApp. Open this file and enter the following content exactly as shown (be aware that XML is case sensitive!):

```
<configuration>
  <runtime>
    <assemblyBinding xmlns="urn:schemas-microsoft-com:asm.v1">
      <probing privatePath="MyLibraries"/>
    </assemblyBinding>
  </runtime>
</configuration>
```

.NET `*.config` files always open with a root element named `<configuration>`. The nested `<runtime>` element may specify an `<assemblyBinding>` element, which nests a further element named `<probing>`. The `privatePath` attribute is the key point in this example, as it is used to specify the subdirectories relative to the application directory where the CLR should probe.

Do note that the `<probing>` element does not specify *which* assembly is located under a given subdirectory. In other words, you cannot say, "CarLibrary is located under the \MyLibraries subdirectory, but MathUtils is located under the \bin subdirectory." The `<probing>` element simply instructs the CLR to investigate all specified subdirectories for the requested assembly until the first match is encountered.

■ **Note** Be very aware that the `privatePath` attribute cannot be used to specify an absolute (C:\SomeFolder\SomeSubFolder) or relative (..\SomeFolder\AnotherFolder) path! If you wish to specify a directory outside the client's application directory, you will need to make use of a completely different XML element named `<codeBase>`, described later in the chapter in the section "Understanding the <codeBase> Element."

Multiple subdirectories can be assigned to the `privatePath` attribute using a semicolon-delimited list. You have no need to do so at this time, but here is an example that informs the CLR to consult the MyLibraries and MyLibraries\Tests client subdirectories:

```
<probing privatePath="MyLibraries;MyLibraries\Tests"/>
```

Once you've finished creating `Vb2008CarClient.exe.config`, run the client by double-clicking the executable in Windows Explorer. You should find that `Vb2008CarClient.exe` executes without a hitch (if this is not the case, double-check it for typos in your XML document).

Next, for testing purposes, change the name of your configuration file (in one way or another) and attempt to run the program once again. The client application should now fail. Remember that `*.config` files must be prefixed with the same name as the related client application. By way of a final test, open your configuration file for editing and capitalize any of the XML elements. Once the file is saved, your client should fail to run once again (as XML is case sensitive).

Configuration Files and Visual Studio 2008

While you are always able to create XML configuration files by hand using your text editor of choice, Visual Studio 2008 allows you to create a configuration file during the development of the client program. To illustrate, load the Vb2008CarClient (or CSharpCarClient for that matter) solution into Visual Studio 2008 and insert a new Application Configuration File item (see Figure 15-13) using the Project ➤ Add New Item menu selection. Before you click the OK button, take note that the file is named `app.config` (don't rename it!). If you look in the Solution Explorer window, you will now find `app.config` has been inserted into your current project.

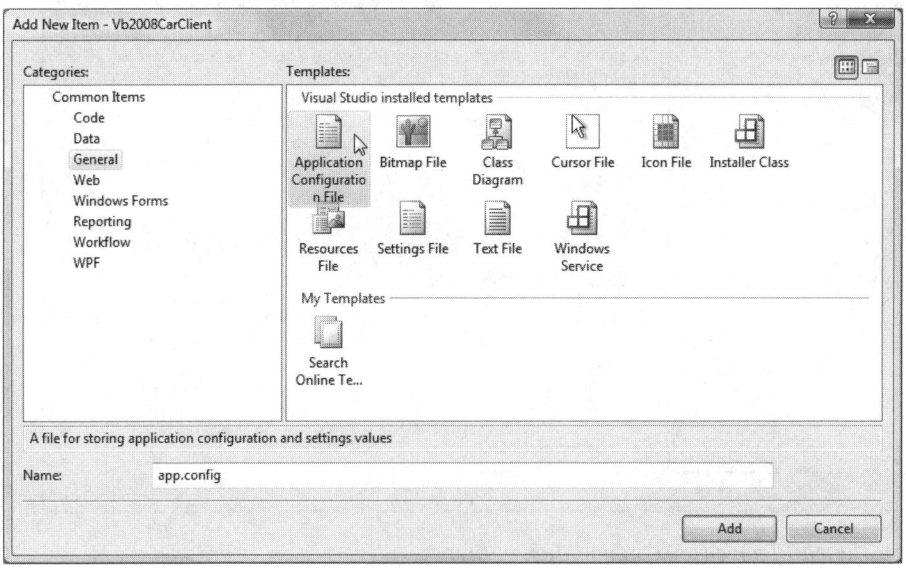

Figure 15-13. *The Visual Studio 2008* `app.config` *file*

At this point, you are free to enter the necessary XML elements for the client you happen to be creating. Now, here is the cool thing. Each time you compile your project, Visual Studio 2008 will automatically copy the data in `app.config` to the \bin\Debug directory using the proper naming convention (such as `Vb2008CarClient.exe.config`). However, this behavior will happen only if your configuration file is indeed named `app.config`.

Using this approach, all you need to do is maintain `app.config`, and Visual Studio 2008 will ensure your application directory contains the latest and greatest content (even if you happen to rename your project).

■ **Note** For better or for worse, when you insert a new `app.config` file into a VB 2008 project, the IDE will add a good deal of data within an element named `<system.diagnostics>`, which has nothing to do with assembly binding. For the remainder of this chapter, I will assume that you will delete this unnecessary XML data and author the XML elements as shown in the remaining code examples.

Introducing the .NET Framework Configuration Utility

Although authoring a `*.config` file by hand is not too traumatic, the .NET Framework SDK does ship with a tool that allows you to build XML configuration files using a friendly GUI editor. You can find the .NET Framework Configuration utility under the Administrative folder of your Control Panel. Once you launch this tool, you will find a number of configuration options, as shown in Figure 15-14.

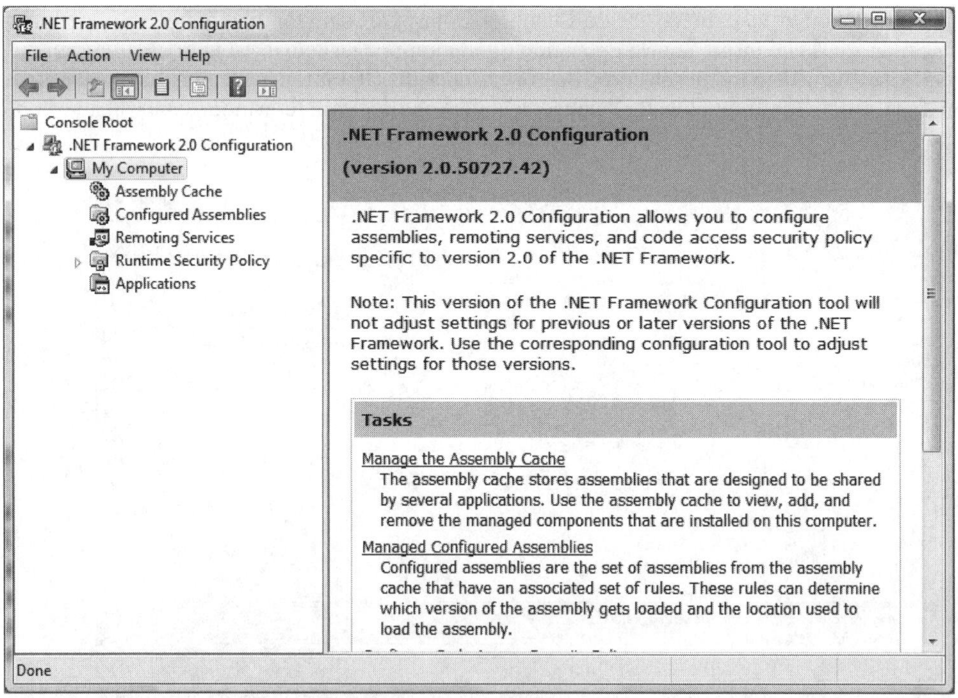

Figure 15-14. *The .NET Framework Configuration utility*

To build a client `*.config` file using this utility, your first step is to add the application to configure by right-clicking the Applications node and selecting Add. In the resulting dialog box, you *may* find the application you wish to configure, provided that you have executed it using Windows Explorer. If this is not the case, click the Other button and navigate to the location of the client program you wish to configure. For this example, assume you have added a client program named `Vb2008CarClient.exe`. Once you have done so, you will now find a new subnode, as shown in Figure 15-15.

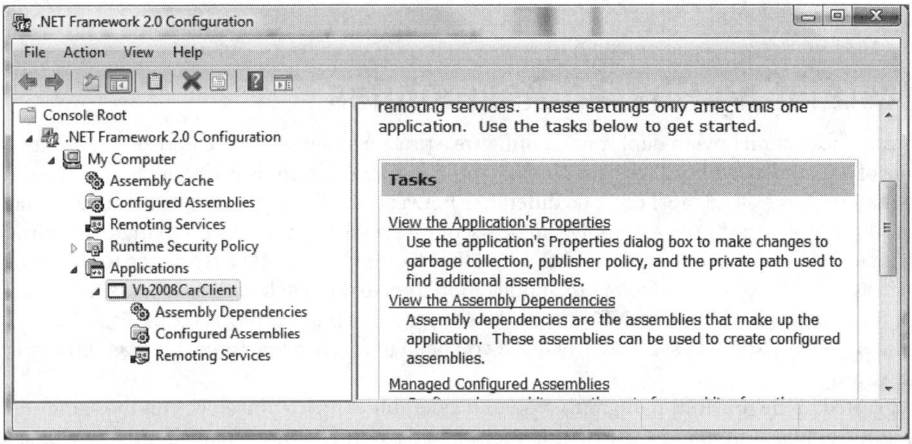

Figure 15-15. *Preparing to configure* `Vb2008CarClient.exe`

If you right-click the Vb2008CarClient node and activate the Properties page, you will notice a text field located at the bottom of the dialog box where you can enter the values to be assigned to the `privatePath` attribute. Just for testing purposes, enter a subdirectory named TestDir (see Figure 15-16).

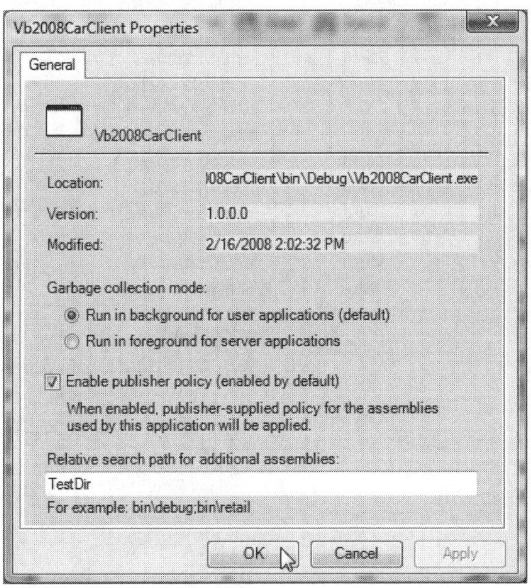

Figure 15-16. *Configuring a private probing path graphically*

Once you click the OK button, you can examine the Vb2008CarClient\bin\Debug directory and find that a new `*.config` file has been updated with the correct `<probing>` element.

■ **Note** As you may guess, you can copy the XML content generated by the .NET Framework Configuration utility into a Visual Studio 2008 `app.config` file for further editing. Using this approach, you can certainly decrease your typing burden by allowing the tool to generate the initial content.

Understanding Shared Assemblies

Now that you understand how to deploy and configure a private assembly, you can begin to examine the role of a *shared assembly*. Like a private assembly, a shared assembly is a collection of types and (optional) resources. The most obvious difference between shared and private assemblies is the fact that a single copy of a shared assembly can be used by several applications on a single machine.

Consider all the applications created in this text that required you to set a reference to `System.Windows.Forms.dll`. If you were to look in the application directory of each of these clients, you would *not* find a private copy of this .NET assembly. The reason is that `System.Windows.Forms.dll` has been deployed as a shared assembly. Clearly, if you need to create a machinewide class library, this is the way to go.

As suggested in the previous paragraph, a shared assembly is not deployed within the same directory as the application making use of it. Rather, shared assemblies are installed into the global assembly cache. The GAC is located under a subdirectory of your Windows directory named "assembly" (e.g., C:\Windows\assembly), as shown in Figure 15-17.

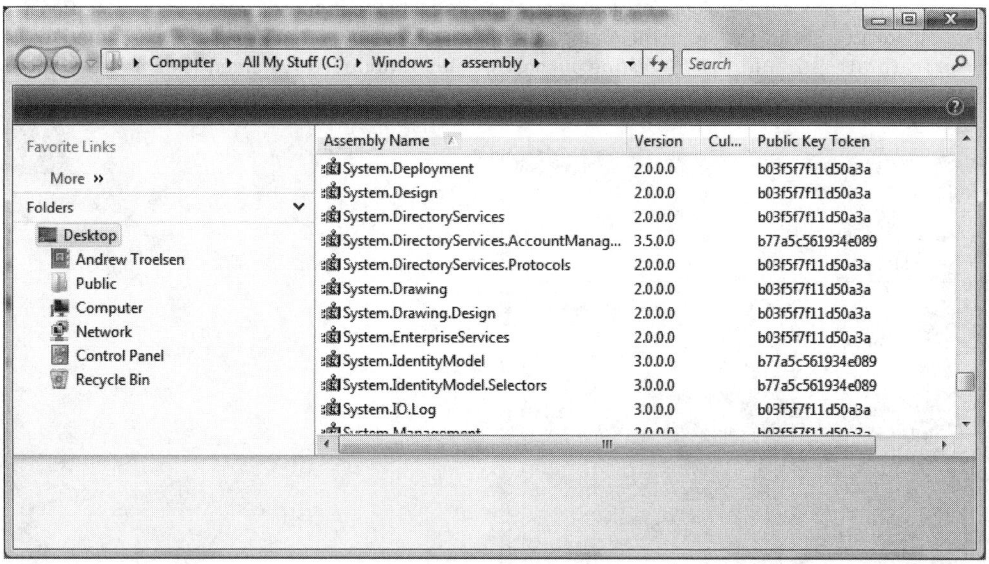

Figure 15-17. *The GAC is located under C:\Windows\assembly.*

Note You cannot install executable assemblies (*.exe) into the GAC. Only assemblies that take the *.dll file extension can be deployed as a shared assembly.

Understanding Strong Names

Before you can deploy an assembly to the GAC, you must assign it a *strong name*, which is used to uniquely identify the publisher of a given .NET binary. Understand that a "publisher" could be an individual programmer, a department within a given company, or an entire company at large.

In some ways, a strong name is the modern-day .NET equivalent of the COM globally unique identifier (GUID) identification scheme. If you have a COM background, you may recall that AppIDs are GUIDs that identify a particular COM application. Unlike COM GUID values (which are nothing more than 128-bit numbers), strong names are based (in part) on two cryptographically related keys (termed the *public key* and the *private key*), which are much more unique and resistant to tampering than a simple GUID.

Formally, a strong name is composed of a set of related data, much of which is specified using assembly-level attributes:

- The friendly name of the assembly (which you recall is the name of the assembly minus the file extension)
- The version number of the assembly (assigned using the <AssemblyVersion()> attribute)
- The public key value (assigned using the <AssemblyKeyFile()> attribute)
- An optional culture identity value for localization purposes (assigned using the <AssemblyCulture()> attribute)
- An embedded *digital signature* created using a hash of the assembly's contents and the private key value

To provide a strong name for an assembly, your first step is to generate public/private key data using the .NET Framework 3.5 SDK's sn.exe utility (which you'll do momentarily). The sn.exe utility responds by generating a file (typically ending with the *.snk [Strong Name Key] file extension) that contains data for two distinct but mathematically related keys, the public key and the private key. Once the VB 2008 compiler is made aware of the location for your *.snk file, it will record the full public key value in the assembly manifest using the .publickey at the time of compilation.

The VB 2008 compiler will also generate a hash code based on the contents of the entire assembly (CIL code, metadata, and so forth). As you recall from Chapter 6, a *hash code* is a numerical value that is unique for a fixed input. Thus, if you modify any aspect of a .NET assembly (even a single character in a string literal), the compiler yields a unique hash code. This hash code is combined with the private key data within the *.snk file to yield a digital signature embedded within the assembly's CLR header data. The process of strongly naming an assembly is illustrated in Figure 15-18.

Understand that the actual *private* key data is not listed anywhere within the manifest, but is used only to digitally sign the contents of the assembly (in conjunction with the generated hash code). Again, the whole idea of making use of public/private key data is to ensure that no two companies, departments, or individuals have the same identity in the .NET universe. In any case, once the process of assigning a strong name is complete, the assembly may be installed into the GAC.

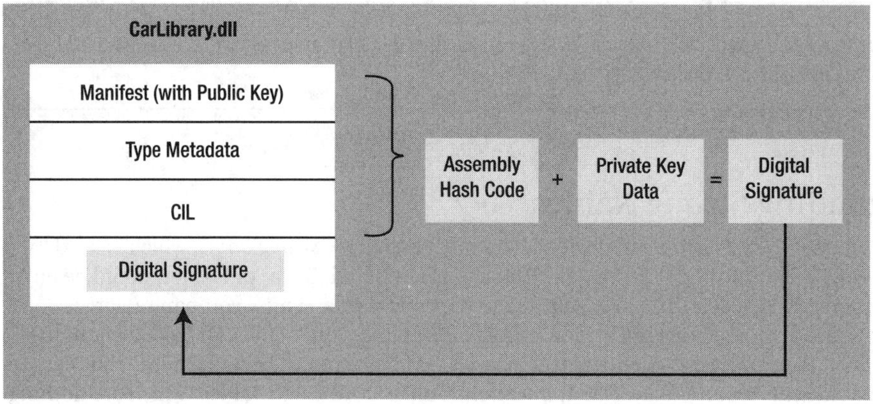

Figure 15-18. *At compile time, a digital signature is generated and embedded into the assembly based in part on public and private key data.*

■ **Note** Strong names also provide a level of protection against potential evildoers tampering with your assembly's contents. Given this point, it is considered a .NET best practice to strongly name every assembly regardless of whether it is deployed to the GAC.

Strongly Naming CarLibrary.dll Using sn.exe

Let's walk through the process of assigning a strong name to the `CarLibrary` assembly created earlier in this chapter (go ahead and open up that project using Visual Studio 2008). The first order of business is to generate the required key data using the `sn.exe` utility. Although this tool has numerous command-line options, all you need to concern yourself with for the moment is the `-k` flag, which instructs the tool to generate a new file containing the public/private key information. Create a new folder on your C drive named MyTestKeyPair and change to that directory using a Visual Studio 2008 command prompt. Now, issue the following command to generate a file named `MyTestKeyPair.snk`:

```
sn -k MyTestKeyPair.snk
```

Now that you have your key data, you need to inform the VB 2008 compiler exactly where `MyTestKeyPair.snk` is located. When you create any new VB 2008 project workspace using Visual Studio 2008, you will receive a project file (located under the My Project node of Solution Explorer) named `AssemblyInfo.vb`. By default, you cannot see this file; however, if you click the Show All Files button in Solution Explorer, you will see this is the case, as shown in Figure 15-19.

This file contains a number of attributes that describe the assembly itself. The `AssemblyKeyFile` assembly-level attribute can be used to inform the compiler of the location of a valid `*.snk` file. Simply specify the path as a string parameter, for example:

```
<Assembly: AssemblyKeyFile("C:\MyTestKeyPair\MyTestKeyPair.snk")>
```

■ **Note** When you add the `<AssemblyKeyFile()>` attribute in a `*.vb` code file, you will find a coding warning is generated. This is because the preferred manner to inform the compiler which `*.snk` file to make use of is via the My Project editor of Visual Studio. You will do so in the next section.

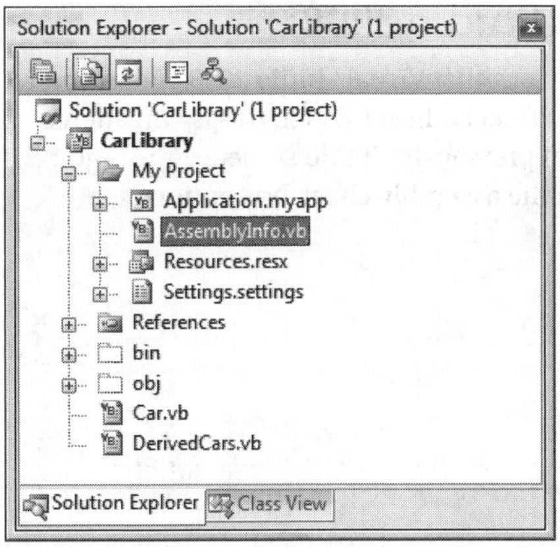

Figure 15-19. *The hidden* `AssemblyInfo.vb` *file*

In the `AssemblyInfo.vb` file, you will find another attribute named `<AssemblyVersion()>`. Initially the value is set to `1.0.0.0`. Recall that a .NET version number is composed of these four parts: *major.minor.build.revision.*

```
<Assembly: AssemblyVersion("1.0.0.0")>
```

At this point, the VB 2008 compiler has all the information needed to generate strong name data (as you are not specifying a unique culture value via the `<AssemblyCulture()>` attribute, you "inherit" the culture of your current machine). Compile your `CarLibrary` code library and open the manifest using `ildasm.exe`. You will now see a new `.publickey` tag is used to document the full public key information, while the `.ver` token records the version specified via the `<AssemblyVersion>` attribute, as shown in Figure 15-20.

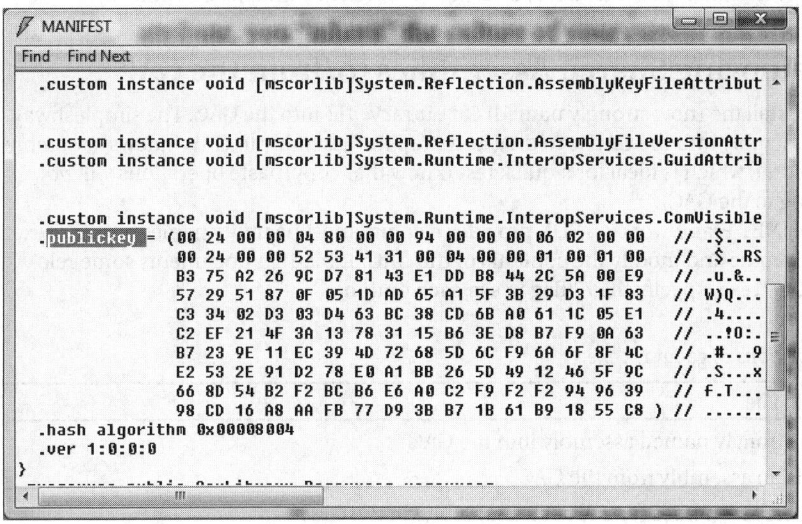

Figure 15-20. *A strongly named assembly records the public key in the manifest.*

Assigning Strong Names Using Visual Studio 2008

Before you deploy `CarLibrary.dll` to the GAC, let me point out that Visual Studio 2008 allows you to specify the location of your `*.snk` file using a project's My Project editor (in fact, this is considered the preferred approach and will not yield the warning seen previously). To do so, select the Signing node, supply the path to the `*.snk` file, and select the Sign the assembly check box option (see Figure 15-21).

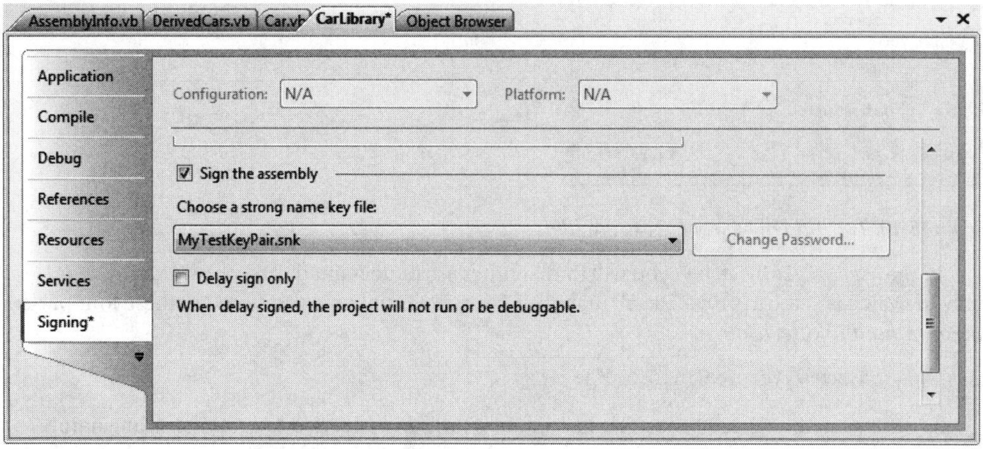

Figure 15-21. *Specifying an `*.snk` file via the Properties page*

Notice that the Signing node also allows you to create a brand-new `*.snk` file directly within the IDE, by selecting the New option of the Choose a strong name key file drop-down list box. By doing so, you do not need to manually generate key files using the `sn.exe` command-line utility.

Installing/Removing Shared Assemblies to/from the GAC

The final step is to install the (now strongly named) `CarLibrary.dll` into the GAC. The simplest way to install a shared assembly into the GAC is to drag and drop the assembly to C:\Windows\assembly using Windows Explorer, which is ideal for a quick test (know that copy/paste operations will *not* work when deploying to the GAC).

In addition, the .NET Framework 3.5 SDK provides a command-line utility named `gacutil.exe` that allows you to examine and modify the contents of the GAC. Table 15-1 documents some relevant options of `gacutil.exe` (specify the `/?` flag to see each option).

Table 15-1. *Various Options of* `gacutil.exe`

Option	Meaning in Life
`/i`	Installs a strongly named assembly into the GAC
`/u`	Uninstalls an assembly from the GAC
`/l`	Displays the assemblies (or a specific assembly) in the GAC

Thus, if you wish, you could also open a Visual Studio 2008 command prompt, navigate to the folder containing the assembly you wish to install (such as `CarLibrary.dll`), and enter the following command set:

```
gacutil -i CarLibrary.dll
```

Using either technique, deploy `CarLibrary.dll` to the GAC. Once you've finished, you should see your library present and accounted for, as shown in Figure 15-22 (your public key token value will differ).

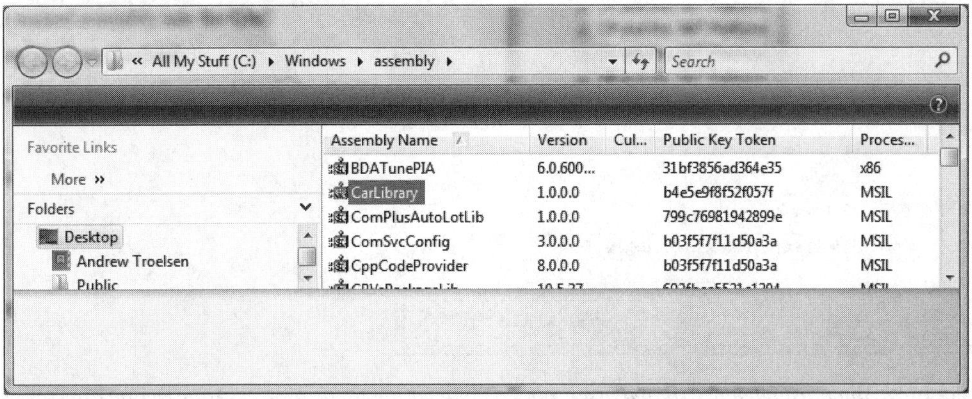

Figure 15-22. *The strongly named, shared* `CarLibrary` *(version 1.0.0.0)*

■ **Note** You may right-click any assembly icon to pull up its Properties page, and you may also uninstall a specific version of an assembly altogether from the right-click context menu (the GUI equivalent of supplying the `/u` flag to `gacutil.exe`).

Consuming a Shared Assembly

When you are building applications that make use of a shared assembly, the only difference from consuming a private assembly is in how you reference the library using Visual Studio 2008. In reality, there is no difference as far as the tool is concerned (you still make use of the Add Reference dialog box). What you must understand is that this dialog box will *not* allow you to reference the assembly by browsing to the GAC folder (e.g., C:\Windows\assembly). Any efforts to do so will be in vain, as you cannot reference the assembly you have highlighted. Rather, you will need to browse to the \bin\Debug directory of the *original* project via the Browse tab, which is shown in Figure 15-23.

This (somewhat annoying) fact aside, create a new VB 2008 Console Application named SharedCarLibClient and exercise your types as you wish:

```
Imports CarLibrary

Module Program
  Sub Main()
    Dim mycar As New SportsCar()
    mycar.TurboBoost()
    Console.ReadLine()
  End Sub
End Module
```

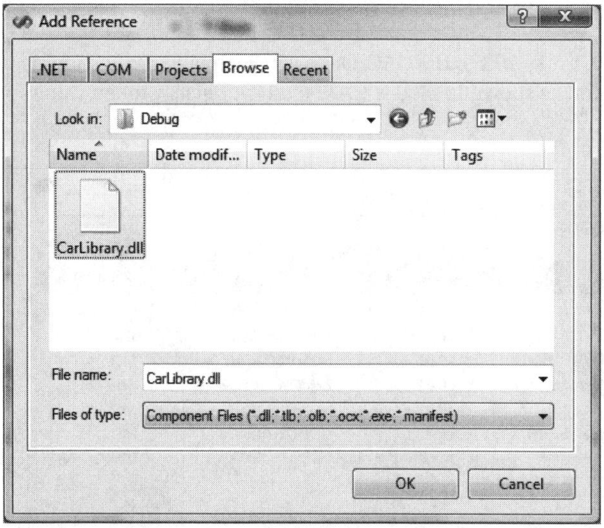

Figure 15-23. *You must reference shared assemblies by navigating to the project's \bin\Debug directory using Visual Studio 2008.*

Once you have compiled your client application, navigate to the directory that contains `SharedCarLibClient.exe` using Windows Explorer and notice that Visual Studio 2008 has *not* copied `CarLibrary.dll` to the client's application directory. When you reference an assembly whose manifest contains a `.publickey` value, Visual Studio 2008 assumes the strongly named assembly will most likely be deployed in the GAC, and therefore does not bother to copy the binary.

Exploring the Manifest of SharedCarLibClient

Recall that when you generate a strong name for an assembly, the entire public key is recorded in the assembly manifest. On a related note, when a client references a strongly named assembly, its manifest records a condensed hash-value of the full public key, denoted by the `.publickeytoken` tag. If you were to open the manifest of `SharedCarLibClient.exe` using `ildasm.exe`, you would find something like the following:

```
.assembly extern CarLibrary
{
  .publickeytoken = (21 9E F3 80 C9 34 8A 38)
  .ver 1:0:0:0
}
```

If you compare the value of the public key token recorded in the client manifest with the public key token value shown in the GAC, you will find a dead-on match. Recall that a public key represents one aspect of the strongly named assembly's identity. Given this, the CLR will only load version 1.0.0.0 of an assembly named `CarLibrary` that has a public key that can be hashed down to the value `219EF380C9348A38`. If the CLR does not find an assembly meeting this description in the GAC (assuming the CLR did not find a private assembly named `CarLibrary` in the client's directory in the first place), a `FileNotFoundException` object is thrown.

■ **Source Code** The SharedCarLibClient application can be found under the Chapter 15 subdirectory.

Configuring Shared Assemblies

Like a private assembly, shared assemblies can be configured using a client `*.config` file. Of course, because shared assemblies are found in a well-known location (the GAC), you will not specify a `<privatePath>` element as you did for private assemblies (although if the client is using both shared and private assemblies, the `<privatePath>` element may still exist in the `*.config` file).

You can use application configuration files in conjunction with shared assemblies whenever you wish to instruct the CLR to bind to a *different* version of a specific assembly, effectively bypassing the value recorded in the client's manifest. This can be useful for a number of reasons. For example, imagine that you have shipped version 1.0.0.0 of an assembly and discover a major bug some time after the fact. One corrective action would be to rebuild the client application to reference the correct version of the bug-free assembly (say, 1.1.0.0) and redistribute the updated client and new library to each and every target machine.

Another option is to ship the new code library and a `*.config` file that automatically instructs the runtime to bind to the new (bug-free) version. As long as the new version has been installed into the GAC, the original client runs without recompilation, redistribution, or fear of having to update your resume.

Here's another example: you have shipped the first version of a bug-free assembly (1.0.0.0), and after a month or two, you add new functionality to the assembly in question to yield version 2.0.0.0. Obviously, existing client applications that were compiled against version 1.0.0.0 have no clue about these new types, given that their code base makes no reference to them.

New client applications, however, wish to make reference to the new functionality found in version 2.0.0.0. Under .NET, you are free to ship version 2.0.0.0 to the target machines, and have version 2.0.0.0 run alongside the older version 1.0.0.0. If necessary, existing clients can be dynamically redirected to load version 2.0.0.0 (to gain access to the implementation refinements), using an application configuration file without needing to recompile and redeploy the client application.

Freezing the Current Shared Assembly

To illustrate how to dynamically bind to a specific version of a shared assembly, open Windows Explorer and copy the current version of CarLibrary (1.0.0.0) into a distinct subdirectory (I called mine "Version 1.0.0.0") off the project root to symbolize the freezing of this version (see Figure 15-24).

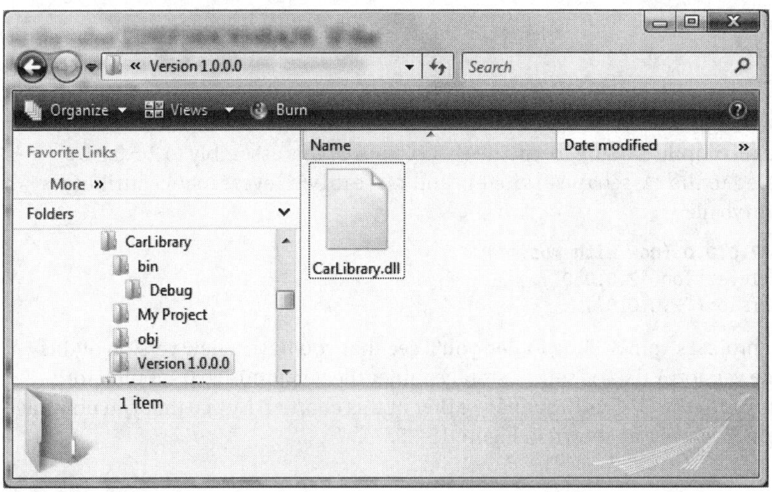

Figure 15-24. *Freezing the current version of* `CarLibrary.dll`

Building Shared Assembly Version 2.0.0.0

Now, update your CarLibrary project to define a new Enum named MusicMedia that defines four possible musical devices:

```
' Holds source of music.
Public Enum MusicMedia
  musicCd
  musicTape
  musicRadio
  musicMp3
End Enum
```

As well, add a new public method to the Car type that allows the caller to turn on one of the given media players (be sure to import the System.Windows.Forms namespace):

```
Public MustInherit Class Car
...
  Public Sub TurnOnRadio(ByVal musicOn As Boolean, ByVal mm As MusicMedia)
    If musicOn Then
      MessageBox.Show(String.Format("Jamming {0}", mm))
    Else
      MessageBox.Show("Quiet time...")
    End If
  End Sub
...
End Class
```

Update the constructors of the Car class to display a MessageBox that verifies you are indeed using CarLibrary 2.0.0.0:

```
Public MustInherit Class Car
...
  Public Sub New()
    MessageBox.Show("Car 2.0.0.0")
  End Sub
  Public Sub New(ByVal carName As String, ByVal max As Short, ByVal curr As Short)
    MessageBox.Show("Car 2.0.0.0")
    name = carName
    max_speed = max
    speed = curr
  End Sub
...
End Class
```

Finally, before you recompile, be sure to update this version of this assembly to 2.0.0.0 by updating the value passed to the <AssemblyVersion()> and <AssemblyFileVersion()> attributes within the AssemblyInfo.vb file:

```
' CarLibrary version 2.0.0.0 (now with music!)
<Assembly: AssemblyFileVersion("2.0.0.0")>
<Assembly: AssemblyVersion("2.0.0.0")>
```

If you look in your project's \bin\Debug folder, you'll see that you have a new version of this assembly (2.0.0.0), while version 1.0.0.0 is safe in storage under the Version 1.0.0.0 subdirectory. Install this new assembly into the GAC as described earlier in this chapter. Notice that you now have two versions of the same assembly, as shown in Figure 15-25.

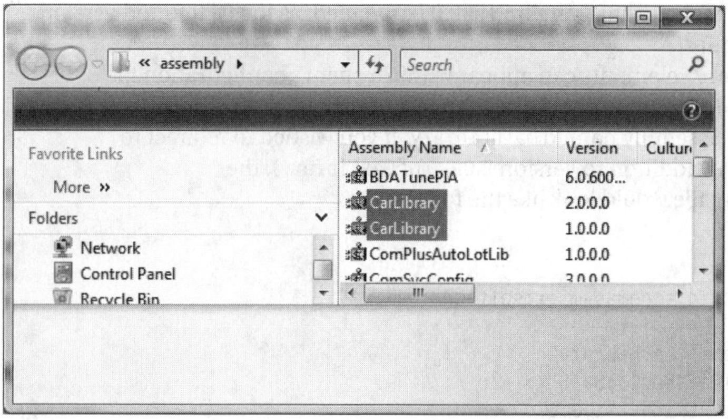

Figure 15-25. *Side-by-side execution*

If you were to run the current SharedCarLibClient.exe program by double-clicking the icon using Windows Explorer, you should *not* see the "Car 2.0.0.0" message box appear, as the manifest is specifically requesting version 1.0.0.0. How then can you instruct the CLR to bind to version 2.0.0.0? Glad you asked.

Dynamically Redirecting to Specific Versions of a Shared Assembly

When you wish to inform the CLR to load a version of a shared assembly other than the version listed in its manifest, you may build a *.config file that contains a <dependentAssembly> element. When doing so, you will need to create an <assemblyIdentity> subelement that specifies the friendly name of the assembly listed in the client manifest (CarLibrary, for this example) and an optional culture attribute (which can be assigned an empty string or omitted altogether if you wish to specify the default culture for the machine). Moreover, the <dependentAssembly> element will define a <bindingRedirect> subelement to specify the version *currently* in the manifest (via the oldVersion attribute) and the version in the GAC to load instead (via the newVersion attribute).

Create a new configuration file in the application directory of SharedCarLibClient named SharedCarLibClient.exe.config that contains the following XML data. Of course, the value of your public key token will be different from what you see in the following code, and it can be obtained either by examining the client manifest using ildasm.exe or via the GAC.

```
<configuration>
  <runtime>
    <assemblyBinding xmlns="urn:schemas-microsoft-com:asm.v1">
      <dependentAssembly>
        <assemblyIdentity name="CarLibrary"
         publicKeyToken="219ef380c9348a38"/>
          <bindingRedirect oldVersion= "1.0.0.0"
          newVersion= "2.0.0.0"/>
      </dependentAssembly>
    </assemblyBinding>
  </runtime>
</configuration>
```

Now run the SharedCarLibClient.exe program. You should see the message that displays version 2.0.0.0 has loaded. If you set the newVersion attribute to 1.0.0.0 (or if you simply deleted the

*.config file), you now see the message that version 1.0.0.0 has loaded, as the CLR found version 1.0.0.0 listed in the client's manifest.

Multiple <dependentAssembly> elements can appear within a client's configuration file. Although you have no need to do so, assume that the manifest of SharedCarLibClient.exe also references version 2.5.0.0 of an assembly named MathLibrary. If you wished to redirect to version 3.0.0.0 of MathLibrary (in addition to version 2.0.0.0 of CarLibrary), the SharedCarLibClient.exe.config file would look like the following:

```
<configuration>
  <runtime>
    <assemblyBinding xmlns="urn:schemas-microsoft-com:asm.v1">
      <dependentAssembly>
        <assemblyIdentity name="CarLibrary"
          publicKeyToken="219ef380c9348a38"/>
        <bindingRedirect oldVersion= "1.0.0.0"
          newVersion= "2.0.0.0"/>
      </dependentAssembly>
      <dependentAssembly>
        <assemblyIdentity name="MathLibrary"
          publicKeyToken="219ef380c9348a38"/>
          <bindingRedirect oldVersion= "2.5.0.0"
          newVersion= "3.0.0.0"/>
      </dependentAssembly>
    </assemblyBinding>
  </runtime>
</configuration>
```

Revisiting the .NET Framework Configuration Utility

As you would hope, you can generate shared assembly–centric *.config files using the graphical .NET Framework 2.0 Configuration utility. Like the process of building a *.config file for private assemblies, the first step is to reference the *.exe to configure. To illustrate, delete the SharedCarLibClient.exe.config you just authored. Now, add a reference to SharedCarLibClient.exe by right-clicking the Applications node. Once you do, expand the plus sign (+) icon and select the Configured Assemblies subnode. From here, click the Configure an Assembly link on the right side of the utility.

At this point, you are presented with a dialog box that allows you to establish a <dependentAssembly> element using a number of friendly UI elements. First, select the "Choose an assembly from the list of assemblies this application uses" radio button (which simply means, "Show me the manifest!") and click the Choose Assembly button.

A dialog box now displays that shows you not only the assemblies specifically listed in the client manifest, but also the assemblies referenced by these assemblies. For this example's purposes, select CarLibrary. When you click the Finish button, you will be shown a Properties page for this one small aspect of the client's manifest. Here, you can generate the <dependentAssembly> using the Binding Policy tab.

Once you select the Binding Policy tab, you can set the oldVersion attribute (1.0.0.0) via the Requested Version text field and the newVersion attribute (2.0.0.0) using the New Version text field. Once you have committed the settings, you will find the following configuration file is generated for you:

```
<?xml version="1.0"?>
<configuration>
   <runtime>
     <assemblyBinding xmlns="urn:schemas-microsoft-com:asm.v1">
```

```
      <dependentAssembly>
        <assemblyIdentity name="CarLibrary"
          publicKeyToken="219ef380c9348a38"/>
        <publisherPolicy apply="yes"/>
        <bindingRedirect oldVersion="1.0.0.0" newVersion="2.0.0.0"/>
      </dependentAssembly>
    </assemblyBinding>
  </runtime>
</configuration>
```

Understanding Publisher Policy Assemblies

The next configuration issue you'll examine is the role of *publisher policy assemblies*. As you've just seen, `*.config` files can be constructed to bind to a specific version of a shared assembly, thereby bypassing the version recorded in the client manifest. While this is all well and good, imagine you're an administrator who now needs to reconfigure all client applications on a given machine to rebind to version 2.0.0.0 of the `CarLibrary.dll` assembly. Given the strict naming convention of a configuration file, you would need to duplicate the same XML content in numerous locations (assuming you are, in fact, aware of the locations of the executables using `CarLibrary`!). Clearly this would be a maintenance nightmare.

Publisher policy allows the publisher of a given assembly (you, your department, your company, or what have you) to ship a binary version of a `*.config` file that is installed into the GAC along with the newest version of the associated assembly. The benefit of this approach is that client application directories do *not* need to contain specific `*.config` files. Rather, the CLR will read the current manifest and attempt to find the requested version in the GAC. However, if the CLR finds a publisher policy assembly, it will read the embedded XML data and perform the requested redirection *at the level of the GAC*.

Publisher policy assemblies are created at the command line using a .NET utility named `al.exe` (the assembly linker). While this tool provides a large number of options, building a publisher policy assembly requires you to pass in only the following input parameters:

- The location of the `*.config` or `*.xml` file containing the redirecting instructions
- The name of the resulting publisher policy assembly
- The location of the `*.snk` file used to sign the publisher policy assembly
- The version numbers to assign the publisher policy assembly being constructed

If you wish to build a publisher policy assembly that controls `CarLibrary.dll`, the command set is as follows (which should be entered on a single line within a Visual Studio 2008 command prompt):

```
al /link:CarLibraryPolicy.xml /out:policy.1.0.CarLibrary.dll
/keyf:C:\MyKey\MyTestKeyPair.snk /v:1.0.0.0
```

Here, the XML content is contained within a file named `CarLibraryPolicy.xml`. The name of the output file (which must be in the format *policy.major.minor.assemblyToConfigure*) is specified using the obvious `/out` flag. In addition, note that the name of the file containing the public/private key pair will also need to be supplied via the `/keyf` option. (Remember, publisher policy files are deployed to the GAC, and therefore must have a strong name!) Last but not least, the `/v` option specifies the version of the policy assembly itself (and has nothing to do with the version binding to or from).

Once the al.exe tool has executed, the result is a new assembly that can be placed into the GAC to force all clients to bind to version 2.0.0.0 of CarLibrary.dll, without the use of a specific client application configuration file.

Disabling Publisher Policy

Now, assume you (as a system administrator) have deployed a publisher policy assembly (and the latest version of the related assembly) to a client machine's GAC. As luck would have it, nine of the ten affected applications rebind to version 2.0.0.0 without error. However, the remaining client application (for whatever reason) blows up when accessing CarLibrary.dll 2.0.0.0 (as we all know, it is next to impossible to build backward-compatible software that works 100 percent of the time).

In such a case, it is possible to build a configuration file for a specific troubled client that instructs the CLR to *ignore* the presence of any publisher policy files installed in the GAC. The remaining client applications that are happy to consume the newest .NET assembly will simply be redirected via the installed publisher policy assembly. To disable publisher policy on a client-by-client basis, author a (properly named) *.config file that makes use of the <publisherPolicy> element and set the apply attribute to no. When you do so, the CLR will load the version of the assembly originally listed in the client's manifest.

```
<configuration>
  <runtime>
    <assemblyBinding xmlns="urn:schemas-microsoft-com:asm.v1">
      <publisherPolicy apply="no" />
    </assemblyBinding>
  </runtime>
</configuration>
```

Understanding the <codeBase> Element

Application configuration files can also specify *code bases*. The <codeBase> element can be used to instruct the CLR to probe for dependent assemblies located at arbitrary locations (such as network share points, or simply a local directory outside a client's application directory).

■Note If the value assigned to a <codeBase> element is located on a remote machine, the assembly will be downloaded on demand to a specific directory in the GAC termed the *download cache*. You can view the content of your machine's download cache by supplying the /ldl option to gacutil.exe.

Given what you have learned about deploying assemblies to the GAC, it should make sense that assemblies loaded from a <codeBase> element will need to be assigned a strong name (after all, how else could the CLR install remote assemblies to the GAC?).

■Note Technically speaking, the <codeBase> element can be used to probe for assemblies that do not have a strong name. However, the assembly's location must be relative to the client's application directory (and thus is little more than an alternative to the <privatePath> element).

Create a new Console Application project named CodeBaseClient, set a reference to CarLibrary.dll version 2.0.0.0, and update the initial file as follows:

```
Imports CarLibrary

Module Program
  Sub Main()
    Console.WriteLine("***** Fun with CodeBases *****")
    Dim c As New SportsCar()
    Console.WriteLine("Sports car has been allocated.")
    Console.ReadLine()
  End Sub
End Module
```

Given that CarLibrary.dll has been deployed to the GAC, you are able to run the program as is. However, to illustrate the use of the <codeBase> element, create a new folder under your C drive (perhaps C:\MyAsms) and place a copy of CarLibrary.dll version 2.0.0.0 into this directory.

Now, add an app.config file to the CodeBaseClient project (as explained earlier in this chapter) and author the following XML content (remember that your .publickeytoken value will differ; consult your GAC as required):

```
<configuration>
  <runtime>
    <assemblyBinding xmlns="urn:schemas-microsoft-com:asm.v1">
      <dependentAssembly>
        <assemblyIdentity name="SharedAssembly" publicKeyToken="219ef380c9348a38" />
        <codeBase version="2.0.0.0" href="file:///C:\MyAsms\CarLibrary.dll" />
      </dependentAssembly>
    </assemblyBinding>
  </runtime>
</configuration>
```

As you can see, the <codeBase> element is nested within the <assemblyIdentity> element, which makes use of the name and publicKeyToken attributes to specify the friendly name as associated publicKeyToken values. The <codeBase> element itself specifies the version and location (via the href property) of the assembly to load. If you were to delete version 2.0.0.0 of CarLibrary.dll from the GAC, this client would still run successfully, as the CLR is able to locate the external assembly under C:\MyAsms.

However, if you were to delete the MyAsms directory from your machine, the client would now fail. Clearly the <codeBase> elements (if present) take precedence over the investigation of the GAC.

■ Note If you place assemblies at random locations on your development machine, you are in effect re-creating the system registry (and the related DLL hell), given that if you move or rename the folder containing your binaries, the current bind will fail. In a nutshell, use <codeBase> with caution.

The <codeBase> element can also be helpful when referencing assemblies located on a remote networked machine. Assume you have permission to access a folder located at http://www.Intertech.com. To download the remote *.dll to the GAC's download cache on your location machine, you could update the <codeBase> element as follows:

```
<codeBase version="2.0.0.0"
  href="http://www.Intertech.com/Assemblies/CarLibrary.dll" />
```

■ Source Code The CodeBaseClient application can be found under the Chapter 15 subdirectory.

The System.Configuration Namespace

Currently, all of the *.config files shown in this chapter have made use of well-known XML elements that are read by the CLR to resolve the location of external assemblies. In addition to these recognized elements, it is perfectly permissible for a client configuration file to contain application-specific data that has nothing to do with binding heuristics. Given this, it should come as no surprise that the .NET Framework provides a namespace that allows you to programmatically read the data within a client configuration file.

The System.Configuration namespace provides a small set of types you may use to read custom data from a client's *.config file. These custom settings must be contained within the scope of an <appSettings> element. The <appSettings> element contains any number of <add> elements that define a key/value pair to be obtained programmatically.

For example, assume you have a *.config file for a Console Application project named AppConfigReaderApp that defines a database connection string and a point of data named timesToSayHello:

```
<configuration>
  <appSettings>
    <add key="appConStr"
        value="server=localhost;uid='sa';pwd='';database=Cars" />
      <add key="timesToSayHello" value="8" />
  </appSettings>
</configuration>
```

Reading these values for use by the client application is as simple as calling the instance-level GetValue() method of the System.Configuration.AppSettingsReader type. As shown in the following code, the first parameter to GetValue() is the name of the key in the *.config file, whereas the second parameter is the underlying type of the key (obtained via the VB 2008 GetType operator):

```
Imports System.Configuration

Module Program
  Sub Main()
    Dim ar As New AppSettingsReader()
    Console.WriteLine(ar.GetValue("appConStr", GetType(String)))
    Dim numbOfTimes As Integer = CType(ar.GetValue("timesToSayHello", _
      GetType(Integer)), Integer)

    For i As Integer = 0 To numbOfTimes
      Console.WriteLine("Yo!")
    Next
    Console.ReadLine()
  End Sub
End Module
```

The AppSettingsReader class type does *not* provide a way to write application-specific data to a *.config file. While this may seem like a limitation at first encounter, it actually makes good sense. The whole idea of a *.config file is that it contains read-only data that is consulted by the CLR (or possibly the AppSettingsReader type) after an application has already been deployed to a target machine.

■ **Note** During our examination of ADO.NET (beginning in Chapter 22), you will learn about the <connectionStrings> configuration element and new types within the System.Configuration namespace. These items provide a standard manner to handle connection string data.

■ **Source Code** The AppConfigReaderApp application can be found under the Chapter 15 subdirectory.

Summary

This chapter drilled down into the details of how the CLR resolves the location of externally referenced assemblies. You began by examining the content within an assembly: headers, metadata, manifests, and CIL. Then you constructed single-file and multifile assemblies and a handful of client applications (written in a language-agnostic manner).

As you have seen, assemblies may be private or shared. Private assemblies are copied to the client's subdirectory, whereas shared assemblies are deployed to the global assembly cache (GAC), provided they have been assigned a strong name. Finally, as you have seen, private and shared assemblies can be configured using a client-side XML configuration file or, alternatively, via a publisher policy assembly.

CHAPTER 16

Type Reflection, Late Binding, and Attribute-Based Programming

As shown in the previous chapter, assemblies are the basic unit of deployment in the .NET universe. Using the integrated object browsers of Visual Studio 2008, you are able to examine the types within a project's referenced set of assemblies. Furthermore, external tools such as `ildasm.exe` allow you to peek into the underlying CIL code, type metadata, and assembly manifest for a given .NET binary. In addition to this design-time investigation of .NET assemblies, you are also able to *programmatically* obtain this same information using the `System.Reflection` namespace. To this end, the first task of this chapter is to define the role of reflection and the necessity of .NET metadata.

The remainder of the chapter examines a number of closely related topics, all of which hinge upon reflection services. For example, you'll learn how a .NET client may employ dynamic loading and late binding to activate types it has no compile-time knowledge of. You'll also learn how to insert custom metadata into your .NET assemblies through the use of system-supplied and custom attributes. To put all of these (seemingly esoteric) topics into perspective, the chapter closes by demonstrating how to build "snap-in objects" that you can plug into an extendable Windows Forms application.

The Necessity of Type Metadata

The ability to fully describe types (classes, interfaces, structures, enumerations, and delegates) using metadata is a key element of the .NET platform. Numerous .NET technologies, such as object serialization, .NET remoting, Windows Communication Foundation (WCF), and XML web services, require the ability to discover the format of types at runtime. Furthermore, COM interoperability, compiler support, and an IDE's IntelliSense capabilities all rely on a concrete description of *type*.

Regardless of (or perhaps due to) its importance, metadata is not a new idea supplied by the .NET Framework. Java, CORBA, and COM all have similar concepts. For example, COM type libraries (which are little more than compiled IDL code) are used to describe the types contained within a COM server. Like COM, .NET code libraries also support type metadata. Of course, .NET metadata has no syntactic similarities to COM IDL. Recall that the `ildasm.exe` utility allows you to view an assembly's type metadata using the Ctrl+M keyboard option (see Chapter 1). Thus, if you were to open any of the `*.dll` or `*.exe` assemblies created over the course of this book (such as `CarLibrary.dll`) using `ildasm.exe` and then press Ctrl+M, you would find the relevant type metadata (see Figure 16-1).

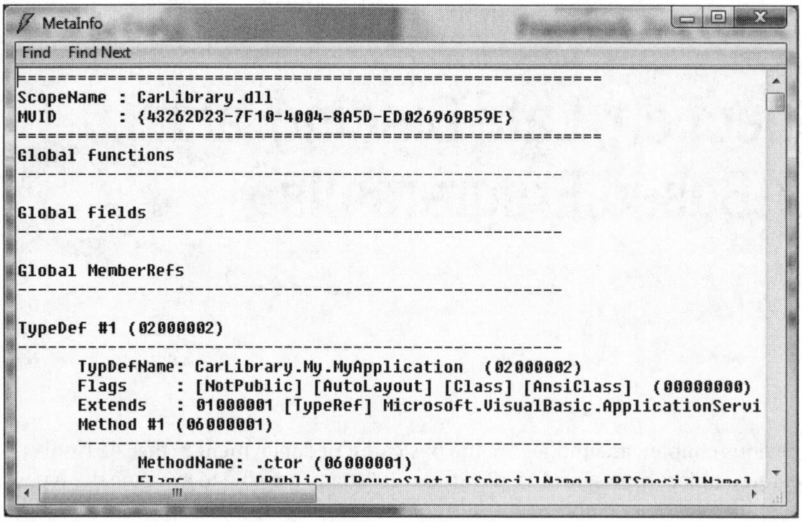

Figure 16-1. *Viewing an assembly's type metadata*

As you can see, ildasm.exe's display of .NET type metadata is very verbose (the actual binary format is much more compact). In fact, if I were to list the entire metadata description representing the CarLibrary.dll assembly, it would span several pages. Given that this act would be a woeful waste of paper, let's just glimpse into some key metadata tokens within the CarLibrary.dll assembly.

Viewing (Partial) Metadata for the EngineState Enumeration

Each type defined within the current assembly is documented using a TypeDef #n token (where TypeDef is short for *type definition*). If the type being described uses a type defined within a separate .NET assembly, the referenced type is documented using a TypeRef #n token (where TypeRef is short for *type reference*). A TypeRef token is a pointer (if you will) to the referenced type's full metadata definition. In a nutshell, .NET metadata is a set of tables that clearly mark all type definitions (TypeDefs) and referenced entities (TypeRefs), all of which can be viewed using ildasm.exe's metadata window.

As far as CarLibrary.dll goes, one TypeDef we encounter is the metadata description of the CarLibrary.EngineState enumeration (your number may differ; TypeDef numbering is based on the order in which the VB 2008 compiler processes the source code files):

```
TypeDef #6 (02000007)
-------------------------------------------------------
  TypDefName: CarLibrary.EngineState  (02000007)
  Flags     : [Public] [AutoLayout] [Class] [Sealed] [AnsiClass]  (00000101)
  Extends   : 01000007 [TypeRef] System.Enum
...
  Field #2 (04000007)
  -------------------------------------------------------
    Field Name: engineAlive (04000007)
    Flags     : [Public] [Shared] [Literal] [HasDefault]  (00008056)
    DefltValue: (I4) 0
    CallCnvntn: [FIELD]
    Field type:  ValueClass CarLibrary.EngineState
...
```

Here, the TypDefName token is used to establish the name of the given type. The Extends metadata token is used to document the base class of a given .NET type (in this case, the referenced type, System.Enum). Each field of an enumeration is marked using the Field #n token. For brevity, I have simply listed the metadata for EngineState.engineAlive.

Viewing (Partial) Metadata for the Car Type

Here is a partial dump of the Car type that illustrates the following:

- How fields are documented in terms of .NET metadata
- How methods are documented via .NET metadata
- How a single type property is mapped to two discrete member functions

```
TypeDef #3
-------------------------------------------------------
  TypDefName: CarLibrary.Car  (02000004)
  Flags     : [Public] [AutoLayout] [Class] [Abstract] [AnsiClass]  (00100081)
  Extends   : 01000002 [TypeRef] System.Object
  Field #1
  -------------------------------------------------------
    Field Name: name (04000008)
    Flags     : [Family]  (00000004)
    CallCnvntn: [FIELD]
    Field type:  String
...
  Method #1
  -------------------------------------------------------
    MethodName: .ctor (06000001)
    Flags     : [Public] [ReuseSlot] [SpecialName]
    [RTSpecialName] [.ctor]  (00001886)
    RVA       : 0x00002050
    ImplFlags : [IL] [Managed]  (00000000)
    CallCnvntn: [DEFAULT]
    hasThis
    ReturnType: Void
    No arguments.
...
  Property #1
  -------------------------------------------------------
    Prop.Name : PetName (17000001)
    Flags     : [none] (00000000)
    CallCnvntn: [PROPERTY]
    hasThis
    ReturnType: String
    No arguments.
    DefltValue:
      Setter    : (06000004) set_PetName
      Getter    : (06000003) get_PetName
      0 Others
 ...
```

First, note that the Car class metadata marks the type's base class and includes various flags that describe how this type was constructed (e.g., [Public], [Abstract], and whatnot). Methods (such as our Car's constructor, denoted by .ctor) are described in regard to their parameters, return value, and name. Finally, note how properties are mapped to their internal get/set methods using the .NET metadata Setter/Getter tokens. As you would expect, the derived Car types (SportsCar and MiniVan) are described in a similar manner.

Examining a TypeRef

Recall that an assembly's metadata will describe not only the set of internal types (Car, EngineState, etc.), but also any external types the internal types reference. For example, given that CarLibrary.dll has defined two enumerations, you find a TypeRef block for the System.Enum type, which is defined in mscorlib.dll:

```
TypeRef #1 (01000001)
-------------------------------------------------------
Token:              0x01000001
ResolutionScope:    0x23000001
TypeRefName:        System.Enum
  MemberRef #1
  -------------------------------------------------------
  Member: (0a00000f) ToString:
  CallCnvntn: [DEFAULT]
  hasThis
  ReturnType: String
  No arguments.
```

Documenting the Defining Assembly

The ildasm.exe metadata window also allows you to view the .NET metadata that describes the assembly itself using the Assembly token. As you can see from the following (partial) listing, information documented within the Assembly table is (surprise, surprise!) the same information that can be viewable via the MANIFEST icon. Here is a partial dump of the manifest of CarLibrary.dll (version 2.0.0.0):

```
Assembly
-------------------------------------------------------
  Token: 0x20000001
  Name : CarLibrary
  Public Key : 00 24 00 00 04 80 00 00  // Etc...

  Hash Algorithm : 0x00008004
  Major Version: 0x00000002
  Minor Version: 0x00000000
  Build Number: 0x00000000
  Revision Number: 0x00000000
  Locale: <null>
  Flags : [PublicKey]  (00000000)
```

Documenting Referenced Assemblies

In addition to the Assembly token and the set of TypeDef and TypeRef blocks, .NET metadata also makes use of AssemblyRef #n tokens to document each external assembly. Given that the CarLibrary.dll makes use of the MessageBox type, you find an AssemblyRef for System.Windows.Forms, for example:

```
AssemblyRef #2
-------------------------------------------------------
  Token: 0x23000002
```

```
Public Key or Token: b7 7a 5c 56 19 34 e0 89
Name: System.Windows.Forms
Version: 2.0.0.0
Major Version: 0x00000002
Minor Version: 0x00000000
Build Number: 0x00000e10
Revision Number: 0x00000000
Locale: <null>
HashValue Blob:
Flags: [none] (00000000)
```

Documenting String Literals

The final point of interest regarding .NET metadata is the fact that each and every string literal in your code base is documented under the User Strings token, for example:

```
User Strings
-------------------------------------------------------
70000001 : (11) L"Car 2.0.0.0"
70000019 : (11) L"Jamming {0} "
70000031 : (13) L"Quiet time..."
7000004d : (14) L"Ramming speed!"
7000006b : (19) L"Faster is better..."
70000093 : (16) L"Time to call AAA"
700000b5 : (16) L"Your car is dead"
```

Now, don't be too concerned with the exact syntax of each and every piece of .NET metadata. The bigger point to absorb is that .NET metadata is very descriptive and lists each internally defined (and externally referenced) type found within a given code base.

The next question on your mind may be (in the best-case scenario) "How can I leverage this information in my applications?" or (in the worst-case scenario) "Why on earth should I care about metadata in the first place?" To address both points of view, allow me to introduce .NET reflection services. Be aware that the usefulness of the topics presented over the pages that follow may be a bit of a head-scratcher until this chapter's endgame. So hang tight.

■ **Note** You will also find a number of `.custom` tokens displayed by the MetaInfo window, which documents the attributes applied within the code base. You'll learn about the role of .NET attributes later in this chapter.

Understanding Reflection

In the .NET universe, *reflection* is the process of runtime type discovery. Using reflection services, you are able to programmatically obtain the same metadata information displayed by ildasm.exe using a friendly object model. For example, through reflection, you can obtain a list of all types contained within a given assembly (or *.netmodule, as discussed in Chapter 15), including the methods, fields, properties, and events defined by a given type. You can also dynamically discover the set of interfaces supported by a given class (or structure), the parameters of a method, and other related details (base class, namespace information, manifest data, and so forth).

Like any namespace, System.Reflection contains a number of related types. Table 16-1 lists some of the core items you should be familiar with.

Table 16-1. *A Sampling of Members of the* System.Reflection *Namespace*

Type	Meaning in Life
Assembly	This class (in addition to numerous related types) contains a number of methods that allow you to load, investigate, and manipulate an assembly programmatically.
AssemblyName	This class allows you to discover numerous details behind an assembly's identity (version information, culture information, and so forth).
EventInfo	This class holds information for a given event.
FieldInfo	This class holds information for a given field.
MemberInfo	This is the abstract base class that defines common behaviors for the EventInfo, FieldInfo, MethodInfo, and PropertyInfo types.
MethodInfo	This class contains information for a given method.
Module	This class allows you to access a given module within a multifile assembly.
ParameterInfo	This class holds information for a given parameter.
PropertyInfo	This class holds information for a given property.

To understand how to leverage the System.Reflection namespace to programmatically read .NET metadata, you need to first come to terms with the System.Type class.

The System.Type Class

The System.Type class defines a number of members that can be used to examine a type's metadata, a great number of which return types from the System.Reflection namespace. For example, Type.GetMethods() returns an array of MethodInfo types, Type.GetFields() returns an array of FieldInfo types, and so on. The complete set of members exposed by System.Type is quite expansive; however, Table 16-2 offers a partial snapshot of the members supported by System.Type (see the .NET Framework 3.5 SDK documentation for full details).

Table 16-2. *Select Members of* System.Type

Type Member	Meaning in Life
IsAbstract IsArray IsClass IsCOMObject IsEnum IsGenericTypeDefinition IsGenericParameter IsInterface IsPrimitive IsNestedPrivate IsNestedPublic IsSealed IsValueType	These properties (among others) allow you to discover a number of basic traits about the Type you are referring to (e.g., whether it is an abstract method, an array, a nested class, and so forth).
GetConstructors() GetEvents() GetFields() GetInterfaces() GetMembers() GetNestedTypes() GetProperties()	These methods (among others) allow you to obtain an array representing the items (interface, method, property, etc.) you are interested in. Each method returns a related array (e.g., GetFields() returns a FieldInfo array, GetMethods() returns a MethodInfo array, etc.). Be aware that each of these methods has a singular form (e.g., GetMethod(), GetProperty(), etc.) that allows you to retrieve a specific item by name, rather than an array of all related items.

Type Member	Meaning in Life
FindMembers()	This method returns an array of MemberInfo types based on search criteria.
GetType()	This shared method returns a Type instance given a string name.
InvokeMember()	This method allows late binding to a given item.

Obtaining a Type Reference Using System.Object.GetType()

You can obtain an instance of the Type class in a variety of ways. However, the one thing you cannot do is directly create a Type object using the New keyword, as Type is an abstract class. Regarding your first choice, recall that System.Object defines a method named GetType(), which returns an instance of the Type class that represents the metadata for the current object:

```
' Obtain type information using a SportsCar instance.
Dim sc As SportsCar = New SportsCar()
Dim t As Type = sc.GetType()
```

Obviously, this approach will only work if you have compile-time knowledge of the type you wish to investigate (SportsCar in this case). Given this restriction, it should make sense that tools such as ildasm.exe do not obtain type information by directly calling a custom type's GetType() method, given that ildasm.exe was not compiled against your custom assemblies!

Obtaining a Type Reference Using System.Type.GetType()

To obtain type information in a more flexible manner, you may call the shared GetType() member of the System.Type class and specify the fully qualified string name of the type you are interested in examining. Using this approach, you do *not* need to have compile-time knowledge of the type you are extracting metadata from, given that Type.GetType() takes an instance of the omnipresent System.String.

The Type.GetType() method has been overloaded to allow you to specify two Boolean parameters, one of which controls whether an exception should be thrown if the type cannot be found, and the other of which establishes the case sensitivity of the string. To illustrate, ponder the following:

```
' Obtain type information using the shared Type.GetType() method
' (don't throw an exception if SportsCar cannot be found and ignore case).
Dim t As Type = Type.GetType("CarLibrary.SportsCar", False, True)
```

In the previous example, notice that the string you are passing into GetType() makes no mention of the assembly containing the type. In this case, the assumption is that the type is defined within the currently executing assembly. However, when you wish to obtain metadata for a type within an external private assembly, the string parameter is formatted using the type's fully qualified name, followed by the friendly name of the assembly containing the type (each of which is separated by a comma):

```
' Obtain type information for a type within an external assembly.
Dim t As Type
t = Type.GetType("CarLibrary.SportsCar, CarLibrary")
```

As well, do know that the string passed into Type.GetType() may specify a plus token (+) to denote a nested type. Assume you wish to obtain type information for an enumeration (SpyOptions) nested within a class named JamesBondCar, defined in an external private assembly named CarLibrary.dll. To do so, you would write the following:

```
' Obtain type information for a nested enumeration
' within the current assembly.
Dim t As Type = _
  Type.GetType("CarLibrary.JamesBondCar+SpyOptions, CarLibrary")
```

Obtaining a Type Reference Using GetType()

The final way to obtain type information is using the VB 2008 GetType operator:

```
' Get the Type using GetType.
Dim t As Type = GetType(SportsCar)
```

Like Type.GetType(), the GetType operator is helpful in that you do not need to first create an object instance to extract type information. However, your code base must still have compile-time knowledge of the type you are interested in examining.

Building a Custom Metadata Viewer

To illustrate the basic process of reflection (and the usefulness of System.Type), let's create a Console Application named MyTypeViewer. Once you have done so, be sure to import the System.Reflection namespace into your initial code file (which I have renamed from Module1.vb to Program.vb). This program will display details of the methods, properties, fields, and supported interfaces (in addition to some other points of interest) for any type within mscorlib.dll (recall all .NET applications have automatic access to this core framework class library) or a type within MyTypeViewer.exe itself.

Reflecting on Methods

The Program module will be updated to define a number of subroutines, each of which takes a single System.Type parameter. First you have ListMethods(), which (as you might guess) prints the name of each method defined by the incoming type. Notice how the GetMethods() method returns an array of System.Reflection.MethodInfo types:

```
' Display method names of type.
Public Sub ListMethods(ByVal t As Type)
  Console.WriteLine("***** Methods *****")
  Dim mi As MethodInfo() = t.GetMethods()
  For Each m As MethodInfo In mi
   Console.WriteLine("->{0}", m.Name)
  Next
  Console.WriteLine()
End Sub
```

Here, you are simply printing the name of the method using the MethodInfo.Name property. Of course, MethodInfo has many additional members that allow you to determine whether the method is shared, virtual, or abstract. As well, the MethodInfo type allows you to obtain the method's return value and parameter set. You'll spruce up the implementation of ListMethods() in just a bit in the section "Reflecting on Method Parameters and Return Values."

Reflecting on Fields and Properties

The implementation of ListFields() is similar. The only notable difference is the call to the GetFields() method and the resulting FieldInfo array. Again, to keep things simple, you are printing out only the name of each field.

```
' Display field names of type.
Public Sub ListFields(ByVal t As Type)
  Console.WriteLine("***** Fields *****")
  Dim fi As FieldInfo() = t.GetFields()
  For Each field As FieldInfo In fi
    Console.WriteLine("->{0}", field.Name)
  Next
  Console.WriteLine()
End Sub
```

The logic to display a type's properties is similar:

```
' Display property names of type.
Public Sub ListProps(ByVal t As Type)
  Console.WriteLine("***** Properties *****")
  Dim pi As PropertyInfo() = t.GetProperties()
  For Each prop As PropertyInfo In pi
    Console.WriteLine("->{0}", prop.Name)
  Next
  Console.WriteLine()
End Sub
```

Reflecting on Implemented Interfaces

Next, you will author a method named `ListInterfaces()` that will print out the names of any interfaces supported on the incoming type. The only point of interest here is that the call to `GetInterfaces()` returns an array of `System.Types`! This should make sense given that interfaces are, indeed, types:

```
' Display implemented interfaces.
Public Sub ListInterfaces(ByVal t As Type)
  Console.WriteLine("***** Interfaces *****")
  Dim ifaces As Type() = t.GetInterfaces()
  For Each i As Type In ifaces
    Console.WriteLine("->{0}", i.Name)
  Next
  Console.WriteLine()
End Sub
```

Displaying Various Odds and Ends

Last but not least, you have one final helper method that will simply display various statistics (indicating whether the type is generic, what the base class is, whether the type is sealed, and so forth) regarding the incoming type:

```
' Just for good measure.
Public Sub ListVariousStats(ByVal t As Type)
  Console.WriteLine("***** Various Statistics *****")
  Console.WriteLine("Base class is: {0}", t.BaseType)
  Console.WriteLine("Is type abstract? {0}", t.IsAbstract)
  Console.WriteLine("Is type sealed? {0}", t.IsSealed)
  Console.WriteLine("Is type generic? {0}", t.IsGenericTypeDefinition)
  Console.WriteLine("Is type a class type? {0}", t.IsClass)
  Console.WriteLine()
End Sub
```

Implementing Main()

The `Main()` method of the `Program` module prompts the user for the fully qualified name of a type. Once you obtain this string data, you pass it into the `Type.GetType()` method and send the extracted `System.Type` into each of your helper methods. This process repeats until the user enters **Q** to terminate the application:

```
' Need to make use of the reflection namespace.
Imports System.Reflection

Module Program
  Sub Main()
    Console.WriteLine("***** Welcome to MyTypeViewer *****")
    Dim typeName As String = String.Empty

    Do
      Console.WriteLine()
      Console.WriteLine("Enter a type name to evaluate")
      Console.Write("or enter Q to quit: ")

      ' Get name of type.
      typeName = Console.ReadLine()

      ' Does user want to quit?
      If typeName.ToUpper() = "Q" Then
        Exit Do
      End If

      ' Try to display type
      Try
        Dim t As Type = Type.GetType(typeName)
        Console.WriteLine()
        ListVariousStats(t)
        ListFields(t)
        ListProps(t)
        ListMethods(t)
        ListInterfaces(t)
      Catch
        Console.WriteLine("Sorry, can't find {0}.", typeName)
      End Try
    Loop
  End Sub
  ' Assume all the helper methods are defined below.
...
End Module
```

At this point, `MyTypeViewer.exe` is ready to take out for a test drive. For example, run your application and enter the following fully qualified names (be aware that the manner in which you invoked `Type.GetType()` requires *case-sensitive* names):

- `System.Int32`
- `System.Collections.ArrayList`
- `System.Threading.Thread`
- `System.Void`
- `System.IO.BinaryWriter`

- `System.Math`
- `System.Console`
- `MyTypeViewer.Program`

Figure 16-2 shows the partial output when specifying `System.Math`.

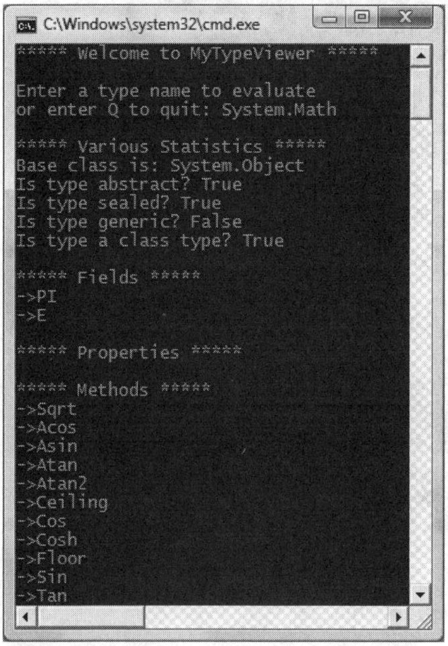

Figure 16-2. *Reflecting on* `System.Math`

Reflecting on Method Parameters and Return Values

So far, so good! Let's make one minor enhancement to the current application. Specifically, you will update the `ListMethods()` helper function to list not only the name of a given method, but also the return value and incoming parameters. The `MethodInfo` type provides the `ReturnType` property and `GetParameters()` method for these very tasks. In the following code, notice that you are building a string type that contains the type and name of each parameter using a nested `For Each` loop:

```
Public Sub ListMethods(ByVal t As Type)
  Console.WriteLine("***** Methods *****")
  Dim mi As MethodInfo() = t.GetMethods()
  For Each m As MethodInfo In mi
    Dim retVal As String = m.ReturnType.FullName()
    Dim paramInfo As String = "( "
    For Each pi As ParameterInfo In m.GetParameters()
      paramInfo &= String.Format("{0} {1} ", pi.ParameterType, pi.Name)
    Next
      paramInfo &= " )"
    Console.WriteLine("->{0} {1} {2}", retVal, m.Name, paramInfo)
  Next
  Console.WriteLine("")
End Sub
```

If you now run this updated application, you will find that the methods of a given type are much more detailed. Figure 16-3 shows the method metadata of the `System.Globalization.GregorianCalendar` type.

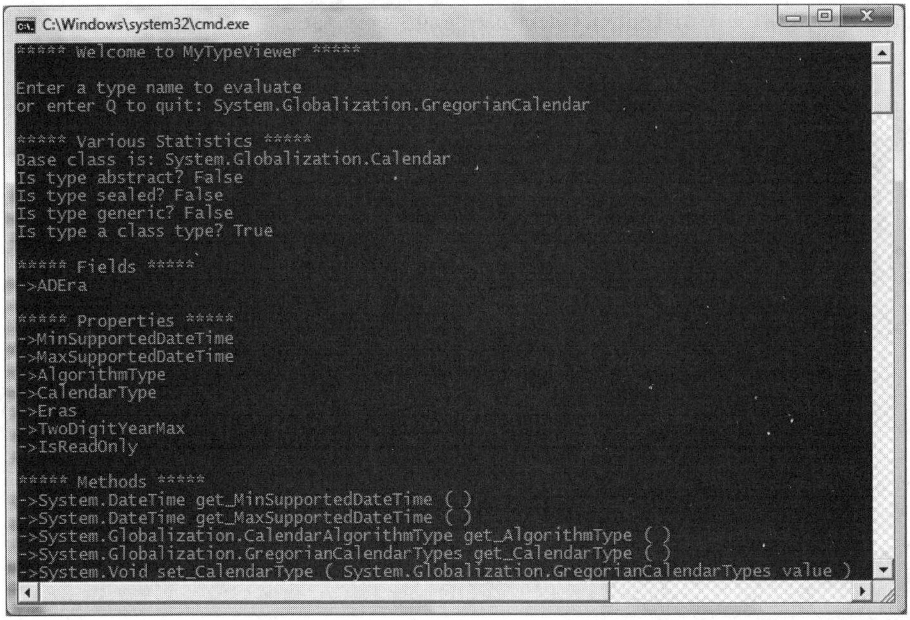

Figure 16-3. *Method details of* `System.Globalization.GregorianCalendar`

Interesting stuff, huh? Clearly the `System.Reflection` namespace and `System.Type` class allow you to reflect over many other aspects of a type beyond what `MyTypeViewer` is currently displaying. For example, you can obtain a type's events, get the list of any generic parameters for a given member and optional arguments, and glean dozens of other details.

Nevertheless, at this point you have created an (somewhat capable) object browser. The major limitation, of course, is that you have no way to reflect beyond the current assembly (`MyTypeViewer.exe`) or the always accessible `mscorlib.dll`. This begs the question, "How can I build applications that can load (and reflect over) external assemblies?"

Source Code The MyTypeViewer project can be found under the Chapter 16 subdirectory.

Dynamically Loading Assemblies

In the previous chapter, you learned all about how the CLR consults the assembly manifest when probing for an externally referenced assembly. While this is all well and good, there will be many times when you need to load assemblies on the fly programmatically, even if there is no record of said assembly in the manifest. Formally speaking, the act of loading external assemblies on demand is known as a *dynamic load*.

`System.Reflection` defines a class named `Assembly`. Using this type, you are able to dynamically load an assembly as well as discover properties about the assembly itself. Using the `Assembly` type, you are able to dynamically load private or shared assemblies, as well as load an assembly located at an arbitrary location on your hard drive. In essence, the `Assembly` class provides methods (`Load()` and `LoadFrom()` in particular) that allow you to programmatically supply the same sort of information found in a client-side `*.config` file.

To illustrate dynamic loading, create a brand-new Console Application named ExternalAssemblyReflector. Your task is to construct a `Main()` method that prompts for the friendly name of an assembly to load dynamically. You will pass the `Assembly` reference in to a helper method named `DisplayTypes()`, which will simply print the names of each class, interface, structure, enumeration, and delegate it contains. The code is refreshingly simple:

```
Imports System.Reflection

Module Program
  Sub Main()
    Console.WriteLine("***** External Assembly Viewer *****")
    Dim asmName As String = String.Empty
    Dim asm As Assembly = Nothing
    Do
      Console.WriteLine()
      Console.WriteLine("Enter an assembly to evaluate")
      Console.Write("or enter Q to quit: ")

      ' Get name of assembly.
      asmName = Console.ReadLine()

      ' Does user want to quit?
      If asmName.ToUpper = "Q" Then
        Exit Do
      End If

      Try ' Try to load assembly.
        asm = Assembly.Load(asmName)
        DisplayTypesInAsm(asm)
      Catch
        Console.WriteLine("Sorry, can't find assembly named {0}.", asmName)
      End Try
    Loop
  End Sub

  Sub DisplayTypesInAsm(ByVal asm As Assembly)
    Console.WriteLine()
    Console.WriteLine("***** Types in Assembly *****")
    Console.WriteLine("->{0}", asm.FullName)
    Dim types As Type() = asm.GetTypes()
    For Each t As Type In types
      Console.WriteLine("Type: {0}", t)
    Next
      Console.WriteLine()
  End Sub
End Module
```

Notice that the shared `Assembly.Load()` method has been passed only the friendly name of the assembly you are interested in loading into memory. Thus, if you wish to reflect over `CarLibrary.dll`, you will need to copy the `CarLibrary.dll` binary to the \bin\Debug directory of the ExternalAssemblyReflector application to run this program. Once you do, you will find output similar to Figure 16-4.

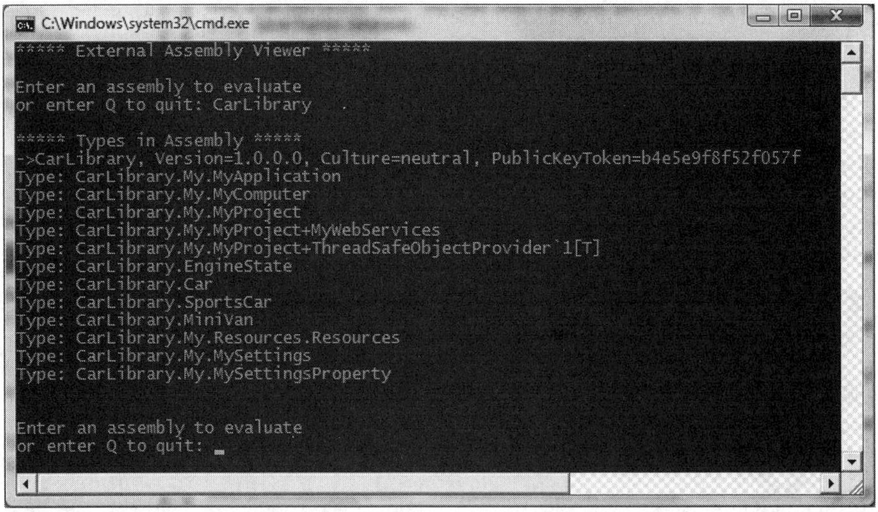

Figure 16-4. *Reflecting on the external* `CarLibrary` *assembly*

Note If you wish to make ExternalAssemblyReflector more flexible, load the external assembly using `Assembly.LoadFrom()` rather than `Assembly.Load()`. By doing so, you can enter an absolute path to the assembly you wish to view (e.g., C:\MyCode\MyApp\MyAsm.dll).

Source Code The ExternalAssemblyReflector project is included in the Chapter 16 subdirectory.

Reflecting on Shared Assemblies

As you may suspect, `Assembly.Load()` has been overloaded a number of times. One variation of the `Assembly.Load()` method allows you to specify a culture value (for localized assemblies) as well as a version number and public key token value (for shared assemblies).

Collectively speaking, the set of items identifying an assembly is termed the *display name*. The format of a display name is a comma-delimited string of name/value pairs that begins with the friendly name of the assembly, followed by optional qualifiers (that may appear in any order). Here is the template to follow (optional items appear in parentheses):

```
Name (,Culture = culture token) (,Version = major.minor.build.revision)
(,PublicKeyToken = public key token)
```

When you're crafting a display name, the convention `PublicKeyToken=null` indicates that binding and matching against a non-strongly named assembly is required. Additionally, `Culture=""` (or `Culture="neutral"`) indicates matching against the default culture of the target machine, for example:

```
' Load version 1.0.0.0 of CarLibrary using the default culture.
Dim a As Assembly = Assembly.Load( _
"CarLibrary, Version=1.0.0.0, PublicKeyToken=null, Culture=""")
```

Also be aware that the `System.Reflection` namespace supplies the `AssemblyName` type, which allows you to represent the preceding string information in a handy object variable. Typically, this class is used in conjunction with `System.Version`, which is an OO wrapper around an assembly's version number. Once you have established the display name, it can then be passed into the overloaded `Assembly.Load()` method:

```
' Make use of AssemblyName to define the display name.
Dim asmName As New AssemblyName()
asmName.Name = "CarLibrary"
Dim v As Version = New Version("1.0.0.0")
asmName.Version = v
Dim a As Assembly = Assembly.Load(asmName)
```

To load a shared assembly from the GAC, the `Assembly.Load()` parameter must specify a `publickeytoken` value. For example, assume you wish to load version 2.0.0.0 of the `System.Windows.Forms.dll` assembly provided by the .NET base class libraries. Given that the number of types in this assembly is very large, the following application simply prints out the names of the first 20 types:

```
Imports System.Reflection

Module Program
  Sub DisplayInfo(ByVal a As Assembly)
    Console.WriteLine("***** Info about Assembly *****")
    Console.WriteLine("Loaded from GAC? {0}", a.GlobalAssemblyCache())
    Console.WriteLine("Asm Name: {0}", a.GetName().Name)
    Console.WriteLine("Asm Version: {0}", a.GetName().Version)
    Console.WriteLine("Asm Culture: {0}", a.GetName().CultureInfo.DisplayName)
    Dim types As Type() = a.GetTypes()

    ' Just print out the first 20 types.
    For i As Integer = 0 To 19
      Try
        Console.WriteLine("Type: {0}", types(i))
      Catch ex As Exception
        Console.WriteLine(ex.Message)
      End Try
    Next
  End Sub

  Sub Main()
    Console.WriteLine("***** The Shared Asm Reflector App *****")
    Console.WriteLine()
    Dim displayName As String = _
    "System.Windows.Forms, Version=2.0.0.0, " & _
      "PublicKeyToken=b77a5c561934e089, Culture=neutral"
    Dim asm As Assembly = Assembly.Load(displayName)
    DisplayInfo(asm)
    Console.ReadLine()
  End Sub
End Module
```

Source Code The SharedAssemblyReflector project is included in the Chapter 16 subdirectory.

Sweet! At this point you should understand how to use some of the core items defined within the `System.Reflection` namespace to discover metadata at runtime. Of course, I realize despite the "cool factor," you likely won't need to build too many custom object browsers at your place of employment. Do recall, however, that reflection services are the foundation for a number of very common (and practical) programming activities, including *late binding*.

Understanding Late Binding

Simply put, *late binding* is a technique in which you are able to create an instance of a given type and invoke its members at runtime without having compile-time knowledge of its existence. When you are building an application that binds late to a type in an external assembly, you have no reason to set a reference to the assembly or import the defining namespace; therefore, the caller's manifest has no direct listing of the assembly.

At first glance, you may not understand the value of late binding. It is true that if you can "bind early" to a type (e.g., set an assembly reference, import the namespace and allocate on object using the VB 2008 `New` keyword), you should opt to do so. For one reason, early binding allows you to determine errors at compile time, rather than at runtime. Nevertheless, late binding does have a critical role in any "extendable application" you may be building.

Late Binding with the System.Activator Class

The `System.Activator` class is the key to the .NET late binding process. For our current example, we are only interested in the `Activator.CreateInstance()` method, which is used to create an instance of a type à la late binding.

This method has been overloaded numerous times to provide a good deal of flexibility. The simplest variation of the `CreateInstance()` member takes a valid `Type` object that describes the entity you wish to allocate on the fly. Create a new Console Application named LateBinding, and update the `Main()` method as follows (be sure to manually place a copy of `CarLibrary.dll` in the project's \bin\Debug directory):

```
Imports System.Reflection
Imports System.IO

Module Program
  Sub Main()
    Console.WriteLine("***** Fun with Late Binding *****")
    ' Try to load a local copy of CarLibrary.
    Dim a As Assembly = Nothing

    Try
      a = Assembly.Load("CarLibrary")
    Catch e As FileNotFoundException
      Console.WriteLine(e.Message)
      Return
    End Try

    ' If we found it, get type information about
    ' the minivan and create an instance.
    Dim miniVan As Type = a.GetType("CarLibrary.MiniVan")
    Dim obj As Object = Activator.CreateInstance(miniVan)
    Console.ReadLine()
  End Sub
End Module
```

Notice that the Activator.CreateInstance() method returns a System.Object reference rather than a strongly typed MiniVan. Therefore, if you apply the dot operator on the obj variable, you will fail to see any members of the MiniVan type. At first glance, you may assume you can remedy this problem with an explicit cast; however, this program has no clue what a MiniVan is in the first place, therefore it would be a compiler error to attempt to use CType() to do so (as you must specify the name of the type to convert to).

Remember that the whole point of late binding is to create instances of objects for which there is no compile-time knowledge. Given this, how can you invoke the underlying methods of the MiniVan object stored in the System.Object variable? The answer, of course, is by using reflection.

Invoking Methods with No Parameters

Assume you wish to invoke the TurboBoost() method of the MiniVan. As you recall, this method will set the state of the engine to "dead" and display an informational message box. The first step is to obtain a MethodInfo type for the TurboBoost() method using Type.GetMethod(). From the resulting MethodInfo, you are then able to call MiniVan.TurboBoost using Invoke(). MethodInfo.Invoke() requires you to send in all parameters that are to be given to the method represented by MethodInfo. These parameters are represented by an array of System.Object types (as the parameters for a given method could be any number of various entities).

Given that TurboBoost() does not require any parameters, you can simply pass Nothing. Update your Main() method like so:

```
Sub Main()
  ' Try to load a local copy of CarLibrary.
...

  ' If we found it, get type information about
  ' the minivan and create an instance.
  Dim miniVan As Type = a.GetType("CarLibrary.MiniVan")
  Dim obj As Object = Activator.CreateInstance(miniVan)

  ' Get info for TurboBoost.
  Dim mi As MethodInfo = miniVan.GetMethod("TurboBoost")

  ' Invoke method (Nothing for no parameters).
  mi.Invoke(obj, Nothing)
End Sub
```

At this point you are happy to see the message box in Figure 16-5.

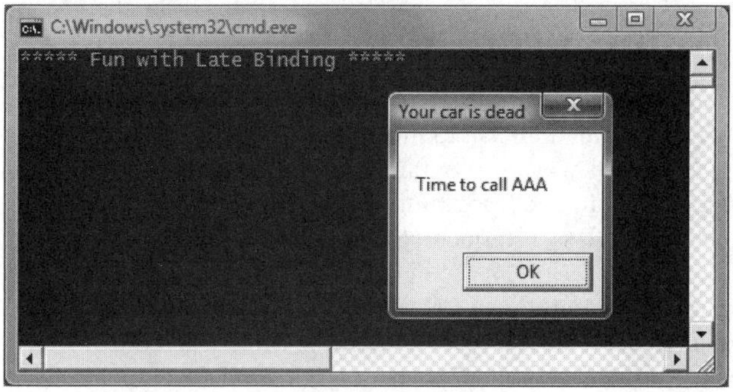

Figure 16-5. *Late-bound method invocation*

Invoking Methods with Parameters

To illustrate how to dynamically invoke a method that does take some number of parameters, assume the MiniVan type defines a method named TellChildToBeQuiet() (feel free to update CarLibrary.dll if you so choose):

```
' Quiet down the troops...
Public Sub TellChildToBeQuiet(ByVal kidName As String, _
  ByVal shameIntensity As Integer)
  For i As Integer = 0 to shameIntensity
    MessageBox.Show(String.Format("Be quiet {0}!!", kidName))
  Next
End Sub
```

TellChildToBeQuiet() takes two parameters: a String representing the child's name and an Integer representing your current level of frustration. When using late binding, parameters are packaged as an array of System.Objects. To invoke the new method (assuming of course you have updated your MiniVan type), add the following code to your Main() method:

```
' Bind late to a method taking params.
Dim args(1) As Object
args(0) = "Fred"
args(1) = 4
mi = miniVan.GetMethod("TellChildToBeQuiet")
mi.Invoke(obj, args)
```

Hopefully at this point you can see the relationships among reflection, dynamic loading, and late binding. Again, you still may wonder exactly when you might make use of these techniques in your own applications. The conclusion of this chapter should shed light on this question; however, the next topic under investigation is the role of .NET attributes.

■ **Note** If Option Strict is disabled (which is the case by default), you can simplify your late binding logic. See the source code for the LateBinding project for details.

■ **Source Code** The LateBinding project is included in the Chapter 16 subdirectory.

Understanding Attributed Programming

As illustrated at the beginning of this chapter, one role of a .NET compiler is to generate metadata descriptions for all defined and referenced types. In addition to this standard metadata contained within any assembly, the .NET platform provides a way for programmers to embed additional metadata into an assembly using *attributes*. In a nutshell, attributes are nothing more than code annotations that can be applied to a given type (class, interface, structure, etc.), member (property, method, etc.), assembly, or module.

The idea of annotating code using attributes is not new. COM IDL provided numerous predefined attributes that allowed developers to describe the types contained within a given COM server. However, COM attributes were little more than a set of keywords. If a COM developer needed to create a custom attribute, they could do so, but it was referenced in code by a 128-bit number (GUID), which was cumbersome at best.

Unlike COM IDL attributes (which again were simply keywords), .NET attributes are class types that extend the abstract `System.Attribute` base class. As you explore the .NET namespaces, you will find many predefined attributes that you are able to make use of in your applications. Furthermore, you are free to build custom attributes to further qualify the behavior of your types by creating a new type deriving from `Attribute`.

Understand that when you apply attributes in your code, the embedded metadata is essentially useless until another piece of software explicitly reflects over the information. If this is not the case, the blurb of metadata embedded within the assembly is ignored and completely harmless.

Attribute Consumers

As you would guess, the .NET Framework 3.5 SDK ships with numerous utilities that are indeed on the lookout for various attributes. The VB 2008 compiler (`vbc.exe`) itself has been preprogrammed to discover the presence of various attributes during the compilation cycle. For example, if the VB 2008 compiler encounters the `<CLSCompilant()>` attribute, it will automatically check the attributed item to ensure it is exposing only CLS-compliant constructs (see Chapter 1). By way of another example, if the VB 2008 compiler discovers an item attributed with the `<Obsolete()>` attribute, it will display a compiler warning in the Visual Studio 2008 Error List window.

In addition to development tools, numerous methods in the .NET base class libraries are preprogrammed to reflect over specific attributes. For example, if you wish to persist the state of an object to a file, all you are required to do is annotate your class with the `<Serializable()>` attribute. If the `Serialize()` method of the `BinaryFormatter` class encounters this attribute, the object's state data is automatically persisted to a stream as a compact binary format (Chapter 21 will examine this topic in detail).

The .NET CLR is also on the prowl for the presence of certain attributes. Perhaps the most famous .NET attribute is `<WebMethod()>`. If you wish to expose a method via HTTP requests and automatically encode the method return value as XML, simply apply `<WebMethod()>` to the method, and the CLR handles the details. Beyond web service development, attributes are critical to the operation of the .NET security system, .NET remoting layer, and COM/.NET interoperability (and so on).

Finally, you are free to build applications that are programmed to reflect over your own custom attributes as well as any attribute in the .NET base class libraries. By doing so, you are essentially able to create a set of "keywords" that are understood by a specific set of assemblies.

Applying Predefined Attributes in VB 2008

As previously mentioned, the .NET base class library provides a number of attributes in various namespaces. Table 16-3 gives a snapshot of some—but by *absolutely* no means all—predefined attributes.

Table 16-3. *A Tiny Sampling of Predefined Attributes*

Attribute	Meaning in Life
`<CLSCompliant()>`	Enforces the annotated item to conform to the rules of the Common Language Specification (CLS). Recall that CLS-compliant types are guaranteed to be used seamlessly across all .NET programming languages.
`<DllImport()>`	Allows .NET code to make calls to any unmanaged C- or C++-based code library, including the API of the underlying operating system. Do note that `<DllImport()>` is not used when communicating with COM-based software.

Continued

Table 16-3. *Continued*

Attribute	Meaning in Life
`<Obsolete()>`	Marks a deprecated type or member. If other programmers attempt to use such an item, they will receive a compiler warning describing the error of their ways.
`<Serializable()>`	Marks a class or structure as being "serializable."
`<NonSerialized()>`	Specifies that a given field in a class or structure should not be persisted during the serialization process.
`<WebMethod()>`	Marks a method as being invokable via HTTP requests and instructs the CLR to serialize the method return value as XML.

To illustrate the process of applying attributes in VB 2008, assume you wish to build a class named `Motorcycle` that can be persisted into a stream for later use. To do so, simply apply the `<Serializable()>` attribute to the class definition. If you have a field that should not be persisted, you may apply the `<NonSerialized()>` attribute:

```
' This class can be saved to a stream.
<Serializable()> _
Public Class Motorcycle
  ' However, this field will not be persisted.
  <NonSerialized()> _
  Private weightOfCurrentPassengers As Single

  ' These fields are still serializable.
  Private hasRadioSystem As Boolean
  Private hasHeadSet As Boolean
  Private hasSissyBar As Boolean
End Class
```

■ **Note** An attribute only applies to the "very next" item. For example, the only nonserialized field of the `Motorcycle` class is `weightOfCurrentPassengers`. The remaining fields are serializable given that the entire class has been annotated with `<Serializable()>`.

At this point, don't concern yourself with the actual process of object serialization (again, Chapter 21 examines the details). Just notice that when you wish to apply an attribute, the name of the attribute is sandwiched between angled brackets.

Once this class has been compiled, you can view the extra metadata using `ildasm.exe`. Notice that these attributes are recorded using the `serializable` and `notserialized` tokens (see Figure 16-6).

As you might guess, a single item can be attributed with multiple attributes. Assume you have a legacy VB 2008 class type (`HorseAndBuggy`) that was marked as serializable, but is now considered obsolete for current development. To apply multiple attributes to a single item, simply use a comma-delimited list:

```
<Serializable(), _
Obsolete("This class is obsolete, use another vehicle!")> _
Public Class HorseAndBuggy
End Class
```

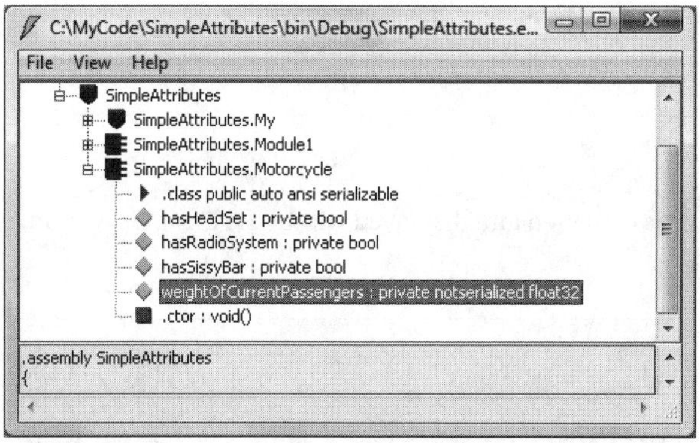

Figure 16-6. *Attributes shown in* `ildasm.exe`

As an alternative, you can also apply multiple attributes on a single item by stacking each attribute as follows (the end result is identical):

```
<Serializable(), _
Obsolete("This class is obsolete, use another vehicle!")> _
Public Class HorseAndBuggy
End Class

<Serializable()> _
<Obsolete("This class is obsolete, use another vehicle!")> _
Public Class HorseAndBuggy
End Class
```

Specifying Constructor Parameters for Attributes

Notice that the `<Obsolete()>` attribute is able to accept what appears to be a constructor parameter. In terms of VB 2008, the formal definition of the `<Obsolete()>` attribute looks something like so:

```
Public NotInheritable Class ObsoleteAttribute
  Inherits System.Attribute
  Public ReadOnly Property IsError() As Boolean
  End Property
  Public ReadOnly Property Message() As String
  End Property
  Public Sub New(ByVal message As String, ByVal error As Boolean)
  End Sub
  Public Sub New(ByVal message As String)
  End Sub
  Public Sub New()
  End Sub
End Class
```

As you can see, this class indeed defines a number of constructors, including one that receives a `System.String`. However, do understand that when you supply constructor parameters to an attribute, the attribute is *not* allocated into memory until the parameters are reflected upon by another type or an external tool. The string data defined at the attribute level is simply stored within the assembly as a blurb of metadata.

The <Obsolete()> Attribute in Action

Now that HorseAndBuggy has been marked as obsolete, if you were to allocate an instance of this type in a VB source code file:

```
Dim buggy As New HorseAndBuggy()
```

you would find that the supplied string data is extracted and displayed within the Error List window of Visual Studio 2008, as you see Figure 16-7.

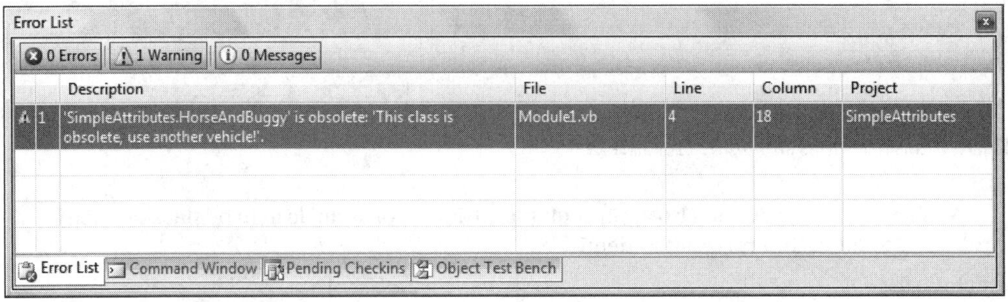

Figure 16-7. *Attributes in action*

In this case, the "other piece of software" that is reflecting on the <Obsolete()> attribute is the VB 2008 compiler.

VB 2008 Attribute Shorthand Notation

If you were reading closely, you may have noticed that the actual class name of the <Obsolete()> attribute is ObsoleteAttribute, not Obsolete. As a naming convention, all .NET attributes (including custom attributes you may create yourself) are suffixed with the Attribute token. However, to simplify the process of applying attributes, the VB 2008 language does not require you to type in the Attribute suffix. Given this, the following iteration of the HorseAndBuggy type is identical to the previous (it just involves a few more keystrokes):

```
<SerializableAttribute()> _
<ObsoleteAttribute("This class is obsolete, use another vehicle!")> _
Public Class HorseAndBuggy
End Class
```

Be aware that this is a courtesy provided by VB 2008. Not all .NET-enabled languages support this feature. In any case, at this point you should hopefully understand the following key points regarding .NET attributes:

- Attributes are classes that derive from System.Attribute.
- Attributes result in embedded metadata.
- Attributes are basically useless until another agent reflects upon them.
- Attributes are applied in VB 2008 using angled brackets.

Next up, let's examine how you can build your own custom attributes and a piece of custom software that reflects over the embedded metadata. After this point, you'll build a complete application that illustrates the real-world application of these rather low-level topics.

Building Custom Attributes

The first step in building a custom attribute is to create a new class deriving from `System.Attribute`. Keeping in step with the automobile theme used throughout this book, assume you have created a brand-new VB 2008 class library named `AttributedCarLibrary`. This library will define a handful of vehicles (some of which you have already seen in this text), each of which is described using a custom attribute named `VehicleDescriptionAttribute`:

```
' A custom attribute.
Public NotInheritable Class VehicleDescriptionAttribute
  Inherits System.Attribute
  Private msgData As String

  Public Sub New(ByVal description As String)
    msgData = description
  End Sub
  Public Sub New()
  End Sub

  Public Property Description() As String
    Get
      Return msgData
    End Get
    Set(ByVal value As String)
      msgData = value
    End Set
  End Property
End Class
```

As you can see, `VehicleDescriptionAttribute` maintains a private internal string (`msgData`) that can be set using a custom constructor and manipulated using a type property (`Description`). Beyond the fact that this class derived from `System.Attribute`, there is nothing unique to this class definition.

■ **Note** For security reasons, it is considered a .NET best practice to design all custom attributes as `NonInheritable`.

Applying Custom Attributes

Given that `VehicleDescriptionAttribute` is derived from `System.Attribute`, you are now able to annotate your vehicles as you see fit. For example, assume you have added the following classes to your current library project:

```
' Assign description using a "named property."
<Serializable()> _
<VehicleDescription(Description:="My rocking Harley")> _
Public Class Motorcycle
End Class

<Serializable()> _
<Obsolete("This class is obsolete, use another vehicle!"), _
VehicleDescription("The old grey Mare she ain't what she used to be...")> _
Public Class HorseAndBuggy
End Class
```

```
<VehicleDescription("A very long, slow but feature rich auto")> _
Public Class Winnebago
End Class
```

Notice that the description of `Motorcycle` is assigned a description using a new bit of attribute-centric syntax termed a *named property*. In the constructor of the first `<VehicleDescription()>` attribute, you set the underlying `System.String` using a name/value pair. If this attribute is reflected upon by an external agent, the value is fed into the `Description` property (named property syntax is legal only if the attribute supplies a writable .NET property). In contrast, the `HorseAndBuggy` and `Winnebago` types are not making use of named property syntax and are simply passing the string data via the custom constructor.

Once you compile the `AttributedCarLibrary` assembly, you can make use of `ildasm.exe` to view the injected metadata descriptions for your type. For example, Figure 16-8 shows an embedded description of the `Winnebago` type.

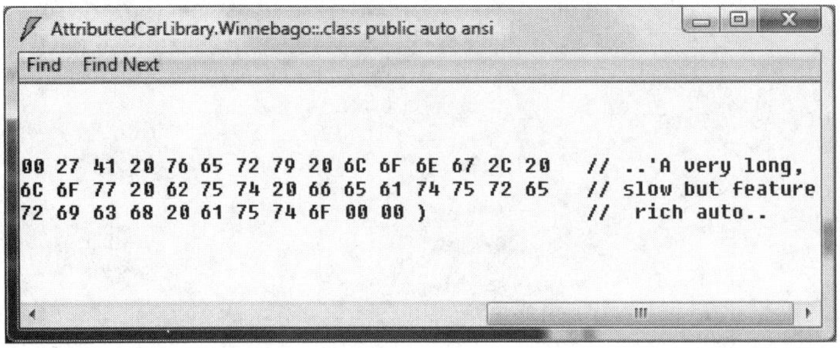

Figure 16-8. *Embedded vehicle description data*

Restricting Attribute Usage

By default, custom attributes can be applied to just about any aspect of your code (methods, classes, properties, and so on). Thus, if it made sense to do so, you could use `VehicleDescription` to qualify methods, properties, or fields (among other things):

```
<VehicleDescription("A very long, slow, but feature-rich auto")> _
Public Class Winnebago
  <VehicleDescription("My rocking CD player")> _
  Public Sub PlayMusic(ByVal isOn As Boolean)
  End Sub
End Class
```

In some cases, this is exactly the behavior you require. Other times, however, you may want to build a custom attribute that can be applied only to select code elements. If you wish to constrain the scope of a custom attribute, you will need to apply the `<AttributeUsage()>` attribute on the definition of your custom attribute. The `<AttributeUsage()>` attribute allows you to supply any combination of values (via an `OR` operation) from the `AttributeTargets` enumeration:

```
' This enumeration defines the possible targets of an attribute.
Public Enum AttributeTargets
  All
  Assembly
  Class
  Constructor
  Delegate
  Enum
```

```
  Event
  Field
  GenericParameter
  Interface
  Method
  Module
  Parameter
  Property
  ReturnValue
  Struct
End Enum
```

Furthermore, <AttributeUsage()> also allows you to optionally set a named property (AllowMultiple) that specifies whether the attribute can be applied more than once on the same item. As well, <AttributeUsage()> allows you to establish whether the attribute should be inherited by derived classes using the Inherited named property.

To establish that the <VehicleDescription()> attribute can be applied only once on a class or structure (and the value is not inherited by derived types), you can update the VehicleDescriptionAttribute definition as follows:

```
<AttributeUsage(AttributeTargets.Class Or _
 AttributeTargets.Struct, AllowMultiple:=False, Inherited:=False)> _
Public NotInheritable Class VehicleDescriptionAttribute
...
End Class
```

With this, if a developer attempted to apply the <VehicleDescription()> attribute on anything other than a class or structure, he or she is issued a compile-time error.

Tip Always get in the habit of explicitly marking the usage flags for any custom attribute you may create, as not all .NET programming languages honor the use of unqualified attributes!

Assembly-Level (and Module-Level) Attributes

It is also possible to apply attributes on all types within a given module or all modules within a given assembly using the <Module:> and <Assembly:> tags, respectively. For example, assume you wish to ensure that every public member of every public type defined within your assembly is CLS-compliant. To do so, simply add the following line in any one of your VB 2008 source code files (do note that assembly-level attributes must be outside the scope of a namespace definition):

```
' Enforce CLS compliance for all public types in this assembly.
<Assembly:System.CLSCompliantAttribute(True)>
```

If you now add a bit of code that falls outside the CLS specification (such as an exposed field of unsigned data) like so:

```
' UInt64 types don't jibe with the CLS.
<VehicleDescription("A very long, slow but feature rich auto")> _
Public Class Winnebago
  Public notCompliant As UInt64
End Class
```

you are issued a compiler warning.

The Visual Studio 2008 AssemblyInfo.vb File

Visual Studio 2008 projects always contain a file named `AssemblyInfo.vb`; however, by default this file is not made visible until you click the Show All Files button of Solution Explorer. Once you do, you can expand the My Project icon to reveal this file, as shown in Figure 16-9.

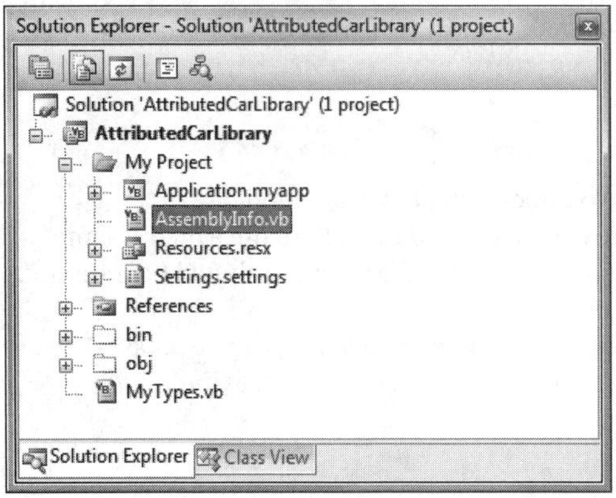

Figure 16-9. *The* `AssemblyInfo.vb` *file*

This file is a handy place to put attributes that are to be applied at the assembly level. Table 16-4 lists some assembly-level attributes to be aware of.

Table 16-4. *Select Assembly-Level Attributes*

Attribute	Meaning in Life
`AssemblyCompany`	Holds basic company information
`AssemblyCopyright`	Holds any copyright information for the product or assembly
`AssemblyCulture`	Provides information on what cultures or languages the assembly supports
`AssemblyDescription`	Holds a friendly description of the product or modules that make up the assembly
`AssemblyKeyFile`	Specifies the name of the file containing the key pair used to sign the assembly (i.e., establish a shared name)
`AssemblyProduct`	Provides product information
`AssemblyTrademark`	Provides trademark information
`AssemblyVersion`	Specifies the assembly's version information, in the format <*major.minor.build.revision*>

■Note While you are free to update `AssemblyInfo.vb` directly, be aware that each of these attributes can be set using various areas of the My Project GUI editor (in fact, this is the preferred manner to establish assembly-level attributes). To do so, open the My Project editor, select the Application tab, and click the Assembly Information button.

Source Code The AttributedCarLibrary project is included in the Chapter 16 subdirectory.

Reflecting on Attributes Using Early Binding

As mentioned in this chapter, an attribute is quite useless until some piece of software reflects over its data. Once a given attribute has been discovered, that piece of software can take whatever course of action necessary. Now, like any application, this "other piece of software" could discover the presence of a custom attribute using either early binding or late binding. If you wish to make use of early binding, you'll require the client application to have a compile-time definition of the attribute in question (VehicleDescriptionAttribute in this case). Given that the AttributedCarLibrary.dll assembly has defined this custom attribute as a public class, early binding is the best option.

To illustrate the process of reflecting on custom attributes, create a new VB 2008 Console Application named VehicleDescriptionReader. Next, set a reference to the AttributedCarLibrary assembly. Finally, update your initial *.vb file with the following code:

```
Imports AttributedCarLibrary

' Reflecting on custom attributes using early binding.
Module Program
  Sub Main()
    ' Get a Type representing the Winnebago.
    Dim t As Type = GetType(Winnebago)

    ' Get all attributes on the Winnebago.
    Dim customAtts As Object() = t.GetCustomAttributes(False)

    ' Print the description.
    Console.WriteLine("***** Value of VehicleDescriptionAttribute *****")
    For Each v As VehicleDescriptionAttribute In customAtts
      Console.WriteLine()
      Console.WriteLine("->{0}.", v.Description)
    Next
    Console.ReadLine()
  End Sub
End Module
```

As the name implies, Type.GetCustomAttributes() returns an object array that represents all the attributes applied to the member represented by the Type (the Boolean parameter controls whether the search should extend up the inheritance chain). Once you have obtained the list of attributes, iterate over each VehicleDescriptionAttribute class and print out the value obtained by the Description property.

Source Code The VehicleDescriptionAttributeReader application is included under the Chapter 16 subdirectory.

Reflecting on Attributes Using Late Binding

The previous example made use of early binding to print out the vehicle description data for the `Winnebago` type. This was possible due to the fact that the `VehicleDescriptionAttribute` class type was defined as a public member in the `AttributedCarLibrary` assembly. It is also possible to make use of dynamic loading and late binding to reflect over attributes.

Create a new Console Application project called VehicleDescriptionReaderLB (where LB stands for late binding) and copy `AttributedCarLibrary.dll` to the project's \bin\Debug directory. Now, update your `Main()` method as follows:

```
Imports System.Reflection

Module Project
  Sub Main()
    Console.WriteLine("***** Descriptions of Your Vehicles *****")
    Console.WriteLine()

    ' Load the local copy of AttributedCarLibrary.
    Dim asm As Assembly = Assembly.Load("AttributedCarLibrary")

    ' Get type info of VehicleDescriptionAttribute.
    Dim vehicleDesc As Type = _
      asm.GetType("AttributedCarLibrary.VehicleDescriptionAttribute")

    ' Get type info of the Description property.
    Dim propDesc As PropertyInfo = vehicleDesc.GetProperty("Description")

    ' Get all types in the assembly.
    Dim types As Type() = asm.GetTypes()

    ' Iterate over each attribute.
    For Each t As Type In types
      Dim objs As Object() = t.GetCustomAttributes(vehicleDesc, False)
        For Each o As Object In objs
          Console.WriteLine("-> {0} : {1}", t.Name, propDesc.GetValue(o, Nothing))
        Next
    Next
    Console.ReadLine()
  End Sub
End Module
```

If you were able to follow along with the examples shown within this chapter, this `Main()` method should be fairly self-explanatory. The only point of interest is the use of the `PropertyInfo.GetValue()` method, which is used to trigger the property's get method. Figure 16-10 shows the output.

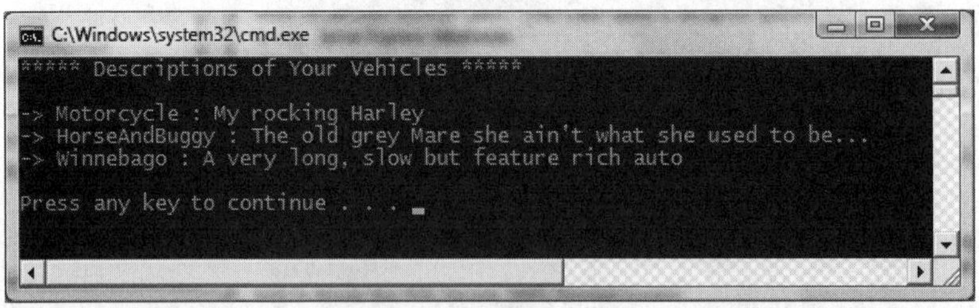

Figure 16-10. *Reflecting on attributes using late binding*

Source Code The `VehicleDescriptionReaderLB` application is included under the Chapter 16 subdirectory.

Putting Reflection, Late Binding, and Custom Attributes in Perspective

Even though you have seen numerous examples of these techniques in action, you may still be wondering when to make use of reflection, dynamic loading, late binding, and custom attributes in your own programs. To be sure, at first glance these topics can seem a bit on the academic side of programming (which may or may not be a bad thing, depending on your point of view). To help map these topics to a real-world situation, you need a solid example. Assume for the moment that you are on a programming team that is building an application with the following requirement:

- The product must be extendable by the use of additional third-party tools.

So, what exactly is meant by *extendable*? Consider Visual Studio 2008. When this application was developed, various "hooks" were inserted to allow other software vendors to snap custom modules into the IDE. Obviously, the Visual Studio 2008 team had no way to set references to external .NET assemblies it had not programmed (thus, no early binding), so how exactly would an application provide the required hooks?

- First, an extendable application must provide some input vehicle to allow the user to specify the module to plug in (such as a dialog box or command-line flag). This requires *dynamic loading*.
- Second, an extendable application must be able to determine whether the module supports the correct functionality (such as a set of required interfaces) in order to be plugged into the environment. This requires *reflection*.
- Finally, an extendable application must obtain a reference to the required infrastructure (e.g., the interface types) and invoke the members to trigger the underlying functionality. This often requires *late binding*.

Simply put, if the extendable application has been preprogrammed to query for specific interfaces, it is able to determine at runtime whether the type can be activated. Once this verification test has been passed, the type in question may support additional interfaces that provide a polymorphic fabric to their functionality. This is the exact approach taken by the Visual Studio 2008 team, and despite what you may be thinking, it is not at all difficult.

Building an Extendable Application

In the sections that follow, I will take you through a complete example that illustrates the process of building an extendable Windows Forms application that can be augmented by the functionality of external assemblies. What I will not do at this point is comment on the process of programming Windows Forms applications (Chapters 27, 28, and 29 will tend to that chore). So, if you are not familiar with the process of building Windows Forms applications, feel free to simply open up the downloadable sample code and follow along (or build a console-based alternative). To serve as a road map, our extendable application entails the following assemblies:

- CommonSnappableTypes.dll: This assembly contains type definitions that will be implemented by each snap-in object as well as referenced by the extendable Windows Forms application.
- VbNetSnapIn.dll: This snap-in, written in Visual Basic 2008, leverages the types of CommonSnappableTypes.dll.
- CSharpSnapIn.dll: This snap-in, written in C#, leverages the types of CommonSnappableTypes.dll. This assembly will allow us to illustrate that any .NET language can be used to build the snap-in.
- MyPluggableApp.exe: This Windows Forms application will be the entity that may be extended by the functionality of each snap-in. Again, this application will make use of dynamic loading, reflection, and late binding to dynamically gain the functionality of assemblies it has no prior knowledge of.

Building CommonSnappableTypes.dll

The first order of business is to create an assembly that contains the types that a given snap-in must leverage to be plugged into your expandable Windows Forms application. The CommonSnappable-Types Class Library project defines two types:

```
Public Interface IAppFunctionality
  Sub DoIt()
End Interface

<AttributeUsage(AttributeTargets.Class)> _
Public NotInheritable Class CompanyInfoAttribute
  Inherits System.Attribute
  Private companyName As String
  Private companyUrl As String

  Public Sub New()
  End Sub
  Public Property Name() As String
    Get
      Return companyName
    End Get
    Set(ByVal value As String)
      companyName = value
    End Set
  End Property
  Public Property Url() As String
    Get
      Return companyUrl
    End Get
    Set(ByVal value As String)
      companyUrl = value
    End Set
  End Property
End Class
```

The IAppFunctionality interface provides a polymorphic interface for all snap-ins that can be consumed by the extendable Windows Forms application. Of course, as this example is purely illustrative in nature, you supply a single method named DoIt(). To map this to a real-world example, imagine an interface (or a set of interfaces) that allows the snapper to generate scripting code, render an image onto the application's toolbox, or integrate into the main menu of the hosting application.

The CompanyInfoAttribute type is a custom attribute that will be applied on any class type that wishes to be snapped into the container. As you can tell by the definition of this class, <CompanyInfo()> allows the developer of the snap-in to provide some basic details about the component's point of origin.

Building the VB 2008 Snap-In

Next up, you need to create a type that implements the IAppFunctionality interface. Again, to focus on the overall design of an extendable application, a trivial type is in order. Assume a new VB 2008 code library named VbNetSnapIn that defines a class type named VbNetSnapInModule. Given that this class must make use of the types defined in CommonSnappableTypes, be sure to set a reference to this binary (as well as System.Windows.Forms.dll to display a noteworthy message) and import the necessary namespaces (which follow). This being said, here is the code:

```
Imports System.Windows.Forms
Imports CommonSnappableTypes

<CompanyInfo(Name:="Chucky's Software", Url:="www.ChuckySoft.com")> _
Public Class VbNetSnapInModule
  Implements IAppFunctionality
  Public Sub DoIt() Implements CommonSnappableTypes.IAppFunctionality.DoIt
    MessageBox.Show("You have just used the VB 2008 snap in!")
  End Sub
End Class
```

Building the C# Snap-In

Now, to simulate the role of a third-party vendor who prefers C# over VB 2008, create a new C# code library (CSharpSnapIn) that references the same external assemblies as the previous VbNetSnapIn project. The code is (again) intentionally simple:

```
using System;
using CommonSnappableTypes;
using System.Windows.Forms;

namespace CSharpSnapIn
{
  [CompanyInfo(Name = "Intertech Training",
  Url = "www.intertechtraining.com")]
  public class CSharpSnapInModule : IAppFunctionality
  {
    void IAppFunctionality.DoIt()
    {
      MessageBox.Show("You have just used the C# snap in!");
    }
  }
}
```

Without getting hung up on the syntax of the C# language, do notice that applying attributes in the syntax of C# requires square brackets ([ ]) rather than angled brackets (< >).

Building an Extendable Windows Forms Application

The final step of this example is to create a new Windows Forms application (MyExtendableApp) that allows the user to select a snap-in using a standard Windows Open dialog box. Next, set a reference to the CommonSnappableTypes.dll assembly, but *not* the CSharpSnapIn.dll or VbNetSnapIn.dll code libraries. Remember that the whole goal of this application is to make use of late binding and reflection to determine the "snapability" of independent binaries created by third-party vendors. Finally, be sure to import the System.Reflection namespace into your initial form's code file.

Again, I won't bother to examine all the details of Windows Forms development at this point in the text. However, assuming you have placed a MenuStrip component onto the Form template, define a topmost menu item named Tools that provides a single submenu named Snap In Module. This Windows Form will also contain a ListBox type (which I renamed as lstLoadedSnapIns) that will be used to display the names of each snap-in loaded by the user. Figure 16-11 shows the final GUI.

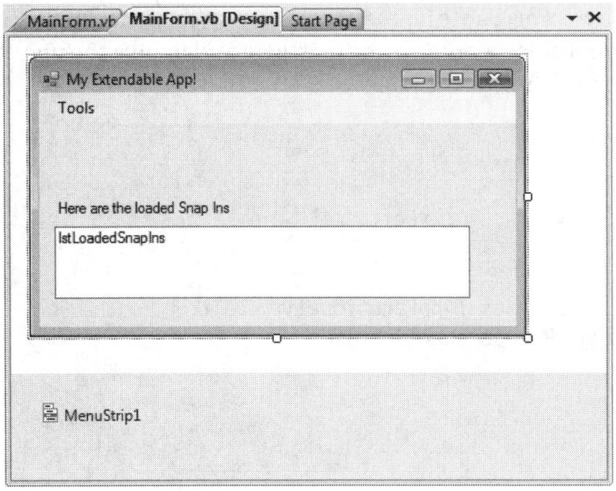

Figure 16-11. *Final GUI for MyExtendableApp*

The code that handles the Click event of the Tools ➤ Snap In Module menu item (which may be created simply by double-clicking the menu item from the design-time editor) displays a File Open dialog box and extracts the path to the selected file.

Provided the user did not attempt to open CommonSnappableTypes.dll, this path is then sent into a helper function named LoadExternalModule() for processing. This method will return False when it is unable to find a class implementing IAppFunctionality:

```
Private Sub SnapInModuleToolStripMenuItem_Click(ByVal sender As System.Object, _
  ByVal e As System.EventArgs) Handles SnapInModuleToolStripMenuItem.Click
  ' Allow user to select an assembly to load.
  Dim dlg As New OpenFileDialog()

  If dlg.ShowDialog = Windows.Forms.DialogResult.OK Then
    If dlg.FileName.Contains("CommonSnappableTypes") Then
      MessageBox.Show("CommonSnappableTypes has no snap-ins!")
    ElseIf LoadExternalModule(dlg.FileName) = False Then
      MessageBox.Show("Nothing implements IAppFunctionality!")
    End If
  End If
End Sub
```

The LoadExternalModule() method performs the following tasks:

- Dynamically loads the assembly into memory
- Determines whether the assembly contains a type implementing IAppFunctionality using a LINQ query

If a type implementing IAppFunctionality is found, the DoIt() method is called, and the fully qualified name of the type is added to the ListBox (note that the For Each loop will iterate over all types in the assembly to account for the possibility that a single assembly has multiple snap-in objects):

```
Private Function LoadExternalModule(ByVal path As String) As Boolean
  Dim foundSnapIn As Boolean = False
  Dim itfAppFx As IAppFunctionality
  Dim theSnapInAsm As Assembly = Nothing

  ' Try to dynamically load the selected assembly.
  Try
    theSnapInAsm = Assembly.LoadFrom(path)
  Catch ex As Exception
    MessageBox.Show(ex.Message)
    Return foundSnapIn
  End Try

  ' Get all IAppFunctionality compatible classes in assembly,
  ' using a LINQ query and implicitly typed data.
  Dim classTypes = From t In theSnapInAsm.GetTypes() Where _
    t.IsClass And (t.GetInterface("IAppFunctionality") _
    IsNot Nothing) Select t

  For Each c As Object In classTypes
    foundSnapIn = True

    ' Use late binding to create the type.
    Dim o As Object = theSnapInAsm.CreateInstance(c.FullName)

    ' Call DoIt() off the interface.
    itfAppFx = CType(o, IAppFunctionality)
    itfAppFx.DoIt()
    lstLoadedSnapIns.Items.Add(c.FullName)

  Next
  Return foundSnapIn
End Function
```

At this point, you can run your application. When you select the CSharpSnapIn.dll or VbNetSnapIn.dll assemblies, you should see the correct message displayed. Figure 16-12 shows one possible run of this Windows Forms application.

Figure 16-12. *Snapping in external assemblies*

The final task is to display the metadata provided by the `<CompanyInfo>`. To do so, simply update `LoadExternalModule()` to call a new helper function named `DisplayCompanyData()` before exiting the `If` scope. Notice this method takes a single `System.Type` parameter.

```
Private Function LoadExternalModule(ByVal path As String) As Boolean
...
  ' Show company info.
  DisplayCompanyData(c)
  Next
  Return foundSnapIn
End Function
```

Using the incoming type, simply reflect over the `<CompanyInfo()>` attribute:

```
Private Sub DisplayCompanyData(ByVal t As Type)
  ' Get <CompanyInfo> type.
  Dim customAtts As Object() = t.GetCustomAttributes(False)
  For Each c As CompanyInfoAttribute In customAtts
    ' Show data.
    MessageBox.Show(c.Url, String.Format _
      ("More info about {0} can be found at", c.Name))
  Next
End Sub
```

Excellent! That wraps up the example application. I hope at this point you can see that the topics presented in this chapter can be quite helpful in the real world and are not limited to the tool builders of the world.

■ **Source Code** The CommonSnappableTypes, CSharpSnapIn, VbNetSnapIn, and MyExtendableApp applications are all included under the Chapter 16 subdirectory.

Summary

Reflection is a very powerful aspect of a robust OO environment. In the world of .NET, the keys to reflection services revolve around the `System.Type` class and the `System.Reflection` namespace. As you have seen, reflection is the process of placing a type under the magnifying glass at runtime to understand the who, what, where, when, why, and how of a given item.

Late binding is the process of creating a type and invoking its members without prior knowledge of the specific names of said members. As shown during this chapter's extendable application example, this is a very powerful technique used by tool builders as well as tool consumers. This chapter also examined the role of attribute-based programming. When you adorn your types with attributes, the result is the augmentation of the underlying assembly metadata.

CHAPTER 17

Processes, AppDomains, and Object Contexts

In the previous two chapters, you examined the steps taken by the CLR to resolve the location of an externally referenced assembly and learned the role of .NET metadata. In this chapter, you'll drill deeper into the details of how an assembly is hosted by the CLR and come to understand the relationship between processes, application domains, and object contexts.

In a nutshell, *application domains* (or, simply, *AppDomains*) are logical subdivisions within a given process that host a set of related .NET assemblies. As you will see, an AppDomain is further subdivided into contextual boundaries, which are used to group together like-minded .NET objects. Using the notion of context, the CLR is able to ensure that objects with special runtime requirements are handled appropriately.

Note This chapter will expose you to a number of lower-level details of the .NET runtime environment. While it is true that much of your .NET programming may not entail directly manipulating processes, application domains, or object contexts, be aware that understanding these concepts is quite important when working with several .NET APIs, such as threading, security, Windows Communication Foundation (WCF), and the .NET remoting layer.

Reviewing Traditional Win32 Processes

The concept of a "process" has existed within Windows-based operating systems well before the release of the .NET platform. Simply put, a *process* is the term used to describe the set of resources (such as external code libraries and the primary thread) and the necessary memory allocations used by a running application. For each `*.exe` loaded into memory, the OS creates a separate and isolated process for use during its lifetime. Using this approach to application isolation, the result is a much more robust and stable runtime environment, given that the failure of one process does not affect the functioning of another.

Now, every Windows process is assigned a unique process identifier (PID) and may be independently loaded and unloaded by the OS as necessary. As you may be aware, the Windows Task Manager utility (activated via the Ctrl+Shift+Esc keystroke combination) allows you to view various statistics regarding the processes running on a given machine, including its PID and image name. Consider Figure 17-1, which shows the Processes tab of the Windows Task Manager.

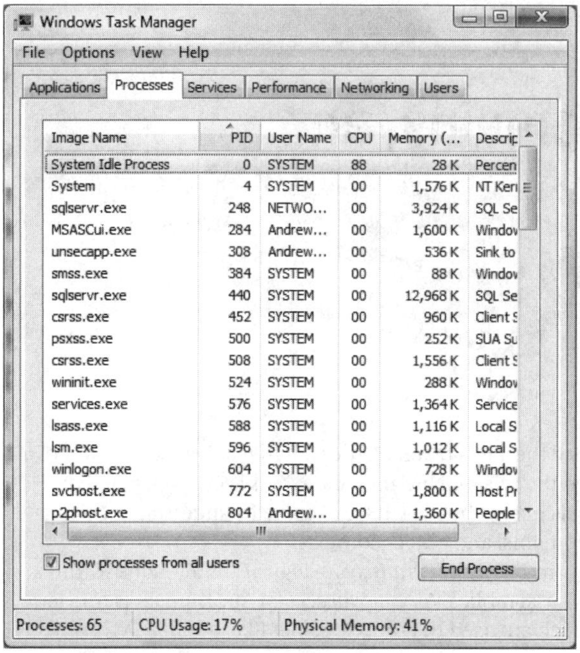

Figure 17-1. *Windows Task Manager*

Note By default, the PID column of the Processes tab is not visible. To view this column, select the View ➤ Select Columns menu option and check the PID (Process Identifier) check box.

An Overview of Threads

Every Windows process has exactly one main "thread" that functions as the entry point for the application. The next chapter examines how to create additional threads and thread-safe code using the `System.Threading` namespace; however, to facilitate the topics presented here, we need a few working definitions. First of all, a *thread* is a path of execution within a process. Formally speaking, the first thread created by a process's entry point (the `Main()` method) is termed the *primary thread.*

Processes that contain a single primary thread of execution are intrinsically *thread safe,* given the fact that there is only one thread that can access the data in the application at a given time. However, a single-threaded application (especially one that is GUI-based, such as a Windows Forms application) may appear a bit unresponsive to the user if this single thread is performing a complex operation (such as printing out a lengthy text file, performing a mathematically intensive calculation, or attempting to connect to a remote server located thousands of miles away).

Given this potential drawback of single-threaded applications, the Windows operating system makes it possible for the primary thread to spawn additional secondary threads, which historically involved calling a handful of C-based Win32 API functions such as `CreateThread()`. Each thread (primary or secondary) becomes a unique path of execution in the process and has concurrent access to all shared points of data.

As you may have guessed, developers typically create additional threads to help improve the program's overall responsiveness. Multithreaded processes provide the illusion that numerous activities are happening at more or less the same time. For example, an application may spawn a worker thread to perform a labor-intensive unit of work (such as printing a large text file). As this secondary thread is churning away, the main thread is still responsive to user input, which gives the entire process the potential of delivering greater performance. However, this may not actually be the case: using too many threads in a single process can actually *degrade* performance, as the CPU must switch between the active threads in the process (which takes time).

In reality, it is always worth keeping in mind that multithreading is most commonly an illusion provided by the OS. Machines that host a single CPU do not have the ability to literally handle multiple threads at the same exact time. Rather, a single CPU will execute one thread for a unit of time (called a *time slice*) based on the thread's priority level. When a thread's time slice is up, the existing thread is suspended to allow another thread to perform its business. For a thread to remember what was happening before it was kicked out of the way, each thread is given the ability to write to Thread Local Storage (TLS) and is provided with a separate call stack, as illustrated in Figure 17-2.

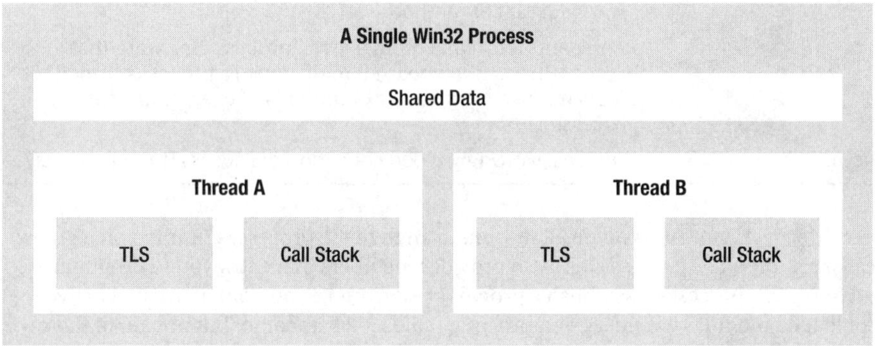

Figure 17-2. *The Win32 process/thread relationship*

■ Note Thread Local Storage (TLS) is an area of memory uniquely allocated to each thread by the OS.

If the subject of threads is new to you, don't sweat the details (again, see Chapter 18). At this point, just remember that a thread is a unique path of execution within a Windows process. Every process has a primary thread (created via the executable's `Main()` method) and may contain additional threads that have been programmatically created.

Interacting with Processes Under the .NET Platform

Although processes and threads are nothing new, the manner in which we interact with these primitives under the .NET platform has changed quite a bit (for the better). To pave the way to understanding the world of building multithreaded assemblies in the next chapter, let's begin by checking out how to interact with processes using the .NET base class libraries.

The `System.Diagnostics` namespace defines a number of types that allow you to programmatically interact with processes and various diagnostic-related types such as the system event log and performance counters. In this chapter, we are only concerned with the process-centric types defined in Table 17-1.

Table 17-1. *Select Members of the* `System.Diagnostics` *Namespace*

Process-Centric Types of the `System.Diagnostics` Namespace	Meaning in Life
`Process`	The `Process` class provides access to local and remote processes and also allows you to programmatically start and stop processes.
`ProcessModule`	This type represents a module (`*.dll` or `*.exe`) that is loaded into a particular process. Understand that the `ProcessModule` type can represent *any* module—COM-based, .NET-based, or traditional C-based binaries.
`ProcessModuleCollection`	Provides a strongly typed collection of `ProcessModule` objects.
`ProcessStartInfo`	Specifies a set of values used when starting a process via the `Process.Start()` method.
`ProcessThread`	Represents a thread within a given process. Be aware that `ProcessThread` is a type used to diagnose a process's thread set and is not used to spawn new threads of execution within a process.
`ProcessThreadCollection`	Provides a strongly typed collection of `ProcessThread` objects.

The `System.Diagnostics.Process` type allows you to analyze the processes running on a given machine (local or remote). The `Process` class also provides members that allow you to programmatically start and terminate processes, establish a process's priority level, and obtain a list of active threads and/or loaded modules within a given process. Table 17-2 lists some (but not all) of the key members of `System.Diagnostics.Process`.

Table 17-2. *Select Members of the* `Process` *Type*

Member	Meaning in Life
`ExitCode`	This property gets the value that the associated process specified when it terminated. Do note that you will be required to handle the `Exited` event (for asynchronous notification) or call the `WaitForExit()` method (for synchronous notification) to obtain this value.
`ExitTime`	This property gets the timestamp associated with the process that has terminated (represented with a `DateTime` type).
`Id`	This property gets the process ID (PID) for the associated process.
`MachineName`	This property gets the name of the computer the associated process is running on.
`MainModule`	This property gets the `ProcessModule` type that represents the main module for a given process.
`MainWindowTitle`	This property gets the caption of the main window of the process (if the process does not have a main window, you receive an empty string).
`Modules`	This property provides access to the strongly typed `ProcessModuleCollection` type, which represents the set of modules (`*.dll` or `*.exe`) loaded within the current process.
`PriorityBoostEnabled`	This property determines whether the OS should temporarily boost the process if the main window has the focus.

Member	Meaning in Life
PriorityClass	This property allows you to read or change the overall priority category for the associated process.
ProcessName	This property gets the name of the process (which, as you would assume, is the name of the application itself).
Responding	This property gets a value indicating whether the user interface of the process is responding (or not).
StartTime	This property gets the time that the associated process was started (via a DateTime type).
Threads	This property gets the set of threads that are running in the associated process (represented via an array of ProcessThread types).
CloseMainWindow()	This method closes a process that has a user interface by sending a close message to its main window.
GetCurrentProcess()	This shared method returns a new Process type that represents the currently active process.
GetProcesses()	This shared method returns an array of new Process components running on a given machine.
GetProcessById()	This shared method returns a single Process object based on a process ID.
Kill()	This method immediately stops the associated process.
Start()	This method starts a process.

Enumerating Running Processes

To illustrate the process of manipulating Process types (pardon the redundancy), assume you have a VB 2008 Console Application named ProcessManipulator, which defines the following method in the initial Module (be sure you import the System.Diagnostics namespace for use within your code file):

```
Public Sub ListAllRunningProcesses()
  ' Get all the processes on the local machine.
  Dim runningProcs As Process() = Process.GetProcesses(".")

  ' Print out PID and name of each process.
  For Each p As Process In runningProcs
    Dim info As String = String.Format("-> PID: {0}" & _
      Chr(9) & "Name: {1}", p.Id, p.ProcessName)
    Console.WriteLine(info)
  Next
  Console.WriteLine("************************************")
  Console.WriteLine()
End Sub
```

Notice how the shared Process.GetProcesses() method returns an array of Process types that represent the running processes on the target machine (the dot notation shown here represents the local computer). Once you have obtained the array of Process types, you are able to access any of the members seen in Table 17-2. Here, you are simply displaying the PID and the name of each process. Assuming the Main() method has been updated to call ListAllRunningProcesses(), you will see something like the output shown in Figure 17-3.

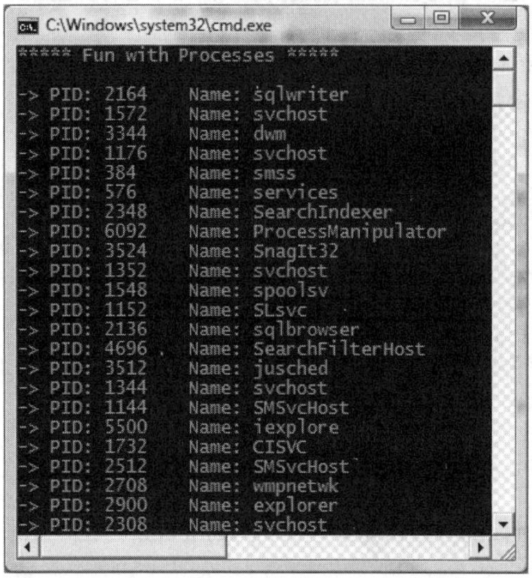

Figure 17-3. *Enumerating running processes*

Investigating a Specific Process

In addition to obtaining a full and complete list of all running processes on a given machine, the shared `Process.GetProcessById()` method allows you to obtain a single `Process` type via the associated PID. If you request access to a nonexistent process ID, an `ArgumentException` exception is thrown. For example, if you were interested in obtaining a `Process` object representing a process with the PID of 987, you could write the following:

```
' If there is no process with the PID of 987, a
' runtime exception will be thrown.
Sub Main()
  Console.WriteLine("***** Fun with Processes *****" & vbLf)
  ListAllRunningProcesses()

  ' Look up a specific process.
  Dim theProc As Process
  Try
    theProc = Process.GetProcessById(987)
    ' Manipulate the process handle...
  Catch  ' Generic catch used for simplicity.
    Console.WriteLine("-> Sorry...bad PID!")
  End Try
  Console.ReadLine()
End Sub
```

Investigating a Process's Thread Set

The `Process` class type also provides a manner to programmatically investigate the set of all threads currently used by a specific process. The set of threads is represented by the strongly typed `ProcessThreadCollection` collection, which contains some number of individual `ProcessThread` types. To illustrate, consider the implementation of the following additional subroutine:

```
Public Sub EnumThreadsForPid(ByVal pID As Integer)
  Dim theProc As Process
  Try
    theProc = Process.GetProcessById(pID)
  Catch
    Console.WriteLine("-> Sorry...bad PID!")
    Console.WriteLine("************************************")
    Console.WriteLine()
    Return
  End Try
  Console.WriteLine("Here are the threads used by: {0}", theProc.ProcessName)

  ' List out stats for each thread in the specified process.
  Dim theThreads As ProcessThreadCollection = theProc.Threads
  For Each pt As ProcessThread In theThreads
    Dim info As String = String.Format("-> Thread ID: {0}" _
      & Chr(9) & "Start Time {1}" & _
      Chr(9) & "Priority {2}", _
      pt.Id, pt.StartTime.ToShortTimeString(), pt.PriorityLevel)
    Console.WriteLine(info)
  Next
  Console.WriteLine("************************************")
  Console.WriteLine()
End Sub
```

As you can see, the Threads property of the System.Diagnostics.Process type provides access to the ProcessThreadCollection class. Here, you are printing out the assigned thread ID, start time, and priority level of each thread in the process specified by the client. Thus, if you update your program's Main() method to prompt the user for a PID to investigate, as follows:

```
Sub Main()
  Console.WriteLine("***** Fun with Processes *****" & vbLf)
  ListAllRunningProcesses()

  ' Prompt user for a PID and print out the set of active threads.
  Console.WriteLine("***** Enter PID of process to investigate *****")
  Console.Write("PID: ")
  Dim pID As String = Console.ReadLine()
  Try
    Dim theProcID As Integer = Integer.Parse(pID)
    EnumThreadsForPid(theProcID)
  Catch ex As Exception
    Console.WriteLine(ex.Message)
  End Try
  Console.ReadLine()
End Sub
```

you would find output along the lines of that shown in Figure 17-4.

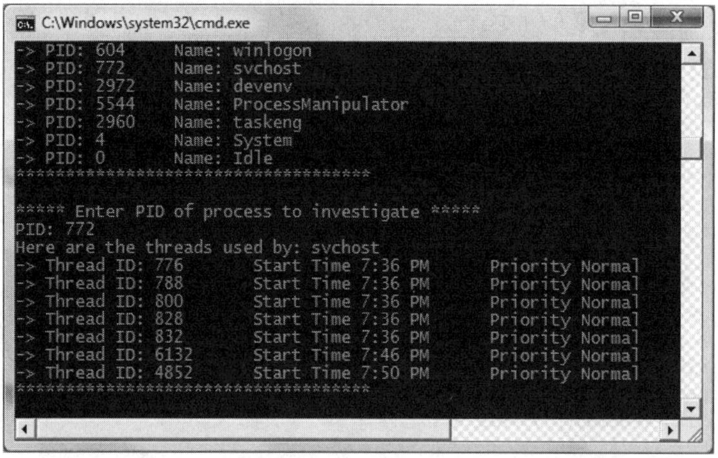

Figure 17-4. *Investigating threads in a process*

The ProcessThread type has additional members beyond Id, StartTime, and PriorityLevel. Table 17-3 documents some members of interest.

Table 17-3. *Select Members of the* ProcessThread *Type*

Member	Meaning in Life
CurrentPriority	Gets the current priority of the thread
Id	Gets the unique identifier of the thread
PriorityLevel	Gets or sets the priority level of the thread
StartTime	Gets the time that the operating system started the thread
ThreadState	Gets the current state of this thread
TotalProcessorTime	Gets the total amount of time that this thread has spent using the processor
WaitReason	Gets the reason that the thread is waiting

Before you read any further, be very aware that the ProcessThread type is *not* the entity used to create, suspend, or kill threads under the .NET platform. Rather, ProcessThread is a vehicle used to obtain diagnostic information for the active Win32 threads within a running process.

Investigating a Process's Module Set

Next up, let's check out how to iterate over the number of loaded *modules* that are hosted within a given process. Recall that a *module* is a generic name used to describe a given *.dll (or the *.exe itself) that is hosted by a specific process. When you access the ProcessModuleCollection via the Process.Modules property, you are able to enumerate over *all modules* hosted within a process: .NET-based, COM-based, or traditional C-based libraries. Ponder the following additional helper function that will enumerate the modules in a specific process based on the PID:

```
Public Sub EnumModsForPid(ByVal pID As Integer)
  Dim theProc As Process
  Try
    theProc = Process.GetProcessById(pID)
```

```
  Catch
    Console.WriteLine("-> Sorry...bad PID!")
    Console.WriteLine("************************************")
    Console.WriteLine()
    Return
  End Try
  Console.WriteLine("Here are the loaded modules for: {0}", theProc.ProcessName)
  Try
    Dim theMods As ProcessModuleCollection = theProc.Modules
    For Each pm As ProcessModule In theMods
      Dim info As String = String.Format("-> Mod Name: {0}", pm.ModuleName)
      Console.WriteLine(info)
    Next
    Console.WriteLine("************************************")
    Console.WriteLine()
  Catch
    Console.WriteLine("No mods!")
  End Try
End Sub
```

To see some possible output, let's check out the loaded modules for the process hosting the current Console Application (ProcessManipulator). To do so, run the application, identify the PID assigned to `ProcessManipulator.exe`, and pass this value to the `EnumModsForPid()` method (be sure to update your `Main()` method accordingly). Once you do, you may be surprised to see the list of `*.dlls` used for a simple console application. Figure 17-5 shows a test run (your output may vary based on which version of the Windows OS you happen to be running).

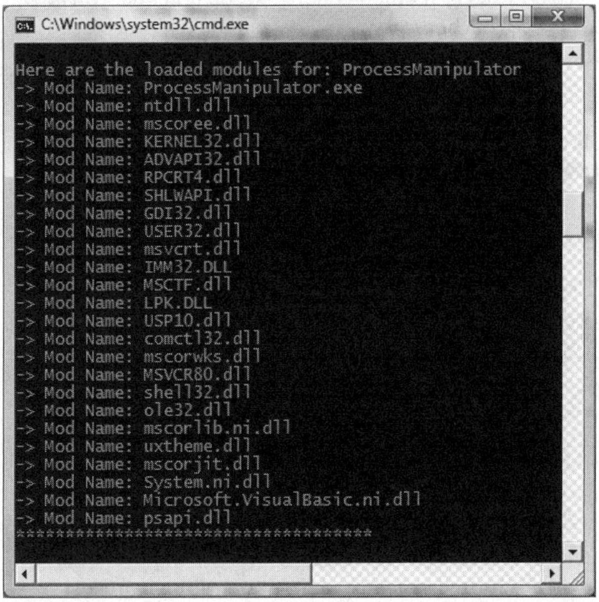

Figure 17-5. *Enumerating the threads within a running process*

Starting and Stopping Processes Programmatically

The final aspects of the System.Diagnostics.Process class examined here are the Start() and Kill() methods. As you can gather by their names, these members provide a way to programmatically launch and terminate a process, respectively. For example, consider the following StartAndKillProcess() method:

```
Public Sub StartAndKillProcess()
  ' Launch Internet Explorer.
  Console.Write("--> Hit a key to launch IE")
  Console.ReadLine()
  Dim ieProc As Process = Process.Start("IExplore.exe", "www.intertech.com")
  Console.Write("--> Hit a key to kill {0}...", ieProc.ProcessName)
  Console.ReadLine()

  ' Kill the IExplorer.exe process.
  Try
    ieProc.Kill()
  Catch  ' In case the user already killed it...
  End Try
End Sub
```

The shared Process.Start() method has been overloaded a few times, however. At minimum, you will need to specify the application name of the process you wish to launch (such as IExplore.exe). This example makes use of a variation of the Start() method that allows you to specify any additional arguments to pass into the program's entry point (i.e., the Main() method), which in this case is the URL to navigate to upon startup.

Regardless of which version of the Process.Start() method you invoke, do note that you are returned a reference to the newly activated process. When you wish to terminate the process, simply call the instance-level Kill() method.

■ **Note** The Start() method also allows you to pass in a System.Diagnostics.ProcessStartInfo type to specify additional bits of information regarding how a given process should come to life. See the .NET Framework 3.5 SDK documentation for full details.

■ **Source Code** The ProcessManipulator application is included under the Chapter 17 subdirectory.

Understanding .NET Application Domains

Now that you understand the role of Win32 processes and how to interact with them from managed code, we are in good position to investigate the concept of a .NET application domain. Under the .NET platform, executables are not hosted directly within a process (as is the case in traditional Win32 applications). Rather, a .NET executable is hosted by a logical partition within a process termed an application domain, or AppDomain. A single process may contain multiple application domains, each of which is capable of hosting a .NET application. This additional subdivision of a traditional Win32 process offers several benefits, some of which are as follows:

- AppDomains are a key aspect of the OS-neutral nature of the .NET platform, given that this logical division abstracts away the differences in how an underlying OS represents a loaded executable.
- AppDomains are far less expensive in terms of processing power and memory than a full-blown process. Thus, the CLR is able to load and unload application domains much quicker than a formal process.
- AppDomains provide a deeper level of isolation for hosting a loaded application. If one AppDomain within a process fails, the remaining AppDomains remain functional.

As suggested in the previous hit list, a single process can host any number of AppDomains, each of which is fully and completely isolated from other AppDomains within this process (or any other process). Given this factoid, be very aware that an application running in one AppDomain is unable to obtain data of any kind within another AppDomain unless it makes use of a distributed programming protocol (such as the .NET remoting layer and the Windows Communication Foundation API).

While a single process *may* host multiple AppDomains, this is not always the case. At the very least, an OS process will host what is termed the *default application domain*. This specific application domain is automatically created by the CLR at the time the process launches. After this point, the CLR creates additional application domains on an as-needed basis.

If the need should arise (which it most likely *will not* for the majority of your .NET endeavors), you are also able to programmatically create application domains at runtime within a given process using various methods of the `System.AppDomain` class. This class is also useful for low-level control of application domains. Key members of this class are shown in Table 17-4.

Table 17-4. *Select Members of* `AppDomain`

Member	Meaning in Life
`BaseDirectory`	This property returns the base directory used to probe for dependent assemblies.
`CreateDomain()`	This shared method creates a new AppDomain in the current process. Understand that the CLR will create new application domains as necessary, and thus the chance of you absolutely needing to call this member is slim to none.
`CreateInstance()`	This method creates an instance of a specified type defined in a specified assembly file.
`ExecuteAssembly()`	This method executes an assembly within an application domain, given its file name.
`GetAssemblies()`	This method gets the set of .NET assemblies that have been loaded into this application domain (COM-based and other unmanaged binaries are ignored).
`Load()`	This method is used to dynamically load an assembly into the current application domain.
`Unload()`	This is another shared method that allows you to unload a specified AppDomain within a given process.

In addition, the `AppDomain` type also defines a small set of events that correspond to various aspects of an application domain's life cycle, as shown in Table 17-5.

Table 17-5. *Events of the* `AppDomain` *Type*

Event	Meaning in Life
`AssemblyLoad`	Occurs when an assembly is loaded
`AssemblyResolve`	Occurs when the resolution of an assembly fails
`DomainUnload`	Occurs when an AppDomain is about to be unloaded
`ProcessExit`	Occurs on the default application domain when the default application domain's parent process exits
`ResourceResolve`	Occurs when the resolution of a resource fails
`TypeResolve`	Occurs when the resolution of a type fails
`UnhandledException`	Occurs when an exception is not caught by an event handler

Enumerating a Process's AppDomains

To illustrate how to interact with .NET application domains programmatically, assume you have a new VB 2008 Console Application named AppDomainManipulator that defines a method named `PrintAllAssembliesInAppDomain()`. This method makes use of `AppDomain.GetAssemblies()` to obtain a list of all .NET assemblies hosted within the application domain in question.

This list is represented by an array of `System.Reflection.Assembly` types, and thus you are required to import the `System.Reflection` namespace (see Chapter 16). Once you acquire the assembly array, you iterate over the array and print out the friendly name and version of each module:

```
Public Sub PrintAllAssembliesInAppDomain(ByVal ad As AppDomain)
  Dim loadedAssemblies As Assembly() = ad.GetAssemblies()
  Console.WriteLine("***** Here are the assemblies loaded in {0} *****", _
    ad.FriendlyName)

  ' Remember! We need to import System.Reflection to use
  ' the Assembly type.
  For Each a As Assembly In loadedAssemblies
    Console.WriteLine("-> Name: {0}", a.GetName.Name)
    Console.WriteLine("-> Version: {0}", a.GetName.Version)
  Next
End Sub
```

Now let's update the `Main()` method to obtain a reference to the current application domain before invoking `PrintAllAssembliesInAppDomain()`, using the `AppDomain.CurrentDomain` property. To make things a bit more interesting, notice that the `Main()` method launches a Windows Forms message box to force the CLR to load the `System.Windows.Forms.dll` (and indirectly the `System.Drawing.dll` and `System.dll` assemblies). Assuming you have set a reference to `System.Windows.Forms.dll` and imported the `System.Windows.Forms` namespace, implement `Main()` as follows:

```
Sub Main()
  Console.WriteLine("***** The Amazing AppDomain app *****" & vbLf)

  ' Get info for current AppDomain.
  Dim defaultAD As AppDomain = AppDomain.CurrentDomain()
  MessageBox.Show("Hello")
  PrintAllAssembliesInAppDomain(defaultAD)
  Console.ReadLine()
End Sub
```

Figure 17-6 shows the output (your version numbers may differ).

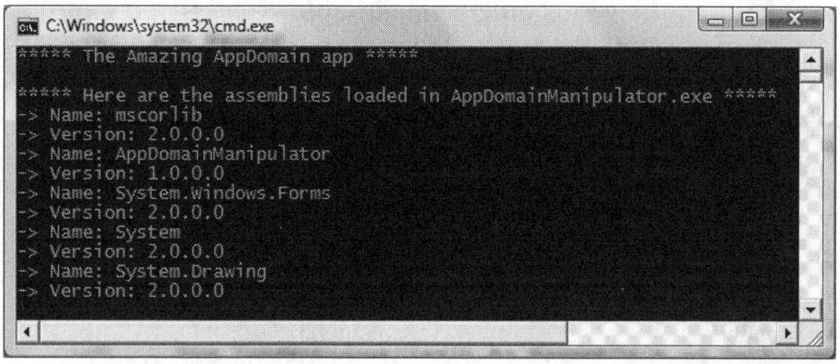

Figure 17-6. *Enumerating assemblies within the current application domain*

Programmatically Creating New AppDomains

Recall that a single process is capable of hosting multiple AppDomains. While it is true that you will seldom (if ever) need to manually create AppDomains in code, you are able to do so via the shared `CreateDomain()` method. As you would guess, `AppDomain.CreateDomain()` has been overloaded a number of times. At minimum, you will specify the friendly name of the new application domain, as shown here:

```
Sub Main()
...
  ' Programmatically make a new app domain.
  Dim anotherAD As AppDomain = AppDomain.CreateDomain("SecondAppDomain")
  PrintAllAssembliesInAppDomain(anotherAD)
  Console.ReadLine()
End Sub
```

Now, if you run the application again, notice that the `System.Windows.Forms.dll`, `System.Drawing.dll`, and `System.dll` assemblies are only loaded within the default application domain, as shown in Figure 17-7. This may seem counterintuitive if you have a background in traditional unmanaged Win32 (as you might suspect, both application domains have access to the same assembly set). Recall, however, that an assembly loads into an *application domain*, not directly into the process itself.

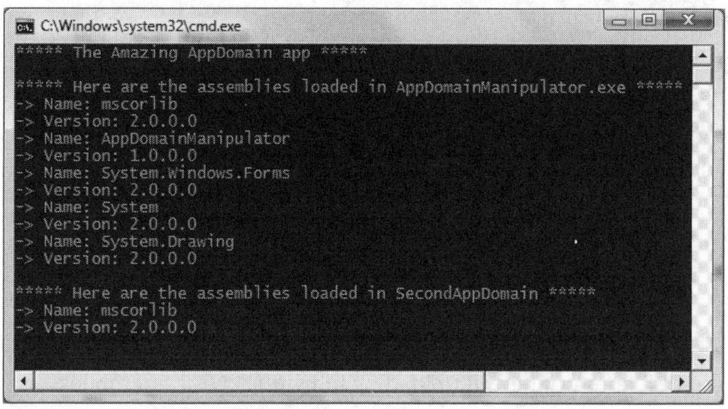

Figure 17-7. *A single process with two application domains*

Next, notice how the SecondAppDomain application domain automatically contains its own copy of `mscorlib.dll`, as this key assembly is automatically loaded by the CLR for each and every application domain. This begs the question, "How can I programmatically load an assembly into an application domain?" Answer: with the `AppDomain.Load()` method (or, alternatively, `AppDomain.ExecuteAssembly()` to load and execute the `Main()` method of an `*.exe` assembly).

Assuming you have copied `CarLibrary.dll` (which you created in Chapter 15) to the application directory of `AppDomainManipulator.exe`, you may load `CarLibrary.dll` into the SecondAppDomain AppDomain like so:

```
Sub Main()
...
  ' Programmatically make a new AppDomain.
  Dim anotherAD As AppDomain = AppDomain.CreateDomain("MySecondAppDomain")

  ' Load CarLibrary.dll into this new AppDomain.
  anotherAD.Load("CarLibrary")
  PrintAllAssembliesInAppDomain(anotherAD)
  Console.ReadLine()
End Sub
```

To solidify the relationship between processes, application domains, and assemblies, Figure 17-8 diagrams the internal composition of the `AppDomainManipulator.exe` process just constructed.

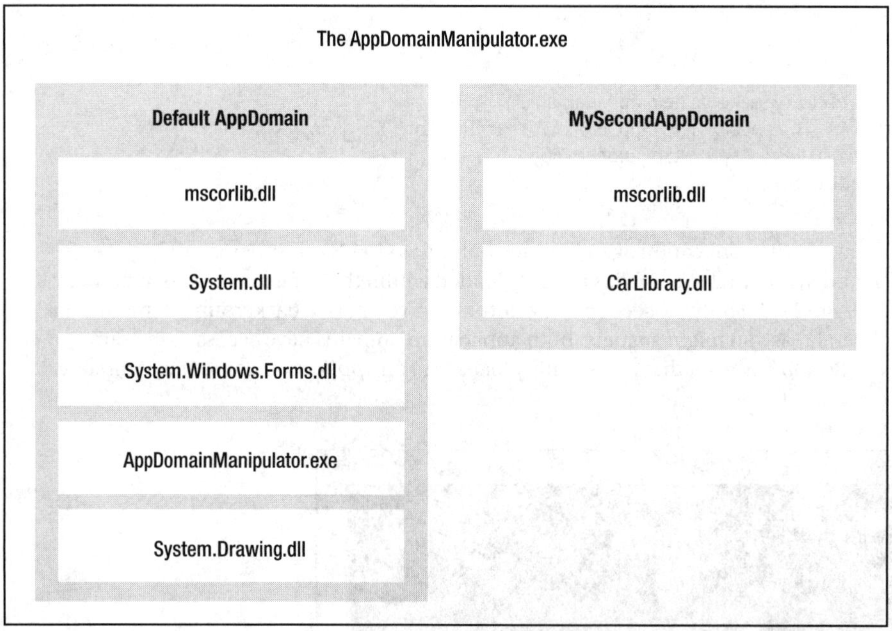

Figure 17-8. *The* `AppDomainManipulator.exe` *process under the hood*

Programmatically Unloading AppDomains

It is important to point out that the CLR does not permit unloading individual .NET assemblies. However, using the `AppDomain.Unload()` method, you are able to selectively unload a given application domain from its hosting process. When you do so, the application domain will unload each assembly in turn.

Recall that the AppDomain type defines a small set of events, one of which is DomainUnload. This event is fired when a (nondefault) AppDomain is unloaded from the containing process. Another event of interest is the ProcessExit event, which is fired when the default application domain is unloaded from the process (which obviously entails the termination of the process itself). Thus, if you wish to programmatically unload anotherAD from the AppDomainManipulator.exe process and be notified when the associated application domain is torn down, you are able to write the following event logic:

```
Sub Main()
...
  ' Hook into DomainUnload event.
  AddHandler anotherAD.DomainUnload, AddressOf anotherAD_DomainUnload

  ' Now unload anotherAD.
  AppDomain.Unload(anotherAD)
  Console.ReadLine()
End Sub
```

Notice that the DomainUnload event works in conjunction with the System.EventHandler delegate, and therefore the format of anotherAD_DomainUnload() takes the following arguments:

```
Public Sub anotherAD_DomainUnload(ByVal sender As Object, ByVal e As EventArgs)
  Console.WriteLine("***** Unloaded anotherAD! *****")
End Sub
```

If you wish to be notified when the default AppDomain is unloaded, modify your Main() method to handle the ProcessEvent event of the default application domain:

```
Sub Main()
...
  ' Hook into DomainUnload event.
  AddHandler anotherAD.DomainUnload, AddressOf anotherAD_DomainUnload
  AppDomain.Unload(anotherAD)

  ' Hook into ProcessExit.
  AddHandler defaultAD.ProcessExit, AddressOf defaultAD_ProcessExit
  Console.ReadLine()
End Sub
```

and define an appropriate event handler:

```
Private Sub defaultAD_ProcessExit(ByVal sender As Object, ByVal e As EventArgs)
  Console.WriteLine("***** Unloaded defaultAD! *****")
End Sub
```

Source Code The AppDomainManipulator project is included under the Chapter 17 subdirectory.

Understanding Object Context Boundaries

As you have just seen, AppDomains are logical partitions within a process used to host .NET assemblies. On a related note, a given application domain may be further subdivided into numerous *context boundaries*. In a nutshell, a .NET context provides a way for a single AppDomain to establish a "specific home" for a given object.

Using context, the CLR is able to ensure that objects that have special runtime requirements are handled in an appropriate and consistent manner by intercepting method invocations into and out of a given context. This layer of interception allows the CLR to adjust the current method invocation to conform to the contextual settings of a given object. For example, if you define a VB class type that requires automatic thread safety (using the `<Synchronization()>` attribute), the CLR will create a "synchronized context" to host the object.

Just as a process defines a default AppDomain, every application domain has a default context. This default context (sometimes referred to as *context 0*, given that it is always the first context created within an application domain) is used to group together .NET objects that have no specific or unique contextual needs. As you may expect, a vast majority of .NET objects are loaded into context 0. If the CLR determines a newly created object has special needs, a new context boundary is created within the hosting application domain. Figure 17-9 illustrates the process/AppDomain/context relationship.

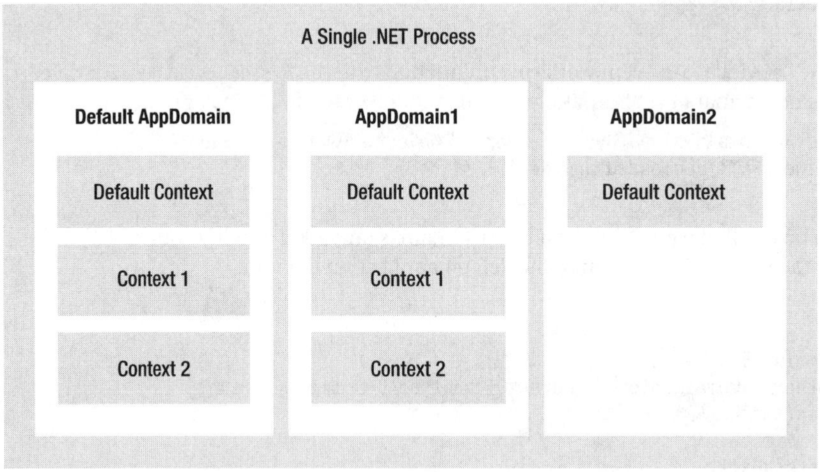

Figure 17-9. *Processes, application domains, and context boundaries*

Context-Agile and Context-Bound Types

.NET types that do not demand any special contextual treatment are termed *context-agile* objects. These objects can be accessed from anywhere within the hosting AppDomain without interfering with the object's runtime requirements. Building context-agile objects is a no-brainer, given that you simply do nothing (specifically, you do not adorn the type with any contextual attributes and do not derive from the `System.ContextBoundObject` base class):

```
' A context-agile object is loaded into context 0.
Public Class SportsCar
End Class
```

On the other hand, objects that do demand contextual allocation are termed *context-bound* objects, and they must derive from the `System.ContextBoundObject` base class. This base class solidifies the fact that the object in question can function appropriately only within the context in which it was created. Given the role of .NET context, it should stand to reason that if a context-bound object were to somehow end up in an incompatible context, bad things would be guaranteed to occur at the most inopportune times.

In addition to deriving from System.ContextBoundObject, a context-sensitive type will also be adorned by a special category of .NET attributes termed (not surprisingly) context attributes. All context attributes derive from the System.Runtime.Remoting.Contexts.ContextAttribute base class.

Given that the ContextAttribute class is not sealed, it is possible for you to build your own custom contextual attribute (simply derive from ContextAttribute and override the necessary virtual methods). Once you have done so, you are able to build a custom piece of software that can respond to the contextual settings. Do be aware that the need to create custom contexts is very slim for a vast majority of your .NET programming assignments, and would only be useful for hooking into lower-level aspects of the .NET runtime environment.

■ **Note** This book doesn't dive into the details of building custom object contexts; however, if you are interested in learning more, check out *Applied .NET Attributes* (Apress, 2003).

Defining a Context-Bound Object

Assume that you wish to define a class (SportsCarTS) that is automatically thread safe in nature, even though you have not hard-coded thread synchronization logic within the member implementations. To do so, derive from ContextBoundObject and apply the <Synchronization()> attribute as follows:

```
Imports System.Runtime.Remoting.Contexts

' This context-bound type will only be loaded into a
' synchronized (hence thread-safe) context.
<Synchronization()> _
Public Class SportsCarTS
  Inherits ContextBoundObject
End Class
```

Types that are attributed with the <Synchronization()> attribute are loaded into a thread-safe context. Given the special contextual needs of the SportsCarTS class type, imagine the problems that would occur if an allocated object were moved from a synchronized context into an unsynchronized context. The object is suddenly no longer thread safe and thus becomes a candidate for massive data corruption, as numerous threads are attempting to interact with the (now thread-volatile) reference object. To ensure the CLR does not move SportsCarTS objects outside of a synchronized context, simply derive from ContextBoundObject and apply the <Synchronization()> attribute.

Inspecting an Object's Context

Although very few of the applications you will write will need to programmatically interact with context, here is an illustrative example. Create a new Console Application named ContextManipulator. This application defines one context-agile class (SportsCar) and a single context-bound type (SportsCarTS, where TS stands for "thread safe"):

```
Imports System.Runtime.Remoting.Contexts   ' For Context type.
Imports System.Threading   ' For Thread type.

' SportsCar has no special contextual
' needs and will be loaded into the
```

```
' default context of the app domain.
Public Class SportsCar
  Public Sub New()
    ' Get context information and print out context ID.
    Dim ctx As Context = Thread.CurrentContext()
    Console.WriteLine("{0} object in context {1}", Me.ToString(), ctx.ContextID)
    For Each prop As IContextProperty In ctx.ContextProperties
      Console.WriteLine("-> Ctx Prop: {0}", prop.Name)
    Next
  End Sub
End Class

' SportsCarTS demands to be loaded in
' a synchronization context.
<Synchronization()> _
Public Class SportsCarTS
  Inherits ContextBoundObject

  Public Sub New()
    ' Get context information and print out context ID.
    Dim ctx As Context = Thread.CurrentContext()
    Console.WriteLine("{0} object in context {1}", Me.ToString(), ctx.ContextID)
    For Each prop As IContextProperty In ctx.ContextProperties
      Console.WriteLine("-> Ctx Prop: {0}", prop.Name)
    Next
  End Sub
End Class
```

Notice that each constructor obtains a Context type from the current thread of execution, via Thread.CurrentContext(). Using the Context object, you are able to print out statistics about the contextual boundary, such as its assigned ID, as well as a set of descriptors obtained via Context.ContextProperties. This property returns an array of objects implementing the IContextProperty interface. This interface exposes each descriptor through the Name property. Now, update Main() to allocate an instance of each class type:

```
Sub Main()
  Console.WriteLine("***** The Amazing Context Application *****")
  Console.WriteLine()

  ' Objects will display contextual info upon creation.
  Dim sport As New SportsCar()
  Console.WriteLine()

  Dim sport2 As New SportsCar()
  Console.WriteLine()

  Dim synchroSport As New SportsCarTS()
  Console.ReadLine()
End Sub
```

As the objects come to life, the class constructors will dump out various bits of context-centric information, as shown in Figure 17-10.

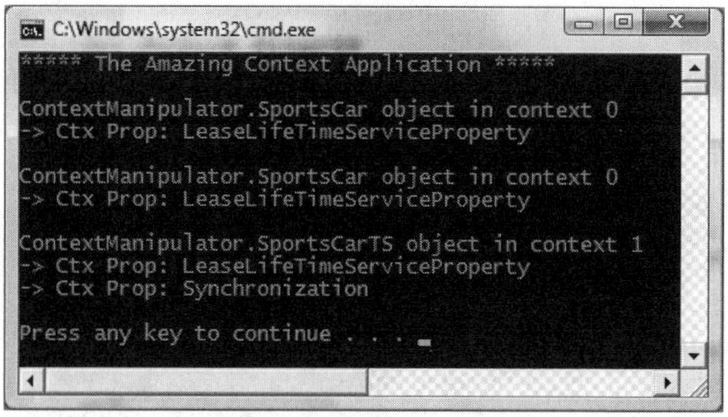

Figure 17-10. *Investigating an object's context*

Given that the SportsCar class has not been qualified with a context attribute, the CLR has allocated sport and sport2 into context 0 (i.e., the default context). However, the SportsCarTS object is loaded into a unique contextual boundary (which has been assigned a context ID of 1), given the fact that this context-bound type was adorned with the <Synchronization()> attribute and derives from ContextBoundObject.

Source Code The ContextManipulator project is included under the Chapter 17 subdirectory.

Summarizing Processes, AppDomains, and Context

At this point, you hopefully have a much better idea about how a .NET assembly is hosted by the CLR. To summarize the key points:

- A .NET process hosts one to many application domains. Each AppDomain is able to host any number of related .NET assemblies and may be independently loaded and unloaded by the CLR (or programmatically via the System.AppDomain type).
- A given AppDomain consists of one to many contexts. Using a context, the CLR is able to place a "special needs" object into a logical container, to ensure that its runtime requirements are honored.

If the previous pages have seemed to be a bit too low level for your liking, fear not. For the most part, the .NET runtime automatically deals with the details of processes, application domains, and contexts on your behalf. The good news, however, is that this information provides a solid foundation for understanding multithreaded programming under the .NET platform beginning in the next chapter.

Summary

The point of this chapter was to examine exactly how a .NET executable image is hosted by the .NET platform. As you have seen, the long-standing notion of a Win32 process has been altered under the hood to accommodate the needs of the CLR. A single process (which can be programmatically manipulated via the `System.Diagnostics.Process` type) is now composed of multiple application domains, which represent isolated and independent boundaries within a process.

As you have seen, a single process can host multiple application domains, each of which is capable of hosting and executing any number of related assemblies. Furthermore, a single application domain can contain any number of contextual boundaries. Using this additional level of type isolation, the CLR can ensure that special-need objects are handled correctly.

CHAPTER 18

Building Multithreaded Applications

In the previous chapter, you examined the relationship between processes, application domains, and contexts. This chapter builds on your newfound knowledge by examining how the Visual Basic language and the .NET platform allow you to build multithreaded applications and how to keep the shared resources of your application thread safe.

You'll begin by revisiting the .NET delegate type and come to understand its intrinsic support for asynchronous method invocations. As you'll see, this technique allows you to invoke a method on a secondary thread of execution automatically. Next, you'll investigate the types within the `System.Threading` namespace. Here you'll examine numerous types (`Thread`, `ThreadStart`, etc.) that allow you to easily create additional threads of execution. As well, you will come to understand the use of the `BackgroundWorker` type, which simplifies the task of performing background operations within the context of a GUI-based application.

As you may know, the complexity of multithreaded development isn't in the creation of threads, but in ensuring that your code base is well equipped to handle concurrent access to shared resources. Given this, the chapter also examines various synchronization primitives that the .NET Framework (and the Visual Basic programming language) provides.

The Process/AppDomain/Context/Thread Relationship

In the previous chapter, a *thread* was defined as a path of execution within an executable application. While many .NET applications can live happy and productive single-threaded lives, an assembly's primary thread (spawned by the CLR when `Main()` executes) may create secondary threads of execution to perform additional units of work. By implementing additional threads, you can build more responsive (but not necessarily faster executing) applications.

The `System.Threading` namespace contains various types that allow you to create multithreaded applications. The `Thread` class is perhaps the core type, as it represents a given thread. If you wish to programmatically obtain a reference to the thread currently executing a given member, simply call the shared `Thread.CurrentThread` property (which of course assumes you have imported `System.Threading`):

```
Private Sub ExtractExecutingThread()
  ' Get the thread currently
  ' executing this method.
  Dim currThread As Thread = Thread.CurrentThread
End Sub
```

Under the .NET platform, there is *not* a direct one-to-one correspondence between application domains and threads. In fact, a given AppDomain can have numerous threads executing within it at any given time. Furthermore, a particular thread is not confined to a single application domain during its lifetime. Threads are free to cross application domain boundaries as the Windows thread scheduler and CLR see fit.

Although active threads can be moved between AppDomain boundaries, a given thread can execute within only a single application domain at any point in time (in other words, it is impossible for a single thread to be doing work in more than one AppDomain). When you wish to programmatically gain access to the AppDomain that is hosting the current thread, call the shared `Thread.GetDomain()` method:

```
Private Sub ExtractAppDomainHostingThread()
  ' Obtain the AppDomain hosting the current thread.
  Dim ad As AppDomain = Thread.GetDomain()
End Sub
```

A single thread may also be moved into a particular context at any given time, and it may be relocated within a new context at the whim of the CLR. When you wish to obtain the current context a thread happens to be executing in, make use of the shared `Thread.CurrentContext` property (recall from Chapter 17 that the `Context` type is defined within `System.Runtime.Remoting.Contexts`):

```
Private Sub ExtractCurrentThreadContext()
  ' Obtain the context under which the
  ' current thread is operating
  Dim ctx As Context = Thread.CurrentContext
End Sub
```

Again, the CLR is the entity that is in charge of moving threads into (and out of) application domains and contexts. As a .NET developer, you can usually remain blissfully unaware where a given thread ends up (or exactly when it is placed into its new boundary). Nevertheless, you should be aware of the various ways of obtaining the underlying primitives.

The Problem of Concurrency and the Role of Thread Synchronization

One of the many "joys" (read: *painful aspects*) of multithreaded programming is that you have little control over how the underlying operating system or the CLR makes use of its threads. For example, if you craft a block of code that creates a new thread of execution, you cannot guarantee that the thread executes immediately. Rather, such code only instructs the OS to execute the thread as soon as possible (which is typically when the thread scheduler gets around to it).

Furthermore, given that threads can be moved between application and contextual boundaries as required by the CLR, you must be mindful of which aspects of your application are *thread volatile* (e.g., subject to multithreaded access) and which operations are *atomic* (thread-volatile operations are the dangerous ones!). To illustrate, assume a thread is executing a method of a specific object. Now assume that this thread is instructed by the thread scheduler to suspend its activity, in order to allow another thread to access the same method of the same object.

If the original thread was not completely finished with the current operation, the second incoming thread may be viewing an object in a partially modified state. At this point, the second thread is basically reading bogus data, which is sure to give way to extremely odd (and very hard to find) bugs, which are even harder to replicate and debug.

Atomic operations, on the other hand, are always safe in a multithreaded environment. Sadly, there are very few operations in the .NET base class libraries that are guaranteed to be atomic. Even the act of assigning a value to a member variable is not atomic! Unless the .NET Framework 3.5 SDK documentation specifically says an operation is atomic, you must assume it is thread volatile and take precautions.

At this point, it should be clear that multithreaded application domains are in themselves quite volatile, as numerous threads can operate on the shared functionality at (more or less) the same time. To protect an application's resources from possible corruption, .NET developers must make use of any number of threading primitives (such as locks, monitors, and the <Synchronization()> attribute) to control access to the data among the executing threads.

Although the .NET platform cannot make the difficulties of building robust multithreaded applications completely disappear, the process has been simplified considerably. Using types defined within the System.Threading namespace, you are able to spawn additional threads with minimal fuss and bother. Likewise, when it is time to lock down shared points of data, you will find additional types that provide the same functionality as the Win32 API threading primitives (using a much cleaner object model).

However, the System.Threading namespace is not the only way to build multithread .NET programs. During our examination of the .NET delegate (see Chapter 11), it was mentioned that all delegates have the ability to invoke members asynchronously. This is a *major* benefit of the .NET platform, given that one of the most common reasons a developer creates threads is for the purpose of invoking methods in a nonblocking (aka asynchronous) manner. Although you could make use of the System.Threading namespace to achieve a similar result, delegates make the whole process much easier.

A Brief Review of the .NET Delegate

Recall that the .NET delegate type is a type-safe, object-oriented function pointer. When you declare a .NET delegate, the VB 2008 compiler responds by building a sealed class that derives from System.MulticastDelegate (which in turn derives from System.Delegate). These base classes provide every delegate with the ability to maintain a list of method addresses, all of which may be invoked at a later time. Consider the BinaryOp delegate first defined in Chapter 11:

```
' A custom delegate type.
Public Delegate Function BinaryOp(ByVal x As Integer, _
  ByVal y As Integer) As Integer
```

Based on its definition, BinaryOp can point to any method taking two Integers as arguments and returning an Integer. Once compiled, the defining assembly now contains a full-blown class definition that is dynamically generated based on the delegate declaration. In the case of BinaryOp, this class definition looks more or less like the following:

```
NotInheritable Class BinaryOp
  Inherits System.MulticastDelegate

  Public Sub New(ByVal target As Object, ByVal functionAddress As System.UInt32)
  End Sub

  Public Function Invoke(ByVal x As Integer, ByVal y As Integer) As Integer
  End Sub

  Public Function BeginInvoke(ByVal x As Integer, ByVal y As Integer, _
    ByVal cb As AsyncCallback, ByVal state As Object) As IAsyncResult
  End Function

  Public Function EndInvoke(ByVal result As IAsyncResult) As Integer
  End Function
End Class
```

Recall that the generated Invoke() method is used to invoke the methods maintained by a delegate object in a synchronous manner. Therefore, the calling thread (such as the primary thread of the application) is forced to wait until the delegate invocation completes. Also recall that in VB 2008, the Invoke() method is called behind the scenes when you apply "normal" method invocation syntax. Consider the following program, which invokes the shared Add() method in a synchronous (aka blocking) manner:

```
' Need this for the Thread.Sleep() call.
Imports System.Threading

' Our custom delegate.
Public Delegate Function BinaryOp(ByVal x As Integer, _
  ByVal y As Integer) As Integer

Module Program
  Sub Main()
    Console.WriteLine("***** Synch Delegate Review *****")
    Console.WriteLine()

    ' Print out the ID of the executing thread.
    Console.WriteLine("Main() invoked on thread {0}.", _
      Thread.CurrentThread.ManagedThreadId)

    ' Invoke Add() in a synchronous manner.
    Dim b As BinaryOp = AddressOf Add
    Dim answer As Integer = b(10, 10)

    ' These lines will not execute until
    ' the Add() method has completed.
    Console.WriteLine("Doing more work in Main()!")
    Console.WriteLine("10 + 10 is {0}.", answer)
    Console.ReadLine()
  End Sub

  Function Add(ByVal x As Integer, ByVal y As Integer) As Integer
    ' Print out the ID of the executing thread.
    Console.WriteLine("Add() invoked on thread {0}.", _
      Thread.CurrentThread.ManagedThreadId)

    '  Pause to simulate a lengthy operation.
    Thread.Sleep(5000)
    Return x + y
  End Function
End Module
```

Notice first of all that this program is making use of the System.Threading namespace. Within the Add() method, you are invoking the shared Thread.Sleep() method to suspend the calling thread for (more or less) 5 seconds to simulate a lengthy task. Given that you are invoking the Add() method in a *synchronous* manner, the Main() method will not print out the result of the operation until the Add() method has completed (again, approximately 5 seconds after the call).

Next, note that the Main() method is obtaining access to the currently executing thread (via Thread.CurrentThread) and printing out its assigned ID. This same logic is repeated in the shared Add() method. As you might suspect, given that all the work in this application is performed exclusively by the primary thread, you find the same ID value displayed to the console, as shown in Figure 18-1.

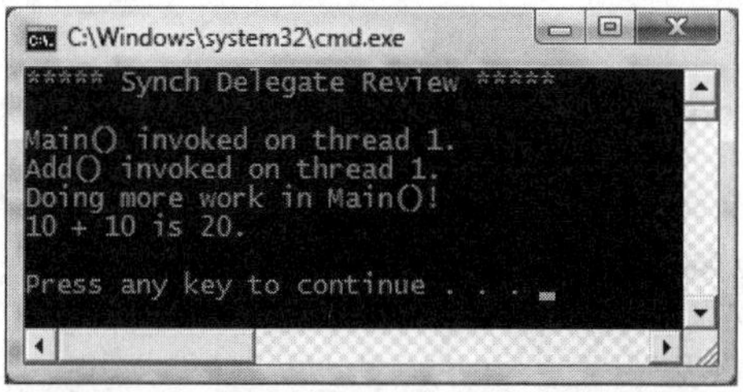

Figure 18-1. *Synchronous method invocations are "blocking" calls.*

When you run this program, you should notice that a 5-second delay takes place before you see the `Console.WriteLine()` logic execute. Although many (if not most) methods may be called synchronously without ill effect, .NET delegates can be instructed to call their methods asynchronously if necessary.

Source Code The SyncDelegate project is located under the Chapter 18 subdirectory.

The Asynchronous Nature of Delegates

If you are new to the topic of multithreading, you may wonder what exactly an *asynchronous* method invocation is all about. As you are no doubt fully aware, some programming operations take time. Although the previous `Add()` was purely illustrative in nature, imagine that you built a single-threaded application that is invoking a method on a remote object, performing a long-running database query, generating a custom report, or executing a lengthy file IO operation. While performing these operations, the application may appear to hang for quite some time. Until the task at hand has been processed, all other aspects of this program (such as menu activation, toolbar clicking, or console output) are unresponsive.

The question therefore is, how can you tell a delegate to invoke a method on a separate thread of execution to simulate numerous tasks performing "at the same time"? The good news is that every .NET delegate type is automatically equipped with this capability. The even better news is that you are *not* required to directly dive into the details of the `System.Threading` namespace to do so (although these entities can quite naturally work hand in hand).

The BeginInvoke() and EndInvoke() Methods

When the VB 2008 compiler processes the `Delegate` keyword, the dynamically generated class defines two methods named `BeginInvoke()` and `EndInvoke()`. Given our definition of the `BinaryOp` delegate, these methods are prototyped as follows:

```
NotInheritable Class BinaryOp
  Inherits System.MulticastDelegate
...
  ' Used to invoke a method asynchronously.
  Public Function BeginInvoke(ByVal x As Integer, ByVal y As Integer, _
    ByVal cb As AsyncCallback, ByVal state As Object) As IAsyncResult
  End Function
```

```
  ' Used to fetch the return value
  ' of the invoked method.
  Public Function EndInvoke(ByVal result As IAsyncResult) As Integer
  End Function
End Class
```

The first stack of parameters passed into BeginInvoke() will be based on the format of the VB 2008 delegate (two Integers in the case of BinaryOp). The final two arguments will always be System.AsyncCallback and System.Object. We'll examine the role of these parameters shortly; for the time being, though, we'll supply Nothing for each.

The System.IAsyncResult Interface

Also note that the BeginInvoke() method always returns an object implementing the IAsyncResult interface, while EndInvoke() requires an IAsyncResult-compatible type as its sole parameter. The IAsyncResult-compatible object returned from BeginInvoke() is basically a coupling mechanism that allows the calling thread to obtain the result of the asynchronous method invocation at a later time via EndInvoke(). The IAsyncResult interface (defined in the System namespace) is defined as follows:

```
Public Interface IAsyncResult
  ReadOnly Property AsyncState() As Object
  ReadOnly Property AsyncWaitHandle() As WaitHandle
  ReadOnly Property CompletedSynchronously() As Boolean
  ReadOnly Property IsCompleted() As Boolean
End Interface
```

In the simplest case, you are able to avoid directly invoking these members. All you have to do is cache the IAsyncResult-compatible object returned by BeginInvoke() and pass it to EndInvoke() when you are ready to obtain the result of the function invocation. As you will see, you are able to invoke the members of an IAsyncResult-compatible object when you wish to become "more involved" with the process of fetching the method's return value.

■ **Note** If you asynchronously invoke a method that does not provide a return value (in other words, a VB subroutine), you can simply "fire and forget." In such cases, you will never need to cache the IAsyncResult-compatible object or call EndInvoke() in the first place (as there is no return value to retrieve).

Invoking a Method Asynchronously

To instruct the BinaryOp delegate to invoke Add() asynchronously, you can update the previous Main() method as follows:

```
Sub Main()
  Console.WriteLine("***** Async Delegate Invocation *****")
  Console.WriteLine()

  ' Print out the ID of the executing thread.
  Console.WriteLine("Main() invoked on thread {0}.", _
    Thread.CurrentThread.ManagedThreadId)
```

```
    ' Invoke Add() on a secondary thread.
    Dim b As BinaryOp = New BinaryOp(AddressOf Add)
    Dim itfAR As IAsyncResult = b.BeginInvoke(10, 10, Nothing, Nothing)

    ' Do other work on primary thread...
    Console.WriteLine("Doing more work in Main()!")

    ' Obtain the result of the Add()
    ' method when ready.
    Dim answer As Integer = b.EndInvoke(itfAR)
    Console.WriteLine("10 + 10 is {0}.", answer)
    Console.ReadLine()
  End Sub
```

If you run this application, you will find that two unique IDs are displayed, given that there are in fact two threads working within the current AppDomain (see Figure 18-2).

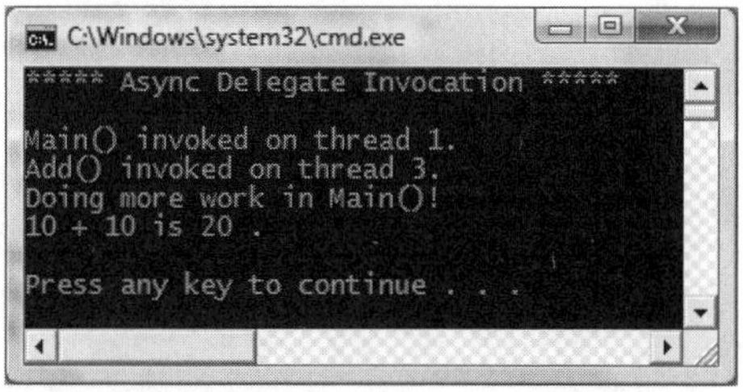

Figure 18-2. *Methods invoked asynchronously are done so on a unique thread.*

In addition to the unique ID values, you will also notice upon running the application that the "Doing more work in Main()!" message displays immediately, while the secondary thread is occupied attending to its business.

Synchronizing the Calling Thread

If you take a moment to ponder the current implementation of `Main()`, you might have realized that the time span between calling `BeginInvoke()` and `EndInvoke()` is clearly less than 5 seconds. Therefore, once "Doing more work in Main()!" prints to the console, the calling thread is now blocked and waiting for the secondary thread to complete before being able to obtain the result of the `Add()` method. Therefore, you are effectively making yet another *synchronous call* (in a very roundabout fashion!):

```
Sub Main()
...
  Dim b As BinaryOp = New BinaryOp(Add)
  Dim itfAR As IAsyncResult = b.BeginInvoke(10, 10, Nothing, Nothing)

  ' This call takes far less than 5 seconds!
  Console.WriteLine("Doing more work in Main()!")

  ' The calling thread is now blocked until
  ' EndInvoke() completes.
  Dim answer As Integer = b.EndInvoke(itfAR)
...
End Sub
```

Obviously, asynchronous delegates would lose their appeal if the calling thread had the potential of being blocked under various circumstances. To allow the calling thread to discover whether the asynchronously invoked method has completed its work, the IAsyncResult interface provides the IsCompleted property.

Using this member, the calling thread is able to determine whether the asynchronous call has indeed completed before calling EndInvoke(). If the method has not completed, IsCompleted returns False, and the calling thread is free to carry on its work. If IsCompleted returns True, the calling thread is able to obtain the result in the "least blocking manner" possible. Ponder the following update to the Main() method:

```
Sub Main()
...
  Dim b As BinaryOp = New BinaryOp(AddressOf Add)
  Dim itfAR As IAsyncResult = b.BeginInvoke(10, 10, Nothing, Nothing)

  ' This message will keep printing until
  ' the Add() method is finished.
  While Not itfAR.IsCompleted
    Console.WriteLine("Doing more work in Main()!")
    ' Just so we don't see hundreds of printouts.
    Thread.Sleep(1000)
  End While

  ' Now we know the Add() method is complete.
  Dim answer As Integer = b.EndInvoke(itfAR)
...
End Sub
```

Here, you enter a loop that will continue processing the Console.WriteLine() statement until the secondary thread has completed. Once this has occurred, you can obtain the result of the Add() method knowing full well the method has indeed completed.

In addition to the IsCompleted property, the IAsyncResult interface provides the AsyncWaitHandle property for more flexible waiting logic. This property returns an instance of the WaitHandle type, which exposes a method named WaitOne(). The benefit of WaitHandle.WaitOne() is that you can specify the maximum wait time. If the specified amount of time is exceeded, WaitOne() returns False. Ponder the following updated While loop:

```
While Not itfAR.AsyncWaitHandle.WaitOne(2000, true)
  Console.WriteLine("Doing more work in Main()!")
  ' Just so we don't see dozens of printouts!
  Thread.Sleep(1000)
End While
```

While these properties of IAsyncResult do provide a way to synchronize the calling thread, they are not the most efficient approach. In many ways, the IsCompleted property is much like a really annoying manager (or classmate) who is constantly asking, "Are you done yet?" Thankfully, delegates provide a number of additional (and more effective) techniques to obtain the result of a method that has been called asynchronously.

■ **Source Code** The AsyncDelegate project is located under the Chapter 18 subdirectory.

The Role of the AsyncCallback Delegate

Rather than polling a delegate to determine whether an asynchronous method has completed, it would be ideal to have the delegate inform the calling thread when the task is finished. When you wish to enable this behavior, you will need to supply an instance of the System.AsyncCallback delegate as a parameter to BeginInvoke(), which up until this point has been Nothing. However, when you do supply an AsyncCallback object, the delegate will call the specified method automatically when the asynchronous call has completed.

Like any delegate, AsyncCallback can only invoke methods that match a specific pattern, which in this case is a method taking IAsyncResult as the sole parameter and returning nothing:

```
Sub MyAsyncCallbackMethod(ByVal itfAR As IAsyncResult)
```

Assume you have another application making use of the BinaryOp delegate. This time, however, you will not poll the delegate to determine whether the Add() method has completed. Rather, you will define a shared method named AddComplete() to receive the notification that the asynchronous invocation is finished:

```
Imports System.Threading

' Our delegate.
Public Delegate Function BinaryOp(ByVal x As Integer, _
  ByVal y As Integer) As Integer

Module Program
  Sub Main()
    Console.WriteLine("*****  AsyncCallbackDelegate Example *****")
    Console.WriteLine()

    Console.WriteLine("Main() invoked on thread {0}.", _
      Thread.CurrentThread.ManagedThreadId)
    Dim b As BinaryOp = New BinaryOp(AddressOf Add)
    Dim itfAR As IAsyncResult = _
      b.BeginInvoke(10, 10, New AsyncCallback(AddressOf AddComplete), _
                    Nothing)

    ' Other work performed here...

    Console.ReadLine()
  End Sub

  Sub AddComplete(ByVal itfAR As IAsyncResult)
    Console.WriteLine("AddComplete() invoked on thread {0}.", _
      Thread.CurrentThread.ManagedThreadId)
    Console.WriteLine("Your addition is complete")
  End Sub

  Function Add(ByVal x As Integer, ByVal y As Integer) As Integer
    Console.WriteLine("Add() invoked on thread {0}.", _
      Thread.CurrentThread.ManagedThreadId)
    Thread.Sleep(5000)
    Return x + y
  End Function
End Module
```

Again, the AddComplete() method will be invoked by the AsyncCallback delegate when the Add() method has completed. If you run this program, you can confirm that the secondary thread is the thread invoking the AddComplete() callback, as shown in Figure 18-3.

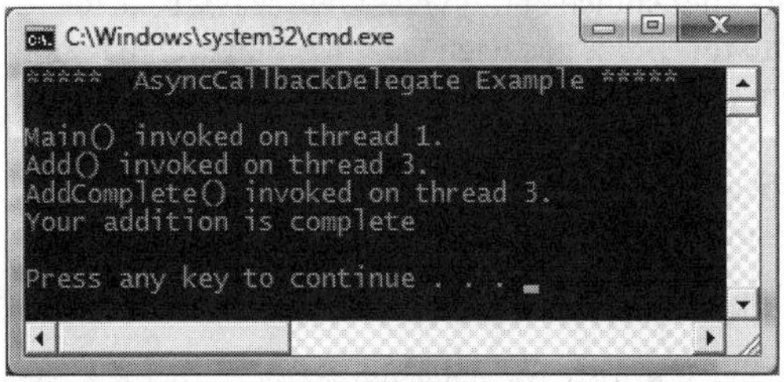

Figure 18-3. *The* AsyncCallback *delegate in action*

The Role of the AsyncResult Class

You may have noticed in the current example that the Main() method is not caching the IAsyncResult type returned from BeginInvoke() and is no longer calling EndInvoke(). The reason is that the target of the AsyncCallback delegate (AddComplete() in this example) does not have access to the original BinaryOp delegate created in the scope of Main(). While you could simply declare the BinaryOp variable as a shared member of the module to allow both methods to access the same object, a more elegant solution is to use the incoming IAsyncResult parameter.

The incoming IAsyncResult parameter passed into the target of the AsyncCallback delegate is actually an instance of the AsyncResult class (note the lack of an I prefix, which identifies interface types) defined in the System.Runtime.Remoting.Messaging namespace. The shared AsyncDelegate property returns a reference to the original asynchronous delegate that was created elsewhere. Therefore, if you wish to obtain a reference to the BinaryOp delegate object allocated within Main(), simply cast the System.Object returned by the AsyncDelegate property into type BinaryOp. At this point, you can trigger EndInvoke() as expected:

```
' Don't forget to import the
' System.Runtime.Remoting.Messaging namespace!
Sub AddComplete(ByVal itfAR As IAsyncResult)
  Console.WriteLine("AddComplete() invoked on thread {0}.", _
    Thread.CurrentThread.ManagedThreadId)
  Console.WriteLine("Your addition is complete")

  ' Now get the result.
  Dim ar As AsyncResult = CType(itfAR, AsyncResult)
  Dim b As BinaryOp = CType(ar.AsyncDelegate, BinaryOp)
  Console.WriteLine("10 + 10 is {0}.", b.EndInvoke(itfAR))
End Sub
```

Passing and Receiving Custom State Data

The final aspect of asynchronous delegates we need to address is the final argument to the BeginInvoke() method (which has been Nothing up to this point). This parameter allows you to pass additional state information to the callback method from the primary thread. Because this argument is prototyped as a System.Object, you can pass in any type of data whatsoever, as long as the callback method knows what to expect. Assume for the sake of demonstration that the primary thread wishes to pass in a custom text message to the AddComplete() method:

```
Sub Main()
...
  Dim b As BinaryOp = New BinaryOp(AddressOf Add)
  Dim itfAR As IAsyncResult = _
    b.BeginInvoke(10, 10, New AsyncCallback(AddressOf AddComplete), _
    "Main() thanks you for adding these numbers.")

  ' Other work performed here...

  Console.ReadLine()
End Sub
```

To obtain this data within the scope of AddComplete(), make use of the AsyncState property of the incoming IAsyncResult parameter:

```
Sub AddComplete(ByVal itfAR As IAsyncResult)
...
  ' Retrieve the informational object and cast it to String
  Dim msg As String = CType(itfAR.AsyncState, String)
  Console.WriteLine(msg)
End Sub
```

Figure 18-4 shows the output of the current application.

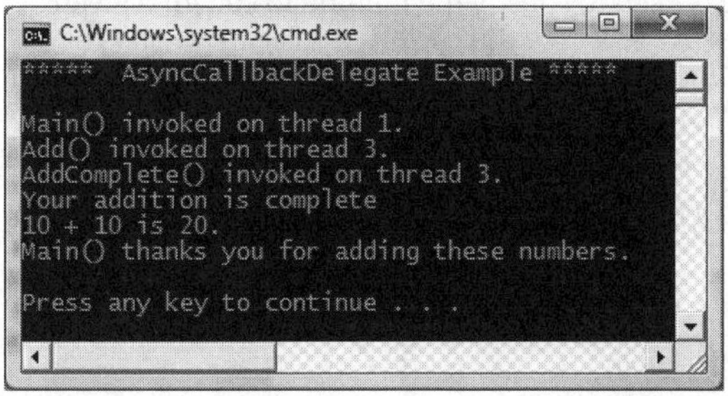

Figure 18-4. *Passing and receiving custom state data*

Cool! Now that you understand how a .NET delegate can be used to automatically spin off a secondary thread of execution to handle an asynchronous method invocation, let's turn our attention to interacting with threads directly using the System.Threading namespace.

■ Source Code The AsyncCallbackDelegate project is located under the Chapter 18 subdirectory.

The System.Threading Namespace

Under the .NET platform, the System.Threading namespace provides a number of types that enable the construction of multithreaded applications. In addition to providing types that allow you to interact with a particular CLR thread, this namespace defines types that allow access to the CLR-maintained thread pool, a simple (non-GUI-based) Timer class, and numerous types used to provide synchronized access to shared resources. Table 18-1 lists some of the core members of this namespace. (Be sure to consult the .NET Framework 3.5 SDK documentation for full details.)

Table 18-1. *Select Types of the* `System.Threading` *Namespace*

Type	Meaning in Life
`Interlocked`	This type provides atomic operations for variables that are shared by multiple threads.
`Monitor`	This type provides the synchronization of threading objects using locks and wait/signals. The VB 2008 `SyncLock` keyword makes use of a `Monitor` type under the hood.
`Mutex`	This synchronization primitive can be used for synchronization between application domain boundaries.
`ParameterizedThreadStart`	This delegate type allows a thread to call methods that take any number of arguments.
`Semaphore`	This type allows you to limit the number of threads that can access a resource, or a particular type of resource, concurrently.
`Thread`	This type represents a thread that executes within the CLR. Using this type, you are able to spawn additional threads in the originating AppDomain.
`ThreadPool`	This type allows you to interact with the CLR-maintained thread pool within a given process.
`ThreadPriority`	This enum represents a thread's priority level (`Highest`, `Normal`, etc.).
`ThreadStart`	This delegate type is used to specify the method to call for a given thread. Unlike the `ParameterizedThreadStart` delegate, targets of `ThreadStart` must match a fixed prototype.
`ThreadState`	This enum specifies the valid states a thread may take (`Running`, `Terminated`, etc.).
`Timer`	This type provides a mechanism for executing a method at specified intervals.
`TimerCallback`	This delegate type is used in conjunction with `Timer` types.

The System.Threading.Thread Class

The most primitive of all types in the `System.Threading` namespace is `Thread`. This class represents an object-oriented wrapper around a given path of execution within a particular AppDomain. This type also defines a number of methods (both shared and instance level) that allow you to create new threads within the current AppDomain, as well as to suspend, stop, and destroy a particular thread. Consider the list of core shared members in Table 18-2.

Table 18-2. *Key Shared Members of the* `Thread` *Type*

Shared Member	Meaning in Life
`CurrentContext`	This read-only property returns the context in which the thread is currently running.
`CurrentThread`	This read-only property returns a reference to the currently running thread.
`GetDomain()` `GetDomainID()`	These methods return a reference to the current AppDomain or the ID of this domain in which the current thread is running.
`ManagedThreadId`	This read-only property returns the assigned ID of the thread allocated by the CLR.
`Sleep()`	This method suspends the current thread for a specified time.

The Thread class also supports several instance-level members, some of which are shown in Table 18-3.

Table 18-3. *Select Instance-Level Members of the Thread Type*

Instance-Level Member	Meaning in Life
IsAlive	Returns a Boolean that indicates whether this thread has been started.
IsBackground	Gets or sets a value indicating whether or not this thread is a "background thread" (more details in just a moment).
Name	Allows you to establish a friendly text name of the thread.
Priority	Gets or sets the priority of a thread, which may be assigned a value from the ThreadPriority enumeration.
ThreadState	Gets the state of this thread, which may be assigned a value from the ThreadState enumeration.
Abort()	Instructs the CLR to terminate the thread as soon as possible.
Interrupt()	Interrupts (e.g., wakes) the current thread from a suitable wait period.
Join()	Blocks the calling thread until the specified thread (the one on which Join() is called) exits.
Resume()	Resumes a thread that has been previously suspended.
Start()	Instructs the CLR to execute the thread ASAP.
Suspend()	Suspends the thread. If the thread is already suspended, a call to Suspend() has no effect.

Obtaining Statistics About the Current Thread

Recall that the entry point of an executable assembly (i.e., the Main() method) runs on the primary thread of execution. To illustrate the basic use of the Thread type, assume you have a new Console Application named ThreadStats. As you know, the shared Thread.CurrentThread property retrieves a Thread object that represents the currently executing thread. Once you have obtained the current thread, you are able to print out various statistics:

```
' Be sure to import the System.Threading namespace.
Sub Main()
  Console.WriteLine("***** Primary Thread stats *****")
  Console.WriteLine()

  ' Obtain and name the current thread.
  Dim primaryThread As Thread = Thread.CurrentThread
  primaryThread.Name = "ThePrimaryThread"

  ' Show details of hosting AppDomain/Context.
  Console.WriteLine("Name of current AppDomain: {0}", _
    Thread.GetDomain().FriendlyName)
  Console.WriteLine("ID of current Context: {0}", _
    Thread.CurrentContext.ContextID)

  ' Print out some stats about this thread.
  Console.WriteLine("Thread Name: {0}", _
    primaryThread.Name)
  Console.WriteLine("Has thread started?: {0}", _
    primaryThread.IsAlive)
```

```
    Console.WriteLine("Priority Level: {0}", _
      primaryThread.Priority)
    Console.WriteLine("Thread State: {0}", _
      primaryThread.ThreadState)
    Console.ReadLine()
  End Sub
```

Figure 18-5 shows the output for the current application.

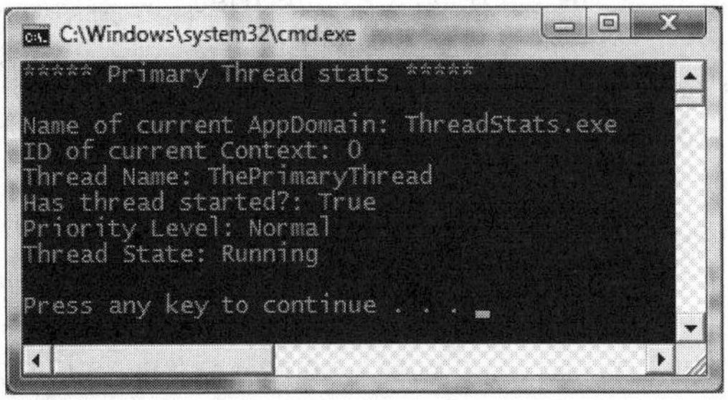

Figure 18-5. *Gathering thread statistics*

The Name Property

While this code is more or less self-explanatory, do notice that the `Thread` class supports a property called `Name`. If you do not set this value, `Name` will return an empty string. However, once you assign a friendly string moniker to a given `Thread` object, you can greatly simplify your debugging endeavors. If you are making use of Visual Studio 2008, you may access the Threads window during a debugging session (select Debug ➤ Windows ➤ Threads). As you can see from Figure 18-6, you can quickly identify the thread you wish to diagnose.

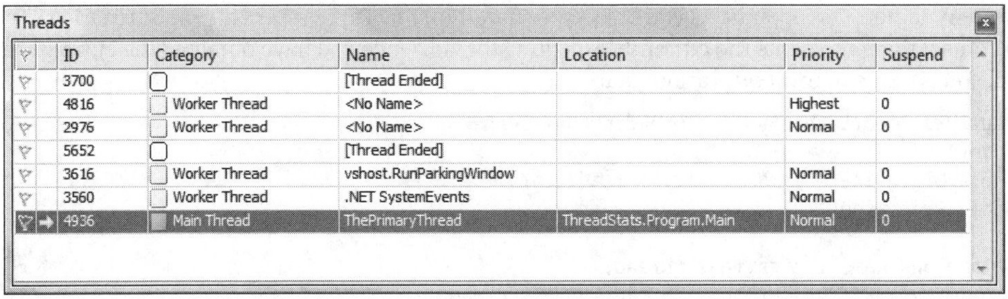

Figure 18-6. *Debugging a thread with Visual Studio 2008*

The Priority Property

Next, notice that the `Thread` type defines a property named `Priority`. By default, all threads have a priority level of `Normal`. However, you can change this at any point in the thread's lifetime using the `ThreadPriority` property and the related `System.Threading.ThreadPriority` enumeration:

```
Public Enum ThreadPriority
  AboveNormal
  BelowNormal
  Highest
```

```
  Lowest
  Normal     ' Default value.
End Enum
```

If you were to assign a thread's priority level to a value other than the default (ThreadPriority.Normal), understand that you would have little control over when the thread scheduler switches between threads. In reality, a thread's priority level offers a hint to the CLR regarding the importance of the thread's activity. Thus, a thread with the value ThreadPriority.Highest is not necessarily guaranteed to given the highest precedence. Again, if the thread scheduler is preoccupied with a given task (e.g., synchronizing an object, switching threads, or moving threads), the priority level will most likely be altered accordingly.

However, all things being equal, the CLR will read these values and instruct the thread scheduler how to best allocate time slices. All things still being equal, threads with an identical thread priority should each receive the same amount of time to perform their work.

In most cases, you will seldom (if ever) need to directly alter a thread's priority level. In theory, it is possible to jack up the priority level on a set of threads, thereby preventing lower-priority threads from executing at their required levels (so use caution).

■ **Source Code** The ThreadStats project is included under the Chapter 18 subdirectory.

Programmatically Creating Secondary Threads

When you wish to programmatically create additional threads to carry on some unit of work, you will follow a very predictable process:

1. Create a method to be the entry point for the new thread.
2. Create a new ParameterizedThreadStart (or ThreadStart) delegate, passing the address of the method defined in step 1 to the constructor.
3. Create a Thread object, passing the ParameterizedThreadStart/ThreadStart delegate as a constructor argument.
4. Establish any initial thread characteristics (name, priority, etc.).
5. Call the Thread.Start() method. This starts the thread at the method referenced by the delegate created in step 2 as soon as possible.

As stated in step 2, you may make use of two distinct delegate types to "point to" the method that the secondary thread will execute. The ThreadStart delegate has been part of the System.Threading namespace since .NET 1.0, and it can point to any subroutine that takes no arguments. This delegate can be helpful when the method is designed to simply run in the background without further interaction.

The obvious limitation of ThreadStart is that you are unable to pass in parameters for processing. As of .NET 2.0 onward, you are provided with the ParameterizedThreadStart delegate type, which allows a single parameter of type System.Object. Given that anything can be represented as a System.Object, you can pass in any number of parameters via a custom class or structure. Do note, however, that like ThreadStart, the ParameterizedThreadStart delegate can only point to.subroutines, not functions.

Working with the ThreadStart Delegate

To illustrate the process of building a multithreaded application (as well as to demonstrate the usefulness of doing so), assume you have a Console Application (SimpleMultiThreadApp) that allows the end user to choose whether the application will perform its duties using the single primary thread or split its workload using two separate threads of execution.

Assuming you have imported the `System.Threading` namespace via the VB 2008 `Imports` keyword, your first step is to define a type method to perform the work of the (possible) secondary thread. To keep focused on the mechanics of building multithreaded programs, this method will simply print out a sequence of numbers to the console window, pausing for approximately 2 seconds with each pass. Here is the full definition of the `Printer` class:

```
Public Class Printer
  Public Sub PrintNumbers()
    ' Display Thread info.
    Console.WriteLine("-> {0} is executing PrintNumbers()", _
      Thread.CurrentThread.Name)

    ' Print out numbers.
    Console.Write("Your numbers: ")
    For i As Integer = 0 To 10
      Console.Write(i & ", ")
      Thread.Sleep(2000)
    Next
    Console.WriteLine()
  End Sub
End Class
```

Now, within `Main()`, you will first prompt the user to determine whether one or two threads will be used to perform the application's work. If the user requests a single thread, you will simply invoke the `PrintNumbers()` method within the primary thread. However, if the user specifies two threads, you will create a `ThreadStart` delegate that points to `PrintNumbers()`, pass this delegate object into the constructor of a new `Thread` object, and call `Start()` to inform the CLR this thread is ready for processing.

To begin, set a reference to the `System.Windows.Forms.dll` assembly, import the `System.Windows.Forms` namespace, and display a message within `Main()` using `MessageBox.Show()` (you'll see the point of doing so once you run the program). Here is the complete implementation of `Main()`:

```
Module Program
  Sub Main()
    Console.WriteLine("***** The Amazing Thread App *****")
    Console.Write("Do you want [1] or [2] threads?")
    Dim threadCount As String = Console.ReadLine()

    ' Name the current thread.
    Dim primaryThread As Thread = Thread.CurrentThread
    primaryThread.Name = "Primary"

    '  Display Thread info.
    Console.WriteLine("-> {0} is executing Main()", Thread.CurrentThread.Name)

    ' Make worker class.
    Dim p As New Printer()
```

```
    ' How many threads does the user want?
    Select Case threadCount
      Case "2"
        ' User wants an extra thread.
        Dim backgroundThread New Thread(New ThreadStart(AddressOf p.PrintNumbers))
        backgroundThread.Name = "Secondary"
        backgroundThread.Start()
      Case "1"
        p.PrintNumbers()
      Case Else
        Console.WriteLine("I don't know what you want...you get 1 thread.")
        p.PrintNumbers()
      End Select

    MessageBox.Show("I'm busy!", "Work on main thread...")
    Console.ReadLine()
  End Sub
End Module
```

Now, if you run this program with a single thread, you will find that the message box will not display until the entire sequence of numbers has printed to the console. As you are explicitly pausing for approximately 2 seconds after each number is printed, this will result in a less-than-stellar end-user experience. However, if you select two threads, the message box displays instantly, given that a unique Thread object is responsible for printing out the numbers to the console (see Figure 18-7).

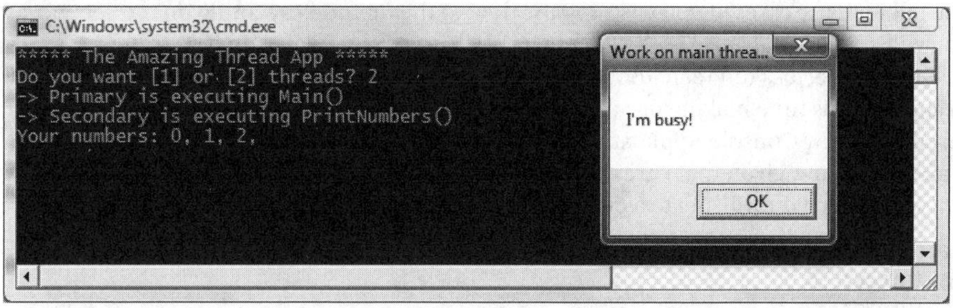

Figure 18-7. *Multithreaded applications result in more responsive applications.*

Before we move on, it is important to note that when you build multithreaded applications (which include the use of asynchronous delegates) on single CPU machines, you do not end up with an application that *runs* any faster, as that is a function of a machine's CPU. When running this application using either one or two threads, the numbers are still displaying at the same pace.

In reality, multithreaded applications result in *more responsive* applications. To the end user, it may appear that the program is "faster," but this is not the case. Threads have no power to make For loops execute quicker, to make paper print faster, or to force numbers to be added together at rocket speed. Multithreaded applications simply allow multiple threads to share the workload.

Source Code The SimpleMultiThreadApp project is included under the Chapter 18 subdirectory.

Creating Threads: A Shorthand Notation

In the previous example, you were shown the five steps the CLR expects you to take when you wish to spin off a new thread of execution. As you would suppose, however, some optional shorthand notations are available. Specifically, if you do not have a need to hold onto the instance of the ThreadStart delegate in your code, you can simply pass in the address of the method the Thread object is pointing to directly. Therefore, the following code:

```
' Directly create the ThreadStart delegate.
Dim backgroundThread As _
  New Thread(New ThreadStart(AddressOf p.PrintNumbers))
backgroundThread.Name = "Secondary"
backgroundThread.Start()
```

could be simplified like so:

```
' Indirectly create the ThreadStart delegate.
Dim backgroundThread As New Thread(AddressOf p.PrintNumbers)
backgroundThread.Name = "Secondary"
backgroundThread.Start()
```

As you might guess, the previous code snippet will force the Thread to create a new instance of the ThreadStart delegate behind the scenes.

Working with the ParameterizedThreadStart Delegate

Recall that the ThreadStart delegate can point only to subroutines that take no arguments. While this may fit the bill in many cases, if you wish to pass data to the method executing on the secondary thread, you will need to make use of the ParameterizedThreadStart delegate type (rather than ThreadStart). To illustrate, let's re-create the logic of the AsyncCallbackDelegate project created earlier in this chapter, this time making use of the ParameterizedThreadStart delegate type.

To begin, create a new Console Application named AddWithThreads and import the System.Threading namespace. Now, given that ParameterizedThreadStart can point to any method taking a System.Object parameter, you will create a custom type containing the numbers to be added:

```
Class AddParams
  Public a As Integer
  Public b As Integer

  Public Sub New(ByVal numb1 As Integer, ByVal numb2 As Integer)
    a = numb1
    b = numb2
  End Sub
End Class
```

Next, create a method in the Module type that will take an AddParams type and print out the summation of each value. The code within Main() is straightforward. Simply use ParameterizedThreadStart rather than ThreadStart. Here is the complete Module definition:

```
Module Program
  Public Sub Add(ByVal data As Object)
    If TypeOf data Is AddParams Then
      Console.WriteLine("ID of thread in Add(): {0}", _
        Thread.CurrentThread.ManagedThreadId)
      Dim ap As AddParams = CType(data, AddParams)
      Console.WriteLine("{0} + {1} is {2}", ap.a, ap.b, ap.a + ap.b)
    End If
  End Sub
```

```
  Sub Main(ByVal args As String())
    Console.WriteLine("***** Adding with Thread objects *****")
    Console.WriteLine("ID of thread in Main(): {0}", _
      Thread.CurrentThread.ManagedThreadId)
    Dim ap As New AddParams(10, 10)
    Dim t As New Thread(New ParameterizedThreadStart(AddressOf Add))
    t.Start(ap)
    Console.ReadLine()
  End Sub
End Module
```

As in the previous example, you have the option of directly creating an instance of the ParameterizedThreadStart delegate, or allowing the Thread type to do so on your behalf. Therefore, we could allocate our new Thread object as follows:

```
' This time, because Add() is a method taking a System.Object,
' a new ParameterizedThreadStart delegate is created
' behind the scenes.
Dim t As New Thread(AddressOf Add)
```

Source Code The AddWithThreads project is included under the Chapter 18 subdirectory.

Foreground Threads and Background Threads

Now that you have seen how to programmatically create new threads of execution using the System.Threading namespace, let's formalize the distinction between foreground threads and background threads:

- *Foreground threads* have the ability to prevent the current application from terminating. The CLR will not shut down an application (which is to say, unload the hosting AppDomain) until all foreground threads have ended.
- *Background threads* (sometimes called *daemon threads*) are viewed by the CLR as expendable paths of execution that can be ignored at any point in time (even if they are currently laboring over some unit of work). Thus, if all foreground threads have terminated, any and all background threads are automatically killed when the application domain unloads.

It is important to note that foreground and background threads are *not* synonymous with primary and worker threads. By default, every thread you create via the Thread.Start() method is automatically a *foreground* thread. Again, this means that the AppDomain will not unload until all threads of execution have completed their units of work. In most cases, this is exactly the behavior you require.

For the sake of argument, however, assume that you wish to invoke Printer.PrintNumbers() on a secondary thread that should behave as a background thread. Again, this means that the method pointed to by the Thread type (via the ThreadStart or ParameterizedThreadStart delegate) should be able to halt safely as soon as all foreground threads are done with their work. Configuring such a thread is as simple as setting the IsBackground property to True:

```
Sub Main()
  Console.WriteLine("***** Background Threads *****")
  Console.WriteLine()
```

```
    Dim p As New Printer()
    Dim bgroundThread As New Thread(AddressOf p.PrintNumbers)
    bgroundThread.IsBackground = True
    bgroundThread.Start()
End Sub
```

Notice that this Main() method is *not* making a call to Console.ReadLine() to force the console to remain visible until you press the Enter key. Thus, when you run the application, it will shut down immediately because the Thread object has been configured as a background thread. Given that the Main() method triggers the creation of the primary *foreground* thread, as soon as the logic in Main() completes, the AppDomain unloads before the secondary thread is able to complete its work.

However, if you comment out the line that sets the IsBackground property, you will find that each number prints to the console, as all foreground threads must finish their work before the AppDomain is unloaded from the hosting process.

For the most part, configuring a thread to run as a background type can be helpful when the worker thread in question is performing a noncritical task that is no longer needed when the main task of the program is finished (for example, periodically checking for e-mails in the background).

■ **Source Code** The BackgroundThread project is included under the Chapter 18 subdirectory.

The Issue of Concurrency

All the multithreaded sample applications you have written over the course of this chapter have been thread safe, given that only a single Thread object was executing the method in question. While some of your applications may be this simplistic in nature, a good deal of your multithreaded applications may contain numerous secondary threads. Given that all threads in an AppDomain have concurrent access to the shared data of the application, imagine what might happen if multiple threads were accessing the same point of data. As the thread scheduler will force threads to suspend their work seemingly at random, what if Thread A is kicked out of the way before it has fully completed its work? Thread B is now reading unstable data.

To illustrate the problem of concurrency, let's build another VB 2008 Console Application named MultiThreadedPrinting. This application will once again make use of the Printer class created previously, but this time the PrintNumbers() method will force the current thread to pause for a randomly generated amount of time:

```
Public Class Printer
  Public Sub PrintNumbers()
    Console.WriteLine("-> {0} is executing PrintNumbers()", _
      Thread.CurrentThread.Name)
    Console.Write("Your numbers: ")
    For i As Integer = 0 To 10
      Dim r As New Random()
      Thread.Sleep(100 * r.Next(5))
      Console.Write(i & ", ")
    Next
    Console.WriteLine()
  End Sub
End Class
```

The `Main()` method is responsible for creating an array of (uniquely named) `Thread` objects, each of which is making calls on the same instance of the `Printer` object:

```
Module Program
  Sub Main()
    Console.WriteLine("***** Synchronizing Threads *****")
    Console.WriteLine()

    Dim p As New Printer()

    ' Make 11 threads that are all pointing to the same
    ' method on the same object.
    Dim threads(10) As Thread
    For i As Integer = 0 To 10
      threads(i) = New Thread(AddressOf p.PrintNumbers)
      threads(i).Name = String.Format("Worker thread #{0}", i)
    Next

    ' Now start each one.
    For Each t As Thread In threads
      t.Start()
    Next
    Console.ReadLine()
  End Sub
End Module
```

Before looking at some test runs, let's recap the problem. The primary thread within this AppDomain begins life by spawning 11 secondary worker threads. Each worker thread is told to make calls on the `PrintNumbers()` method on the *same* `Printer` instance. Given that you have taken no precautions to lock down this object's shared resources (the console), there is a good chance that the current thread will be kicked out of the way before the `PrintNumbers()` method is able to print out the complete results. Because you don't know exactly when (or if) this might happen, you are bound to get unpredictable results. For example, you might find the output shown in Figure 18-8.

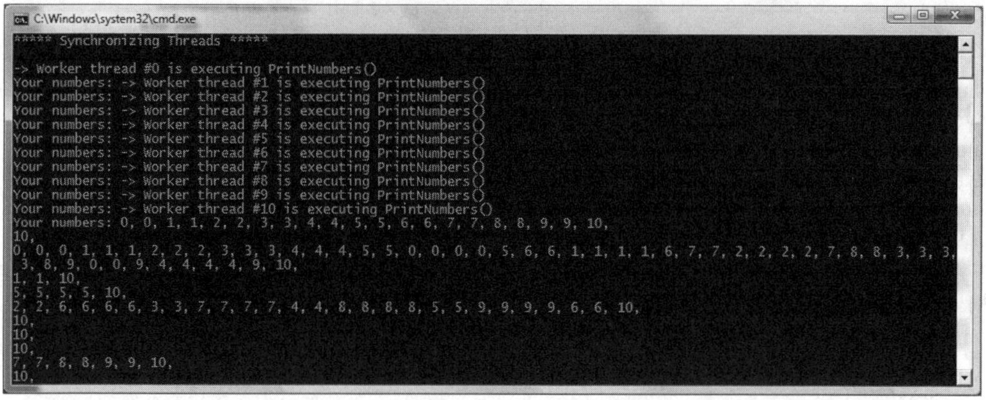

Figure 18-8. *Concurrency in action, take one*

Now run the application a few more times. Figure 18-9 shows another possibility (your results will obviously differ).

Figure 18-9. *Concurrency in action, take two*

There are clearly some problems here. As each thread is telling the `Printer` to print out the numerical data, the thread scheduler is happily swapping threads in the background. The result is inconsistent output. What we need is a way to programmatically enforce synchronized access to the shared resources. As you would guess, the `System.Threading` namespace provides a number of synchronization-centric types. The VB 2008 programming language also provides a particular keyword for the very task of synchronizing shared data in multithreaded applications.

■ **Note** If you are unable to generate unpredictable outputs, increase the number of secondary threads to 100 (for example) or introduce a call to `Thread.Sleep()` within your program. Eventually, you will encounter a concurrency issue.

Synchronization Using the SyncLock Keyword

The first technique you can use to synchronize access to shared resources is the VB `SyncLock` keyword. This keyword allows you to define a scope of statements that must be synchronized between threads. By doing so, incoming threads cannot interrupt the current thread, preventing it from finishing its work. The `SyncLock` keyword requires you to specify a *token* (an object reference) that must be acquired by a thread to enter within the lock scope. When you are attempting to lock down a *private* instance-level method, you can simply pass in a reference to the current object instance:

```
Private Sub SomePrivateMethod()
  ' Use the current object as the thread token.
  SyncLock Me
    ' All code within this scope is thread safe.
  End SyncLock
End Sub
```

However, if you are locking down a region of code within a *public* member, it is safer (and a best practice) to declare a private Object member variable to serve as the lock token:

```
Public Class Printer
  ' Lock token.
  Private threadLock As New Object()

  Public Sub PrintNumbers()
    ' Use the lock token.
    SyncLock threadLock
      ...
    End SyncLock
  End Sub
End Class
```

In any case, if you examine the PrintNumbers() method, you can see that the shared resource the threads are competing to gain access to is the console window. Therefore, if you scope all interactions with the Console type within a lock scope as follows:

```
Public Sub PrintNumbers()

  SyncLock threadLock
    Console.WriteLine("-> {0} is executing PrintNumbers()", _
      Thread.CurrentThread.Name)
    Console.Write("Your numbers: ")
    For i As Integer = 0 To 10
      Dim r As New Random()
      Thread.Sleep(100 * r.Next(5))
      Console.Write(i & ", ")
    Next
    Console.WriteLine()
  End SyncLock

End Sub
```

you have effectively designed a method that will allow the current thread to complete its task. Once a thread enters into a lock scope, the lock token (in this case, a reference to the current object) is inaccessible by other threads until the lock is released once the lock scope has exited. Thus, if Thread A has obtained the lock token, other threads are unable to enter the scope until Thread A relinquishes the lock token.

Note If you are attempting to lock down code in a shared method, simply declare a private shared Object member variable to serve as the lock token.

If you now run the application, you can see that each thread has ample opportunity to finish its business, as shown in Figure 18-10.

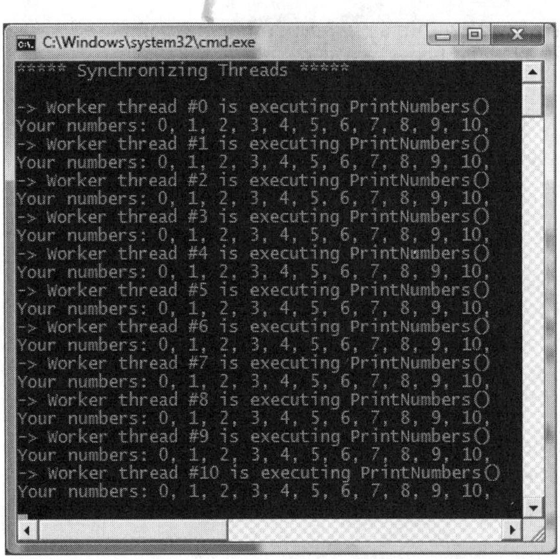

Figure 18-10. *Concurrency in action, take three*

Source Code The MultiThreadedPrinting application is included under the Chapter 18 subdirectory.

Synchronization Using the System.Threading.Monitor Type

The VB 2008 `SyncLock` statement is really just a shorthand notation for working with the `System.Threading.Monitor` class type. Once processed by the VB 2008 compiler, a `SyncLock` scope actually resolves to the following (which you can verify using `ildasm.exe`):

```
Public Sub PrintNumbers()
  Monitor.Enter(threadLock)
  Try
    Console.WriteLine("-> {0}  is executing PrintNumbers()", _
      Thread.CurrentThread.Name)
    Console.Write("Your numbers: ")
    For i As Integer = 0 To 10
      Dim r As New Random()
      Thread.Sleep(100 * r.Next(5))
      Console.Write(i & ", ")
    Next
    Console.WriteLine()
  Finally
    Monitor.Exit(threadLock)
  End Try
End Sub
```

First, notice that the `Monitor.Enter()` method is the ultimate recipient of the thread token you specified as the argument to the `SyncLock` keyword. Next, all code within a lock scope is wrapped within a `Try` block. The corresponding `Finally` clause ensures that the thread token is released (via the `Monitor.Exit()` method), regardless of any possible runtime exception. If you were to modify the MultiThreadedPrinting program to make direct use of the `Monitor` type (as just shown), you will find the output is identical.

Now, given that the SyncLock keyword seems to require less code than making explicit use of the System.Threading.Monitor type, you may wonder about the benefits of using the Monitor type directly. The short answer is control. If you make use of the Monitor type, you are able to instruct the active thread to wait for some duration of time (via the Wait() method), inform waiting threads when the current thread is completed (via the Pulse() and PulseAll() methods), and so on.

As you would expect, in a great number of cases, the VB 2008 SyncLock keyword will fit the bill. However, if you are interested in checking out additional members of the Monitor class, consult the .NET Framework 3.5 SDK documentation.

Synchronization Using the System.Threading.Interlocked Type

Although it always is hard to believe until you look at the underlying CIL code, assignments and simple arithmetic operations are *not atomic*! For this reason, the System.Threading namespace provides a type that allows you to operate on a single point of data atomically with less overhead than with the Monitor type. The Interlocked class type defines various shared members, some of which are presented in Table 18-4.

Table 18-4. *Select members of the* System.Threading.Interlocked *Type*

Member	Meaning in Life
CompareExchange()	Safely tests two values for equality and, if equal, changes one of the values with a third
Decrement()	Safely decrements a value by 1
Exchange()	Safely sets a variable to a specified value
Increment()	Safely increments a value by 1

Although it might not seem like it from the onset, the process of atomically altering a single value is quite common in a multithreaded environment. Assume you have a method named AddOne() that increments an integer member variable named intVal. Rather than writing synchronization code such as the following:

```
Public Sub AddOne()
  SyncLock Me
    intVal = intVal + 1
  End SyncLock
End Sub
```

you can simplify your code via the shared Interlocked.Increment() method. Simply pass in the variable to increment by reference. Do note that the Increment() method not only adjusts the value of the incoming parameter, but also returns the new value:

```
Public Sub AddOne()
  Dim newVal As Integer = Interlocked.Increment(intVal)
End Sub
```

In addition to Increment() and Decrement(), the Interlocked type allows you to atomically assign numerical and object data. For example, if you wish to assign a member variable to the value 83, you can avoid the need to use an explicit SyncLock statement (or explicit Monitor logic) and make use of the Interlocked.Exchange() method:

```
Public Sub SafeAssignment()
  Interlocked.Exchange(intVal, 83)
End Sub
```

Finally, if you wish to test two values for equality to change the point of comparison in a thread-safe manner, you are able to leverage the Interlocked.CompareExchange() method as follows:

```
Public Sub CompareAndExchange()
  ' If the value of intVal is currently 83, change i to 99.
  Interlocked.CompareExchange(intVal, 99, 83)
End Sub
```

Synchronization Using the <Synchronization()> Attribute

The final synchronization primitive examined here is the <Synchronization()> attribute, which is a member of the System.Runtime.Remoting.Contexts namespace. In essence, this class-level attribute effectively locks down *all* instance member code of the object for thread safety. When the CLR allocates objects attributed with <Synchronization()>, it will place the object within a synchronized context (see Chapter 17). As you may recall, objects that should not be removed from a contextual boundary should derive from ContextBoundObject. Therefore, if you wish to make the Printer class type thread safe (without explicitly writing thread-safe code within the class members), you could update the definition like so:

```
Imports System.Runtime.Remoting.Contexts
...

' All methods of Printer are now thread safe!
<Synchronization()> _
Public Class Printer
  Inherits ContextBoundObject
  Public Sub PrintNumbers()
    ...
  End Sub
End Class
```

In some ways, this approach can be seen as the lazy way to write thread-safe code, given that you are not required to dive into the details about which aspects of the type are truly manipulating thread-sensitive data. The major downfall of this approach, however, is that even if a given method is not making use of thread-sensitive data, the CLR will *still* lock invocations to the method. Obviously, this could degrade the overall functionality of the type, so use this technique with care.

At this point, you have seen a number of ways you are able to provide synchronized access to shared data. To be sure, additional types are available under the System.Threading namespace, which I will encourage you to explore at your leisure. To wrap up our examination of thread programming, allow me to introduce three additional types: TimerCallback, Timer, and ThreadPool. After this point, you'll examine how to control threads from within a graphical user interface using the BackgroundWorker. component.

Programming with Timer Callbacks

Many applications have the need to call a specific method during regular intervals of time. For example, you may have an application that needs to display the current time on a status bar via a given helper function. As another example, you may wish to have your application call a helper function every so often to perform noncritical background tasks such as checking for new e-mail messages. For situations such as these, you can use the System.Threading.Timer type in conjunction with a related delegate named TimerCallback.

To illustrate, assume you have a Console Application that will print the current time every second until the user presses a key to terminate the application. Assuming you have imported the `System.Threading` namespace, the first step is to write the method that will be called by the `Timer` type:

```
Sub PrintTime(ByVal state As Object)
  Console.WriteLine("Time is: {0}", _
    DateTime.Now.ToLongTimeString())
End Sub
```

Notice how this method has a single parameter of type `System.Object` and is a subroutine, rather than a function. This is not optional, given that the `TimerCallback` delegate can only call methods that match this signature. The value passed into the target of your `TimerCallback` delegate can be any bit of information whatsoever (in the case of the e-mail example, this parameter might represent the name of the Microsoft Exchange server to interact with during the process). Also note that given that this parameter is indeed a `System.Object`, you are able to pass in multiple arguments using a `System.Array` or custom class/structure.

The next step is to configure an instance of the `TimerCallback` delegate and pass it into the `Timer` object. In addition to configuring a `TimerCallback` delegate, the `Timer` constructor allows you to specify the optional parameter information to pass into the delegate target (defined as a `System.Object`), the interval to poll the method, and the amount of time to wait (in milliseconds) before making the first call, for example:

```
Sub Main()
  Console.WriteLine("***** Working with Timer type *****")
  Console.WriteLine()

  ' Create the delegate for the Timer type.
  Dim timeCB As TimerCallback = AddressOf PrintTime

  ' Pass in the delegate instance, data to send the
  ' method "pointed to," time to wait before starting,
  ' and interval of time between calls.
  Dim t As New Timer(timeCB, Nothing, 0, 1000)

  Console.WriteLine("Hit Enter key to terminate...")
  Console.ReadLine()
End Sub
```

As you would guess, if you don't need to use the `TimerCallback` delegate object directly, you can simply create your `Timer` object as follows:

```
Dim t As New Timer(AddressOf PrintTime, Nothing, 0, 1000)
```

In any case, the `PrintTime()` method will be called roughly every second and will pass in no additional information to said method. If you did wish to send in some information for use by the delegate target, simply substitute the `Nothing` value of the second constructor parameter with the appropriate information:

```
Dim t As New Timer(AddressOf PrintTime, "Hi", 0, 1000)
```

We could now make use of this data within the `PrintTime()` method. Consider the following updates:

```
Sub PrintTime(ByVal state As Object)
  Console.WriteLine("Time is: {0}, Param is: {1}", _
    DateTime.Now.ToLongTimeString, state.ToString())
End Sub
```

Figure 18-11 shows the output.

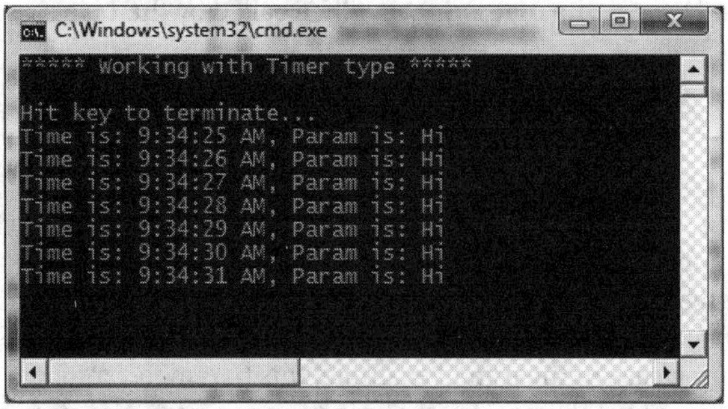

Figure 18-11. *Timers at work*

■ **Source Code** The TimerApp application is included under the Chapter 18 subdirectory.

Understanding the CLR ThreadPool

The next thread-centric topic we will examine in this chapter is the CLR thread pool. When you invoke a method asynchronously using delegate types (via the `BeginInvoke()` method), the CLR does not literally create a brand-new thread. For purposes of efficiency, a delegate's `BeginInvoke()` method leverages a pool of worker threads that is maintained by the runtime. To allow you to interact with this pool of waiting threads, the `System.Threading` namespace provides the `ThreadPool` class type.

If you wish to queue a method call for processing by a worker thread in the pool, you can make use of the `ThreadPool.QueueUserWorkItem()` method. This method has been overloaded to allow you to specify an optional `System.Object` for custom state data in addition to an instance of the `WaitCallback` delegate.

The `WaitCallback` delegate can point to any subroutine that takes a `System.Object` as its sole parameter (which represents the optional state data). Do note that if you do not provide a `System.Object` when calling `QueueUserWorkItem()`, the CLR automatically passes the value `Nothing`. To illustrate queuing methods for use by the CLR thread pool, consider the following program, which makes use of the `Printer` type once again. In this case, however, you are not manually creating an array of `Thread` types; rather, you are assigning members of the pool to the `PrintNumbers()` method:

```
Module Program
  Sub Main()
    Console.WriteLine("Main thread started. ThreadID = {0}", _
      Thread.CurrentThread.ManagedThreadId)
    Dim p As New Printer()
    Dim workItem As WaitCallback = AddressOf PrintTheNumbers

    ' Queue the method 10 times
    For i As Integer = 0 To 9
      ThreadPool.QueueUserWorkItem(workItem, p)
    Next
```

```
    Console.WriteLine("All tasks queued")
    Console.ReadLine()
  End Sub

  Sub PrintTheNumbers(ByVal state As Object)
    Dim task As Printer = CType(state, Printer)
    task.PrintNumbers()
  End Sub
End Module
```

At this point, you may be wondering whether it would be advantageous to make use of the CLR-maintained thread pool rather than explicitly creating `Thread` objects. Consider these major benefits of leveraging the thread pool:

- The thread pool manages threads efficiently by minimizing the number of threads that must be created, started, and stopped.
- By using the thread pool, you can focus on your business problem rather than the application's threading infrastructure.

However, using manual thread management is preferred in some cases, for example:

- If you require foreground threads or must set the thread priority. Pooled threads are *always* background threads with default priority (`ThreadPriority.Normal`).
- If you require a thread with a fixed identity in order to abort it, suspend it, or discover it by name.

■ **Source Code** The ThreadPoolApp application is included under the Chapter 18 subdirectory.

The Role of the BackgroundWorker Component

The final threading type we will examine here is `BackgroundWorker`, defined in the `System.ComponentModel` namespace (of `System.dll`). `BackgroundWorker` is a class that is very helpful when you are building a graphical Windows Forms desktop application and need to execute a long-running task (invoking a remote web service, performing a database transaction, downloading a large file, etc.) on a thread different from your application's main UI thread.

While you are most certainly able to build multithreaded GUI applications by making direct use of the `System.Threading` types as seen in this chapter, `BackgroundWorker` allows you to get the job done with much less fuss and bother. Thankfully, the programming model of this type leverages much of the same threading syntax we find with asynchronous delegates, so learning how to use this type is very straightforward.

To use a `BackgroundWorker`, you simply tell it what method to execute in the background and call `RunWorkerAsync()`. The calling thread (typically the primary thread) continues to run normally while the worker method runs asynchronously. When the time-consuming method has completed, the `BackgroundWorker` type informs the calling thread by firing the `RunWorkerCompleted` event. The associated event hander provides an incoming argument that allows you to obtain the results of the operation (if any exist).

■ **Note** The following example assumes you have some familiarity with GUI desktop development using Windows Forms. If this is not the case, you may wish to return to this section once you have completed reading Chapter 27.

Working with the BackgroundWorker Type

To illustrate using this UI threading component, begin by creating a new Windows Forms application named WinFormsBackgroundWorkerThread. Staying true to the same numerical operation examples used here, construct a simple UI that allows the user to input two values to process (via `TextBox` controls) and a `Button` control to begin the background operation. Be sure to give each UI element a fitting name using the `Name` property of the Properties window. Figure 18-12 shows one possible layout.

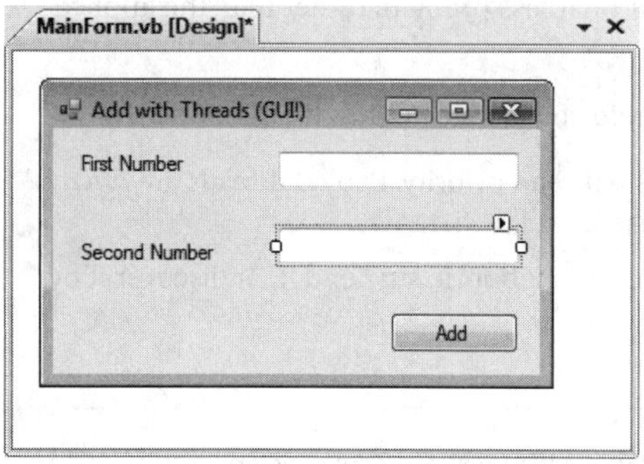

Figure 18-12. *Layout of the Windows Forms UI application*

After you have designed your UI layout, handle the `Click` event of the `Button` control by double-clicking the control on the form designer. This will result in a new event handler that we will implement in just a bit:

```
Private Sub btnAdd_Click(ByVal sender As System.Object, _
  ByVal e As System.EventArgs) Handles btnAdd.Click

End Sub
```

Now, open the Components region of your Toolbox, locate the `BackgroundWorker` component (see Figure 18-13), and drag an instance of this type onto your form designer.

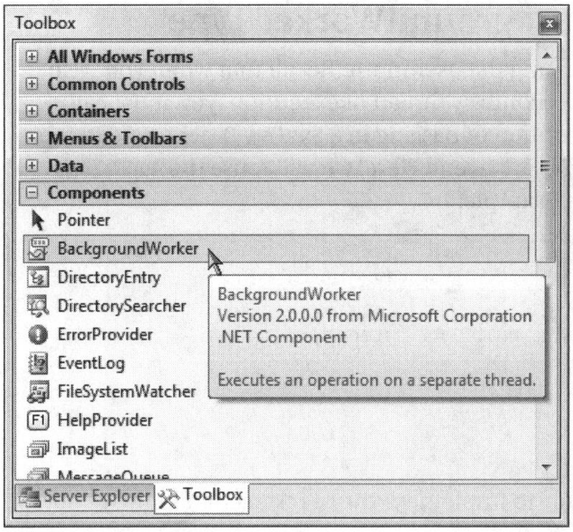

Figure 18-13. *The* `BackgroundWorker` *type*

You will now see a variable of this type on the designer's component tray. Using the Properties window, rename this component to `ProcessNumbersBackgroundWorker`. Now, switch to the Event pane of the Properties window (by clicking the "lightning bolt" icon) and handle the `DoWork` and `RunWorkerCompleted` events by double-clicking each event name. This will result in the following new handlers added to your initial `Form`-derived type:

```
Private Sub ProcessNumbersBackgroundWorker_DoWork(ByVal sender As System.Object, _
     ByVal e As System.ComponentModel.DoWorkEventArgs) Handles _
     ProcessNumbersBackgroundWorker.DoWork

End Sub

Private Sub ProcessNumbersBackgroundWorker_RunWorkerCompleted( _
  ByVal sender As System.Object, _
  ByVal e As System.ComponentModel.RunWorkerCompletedEventArgs) Handles _
  ProcessNumbersBackgroundWorker.RunWorkerCompleted

End Sub
```

The `DoWork` event handler represents the method that will be called by the `BackgroundWorker` on the secondary thread of execution. Notice that the second parameter of the handler is a `DoWorkEventArgs` type, which will contain any arguments required by the secondary thread to complete its work. As you'll see in just a moment, when you call the `RunWorkerAsync()` method to spawn this thread, you have the option of passing in this related data (quite similar to working with the `ParameterizedThreadStart` delegate type used previously in this chapter).

The `RunWorkerCompleted` event represents the method that the `BackgroundWorker` will invoke once the background operation has completed. Using the `RunWorkerCompletedEventArgs` type, you are able to scrape out any return value of the asynchronous operation.

Processing Our Data with the BackgroundWorker Type

At this point, we can flesh out the details of processing the user input. Recall that when you wish to inform the BackgroundWorker type to spin up a secondary thread of execution, you must call RunWorkerAsync(). When you do so, you have the option of passing in a System.Object type to represent any data to pass the method invoked by the DoWork event. Here, we will reuse the AddParams class we created in the ParameterizedThreadStart example:

```
Class AddParams
  Public a, b As Integer

  Public Sub New (ByVal numb1 As Integer, ByVal numb2 As Integer)
    a = numb1
    b = numb2
  End Sub
End Class
```

With this helper class in place, we are now able to implement the Click event handler of our Button control as follows:

```
Private Sub btnAdd_Click(ByVal sender As System.Object, _
  ByVal e As System.EventArgs) Handles btnAdd.Click
  Try
    ' First get the user data (as numerical).
    Dim numbOne As Integer = Integer.Parse(txtNumbOne.Text)
    Dim numbTwo As Integer = Integer.Parse(txtNumbTwo.Text)
    Dim args As New AddParams(numbOne, numbTwo)

    ' Now spin up the new thread and pass args variable.
    ProcessNumbersBackgroundWorker.RunWorkerAsync(args)
  Catch ex As Exception
    MessageBox.Show(ex.Message)
  End Try
End Sub
```

As soon as you call RunWorkerAsync(), the DoWork event fires, which will be captured by your handler. Implement this type to scrape out the AddParams object using the Argument property of the incoming DoWorkEventArgs. Again, to simulate a lengthy operation, we will put the current thread to sleep for approximately 5 seconds. After this point, we will return the value by setting the Result property of the DoWorkEventArgs type:

```
Private Sub ProcessNumbersBackgroundWorker_DoWork(ByVal sender As System.Object, _
  ByVal e As System.ComponentModel.DoWorkEventArgs) _
  Handles ProcessNumbersBackgroundWorker.DoWork
  ' Get the incoming AddParam object.
  Dim args As AddParams = DirectCast(e.Argument, AddParams)

  ' Artifical lag.
  System.Threading.Thread.Sleep(5000)

  ' Return the value.
  e.Result = args.a + args.b
End Sub
```

Finally, once the BackgroundWorker type has exited the scope of the DoWork handler, the RunWorkerCompleted event will fire. Our registered handler will simply display the result of the operation using the RunWorkerCompletedEventArgs.Result property:

```
Private Sub ProcessNumbersBackgroundWorker_RunWorkerCompleted( _
  ByVal sender As System.Object, _
  ByVal e As System.ComponentModel.RunWorkerCompletedEventArgs) Handles _
  ProcessNumbersBackgroundWorker.RunWorkerCompleted
  MessageBox.Show(e.Result.ToString(), "Your result is")
End Sub
```

If you were to now run your application, you would find that while the data is being processed, the thread hosting the UI is still completely responsive (for example, the window can be resized, moved, minimized, etc.). If you wish to accentuate this point, you might want to add a new `TextBox` to the form and verify you are able to enter data within the UI area while the 5-second addition operation performs asynchronously in the background.

■ **Source Code** The WinFormsBackgroundWorkerThread project is included under the Chapter 18 subdirectory.

That wraps up our examination of multithreaded programming under .NET. To be sure, the `System.Threading` namespace defines numerous types beyond what I had the space to cover in this chapter. Nevertheless, at this point you should have a solid foundation to build on.

Summary

This chapter began by examining how .NET delegate types can be configured to execute a method in an asynchronous manner. As you have seen, the `BeginInvoke()` and `EndInvoke()` methods allow you to indirectly manipulate a background thread with minimum fuss and bother. During this discussion, you were also introduced to the `IAsyncResult` interface and `AsyncResult` class type. As you learned, these types provide various ways to synchronize the calling thread and obtain possible method return values.

The remainder of this chapter examined the role of the `System.Threading` namespace. As you learned, when an application creates additional threads of execution, the result is that the program in question is able to carry out numerous tasks at (what appears to be) the same time. You also examined several manners in which you can protect thread-sensitive blocks of code to ensure that shared resources do not become unusable units of bogus data.

This chapter also pointed out that the CLR maintains an internal pool of threads for the purposes of performance and convenience. Last but not least, you examined the use of the `BackgroundWorker` type, which allows you to easily spin up new threads of execution within a GUI-based application.

Summary

CHAPTER 19

.NET Interoperability Assemblies

By this point in the text, you've gained a solid foundation in the VB language and .NET type system. I suspect that when you contrast the object model provided by .NET to that of classic COM and VB6, you'll no doubt be convinced that these are two entirely unique systems. Regardless of the fact that COM is now considered to be a legacy framework, few of us are in a position to completely abandon the ways of COM and Visual Basic 6.0 (after all, we'll always have legacy systems to maintain). The truth is that people have spent hundreds of thousands of hours building systems that make substantial use of these legacy technologies.

Thankfully, the .NET platform provides various types, tools, and namespaces that make the process of COM and .NET interoperability quite straightforward. This chapter begins by examining the process of .NET to COM interoperability and the related Runtime Callable Wrapper (RCW). The latter part of this chapter examines the opposite situation: a COM type communicating with a .NET type using a COM Callable Wrapper (CCW).

Note A full examination of the .NET interoperability layer would require a book unto itself. If you require more details than presented in this chapter, check out my book *COM and .NET Interoperability* (Apress, 2002).

The Scope of .NET Interoperability

Recall that when you build assemblies using a .NET-aware compiler, you are creating *managed code* that can be hosted by the common language runtime (CLR). Managed code offers a number of benefits such as automatic memory management, a unified type system (the CTS), self-describing assemblies, and so forth. As you have also seen, .NET assemblies have a particular internal composition. In addition to CIL instructions and type metadata, assemblies contain a manifest that fully documents any required external assemblies as well as other file-related details (strong naming, version, etc.).

On the other side of the spectrum are legacy COM servers (which are, of course, *unmanaged code*). These binaries bear no relationship to .NET assemblies beyond a shared file extension (`*.dll` or `*.exe`). First of all, COM servers contain platform-specific machine code, not platform-agnostic CIL instructions, and work with a unique set of data types (often termed *oleautomation* or *variant-compliant* data types), none of which are directly understood by the CLR. In addition to the necessary COM-centric infrastructure required by all COM binaries (such as registry entries and support for core COM interfaces like `IUnknown`) is the fact that COM types demand to be *reference counted* in order to correctly control the lifetime of a COM object. This is in stark contrast, of course, to a .NET object, which is allocated on a managed heap and handled by the CLR garbage collector.

Given that .NET types and COM types have so little in common, you may wonder how these two architectures can make use of each others' services. Unless you are lucky enough to work for a company dedicated to "100% Pure .NET" development, you will most likely need to build .NET solutions that use legacy COM types. As well, you may find that a legacy COM server might like to communicate with the types contained within a shiny new .NET assembly.

The bottom line is that for some time to come, COM and .NET must learn how to get along. This chapter examines the process of managed and unmanaged types living together in harmony using the .NET interoperability layer. In general, the .NET Framework supports two core flavors of interoperability:

- .NET types using COM types
- COM types using .NET types

As you see throughout this chapter, the .NET Framework 3.5 SDK and Visual Studio supply a number of tools that help bridge the gap between these unique architectures. As well, the .NET base class library defines a namespace (`System.Runtime.InteropServices`) dedicated solely to the issue of interoperability. However, before diving in too far under the hood, let's look at a very simple example of .NET to COM interoperability.

■ **Note** The .NET platform also makes it very simple for a .NET assembly to call into the underlying API of the operating system (as well as any C-based unmanaged `*.dll`) using a technology termed *platform invocation* (or simply *PInvoke*). From a VB point of view, working with PInvoke looks very similar to working with VB6, as we can simply use the `Declare` statement. As an alternative, the .NET platform provides the language-neutral `<DllImport()>` attribute, which performs the same function as the VB-specific `Declare` statement. Although PInvoke is not examined in this chapter, check out the `Declare` keyword (and `<DllImport()>` attribute) using the .NET Framework 3.5 SDK documentation for further details.

A Simple Example of .NET to COM Interop

To begin our exploration of interoperability services, let's see just how simple things appear on the surface. The goal of this section is to build a VB6 ActiveX `*.dll` server, which is then consumed by a VB .NET application. Fire up VB6, create a new ActiveX `*.dll` project (which we will save using the name SimpleComServer), rename your initial class file to `ComCalc.cls`, and name the class itself `ComCalc`. As you may know, the name of your project and the names assigned to the contained classes will be used to define the programmatic identifier (ProgID) of the COM types (`SimpleComServer.ComCalc`, in this case). Now, define the following methods within `ComCalc.cls`:

```
' The VB6 COM object.
Option Explicit

Public Function Add(ByVal x As Integer, ByVal y As Integer) As Integer
  Add = x + y
End Function

Public Function Subtract(ByVal x As Integer, ByVal y As Integer) As Integer
  Subtract = x - y
End Function
```

At this point, compile your `*.dll` (via the File ➤ Make menu option) and, just to keep things peaceful in the world of COM, establish binary compatibility (via the Component tab of the project's Property page) before you exit the VB6 IDE. This will ensure that if you recompile the application, VB6 will preserve the assigned globally unique identifiers (GUIDs).

Source Code The SimpleComServer is located under the Chapter 19 subdirectory.

Building the VB 2008 Client

Now open up Visual Studio 2008 and create a new VB 2008 Console Application project named VbNetSimpleComClient, and rename your initial module to `Program`. When you are building a .NET application that needs to communicate with a legacy COM application, the first step is to reference the COM server within your project (much like you reference a .NET assembly).

To do so, simply access the Project ➤ Add Reference menu selection and select the COM tab from the Add Reference dialog box. The name of your COM server will be listed alphabetically, as the VB6 compiler updated the system registry with the necessary listings when you compiled your COM server. Go ahead and select the `SimpleComServer.dll` as shown in Figure 19-1 and close the dialog box.

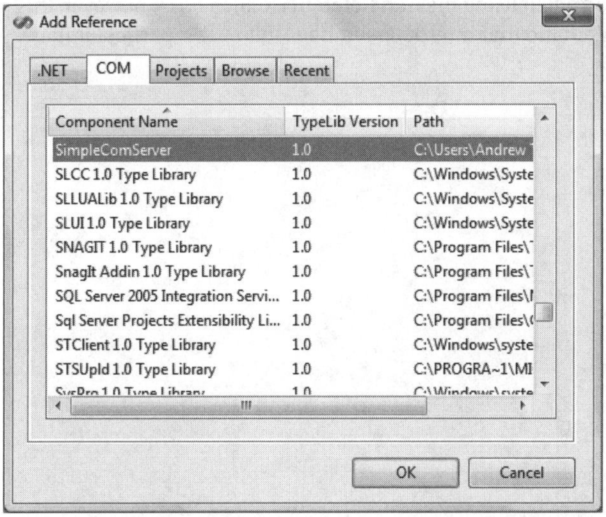

Figure 19-1. *Referencing a COM server using Visual Studio 2008*

Now, if you click the Show All Files button on Solution Explorer, you see what looks to be a new .NET assembly reference (named SimpleComServer) added to your project, as illustrated in Figure 19-2. Formally speaking, assemblies that are generated when referencing a COM server are termed *interop assemblies*. Without getting too far ahead of ourselves at this point, simply understand that interop assemblies contain .NET descriptions of COM types.

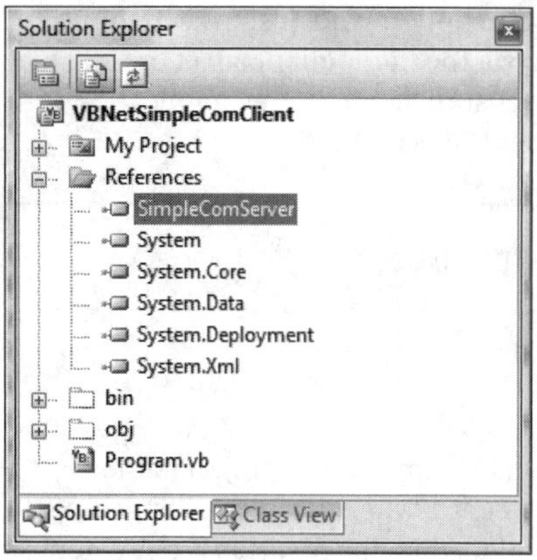

Figure 19-2. *The referenced interop assembly*

Although we have not added any code to our initial module, if you compile your application and examine the project's bin\Debug directory (be sure to hit the Refresh button of Solution Explorer), you will find that a local copy of the generated interop assembly has been placed in the application directory (see Figure 19-3). Notice that Visual Studio 2008 automatically prefixes `Interop.` to interop assemblies generated when using the Add Reference dialog box—however, this is only a convention; the CLR does not demand that interop assemblies follow this particular naming convention.

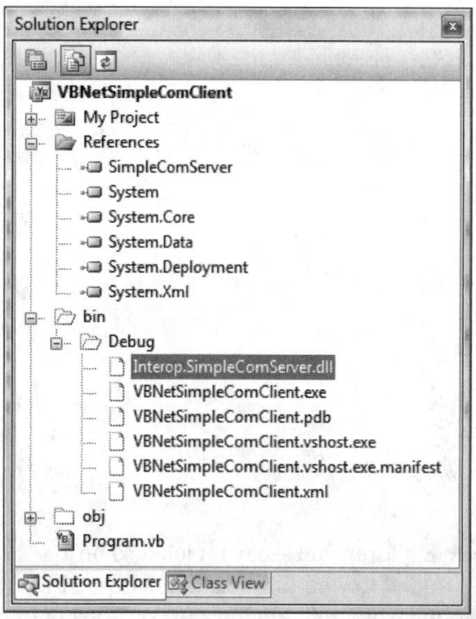

Figure 19-3. *The autogenerated interop assembly*

To complete this initial example, update the `Main()` method of your module to invoke the `Add()` method from a `ComCalc` object and display the result. For example:

```
Imports SimpleComServer

Module Program
  Sub Main()
    Console.WriteLine("***** The .NET COM Client App *****")
    Dim comObj As New ComCalc()
    Console.WriteLine("COM server says 10 + 832 is {0}", _
      comObj.Add(10, 832))
    Console.ReadLine()
  End Sub
End Module
```

As you can see from the previous code example, the namespace that contains the `ComCalc` COM object is named identically to the original VB6 project (notice the `Imports` statement). The output shown in Figure 19-4 is as you would expect.

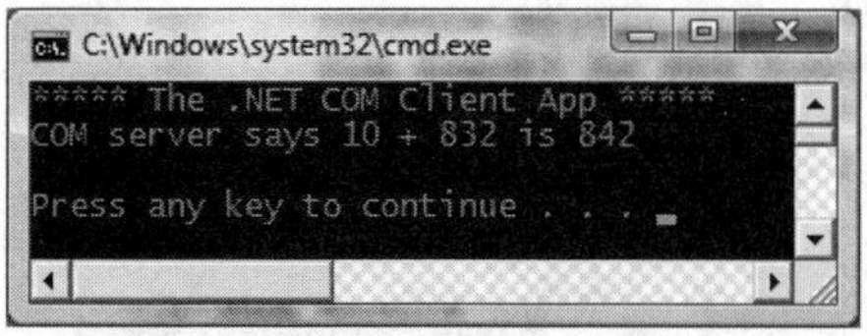

Figure 19-4. *Behold! .NET to COM interoperability*

As you can see, consuming a COM type from a .NET application can be a very transparent operation indeed. As you might imagine, however, a number of details are occurring behind the scenes to make this communication possible, the gory details of which you will explore throughout this chapter, beginning with taking a deeper look into the interop assembly itself.

Investigating a .NET Interop Assembly

As you have just seen, when you reference a COM server using the Visual Studio 2008 Add Reference dialog box, the IDE responds by generating a brand-new .NET assembly taking an `Interop.` prefix (such as `Interop.SimpleComServer.dll`). Just like an assembly that you would create yourself, interop assemblies contain type metadata, an assembly manifest, and under some circumstances *may* contain CIL code. As well, just like a "normal" assembly, interop assemblies can be deployed privately (e.g., within the directory of the client assembly) or assigned a strong name to be deployed to the GAC.

Interop assemblies are little more than containers to hold .NET metadata descriptions of the original COM types. In many cases, interop assemblies do not contain CIL instructions to implement their methods, as the real work is taking place in the COM server itself. The only time an interop assembly contains executable CIL instructions is if the COM server contains COM objects that have the ability to fire events to the client. In this case, the CIL code within the interop assembly is used by the CLR to manage the event handling logic.

At first glance, it may seem that interop assemblies are not entirely useful, given that they do not contain any implementation logic. However, the metadata descriptions within an interop assembly are extremely important, as it will be consumed by the CLR at runtime to build a runtime proxy (termed the *Runtime Callable Wrapper*, or simply *RCW*) that forms a bridge between the .NET application and the COM object it is communicating with.

You'll examine the details of the RCW in the next several sections; however, for the time being, open up the `Interop.SimpleComServer.dll` assembly using `ildasm.exe`, as you see in Figure 19-5.

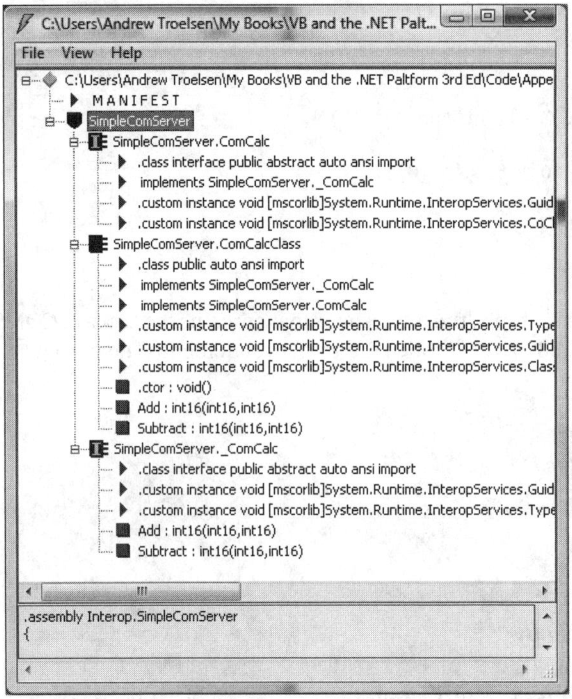

Figure 19-5. *The guts of the* `Interop.SimpleComServer.dll` *interop assembly*

As you can see, although the original VB6 project only defined a single COM class (`ComCalc`), the interop assembly contains *three* types (`ComCalc`, `ComCalcClass`, and `_ComCalc`). To make things even more confusing, if you were to examine the interop assembly using Visual Studio 2008, you only see a single type named `ComCalc`. Rest assured that `ComCalcClass` and `_ComCalc` are within the interop assembly. To view them, you simply need to elect to view hidden types with the VS 2008 Object Browser (see Figure 19-6).

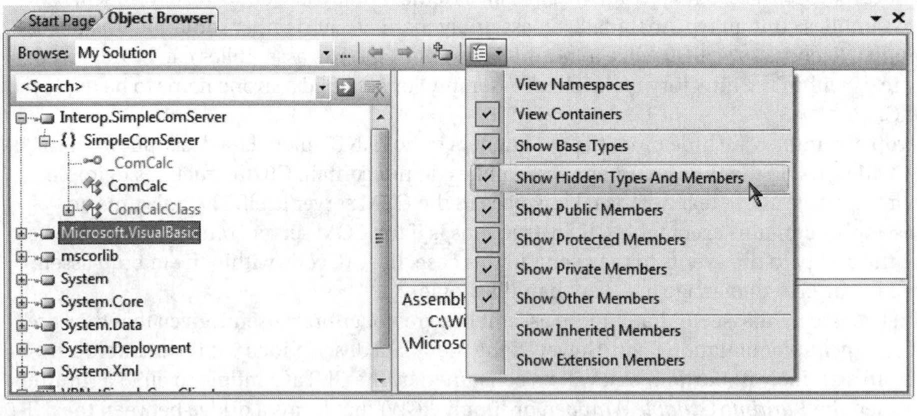

Figure 19-6. *Viewing hidden types within our interop assembly*

Simply put, each COM class is represented by three distinct .NET types. First, you have a .NET class that is identically named to the original COM type (`ComCalc`, in this case). Next, you have a second .NET class that takes a `Class` suffix (`ComCalcClass`). These types are very helpful when you have a COM type that implements several custom interfaces, in that the `Class`-suffixed types expose *all* members from *each* COM interface supported by the COM type. Thus, from a .NET programmer's point of view, there is no need to manually obtain a reference to a specific COM interface before invoking its functionality. Although `ComCalc` did not implement multiple custom interfaces, we are able to invoke the `Add()` and `Subtract()` methods from a `ComCalcClass` object (rather than a `ComCalc` object) as follows:

```
Module Program
  Sub Main()
    Console.WriteLine("***** The .NET COM Client App *****")

    ' Now using the Class-suffixed type.
    Dim comObj As New ComCalcClass()
    Console.WriteLine("COM server says 10 + 832 is {0}", _
      comObj.Add(10, 832))
    Console.ReadLine()
  End Sub
End Module
```

Finally, interop assemblies define .NET equivalents of any original COM interfaces defined within the COM server. In this case, we find a .NET interface named `_ComCalc`. Unless you are well versed in the mechanics of VB6 COM, this is certain to appear strange, given that we never directly created an interface in our SimpleComServer project (let alone the oddly named `_ComCalc` interface). The role of these underscore-prefixed interfaces will become clear as you move throughout this chapter; for now, simply know that if you really wanted to, you could make use of interface-based programming techniques to invoke `Add()` or `Subtract()`:

```
Module Program
  Sub Main()
    Console.WriteLine("***** The .NET COM Client App *****")

    ' Now manually obtain the hidden interface.
    Dim i As _ComCalc
    Dim c As New ComCalc()
    i = c
    Console.WriteLine("COM server says 10 + 832 is {0}", _
      i.Add(10, 832))
    Console.ReadLine()
  End Sub
End Module
```

Now, do understand that invoking a method using the `Class`-suffixed or underscore-prefixed interface is seldom necessary (which is exactly why the Visual Studio 2008 Object Browser hides these types by default). However, as you build more complex .NET applications that need to work with COM types in more sophisticated manners, having knowledge of these types is critical.

Source Code The VbNetSimpleComClient project is located under the Chapter 19 subdirectory.

Understanding the Runtime Callable Wrapper

As mentioned, at runtime the CLR will make use of the metadata contained within a .NET interop assembly to create a proxy that will manage the process of .NET to COM communication. The proxy to which I am referring is the Runtime Callable Wrapper (RCW), which is little more than a bridge to the real COM object. Every COM object accessed by a .NET client requires a corresponding RCW. Thus, if you have a single .NET application that uses three COM objects, you end up with three distinct RCWs that map .NET calls into COM requests. Figure 19-7 illustrates the big picture.

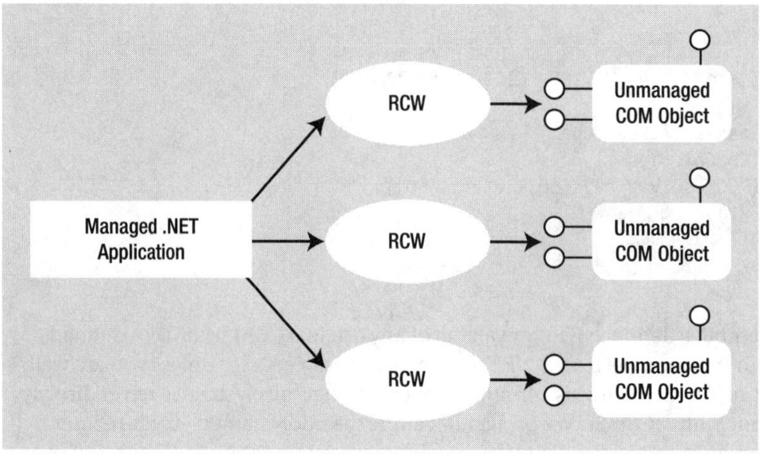

Figure 19-7. *RCWs sit between the .NET caller and the COM object.*

■ **Note** There is always a single RCW per COM object, regardless of how many interfaces the .NET client has obtained from the COM type (you'll examine a multi-interfaced VB6 COM object a bit later in this chapter). Using this technique, the RCW can maintain the correct COM identity (and reference count) of the COM object.

Again, the good news is that the RCW is created automatically when required by the CLR. The other bit of good news is that legacy COM servers do not require any modifications to be consumed by a .NET-aware language. The intervening RCW takes care of the internal work. To see how this is achieved, let's formalize some core responsibilities of the RCW.

The RCW: Exposing COM Types As .NET Types

The RCW is in charge of transforming COM data types into .NET equivalents (and vice versa). As a simple example, assume you have a VB6 COM subroutine defined as follows:

```
' VB6 COM method definition.
Public Sub DisplayThisString(ByVal s as String)
```

The interop assembly defines the method parameter as a .NET `System.String`:

```
' VB 2008 mapping of COM method.
Public Sub DisplayThisString(ByVal s as System.String)
```

When this method is invoked by the .NET code base, the RCW automatically takes the incoming `System.String` and transforms it into a VB6 `String` data type (which, as you may know, is in fact a COM `BSTR`). As you would guess, all VB6 COM data types have a corresponding .NET equivalent. To help you gain your bearings, Table 19-1 documents the mapping taking place between COM IDL (interface definition language) data types, the related .NET `System` data types, and the corresponding VB 2008 keyword.

Table 19-1. *Mapping Intrinsic COM Types to .NET Types*

COM IDL Data Type	`System` Types	Visual Basic 2008 Data Type
`wchar_t`, `short`	`System.Int16`	`Short`
`long`, `int`	`System.Int32`	`Integer`
`Hyper`	`System.Int64`	`Long`
`unsigned char`, `byte`	`System.Byte`	`Byte`
`single`	`System.Single`	`Single`
`double`	`System.Double`	`Double`
`VARIANT_BOOL`	`System.Boolean`	`Boolean`
`BSTR`	`System.String`	`String`
`VARIANT`	`System.Object`	`Object`
`DECIMAL`	`System.Decimal`	`Decimal`
`DATE`	`System.DateTime`	`DateTime`
`GUID`	`System.Guid`	`Guid`
`CURRENCY`	`System.Decimal`	`Decimal`
`IUnknown`	`System.Object`	`Object`
`IDispatch`	`System.Object`	`Object`

Note You will come to understand the importance of having some knowledge of IDL data types as you progress through this chapter.

The RCW: Managing a Coclass's Reference Count

Another important duty of the RCW is to manage the reference count of the COM object. As you may know from your experience with COM, the COM reference-counting scheme is a joint venture between coclass and client and revolves around the proper use of `AddRef()` and `Release()` calls. COM objects self-destruct when they detect that they have no outstanding references (thankfully, VB6 would call these low-level COM methods behind the scenes).

However, .NET types do not use the COM reference-counting scheme, and therefore a .NET client should not be forced to call `Release()` on the COM types it uses. To keep each participant happy, the RCW caches all interface references internally and triggers the final release when the type is no longer used by the .NET client. The bottom line is that similar to VB6, .NET clients never explicitly call `AddRef()`, `Release()`, or `QueryInterface()`.

Note If you wish to directly interact with a COM object's reference count from a .NET application, the `System.Runtime.InteropServices` namespace provides a type named `Marshal`. This class defines a number of shared methods, many of which can be used to manually interact with a COM object's lifetime. Although you will typically not need to make use of `Marshal` in most of your applications, consult the .NET Framework 3.5 SDK documentation for further details.

The RCW: Hiding Low-Level COM Interfaces

The final core service provided by the RCW is to consume a number of low-level COM interfaces. Because the RCW tries to do everything it can to fool the .NET client into thinking it is communicating with a native .NET type, the RCW must hide various low-level COM interfaces from view.

For example, when you build a COM class that supports `IConnectionPointContainer` (and maintains a subobject or two supporting `IConnectionPoint`), the coclass in question is able to fire events back to the COM client. VB6 hides this entire process from view using the `Event` and `RaiseEvent` keywords. In the same vein, the RCW also hides such COM "goo" from the .NET client. Table 19-2 outlines the role of these hidden COM interfaces consumed by the RCW.

Table 19-2. *Hidden COM Interfaces*

Hidden COM Interface	Meaning in Life
`IConnectionPointContainer` `IConnectionPoint`	These interfaces enable a coclass to send events back to an interested client. VB6 automatically provides a default implementation of each of these interfaces.
`IDispatch` `IProvideClassInfo`	These interfaces facilitate "late binding" to a coclass. Again, when you are building VB6 COM types, these interfaces are automatically supported by a given COM type.

`IErrorInfo`
`ISupportErrorInfo`
`ICreateErrorInfo`
	These interfaces enable COM clients and COM objects to send and respond to COM errors.

`IUnknown`	The granddaddy of COM. This interface manages the reference count of the COM object and allows clients to obtain interfaces from the coclass.

The Role of COM IDL

At this point you hopefully have a solid understanding of the role of the interop assembly and the RCW. Before you go much further into the COM to .NET conversion process, it is necessary to review some of the basic details of COM IDL. Understand, of course, that this chapter is *not* intended to function as a complete COM IDL tutorial; however, to better understand the interop layer, you only need to be aware of a few IDL constructs.

As you saw in Chapter 16, a .NET assembly contains *metadata*. Formally speaking, metadata is used to describe each and every aspect of a .NET assembly, including the internal types (their members, base class, and so on), assembly version, and optional assembly-level information (strong name, culture, and so on).

In many ways, .NET metadata is the big brother of an earlier metadata format used to describe classic COM servers. Classic ActiveX COM servers (`*.dlls` or `*.exes`) document their internal types using a *type library*, which may be realized as a stand-alone `*.tlb` file or bundled into the COM server as an internal resource (which is the default behavior of VB6). COM type libraries are themselves created using a metadata language called the Interface Definition Language and a special compiler named `midl.exe` (the Microsoft IDL compiler).

VB6 does a fantastic job of hiding type libraries and IDL from view. In fact, many skilled VB COM programmers can live a happy and productive life ignoring the syntax of IDL altogether. Nevertheless, whenever you compile ActiveX project workspace types, VB automatically generates and embeds the type library within the physical `*.dll` or `*.exe` COM server. Furthermore, VB6 ensures that the type library is automatically registered under a very particular part of the system registry: HKEY_CLASSES_ROOT\TypeLib (see Figure 19-8).

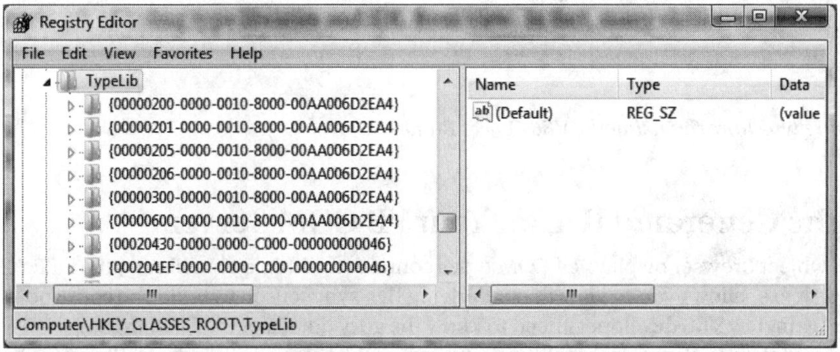

Figure 19-8. *HKCR\TypeLib lists all registered type libraries on a given machine.*

Type libraries are referenced all the time by numerous IDEs. For example, whenever you access the Project ➤ References menu selection of VB6, the IDE consults HKEY_CLASSES_ROOT\TypeLib to determine each and every registered type library, as shown in Figure 19-9.

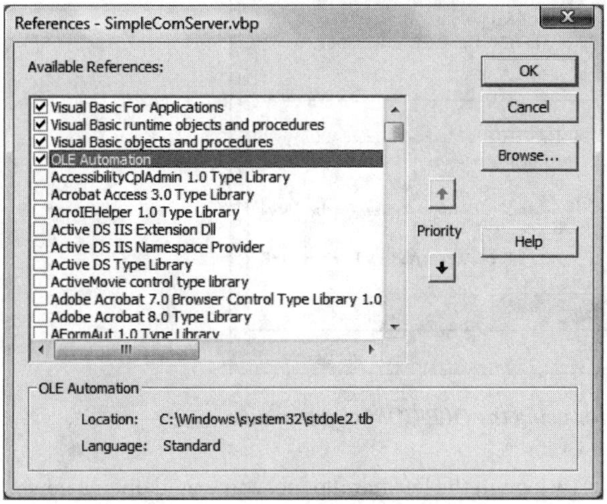

Figure 19-9. *Referencing COM type information from VB6*

Likewise, when you open the VB6 Object Browser, the VB6 IDE reads the type information and displays the contents of the COM server using a friendly GUI, as shown in Figure 19-10.

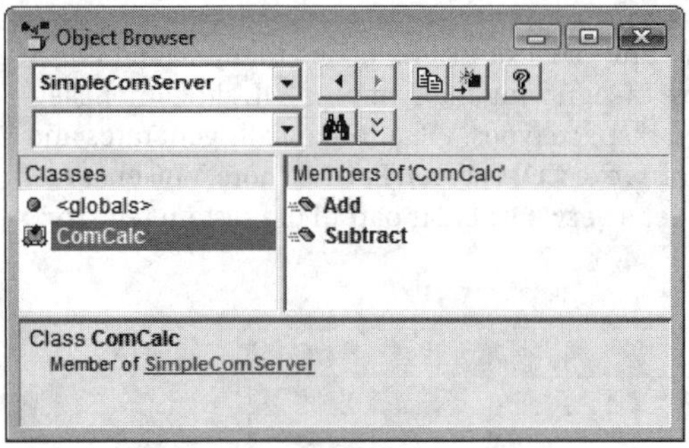

Figure 19-10. *Viewing type libraries using the VB6 Object Browser*

Observing the Generated IDL for Your VB COM Server

Although the VB6 Object Browser displays all COM types contained within a type library, the OLE View utility (`oleview.exe`) allows you to view the underlying IDL syntax used to build the correspon-ding type library. Again, few VB6 developers need to know the gory details of the IDL language; however, to better understand the interoperability layer, open OLE View (via Start ➤ All Programs ➤ Microsoft Visual Studio 6.0 ➤ Microsoft Visual Studio 6.0 Tools) and locate the SimpleComServer server under the Type Libraries node of the tree view control, as shown in Figure 19-11.

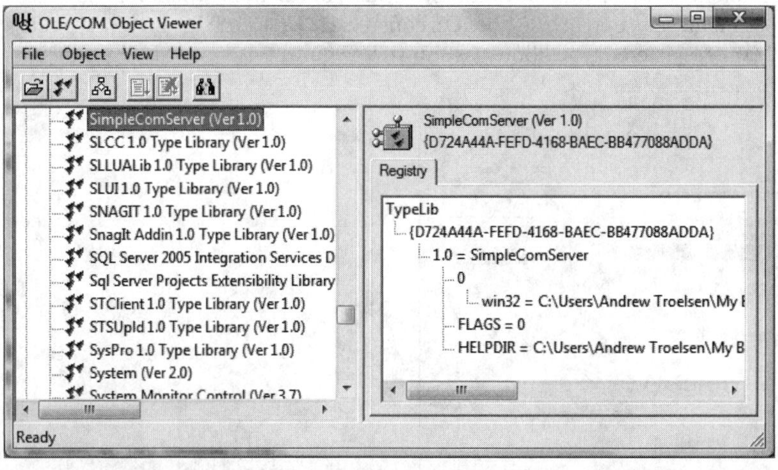

Figure 19-11. *Hunting down SimpleComServer using the OLE/COM object viewer*

If you were to double-click the type library icon in the left-hand pane, you would open a new window that shows you all of the IDL tokens that constitute the type library generated by the VB6 compiler. Here is the relevant—and slightly reformatted—IDL (your `[uuid]` values will differ):

```
[uuid(8AED93CB-7832-4699-A2FC-CAE08693E720), version(1.0)]
library SimpleComServer
{
```

```
  importlib("stdole2.tlb");
  interface _ComCalc;

  [odl, uuid(5844CD28-2075-4E77-B619-9B65AA0761A3), version(1.0),
   hidden, dual, nonextensible, oleautomation]
  interface _ComCalc : IDispatch {
    [id(0x60030000)]
    HRESULT Add([in] short x, [in] short y,
                [out, retval] short*);
    [id(0x60030001)]
    HRESULT Subtract([in] short x, [in] short y,
                     [out, retval] short*);
    };

    [uuid(012B1485-6834-47FF-8E53-3090FE85050C), version(1.0)]
    coclass ComCalc {
        [default] interface _ComCalc;
    };
};
```

IDL Attributes

To begin parsing out this IDL, notice that IDL syntax contains blocks of code placed in square brackets ([...]). Within these brackets is a comma-delimited set of IDL keywords, which are used to disambiguate the "very next thing" (the item to the right of the block or the item directly below the block). These blocks are IDL *attributes* that serve the same purpose as .NET attributes (i.e., they describe something). One key IDL attribute is [uuid], which is used to assign the globally unique identifier (GUID) of a given COM type. As you may already know, just about everything in COM is assigned a GUID (interfaces, COM classes, type libraries, and so on), which is used to uniquely identify a given item.

The IDL Library Statement

Starting at the top, you have the COM "library statement," which is marked using the IDL library keyword. Contained within the library statement are each and every interface and COM class, and any enumeration (through the VB6 Enum keyword) and user-defined type (through the VB6 Type keyword). In the case of SimpleComServer, the type library lists exactly one COM class, ComCalc, which is marked using the *coclass* (i.e., COM class) keyword.

The Role of the [default] Interface

According to the laws of COM, the only possible way in which a COM client can communicate with a COM class is to use an interface reference (not an object reference). If you have created C++-based COM clients, you are well aware of the process of querying for a given interface, releasing the interface when it is no longer used, and so forth. However, when you make use of VB6 to build COM clients, you receive a *default interface* on the COM class automatically.

When you build VB6 COM servers, any public member on a *.cls file (such as your Add() function) is placed onto the "default interface" of the COM class. Now, if you examine the class definition of ComCalc, you can see that the name of the default interface is _ComCalc:

```
[uuid(012B1485-6834-47FF-8E53-3090FE85050C), version(1.0)]
coclass ComCalc {
  [default] interface _ComCalc;
};
```

In case you are wondering, the name of the default interface VB6 constructs in the background is always _NameOfTheClass (the underscore is a naming convention used to specify a hidden interface, the very interface the VS 2008 Object Browser did not show by default). Thus, if you have a class named Car, the default interface is _Car, a class named DataConnector has a default interface named _DataConnector, and so forth.

Under VB6, the default interface is completely hidden from view. However, when you write the following VB6 code:

```
' VB6 COM client code.
Dim c As ComCalc
Set c = New ComCalc ' [default] _ComCalc interface returned automatically!
```

the VB runtime automatically queries the object for the default interface (as specified by the type library) and returns it to the client. Because VB always returns the default interface on a COM class, you can pretend that you have a true object reference. However, this is only a bit of syntactic sugar provided by VB6. In COM, there is no such thing as a direct object reference. You always have an interface reference (even if it happens to be the default).

The Role of IDispatch

If you examine the IDL description of the default _ComCalc interface, you see that this interface derives from a standard COM interface named IDispatch. While a full discussion concerning the role of IDispatch is well outside of the scope of this chapter, simply understand that this is the interface that makes it possible to interact with COM objects on the Web from within a classic Active Server Page, as well as anywhere else where late binding is required.

When you use VB proper (as opposed to VBScript), 99 percent of the time you want to avoid the use of IDispatch (it is slower, and errors are discovered at runtime rather than at compile time). However, just to illustrate, say you call the VB6 CreateObject() method as follows:

```
' VB6 late binding.
Dim o As Object
Set o = CreateObject("SimpleComServer.ComCalc")
```

You have actually instructed the VB runtime to query the COM type for the IDispatch interface. However, be aware that calling CreateObject() alone does not automatically obtain the IDispatch interface. In addition, you must store the return value in a VB6 Object data type.

IDL Parameter Attributes

The final bit of IDL that you need to be aware of is how VB6 parameters are expressed under the hood. As you know, under VB6 all parameters are passed by reference, unless the ByVal keyword is used explicitly, which is represented using the IDL [in] attribute. Furthermore, a function's return value is marked using the [out, retval] attributes. Thus, the following VB6 function:

```
' VB6 function
Public Function Add(ByVal x as Integer, ByVal y as Integer) as Integer
  Add = x + y
End Function
```

would be expressed in IDL like so:

```
HRESULT Add([in] short x, [in] short y, [out, retval] short*);
```

On the other hand, if you do not mark a parameter using the VB6 ByVal keyword, ByRef is assumed:

```
' These parameters are passed ByRef under VB6!
Public Function Subtract(x As Integer, y As Integer) As Integer
  Subtract = x - y
End Function
```

ByRef parameters are marked in IDL via the [in, out] attributes:

```
HRESULT Subtract([in, out] short* x,  [in, out] short* y,  [out, retval] short*);
```

Using a Type Library to Build an Interop Assembly

To be sure, the VB6 compiler generates many other IDL attributes under the hood, and you see additional bits and pieces where appropriate. However, at this point, I am sure you are wondering exactly why I spent the last several pages describing the COM IDL. The reason is simple: when you add a reference to a COM server using Visual Studio 2008, the IDE reads the type library to build the corresponding interop assembly. While VS 2008 does a very good job of generating an interop assembly, the Add Reference dialog box follows a default set of rules regarding how the interop assembly will be constructed and does not allow you to fine-tune this construction.

If you require a greater level of flexibility, you have the option of generating interop assemblies at the command prompt, using a .NET tool named `tlbimp.exe` (the type library importer utility). Among other things, `tlbimp.exe` allows you to control the name of the .NET namespace that will contain the types and the name of the output file. Furthermore, if you wish to assign a strong name to your interop assembly in order to deploy it to the GAC, `tlbimp.exe` provides the `/keyfile` flag to specify the `*.snk` file (see Chapter 15 for details regarding strong names). To view all of your options, simply type **tlbimp** at a Visual Studio 2008 command prompt and hit the Enter key, as shown in Figure 19-12.

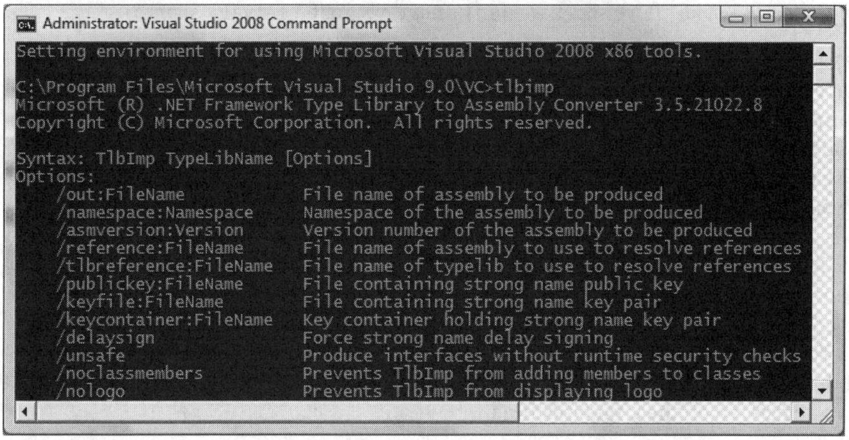

Figure 19-12. *Options of* `tlbimp.exe`

While this tool has numerous options, the following command could be used to generate a strongly named interop assembly named `CalcInteropAsm.dll`:

```
tlbimp SimpleComServer.dll /keyfile:myKeyPair.snk /out:CalcInteropAsm.dll
```

Again, if you are happy with the interop assembly created by Visual Studio 2008, you are not required to directly make use of `tlbimp.exe`.

Late Binding to the CoCalc Coclass

Once you have generated an interop assembly (using `tlbimp.exe` or Visual Studio), your .NET applications are now able to make use of their types using early binding or late binding techniques. Given that you have already seen how to create a COM type using early binding at the opening of this chapter (via the VB 2008 `New` keyword), let's turn our attention to activating a COM object using late binding.

As you recall from Chapter 16, the `System.Reflection` namespace provides a way for you to programmatically inspect the types contained in a given assembly at runtime. In COM, the same sort of functionality is supported through the use of a set of standard interfaces (e.g., `ITypeLib`, `ITypeInfo`, and so on). When a client binds to a member at runtime (rather than at compile time), the client is said to exercise "late" binding.

By and large, you should always prefer the early binding technique using the VB 2008 `New` keyword. There are times, however, when you must use late binding to a COM object. For example, some legacy COM servers may have been constructed in such a way that they provide no type information whatsoever. If this is the case, it should be clear that you cannot run the `tlbimp.exe` utility in the first place. For these rare occurrences, you can access classic COM types using .NET reflection services.

The process of late binding begins with a client obtaining the `IDispatch` interface from a given COM object. This standard COM interface defines a total of four methods, only two of which you need to concern yourself with at the moment. First, you have `GetIDsOfNames()`. This method allows a late bound client to obtain the numerical value (called the `dispatch ID`, or `DISPID`) used to identify the method it is attempting to invoke.

In COM IDL, a member's DISPID is assigned using the `[id]` attribute. If you examine the IDL code generated by Visual Basic (using the OLE View tool), you will see that the DISPID of the `Add()` method has been assigned a DISPID such as the following:

```
[id(0x60030000)] HRESULT Add( [in] short x, [in] short y, [out, retval] short*);
```

This is the value that `GetIDsOfNames()` returns to the late bound client. Once the client obtains this value, it makes a call to the next method of interest, `Invoke()`. This method of `IDispatch` takes a number of arguments, one of which is the DISPID obtained using `GetIDsOfNames()`. In addition, the `Invoke()` method takes an array of `COM VARIANT` types that represent the parameters passed to the function. In the case of the `Add()` method, this array contains two `shorts` (of some value). The final argument of `Invoke()` is another `VARIANT` that holds the return value of the method invocation (again, a `short`).

Although a .NET client using late binding does not directly use the `IDispatch` interface, the same general functionality comes through using the `System.Reflection` namespace. To illustrate, the following is another VB 2008 client that uses late binding to trigger the `Add()` logic. Notice that this application does *not* make reference to the assembly in any way and therefore does not require the use of the `tlbimp.exe` utility. All that is required for late binding to occur is that the original COM server is correctly registered on the target machine.

```
Imports System.Reflection

Module Program
  Sub Main()
    Console.WriteLine("***** The Late Bound .NET Client *****")

    ' First get IDispatch reference from coclass.
    Dim calcObj As Type = _
      Type.GetTypeFromProgID("SimpleCOMServer.ComCalc")
    Dim calcDisp As Object = Activator.CreateInstance(calcObj)
```

```
    ' Make the array of args.
    Dim addArgs() As Object = {100, 24}

    ' Invoke the Add() method and obtain summation.
    Dim sum As Object
    sum = calcObj.InvokeMember("Add", BindingFlags.InvokeMethod, _
      Nothing, calcDisp, addArgs)

    ' Display result.
    Console.WriteLine("Late bound adding: 100 + 24 is: {0}", sum)
  End Sub
End Module
```

Finally, be aware that VB 2008 does allow you to simplify your late binding code by making use of the legacy `CreateObject()` method. However, the following VB 2008 late binding code would *only* work if `Option Strict` is disabled:

```
' This will only compile if Option Strict is disabled.
Dim c As Object = CreateObject("SimpleCOMServer.ComCalc")
Console.WriteLine("10 + 10 = {0}", c.Add(10, 10))
```

■ **Source Code** The VbNetComClientLateBinding application is included under the Chapter 19 subdirectory.

Building a More Interesting VB6 COM Server

So much for Math 101. It's time to build a more exotic VB6 ActiveX server that makes use of more elaborate COM programming techniques. Create a brand-new ActiveX `*.dll` workspace and save it under the name of Vb6ComCarServer. Rename your initial class file to `CoCar.cls`, which is implemented like so:

```
Option Explicit

' A COM enum.
Enum CarType
  Viper
  Colt
  BMW
End Enum

' A COM Event.
Public Event BlewUp()

' Member variables.
Private currSp As Integer
Private maxSp As Integer
Private make As CarType

' Remember! All Public members
' are exposed by the default interface!
Public Property Get CurrentSpeed() As Integer
  CurrentSpeed = currSp
End Property
```

```
Public Property Get CarMake() As CarType
  CarMake = make
End Property

Public Sub SpeedUp()
  currSp = currSp + 10
  If currSp > maxSp Then
    RaiseEvent BlewUp  ' Fire event If you max out the engine.
  End If
End Sub

Private Sub Class_Initialize()
  MsgBox "Init COM car"
End Sub

Public Sub Create(ByVal maximumSpeed As Integer, _
  ByVal currentSpeed As Integer, ByVal carMake As CarType)
  maxSp = maximumSpeed
  currSp = currentSpeed
  make = carMake
End Sub
```

As you can see, this is a simple COM class that mimics the functionality of the VB 2008 `Car` class used throughout this text. The only point of interest is the `Create()` subroutine, which allows the caller to pass in the state data representing the `Car` object. (Remember, VB6 has no support for class constructors!)

Supporting an Additional COM Interface

Now that you have fleshed out the details of building a COM class with a single (default) interface, insert a new `*.cls` file that defines the following `IDriverInfo` interface:

```
Option Explicit

' Driver has a name
Public Property Let DriverName(ByVal s As String)
End Property

Public Property Get DriverName() As String
End Property
```

If you have created COM objects supporting multiple interfaces, you are aware that VB6 provides the `Implements` keyword. Assume you have added a private `String` variable (`driverName`) to the `CoCar` class type and implemented the `IDriverInfo` interface as follows:

```
' Implemented interfaces
Implements IDriverInfo
...

' ***** IDriverInfo impl ***** '
Private Property Let IDriverInfo_DriverName(ByVal RHS As String)
  driverName = RHS
End Property

Private Property Get IDriverInfo_DriverName() As String
  IDriverInfo_driverName = driverName
End Property
```

To wrap up this interface implementation, set the Instancing property of IDriverInfo to PublicNotCreatable (given that the outside world should not be able to "New" an interface reference). To do so, select IDriverInfo in the Project window, and then in the Properties window locate the Instancing property. Set it to PublicNotCreatable.

Exposing an Inner Object

Under VB6 (as well as COM itself), we do not have the luxury of classical implementation inheritance. Rather, you are limited to the use of the containment/delegation model (the "has-a" relationship). For testing purposes, add a final *.cls file to your current VB6 project named Engine, and set its instancing property to PublicNotCreatable (as you want to prevent the user from directly creating an Engine object).

The default public interface of Engine is short and sweet. Define a single function that returns an array of strings to the outside world representing pet names for each cylinder of the engine (okay, no right-minded person gives friendly names to his or her cylinders, but hey . . .):

```
Option Explicit

Public Function GetCylinders() As String()
  Dim c(3) As String
  c(0) = "Grimey"
  c(1) = "Thumper"
  c(2) = "Oily"
  c(3) = "Crusher"
  GetCylinders = c
End Function
```

Finally, add a method to the default interface of CoCar named GetEngine(), which returns an instance of the contained Engine (I assume you will create a Private member variable named eng of type Engine for this purpose):

```
' Member variables.
Private eng As Engine
...

Public Sub Create(ByVal maximumSpeed As Integer, _
  ByVal currentSpeed As Integer, ByVal carMake As CarType)
  Set eng = New Engine
  ...
End Sub

Public Function GetEngine() As Engine
  Set GetEngine = eng
End Function
```

At this point you have an ActiveX server that contains a COM class supporting two interfaces. As well, you are able to return an internal COM type using the [default] interface of the CoCar and interact with some common programming constructs (enumerations and COM arrays). Go ahead and compile your server (setting binary compatibility, once finished), and then close down your current VB6 workspace.

Source Code The Vb6ComCarServer project is included under the Chapter 19 subdirectory.

Examining the Interop Assembly

Rather than making use of the `tlbimp.exe` utility to generate our interop assembly, simply create a new console project (named VbNetCarClient) using Visual Studio 2008 and set a reference to the `Vb6ComCarServer.dll` using the COM tab of the Add Reference dialog box. Now, examine the interop assembly using the VS 2008 Object Browser utility, as shown in Figure 19-13.

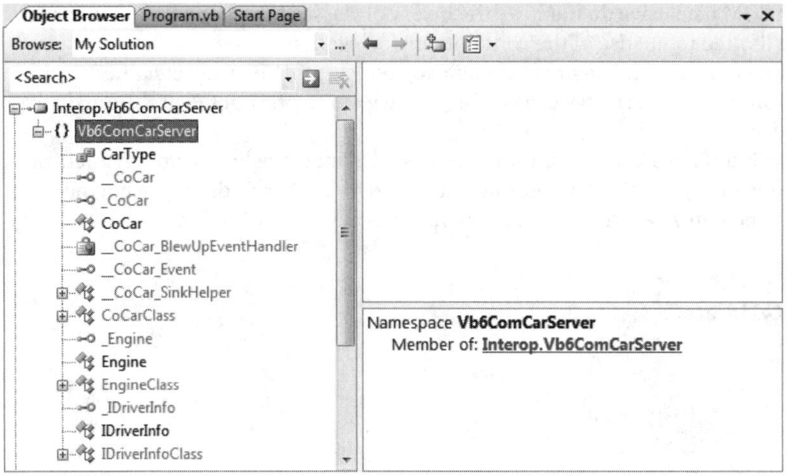

Figure 19-13. *The* `Interop.VbComCarServer.dll` *assembly*

Assuming you have configured the Object Browser to show hidden types, you will find that you once again have a number of `Class`-suffixed and underscore-prefixed interface types, as well as a number of new items we have not yet examined, whose names suggest they may be used to handle COM to .NET event notifications (`__CoCar_Event`, `__CoCar_SinkHelper`, and `__CoCarBlewUpEventHandler` in particular). Recall from earlier in this chapter, I mentioned that when a COM object exposes COM events, the interop assembly will contain additional CIL code that is used by the CLR to map COM events to .NET events (you'll see them in action in just a bit).

Building Our VB 2008 Client Application

Given that the CLR will automatically create the necessary RCW at runtime, our VB 2008 application can program directly against the `CoCar`, `CarType`, `Engine`, and `IDriveInfo` types as if they were all implemented using managed code. Here is the complete module, with analysis to follow:

```
Imports Vb6ComCarServer

Module Program
  ' Create the COM class using
  ' Early binding.
  Public WithEvents myCar As New CoCar()

  Sub Main()
    Console.WriteLine("***** CoCar Client App *****")

    ' Call the Create() method.
    myCar.Create(50, 10, CarType.BMW)
```

```
    ' Set name of driver.
    Dim itf As IDriverInfo
    itf = myCar
    itf.driverName = "Fred"
    Console.WriteLine("Driver is named: {0}", itf.driverName)

    ' Print type of car.
    Console.WriteLine("Your car is a {0}.", myCar.CarMake())
    Console.WriteLine()

    ' Get the Engine and print name of all Cylinders.
    Dim eng As Engine = myCar.GetEngine()
    Console.WriteLine("Your Cylinders are named:")
    Dim names() As String = eng.GetCylinders()
    For Each s As String In names
      Console.WriteLine(s)
    Next
    Console.WriteLine()

    ' Speed up car to trigger event.
    For i As Integer = 0 To 3
      myCar.SpeedUp()
    Next
    Console.ReadLine()
  End Sub

  Private Sub myCar_BlewUp() Handles myCar.BlewUp
    Console.WriteLine("***** Ek!  Car is doomed...! *****")
  End Sub
End Module
```

Interacting with the CoCar Type

Recall that when we created the VB6 CoCar, we defined and implemented a custom COM interface named IDriverInfo, in addition to the automatically generated default interface (_CoCar) created by the VB6 compiler. When our Main() method creates an instance of CoCar, we only have direct access to the members of the _CoCar interface, which as you recall will be composed by each public member of the COM class:

```
' Here, you are really working with the [default] interface.
myCar.Create(50, 10, CarType.BMW)
```

Given this fact, in order to invoke the driverName property of the IDriverInfo interface, we must explicitly cast the CoCar object to an IDriverInfo interface as follows (unless you set Option Strict to Off, in which case you could make use of a direct assignment):

```
' Set name of driver.
Dim itf As IDriverInfo
itf = CType(myCar, IDriverInfo)
itf.driverName = "Fred"
Console.WriteLine("Driver is named: {0}", itf.driverName)
```

Recall, however, that when a type library is converted into an interop assembly, it will contain Class-suffixed types that expose every member of every interface. Therefore, if you so choose, you could simplify your programming if you create and make use of a CoCarClass object, rather than a CoCar object. For example, consider the following subroutine, which makes use of members of the default interface of CoCar as well as members of IDriverInfo:

```
Sub UseCar()
  Dim c As New CoCarClass()

  ' This property is a member of IDriverInfo.
  c.driverName = "Mary"

  ' This method is a member of _CoCar.
  c.SpeedUp()
End Sub
```

■ **Note** Remember, because the `Class`-suffixed types are hidden by default, they will not appear in the Visual Studio 2008 IntelliSense.

If you are wondering exactly how this single type is exposing members of each implemented interface, check out the list of implemented interfaces and the base class of `CoCarClass` using the Visual Studio 2008 Object Browser (see Figure 19-14).

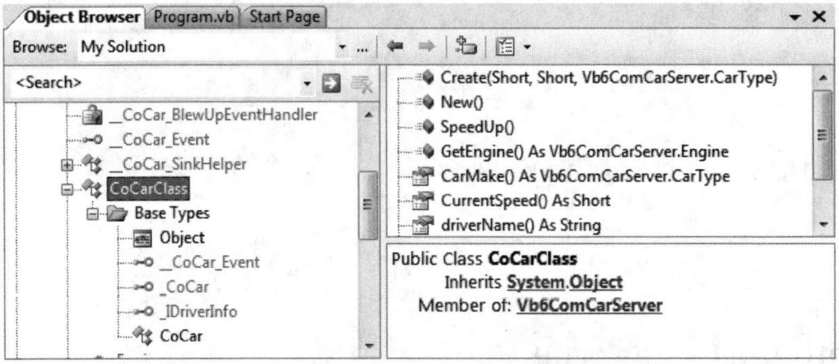

Figure 19-14. *The composition of* `CoCarClass`

As you can see, this type implements the hidden `_CoCar` and `_IDriverInfo` interfaces and exposes them as "normal" public members.

Intercepting COM Events

In Chapter 11, you learned about the .NET event model. Recall that this architecture is based on delegating the flow of logic from one part of the application to another. The entity in charge of forwarding a request is a type deriving from `System.MulticastDelegate`, which we create indirectly in VB 2008 using the `Delegate` keyword.

When the `tlbimp.exe` utility encounters event definitions in the COM server's type library, it responds by creating a number of managed types that wrap the low-level COM connection point architecture. Using these types, you can pretend to add a member to a `System.MulticastDelegate`'s internal list of methods. Under the hood, of course, the proxy is mapping the incoming COM event to their managed equivalents. Table 19-3 briefly describes these types.

Table 19-3. *COM Event Helper Types*

Generated Type (Based on the `_CarEvents [source]` Interface)	Meaning in Life
`__CoCar_Event`	This is a managed interface that defines the add and remove members used to add (or remove) a method to (or from) the `System.MulticastDelegate`'s linked list.
`__CoCar_BlewUpEventHandler`	This is the managed delegate (which derives from `System.MulticastDelegate`).
`__CoCar_SinkHelper`	This generated class is used internally to map COM events to .NET events.

As you would hope, the VB 2008 language does not require you to make direct use of these types. Rather, you are able to handle the incoming COM events in the same way you handle events based on the .NET delegation architecture. Simply declare the COM object `WithEvents`, and use the `Handles` keyword to map the event to a given method (or make use of the `AddHandler`/`RemoveHandler` statements).

```
Module Program
  Public WithEvents myCar As New CoCar()
...
  Private Sub myCar_BlewUp() Handles myCar.BlewUp
    Console.WriteLine("***** Ek!  Car is doomed...! *****")
  End Sub
End Module
```

■ **Source Code** The VbNetCarClient project is included under the Chapter 19 subdirectory.

That wraps up our investigation of how a .NET application can communicate with a legacy COM application. Now be aware that the techniques you have just learned would work for *any* COM server at all. This is important to remember, given that many COM servers might never be rewritten as native .NET applications. For example, the object models of Microsoft Outlook and Microsoft Office products are currently exposed only through a COM interop assembly. Thus, if you needed to build a .NET program that interacted with these products, the interoperability layer is (currently) mandatory.

■ **Note** Be aware that many COM component vendors (including Microsoft) have already created "primary interop assemblies" for commonly used COM applications (such as Office and Outlook). These primary interop assemblies have been optimized to ensure the best performance and will typically be listed within the COM tab of the Visual Studio 2008 Add Reference dialog box.

Understanding COM to .NET Interoperability

The next topic of this chapter is to examine the process of a COM application communicating with a .NET type. This "direction" of interop allows legacy COM code bases (such as your existing VB6 projects) to make use of functionality contained within newer .NET assemblies. As you might imagine, this situation is less likely to occur than .NET to COM interop; however, it is still worth exploring. For example, using this direction of interop, it would be possible to consume a custom .NET Windows Forms control library from within a VB6 Windows application.

In order for a COM application to make use of a .NET type, we somehow need to fool the COM program into believing that the managed .NET type is in fact *unmanaged*. In essence, you need to allow the COM application to interact with the .NET type using the functionality required by the COM architecture. For example, the COM type should be able to obtain new interfaces through `QueryInterface()` calls, simulate unmanaged memory management using `AddRef()` and `Release()`, make use of the COM connection point protocol, and so on. Again, although VB6 does not expose this level of COM infrastructure to the surface, it must exist nonetheless.

Beyond fooling the COM client, COM to .NET interoperability also involves fooling the COM runtime. As you know, a COM server is activated using the COM runtime rather than the CLR. For this to happen, the COM runtime must look up numerous bits of information in the system registry (ProgIDs, CLSIDs, IIDs, and so forth). The problem, of course, is that .NET assemblies are not registered in the registry in the first place!

In a nutshell, to make your .NET assemblies available to COM clients, you must take the following steps:

1. Register your .NET assembly in the system registry to allow the COM runtime to locate it.
2. Generate a COM type library (`*.tlb`) file (based on the .NET metadata) to allow the COM client to interact with the public types.
3. Deploy the assembly in the same directory as the COM client or (more typically) install it into the GAC.

As you will see, these steps can be performed using Visual Studio 2008 or at the command line using various tools that ship with the .NET Framework 3.5 SDK.

The Attributes of System.Runtime.InteropServices

In addition to performing these steps, you will typically also need to decorate your VB 2008 types with various .NET attributes, all of which are defined in the `System.Runtime.InteropServices` namespace. These attributes ultimately control how the COM type library is created and therefore control how the COM application is able to interact with your managed types. Table 19-4 documents some (but not all) of the attributes you can use to control the generated COM type library.

Table 19-4. *Select Attributes of* `System.Runtime.InteropServices`

.NET Interop Attribute	Meaning in Life
`<ClassInterface()>`	This attribute is used to create a default COM interface for a .NET class type.
`<ComClass()>`	This attribute is similar to `<ClassInterface()>`, except it also provides the ability to establish the GUIDs used for the class ID (CLSID) and interface IDs of the COM types within the type library.
`<DispId()>`	This attribute is used to hard-code the DISPID values assigned to a member for purposes of late binding.
`<Guid()>`	This attribute is used to hard-code a GUID value in the COM type library.
`<In()>`	This attribute exposes a member parameter as an input parameter in COM IDL.
`<InterfaceType()>`	This attribute is used to control how a .NET interface should be exposed to COM (`IDispatch`-only, dual, or `IUnknown`-only).
`<Out()>`	This attribute exposes a member parameter as an output parameter in COM IDL.

Now do be aware that for simple COM to .NET interop scenarios, you are not required to adorn your .NET code base with dozens of attributes in order to control how the underlying COM type library is defined. However, when you need to be very specific regarding how your .NET types will be exposed to COM, the more you understand COM IDL attributes, the better, given that the attributes defined in `System.Runtime.InteropServices` are little more than managed definitions of these IDL keywords.

The Role of the CCW

Before we walk through the steps of exposing a .NET type to COM, let's take a look at exactly how COM programs interact with .NET types using a COM Callable Wrapper, or CCW. As you have seen, when a .NET program communicates with a COM type, the CLR creates a Runtime Callable Wrapper. In a similar vein, when a COM client accesses a .NET type, the CLR makes use of an intervening proxy termed the COM Callable Wrapper to negotiate the COM to .NET conversion (see Figure 19-15).

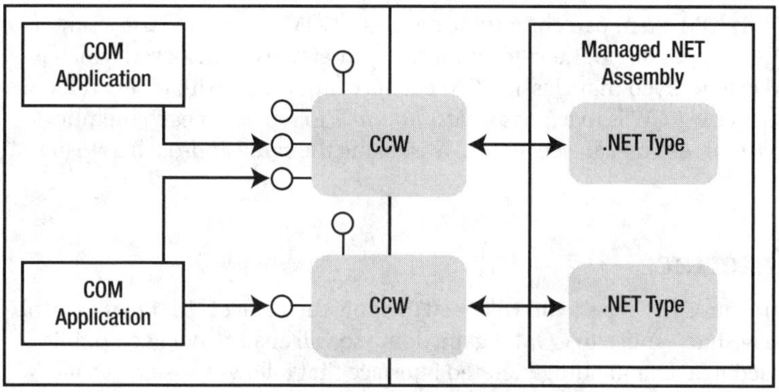

Figure 19-15. *COM types talk to .NET types using a CCW.*

Like any COM object, the CCW is a reference-counted entity. This should make sense, given that the COM client is assuming that the CCW is a real COM type and thus must abide by the rules of `AddRef()` and `Release()`. When the COM client has issued the final release, the CCW releases its reference to the real .NET type, at which point it is ready to be garbage collected.

The CCW implements a number of COM interfaces automatically to further the illusion that the proxy represents a genuine coclass. In addition to the set of custom interfaces defined by the .NET type (including an entity termed the *class interface* that you will examine in just a moment), the CCW provides support for the standard COM behaviors described in Table 19-5.

Table 19-5. *The CCW Supports Many Core COM Interfaces*

CCW-implemented Interface	Meaning in Life
`IConnectionPointContainer` `IConnectionPoint`	If the .NET type supports any events, they are represented as COM connection points.
`IEnumVariant`	If the .NET type supports the `IEnumerable` interface, it appears to the COM client as a standard COM enumerator, `IEnumVariant`.

Continued

Table 19-5. *Continued*

CCW-implemented Interface	Meaning in Life
`ISupportErrorInfo` `IErrorInfo`	These interfaces allow COM objects to send COM error objects.
`ITypeInfo` `IProvideClassInfo`	These interfaces allow the COM client to pretend to manipulate an assembly's COM type information. In reality, the COM client is interacting with .NET metadata.

`IUnknown`
`IDispatch`
`IDispatchEx`
	These COM interfaces provide support for early and late binding to the .NET type.

The Role of the .NET Class Interface

In classic COM, the only way a COM client can communicate with a COM object is to use an interface reference. In contrast, .NET types do not need to support any interfaces whatsoever, which is clearly a problem for a COM caller. Given that classic COM clients cannot work with object references, another responsibility of the CCW is to expose a *class interface* to represent each member defined by the type's public sector. As you can see, the CCW is taking the same approach as Visual Basic 6.0!

Defining a Class Interface

To define a class interface for your .NET types, you will need to apply the `<ClassInterface()>` attribute on each public class you wish to expose to COM. Again, doing so will ensure that each public member of the class is exposed to a default autogenerated interface that follows the same exact naming convention as VB6 (`_NameOfTheClass`). Technically speaking, applying this attribute is optional; however, you will almost always wish to do so. If you do not, the only way the COM caller can communicate with the type is using late binding (which is far less type safe and typically results in slower performance).

The `<ClassInterface()>` attribute provides a constructor taking a `ClassInterfaceType` enumeration that controls exactly how this default interface should appear in the COM type library. Table 19-6 defines the possible settings.

Table 19-6. *Values of the* `ClassInterfaceType` *Enumeration*

`ClassInterfaceType` **Member Name**	**Meaning in Life**
`AutoDispatch`	Indicates the autogenerated default interface will only support late binding, and is equivalent to not applying the `<ClassInterface()>` attribute at all.
`AutoDual`	Indicates that the autogenerated default interface is a "dual interface" and can therefore be interacted with using early binding or late binding. This would be the same behavior taken by VB6 when it defines a default COM interface.
`None`	Indicates that no interface will be generated for the class. This can be helpful when you have defined your own strongly typed .NET interfaces that will be exposed to COM, and do not wish to have the "freebie" interface.

In the next example, you specify ClassInterfaceType.AutoDual as the class interface designation. In this way, late binding clients such as VBScript can access the Add() and Subtract() methods using IDispatch, while early bound clients (such as VB6 or C++) can use the class interface.

Building Your .NET Types

To illustrate a COM type communicating with managed code, assume you have created a simple VB 2008 Class Library project named ComUsableDotNetServer, which defines a class named DotNetCalc. This class will define two simple methods named Add() and Subtract(). The implementation logic is trivial; however, notice the use of the <ClassInterface()> attribute:

```
' We need this to obtain the necessary
' interop attributes.
Imports System.Runtime.InteropServices

<ClassInterface(ClassInterfaceType.AutoDual)> _
Public Class DotNetCalc
  Public Function Add(ByVal x As Integer, ByVal y As Integer) As Integer
    Return x + y
  End Function

  Public Function Subtract(ByVal x As Integer, ByVal y As Integer) As Integer
    Return x - y
  End Function
End Class
```

As mentioned earlier in this chapter, in the world of COM, just about everything is identified using a 128-bit number termed a GUID. These values are recorded into the system registry in order to define an identity of the COM type. Here, we have not specifically defined GUID values for our DotNetCalc class, and therefore the type library exporter tool (tlbexp.exe) will generate GUIDs on the fly. The problem with this approach, of course, is that each time you generate the type library (which we will do shortly), you receive unique GUID values, which can break existing COM clients.

To define specific GUID values, you may make use of the guidgen.exe utility, which is accessible from the Tools ➤ Create GUID menu item of Visual Studio 2008. Although this tool provides four GUID formats, the <Guid()> attribute demands the GUID value be defined using the Registry Format option, as shown in Figure 19-16.

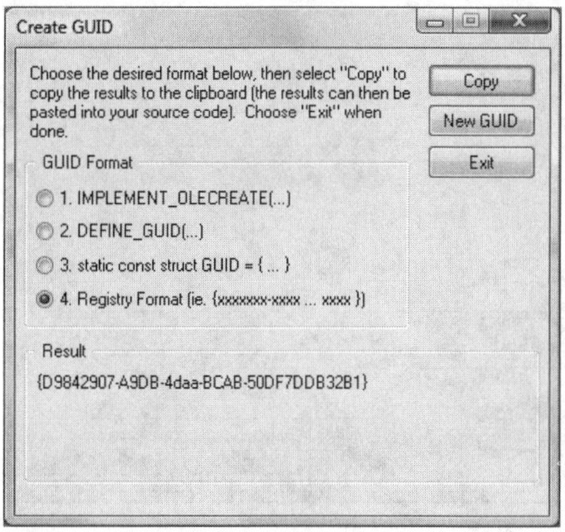

Figure 19-16. *Obtaining a GUID value*

Once you copy this value to your clipboard (via the Copy GUID button), you can then paste it in as an argument to the `<Guid()>` attribute. Be aware that you must remove the curly brackets from the GUID value! This being said, here is our updated `DotNetCalc` class type:

```
<ClassInterface(ClassInterfaceType.AutoDual)> _
<Guid("88737214-2E55-4d1b-A354-7A538BD9AB2D")> _
Public Class DotNetCalc
  Public Function Add(ByVal x As Integer, ByVal y As Integer) As Integer
    Return x + y
  End Function

  Public Function Subtract(ByVal x As Integer, ByVal y As Integer) As Integer
    Return x - y
  End Function
End Class
```

On a related note, click the Show All Files button on Solution Explorer and open up the `AssemblyInfo.vb` file located under the My Project icon. By default, all Visual Studio 2008 project workspaces are provided with an assembly-level `<Guid()>` attribute used to identify the GUID of the type library generated based on the .NET server (if exposed to COM).

```
' The following GUID is for the ID of the typelib if this project is exposed to COM.
<Assembly: Guid("EB268C4F-EB36-464C-8A25-93212C00DC89")>
```

Inserting a COM Class Using Visual Studio 2008

While you are always able to manually add attributes to a .NET type for purposes of COM interop, Visual Studio 2008 provides a project item named Com Class, which can be inserted using the Project ➤ Add New Item dialog box. To illustrate, insert a new COM type named `DotNetPerson`, as you see in Figure 19-17.

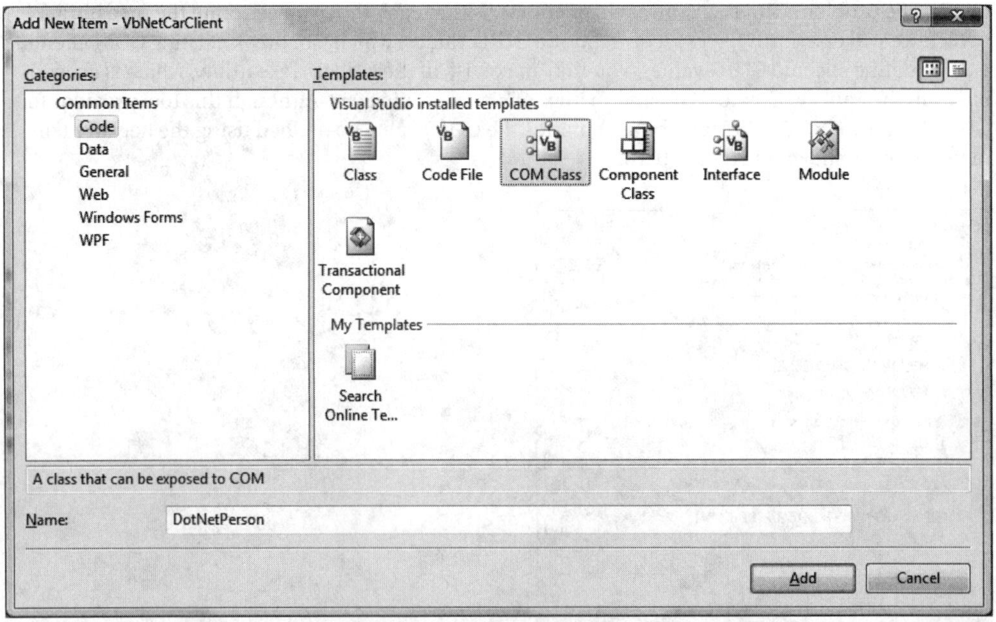

Figure 19-17. *Inserting a COM Class using Visual Studio 2008*

Although the name of this project item is termed *COM Class*, it should be clear that what you are really inserting into your project is a .NET class type that is adorned with several attributes that expose this type to COM. Here is the initial code definition of the DotNetPerson:

```
<ComClass(DotNetPerson.ClassId, _
  DotNetPerson.InterfaceId, DotNetPerson.EventsId)> _
Public Class DotNetPerson

#Region "COM GUIDs"
  ' These GUIDs provide the COM identity for this class
  ' and its COM interfaces. If you change them, existing
  ' clients will no longer be able to access the class.
  Public Const ClassId As String = "ec2a6ec2-a681-41a1-a644-30c16c7409a9"
  Public Const InterfaceId As String = "ea905f17-5f7f-4958-b8c6-a95f419063a8"
  Public Const EventsId As String = "57c3d0e3-9e15-4b6a-a96e-b4c6736c7b6d"
#End Region

  ' A creatable COM class must have a Public Sub New()
  ' with no parameters; otherwise, the class will not be
  ' registered in the COM registry and cannot be created
  ' via CreateObject.
  Public Sub New()
    MyBase.New()
  End Sub
End Class
```

As you can see, DotNetPerson has been attributed with the <ComClass()> attribute, rather than the <ClassInterface()> attribute used previously. One benefit of <ComClass()> is that it allows us to establish the necessary GUIDs as direct arguments, as opposed to making use of additional attributes (such as <Guid()>) individually. As well, notice that we have already been provided with a set of GUID values, and thus have no need to manually run the guidgen.exe utility.

■ **Note** As explained in the generated code comments, all .NET types exposed to COM must have a default constructor. Recall that when you define a custom constructor, the default is *removed* from the class definition. Here, the COM Class template ensures this does not happen by explicitly defining the default constructor in the initial code.

For testing purposes, add a single method to your DotNetPerson type that returns a hard-coded string.

```
Public Function GetMessage() As String
  Return "I am alive..."
End Function
```

Defining a Strong Name

As a best practice, all .NET assemblies that are exposed to COM should be assigned a strong name and installed into the global assembly cache (the GAC). Technically speaking, this is not required; however, if you do not deploy the assembly to the GAC, you will need to copy this assembly into the same folder as the COM application making use of it.

Given that Chapter 15 already walked you through the details of defining a strongly named assembly, simply generate a new *.snk file for signing purposes using the Signing tab of the My Project editor (see Figure 19-18).

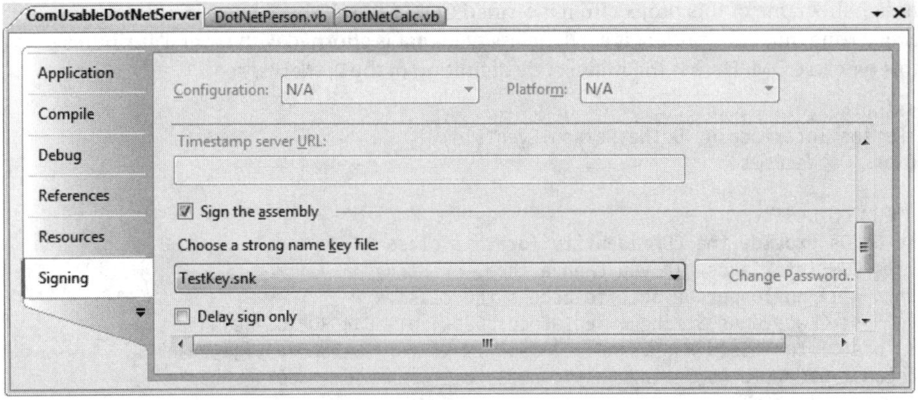

Figure 19-18. *Generating a strong name using Visual Studio 2008*

At this point, you can compile your assembly and install `ComUsableDotNetServer.dll` into the GAC using `gacutil.exe` (again, see Chapter 15 for details).

```
gacutil -i ComUsableDotNetServer.dll
```

Generating the Type Library and Registering the .NET Types

At this point, we are ready to generate the necessary COM type library and register our .NET assembly into the system registry for use by COM. To do so, you can take two possible approaches. Your first approach is to use a command-line tool named `regasm.exe`, which ships with the .NET Framework 3.5 SDK. This tool will add several listings to the system registry, and when you specify the `/tlb` flag, it will also generate the required type library, as shown here:

```
regasm ComUsableDotNetServer.dll /tlb:VbDotNetCalc.tlb
```

■ **Note** The .NET Framework 3.5 SDK also provides a tool named `tlbexp.exe`. Like `regasm.exe`, this tool will generate type libraries from a .NET assembly; however, it does not add the necessary registry entries. Given this, it is more common to simply use `regasm.exe` to perform each required step.

While `regasm.exe` provides the greatest level of flexibility regarding how the COM type library is to be generated, Visual Studio 2008 provides a handy alternative. Using the My Project editor, simply check the Register for COM interop option on the Compile tab, as shown in Figure 19-19, and recompile your assembly.

Once you have run `regasm.exe` or enabled the Register for COM Interop option, you will find that your bin\Debug folder now contains a COM type library file (taking a `*.tlb` file extension).

■ **Source Code** The ComUsableDotNetServer application is included under the Chapter 19 subdirectory.

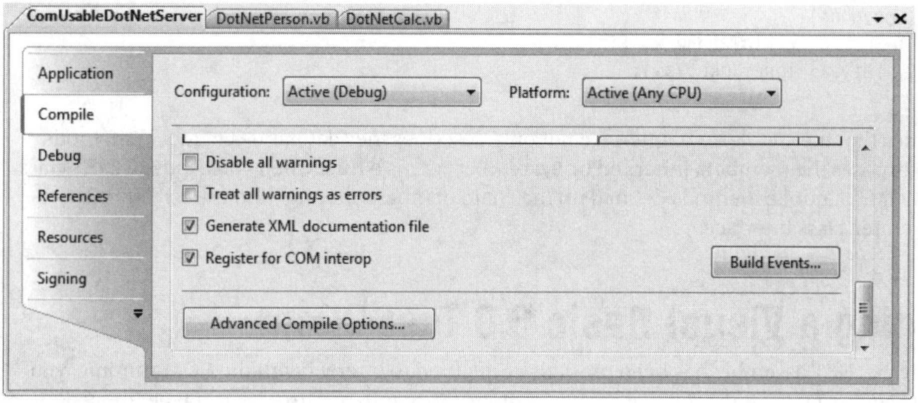

Figure 19-19. *Registering an assembly for COM interop using Visual Studio 2008*

Examining the Exported Type Information

Now that you have generated the corresponding COM type library, you can view its contents using the OLE View utility by loading the `*.tlb` file. If you load `VbDotNetCalc.tlb` (via the File ➤ View Type Library menu option), you will find the COM type descriptions for each of your .NET class types. For example, the `DotNetCalc` type has been defined to support the default `_DotNetClass` interface (due to the `<ClassInterface()>` attribute), as well as an interface named (surprise, surprise) `_Object`. As you would guess, this is an unmanaged definition of the functionality defined by `System.Object`:

```
[uuid(88737214-2E55-4D1B-A354-7A538BD9AB2D),
 version(1.0), custom({0F21F359-AB84-41E8-9A78-36D110E6D2F9},
 "ComUsableDotNetServer.DotNetCalc")]
coclass DotNetCalc {
  [default] interface _DotNetCalc;
  interface _Object;
};
```

As specified by the `<ClassInterface()>` attribute, the default interface has been configured as a dual interface, and can therefore be accessed using early or late binding:

```
[odl, uuid(AC807681-8C59-39A2-AD49-3072994C1EB1), hidden,
 dual, nonextensible, oleautomation,
 custom({0F21F359-AB84-41E8-9A78-36D110E6D2F9},
 "ComUsableDotNetServer.DotNetCalc")]
interface _DotNetCalc : IDispatch {
  [id(00000000), propget,
   custom({54FC8F55-38DE-4703-9C4E-250351302B1C}, "1")]
  HRESULT ToString([out, retval] BSTR* pRetVal);
  [id(0x60020001)]
  HRESULT Equals( [in] VARIANT obj,
    [out, retval] VARIANT_BOOL* pRetVal);
  [id(0x60020002)]
  HRESULT GetHashCode([out, retval] long* pRetVal);
  [id(0x60020003)]
  HRESULT GetType([out, retval] _Type** pRetVal);
  [id(0x60020004)]
  HRESULT Add([in] long x, [in] long y,
    [out, retval] long* pRetVal);
```

```
  [id(0x60020005)]
  HRESULT Subtract( [in] long x, [in] long y,
    [out, retval] long* pRetVal);
};
```

Notice that the `_DotNetCalc` interface not only describes the `Add()` and `Subtract()` methods, but also exposes the members inherited by `System.Object`! As a rule, when you expose a .NET class type to COM, all public methods defined up the chain of inheritance are also exposed through the autogenerated class interface.

Building a Visual Basic 6.0 Test Client

Now that the .NET assembly has been properly configured to interact with the COM runtime, you can build some COM clients. You can create a simple VB6 Standard `*.exe` project type (named VB6_DotNetClient) and set a reference to the new generated type library via the dialog box launched using the Project ➤ References menu option (see Figure 19-20).

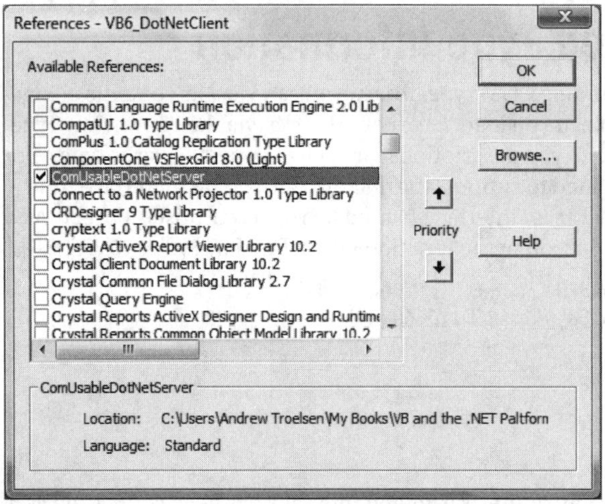

Figure 19-20. *Referencing your .NET server from VB6*

As for the GUI front end, keep things really simple. A single `Button` object (named `btnUseDotNetObject`) will be used to manipulate the `DotNetCalc` .NET type. Here is the code (notice that you are also invoking `ToString()`, defined by the `_Object` interface):

```
Private Sub btnUseDotNetObject_Click()
  ' Create the .NET object.
  Dim c As New DotNetCalc
  MsgBox c.Add(10, 10), , "Adding with .NET"

  ' Invoke some members of System.Object.
  MsgBox c.ToString, , "ToString value"
End Sub
```

Source Code The Vb6_DotNetClient application is included under the Chapter 19 subdirectory.

So, at this point you have seen the process of building .NET applications that talk to COM types and COM applications that talk to .NET types. Again, while there are many additional topics regarding the role of interop services, you should be in a solid position for further exploration.

Summary

.NET is a wonderful thing. Nevertheless, managed and unmanaged code must learn to work together for some time to come. Given this fact, the .NET platform provides various techniques that allow you to blend the best of both worlds.

A major section of this chapter focused on the details of .NET types using legacy COM components. As you have seen, the process begins by generating an assembly proxy for your COM types. The RCW forwards calls to the underlying COM binary and takes care of the details of mapping COM types to their .NET equivalents.

The chapter concluded by examining how COM types can call on the services of newer .NET types. As you have seen, this requires that the creatable types in the .NET assembly are registered for use by COM, and that the .NET types are described via a COM type library.

PART 5

Introducing the .NET Base Class Libraries

CHAPTER 20

File and Directory Manipulation

When you are creating full-blown desktop applications, the ability to save information between user sessions is imperative. This chapter examines a number of I/O-related topics as seen through the eyes of the .NET Framework. The first order of business is to explore the core types defined in the System.IO namespace and come to understand how to programmatically modify a machine's directory and file structure. Once you can do so, the next task is to explore various ways to read from and write to character-based, binary-based, string-based, and memory-based data stores.

Exploring the System.IO Namespace

In the framework of .NET, the System.IO namespace is the region of the base class libraries devoted to file-based (and memory-based) input and output (I/O) services. Like any namespace, System.IO defines a set of classes, interfaces, enumerations, structures, and delegates, most of which are contained in mscorlib.dll. In addition to the types contained within mscorlib.dll, the System.dll assembly defines additional types of the System.IO namespace (given that all Visual Studio 2008 projects automatically set a reference to both assemblies, you should be ready to go).

Many of the types within the System.IO namespace focus on the programmatic manipulation of physical directories and files. However, additional types provide support to read data from and write data to string buffers as well as raw memory locations. To give you a road map of the functionality in System.IO, Table 20-1 outlines the core (nonabstract) classes.

Table 20-1. *Key Members of the* System.IO *Namespace*

Nonabstract I/O Class Type	Meaning in Life
BinaryReader BinaryWriter	These types allow you to store and retrieve primitive data types (Integers, Booleans, Strings, and whatnot) as a binary value.
BufferedStream	This type provides temporary storage for a stream of bytes that may be committed to storage at a later time.
Directory DirectoryInfo	These types are used to manipulate a machine's directory structure. The Directory type exposes functionality primarily as *shared methods*. The DirectoryInfo type exposes similar functionality from a valid *object variable*.
DriveInfo	This type provides detailed information regarding the drives on a given machine.
File FileInfo	These types are used to manipulate a machine's set of files. The File type exposes functionality primarily as *shared methods*. The FileInfo type exposes similar functionality from a valid *object variable*.

Continued

Table 20-1. *Continued*

Nonabstract I/O Class Type	Meaning in Life
FileStream	This type allows for random file access (e.g., seeking capabilities) with data represented as a stream of bytes.
FileSystemWatcher	This type allows you to monitor the modification of a given file on the hard drive.
MemoryStream	This type provides random access to streamed data stored in memory rather than a physical file.
Path	This type performs operations on System.String types that contain file or directory path information in a platform-neutral manner.
StreamWriter StreamReader	These types are used to store (and retrieve) textual information to (or from) a file. These types do not support random file access.
StringWriter StringReader	Like the StreamReader/StreamWriter types, these classes also work with textual information. However, the underlying storage is a string buffer rather than a physical file.

In addition to these creatable class types, System.IO contains a number of enumerations, as well as a set of abstract classes (Stream, TextReader, TextWriter, and so forth), that define a polymorphic interface to all descendents. You will read about many of these types in this chapter.

The Directory(Info) and File(Info) Types

System.IO provides four types that allow you to manipulate individual files, as well as interact with a machine's directory structure. The first two types, Directory and File, expose creation, deletion, copying, and moving operations using various shared members. The closely related DirectoryInfo and FileInfo types expose similar functionality as instance-level methods (and therefore these types must be instantiated with the VB 2008 New keyword). In Figure 20-1, notice that the Directory and File types directly extend System.Object, while DirectoryInfo and FileInfo derive from the abstract FileSystemInfo type.

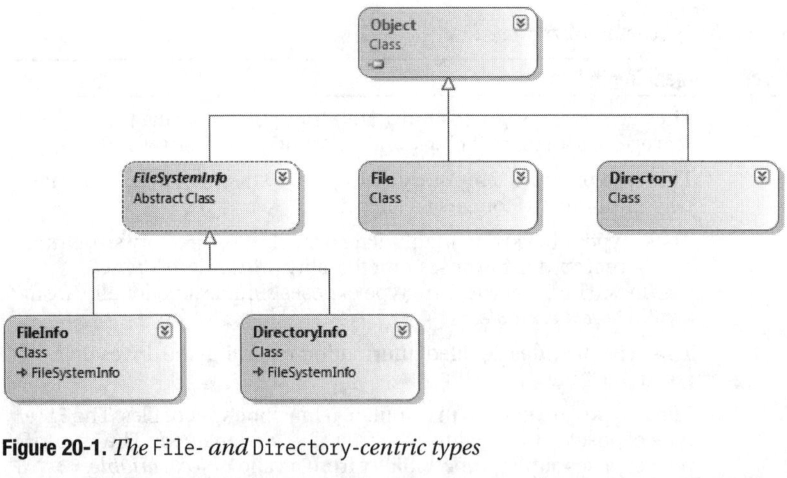

Figure 20-1. *The* File- *and* Directory-*centric types*

Generally speaking, FileInfo and DirectoryInfo are better choices for recursive operations (such as enumerating all subdirectories under a given root), as the Directory and File class members tend to return String values rather than strongly typed objects. However, as you will see, in many cases File and FileInfo (as well as Directory and DirectoryInfo) offer similar functionality.

The Abstract FileSystemInfo Base Class

The DirectoryInfo and FileInfo types receive many behaviors from the abstract FileSystemInfo base class. For the most part, the members of the FileSystemInfo class are used to discover general characteristics (such as time of creation, various attributes, and so forth) about a given file or directory. Table 20-2 lists some core properties of interest.

Table 20-2. FileSystemInfo *Properties*

Property	Meaning in Life
Attributes	Gets or sets the attributes associated with the current file that are represented by the FileAttributes enumeration.
CreationTime	Gets or sets the time of creation for the current file or directory.
Exists	Can be used to determine whether a given file or directory exists.
Extension	Retrieves a file's extension.
FullName	Gets the full path of the directory or file.
LastAccessTime	Gets or sets the time the current file or directory was last accessed.
LastWriteTime	Gets or sets the time when the current file or directory was last written to.
Name	For files, gets the name of the file. For directories, gets the name of the last directory in the hierarchy if a hierarchy exists. Otherwise, the Name property gets the name of the directory.

The FileSystemInfo type also defines the Delete() method. This is implemented by derived types to delete a given file or directory from the hard drive. As well, Refresh() can be called prior to obtaining attribute information to ensure that the statistics regarding the current file (or directory) are not outdated.

Working with the DirectoryInfo Type

The first creatable I/O-centric type you will examine is the DirectoryInfo class. This class contains a set of members used for creating, moving, deleting, and enumerating over directories and subdirectories. In addition to the functionality provided by its base class (FileSystemInfo), DirectoryInfo offers the key members in Table 20-3.

Table 20-3. *Key Members of the* DirectoryInfo *Type*

Member	Meaning in Life
Create() CreateSubdirectory()	Create a directory (or set of subdirectories), given a path name
Delete()	Deletes a directory and all its contents
GetDirectories()	Returns an array of strings that represent all subdirectories in the current directory
GetFiles()	Retrieves an array of FileInfo objects that represent a set of files in the given directory

Continued

Table 20-3. *Continued*

Member	Meaning in Life
MoveTo()	Moves a directory and its contents to a new path
Parent	Retrieves the parent directory of the specified path
Root	Gets the root portion of a path

You begin working with the DirectoryInfo type by specifying a particular directory path as a constructor parameter. If you want to obtain access to the current application directory (i.e., the directory of the executing application), use the "." notation. Here are some examples:

```
' Bind to the current application directory.
Dim dir1 As New DirectoryInfo(".")

' Bind to C:\Windows.
Dim dir2 As New DirectoryInfo("C:\Windows")
```

In the second example, you are making the assumption that the path passed into the constructor (C:\Windows) already exists on the physical machine. However, if you attempt to interact with a nonexistent directory, a System.IO.DirectoryNotFoundException is thrown. Thus, if you specify a directory that is not yet created, you will need to call the Create() method before proceeding:

```
' Bind to a nonexistent directory, then create it.
Dim dir3 As New DirectoryInfo("C:\Windows\Testing")
dir3.Create()
```

Once you have created a DirectoryInfo object, you can investigate the underlying directory contents using any of the properties inherited from FileSystemInfo. To illustrate, create a new Console Application project named MyDirectoryApp. The following helper method (which is called from within Main()) creates a new DirectoryInfo object mapped to C:\Windows (adjust your path if need be) and displays a number of interesting statistics (see Figure 20-2 for the corresponding output):

```
Imports System.IO

Module Program
  Sub Main()
    Console.WriteLine("***** Fun with Directory(Info) *****")
    Console.WriteLine()

    ShowWindowsDirectoryInfo()
    Console.ReadLine()
  End Sub

  Sub ShowWindowsDirectoryInfo()
    ' Get basic info about C:\Windows
    Dim dir As New DirectoryInfo("C:\Windows")
    Console.WriteLine("***** Directory Info *****")
    Console.WriteLine("FullName: {0}  ", dir.FullName)
    Console.WriteLine("Name: {0}  ", dir.Name)
    Console.WriteLine("Parent: {0}  ", dir.Parent)
    Console.WriteLine("Creation: {0}  ", dir.CreationTime)
    Console.WriteLine("Attributes: {0}  ", dir.Attributes)
    Console.WriteLine("Root: {0}  ", dir.Root)
    Console.WriteLine("**************************")
```

```
    Console.WriteLine()
  End Sub
End Module
```

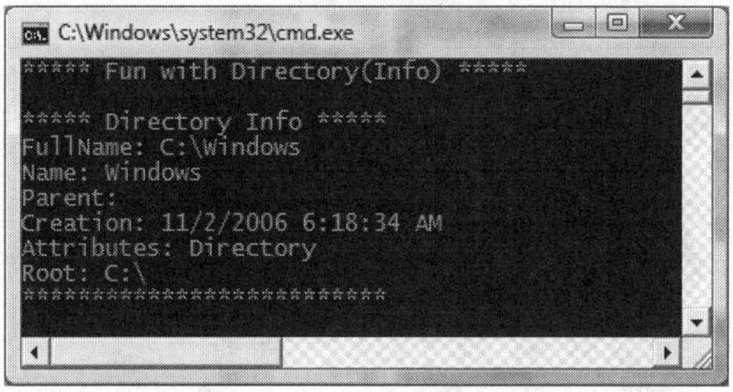

Figure 20-2. *Information about your Windows directory*

Enumerating Files with the DirectoryInfo Type

In addition to obtaining basic details of an existing directory, you can extend the current example to use some methods of the `DirectoryInfo` type. First, let's leverage the `GetFiles()` method to obtain information about all `*.jpg` files located under the C:\Windows\Web\Wallpaper directory. This method returns an array of `FileInfo` types, each of which exposes details of a particular file (full details of the `FileInfo` type are explored later in this chapter). Assume the following method of the `Program` module, called from within `Main()`:

```
Sub DisplayImageFiles()
  ' Get all files with a *.jpg extension.
  Dim dir As New DirectoryInfo("C:\Windows\Web\Wallpaper")
  Dim bitmapFiles As FileInfo() = dir.GetFiles("*.jpg")
  Console.WriteLine("Found {0} *.jpg files", bitmapFiles.Length)

  For Each f As FileInfo In bitmapFiles
    Console.WriteLine()
    Console.WriteLine("File name: {0}", f.Name)
    Console.WriteLine("File size: {0}", f.Length)
    Console.WriteLine("Creation: {0}", f.CreationTime)
    Console.WriteLine("Attributes: {0}", f.Attributes)
    Console.WriteLine()
    Console.WriteLine("**************************")
  Next
End Sub
```

■ **Note** C:\Windows\Web\Wallpaper is a Vista-specific directory. If you are running under XP, retrofit this code example to read all `*.bmp` files from the C:\Windows directory.

Once you run the application, you see a listing something like the one shown in Figure 20-3. (Your file names may vary!)

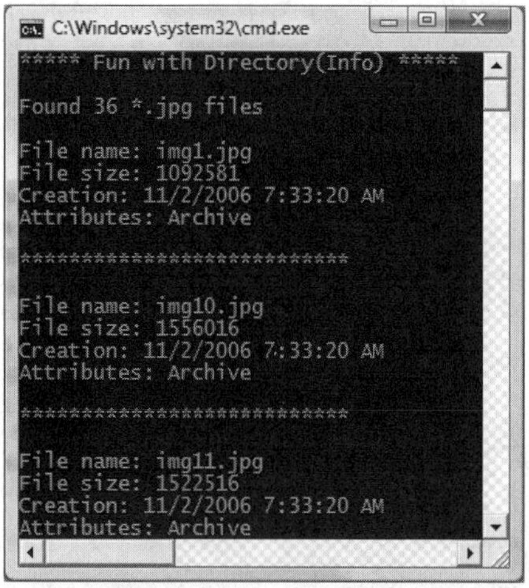

Figure 20-3. *Image file information*

Creating Subdirectories with the DirectoryInfo Type

You can programmatically extend a directory structure using the `DirectoryInfo.CreateSubdirectory()` method. This method can create a single subdirectory, as well as multiple nested subdirectories, in a single function call. To illustrate, here is a method that extends the directory structure of C:\Windows with some custom subdirectories:

```
Sub ModifyWindowsDirectory()
  Dim dir As New DirectoryInfo("C:\Windows")

  ' Create \MyFolder off initial directory.
  dir.CreateSubdirectory("MyFolder")

  ' Create \MyFolder2\Data off initial directory.
  dir.CreateSubdirectory("MyFolder2\Data")
End Sub
```

If you examine your Windows directory using Windows Explorer, you will see that the new subdirectories are present and accounted for (see Figure 20-4).

Although you are not required to capture the return value of the `CreateSubdirectory()` method, be aware that a `DirectoryInfo` type representing the newly created item is passed back on successful execution:

```
' CreateSubdirectory() returns a DirectoryInfo item representing the new item.
Dim d As DirectoryInfo = dir.CreateSubdirectory("MyFolder")
Console.WriteLine("Created: {0}", d.FullName)

d = dir. CreateSubdirectory("MyFolder2\Data")
Console.WriteLine("Created: {0}", d.FullName)
```

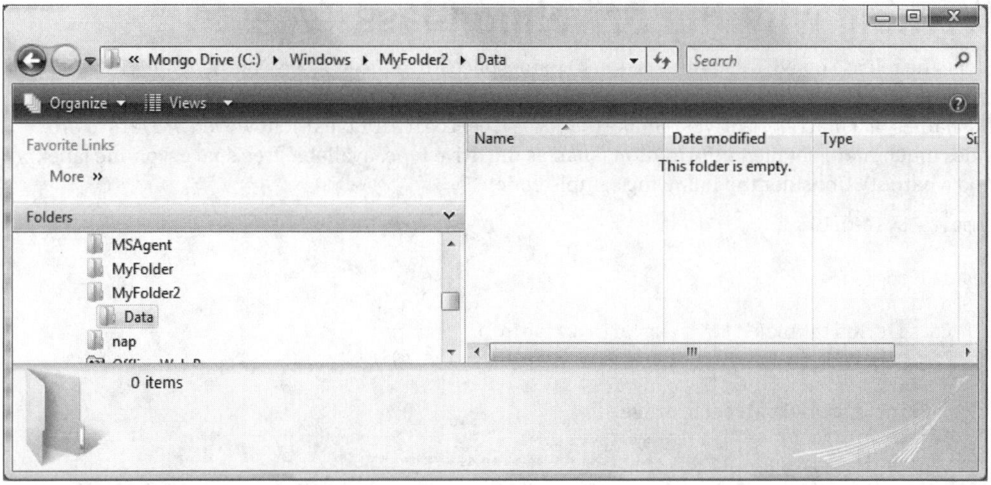

Figure 20-4. *Creating subdirectories*

Working with the Directory Type

Now that you have seen the DirectoryInfo type in action, you can learn about the Directory type. For the most part, the members of Directory mimic the functionality provided by the instance-level members defined by DirectoryInfo. Recall, however, that the members of Directory typically return String types rather than strongly typed FileInfo/DirectoryInfo types.

To illustrate some functionality of the Directory type, the final iteration of this example displays the names of all drives mapped to the current computer (via the Directory.GetLogicalDrives() method) and uses the shared Directory.Delete() method to remove the \MyFolder and \MyFolder2\Data subdirectories previously created:

```
Sub FunWithDirectoryType()
  ' Use Directory type.
  Dim drives As String() = Directory.GetLogicalDrives()
  Console.WriteLine("Here are your drives:")
  For Each s As String In drives
    Console.WriteLine("->{0}", s)
  Next

  ' Delete the directories we created.
  Console.WriteLine("Press Enter to delete directories")
  Console.ReadLine()
  Try
    Directory.Delete("C:\Windows\MyFolder")
    Directory.Delete("C:\Windows\MyFolder2\Data")
  Catch e As IOException
    Console.WriteLine(e.Message)
  End Try
End Sub
```

Source Code The MyDirectoryApp project is located under the Chapter 20 subdirectory.

Working with the DriveInfo Class Type

Since the release of .NET 2.0, the `System.IO` namespace introduced a class named `DriveInfo`. Like `Directory.GetLogicalDrives()`, the shared `DriveInfo.GetDrives()` method allows you to discover the names of a machine's drives. Unlike `Directory.GetLogicalDrives()`, however, `DriveInfo` provides much more detailed information (such as the drive type, available free space, volume label, and whatnot). Consider the following sample code:

```
Imports System.IO

Module Program
  Sub Main()
    Console.WriteLine("***** Fun with DriveInfo *****")
    Dim myDrives As DriveInfo() = DriveInfo.GetDrives()

    ' Print stats about each drive.
    For Each d As DriveInfo In myDrives
      Console.WriteLine("******************************")
      Console.WriteLine("-> Name: {0}", d.Name)
      Console.WriteLine("-> Type: {0}", d.DriveType)

      ' Is the drive mounted?
      If d.IsReady Then
        Console.WriteLine("-> Free space: {0}", d.TotalFreeSpace)
        Console.WriteLine("-> Format: {0}", d.DriveFormat)
        Console.WriteLine("-> Label: {0}", d.VolumeLabel)
      End If
    Next
    Console.ReadLine()
  End Sub
End Module
```

Figure 20-5 shows the output based on my current machine.

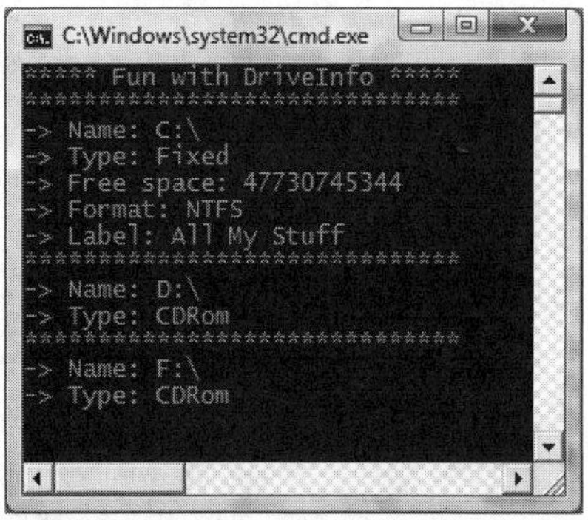

Figure 20-5. *Gather drive details via* `DriveInfo`.

At this point, you have investigated some core behaviors of the `Directory`, `DirectoryInfo`, and `DriveInfo` classes. Next, you'll learn how to create, open, close, and destroy the files that populate a given directory.

Source Code The DriveTypeApp project is located under the Chapter 20 subdirectory.

Working with the FileInfo Class

As shown in the MyDirectoryApp example, the `FileInfo` class allows you to obtain details regarding existing files on your hard drive (time created, size, file attributes, and so forth) and aids in the creation, copying, moving, and destruction of files. In addition to the set of functionality inherited by `FileSystemInfo` are some core members unique to the `FileInfo` class, which are described in Table 20-4.

Table 20-4. `FileInfo` *Core Members*

Member	Meaning in Life
`AppendText()`	Creates a `StreamWriter` object (described later) that appends text to a file
`CopyTo()`	Copies an existing file to a new file
`Create()`	Creates a new file and returns a `FileStream` object (described later) to interact with the newly created file
`CreateText()`	Creates a `StreamWriter` object that writes a new text file
`Delete()`	Deletes the file to which a `FileInfo` instance is bound
`Directory`	Gets an instance of the parent directory
`DirectoryName`	Gets the full path to the parent directory
`Length`	Gets the size of the current file
`MoveTo()`	Moves a specified file to a new location, providing the option to specify a new file name
`Name`	Gets the name of the file
`Open()`	Opens a file with various read/write and sharing privileges
`OpenRead()`	Creates a read-only `FileStream`
`OpenText()`	Creates a `StreamReader` object (described later) that reads from an existing text file
`OpenWrite()`	Creates a write-only `FileStream` object

It is important to understand that a majority of the members of the `FileInfo` class return a specific I/O-centric object (`FileStream`, `StreamWriter`, and so forth) that allows you to begin reading and writing data to (or reading from) the associated file in a variety of formats. You will check out these types in just a moment, but until then, let's examine various ways to obtain a file handle using the `FileInfo` class type.

The FileInfo.Create() Method

The first way you can create a file handle is to make use of the `FileInfo.Create()` method:

```
Imports System.IO

Module Program
  Sub Main()
```

```
    ' Make a new file on the C drive.
    Dim f As New FileInfo("C:\Test.dat")
    Dim fs As FileStream = f.Create()

    ' Use the FileStream object...

    ' Close down file stream.
    fs.Close()
  End Sub
End Module
```

Notice that the FileInfo.Create() method returns a FileStream type, which exposes synchronous and asynchronous write/read operations to/from the underlying file (more details in a moment). Be aware that the FileStream object returned by FileInfo.Create() grants full read/write access to all users.

Also notice that after we are done with the current FileStream object, we make sure to close down the handle to release the underlying unmanaged resources of the stream. Given that FileStream implements IDisposable, you can make use of the VB Using scope to allow the compiler to generate the teardown logic (see Chapter 8 for details):

```
Sub Main()
  ' Defining a "Using scope" for file I/O
  ' types is ideal.
  Dim f As New FileInfo("C:\Test.dat")
  Using fs As FileStream = f.Create()
    ' Use the FileStream object...
  End Using
End Sub
```

The FileInfo.Open() Method

You can use the FileInfo.Open() method to open existing files as well as create new files with far more precision than FileInfo.Create(). Once the call to Open() completes, you are returned a FileStream object. Ponder the following logic:

```
Imports System.IO

Module Program
  Sub Main()
    ' Make a new file via FileInfo.Open().
    Dim f2 As New FileInfo("C:\Test2.dat")
    Using fs2 As FileStream = f2.Open(FileMode.OpenOrCreate, _
      FileAccess.ReadWrite, FileShare.None)

    ' Use the FileStream object...

    End Using
  End Sub
End Module
```

This version of the overloaded Open() method requires three parameters. The first parameter specifies the general flavor of the I/O request (e.g., make a new file, open an existing file, append to a file, etc.), which is specified using the FileMode enumeration (see Table 20-5 for details):

```
Enum FileMode
  CreateNew
  Create
```

```
  Open
  OpenOrCreate
  Truncate
  Append
End Enum
```

Table 20-5. *Members of the* `FileMode` *Enumeration*

Member	Meaning in Life
`CreateNew`	Informs the OS to make a new file. If it already exists, an `IOException` is thrown.
`Create`	Informs the OS to make a new file. If it already exists, it will be overwritten.
`Open`	Opens an existing file. If the file does not exist, a `FileNotFoundException` is thrown.
`OpenOrCreate`	Opens the file if it exists; otherwise, a new file is created.
`Truncate`	Opens a file and truncates the file to zero bytes in size.
`Append`	Opens a file, moves to the end of file, and begins write operations (this flag can only be used with a write-only stream). If the file does not exist, a new file is created.

The second parameter to the `Open()` method is a value from the `FileAccess` enumeration, used to determine the read/write behavior of the underlying stream:

```
Enum FileAccess
  Read
  Write
  ReadWrite
End Enum
```

Finally, you have the third parameter to the `Open()` method, `FileShare`, which specifies how the file is to be shared among other file handlers. Here are the core names:

```
Enum FileShare
  None
  Read
  Write
  ReadWrite
End Enum
```

The FileInfo.OpenRead() and FileInfo.OpenWrite() Methods

While the `FileInfo.Open()` method allows you to obtain a file handle in a very flexible manner, the `FileInfo` class also provides members named `OpenRead()` and `OpenWrite()`. As you might imagine, these methods return a properly configured read-only or write-only `FileStream` type, without the need to supply various enumeration values. Like `FileInfo.Create()` and `FileInfo.Open()`, `OpenRead()` and `OpenWrite()` return a `FileStream` object:

```
Sub Main()
...
  ' Get a FileStream object with read-only permissions.
  Dim f3 As New FileInfo("C:\Test3.dat")
  Using readOnlyStream As FileStream = f3.OpenRead()
    ' Use FileStream...
  End Using
```

```
  ' Get a FileStream object with write-only permissions.
  Dim f4 As New FileInfo("C:\Test4.dat")
  Using writeOnlyStream As FileStream = f4.OpenWrite()
    ' Use FileStream...
  End Using
End Sub
```

The FileInfo.OpenText() Method

Another open-centric member of the FileInfo type is OpenText(). Unlike Create(), Open(), OpenRead(), and OpenWrite(), the OpenText() method returns an instance of the StreamReader type, rather than an instance of a FileStream type:

```
Sub Main()
...
  ' Get a StreamReader object.
  Dim f5 As New FileInfo("C:\boot.ini")
  Using sreader As StreamReader = f5.OpenText()
    ' Use the StreamReader object...
  End Using
End Sub
```

As you will see shortly, the StreamReader type provides a way to read character data from the underlying file.

The FileInfo.CreateText() and FileInfo.AppendText() Methods

The final two methods of interest at this point are CreateText() and AppendText(), both of which return a StreamWriter reference, as shown here:

```
Sub Main()
...
  Dim f6 As New FileInfo("C:\Test5.txt")
  Using swriter As StreamWriter = f6.CreateText()
    ' Use the StreamWriter object...
  End Using

  Dim f7 As New FileInfo("C:\FinalTest.txt")
  Using swriterAppend As StreamWriter = f7.AppendText()
    ' Use the StreamWriter object...
  End Using
End Sub
```

As you would guess, the StreamWriter type provides a way to write character data to the underlying file.

Working with the File Type

The File type provides functionality almost identical to that of the FileInfo type, using a number of shared members. Like FileInfo, File supplies the AppendText(), Create(), CreateText(), Open(), OpenRead(), OpenWrite(), and OpenText() methods. In fact, in many cases, the File and FileStream types may be used interchangeably. To illustrate, each of the previous FileStream examples can be simplified by using the File type instead:

```
Sub Main()
  ' Obtain FileStream object via File.Create().
  Using fs As FileStream = File.Create("C:\Test.dat")
  End Using

  ' Obtain FileStream object via File.Open().
  Using fs2 As FileStream = File.Open("C:\Test2.dat", _
    FileMode.OpenOrCreate, _
    FileAccess.ReadWrite, FileShare.None)
  End Using

  ' Get a FileStream object with read-only permissions.
  Using readOnlyStream As FileStream = File.OpenRead("C:\Test3.dat")
  End Using

  ' Get a FileStream object with write-only permissions.
  Using writeOnlyStream As FileStream = File.OpenWrite("C:\Test4.dat")
  End Using

  ' Get a StreamReader object.
  Using sreader As StreamReader = File.OpenText("C:\boot.ini")
  End Using

  ' Get some StreamWriters.
  Using swriter As StreamWriter = File.CreateText("C:\Test3.txt")
  End Using
  Using swriterAppend As StreamWriter = File.AppendText("C:\FinalTest.txt")
  End Using
End Sub
```

Additional File-Centric Members

Unlike `FileInfo`, the `File` type supports a few additional members, shown in Table 20-6, which can greatly simplify the processes of reading and writing textual data.

Table 20-6. *Methods of the* `File` *Type*

Method	Meaning in Life
`ReadAllBytes()`	Opens the specified file, returns the binary data as an array of bytes, and then closes the file
`ReadAllLines()`	Opens a specified file, returns the character data as an array of strings, and then closes the file
`ReadAllText()`	Opens a specified file, returns the character data as a `System.String`, and then closes the file
`WriteAllBytes()`	Opens the specified file, writes out the byte array, and then closes the file
`WriteAllLines()`	Opens a specified file, writes out an array of strings, and then closes the file
`WriteAllText()`	Opens a specified file, writes the character data, and then closes the file

Using these new methods of the `File` type, you are able to read and write batches of data in just a few lines of code. Even better, each of these members automatically closes down the underlying file handle. For example, the following Console Application project (named SimpleFileIO) will persist the textual data into a new file on the C drive (and read it into memory) with minimal fuss:

```
Imports System.IO

Module Program
  Sub Main()
    ' Write these strings to a new file on the C drive.
    Dim myTasks As String() = {"Fix bathroom sink", _
      "Call Dave", "Call Mom and Dad", _
      "Play Xbox 360"}
    File.WriteAllLines("C:\tasks.txt", myTasks)

    ' Now read in each one and print to the console.
    For Each task As String In File.ReadAllLines("C:\tasks.txt")
      Console.WriteLine("TODO: {0}.", task)
    Next
    Console.ReadLine()
  End Sub
End Module
```

Clearly, when you wish to quickly obtain a file handle, the `File` type will save you some keystrokes. However, one benefit of first creating a `FileInfo` object is that you are able to investigate the file using the members of the abstract `FileSystemInfo` base class.

Source Code The SimpleFileIO project is located under the Chapter 20 subdirectory.

The Abstract Stream Class

At this point, you have seen numerous ways to obtain `FileStream`, `StreamReader`, and `StreamWriter` objects, but you have yet to read data from, or write data to, a file using these types. To understand how to do so, you'll need to become familiar with the concept of a *stream*.

In the world of I/O manipulation, a stream represents a chunk of data. Streams provide a common way to interact with a *sequence of bytes*, regardless of what kind of device (file, network connection, printer, etc.) is storing or displaying the bytes in question.

The abstract `System.IO.Stream` class defines a number of members that provide support for synchronous and asynchronous interactions with the storage medium (e.g., an underlying file or memory location). Figure 20-6 shows a few descendents of the `Stream` type, seen through the eyes of the Visual Studio 2008 Object Browser.

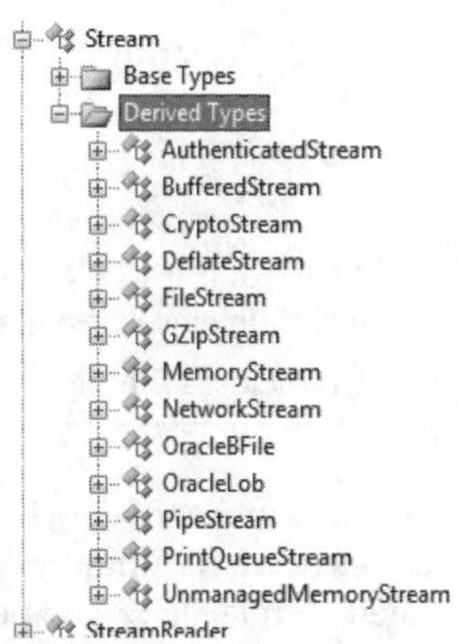

Figure 20-6. *Stream-derived types*

■ **Note** Be aware that the concept of a stream is not limited to files or memory locations. To be sure, the .NET libraries provide stream access to networks and other stream-centric abstractions.

Again, `Stream` descendents represent data as a raw stream of bytes; therefore, working with raw streams can be quite cryptic. Some `Stream`-derived types support *seeking*, which refers to the process of obtaining and adjusting the current position in the stream. To begin understanding the functionality provided by the `Stream` class, take note of the core members described in Table 20-7.

Table 20-7. *Abstract Members of the* `Stream` *Class*

Member	Meaning in Life
`CanRead` `CanSeek` `CanWrite`	Determine whether the current stream supports reading, seeking, and/or writing.
`Close()`	Closes the current stream and releases any resources (such as sockets and file handles) associated with the current stream.
`Flush()`	Updates the underlying data source or repository with the current state of the buffer and then clears the buffer. If a stream does not implement a buffer, this method does nothing.
`Length`	Returns the length of the stream, in bytes.
`Position`	Gets or sets the position in the current stream.
`Read()` `ReadByte()`	Read a sequence of bytes (or a single byte) from the current stream and advance the current position in the stream by the number of bytes read.
`Seek()`	Sets the position in the current stream.
`SetLength()`	Sets the length of the current stream.
`Write()` `WriteByte()`	Write a sequence of bytes (or a single byte) to the current stream and advance the current position in this stream by the number of bytes written.

Working with FileStreams

The `FileStream` class provides an implementation for the abstract `Stream` members in a manner appropriate for file-based streaming. It is a fairly primitive stream; it can read or write only a single byte or an array of bytes. In reality, you will not often need to directly interact with the members of the `FileStream` type. Rather, you will most likely make use of various *stream wrappers*, which make it easier to work with textual data or .NET types. Nevertheless, for illustrative purposes, let's experiment with the synchronous read/write capabilities of the `FileStream` type.

Assume you have a new Console Application named FileStreamApp. Your goal is to write a simple text message to a new file named `myMessage.dat`. However, given that `FileStream` can operate only on raw bytes, you will be required to encode the `System.String` type into a corresponding byte array. Luckily, the `System.Text` namespace defines a type named `Encoding`, which provides members that encode and decode strings to (or from) an array of bytes (check out the .NET Framework 3.5 SDK documentation for full details of the `Encoding` type).

Once encoded, the byte array is persisted to the file using the `FileStream.Write()` method. To read the bytes back into memory, you must reset the internal position of the stream (via the `Position` property) and call the `ReadByte()` method. Finally, you display the raw byte array and the decoded string to the console. Here is the complete code for the sample application:

```
Imports System.IO
Imports System.Text

Module Program
  Sub Main()
    Console.WriteLine("***** Fun with FileStreams *****")
    Console.WriteLine()

    ' Obtain a FileStream object.
    Using fStream As FileStream = File.Open("C:\myMessage.dat", FileMode.Create)

      ' Encode a string as an array of bytes.
      Dim msg As String = "Hello!"
      Dim msgAsByteArray As Byte() = Encoding.Default.GetBytes(msg)

      ' Write array of bytes to file.
      fStream.Write(msgAsByteArray, 0, msgAsByteArray.Length)

      ' Reset internal position of stream.
      fStream.Position = 0

      ' Read the types from file and display to console.
      Console.Write("Your message as an array of bytes: ")
      Dim bytesFromFile(msgAsByteArray.Length) As Byte
      Dim i As Integer = 0
      While i < msgAsByteArray.Length
        bytesFromFile(i) = CType(fStream.ReadByte, Byte)
        Console.Write(bytesFromFile(i))
        i = i + 1
      End While

      ' Display decoded messages.
      Console.WriteLine()
      Console.Write("Decoded Message: ")
      Console.WriteLine(Encoding.Default.GetString(bytesFromFile))
    End Using
    Console.ReadLine()
  End Sub
End Module
```

While this example does indeed populate the file with data, it punctuates the major downfall of working directly with the `FileStream` type: it demands to operate on raw bytes. Other `Stream`-derived types operate in a similar manner. For example, if you wish to write a sequence of bytes to a region of memory, you can allocate a `MemoryStream`. Likewise, if you wish to push an array of bytes through a network connection, you can make use of the `NetworkStream` type.

Thankfully, the `System.IO` namespace provides a number of "reader" and "writer" types that encapsulate the details of working with `Stream`-derived types.

■ **Source Code** The FileStreamApp project is included under the Chapter 20 subdirectory.

Working with StreamWriters and StreamReaders

The `StreamWriter` and `StreamReader` classes are useful whenever you need to read or write character-based data (e.g., `Strings`). Both of these types work by default with Unicode characters; however, you can change the underlying character encoding by supplying a properly configured `System.Text.Encoding` object reference. To keep things simple, let's assume that the default Unicode encoding fits the bill (as will be the case for many of your .NET applications).

`StreamReader` derives from an abstract type named `TextReader`, as does the related `StringReader` type (discussed later in this chapter). The `TextReader` base class provides a very limited set of functionality to each of these descendents, specifically the ability to read and peek into a character stream.

The `StreamWriter` type (as well as `StringWriter`, also examined later in this chapter) derives from an abstract base class named `TextWriter`. This class defines members that allow derived types to write textual data to a given character stream.

To aid in your understanding of the core writing capabilities of the `StreamWriter` and `StringWriter` classes, Table 20-8 describes the core members of the abstract `TextWriter` base class.

Table 20-8. *Core Members of* `TextWriter`

Member	Meaning in Life
`Close()`	Closes the writer and frees any associated resources. In the process, the buffer is automatically flushed.
`Flush()`	Clears all buffers for the current writer and causes any buffered data to be written to the underlying device, but does not close the writer.
`NewLine`	Indicates the newline constant for the derived writer class. The default line terminator is a carriage return followed by a line feed (the equivalent to the VB `vbCrLf` constant).
`Write()`	Writes a line to the text stream without a newline constant.
`WriteLine()`	Writes a line to the text stream with a newline constant.

■ **Note** The last two members of the `TextWriter` class probably look familiar to you. If you recall, the `System.Console` type has `Write()` and `WriteLine()` members that push textual data to the standard output device. In fact, the `Console.In` property wraps a `TextReader`, and the `Console.Out` property wraps a `TextWriter`.

The derived `StreamWriter` class provides an appropriate implementation for the `Write()`, `Close()`, and `Flush()` methods, and it defines the additional `AutoFlush` property. This property, when set to `True`, forces `StreamWriter` to flush all data every time you perform a write operation. Be aware that you can gain better performance by setting `AutoFlush` to `False`, provided you always call `Close()` when you are done writing with a `StreamWriter`.

Writing to a Text File

To see the `StreamWriter` type in action, create a new Console Application named StreamWriterReaderApp. The following code creates a new file named `reminders.txt` using the `File.CreateText()` method. Using the obtained `StreamWriter` object, you add some textual data to the new file, as shown here:

```
Imports System.IO

Module Program
  Sub Main()
    Console.WriteLine("***** Fun with StreamWriter / StreamReader *****")
    Console.WriteLine()

    ' Get a StreamWriter and write string data.
    Using writer As StreamWriter = File.CreateText("reminders.txt")
      writer.WriteLine("Don't forget Mother's Day this year...")
      writer.WriteLine("Don't forget Father's Day this year...")
      writer.WriteLine("Don't forget these numbers:")
      For i As Integer = 0 To 10
        writer.Write(String.Format("{0},", i))
      Next

      ' Insert a new line and close.
      writer.Write(writer.NewLine)
    End Using
    Console.WriteLine("Created file and wrote some thoughts...")
    Console.ReadLine()
  End Sub
End Module
```

Notice that the parameter to `File.CreateTest()` is the full path of the file you wish to create. Here, however, I simply specified the file name itself, and therefore the file will be created in the application directory of the assembly (which will be under your bin\Debug folder). In any case, once you run this program, you can examine the contents of this new file, which should resemble what you see in Figure 20-7.

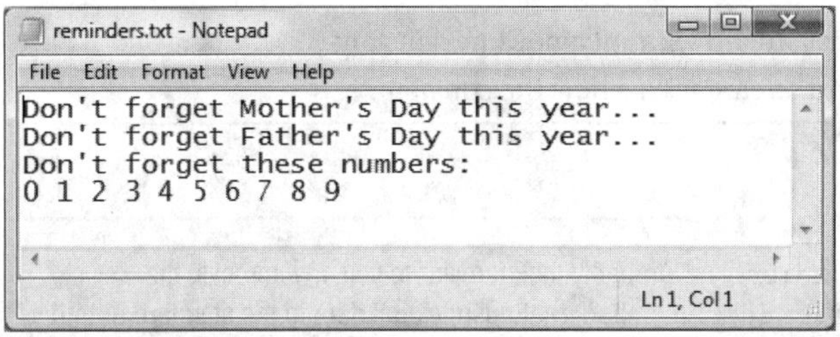

Figure 20-7. *The contents of your* `*.txt` *file*

Reading from a Text File

Now you need to understand how to programmatically read data from a file using the corresponding `StreamReader` type. As you recall, this class derives from the abstract `TextReader` class, which offers the functionality described in Table 20-9.

Table 20-9. TextReader *Core Members*

Member	Meaning in Life
Peek()	Returns the next available character without actually changing the position of the reader. A value of -1 indicates you are at the end of the stream (or that the stream does not support seeking capabilities).
Read()	Reads data from an input stream.
ReadBlock()	Reads up to a maximum number of characters from the current stream and writes the data to a buffer, beginning at specified index.
ReadLine()	Reads a line of characters from the current stream and returns the data as a String (Nothing indicates EOF).
ReadToEnd()	Reads all characters from the current position to the end of the stream and returns them as a single String.

If you now extend the example to use a StreamReader, you can read in the textual data from the reminders.txt file as shown here:

```
Sub Main()
  Console.WriteLine("***** Fun with StreamWriter / StreamReader *****")
...
  Console.WriteLine("Here are your thoughts:")
  Using sr As StreamReader = File.OpenText("reminders.txt")
    Console.WriteLine(sr.ReadToEnd())
  End Using
  Console.ReadLine()
End Sub
```

Once you run the program, you will see the character data within reminders.txt displayed to the console.

Directly Creating StreamWriter/StreamReader Objects

One of the slightly confusing aspects of working with the types within System.IO is that you can often achieve an identical result using numerous approaches. For example, you have already seen that you can obtain a StreamWriter via the File or FileInfo type using the CreateText() method. In reality, there is yet another way in which you can work with StreamWriters and StreamReaders: create them directly. For example, the current application could be retrofitted as follows:

```
Sub Main()
  Console.WriteLine("***** Fun with StreamWriter / StreamReader *****")
  ' Get a StreamWriter and write string data.
  Using writer As New StreamWriter("reminders.txt")
    ...
  End Using

  ' Now read data from file.
  Using sr As New StreamReader("reminders.txt")
  ...
  End Using
End Sub
```

Although it can be a bit confusing to see so many seemingly identical approaches to file I/O, keep in mind that the end result is greater flexibility. In any case, now that you have seen how to move character data to and from a given file using the StreamWriter and StreamReader types, you will next examine the role of the StringWriter and StringReader classes.

Source Code The StreamWriterReaderApp project is included under the Chapter 20 subdirectory.

Working with StringWriters and StringReaders

Using the StringWriter and StringReader types, you can treat textual information as a stream of in-memory characters. This can prove helpful when you wish to append character-based information to an existing buffer. To illustrate, the following Console Application (named StringReaderWriter-App) writes a block of string data to a StringWriter object rather than a file on the local hard drive:

```
Module Program
  Sub Main()
    Console.WriteLine("***** Fun with StringWriter / StringReader *****")
    Console.WriteLine()

    ' Create a StringWriter and emit character data
    ' to memory.
    Using strWriter As New StringWriter()
      strWriter.Write("Don't forget Mother's Day this year...")
      ' Get a copy of the contents (stored in a string) and pump
      ' to console.
      Console.WriteLine("Contents of StringWriter: {0}", strWriter)
    End Using

    Console.ReadLine()
  End Sub
End Module
```

Because StringWriter and StreamWriter both derive from the same base class (TextWriter), the writing logic is more or less identical. However, given that nature of StringWriter, be aware that this class allows you to extract a System.Text.StringBuilder object via the GetStringBuilder() method:

```
Using strWriter As New StringWriter()
  strWriter.Write("Don't forget Mother's Day this year...")
  ' Get a copy of the contents (stored in a String) and pump
  ' to console.
  Console.WriteLine("Contents of StringWriter: {0}", strWriter)

  ' Get the internal StringBuilder.
  Dim sb As StringBuilder = strWriter.GetStringBuilder()
  sb.Insert(0, "Hey!! ")
  Console.WriteLine("-> {0}", sb.ToString())

  ' Remove the inserted String.
  sb.Remove(0, "Hey!! ".Length)
  Console.WriteLine("-> {0}", sb.ToString())
End Using
```

When you wish to read from a stream of character data, make use of the corresponding StringReader type, which (as you would expect) functions identically to the related StreamReader class. In fact, the StringReader class does nothing more than override the inherited members to read from a block of character data, rather than a file, as shown here:

```
Using strWriter As New StringWriter()
  strWriter.Write("Don't forget Mother's Day this year...")
  ' Get a copy of the contents (stored in a string) and pump
  ' to console.
  Console.WriteLine("Contents of StringWriter: {0}", strWriter)

  ' Get the internal StringBuilder.
  Dim sb As StringBuilder = strWriter.GetStringBuilder()
  sb.Insert(0, "Hey!! ")
  Console.WriteLine("-> {0}", sb.ToString())

  ' Remove the inserted string.
  sb.Remove(0, "Hey!! ".Length)
  Console.WriteLine("-> {0}", sb.ToString())

  ' Now dump using a StringReader.
  Console.WriteLine("-> Here are your thoughts:")
  Using strReader As New StringReader(strWriter.ToString())
    Dim input As String = strReader.ReadToEnd()
    Console.WriteLine(input)
  End Using
End Using
```

Source Code The StringReaderWriterApp is included under the Chapter 20 subdirectory.

Working with BinaryWriters and BinaryReaders

The final writer/reader sets you will examine here are `BinaryReader` and `BinaryWriter`, both of which derive directly from `System.Object`. These types allow you to read and write discrete *data types* to an underlying stream in a compact binary format. The `BinaryWriter` class defines a highly overloaded `Write()` method to place a data type in the underlying stream. In addition to `Write()`, `BinaryWriter` provides additional members that allow you to get or set the internal `Stream`-derived type and offers support for random access to the data (see Table 20-10).

Table 20-10. `BinaryWriter` *Core Members*

Member	Meaning in Life
`BaseStream`	Provides access to the underlying stream used with the `BinaryWriter` object. This property is read-only.
`Close()`	Closes the binary stream.
`Flush()`	Flushes the binary stream.
`Seek()`	Sets the position in the current stream.
`Write()`	Writes a value to the current stream.

The `BinaryReader` class complements the functionality offered by `BinaryWriter` with the members described in Table 20-11.

Table 20-11. BinaryReader *Core Members*

Member	Meaning in Life
BaseStream	This read-only property provides access to the underlying stream used with the BinaryReader object.
Close()	This method closes the binary reader.
PeekChar()	This method returns the next available character without actually advancing the position in the stream.
Read()	This method reads a given set of bytes or characters and stores them in the incoming array.
ReadXXXX()	The BinaryReader class defines numerous ReadXXXX() methods that grab the next type from the stream (ReadBoolean(), ReadByte(), ReadInt32(), and so forth).

The following example (a Console Application named BinaryWriterReader) writes a number of data values to a new *.dat file:

```
Sub Main()
  Console.WriteLine("***** Fun with Binary Writers / Readers *****" & vbLf)

  ' Open a binary writer for a file.
  Dim f As New FileInfo("BinFile.dat")

  Using bw As New BinaryWriter(f.OpenWrite())
    ' Print out the type of BaseStream.
    ' (System.IO.FileStream in this case).
    Console.WriteLine("Base stream is: {0}", bw.BaseStream)

    ' Create some data to save in the file
    Dim aDouble As Double = 1234.67
    Dim anInt As Integer = 34567
    Dim aString As String = "A, B, C"

    ' Write the data
    bw.Write(aDouble)
    bw.Write(anInt)
    bw.Write(aString)
  End Using
  Console.ReadLine()
End Sub
```

Notice how the FileStream object returned from FileInfo.OpenWrite() is passed to the constructor of the BinaryWriter type. Using this technique, it is very simple to "layer in" a stream before writing out the data. Do understand that the constructor of BinaryWriter takes any Stream-derived type (e.g., FileStream, MemoryStream, or BufferedStream). Thus, if you would rather write binary data to memory, simply supply a valid MemoryStream object.

To read the data out of the BinFile.dat file, the BinaryReader type provides a number of options. Here, you will call various read-centric members to pluck each chunk of data from the file stream:

```
Sub Main()
  Console.WriteLine("***** Fun with Binary Writers / Readers *****" & vbLf)
...
  ' Read the data as raw bytes
  Using br As New BinaryReader(f.OpenRead())
    Console.WriteLine(br.ReadDouble())
```

```
    Console.WriteLine(br.ReadInt32())
    Console.WriteLine(br.ReadString())
  End Using
  Console.ReadLine()
End Sub
```

■ **Source Code** The BinaryWriterReader application is included under the Chapter 20 subdirectory.

Programmatically "Watching" Files

Now that you have a better handle on the use of various readers and writers, next you'll look at the role of the `FileSystemWatcher` class. This type can be quite helpful when you wish to programmatically monitor (or "watch") files on your system. Specifically, the `FileSystemWatcher` type can be instructed to monitor files for any of the actions specified by the `NotifyFilters` enumeration (while many of these members are self-explanatory, check the .NET Framework 3.5 SDK documentation for further details):

```
Enum NotifyFilters
  Attributes
  CreationTime
  DirectoryName
  FileName
  LastAccess
  LastWrite
  Security
  Size
End Enum
```

The first step you will need to take to work with the `FileSystemWatcher` type is to set the `Path` property to specify the name (and location) of the directory that contains the files to be monitored, as well as the `Filter` property that defines the file extensions of the files to be monitored.

At this point, you may choose to handle the `Changed`, `Created`, `Deleted`, and `Renamed` events, all of which work in conjunction with the `FileSystemEventHandler` delegate. This delegate can call any method matching the following pattern:

```
' The FileSystemEventHandler delegate must point
' to methods matching the following signature.
Sub MyNotificationHandler(ByVal sender As Object, ByVal e As FileSystemEventArgs)
```

As well, the `Renamed` event may also be handled via the `RenamedEventHandler` delegate type, which can call methods matching the following signature:

```
' The RenamedEventHandler delegate must point
' to methods matching the following signature.
Sub MyNotificationHandler(ByVal sender As Object, ByVal e As RenamedEventArgs)
```

To illustrate the process of watching a file, assume you have created a new directory on your C drive named MyFolder that contains various `*.txt` files (named whatever you wish). The following Console Application (named MyDirectoryWatcher) will monitor the `*.txt` files within MyFolder and print out messages in the event that the files are created, deleted, modified, or renamed:

```
Sub Main()
  Console.WriteLine("***** The Amazing File Watcher App *****")

  ' Create and configure the watcher.
  Dim watcher As New FileSystemWatcher()
  Try
    watcher.Path = "C:\MyFolder"
  Catch ex As ArgumentException
    Console.WriteLine(ex.Message)
    Return
  End Try
  watcher.NotifyFilter = NotifyFilters.LastAccess Or _
                         NotifyFilters.LastWrite Or _
                         NotifyFilters.FileName Or _
                         NotifyFilters.DirectoryName
  watcher.Filter = "*.txt"

  ' Establish event handlers.
  AddHandler watcher.Changed, AddressOf OnFileModified
  AddHandler watcher.Created, AddressOf OnFileModified
  AddHandler watcher.Deleted, AddressOf OnFileModified
  AddHandler watcher.Renamed, AddressOf OnFileRenamed
  watcher.EnableRaisingEvents = True

  ' Keep alive until user hits enter key.
  Console.WriteLine("Press ''Enter to quit app.")
  Console.ReadLine()
End Sub
```

The two event handlers simply print out the current file modification:

```
' Event handlers.
Sub OnFileModified(ByVal source As Object, ByVal e As FileSystemEventArgs)
  ' Specify what is done when a file is changed, created, or deleted.
  Console.WriteLine("File: {0} {1}!", e.FullPath, e.ChangeType)
End Sub

Sub OnFileRenamed(ByVal source As Object, ByVal e As RenamedEventArgs)
  ' Specify what is done when a file is renamed.
  Console.WriteLine("File: {0} renamed to {1}.", e.OldFullPath, e.FullPath)
End Sub
```

To test this program, run the application and open Windows Explorer. Try renaming your files, creating a `*.txt` file, deleting a `*.txt` file, or whatnot. You will see the console application print out various bits of information regarding the state of the text files within MyFolder, as shown in Figure 20-8.

Source Code The MyDirectoryWatcher application is included under the Chapter 20 subdirectory.

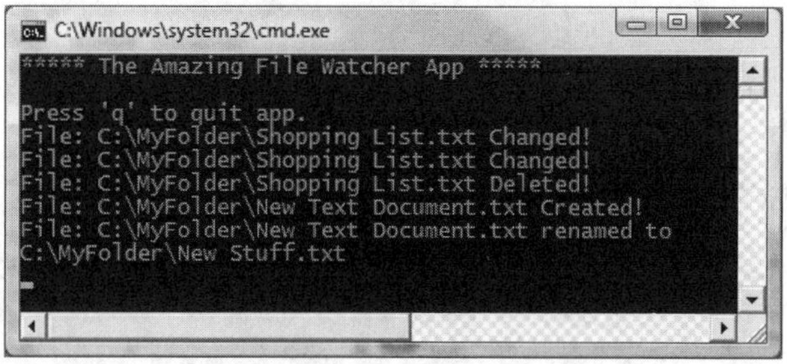

Figure 20-8. *Watching some text files*

Performing Asynchronous File I/O

To conclude our examination of the `System.IO` namespace, let's see how to interact with `FileStream` types asynchronously. You have already seen the asynchronous support provided by the .NET Framework during the examination of multithreading (see Chapter 18). Because I/O can be a lengthy task, all types deriving from `System.IO.Stream` inherit a set of methods (`BeginRead()`, `BeginWrite()`, `EndRead()`, and `EndWrite()`, specifically) that enable asynchronous processing of the data. As you would expect, these methods work in conjunction with the `IAsyncResult` type (again, see Chapter 18). Here are the prototypes of the members in question:

```
Public Class Stream
  Inherits MarshalByRefObject
...
  Public Overridable Function BeginRead(ByVal array As Byte(), _
    ByVal offset As Integer, ByVal numBytes As Integer,
    ByVal userCallback As AsyncCallback,
    ByVal stateObject As Object) As IAsyncResult

  Public Overridable Function BeginWrite(ByVal array As Byte(), _
    ByVal offset As Integer, ByVal numBytes As Integer, _
    ByVal userCallback As AsyncCallback, _
    ByVal stateObject As Object) As IAsyncResult

  Public Overridable Function EndRead(ByVal asyncResult As IAsyncResult) _
    As Integer

  Public Overridable Sub EndWrite(ByVal asyncResult As IAsyncResult)
...
End Class
```

The process of working with the asynchronous behavior of `Stream`-derived types is identical to working with asynchronous delegates and asynchronous remote method invocations. While it's unlikely that asynchronous behaviors will greatly improve file access, other streams (e.g., socket-based streams) are much more likely to benefit from asynchronous handling. In any case, the following example (a Console Application named AsyncFileStream) illustrates one manner in which you can asynchronously interact with a `FileStream` type:

```
Imports System.IO
Imports System.Text
Imports System.Threading
```

```
Module Program
  Sub Main()
    Console.WriteLine("**** Asynch File IO *****")
    Console.WriteLine()

    Console.WriteLine("Main thread started. ThreadID = {0}", _
     Thread.CurrentThread.GetHashCode)

    ' Must use this ctor to get a FileStream with asynchronous
    ' read or write access.
    Dim fs As New FileStream("logfile.txt", FileMode.Append, _
      FileAccess.Write, FileShare.None, 4096, True)
    Dim msg As String = "this is a test"
    Dim buffer As Byte() = Encoding.ASCII.GetBytes(msg)

    ' Start the asynchronous write. WriteDone invoked when finished.
    ' Note that the FileStream object is passed as state info to the
    ' callback method.
    fs.BeginWrite(buffer, 0, buffer.Length, AddressOf WriteDone, fs)
  End Sub

  Private Sub WriteDone(ByVal ar As IAsyncResult)
    Console.WriteLine("AsyncCallback method on ThreadID = {0}", _
      Thread.CurrentThread.GetHashCode)
    Dim s As Stream = CType(ar.AsyncState, Stream)
    s.EndWrite(ar)
    s.Close()
  End Sub
End Module
```

The only point of interest in this example (assuming you recall the process of working with delegates!) is that in order to enable the asynchronous behavior of the `FileStream` type, you must make use of a specific constructor (shown here). The final `System.Boolean` parameter (when set to `True`) informs the `FileStream` object to perform its work on a secondary thread of execution.

■ **Source Code** The AsyncFileStream application is included under the Chapter 20 subdirectory.

Summary

This chapter began by examining the use of the `Directory(Info)` and `File(Info)` types. As you learned, these classes allow you to manipulate a physical file or directory on your hard drive. Next, you examined a number of types derived from the abstract `Stream` class, specifically `FileStream`. Given that `Stream`-derived types operate on a raw stream of bytes, the `System.IO` namespace provides numerous reader/writer types (`StreamWriter`, `StringWriter`, `BinaryWriter`, etc.) that simplify the process. Along the way, you also checked out the functionality provided by `DriveInfo`, and you learned how to monitor files using the `FileSystemWatcher` type and how to interact with streams in an asynchronous manner.

CHAPTER 21

Introducing Object Serialization

In Chapter 20, you learned about the functionality provided by the System.IO namespace. As shown, this namespace provides numerous reader/writer types that can be used to persist data to a given location (in a given format). This chapter examines the related topic of *object serialization*. Using object serialization, you are able to persist and retrieve the state of an object to (or from) any System.IO.Stream-derived type.

As you might imagine, the ability to serialize types is critical when you attempt to copy an object to a remote machine or when you need to persist the state of any custom object for a later user session. Over the course of this chapter, you will be exposed to numerous aspects of the .NET serialization scheme, including a set of attributes (and the legacy ISerializable interface) that allows you to customize the process.

Understanding Object Serialization

The term *serialization* describes the process of persisting (and possibly transferring) the state of an object to a stream. The persisted data sequence contains all necessary information needed to reconstruct (or *deserialize*) the state of the object for use later. Using this technology, it is trivial to save vast amounts of data (in various formats) with minimal fuss and bother. In fact, in many cases, saving application data using serialization services is much less cumbersome than making direct use of the readers/writers found within the System.IO namespace.

For example, assume you have created a GUI-based desktop application and wish to provide a way for end users to save their preferences. To do so, you might define a class named UserPrefs that encapsulates 20 or so pieces of field data, for example:

```
Public Class UserPrefs
  ' Assume this class has 20 unique pieces of data.
  Public WindowColor As String
  Public FontSize As Integer
  Public IsPowerUser As Boolean
...
End Class
```

If you were to make use of a System.IO.BinaryWriter type, you would need to *manually* save each field of a UserPrefs object. Likewise, when you wish to load the data from the file back into memory, you would need to make use of a System.IO.BinaryReader and (once again) *manually* read in each value to reconfigure a new UserPrefs object.

While this is certainly doable, you would save yourself a good amount of time simply by marking the UserPrefs class with the <Serializable()> attribute, and allow the .NET serialization layer to take care of the details of saving the state of a UserPrefs object:

```
' Classes (or structures) marked as serializable can be
' persisted into a stream using various formatters.
<Serializable()> _
Class UserPrefs
  Public WindowColor As String
  Public FontSize As Integer
  Public IsPowerUser As Boolean
...
End Class
```

In this case, the entire state of the object can be persisted out using a few lines of code. We will dive into various details during the remainder of this chapter; however, consider the following `Main()` method:

```
Sub Main()
  ' Create a UserPrefs object and set the values to save.
  Dim userData As New UserPrefs()
  userData.WindowColor = "Yellow"
  userData.FontSize = "50"
  userData.IsPowerUser = False

  ' Create a new binary formatter to perform the persistence.
  Dim binFormat As New BinaryFormatter()

  ' Place object state into a file named user.dat.
  Using fStream As Stream = New FileStream("user.dat", _
    FileMode.Create, FileAccess.Write, FileShare.None)
    binFormat.Serialize(fStream, userData)
  End Using

  Console.ReadLine()
End Sub
```

While it is quite simple to persist objects using .NET object serialization, the processes used behind the scenes are quite sophisticated. For example, when an object is persisted to a stream, all associated data (base classes, contained objects, etc.) are automatically serialized as well. Therefore, if you are attempting to persist a derived class, all data up the chain of inheritance comes along for the ride. As you will see in just a moment, a set of interrelated objects is represented using an *object graph*.

.NET serialization services also allow you to persist an object graph in a variety of formats. The previous partial-code example made use of the `BinaryFormatter` type; therefore, the state of the `UserPrefs` object was persisted as a compact binary format. You are also able to persist an object graph into a Simple Object Access Protocol (SOAP) or XML format using other formatting types.

■ **Note** The SOAP and XML formats can be quite helpful when you wish to ensure that your persisted objects travel well across operating systems, languages, and architectures. A binary format will tie you to the Windows OS and the .NET platform (unless you were to undertake Herculean efforts to reconstruct the data manually).

Finally, do know that an object graph can be persisted into *any* `System.IO.Stream`-derived type. In the previous example, you persisted a `UserPrefs` object into a local file via the `FileStream` type. However, if you would rather persist an object to memory, you could make use of a `MemoryStream` type instead. All that matters is the fact that the sequence of data correctly represents the state of objects within the graph.

The Role of Object Graphs

As mentioned, when an object is serialized, the CLR will account for all related objects. The set of related objects is collectively referred to as an *object graph*. Object graphs provide a simple way to document how a set of objects refer to each other and do not necessarily map to classic OO relationships (such as the "is-a" or "has-a" relationship), although they do model this paradigm quite well.

Each object in an object graph is assigned a unique numerical value. Keep in mind that the numbers assigned to the members in an object graph are arbitrary and have no real meaning to the outside world. Once all objects have been assigned a numerical value, the object graph can record each object's set of dependencies.

As a simple example, assume you have created a set of classes that model some automobiles (of course). You have a base class named `Car`, which "has-a" `Radio`. Another class named `JamesBondCar` extends the `Car` base type. Figure 21-1 shows a possible object graph that models these relationships.

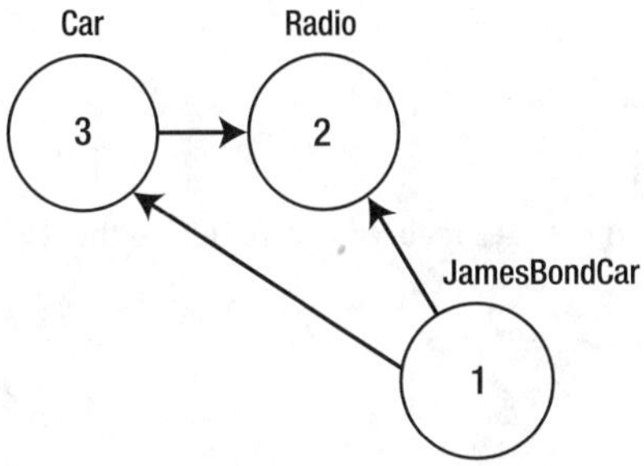

Figure 21-1. *A simple object graph*

When reading object graphs, you can use the phrase "depends on" or "refers to" when connecting the arrows. Thus, in Figure 21-1 you can see that the `Car` class refers to the `Radio` class (given the "has-a" relationship). `JamesBondCar` refers to `Car` (given the "is-a" relationship) as well as `Radio` (as it inherits this member variable).

Of course, the CLR does not paint pictures in memory to represent a graph of related objects. Rather, the relationship documented in the previous diagram is represented by a flattened mathematical formula that looks something like this:

```
[Car 3, ref 2], [Radio 2], [JamesBondCar 1, ref 3, ref 2]
```

If you parse this formula, you can again see that object 3 (the `Car`) has a dependency on object 2 (the `Radio`). Object 2, the `Radio`, is a lone wolf and requires nobody. Finally, object 1 (the `JamesBondCar`) has a dependency on object 3 as well as object 2. In any case, when you serialize or deserialize an instance of `JamesBondCar`, the object graph ensures that the `Radio` and `Car` types also participate in the process.

The beautiful thing about the serialization process is that the graph representing the relationships among your objects is established automatically behind the scenes. As you will see later in this chapter, however, if you do wish to become more involved in the construction of a given object graph, it is possible to do so.

Configuring Objects for Serialization

To make an object available to .NET serialization services, all you need to do is decorate each type of the object graph with the `<Serializable()>` attribute. That's it (really). If you determine that a given class has some member data that should not (or perhaps cannot) participate in the serialization scheme, you can mark such fields with the `<NonSerialized()>` attribute. This can be helpful if you have member variables in a serializable class that do not need to be "remembered" (e.g., fixed values, random values, transient data, etc.) and you wish to reduce the size of the persisted graph.

To get the ball rolling, create a new Console Application project named SimpleSerialization. Now, define the following `Radio` class, which has been marked `<Serializable()>`. Note that one of the member variables (`radioID`) has been marked `<NonSerialized()>` and will therefore not be persisted into the specified data stream:

```
<Serializable()> _
Public Class Radio
  Public hasTweeters As Boolean
  Public hasSubWoofers As Boolean
  Public stationPresets() As Double
  <NonSerialized()> _
  Public radioID As String = "XF-552RR6"
End Class
```

The `JamesBondCar` class and `Car` base class are also marked `<Serializable()>` and define the following pieces of field data:

```
<Serializable()> _
Public Class Car
  Public theRadio As New Radio()
  Public isHatchBack As Boolean
End Class

<Serializable()> _
Public Class JamesBondCar
  Inherits Car
  Public canFly As Boolean
  Public canSubmerge As Boolean
End Class
```

Be aware that the `<Serializable()>` attribute (like any attribute) cannot be inherited. Therefore, if you derive a class from a type marked `<Serializable()>`, the child class must be marked `<Serializable()>` as well, or it cannot be persisted. In fact, all objects in an object graph must be marked with the `<Serializable()>` attribute. If you attempt to serialize a nonserializable object using the `BinaryFormatter` or `SoapFormatter`, you will receive a `SerializationException` at runtime. Oddly enough, if you serialize an object using the `XmlSerializer`, you will *not* receive a runtime error, even if the type has not been marked `<Serializable()>`.

Public Fields, Private Fields, and Public Properties

Notice that in each of these classes, I have defined the field data using the `Public` keyword, just to simplify the example. Of course, private data exposed using public properties would be preferable from an OO point of view. Also, for the sake of simplicity, I have not defined any custom constructors on these types, and therefore all unassigned field data will receive the expected default values.

OO design principles aside, you may wonder how the various formatters expect a type's field data to be defined in order to be serialized into a stream. The answer is, it depends. If you are persisting an object using the `BinaryFormatter` or `SoapFormatter`, it makes absolutely no difference.

These formatters are programmed to serialize *all* serializable fields of a type, regardless of whether they are public fields, private fields, or private fields exposed through public properties.

The situation is quite different if you make use of the XmlSerializer type, however. These types will *only* serialize public pieces of field data or private data exposed through public properties.

Do recall, however, that if you have points of data that you do not want to be persisted into the object graph, you can selectively mark public or private fields as <NonSerialized()>, as done with the String field of the Radio type.

Choosing a Serialization Formatter

Once you have configured your types to participate in the .NET serialization scheme, your next step is to choose which format should be used when persisting your object graph. As of .NET 3.5, you have three choices out of the box:

- BinaryFormatter
- SoapFormatter
- XmlSerializer

The BinaryFormatter type serializes your object graph to a stream using a compact binary format. This type is defined within the System.Runtime.Serialization.Formatters.Binary namespace that is part of mscorlib.dll. Therefore, to serialize your objects using a binary format, all you need to do is specify the following VB 2008 Imports directive:

```
' Gain access to the BinaryFormatter in mscorlib.dll.
Imports System.Runtime.Serialization.Formatters.Binary
```

The SoapFormatter type represents your graph as a SOAP message. This type is defined within the System.Runtime.Serialization.Formatters.Soap namespace that is defined within a *separate assembly*. Thus, to format your object graph into a SOAP message, you must set a reference to System.Runtime.Serialization.Formatters.Soap.dll and specify the following VB 2008 Imports directive:

```
' Must reference System.Runtime.Serialization.Formatters.Soap.dll!
Imports System.Runtime.Serialization.Formatters.Soap
```

Finally, if you wish to persist an object graph as an XML document, you will need to specify that you are using the System.Xml.Serialization namespace, which is also defined in a separate assembly: System.Xml.dll. As luck would have it, all Visual Studio 2008 project templates automatically reference System.Xml.dll, therefore you will simply need to import the following namespace:

```
' Defined within System.Xml.dll.
Imports System.Xml.Serialization
```

The IFormatter and IRemotingFormatting Interfaces

Regardless of which formatter you choose to make use of, be aware that each of them derives directly from System.Object, and therefore they do not share a common set of members beyond ToString(), GetHashCode(), Equals(), and GetType(). However, the BinaryFormatter and SoapFormatter types do support common members through the implementation of the IFormatter and IRemotingFormatter interfaces (of which XmlSerializer implements neither).

System.Runtime.Serialization.IFormatter defines the core Serialize() and Deserialize() methods, which do the grunt work to move your object graphs into and out of a specific stream. Beyond these members, IFormatter defines a few properties that are used behind the scenes by the implementing type:

```
Public Interface IFormatter
  Function Deserialize(ByVal serializationStream As Stream) As Object
  Sub Serialize(ByVal serializationStream As Stream, ByVal graph As Object)

  Property Binder() As SerializationBinder
  Property Context() As StreamingContext
  Property SurrogateSelector() As ISurrogateSelector
End Interface
```

The `System.Runtime.Remoting.Messaging.IRemotingFormatter` interface (which is leveraged internally by the .NET remoting layer) overloads the `Serialize()` and `Deserialize()` members into a manner more appropriate for distributed persistence. Note that `IRemotingFormatter` derives from the more general `IFormatter` interface:

```
Public Interface IRemotingFormatter
  Inherits IFormatter
  Function Deserialize(ByVal serializationStream As Stream, _
                     ByVal handler As HeaderHandler) As Object
  Sub Serialize(ByVal serializationStream As Stream, _
              ByVal graph As Object, ByVal headers As Header())
End Interface
```

Although you may not need to directly interact with these interfaces for most of your serialization endeavors, recall that interface-based polymorphism allows you to hold an instance of `BinaryFormatter` or `SoapFormatter` using an `IFormatter` reference. Therefore, if you wish to build a method that can serialize an object graph using either of these classes, you could write the following:

```
Sub SerializeObjectGraph(ByVal itfFormat As IFormatter, _
 ByVal destStream As Stream, ByVal graph As Object)
  ' Serialize the object graph here!
  itfFormat.Serialize(destStream, graph)
End Sub
```

Type Fidelity Among the Formatters

The most obvious difference among the three formatters is how the object graph is persisted to the stream (binary, SOAP, or pure XML). You should be aware of a few more subtle points of distinction, specifically how the formatters contend with *type fidelity*. When you make use of the `BinaryFormatter` type, it will not only persist the serializable field data of the objects in the graph, but also each type's fully qualified name and the full name of the defining assembly. These extra points of data make the `BinaryFormatter` an ideal choice when you wish to transport objects by value (e.g., as a full copy) across machine boundaries using the .NET remoting APIs.

The `SoapFormatter` and `XmlSerializer`, on the other hand, do *not* attempt to preserve full type fidelity and therefore do not record the type's fully qualified name. While this may seem like a limitation at first glance, the reason has to do with the open-ended nature of XML data representation. If you wish to persist object graphs that can be used by any operating system (Windows, Mac OS X, and Unix distributions), application framework (.NET, Java EE, COM, etc.), or programming language, you do not want to maintain full type fidelity, as you cannot assume all possible recipients can understand .NET-specific data types. Given this, `SoapFormatter` and `XmlSerializer` are ideal choices when you wish to ensure as broad a reach as possible for the persisted object graph.

Note Strictly speaking, the SoapFormatter will use assembly data (friendly name, version, public key token, and culture identifier) to generate an XML namespace to wrap your custom types within the SOAP envelope.

Serializing Objects Using the BinaryFormatter

To illustrate how easy it is to persist an instance of the JamesBondCar to a physical file, let's make use of the BinaryFormatter type. Again, the two key methods of the BinaryFormatter type to be aware of are Serialize() and Deserialize():

- Serialize(): Persists an object graph to a specified stream as a sequence of bytes
- Deserialize(): Converts a persisted sequence of bytes to an object graph

Assume you have created an instance of JamesBondCar, modified some state data, and want to persist your spy-mobile into a *.dat file. The first task is to create the *.dat file itself. This can be achieved by creating an instance of the System.IO.FileStream type (see Chapter 20). At this point, simply create an instance of the BinaryFormatter and pass in the FileStream and object graph to persist:

```
Imports System.Runtime.Serialization.Formatters.Binary
Imports System.IO

Module Program
  Sub Main()
    Console.WriteLine("***** Fun with Object Serialization *****")
    ' Make a new object to persist.
    Dim jbc As New JamesBondCar()
    jbc.canFly = True
    jbc.canSubmerge = False
    jbc.theRadio.stationPresets = New Double() {89.3, 105.1, 97.1}
    jbc.theRadio.hasTweeters = True

    ' Save the object in a binary format to
    ' a local file.
    Dim binFormat As New BinaryFormatter()
    Dim fStream As Stream = New FileStream("CarData.dat", FileMode.Create, _
      FileAccess.Write, FileShare.None)
    binFormat.Serialize(fStream, jbc)
    fStream.Close()
    Console.ReadLine()
  End Sub
End Module
```

As you can see, the BinaryFormatter.Serialize() method is the member responsible for composing the object graph and moving the byte sequence to some Stream-derived type. In this case, the stream happens to be a physical file. However, you could also serialize your object types to any Stream-derived type such as a memory location, given that MemoryStream is a descendent of the Stream type. At this point, you can open the CarData.dat file (in Visual Studio if you like) to view the binary data that represents this instance of the JamesBondCar, as shown in Figure 21-2.

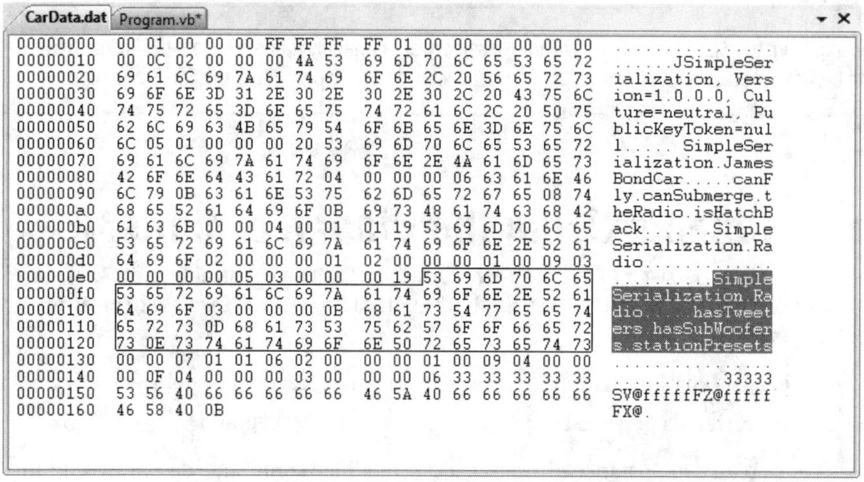

Figure 21-2. `JamesBondCar` *serialized using a* `BinaryFormatter`

Deserializing Objects Using the BinaryFormatter

Now suppose you want to read the persisted `JamesBondCar` from the binary file back into an object for use within your program. Once you have programmatically opened `CarData.dat` (via the `File.OpenRead()` method), simply call the `Deserialize()` method of the `BinaryFormatter`. Be aware that `Deserialize()` returns a `System.Object` type, so you need to impose an explicit cast, as shown here:

```
Sub Main()
...
  ' Now read the JamesBondCar from the binary file.
  fStream = File.OpenRead("CarData.dat")
  Dim carFromDisk As JamesBondCar = _
    CType(binFormat.Deserialize(fStream), JamesBondCar)

  Console.WriteLine("Can this car fly? : {0}", carFromDisk.canFly)
  fStream.Close()
  Console.ReadLine()
End Sub
```

Notice that when you call `Deserialize()`, you pass the `Stream`-derived type that represents the location of the persisted object graph (again, a file stream in this case). Now if that is not painfully simple, I'm not sure what is. In a nutshell, mark each class you wish to persist to a stream with the `<Serializable()>` attribute. After this point, use the `BinaryFormatter` type to move your object graph to and from a binary stream.

Serializing Objects Using the SoapFormatter

Your next choice of formatter is the `SoapFormatter` type. The `SoapFormatter` will persist an object graph into a SOAP message, which makes this formatter a solid choice when you wish to distribute objects remotely using HTTP. If you are unfamiliar with the SOAP specification, don't sweat the details right now. In a nutshell, SOAP defines a standard process in which methods may be invoked in a platform- and OS-neutral manner.

Note Chapter 25 will provide an introduction into the role of SOAP and the nature of Service-Oriented Architectures using Windows Communication Foundation.

Assuming you have referenced the System.Runtime.Serialization.Formatters.Soap.dll assembly, you could persist and retrieve a JamesBondCar as a SOAP message simply by replacing each occurrence of BinaryFormatter with SoapFormatter. Consider the following code, which serializes an object to a local file named CarData.soap:

```
Imports System.Runtime.Serialization.Formatters.Soap
...
Sub Main()
...
  ' Save object to a file named CarData.soap in SOAP format.
  Dim soapFormat As New SoapFormatter()
  fStream = New FileStream("CarData.soap", _
    FileMode.Create, FileAccess.Write, FileShare.None)
  soapFormat.Serialize(fStream, jbc)
  fStream.Close()
  Console.ReadLine()
End Sub
```

As before, simply use Serialize() and Deserialize() to move the object graph in and out of a valid stream. If you open the resulting *.soap file, you can locate the XML elements that mark the stateful values of the current JamesBondCar as well as the relationship between the objects in the graph via the #ref tokens. Consider the following end result (the XML namespaces have been snipped for brevity):

```
<SOAP-ENV:Envelope xmlns:xsi="...">
  <SOAP-ENV:Body>
    <a1:JamesBondCar id="ref-1" xmlns:a1="...">
      <canFly>true</canFly>
      <canSubmerge>false</canSubmerge>
      <theRadio href="#ref-3"/>
      <isHatchBack>false</isHatchBack>
    </a1:JamesBondCar>
    <a1:Radio id="ref-3" xmlns:a1="...">
      <hasTweeters>true</hasTweeters>
      <hasSubWoofers>false</hasSubWoofers>
      <stationPresets href="#ref-4"/>
    </a1:Radio>
    <SOAP-ENC:Array id="ref-4" SOAP-ENC:arrayType="xsd:double[3]">
      <item>89.3</item>
      <item>105.1</item>
      <item>97.1</item>
    </SOAP-ENC:Array>
  </SOAP-ENV:Body>
</SOAP-ENV:Envelope>
```

Serializing Objects Using the XmlSerializer

In addition to the SOAP and binary formatters, the System.Xml.dll assembly provides a third formatter, System.Xml.Serialization.XmlSerializer, which can be used to persist the state of a given object as pure XML, as opposed to a SOAP message. Working with this type is a bit different from working with the SoapFormatter or BinaryFormatter type. Consider the following code:

```
Imports System.Xml.Serialization
...
Sub Main()
...
  ' Save object to a file named CarData.xml in XML format.
  Dim xmlFormat As = New XmlSerializer(GetType(JamesBondCar), _
    New Type() {GetType(Radio), GetType(Car)})
  fStream = New FileStream("CarData.xml", FileMode.Create, _
    FileAccess.Write, FileShare.None)
  xmlFormat.Serialize(fStream, jbc)
  fStream.Close()
  Console.ReadLine()
End Sub
```

The key difference is that the XmlSerializer type requires you to specify type information (which can be obtained using GetType()) that represents the items in the object graph. Notice that the first constructor argument of the XmlSerializer defines the root element of the XML file, while the second argument is an array of System.Type types that hold metadata regarding the subelements. If you were to look within the newly generated CarData.xml file, you would find the following (abbreviated) XML data:

```
<?xml version="1.0" encoding="utf-8"?>
<JamesBondCar xmlns:xsi="...">
  <theRadio>
    <hasTweeters>true</hasTweeters>
    <hasSubWoofers>false</hasSubWoofers>
    <stationPresets>
      <double>89.3</double>
      <double>105.1</double>
      <double>97.1</double>
    </stationPresets>
   <radioID>XF-552RR6</radioID>
  </theRadio>
  <isHatchBack>false</isHatchBack>
  <canFly>true</canFly>
  <canSubmerge>false</canSubmerge>
</JamesBondCar>
```

■ **Note** XmlSerializer demands that all serialized types in the object graph support a default constructor (so be sure to add it back if you define custom constructors). If this is not the case, you will receive an InvalidOperationException at runtime.

Controlling the Generated XML Data

If you have a background in XML technologies, you are well aware that it is often critical to ensure the elements within an XML document conform to a set of rules that establish the "validity" of the data. Understand that a "valid" XML document does not have to do with the syntactic well-being of the XML elements (e.g., all opening elements must have a closing element). Rather, valid documents conform to agreed-upon formatting rules (e.g., field *x* must be expressed as an attribute and not a subelement), which are typically defined by an XML schema or document-type definition (DTD) file.

By default, the `XmlSerializer` will format all field data of a type as element data rather than XML attributes. If you wish to control how the `XmlSerializer` generates the resulting XML document, you may decorate your `<Serializable()>` types with any number of additional attributes from the `System.Xml.Serialization` namespace. Table 21-1 documents some (but not all) of the attributes that influence how XML data is encoded to a stream.

Table 21-1. *Serialization-Centric Attributes of the* `System.Xml.Serialization` *Namespace*

Attribute	Meaning in Life
`<XmlAttribute()>`	Serializes the member as an XML attribute
`<XmlElement()>`	Serializes the field or property as an XML element
`<XmlEnum()>`	Represents the element name of an enumeration member
`<XmlRoot()>`	Specifies the namespace and element name for the root namespace
`<XmlText()>`	Serializes the property or field as XML text
`<XmlType()>`	Represents the name and namespace of the XML type

By way of a simple example, first consider how the field data of `JamesBondCar` is currently persisted as XML:

```
<?xml version="1.0" encoding="utf-8"?>
<JamesBondCar xmlns:xsi="http://www.w3.org/2001/XMLSchema-instance"
  xmlns:xsd="http://www.w3.org/2001/XMLSchema">
...
  <canFly>true</canFly>
  <canSubmerge>false</canSubmerge>
</JamesBondCar>
```

If you wished to specify a custom XML namespace that qualifies the `JamesBondCar` as well as encodes the `canFly` and `canSubmerge` values as XML attributes, you can do so by modifying the VB 2008 definition of `JamesBondCar` as follows (be sure to import the `System.Xml.Serialization` into your file if necessary):

```
<Serializable(), XmlRoot(Namespace:="http://www.intertechtraining.com")> _
Public Class JamesBondCar
  Inherits Car
  <XmlAttribute()> _
  Public canFly As Boolean
  <XmlAttribute()> _
  Public canSubmerge As Boolean
End Class
```

This would yield the following XML document (note the opening `<JamesBondCar>` element):

```
<?xml version="1.0" encoding="utf-8"?>
<JamesBondCar xmlns:xsi="http://www.w3.org/2001/XMLSchema-instance"
  xmlns:xsd="http://www.w3.org/2001/XMLSchema"
  canFly="true" canSubmerge="false"
  xmlns="http://www.intertechtraining.com">
...
</JamesBondCar>
```

Of course, there are numerous other attributes that can be used to control how the XmlSerializer generates the resulting XML document. If you wish to see all of your options, look up the System.Xml.Serialization namespace using the .NET Framework 3.5 SDK documentation.

Persisting Collections of Objects

Now that you have seen how to persist a single object to a stream, let's examine how to save a set of objects. As you may have noticed, the Serialize() method of the IFormatter interface does not provide a way to specify an arbitrary number of objects (only a single System.Object). On a related note, the return value of Deserialize() is, again, a single System.Object:

```
Public Interface IFormatter
  Function Deserialize(ByVal serializationStream As Stream) As Object
  Sub Serialize(ByVal serializationStream As Stream, ByVal graph As Object)
...
End Interface
```

Recall that the System.Object parameter and return value found in these methods in fact represent a complete object graph. Given this, if you pass in an object that has been marked as <Serializable()> and contains other <Serializable()> objects, the entire set of objects is persisted right away. As luck would have it, most of the types found within the System.Collections and System.Collections.Generic namespaces have already been marked as <Serializable()>. Therefore, if you wish to persist a set of objects, simply add the set to the container (such as an ArrayList or generic List(Of T)) and serialize the container to your stream of choice.

Assume you have updated the JamesBondCar class with a two-argument constructor to set a few pieces of state data (note that you add back the default constructor, as required by the XmlSerializer):

```
<Serializable(), XmlRoot(Namespace:="http://www.intertechtraining.com")> _
Public Class JamesBondCar
  Inherits Car

  Public Sub New(ByVal SkyWorthy As Boolean, ByVal SeaWorthy As Boolean)
    canFly = SkyWorthy
    canSubmerge = SeaWorthy
  End Sub

  ' The XmlSerializer demands a default constructor!
  Public Sub New()
  End Sub

  <XmlAttribute()> _
  Public canFly As Boolean
  <XmlAttribute()> _
  Public canSubmerge As Boolean
End Class
```

With this, you are now able to persist any number of JamesBondCars like so:

```
Sub Main()
...
  ' Now persist a List(Of T) of JamesBondCars.
  Dim myCars As New List(Of JamesBondCar)()
  myCars.Add(New JamesBondCar(True, True))
  myCars.Add(New JamesBondCar(True, False))
```

```
  myCars.Add(New JamesBondCar(False, True))
  myCars.Add(New JamesBondCar(False, False))

  fStream = New FileStream("CarCollection.xml", _
    FileMode.Create, FileAccess.Write, FileShare.None)
  xmlFormat = New XmlSerializer(GetType(List(Of JamesBondCar)), _
                                New Type() {GetType(JamesBondCar), _
                                GetType(Car), GetType(Radio)})
  xmlFormat.Serialize(fStream, myCars)
  fStream.Close()
  Console.ReadLine()
End Sub
```

Again, because you made use of the `XmlSerializer`, you are required to specify type information for each of the subobjects within the root object (which in this case is the `List(Of T)`). Had you made use of the `BinaryFormatter` type, the logic would be even more straightforward, for example:

```
Sub Main()
...
  ' Save List object (myCars) as binary.
  Dim myCars As New List(Of JamesBondCar)()
...
  Dim binFormat As New BinaryFormatter()
  Dim fStream As Stream = New FileStream("CarData.dat", FileMode.Create, _
    FileAccess.Write, FileShare.None)
  binFormat.Serialize(fStream, myCars)
  fStream.Close()
  Console.ReadLine()
End Sub
```

Excellent! At this point, you should see how you can use object serialization services to simplify the process of persisting and resurrecting your application's data. Next up, allow me to illustrate how you can customize the default serialization process.

Source Code The SimpleSerialize application is located under the Chapter 21 subdirectory.

Customizing the Serialization Process

In a vast majority of cases, the default serialization scheme just examined will fit the bill. Simply apply the `<Serializable()>` attribute accordingly and pass the object graph to your formatter of choice. In some cases, however, you may wish to become more involved with how an object graph is handled during the serialization process in order to customize the formatting of the data (among other tasks).

For example, maybe you have a business rule that says all field data must be persisted in a given text format, or perhaps you wish to add additional bits of data to the stream that do not directly map to fields in the object being persisted (time stamps, unique identifiers, or whatnot) or interact with an external log file.

When you wish to become more involved with the process of object serialization, the `System.Runtime.Serialization` namespace provides several types that allow you to do so. Table 21-2 describes some of the core types to be aware of.

Table 21-2. `System.Runtime.Serialization` *Namespace Core Types*

Type	Meaning in Life
`ISerializable`	Before the release of .NET 2.0, implementing this interface was the preferred way to perform custom serialization. As of .NET 2.0 and higher, however, the preferred way to customize the serialization process is to apply a new set of serialization-centric attributes (described in just a bit).
`<OnDeserialized()>`	This attribute allows you to specify a method that will be called immediately after the object has been deserialized.
`<OnDeserializing()>`	This attribute allows you to specify a method that will be called during the deserialization process.
`<OnSerialized()>`	This attribute allows you to specify a method that will be called immediately after the object has been serialized.
`<OnSerializing()>`	This attribute allows you to specify a method that will be called during the serialization process.
`<OptionalField()>`	This attribute allows you to define a field on a type that can be missing from the specified stream.
`SerializationInfo`	In essence, this class is a "property bag" that maintains name/value pairs representing the state of an object during the serialization process.

A Deeper Look at Object Serialization

Before we examine various ways in which you can customize the serialization process, it will be helpful to take a deeper look at what takes place behind the scenes. When the `BinaryFormatter` serializes an object graph, it is in charge of transmitting the following information into the specified stream:

- The fully qualified name of the objects in the graph (e.g., `MyApp.JamesBondCar`)
- The name of the assembly defining the object graph (e.g., `MyApp.exe`)
- An instance of the `SerializationInfo` class that contains all stateful data maintained by the members in the object graph

During the deserialization process, the `BinaryFormatter` uses this same information to build an identical copy of the object, using the information extracted from the underlying stream. The actual state of the object graph itself is represented by an instance of the `SerializationInfo` type, which is created and populated automatically by the formatter when required.

■ Note Recall that `SoapFormatter` and `XmlSerializer` do not persist a type's fully qualified name.

The big picture can be visualized as shown in Figure 21-3.

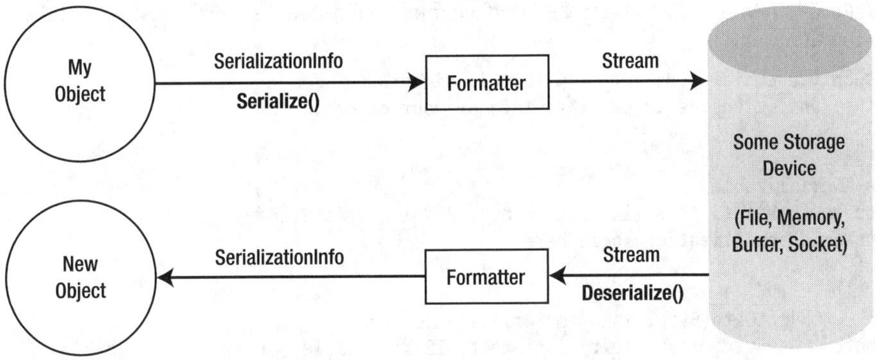

Figure 21-3. *The serialization process*

Beyond moving the required data into and out of a stream, formatters also analyze the members in the object graph for the following pieces of infrastructure:

- A check is made to determine whether the object is marked with the `<Serializable()>` attribute. If the object is not, a `SerializationException` is thrown.
- If the object is marked `<Serializable()>`, a check is made to determine whether the object implements the `ISerializable` interface. If this is the case, `ISerializable.GetObjectData()` is called on the object.
- If the object does not implement `ISerializable`, the default serialization process is used, serializing all fields not marked as `<NonSerialized()>`.

In addition to determining whether the type supports `ISerializable`, formatters are also responsible for discovering whether the types in question support members that have been adorned with the `<OnSerializing()>`, `<OnSerialized()>`, `<OnDeserializing()>`, or `<OnDeserialized()>` attribute. We'll examine the role of these attributes in just a bit, but first let's look at the role of `ISerializable`.

Customizing Serialization Using ISerializable

Objects that are marked `<Serializable()>` have the option of implementing the `ISerializable` interface. By doing so, you are able to "get involved" with the serialization process and perform any pre-data formatting. This interface is quite simple, given that it defines only a single method, `GetObjectData()`, which is called by the formatter when the object is being serialized into a stream:

```
' The formatter will call this method when serializing
' an object.
Public Interface ISerializable
  Sub GetObjectData(ByVal info As SerializationInfo, _
  ByVal context As StreamingContext)
End Interface
```

The implementation of this method populates the incoming `SerializationInfo` parameter with a series of name/value pairs that (typically) map to the field data of the object being persisted. `SerializationInfo` defines numerous variations on the overloaded `AddValue()` method, in addition to a small set of properties that allow the type to get and set the type's name, defining assembly, and member count.

Types that implement the ISerializable interface must also define a special constructor taking the following signature:

```
' You must supply a custom constructor with this signature
' to allow the runtime engine to set the state of your object.
<Serializable()> _
Class SomeClass
  Implements ISerializable
  Private Sub New(ByVal si As SerializationInfo, ByVal ctx As StreamingContext)
    ' Add custom deserialization logic here.
  End Sub

  Public Sub GetObjectData(ByVal info As SerializationInfo, _
    ByVal context As StreamingContext) Implements ISerializable.GetObjectData
    ' Add custom serialization logic here.
  End Sub
End Class
```

This special constructor is only intended to be called by a given formatter when the object is being deserialized, and therefore best practice is to define the visibility of this constructor as Private. This is permissible given that the formatter will have access to this member regardless of its visibility. As you can see, the first parameter of this constructor must be an instance of the SerializationInfo type (which again holds the state of the object's members).

The second parameter of this special constructor is a StreamingContext type, which contains information regarding the source or destination of the bits. The most informative member of this type is the State property, which represents a value from the StreamingContextStates enumeration. The values of this enumeration represent the basic composition of the current stream. To be honest, unless you are implementing some low-level custom remoting services, you will seldom need to deal with this enumeration directly. Nevertheless, here are the possible names of the StreamingContextStates enum (consult the .NET Framework 3.5 SDK documentation for full details):

```
Enum StreamingContextStates
  CrossProcess
  CrossMachine
  File
  Persistence
  Remoting
  Other
  Clone
  CrossAppDomain
  All
End Enum
```

To illustrate customizing the serialization process using ISerializable, assume you have a class type that defines two points of string data. Furthermore, assume that you must ensure the string values are serialized to the stream in all uppercase and deserialized from the stream in all lowercase. To account for such rules, you could implement ISerializable as follows (be sure to import the System.Runtime.Serialization namespace):

```
<Serializable()> _
Class MyStringData
  Implements ISerializable
```

```
  Public dataItemOne As String
  Public dataItemTwo As String

  Public Sub New()
  End Sub

  ' Called by formatter when object graph is being deserialized.
  Private Sub New(ByVal si As SerializationInfo, ByVal ctx As StreamingContext)
    dataItemOne = si.GetString("First_Item").ToLower()
    dataItemTwo = si.GetString("dataItemTwo").ToLower()
  End Sub

  ' Called by formatter when object is being serialized.
  Public Sub GetObjectData(ByVal info As SerializationInfo, _
    ByVal context As StreamingContext) Implements ISerializable.GetObjectData
    info.AddValue("First_Item", dataItemOne.ToUpper())
    info.AddValue("dataItemTwo", dataItemTwo.ToUpper())
  End Sub
End Class
```

Notice that when you are filling the `SerializationInfo` object from within the `GetObjectData()` method, you are not required to name the data points identically to the type's internal member variables. This can obviously be helpful if you need to further decouple the type's data from the persisted format. Do be aware, however, that you will need to obtain the values from within the private constructor using the same names assigned within `GetObjectData()`.

To test your customization, assume you have persisted an instance of `MyStringData` using a `SoapFormatter`. When you view the resulting `*.soap` file, you will note that the string fields have indeed been persisted in uppercase:

```
<SOAP-ENV:Envelope xmlns:xsi="...">
  <SOAP-ENV:Body>
    <a1:MyStringData id="ref-1" xmlns:a1="...">
      <First_Item id="ref-3">THIS IS SOME DATA.</First_Item>
      <dataItemTwo id="ref-4">HERE IS SOME MORE DATA.</dataItemTwo>
    </a1:MyStringData>
  </SOAP-ENV:Body>
</SOAP-ENV:Envelope>
```

When deserializing these same values, they would be converted back into lowercase given the custom code within the "special hidden" constructor. While this example was intended to be only illustrative in nature, it does point out the fact that customizing how your object's data is (de)serialized involves support of the `ISerializable` interface and support for a specific hidden constructor invoked behind the scenes by the formatter.

Customizing Serialization Using Attributes

Although the previously examined approach to customizing the object serialization process is still possible under .NET 3.5, the preferred manner to do so is to define methods that are attributed with any of the new serialization-centric attributes: `<OnSerializing()>`, `<OnSerialized()>`, `<OnDeserializing()>`, or `<OnDeserialized()>`. The roles of each of these new attributes are documented in Table 21-3.

Table 21-3. *Custom Serialization Attributes*

Serialization Attribute	Meaning in Life
<OnDeserializing()>	The method marked with this attribute will be called before the deserialization process begins. Here you can initialize default values for optional fields (these being fields marked with the <OptionalField()> attribute).
<OnDeserialized()>	The method marked with this attribute will be called once the deserialization process is complete. Here you are able to establish optional field values based on the contents of other fields.
<OnSerializing()>	The method marked with this attribute will be called before the serialization process begins. Here you can prep for the serialization process (e.g., create optional data structures, write to event logs, etc.).
<OnSerialized()>	The method marked with this attribute will be called after the serialization process is complete. Typically, this method would be used to log serialization events.

Using these attributes to control object serialization is typically less cumbersome than implementing ISerializable (and the obligatory private "special constructor"), given that you do not need to manually interact with an incoming SerializationInfo parameter. Instead, you are able to directly modify your state data while the formatter is operating on the type. Also be aware that you are not required to capture each step of the serialization/deserialization process. Thus, if you are interested only in attributing methods with the <OnDeserialized()> and <OnSerialized()> attributes (to account for when the object is fully serialized or deserialized), you are free to do so.

The subroutines that are decorated with any of the attributes described in Table 21-3 must be defined to receive a StreamingContext parameter as their only parameter (otherwise, you will receive a runtime exception). To illustrate, here is a new <Serializable()> type that has the same requirements as MyStringData, this time accounted for using the <OnSerializing()> and <OnDeserialized()> attributes:

```
<Serializable()> _
Class MoreStringData
  Public dataItemOne As String
  Public dataItemTwo As String

  ' This method is called by the formatter when the
  ' object is being serialized.
  <OnSerializing()> _
  Private Sub OnSerializing(ByVal context As StreamingContext)
    dataItemOne = dataItemOne.ToUpper()
    dataItemTwo = dataItemTwo.ToUpper()
  End Sub

  ' This method is called by the formatter when the
  ' object is being deserialized.
  <OnDeserialized()> _
  Private Sub OnDeserialized(ByVal context As StreamingContext)
    dataItemOne = dataItemOne.ToLower()
    dataItemTwo = dataItemTwo.ToLower()
  End Sub
End Class
```

If you were to serialize this new type, you would again find that the data has been persisted as uppercase and deserialized as lowercase.

Source Code The CustomSerialization project is included under the Chapter 21 subdirectory.

Note The .NET platform provides another serialization-centric attribute named <OptionalField()>. This attribute can be applied to new fields of a previously serializable type to help safely version an object (and prevent the CLR from throwing runtime exceptions when incompatibilities are found). Look up the topic "Version Tolerant Serialization" within the .NET Framework 3.5 SDK documentation for further information.

Summary

This chapter introduced the topic of object serialization services. As you have seen, the .NET platform makes use of an object graph to correctly account for the full set of related objects that are to be persisted to a stream. As long as each type in the object graph has been marked with the <Serializable()> attribute, the data is persisted using your format of choice (binary, SOAP, or XML).

You also learned that it is possible to customize the out-of-the-box serialization process using two possible approaches. First, you learned how to implement the ISerializable interface (and support a special private constructor) to become more involved with how formatters persist the supplied data. Next, you came to know a set of attributes that simplifies the process of custom serialization. Just apply the <OnSerializing()>, <OnSerialized()>, <OnDeserializing()>, or <OnDeserialized()> attribute on members taking a StreamingContext parameter, and the formatters will invoke them accordingly.

CHAPTER 22

ADO.NET Part I: The Connected Layer

As you would expect, the .NET platform defines a number of namespaces that allow you to interact with machine local and remote relational databases. Collectively speaking, these namespaces are known as *ADO.NET*. In this chapter, once I frame the overall role of ADO.NET, I'll move on to discuss the topic of ADO.NET data providers. As you will see, the .NET platform supports numerous data providers, each of which is optimized to communicate with a specific database management system (Microsoft SQL Server, Oracle, MySQL, etc.).

After you understand the common functionality provided by various data providers, you will then examine the data provider factory pattern. As you will see, using types within the `System.Data.Common` namespace (and a related `App.config` file), you are able to build a single code base that can dynamically pick and choose the underlying data provider without the need to recompile or redeploy the application's code base.

Perhaps most important, this chapter will give you the chance to build a custom data access library assembly (`AutoLotDAL.dll`) that will encapsulate various database operations performed on a custom database named AutoLot. This library will be expanded upon (in Chapter 23) and leveraged over many of this text's remaining chapters. We wrap things up by examining how to communicate with Microsoft SQL Server in an asynchronous manner using the types within the `System.Data.SqlClient` namespace and introduce the topic of database transactions.

Note This chapter is one of three that deal with the topic of data access under the .NET platform. Chapter 23 examines the disconnected layer of ADO.NET, while Chapter 24 examines the role of LINQ to ADO.

A High-Level Definition of ADO.NET

If you have a background in Microsoft's previous COM-based data access model (Active Data Objects, or ADO), understand that ADO.NET has very little to do with ADO beyond the letters "A," "D," and "O." While it is true that there is some relationship between the two systems (e.g., each has the concept of connection and command objects), some familiar ADO types (e.g., the `Recordset`) no longer exist. Furthermore, there are a number of new ADO.NET types that have no direct equivalent under classic ADO (e.g., the data adapter).

Unlike classic ADO, which was primarily designed for tightly coupled client/server systems, ADO.NET was built with the disconnected world in mind, using `DataSets`. This class represents a local copy of any number of related data tables, each of which contains a collection of rows and columns. Using the `DataSet`, the calling assembly (such as a web page, a WCF service or desktop executable) is able to manipulate and update a `DataSet`'s contents while disconnected from the data source, and send modified data back for processing using a related data adapter.

Another major difference between classic ADO and ADO.NET is that ADO.NET has deep support for XML data representation. In fact, the data obtained from a data store is serialized (by default) as XML when accessed across application domain boundaries. Given that XML is often transported between layers using standard HTTP, ADO.NET is not limited by firewall constraints.

Perhaps the most fundamental difference between classic ADO and ADO.NET is that ADO.NET is a managed library of code, therefore it plays by the same rules as any managed library. The types that make up ADO.NET use the CLR memory management protocol, adhere to the same type system (classes, interfaces, enums, structures, and delegates), and can be accessed by any .NET language.

From a programmatic point of view, the bulk of ADO.NET is represented by a core assembly named `System.Data.dll`. Within this binary, you will find a good number of namespaces (see Figure 22-1), many of which represent the types of a particular ADO.NET data provider (defined shortly).

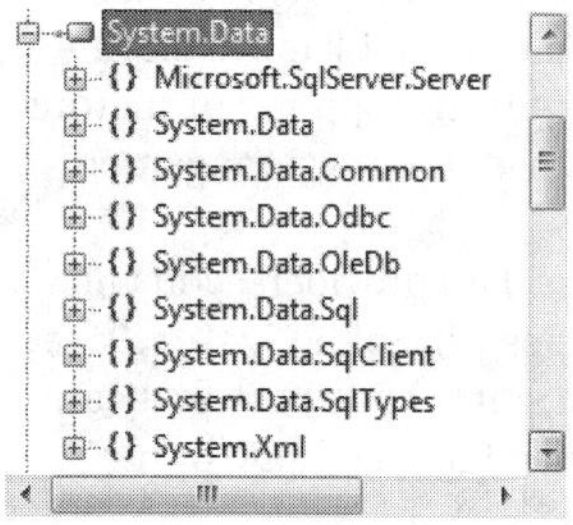

Figure 22-1. `System.Data.dll` *is the core ADO.NET assembly.*

As it turns out, all Visual Basic projects created with Visual Studio 2008 reference this key data access library. Furthermore, the References tab of the My Project editor (see Chapter 2) automatically imports the `System.Data` namespace into each `*.vb` file. However, you will need to update your code files to import any additional ADO.NET namespaces you wish to use.

Also understand that there are other ADO.NET-centric assemblies beyond `System.Data.dll` (such as `System.Data.OracleClient.dll`) that you may need to manually reference in your current project using the Add Reference dialog box.

■ **Note** With the release of .NET 3.5, ADO.NET has received many additional assemblies/namespaces that facilitate ADO.NET/LINQ integration (see Chapter 24).

The Two Faces of ADO.NET

The ADO.NET libraries can be used in two conceptually unique manners: connected or disconnected. When you are making use of the *connected layer*, your code base will explicitly connect to and disconnect from the underlying data store. When you are using ADO.NET in this manner, you typically interact with the data store using connection objects, command objects, and data reader objects.

The disconnected layer, which is the subject of Chapter 23, allows you to manipulate a set of `DataTable` objects (contained within a `DataSet`) that functions as a client-side copy of the external data. When you obtain a `DataSet` using a related data adapter object, the connection is automatically opened and closed on your behalf. As you would guess, this approach helps quickly free up connections for other callers and goes a long way toward increasing the scalability of your systems.

Once a caller receives a DataSet, it is able to traverse and manipulate the contents without incurring the cost of network traffic. As well, if the caller wishes to submit the changes back to the data store, the data adapter (in conjunction with a set of SQL statements) is used once again to update the data source, at which point the connection is closed immediately.

Understanding ADO.NET Data Providers

Unlike classic ADO, ADO.NET does not provide a single set of types that communicate with multiple database management systems (DBMSs). Rather, ADO.NET supports multiple *data providers*, each of which is optimized to interact with a specific DBMS. The first benefit of this approach is that a specific data provider is programmed to access any unique features of a particular DBMS. Another benefit is that a specific data provider is able to directly connect to the underlying engine of the DBMS in question without an intermediate mapping layer standing between the tiers.

Programmatically speaking, a data provider is a set of types defined in a given namespace that understand how to communicate with a specific data source. Regardless of which data provider you make use of, each defines a set of class types that provide core functionality. Table 22-1 documents some of the core common objects, their base class (all defined in the System.Data.Common namespace), and the data-centric interfaces (each defined in the System.Data namespace) they implement.

Table 22-1. *Core Objects of an ADO.NET Data Provider*

Common Object	Base Class	Implemented Interfaces	Meaning in Life
Connection	DbConnection	IDbConnection	Provides the ability to connect to and disconnect from the data store. Connection objects also provide access to a related transaction object.
Command	DbCommand	IDbCommand	Represents a SQL query or a stored procedure. Command objects also provide access to the provider's data reader object.
DataReader	DbDataReader	IDataReader, IDataRecord	Provides forward-only, read-only access to data using a server-side cursor.
DataAdapter	DbDataAdapter	IDataAdapter, IDbDataAdapter	Transfers DataSets between the caller and the data store. Data adapters contain a connection and a set of four internal command objects used to select, insert, update, and delete information from the data store.
Parameter	DbParameter	IDataParameter, IDbDataParameter	Represents a named parameter within a parameterized query.
Transaction	DbTransaction	IDbTransaction	Encapsulates a database transaction.

Although the specific names of these core objects will differ among data providers (e.g., SqlConnection versus OracleConnection versus OdbcConnection versus MySqlConnection), each object derives from the same base class (DbConnection in the case of connection objects) that implements identical interfaces (such as IDbConnection). Given this, you are correct to assume that once you learn how to work with one data provider, the remaining providers are quite straightforward.

■ **Note** Understand that under ADO.NET, when speaking of a "connection object," one is really referring to a specific `DbConnection`-derived type; there is no class literally named `Connection`. The same idea holds true for a "command object," "data adapter object," and so forth. As a naming convention, the objects in a specific data provider are prefixed with the name of the related DBMS (e.g., `SqlConnection`, `SqlCommand`, `OracleConnection`, etc.).

Figure 22-2 illustrates the big picture behind ADO.NET data providers. Note that in the diagram, the "Client Assembly" can literally be any type of .NET application: console program, Windows Forms application, ASP.NET web page, XML web service, .NET code library, and so on.

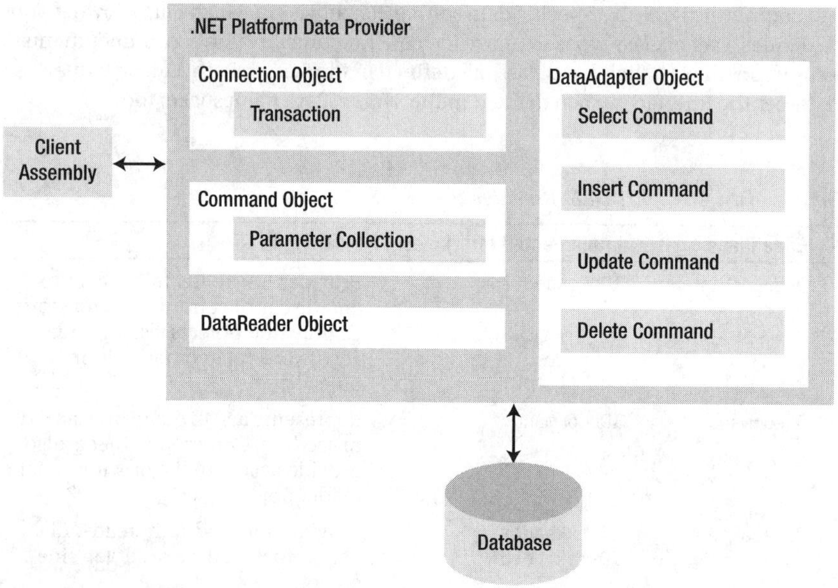

Figure 22-2. *ADO.NET data providers provide access to a given DBMS.*

Now, to be sure, a data provider will supply you with other types beyond the handful of objects shown in Figure 22-2. However, these core objects define a common baseline across all data providers.

The Microsoft-Supplied ADO.NET Data Providers

Microsoft's .NET distribution ships with numerous data providers, including a provider for Oracle, SQL Server, and OLE DB/ODBC-style connectivity. Table 22-2 documents the namespace and containing assembly for each Microsoft ADO.NET data provider.

Table 22-2. *Microsoft ADO.NET Data Providers*

Data Provider	Namespace	Assembly
OLE DB	`System.Data.OleDb`	`System.Data.dll`
Microsoft SQL Server	`System.Data.SqlClient`	`System.Data.dll`
Microsoft SQL Server Mobile	`System.Data.SqlServerCe`	`System.Data.SqlServerCe.dll`
ODBC	`System.Data.Odbc`	`System.Data.dll`
Oracle	`System.Data.OracleClient`	`System.Data.OracleClient.dll`

■ **Note** There is no specific data provider that maps directly to the Jet engine (and therefore Microsoft Access). If you wish to interact with an Access data file, you can do so using the OLE DB or ODBC data provider.

The OLE DB data provider, which is composed of the types defined in the `System.Data.OleDb` namespace, allows you to access data located in any data store that supports the classic COM-based OLE DB protocol. Using this provider, you may communicate with any OLE DB–compliant database simply by tweaking the `Provider` segment of your connection string.

Be aware, however, that the OLE DB provider interacts with various COM objects behind the scenes, which can affect the performance of your application. By and large, the OLE DB data provider is only useful if you are interacting with a DBMS that does not define a specific .NET data provider. However, given the fact that these days any DBMS worth its salt should have a custom ADO.NET data provider for download, `System.Data.OleDb` should be considered a legacy namespace that has little use in the .NET 3.5 world (this is even more the case with the advent of the data provider factory model introduced under .NET 2.0).

■ **Note** There is one case in which using the types of `System.Data.OleDb` is necessary; specifically if you need to communicate with Microsoft SQL Server version 6.5 or earlier. The `System.Data.SqlClient` namespace can only communicate with Microsoft SQL Server version 7.0 or higher.

The Microsoft SQL Server data provider offers direct access to Microsoft SQL Server data stores, and *only* SQL Server data stores (version 7.0 and greater) as well as SQL Server 2005 Express Edition. The `System.Data.SqlClient` namespace contains the types used by the SQL Server provider and offers the same basic functionality as the OLE DB provider. The key difference is that the SQL Server provider bypasses the OLE DB layer and thus gives numerous performance benefits. As well, the Microsoft SQL Server data provider allows you to gain access to the unique features of this particular DBMS.

The remaining Microsoft-supplied providers (`System.Data.OracleClient`, `System.Data.Odbc`, and `System.Data.SqlClientCe`) provide access to Oracle databases, interactivity with ODBC connections, and the SQL Server Compact edition DBMS (commonly used by handheld devices, such as a Pocket PC). The ODBC types defined within the `System.Data.Odbc` namespace are typically only useful if you need to communicate with a given DBMS for which there is no custom .NET data provider (in that ODBC is a widespread model that provides access to a number of data stores).

Obtaining Third-Party ADO.NET Data Providers

In addition to the data providers that ship from Microsoft, numerous third-party data providers exist for various open source and commercial databases. While you will most likely be able to obtain an ADO.NET data provider directly from the database vendor, you should be aware of the following site (please note that this URL is subject to change): `http://www.sqlsummit.com/DataProv.htm`.

This website is one of many that document each known ADO.NET data provider and provide links for more information and downloads. Here you will find numerous ADO.NET providers, including SQLite, DB2, MySQL, PostgreSQL, and Sybase (among others).

Given the large number of ADO.NET data providers, the examples in this chapter will make use of the Microsoft SQL Server data provider (`System.Data.SqlClient.dll`). Recall that this provider allows you to communicate with Microsoft SQL Server version 7.0 and higher, including SQL Server 2005 Express Edition. If you intend to use ADO.NET to interact with another DBMS, you should have no problem doing so once you understand the material presented in the pages that follow.

Additional ADO.NET Namespaces

In addition to the .NET namespaces that define the types of a specific data provider, the .NET base class libraries provide a number of additional ADO.NET-centric namespaces, some of which are shown in Table 22-3.

Table 22-3. *Select Additional ADO.NET-Centric Namespaces*

Namespace	Meaning in Life
`Microsoft.SqlServer.Server`	This namespace provides types that facilitate CLR and SQL Server 2005 integration services.
`System.Data`	This namespace defines the core ADO.NET types used by all data providers, including common interfaces and numerous types that represent the disconnected layer (`DataSet`, `DataTable`, etc.).
`System.Data.Common`	This namespace contains types shared between all ADO.NET data providers, including the common abstract base classes.
`System.Data.Sql`	This namespace contains types that allow you to discover Microsoft SQL Server instances installed on the current local network.
`System.Data.SqlTypes`	This namespace contains native data types used by Microsoft SQL Server. Although you are always free to use the corresponding CLR data types, the `SqlTypes` are optimized to work with SQL Server.

Do understand that this chapter will not examine each and every type within each and every ADO.NET namespace (that task would require a large book in and of itself). However, it is quite important for you to understand the types within the `System.Data` namespace.

The Types of the System.Data Namespace

Of all the ADO.NET namespaces, `System.Data` is the lowest common denominator. You simply cannot build ADO.NET applications without specifying this namespace in your data access applications. This namespace contains types that are shared among all ADO.NET data providers, regardless of the underlying data store. In addition to a number of database-centric exceptions (`NoNullAllowedException`, `RowNotInTableException`, `MissingPrimaryKeyException`, and the like), `System.Data` contains types that represent various database primitives (tables, rows, columns, constraints, etc.), as well as the common interfaces implemented by data provider objects. Table 22-4 lists some of the core types to be aware of.

Table 22-4. *Core Members of the* System.Data *Namespace*

Type	Meaning in Life
Constraint	Represents a constraint for a given DataColumn object
DataColumn	Represents a single column within a DataTable object
DataRelation	Represents a parent/child relationship between two DataTable objects
DataRow	Represents a single row within a DataTable object
DataSet	Represents an in-memory cache of data consisting of any number of interrelated DataTable objects
DataTable	Represents a tabular block of in-memory data
DataTableReader	Allows you to treat a DataTable as a fire-hose cursor (forward only, read-only data access)
DataView	Represents a customized view of a DataTable for sorting, filtering, searching, editing, and navigation
IDataAdapter	Defines the core behavior of a data adapter object
IDataReader	Defines the core behavior of a data reader object
IDbCommand	Defines the core behavior of a command object
IDbConnection	Defines the core behavior of a connection object
IDbDataAdapter	Extends IDataAdapter to provide additional functionality of a data adapter object
IDbDataParameter	Defines the core behavior of a parameter object
IDbTransaction	Defines the core behavior of a transaction object

A vast majority of the classes within System.Data are used when programming against the disconnected layer of ADO.NET. In the next chapter, you will get to know the details of the DataSet and its related cohorts (DataTable, DataRelation, DataRow, etc.) and how to use them (and a related data adapter) to represent and manipulate client-side copies of remote data.

However, your next task is to examine the core interfaces of System.Data at a high level, to better understand the common functionality offered by any data provider. You will learn specific details throughout this chapter, so for the time being let's simply focus on the overall behavior of each interface type.

The Role of the IDbConnection Interface

First up is the IDbConnection type, which is implemented by a data provider's *connection object*. This interface defines a set of members used to configure a connection to a specific data store, and it also allows you to obtain the data provider's transactional object. Here is the formal definition of IDbConnection:

```
Public Interface IDbConnection
  Inherits IDisposable
  Property ConnectionString() As String
  ReadOnly Property ConnectionTimeout() As Integer
  ReadOnly Property Database() As String
  ReadOnly Property State() As ConnectionState
  Function BeginTransaction() As IDbTransaction
  Function BeginTransaction(ByVal il As IsolationLevel) As IDbTransaction
  Sub ChangeDatabase(ByVal databaseName As String)
  Sub Close()
```

```
  Function CreateCommand() As IDbCommand
  Sub Open()
End Interface
```

■Note Like many other types in the .NET base class libraries, the `Close()` method is functionally equivalent to calling the `Dispose()` method directly or indirectly within a `Using` scope (see Chapter 8).

The Role of the IDbTransaction Interface

As you can see, the overloaded `BeginTransaction()` method defined by `IDbConnection` provides access to the provider's *transaction object*. Using the members defined by `IDbTransaction`, you are able to programmatically interact with a transactional session and the underlying data store:

```
Public Interface IDbTransaction
  Inherits IDisposable
  ReadOnly Property Connection() As IDbConnection
  ReadOnly Property IsolationLevel() As IsolationLevel
  Sub Commit()
  Sub Rollback()
End Interface
```

The Role of the IDbCommand Interface

Next, we have the `IDbCommand` interface, which will be implemented by a data provider's *command object*. Like other data access object models, command objects allow programmatic manipulation of SQL statements, stored procedures, and parameterized queries. In addition, command objects provide access to the data provider's data reader type via the overloaded `ExecuteReader()` method:

```
Public Interface IDbCommand
  Inherits IDisposable
  Property CommandText() As String
  Property CommandTimeout() As Integer
  Property CommandType() As CommandType
  Property Connection() As IDbConnection
  ReadOnly Property Parameters() As IDataParameterCollection
  Property Transaction() As IDbTransaction
  Property UpdatedRowSource() As UpdateRowSource
  Sub Cancel()
  Function CreateParameter() As IDbDataParameter
  Function ExecuteNonQuery() As Integer
  Function ExecuteReader() As IDataReader
  Function ExecuteReader(ByVal behavior As CommandBehavior) As IDataReader
  Function ExecuteScalar() As Object
  Sub Prepare()
End Interface
```

The Role of the IDbDataParameter and IDataParameter Interfaces

Notice in the previous code sample that the `Parameters` property of `IDbCommand` returns a strongly typed collection that implements `IDataParameterCollection`. This interface provides access to a set of parameter objects, each of which implements `IDbDataParameter`:

```
Public Interface IDbDataParameter
  Inherits IDataParameter
  Property Precision() As Byte
  Property Scale() As Byte
  Property Size() As Integer
End Interface
```

IDbDataParameter extends the IDataParameter interface to obtain the following additional operations:

```
Public Interface IDataParameter
  Property DbType() As DbType
  Property Direction() As ParameterDirection
  ReadOnly Property IsNullable() As Boolean
  Property ParameterName() As String
  Property SourceColumn() As String
  Property SourceVersion() As DataRowVersion
  Property Value() As Object
End Interface
```

As you will see, the functionality of the IDbDataParameter and IDataParameter interfaces allows you to represent parameters within a SQL command (including stored procedures) via specific ADO.NET parameter objects rather than hard-coded string literals.

The Role of the IDbDataAdapter and IDataAdapter Interfaces

Data adapters are used to push and pull DataSets to and from a given data store. Given this, the IDbDataAdapter interface defines a set of properties that are used to maintain the SQL statements for the related select, insert, update, and delete operations:

```
Public Interface IDbDataAdapter
  Inherits IDataAdapter
  Property DeleteCommand() As IDbCommand
  Property InsertCommand() As IDbCommand
  Property SelectCommand() As IDbCommand
  Property UpdateCommand() As IDbCommand
End Interface
```

In addition to these four properties, an ADO.NET data adapter also picks up the behavior defined in the base interface, IDataAdapter. This interface defines the key function of a data adapter type: the ability to transfer DataSets between the caller and underlying data store using the Fill() and Update() methods. As well, the IDataAdapter interface allows you to map database column names to more user-friendly display names via the TableMappings property:

```
Public Interface IDataAdapter
  Property MissingMappingAction() As MissingMappingAction
  Property MissingSchemaAction() As MissingSchemaAction
  ReadOnly Property TableMappings() As ITableMappingCollection
  Function Fill(ByVal dataSet As DataSet) As Integer
  Function FillSchema(ByVal dataSet As DataSet, _
    ByVal schemaType As SchemaType) As DataTable()
  Function GetFillParameters() As IDataParameter()
  Function Update(ByVal dataSet As DataSet) As Integer
End Interface
```

The Role of the IDataReader and IDataRecord Interfaces

The next key interface to be aware of is IDataReader, which represents the common behaviors supported by a given data reader object. When you obtain an IDataReader-compatible type from an ADO.NET data provider, you are able to iterate over the result set in a forward-only, read-only manner.

```
Public Interface IDataReader
  Inherits IDisposable
  Inherits IDataRecord
  ReadOnly Property Depth() As Integer
  ReadOnly Property IsClosed() As Boolean
  ReadOnly Property RecordsAffected() As Integer
  Sub Close()
  Function GetSchemaTable() As DataTable
  Function NextResult() As Boolean
  Function Read() As Boolean
  ' Indexers to get table data.
  Default Public ReadOnly Property Item(ByVal i As Integer) As Object
  Default Public ReadOnly Property Item(ByVal name As String) As Object
End Interface
```

Finally, as you can see, IDataReader extends IDataRecord, which defines a good number of members that allow you to extract a strongly typed value from the stream, rather than casting the generic System.Object retrieved from the data reader's overloaded Item property. Here is a partial listing of the various Get*XXX*() methods defined by IDataRecord (see the .NET Framework 3.5 SDK documentation for a complete listing):

```
Public Interface IDataRecord
  ReadOnly Property FieldCount() As Integer
  Function GetBoolean(ByVal i As Integer) As Boolean
  Function GetByte(ByVal i As Integer) As Byte
  Function GetChar(ByVal i As Integer) As Char
  Function GetDateTime(ByVal i As Integer) As DateTime
  Function GetDecimal(ByVal i As Integer) As Decimal
  Function GetFloat(ByVal i As Integer) As Single
  Function GetInt16(ByVal i As Integer) As Short
  Function GetInt32(ByVal i As Integer) As Integer
  Function GetInt64(ByVal i As Integer) As Long
...
  Function IsDBNull(ByVal i As Integer) As Boolean

  Default ReadOnly Property Item(ByVal name As String) As Object
  Default ReadOnly Property Item(ByVal i As Integer) As Object

End Interface
```

■ **Note** The IDataReader.IsDBNull() method can be used to programmatically discover if a specified field is set to Nothing before obtaining a value from the data reader (to avoid a runtime exception). Also recall that VB supports nullable data types (see Chapter 10), which are ideal for interacting with data columns that could be empty.

Abstracting Data Providers Using Interfaces

At this point, you should have a better idea of the common functionality found among all .NET data providers. Recall that even though the exact names of the implementing types will differ among data providers, you are able to program against these types in a similar manner—that's the beauty of interface-based polymorphism. For example, if you define a method that takes an `IDbConnection` parameter, you can pass in any ADO.NET connection object:

```
Public Sub OpenConnection(ByVal cn As IDbConnection)
  ' Open the incoming connection for the caller.
  cn.Open()
End Sub
```

Note Interfaces are not strictly required to access common functionality of ADO.NET objects; a similar result could be achieved using abstract base classes (such as `DbConnection`) as parameters or return values.

The same holds true for member return values. For example, consider the following VB Console Application project (named MyConnectionFactory), which allows you to obtain a specific connection object based on the value of a custom enumeration. For diagnostic purposes, we will simply print out the underlying connection object via reflection services:

```
' Need these to get definitions
' of various connection objects for our test.
Imports System.Data.SqlClient
Imports System.Data.Odbc
Imports System.Data.OleDb

' Need to reference System.Data.OracleClient.dll to nab this namespace!
Imports System.Data.OracleClient

' A list of possible providers.
Enum DataProvider
  SqlServer
  OleDb
  Odbc
  Oracle
  None
End Enum

Module Program
  Sub Main()
    Console.WriteLine("**** Very Simple Connection Factory *****" & vblf)

    ' Get a specific connection.
    Dim myCn As IDbConnection = GetConnection(DataProvider.SqlServer)
    Console.WriteLine("Your connection is a {0}", myCn.GetType().Name)

    ' Open, use, and close connection...

    Console.ReadLine()
  End Sub

  ' This method returns a specific connection object
  ' based on the value of a DataProvider enum.
```

```
  Private Function GetConnection(ByVal dp As DataProvider) As IDbConnection
    Dim conn As IDbConnection = Nothing
    Select Case dp
      Case DataProvider.SqlServer
        conn = New SqlConnection()
        Exit Select
      Case DataProvider.OleDb
        conn = New OleDbConnection()
        Exit Select
      Case DataProvider.Odbc
        conn = New OdbcConnection()
        Exit Select
      Case DataProvider.Oracle
        conn = New OracleConnection()
        Exit Select
    End Select
    Return conn
  End Function
End Module
```

The benefit of working with the general interfaces of `System.Data` (or for that matter, the abstract base classes of `System.Data.Common`) is that you have a much better chance of building a flexible code base that can evolve over time. For example, perhaps today you are building an application targeting Microsoft SQL Server, but what if your company switches to Oracle months down the road? If you build a solution that hard-codes the Microsoft SQL Server–specific types of `System.Data.SqlClient`, you will obviously need to edit, recompile, and redeploy the assembly should the back-end DBMS change.

Increasing Flexibility Using Application Configuration Files

To further increase the flexibility of your ADO.NET applications, you could incorporate a client-side `*.config` file that makes use of custom key/value pairs within the `<appSettings>` element. Recall from Chapter 15 that custom data stored within a `*.config` file can be programmatically obtained using types within the `System.Configuration` namespace. For example, assume you have specified a data provider value within a configuration file as follows:

```
<configuration>
  <appSettings>
    <!-- This key value maps to one of our enum values -->
    <add key="provider" value="SqlServer"/>
  </appSettings>
</configuration>
```

With this, you could update `Main()` to programmatically obtain the underlying data provider. By doing so, you have essentially built a *connection object factory* that allows you to change the provider without requiring you to recompile your code base (simply change the `*.config` file and restart the program). Here are the relevant updates to `Main()`:

```
Sub Main()
  Console.WriteLine("**** Very Simple Connection Factory *****" & vblf)

  ' Read the provider key.
  Dim dataProvString As String = ConfigurationManager.AppSettings("provider")

  ' Transform string to enum.
  Dim dp As DataProvider = DataProvider.None
  If [Enum].IsDefined(GetType(DataProvider), dataProvString) Then
```

```
    dp = DirectCast([Enum].Parse(GetType(DataProvider), _
      dataProvString), DataProvider)
  Else
    Console.WriteLine("Sorry, no provider exists!")
  End If

  ' Get a specific connection.
  Dim myCn As IDbConnection = GetConnection(dp)
  If myCn IsNot Nothing Then
    Console.WriteLine("Your connection is a {0}", myCn.GetType().Name)
  End If

  ' Open, use, and close connection.

  Console.ReadLine()
End Sub
```

■ **Note** To use the `ConfigurationManager` type, be sure to set a reference to the `System.Configuration.dll` assembly and import the `System.Configuration` namespace.

At this point we have authored some ADO.NET code that allows us to specify the underlying connection dynamically. One obvious problem, however, is that this abstraction is only used within the `MyConnectionFactory.exe` application. If we were to rework this example within a .NET code library (e.g., `MyConnectionFactory.dll`), we would be able to build any number of clients that could obtain various connection objects using layers of abstraction.

However, obtaining a connection object is only one aspect of working with ADO.NET. To make a worthwhile data provider factory library, we would also have to account for command objects, data readers, data adapters, transaction objects, and other data-centric types. While building such a code library would not necessarily be difficult, it would require a good amount of code and a considerable amount of time.

Thankfully, since the release of .NET 2.0, the kind folks in Redmond have built this very functionality directly within the .NET base class libraries. We will examine this formal API in just a moment, but first we need to create a custom database for use throughout this chapter, as well as many chapters to come.

■ **Source Code** The MyConnectionFactory project is included under the Chapter 22 subdirectory.

Creating the AutoLot Database

As we work through this chapter we will execute queries against a simple SQL Server test database named AutoLot. In keeping with the automotive theme used throughout this text, this database will contain three interrelated tables (Inventory, Orders, and Customers) that contain various bits of data representing order information for a fictional automobile sales company.

The assumption in this text is that you have a copy of Microsoft SQL Server (7.0 or higher) or a copy of Microsoft SQL Server 2005 Express Edition (which can be downloaded for free from `http://www.microsoft.com/sql/editions/express/`). This lightweight database server is perfect for our needs, in that (a) it is free, (b) it provides a GUI front end (the SQL Server Management Tool) to create and administer your databases, and (c) it integrates with Visual Studio 2008/Visual Basic 2008 Express Edition.

To illustrate the last point, the remainder of this section will walk you through the construction of the AutoLot database using Visual Studio 2008. If you are using Visual Basic 2008 Express, you can perform similar operations to what is explained here, using the Server Explorer window (which can be loaded from the View ➤ Other Windows menu option).

■ **Note** Do be aware that the AutoLot database will be used throughout the remainder of this text.

Creating the Inventory Table

To begin building our testing database, launch Visual Studio 2008 and open the Server Explorer perspective using the View menu of the IDE. Next, right-click the Data Connections node and select the Create New SQL Server Database menu option. Within the resulting dialog box, connect to your SQL Server installation on your local machine and specify AutoLot as the database name (Windows Authentication should be fine—see Figure 22-3).

Figure 22-3. *Creating a new SQL Server 2005 Express database using Visual Studio 2008*

At this point, the AutoLot database is completely devoid of any custom database objects (tables, stored procedures, views, etc.). To insert the Inventory table, simply right-click the Tables node and select Add New Table (see Figure 22-4).

Using the table editor, add four data columns: CarID, Make, Color, and PetName. Ensure that the CarID column has been set to the Primary Key (right-click the CarID row and select Set Primary Key). Note the key icon in Figure 22-5, which shows the final table settings.

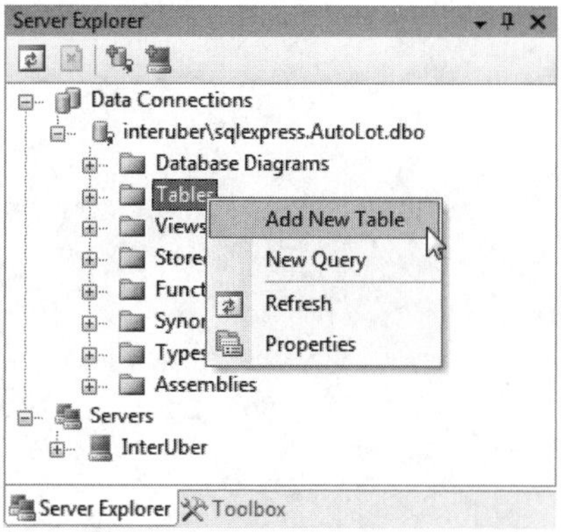

Figure 22-4. *Adding the Inventory table*

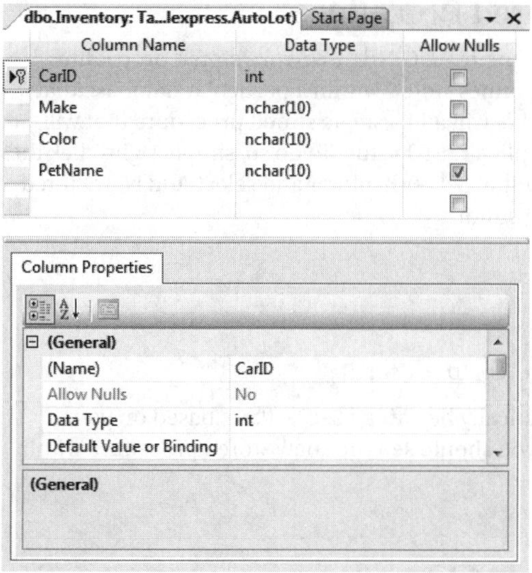

Figure 22-5. *Designing the Inventory table*

■ **Note** Many of the Visual Studio IDE data tools will only work to their full potential if a database table has been assigned a primary key.

Save (and then close) your new table and be sure you name this new database object as Inventory. At this point, you should see the Inventory table under the Tables node of Server Explorer.

Now, right-click the Inventory table icon and select Show Table Data. Enter a handful of new automobiles of your choosing (to make it interesting, be sure to have some cars that have identical colors and makes). Figure 22-6 shows one possible inventory list.

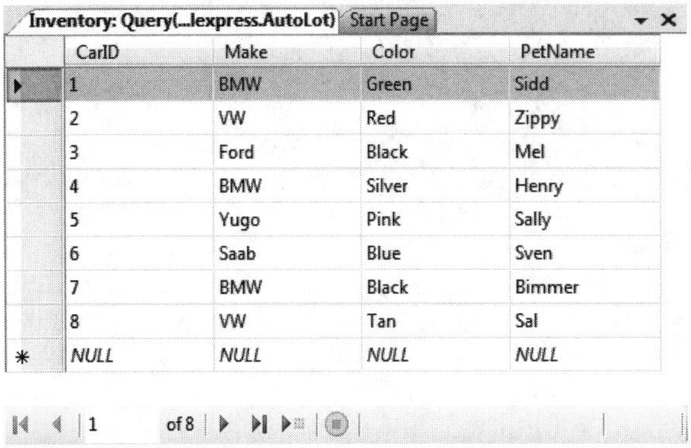

Figure 22-6. *Populating the Inventory table*

Authoring the GetPetName() Stored Procedure

Later in this chapter, we will examine how to make use of ADO.NET to invoke stored procedures. As you may already know, stored procedures are routines stored within a particular database that operate often on table data to yield a return value. We will add a single stored procedure that will return an automobile's pet name based on the supplied CarID value. To do so, simply right-click the Stored Procedures node of the AutoLot database within Server Explorer and select Add New Stored Procedure. Enter the following within the resulting editor:

```
CREATE PROCEDURE GetPetName
@carID int,
@petName char(10) output
AS
SELECT @petName = PetName from Inventory where CarID = @carID
```

When you save your procedure, it will automatically be named `GetPetName`, based on your `CREATE PROCEDURE` statement. Once you are done, you should see your new stored procedure within Server Explorer (see Figure 22-7).

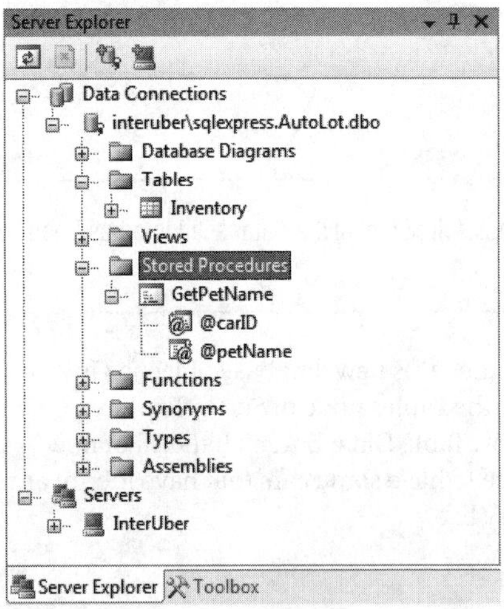

Figure 22-7. *The* `GetPetName` *stored procedure*

■ **Note** Stored procedures are not required to return data using output parameters as shown here; however, doing so will set the stage for talking about the `Direction` property of the `SqlParameter` type later in this chapter.

Creating the Customers and Orders Tables

Our testing database will have two additional tables. The Customers table (as the name suggests) will contain a list of customers, which will be represented by three columns: CustID (which should be set as the primary key), FirstName, and LastName. Taking the same steps you took to create the Inventory table, create the Customers table using the following schema (see Figure 22-8).

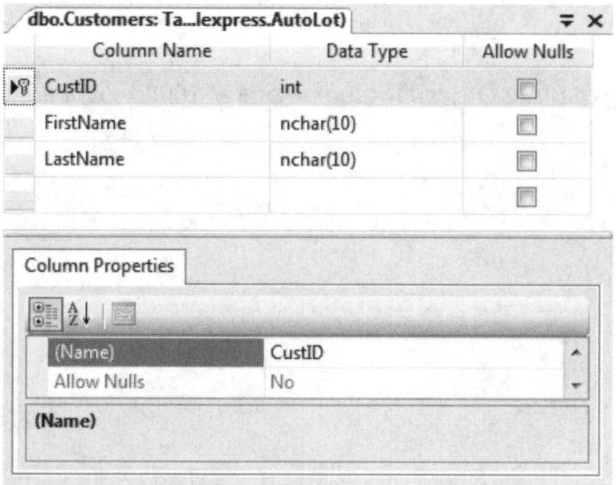

Figure 22-8. *Designing the Customers table*

Once you have saved your table, add a handful of customer records (see Figure 22-9).

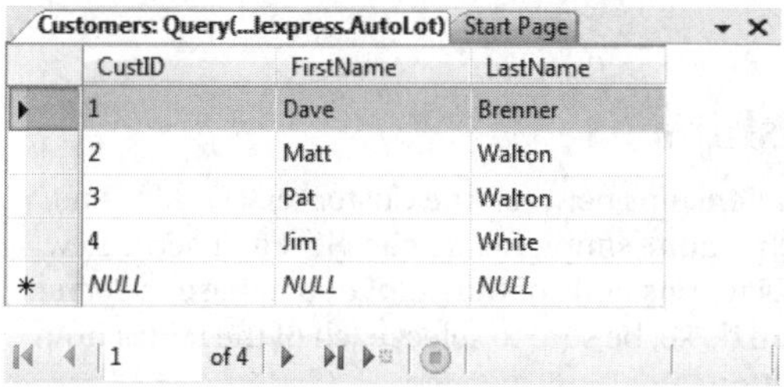

Figure 22-9. *Populating the Customers table*

Our final table, Orders, will be used to represent the automobile a given customer is interested in purchasing by mapping OrderID values to CarID/CustID values. Figure 22-10 shows the structure of our final table (again note that OrderID is the primary key).

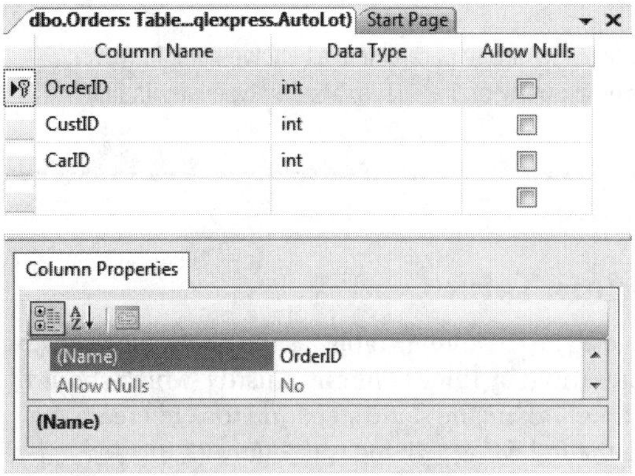

Figure 22-10. *Designing the Orders table*

Now, add data to your Orders table. Assuming that the OrderID value begins at 1000, select a unique CarID for each CustID value (see Figure 22-11).

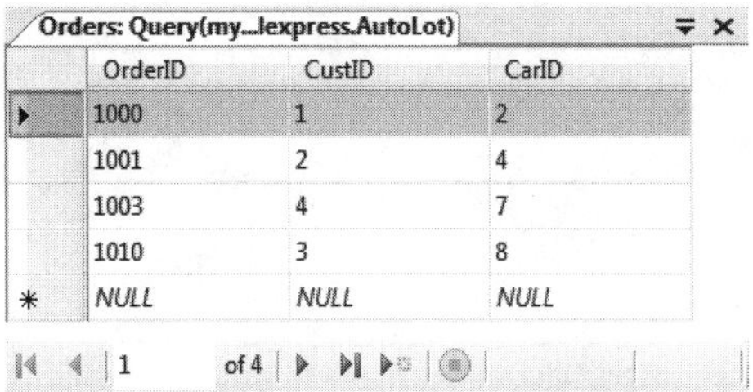

Figure 22-11. *Populating the Orders table*

Given the table data used in this text, we can see that Dave Brenner (CustID = 1) is interested in the red Volkswagen (CarID = 2), while Pat Walton (CustID = 3) has her eye on the tan Volkswagen (CarID = 8).

Visually Creating Table Relationships

The final task is to establish parent/child table relationships between the Customers, Orders, and Inventory tables. Doing so using Visual Studio 2008 is quite simple, as we can elect to insert a new database diagram by right-clicking the Database Diagrams node of the AutoLot database in Server Explorer and selecting Add New Diagram. Once you do so, be sure to select each of the tables from the resulting dialog box before clicking the Add button.

To establish the relationships between the tables, begin by clicking the CarID key of the Inventory table and (while holding down the mouse button) drag to the CarID field of the Orders table. Once you release the mouse, accept all defaults from the resulting dialog boxes.

Repeat the same process to map the CustID key of the Customers table to the CustID field of the Orders table. Once you are finished, you should find the class dialog box shown in Figure 22-12 (note that I enabled the display of the table relationships by right-clicking the designer and selecting Show Relationship Labels).

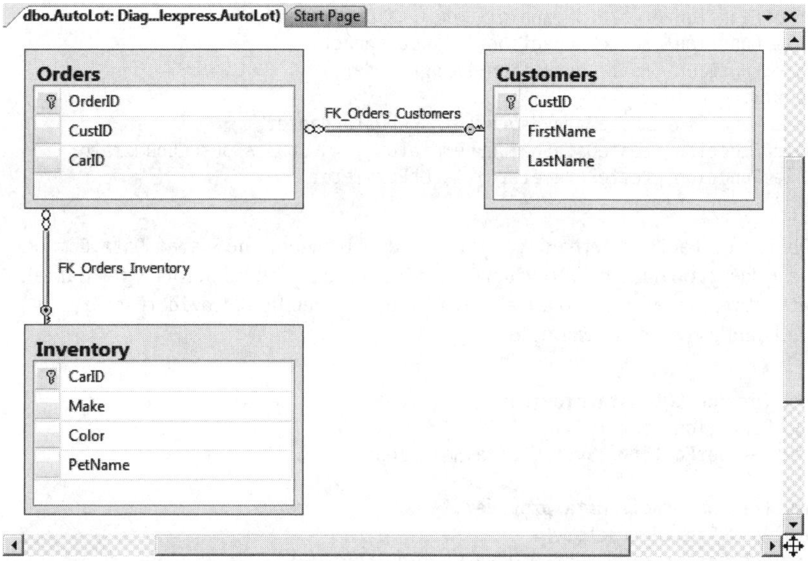

Figure 22-12. *The interconnected Orders, Inventory, and Customers tables*

With this, the AutoLot database is complete! While it is a far cry from a real-world corporate database, it will most certainly serve our purposes over the remainder of this book. Now that we have a database to test with, let's dive into the details of the ADO.NET data provider factory model.

The ADO.NET Data Provider Factory Model

The .NET data provider factory pattern allows us to build a single code base using generalized data access types. Furthermore, using application configuration files (and the `<connectionStrings>` subelement), we are able to obtain providers and connection strings declaratively without the need to recompile or redeploy the assembly.

To understand the data provider factory implementation, recall from Table 22-1 that the objects within a data provider derive from the same base classes defined within the `System.Data.Common` namespace:

- `DbCommand`: Abstract base class for all command objects
- `DbConnection`: Abstract base class for all connection objects
- `DbDataAdapter`: Abstract base class for all data adapter objects
- `DbDataReader`: Abstract base class for all data reader objects
- `DbParameter`: Abstract base class for all parameter objects
- `DbTransaction`: Abstract base class for all transaction objects

In addition, each of the Microsoft-supplied data providers contains a class type deriving from `System.Data.Common.DbProviderFactory`. This base class defines a number of methods that retrieve provider-specific data objects. Here is a snapshot of the relevant members of `DbProviderFactory`:

```
Public MustInherit Class DbProviderFactory
  ...
  Public Overridable Function CreateCommand() As DbCommand
```

```
  Public Overridable Function CreateCommandBuilder() As DbCommandBuilder
  Public Overridable Function CreateConnection() As DbConnection
  Public Overridable Function CreateConnectionStringBuilder() _
    As DbConnectionStringBuilder
  Public Overridable Function CreateDataAdapter() As DbDataAdapter
  Public Overridable Function CreateDataSourceEnumerator() As DbDataSourceEnumerator
  Public Overridable Function CreateParameter() As DbParameter
End Class
```

To obtain the DbProviderFactory-derived type for your data provider, the System.Data.Common namespace provides a class type named DbProviderFactories (note the plural in this type's name). Using the shared GetFactory() method, you are able to obtain the specific DbProviderFactory object of the specified data provider, for example:

```
Sub Main()
  ' Get the factory for the SQL data provider.
  Dim sqlFactory As DbProviderFactory = _
    DbProviderFactories.GetFactory("System.Data.SqlClient")
...
  ' Get the factory for the Oracle data provider.
  Dim oracleFactory As DbProviderFactory = _
    DbProviderFactories.GetFactory("System.Data.OracleClient")
...
End Sub
```

Of course, rather than obtaining a factory using a hard-coded string literal, you could read in this information from a client-side *.config file (much like the previous MyConnectionFactory example). You will do so in just a bit. However, in any case, once you have obtained the factory for your data provider, you are able to obtain the associated provider-specific data objects (connections, commands, data readers, etc.).

Registered Data Provider Factories

Before you build a full example of working with ADO.NET data provider factories, it is important to note that the DbProviderFactories type is able to fetch factories for only a subset of all possible data providers. The list of valid provider factories is recorded within the <DbProviderFactories> element within the machine.config file for your .NET 3.5 installation (which confusingly is located under C:\Windows\Microsoft.NET\Framework\v2.0.50727\CONFIG). Note that the value of the invariant attribute is identical to the value passed into the DbProviderFactories.GetFactory() method:

```
<system.data>
  <DbProviderFactories>
    <add name="Odbc Data Provider" invariant="System.Data.Odbc"
      description=".Net Framework Data Provider for Odbc"
      type="System.Data.Odbc.OdbcFactory,
      System.Data, Version=2.0.0.0, Culture=neutral,
      PublicKeyToken=b77a5c561934e089" />
    <add name="OleDb Data Provider" invariant="System.Data.OleDb"
      description=".Net Framework Data Provider for OleDb"
      type="System.Data.OleDb.OleDbFactory,
      System.Data, Version=2.0.0.0, Culture=neutral,
      PublicKeyToken=b77a5c561934e089" />
    <add name="OracleClient Data Provider" invariant="System.Data.OracleClient"
      description=".Net Framework Data Provider for Oracle"
      type="System.Data.OracleClient.OracleClientFactory, System.Data.OracleClient,
      Version=2.0.0.0, Culture=neutral, PublicKeyToken=b77a5c561934e089" />
    <add name="SqlClient Data Provider" invariant="System.Data.SqlClient"
```

```
      description=".Net Framework Data Provider for SqlServer"
      type="System.Data.SqlClient.SqlClientFactory, System.Data,
      Version=2.0.0.0, Culture=neutral, PublicKeyToken=b77a5c561934e089" />
    <add name="Microsoft SQL Server Compact Data Provider"
     invariant="System.Data.SqlServerCe.3.5"
     description=".NET Framework Data Provider for Microsoft SQL Server Compact"
     type="System.Data.SqlServerCe.SqlCeProviderFactory,
          System.Data.SqlServerCe,
     Version=3.5.0.0, Culture=neutral, PublicKeyToken=89845dcd8080cc91"/>
  </DbProviderFactories>
</system.data>
```

■ **Note** If you wish to leverage a similar data provider factory pattern for DMBSs not accounted for in the `machine.config` file, it is technically possible to add new invariant values that point to shared assemblies in the GAC. However, you must ensure that the data provider is ADO.NET 2.0 compliant and works with the data provider factory model.

A Complete Data Provider Factory Example

For a complete example, let's create a new Console Application (named DataProviderFactory) that prints out the automobile inventory of the AutoLot database. For this initial example, we will hard-code the data access logic directly within the `DataProviderFactory.exe` assembly (just to keep things simple for the time being). However, once we begin to dig into the details of the ADO.NET programming model, we will isolate our data logic to a specific .NET code library that will be used throughout the remainder of this text.

First, add a reference to the `System.Configuration.dll` assembly and import the `System.Configuration` namespace. Next, insert an `App.config` file to the current project and define an empty `<appSettings>` element. Add a new key named `provider` that maps to the namespace name of the data provider you wish to obtain (`System.Data.SqlClient`). As well, define a connection string that represents a connection to the AutoLot database (which may differ based on your version of SQL Server; see the following note for a helpful shortcut):

```
<?xml version="1.0" encoding="utf-8" ?>
<configuration>
 <appSettings>
  <!-- Which provider? -->
  <add key="provider" value="System.Data.SqlClient" />
  <!-- Which connection string? -->
  <add key="cnStr" value=
  "Data Source=(local)\SQLEXPRESS;Initial Catalog=AutoLot;
  Integrated Security=True"/>
 </appSettings>
</configuration>
```

■ **Note** We will examine connection strings in more detail in just a bit, including the role of the `<connectionStrings>` element. However, be aware that if you select your AutoLot database icon within Server Explorer, you can copy and paste the correct connection string from the Connection String property of the Visual Studio 2008 Properties window.

Now that you have a proper *.config file, you can read in the provider and cnStr values using the ConfigurationManager.AppSettings() method. The provider value will be passed to DbProviderFactories.GetFactory() to obtain the data provider–specific factory type. The cnStr value will be used to set the ConnectionString property of the DbConnection-derived type. Assuming you have imported the System.Data.Common namespace, update your Main() method as follows:

```
Sub Main()
  Console.WriteLine("***** Fun with Data Provider Factories *****" & vblf)

  ' Get Connection string/provider from *.config.
  Dim dp As String = ConfigurationManager.AppSettings("provider")
  Dim cnStr As String = ConfigurationManager.AppSettings("cnStr")

  ' Get the factory provider.
  Dim df As DbProviderFactory = DbProviderFactories.GetFactory(dp)

  ' Now make connection object.
  Dim cn As DbConnection = df.CreateConnection()
  Console.WriteLine("Your connection object is a: {0}", cn.GetType().FullName)
  cn.ConnectionString = cnStr
  cn.Open()

  ' Make command object.
  Dim cmd As DbCommand = df.CreateCommand()
  Console.WriteLine("Your command object is a: {0}", cmd.GetType().FullName)
  cmd.Connection = cn
  cmd.CommandText = "Select * From Inventory"

  ' Print out data with data reader.
  ' Because we specified CommandBehavior.CloseConnection, we
  ' don't need to explicitly call Close() on the connection.
  Dim dr As DbDataReader = cmd.ExecuteReader(CommandBehavior.CloseConnection)
  Console.WriteLine("Your data reader object is a: {0}", dr.GetType().FullName)

  Console.WriteLine(vblf & "***** Current Inventory *****")
  While dr.Read()
    Console.WriteLine("-> Car #{0} is a {1}.", _
      dr("CarID"), dr("Make").ToString().Trim())
  End While

  dr.Close()
  Console.ReadLine()
End Sub
```

Notice that for diagnostic purposes, you are printing out the fully qualified name of the underlying connection, command, and data reader using reflection services. If you run this application, you will find that the Microsoft SQL Server provider has been used to read data from the Inventory table of the AutoLot database (see Figure 22-13).

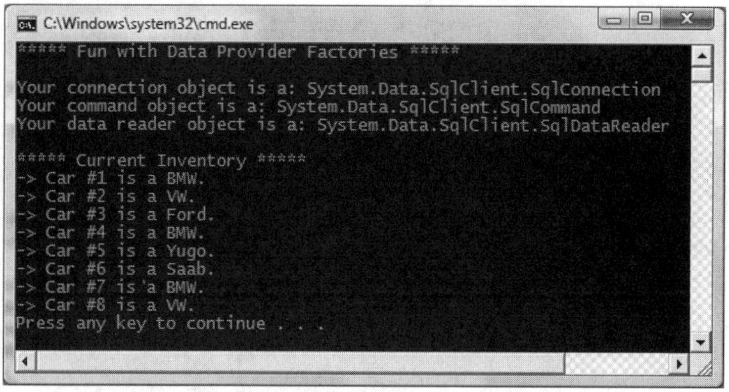

Figure 22-13. *Obtaining the SQL Server data provider factory*

Now, if you change the `*.config` file to specify `System.Data.OleDb` as the data provider (and update your connection string with a `Provider` segment) as follows:

```
<configuration>
 <appSettings>
  <!-- Which provider? -->
  <add key="provider" value="System.Data.OleDb" />
  <!-- Which connection string? -->
  <add key="cnStr" value=
  "Provider=SQLOLEDB;Data Source=(local)\SQLEXPRESS;
  Integrated Security=SSPI;Initial Catalog=AutoLot"/>
 </appSettings>
</configuration>
```

you will find the `System.Data.OleDb` types are used behind the scenes (see Figure 22-14).

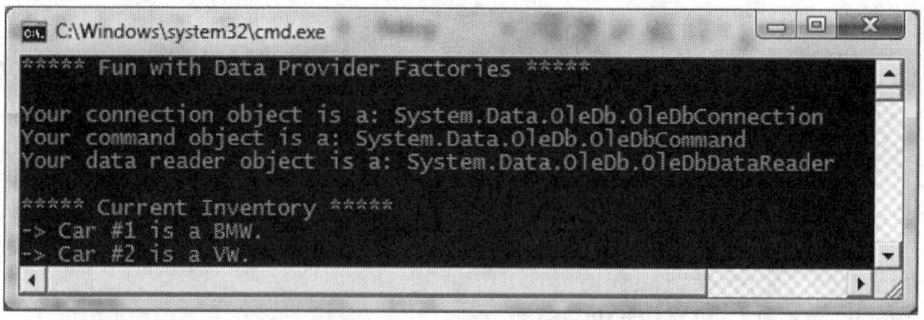

Figure 22-14. *Obtaining the OLE DB data provider factory*

Of course, based on your experience with ADO.NET, you may be a bit unsure exactly what the connection, command, and data reader objects are actually doing. Don't sweat the details for the time being (quite a few pages remain in this chapter, after all!). At this point, just understand that with the ADO.NET data provider factory model, it is possible to build a single code base that can consume various data providers in a declarative manner.

A POTENTIAL DRAWBACK TO THE PROVIDER FACTORY MODEL

Although the provider factory model is very powerful, you must make sure that the code base does indeed make use only of types and methods that are common to all providers via the members of the abstract base classes. Therefore, when authoring your code base, you will be limited to the members exposed by DbConnection, DbCommand, and the other types of the System.Data.Common namespace.

You may find that this "generalized" approach will prevent you from directly accessing some of the bells and whistles of a particular DBMS. If you must be able to invoke specific members of the underlying provider (e.g., SqlConnection), you can do so via an explicit cast. When doing so, however, your code base will become a bit harder to maintain (and far less flexible), given that you must add a number of runtime checks to determine the underlying ADO.NET type.

The <connectionStrings> Element

Currently our connection string data is within the <appSettings> element of our *.config file. Application configuration files may define an element named <connectionStrings>. Within this element, you are able to define any number of name/value pairs that can be programmatically read into memory using the ConfigurationManager.ConnectionStrings indexer. One advantage of this approach (rather than using the <appSettings> element and the ConfigurationManager.AppSettings indexer) is that you can define multiple connection strings for a single application in a consistent manner.

To illustrate, update your current App.config file as follows (note that each connection string is documented using the name and connectionString attributes rather than the key and value attributes as found in <appSettings>):

```
<configuration>
 <appSettings>
  <!-- Which provider? -->
  <add key="provider" value="System.Data.SqlClient" />
 </appSettings>

 <!-- Here are the connection strings -->
 <connectionStrings>
  <add name ="AutoLotSqlProvider" connectionString =
    "Data Source=(local)\SQLEXPRESS;Integrated Security=SSPI;
    Initial Catalog=AutoLot"/>

  <add name ="AutoLotOleDbProvider" connectionString =
    "Provider=SQLOLEDB;Data Source=(local)\SQLEXPRESS;
    Integrated Security=SSPI;Initial Catalog=AutoLot"/>

 </connectionStrings>
</configuration>
```

With this, you can now update your Main() method as follows:

```
Sub Main()
  Console.WriteLine("***** Fun with Data Provider Factories *****" & vblf)
  Dim dp As String = _
    ConfigurationManager.AppSettings("provider")
  Dim cnStr As String = _
    ConfigurationManager.ConnectionStrings("AutoLotSqlProvider").ConnectionString
...
End Sub
```

At this point, you have an application that is able to display the results of the Inventory table of the AutoLot database using a neutral code base. As you have seen, by offloading the provider name and connection string to an external `*.config` file, the data provider factory model will dynamically load the correct provider in the background. With this first example behind us, we can now dive into the details of working with the connected layer of ADO.NET.

Note Now that you understand the role of ADO.NET data provider factories, the remaining examples in this book will make explicit use of the types within the `System.Data.SqlClient` namespace just to keep focused on the task at hand. If you are using a different database management system (such as Oracle), you will need to update your code base accordingly.

Source Code The DataProviderFactory project is included under the Chapter 22 subdirectory.

Understanding the Connected Layer of ADO.NET

Recall that the *connected layer* of ADO.NET allows you to interact with a database using the connection, command, and data reader objects of your data provider. Although you have already made use of these objects in the previous DataProviderFactory application, let's walk through the process once again in detail using an expanded example. When you wish to connect to a database and read the records using a data reader object, you need to perform the following steps:

1. Allocate, configure, and open your connection object.
2. Allocate and configure a command object, specifying the connection object as a constructor argument or via the `Connection` property.
3. Call `ExecuteReader()` on the configured command object.
4. Process each record using the `Read()` method of the data reader.

To get the ball rolling, create a brand-new Console Application named AutoLotDataReader and import the `System.Data.SqlClient` namespace. The goal is to open a connection (via the `SqlConnection` object) and submit a SQL query (via the `SqlCommand` object) to obtain all records within the Inventory table. At this point, you will use a `SqlDataReader` to print out the results using the type indexer. Here is the complete code, with analysis to follow:

```
Imports System.Data.SqlClient

Module Program
  Sub Main()
    Console.WriteLine("***** Fun with Data Readers *****" & vblf)

    ' Create and open a connection.
    Dim cn As New SqlConnection()
    cn.ConnectionString = "Data Source=(local)\SQLEXPRESS;" & _
      "Integrated Security=SSPI;Initial Catalog=AutoLot"
    cn.Open()

    ' Create a SQL command object.
    Dim strSQL As String = "Select * From Inventory"
    Dim myCommand As New SqlCommand(strSQL, cn)
```

```
    ' Obtain a data reader a la ExecuteReader().
    Dim myDataReader As SqlDataReader
    myDataReader = myCommand.ExecuteReader(CommandBehavior.CloseConnection)

    ' Loop over the results.
    While myDataReader.Read()
      Console.WriteLine("-> Make: {0}, PetName: {1}, Color: {2}.", _
        myDataReader("Make").ToString().Trim(), _
        myDataReader("PetName").ToString().Trim(), _
        myDataReader("Color").ToString().Trim())
    End While

    ' Because we specified CommandBehavior.CloseConnection, we
    ' don't need to explicitly call Close() on the connection.
    myDataReader.Close()
    Console.ReadLine()
  End Sub
End Module
```

Working with Connection Objects

The first step to take when working with a data provider is to establish a session with the data source using the connection object (which, as you recall, derives from DbConnection). .NET connection types are provided with a formatted *connection string*, which contains a number of name/value pairs separated by semicolons. This information is used to identify the name of the machine you wish to connect to, required security settings, the name of the database on that machine, and other data provider–specific information.

As you can infer from the preceding code, the Initial Catalog name refers to the database you are attempting to establish a session with. The Data Source name identifies the name of the machine that maintains the database. Here, (local) allows you to define a single token to specify the current local machine (regardless of the literal name of said machine), while the \SQLEXPRESS token informs the SQL Server provider you are connecting to the default SQL Server Express Edition installation (if you created AutoLot on a full version of SQL Server 7.0 or above, simply specify Data Source=(local)).

Beyond this you are able to supply any number of tokens that represent security credentials. Here, we are setting Integrated Security to SSPI (which is equivalent to true), which uses the current Windows account credentials for user authentication.

■Note Look up the ConnectionString property of your data provider's connection object in the .NET Framework 3.5 SDK documentation to learn about each name/value pair for your specific DBMS. As you will quickly notice, a single segment (such as Integrated Security) can be set to multiple, redundant values (e.g., SSPI, true, and yes behave identically for the Integrated Security value of the SQL Server provider). Furthermore, you may find multiple terms for the same task (e.g., Initial Catalog and Database are interchangeable).

Once your construction string has been established, a call to Open() establishes your connection with the DBMS. In addition to the ConnectionString, Open(), and Close() members, a connection object provides a number of members that let you configure additional settings regarding your connection, such as timeout settings and transactional information. Table 22-5 lists some (but not all) members of the DbConnection base class.

Table 22-5. *Members of the* DbConnection *Type*

Member	Meaning in Life
BeginTransaction()	This method is used to begin a database transaction.
ChangeDatabase()	This method changes the database on an open connection.
ConnectionTimeout	This read-only property returns the amount of time to wait while establishing a connection before terminating and generating an error (the default value differs among providers). If you wish to change the default, specify a Connect Timeout segment in the connection string (e.g., Connect Timeout=30).
Database	This property gets the name of the database maintained by the connection object.
DataSource	This property gets the location of the database server maintained by the connection object.
GetSchema()	This method returns a DataTable that contains schema information from the data source.
State	This property gets the current state of the connection, represented by the ConnectionState enumeration.

As you can see, the properties of the DbConnection type are typically read-only in nature and are only useful when you wish to obtain the characteristics of a connection at runtime. When you wish to override default settings, you must alter the construction string itself. For example, the connection string sets the connection timeout setting from 15 seconds to 30 seconds:

```
Sub Main()
  Console.WriteLine("***** Fun with Data Readers *****" & vblf)

  ' Create an open a connection.
  Dim cn As New SqlConnection()
  cn.ConnectionString = "Data Source=(local)\SQLEXPRESS;" & _
    "Integrated Security=SSPI;Initial Catalog=AutoLot;Connect Timeout=30"
  cn.Open()

  ' New helper function (see below).
  ShowConnectionStatus(cn)
...
End Sub
```

In the preceding code, notice you have now passed your connection object as a parameter to a new helper method in the Program class named ShowConnectionStatus(), implemented as follows (be sure to import the System.Data.Common namespace to get the definition of DbConnection):

```
Sub ShowConnectionStatus(ByVal cn As DbConnection)
  ' Show various stats about current connection object.
  Console.WriteLine("***** Info about your connection *****")
  Console.WriteLine("Database location: {0}", cn.DataSource)
  Console.WriteLine("Database name: {0}", cn.Database)
  Console.WriteLine("Timeout: {0}", cn.ConnectionTimeout)
  Console.WriteLine("Connection state: {0}" & Chr(10), cn.State.ToString())
End Sub
```

While most of these properties are self-explanatory, the State property is worth special mention. Although this property may be assigned any value of the ConnectionState enumeration:

```
Public Enum ConnectionState
  Broken
  Closed
  Connecting
  Executing
  Fetching
  Open
End Enum
```

the only valid `ConnectionState` values are `ConnectionState.Open` and `ConnectionState.Closed` (the remaining members of this enum are reserved for future use). Also, understand that it is always safe to close a connection whose connection state is currently `ConnectionState.Closed`.

Working with ConnectionStringBuilder Objects

Working with connection strings programmatically can be a bit cumbersome, given that they are often represented as string literals, which are difficult to maintain and error-prone at best. The Microsoft-supplied ADO.NET data providers support *connection string builder objects*, which allow you to establish the name/value pairs using strongly typed properties. Consider the following update to the current `Main()` method:

```
Sub Main()
  Console.WriteLine("***** Fun with Data Readers *****" & vblf)

  ' Create a connection string via the builder object.
  Dim cnStrBuilder  As New SqlConnectionStringBuilder()
  cnStrBuilder.InitialCatalog = "AutoLot"
  cnStrBuilder.DataSource = "(local)\SQLEXPRESS"
  cnStrBuilder.ConnectTimeout = 30
  cnStrBuilder.IntegratedSecurity = True

  Dim cn As New SqlConnection()
  cn.ConnectionString = cnStrBuilder.ConnectionString
  cn.Open()

  ShowConnectionStatus(cn)
...
End Sub
```

In this iteration, you create an instance of `SqlConnectionStringBuilder`, set the properties accordingly, and obtain the internal string via the `ConnectionString` property. Also note that you make use of the default constructor of the type. If you so choose, you can also create an instance of your data provider's connection string builder object by passing in an existing connection string as a starting point (which can be helpful when you are reading these values dynamically from an `App.config` file). Once you have hydrated the object with the initial string data, you can change specific name/value pairs using the related properties, for example:

```
Sub Main()
  Console.WriteLine("***** Fun with Data Readers *****" & vblf)

  ' Assume you really obtained the cnStr value from a *.config file.
  Dim cnStr As String = "Data Source=(local)\SQLEXPRESS;" & _
  "Integrated Security=SSPI;Initial Catalog=AutoLot"

  Dim cnStrBuilder As New SqlConnectionStringBuilder(cnStr)
```

```
    ' Change timeout value.
    cnStrBuilder.ConnectTimeout = 5
...
End Sub
```

Working with Command Objects

Now that you better understand the role of the connection object, the next order of business is to check out how to submit SQL queries to the database in question. The SqlCommand type (which derives from DbCommand) is an OO representation of a SQL query, table name, or stored procedure. The type of command is specified using the CommandType property, which may take any value from the CommandType enum:

```
Public Enum CommandType
  StoredProcedure
  TableDirect
  Text   ' Default value.
End Sub
```

When creating a command object, you may establish the SQL query as a constructor parameter or directly via the CommandText property. Also when you are creating a command object, you need to specify the connection to be used. Again, you may do so as a constructor parameter or via the Connection property:

```
Sub Main()
...
  Dim cn As New SqlConnection()
...
  ' Create command object via ctor args.
  Dim strSQL As String = "Select * From Inventory"
  Dim myCommand As New SqlCommand(strSQL, cn)

  ' Create another command object via properties.
  Dim testCommand As New SqlCommand()
  testCommand.Connection = cn
  testCommand.CommandText = strSQL
...
End Sub
```

Realize that at this point, you have not literally submitted the SQL query to the AutoLot database, but rather prepared the state of the command object for future use. Table 22-6 highlights some additional members of the DbCommand type.

Table 22-6. *Members of the* DbCommand *Type*

Member	Meaning in Life
CommandTimeout	Gets or sets the time to wait while executing the command before terminating the attempt and generating an error.
Connection	Gets or sets the DbConnection used by this instance of the DbCommand.
Parameters	Gets the collection of DbParameter objects used for a parameterized query.
Cancel()	Cancels the execution of a command.
ExecuteReader()	Returns the data provider's DbDataReader object, which provides forward-only, read-only access to the underlying data.

Continued

Table 22-6. *Continued*

Member	Meaning in Life
ExecuteNonQuery()	Issues the command text to the data store where no results are expected or desired.
ExecuteScalar()	A lightweight version of the ExecuteReader() method, designed specifically for singleton queries (such as obtaining a record count).
Prepare()	Creates a prepared (or compiled) version of the command on the data source. As you may know, a *prepared query* executes slightly faster and is useful when you wish to execute the same query multiple times.

■ **Note** As illustrated later in this chapter, the SqlCommand object defines additional members that facilitate asynchronous database interactions.

Working with Data Readers

Once you have established the active connection and SQL command, the next step is to submit the query to the data source. As you might guess, you have a number of ways to do so. The DbDataReader type (which implements IDataReader) is the simplest and fastest way to obtain information from a data store. Recall that data readers represent a read-only, forward-only stream of data returned one record at a time. Given this, it should stand to reason that data readers are useful only when submitting SQL selection statements to the underlying data store.

Data readers are useful when you need to iterate over large amounts of data very quickly and have no need to maintain an in-memory representation. For example, if you request 20,000 records from a table to store in a text file, it would be rather memory-intensive to hold this information in a DataSet. A better approach is to create a data reader that spins over each record as rapidly as possible. Be aware, however, that data reader objects (unlike data adapter objects, which you'll examine later) maintain an open connection to their data source until you explicitly close the session.

Data reader objects are obtained from the command object via a call to ExecuteReader(). When invoking this method, you may optionally instruct the reader to automatically close down the related connection object by specifying CommandBehavior.CloseConnection.

The following use of the data reader leverages the Read() method to determine when you have reached the end of your records (via a False return value). For each incoming record, you are making use of the type indexer to print out the make, pet name, and color of each automobile. Also note that you call Close() as soon as you are finished processing the records, to implicitly free up the underlying connection object used by the command object:

```
Sub Main()
...
  ' Obtain a data reader a la ExecuteReader().
  Dim myDataReader As SqlDataReader
  myDataReader = myCommand.ExecuteReader(CommandBehavior.CloseConnection)

  ' Loop over the results.
  While myDataReader.Read()
    Console.WriteLine("-> Make: {0}, PetName: {1}, Color: {2}.", _
      myDataReader("Make").ToString().Trim(), _
      myDataReader("PetName").ToString().Trim(), _
```

```
      myDataReader("Color").ToString().Trim())
  End While

  ' Because we specified CommandBehavior.CloseConnection, we
  ' don't need to explicitly call Close() on the connection.
  myDataReader.Close()
  Console.ReadLine()
End Sub
```

Note The trimming of the string data shown here is only used to remove trailing blank spaces in the database entries; it is not directly related to ADO.NET! Whether this is necessary or not depends on the column definitions and the data placed in the table, and isn't always required.

The indexer of a data reader object has been overloaded to take either a `String` (representing the name of the column) or an `Integer` (representing the column's ordinal position). Thus, you could clean up the current reader logic (and avoid hard-coded string names) with the following update (note the use of the `FieldCount` property):

```
While myDataReader.Read()
  Console.WriteLine("***** Record *****")
  For i As Integer = 0 To myDataReader.FieldCount - 1
    Console.WriteLine("{0} = {1} ", myDataReader.GetName(i), _
    myDataReader.GetValue(i).ToString().Trim())
  Next
  Console.WriteLine()
End While
```

If you compile and run your project, you should be presented with a list of all automobiles in the Inventory table of the AutoLot database (see Figure 22-15).

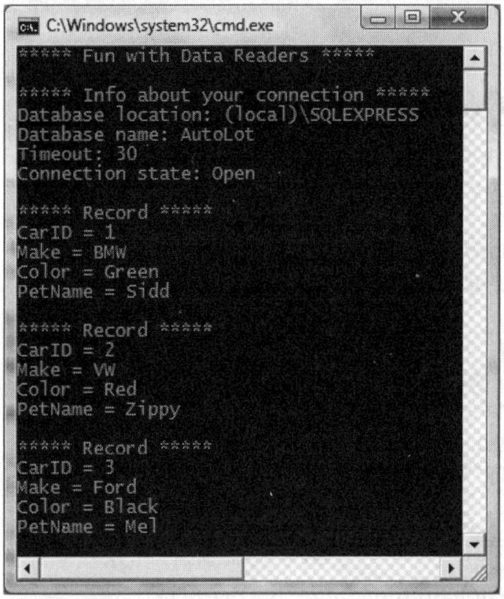

Figure 22-15. *Fun with data reader objects*

Obtaining Multiple Result Sets Using a Data Reader

Data reader objects are able to obtain multiple result sets using a single command object. For example, if you are interested in obtaining all rows from the Inventory table as well as all rows from the Customers table, you are able to specify both SQL SELECT statements using a semicolon delimiter:

```
Dim strSQL As String = "Select * From Inventory;Select * from Customers"
```

Once you obtain the data reader, you are able to iterate over each result set via the `NextResult()` method. Do be aware that you are always returned the first result set automatically. Thus, if you wish to read over the rows of each table, you will be able to build the following iteration construct:

```
Do
  While myDataReader.Read()
    Console.WriteLine("***** Record *****")
    For i As Integer = 0 To myDataReader.FieldCount - 1
      Console.WriteLine("{0} = {1}", myDataReader.GetName(i), _
        myDataReader.GetValue(i).ToString().Trim())
    Next
    Console.WriteLine()
  End While
Loop While myDataReader.NextResult()
```

So, at this point, you should be more aware of the functionality data reader objects bring to the table. Always remember that a data reader can only process SQL `Select` statements and cannot be used to modify an existing database table via `Insert`, `Update`, or `Delete` requests. To understand how to modify an existing database requires a further investigation of command objects.

■ **Source Code** The AutoLotDataReader project is included under the Chapter 22 subdirectory.

Building a Reusable Data Access Library

As you have just seen, the `ExecuteReader()` method extracts a data reader object that allows you to examine the results of a SQL `Select` statement using a forward-only, read-only flow of information. However, when you wish to submit SQL commands that result in the modification of a given table, you will call the `ExecuteNonQuery()` method of your command object. This single method will perform inserts, updates, and deletes based on the format of your command text.

■ **Note** Technically speaking, a *nonquery* is a SQL statement that does not return a result set. Thus, `Select` statements are queries, while `Insert`, `Update`, and `Delete` statements are not. Given this, `ExecuteNonQuery()` returns an `Integer` that represents the number of rows affected, not a new set of records. You can also use `ExecuteNonQuery()` to execute catalog commands such as `CREATE TABLE` and `DROP TABLE`, plus DCL commands such as `GRANT PERMISSION` and `REVOKE PERMISSION`.

To illustrate how to modify an existing database using nothing more than a call to `ExecuteNonQuery()`, your next goal is to build a custom data access library that will encapsulate the process of operating upon the AutoLot database. In a production-level environment, your ADO.NET logic will almost always be isolated to a .NET `*.dll` assembly for one simple reason: code reuse! The first examples of this chapter did not do so, just to keep focused on the task at hand; however, as you might imagine, it would be a waste of time to author the *same* connection logic, the *same* data reading logic, and the *same* command logic for every application that needs to interact with the AutoLot database.

By isolating data access logic to a .NET code library, multiple applications using any sort of front end (console based, desktop based, web based, etc.) can reference the library at hand in a language-independent manner. Thus, if you author your data library using VB, other .NET programmers would be able to build a UI in their language of choice (C#, C++/CLI, etc.).

In this chapter, our data library (`AutoLotDAL.dll`) will contain a single namespace (`AutoLotConnectedLayer`) that interacts with AutoLot using the connected layer. The next chapter will add a new namespace (`AutoLotDisconnectionLayer`) to this same `*.dll` that contains types to communicate with AutoLot using the disconnected layer. This library will then be used by numerous applications over the remainder of the text.

To begin, create a new VB Class Library project named AutoLotDAL (short for AutoLot Data Access Layer) and rename your initial VB code file to `AutoLotConnDAL.vb`. Next, define a namespace scope named `AutoLotConnectedLayer` and change the name of your initial class to `InventoryDAL`, as this class will define various members to interact with the Inventory table of the AutoLot database. Finally, import the `System.Data.SqlClient` namespace:

```
' We will make use of the SQL server
' provider; however, it would also be
' permissible to make use of the ADO.NET
' factory pattern for greater flexibility.
Imports System.Data.SqlClient

Namespace AutoLotConnectedLayer
  Public Class InventoryDAL
  End Class
End Namespace
```

■ **Note** Recall from Chapter 8 that when objects make use of types managing raw resources (such as a database connection), it is a good practice to implement `IDisposable` and author a proper finalizer. In a production environment, classes such as `InventoryDAL` would do the same; however, I'll avoid doing so to stay focused on the particulars of ADO.NET.

Now, recall from Chapter 15 that every VB project created with Visual Studio receives a default root namespace, which is identically named to the project you are creating. Therefore, at this point, the `InventoryDAL` class is defined within the nested `AutoLotDAL.AutoLotConnectedLayer` namespace.

To simplify how others can import the `InventoryDAL` type into their projects, open the My Project editor, select the Application tab, and delete the current value within the Root Namespace text box. Given that the Root Namespace is now empty, the fully qualified name of our class is simply `AutoLotConnectedLayer.InventoryDAL`.

Adding the Connection Logic

The first task is to define some methods that allow the caller to connect to and disconnect from the data source using a valid connection string. Because our `AutoLotDAL.dll` assembly will be hard-coded to make use of the types of `System.Data.SqlClient`, define a private member variable of `SqlConnection` that is allocated at the time the `InventoryDAL` object is created. As well, define a method named `OpenConnection()` and another named `CloseConnection()` that interact with this member variable as follows:

```
Public Class InventoryDAL
  ' This member will be used by all methods.
  Private sqlCn As New SqlConnection()

  Public Sub OpenConnection(ByVal connectionString As String)
    sqlCn.ConnectionString = connectionString
    sqlCn.Open()
  End Sub

  Public Sub CloseConnection()
    sqlCn.Close()
  End Sub
End Class
```

For the sake of brevity, our InventoryDAL type will not test for possible exceptions, nor will it throw custom exceptions under various circumstances (such as a malformed connection string). If you were to build an industrial-strength data access library, you would most certainly want to make use of structured exception handling techniques to account for any runtime anomalies.

Adding the Insertion Logic

Inserting a new record into the Inventory table is as simple as formatting the SQL Insert statement (based on user input) and calling the ExecuteNonQuery() method using your command object. To illustrate, add a public method to your InventoryDAL type named InsertAuto() that takes four parameters that map to the four columns of the Inventory table (CarID, Color, Make, and PetName). Using the arguments, format a string type to insert the new record. Finally, using your SqlConnection object, create a SqlCommand object and execute the SQL statement:

```
Public Sub InsertAuto(ByVal id As Integer, ByVal color As String, _
                      ByVal make As String, ByVal petName As String)
  ' Format and execute SQL statement.
  Dim sql As String = String.Format("Insert Into Inventory" & _
  "(CarID, Make, Color, PetName) Values" & _
  "('{0}', '{1}', '{2}', '{3}')", id, make, color, petName)

  ' Execute using our connection.
  Using cmd As New SqlCommand(sql, Me.sqlCn)
    cmd.ExecuteNonQuery()
  End Using
End Sub
```

■ **Note** As you may know, building a SQL statement using string concatenation can be risky from a security point of view (think SQL injection attacks). The preferred way to build command text is using a parameterized query, which I describe shortly.

Of course, when you are constructing a data access library, it is certainly possible to build additional public types to represent the data for a new record. Thus, if you wish, you could build a custom public class or structure named (for example) NewAutoRecord, which contains properties to represent the ID, color, make, and pet name. In this case, our InsertAuto() method would only need a single parameter of type NewAutoRecord. We have no need to do so for this example, but points such as this highlight the fact that building a production-level data access library does demand some up-front design.

Adding the Deletion Logic

Deleting an existing record is as simple as inserting a new record. Unlike the code listing for InsertAuto(), I will show one important Try/Catch scope that handles the possibility of attempting to delete a car that is currently on order for an individual in the Customers table. Add the following method to the InventoryDAL class type:

```
Public Sub DeleteCar(ByVal id As Integer)
  ' Get ID of car to delete, then do so.
  Dim sql As String = String.Format("Delete from Inventory where CarID = '{0}'", id)
  Using cmd As New SqlCommand(sql, Me.sqlCn)
    Try
      cmd.ExecuteNonQuery()
    Catch ex As SqlException
      Dim er As New Exception("Sorry!  That car is on order!", ex)
      Throw er
    End Try
  End Using
End Sub
```

Adding the Updating Logic

When it comes to the act of updating an existing record in the Inventory table, the first obvious question is what exactly do we wish to allow the caller to change? The car's color? The pet name or make? All of the above? Of course, one way to allow the caller complete flexibility is to simply define a method that takes a string type to represent any sort of SQL statement, but that is risky at best. Ideally, we would have a set of methods that allow the caller to update a record in a variety of manners. However, for our simple data access library, we will define a single method that allows the caller to update the pet name of a given automobile:

```
Public Sub UpdateCarPetName(ByVal id As Integer, ByVal newPetName As String)
  ' Get ID of car to modify and new pet name.
  Dim sql As String = String.Format _
  ("Update Inventory Set PetName = '{0}' Where CarID = '{1}'", newPetName, id)
  Using cmd As New SqlCommand(sql, Me.sqlCn)
    cmd.ExecuteNonQuery()
  End Using
End Sub
```

Adding the Selection Logic

The next method to add is a selection method. As seen earlier in this chapter, a data provider's data reader object allows for a selection of records using a read-only, forward-only server-side cursor. As you call the Read() method, you are able to process each record in a fitting manner. While this is all well and good, we need to contend with the issue of how to return these records to the calling tier of our application.

One approach would be to populate and return a multidimensional array, an array of custom objects representing a single record, or other such object, like a generic List(Of T) with the data obtained by the Read() method. While this approach would certainly work, the code could end up being a bit grungy on both sides of the equation. A cleaner approach is to return a System.Data.DataTable object, which is actually part of the disconnected layer of ADO.NET.

Full coverage of the DataTable type can be found in the next chapter; however, for the time being, simply understand that a DataTable is a class type that represents a tabular block of data (like a grid on a spreadsheet). To do so, the DataTable type maintains a collection of rows and columns. While these collections can be filled programmatically, the DataTable type provides a method named Load(), which will automatically populate these collections using a data reader object! Consider the following:

```
Public Function GetAllInventory() As DataTable
  ' This will hold the records.
  Dim inv As New DataTable()

  ' Prep command object.
  Dim sql As String = "Select * From Inventory"
  Using cmd As New SqlCommand(sql, Me.sqlCn)
    Dim dr As SqlDataReader = cmd.ExecuteReader()
    ' Fill the DataTable with data from the reader and clean up.
    inv.Load(dr)
    dr.Close()
  End Using
  Return inv
End Function
```

Working with Parameterized Command Objects

Currently, the insert, update, and delete logic for the InventoryDAL type uses hard-coded string literals for each SQL query. As you may know, a *parameterized query* can be used to treat SQL parameters as objects, rather than a simple blob of text. Treating SQL queries in a more object-oriented manner not only helps reduce the number of typos (given strongly typed properties), but parameterized queries typically execute much faster than a literal SQL string, in that they are parsed exactly once (rather than each time the SQL string is assigned to the CommandText property). Furthermore, parameterized queries also help protect against SQL injection attacks (a well-known data access security issue).

To support parameterized queries, ADO.NET command objects maintain a collection of individual parameter objects. By default, this collection is empty, but you are free to insert any number of objects that map to a "placeholder parameter" in the SQL query. When you wish to associate a parameter within a SQL query to a member in the command object's parameters collection, prefix the SQL text parameter with an at (@) symbol (at least when using Microsoft SQL Server; not all DBMSs support this notation).

Specifying Parameters Using the DbParameter Type

Before building a parameterized query, let's get to know the DbParameter type (which is the base class to a provider's specific parameter object). This class maintains a number of properties that allow you to configure the name, size, and data type of the parameter, as well as other characteristics such as the parameter's direction of travel. Table 22-7 describes some key properties of the DbParameter type.

Table 22-7. *Key Properties of the* DbParameter *Type*

Property	Meaning in Life
DbType	Gets or sets the native data type from the data source, represented as a CLR data type
Direction	Gets or sets whether the parameter is input-only, output-only, bidirectional, or a return value parameter
IsNullable	Gets or sets whether the parameter accepts null values
ParameterName	Gets or sets the name of the DbParameter

Property	Meaning in Life
Size	Gets or sets the maximum parameter size of the data (only truly useful for textual data)
Value	Gets or sets the value of the parameter

To illustrate how to populate a command object's collection of DBParameter-compatible objects, let's rework the previous InsertAuto() method to make use of parameter objects (a similar reworking could also be performed for your remaining SQL-centric methods; however, it is not necessary for this example):

```
Public Sub InsertAuto(ByVal id As Integer, ByVal color As String, _
  ByVal make As String, ByVal petName As String)
  ' Note the 'placeholders' in the SQL query.
  Dim sql As String = String.Format("Insert Into Inventory" & _
  "(CarID, Make, Color, PetName) Values (@CarID, @Make, @Color, @PetName)")

  ' This command will have internal parameters.
  Using cmd As New SqlCommand(sql, Me.sqlCn)
    ' Fill params collection.
    Dim param As New SqlParameter()
    param.ParameterName = "@CarID"
    param.Value = id
    param.SqlDbType = SqlDbType.Int
    cmd.Parameters.Add(param)

    param = New SqlParameter()
    param.ParameterName = "@Make"
    param.Value = make
    param.SqlDbType = SqlDbType.Char
    param.Size = 10
    cmd.Parameters.Add(param)

    param = New SqlParameter()
    param.ParameterName = "@Color"
    param.Value = color
    param.SqlDbType = SqlDbType.Char
    param.Size = 10
    cmd.Parameters.Add(param)

    param = New SqlParameter()
    param.ParameterName = "@PetName"
    param.Value = petName
    param.SqlDbType = SqlDbType.Char
    param.Size = 10
    cmd.Parameters.Add(param)

    cmd.ExecuteNonQuery()
  End Using
End Sub
```

First, notice that our SQL query consists of four embedded placeholder symbols, each of which is prefixed with the @ token. Using the SqlParameter type, we are able to map each placeholder using the ParameterName property and specify various details (its value, data type, size, etc.) in a strongly typed matter. Once each parameter object is hydrated, it is added to the command object's parameters collection via a call to Add().

■ **Note** Here, I made use of various properties to establish a parameter object. Do know, however, that parameter objects support a number of overloaded constructors that allow you to set the values of various properties (which will result in a more compact code base). Also be aware that Visual Studio 2008 provides numerous graphical designers that will generate a good deal of this grungy parameter-centric code on your behalf.

While building a parameterized query often requires a larger amount of code, the end result is a more convenient way to tweak SQL statements programmatically as well as better overall performance. While you are free to make use of this technique whenever a SQL query is involved, parameterized queries are most helpful when you wish to call a stored procedure.

Executing a Stored Procedure Using DbCommand

Recall that a *stored procedure* is a named block of SQL code stored in the database. Stored procedures can be constructed to return a set of rows or scalar data types and may take any number of optional parameters. The end result is a unit of work that behaves like a typical function, with the obvious difference of being located on a data store rather than a binary business object. Currently our AutoLot database defines a single stored procedure named GetPetName, which was defined as follows:

```
CREATE PROCEDURE GetPetName
@carID int,
@petName char(10) output
AS
SELECT @petName = PetName from Inventory where CarID = @carID
```

Now, consider the following final method of the InventoryDAL type, which invokes our stored procedure:

```
Public Function LookUpPetName(ByVal carID As Integer) As String
  Dim carPetName As String = String.Empty

  ' Establish name of stored proc.
  Using cmd As New SqlCommand("GetPetName", Me.sqlCn)
    cmd.CommandType = CommandType.StoredProcedure

    ' Input param.
    Dim param As New SqlParameter()
    param.ParameterName = "@carID"
    param.SqlDbType = SqlDbType.Int
    param.Value = carID
    param.Direction = ParameterDirection.Input
    cmd.Parameters.Add(param)

    ' Output param.
    param = New SqlParameter()
    param.ParameterName = "@petName"
    param.SqlDbType = SqlDbType.Char
    param.Size = 10
    param.Direction = ParameterDirection.Output
    cmd.Parameters.Add(param)

    ' Execute the stored proc.
    cmd.ExecuteNonQuery()
```

```
    ' Return output param.
    carPetName = DirectCast(cmd.Parameters("@petName").Value, String).Trim()
  End Using
  Return carPetName
End Function
```

The first important aspect of invoking a stored procedure is to recall that a command object can represent a SQL statement (the default) *or* the name of a stored procedure. When you wish to inform a command object that it will be invoking a stored procedure, you pass in the name of the procedure (as a constructor argument or via the CommandText property), and you must set the CommandType property to the value CommandType.StoredProcedure (if you fail to do so, you will receive a runtime exception, as the command object is expecting a SQL statement by default):

```
Dim cmd As New SqlCommand("GetPetName", Me.sqlCn)
cmd.CommandType = CommandType.StoredProcedure
```

Next, notice that the Direction property of a parameter object allows you to specify the direction of travel for each parameter passed to the stored procedure (e.g., input parameters and the output parameter). As before, each parameter object is added to the command object's parameters collection:

```
' Input param.
Dim param As New SqlParameter()
param.ParameterName = "@carID"
param.SqlDbType = SqlDbType.Int
param.Value = carID
param.Direction = ParameterDirection.Input
cmd.Parameters.Add(param)
```

Finally, once the stored procedure completes via a call to ExecuteNonQuery(), you are able to obtain the value of the output parameter by investigating the command object's parameters collection and casting accordingly:

```
' Return output param.
carPetName = DirectCast(cmd.Parameters("@petName").Value, String).Trim()
```

■ Note You are able to call stored procedures by calling ExecuteReader() and ExecuteSclar(), in addition to calling ExecuteNonQuery().

At this point, our first iteration of the AutoLotDAL.dll data access library is complete! To be sure, we could add many more methods to InventoryDAL to account for other database operations. As well, we could build additional public classes (such as CustomersDAL and OrdersDAL) to deal with placing orders, updating orders, and changing customer record information and myriad other details.

In Chapters 23 and 24, you will learn about various database access tools of Visual Studio 2008 that will generate a good deal of this very type of code automatically. Using these tools, you will be able to generate a large amount of VB based on the schema of the database you are attempting to communicate with, at which point you can tweak the code as you see fit.

■ Source Code The AutoLotDAL project is included under the Chapter 22 subdirectory.

Creating a Console UI–Based Front End

Using AutoLotDAL.dll, we can now build any sort of front end to display and edit our data (console based, Windows Forms based, a Windows Presentation Foundation, or an HTML-based web application). Given that we have not yet examined how to build graphical user interfaces, we will test our data library from a new Console Application named AutoLotCUIClient. Once you create your new project, be sure to add a reference to your AutoLotDAL.dll assembly as well as System.Configuration.dll and update your Imports statements as follows:

```
Imports AutoLotConnectedLayer
Imports System.Configuration
```

Next, insert a new App.config file into your project that contains a <connectionStrings> element (which again may differ from what is shown here based on your version of SQL Server) used to connect to your instance of the AutoLot database, for example:

```
<configuration>
  <connectionStrings>
    <add name ="AutoLotSqlProvider" connectionString =
    "Data Source=(local)\SQLEXPRESS;Integrated Security=SSPI;
     Initial Catalog=AutoLot"/>
  </connectionStrings>
</configuration>
```

Implementing the Main() Method

The Main() method is responsible for prompting the user for a specific course of action and executing that request via a Select statement. This program will allow the user to enter the following commands:

- I: Inserts a new record into the Inventory table
- U: Updates an existing record in the Inventory table
- D: Deletes an existing record from the Inventory table
- L: Displays the current inventory using a data reader
- S: Shows these options to the user
- C: Clears the console window and shows instructions
- P: Looks up the pet name from the car ID
- Q: Quits the program

Each possible option is handled by a unique method within the Program class. Here is the complete implementation of Main(). Notice that each method invoked from the Do/While loop (with the exception of the ShowInstructions() method) takes an InventoryDAL object as its sole parameter:

```
Sub Main()
  Console.WriteLine("***** The AutoLot Console UI *****" & vbLf)

  ' Get connection string from App.config.
  Dim cnStr As String = _
    ConfigurationManager.ConnectionStrings("AutoLotSqlProvider").ConnectionString
  Dim userDone As Boolean = False
  Dim userCommand As String = String.Empty
```

```
  ' Create our InventoryDAL object.
  Dim invDAL As New InventoryDAL()
  invDAL.OpenConnection(cnStr)

  ' Keep asking for input until user presses the Q key.
  Try
    ShowInstructions()
    Do
      Console.Write("Please enter your command: ")
      userCommand = Console.ReadLine()
      Console.WriteLine()
      Select Case userCommand.ToUpper()
        Case "I"
          InsertNewCar(invDAL)
          Exit Select
        Case "U"
          UpdateCarPetName(invDAL)
          Exit Select
        Case "D"
          DeleteCar(invDAL)
          Exit Select
        Case "L"
          ListInventory(invDAL)
          Exit Select
        Case "S"
          ShowInstructions()
          Exit Select
        Case "C"
          ClearConsole()
          Exit Select
        Case "P"
          LookUpPetName(invDAL)
          Exit Select
        Case "Q"
          userDone = True
          Exit Select
        Case Else
          Console.WriteLine("Bad data!  Try again")
        Exit Select
      End Select
    Loop While Not userDone
  Catch ex As Exception
    Console.WriteLine(ex.Message)
  Finally
    invDAL.CloseConnection()
  End Try
End Sub
```

Implementing the ShowInstructions() and ClearConsole() Methods

The ShowInstructions() method does what you would expect:

```
Private Sub ShowInstructions()
  Console.WriteLine("I: Inserts a new car.")
  Console.WriteLine("U: Updates an existing car.")
```

```
  Console.WriteLine("D: Deletes an existing car.")
  Console.WriteLine("L: Lists current inventory.")
  Console.WriteLine("S: Shows these instructions.")
  Console.WriteLine("C: Clears console and show instructions.")
  Console.WriteLine("P: Looks up pet name.")
  Console.WriteLine("Q: Quits program.")
End Sub
```

ClearConsole() is also very straightforward:

```
Private Sub ClearConsole()
  Console.Clear()
  ShowInstructions()
End Sub
```

Implementing the ListInventory() Method

The ListInventory() method obtains the DataTable returned from the GetAllInventory() method of the InventoryDAL object. After this point, we call a (yet to be created) function named DisplayTable():

```
Private Sub ListInventory(ByVal invDAL As InventoryDAL)
  Dim dt As DataTable = invDAL.GetAllInventory()
  DisplayTable(dt)
End Sub
```

The DisplayTable() helper method displays the table data using the Rows and Columns properties of the incoming DataTable (again, full details of the DataTable class appear in the next chapter, so don't fret over the details):

```
Private Sub DisplayTable(ByVal dt As DataTable)
  For curCol As Integer = 0 To dt.Columns.Count - 1
    ' Print out the column names.
    Console.Write(dt.Columns(curCol).ColumnName.Trim() & vbTab)
  Next
  Console.WriteLine(vbLf & "----------------------------------")
  For curRow As Integer = 0 To dt.Rows.Count - 1
    ' Print the DataTable.
    For curCol As Integer = 0 To dt.Columns.Count - 1
      Console.Write(dt.Rows(curRow)(curCol).ToString().Trim() & vbTab)
    Next
    Console.WriteLine()
  Next
End Sub
```

Implementing the DeleteCar() Method

Deleting an existing automobile is as simple as asking the user for the ID of the car to blow out of the data table and passing this to the DeleteCar() method of the InventoryDAL type:

```
Private Sub DeleteCar(ByVal invDAL As InventoryDAL)
  ' Get ID of car to delete.
  Console.Write("Enter ID of Car to delete: ")
  Dim id As Integer = Integer.Parse(Console.ReadLine())

  ' Just in case we have a primary key
  ' violation!
  Try
```

```
    invDAL.DeleteCar(id)
  Catch ex As Exception
    Console.WriteLine(ex.Message)
  End Try
End Sub
```

■Note Here we are making use of `Try/Catch` logic when calling `DeleteCar()`. The reason is that if we attempt to delete from the Inventory table a car that is currently referenced by other tables (Customers or Orders), the runtime will throw a primary key violation exception.

Implementing the InsertNewCar() Method

Inserting a new record into the Inventory table is simply a matter of asking the user for the new bits of data (via `Console.ReadLine()` calls) and passing this data into the `InsertAuto()` method of `InventoryDAL`:

```
Private Sub InsertNewCar(ByVal invDAL As InventoryDAL)
  ' First get the user data.
  Dim newCarID As Integer
  Dim newCarColor As String, newCarMake As String, newCarPetName As String

  Console.Write("Enter Car ID: ")
  newCarID = Integer.Parse(Console.ReadLine())
  Console.Write("Enter Car Color: ")
  newCarColor = Console.ReadLine()
  Console.Write("Enter Car Make: ")
  newCarMake = Console.ReadLine()
  Console.Write("Enter Pet Name: ")
  newCarPetName = Console.ReadLine()

  ' Now pass to data access library.
  invDAL.InsertAuto(newCarID, newCarColor, newCarMake, newCarPetName)
End Sub
```

Implementing the UpdateCarPetName() Method

The implementation of `UpdateCarPetName()` is very similar:

```
Private Sub UpdateCarPetName(ByVal invDAL As InventoryDAL)
  ' First get the user data.
  Dim carID As Integer
  Dim newCarPetName As String

  Console.Write("Enter Car ID: ")
  carID = Integer.Parse(Console.ReadLine())
  Console.Write("Enter New Pet Name: ")
  newCarPetName = Console.ReadLine()

  ' Now pass to data access library.
  invDAL.UpdateCarPetName(carID, newCarPetName)
End Sub
```

Invoking Our Stored Procedure

Obtaining the pet name of a given automobile is also very similar to the previous methods, given that the data access library has encapsulated all of the lower-level ADO.NET calls:

```
Private Sub LookUpPetName(ByVal invDAL As InventoryDAL)
  ' Get ID of car to look up.
  Console.Write("Enter ID of Car to look up: ")
  Dim id As Integer = Integer.Parse(Console.ReadLine())
  Console.WriteLine("Petname of {0} is {1}.", id, invDAL.LookUpPetName(id))
End Sub
```

With this, our console-based front end is finished. Figure 22-16 shows a test run.

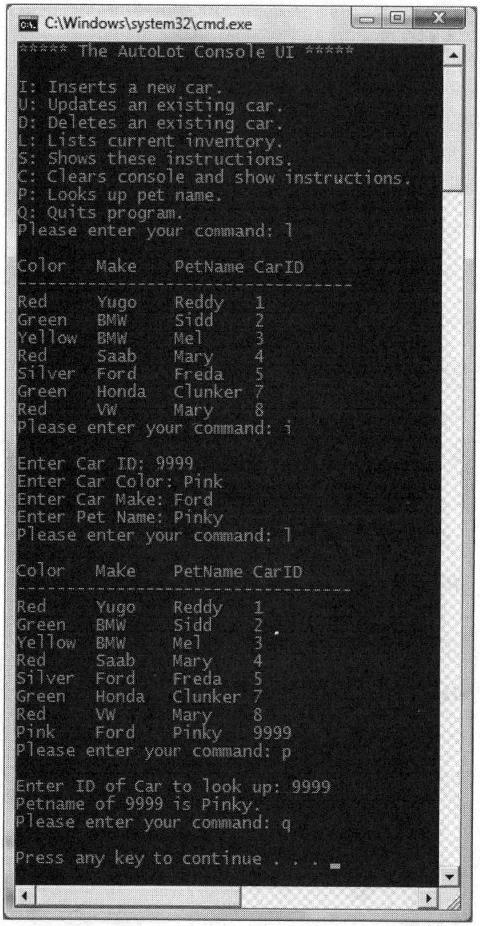

Figure 22-16. *Inserting, updating, and deleting records via command objects*

■ **Source Code** The AutoLotCUIClient application is included under the Chapter 22 subdirectory.

Asynchronous Data Access Using SqlCommand

Currently, all of our data access logic is happening on a single thread of execution. However, allow me to point out that since the release of .NET 2.0, the Microsoft SQL Server data provider has been enhanced to support asynchronous database interactions via the following new members of `SqlCommand`:

- `BeginExecuteReader()/EndExecuteReader()`
- `BeginExecuteNonQuery()/EndExecuteNonQuery()`
- `BeginExecuteXmlReader()/EndExecuteXmlReader()`

Given your work in Chapter 18, the naming convention of these method pairs may ring a bell. Recall that the .NET asynchronous delegate pattern makes use of a "begin" method to execute a task on a secondary thread, whereas the "end" method can be used to obtain the result of the asynchronous invocation using the members of `IAsyncResult` and the optional `AsyncCallback` delegate. Because the process of working with asynchronous commands is modeled after the standard delegate patterns, a simple example should suffice (so be sure to consult Chapter 18 for full details of asynchronous delegates).

Assume you wish to select the records from the Inventory table on a secondary thread of execution using a data reader object. Here is a completely new Console Application (which does not make use of our `InventoryDAL.dll` assembly) named AsyncCmdObjectApp:

Note When you wish to enable access data in an asynchronous manner, you must update your connection string with `Asynchronous Processing=True` (the default value is, in fact, `False`).

```
Imports System.Data.SqlClient
Imports System.Threading

Module Program
  Sub Main()
    Console.WriteLine("***** Fun with ASNYC Data Readers *****" & vbLf)

    ' Create and open a connection that is async-aware.
    Dim cn As New SqlConnection()
    cn.ConnectionString = "Data Source=(local)\SQLEXPRESS" & _
      ";Integrated Security=SSPI;" & _
      "Initial Catalog=AutoLot;Asynchronous Processing=true"
    cn.Open()

    ' Create a SQL command object that waits for approx. 2 seconds.
    Dim strSQL As String = "WaitFor Delay '00:00:02';Select * From Inventory"
    Dim myCommand As New SqlCommand(strSQL, cn)

    ' Execute the reader on a second thread.
    Dim itfAsynch As IAsyncResult
    itfAsynch = myCommand.BeginExecuteReader(CommandBehavior.CloseConnection)

    ' Do something while other thread works.
    While Not itfAsynch.IsCompleted
      Console.WriteLine("Working on main thread...")
      Thread.Sleep(1000)
```

```
    End While
    Console.WriteLine()

    ' All done! Get reader and loop over results.
    Dim myDataReader As SqlDataReader = myCommand.EndExecuteReader(itfAsynch)
    While myDataReader.Read()
      Console.WriteLine("-> Make: {0}, PetName: {1}, Color: {2}.", _
                        myDataReader("Make").ToString().Trim(), _
                        myDataReader("PetName").ToString().Trim(), _
                        myDataReader("Color").ToString().Trim())
    End While
    myDataReader.Close()
  End Sub
End Module
```

The first point of interest is the fact that you need to enable asynchronous activity using the new `Asynchronous Processing` segment of the connection string. Also note that you have padded into the command text of your `SqlCommand` object a `WaitFor Delay` segment simply to simulate a long-running database interaction.

Beyond these points, notice that the call to `BeginExecuteReader()` returns the expected `IAsyncResult`-compatible type, which is used to synchronize the calling thread (via the `IsCompleted` property) as well as obtain the `SqlDataReader` once the query has finished executing.

■ **Source Code** The AsyncCmdObjectApp application is included under the Chapter 22 subdirectory.

An Introduction to Database Transactions

To wrap up our examination of the connected layer of ADO.NET, we will take a look at the concept of a database transaction. Simply put, a *transaction* is a set of database operations that must either *all* work or *all* fail as a whole. As you might imagine, transactions are quite important to ensure that table data is safe, valid, and consistent.

Transactions are very important when a database operation involves interacting with multiple tables or multiple stored procedures (or a combination of database atoms). The classic transaction example involves the process of transferring monetary funds between two bank accounts. For example, if you were to transfer $500.00 from your savings account into your checking account, the following steps should occur in a transactional manner:

- The bank should remove $500.00 from your savings account.
- The bank should then add $500.00 to your checking account.

It would be a very bad thing indeed if the money was removed from the savings account, yet was not transferred to the checking account (due to some error on the bank's part), as you are now out $500.00! However, if these steps were wrapped up into a database transaction, the DBMS would ensure that all related steps occur as a single unit. If any part of the transaction fails, the entire operation is "rolled back" to the original state. On the other hand, if all steps succeed, the transaction is "committed."

■ **Note** You may have heard of the acronym ACID when examining transactional literature. This represents the four key properties of a prim-and-proper transaction, specifically **A**tomic (all or nothing), **C**onsistent (data remains stable throughout the transaction), **I**solated (transactions do not step on each other's feet), and **D**urable (transactions are saved and logged).

As it turns out, the .NET platform supports transactions in a variety of ways. Most important for this chapter is the transaction object of your ADO.NET data provider (`SqlTransaction` in the case of `System.Data.SqlClient`). In addition, the .NET base class libraries provide transactional supports within numerous APIs, including the following:

- `System.EnterpriseServices`: This namespace provides types that allow you to integrate with the COM+ runtime layer, including its support for distributed transactions.
- `System.Transactions`: This namespace contains classes that allow you to write your own transactional applications and resource managers for a variety of services (MSMQ, ADO.NET, COM+, etc.).
- *Windows Communication Foundation (WCF)*: The WCF API provides services to facilitate transactions.
- *Windows Workflow Foundation (WF)*: The WF API provides transactional support for workflow activities.

In addition to the baked-in transactional support found within the .NET base class libraries, it is also possible to make use of the SQL language itself of your DBMS. For example, you could author a stored procedure that makes use of the `BEGIN TRANSACTION`, `ROLLBACK`, and `COMMIT` statements.

Key Members of an ADO.NET Transaction Object

While transactional functionality exists throughout the base class libraries, we will focus on transaction objects found within an ADO.NET data provider, all of which derive from `DBTransaction` and implement the `IDbTransaction` interface. Recall from the beginning of this chapter that `IDbTransaction` defines a handful of members:

```
Public Interface IDbTransaction
  Inherits IDisposable
  ReadOnly Property Connection() As IDbConnection
  ReadOnly Property IsolationLevel() As IsolationLevel
  Sub Commit()
  Sub Rollback()
End Interface
```

Notice first of all the `Connection` property, which will return to you a reference to the connection object that initiated the current transaction (as you'll see, you obtain a transaction object from a given connection object). The `Commit()` method is called when each of your database operations has succeeded, so that each of the pending changes will be persisted in the data store. Conversely, the `Rollback()` method can be called in the event of a runtime exception, which will inform the DMBS to disregard any pending changes, leaving the original data intact.

■ **Note** The IsolationLevel property of a transaction object allows you to specify how aggressively a transaction should be guarded against the activities of other parallel transactions. By default, transactions are isolated completely until committed. Consult the .NET Framework 3.5 SDK documentation for full details regarding the values of the IsolationLevel enumeration.

Beyond the members defined by the IDbTransaction interface, the SqlTransaction type defines an additional member named Save(), which allows you to define *save points*. This concept allows you to roll back a failed transaction up until a named point, rather than rolling back the entire transaction. Essentially, when you call Save() using a SqlTransaction object, you are able to specify a friendly string moniker. When calling Rollback(), you are able to specify this same moniker as an argument to effectively do a "partial rollback." When calling Rollback() with no arguments, all of the pending changes will indeed be rolled back.

Adding a Transaction Method to InventoryDAL

To illustrate the use of the ADO.NET transactions, begin by using Visual Studio 2008's Server Explorer to add a new table named CreditRisks to the AutoLot database, which has the same exact columns (CustID [which is the primary key], FirstName, and LastName) as the Customers table created earlier in this chapter. As suggested by the name, CreditRisks is where the undesirable customers are banished if they fail a credit check.

■ **Note** We will be using this new transactional functionality in Chapter 26 when we examine the Windows Workflow Foundation API, so be sure to add the CreditRisks table to the AutoLot database as just described.

Much like the savings-to-checking-account money transfer example described previously, the act of moving a risky customer from the Customers table into the CreditRisks table should occur under the watchful eye of a transactional scope (after all, we will want to remember the ID and names of those who are not credit worthy). Specifically, we need to ensure that *either* we successfully delete the current credit risks from the Customers table and add them to the CreditRisks table *or* neither of these database operations occurs.

To illustrate how to programmatically work with ADO.NET transactions, open the AutoLotDAL Code Library project you created earlier in this chapter. Add a new public method named ProcessCreditRisk() to the InventoryDAL class that will deal with a perceived a credit risk as follows:

```
' A new member of the InventoryDAL class.
Public Sub ProcessCreditRisk(ByVal throwEx As Boolean, ByVal custID As Integer)
  ' First, look up current name based on customer ID.
  Dim fName As String = String.Empty
  Dim lName As String = String.Empty

  Dim cmdSelect As New SqlCommand(String.Format _
    ("Select * from Customers where CustID = {0}", custID), sqlCn)
  Using dr As SqlDataReader = cmdSelect.ExecuteReader()
    While dr.Read()
      fName = DirectCast(dr("FirstName"), String)
      lName = DirectCast(dr("LastName"), String)
    End While
  End Using
```

```
  ' Create command objects that represent each step of the operation.
  Dim cmdRemove As New SqlCommand(String.Format _
    ("Delete from Customers where CustID = {0}", custID), sqlCn)

  Dim cmdInsert As New SqlCommand(String.Format("Insert Into CreditRisks" & _
    "(CustID, FirstName, LastName) Values" & _
    "({0}, '{1}', '{2}')", custID, fName, lName), sqlCn)

  ' We will get this from the Connection object.
  Dim tx As SqlTransaction = Nothing
  Try
    tx = sqlCn.BeginTransaction()

    ' Enlist the commands into this transaction.
    cmdInsert.Transaction = tx
    cmdRemove.Transaction = tx

    ' Execute the commands.
    cmdInsert.ExecuteNonQuery()
    cmdRemove.ExecuteNonQuery()

    ' Simulate error.
    If throwEx Then
      Throw New ApplicationException("Sorry!  Database error! Tx failed...")
    End If

    ' Commit it!
    tx.Commit()
  Catch ex As Exception
    Console.WriteLine(ex.Message)
    ' Any error will roll back the transaction.
    tx.Rollback()
  End Try
End Sub
```

Here, we are using an incoming Boolean parameter to represent whether we will throw an arbitrary exception when attempting to process the offending customer. This will allow us to easily simulate an unforeseen circumstance that will cause the database transaction to fail. Obviously, this is done here only for illustrative purposes; a true database transaction method would certainly not want to allow the caller to force the logic to fail at its whim!

Once we obtain the customer's first and last name based on the incoming custID parameter, note that we are using two SqlCommand objects that represent each step in the transaction we will be kicking off, and we obtain a valid SqlTransaction object from the connection object via BeginTransaction(). Next, and most important, we must *enlist each command object* by assigning the Transaction property to the transaction object we have just obtained. If we fail to do so, the insert/delete logic will not be under a transactional context.

After we call ExecuteNonQuery() on each command, we will throw an exception if (and only if) the value of the Boolean parameter is True. In this case, all pending database operations are rolled back. If we do not throw an exception, both steps will be committed to the database tables once we call Commit(). Compile your modified AutoLotDAL Code Library project to ensure you do not have any typos.

Testing Our Database Transaction

While you could update the previous AutoLotCUIClient application with a new option to invoke the `ProcessCreditRisk()` method, let's create a new Console Application named AdoNetTransaction to do so. Set a reference to your `AutoLotDAL.dll` assembly, and import the `AutoLotConnectedLayer` namespace.

Next, open your Customers table for data entry by right-clicking the table icon from Server Explorer and selecting Show Table Data. Add a new customer who will be the victim of a low credit score, for example:

- *CustID*: 333
- *FirstName*: Homer
- *LastName*: Simpson

Now, update your `Main()` method as follows:

```
Sub Main()
  Console.WriteLine("***** Simple Transaction Example *****" & vbLf)

  ' A simple way to allow the tx to work or not.
  Dim throwEx As Boolean = True
  Dim userAnswer As String = String.Empty

  Console.Write("Do you want to throw an exception (Y or N): ")
  userAnswer = Console.ReadLine()
  If userAnswer.ToLower() = "n" Then
    throwEx = False
  End If

  Dim dal As New InventoryDAL()
  dal.OpenConnection("Data Source=(local)\SQLEXPRESS;Integrated Security=SSPI;" & _
                     "Initial Catalog=AutoLot")

  ' Process customer 333.
  dal.ProcessCreditRisk(throwEx, 333)
  Console.ReadLine()
End Sub
```

If you were to run your program and elect to throw an exception, you would find that Homer is *not* removed from the Customers table, as the entire transaction has been rolled back. However, if you did not throw an exception, you would find that Customer ID 333 is no longer in the Customers table and has been placed in the CreditRisks table (see Figure 22-17).

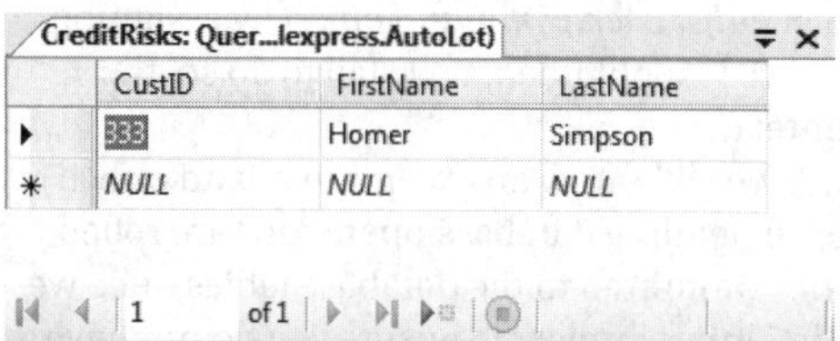

Figure 22-17. *The result of our database transaction*

Source Code The AdoNetTransaction project is included under the Chapter 22 subdirectory.

Summary

ADO.NET is the native data access technology of the .NET platform, which can be used in two distinct manners: connected or disconnected. In this chapter, you examined the connected layer and came to understand the role of data providers, which are essentially concrete implementations of several abstract base classes (in the `System.Data.Common` namespace) and interface types (in the `System.Data` namespace). As you have seen, it is possible to build a provider-neutral code base using the ADO.NET data provider factory model.

Using connection objects, transaction objects, command objects, and data reader objects of the connected layer, you are able to select, update, insert, and delete records. Also recall that command objects support an internal parameters collection, which can be used to add some type safety to your SQL queries and are quite helpful when triggering stored procedures.

CHAPTER 23

ADO.NET Part II: The Disconnected Layer

This chapter picks up where the previous one left off and digs deeper into the .NET database APIs. Here, you will be introduced to the *disconnected layer* of ADO.NET. When you use this facet of ADO.NET, you are able to model database data in memory within the calling tier using numerous members of the System.Data namespace (most notably, DataSet, DataTable, DataRow, DataColumn, DataView, and DataRelation). By doing so, you are able to provide the illusion that the calling tier is continuously connected to an external data source, while in reality it is simply operating on a local copy of relational data.

While it is completely possible to use this "disconnected" aspect of ADO.NET without ever making a literal connection to a relational database, you will most often obtain populated DataSet objects using the data adapter object of your data provider. As you will see, data adapter objects function as a bridge between the client tier and a relational database. Using these objects, you are able to obtain DataSet objects, manipulate their contents, and send modified rows back for processing. The end result is a highly scalable data-centric .NET application.

To showcase the usefulness of the disconnected layer, you will be updating the AutoLotDAL.dll data library created in Chapter 22 with a new namespace that makes use of disconnected types. As well, you will come to understand the role of data binding and various UI elements within the Windows Forms API that allow you to display and update client-side local data. We wrap things up by examining the role of strongly typed DataSet objects and see how they can be used to expose data using a more object-oriented model.

Understanding the Disconnected Layer of ADO.NET

As you saw in the previous chapter, working with the connected layer allows you to interact with a database using the primary connection, command, and data reader objects. With this handful of types, you are able to select, insert, update, and delete records to your heart's content (as well as invoke stored procedures). However, you have seen only half of the ADO.NET story. Recall that the ADO.NET object model can be used in a disconnected manner.

Using the disconnected types, it is possible to model relational data via an in-memory object model. Far beyond simply modeling a tabular block of rows and columns, the types within System.Data allow you to represent table relationships, column constraints, primary keys, views, and other database primitives. Furthermore, once you have modeled the data, you are able to apply filters, submit in-memory queries, and persist (or load) your data in XML and binary formats. You can do all of this without ever making a literal connection to a DBMS (hence the term *disconnected layer*).

While you could indeed use the disconnected types without ever connecting to a database, you will most often still make use of connection and command objects. In addition, you will leverage a specific object, the *data adapter* (which extends the abstract DbDataAdapter), to fetch and update data. Unlike the connected layer, data obtained via a data adapter is not processed using data reader objects. Rather, data adapter objects make use of DataSet objects to move data between the caller and data source. The DataSet type is a container for any number of DataTable objects, each of which contains a collection of DataRow and DataColumn objects.

The data adapter object of your data provider handles the database connection automatically. In an attempt to increase scalability, data adapters keep the connection open for the shortest amount of time possible. Once the caller receives the DataSet object, the calling tier is completely disconnected from the database and left with a local copy of the remote data. The caller is free to insert, delete, or update rows from a given DataTable, but the physical database is not updated until the caller explicitly passes the DataSet to the data adapter for updating. In a nutshell, DataSets allow the clients to pretend they are indeed always connected, when in fact they are operating on an in-memory database (see Figure 23-1).

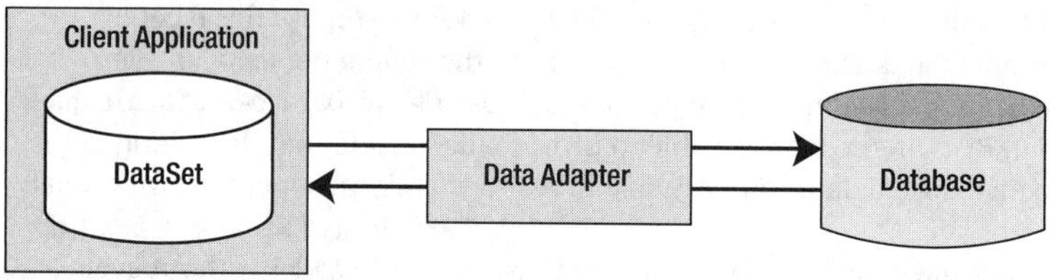

Figure 23-1. *Data adapter objects move* DataSet*s to and from the client tier.*

Given that the centerpiece of the disconnected layer is the DataSet type, the first task of this chapter is to learn how to manipulate a DataSet manually. Once you understand how to do so, you will have no problem manipulating the contents of a DataSet retrieved via a data adapter object.

Understanding the Role of the DataSet

As stated earlier, a DataSet is an in-memory representation of relational data. More specifically, a DataSet is a class type that maintains three internal strongly typed collections (see Figure 23-2).

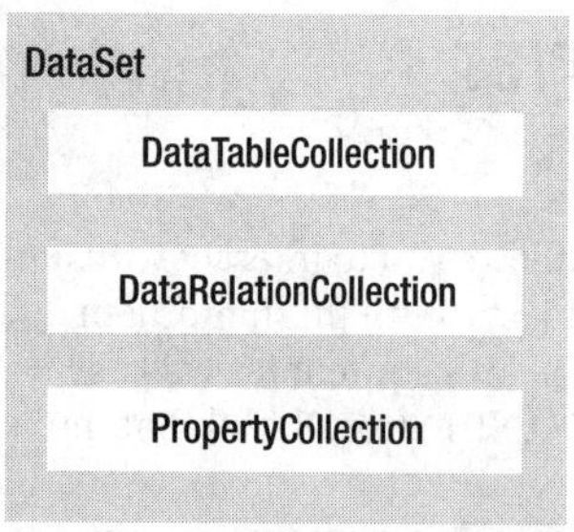

Figure 23-2. *The anatomy of a* DataSet

The Tables property of the DataSet allows you to access the DataTableCollection that contains the individual DataTables. Another important collection used by the DataSet is the

DataRelationCollection, which is accessible via the Relations property. Given that a DataSet is a disconnected version of a database schema, it can be used to programmatically represent the parent/child relationships between its tables. For example, a relation can be created between two tables to model a foreign key constraint using the DataRelation type. This object can then be added to the DataRelationCollection through the Relations property. At this point, you can navigate between the connected tables as you search for data. You will see how this is done a bit later in the chapter.

The ExtendedProperties property of the DataSet provides access to the PropertyCollection object, which allows you to associate any extra information to the DataSet as name/value pairs. This information can literally be anything at all, even if it has no bearing on the data itself. For example, you can associate your company's name to a DataSet, which can then function as in-memory metadata. Other examples of extended properties might include timestamps, an encrypted password that must be supplied to access the contents of the DataSet, a number representing a data refresh rate, and so forth.

■ **Note** The DataTable class also supports extended properties via the ExtendedProperties property.

Key Properties of the DataSet

Before exploring too many other programmatic details, let's take a look at some core members of the DataSet. Beyond the Tables, Relations, and ExtendedProperties properties, Table 23-1 describes some additional properties of interest.

Table 23-1. *Selected Properties of the Mighty* DataSet

Property	Meaning in Life
CaseSensitive	Indicates whether string comparisons in DataTable objects are case sensitive (or not).
DataSetName	Represents the friendly name of this DataSet. Typically this value is established as a constructor parameter.
EnforceConstraints	Gets or sets a value indicating whether constraint rules are followed when attempting any update operation.
HasErrors	Gets a value indicating whether there are errors in any of the rows in any of the DataTables of the DataSet.
RemotingFormat	Allows you to define how the DataSet should serialize its content (binary or XML).

Key Methods of the DataSet

The methods of the DataSet work in conjunction with some of the functionality provided by the aforementioned properties. In addition to interacting with XML streams, the DataSet provides methods that allow you to copy the contents of your DataSet, navigate between the internal tables, and establish the beginning and ending points of a batch of updates. Table 23-2 describes some core methods.

Table 23-2. *Selected Methods of the Mighty* DataSet

Methods	Meaning in Life
AcceptChanges()	Commits all the changes made to this DataSet since it was loaded or the last time AcceptChanges() was called.
Clear()	Completely clears the DataSet data by removing every row in each DataTable.
Clone()	Clones the structure of the DataSet, including all DataTables, as well as all relations and any constraints.
Copy()	Copies both the structure and data for this DataSet.
GetChanges()	Returns a copy of the DataSet containing all changes made to it since it was last loaded or since AcceptChanges() was called.
HasChanges()	Gets a value indicating whether the DataSet has changes, including new, deleted, or modified rows.
Merge()	Merges this DataSet with a specified DataSet.
ReadXml() ReadXmlSchema()	Allow you to read XML data from a valid stream (file based, memory based, or network based) into the DataSet.
RejectChanges()	Rolls back all the changes made to this DataSet since it was created or the last time AcceptChanges() was called.
WriteXml() WriteXmlSchema()	Allow you to write out the contents of a DataSet into a valid stream.

Building a DataSet

Now that you have a better understanding of the role of the DataSet (and some idea of what you can do with one), create a new Console Application named SimpleDataSet.

■ **Note** The SimpleDataSet project will give you a chance to create and populate a DataSet object completely by hand, in order to solidify the underlying object model. However, recall that in a vast majority of cases, DataSet objects will be constructed for you via the "data adapter" of your ADO.NET provider or using various data access tools of Visual Studio 2008. You will see each of these approaches later in this chapter.

Within the Main() method, define a new DataSet object that contains three extended properties representing your company name, a unique identifier (represented as a System.Guid type), and a timestamp:

```
Sub Main()
  Console.WriteLine("***** Fun with DataSets *****" & vbLf)

  ' Create the DataSet object and add a few properties.
  Dim carsInventoryDS As New DataSet("Car Inventory")

  carsInventoryDS.ExtendedProperties("TimeStamp") = DateTime.Now
  carsInventoryDS.ExtendedProperties("DataSetID") = Guid.NewGuid()
  carsInventoryDS.ExtendedProperties("Company") = "Intertech Training"
  Console.ReadLine()
End Sub
```

If you are unfamiliar with the concept of a globally unique identifier (GUID), simply understand that it is a statistically unique 128-bit number. While GUIDs are used throughout the COM framework to identify numerous COM-atoms (classes, interfaces, applications, etc.), the System.Guid type is still very helpful under .NET when you need to quickly generate a unique identifier.

In any case, a DataSet object is not terribly interesting until you insert any number of DataTables. Therefore, the next task is to examine the internal composition of the DataTable, beginning with the DataColumn type.

Working with DataColumns

The DataColumn type represents a single column within a DataTable. Collectively speaking, the set of all DataColumn types bound to a given DataTable represents the foundation of a table's *schema* information. For example, if you were to model the Inventory table of the AutoLot database (see Chapter 22), you would create four DataColumns, one for each column (CarID, Make, Color, and PetName). Once you have created your DataColumn objects, they are typically added into the columns collection of the DataTable type (via the Columns property).

Based on your background, you may know that a given column in a database table can be assigned a set of constraints (e.g., configured as a primary key, assigned a default value, configured to contain read-only information, etc.). Also, every column in a table must map to an underlying data type. For example, the Inventory table's schema requires that the CarID column map to an integer, while Make, Color, and PetName map to an array of characters. The DataColumn class has numerous properties that allow you to configure these very things. Table 23-3 provides a rundown of some core properties.

Table 23-3. *Select Properties of the* DataColumn

Properties	Meaning in Life
AllowDBNull	This property is used to indicate if a row can specify Nothing values in this column. The default value is True.
AutoIncrement AutoIncrementSeed AutoIncrementStep	These properties are used to configure the autoincrement behavior for a given column. This can be helpful when you wish to ensure unique values in a given DataColumn (such as a primary key). By default, a DataColumn does not support autoincrement behavior.
Caption	This property gets or sets the caption to be displayed for this column. This allows you to define a user-friendly version of a literal database column name.
ColumnMapping	This property determines how a DataColumn is represented when a DataSet is saved as an XML document using the DataSet.WriteXml() method.
ColumnName	This property gets or sets the name of the column in the Columns collection (meaning how it is represented internally by the DataTable). If you do not set the ColumnName explicitly, the default values are Column with (*n*+1) numerical suffixes (i.e., Column1, Column2, Column3, etc.).
DataType	This property defines the data type (Boolean, String, Double, etc.) stored in the column.
DefaultValue	This property gets or sets the default value assigned to this column when inserting new rows. This default value is used if not otherwise specified.
Expression	This property gets or sets the expression used to filter rows, calculate a column's value, or create an aggregate column.
Ordinal	This property gets the numerical position of the column in the columns collection maintained by the DataTable.

Continued

Table 23-3. *Continued*

Properties	Meaning in Life
ReadOnly	This property determines if this column can be modified once a row has been added to the table. The default is False.
Table	This property gets the DataTable that contains this DataColumn.
Unique	This property gets or sets a value indicating whether the values in each row of the column must be unique or if repeating values are permissible. If a column is assigned a primary key constraint, the Unique property should be set to True.

Building a DataColumn

To continue with the SimpleDataSet project (and illustrate the use of the DataColumn), assume you wish to model the columns of the Inventory table. Given that the CarID column will be the table's primary key, you will configure the DataColumn object as read-only, unique, and non-null (using the ReadOnly, Unique, and AllowDBNull properties). Update the Main() method to build four DataColumn objects:

```
Sub Main()
...
  ' Create data columns that map to the
  ' 'real' columns in the Inventory table
  ' of the AutoLot database.
  Dim carIDColumn As New DataColumn("CarID", GetType(Integer))
  carIDColumn.Caption = "Car ID"
  carIDColumn.ReadOnly = True
  carIDColumn.AllowDBNull = False
  carIDColumn.Unique = True

  Dim carMakeColumn As New DataColumn("Make", GetType(String))
  Dim carColorColumn As New DataColumn("Color", GetType(String))
  Dim carPetNameColumn As New DataColumn("PetName", GetType(String))
  carPetNameColumn.Caption = "Pet Name"
  Console.ReadLine()
End Sub
```

Notice that when configuring the carIDColumn object, you have assigned a value to the Caption property. This property is very helpful in that it allows you to define a string value for display purposes, which can be distinct from the literal column name (column names in a literal database table are typically better suited for programming purposes [e.g., au_fname] than display purposes [e.g., Author First Name]).

Enabling Autoincrementing Fields

One aspect of the DataColumn you may choose to configure is its ability to *autoincrement*. Simply put, an autoincrementing column is used to ensure that when a new row is added to a given table, the value of this column is assigned automatically, based on the current step of the increase. This can be helpful when you wish to ensure that a column has no repeating values (such as a primary key).

This behavior is controlled using the AutoIncrement, AutoIncrementSeed, and AutoIncrementStep properties. The seed value is used to mark the starting value of the column, whereas the step value identifies the number to add to the seed when incrementing. Consider the following update to the construction of the carIDColumn DataColumn:

```
Sub Main()
...
  Dim carIDColumn As New DataColumn("CarID", GetType(Integer))
  carIDColumn.Caption = "Car ID"
  carIDColumn.ReadOnly = True
  carIDColumn.AllowDBNull = False
  carIDColumn.Unique = True
  carIDColumn.AutoIncrement = True
  carIDColumn.AutoIncrementSeed = 0
  carIDColumn.AutoIncrementStep = 1
...
End Sub
```

Here, the carIDColumn object has been configured to ensure that as rows are added to the respective table, the value for this column is incremented by 1. Because the seed has been set at 0, this column would be numbered 0, 1, 2, 3, and so forth.

Adding DataColumn Objects to a DataTable

The DataColumn type does not typically exist as a stand-alone entity, but is instead inserted into a related DataTable. To illustrate, create a new DataTable object (fully detailed in just a moment) and insert each DataColumn object in the columns collection using the Columns property:

```
Sub Main()
...
  ' Now add DataColumns to a DataTable.
  Dim inventoryTable As New DataTable("Inventory")
  inventoryTable.Columns.AddRange(New DataColumn() {carIDColumn, carMakeColumn, _
    carColorColumn, carPetNameColumn})
  Console.ReadLine()
End Sub
```

At this point, the DataTable object contains four DataColumn objects that represent the schema of the in-memory Inventory table. However, the table is currently devoid of data, and the table is currently outside of the table collection maintained by the DataSet. We will deal with both of these shortcomings, beginning with populating the table with data via DataRow objects.

Working with DataRows

As you have seen, a collection of DataColumn objects represents the schema of a DataTable. In contrast, a collection of DataRow types represents the actual data in the table. Thus, if you have 20 rows in the Inventory table of the AutoLot database, you can represent these records using 20 DataRow objects. Using the members of the DataRow class, you are able to insert, remove, evaluate, and manipulate the values in the table. Table 23-4 documents some (but not all) of the members of the DataRow type.

Table 23-4. *Select members of the* `DataRow` *Type*

Members	Meaning in Life
HasErrors GetColumnsInError() GetColumnError() ClearErrors() RowError	The HasErrors property returns a Boolean value indicating if there are errors. If so, the GetColumnsInError() method can be used to obtain the offending members, and GetColumnError() can be used to obtain the error description, while the ClearErrors() method removes each error listing for the row. The RowError property allows you to configure a textual description of the error for a given row.
ItemArray	This property gets or sets all of the values for this row using an array of objects.
RowState	This property is used to pinpoint the current "state" of the DataRow using values of the RowState enumeration.
Table	This property is used to obtain a reference to the DataTable containing this DataRow.
AcceptChanges() RejectChanges()	These methods commit or reject all changes made to this row since the last time AcceptChanges() was called.
BeginEdit() EndEdit() CancelEdit()	These methods begin, end, or cancel an edit operation on a DataRow object.
Delete()	This method marks this row to be removed when the AcceptChanges() method is called.
IsNull()	This method gets a value indicating whether the specified column contains a null (e.g., Nothing) value.

Working with a DataRow is a bit different from working with a DataColumn, because you cannot create a direct instance of this type, as there is no public constructor:

```
' Error!  No public constructor!
Dim r As New DataRow()
```

Rather, you obtain a DataRow reference from a given DataTable. For example, assume you wish to insert two rows in the Inventory table. The DataTable.NewRow() method allows you to obtain the next slot in the table, at which point you can fill each column with new data via the type indexer. When doing so, you can specify either the string name assigned to the DataColumn or its ordinal position:

```
Sub Main()
...
  ' Now add some rows to the Inventory Table.
  Dim carRow As DataRow = inventoryTable.NewRow()
  carRow("Make") = "BMW"
  carRow("Color") = "Black"
  carRow("PetName") = "Hamlet"
  inventoryTable.Rows.Add(carRow)

  carRow = inventoryTable.NewRow()
  ' Column 0 is the autoincremented ID field,
  ' so start at 1.
  carRow(1) = "Saab"
  carRow(2) = "Red"
  carRow(3) = "Sea Breeze"
  inventoryTable.Rows.Add(carRow)
  Console.ReadLine()
End Sub
```

■Note If you pass the `DataRow`'s indexer method an invalid column name or ordinal position, you will receive a runtime exception.

At this point, you have a single `DataTable` containing two rows. Of course, you can repeat this general process to create a number of `DataTables` to define the schema and data content. Before you insert the `inventoryTable` object into your `DataSet` object, let's check out the all-important `RowState` property.

Understanding the RowState Property

The `RowState` property is useful when you need to programmatically identify the set of all rows in a table that have changed from their original value, have been newly inserted, and so forth. This property may be assigned any value from the `DataRowState` enumeration, as shown in Table 23-5.

Table 23-5. *Values of the* `DataRowState` *Enumeration*

Value	Meaning in Life
`Added`	The row has been added to a `DataRowCollection`, and `AcceptChanges()` has not been called.
`Deleted`	The row has been marked for deletion via the `Delete()` method of the `DataRow`, and `AcceptChanges()` has not been called.
`Detached`	The row has been created but is not part of any `DataRowCollection`. A `DataRow` is in this state immediately after it has been created and before it is added to a collection, or if it has been removed from a collection.
`Modified`	The row has been modified, and `AcceptChanges()` has not been called.
`Unchanged`	The row has not changed since `AcceptChanges()` was last called, or since the row was first added to the table.

While you are programmatically manipulating the rows of a given `DataTable`, the `RowState` property is set automatically. By way of example, add a new method to your initial module, which operates on a local `DataRow` object, printing out its row state along the way:

```
Private Sub ManipulateDataRowState()
  Console.WriteLine("***** Fun with RowState *****" & vbLf)
  ' Create a temp DataTable for testing.
  Dim temp As New DataTable("Temp")
  temp.Columns.Add(New DataColumn("TempColumn", GetType(Integer)))

  ' RowState = Detatched.
  Dim row As DataRow = temp.NewRow()
  Console.WriteLine("After calling NewRow(): {0}", row.RowState)

  ' RowState = Added.
  temp.Rows.Add(row)
  Console.WriteLine("After calling Rows.Add(): {0}", row.RowState)

  ' RowState = Added.
  row("TempColumn") = 10
  Console.WriteLine("After first assignment: {0}", row.RowState)
```

```
    ' RowState = Unchanged.
    temp.AcceptChanges()
    Console.WriteLine("After calling AcceptChanges: {0}", row.RowState)

    ' RowState = Modified.
    row("TempColumn") = 11
    Console.WriteLine("After second assignment: {0}", row.RowState)

    ' RowState = Deleted.
    temp.Rows(0).Delete()
    Console.WriteLine("After calling Delete: {0}", row.RowState)
End Sub
```

As you can see, the ADO.NET DataRow is smart enough to remember its current state of affairs. Given this, the owning DataTable is able to identify which rows have been modified. This is a key feature of the DataSet, as when it comes time to send updated information to the data store, only the modified data is submitted.

Understanding the DataRowVersion Property

Beyond maintaining the current state of a row via the RowState property, a DataRow object maintains three possible versions of the data it contains via the DataRowVersion property. When a DataRow object is first constructed, it contains only a single copy of data, represented as the "current version." However, as you programmatically manipulate a DataRow object (via various method calls), additional versions of the data spring to life. Specifically, the DataRowVersion property can be set to any value of the related DataRowVersion enumeration (see Table 23-6).

Table 23-6. *Values of the* DataRowVersion *Enumeration*

Value	Meaning in Life
Current	Represents the current value of a row, even after changes have been made.
Default	The default version of DataRowState. For a DataRowState value of Added, Modified, or Deleted, the default version is Current. For a DataRowState value of Detached, the version is Proposed.
Original	Represents the value first inserted into a DataRow, or the value the last time AcceptChanges() was called.
Proposed	The value of a row currently being edited due to a call to BeginEdit().

As suggested in Table 23-6, the value of the DataRowVersion property is dependent on the value of the DataRowState property in a good number of cases. As mentioned, the DataRowVersion property will be changed behind the scenes when you invoke various methods on the DataRow (or, in some cases, the DataTable) object. Here is a breakdown of the methods that can affect the value of a row's DataRowVersion property:

- If you call the DataRow.BeginEdit() method and change the row's value, the Current and Proposed values become available.
- If you call the DataRow.CancelEdit() method, the Proposed value is deleted.
- After you call DataRow.EndEdit(), the Proposed value becomes the Current value.

- After you call the DataRow.AcceptChanges() method, the Original value becomes identical to the Current value. The same transformation occurs when you call DataTable.AcceptChanges().
- After you call DataRow.RejectChanges(), the Proposed value is discarded, and the version becomes Current.

Yes, this is a bit convoluted—especially due to the fact that a DataRow may or may not have all versions at any given time (you'll receive runtime exceptions if you attempt to obtain a row version that is not currently tracked). Regardless of the complexity, given that the DataRow maintains three copies of data, it becomes very simple to build a front end that allows an end user to alter values, change his or her mind and "roll back" values, or commit values permanently. You'll see various examples of manipulating these methods over the remainder of this chapter.

Working with DataTables

The DataTable type defines a good number of members, many of which are identical in name and functionality to those of the DataSet. Table 23-7 describes some core members of the DataTable type beyond Rows and Columns.

Table 23-7. *Select Members of the* DataTable *Type*

Member	Meaning in Life
CaseSensitive	Indicates whether string comparisons within the table are case sensitive (or not). The default value is False.
ChildRelations	Returns the collection of child relations for this DataTable (if any).
Constraints	Gets the collection of constraints maintained by the table.
Copy()	A method that copies the schema and data of a given DataTable into a new instance.
DataSet	Gets the DataSet that contains this table (if any).
DefaultView	Gets a customized view of the table that may include a filtered view or a cursor position.
MinimumCapacity	Gets or sets the initial number of rows in this table (the default is 50).
ParentRelations	Gets the collection of parent relations for this DataTable.
PrimaryKey	Gets or sets an array of columns that function as primary keys for the data table.
RemotingFormat	Allows you to define how the DataTable should serialize its content (binary or XML) content (binary or XML).
TableName	Gets or sets the name of the table. This same property may also be specified as a constructor parameter.

To continue with our current example, let's set the PrimaryKey property of the DataTable to the carIDColumn DataColumn object. Be aware that the PrimaryKey property is assigned a collection of DataColumn objects, to account for a multicolumned key. In our case, however, we need to specify only the CarID column (being the first ordinal position in the table):

```
Sub Main()
...
  ' Mark the primary key of this table.
  inventoryTable.PrimaryKey = New DataColumn() {inventoryTable.Columns(0)}
...
End Sub
```

Inserting DataTables into DataSets

At this point, our DataTable object is complete. The final step is to insert the DataTable into the carsInventoryDS DataSet object using the Tables collection. Assume that you have updated Main() to do so, and pass the DataSet object into a new (yet to be written) helper method named PrintDataSet():

```
Sub Main()
...
  ' Finally, add our table to the DataSet.
  carsInventoryDS.Tables.Add(inventoryTable)

  ' Now print the DataSet.
  PrintDataSet(carsInventoryDS)
  Console.ReadLine()
End Sub
```

The PrintDataSet() method simply iterates over the DataSet metadata (via the ExtendedProperties collection) and each DataTable in the DataSet, printing out the column names and row values using the type indexers:

```
Private Sub PrintDataSet(ByVal ds As DataSet)
  ' Print out any name and extended properties.
  Console.WriteLine("DataSet is named: {0}", ds.DataSetName)
  For Each de As System.Collections.DictionaryEntry In ds.ExtendedProperties
    Console.WriteLine("Key = {0}, Value = {1}", de.Key, de.Value)
  Next
  Console.WriteLine()

  For Each dt As DataTable In ds.Tables
    Console.WriteLine("=> {0} Table:", dt.TableName)
    For curCol As Integer = 0 To dt.Columns.Count - 1

      ' Print out the column names.
      Console.Write(dt.Columns(curCol).ColumnName + "" & vbTab)
    Next
    Console.WriteLine(vbLf & "---------------------------------")
    For curRow As Integer = 0 To dt.Rows.Count - 1
      ' Print the DataTable.
      For curCol As Integer = 0 To dt.Columns.Count - 1
        Console.Write(dt.Rows(curRow)(curCol).ToString() & vbTab)
      Next
      Console.WriteLine()
    Next
  Next
End Sub
```

Figure 23-3 shows the program's output.

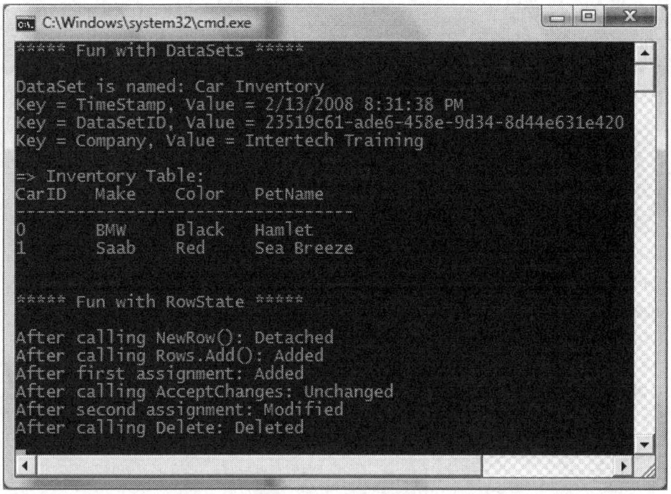

Figure 23-3. *Contents of the example's* DataSet *object*

Processing DataTable Data Using DataTableReader Objects

Given your work in the previous chapter, you are sure to notice that the manner in which you process data using the connected layer (e.g., data reader objects) and the disconnected layer (e.g., DataSet objects) is quite different. Working with a data reader typically involves establishing a While loop, calling the Read() method, and using an indexer to pluck out the name/value pairs. On the other hand, DataSet processing typically involves a series of iteration constructs to drill into the data within the tables, rows, and columns.

Since the release of .NET 2.0, DataTables were provided with a method named CreateDataReader(). This method allows you to obtain the data within a DataTable using a data reader–like navigation scheme (forward-only, read-only). The major benefit of this approach is that you now use a single model to process data, regardless of which "layer" of ADO.NET you use to obtain it. Assume you have authored the following helper function named PrintTable(), implemented as so:

```
Private Sub PrintTable(ByVal dt As DataTable)
  ' Get the DataTableReader type.
  Dim dtReader As DataTableReader = dt.CreateDataReader()

  ' The DataTableReader works just like the DataReader.
  While dtReader.Read()
    For i As Integer = 0 To dtReader.FieldCount - 1
      Console.Write("{0}" & vbTab, dtReader.GetValue(i).ToString().Trim())
    Next
    Console.WriteLine()
  End While
  dtReader.Close()
End Sub
```

Notice that the DataTableReader works identically to the data reader object of your data provider. Using a DataTableReader can be an ideal choice when you wish to quickly pump out the data within a DataTable without needing to traverse the internal row and column collections. Now, assume you have updated the previous PrintDataSet() method to invoke PrintTable(), rather than drilling into data using the Rows and Columns properties:

```
Private Sub PrintDataSet(ByVal ds As DataSet)
  ' Print out any name and extended properties.
  Console.WriteLine("DataSet is named: {0}", ds.DataSetName)
  For Each de As System.Collections.DictionaryEntry In ds.ExtendedProperties
    Console.WriteLine("Key = {0}, Value = {1}", de.Key, de.Value)
  Next
  Console.WriteLine()

  For Each dt As DataTable In ds.Tables
    Console.WriteLine("=> {0} Table:", dt.TableName)
    For curCol As Integer = 0 To dt.Columns.Count - 1
      ' Print out the column names.
      Console.Write(dt.Columns(curCol).ColumnName + "" & vbTab)
    Next
    Console.WriteLine("" & vbLf & "----------------------------------")
    PrintTable(dt)
  Next
End Sub
```

When you run the application, the output is identical to that of Figure 23-3. The only difference is how you are internally accessing the DataTable's contents.

Serializing DataTable/DataSet Objects As XML

DataSets and DataTables both support the WriteXml() and ReadXml() methods. WriteXml() allows you to persist the object's content to a local file (as well as into any System.IO.Stream-derived type) as an XML document. ReadXml() allows you to hydrate the state of a DataSet (or DataTable) from a given XML document. In addition, DataSets and DataTables both support WriteXmlSchema() and ReadXmlSchema() to save or load an *.xsd file.

To test this out for yourself, update your Main() method to call the following final helper function (notice you will pass in a DataSet as the sole parameter):

```
Private Sub DataSetAsXml(ByVal carsInventoryDS As DataSet)
  ' Save this DataSet as XML.
  carsInventoryDS.WriteXml("carsDataSet.xml")
  carsInventoryDS.WriteXmlSchema("carsDataSet.xsd")

  ' Clear out DataSet.
  carsInventoryDS.Clear()

  ' Load DataSet from XML file.
  carsInventoryDS.ReadXml("carsDataSet.xml")
End Sub
```

If you open the carsDataSet.xml file (located under the \bin\Debug folder of your project), you will find that each column in the table has been encoded as an XML element:

```
<?xml version="1.0" standalone="yes"?>
<Car_x0020_Inventory>
  <Inventory>
    <CarID>0</CarID>
    <Make>BMW</Make>
    <Color>Black</Color>
    <PetName>Hamlet</PetName>
  </Inventory>
  <Inventory>
    <CarID>1</CarID>
```

```
    <Make>Saab</Make>
    <Color>Red</Color>
    <PetName>Sea Breeze</PetName>
  </Inventory>
</Car_x0020_Inventory>
```

Serializing DataTable/DataSet Objects in a Binary Format

It is also possible to persist the contents of a DataSet (or an individual DataTable) as a compact binary format. This can be especially helpful when a DataSet object needs to be passed across a machine boundary (in the case of a distributed application); one drawback of XML data representation is that its very descriptive nature can result in a good deal of overhead.

In order to persist DataTables or DataSets in a binary format, simply set the RemotingFormat property to SerializationFormat.Binary. After this point, you can make use of the BinaryFormatter type (see Chapter 21) as expected. Consider the following final method of the SimpleDataSet project (don't forget to import the System.IO and System.Runtime.Serialization.Formatters.Binary namespaces):

```
Private Sub DataSetAsBinary(ByVal carsInventoryDS As DataSet)
  ' Set binary serialization flag.
  carsInventoryDS.RemotingFormat = SerializationFormat.Binary

  ' Save this DataSet as binary.
  Dim fs As New FileStream("BinaryCars.bin", FileMode.Create)
  Dim bFormat As New BinaryFormatter()
  bFormat.Serialize(fs, carsInventoryDS)
  fs.Close()

  ' Clear out DataSet.
  carsInventoryDS.Clear()

  ' Load DataSet from binary file.
  fs = New FileStream("BinaryCars.bin", FileMode.Open)
  Dim data As DataSet = DirectCast(bFormat.Deserialize(fs), DataSet)
End Sub
```

Figure 23-4 shows the contents of the BinaryCars.bin file.

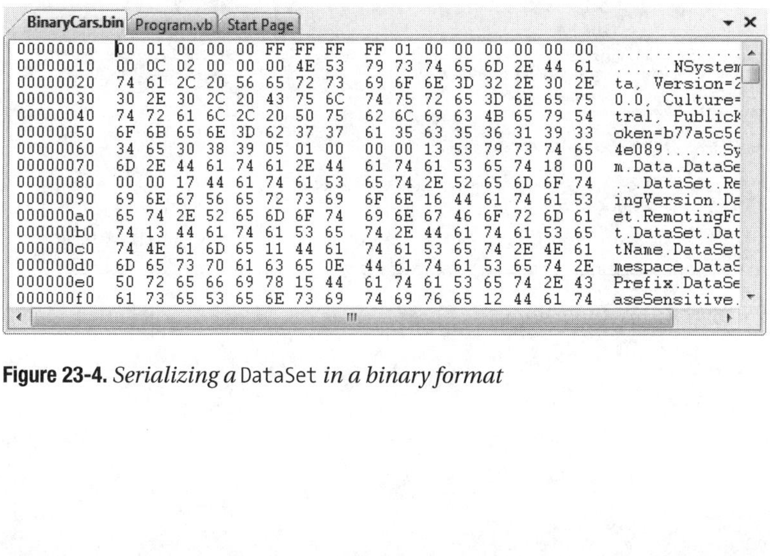

Figure 23-4. *Serializing a* DataSet *in a binary format*

Source Code The SimpleDataSet application is included under the Chapter 23 subdirectory.

Binding DataTable Objects to User Interfaces

At this point in the chapter, you have examined how to manually create, hydrate, and iterate over the contents of a `DataSet` object using the inherit object model of ADO.NET. While understanding how to do these things is quite important, the .NET platform ships with numerous APIs that have the ability to "bind" data to user interface elements automatically.

For example, the original GUI toolkit of .NET, Windows Forms, supplies a control named `DataGridView` that has the built-in ability to display the contents of a `DataSet` or `DataTable` object using just a few lines of code. ASP.NET (.NET's web development API) and the Windows Presentation Foundation API (the new, supercharged GUI API introduced with .NET 3.0) also support the notion of data binding in one form or another.

To continue our investigation of the disconnected layer of ADO.NET, our next task is to build a Windows Forms application that will display the contents of a `DataTable` object within its user interface. Along the way, we will also examine how to filter and change table data, and we'll come to know the role of the `DataView` object. To begin, create a brand-new Windows Forms project workspace named WindowsFormsDataTableViewer, as shown in Figure 23-5.

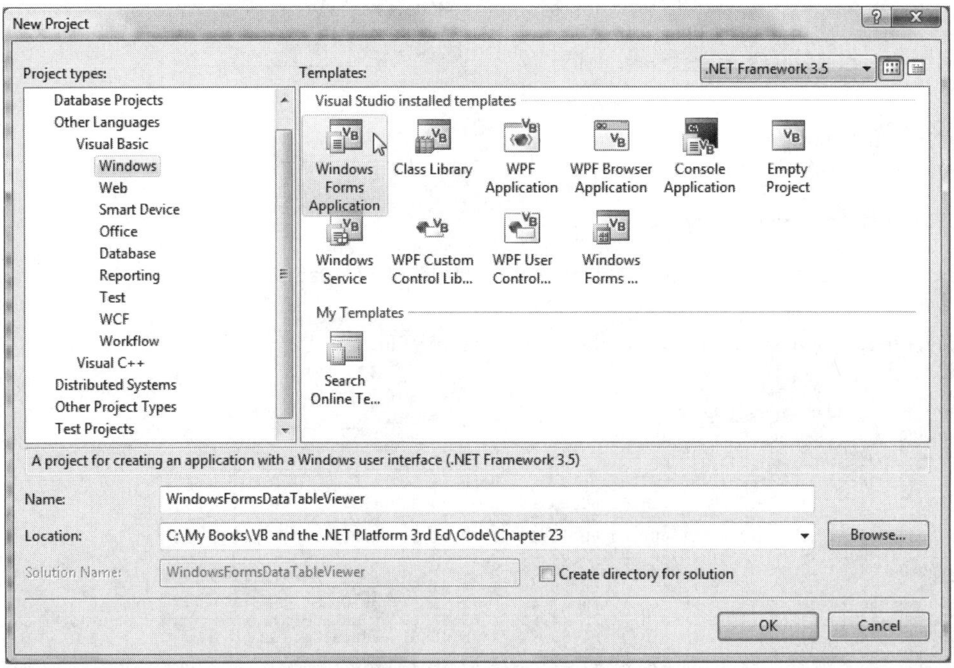

Figure 23-5. *Creating a Windows Forms Application*

■ **Note** The current example assumes you have some experience using Windows Forms to build graphical user interfaces. If this is not the case, you may wish to simply open the solution and follow along, or return to this section once you have read Chapter 27, where you will begin to formally investigate the Windows Forms API.

Rename your initial `Form1.vb` file to the more fitting `MainForm.vb`. Next, using the Visual Studio 2008 Toolbox, drag a `DataGridView` control (renamed to `carInventoryGridView` via the `(Name)` property of the Properties window) onto the designer surface. You may notice that when you place the control on the designer, you activate a context menu that allows you to connect to a physical data source. For the time being, completely ignore this aspect of the designer, as you will be binding your `DataTable` object programmatically. Finally, add a descriptive `Label` to your designer for information purposes. Figure 23-6 shows one possible look and feel.

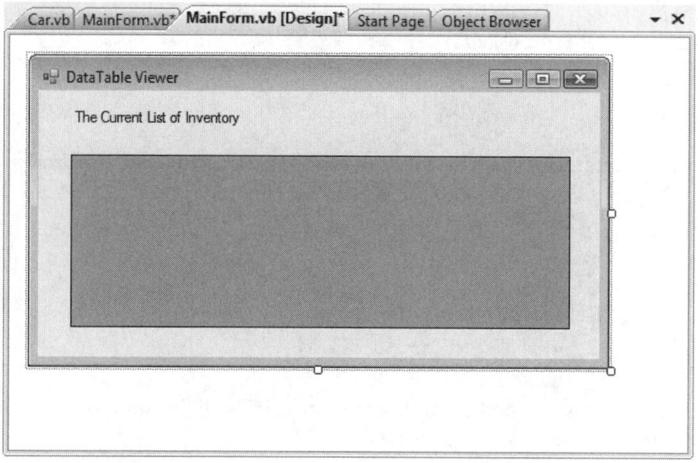

Figure 23-6. *The initial UI*

Hydrating a DataTable from a Generic List(Of T)

Similar to the previous SimpleDataSet example, the WindowsFormsDataTableViewer application will construct a `DataTable` that contains a set of `DataColumns` representing various columns and rows of data. This time, however, you will fill the rows using your generic `List(Of T)` member variable. First, insert a new VB class into your project (named `Car`), defined as follows:

```
Class Car
  ' Public for simplicity.
  Public carPetName As String
  Public carMake As String
  Public carColor As String

  Public Sub New(ByVal petName As String, ByVal make As String, _
    ByVal color As String)
    carPetName = petName
    carColor = color
    carMake = make
  End Sub
End Class
```

Now, within the default constructor of the MainForm class, populate a List(Of T) member variable (named listCars) with a set of new Car objects:

```
Public Class MainForm
  ' A collection of Car objects.
  Private listCars As New List(Of Car)()

  Public Sub New()
    InitializeComponent()

    ' Fill the list with some cars.
    listCars.Add(New Car("Chucky", "BMW", "Green"))
    listCars.Add(New Car("Tiny", "Yugo", "White"))
    listCars.Add(New Car("Ami", "Jeep", "Tan"))
    listCars.Add(New Car("Pain Inducer", "Caravan", "Pink"))
    listCars.Add(New Car("Fred", "BMW", "Pea Soup Green"))
    listCars.Add(New Car("Sidd", "BMW", "Black"))
    listCars.Add(New Car("Mel", "Firebird", "Red"))
    listCars.Add(New Car("Sarah", "Colt", "Black"))
  End Sub
End Class
```

Next, add a new member variable named inventoryTable of type DataTable to your MainForm class type:

```
Public Class MainForm

  ' Our DataTable.
  Private inventoryTable As New DataTable("Inventory")
...
End Class
```

Add a new helper function to your class named CreateDataTable(), and call this method within the default constructor of the MainForm class:

```
Private Sub CreateDataTable()
  ' Create table schema
  Dim carMakeColumn As New DataColumn("Make", GetType(String))
  Dim carColorColumn As New DataColumn("Color", GetType(String))
  Dim carPetNameColumn As New DataColumn("PetName", GetType(String))
  carPetNameColumn.Caption = "Pet Name"
  inventoryTable.Columns.AddRange(New DataColumn() {carMakeColumn, _
    carColorColumn, carPetNameColumn})

  ' Iterate over the list to make rows.
  For Each c As Car In listCars
    Dim newRow As DataRow = inventoryTable.NewRow()
    newRow("Make") = c.carMake
    newRow("Color") = c.carColor
    newRow("PetName") = c.carPetName
    inventoryTable.Rows.Add(newRow)
  Next

  ' Bind the DataTable to the carInventoryGridView.
  carInventoryGridView.DataSource = inventoryTable
End Sub
```

The method implementation begins by creating the schema of the DataTable by creating three DataColumn objects (for simplicity, I did not bother to add the autoincrementing CarID field), after which point they are added to the DataTable member variable. The row data is mapped from the List(Of T) field into the DataTable using a For Each iteration construct and the native ADO.NET object model.

However, notice that the final code statement within the CreateDataTable() method assigns the inventoryTable to the DataSource property. This single property is all you need to set to bind a DataTable to a DataGridView object. Under the hood, this GUI control is reading the row and column collections internally, much like you did with the PrintDataSet() method of the SimpleDataSet example. At this point, you should be able to run your application and see the DataTable within the DataGridView control, as shown in Figure 23-7.

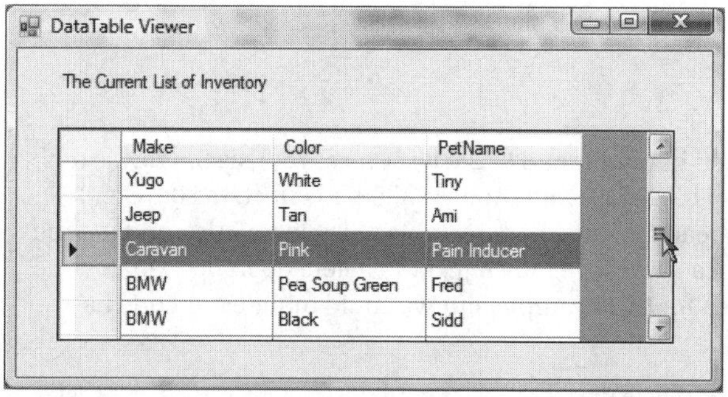

Figure 23-7. *Binding a* DataTable *to a Windows Forms* DataGridView

Programmatically Deleting Rows

Now, assume you wish to update your graphical interface to allow the user to delete a row from the DataTable that is bound to the DataGridView. One approach is to call the Delete() method of the DataRow object that represents the row to terminate. Simply specify the index (or DataRow object) representing the row to remove. To allow the user to specify which row to delete, add a TextBox (named txtRowToRemove) and a Button control (named btnRemoveRow) to the current designer, as shown in Figure 23-8.

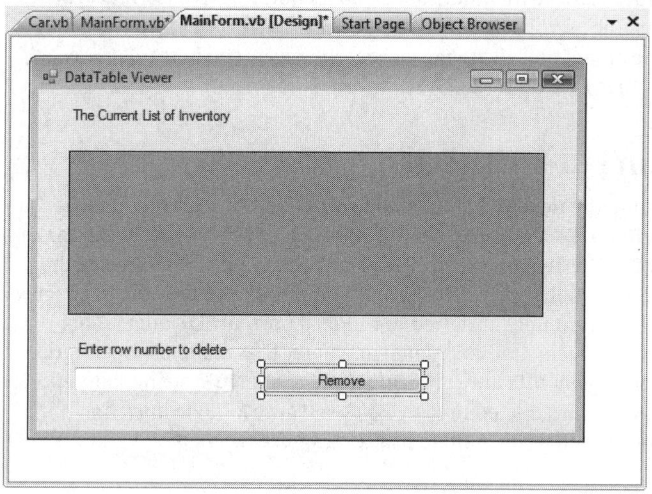

Figure 23-8. *Updating the UI to enable removal of rows from the underlying* DataTable

The following logic behind the new Button's Click event handler removes the user-specified row from your in-memory DataTable. Note that we are wrapping the deletion logic within a Try scope, to account for the possibility the user has entered a row number not currently in the DataGridView:

```
' Remove this row from the DataRowCollection.
Private Sub btnRemoveRow_Click(ByVal sender As System.Object, _
  ByVal e As System.EventArgs) Handles btnRemoveRow.Click
  Try
    inventoryTable.Rows((Integer.Parse(txtRowToRemove.Text))).Delete()
    inventoryTable.AcceptChanges()
  Catch ex As Exception
    MessageBox.Show(ex.Message)
  End Try
End Sub
```

The Delete() method might have been better named MarkedAsDeletable(), as the row is not literally removed until the DataTable.AcceptChanges() method is called. In effect, the Delete() method simply sets a flag that says, "I am ready to die when my table tells me to." Also understand that if a row has been marked for deletion, a DataTable may reject the delete operation via RejectChanges(). We have no need to do so for this example, but we could update our code base as follows:

```
' Mark a row as deleted, but reject the changes.
Private Sub btnRemoveRow_Click(ByVal sender As System.Object, _
  ByVal e As System.EventArgs) Handles btnRemoveRow.Click
    inventoryTable.Rows((Integer.Parse(txtRowToRemove.Text))).Delete()

  ' Do more work
  ...

  ' Restore previous RowState value.
  inventoryTable.RejectChanges()
  ...
End Sub
```

You should now be able to run your application and specify a row to delete from the DataTable, based on a given row of the DataGridView (note the internal row collection is zero based). As you remove DataRow objects from the DataTable, you will notice that the grid's UI is updated immediately, as it is bound to the state of the object. Recall, however, that the row is still in the DataTable, but the grid chooses not to display it because of the RowState value.

Selecting Rows Based on Filter Criteria

Many data-centric applications require the need to view a small subset of a DataTable's data, as specified by some sort of filtering criteria. For example, what if you wish to see only a certain make of automobile from the in-memory DataTable (such as only BMWs)? The Select() method of the DataTable class provides this very functionality. Using the Select() method, you are able to specify search criteria that support a syntax intentionally designed to model a normal SQL query. This method will return an array of DataRow objects that represent each entry that matches the criteria.

To illustrate, update your UI once again, this time allowing users to specify a string that represents the make of the automobile they are interested in viewing (see Figure 23-9) using a new TextBox (named txtMakeToView) and a new Button (named btnDisplayMakes).

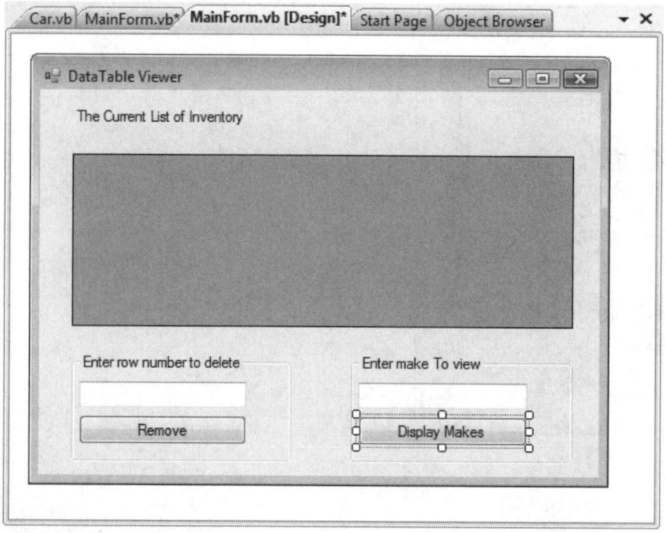

Figure 23-9. *Updating the UI to enable row filtering*

The `Select()` method has been overloaded a number of times to provide different selection semantics. At its most basic level, the parameter sent to `Select()` is a string that contains some conditional operation. To begin, observe the following logic for the `Click` event handler of your new button:

```
Private Sub btnDisplayMakes_Click(ByVal sender As System.Object, _
  ByVal e As System.EventArgs) Handles btnDisplayMakes.Click
  ' Build a filter based on user input.
  Dim filterStr As String = String.Format("Make= '{0}'", txtMakeToView.Text)

  ' Find all rows matching the filter.
  Dim makes As DataRow() = inventoryTable.Select(filterStr)

  ' Show what we got!
  If makes.Length = 0 Then
    MessageBox.Show("Sorry, no cars...", "Selection error!")
  Else
    Dim strMake As String = String.Empty
    For i As Integer = 0 To makes.Length - 1
      Dim temp As DataRow = makes(i)
      strMake &= temp("PetName") & vbLf
    Next
    MessageBox.Show(strMake, String.Format("{0} type(s):", txtMakeToView.Text))
  End If
End Sub
```

Here, you first build a simple filter based on the value in the associated `TextBox`. If you specify BMW, your filter is `Make = 'BMW'`. When you send this filter to the `Select()` method, you get back an array of `DataRow` types that represent each row that matches the filter (see Figure 23-10).

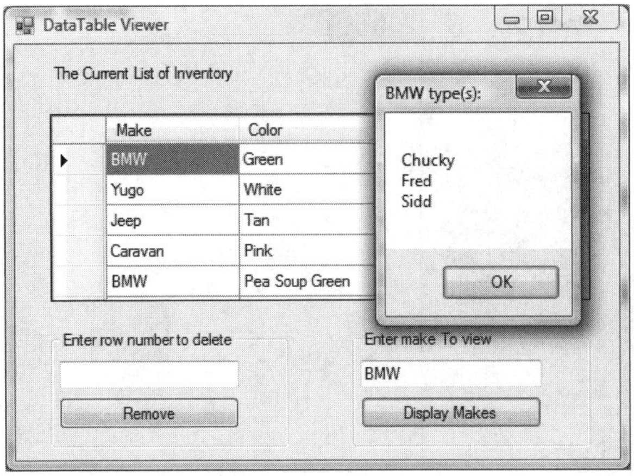

Figure 23-10. *Displaying filtered data*

Again, filtering logic is standard SQL syntax. To prove the point, assume you wish to obtain the results of the previous `Select()` invocation alphabetically based on pet name. In terms of SQL, this translates into a sort based on the PetName column. Luckily, the `Select()` method has been overloaded to send in a sort criterion, as shown here:

```
' Sort by PetName.
makes = inventoryTable.Select(filterStr, "PetName")
```

If you want the results in descending order, call `Select()` as so:

```
' Return results in descending order.
makes = inventoryTable.Select(filterStr, "PetName DESC")
```

In general, the sort string contains the column name followed by `ASC` (ascending, which is the default) or `DESC` (descending). If need be, multiple columns can be separated by commas. Finally, understand that a filter string can be composed of any number of relational operators. For example, assume that your `DataTable` also defined a column representing the ID of a vehicle. What if you want to find all cars with an ID greater than 5? Here is a helper function that does this very thing:

```
Private Sub ShowCarsWithIdGreaterThanFive()
  ' Now show the pet names of all cars with ID greater than 5.
  Dim properIDs As DataRow()
  Dim newFilterStr As String = "ID > 5"
  properIDs = inventoryTable.Select(newFilterStr)

  Dim strIDs As String = String.Empty
  For i As Integer = 0 To properIDs.Length - 1
    Dim temp As DataRow = properIDs(i)
    strIDs &= temp("PetName") & " is ID " & temp("ID") & vbLf
  Next
  MessageBox.Show(strIDs, "Pet names of cars where ID > 5")
End Sub
```

Updating Rows

The final aspect of the `DataTable` you should be aware of is the process of updating an existing row with new values. One approach is to first obtain the row(s) that match a given filter criterion using the Select() method. Once you have the DataRow(s) in question, modify them accordingly. For example, assume you have a new Button on your form-derived type named btnChangeBeemersToYugos that (when clicked) searches the DataTable for all rows where Make is equal to BMW. Once you identify these items, you change the Make from BMW to Yugo:

```
' Find the rows you want to edit with a filter.
Private Sub btnChangeBeemersToYugos_Click(ByVal sender As System.Object, _
  ByVal e As System.EventArgs) Handles btnChangeBeemersToYugos.Click
  ' Make sure user has not lost his or her mind.
  If DialogResult.Yes = _
    MessageBox.Show("Are you sure?? BMWs are much nicer than Yugos!", _
    "Please Confirm!", MessageBoxButtons.YesNo) Then
    ' Build a filter.
    Dim filterStr As String = "Make='BMW'"

    ' Find all rows matching the filter.
    Dim makes As DataRow() = inventoryTable.Select(filterStr)
    For i As Integer = 0 To makes.Length - 1
      ' Change all Beemers to Yugos!
      makes(i)("Make") = "Yugo"
    Next
  End If
End Sub
```

The DataRow class also provides the BeginEdit(), EndEdit(), and CancelEdit() methods, which allow you to edit the content of a row while temporarily suspending any associated validation rules. In the previous logic, each row was validated with each assignment. (Also, if you handle any events from the DataRow, they fire with each modification.) When you call BeginEdit() on a given DataRow, the row is placed in edit mode. At this point you can make your changes as necessary and call either EndEdit() to commit these changes or CancelEdit() to roll back the changes to the original version, for example:

```
Sub UpdateSomeRow()
  ' Assume you have obtained a row to edit.
  ' Now place this row in edit mode.
  rowToUpdate.BeginEdit()

  ' Send the row to a helper function, which returns a Boolean.
  If ChangeValuesForThisRow(rowToUpdate)
    rowToUpdate.EndEdit()      ' OK!
  Else
    rowToUpdate.CancelEdit()   ' Forget it.
  End If
End Sub
```

Although you are free to manually call these methods on a given DataRow, these members are automatically called when you edit a DataGridView widget that has been bound to a DataTable. For example, when you select a row to edit from a DataGridView, that row is automatically placed in edit mode. When you shift focus to a new cell, EndEdit() is called automatically.

Working with the DataView Type

In database nomenclature, a *view object* is an alternative representation of a table (or set of tables). For example, using Microsoft SQL Server, you could create a view for your Inventory table that returns a new table containing automobiles only of a given color. In ADO.NET, the DataView type allows you to programmatically extract a subset of data from the DataTable into a stand-alone object.

One great advantage of holding multiple views of the same table is that you can bind these views to various GUI widgets (such as the DataGridView). For example, one DataGridView might be bound to a DataView showing all autos in the Inventory, while another might be configured to display only green automobiles.

To illustrate, update the current UI with an additional DataGridView type named dataGridColtsView and a descriptive Label. Next, define a member variable named coltsOnlyView of type DataView:

```
Public Class MainForm
  ' A collection of Car objects.
  Private listCars As New List(Of Car)()

  ' View of the DataTable.
  Private coltsOnlyView As DataView
...
End Class
```

Now, create a new helper function named CreateDataView(), and call this method within the form's default constructor directly after the DataTable has been fully constructed, as shown here:

```
Sub New()
...
  ' Make a data table.
  CreateDataTable()

  ' Make a view.
  CreateDataView()
End Sub
```

Here is the implementation of this new helper function. Notice that the constructor of each DataView has been passed the DataTable that will be used to build the custom set of data rows.

```
Private Sub CreateDataView()
  ' Set the table that is used to construct this view.
  coltsOnlyView = New DataView(inventoryTable)

  ' Now configure the views using a filter.
  coltsOnlyView.RowFilter = "Make = 'Colt'"

  ' Bind to the new grid.
  dataGridColtsView.DataSource = coltsOnlyView
End Sub
```

As you can see, the DataView class supports a property named RowFilter, which contains the string representing the filtering criteria used to extract matching rows. Once you have your view established, set the grid's DataSource property accordingly. Figure 23-11 shows the completed application in action.

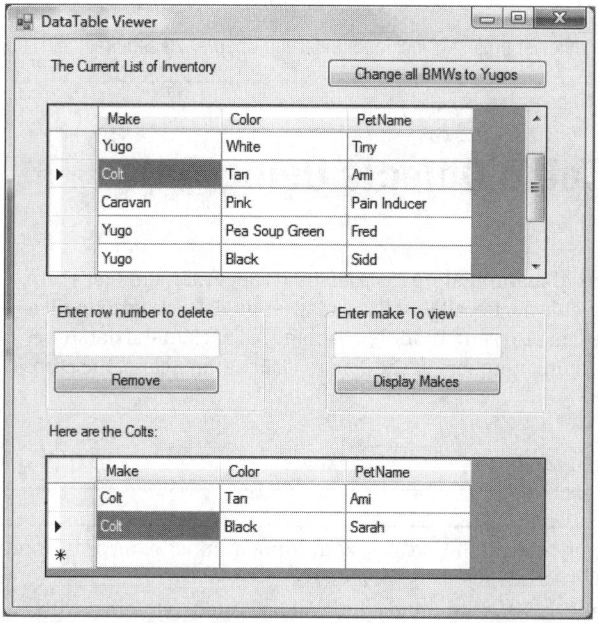

Figure 23-11. *Displaying a unique view of our data*

One Final UI Enhancement: Rendering Row Numbers

Before wrapping up this example, let's add one small enhancement to the current application. Currently, the grids on this window do not provide any sort of visual cue to the end user about which row number he or she is editing (or possibly deleting). If you wish to display row numbers on a `DataGridView`, your first step is to handle the `RowPostPaint` event on the grid itself. This event will fire after all of the data in the grid's cells have been rendered in the UI, and it gives you a chance to finalize the graphical look and feel of the rows before they are presented to the user.

Once you have handled this event, you are able to take the incoming `DataGridViewRowPostPaintEventArgs` parameter to obtain a `Graphics` object. As you will see in Chapter 28, the `Graphics` type is part of the GDI+ API, which is the native Windows Forms 2D rendering toolkit. Using this `Graphics` object, you are able invoke various methods (such as `DrawString()`, which is appropriate for this example) to render content. Again, Chapter 28 will examine GDI+; however, here is an implementation of the `RowPostPaint` event that will paint the numbers of each row on the `carInventoryGridView` object (you could, of course, handle the same event on the `dataGridColtsView` object for a similar effect):

```
Private Sub carInventoryGridView_RowPostPaint(ByVal sender As Object, _
  ByVal e As DataGridViewRowPostPaintEventArgs) _
  Handles carInventoryGridView.RowPostPaint

  ' This extra code will simply make it easier to visualize the # of the rows.
  Using b As New SolidBrush(Color.Black)
    e.Graphics.DrawString((e.RowIndex).ToString(), _
                          e.InheritedRowStyle.Font, b, _
                          e.RowBounds.Location.X + 15, _
                          e.RowBounds.Location.Y + 4)
  End Using
End Sub
```

■ **Source Code** The WindowsFormsDataTableViewer project is included under the Chapter 23 subdirectory.

Filling DataSet/DataTable Objects Using Data Adapters

Now that you understand the ins and outs of manipulating ADO.NET DataSets manually, let's turn our attention to the topic of data adapter objects. Recall that data adapter objects are used to fill a DataSet with DataTable objects, and they can also send modified DataTables back to the database for processing. Table 23-8 documents the core members of the DbDataAdapter base class, the common parent to every data adapter object.

Table 23-8. *Core Members of the* DbDataAdapter *Class*

Members	Meaning in Life
Fill()	This method fills a given table in the DataSet with some number of records from a database based on the command object–specified SelectCommand.
SelectCommand InsertCommand UpdateCommand DeleteCommand	These properties establish SQL commands that will be issued to interact with the data store when the Fill() and Update() methods are called.
Update()	This method updates a database using command objects within the InsertCommand, UpdateCommand, or DeleteCommand property. The exact command that is executed is based on the RowState value for a given DataRow in a given DataTable (of a given DataSet).

First of all, notice that a data adapter defines four properties (SelectCommand, InsertCommand, UpdateCommand, and DeleteCommand), each of which operates upon discrete command objects. When you create the data adapter object for your particular data provider (e.g., SqlDataAdapter), you are able to pass in a string type that represents the command text used by the SelectCommand's command object. However, the remaining three command objects (used by the InsertCommand, UpdateCommand, and DeleteCommand properties) must be configured manually.

Assuming each of the four command objects has been properly configured, you are then able to call the Fill() method to obtain a DataSet (or a single DataTable, if you wish). To do so, the data adapter will use whichever command object is found via the SelectCommand property. In a similar manner, when you wish to pass a modified DataSet (or DataTable) object back to the database for processing, you can call the Update() method on the data adapter, which will make use of any of the remaining command objects based on the state of each row in the DataTable (more details in just a bit).

One of the strangest aspects of working with a data adapter object is the fact that you are never required to open or close a connection to the database. Rather, the underlying connection to the database is managed on your behalf. However, you will still need to supply the data adapter with a valid connection object or a connection string (which will be used to build a connection object internally) to inform the data adapter exactly which database you wish to communicate with.

A Simple Data Adapter Example

Before we add new functionality to the AutoLotDAL.dll assembly created in Chapter 22, let's begin with a very simple example that fills a DataSet with a single table using an ADO.NET data adapter object. Create a new Console Application named FillDataSetWithSqlDataAdapter, and import the System.Data.SqlClient namespace into your initial VB code file.

Now, update your Main() method as follows (for reasons of simplicity, feel free to make use of a hard-coded connection string, as shown here):

```
Sub Main()
  Console.WriteLine("***** Fun with Data Adapters *****" & vbLf)

  ' Hard-coded connection string.
  Dim cnStr As String = _
  "Integrated Security = SSPI;Initial Catalog=AutoLot;" & _
  "Data Source=(local)\SQLEXPRESS"

  ' Caller creates the DataSet object.
  Dim ds As New DataSet("AutoLot")

  ' Inform adapter of the Select command text and connection.
  Dim dAdapt As New SqlDataAdapter("Select * From Inventory", cnStr)

  ' Fill our DataSet with a new table, named Inventory.
  dAdapt.Fill(ds, "Inventory")

  ' Display contents of DataSet.
  PrintDataSet(ds)
  Console.ReadLine()
End Sub
```

Notice that the data adapter has been constructed by specifying a string literal that will map to the SQL SELECT statement. This value will be used to build a command object internally, which can be later obtained via the SelectCommand property.

Next, notice that it is the job of the caller to create an instance of the DataSet type, which is passed into the Fill() method of the data adapter. Optionally, the Fill() method can be passed as a second argument a string name that will be used to set the TableName property of the new DataTable (if you do not specify a table name, the data adapter will simply name the table Table). While in most cases the name you assign a DataTable will be identical to the name of the physical table in the relational database, this is not required.

Note The Fill() method returns a numeric value that represents the number of rows returned by the SQL query.

Finally, notice that nowhere in the Main() method are you explicitly opening or closing the connection to the database. The Fill() method of a given data adapter has been preprogrammed to open and then close the underlying connection before returning from the Fill() method. Therefore, when you pass the DataSet to the PrintDataSet() method (implemented earlier in this chapter), you are operating on a local copy of disconnected data, incurring no round-trips to fetch the data.

Mapping Database Names to Friendly Names

As mentioned earlier, database administrators tend to create table and column names that can be less than friendly to end users (e.g., au_id, au_fname, au_lname, etc.). The good news is that data adapter objects maintain an internal strongly typed collection (named `DataTableMappingCollection`) of `System.Data.Common.DataTableMapping` types. This collection can be accessed via the `TableMappings` property of your data adapter object.

If you so choose, you may manipulate this collection to inform a `DataTable` which "display names" it should use when asked to print its contents. For example, assume that you wish to map the table name Inventory to Current Inventory for display purposes. Furthermore, say you wish to display the CarID column name as Car ID (note the extra space) and the PetName column name as Name of Car. To do so, add the following code before calling the `Fill()` method of your data adapter object (and be sure to import the `System.Data.Common` namespace to gain the definition of the `DataTableMapping` type):

```
Sub Main()
...
  ' Now map DB column names to user-friendly names.
  Dim custMap As DataTableMapping = _
    dAdapt.TableMappings.Add("Inventory", "Current Inventory")
  custMap.ColumnMappings.Add("CarID", "Car ID")
  custMap.ColumnMappings.Add("PetName", "Name of Car")
  dAdapt.Fill(ds, "Inventory")
...
End Sub
```

If you were to run this program once again, you would find that the `PrintDataSet()` method now displays the "friendly names" of the `DataTable` and `DataRow` objects, rather than the names established by the database schema. Figure 23-12 shows the output of the current example.

Figure 23-12. `DataTable` *objects with custom mappings*

Source Code The FillDataSetWithSqlDataAdapter project is included under the Chapter 23 subdirectory.

Revisiting AutoLotDAL.dll

To illustrate the process of using a data adapter to push modifications in a `DataTable` back to the database for processing, we will now update the `AutoLotDAL.dll` assembly created back in Chapter 22 to include a new namespace (named `AutoLotDisconnectedLayer`). This namespace will contain a new class, `InventoryDALDisLayer`, that will make use of a data adapter to interact with a `DataTable`.

Defining the Initial Class Type

Open the AutoLotDAL project in Visual Studio 2008, insert a new class type named `InventoryDALDisLayer` using the Project ➤ Add New Item menu option, and ensure you have a *public* class type in your new code file, wrapped in a new namespace named `AutoLotDisconnectedLayer`. Unlike the connection-centric `InventoryDAL` type, this new class will not need to provide custom open/close methods, as the data adapter will handle the details automatically.

To begin, add a custom constructor that sets a private `String` variable representing the connection string. As well, define a private `SqlDataAdapter` member variable, which will be configured by calling a (yet to be created) helper method called `ConfigureAdapter()`, which takes a `SqlDataAdapter` parameter by reference:

```
Imports System.Data.SqlClient

Namespace AutoLotDisconnectedLayer
  Public Class InventoryDALDisLayer
    ' Field data.
    Private cnString As String = String.Empty
    Private dAdapt As SqlDataAdapter = Nothing

    Public Sub New(ByVal connectionString As String)
      cnString = connectionString

      ' Configure the SqlDataAdapter.
      ConfigureAdapter(dAdapt)
    End Sub
  End Class
End Namespace
```

Configuring the Data Adapter Using the SqlCommandBuilder

When you are using a data adapter to modify a database based on the contents of a `DataSet`, the first order of business is to assign the `UpdateCommand`, `DeleteCommand`, and `InsertCommand` properties with valid command objects (until you do so, these properties return `Nothing` references). By "valid" command objects, I am referring to the set of command objects used in conjunction with the table you are attempting to update (the Inventory table in our example).

To fill up our adapter with the necessary data can entail a good amount of code, especially if we make use of parameterized queries. Recall from Chapter 22 that a parameterized query allows us to build a SQL statement using a set of parameter objects. Thus, if we were to take the long road, we could implement `ConfigureAdapter()` to manually create three new `SqlCommand` objects, each of which contains a set of `SqlParameter` objects. After this point, we could set each object to the `UpdateCommand`, `DeleteCommand`, and `InsertCommand` properties of the adapter.

Thankfully, Visual Studio 2008 provides a number of designer tools to take care of this mundane and tedious code on our behalf. You'll see some of these shortcuts in action at the conclusion of this chapter. Rather than forcing you to author the numerous code statements to fully configure a data adapter, let's take a massive shortcut by implementing `ConfigureAdapter()` as so:

```
Private Sub ConfigureAdapter(ByRef dAdapt As SqlDataAdapter)
  ' Create the adapter and set up the SelectCommand.
  dAdapt = New SqlDataAdapter("Select * From Inventory", cnString)

  ' Obtain the remaining Command objects dynamically at runtime
  ' using the SqlCommandBuilder.
  Dim builder As New SqlCommandBuilder(dAdapt)
End Sub
```

To help simplify the construction of data adapter objects, each of the Microsoft-supplied ADO.NET data providers provides a *command builder* type. The `SqlCommandBuilder` automatically generates the values contained within the `SqlDataAdapter`'s `InsertCommand`, `UpdateCommand`, and `DeleteCommand` properties based on the initial `SelectCommand`. Clearly, the benefit is that you have no need to build all the `SqlCommand` and `SqlParameter` types by hand.

An obvious question at this point is how a command builder is able to build these SQL command objects on the fly. The short answer is metadata. At runtime, when you call the `Update()` method of a data adapter, the related command builder will read the database's schema data to autogenerate the underlying insert, delete, and update command objects.

Obviously, doing so requires additional round-trips to the remote database, and therefore it will certainly hurt performance if you use the `SqlCommandBuilder` numerous times in a single application. Here, we are minimizing the negative effect by calling our `ConfigureAdapter()` method at the time the `InventoryDALDisLayer` object is constructed, and retaining the configured `SqlDataAdapter` for use throughout the object's lifetime.

In the previous code, notice that we made no use of the command builder object (`SqlCommandBuilder` in this case) beyond passing in the data adapter object as a constructor parameter. As odd as this may seem, this is all we are required to do (at a minimum). Under the hood, this type will configure the data adapter with the remaining command objects.

Now, while you may love the idea of getting something for nothing, do understand that command builders come with some critical restrictions. Specifically, a command builder is only able to autogenerate SQL commands for use by a data adapter if all of the following conditions are true:

- The SQL `SELECT` command interacts with only a single table (e.g., no joins).
- The single table has been attributed with a primary key.
- The table must have a column(s) representing a primary key.

Based on the way we constructed our AutoLot database, these restrictions pose no problem. However, in a more industrial-strength database, you will need to consider if this type is at all useful (if not, remember that Visual Studio 2008 will autogenerate a good deal of the required code, as you'll see at the end of this chapter).

Implementing GetAllInventory()

Now that our data adapter is ready to go, the first method of our new class type will simply use the `Fill()` method of the `SqlDataAdapter` object to fetch a `DataTable` representing all records in the Inventory table of the AutoLot database:

```
Public Function GetAllInventory() As DataTable
  Dim inv As New DataTable("Inventory")
  dAdapt.Fill(inv)
  Return inv
End Function
```

Implementing UpdateInventory()

The UpdateInventory() method is very simple:

```
Public Sub UpdateInventory(ByVal modifiedTable As DataTable)
  dAdapt.Update(modifiedTable)
End Sub
```

Here, the data adapter object will examine the RowState value of each row of the incoming DataTable. Based on this value (RowState.Added, RowState.Deleted, or RowState.Modified), the correct command object will be leveraged behind the scenes.

Source Code The AutoLotDAL (Part 2) project is included under the Chapter 23 subdirectory.

Building a Windows Forms Front End

At this point we can build a front end to test our new InventoryDALDisLayer object, which will be a Windows Forms application named WindowsFormsInventoryUI. Once you have created the project, set a reference to your updated AutoLotDAL.dll and the System.Configuration.dll assembly and import the following namespaces:

```
Imports AutoLotDisconnectedLayer
Imports System.Configuration
```

Next, insert an app.config file that contains a <connectionStrings> element specifying a connection string value named AutoLotSqlProvider (see Chapter 22 for details):

```
<?xml version="1.0" encoding="utf-8" ?>
<configuration>
  <connectionStrings>
    <add name ="AutoLotSqlProvider"  connectionString =
    "Data Source=(local)\SQLEXPRESS;
     Integrated Security=SSPI;Initial Catalog=AutoLot"/>
  </connectionStrings>
</configuration>
```

The design of the form consists of a single Label, DataGridView (named inventoryGrid), and Button (named btnUpdateInventory), which has been configured to handle the Click event. Here is the definition of the form (which does not contain error-handling logic for simplicity; feel free to add Try/Catch logic if you so choose):

```
Imports AutoLotDisconnectedLayer
Imports System.Configuration

Public Class MainForm
  Private dal As InventoryDALDisLayer = Nothing

  Sub New()

    ' This call is required by the Windows Form Designer.
    InitializeComponent()

    ' Add any initialization after the InitializeComponent() call.
    ' Assume we have an app.config file
    ' storing the connection string.
```

```
    Dim cnStr As String = ConfigurationManager.ConnectionStrings _
      ("AutoLotSqlProvider").ConnectionString

    ' Create our data access object.
    dal = New InventoryDALDisLayer(cnStr)

    ' Fill up our grid!
    inventoryGrid.DataSource = dal.GetAllInventory()
  End Sub

  Private Sub btnUpdateInventory_Click(ByVal sender As System.Object, _
    ByVal e As System.EventArgs) Handles btnUpdateInventory.Click
    Dim changedDT As DataTable = DirectCast(inventoryGrid.DataSource, DataTable)
    ' Commit our changes.
    dal.UpdateInventory(changedDT)
  End Sub
End Class
```

Once we create the InventoryDALDisLayer object, we bind the DataTable returned from GetAllInventory() to the DataGridView object. When the end user clicks the Update button, we extract out the modified DataTable from the grid (via the DataSource property) and pass it into our UpdateInventory() method.

That's it! Once you run this application, add a set of new rows to the grid and update/delete a few others. Assuming you click the Button control, you will see your changes have persisted into the AutoLot database.

Source Code The updated WindowsFormsInventoryUI project is included under the Chapter 23 subdirectory.

Navigating Multitabled DataSet Objects

So far, all of this chapter's examples have operated on a single DataTable object. However, the power of the disconnected layer really comes to light when a DataSet object contains numerous interrelated DataTables. In this case, you are able to insert any number of DataRelation objects into the DataSet's DataRelations collection to account for the interdependencies of the tables. Using these objects, the client tier is able to navigate between the table data without incurring network round-trips.

Note Rather than updating AutoLotDAL.dll yet again in order to account for the Customers and Orders tables, this example isolates all of the data access logic within a new Windows Forms project. However, intermixing UI and data logic in a production-level application is certainly not recommended. The final examples of this chapter leverage various database design tools to decouple the UI and data logic code.

Begin this example by creating a new Windows Forms application named MultitabledDataSetApp. The GUI is simple enough. In Figure 23-13 you can see three DataGridView widgets that hold the data retrieved from the Inventory, Orders, and Customers tables of the AutoLot database. In addition, the initial Button (named btnUpdateDatabase) submits any and all changes entered within the grids back to the database for processing via data adapter objects.

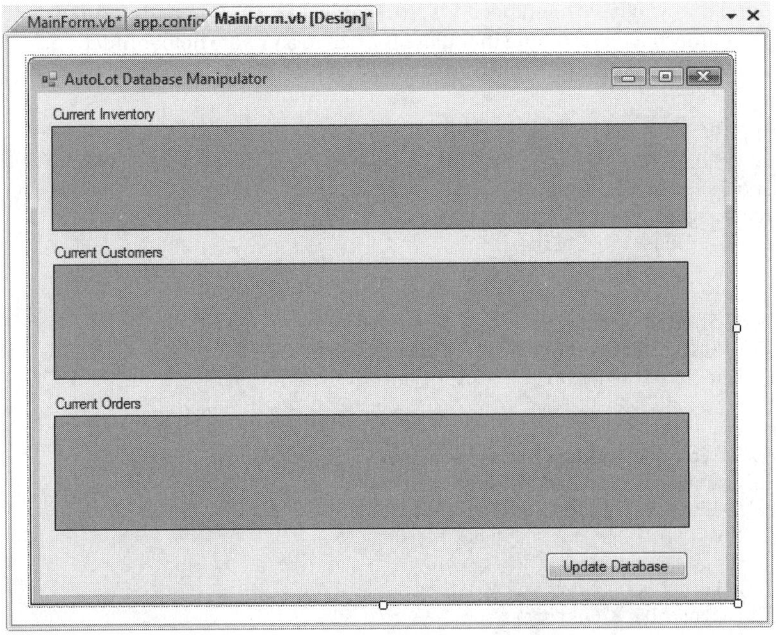

Figure 23-13. *The initial UI will display data from each table of the AutoLot database.*

Prepping the Data Adapters

To keep the data access code as simple as possible, the `MainForm` will make use of command builder objects to autogenerate the SQL commands for each of the three `SqlDataAdapters` (one for each table). Here is the initial update to the `Form`-derived type:

```
Imports System.Data.SqlClient
Imports System.Configuration

Public Class MainForm
  ' Formwide DataSet.
  Private autoLotDS As New DataSet("AutoLot")

  ' Make use of command builders to simplify data adapter configuration.
  Private sqlCBInventory As SqlCommandBuilder
  Private sqlCBCustomers As SqlCommandBuilder
  Private sqlCBOrders As SqlCommandBuilder

  ' Our data adapters (for each table).
  Private invTableAdapter As SqlDataAdapter
  Private custTableAdapter As SqlDataAdapter
  Private ordersTableAdapter As SqlDataAdapter

  ' Formwide connection string.
  Private cnStr As String = String.Empty
End Class
```

The constructor does the grunge work of creating your data-centric member variables and filling the `DataSet`. Here, I am assuming you have authored an `app.config` file that contains the correct connection string data (and that you have referenced System.Configuration.dll and imported the System.Configuration namespace). Also note that there is a call to a private helper function, BuildTableRelationship(), as shown here:

```
Public Sub New()
  InitializeComponent()

  ' Get connection string.
  cnStr = ConfigurationManager.ConnectionStrings _
    ("AutoLotSqlProvider").ConnectionString

  ' Create adapters.
  invTableAdapter = New SqlDataAdapter("Select * from Inventory", cnStr)
  custTableAdapter = New SqlDataAdapter("Select * from Customers", cnStr)
  ordersTableAdapter = New SqlDataAdapter("Select * from Orders", cnStr)

  ' Autogenerate commands.
  sqlCBInventory = New SqlCommandBuilder(invTableAdapter)
  sqlCBOrders = New SqlCommandBuilder(ordersTableAdapter)
  sqlCBCustomers = New SqlCommandBuilder(custTableAdapter)

  ' Add tables to DS.
  invTableAdapter.Fill(autoLotDS, "Inventory")
  custTableAdapter.Fill(autoLotDS, "Customers")
  ordersTableAdapter.Fill(autoLotDS, "Orders")

  ' Build relations between tables.
  BuildTableRelationship()

  ' Bind to grids.
  dataGridViewInventory.DataSource = autoLotDS.Tables("Inventory")
  dataGridViewCustomers.DataSource = autoLotDS.Tables("Customers")
  dataGridViewOrders.DataSource = autoLotDS.Tables("Orders")
End Sub
```

Building the Table Relationships

The BuildTableRelationship() helper function does the grunt work to add two DataRelation objects into the autoLotDS object. Recall from Chapter 22 that the AutoLot database expresses a number of parent/child relationships, accounted for with the following code:

```
Private Sub BuildTableRelationship()
  ' Create CustomerOrder data relation object.
  Dim dr As New DataRelation("CustomerOrder", _
    autoLotDS.Tables("Customers").Columns("CustID"), _
    autoLotDS.Tables("Orders").Columns("CustID"))
  autoLotDS.Relations.Add(dr)

  ' Create InventoryOrder data relation object.
  dr = New DataRelation("InventoryOrder", _
    autoLotDS.Tables("Inventory").Columns("CarID"), _
    autoLotDS.Tables("Orders").Columns("CarID"))
  autoLotDS.Relations.Add(dr)
End Sub
```

Note that when creating a DataRelation object, you establish a friendly string moniker with the first parameter (you'll see the usefulness of doing so in just a minute) as well as the keys used to build the relationship itself. Notice that the parent table (the second constructor parameter) is specified before the child table (the third constructor parameter).

Updating the Database Tables

Now that the DataSet has been filled and disconnected from the data source, you can manipulate each DataTable locally. To do so, simply insert, update, or delete values from any of the three DataGridViews. When you are ready to submit the data back for processing, click the Update button. The code behind the related Click event should be clear at this point:

```
Private Sub btnUpdateDatabase_Click(ByVal sender As System.Object, _
  ByVal e As System.EventArgs) Handles btnUpdateDatabase.Click
  Try
    invTableAdapter.Update(autoLotDS, "Inventory")
    custTableAdapter.Update(autoLotDS, "Customers")
    ordersTableAdapter.Update(autoLotDS, "Orders")
  Catch ex As Exception
    MessageBox.Show(ex.Message)
  End Try
End Sub
```

Now run your application and perform various updates. When you rerun the application, you should find that your grids are populated with the recent changes.

Navigating Between Related Tables

To illustrate how a DataRelation allows you to move between related tables programmatically, extend your UI to include a new Button (named btnGetOrderInfo), a related TextBox (named txtCustID), and a descriptive Label (I grouped these controls within a GroupBox simply for visual appeal). Figure 23-14 shows one possible UI of the application.

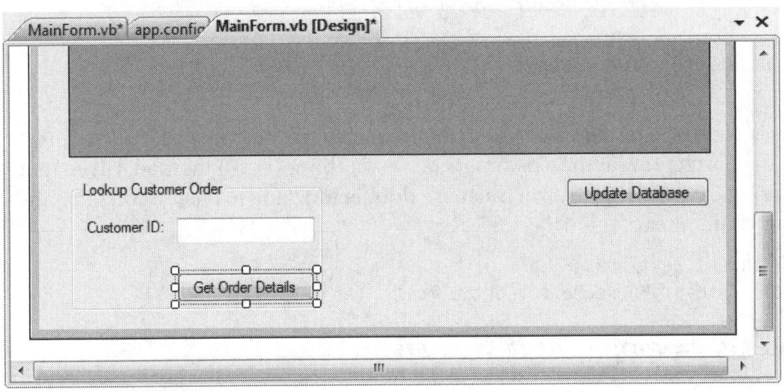

Figure 23-14. *The updated UI allows the user to look up customer order information.*

Using this updated UI, the end user is able to enter the ID of a customer and retrieve all the relevant information about that customer's order (name, order ID, car order, etc.), which will be formatted into a String variable that is eventually displayed within a message box. Ponder the code behind the new Button's Click event handler:

```
Private Sub btnGetOrderInfo_Click(ByVal sender As System.Object, _
  ByVal e As System.EventArgs) Handles btnGetOrderInfo.Click
  Dim strOrderInfo As String = String.Empty
  Dim drsCust As DataRow() = Nothing
  Dim drsOrder As DataRow() = Nothing

  ' Get the customer ID in the text box.
  Dim custID As Integer = Integer.Parse(Me.txtCustID.Text)

  ' Now based on custID, get the correct row in Customers table.
  drsCust = autoLotDS.Tables("Customers").Select( _
    String.Format("CustID = {0}", custID))

  strOrderInfo &= String.Format("Customer {0}: {1} {2}" & vbLf, _
    drsCust(0)("CustID").ToString(), _
    drsCust(0)("FirstName").ToString().Trim(), _
    drsCust(0)("LastName").ToString().Trim())

  ' Navigate from Customers table to Orders table.
  drsOrder = drsCust(0).GetChildRows(autoLotDS.Relations("CustomerOrder"))

  ' Get order number.
  For Each r As DataRow In drsOrder
    strOrderInfo &= String.Format("Order Number: {0}" & vbLf, r("OrderID"))
  Next

  ' Now navigate from Orders table to Inventory table.
  Dim drsInv As DataRow() = _
    drsOrder(0).GetParentRows(autoLotDS.Relations("InventoryOrder"))

  ' Get car info.
  For Each r As DataRow In drsInv
    strOrderInfo &= String.Format("Make: {0}" & vbLf, r("Make"))
    strOrderInfo &= String.Format("Color: {0}" & vbLf, r("Color"))
    strOrderInfo &= String.Format("Pet Name: {0}" & vbLf, r("PetName"))
  Next
  MessageBox.Show(strOrderInfo, "Order Details")
End Sub
```

Let's break down this code step by step. First, you obtain the correct customer ID from the text box and use it to select the correct row in the Customers table, via the `Select()` method. Given that `Select()` returns an *array* of `DataRow` objects, you must use double indexing to ensure you fetch the data for the first (and only) member of this array:

```
' Get the customer ID in the text box.
Dim custID As Integer = Integer.Parse(Me.txtCustID.Text)

' Now based on custID, get the correct row in Customers table.
drsCust = autoLotDS.Tables("Customers").Select( _
  String.Format("CustID = {0}", custID))

strOrderInfo &= String.Format("Customer {0}: {1} {2}" & vbLf, _
  drsCust(0)("CustID").ToString(), _
  drsCust(0)("FirstName").ToString().Trim(), _
  drsCust(0)("LastName").ToString().Trim())
```

Next, you navigate from the Customers table to the Orders table, using the CustomerOrder data relation. Notice that the `DataRow.GetChildRows()` method allows you to grab rows from your child table. Once you do, you can read information out of the table:

```
' Navigate from Customers table to Orders table.
drsOrder = drsCust(0).GetChildRows(autoLotDS.Relations("CustomerOrder"))

' Get order number.
For Each r As DataRow In drsOrder
  strOrderInfo &= String.Format("Order Number: {0}" & vbLf, r("OrderID"))
Next
```

The final step is to navigate from the Orders table to its parent table (Inventory), using the `GetParentRows()` method. At this point, you can read information from the Inventory table using the Make, PetName, and Color columns, as shown here:

```
' Now navigate from Orders table to Inventory table.
Dim drsInv As DataRow() = _
  drsOrder(0).GetParentRows(autoLotDS.Relations("InventoryOrder"))

' Get car info.
For Each r As DataRow In drsInv
  strOrderInfo &= String.Format("Make: {0}" & vbLf, r("Make"))
  strOrderInfo &= String.Format("Color: {0}" & vbLf, r("Color"))
  strOrderInfo &= String.Format("Pet Name: {0}" & vbLf, r("PetName"))
Next
```

Figure 23-15 shows one possible output when specifying a customer ID with the value of 2 (Matt Walton in my copy of the AutoLot database).

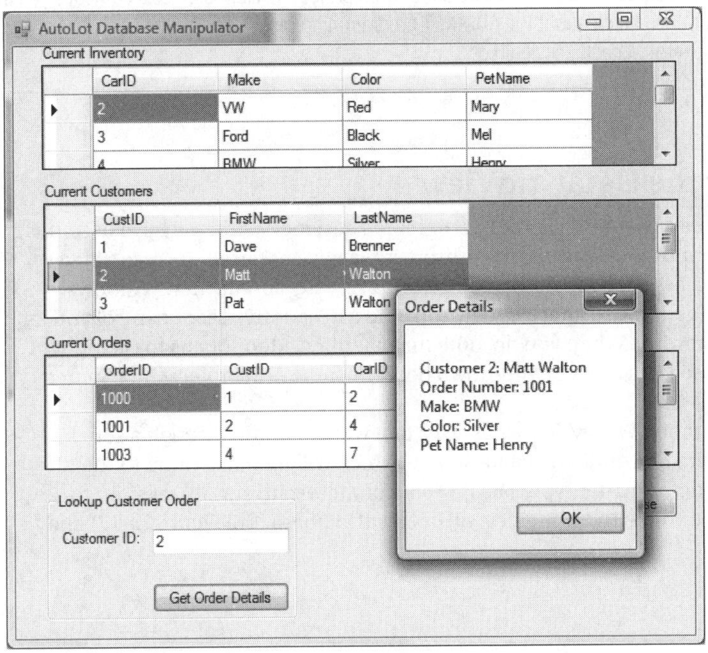

Figure 23-15. *Navigating data relations*

Hopefully, this last example has you convinced of the usefulness of the `DataSet` type. Given that a `DataSet` is completely disconnected from the underlying data source, you can work with an in-memory copy of data and navigate around each table to make any necessary updates, deletes, or inserts. Once you've finished, you can submit your changes to the data store for processing. The end result is a very scalable and robust application.

Source Code The MultitabledDataSetApp project is included under the Chapter 23 subdirectory.

The Data Access Tools of Visual Studio 2008

All of the ADO.NET examples in this text thus far have involved a fair amount of elbow grease, in that we were authoring all data access logic by hand. While we did offload a good amount of said code to a .NET code library (`AutoLotDAL.dll`) for reuse in later chapters of the book, we were still required to manually create the various objects of our data provider before interacting with the relational database.

To wrap up our examination of the disconnected layer of ADO.NET, we will now take a look at a number of tools provided by Visual Studio 2008 that can assist you in authoring data access logic. As you might suspect, this IDE supports a number of visual designers and code generation tools (aka wizards) that can produce a good deal of starter code.

Note Don't get lulled into the belief that you will never be required to author ADO.NET logic by hand, or that the wizard-generated code will always fit the bill 100 percent for your current project. While these tools can save you a significant amount of time, the more you know about the ADO.NET programming model, the better, as this enables you to customize and tweak the generated code as required.

Visually Designing the DataGridView

The first data access shortcut can be found via the `DataGridView` designer. While we have used this widget in previous examples for display and editing purposes, we have not used the associated wizard that will render data access code on our behalf. To begin, create a brand-new Windows Forms Application project named VisualDataGridViewApp. Add a descriptive `Label` control and an instance of the `DataGridView` control. When you do, note that an inline editor opens to the right of the UI widget. From the Choose Data Source drop-down box, select the Add Project Data Source link (see Figure 23-16).

The Data Source Configuration Wizard launches. This tool will guide you through a series of steps that allow you to select and configure a data source, which will then be bound to the `DataGridView` using a custom data adapter type. The first step of the wizard simply asks you to identify the type of data source you wish to interact with. Select Database (see Figure 23-17) and click the Next button.

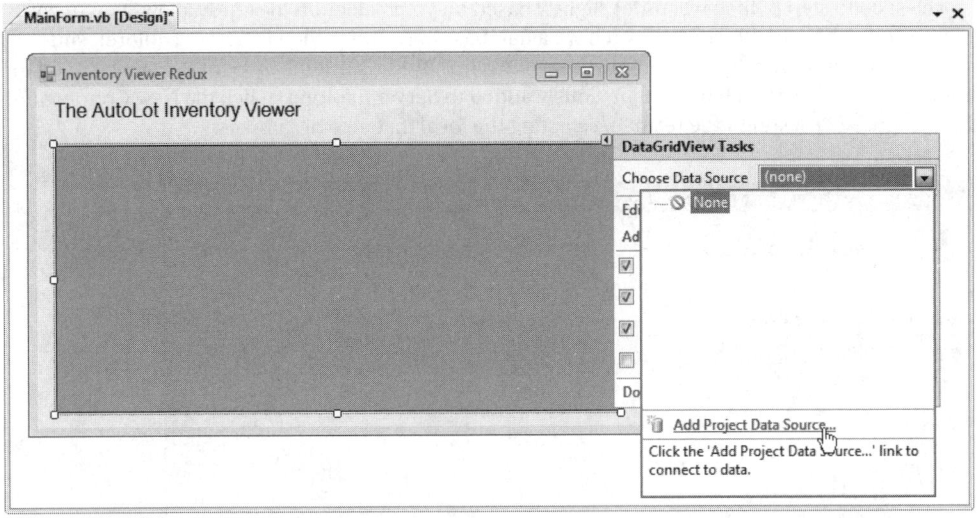

Figure 23-16. *The* `DataGridView` *editor*

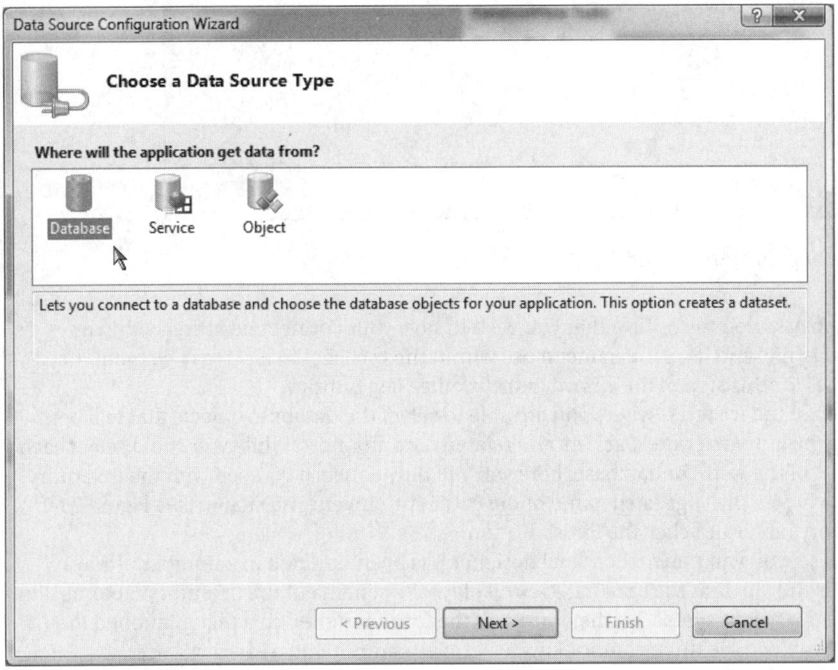

Figure 23-17. *Selecting the type of data source*

■ **Note** This step of the wizard also allows you to connect data that comes from an external XML web service or a custom business object within a separate .NET assembly.

The second step (which will differ slightly based on your selection in step 1) allows you to configure your database connection. If you have a database currently added to Server Explorer, you should find it automatically listed in the drop-down list. If this is not the case (or if you ever need to connect to a database you have not previously added to Server Explorer), click the New Connection button. Figure 23-18 shows the result of selecting the local instance of AutoLot.

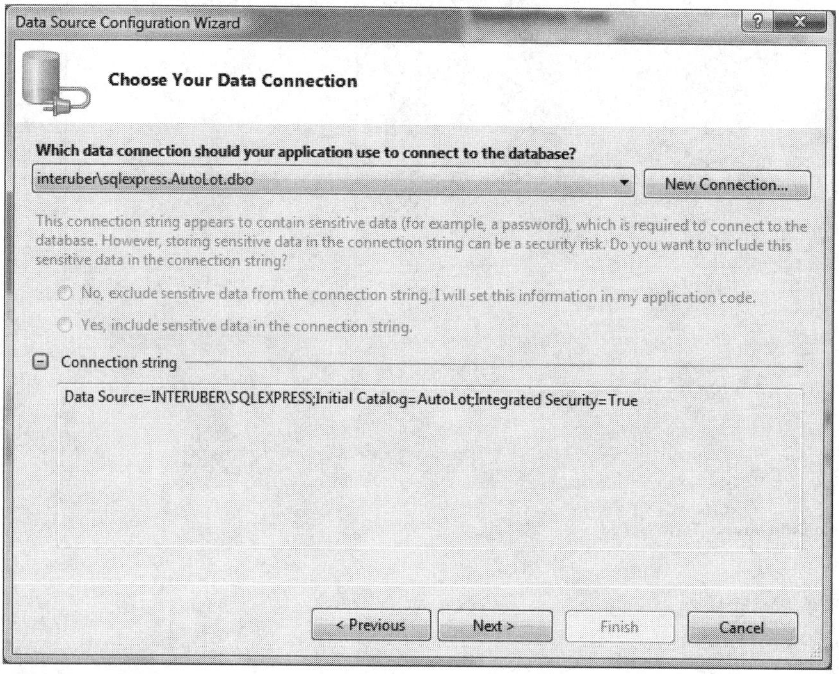

Figure 23-18. *Selecting the AutoLot database*

The third step asks you to confirm that you wish to save your connection string within an external `app.config` file, and if so, the name to use within the `<connectionStrings>` element. Keep the default settings for this step of the wizard and click the Next button.

The final step of the wizard is where you are able to select the database objects that will be accounted for by the autogenerated `DataSet` and related data adapters. While you could select each of the data objects of the AutoLot database, here you will only concern yourself with the Inventory table. Given this, change the suggested name of the `DataSet` to InventoryDataSet (see Figure 23-19), check the Inventory table, and click the Finish button.

Once you do so, you will notice the visual designer has been updated in a number of ways. Most noticeable is the fact that the `DataGridView` displays the schema of the Inventory table, as illustrated by the column headers. Also, on the bottom of the form designer (in a region dubbed the *component tray*), you will see three components: a `DataSet` component, a `BindingSource` component, and a `TableAdapter` component (see Figure 23-20).

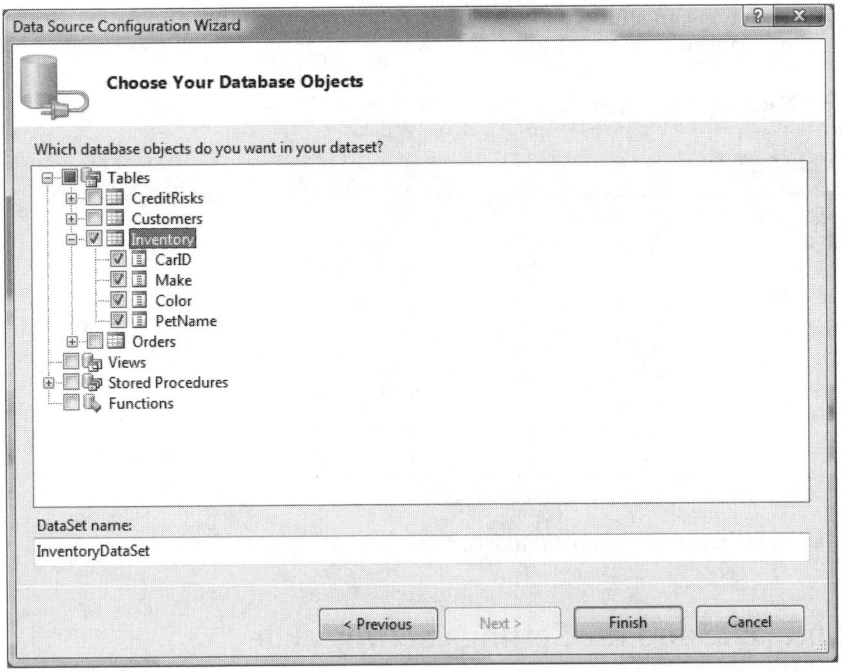

Figure 23-19. *Selecting the Inventory table*

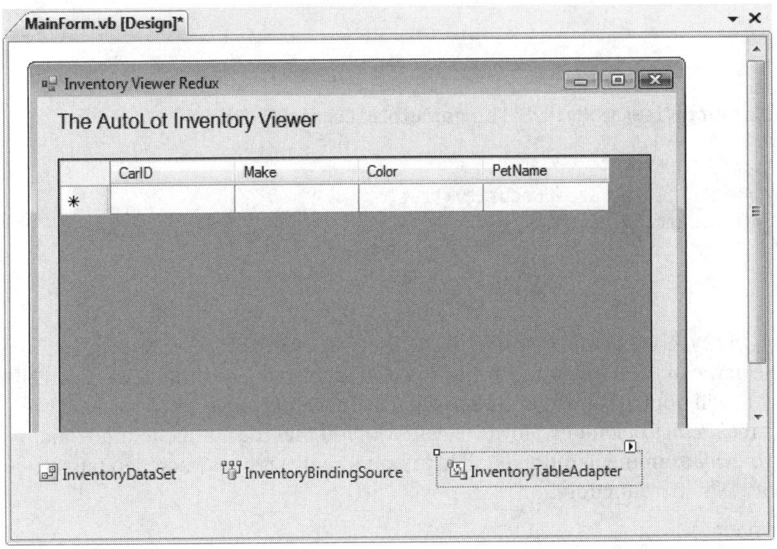

Figure 23-20. *Our Windows Forms project, after running the Data Source Configuration Wizard*

At this point you can run your application, and lo and behold, the grid is filled with the records of the Inventory table, as shown in Figure 23-21.

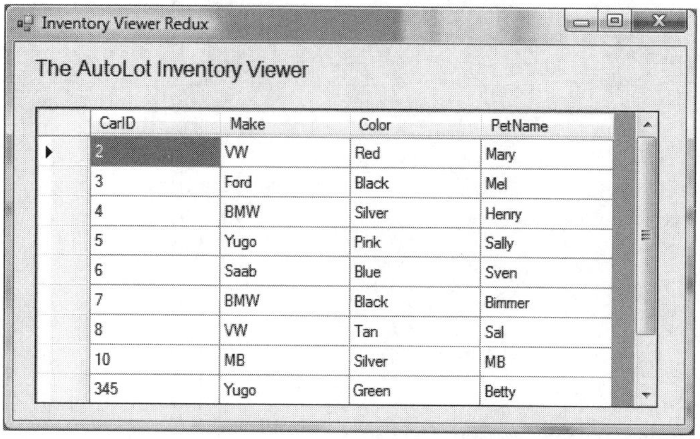

Figure 23-21. *A populated* DataGridView*—no manual coding required!*

The app.config File and the Settings.Settings File

If you examine your Solution Explorer, you will find your project now contains an `app.config` file. If you open this file, you will notice the `name` attribute of the `<add>` element used in previous examples:

```
<?xml version="1.0" encoding="utf-8" ?>
<configuration>
  <configSections>
  </configSections>
  <connectionStrings>
    <add name="VisualDataGridViewApp.My.MySettings.AutoLotConnectionString"
      connectionString=
      "Data Source=(local)\SQLEXPRESS;
      Initial Catalog=AutoLot;Integrated Security=True"
      providerName="System.Data.SqlClient" />
  </connectionStrings>
...
</configuration>
```

Specifically, the lengthy `"VisualDataGridViewApp.My.MySettings.AutoLotConnectionString"` value has been set as the name of the connection string. Even stranger is the fact that if you scan all of the generated code, you will not find any reference to the `ConfigurationManager` type to read the value from the `<connectionStrings>` element. However, you will find that the autogenerated data adapter object (which you will examine in more detail in just a moment) is constructed in part by calling the following private helper function:

```
Private Sub InitConnection()
  Me._connection = New Global.System.Data.SqlClient.SqlConnection
  Me._connection.ConnectionString = _
  Global.VisualDataGridViewApp.My.MySettings.Default.AutoLotConnectionString
End Sub
```

As you can see, the `ConnectionString` property is set via a call to `MySettings.Default`. As it turns out, every Visual Studio 2008 project type maintains a set of application-wide settings that are burned into your assembly as metadata when you compile the application. The short answer is that if you open your compiled application using `reflector.exe` (see Chapter 2), you can view this internal type (see Figure 23-22).

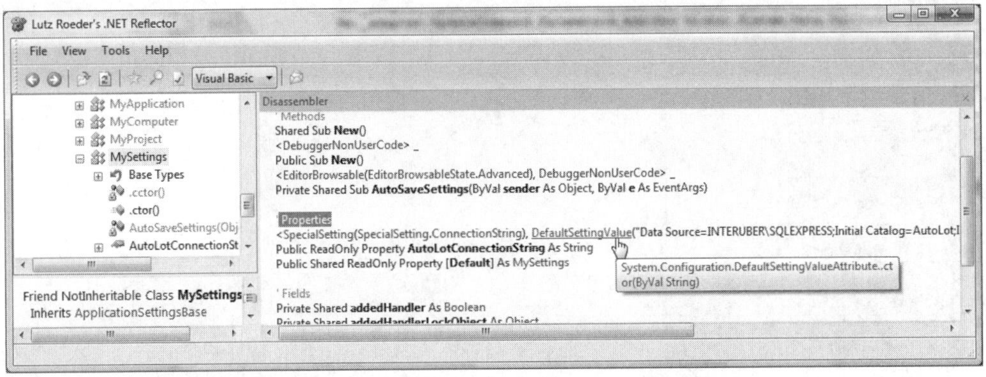

Figure 23-22. *The* `Settings` *object contains an embedded connection string value.*

Given the previous point, it would be possible to deploy your application *without* shipping the `*.config` file, as the embedded value will be used by default if a client-side `*.config` file is not present.

Note The Visual Studio 2008 settings programming model is really quite interesting; however, full coverage is outside of the scope of this chapter (and this edition of the text, for that matter). If you are interested in learning more, look up the topic "Managing Application Settings" in the .NET Framework 3.5 SDK documentation.

Examining the Generated DataSet

Now let's take a look at some of the core aspects of this generated code. First of all, insert a new class diagram type into your project by right-clicking the project icon in Solution Explorer and clicking the View Class Diagram button. Notice that the wizard has created a new `DataSet` type based on your input, which in this case is named `InventoryDataSet`. As you can see, this class defines a handful of members, the most important of which is a property named `Inventory` (see Figure 23-23).

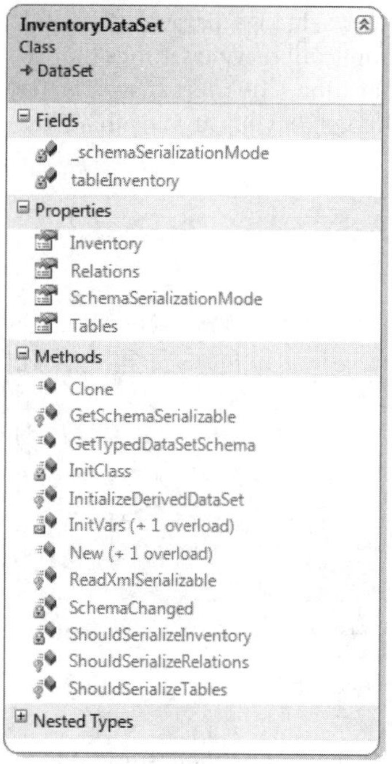

Figure 23-23. *The Data Source Configuration Wizard created a strongly typed* `DataSet`.

If you double-click the `InventoryDataSet.xsd` file within Solution Explorer, you will load the Visual Studio 2008 Dataset Designer (more details on this designer in just a bit). If you right-click on the InventoryDataSet.xsd file within Solution Explorer and select the View Code option, you will notice a fairly empty partial class definition:

```
Partial Class InventoryDataSet
End Class
```

The real action is taking place within the designer-maintained file, `InventoryDataSet.Designer.vb`, which can be viewed once you click the Show All button of Solution Explorer and expand the `*.xsd` file icon. If you open this file using Solution Explorer, you will notice that `InventoryDataSet` is actually extending the `DataSet` class type. When you (or a wizard) create a class extending `DataSet`, you are building what is termed a *strongly typed* `DataSet`. One benefit of using strongly typed `DataSet` objects is that they contain a number of properties that map directly to the database tables' names. Thus, rather than having to drill into the collection of tables using the `Tables` property, you can simply use the `Inventory` property. Consider the following partial code, commented for clarity:

```
' This is all designer-generated code!
Partial Public Class InventoryDataSet
  Inherits Global.System.Data.DataSet

  Private tableInventory As InventoryDataTable
```

```
  ' Each constructor calls a helper method named InitClass().
  Public Sub New()
  ...
    Me.InitClass()
...
  End Sub

  ' InitClass() preps the DataSet and adds the InventoryDataTable
  ' to the Tables collection.
  Private Sub InitClass()
    Me.DataSetName = "InventoryDataSet"
    Me.Prefix = ""
    Me.Namespace = "http://tempuri.org/InventoryDataSet.xsd"
    Me.EnforceConstraints = true
    Me.SchemaSerializationMode = _
      Global.System.Data.SchemaSerializationMode.IncludeSchema
    Me.tableInventory = New InventoryDataTable
    MyBase.Tables.Add(Me.tableInventory)
  End Sub

  ' The read-only Inventory property returns
  ' the InventoryDataTable member variable.
  Public ReadOnly Property Inventory() As InventoryDataTable
    Get
      Return Me.tableInventory
    End Get
  End Property
End Class
```

In addition to wrapping the details of maintaining a DataTable object, the designer-generated strongly typed DataSet could contain similar logic to expose any DataRelation objects (which we do not currently have) that represent the connections between each of the tables.

Examining the Generated DataTable and DataRow

In a similar fashion, the wizard created a *strongly typed* DataTable class and a *strongly typed* DataRow class, both of which have been nested within the InventoryDataSet class. The InventoryDataTable class (which is the same type as the member variable of the strongly typed DataSet we just examined) defines a set of properties that are based on the column names of the physical Inventory table (CarIDColumn, ColorColumn, MakeColumn, and PetNameColumn) as well as a custom indexer and a Count property to obtain the current number of records.

More interestingly, this strongly typed DataTable class defines a set of methods (see Figure 23-24) that allow you to insert, locate, and delete rows within the table using strongly typed members (an attractive alternative to manually navigating the Rows and Columns indexers).

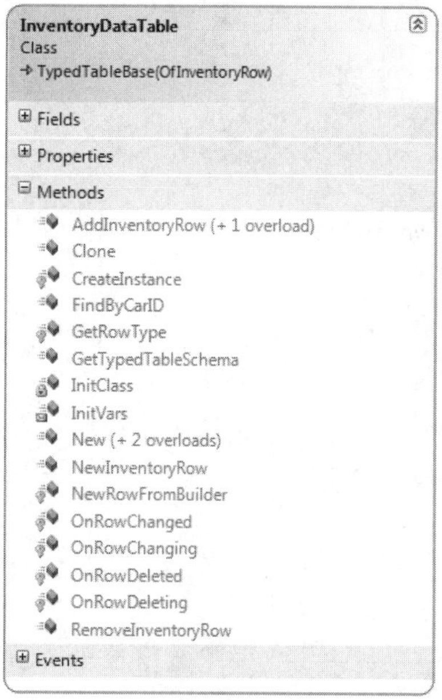

Figure 23-24. *The custom* `DataTable` *type*

■Note The strongly typed `DataTable` also defines a handful of events you can handle to monitor changes to your table data.

The custom `DataRow` type is far less exotic than the generated `DataSet` or `DataTable`. As shown in Figure 23-25, this class extends `DataRow` and exposes properties that map directly to the schema of the Inventory table (also be aware that the columns are appropriately typed).

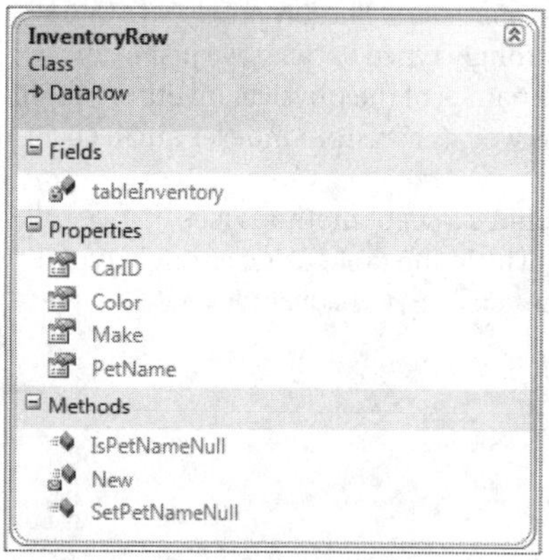

Figure 23-25. *The custom* `DataRow` *type*

Examining the Generated Data Adapter

Having some strong typing for our disconnected types is a solid benefit of using the Data Source Configuration Wizard, given that adding strongly typed classes by hand would be tedious (but entirely possible). This same wizard was kind enough to generate a strongly typed data adapter object that is able to fill and update the `InventoryDataSet` and `InventoryDataTable` class types (see Figure 23-26).

The autogenerated `InventoryTableAdapter` type maintains a collection of `SqlCommand` objects, each of which has a fully populated set of `SqlParameter` objects (this alone is a massive time-saver). Furthermore, this strongly typed data adapter provides a set of properties to extract the underlying connection, transaction, and data adapter objects, as well as a property to obtain an array representing each command type. The obvious benefit is you did not have to author the code!

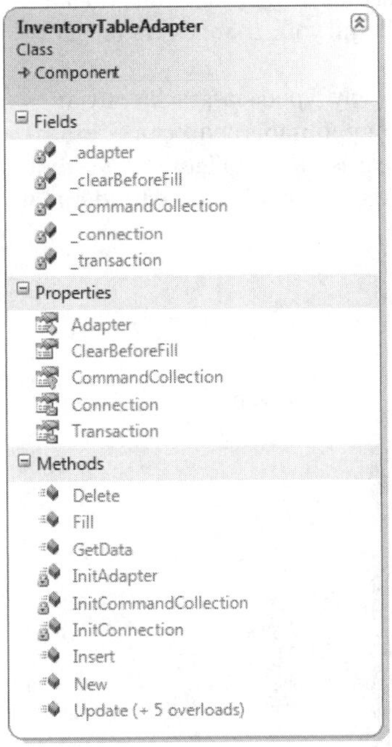

Figure 23-26. *A strongly typed data adapter that operates on the strongly typed types*

Using the Generated Types in Code

If you examine the `Load` event handler of the form-derived type, you will find that the `Fill()` method of the custom data adapter is called upon startup, passing in the custom `DataTable` maintained by the custom `DataSet`:

```
Public Class MainForm
  Private Sub MainForm_Load(ByVal sender As System.Object, _
  ByVal e As System.EventArgs) Handles MyBase.Load
  'TODO: This line of code loads data into
  ' the 'InventoryDataSet.Inventory' table. You can move, or remove it, as needed.
  Me.InventoryTableAdapter.Fill(Me.InventoryDataSet.Inventory)
  End Sub
End Class
```

You can use this same custom data adapter object to update changes to the grid. Update the UI of your form with a single Button control (named btnUpdateInventory). Handle the Click event, and author the following code within the event handler:

```
Private Sub btnUpdateInventory_Click(ByVal sender As System.Object, _
  ByVal e As System.EventArgs) Handles btnUpdateInventory.Click
  ' This will push any changes within the Inventory table back to
  ' the database for processing.
  Me.InventoryTableAdapter.Update(Me.InventoryDataSet.Inventory)

  ' Get fresh copy for grid.
  Me.InventoryTableAdapter.Fill(Me.InventoryDataSet.Inventory)
End Sub
```

Run your application once again; add, delete, or update the records displayed in the grid; and click the Update button. When you run the program again, you will find your changes are present and accounted for.

Understand that you are able to make use of each of these strongly typed classes directly in your code, in (more or less) the same way you have been doing throughout this chapter. For example, assume you have updated your form with a new chunk of UI real estate (see Figure 23-27) that allows the user to enter a new record using a series of text boxes (granted, this is a bit redundant for this example, as the DataGridView will do so on your behalf).

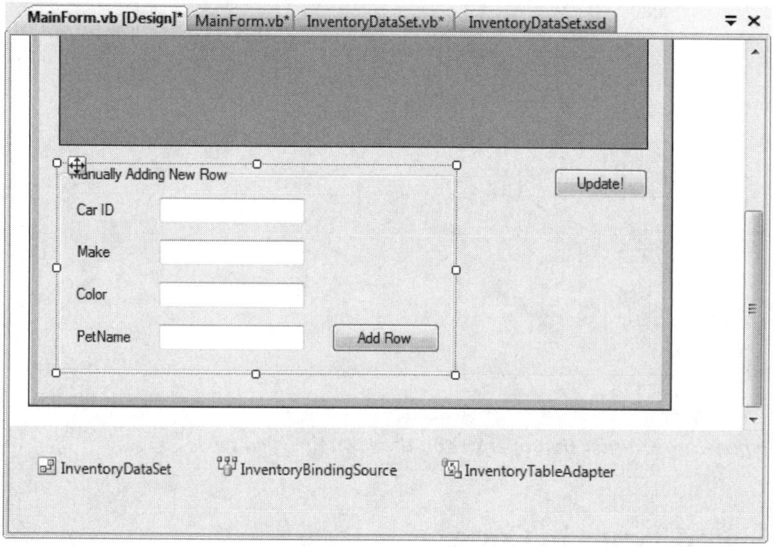

Figure 23-27. *A simple update to the form type*

Within the Click event handler of the new Button, you could author the following code:

```
Private Sub btnAddRow_Click(ByVal sender As System.Object, _
  ByVal e As System.EventArgs) Handles btnAddRow.Click
  ' Get data from widgets.
  Dim id As Integer = Integer.Parse(txtCarID.Text)
  Dim make As String = txtMake.Text
  Dim color As String = txtColor.Text
  Dim petName As String = txtPetName.Text
```

```
    ' Use custom adapter to add row to the database.
    InventoryTableAdapter.Insert(id, make, color, petName)

    ' Refill table data from the database.
    Me.InventoryTableAdapter.Fill(Me.InventoryDataSet.Inventory)
End Sub
```

Or, if you so choose, you can manually add a new row:

```
Private Sub btnAddRow_Click(ByVal sender As Object, _
  ByVal e As EventArgs) Handles btnAddRow.Click
  ' Get new Row.
  Dim newRow As InventoryDataSet.InventoryRow = _
    InventoryDataSet.Inventory.NewInventoryRow()
  newRow.CarID = Integer.Parse(txtCarID.Text)
  newRow.Make = txtMake.Text
  newRow.Color = txtColor.Text
  newRow.PetName = txtPetName.Text
  InventoryDataSet.Inventory.AddInventoryRow(newRow)

  ' Use custom adapter to add row.
  InventoryTableAdapter.Update(InventoryDataSet.Inventory)

  ' Refill table data.
  Me.InventoryTableAdapter.Fill(Me.InventoryDataSet.Inventory)
End Sub
```

Source Code The VisualDataGridViewApp project is included under the Chapter 23 subdirectory.

Decoupling Autogenerated Code from the UI Layer

To close, allow me to point out that while the Data Source Configuration Wizard launched by the DataGridView has done a fantastic job of authoring a ton of grungy code on our behalf, the previous example hard-coded the data access logic directly within the user interface layer—a major design faux pas. Ideally, this sort of code belongs in our AutoLotDAL.dll assembly (or some other data access library). However, you may wonder how to harvest the code generated via the DataGridView's associated wizard in a Class Library project, given that there certainly is no Forms designer for this project type by default.

Thankfully, you can activate the data design tools of Visual Studio 2008 from any sort of project (UI based or otherwise) without the need to copy and paste massive amounts of code between projects. To illustrate some of your options, open your AutoLotDAL project once again and insert into your project a new DataSet type (named AutoLotDataSet) via the Project ➤ Add New Item menu option (see Figure 23-28).

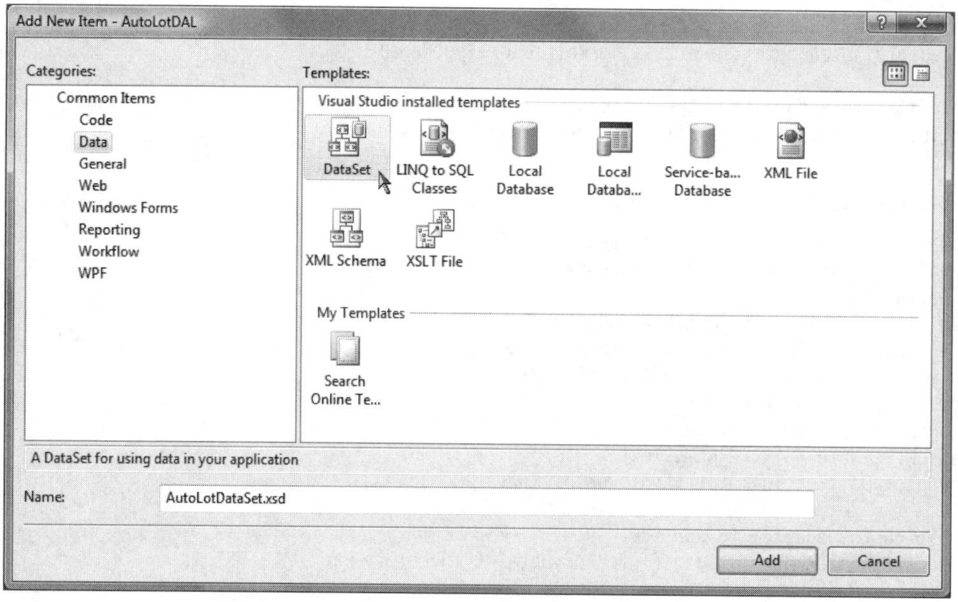

Figure 23-28. *Inserting a new* `DataSet`

This will open a blank Dataset Designer surface. At this point, use Server Explorer to connect to a given database (you should already have a connection to AutoLot), and drag and drop each database object (here, I did not bother to drag over the CreditRisk table) you wish to generate onto the surface. In Figure 23-29, you can see each of the custom aspects of AutoLot is now accounted for (be sure to right-click the designer surface and select Show Relation Labels).

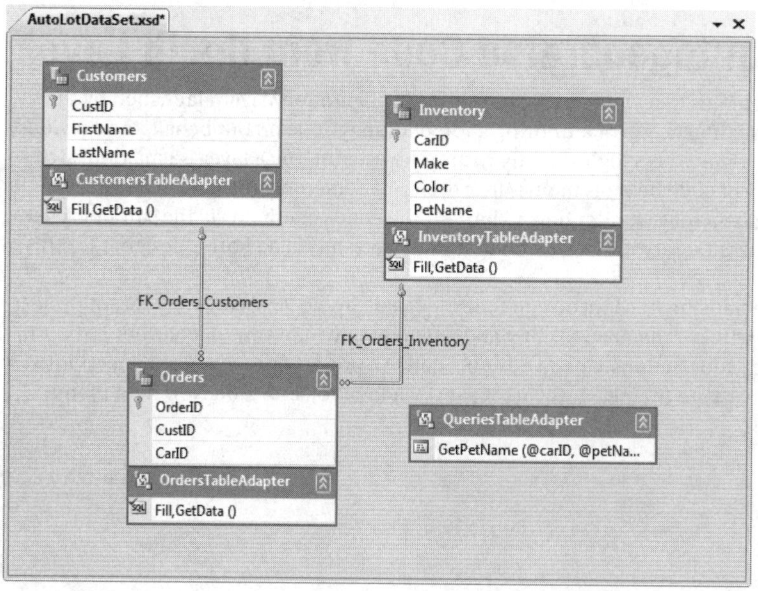

Figure 23-29. *Our custom strongly typed types, this time within a Class Library project*

If you look at the generated code, you will find a new batch of strongly typed `DataSets`, `DataTables`, and `DataRows`, and a custom data adapter object for each table. Because the `AutoLotDataSet` type contains code to fill and update all of the tables of the AutoLot database, the amount of code autogenerated is more than an eye-popping 3,000 lines! However, much of this is grungy infrastructure you can remain blissfully unaware of. As you can see in Figure 23-30, the `AutoLotDataSet` type is constructed in a way that is very close to the previous `InventoryDataSet` type.

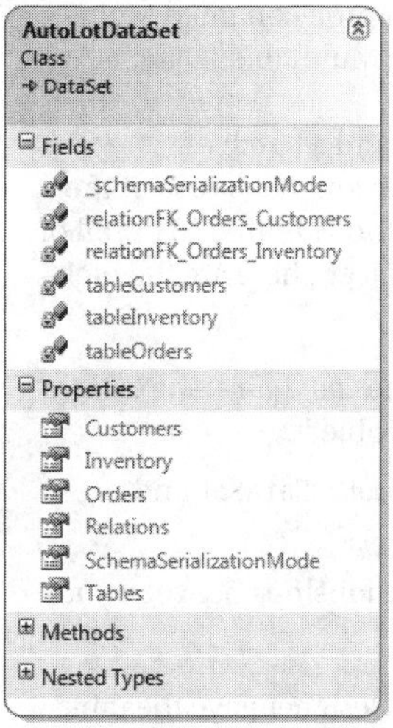

Figure 23-30. *The* `AutoLotDataSet`

As well, you will find a strongly typed data adapter object for each of the database objects you dragged onto the Dataset Designer surface as well as a helpful type named `TableAdapterManager` that provides a single entry point to each object (see Figure 23-31).

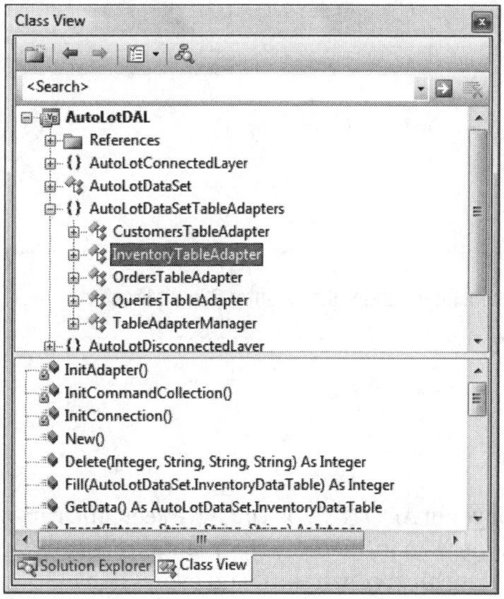

Figure 23-31. *The autogenerated data adapter objects*

■ **Source Code** The AutoLotDAL (Part 3) project is included under the Chapter 23 subdirectory.

A UI Front End: MultitabledDataSetApp (Redux)

Using these autogenerated types is quite simple, provided you are comfortable working with the disconnected layer. The downloadable source code for this text contains a project named MultitabledDataSetApp-Redux, which, as the name implies, is an update to the MultitabledDataSetApp project you created earlier in this chapter.

Recall that the original example made use of a loosely typed `DataSet` and a batch of `SqlDataAdapter` objects to move the table data to and fro. This updated version makes use of the third iteration of `AutoLotDAL.dll` and the wizard-generated types. While I won't bother to list all of the code here (as it is more or less the same as the first iteration of this project), here are the highlights:

- You no longer need to manually author an `app.config` file or use the `ConfigurationManager` to obtain the connection string, as this is handled via the `Settings` object.
- You are now making use of the strongly typed classes within the `AutoLotDataSet` and `AutoLotDataSetTableAdapters` namespaces.
- You are no longer required to manually create or configure the relationships between your tables, as the Dataset Designer has done so automatically.

Regarding the last bullet point, be aware that the names the Dataset Designer gave the table relationships are *different* from the names we gave to them in the first iteration of this project. Therefore, the `btnGetOrderInfo_Click()` method must be updated to use the correct relationship names (which can be seen on the designer surface of the Dataset Designer), for example:

```
Private Sub btnGetOrderInfo_Click(ByVal sender As System.Object, _
  ByVal e As System.EventArgs) Handles btnGetOrderInfo.Click
...
  ' Need to update relationship name!
  drsOrder = drsCust(0).GetChildRows(autoLotDS.Relations("FK_Orders_Customers"))
...
  ' Need to update relationship name!
  Dim drsInv() As DataRow = _
    drsOrder(0).GetParentRows(autoLotDS.Relations("FK_Orders_Inventory"))
...
End Sub
```

■ **Source Code** The MultitabledDataSetApp-Redux project is included under the Chapter 23 subdirectory.

Summary

This chapter dove into the details of the disconnected layer of ADO.NET. As you have seen, the centerpiece of the disconnected layer is the `DataSet`. This type is an in-memory representation of any number of tables and any number of optional interrelationships, constraints, and expressions.

The beauty of establishing relations on your local tables is that you are able to programmatically navigate between them while disconnected from the remote data store.

You also examined the role of the data adapter type in this chapter. Using this type (and the related `SelectCommand`, `InsertCommand`, `UpdateCommand`, and `DeleteCommand` properties), the adapter can resolve changes in the `DataSet` with the original data store. As well, you learned how to navigate the object model of a `DataSet` using the brute-force manual approach, as well as via strongly typed objects, typically generated by the data designer tools of Visual Studio 2008.

CHAPTER 24

Programming with the LINQ APIs

Now that you have spent the previous two chapters examining the ADO.NET programming model, we are in a position to return to the topic of Language Integrated Query (LINQ). Here, you will begin by examining the role of *LINQ to ADO.NET*. This particular term is used to describe two related facets of the LINQ programming model, specifically LINQ to DataSet and LINQ to SQL. As you would expect, these APIs allow you to apply LINQ queries to relational databases and ADO.NET `DataSet` objects.

This chapter examines the role of LINQ to XML. This aspect of LINQ not only allows you to extract data from an XML document using the expected set of query operators, but also enables you to load, save, and generate XML documents in an extremely straightforward manner (much more so than working with the types packaged in the `System.Xml.dll` assembly).

On a related note, this chapter also examines several new aspects of Visual Basic 2008 that facilitate the construction and manipulation of XML data. As you will see, the latest version of VB now allows you to define XML elements (and their attributes, processing instructions, etc.) directly within a `*.vb` code file using *XML literals*. Furthermore, XML literals may be manipulated via *XML axis properties*. In a nutshell, these language features can simplify how you interact with LINQ to XML, as the compiler will transform your XML literals into the equivalent LINQ to XML object model.

Note This chapter assumes you are already comfortable with the LINQ programming model as described in Chapter 14.

The Role of LINQ to ADO.NET

As explained in Chapter 14, LINQ is a programming model that allows programmers to build strongly typed query expressions that can be applied to a wide variety of data stores (arrays, collections, databases, XML documents). While it is true that you always use the same query operators regardless of the target of your LINQ query, the LINQ to ADO.NET API provides some additional types and infrastructure to enable LINQ/database integration.

LINQ to ADO.NET is a blanket term that describes two database-centric aspects of LINQ. First we have LINQ to DataSet. This API is essentially a set of extensions to the standard ADO.NET DataSet programming model that allows `DataSets`, `DataTables`, and `DataRows` to be a natural target for a LINQ query expression. Beyond using the types of `System.Core.dll`, LINQ to DataSet requires your projects to make use of auxiliary types within the `System.Data.DataSetExtensions.dll` assembly.

The second component of LINQ to ADO.NET is LINQ to SQL. This API allows you to interact with a relational database by abstracting away the underlying ADO.NET data types (connections, commands, data adapters, etc.) through the use of *entity classes*. Through these entity classes, you are able to represent relational data using an intuitive object model and manipulate the data using LINQ queries. The LINQ to SQL functionality is contained within the `System.Data.Linq.dll` assembly.

■ **Note** As of .NET 3.5, LINQ to SQL does not support a data provider factory model (see Chapter 22). Therefore, when using this API, your data must be contained within Microsoft SQL Server. The LINQ to DataSet API, however, is agnostic in nature, as the `DataSet` being manipulated can come from any relational database.

Programming with LINQ to DataSet

Recall from the previous chapter that the `DataSet` type is the centerpiece of the disconnected layer and is used to represent a cached copy of interrelated `DataTable` objects and (optionally) the relationships between them. On a related note, you may also recall that the data within a `DataSet` can be manipulated in three distinct manners:

- Indexer syntax
- Data table readers
- Strongly typed data members

When you make use of the various indexers of the `DataSet` and `DataTable` types, you are able to interact with the contained data in a fairly straightforward but very loosely typed manner. Recall that this approach requires you to treat the data as a tabular block of cells. For example:

```
Sub PrintDataWithIndxers(ByVal dt As DataTable)
  For curRow As Integer = 0 To dt.Rows.Count - 1
    ' Print the DataTable using indexer syntax.
    For curCol As Integer = 0 To dt.Columns.Count - 1
      Console.Write(dt.Rows(curRow)(curCol).ToString() & vbTab)
    Next
    Console.WriteLine()
  Next
End Sub
```

The `CreateDataReader()` method of the `DataTable` type offers a second approach, where you are able to treat the data in the `DataTable` as a linear set of rows to be processed in a sequential manner:

```
Sub PrintDataWithDataTableReader(ByVal dt As DataTable)
  ' Get the DataTableReader type.
  Dim dtReader As DataTableReader = dt.CreateDataReader()
  While dtReader.Read()
    For i As Integer = 0 To dtReader.FieldCount - 1
      Console.Write("{0}" & vbTab, dtReader.GetValue(i))
    Next
    Console.WriteLine()
  End While
  dtReader.Close()
End Sub
```

Finally, using a strongly typed DataSet yields a code base that allows you to interact with data in the object using properties that map to the actual column names in the relational database. Recall from Chapter 23 that we used strongly typed objects to allow us to author record insertion code such as the following:

```
Sub AddRowWithTypedDataSet()
  Dim invDA As New InventoryTableAdapter()
  Dim inv As AutoLotDataSet.InventoryDataTable = invDA.GetData()
  inv.AddInventoryRow(999, "Ford", "Yellow", "Sal")
  invDA.Update(inv)
End Sub
```

While all of these approaches have their place, LINQ to DataSet provides yet another option to manipulate the contained data using LINQ query expressions. To understand how to do so requires examining the types of System.Data.DataSetExtensions.dll.

The Role of the DataSet Extensions

The System.Data.DataSetExtensions.dll assembly extends the System.Data namespace with a handful of new types (see Figure 24-1).

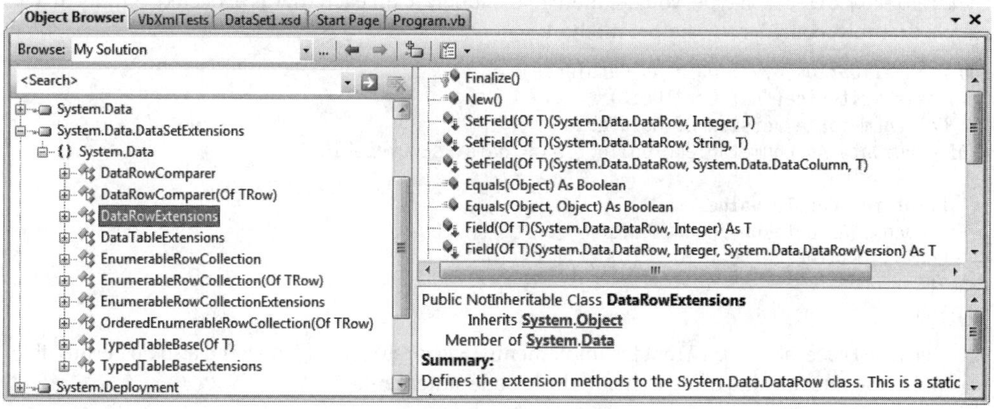

Figure 24-1. *The* System.Data.DataSetExtensions.dll *assembly*

Far and away the two most useful types are DataTableExtensions and DataRowExtensions. As their names imply, these types extend the functionality of DataTable and DataRow using a set of extension methods. The other key type is TypedTableBaseExtensions, which defines extension methods that can be applied to strongly typed DataSet objects to make the internal DataTable objects LINQ aware. All of the remaining members within the System.Data.DataSetExtensions.dll assembly are pure infrastructure and not intended to be used directly in your code base.

Obtaining a LINQ-Compatible DataTable

To illustrate using the DataSet extensions, assume you have a new VB Console Application named LinqOverDataSet. Be aware that when you create projects that target .NET 3.5, you will automatically be given a reference to System.Core.dll and System.Data.DataSetExtensions.dll; however, for this example, add an additional assembly reference to the AutoLotDAL.dll assembly you created in Chapter 23, and update your initial code file with the following logic:

```
Imports AutoLotDisconnectedLayer

Module Program
  Sub Main()
    Console.WriteLine("***** LINQ over DataSet *****" & vbLf)
    ' Get a DataTable containing the current Inventory
    ' of the AutoLot database (modify connection string if necessary).
    Dim dal As New InventoryDALDisLayer _
      ("Data Source=(local)\SQLEXPRESS;Initial Catalog=AutoLot;" & _
       "Integrated Security=True")
    Dim data As DataTable = dal.GetAllInventory()

    ' We will add methods to invoke here!

    Console.ReadLine()
  End Sub
End Module
```

When you wish to transform an ADO.NET DataTable into a LINQ-compatible object, you can call the AsEnumerable() extension method defined by the DataTableExtensions type. This will return to you an EnumerableRowCollection object, which contains a collection of DataRows. Using the EnumerableRowCollection type, you are then able to operate on each row as expected. By way of a simple example, consider this helper method:

```
Sub PrintAllCarIDs(ByVal data As DataTable)
  Console.WriteLine("All Car IDs:")
  ' Get enumerable version of DataTable.
  Dim enumData As EnumerableRowCollection = data.AsEnumerable()

  ' Print the car ID values.
  For Each r As DataRow In enumData
    Console.WriteLine("Car ID = {0}", r("CarID"))
  Next
End Sub
```

Because EnumerableRowCollection implements IEnumerable(Of T), it would also be permissible to capture the return value using either of these code statements:

```
' Store return value as IEnumerable(Of T).
Dim enumData As IEnumerable(Of DataRow) = data.AsEnumerable()

' Store return value implicitly.
Dim enumData = data.AsEnumerable()
```

At this point, we have not actually applied a LINQ query; the point is that the enumData object is now able to be the target of a LINQ query expression. Do notice, however, that the EnumerableRowCollection does indeed contain a collection of DataRow objects, as we are applying a type indexer against each subobject to print out the value of the CarID column.

In most cases, you will not need to declare a variable of type EnumerableRowCollection to hold the return value of AsEnumerable(). Rather, you can invoke this method from within the query expression itself. Here is a more interesting method, which obtains a projection of CarIDs/Colors from all entries in the DataTable where the CarID is greater than the value of 5:

```
Sub ApplyLinqQuery(ByVal data As DataTable)
  ' Project a new result set containing
  ' the ID/color for rows with a CarID > 5
  Dim cars = From car In data.AsEnumerable() Where _
             CType(car("CarID"), Integer) > 5 _
```

```
            Select New With _
            { _
              .ID = CType(car("CarID"), Integer), _
              .Color = CType(car("Color"), String) _
            }

  Console.WriteLine("Cars with ID greater than 5:")
  For Each item In cars
    Console.WriteLine("-> CarID = {0} is {1}", item.ID, item.Color)
  Next
End Sub
```

Implicit Inference of EnumerableRowCollection

As just described, an ADO.NET DataTable cannot be the direct target of a LINQ query until you obtain an enumerable-compatible version of the data via a call to the AsEnumerable() extension method. However, as a convenience, the Visual Basic 2008 programming language will allow you to build a LINQ query that makes this fact appear otherwise. For example, the previous LINQ query could be represented as so (notice we are no longer calling AsEnumerable() off the data variable):

```
' VB will assume the call to AsEnumerable
' when a DataTable is the target of a LINQ query.
Dim cars = From car In data Where _
  CType(car("CarID"), Integer) > 5 _
  Select New With _
  { _
    .ID = CType(car("CarID"), Integer), _
    .Color = CType(car("Color"), String) _
  }
```

If you use a disassembly tool such as ildasm.exe or reflector.exe to view the internal representation of this LINQ query, you will find that the compiler has inserted a call to AsEnumerable() on your behalf! This will work just fine, even when you enable Option Explicit or Option Strict (or for that matter, disable Option Infer).

Given this freebie, you can save yourself a bit of typing time by simply using your DataTable object as is within a LINQ query. Do always be aware, however, that in the background the AsEnumerable() extension method has been called internally.

■ **Note** This level of inference is not found in all .NET programming languages. For example, if you apply a LINQ query to a DataTable using C#, calling AsEnumerable() is mandatory.

The Role of the DataRowExtensions.Field(Of T)() Extension Method

One undesirable aspect of the current LINQ query expression is that we are making use of numerous casting operations and DataRow indexers to gather the result set, which could result in runtime exceptions if we attempt to cast to an incompatible data type (assuming Option Strict is enabled). To inject some strong typing into our query, we can make use of the Field(Of T)() extension method of the DataRow type. By doing so, we increase the type safety of our query, as the compatibility of data types is checked at compile time. Consider the following update:

```
Dim cars = From car In data Where _
  car.Field(Of Integer)("CarID") > 5 _
  Select New With _
  { _
    .ID = car.Field(Of Integer)("CarID"), _
    .Color = car.Field(Of String)("Color") _
  }
```

Notice in this case we are able to invoke `Field(Of T)()` and specify a type parameter to represent the underlying data type of the column. As an argument to this method, we pass in the column name itself. Given the additional compile-time checking, consider it a best practice to make use of `Field(Of T)()` when processing the roles of a `EnumerableRowCollection`, rather than the `DataRow` indexer.

Note When `Option Strict` is disabled, it is possible in some cases to directly process the columns within a `DataRow` without using explicit casting and without calling `Field(Of T)`. Recall that when `Option Strict` is `Off`, all variables not defined with an `As` clause default to `System.Object`. Therefore, if you do not explicitly call `Field(Of T)` or call it using an explicit cast, you will incur some performance penalties (and in some cases, you will generate coding errors, such as when you apply VB operators directly to the implicitly typed column).

Beyond the fact that the `AsEnumerable()` method transforms a `DataTable` into a LINQ-compatible object, the overall format of the LINQ query is identical to what you have already seen in Chapter 14. Given this point, I won't bother to repeat the details of the various LINQ operators here. If you wish to see additional examples, look up the topic "LINQ to DataSet Examples" in the .NET Framework 3.5 SDK documentation.

Hydrating New DataTables from LINQ Queries

It is also possible to easily populate the data of a new `DataTable` based on the results of a LINQ query, provided that you are *not* using projections. When you have a result set where the underlying type can be represented as `IEnumerable(Of T)`, you can call the `CopyToDataTable(Of T)()` extension method on the result, for example:

```
Sub BuildDataTableFromQuery(ByVal data As DataTable)
  Dim cars = From car In data _
    Where car.Field(Of Integer)("CarID") > 5 Select car

  ' Use this result set to build a new DataTable.
  Dim newTable As DataTable = cars.CopyToDataTable()
  For curRow As Integer = 0 To newTable.Rows.Count - 1
    ' Print the DataTable.
    For curCol As Integer = 0 To newTable.Columns.Count - 1
      Console.Write(newTable.Rows(curRow)(curCol).ToString().Trim() & vbTab)
    Next
      Console.WriteLine()
  Next
End Sub
```

Note It is also possible to transform a LINQ query to a `DataView` type, via the `AsDataView(Of T)()` extension method.

This approach can be very helpful when you wish to use the result of a LINQ query as the source of a data binding operation. For example, the `DataGridView` of Windows Forms (as well as the `GridView` of ASP.NET) supports a property named `DataSource`. You could bind a LINQ result to the grid as follows:

```
' Assume myDataGrid is a GUI-based grid object.
myDataGrid.DataSource = (From car In data _
  Where car.Field(Of Integer)("CarID") > 5 _
  Select car).CopyToDataTable()
```

Now that you have seen the role of LINQ to DataSet, let's turn our attention to LINQ to SQL.

Source Code The LinqOverDataSet project can be found under the Chapter 24 subdirectory.

Programming with LINQ to SQL

LINQ to SQL is an API that allows you to apply well-formed LINQ query expressions to data held within relational databases. LINQ to SQL provides a number of types (within the `System.Data.Linq.dll` assembly) that facilitate the communication between your code base and the physical database engine.

The major goal of LINQ to SQL is to provide consistency between relational databases and the programming logic used to interact with them. For example, rather than representing database queries using a big clunky SQL string, we can use strongly typed LINQ queries. As well, rather than having to treat relational data as a stream of records, we are able to interact with the data using standard object-oriented programming techniques. Given the fact that LINQ to SQL allows us to integrate data access directly within our VB code base, the need to manually build dozens of custom classes and data access libraries that hide ADO.NET grunge from view is greatly minimized.

When programming with LINQ to SQL, you see no trace of common ADO.NET types such as `SqlConnection`, `SqlCommand`, or `SqlDataAdapter`. Using LINQ query expressions, entity classes (defined shortly), and the `DataContext` type, you are able to perform all the expected database operations, as well as define transactional contexts, create new database entities (or entire databases), invoke stored procedures, and perform other database-centric activities.

Furthermore, the LINQ to SQL types (again, such as `DataContext`) have been developed to integrate with standard ADO.NET data types. For example, one of the overloaded constructors of `DataContext` takes as an input an `IDbConnection`-compatible object, which as you may recall is a common interface supported by all ADO.NET connection objects.

In this way, existing ADO.NET data access libraries can integrate with Visual Basic 2008 LINQ query expressions (and vice versa). In reality, as far as Microsoft is concerned, LINQ to SQL is simply a new member of the ADO.NET family.

The Role of Entity Classes

When you wish to make use of LINQ to SQL within your applications, the first step is to define *entity classes*. In a nutshell, entity classes are types that represent the relational data you wish to interact with. Programmatically speaking, entity classes are class definitions that are annotated with various LINQ to SQL attributes (such as `<Table()>` and `<Column()>`) that map to a physical table in a specific database. In addition to various enumerations and basic class types, numerous LINQ to SQL attributes are defined with the `System.Data.Linq.Mapping` namespace (see Figure 24-2).

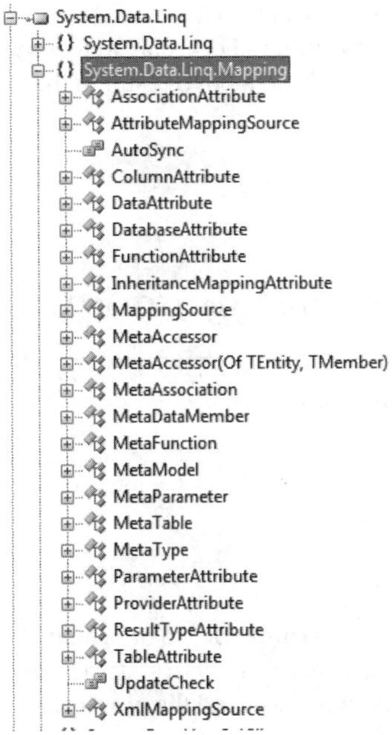

Figure 24-2. *The* `System.Data.Linq.Mapping` *namespace defines numerous LINQ to SQL attributes.*

As you will see in just a bit, the .NET Framework 3.5 SDK (as well as Visual Studio 2008) ships with tools that automate the construction of the entity types required by your application. Until that point, our first LINQ to SQL example will illustrate how to build entity classes by hand.

The Role of the DataContext Type

Once you have defined your entity classes, you are then able to pass your query expressions to the relational database using a `DataContext` object. This LINQ to SQL–specific class type is in charge of translating your LINQ query expressions into proper SQL queries as well as communicating with the specified database. In some ways, the `DataContext` looks and feels like an ADO.NET connection object, in that it requires a connection string. However, unlike a typically connection object, the `DataContext` type has numerous members that will map the results of your query expressions back into the entity classes you define.

Furthermore, the `DataContext` type defines a factory pattern to obtain instances of the entity classes used within your code base. Once you obtain an entity instance, you are free to change its state in any way you desire (adding records, updating records, etc.) and submit the modified object back for processing. In this way, the `DataContext` is similar to an ADO.NET data adapter type.

A Simple LINQ to SQL Example

Before we dive into too many details, let's see a simple example of using LINQ to SQL to interact with the Inventory table of the AutoLot database created in Chapter 22. In this example, we will not make use of our `AutoLotDAL.dll` library, but will instead author all the code by hand. Create a new Console Application named SimpleLinqToSqlApp and reference the `System.Data.Linq.dll` assembly.

Next, insert a new VB class file named `Inventory.vb`. This file will define our entity class, which requires decorating the type with various LINQ-centric attributes; therefore, be sure to import the

System.Data.Linq.Mapping and System.Data.Linq namespaces. With this detail out of the way, here is the definition of the Inventory type:

```
<Table()> _
Public Class Inventory
  <Column()> _
  Public Make As String
  <Column()> _
  Public Color As String
  <Column()> _
  Public PetName As String

  ' Identify the primary key.
  <Column(IsPrimaryKey := True)> _
  public CarID As Integer

  Public Overrides Function ToString() As String
    Return String.Format("ID = {0}; Make = {1}; Color = {2}; PetName = {3}", _
      CarID, Make.Trim(), Color.Trim(), PetName.Trim())
  End Function
End Class
```

First of all, notice that our entity class has been adorned with the <Table()> attribute, while each public field has been marked with <Column()>. In both cases, the names are a direct mapping to the physical database table. However, this is not a strict requirement, as the TableAttribute and ColumnAttribute types both support a Name property that allows you to decouple your programmatic representation of the data table from the physical table itself. Also notice that the CarID field has been further qualified by setting the IsPrimaryKey property of the ColumnAttribute type using named property syntax.

Here, for simplicity, each field has been declared publicly. If you require stronger encapsulation, you could most certainly define private fields wrapped by public properties. If you do so, the *property*—not the fields—will be marked with the <Column()> attribute.

It is also worth pointing out that an entity class can contain any number of members that do not map to the data table it represents. As far as the LINQ runtime is concerned, only items marked with LINQ to SQL attributes will be used during the data exchange. For example, this Inventory class definition provides a custom implementation of ToString() to allow the application to quickly display its state.

Now that we have an entity class, we can make use of the DataContext type to submit (and translate) our LINQ query expressions to the specified database. Ponder the following Main() method, which will display the result of all items in the Inventory table maintained by the AutoLot database:

```
Imports System.Data.Linq

Module Program
  Const cnStr As String = _
    "Data Source=(local)\SQLEXPRESS;Initial Catalog=AutoLot;" & _
    "Integrated Security=True"

  Sub Main()
    Console.WriteLine("***** LINQ to SQL Sample App *****")
    ' Create a DataContext object.
    Dim db As New DataContext(cnStr)

    ' Now create a Table(Of T) type.
    Dim invTable As Table(Of Inventory) = db.GetTable(Of Inventory)()
```

```
    ' Show all data using a LINQ query.
    Console.WriteLine("-> Contents of Inventory Table from AutoLot database:")
    For Each car In From c In invTable Select c
      Console.WriteLine(car.ToString())
    Next
    Console.ReadLine()
  End Sub
End Module
```

Notice that when you create a DataContext object, you will feed in a proper connection string, which is represented here as a simple string constant. Of course, you are free to store this in an application configuration file and/or make use of the SqlConnectionStringBuilder type to treat this string type in a more object-oriented manner.

Next up, we obtain an instance of our Inventory entity class by calling the generic GetTable(Of T)() method of the DataContext type, specifying the entity class as the type parameter when doing so. Finally, we build a LINQ query expression and apply it to the invTable object. As you would expect, the end result is a display of each item in the Inventory table.

Building a Strongly Typed DataContext

While our first example is strongly typed as far as the database query is concerned, we do have a bit of a disconnect between the DataContext and the Inventory entity class it is maintaining. To remedy this situation, it is typically preferable to create a class that extends the DataContext type that defines member variables for each table it operates upon. Insert a new class called AutoLotDatabase, specify you have imported the System.Data.Linq namespace, and implement the type as follows:

```
Imports System.Data.Linq

Class AutoLotDatabase
  Inherits DataContext

  ' Define a member variable representing
  ' the table in the database.
  Public Inventory As Table(Of Inventory)

  ' Pass connection string to base class.
  Public Sub New(ByVal connectionString As String)
    MyBase.New(connectionString)
  End Sub
End Class
```

With this new class type, we are now able to simplify the code within Main() quite a bit:

```
Sub Main()
  Console.WriteLine("***** LINQ to SQL Sample App *****")

  ' Create an AutoLotDatabase object.
  Dim db As New AutoLotDatabase(cnStr)

  ' Note we can now use the Inventory field of AutoLotDatabase.
  Console.WriteLine("-> Contents of Inventory Table from AutoLot database:")
  For Each car In From c in db.Inventory Select c
    Console.WriteLine(car.ToString())
  Next
  Console.ReadLine()
End Sub
```

One aspect of building a strongly typed data context that may surprise you is that the `DataContext`-derived type (`AutoLotDatabase` in this example) does not directly create the `Table(Of T)` member variables and has no trace of the expected `GetTable()` method call. At runtime, however, when you iterate over your LINQ result set, the `DataContext` will create the `Table(Of T)` type transparently in the background.

Of course, any LINQ query can be used to obtain a given result set. Assume we have authored the following helper method that is called from `Main()` before exiting (note this method expects us to pass in a `AutoLotDatabase` instance):

```
Sub ShowOnlyBimmers(ByVal db As AutoLotDatabase)
  Console.WriteLine("***** Only BMWs *****")

  ' Get the BMWs.
  Dim bimmers = From s In db.Inventory _
    Where (s.Make = "BMW") _
    Order By s.CarID Select s

  For Each c In bimmers
    Console.WriteLine(c.ToString())
  Next
End Sub
```

Figure 24-3 shows the output of this first LINQ to SQL example.

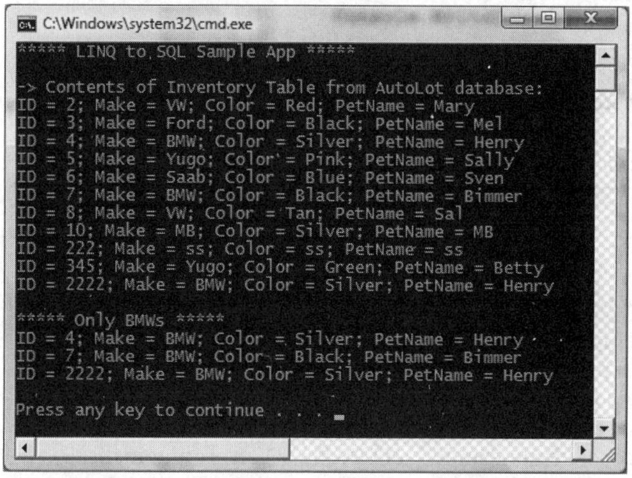

Figure 24-3. *A first look at LINQ to SQL*

Source Code The SimpleLinqToSqlApp project can be found under the Chapter 24 subdirectory.

The <Table()> and <Column()> Attributes: Further Details

As you have seen, entity classes are adorned with various attributes that are used by LINQ to SQL to translate queries for your objects into SQL queries against the database. At absolute minimum, you will make use of the `<Table()>` and `<Column()>` attributes; however, additional attributes exist to mark the methods that perform SQL insert, update, and delete commands. As well, each of the LINQ to SQL attributes defines a set of properties that further qualify to the LINQ to SQL runtime engine how to process the annotated item.

The <Table()> attribute is very simple, given that it defines only a single property of interest: Name. As mentioned, this allows you to decouple the name of the entity class from the physical table. If you do not set the Name property at the time you apply the <Table()> attribute, LINQ to SQL assumes the entity class and database table names are one and the same.

The <Column()> attribute provides a bit more meat than <Table()>. Beyond the IsPrimaryKey property, ColumnAttribute defines additional members that allow you to fully qualify the details of each field in the entity class and how it maps to a particular column in the physical database table. Table 24-1 documents the additional properties of interest.

Table 24-1. *Select Properties of the* <Column()> *Attribute*

ColumnAttribute Property	Meaning in Life
CanBeNull	This property indicates that the column can contain Nothing values.
DbType	LINQ to SQL will automatically infer the data types to pass to the database engine based on declaration of your field data. Given this, it is typically only necessary to set DbType directly if you are dynamically creating databases using the CreateDatabase() method of the DataContext type.
IsDbGenerated	This property establishes that a field's value is autogenerated by the database (e.g., identity columns).
IsVersion	This property identifies that the column type is a database timestamp or a version number. Version numbers are incremented and timestamp columns are updated every time the associated row is updated.
UpdateCheck	This property controls how LINQ to SQL should handle database conflicts via optimistic concurrency.

Generating Entity Classes Using sqlmetal.exe

Our first LINQ to SQL example was fairly simplistic, partially due to the fact that our DataContext was operating on a single data table. A production-level LINQ to SQL application may instead be operating on multiple interrelated data tables, each of which could define dozens of columns. In these cases, it would be very tedious to author each and every required entity class by hand. Thankfully, we do have two approaches to generate these important LINQ to SQL types automatically.

The first option is to make use of the sqlmetal.exe command-line utility, which can be executed using a Visual Studio 2008 command prompt. This tool automates the creation of entity classes by generating an appropriate VB class type from the database metadata. While this tool has numerous command-line options, Table 24-2 documents the major flags of interest.

Table 24-2. *Various Options of the* sqlmetal.exe *Command*

sqlmetal.exe Command-Line Option	Meaning in Life
/server	Specifies the server hosting the database
/database	Specifies the name of the database to read metadata from
/user	Specifies the user ID to log in to the server
/password	Specifies the password to log in to the server

sqlmetal.exe Command-Line Option	Meaning in Life
/views	Informs sqlmetal.exe to generate code based on existing database views
/functions	Informs sqlmetal.exe to extract database functions
/sprocs	Informs sqlmetal.exe to extract stored procedures
/code	Informs sqlmetal.exe to output results as a VB code file
/namespace	Specifies the namespace to define the generated types

By way of an example, the following command set will generate entity classes for each table within the AutoLot database, expose the `GetPetName` stored procedure, and wrap all generated VB code within a namespace named `AutoLotDatabase` (of course, this would be entered on a single line within a Visual Studio 2008 command prompt):

```
sqlmetal /server:(local)\SQLEXPRESS /database:AutoLot /namespace:AutoLotDatabase
        /code:autoLotDB.vb /sprocs
```

Once you have executed the command, create a new Console Application named LinqWithSqlMetalGenedCode, reference the `System.Data.Linq.dll` assembly, and include the `autoLotDB.vb` file into your project using the Project ➤ Add Existing Item menu option. As well, insert a new class diagram into your project (as described in Chapter 2) and expand each of the AutoLot-centric generated classes (see Figure 24-4).

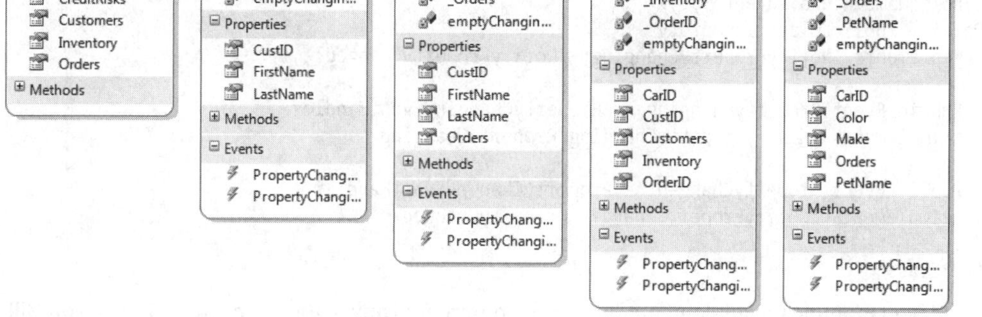

Figure 24-4. *The* `sqlmetal.exe`*-generated entity classes*

Notice that you have a new type extending `DataContext` that contains properties for each data table in the specified database. (As well, if you examine the methods of your custom `DataContext`, you'll notice that the `GetPetName()` stored procedure is represented by a public method of the same name.) Before we program against these new types, let's examine this autogenerated code in a bit more detail.

Examining the Generated Entity Classes

sqlmetal.exe defines a separate entity class for each table in the AutoLot database (Inventory, Customers, Orders, CreditRisks), with each column encapsulated by a type property. In addition, notice that each entity class implements two interfaces (INotifyPropertyChanging and INotifyPropertyChanged), each of which defines a single event:

```
Namespace System.ComponentModel
  Public Interface INotifyPropertyChanging
    ' This event fires when a property is being changed.
    Event PropertyChanging As PropertyChangingEventHandler
  End Interface
End Namespace

Namespace System.ComponentModel
  Public Interface INotifyPropertyChanged
    ' This event fires when a property value has changed.
    Event PropertyChanged As PropertyChangedEventHandler
  End Interface
End Namespace
```

Collectively, these interfaces define a total of two events named PropertyChanging and PropertyChanged. The PropertyChanging event works in conjunction with the PropertyChangingEventHandler delegate, which can point to any method taking an Object as the first parameter and a PropertyChangingEventArgs as the second:

```
Public Delegate Sub PropertyChangingEventHandler(ByVal sender As Object, _
  ByVal e As PropertyChangingEventArgs)
```

The PropertyChanged event has been defined in terms of the PropertyChangedEventHandler delegate defined as so:

```
Public Delegate Sub PropertyChangedEventHandler(ByVal sender As Object, _
  ByVal e As PropertyChangedEventArgs)
```

Given the interface contracts, each entity class supports the following members:

```
<Table(Name:="dbo.Inventory")> _
Partial Public Class Inventory
  Implements INotifyPropertyChanging, INotifyPropertyChanged

  Public Event PropertyChanging As PropertyChangingEventHandler _
    Implements INotifyPropertyChanging.PropertyChanging

  Public Event PropertyChanged As PropertyChangedEventHandler _
    Implements INotifyPropertyChanged.PropertyChanged
...
End Class
```

If you examine the implementation of the properties of any of the three entity classes, you will note that each property setter fires each event to any interested listener. By way of an example, here is the PetName property of the Inventory type:

```
Public Property PetName() As String
  Get
    Return Me._PetName
  End Get
  Set
    If (String.Equals(Me._PetName, value) = false) Then
      Me.OnPetNameChanging(value)
```

```
      Me.SendPropertyChanging
      Me._PetName = value
      Me.SendPropertyChanged("PetName")
      Me.OnPetNameChanged()
    End If
  End Set
End Property
```

Notice that the property setter invokes the `OnPetNameChanging()` and `OnPetNameChanged()` methods on the entity class type to actually fire the events themselves.

Defining Relationships Using Entity Classes

Beyond simply defining properties with backing fields to represent data table columns, the `sqlmetal.exe` utility will also model the relationships between interrelated tables using the `EntitySet(Of T)` type. Recall from Chapter 22 that the AutoLot database defined three interrelated tables connected by primary and foreign keys. Rather than forcing us to author SQL-centric syntax to navigate between these tables, LINQ to SQL allows us to navigate using the object-centric VB dot operator.

To account for this sort of table relationship, the parent entity class may encode the child table as property references. This property is marked with the `<Association()>` attribute to establish an *association relationship* made by matching column values between tables. For example, consider the (partial) generated code for the `Customer` type, which can have any number of orders:

```
<Table(Name:="dbo.Customers")> _
Partial Public Class Customers
  Implements INotifyPropertyChanging, INotifyPropertyChanged

  Private _Orders As EntitySet(Of Orders)

  <Association(Name:="FK_Orders_Customers", _
   Storage:="_Orders", OtherKey:="CustID", DeleteRule:="NO ACTION")> _
  Public Property Orders() As EntitySet(Of Orders)
    Get
      Return Me._Orders
    End Get
    Set
      Me._Orders.Assign(value)
    End Set
  End Property
...
End Class
```

Here, the `Orders` property is understood by the LINQ to SQL runtime engine as the member that allows navigation *from* the Customers table *to* the Orders table via the column defined by the `OtherKey` named property. The `EntitySet(Of T)` member variable is used to represent the one-to-many nature of this particular relationship.

The Strongly Typed DataContext

The final aspect of the `sqlmetal.exe`-generated code to be aware of is the `DataContext`-derived type. Like the `AutoLotDatabase` class we authored in the previous example, each table is represented by a `Table(Of T)`-compatible property. As well, this class has a series of constructors, one of which takes an object implementing `IDbConnection`, which represents an ADO.NET connection object (remember, LINQ to SQL and ADO.NET types can be intermixed within a single application).

As well, this DataContext-derived class is how we are able to interact with the stored procedures defined by the database. Given the fact that we supplied the /sprocs flag as part of our sqlmetal.exe command set, we find a method named GetPetName() in the AutoLot class:

```
<FunctionAttribute(Name:="dbo.GetPetName")> _
Public Function GetPetName( _
  <Parameter(DbType:="Int")> ByVal carID As System.Nullable(Of Integer), _
  <Parameter(DbType:="Char(10)")> ByRef petName As String) As Integer

  Dim result As IExecuteResult = _
    Me.ExecuteMethodCall(Me, _
      CType(MethodInfo.GetCurrentMethod, MethodInfo), carID, petName)

  petName = CType(result.GetParameterValue(1), String)
  Return CType(result.ReturnValue, Integer)
End Function
```

Notice that the GetPetName() method is marked with the <Function()>attribute, while each parameter is marked with the <Parameter()> attribute. The implementation makes use of the inherited ExecuteMethodCall() method (and a bit of reflection services) to take care of the details of invoking the stored procedure and returning the result to the caller.

Programming Against the Generated Types

Now that you have a better idea regarding the code authored by sqlmetal.exe, consider the following implementation of the Program type, which invokes our stored procedure:

```
Imports LinqWithSqlMetalGenedCode.AutoLotDatabase

Module Program
  Const cnStr As String = "Data Source=(local)\SQLEXPRESS;" & _
    "Initial Catalog=AutoLot;Integrated Security=True"

  Sub Main()
    Console.WriteLine("***** More Fun with LINQ to SQL *****" & vbLf)
    Dim carsDB As New AutoLot(cnStr)
    InvokeStoredProc(carsDB)
    Console.ReadLine()
  End Sub

  Sub InvokeStoredProc(ByVal carsDB As AutoLot)
    Dim carID As Integer = 0
    Dim petName As String = ""
    Console.Write("Enter ID: ")
    carID = Integer.Parse(Console.ReadLine())

    ' Invoke stored proc and print out the petname.
    carsDB.GetPetName(carID, petName)
    Console.WriteLine("Car ID {0} has the petname: {1}", carID, petName)
  End Sub
End Module
```

Notice that LINQ to SQL completely hides the underlying stored procedure logic from view. Here, we have no need to manually create a `SqlCommand` object, fill the parameters collection, or call `ExecuteNonQuery()`. Instead, we simply invoke the `GetPetName()` method of our `DataContext`-derived type.

Now assume we have a second helper function (also called from within `Main()`) named `PrintOrderForCustomer()`. This method will print out some order details for the specified customer as well as the first and last name of the customer:

```
Sub PrintOrderForCustomer(ByVal carsDB As AutoLot)
  Dim custID As Integer = 0
  Console.Write("Enter customer ID: ")
  custID = Integer.Parse(Console.ReadLine())

  Dim customerOrders = _
    From cust In carsDB.Customers() _
    From o In cust.Orders() _
    Where cust.CustID = custID _
    Select New With {cust, o}

  Console.WriteLine("***** Order Info for Customer ID: {0}. *****", custID)
  For Each q In customerOrders
    Console.WriteLine("{0} {1} is order ID # {2}.", _
      q.cust.FirstName.Trim(), _
      q.cust.LastName.Trim(), _
      q.o.OrderID)
    Console.WriteLine("{0} bought Car ID # {1}.", _
      q.cust.FirstName.Trim(), q.o.CarID)
  Next
End Sub
```

Figure 24-5 shows the output (for my instance of AutoLot) when querying about the customer assigned the ID of 1.

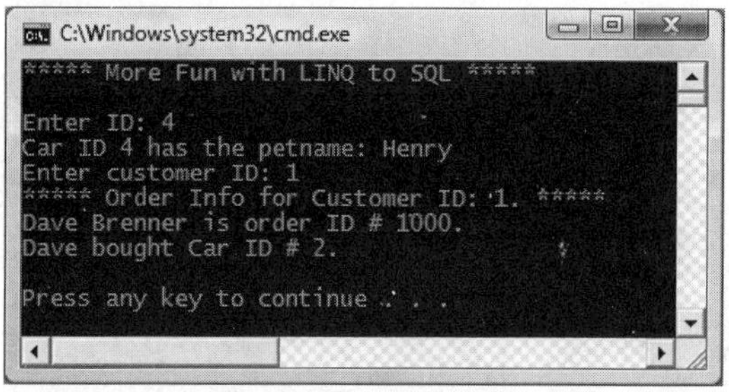

Figure 24-5. *Printing our order details for a specified customer*

Again, the benefit of LINQ to SQL is that we are able to interact with relational databases using a consistent, object-based model. Just to shed some more light on our LINQ query expression, add the following code statement at the end of your `PrintOrderForCustomer()` method:

```
Console.WriteLine("customerOrders as a string: {0}", customerOrders)
```

When you run your program once again, you may be surprised to find that the stringified value of your query expression reveals the underlying SQL query:

```
customerOrders as a string: SELECT [t0].[CustID], [t0].[FirstName],
[t0].[LastName], [t1].[OrderID], [t1].[CustID] AS [Cus
tID2], [t1].[CarID]
FROM [dbo].[Customers] AS [t0], [dbo].[Orders] AS [t1]
WHERE ([t0].[CustID] = @p0) AND ([t1].[CustID] = [t0].[CustID])
```

■ **Source Code** The LinqWithSqlMetalGenedCode project can be found under the Chapter 24 subdirectory.

Building Entity Classes Using Visual Studio 2008

To wrap up our look at LINQ to SQL, create a new Console Application named LinqToSqlCrud and reference the `System.Data.Linq.dll` assembly. This time, rather than running `sqlmetal.exe` to generate our entity classes, we will allow Visual Studio 2008 to do the grunt work. To do so, select Project ➤ Add New Item, and add a new LINQ to SQL Classes item named AutoLotObjects (see Figure 24-6).

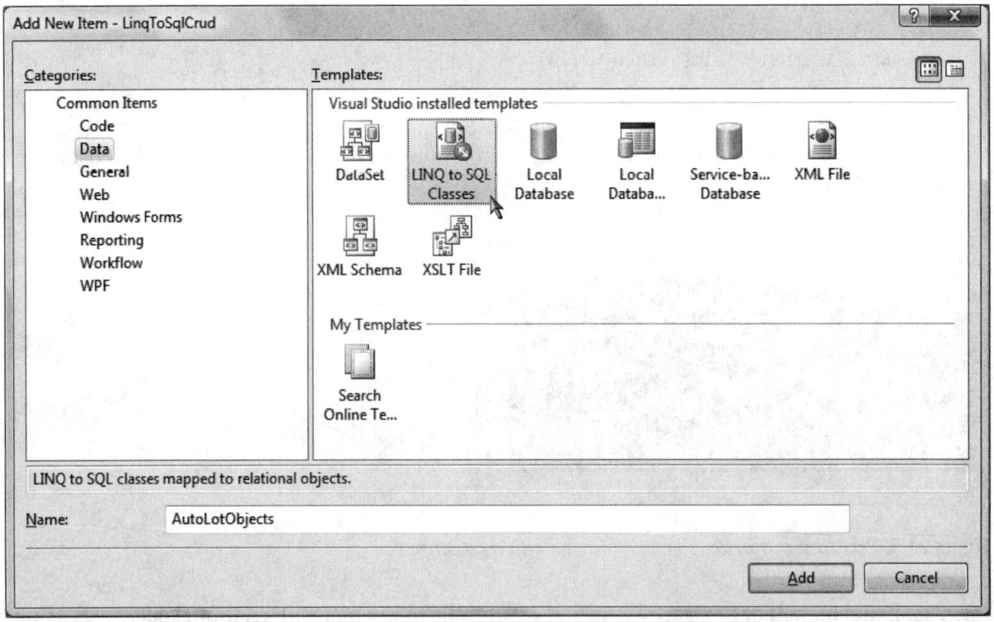

Figure 24-6. *The LINQ to SQL Classes item performs the same duties as* `sqlmetal.exe`.

Open Server Explorer and ensure you have an active connection to the AutoLot database (if not, right-click the Data Connections icon and select Add Connection). At this point, select each table and drag it onto the LINQ to SQL designer surface. Once you are done, your screen should resemble Figure 24-7.

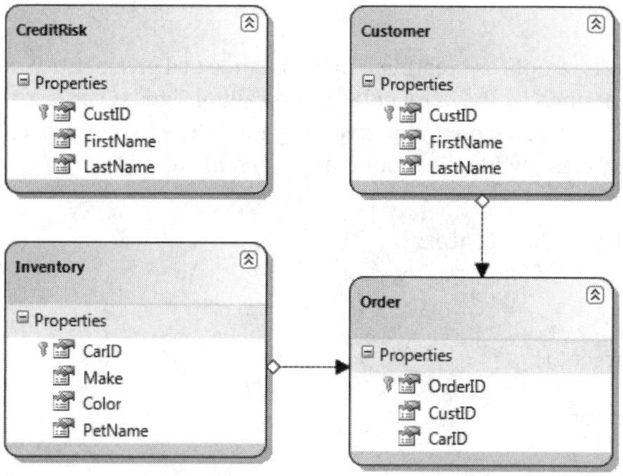

Figure 24-7. *Creating entity classes using the LINQ to SQL designer*

■Note You can also drag stored procedures from Server Explorer onto the designer surface to autogenerate the related code to invoke them.

Once you perform your initial compile, go to Solution Explorer and open the related `*.vb` file (see Figure 24-8, which assumes you have clicked the Show All Files button). As you look over the generated VB code, you'll quickly notice it is the same overall code generated by the `sqlmetal.exe` command-line utility. Also note that the visual LINQ to SQL designer added an `app.config` file to your project to store the necessary connection string data.

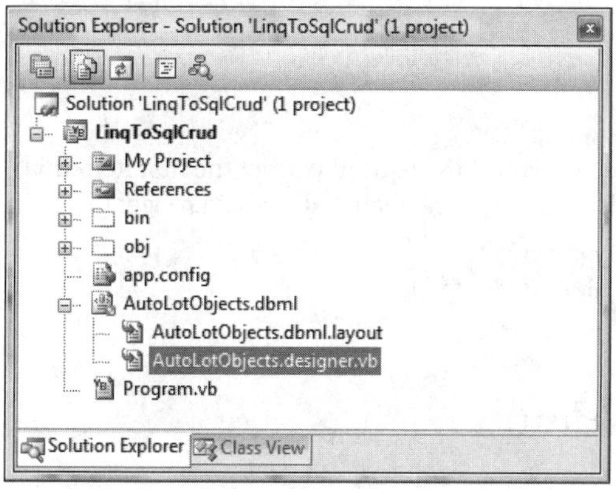

Figure 24-8. *The generated LINQ to SQL code*

Now that all the generated types are accounted for, here is a `Program` class that illustrates inserting, updating, and deleting data on the Inventory table.

Inserting New Items

Adding new items to a relational database is as simple as creating a new instance of a given entity class, adding into the `Table(Of T)` type maintained by the `DataContext` and calling `SubmitChanges()`. The following `InsertNewCars()` method adds two new cars to the Inventory table. The first approach directly sets each field of the `Inventory` entity class, while the second approach makes use of the more compact object initialization syntax:

```
Sub InsertNewCars(ByVal ctx As AutoLotObjectsDataContext)
  Console.WriteLine("***** Adding 2 Cars *****")
  Dim newCarID As Integer = 0
  Console.Write("Enter ID for Betty: ")
  newCarID = Integer.Parse(Console.ReadLine())

  ' Add a new row using "longhand" notation.
  Dim newCar As New Inventory()
  newCar.Make = "Yugo"
  newCar.Color = "Pink"
  newCar.PetName = "Betty"
  newCar.CarID = newCarID
  ctx.Inventories.InsertOnSubmit(newCar)
  ctx.SubmitChanges()

  Console.Write("Enter ID for Henry: ")
  newCarID = Integer.Parse(Console.ReadLine())

  ' Add another row using "shorthand" object init syntax.
  newCar = New Inventory With {.Make = "BMW", .Color = "Silver", _
    .PetName = "Henry", .CarID = newCarID}

  ctx.Inventories.InsertOnSubmit(newCar)
  ctx.SubmitChanges()
End Sub
```

Updating Existing Items

Updating an item is also very straightforward. Based on your LINQ query, extract the first item that meets the search criteria. Once you update the object's state, once again call `SubmitChanges()`.

```
Sub UpdateCar(ByVal ctx As AutoLotObjectsDataContext)
  Console.WriteLine("***** Updating color of 'Betty' *****")

  ' Update Betty's color to light pink.
  Dim betty = (From c In ctx.Inventories Where _
               (c.PetName = "Betty") Select c).First()
  betty.Color = "Pink"
  ctx.SubmitChanges()
End Sub
```

Deleting Existing Items

And finally, if you wish to delete an item from the relational database table, simply build a LINQ query to locate the item you are no longer interested in, and remove it from the correct `Table(Of T)` member variable of the `DataContext` using the `DeleteOnSubmit()` method. Once you have done so, again call `SubmitChanges()`:

```
Sub DeleteCar(ByVal ctx As AutoLotObjectsDataContext)
  Dim carToDelete As Integer = 0
  Console.Write("Enter ID of car to delete: ")
  carToDelete = Integer.Parse(Console.ReadLine())

  ' Remove specified car.
  ctx.Inventories.DeleteOnSubmit((from c in ctx.Inventories _
    where c.CarID = carToDelete _
    select c).First())
  ctx.SubmitChanges()
End Sub
```

At this point you can call each method from within `Main()` to verify the output:

```
Sub Main()
  Console.WriteLine("***** CRUD with LINQ to SQL *****")

  Dim ctx As New AutoLotObjectsDataContext()
  InsertNewCars(ctx)
  UpdateCar(ctx)
  DeleteCar(ctx)
  Console.ReadLine()
End Sub
```

That wraps up our look at LINQ to SQL. Obviously, there is much more to the story than you have seen here; however, hopefully at this point you feel you are better equipped to dive into further details as you see fit.

Source Code The LinqToSqlCrud project can be found under the Chapter 24 subdirectory.

Programming with LINQ to XML

The final task of this chapter is to examine the role of LINQ to XML, which as you recall allows you to apply LINQ query expressions against XML-based data. Although this edition of this book does not provide a chapter solely dedicated to programming with .NET's XML APIs, by now you have probably picked up on how deeply XML data representation has been integrated into the .NET Framework.

Application and web-based configuration files store data as XML. ADO.NET `DataSets` can easily save out (or load in) data as XML. Windows Presentation Foundation makes use of an XML-based grammar (XAML) to represent desktop UIs, and Windows Communication Foundation (as well as the previous .NET remoting APIs) also stores numerous settings as the well-formatted string we call XML.

Although XML is indeed everywhere, programming with XML has historically been very tedious, very verbose, and very complex if one is not well versed in a great number of XML technologies (XPath, XQuery, XSLT, DOM, SAX, etc.). Since the inception of the .NET platform, Microsoft has provided a specific assembly devoted to programming with XML documents named `System.Xml.dll`. Within this binary are a number of namespaces and types to various XML programming techniques, as well as a few .NET-specific XML APIs such as the `XmlReader`/`XmlWriter` models.

LINQ to XML As a Better DOM

Just as LINQ to ADO.NET intends to integrate relational database manipulation directly within .NET programming languages, LINQ to XML aspires to the same goals for XML data processing. Not only can you use LINQ to XML as a vehicle to obtain subsets of data from an existing XML document via LINQ queries, but you can also use this same API to create, copy, and parse XML data. To this end, LINQ to XML can be thought of as a "better DOM" programming model. As well, just as LINQ to ADO.NET can interoperate with ADO.NET types, LINQ to XML can also interoperate with many members of the `System.Xml.dll` assemblies.

The System.Xml.XLinq Namespace

Somewhat surprisingly, the core LINQ to XML assembly (`System.Xml.Linq.dll`) defines a very small number of types in three distinct namespaces (see Figure 24-9).

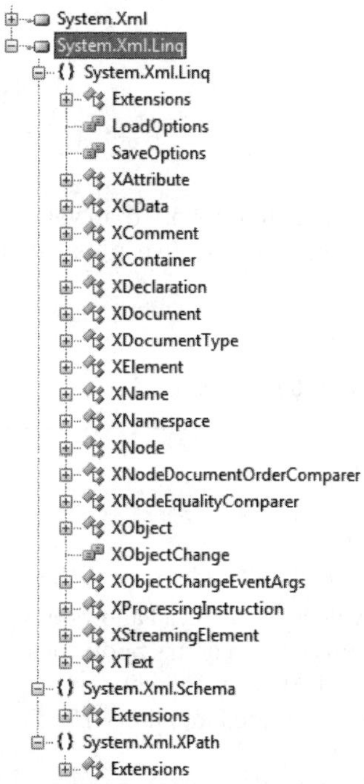

Figure 24-9. *The namespaces of* `System.Xml.Linq.dll`

The core namespace, `System.Xml.Linq`, contains a very manageable set of types that represents various aspects of an XML document (its elements and their attributes, XML namespaces, XML comments, processing instructions, etc.). Table 24-3 documents the core types of `System.Xml.Linq`.

Table 24-3. *Select Types of the* `System.Xml.Linq` *Namespace*

Member	Meaning in Life
`XAttribute`	Represents an XML attribute on a given XML element
`XComment`	Represents an XML comment
`XDeclaration`	Represents the opening declaration of an XML document
`XDocument`	Represents the document node of an XML document
`XElement`	Represents a given element within an XML document
`XName`	Represents the name of a given element or attribute within an XML document
`XNamespace`	Provides a simple manner to define and reference XML namespaces

While you'll see many of these types in action throughout the remainder of this chapter, it may surprise you to know that as a Visual Basic programmer, you may in fact make use of them indirectly! This is due to the intrinsic XML data type support offered by Visual Basic 2008.

The Integrated XML Support of Visual Basic 2008

While VB developers are free to make direct use of the types of the `System.Xml.Linq` namespace, the Visual Basic 2008 language provides a number of unique features that greatly simplify your LINQ to XML programming tasks. Specifically, Visual Basic 2008 allows you to author XML markup *directly* within a `*.vb` code file using *XML literals*.

When you make use of XML literal syntax, you are essentially able to author XML data structures (which, for the most part, are compliant with the XML 1.0 specification) that can be intermixed with LINQ queries, function calls, and the use of data variables. Without getting too hung up on the details at this point, consider the following code example that makes use of an XML literal:

```
' Define an XML literal held within an XElement.
Dim car1 As XElement = _
  <Automobile>
    <petname>Mel</petname>
    <color type="interior">Black</color>
    <color type="exterior">Black</color>
  </Automobile>
```

Notice that when you are creating the XML literal content, you are *not* required to use a line continuation character (which is in fact mandatory when splitting a VB code statement across multiple lines). This very fact alone makes XML literal syntax extremely useful, as lengthy XML document descriptions may involve numerous elements, attributes, and textual values. In stark contrast, authoring XML data types using the object model of LINQ to XML, you *must* use line continuation characters whenever your VB code statements are separated by multiple lines (which will most always be the case when working with the `System.Xml.Linq` data types).

Also notice that the variable data type holding our XML literal is a LINQ to XML data type (`XElement` in this case). When you store an XML literal in a proper LINQ to XML data type, at compile time, the XML literal data is mapped into a related object model using the same types found in the `System.Xml.Linq` namespace (which greatly simplify your coding efforts). If you were to print the contents of the `car1` variable to the console, you would find that the strong typing of the XML data is preserved (see Figure 24-10).

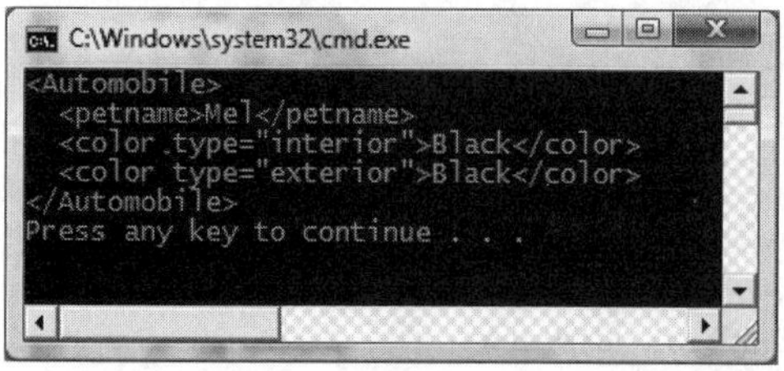

Figure 24-10. *The result of calling* `ToString()` *on our* `XElement` *type*

Storing XML Literals in String Data Types

It is not mandatory to store an XML literal within a LINQ to XML data type, however. If you wish, you could also store the data of an XML literal within a `System.String` variable. When you do so, the `String` will *not* contain any of the declared XML elements or XML attributes. Rather, the `String` variable will only contain the "inner text" of each element (ignoring white space). Thus, if you were to execute the following code:

```
Module Program
  Sub Main()
    ' Store XML literal in a String.
    Dim car1 As String = _
  <Automobile>
    <petname>Mel</petname>
    <color type="interior">Black</color>
    <color type="exterior">Black</color>
  </Automobile>

    ' ToString() is called automatically on car1.
    Console.WriteLine(car1)
  End Sub
End Module
```

the following would print out to the console:

```
MelBlackBlack
```

Given this point, you will almost always want to store an XML literal within a valid LINQ to XML data type.

Blending Programming Constructs Within an XML Literal

An XML literal can also be composed using VB coding constructs, such as method calls (to receive some data), member variables/local variables (to fill in the values of an XML element or property dynamically), or with the result of a LINQ query. Again, while you could do the same operations using the LINQ to XML object model, XML literals make the process a bit more streamlined. Consider the following code example (defined within a Console Application named SimpleXmlLiteral):

```
Module Program
  Sub Main()

    Dim interiorColor As String = "White"
    Dim exteriorColor As String = "Blue"
```

```
    ' Note the 'inlined' code blocks.
    Dim car1 As XElement = _
  <Automobile>
    <petname><%= GetPetName() %></petname>
    <color type="interior"><%= interiorColor %></color>
    <color type="exterior"><%= exteriorColor %></color>
  </Automobile>

    Console.WriteLine(car1)
  End Sub

  Function GetPetName() As String
    Return "Sidd"
  End Function
End Module
```

Notice that our XML literal has a series of embedded <%= %> tokens, which may look familiar if you have a background in ASP or ASP.NET. Within the scope of this syntax, you are able to "inline" any valid VB code statements to build your XML literal dynamically. Here, we have used two `String` variables to represent the value of the `<color>` elements and a call to the `GetPetName()` function to fill the value of the `<petname>` element.

Source Code The SimpleXmlLiteral project can be found under the Chapter 24 subdirectory.

In any case, do be aware that when you use XML literals in your VB code base, you are really making use of the LINQ to XML data types in the background (which can be verified using a tool such as `ildasm.exe` or `reflector.exe`). Thus, while you could author all of your code using the underlying LINQ to XML object model (`XElement`, `XName`, etc.), using XML literals makes the process much easier. You'll see both approaches in the examples that follow.

Note As of .NET 3.5, XML literal syntax is unique to Visual Basic. Other .NET languages (such as C#) must always make use of the LINQ to XML object model.

Programmatically Creating XML Elements

To begin our investigation of the LINQ to XML object model (and continue to explore VB 2008 XML literals), create a new Console Application named FunWithLinqToXml. Be aware that the `System.Xml.Linq.dll` assembly is automatically referenced for new Visual Studio projects and the `System.Xml.Linq` namespace is available to all VB code files.

Unlike the original .NET XML programming model (à la `System.Xml.dll`), manipulating an XML document using LINQ can be achieved in a very functional manner. Thus, rather than building a document in memory using the very verbose XML DOM API, LINQ to XML allows you to go "DOM free" if you so choose.

Not only does this greatly reduce the amount of required code, but also the programming model maps almost directly to the format of well-formed XML data. To illustrate, add a method to your `Program` module named `CreateXmlElementWithObjectModel()`, implemented as follows:

```
Sub CreateXmlElementWithObjectModel()
  ' Use the types of System.Xml.Data to
  ' generate an in-memory XML element.
  Dim inventory As XElement = _
    New XElement("Inventory", _
      New XElement("Car", New XAttribute("ID", "1"), _
        New XElement("Color", "Green"), _
        New XElement("Make", "BMW"), _
        New XElement("PetName", "Stan") _
    ) _
  )

  ' Call ToString() on our XElement.
  Console.WriteLine(inventory)
End Sub
```

Although this method is making use of several LINQ to XML data types, in reality we are declaring only a single local variable of type `XElement`. However, in the constructor of the inventory `XElement` object is in fact a tree of additional `XElements` and `XAttributes`. As you can see, by mindfully indenting our code statements (and using the line continuation character), our code base has a similar look and feel to the XML document itself.

While understanding the underlying object model is important when working with LINQ to XML, given that VB supports XML literals, we would generate the same XML data in a more functional manner as so:

```
Sub CreateXmlElementWithXmlLiteral()
  Dim inventory As XElement = _
    <Inventory>
      <Car ID="1">
        <Color>Green</Color>
        <Make>BMW</Make>
        <PetName>Stan</PetName>
      </Car>
    </Inventory>

  ' Call ToString() on our XElement.
  Console.WriteLine(inventory)
End Sub
```

As you most likely agree, XML literal syntax is a much cleaner mapping to the XML itself and is less cumbersome than working with the LINQ to XML object model. If we were to call both of these methods from within our `Main()` method, it should come as no surprise that the output is identical (Figure 24-11).

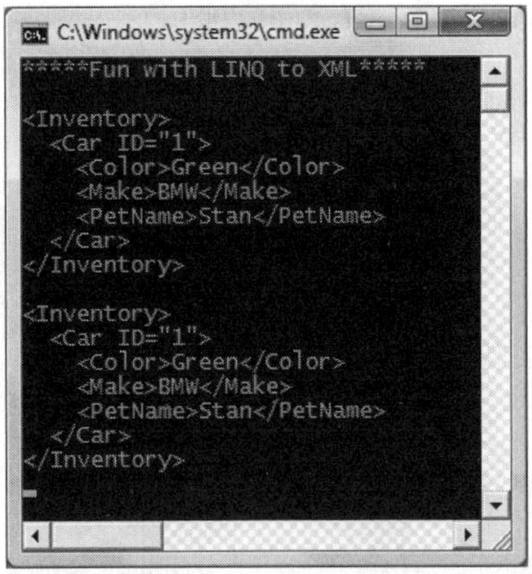

Figure 24-11. *Two approaches to generating a new XML element using LINQ to XML*

Programmatically Creating XML Documents

Currently, we have created only a single XML element. To create an entire XML document in memory (with comments, processing instructions, opening declarations, etc.), you can load the object tree into the constructor of an `XDocument` type. Consider the following `CreateFunctionalXmlDoc()` method, which first creates an in-memory document and then saves it to a local file using the LINQ to XML object model:

```
Sub CreateFunctionalXmlDoc()
  ' Create an in-memory XML document.
  Dim inventoryDoc As XDocument = _
    New XDocument( _
      New XDeclaration("1.0", "utf-8", "yes"), _
      New XComment("Current Inventory of AutoLot"), _
        New XElement("Inventory", _
          New XElement("Car", New XAttribute("ID", "1"), _
            New XElement("Color", "Green"), _
            New XElement("Make", "BMW"), _
            New XElement("PetName", "Stan") _
          ), _
          New XElement("Car", New XAttribute("ID", "2"), _
            New XElement("Color", "Pink"), _
            New XElement("Make", "Yugo"), _
            New XElement("PetName", "Melvin") _
          ) _
        ) _
    )
  ' Display the document and save to disk.
  Console.WriteLine(inventoryDoc)
  inventoryDoc.Save("SimpleInventory.xml")
End Sub
```

Figure 24-12 shows the SimpleInventory.xml file opened within Visual Studio 2008.

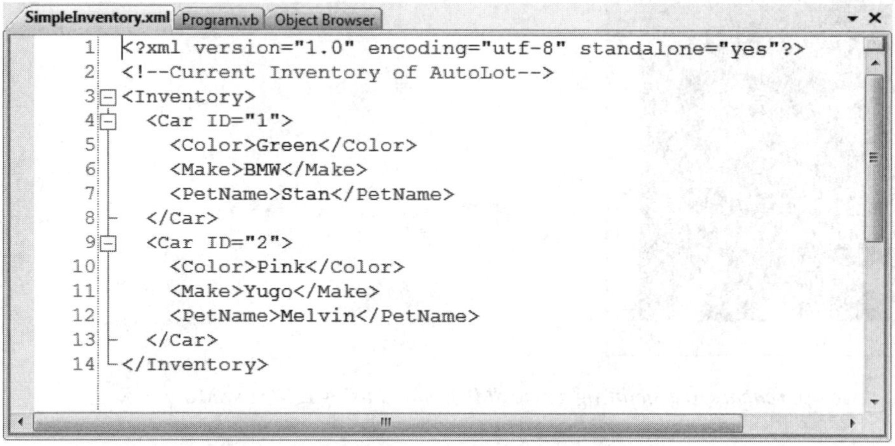

Figure 24-12. *The persisted XML document*

The XElement and XDocument types each define a constructor that takes an XName as the first parameter and a parameter array of objects as the second. The XName type is used in LINQ to SQL to represent (obviously) the name of the item you are creating, while the parameter array of objects can consist of any number of additional LINQ to XML types (XComment, XProcessingInstruction, XElement, XAttribute, etc.), as well as simple strings (for element content) or an object implementing IEnumerable.

Of course, the same XML document can be represented using XML literal syntax as so:

```
Sub CreateFunctionalXmlDocWithLiteral()
  ' Create an in-memory XML document using
  ' an XML literal.
  Dim inventoryDoc As XDocument = _
  <?xml version="1.0" encoding="utf-8" standalone="yes"?>
  <!--Current Inventory of AutoLot-->
  <Inventory>
    <Car ID="1">
      <Color>Green</Color>
      <Make>BMW</Make>
      <PetName>Stan</PetName>
    </Car>
    <Car ID="2">
      <Color>Pink</Color>
      <Make>Yugo</Make>
      <PetName>Melvin</PetName>
    </Car>
  </Inventory>

  ' Display the document and save to disk.
  Console.WriteLine(inventoryDoc)
  inventoryDoc.Save("SimpleInventory.xml")
End Sub
```

Generating Documents from LINQ Queries

Recall that you are able to incorporate coding constructs (LINQ queries, method calls, etc.) when you are building an in-memory XML document. Assume we have a generic List of Car objects (each of which supports the PetName and ID properties). We could now build a LINQ query that will select each item in the List(Of Car) object to dynamically build a new XElement:

```
Sub CreateXmlDocFromArray()
  ' Create a List of Car types.
  Dim data As New List(Of Car)
  data.Add(New Car With {.PetName = "Melvin", .ID = 10})
  data.Add(New Car With {.PetName = "Pat", .ID = 11})
  data.Add(New Car With {.PetName = "Danny", .ID = 12})
  data.Add(New Car With {.PetName = "Clunker", .ID = 13})

  ' Now enumerate over the array to build
  ' an XElement via a LINQ query.
  Dim vehicles As XElement = _
    New XElement("Inventory", _
      From c In data _
        Select New XElement("Car", _
         New XAttribute("ID", c.ID), _
         New XElement("PetName", c.PetName) _
      ) _
    )
  Console.WriteLine(vehicles)
End Sub
```

Note that into the constructor of the XElement, we pass in a LINQ query that dynamically builds the following XML data:

```
<Inventory>
  <Car ID="10">
    <PetName>Melvin</PetName>
  </Car>
  <Car ID="11">
    <PetName>Pat</PetName>
  </Car>
  <Car ID="12">
    <PetName>Danny</PetName>
  </Car>
  <Car ID="13">
    <PetName>Clunker</PetName>
  </Car>
</Inventory>
```

If we use XML literal syntax, the process of building our XElement is even more streamlined:

```
Sub CreateXmlDocFromArrayUsingLiteral()
  ' Create a List of Car types.
  Dim data As New List(Of Car)
  data.Add(New Car With {.PetName = "Melvin", .ID = 10})
  data.Add(New Car With {.PetName = "Pat", .ID = 11})
  data.Add(New Car With {.PetName = "Danny", .ID = 12})
  data.Add(New Car With {.PetName = "Clunker", .ID = 13})

  ' Inline the LINQ query within our XML literal.
  Dim vehicles As XElement = _
```

```
    <Inventory>
      <%= From c In data _
          Select <Car ID=<%= c.ID %>>
                     <PetName><%= c.PetName %></PetName>
                 </Car> %>
    </Inventory>

  Console.WriteLine(vehicles)
End Sub
```

Here, within the scope of the root `<Inventory>` element, we have embedded our LINQ query using the inline code markers (`<%= %>`). As with any XML literal, rather than making direct use of LINQ to XML data types (`XElement`, `XAttribute`, etc.), we are able to define these tokens as raw XML and fill in the blanks on the fly.

Loading and Parsing XML Content

The `XElement` and `XDocument` types both support `Load()` and `Parse()` methods, which allow you to hydrate an XML object model from `String` variables or external files. Consider the following method, which illustrates both approaches:

```
Sub LoadExistingXml()

  ' Build an XElement from string.
  Dim myElement As String = _
    "<Car ID='3'>" & _
      "<Color>Yellow</Color>" & _
      "<Make>Yugo</Make>" & _
    "</Car>"

  Dim newElement As XElement = XElement.Parse(myElement)
  Console.WriteLine(newElement)
  Console.WriteLine()

  ' Load the SimpleInventory.xml file.
  Dim myDoc As XDocument = XDocument.Load("SimpleInventory.xml")
  Console.WriteLine(myDoc)
End Sub
```

Notice that the `myElement` variable is a true string literal, *not* an XML literal. This is important, as the `Parse()` method expects a `String` containing well-formed XML, which would not be the case if we were to author the following XML literal:

```
Dim myBadElement As String = _
  <Car ID='3'>
    <Color>Yellow</Color>
    <Make>Yugo</Make>
  </Car>
```

Recall from earlier in this chapter that storing an XML literal within a `String` type strips out all of the XML elements and attributes, leaving only the values of the XML element data. In this case, passing in `myBadElement` to the `XElement.Parse()` method results in a runtime error.

■ Source Code The FunWithLinqToXml project can be found under the Chapter 24 subdirectory.

Navigating an In-Memory XML Document

So, at this point you have seen various ways in which LINQ to XML can be used to create, save, parse, and load XML data. The next aspect of LINQ to XML we need to examine is how to navigate a given document to locate specific elements/attributes. While the LINQ to XML object model provides a number of methods that can be used to programmatically navigate a document, not too surprisingly LINQ query expressions can also be used for this very purpose.

Since you have already seen numerous examples of building query expressions, the next example will be short and sweet. First, create a new Console Application named NavigationWithLinqToXmlObjectModel and import the `System.Xml.Linq` namespace. Next, add a new XML document into your current project named `Inventory.xml`, which supports a small set of entries within the root `<Inventory>` element. Here is one possibility:

```
<?xml version="1.0" encoding="utf-8"?>
<Inventory>
  <Car carID ="0">
    <Make>Ford</Make>
    <Color>Blue</Color>
    <PetName>Chuck</PetName>
  </Car>
  <Car carID ="1">
    <Make>VW</Make>
    <Color>Silver</Color>
    <PetName>Mary</PetName>
  </Car>
  <Car carID ="2">
    <Make>Yugo</Make>
    <Color>Pink</Color>
    <PetName>Gipper</PetName>
  </Car>
  <Car carID ="55">
    <Make>Ford</Make>
    <Color>Yellow</Color>
    <PetName>Max</PetName>
  </Car>
  <Car carID ="98">
    <Make>BMW</Make>
    <Color>Black</Color>
    <PetName>Zippy</PetName>
  </Car>
</Inventory>
```

Now, select this file within Solution Explorer and use the Properties window to set the Copy to Output Directory property to Copy Always (to ensure a copy of the file ends up in your Bin folder). Finally, update your `Main()` method to load this file into memory using `XElement.Load()`. The local `doc` variable will be passed into various helper methods to modify the data in various manners:

```
Sub Main()
  Console.WriteLine("***** Fun with LINQ to XML *****")

  ' Load the Inventory.xml document into memory.
  Dim doc As XElement = XElement.Load("Inventory.xml")

  ' We will author each of these next...
  PrintAllPetNames(doc)
  Console.WriteLine()
```

```
  GetAllFords(doc)
  Console.ReadLine()
End Sub
```

The PrintAllPetNames() method illustrates the use of the XElement.Descendants() method, which allows you to directly specify a given descendant node you wish to navigate to in order to apply a LINQ query expression. Here we are selecting each PetName value and printing out the contents to the console:

```
Sub PrintAllPetNames(ByVal doc As XElement)
  Dim petNames = From pn In doc.Descendants("PetName") _
                 Select pn.Value

  For Each name in petNames
    Console.WriteLine("Name: {0}", name)
  Next
End Sub
```

The GetAllFords() method is very similar in nature. Given the incoming XElement, we define a Where operator and select all the XElements where the Make element is equal to the value "Ford":

```
Sub GetAllFords(ByVal doc As XElement)
  Dim fords = From c In doc.Descendants("Make") _
              Where c.Value = "Ford" _
              Select c

  For Each f in fords
    Console.WriteLine(f)
  Next
End Sub
```

Figure 24-13 shows the output of this program.

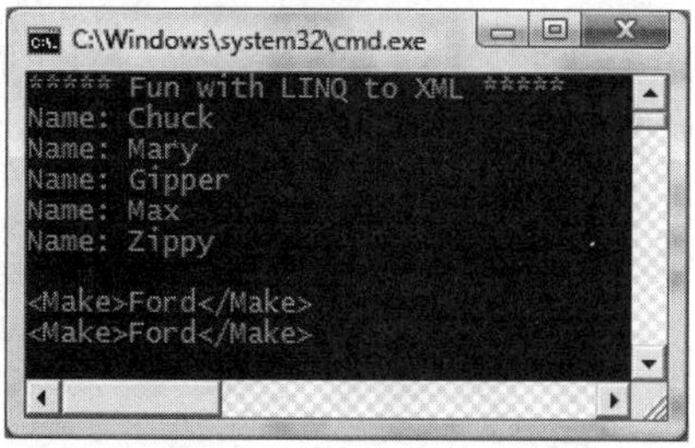

Figure 24-13. *Obtaining data from an XML document using LINQ*

Modifying Data in an XML Document

As you would hope, LINQ to XML provides numerous ways to insert, delete, copy, and update XML content. Adding new XElements to an existing XElement (or XDocument) is no harder than calling the Add() method, which adds the data to the end of the element/document. As an alternative, you can call AddFirst() to add the item to the top of the element/document or AddAfterThis()/AddBeforeThis() to insert data at a specific location.

Updating or deleting content is also very straightforward. After constructing a LINQ query statement to identify the item (or items) you wish to tinker with, simply call ReplaceContent() (for updating) or Remove()/RemoveContent() (for deletion of data). By way of a simple example, consider the following code, which adds a set of new <Car> elements to the incoming XElement parameter:

```
Sub AddNewElements(ByVal doc As XElement)
  For i As Integer = 0 To 4
    ' Add 5 new green Fords to the incoming document.
    ' Create a new XElement.
    Dim newCar As New XElement("Car", _
      New XAttribute("ID", i + 1000), _
        New XElement("Color", "Green"), _
        New XElement("Make", "Ford"), _
        New XElement("PetName", ""))
    ' Add to doc.
    doc.Add(newCar)
  Next
  ' Show the updates.
  Console.WriteLine(doc)
End Sub
```

As you might suspect, Visual Basic 2008 provides additional syntax that can be used within an XML literal to simplify the manner in which we navigate and modify XML data, using *XML axis property syntax*.

Source Code The NavigationWithLinqToXmlObjectModel project can be found under the Chapter 24 subdirectory.

The Role of XML Axis Properties

We can also construct XML literals that allow us to navigate within in-memory XML documents in a functional manner. Using XML axis property syntax, we have no need to directly make method calls on LINQ to XML objects; rather, we can make use of some specialized XML literal tokens, as shown in Table 24-4.

Table 24-4. *XML Axis Property Tokens*

Axis Property Token	Meaning in Life
`.@attribute`	Provides access to the value of an attribute for an `XElement` object
`.<child>`	Provides access to the children of a given `XElement` or `XDocument` object
`...<descendant>`	Provides access to the descendants of an `XElement` or `XDocument` object
`object(index)`	Allows you to apply an indexer syntax to an XML literal to access subitems
`Value`	Can be applied to an `XElement` to obtain the value of the element

In Table 24-4, each italicized token is described in generalized terms. For example, `.<child>` is referring to a child element of the object to the left of the dot operator, `.@attribute` refers to an attribute of the object to the left of the dot operator, and so on.

To see these tokens in action, create a final Console Application named NavigationWithAxis-Properties and insert the `Inventory.xml` file created in the previous example using the Project ➤ Add Existing Item menu option (don't forget to set the Copy to Output Directory property to Copy Always).

Our goal is to re-create the some of the methods of the previous example using the XML axis property token syntax, rather than directly using types of the `System.Xml.Linq` namespace. First, consider the following version of PrintAllPetNames(), which uses the descendant axis property token to navigate to the <PetName> element of the incoming XElement parameter:

```
Sub PrintAllPetNames(ByVal doc As XElement)
  ' Use XML descendant axis property to
  ' navigate to <PetName> descendant.
  Dim petNames = From pn In doc...<PetName> _
    Select pn.Value

  For Each name In petNames
    Console.WriteLine("Name: {0}", name)
  Next
End Sub
```

Notice that the recursive descent operator can be used to navigate to any descendant from the base object. For example, if we wish to navigate to the <Make> element, we could provide the following version of GetAllFords():

```
Sub GetAllFords(ByVal doc As XElement)
  Dim fords = From c In doc...<Make> _
    Where c.Value = "Ford" _
    Select c

  For Each f In fords
    Console.WriteLine("Name: {0}", f)
  Next
End Sub
```

To illustrate the use of the attribute axis property token, assume we wish to print out the value of each carID attribute within the document. Here is one possible way to do so:

```
Sub GetAllIds(ByVal doc As XElement)
  ' Navigate to <Car> element and
  ' get carID attribute.
  Dim ids = From c In doc.<Car> _
    Select c.@carID

  For Each id In ids
    Console.WriteLine(id)
  Next
End Sub
```

Last but not least, here is a final method that illustrates how to extract the values from an XElement using indexer syntax and the Value property:

```
Sub PrintAllColors(ByVal doc As XElement)
  ' Get value of each color using indexer.
  For i As Integer = 0 To doc.Nodes.Count - 1
    Console.WriteLine(doc.<Car>(i).<Color>.Value)
  Next
End Sub
```

Here, we obtain the number of nodes within the incoming XElement via the Count property of the Nodes collection. Knowing this value, we are then able to loop over each <Car> subelement within the <Inventory> root, printing out its <Color> value (via the Value property).

Now, assuming you have called each of these methods from within your `Main()` method, as so:

```
Sub Main()
  Console.WriteLine("***** Fun with XML Axis Properties *****")

  ' Load the Inventory.xml document into memory.
  Dim doc As XElement = XElement.Load("Inventory.xml")

  PrintAllPetNames(doc)
  Console.WriteLine()
  GetAllFords(doc)

  Console.WriteLine()
  GetAllIds(doc)

  Console.WriteLine()
  PrintAllColors(doc)

  Console.ReadLine()
End Sub
```

you would find the output shown in Figure 24-14.

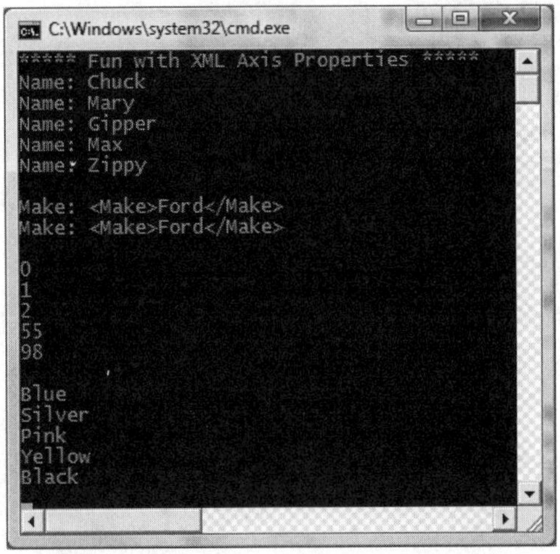

Figure 24-14. *XML axis properties in action*

That wraps up our look at the major LINQ APIs that ship with .NET 3.5, and this chapter as well! Over the remainder of this book, you will find various LINQ queries where appropriate; however, be aware that the APIs examined here (LINQ to DataSet, LINQ to SQL, and LINQ to XML) are extensively documented in the .NET Framework 3.5 SDK documentation.

Source Code The NavigationWithAxisProperties example can be found under the Chapter 24 subdirectory.

Summary

This chapter extended your understanding of LINQ by introducing three LINQ-centric APIs. We began by examining how to transform an ADO.NET `DataSet` into a LINQ-compatible container using the `AsEnumerable()` extension method. Once you have extracted an `IEnumerable(Of T)` type, you are able to apply any flavor of LINQ query.

Closely related to LINQ to DataSet is the LINQ to SQL API. This aspect of LINQ not only allows you to apply query expressions to data held within relational databases, it also provides infrastructure that essentially encapsulates all trace of the underlying ADO.NET data types. As you have seen, the `DataContext` type can be used to perform all of the expected database operations, including invoking stored procedures.

We wrapped up by examining LINQ to XML. Similar to LINQ to SQL, this API can be used either to apply LINQ queries to data within an XML document or to build XML documents in a functional manner. As a bonus, you examined how the Visual Basic programming language simplified the use of LINQ to XML even further using XML literal notation and axis property syntax.

CHAPTER 25

Introducing Windows Communication Foundation

.NET 3.0 introduced an API specifically for the process of building distributed systems named Windows Communication Foundation (WCF). Unlike other distributed APIs you may have used in the past (DCOM, .NET remoting, XML web services, etc.), WCF provides a single, unified, and extendable programming object model that can be used to interact with a number of previously diverse distributed technologies.

This chapter begins by framing the need for WCF and examining the problems it intends to solve by way of a quick review of previous distributed computing APIs. After we look at the services provided by WCF, we'll turn to examine the .NET assemblies (and core types) that represent this programming model. Over the remainder of this chapter, we'll build several WCF services, hosts, and clients using various WCF development tools.

Note This chapter will provide you with a firm foundation in WCF development. However, if you require a comprehensive treatment of the subject, check out *Pro WCF: Practical Microsoft SOA Implementation* by Chris Peiris and Dennis Mulder (Apress, 2007).

A Potpourri of Distributed Computing APIs

The Windows operating system has historically provided a number of APIs for building distributed systems. While it is true that most people consider a "distributed system" to involve at the very least two networked computers, this term in the broader sense can simply refer to two executables that need to exchange data, even if they happen to be running on the same physical machine. Using this definition, selecting a distributed API for your current programming task typically involves asking the following pivotal question:

> *Will this system be used exclusively "in house," or will external users require access to the application's functionality?*

If you are building a distributed system for in-house use, you have a far greater chance of ensuring that each connected computer is running the same operating system, using the same programming framework (.NET, COM, Java EE, etc.), and you will be able to leverage your existing security system for purposes of authentication, authorization, and so forth. In this situation, you may be willing to select a particular distributed API that will tie you to a specific operating system/programming framework for the purposes of performance.

In contrast, if you are building a system that must be reached by those outside of your walls, you have a whole other set of issues to contend with. First of all, you will most likely *not* be able to dictate to external users which operating system they make use of, which programming framework they use to build their software, or how they configure their security settings.

Furthermore, if you happen to work for a larger company or in a university setting that makes use of numerous operating systems and programming technologies, an in-house application suddenly faces the same challenges as an outward-facing application. In either of these cases, you need to limit yourself to a more flexible distributed API to ensure the furthest "reach" of your application.

Based on the answer to this key distributed computing question, the next task is to pinpoint exactly which API (or set of APIs) to make use of. By way of a painless overview, the following sections present a quick recap of some of the major distributed APIs historically used by Windows software developers. Once you finish this brief history lesson, you will easily be able to see the usefulness of Windows Communication Foundation.

■ Note Just to make sure we are all on the same page here, I feel compelled to point out that WCF (and the technologies it encompasses) has nothing to do with building an HTML-based web application. While it is true that web applications can be considered "distributed" in that two machines are typically involved in the exchange, WCF is about establishing connections to machines to share the functionality of remote components—not for displaying HTML in a web browser. Chapter 33 will begin your examination of building websites with the .NET platform.

The Role of DCOM

Prior to the release of the .NET platform, Distributed Component Object Model (DCOM) was the remoting API of choice for Microsoft-centric development endeavors. Using DCOM, it was possible to build distributed systems using COM objects, the system registry, and a good amount of elbow grease. One benefit of DCOM was that it allowed for *location transparency* of components. Simply put, this allowed client software to be programmed in such a way that the physical locations of the remote objects were not hard-coded. Regardless of whether the remote object was on the same machine or a secondary networked machine, the code base could remain neutral, as the actual location was recorded externally in the system registry.

While DCOM did enjoy some degree of success, for all practical purposes it was a Windows-centric API. Even though DCOM was ported to a few other operating systems, DCOM alone did not provide a fabric to build comprehensive solutions involving multiple operating systems (Windows, Unix, Mac) or promote sharing of data between diverse architectures (COM, Java EE, CORBA, etc.).

■ Note There were some attempts to port DCOM to run on various flavors of Unix/Linux, but the end result was lackluster and eventually became a technology footnote.

By and large, DCOM was best suited for in-house application development, as exposing COM types outside company walls entailed a set of additional complications (firewalls and so forth). With the release of the .NET platform, DCOM quickly became a legacy programming model, and unless you are maintaining legacy DCOM systems, you can consider it a deprecated technology.

The Role of COM+/Enterprise Services

DCOM alone did little more than define a way to establish a communication channel between two pieces of COM-based software. To fill in the missing pieces required for building a feature-rich distributed computing solution, Microsoft eventually released Microsoft Transaction Server (MTS), which was subsequently renamed to COM+ at a later release.

Despite its name, COM+ is not only used by COM programmers—it is completely accessible to .NET professionals. Since the first release of the .NET platform, the base class libraries provided a namespace named `System.EnterpriseServices`. Here, .NET programmers could build managed libraries that could be installed into the COM+ runtime in order to access the same set of services as a traditional COM+-aware COM server. In either case, once a COM+-aware library is installed into the COM+ runtime, it is termed a *serviced component*.

COM+ provides a number of features that serviced components can leverage, including transaction management, object lifetime management, pooling services, a role-based security system, a loosely coupled event model, and so on. This was a major benefit at the time COM+ was released, given that most distributed systems require the same set of services. Rather than forcing developers to code these services by hand, COM+ provided an out-of-the-box solution.

One of the compelling aspects of COM+ was the fact that all of these settings could be configured in a declarative manner using administrative tools. Thus, if you wished to ensure an object was monitored under a transactional context or belonged to a particular security role, you simply needed to select the correct check boxes.

While COM+/Enterprise Services is still in use today, this technology is a Windows-only solution that is best suited for in-house application development or as a back-end service indirectly manipulated by more agonistic front ends (e.g., a public website that makes calls on serviced components [aka COM+ objects] in the background).

■ **Note** WCF does not currently provide a way to build serviced components. However, it does provide a way for WCF services to communicate with existing COM+ objects. If you need to build serviced components using VB, you will need to make direct use of the `System.EnterpriseServices` namespace. Consult the .NET Framework 3.5 SDK documentation for details.

The Role of MSMQ

The Microsoft Message Queuing (MSMQ) API allows developers to build distributed systems that need to ensure reliable delivery of message data on the network. As we all know too well, in any distributed system there is the risk that a network server is down, a database is offline, or connections are lost for mysterious reasons. Furthermore, a number of applications need to be constructed in such a way that they hold message data for delivery at a later time (known as *queuing data*).

At first, MSMQ was packaged as a set of low-level C-based APIs and COM objects. As well, using the `System.Messaging` namespace, .NET programmers could hook into MSMQ and build software that communicated with intermittently connected applications in a dependable fashion. Last but not least, the COM+ layer incorporated MSMQ functionality into the runtime (in a simplified format) using a technology termed Queued Components (QC).

Regardless of which programming model you used to interact with the MSMQ runtime, the end result ensured that applications could deliver messages in a reliable and timely fashion. Like COM+, MSMQ is still certainly part of the fabric of building distributed software on the Windows operating system.

The Role of .NET Remoting

As mentioned, with the release of the .NET platform, DCOM quickly became a legacy distributed API. In its place, the .NET base class libraries shipped with the .NET remoting layer, represented by the `System.Runtime.Remoting` namespace (and numerous related subnamespaces). This API allows multiple computers to distribute objects, provided they are all running the applications under the .NET platform.

The .NET remoting APIs provide a number of very useful features. Most important is the use of XML-based configuration files to declaratively define the underlying plumbing used by the client and the server software. Using `*.config` files, it is very simple to radically alter the functionality of your distributed system simply by changing the content of the configuration files and restarting the application.

As well, given the fact that this API is useable only by .NET applications, you can gain various performance benefits, as data can be encoded in a compact binary format, and you can make use of the Common Type System (CTS) when defining parameters and return values. While it is possible to make use of .NET remoting to build distributed systems that span multiple operating systems (via Mono, briefly mentioned in Chapter 1), interoperability between other programming architectures (such as Java EE) is still not directly possible.

■ **Note** Previous editions of this text included an entire chapter devoted to the topic of the .NET remoting APIs. With the release of WCF, however, I have decided not to include that chapter in this edition.

The Role of XML Web Services

Each of the previously mentioned distributed APIs provide little (if any) support to allow external callers to access the supplied functionality in an *agnostic manner*. When you need to expose the services of remote objects to *any* operating system and *any* programming model, XML web services provide the most straightforward way of doing so.

Unlike a traditional browser-based web application, a web service is simply a way to expose the functionality of remote components via standard web protocols. Since the initial release of .NET, programmers have been provided with superior support for building and consuming XML web services via the `System.Web.Services` namespace. In fact, in many cases, building a feature-complete web service is no more complicated than applying the `<WebMethod()>` attribute to each public method you wish to provide access to. Furthermore, Visual Studio 2008 allows you to connect to a remote web service with the click of a button (or two).

Web services allow developers to build .NET assemblies containing types that can be accessed via simple HTTP. Furthermore, a web service encodes its data as simple XML. Given the fact that web services are based on open industry standards (HTTP, XML, SOAP, etc.) rather than proprietary type systems and proprietary wire formats (as is the case with DCOM or .NET remoting), they allow for a high degree of interoperability and data exchange. Figure 25-1 illustrates the agnostic nature of XML web services.

Of course, no distributed API is perfect. One potential drawback of web services is the fact that they can suffer from some performance issues (given the use of HTTP and XML data representation), and they may not be an ideal solution for in-house applications where a TCP-based protocol and binary formatting of data could be used without penalty.

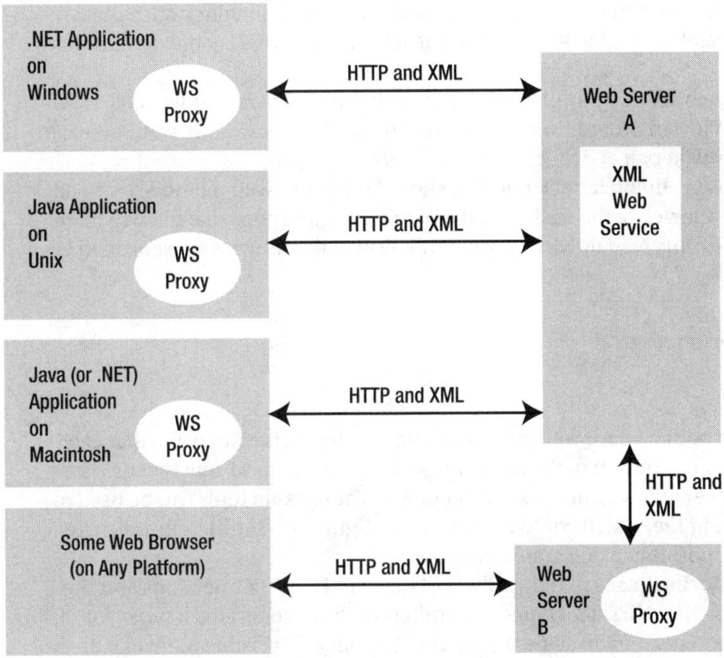

Figure 25-1. *XML web services allow for a very high degree of interoperability.*

A .NET Web Service Example

For many years now, .NET programmers have created web services using the ASP.NET Web Service project template of Visual Studio, which can be accessed using the File ➤ New ➤ Web Site dialog box. This particular project template creates a commonly used directory structure and a handful of initial files to represent the web service itself. While this project template is very helpful to get you up and running, you are able to build a .NET XML web service using a simple text editor and test it immediately using the ASP.NET development web server, `WebDev.WebServer.exe` (Chapter 33 examines this utility in more detail).

By way of a quick example, assume you have authored the following programming logic (using a simple text editor) in a new file named `HelloWebService.asmx` (`*.asmx` is the default file extension for a .NET XML web service file). Once you have done so, save it into C:\HelloWebService.

```
<%@ WebService Language="VB" Class="HelloWebService" %>
Imports System
Imports System.Web.Services

Public Class HelloWebService
  <WebMethod()> _
  Public Function HelloWorld() As String
    Return "Hello World"
  End Function
End Class
```

While this simple service is hardly doing anything terribly useful, notice that the file opens with the `WebService` directive, which is used to specify which .NET programming language is used in the file, and the name of the class type representing the service. Beyond this, the only point of interest is that the `HelloWorld()` method has been decorated with the `<WebMethod()>` attribute. In many cases, this is all you need to do to expose a method to external callers via HTTP. Finally, notice that you do not need to do anything special to encode the return value into XML, as this is done so automatically by the runtime.

If you wish to test this web service, simply open up this file within Visual Studio 2008, right-click the file, and select the View in Browser menu option. This will host your XML web service in the ASP.NET development web server.

At this point, your browser should launch and you should see each "web method" exposed from this endpoint. You can then click the HelloWorld link to view a test page that allows you to invoke the method via HTTP. Once you do, the browser will display the return value encoded as XML:

```
<?xml version="1.0" encoding="utf-8" ?>
<string xmlns="http://tempuri.org/">
  Hello World
</string>
```

Simple stuff, huh? Even better, when you wish to generate a client-side proxy file that can be used to invoke web methods, you can make use of the `wsdl.exe` command-line tool or Visual Studio's Add Service Reference option under the Project menu. These same tools can be used to generate a client-side `*.config` file, which contains various configuration settings for the proxy (such as the web service endpoint) in a declarative manner.

This proxy code will hide the details of manually working with HTTP connections and the translation of XML data back into .NET data types. Assuming you have generated a proxy for this simple web service (there is no need to do so here), the client application is able to invoke the web method in a painfully simple manner, for example:

```
Sub Main()
  ' The proxy type contains code to read the *.config file
  ' to resolve the location of the web service.
  Dim proxy As New HelloWebServiceProxy()
  Console.WriteLine(proxy.HelloWorld())
End Sub
```

■ **Note** Previous editions of this text included an entire chapter devoted to the topic of .NET XML web services. With the release of WCF, however, I have decided not to include that chapter in this edition.

While it is still perfectly possible to build this "traditional" flavor of XML web service under .NET 3.5, most new service projects will benefit from instead making use of the WCF templates. As you will see, you have many HTTP-based bindings to choose from, which allow you to essentially build a web service without selecting a specific "web service" project template.

■ **Source Code** The HelloWebService project is located under the Chapter 25 subdirectory.

Web Service Standards

A major problem that web services faced early on was the fact that all of the big industry players (Microsoft, IBM, and Sun Microsystems) created web service implementations that were not 100 percent compatible with other web service implementations. Obviously, this was an issue, given that the whole point of web services was to achieve a very high degree of interoperability across platforms and operating systems!

In order to ensure the interoperability of web services, groups such as the World Wide Web Consortium (W3C; `http://www.w3.org`) and the Web Services Interoperability Organization (WS-I; `http://www.ws-i.org`) began to author several specifications that laid out the details of how a software vendor (again, such as Microsoft, IBM, or Sun Microsystems) should build web service–centric software libraries to ensure compatibility.

Collectively all of these specifications are given the blanket name WS-* and cover the issues of security, attachments, the description of web services (via the Web Service Description Language, or WSDL), policies, SOAP formats, and a slew of other important details.

As you may know, Microsoft's implementation of most of these standards (for both managed and unmanaged code) is embodied in the Web Services Enhancements (WSE) 3.0 toolkit, which can be downloaded free of charge from the supporting website: `http://msdn2.microsoft.com/en-us/webservices`.

When you are building WCF service applications, you will not need to make direct use of the assemblies that are part of the WSE 3.0 toolkit. Rather, if you build a WCF service that makes use of an HTTP-based binding, these same WS-* specifications will be given to you out of the box (exactly which ones will be based on the binding you choose).

Named Pipes, Sockets, and P2P

As if choosing among DCOM, .NET remoting, web services, COM+, and MSMQ was not challenging enough, the list of distributed APIs continues. Programmers can also make use of additional interprocess communication APIs such as named pipes, sockets, and peer-to-peer (P2P) services. These lower-level APIs typically provide better performance (especially for machines on the same LAN); however, using these APIs becomes more complex (if not impossible) for outward-facing applications.

If you are building a distributed system involving a set of applications running on the same physical machine, you can make use of the named pipes API via the `System.IO.Pipes` namespace (which is new to .NET 3.5). This approach can provide the absolute fastest way to push data between applications on the same machine.

As well, if you are building an application that requires absolute control over how network access is obtained and maintained, sockets and P2P functionality can be achieved under the .NET platform using the `System.Net.Sockets` and `System.Net.PeerToPeer` namespaces, respectively.

The Role of WCF

As I am sure you already figured out from the previous few pages, the wide array of distributed technologies makes it very difficult to pick the right tool for the job. This is further complicated by the fact that several of these technologies overlap in the features they provide (most notably in the areas of transactions and security).

Even when a .NET developer has selected what appear to be the "correct" technologies for the task at hand, building, maintaining, and configuring such an application is complex at best. Each API has its own programming model, its own unique set of configuration utilities, and so forth.

Because of this, prior to .NET 3.0, it was very difficult to "plug and play" distributed APIs without authoring a considerable amount of custom infrastructure. For example, if you build your system using the .NET remoting APIs, and you later decide that XML web services are a more appropriate solution, you need to reengineer your code base make use of them.

WCF is a distributed computing toolkit introduced with .NET 3.0 that integrates these previous independent distributed technologies into a streamlined API represented primarily via the `System.ServiceModel` namespace. Using WCF, you are able to expose services to callers using a wide variety of techniques. For example, if you are building an in-house application where all connected machines are Windows based, you can make use of various TCP protocols to ensure the fastest possible performance. This same service can also be exposed using an XML web service–based protocol to allow external callers to leverage its functionality regardless of the programming language or operating system.

Given the fact that WCF allows you to pick the correct protocol for the job (using a common programming model), you will find that it becomes quite easy to plug and play the underlying plumbing of your distributed application. In most cases, you can do so without being required to recompile or redeploy the client/service software, as the grungy details are often relegated to application configuration files (much like the older .NET remoting APIs).

An Overview of WCF Features

Interoperability and integration of diverse APIs are only two (very important) aspects of WCF. In addition, WCF provides a rich software fabric that complements the remoting technologies it exposes. Consider the following list of major WCF features:

- Support for strongly typed *as well as* untyped messages. This approach allows .NET applications to share custom types efficiently, while software created using other platforms (such as Java EE) can consume streams of loosely typed XML.
- Support for several *bindings* (raw HTTP, TCP, MSMQ, and named pipes) to allow you to choose the most appropriate plumbing to transport message data to and fro.
- Support for the latest and greatest web service specifications (WS-*).
- A fully integrated security model encompassing both native Windows/.NET security protocols and numerous neutral security techniques built upon web service standards.
- Support for sessionlike state management techniques, as well as support for one-way stateless messages.

As impressive as this list of features may be, it really only scratches the surface of the functionality WCF provides. WCF also offers tracing and logging facilities, performance counters, a publish and subscribe event model, and transactional support, among other features.

An Overview of Service-Oriented Architecture

Yet another benefit of WCF is that it is based on the design principles established by *service-oriented architecture* (SOA). To be sure, SOA is a major buzzword in the industry, and like most buzzwords, SOA can be defined in numerous ways. Simply put, SOA is a way to design a distributed system where several autonomous *services* work in conjunction by passing *messages* across boundaries (either networked machines or simply two processes on the same machine) using well-defined *interfaces.*

In the world of WCF, these "well-defined interfaces" are typically created using actual CLR interface types (see Chapter 9). In a more general sense, however, the interface of a service simply describes the set of members that may be invoked by external callers.

When WCF was designed, the WCF team did so by observing four tenets of SOA design. While these tenets are typically honored automatically simply by building a WCF application, understanding these four cardinal design rules of SOA can further help put WCF into perspective. The sections that follow provide a brief overview of each tenet.

Tenet 1: Boundaries Are Explicit

This tenet reiterates the fact that the functionality of a WCF service is expressed using well-defined interfaces (e.g., descriptions of each member, its parameters, and its return values). The only way that an external caller is able to communicate with a WCF service is via the interface, and the external caller remains blissfully unaware of the underlying implementation details.

Tenet 2: Services Are Autonomous

When speaking of services as "autonomous" entities, we are referring to the fact that a given WCF service is (as much as possible) an island unto itself. An autonomous service should be independent with regard to version issues, deployment issues, and installation issues. To help promote this tenet, we yet again fall back on a key aspect of interface-based programming. Once an interface is in production, it should never be changed (or you risk breaking existing clients). When you need to extend the functionality of your WCF service, simply author new interfaces that model the desired functionality.

Tenet 3: Services Communicate via Contract, Not Implementation

The third tenet is yet another byproduct of interface-based programming in that the implementation details of a WCF service (which language it was written in, how it gets its work accomplished, etc.) are of no concern to the external caller. WCF clients interact with services solely through their exposed public interfaces. Furthermore, if the members of a service interface expose custom complex types, they need to be fully detailed as a *data contract* to ensure all callers can map the content into a particular data structure.

Tenet 4: Service Compatibility Is Based on Policy

Because CLR interfaces provide strongly typed contracts for all WCF clients (and may also be used to generate a related WSDL document based on your choice of binding), it is important to point out that interfaces/WSDL alone is not expressive enough to detail aspects of what the service is capable of doing. Given this, SOA allows us to define "policies" that further qualify the semantics of the service (e.g., the expected security requirements used to talk to the service). Using these policies, we are able to basically separate the low-level syntactic description of our service (the exposed interfaces) from the semantic details of how the service works and how it needs to be invoked.

WCF: The Bottom Line

Hopefully this little history lesson has illustrated that WCF is the preferred approach for building distributed applications under .NET 3.0 and higher. Whether you are attempting to build an in-house application using TCP protocols, are moving data between programs on the same machine using named pipes, or are exposing data to the world at large using web service protocols, WCF is the recommended API to do so.

This is not to say you cannot use the original .NET distributed-centric namespaces (`System.Runtime.Remoting`, `System.Messaging`, `System.EnterpriseServices`, `System.Web.Services`, etc.) in new development efforts. In fact, in some cases (specifically if you need to build COM+ objects), you will be required to do so. In any case, if you have used these APIs in previous projects, you will find learning WCF straightforward. Like the technologies that preceded it, WCF makes considerable use of XML-based configuration files, .NET attributes, and proxy generation utilities.

With this introductory foundation behind us, we can now turn to the topic of actually building WCF applications. Again, do understand that full coverage of WCF would require an entire book, as each of the supported services (MSMQ, COM+, P2P, named pipes, etc.) could easily be a chapter unto itself. Here, you will learn the overall process of building WCF programs using HTTP-based (e.g., web service) protocols. This should put you in a good position for future study as you see fit.

Investigating the Core WCF Assemblies

As you would expect, the programming fabric of WCF is represented by a set of .NET assemblies installed into the GAC. Table 25-1 describes the overall role of the core WCF assemblies you will need to make use of in just about any WCF application.

Table 25-1. *Core WCF Assemblies*

Assembly	Meaning in Life
`System.Runtime.Serialization.dll`	Defines namespaces and types that can be used for serializing and deserializing objects within the WCF framework
`System.ServiceModel.dll`	The core assembly that contains the types used to build any sort of WCF application

These two assemblies define a number of new namespaces and types. While you should consult the .NET Framework 3.5 SDK documentation for complete details, Table 25-2 documents the roles of some of the important namespaces to be aware of.

Table 25-2. *Core WCF Namespaces*

Namespace	Meaning in Life
`System.Runtime.Serialization`	Defines numerous types used to control how data is serialized and deserialized within the WCF framework
`System.ServiceModel`	The primary WCF namespace that defines binding and hosting types, as well as basic security and transactional types
`System.ServiceModel.Configuration`	Defines numerous types that provide programmatic access to WCF configuration files
`System.ServiceModel.Description`	Defines types that provide an object model to the addresses, bindings, and contracts defined within WCF configuration files
`System.ServiceModel.MsmqIntegration`	Contains types to integrate with the MSMQ service
`System.ServiceModel.Security`	Defines numerous types to control aspects of the WCF security layers

A BRIEF WORD REGARDING CARDSPACE

In addition to `System.ServiceModel.dll` and `System.Runtime.Serialization.dll`, WCF provides a third WCF assembly named `System.IdentityModel.dll`. Here you will find a number of additional namespaces and types that support the WCF CardSpace API. This technology allows you to establish and manage digital identities within a WCF application. Essentially, the CardSpace API provides a unified programming model to account for various security-related details for WCF applications, such as caller identity, user authentication/authorization services, and whatnot.

We will not examine CardSpace further in this edition of the text, so be sure to consult the .NET Framework 3.5 SDK documentation if you are interested in learning more.

The Visual Studio WCF Project Templates

As will be explained in more detail later in this chapter, a WCF application is typically represented by three interrelated assemblies, one of which is a `*.dll` that contains the types that external callers can communicate with (in other words, the WCF service itself). When you wish to build a WCF service, it is perfectly permissible to select a standard Class Library project template (see Chapter 15) as a starting point and manually reference the WCF assemblies.

Alternatively, you can create a new WCF service by selecting the WCF Service Library project template of Visual Studio 2008 (see Figure 25-2). This project type automatically sets references to the required WCF assemblies; however, it also generates a good deal of "starter code," which you will more likely than not simply delete.

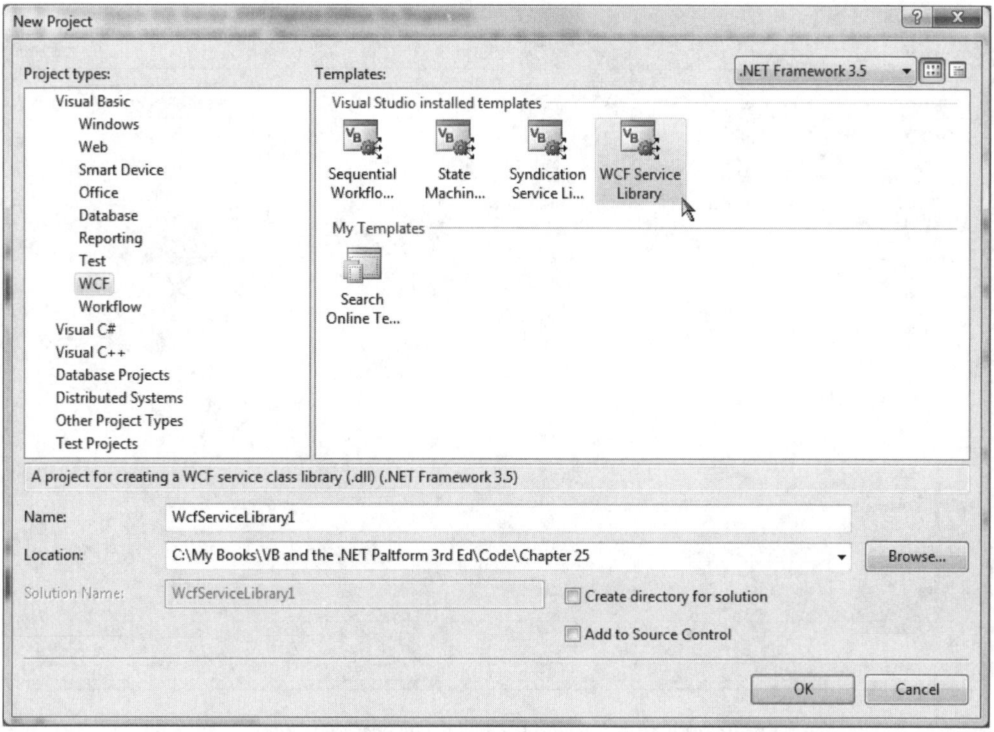

Figure 25-2. *The Visual Studio 2008 WCF Service Library project template*

One benefit of selecting the WCF Service Library project template is that it also supplies you with an `App.config` file, which may seem strange since we are building a .NET `*.dll`, not a .NET `*.exe`. This file, however, is very useful in that when you debug or run your WCF Service Library project, the Visual Studio IDE will automatically launch the WCF Test Client application. This program (`WcfTestClient.exe`) will read the settings in the `App.config` file in order to host your service for testing purposes. You'll learn more about the WCF Test Client later in this chapter.

■ **Note** The `App.config` file of the WCF Service Library project is also useful in that it shows you the bare-bones settings used to configure a WCF host application. In fact, you can copy and paste much of this code into your host's actual configuration file.

In addition to the basic WCF Service Library template, the WCF project category of the New Project dialog box defines two WCF library projects that integrate Windows Workflow Foundation functionality into a WCF service as well as a template to build an RSS library (all of which are also seen in Figure 25-2). The next chapter will introduce you to Windows Workflow Foundation, so I'll ignore these particular WCF project templates for the time being (and I'll leave it to the interested reader to dig into the RSS feed project template).

The WCF Service Website Project Template

Truth be told, there is yet another Visual Studio 2008 WCF-centric project template that you will find in the New Web Site dialog box, activated via the File ➤ New ➤ Web Site menu option (see Figure 25-3).

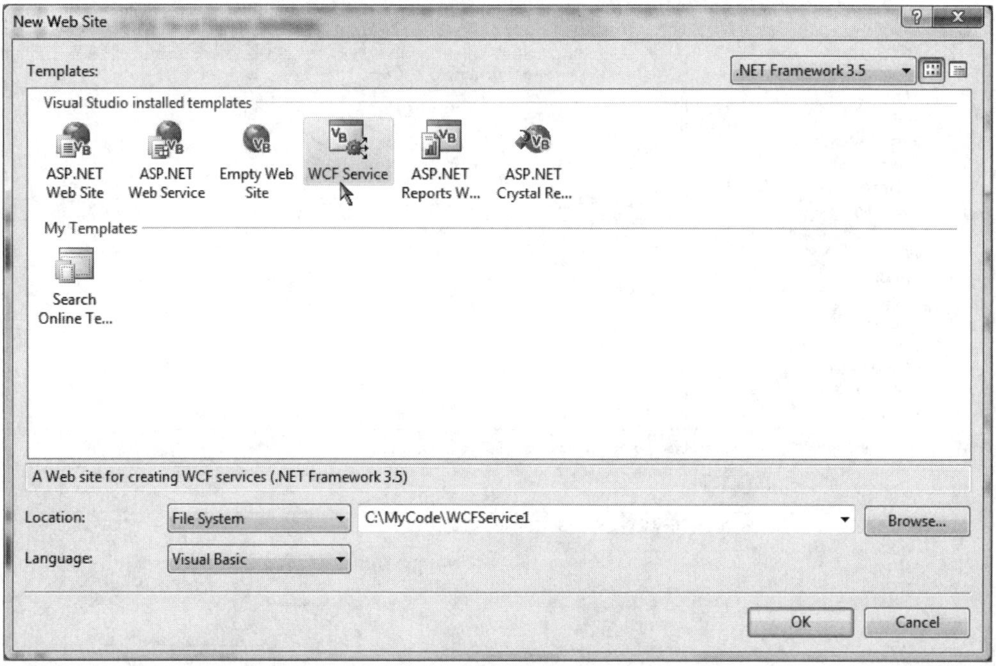

Figure 25-3. *The Visual Studio 2008 web-based WCF Service project template*

This WCF Service project template is useful when you know from the outset that your WCF service will make use of web service–based protocols rather than, for example, named pipes. This option can automatically create a new Internet Information Services (IIS) virtual directory to contain your WCF program files, create a proper `web.config` file to expose the service via HTTP, and author the necessary `*.svc` file (more about `*.svc` files later in this chapter). In this light, the web-based WCF Service project is simply a time-saver, as the IDE will automatically set up the required IIS infrastructure.

In contrast, if you build a new WCF service using the WCF Service Library option, you have the ability to host the service in a variety of ways (custom host, Windows service, manually built IIS virtual directory, etc.). This option is more appropriate when you wish to build a custom host for your WCF service.

The Basic Composition of a WCF Application

When you are building a WCF distributed system, you will typically do so by creating three interrelated assemblies:

- *The WCF service assembly*: This `*.dll` contains the classes and interfaces that represent the overall functionality you are exposing to external callers.
- *The WCF service host*: This software module is the entity that hosts your WCF service assembly.
- *The WCF client*: This is the application that accesses the service's functionality through an intervening proxy.

As mentioned, the WCF service assembly is a .NET class library that contains a number of WCF contracts and their implementations. The one key difference is that the interface contracts are adorned with various attributes that control data type representation, how the WCF runtime interacts with the exposed types, and so forth.

The second assembly, the WCF service host, can literally be any .NET executable. As you will see in this chapter, WCF was set up in such a way that services can be easily exposed from any type of application (Windows Forms, a Windows service, WPF applications, etc.). When you are building a custom host, you will make use of the `ServiceHost` type and a related `*.config` file, which contains details regarding the server-side plumbing you wish to make use of. However, if you are using IIS as the host for your WCF service, there is no need to programmatically build a custom host, as IIS will make use of the `ServiceHost` type behind the scenes.

■ **Note** It is also possible to host a WCF service using the Vista-specific Windows Activation Service (WAS). Consult the .NET Framework 3.5 SDK documentation for details.

The final assembly represents the client that is making calls into the WCF service. As you might expect, this client could be any type of .NET application. Similar to the host, client applications also typically make use of a client-side `*.config` file that defines the client-side plumbing.

Figure 25-4 illustrates (from a very high level) the relationship between these three interrelated WCF assemblies. As you would assume, behind the scenes are several lower-level details used to represent the required plumbing (factories, channels, listeners, etc.). These low-level details are most often hidden from view; however, they can be extended or customized if required. Thankfully, in most cases, the default plumbing will fit the bill.

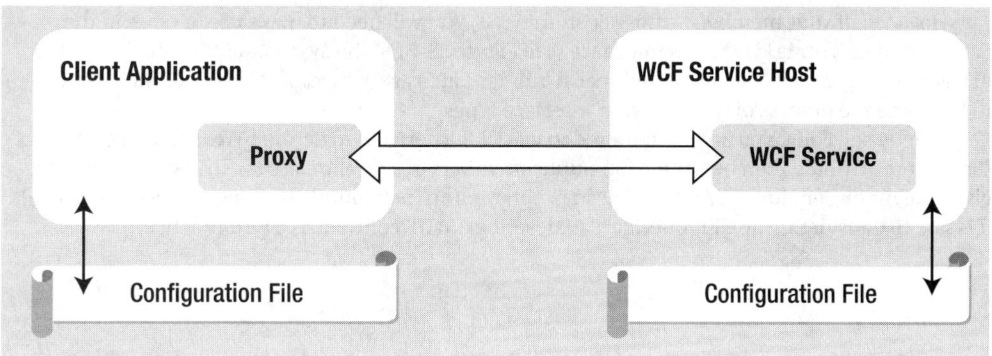

Figure 25-4. *A high-level look at a typical WCF application*

It is also worth pointing out that the use of a server-side or client-side `*.config` file is technically optional. If you wish, you can hard-code the host (as well as the client) to specify the necessary plumbing (endpoints, binding, addresses, etc.). The obvious problem with this approach is that if you need to change the plumbing details, you will be required to recode, recompile, and redeploy a number of assemblies. Using a `*.config` file keeps your code base much more flexible, as changing the plumbing is as simple as updating the file's content and restarting the application.

The ABCs of WCF

Hosts and clients communicate with each other by agreeing on the ABCs, a friendly mnemonic for remembering the core building blocks of a WCF application, specifically *address, binding,* and *contract.*

- *Address*: The location of the service. In code, this is represented with a `System.Uri` type; however, the value is typically stored in `*.config` files.
- *Binding*: WCF ships with a number of different bindings that specify network protocols, encoding mechanisms, and the transport layer.
- *Contract*: A description of each method exposed from the WCF service.

Do understand that the ABC abbreviation does not imply that a developer must define the address first, followed by binding, and ending with the contract. In many cases, a WCF developer begins by defining a contract for the service, followed by establishing an address and bindings (but any order will do, so long as each aspect is accounted for). Before we build our first WCF application, here is a more detailed walk-through of the ABCs.

Understanding WCF Contracts

The notion of a *contract* is the key to building a WCF service. While not mandatory, the vast majority of your WCF applications will begin by defining a set of .NET interface types that are used to represent the set of members a given WCF type will support. Specifically, interfaces that represent a WCF contract are termed *service contracts.* The classes (or structures) that implement them are termed *service types.*

WCF service contracts are adorned with various attributes, the most common of which are defined in the `System.ServiceModel` namespace. When the members of a service contract contain only simple data types (such as numerical data, Booleans, and string data), you can build a complete WCF service using nothing more than the `<ServiceContract()>` and `<OperationContract()>` attributes.

However, if your members expose custom types, you will need to make use of types in the `System.Runtime.Serialization` namespace (see Figure 25-5) of the `System.Runtime.Serialization.dll` assembly. Here you will find additional attributes (such as `<DataMember()>` and `<DataContract()>`) to fine-tune the process of defining your interface types.

Strictly speaking, you are not required to use CLR interfaces to define a WCF contract. Many of these same attributes can be applied on public members of a public class (or structure). However, given the many benefits of interface-based programming (polymorphism, elegant versioning, etc.), it is safe to consider using CLR interfaces to describe a WCF contract as a best practice.

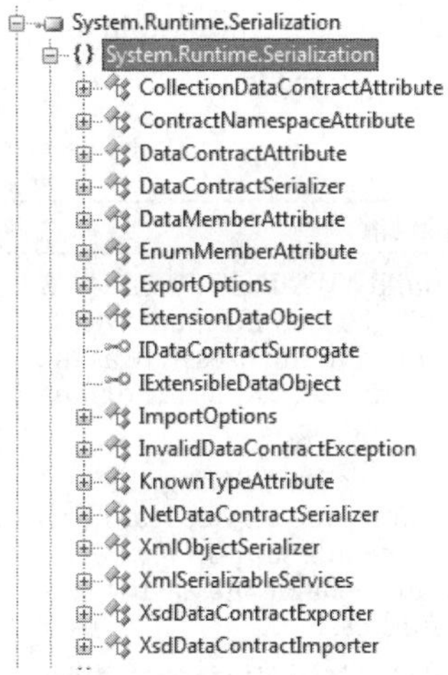

Figure 25-5. `System.Runtime.Serialization` *defines a number of attributes used when building WCF data contracts.*

Understanding WCF Bindings

Once a contract (or a set of contracts) has been defined and implemented within your service library, the next logical step is to build a hosting agent for the WCF service itself. As mentioned, you have a variety of possible hosts to choose from, all of which must specify the *bindings* used by remote callers to gain access to the service type's functionality.

Choosing a set of bindings is one area that makes WCF development quite different from .NET remoting and/or XML web service development in that WCF ships with a number of binding choices, each of which is tailored to a specific need. If none of the out-of-the-box bindings fits the bill, it is possible to create your own by extending the `CustomBinding` type (something we will not do in this chapter). Simply put, a WCF binding can specify the following characteristics:

- The contracts implemented by the service
- The transport layer used to move data (HTTP, MSMQ, named pipes, TCP)
- The channels used by the transport (one-way, request-reply, duplex)
- The encoding mechanism used to deal with the data itself (XML, binary, etc.)
- Any supported web service protocols (if permitted by the binding) such as WS-Security, WS-Transactions, WS-Reliability, and so on

Let's take a look at our choices.

HTTP-Based Bindings

The `BasicHttpBinding`, `WSHttpBinding`, `WSDualHttpBinding`, and `WSFederationHttpBinding` options are geared toward exposing contract types via XML web service protocols. Clearly, if you require the furthest reach possible for your service (multiple operating systems and multiple programming architectures), these are the bindings to focus on, because all of these binding types encode data based on XML representation and use HTTP on the wire.

In Table 25-3, note that a WCF binding can be represented in code (via class types within the `System.ServiceModel` namespace) or as XML attributes defined within `*.config` files.

Table 25-3. *The HTTP-Centric WCF Bindings*

Binding Class	Binding Element	Meaning in Life
`BasicHttpBinding`	<basicHttpBinding>	Used to build a WS-Basic Profile (WS-I Basic Profile 1.1)–conformant WCF service. This binding uses `HTTP` as the transport and `Text/XML` as the default message encoding.
`WSHttpBinding`	<wsHttpBinding>	Similar to `BasicHttpBinding`, but provides more web service features. This binding adds support for transactions, reliable messaging, and WS-Addressing.
`WSDualHttpBinding`	<wsDualHttpBinding>	Similar to `WSHttpBinding`, but for use with duplex contracts (e.g., the service and client can send messages back and forth). This binding supports only SOAP security and requires reliable messaging.
`WSFederationHttpBinding`	<wsFederationHttpBinding>	A secure and interoperable binding that supports the WS-Federation protocol, enabling organizations that are in a federation to efficiently authenticate and authorize users.

As the name suggests, `BasicHttpBinding` is the simplest of all web service–centric protocols. Specifically, this binding will ensure that your WCF service conforms to a specification named WS-I Basic Profile 1.1 defined by WS-I. The main reason to use this binding is to maintain backward compatibility with applications that were previously built to communicate with ASP.NET web services (which have been part of the .NET libraries since version 1.0).

The `WSHttpBinding` protocol not only incorporates support for a subset of the WS-* specification (transactions, security, and reliable sessions), but also supports the ability to handle binary data encoding using Message Transmission Optimization Mechanism (MTOM).

The main benefit of `WSDualHttpBinding` is that it adds the ability to allow the caller and sender to communicate using *duplex messaging*, which is just a fancy way of saying they can engage in a two-way conversation. When selecting `WSDualHttpBinding`, you can hook into the WCF publish/subscribe event model.

Finally, `WSFederationHttpBinding` is the web service–based protocol you may wish to consider when security is of the utmost importance. This binding supports the WS-Trust, WS-Security, and WS-SecureConversation specifications, which are represented by the WCF CardSpace APIs.

TCP-Based Bindings

If you are building a distributed application involving a set of networked machines configured with the .NET 3.0/3.5 libraries (in other words, all machines are running Windows XP, Windows Server 2003, or Windows Vista), you can gain performance benefits bypassing web service bindings and opting for a TCP binding, which ensures all data is encoded in a compact binary format rather than XML. Again, when using the bindings shown in Table 25-4, the client and host must be .NET applications.

Table 25-4. *The TCP-Centric WCF Bindings*

Binding Class	Binding Element	Meaning in Life
NetNamedPipeBinding	<netNamedPipeBinding>	A secure, reliable, optimized binding for on-the-same-machine communication between .NET applications
NetPeerTcpBinding	<netPeerTcpBinding>	Provides a secure binding for peer-to-peer (P2P) network applications
NetTcpBinding	<netTcpBinding>	A secure and optimized binding suitable for cross-machine communication between .NET applications

The NetTcpBinding class uses TCP to move binary data between the client and WCF service. As mentioned, this will result in higher performance than the web service protocols, but you are limited to an in-house Windows solution. On the plus side, NetTcpBinding does support transactions, reliable sessions, and secure communications.

Like NetTcpBinding, NetNamedPipeBinding supports transactions, reliable sessions, and secure communications, but it has no ability to make cross-machine calls. If you are looking for the fastest way to push data between WCF applications on the same machine (e.g., cross-application domain communications), NetNamedPipeBinding is the binding choice of champions. As far as NetPeerTcpBinding is concerned, consult the .NET Framework 3.5 documentation for details regarding P2P networking.

MSMQ-Based Bindings

Finally, if you are attempting to integrate with a Microsoft MSMQ server, the NetMsmqBinding and MsmqIntegrationBinding bindings are of immediate interest. We will not examine the details of using MSMQ bindings in this chapter, but Table 25-5 documents the basic role of each.

Table 25-5. *The MSMQ-Centric WCF Bindings*

Binding Class	Binding Element	Meaning in Life
MsmqIntegrationBinding	<msmqIntegrationBinding>	This binding can be used to enable WCF applications to send and receive messages to and from existing MSMQ applications that use COM, native C++, or the types defined in the System.Messaging namespace.
NetMsmqBinding	<netMsmqBinding>	This queued binding is suitable for cross-machine communication between .NET applications.

A BRIEF NOTE ON COMMUNICATING WITH COM+ OBJECTS

Notice that there is not a specific binding to interact with COM+ objects. Communicating with COM+ components via WCF is entirely possible; however, doing so involves exposing the COM+ types through a XML web service binding via the ComSvcConfig.exe command-line tool that ships with the .NET Framework 3.5 SDK or by using the SvcConfigEditor.exe utility (which we will examine later in this chapter).

Understanding WCF Addresses

Once the contracts and bindings have been established, the final piece of the puzzle is to specify an *address* for the WCF service. This is obviously quite important, as remote callers will be unable to communicate with the remote types if they cannot locate them! Like most aspects of WCF, an address can be hard-coded in an assembly (via the `System.Uri` type) or offloaded to a `*.config` file.

In either case, the exact format of the WCF address will differ based on your choice of binding (HTTP based, named pipes, TCP based, or MSMQ based). From a high level, WCF addresses can specify the following bits of information:

- `Scheme`: The transport protocol (HTTP, etc.).
- `machineName`: The fully qualified domain of the machine.
- `Port`: This is optional in many cases. For example, the default for HTTP bindings is port 80.
- `Path`: The path to the WCF service.

This information can be represented by the following generalized template (the `Port` value is optional, as some bindings make no use of it):

```
scheme://<machineName>[:Port]/Path
```

When you are using a web service–based binding (`basicHttpBinding`, `wsHttpBinding`, `wsDualHttpBinding`, or `wsFederationHttpBinding`), the address breaks down as so (recall that if you do not specify a port number, HTTP-based protocols will default to port 80):

```
http://localhost:8080/MyWCFService
```

■ Note If you wish to make use of Secure Sockets Layer (SSL), simply replace `http` with `https`.

If you are making use of TCP-centric bindings (such as `NetTcpBinding` or `NetPeerTcpBinding`), the URI takes the following format:

```
net.tcp://localhost:8080/MyWCFService
```

The MSMQ-centric bindings (`NetMsmqBinding` and `MsmqIntegrationBinding`) are a bit unique in their URI format, given that MSMQ can make use of public or private queues (which are available only on the local machine) and port numbers have no meaning within an MSMQ-centric URI. Consider the following URI, which describes a private queue named `MyPrivateQ`:

```
net.msmq://localhost/private$/MyPrivateQ
```

Last but not least, the address format used for the named-pipe binding, `NetNamedPipeBinding`, breaks down as so (recall that named pipes allow for interprocess communication for applications on the same physical machine):

```
net.pipe://localhost/MyWCFService
```

While a single WCF service might expose only a single address (based on a single binding), it is possible to configure a collection of unique addresses (with different bindings). This can be done within a `*.config` file by defining multiple `<endpoint>` elements. Here, you can specify any number of ABCs for the same service. This approach can be helpful when you want to allow callers to select which protocol they would like to use when communicating with the service.

Building a WCF Service

Now that you have a better understanding about the building blocks of a WCF application, let's create our first sample application to see how the ABCs are accounted for in code. Our first step is to define our WCF service library consisting of the contracts and their implementations.

This first example will not use the Visual Studio WCF project templates, in order to keep focused on the specific steps involved in making a WCF service. To begin, create a new VB Class Library project named MagicEightBallServiceLib. Once you have done so, rename your initial file from `Class1.vb` to `MagicEightBallService.vb` and add a reference to the `System.ServiceModel.dll` assembly. In the initial code file, specify that you are using the `System.ServiceModel` namespace. At this point, your VB file should look like so:

```
' The key WCF namespace.
Imports System.ServiceModel

Public Class MagicEightBallService
End Class
```

Our class type will implement a single WCF service contract represented by a strongly typed CLR interface named `IEightBall`. As you may know, the Magic 8-Ball is a toy that allows you to view one of a handful of fixed answers to a question you may ask. Our interface will define a single method that allows the caller to pose a question to the Magic 8-Ball to obtain a random answer.

WCF service interfaces are adorned with the `<ServiceContract()>` attribute, while each interface member is decorated with the `<OperationContract()>` attribute (more details regarding these two attributes in just a moment). Here is the definition of the `IEightBall` interface:

```
<ServiceContract()> _
Public Interface IEightBall
  ' Ask a question, receive an answer!
  <OperationContract()> _
  Function ObtainAnswerToQuestion(ByVal userQuestion As String) As String
End Interface
```

■ **Note** It is permissible to define a service contract interface that contains methods not adorned with the `<OperationContract()>` attribute. However, such members will not be exposed through the WCF runtime.

As you know from your study of the interface type (see Chapter 9), interfaces are quite useless until they are implemented by a class or structure, in order to flesh out their functionality. Like a real Magic 8-Ball, the implementation of our service type (`MagicEightBallService`) will randomly return a canned answer from an array of strings. Also, our default constructor will display an information message that will be (eventually) displayed within the host's console window (for diagnostic purposes):

```
Public Class MagicEightBallService
  Implements IEightBall
  ' Just for display purposes on the host.
  Public Sub New()
    Console.WriteLine("The 8-Ball awaits your question...")
  End Sub

  Public Function ObtainAnswerToQuestion(ByVal userQuestion As String) As String _
  Implements IEightBall.ObtainAnswerToQuestion
    Dim answers As String() = {"Future Uncertain", "Yes", "No", _
                               "Hazy", "Ask again later", "Definitely"}
```

```
    ' Return a random response.
    Dim r As New Random()
    Return String.Format("{0}? {1}.", userQuestion, answers(r.Next(answers.Length)))
  End Function
End Class
```

At this point, our WCF service library is complete. However, before we construct a host for this service, let's examine some additional details of the `<ServiceContract()>` and `<OperationContract()>` attributes.

The <ServiceContract()> Attribute

In order for a CLR interface to participate in the services provided by WCF, it must be adorned with the `<ServiceContract()>` attribute. Like many other .NET attributes, the `ServiceContractAttribute` type supports a number of properties to further qualify its intention. Two properties, `Name` and `Namespace`, can be set to control the name of the service type and the name of the XML namespace defining the service type. If you are using a web service–specific binding, these values are used to define the `<portType>` elements of the related WSDL document.

Here, we have not bothered to assign a `Name` value, given that the default name of the service type is directly based on the VB class name. However, the default name for the underlying XML namespace is simply `http://tempuri.org` (which really should be changed for all of your WCF services).

When you are building a WCF service that will send and receive custom data types (which we are currently not doing), it is important to establish a meaningful value to the underlying XML namespace, as this will make sure that your custom types are unique. As you may know from your experience building XML web services, XML namespaces provide a way to wrap your custom types in a unique container to ensure that your types do not clash with types in another organization.

For this reason, we can update our interface definition with a more fitting definition, which, much like the process of defining an XML namespace in a .NET Web Service project, is typically the URI of the service's point of origin, for example:

```
<ServiceContract(Namespace := "http://Intertech.com")> _
Public Interface IEightBall
  ...
End Interface
```

Beyond `Namespace` and `Name`, the `<ServiceContract()>` attribute can be configured with the additional properties shown in Table 25-6. Be aware that some of these settings will be ignored depending on your selection of binding.

Table 25-6. *Various Named Properties of the* `<ServiceContract()>` *Attribute*

Property	Meaning in Life
`CallbackContract`	Specifies if this service contract requires callback functionality for two-way message exchange.
`ConfigurationName`	The name used to locate the service element in an application configuration file. The default is the name of the service implementation class.
`ProtectionLevel`	Allows you to specify the degree to which the contract binding requires encryption, digital signatures, or both for endpoints that expose the contract.
`SessionMode`	Used to establish if per-user sessions are allowed, not allowed, or required by this service contract.

The <OperationContract()> Attribute

Methods that you wish to be used within the WCF framework must be attributed with the `<OperationContract()>` attribute, which may also be configured with various named properties. Using the properties shown in Table 25-7, you are able to declare that a given method is intended to be one-way in nature, supports asynchronous invocation, requires encrypted message data, and so forth (again, many of these values may be ignored based on your binding selection).

Table 25-7. *Various Named Properties of the* `<OperationContract()>` *Attribute*

Property	Meaning in Life
`Action`	Gets or sets the WS-Addressing action of the request message.
`AsyncPattern`	Indicates if the operation is implemented asynchronously using a `Begin`/`End` method pair on the service. This allows the service to offload processing to another server-side thread; this has nothing to do with the client calling the method asynchronously!
`IsInitiating`	Specifies if this operation can be the initial operation in a session.
`IsOneWay`	Indicates if the operation consists of only a single input message (and no associated output).
`IsTerminating`	Specifies if the WCF runtime should attempt to terminate the current session after the operation completes.

For this initial example, we don't need to configure the `ObtainAnswerToQuestion()` method with additional traits, so the `<OperationContract()>` attribute can be used as currently defined.

Service Types As Operational Contracts

Finally, recall that the use of interfaces is not required when building WCF service types. It is in fact possible to apply the `<ServiceContract()>` and `<OperationContract()>` attributes directly on the service type itself:

```
' This is only for illustrative purposes
' and not used for the current example.
<ServiceContract(Namespace := "http://intertech.com")> _
Public Class ServiceTypeAsContract
  <OperationContract()> _
  Public Sub SomeMethod()
  End Sub

  <OperationContract()> _
  Public Sub AnotherMethod()
  End Sub
End Class
```

Although this approach is possible, there are many benefits to explicitly defining an interface type to represent the service contract. The most obvious benefit is that a given interface can be applied to multiple service types (authored in a variety of languages and architectures) to achieve a high degree of polymorphism. Another benefit is that a service contract interface can be used as the basis of new contracts (via interface inheritance), without having to carry any implementation baggage.

In any case, at this point our first WCF service library is complete. Compile your project to ensure you do not have any typos.

■ **Source Code** The MagicEightBallServiceLib project is located under the Chapter 25 subdirectory.

Hosting the WCF Service

We are now ready to define a host. Although a production-level service would be hosted from a Windows service or an IIS virtual directory, our first host will be a simple Console Application named MagicEightBallServiceHost.

Once you have created this new project, add a reference to the `System.ServiceModel.dll` and `MagicEightBallServiceLib.dll` assemblies, and update your initial code file by importing the `System.ServiceModel` and `MagicEightBallServiceLib` namespaces:

```
Imports System.ServiceModel
Imports MagicEightBallServiceLib

Module Program

  Sub Main()
    Console.WriteLine("***** Console Based WCF Host *****")
    Console.ReadLine()
  End Sub

End Module
```

The first step you must take when building a host for a WCF service type is to decide whether you want to define the necessary hosting logic completely in code or to relegate several low-level details to an application configuration file. As mentioned, the benefit of `*.config` files is that the host is able to change the underlying plumbing without requiring you to recompile and redeploy the executable. However, always remember this is strictly optional, as you can hard-code the hosting logic using the types within the `System.ServiceModel.dll` assembly.

This console-based host will indeed make use of an application configuration file, so insert a new Application Configuration File into your current project using the Project ➤ Add New Item menu option.

■ **Note** Recall from Chapter 15 that the `App.config` file inserted into Visual Basic projects includes a good number of (unnecessary) starter elements. As you work through this chapter, my assumption is that you will delete all of the initial markup within a new `App.config` file and enter the markup shown in the following examples.

Establishing the ABCs Within an App.config File

When you are building a host for a WCF service type, you will follow a very predictable set of steps—some via configuration and some via code:

1. Define the *endpoint* for the WCF service being hosted within the host's configuration file.
2. Programmatically make use of the `ServiceHost` type to expose the service types available from this endpoint.
3. Ensure the host remains running to service incoming client request. Obviously, this step is not required if you are hosting your service types using a Windows service or IIS.

In the world of WCF, the term "endpoint" simply represents the address, binding, and contract rolled together in a nice tidy package. In XML, an endpoint is expressed using the <endpoint> element and the address, binding, and contract attributes. Update your *.config file to specify a single endpoint (reachable via port 8080) exposed by this host:

```
<?xml version="1.0" encoding="utf-8" ?>
<configuration>
  <system.serviceModel>
    <services>
      <service name="MagicEightBallServiceLib.MagicEightBallService">
        <endpoint address ="http://localhost:8080/MagicEightBallService"
                  binding="basicHttpBinding"
                  contract="MagicEightBallServiceLib.IEightBall"/>
      </service>
    </services>
  </system.serviceModel>
</configuration>
```

Notice that the <system.serviceModel> element is the root for all of a host's WCF settings. Each service exposed by the host is represented by a <service> element, wrapped within the <services> container element. Here, our single <service> element makes use of the (optional) name attribute to specify the friendly name of the service type.

The nested <endpoint> element handles the task of defining the address, the binding model (basicHttpBinding in this example), and the fully qualified name of the interface type defining the WCF service contract (IEightBall). Because we are using an HTTP-based binding, we make use of the http:// scheme, specifying an arbitrary port ID.

Coding Against the ServiceHost Type

With the current configuration file in place, the actual programming logic required to complete the host is painfully simple. When our executable starts up, we will create an instance of the ServiceHost type. At runtime, this object will automatically read the data within the scope of the <system.serviceModel> element of the host's *.config file to determine the correct address, binding, and contract, and create the necessary plumbing:

```
Sub Main()
  Console.WriteLine("***** Console Based WCF Host *****")

  Using svcHost As New ServiceHost(GetType(MagicEightBallService))
    ' Open the host and start listening for incoming messages.
    svcHost.Open()

    ' Keep the service running until the Enter key is pressed.
    Console.WriteLine("The service is ready.")
    Console.WriteLine("Press the Enter key to terminate service.")
    Console.ReadLine()
  End Using
End Sub
```

If you now run this application, you will find that the host is alive in memory, ready to take incoming requests from remote clients (see Figure 25-6).

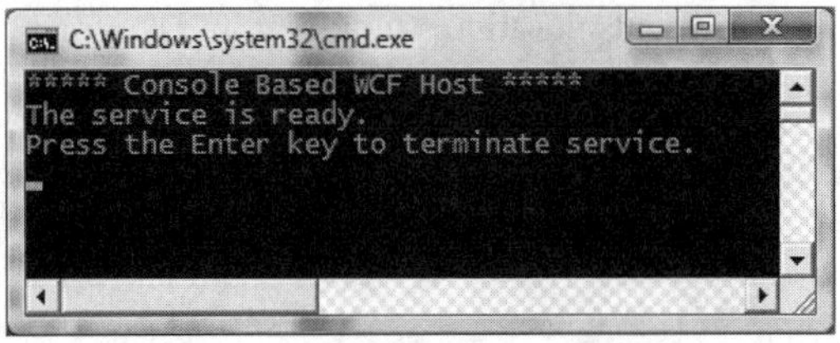

Figure 25-6. *Our host, ready for external calls via basic HTTP binding*

Host Coding Options

We are creating our `ServiceHost` using a constructor that simply requires the service's type information. However, it is also possible to pass in an array of `System.Uri` objects as a constructor argument to represent the collection of addresses this service is accessible from. Currently, the address is found via the `*.config` file; however, if we were to update the `Using` scope as so:

```
Using svcHost As New ServiceHost(GetType(MagicEightBallService), _
  New Uri() {New Uri("http://localhost:8080/MagicEightBallService")})
  ...
End Using
```

we would be able to define our endpoint as so:

```
<endpoint address =""
          binding="basicHttpBinding"
          contract="MagicEightBallServiceLib.IEightBall"/>
```

Of course, too much hard-coding within a host's code base decreases flexibility, so for the purposes of this current host example, assume we are creating the service host simply by supplying the type information as we did before:

```
Using svcHost As New ServiceHost(GetType(MagicEightBallService))
  ...
End Using
```

One of the (slightly frustrating) aspects of authoring host `*.config` files is that you have a number of ways to construct the XML descriptors, based on the amount of hard-coding you have in the code base (as you have just seen in the case of the optional `Uri` array). To show yet another way to author `*.config` files, rework your `App.config` file as so:

```
<?xml version="1.0" encoding="utf-8" ?>
<configuration>
  <system.serviceModel>
    <services>
      <service name="MagicEightBallServiceLib.MagicEightBallService">

        <!-- Address obtained from <baseAddresses> -->
        <endpoint address =""
                  binding="basicHttpBinding"
                  contract="MagicEightBallServiceLib.IEightBall"/>

        <!-- List all of the base addresses in a dedicated section -->
        <host>
          <baseAddresses>
            <add baseAddress ="http://localhost:8080/MagicEightBallService"/>
          </baseAddresses>
```

```
      </host>
    </service>
  </services>
 </system.serviceModel>
</configuration>
```

In this case, the address attribute of the <endpoint> element is still empty, and regardless of the fact that we are not specifying an array of Uri objects in code when creating the ServiceHost, the application runs as before as the value is pulled from the baseAddresses scope. The benefit of storing the base address in a <host>'s <baseAddresses> region is that other parts of a *.config file (such as MEX, described shortly) also need to know the address of the service's endpoint. Thus, rather than having to copy and paste address values within a single *.config file, we can isolate the single value as shown here.

Note In the next example, I'll introduce you to a graphical configuration tool that allows you to author configuration files in a less tedious manner.

In any case, before we build a client application to communicate with our service, let's dig a bit deeper into the role of the ServiceHost class type and <service.serviceModel> element as well as the role of metadata exchange (MEX) services.

Details of the ServiceHost Type

The ServiceHost class type is used to configure and expose a WCF service from the hosting executable. However, be aware that you will only make direct use of this type when building a custom *.exe to host your services. If you are using IIS (or the Vista-specific WAS) to expose a service, the ServiceHost object is created automatically on your behalf.

As you have seen, this type requires a complete service description, which is obtained dynamically through the configuration settings of the host's *.config file. While this happens automatically upon object creation, it is possible to manually configure the state of your ServiceHost object using a number of members. In addition to Open() and Close() (which communicate with your service in a synchronous manner), Table 25-8 illustrates some further members of interest.

Table 25-8. *Select Members of the* ServiceHost *Type*

Members	Meaning in Life
Authorization	This property gets the authorization level for the service being hosted.
AddServiceEndpoint()	This method allows you to programmatically add a service endpoint to the host.
BaseAddresses	This property obtains the list of registered base addresses for the current service.
BeginOpen() BeginClose()	These methods allow you to asynchronously open and close a ServiceHost object, using the standard asynchronous .NET delegate syntax.
CloseTimeout	This property allows you to set and get the time allowed for the service to close down.
Credentials	This property obtains the security credentials used by the current service.

Continued

Table 25-8. *Continued*

Members	Meaning in Life
`EndOpen()` `EndClose()`	These methods are the asynchronous counterparts to `BeginOpen()` and `BeginClose()`.
`OpenTimeout`	This property allows you to set and get the time allowed for the service to start up.
`State`	This property gets a value that indicates the current state of the communication object, represented by the `CommunicationState` enum (opened, closed, created, etc.).

To illustrate some additional aspects of `ServiceHost`, update your `Program` module with a new method that prints out various aspects of the current host:

```
Private Sub DisplayHostInfo(ByVal host As ServiceHost)
  Console.WriteLine()
  Console.WriteLine("***** Host Info *****")

  Console.WriteLine("Name: {0}", host.Description.ConfigurationName)
  Console.WriteLine("Port: {0}", host.BaseAddresses(0).Port)
  Console.WriteLine("LocalPath: {0}", host.BaseAddresses(0).LocalPath)
  Console.WriteLine("Uri: {0}", host.BaseAddresses(0).AbsoluteUri)
  Console.WriteLine("Scheme: {0}", host.BaseAddresses(0).Scheme)
  Console.WriteLine("**********************")
  Console.WriteLine()
End Sub
```

Assuming you call this new method from within `Main()` after opening your host, you will see the statistics shown in Figure 25-7.

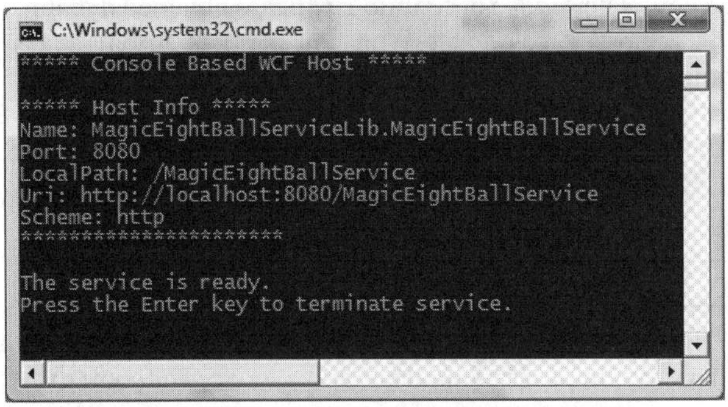

Figure 25-7. *Details of our host*

Details of the <system.serviceModel> Element

Like any XML element, `<system.serviceModel>` can define a set of subelements, each of which can be qualified via numerous attributes. While you should consult the .NET Framework 3.5 SDK documentation for full details regarding the set of possible attributes, here is a skeleton that lists the valid subelements:

```
<system.serviceModel>
  <behaviors>
  </behaviors>
  <client>
  </client>
  <commonBehaviors>
  </commonBehaviors>
  <diagnostics>
  </diagnostics>
  <serviceHostingEnvironment>
  </serviceHostingEnvironment>
  <comContracts>
  </comContracts>
  <services>
  </services>
  <bindings>
  </bindings>
</system.serviceModel>
```

You'll see more exotic configuration files as you move through the chapter; however, the crux of each subelement can be discovered in Table 25-9.

Table 25-9. *Subelements of* `<service.serviceModel>`

Subelement	Meaning in Life
`behaviors`	WCF supports various endpoint and service behaviors. In a nutshell, a *behavior* allows you to further qualify the functionality of a host or client.
`bindings`	This element allows you to fine-tune each of the WCF-supplied bindings (`basicHttpBinding`, `netMsmqBinding`, etc.) as well as specify any custom bindings used by the host.
`client`	This element contains a list of endpoints a client uses to connect to a service. Obviously, this is not terribly useful in a host's `*.config` file.
`comContracts`	This element defines COM contracts enabled for WCF and COM interoperability.
`commonBehaviors`	This element can only be set within a `machine.config` file. It can be used to define all of the behaviors used by each WCF service on a given machine.
`diagnostics`	This element contains settings for the diagnostic features of WCF. The user can enable/disable tracing, performance counters, and the WMI provider, and can add custom message filters.
`serviceHostingEnvironment`	This element specifies if this operation can be the initial operation in a session.
`services`	This element contains a collection of WCF services exposed from the host.

Enabling Metadata Exchange

Recall that WCF client applications communicate with the WCF service via an intervening proxy type. While you could most certainly author the proxy code completely by hand, doing so would be tedious and error-prone. Ideally, a tool could be used to generate the necessary grunge code (including the client-side `*.config` file). Thankfully, the .NET Framework 3.5 SDK provides a command-line tool (`svcutil.exe`) for this very purpose. As well, Visual Studio 2008 provides similar functionality via the Project ➤ Add Service Reference menu option.

However, in order for these tools to generate the necessary proxy code/`*.config` file, they must be able to discover the format of the WCF service interfaces and any defined data contracts (the method names, types of parameters, etc.).

Metadata exchange (MEX) is a WCF *service behavior* that can be specified to fine-tune how the WCF runtime handles your service. Simply put, each `<behavior>` element can define a set of activities a given service can subscribe to. WCF provides numerous behaviors out of the box, and it is possible to build your own.

The MEX behavior (which is disabled by default) will intercept any metadata requests sent via HTTP GET. If you want to allow `svcutil.exe` or Visual Studio 2008 to automate the creation of the required client-side proxy/`*.config` file, you must enable MEX.

Enabling MEX is a matter of tweaking the host's `*.config` file with the proper settings (or authoring the corresponding VB code). First, you must add a new `<endpoint>` just for MEX. Second, you need to define a WCF behavior to allow HTTP GET access. Third, you need to associate this behavior by name to your service via the `behaviorConfiguration` attribute on the opening `<service>` element. Finally, you need to add a `<host>` element to define the base address of this service (MEX will look here to figure out the locations of the types to describe).

■ **Note** This final step can be bypassed if you pass in a `System.Uri` object to represent the base address as a parameter to the `ServiceHost` constructor.

Consider the following updated host `*.config` file, which creates a custom `<behavior>` element (named `EightBallServiceMEXBehavior`) that is associated to our service via the `behaviorConfiguration` attribute within the `<service>` definition:

```
<?xml version="1.0" encoding="utf-8" ?>
<configuration>
  <system.serviceModel>
    <services>
      <service name="MagicEightBallServiceLib.MagicEightBallService"
               behaviorConfiguration = "EightBallServiceMEXBehavior">
        <endpoint address =""
                  binding="basicHttpBinding"
                  contract="MagicEightBallServiceLib.IEightBall"/>

        <!-- Enable the MEX endpoint -->
        <endpoint address="mex"
                  binding="mexHttpBinding"
                  contract="IMetadataExchange" />

        <!-- Need to add this so MEX knows the address of our service -->
        <host>
          <baseAddresses>
            <add baseAddress ="http://localhost:8080/MagicEightBallService"/>
          </baseAddresses>
        </host>
      </service>
    </services>
```

```
    <!-- A behavior definition for MEX -->
    <behaviors>
      <serviceBehaviors>
        <behavior name="EightBallServiceMEXBehavior" >
          <serviceMetadata httpGetEnabled="true" />
        </behavior>
      </serviceBehaviors>
    </behaviors>
  </system.serviceModel>
</configuration>
```

You are now able to restart the service and view its metadata description using the web browser of your choice. To do so, while the host is still running simply enter the address as the URL:

```
http://localhost:8080/MagicEightBallService
```

Once you are at the homepage for your WCF service (see Figure 25-8), you are provided with basic details regarding how to interact with this service programmatically as well as a way to view the WSDL contract by clicking the hyperlink at the top of the page. Recall that Web Service Description Language (WSDL) is a grammar that describes the structure of web services at a given endpoint.

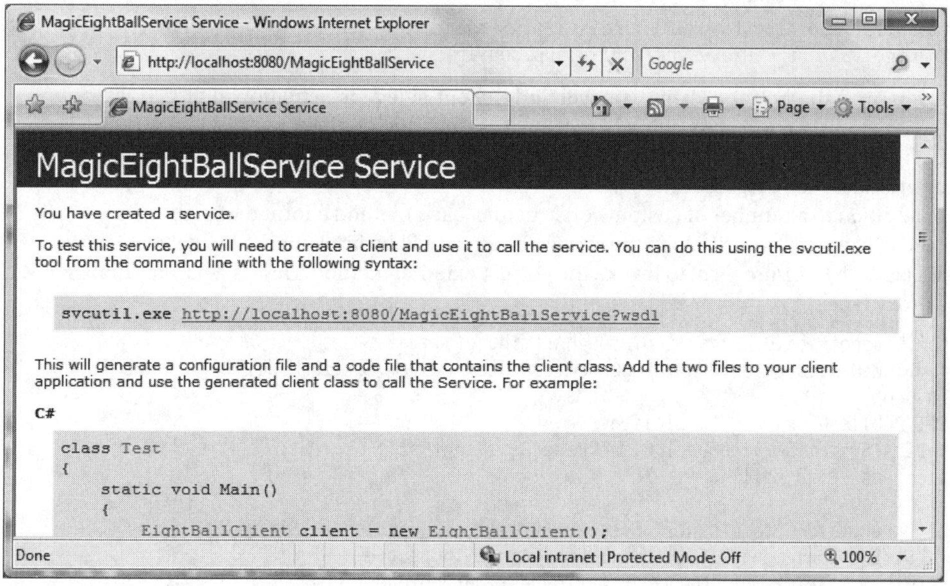

Figure 25-8. *Ready to view metadata, via MEX*

Source Code The MagicEightBallServiceHost project is located under the Chapter 25 subdirectory.

Building the WCF Client Application

Now that our host is in place, the final task is to build a piece of software to communicate with this WCF service type. While we could take the long road and build the necessary infrastructure by hand (a feasible but labor-intensive task), the .NET Framework 3.5 SDK provides several approaches to quickly generate a client-side proxy. To begin, create a new Console Application named MagicEightBallServiceClient.

Generating Proxy Code Using svcutil.exe

The first way you can build a client-side proxy is to make use of the svcutil.exe command-line tool using a Visual Studio 2008 command prompt. Using svcutil.exe, you can generate a new VB language file that represents the proxy code itself as well as a client-side configuration file. To do so, simply specify the service's endpoint as the first parameter. The /language: file allows you to specify that you wish to generate VB code (rather than the default, which is C#). The /out: flag is used to define the name of the *.vb file containing the proxy, while the /config: option specifies the name of the generated client-side *.config file.

Assuming your service is currently running, the following command set passed into svcutil.exe will generate two new files in the working directory (which should, of course, be entered as a single line within a Visual Studio 2008 command prompt):

```
svcutil http://localhost:8080/MagicEightBallService
  /language:VB /out:myProxy.vb /config:app.config
```

If you open the myProxy.vb file, you will find a client-side representation of the IEightBall interface, as well as a new class named EightBallClient, which is the proxy class itself. This class derives from the generic class, System.ServiceModel.ClientBase(Of T), where T is the registered service interface (i.e., IEightBall).

In addition to a number of custom constructors, each method adorned with the <OperationContract()> attribute in the service interface will be implemented to delegate to the parent class's Channel property to invoke the correct external method. Here is a partial snapshot of the proxy type:

```
<System.Diagnostics.DebuggerStepThroughAttribute(), _
 System.CodeDom.Compiler.GeneratedCodeAttribute("System.ServiceModel", _
  "3.0.0.0")> _
Partial Public Class EightBallClient
  Inherits System.ServiceModel.ClientBase(Of IEightBall)
  Implements IEightBall
...
  Public Function ObtainAnswerToQuestion(ByVal userQuestion As String) _
    As String Implements IEightBall.ObtainAnswerToQuestion
    Return MyBase.Channel.ObtainAnswerToQuestion(userQuestion)
  End Function
End Class
```

When you create an instance of the proxy type, the base class will establish a connection to the endpoint using the settings specified in the client-side application configuration file. Much like the server-side configuration file, the generated client-side App.config file contains an <endpoint> element and details regarding the basicHttpBinding used to communicate with the service.

In addition, you will find the following <client> element, which (once again) establishes the ABCs from the client's perspective:

```
<client>
  <endpoint
   address="http://localhost:8080/MagicEightBallService"
```

```
    binding="basicHttpBinding" bindingConfiguration="BasicHttpBinding_IEightBall"
    contract="IEightBall" name="BasicHttpBinding_IEightBall" />
</client>
```

At this point, you could include these two files into your project (and reference the System.ServiceModel.dll assembly) and use the proxy type to communicate with the remote WCF service. However, rather than doing so, let's see how Visual Studio can help to further automate the creation of client-side proxy files.

Generating Proxy Code Using Visual Studio 2008

Like any good command-line tool, svcutil.exe provides a great number of options that can be used to control how the client proxy is generated. If you do not require these advanced options, you are able to generate the same two files using the Visual Studio 2008 IDE. Simply select the Add Service Reference option from the Project menu.

Once you activate this menu option, you will be prompted to enter the service URI. At this point click the Go button to see the service description (see Figure 25-9).

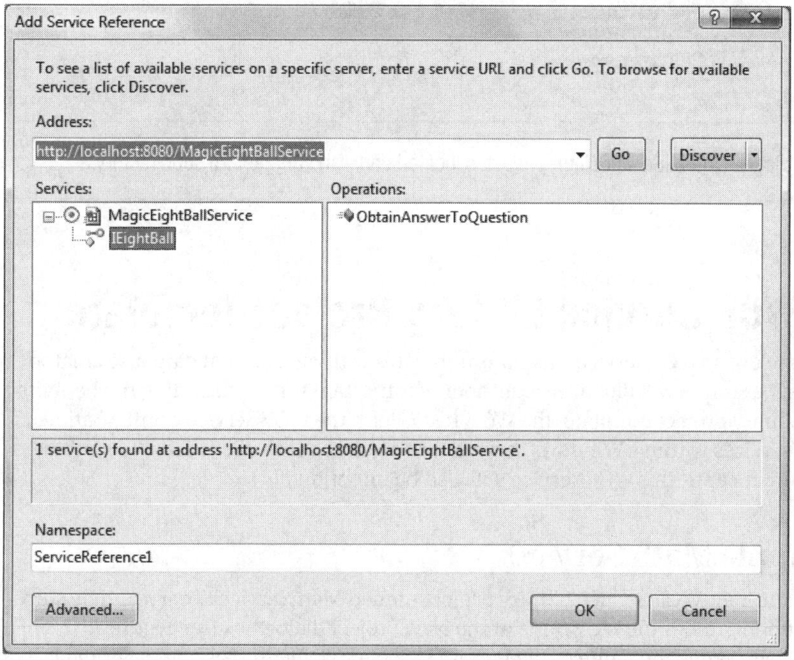

Figure 25-9. *Generating the proxy files using Visual Studio 2008*

Beyond creating and inserting the proxy files into your current project, this tool is kind enough to reference the WCF assemblies automatically on your behalf. As a naming convention, the proxy class is defined within a namespace called ServiceReference1, which is nested in the client's namespace (to avoid possible name clashes). Here, then, is the complete client code:

```
Imports MagicEightBallServiceClient.ServiceReference1

Module Program
  Sub Main()
    Console.WriteLine("***** Ask the Magic 8 Ball *****" & Vblf)
```

```
    Using ball As New EightBallClient()
      Console.Write("Your question: ")
      Dim question As String = Console.ReadLine()
      Dim answer As String = ball.ObtainAnswerToQuestion(question)
      Console.WriteLine("8-Ball says: {0}", answer)
    End Using
    Console.ReadLine()
  End Sub
End Module
```

Now, assuming your WCF host is currently running, you can execute the client. Figure 25-10 shows one possible response.

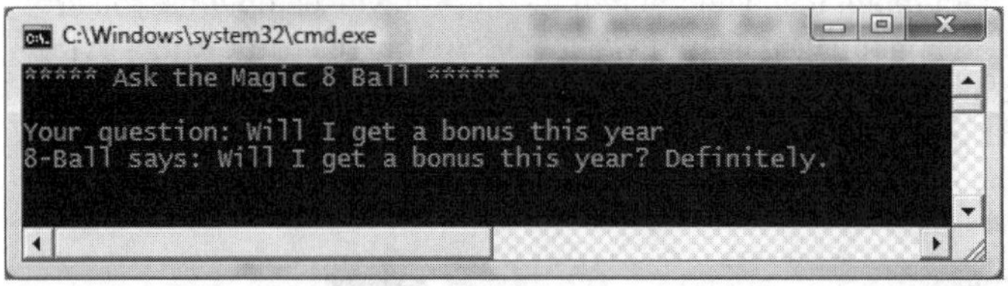

Figure 25-10. *The completed WCF client host*

■ **Source Code** The MagicEightBallServiceClient project is located under the Chapter 25 subdirectory.

Using the WCF Service Library Project Template

Before we build a more exotic WCF service that communicates with our AutoLot database created in Chapter 22, the next example will illustrate a number of important topics, including the benefits of the WCF Service Library project template, the WCF Test Client, the WCF Service Configuration Editor, hosting WCF services within a Windows service, and asynchronous client calls. To stay focused on these new concepts, this WCF service will also be intentionally simple.

Building a Simple Math Service

To begin, create a brand-new WCF Service Library project named MathServiceLibrary, and be sure to select the correct option under the WCF node of the New Project dialog box (see Figure 25-2 if you need a nudge). Now change the name of the initial `IService1.vb` file to `IBasicMath.vb`. Once you have done so, *delete* all of the example code within the code file and replace it with the following:

```
<ServiceContract(Namespace :="www.intertech.com")> _
Public Interface IBasicMath
  <OperationContract()> _
  Function Add(ByVal x As Integer, ByVal y As Integer) As Integer
End Interface
```

Next, change the name of the `Service1.vb` file to `MathService.vb`, and (once again) delete all the example code within the code file and implement your service contract as so:

```
Public Class MathService
  Implements IBasicMath

  Public Function Add(ByVal x As Integer, ByVal y As Integer) _
    As Integer Implements IBasicMath.Add
    Return x + y
  End Function
End Class
```

Finally, open the supplied `App.config` file and replace all occurrences of `IService1` with `IBasicMath`, and all occurrences of `Service1` with `MathService`. As well, take a moment to notice that this `*.config` file has already been enabled to support MEX, and by default it is making use of the `wsHttpBinding` protocol.

Testing the WCF Service with WcfTestClient.exe

One benefit of using the WCF Service Library project template is that when you debug or run your library, it will read the settings in the `*.config` file and use them to load the WCF Test Client application (`WcfTestClient.exe`). This GUI-based application allows you to test each member of your service interface as you build the WCF service, rather than having to manually build a host/client as you did previously simply for testing purposes.

Figure 25-11 shows the testing environment for `MathService`. Notice that when you double-click an interface method, you are able to specify input parameters and invoke the member.

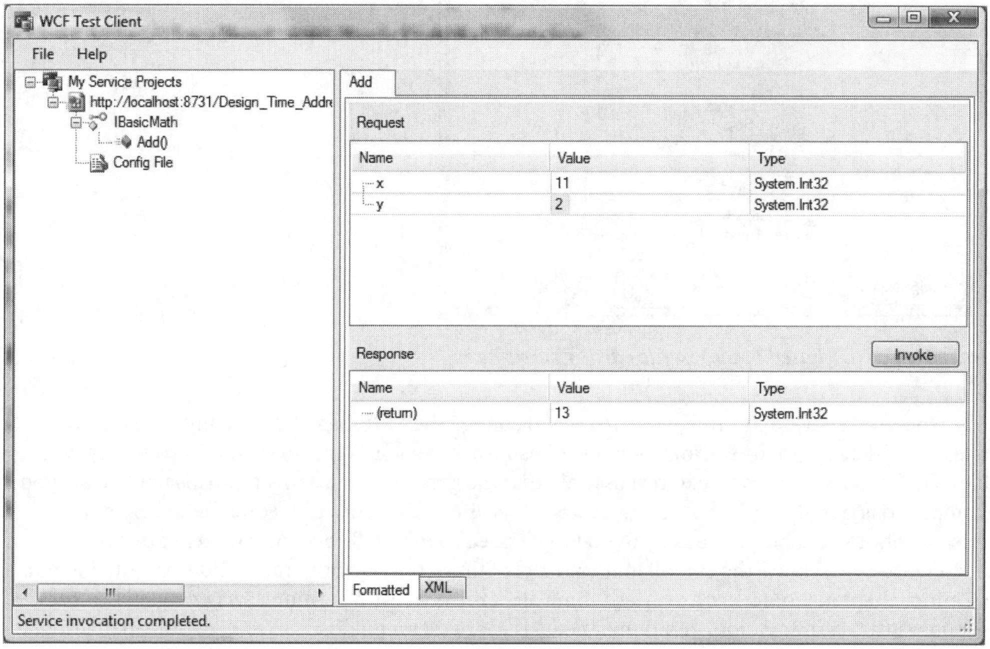

Figure 25-11. *Testing the WCF service using* `WcfTestClient.exe`

While this utility works out of the box when you have created a WCF Service Library project, be aware that you can use this tool to test any WCF service when you start it at the command line by specifying a MEX endpoint. For example, if you were to start the `MagicEightBallServiceHost.exe` application, you would be able to specify the following command within a Visual Studio 2008 command prompt:

```
wcftestclient http://localhost:8080/MagicEightBallService
```

Once you do, you will be able to invoke `ObtainAnswerToQuestion()` in a similar manner.

Altering Configuration Files Using SvcConfigEditor.exe

Another benefit of making use of the WCF Service Library project is that you are able to right-click the `App.config` file within Solution Explorer and select Edit WCF Configuration to activate the GUI-based Service Configuration Editor, `SvcConfigEditor.exe` (see Figure 25-12). This same technique can be used from a client application that has referenced a WCF service.

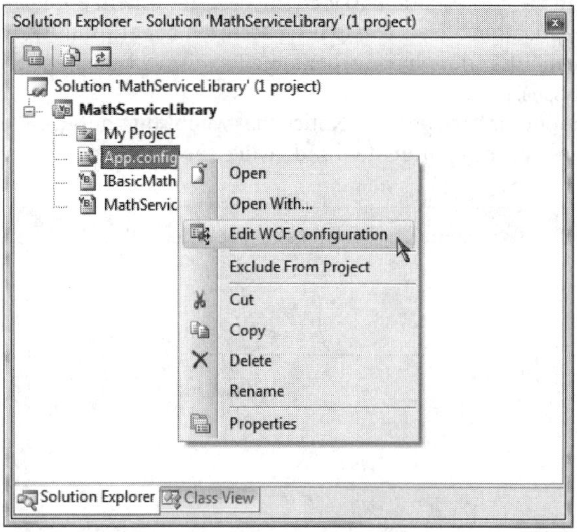

Figure 25-12. *GUI-based* `*.config` *file editing starts here.*

Once you activate this tool, you are able to change the XML-based data using a friendly user interface. There are many obvious benefits of using a tool such as this to maintain your `*.config` files. First and foremost, you can rest assured that the generated markup conforms to the expected format and is typo-free. Next, it is a great way to *see* the valid values that could be assigned to a given attribute. Last but not least, you no longer need to manually author tedious XML data.

Figure 25-13 shows the overall look and feel of the Service Configuration Editor. Truth be told, an entire chapter could be written describing all of the interesting options `SvcConfigEditor.exe` supports (COM+ integration, creation of new `*.config` files, etc.). Be sure to take time to investigate this tool, and be aware that you can access a fairly detailed help system by pressing F1.

■Note The `SvcConfigEditor.exe` utility can edit (or create) configuration files even if you do not select an initial WCF Service Library project. Using a Visual Studio 2008 command window, launch the tool and make use of the File ➤ Open menu option to load an existing `*.config` file for editing.

We have no need to further configure our WCF `MathService`, so at this point we can move on to the task of building a custom host.

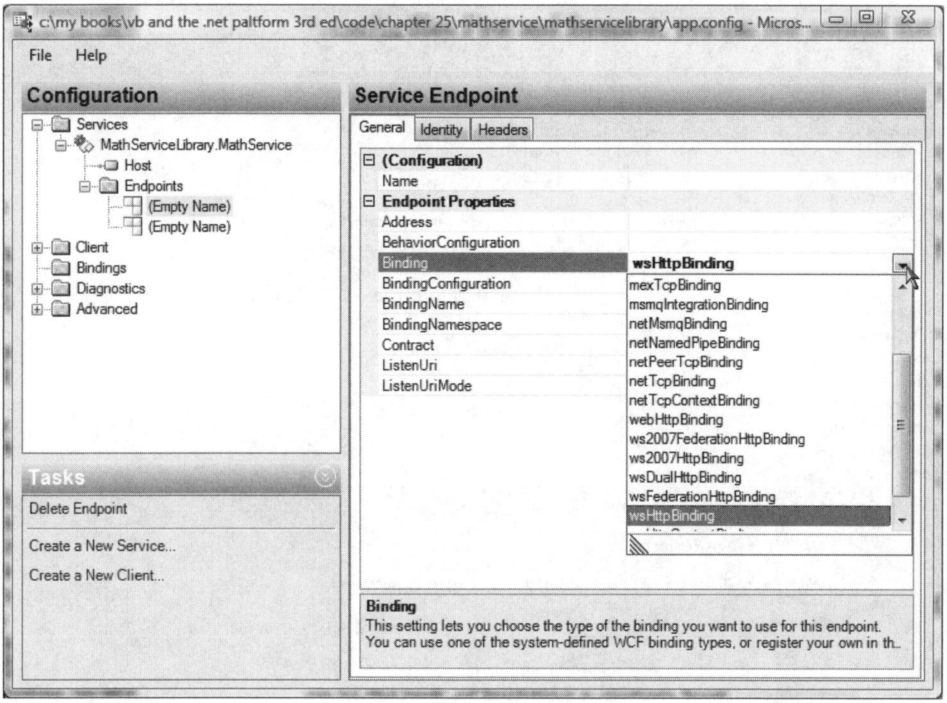

Figure 25-13. *Working with the WCF Service Configuration Editor*

Hosting the WCF Service As a Windows Service

As you might agree, hosting a WCF service from within a console application (or within a GUI desktop application, for that matter) is not an ideal choice for a production-level server, given that the host must remain running visibly in the background to service clients. Even if you were to minimize the hosting application to the Windows taskbar, it would still be far too easy to accidentally shut down the host, thereby terminating the connection with any client applications.

Note While it is true that a desktop Windows application does not *have* to show a main window, a typical `*.exe` does require user interaction to load the executable. A Windows service (described next) can be configured to run even if no users are currently logged on to the workstation.

If you are building an in-house WCF application, another alternative is to host your WCF service library from within a dedicated Windows service. One benefit of doing so is that a Windows service can be configured to automatically start when the target machine boots up. Another benefit is that Windows services run invisibly in the background (unlike our console application) and do not require user interactivity.

To illustrate how to build such a host, begin by creating a new Windows Service project named MathWindowsServiceHost (see Figure 25-14). Once you have done so, rename your initial `Service1.vb` file to `MathWinService.vb` using Solution Explorer.

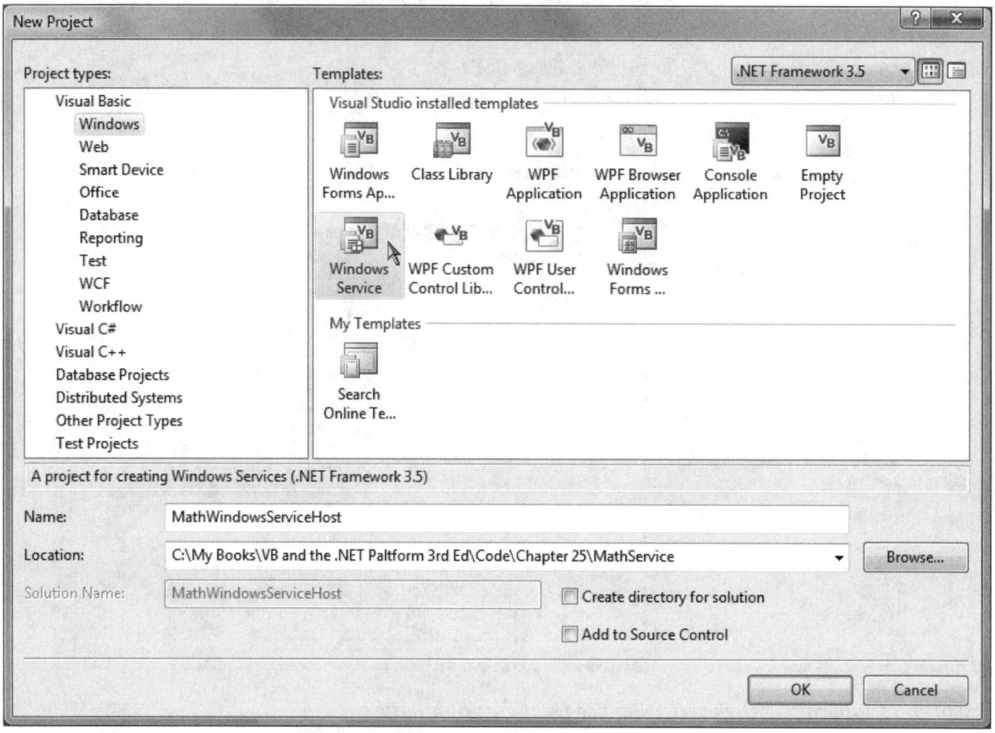

Figure 25-14. *Creating a Windows service to host our WCF service*

Specifying the ABCs in Code

Now, assuming you have set a reference to your `MathServiceLibrary.dll` and `System.ServiceModel.dll` assemblies, all you need to do is make use of the `ServiceHost` type within the `OnStart()` and `OnStop()` methods of your Windows service type. Open the code file for your service host class (by right-clicking the designer and selecting View Code), and add the following logic:

```
' Be sure to import these namespaces:
Imports MathServiceLibrary
Imports System.ServiceModel

Partial Public Class MathWinService
  ' A member variable of type ServiceHost.
  Private myHost As ServiceHost

  Public Sub New()
    InitializeComponent()
  End Sub
```

```
  Protected Overrides Sub OnStart(ByVal args As String())
    ' Just to be really safe.
    If myHost IsNot Nothing Then
      myHost.Close()
      myHost = Nothing
    End If

    ' Create the host.
    myHost = New ServiceHost(GetType(MathService))

    ' The ABCs in code!
    Dim address As New Uri("http://localhost:8080/MathServiceLibrary")
    Dim binding As New WSHttpBinding()
    Dim contract As Type = GetType(IBasicMath)

    ' Add this endpoint.
    myHost.AddServiceEndpoint(contract, binding, address)

    ' Open the host.
    myHost.Open()
  End Sub

  Protected Overrides Sub OnStop()
    ' Shut down the host.
    If myHost IsNot Nothing Then
      myHost.Close()
    End If
  End Sub
End Class
```

While nothing is preventing you from using a configuration file when building a Windows service host for a WCF service, here (for a change of pace) notice that you are programmatically establishing the endpoint using the `Uri`, `WSHttpBinding`, and `Type` classes, rather than making use of a `*.config` file. Once you have created each aspect of the ABCs, you inform the host programmatically by calling `AddServiceEndpoint()`.

Enabling MEX

While we could enable MEX programmatically as well, we will opt for a configuration file. Insert a new `App.config` file into your Windows Service project that contains the following MEX settings:

```
<?xml version="1.0" encoding="utf-8" ?>
<configuration>
  <system.serviceModel>
    <services>
      <service name="MathServiceLibrary.MathService"
               behaviorConfiguration = "MathServiceMEXBehavior">

      <!-- Enable the MEX endpoint -->
      <endpoint address="mex"
                binding="mexHttpBinding"
                contract="IMetadataExchange" />
```

```
      <!-- Need to add this so MEX knows the address of our service -->
      <host>
        <baseAddresses>
          <add baseAddress ="http://localhost:8080/MathService"/>
        </baseAddresses>
      </host>
    </service>
  </services>

    <!-- A behavior definition for MEX -->
    <behaviors>
      <serviceBehaviors>
        <behavior name="MathServiceMEXBehavior" >
          <serviceMetadata httpGetEnabled="true" />
        </behavior>
      </serviceBehaviors>
    </behaviors>
  </system.serviceModel>
</configuration>
```

Creating a Windows Service Installer

In order to register your Windows service with the operating system, you need to add an installer to your project that will contain the necessary code to allow you to register the service. To do so, simply right-click the Windows service designer surface and select Add Installer (see Figure 25-15).

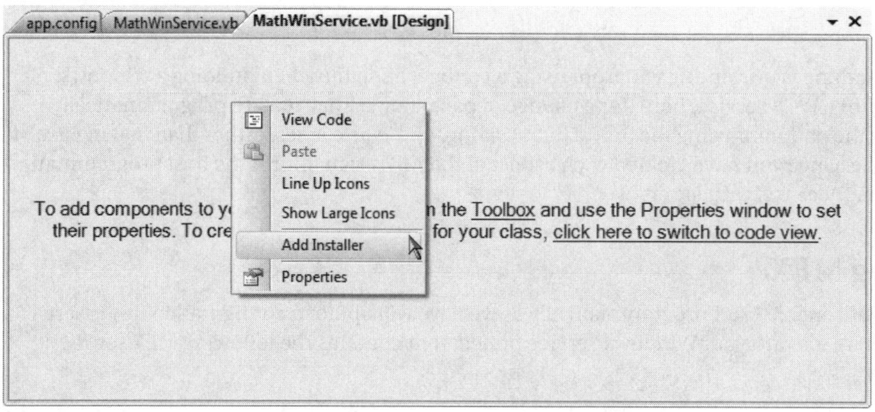

Figure 25-15. *Adding an installer for the Windows service*

Once you have done so, you will see two components have been added to a new designer surface. The first component (named `ServiceProcessInstaller1` by default) represents a type that is able to install a new Windows service on the target machine. Select this type on the designer and use the Properties window to set the `Account` property to `LocalSystem`.

The second component (named `ServiceInstaller1`) represents a type that will install your particular Windows service. Again, using the Properties window, change the `ServiceName` property to Math Service (as you might have guessed, this represents the friendly display name of the registered Windows service), set the `StartType` property to `Automatic`, and add a friendly description of your Windows service via the `Description` property. At this point you can compile your application.

Installing the Windows Service

A Windows service can be installed on the host machine using a traditional setup program (such as an `*.msi` installer) or via the `installutil.exe` command-line tool. Using a Visual Studio 2008 command prompt, change into the \bin\Debug folder of your MathWindowsServiceHost project. Now, enter the following command:

```
installutil MathWindowsServiceHost.exe
```

Assuming the installation succeeded, you can now open the Services applet located under the Administrative Tools folder of your Control Panel. You should see the friendly name of your Windows service listed alphabetically. Once you locate it, you can start the service on your local machine by clicking the Start the Service link (see Figure 25-16).

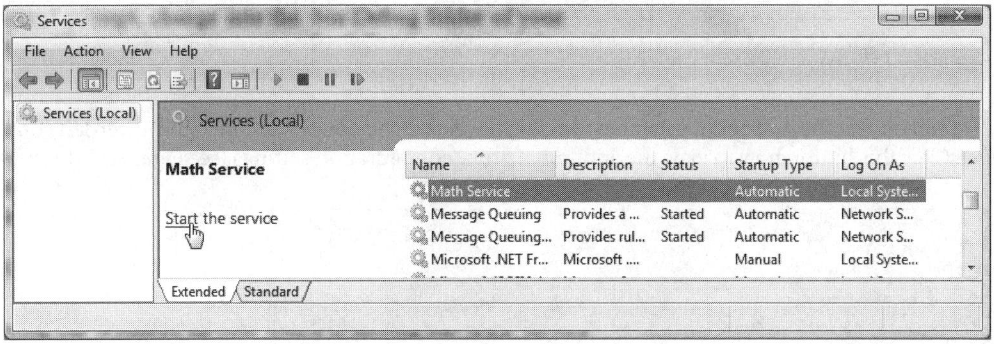

Figure 25-16. *Viewing our Windows service, which is hosting our WCF service*

Now that the service is alive and kicking, the last step is to build a client application to consume its services.

Source Code The MathWindowsServiceHost project is located under the Chapter 25 subdirectory.

Invoking a Service Asynchronously

Create a new Console Application named MathClient and set a Service Reference to your running WCF service that is current hosted by the Windows service running in the background using the Add Service Reference option of Visual Studio. Don't click the OK button yet, however (see Figure 25-17).

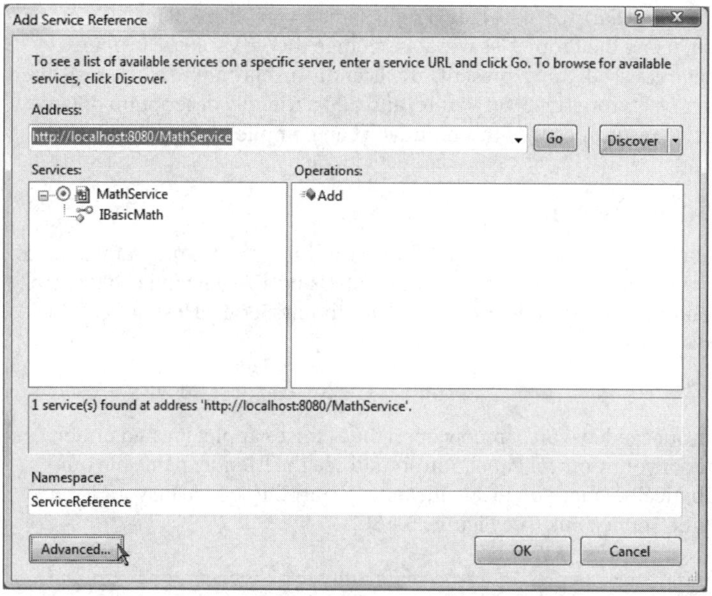

Figure 25-17. *Referencing our* `MathService`

Notice that the Add Service Reference dialog box has an Advanced button in the lower-left corner. Click this button now to view the additional proxy configuration settings (see Figure 25-18).

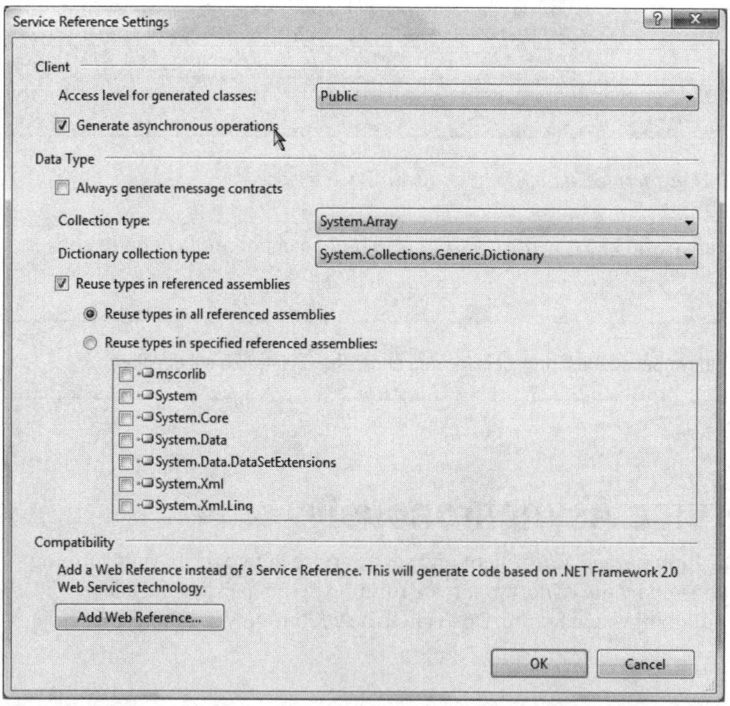

Figure 25-18. *Advanced client-side proxy configuration options*

Using this dialog box, we can elect to generate code that allows us to call the remote methods in an asynchronous manner, provided we check the "Generate asynchronous operations" check box. Go ahead and check this option for the time being.

The other option on this dialog box you should be aware of is the Add Web Reference button. If you have a background in building XML web services in Visual Studio 2005 or earlier, you may recall that you had an Add Web Reference option rather than an Add Service Reference option. If you click this particular button, you will be able to receive proxy code that will allow you to communicate with a traditional web service described within an `*.asmx` file.

The remaining options of this dialog box are used to control the generation of data contracts, which we will examine a bit later in this chapter. In any case, be sure you did indeed check the "Generate asynchronous operations" check box and click OK on each dialog box to return to the Visual Studio IDE.

At this point, the proxy code will contain additional methods that allow you to invoke each member of the service contract using the expected `Begin`/`End` asynchronous invocation pattern described in Chapter 18. Here is a simple implementation:

```
Imports MathClient.ServiceReference1
Imports System.Threading

Module Program
  Private proxy As New BasicMathClient()

  Sub Main()
    Console.WriteLine("***** The Async Math Client *****")

    proxy.Open()

    Dim result As IAsyncResult = proxy.BeginAdd(10, 10, _
      New AsyncCallback(AddressOf AddCallback), Nothing)

    While Not result.IsCompleted
      Thread.Sleep(200)
    End While

    proxy.Close()
    Console.ReadLine()
  End Sub

  Sub AddCallback(ByVal i As IAsyncResult)
    Console.WriteLine("10 + 10 = {0}", proxy.EndAdd(i))
  End Sub
End Module
```

Source Code The MathClient project is located under the Chapter 25 subdirectory.

Designing WCF Data Contracts

This chapter's final example involves the construction of WCF *data contracts*. The previous WCF services defined very simple methods that operate on primitive CLR data types. When you are making use of any of the web service–centric binding types (`basicHttpBinding`, `wsHttpBinding`, etc.), incoming and outgoing data types are automatically formatted into XML elements. On a related note, if you make use of a TCP-based binding (such as `netTcpBinding`), the parameters and return values of simple data types are transmitted using a compact binary format.

Note The WCF runtime will also automatically encode any type marked with the `<Serializable()>` attribute.

However, when you define service contracts that make use of custom types as parameters or return values, these types must be defined using a data contract. Simply put, a data contract is a type adorned with the `<DataContract()>` attribute. Each field you expect to be used as part of the proposed contract is likewise marked with the `<DataMember()>` attribute.

Note If a data contract contains a field not marked with the `<DataMember()>` attribute, the field will not be serialized by the WCF runtime.

To illustrate the construction of data contracts, let's create a brand-new WCF service that interacts with the AutoLot database created back in Chapter 22. As well, this final WCF service will be created using the web-based WCF Service template. Recall that this type of WCF service will automatically be placed into an IIS virtual directory, and it will function in a similar fashion to a traditional .NET XML web service. Once you understand the composition of such a WCF service, you should have little problem porting an existing WCF service into a new IIS virtual directory.

Note This example assumes you are somewhat comfortable with the structure of an IIS virtual directory (and IIS itself). If this is not the case, Chapter 33 will examine the details.

Using the Web-Centric WCF Service Project Template

Using the File ➤ New ➤ Web Site menu option, create a new WCF Service named VbAutoLot-WCFService, exposed from the following URI: `http://localhost/VbAutoLotWCFService` (see Figure 25-19). Be sure the Location drop-down list has HTTP as the active selection.

Once you have done so, set a reference to the `AutoLotDAL.dll` assembly you created in Chapter 22 (via the Website ➤ Add Reference menu option). Much like a WCF Service Library project, you have been given some example starter code (located under the App_Code folder), which you will obviously want to delete. To begin, rename the initial `IService.vb` file to `IAutoLotService.vb`, and define the initial service contract within your newly named file:

```
<ServiceContract()> _
Public Interface IAutoLotService
  <OperationContract()> _
  Sub InsertCar(ByVal id As Integer, ByVal make As String, _
    ByVal color As String, ByVal petname As String)

  <OperationContract()> _
  Sub InsertCar(ByVal car As InventoryRecord)

  <OperationContract()> _
  Function GetInventory() As InventoryRecord()
End Interface
```

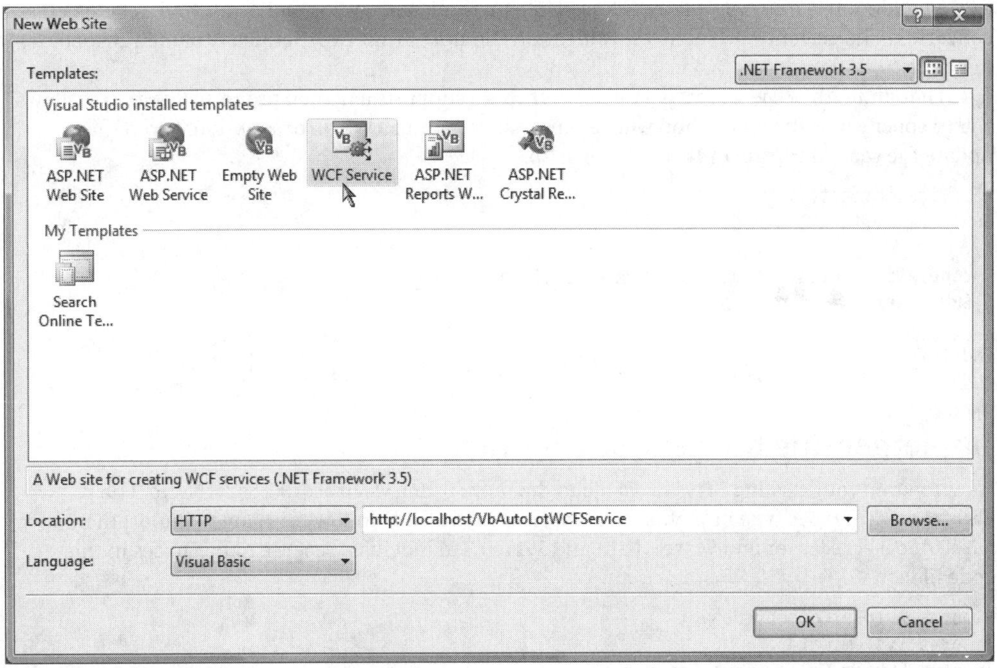

Figure 25-19. *Creating a web-centric WCF Service*

This interface defines three methods, one of which returns an array of (the yet-to-be-created) `InventoryRecord` type. You may recall that the `GetInventory()` method of `InventoryDAL` simply returned a `DataTable` object, which might make you question why our service's `GetInventory()` method does not do the same.

While it would work to return a `DataTable` from a WCF service method, recall that WCF was built to honor the use of SOA principles, one of which is to program against contracts, not implementations. Therefore, rather than returning the .NET-specific `DataTable` type to an external caller, we will return a custom data contract (`InventoryRecord`) that will be correctly expressed in the contained WSDL document in an agnostic manner.

Also note that this interface defines an overloaded method named `InsertCar()`. The first version takes four incoming parameters, while the second version takes an `InventoryRecord` type as input. This data contract can be defined as so:

```
<DataContract()> _
Public Class InventoryRecord
  <DataMember()> _
  Public ID As Integer
  <DataMember()> _
  Public Make As String
  <DataMember()> _
  Public Color As String
  <DataMember()> _
  Public PetName As String
End Class
```

If you were to implement this interface as it now stands, build a host, and attempt to call these methods from a client, you might be surprised to find a runtime exception. The reason has to do with the fact that one of the requirements of a WSDL description is that each method exposed from a given endpoint is *uniquely named*. Thus, while method overloading works just fine as far as VB is concerned, the current web service specifications do not permit two identically named InsertCar() methods.

Thankfully, the <OperationContract()> attribute supports a named property (Name) that allows you to specify how the VB method will be represented within a WSDL description. Given this, update the second version of InsertCar() as so:

```
<ServiceContract()> _
Public Interface IAutoLotService
...
  <OperationContract(Name:="InsertCarWithDetails")> _
  Sub InsertCar(ByVal car As InventoryRecord)
...
End Interface
```

Implementing the Service Contract

Now, rename your existing Service.vb file to the more fitting VbAutoLotWCFService.vb. The VbAutoLotWCFService type implements the service interface as follows (be sure to import the AutoLotConnectedLayer and System.Data and System.Collections.Generic namespaces in this code file):

```
Imports AutoLotConnectedLayer
Imports System.Data
Imports System.Collections.Generic

Public Class VbAutoLotWCFService
  Implements IAutoLotService
  Private Const ConnString As String = _
    "Data Source=(local)\SQLEXPRESS;Initial Catalog" & _
    "=AutoLot;Integrated Security=True"

  Public Sub InsertCar(ByVal id As Integer, ByVal make As String, _
    ByVal color As String, ByVal petname As String) _
    Implements IAutoLotService.InsertCar
    Dim d As New InventoryDAL()
    d.OpenConnection(ConnString)
    d.InsertAuto(id, color, make, petname)
    d.CloseConnection()
  End Sub

  Public Sub InsertCarWithDetails(ByVal car As InventoryRecord) _
    Implements IAutoLotService.InsertCar
    Dim d As New InventoryDAL()
    d.OpenConnection(ConnString)
    d.InsertAuto(car.ID, car.Color, car.Make, car.PetName)
    d.CloseConnection()
  End Sub

  Public Function GetInventory() As InventoryRecord() _
    Implements IAutoLotService.GetInventory
    ' First, get the DataTable from the database.
    Dim d As New InventoryDAL()
    d.OpenConnection(ConnString)
    Dim dt As DataTable = d.GetAllInventory()
    d.CloseConnection()
```

```
    ' Now make a List to contain the records.
    Dim records As New List(Of InventoryRecord)()

    ' Copy the data table into List of custom contracts.
    Dim reader As DataTableReader = dt.CreateDataReader()
    While reader.Read()
      Dim r As New InventoryRecord()
      r.ID = CInt(reader("CarID"))
      r.Color = DirectCast(reader("Color"), String).Trim()
      r.Make = DirectCast(reader("Make"), String).Trim()
      r.PetName = DirectCast(reader("PetName"), String).Trim()
      records.Add(r)
    End While

    ' Transform List to array of InventoryRecord types.
    Return DirectCast(records.ToArray(), InventoryRecord())
  End Function
End Class
```

Not too much to say here. For simplicity, we are hard-coding the connection string value (which you may need to adjust based on your machine settings) rather than storing it in our web.config file. Given that our data access library does all the real work of communicating with the AutoLot database, all we need to do is pass the incoming parameters to the InsertAuto() method of the InventoryDAL class type. The only other point of interest is the act of mapping the DataTable object's values into a generic list of InventoryRecord types (using a DataTableReader to do so) and then transforming the List(Of T) into an array of InventoryRecord types.

The Role of the *.svc File

When you create a web-centric WCF service, you will find your project contains a specific file with an *.svc file extension. This particular file is required for any WCF service hosted by IIS; it describes the name and location of the service implementation within the install point. Because we have changed the names of our starter files and WCF types, we must now update the contents of the Service.svc file as so:

```
<%@ ServiceHost Language="VB" Debug="true"
  Service=" VbAutoLotWCFService" CodeBehind="~/App_Code/ VbAutoLotWCFService.vb" %>
```

Updating the web.config File

Before we can take this service out for a test drive, the final task is to update the <system.serviceModel> section of the web.config file. As described in more detail during our examination of ASP.NET later in this book, the web.config file serves a similar purpose to an executable's *.config file; however, it also controls a number of web-specific settings. For this example, all we need to do is update WCF-specific section of the file as follows:

```
<system.serviceModel>
  <services>
    <service name=" VbAutoLotWCFService" behaviorConfiguration="ServiceBehavior">
      <endpoint address="" binding="wsHttpBinding" contract="IAutoLotService"/>

      <endpoint address="mex" binding="mexHttpBinding"
                contract="IMetadataExchange"/>
    </service>
  </services>
```

```
    <behaviors>
      <serviceBehaviors>
        <behavior name="ServiceBehavior">
          <serviceMetadata httpGetEnabled="true"/>
          <serviceDebug includeExceptionDetailInFaults="false"/>
        </behavior>
      </serviceBehaviors>
    </behaviors>
  </system.serviceModel>
```

Testing the Service

Now you are free to build any sort of client to test your service, including passing in the endpoint of the `*.svc` file to the `WcfTestClient.exe` application:

```
WcfTestClient http://localhost/VbAutoLotWCFService/Service.svc
```

Consider Figure 25-20, which illustrates the result of invoking `GetInventory()`.

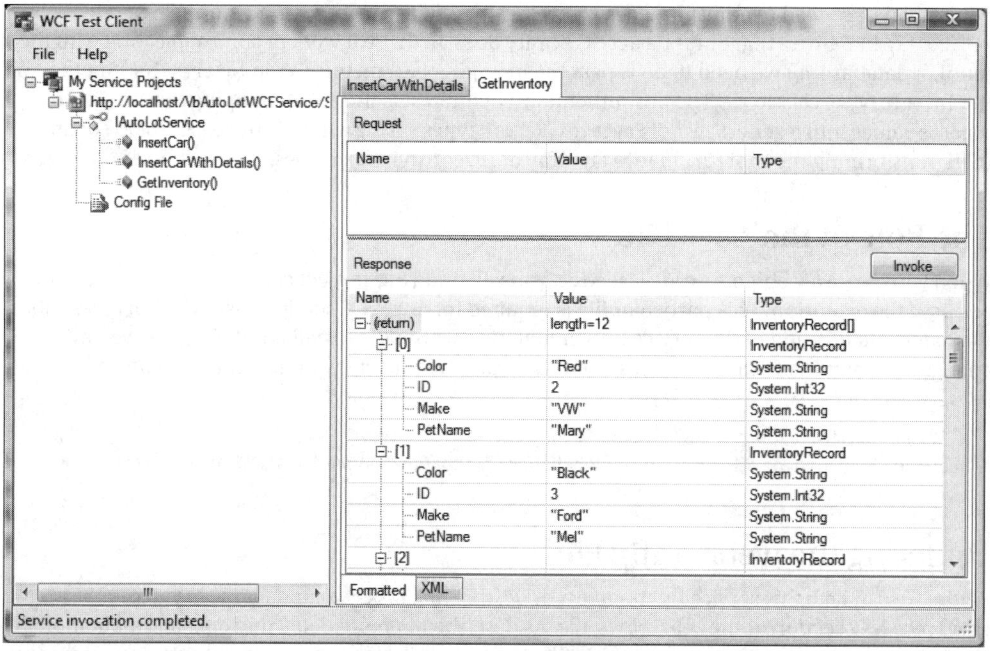

Figure 25-20. *Interacting with a WCF Service using the WCF Test Client*

If you wish to build a custom client application, simply use the Add Service Reference dialog box as you did for the MagicEightBallServiceClient and MathClient project examples earlier in this chapter.

Source Code The VbAutoLotWCFService files are located under the Chapter 25 subdirectory.

Summary

This chapter introduced you to the Windows Communication Foundation (WCF) API, which has been part of the base class libraries since .NET 3.0. As explained, the major motivation behind WCF is to provide a unified object model that exposes a number of (previously unrelated) distributed computing APIs under a single umbrella. Furthermore, as you saw at the onset of this chapter, a WCF service is represented by specified addresses, bindings, and contracts (easily remembered by the friendly abbreviation ABC).

As you have seen, a typical WCF application involves the use of three interrelated assemblies. The first assembly defines the service contracts and service types that represent the services functionality. This assembly is then hosted by a custom executable, an IIS virtual directory, or a Windows service. Finally, the client assembly makes use of a generated code file defining a proxy type (and settings within the application configuration file) to communicate with the remote type.

The chapter also examined using a number of WCF programming tools such as `SvcConfigEditor.exe` (which allows you modify `*.config` files), the `WcfTestClient.exe` application (to quickly test a WCF service), and various Visual Studio 2008 WCF project templates.

CHAPTER 26

Introducing Windows Workflow Foundation

.NET 3.0 shipped with a particular programming framework named Windows Workflow Foundation (WF). This API allows you to model, configure, monitor, and execute the *workflows* (which, for the time being, can simply be regarded as a collection of related tasks) used internally by a given application. The out-of-the-box solution provided by WF is a huge benefit when building software, as we are no longer required to manually develop complex infrastructure to support *workflow-enabled applications*.

This chapter begins by defining the role of *business processes* and describes how they relate to the WF API. As well, you will be exposed to the concept of a WF *activity*, the two major flavors of workflows (*sequential* and *state machine*), and various WF assemblies, project templates, and programming tools. Once we've covered the basics, we'll build several example programs that illustrate how to leverage the WF programming model to establish business processes that execute under the watchful eye of the WF runtime engine.

Note The entirety of WF cannot be covered in a single introductory chapter. If you require a deeper treatment of the topic than presented here, check out *Pro WF: Windows Workflow in .NET 3.0* by Bruce Bukovics (Apress, 2007).

Defining a Business Process

Any real-world application must be able to model various business processes. Simply put, a *business process* is a conceptual grouping of tasks that logically work as a collective whole. For example, assume you are building an application that allows a user to purchase an automobile online. Once the user submits the order, a large number of activities are set in motion. We might begin by performing a credit check. If the user passes our credit verification, we might start a database transaction in order to remove the entry from an Inventory table, add a new entry to an Orders table, and update the customer account information. After the database transaction has completed, we still might need to send a confirmation e-mail to the buyer, and then invoke a remote XML web service (or Windows Communication Foundation [WCF] service) to place the order at the dealership. Collectively, all of these tasks could represent a single business process.

Historically speaking, modeling a business process was yet another detail that programmers had to account for, often by authoring custom code to ensure that a business process was not only modeled correctly, but also executed correctly within the application itself. For example, you may need to author code to account for points of failure, tracing, and logging support (to see what a given business process is up to); persistence support (to save the state of long-running processes);

and whatnot. As you may know firsthand, building this sort of infrastructure from scratch entails a great deal of time and manual labor.

Assuming that a development team did, in fact, build a custom business process framework for their applications, their work was not yet complete. Simply put, a raw VB code base cannot be easily explained to nonprogrammers on the team who *also* need to understand the business process. The truth of the matter is that subject matter experts (SMEs), managers, salespeople, and members of a graphical design team often do not speak the language of code. Given this, we were required to make use of other modeling tools (such as Microsoft Visio) to graphically represent our processes using skill set–neutral terms. The obvious problem here is we now have two entities to keep in sync: If we change the code, we need to update the diagram. If we change the diagram, we need to update the code.

Furthermore, when building a sophisticated workflow-enabled application using the "100% code approach," the code base has very little trace of the internal "flow" of the application. For example, a typical .NET program might be composed of hundreds of custom types (not to mention the numerous types used by the base class libraries). While programmers may have a feel for which objects are making calls on other objects, the code itself is a far cry from a living document that explains the overall sequence of activity. While the development team may build external documentation and workflow charts, again we run into the problem of multiple representations of the same process.

The Role of WF

Since the release of .NET 3.0, we were provided with the Windows Workflow Foundation API. In essence, WF allows programmers to declaratively and graphically design business processes using a prefabricated set of *activities*. Thus, rather than building a custom set of assemblies to represent a given business activity and the necessary infrastructure, we can make use of the WF designers of Visual Studio 2008 to create our business process at design time. In this respect, WF allows us to build the skeleton of a business process, which can be fleshed out through code.

When programming with the WF API, a single entity can then be used to represent the overall business process as well as the code that defines it. Since a single WF document is used to represent the code driving the process in addition to being a friendly visual representation of the process, we no longer need to worry about multiple documents falling out of sync. Better yet, this WF document will clearly illustrate the process itself.

■ **Note** Strictly speaking, you could model a workflow using nothing but VB code, avoiding designers altogether. Using this "100% code approach" would not account for a visual representation of the workflow process.

The Building Blocks of WF

As you build a workflow-enabled application, you will undoubtedly notice that it "feels different" from building a typical .NET application. For example, up until this point in the text, every code example began by creating a new project workspace (most often a Console Application project) and involved authoring code to represent the program at large. A WF application also consists of custom code; however, in addition, you are building *directly into the assembly* the business process itself.

You'll learn how to create a WF project in just a moment; however, consider Figure 26-1, which illustrates the initial workflow diagram generated by Visual Studio 2008 when selecting a new Sequential Workflow Console Application project workspace.

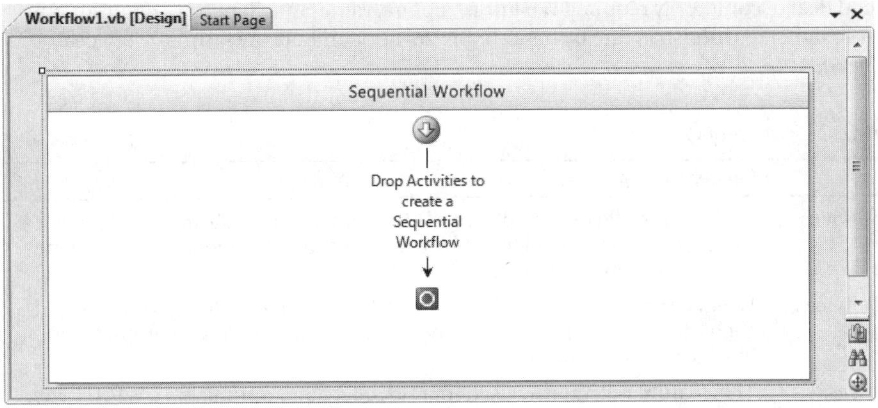

Figure 26-1. *An empty sequential workflow diagram designer*

Using this designer (and the various WF-centric tools integrated into Visual Studio) you are able to model your business process and eventually author code to execute it under the appropriate circumstances. You'll examine these tools in more detail a bit later in this chapter.

Understand that WF is far more than a pretty designer that allows you to model the activities of a business process. As you are building your WF diagram, the designer tools are authoring code to represent the skeleton of your process. Thus, the first thing to be aware of is that a visual WF diagram is executable code, not just simply a Visio-like static image. As such, WF is represented by a set of .NET assemblies, namespaces, and types, just like any other .NET technology.

The WF Runtime Engine

Given the fact that a WF diagram equates to real types and custom code, the next thing to understand is that the WF API also consists of a runtime engine to load, execute, unload, and in other ways manipulate a workflow process. The WF runtime engine can be hosted within any .NET application domain; however, be aware that a single application domain can only have one running instance of the WF engine.

Recall from Chapter 17 that an AppDomain is a partition within a Win32 process that plays host to a .NET application and any external code libraries. As such, the WF engine can be embedded within a simple console program, a GUI desktop application (Windows Forms or Windows Presentation Foundation [WPF]), and an ASP.NET web application, or exposed from a WCF service or XML web service.

If you are modeling a business process that needs to be used by a wide variety of systems, you also have the option of authoring your workflows within a VB Class Library project. In this way, new applications can simply reference your `*.dll` to reuse a predefined collection of business processes. This is obviously helpful in that you would not want to have to re-create the same workflow instances multiple times.

In any case, at this point understand that the WF API provides a full-blown object model that allows you to programmatically interact with the runtime engine as well as the workflows you have designed.

The Core Services of WF

In addition to designer tools and a runtime engine, WF provides a set of out-of-the-box services that completes the overall framework of a workflow-enabled application. Using these services, we can "inherit" a good deal of commonly required WF infrastructure, rather than having to commit time and resources to build this infrastructure by hand. Table 26-1 documents the intrinsic services baked into the WF API.

Table 26-1. *Intrinsic Services of WF*

Services	Meaning in Life
Persistence services	This feature allows you to save a WF instance to an external source (such as a database). This can be useful if a long-running business process will be idle for some amount of time.
Transaction services	WF instances can be monitored in a transactional context, to ensure that each aspect of your workflow—or a subset of a workflow—completes (or fails) as a singular atomic unit.
Tracking services	This feature is primarily used for debugging and optimizing a WF activity; it allows you to monitor the activities of a given workflow.
Scheduling services	This feature allows you to control how the WF runtime engine manages threads for your workflows.

Collectively, the four intrinsic services seen in Table 26-1 are termed the *core services*. The WF APIs provide default implementations of each of these services, two of which (scheduling and transactions) are registered with the WF runtime automatically, while tracking and persistence services are optional and not registered with the runtime by default.

While the .NET base class libraries do provide types that support each core service, you are able to exchange them with your own custom implementations. Thus, if you wish to customize the way in which a long-running workflow should be persisted, you can do so. As well, if you wish to extend the basic functionality of a core service with new functionality, it is possible to do so.

When you create an instance of the WF runtime engine in order to execute one of your workflows, you have the option of calling the `AddService()` method to plug in tracking or persistence service objects (such as `SqlWorkflowPersistanceService` and `SqlTrackingService`) as well as any customized service you may have designed. At this point you are able to execute a given workflow instance and allow these auxiliary services to further monitor its lifetime.

In this introductory chapter, we will not build custom implementations of the core services, nor will we dive too deeply into the default functionality of them. Here, we will focus on the building blocks of a workflow-enabled application, and we will examine numerous WF activities. Be sure to check out the .NET Framework 3.5 SDK documentation for further details of the core services.

A First Look at WF Activities

Recall that the purpose of WF is to allow you to model a business process in a declarative manner, which is then executed by the WF runtime engine. In the vernacular of WF, a business process is composed of any number of *activities*. Simply put, a WF activity is a "step" in the overall process. When you create a new WF-enabled application using Visual Studio 2008, you will find a Windows Workflow area of the Toolbox that contains iconic representations of the built-in activities (see Figure 26-2).

Note Visual Studio 2008 divides the set of activities into .NET 3.0 and .NET 3.5 activity categories. The activities under the Windows Workflow v3.5 node allow you to interact with WCF services.

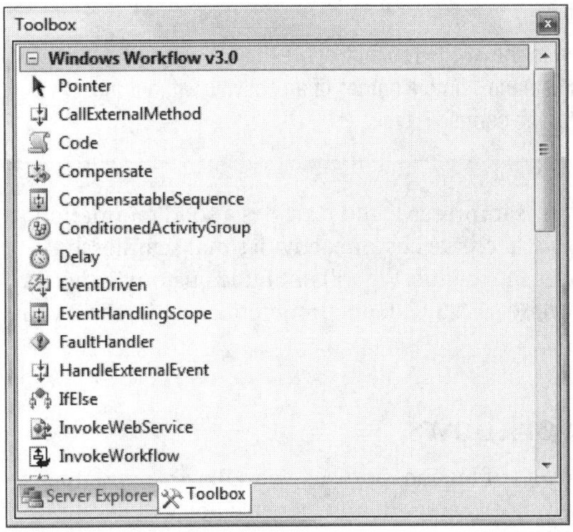

Figure 26-2. *The Windows Workflow Toolbox*

.NET 3.5 provides numerous out-of-the-box activities that you can use to model your business process, each of which maps to real types within the `System.Workflow.Activities` namespace and therefore can be represented by, and driven from, code. You'll make use of several of these baked-in activities over the course of this chapter. Table 26-2 describes the high-level functionality of some useful activities within `System.Workflow.Activities`, grouped by related functionality.

Table 26-2. *A Sampling of Intrinsic WF Activities*

Activity	Meaning in Life
`CodeActivity`	This activity represents a unit of custom code to execute within the workflow.
`IfElseActivity` `WhileActivity`	These activities provide basic looping and decision support within a workflow.

`InvokeWebServiceActivity`
`WebServiceInputActivity`
`WebServiceOutputActivity`
`WebServiceFaultActivity`
	These activities allow your workflow to interact with XML web services.

`SendActivity` `ReceiveActivity`	These activities allow you to interact with Windows Communication Foundation services. Be aware that these two activities are .NET 3.5 specific.
`ConditionedActivityGroup`	This activity allows you to define a group of related activities that execute when a given condition is true.

`DelayActivity`
`SuspendActivity`
`TerminateActivity`
	These activities allow you to define wait periods as well as pause or terminate a course of action within a workflow.

`EventDrivenActivity` `EventHandlingScopeActivity`	These activities allow you to associate CLR events to a given activity within the workflow.
`ThrowActivity` `FaultHandlerActivity`	These activities allow you to raise and handle exceptions within a workflow.
`ParallelActivity` `SequenceActivity`	These activities allow you to execute a set of activities in parallel or in sequence.

Note As a naming convention, an activity class ends with the `Activity` suffix (`IfElseActivity`, `CodeActivity`, etc.). However, the Visual Studio toolbox lists the "simple name" of an activity, without the suffix (IfElse, Code, etc.). Under the covers, they are in fact the same WF type.

While the current number of intrinsic activities is impressive and provides a solid foundation for many WF-enabled applications, you are also able to create custom activities that seamlessly integrate into the Visual Studio IDE and the WF runtime engine. We will not build custom activities in this introductory chapter; consult the .NET Framework 3.5 SDK documentation for details if you are interested.

Sequential and State Machine Workflows

The WF API provides support for modeling two flavors of business process workflows: sequential workflows and state machine workflows. Ultimately, both categories are constructed by piecing together any number of related activities; however, exactly *how* they execute is what sets them apart.

The most straightforward workflow type is *sequential*. As its name implies, a sequential workflow allows you to model a business process where each activity executes in sequence until the final activity completes. This is not to say that a sequential workflow is necessarily linear or predictable in nature—it is entirely possible to build a sequential workflow that contains various branching and looping activities, as well as a set of activities that execute in parallel on separate threads.

The key aspect of a sequential workflow is that it has a crystal-clear beginning and ending point. Within the Visual Studio 2008 workflow designer, the path of execution begins at the top of the WF diagram and proceeds downward to the end point. Figure 26-3 shows a simple sequential workflow that models a partial business process for verifying a given automobile is in stock.

Sequential workflows work well when the workflow models interactions with various system level atoms, and when there is no requirement for backtracking in the process. For example, the business process modeled in Figure 26-3 has two possible outcomes: the car is in stock or it isn't. If the car is indeed in stock, the order is processed using some block of custom code (whatever that may be). If the car isn't in stock, we send a notification e-mail, provided that we have the client's e-mail address at our disposal.

In contrast to sequential workflows, *state machine workflows* do not model activities using a simple linear path. Instead, the workflow defines a number of *request states* and a set of related *events* that trigger transitions between these states. Figure 26-4 illustrates a simple state machine WF diagram that represents the processing of an order. Don't worry about the details of what each activity is doing behind the scenes, but do notice that each request state in the workflow can flow across various states based on some internal event.

State machine workflows can be very helpful when you need to model a business process that can be in various states of completion, typically due to the fact that human interaction is involved to move between states. Here, we have a request state that is waiting for an order to be created. Once that occurs, an event forces the flow of activity to the order open state, which may trigger an order processed state (or loop back to the previous open state), and so forth.

Note In this introductory chapter, I don't dig into the details of building state machine workflows. Consult the .NET Framework 3.5 SDK documentation for further information if you are interested.

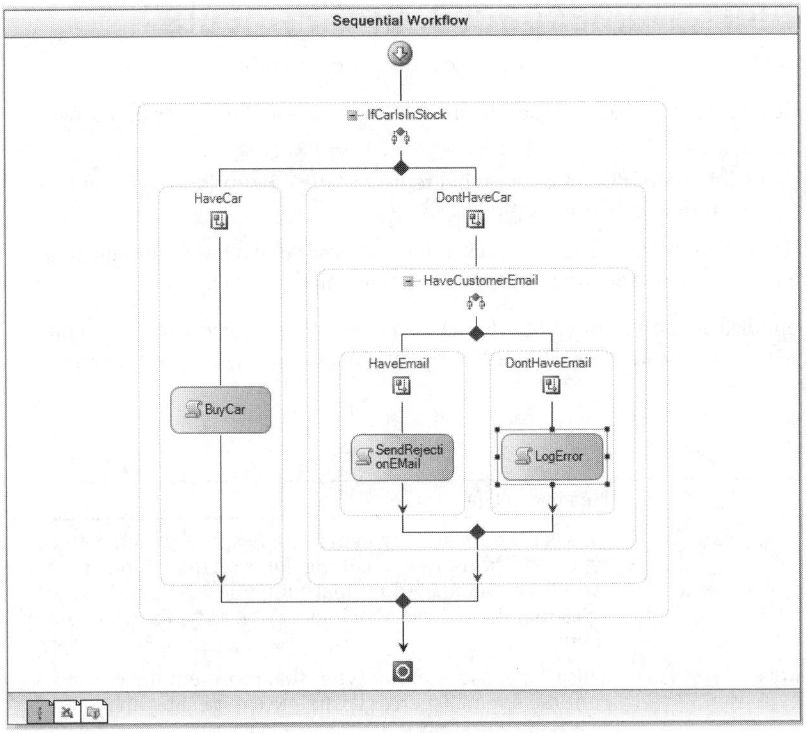

Figure 26-3. *Sequential workflows have a clear starting point and ending point.*

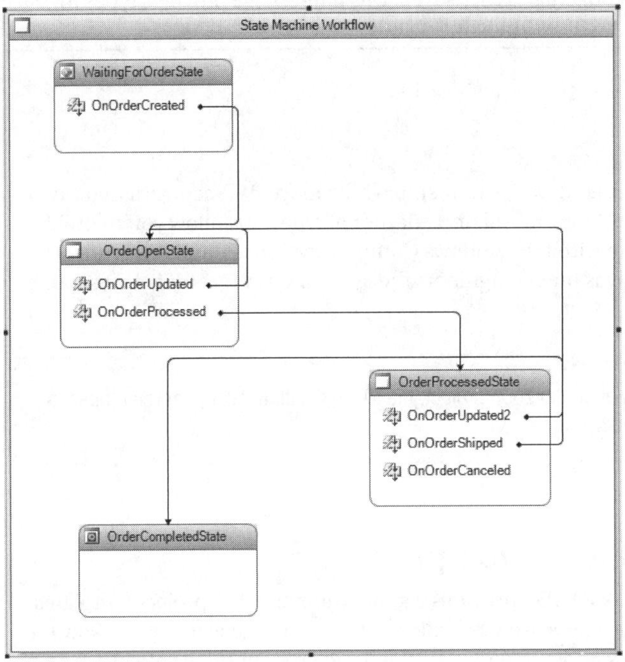

Figure 26-4. *State machine workflows do not follow a fixed, linear path.*

WF Assemblies, Namespaces, and Projects

From a programmer's point of view, WF is represented by three core assemblies:

- `System.Workflow.Activities.dll`: Defines the intrinsic activities and the rules that drive them
- `System.Workflow.Runtime.dll`: Defines types that represent the WF runtime engine and instances of your custom workflows
- `System.Workflow.ComponentModel.dll`: Defines numerous types that allow for design-time support of WF applications, including construction of custom designer hosts

While these assemblies define a number of .NET namespaces, many of them are used behind the scenes by various WF visual design tools. Table 26-3 documents some key WF-centric namespaces to be aware of.

Table 26-3. *Core WF Namespaces*

Namespace	Meaning in Life
`System.Workflow.Activities`	This is the core activity-centric namespace, which defines type definitions for each of the items on the Windows Workflow Toolbox. Additional subnamespaces define the rules that drive these activities as well as types to configure them.
`System.Workflow.Runtime`	This namespace defines types that represent the WF runtime engine (such as `WorkflowRuntime`) and an instance of a given workflow (via `WorkflowInstance`).
`System.Workflow.Runtime.Hosting`	This namespace provides types to build a host for the WF runtime, which make use of custom WF services (tracking, logging, etc.). As well, this namespace provides types to represent the out-of-the-box core WF services.

.NET 3.5 WF Support

With the release of .NET 3.5, the base class libraries now ship with a fourth WF-centric assembly named `System.WorkflowServices.dll`. Here you will find additional types that allow you to build WF-enabled applications that integrate with the Windows Communications Foundation APIs. The most important aspect of this assembly is that it augments the `System.Workflow.Activities` namespace with new types to support WCF integration.

■ **Note** When you build any WF-aware Visual Studio 2008 project, the IDE will automatically set references to each of the Windows Workflow Foundation assemblies.

Visual Studio Workflow Project Templates

As you would expect, the Visual Studio 2008 IDE provides a good number of WF project templates. First and foremost, when you select the File ➤ New ➤ Project menu option to activate the New Project dialog box, you will find a Workflow node under the Visual Basic programming category (see

Figure 26-5). Here you will find projects that allow you to build sequential and state machine workflows.

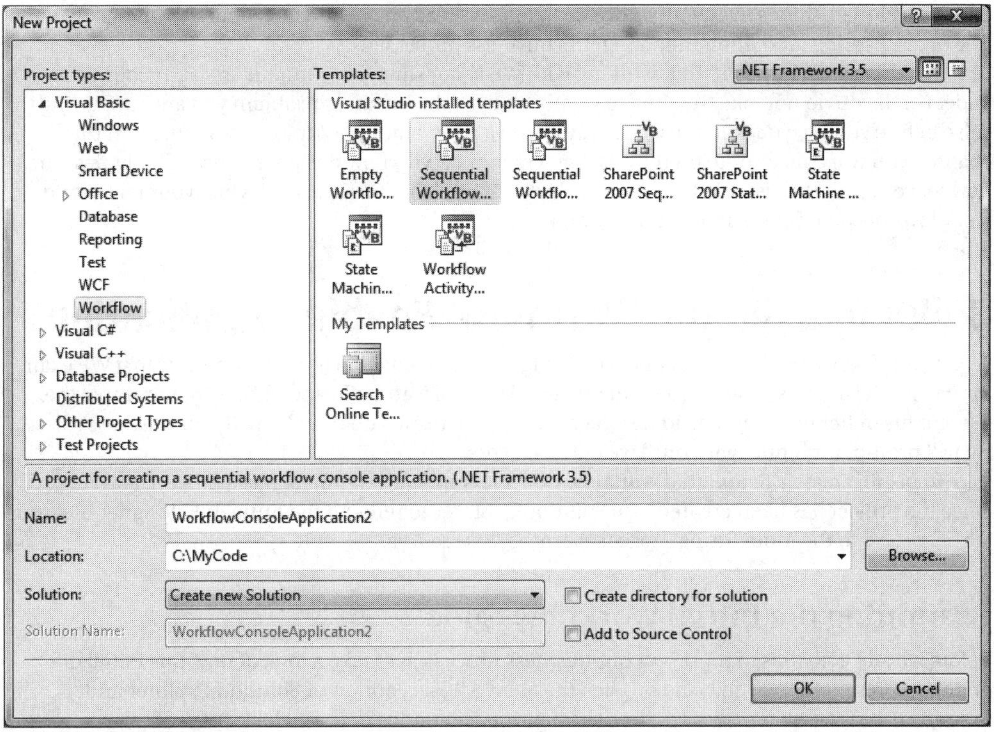

Figure 26-5. *The core WF project templates*

In addition, you may recall from Chapter 25 that the Windows Communication Foundation (WCF) node of the New Project dialog box also provides a set of WF templates. Here you will find two project templates (Sequential Workflow Service Library and State Machine Workflow Service Library) that allow you to build a WCF service that internally makes use of workflows. We will not make use of this group of WF project templates in this chapter; however, do remember that when you are building WCF services, you can elect to integrate WF functionality when creating a new project.

Getting into the Flow of Workflow

Before we dive into our first code example, allow me to point out a few final thoughts regarding the "workflow mind-set." When programming with the WF API, you must keep in mind that you are ultimately attempting to model a *business process*; therefore, the first step is to investigate the business process itself, including all the substeps within the process and each of the possible outcomes. For example, assume you are modeling the process of registering for a training class online. When a request comes in, what should you do if the salesperson is out of the office? What if the class is currently full? What if the class has been canceled or moved to a new date? How can you determine whether the trainer is available, is not on vacation, is not teaching a class that same week, or whatnot?

Depending on your current background, the process of gathering these requirements may be a very new task, as figuring out a business process may be "someone else's problem." However, in small companies, the act of determining the necessary business processes may fall on the shoulders of the developers themselves. Larger organizations typically have business analysts who take on the role of discovering (and often modeling) the business processes.

In any case, do be aware that working with WF is not simply a "jump in and start coding" endeavor. If you do not take the time to clearly analyze the business problem you are attempting to solve before coding, you will most certainly create a good amount of unnecessary pain. In this chapter, you will concentrate on the basic mechanics of workflow design, the use of activities, and how to work with the visual WF designers. However, don't be too surprised when your real-world workflows become substantially more complex.

Building a Simple Workflow-Enabled Application

To get your feet wet with the process of building workflow-enabled applications, this first WF example will model a very simple sequential process. The goal is to build a workflow that prompts the user for his or her name and validates the results. If the results do not jibe with our business rules, we will prompt for input again until we reach success.

To begin, create a Sequential Workflow Console Application project named UserDataWFApp. Once the project has been created, use Solution Explorer to rename the initial WF designer file from `Workflow1.vb` to the more fitting `ProcessUsernameWorkflow.vb`.

Examining the Initial Workflow Code

Before we add activities to represent our business process, let's take a look at how this initial diagram is represented internally. If you click the Show All Files option of Solution Explorer and examine the `ProcessUsernameWorkflow.vb` icon, you will notice that much like other designer-maintained files (forms, windows, web pages), a WF diagram consists of a designer-maintained file. When you right-click the `ProcessUsernameWorkflow.vb` file and choose the View Code option, you will find a class type that extends the `SequentialWorkflowActivity` type:

```
Public Class ProcessUsernameWorkflow
  Inherits SequentialWorkflowActivity
End Class
```

If you now open the related `*.designer.vb` file, you will find that the `InitializeComponent()` method (called automatically upon object construction) has set the `Name` property accordingly:

```
Partial Class ProcessUsernameWorkflow
  <System.Diagnostics.DebuggerNonUserCode()> _
  Private Sub InitializeComponent()
    Me.Name = "Workflow1"
  End Sub
End Class
```

As you make use of the Windows Workflow Toolbox to drag various activities onto the designer surface and configure them using the Properties window (or the inline smart tags), the `*.designer.vb` file will be updated automatically. Like other IDE-maintained files, you can typically ignore the code within this file completely and keep focused on authoring code within the primary `*.vb` file.

Adding a Code Activity

The first activity you will add in the sequence is a Code activity. To do so, activate the designer, drag a Code activity component from the Windows Workflow Toolbox, and drop it onto the line connecting the starting and ending points of the workflow. Next, use the Properties window to rename this activity as ShowInstructionsActivity using the (Name) property. At this point, your designer should look like Figure 26-6.

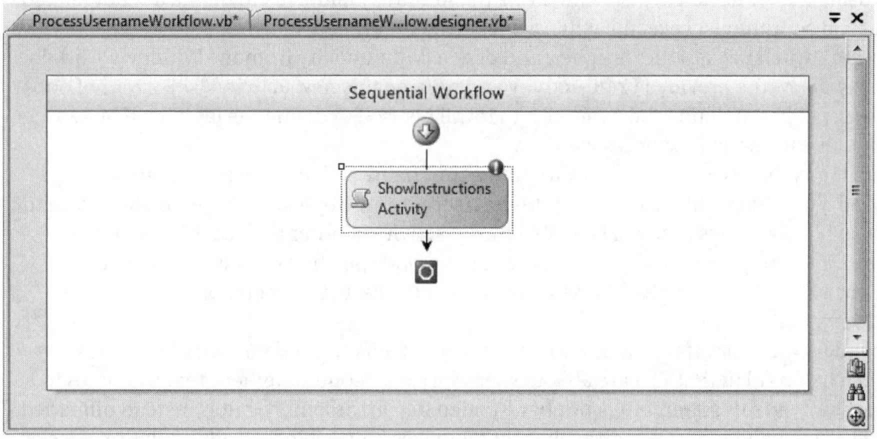

Figure 26-6. *A (not quite ready for prime time) Code activity*

As you can see, the designer is currently reporting an error, which you can view by clicking the red exclamation point on top of the Code activity. The error informs you that the ExecuteCode value has not been set, which is a mandatory step for all Code activity types. Not too surprisingly, ExecuteCode establishes the name of the method to execute when this task is encountered by the WF runtime engine.

Using the Properties window, set the value of ExecuteCode to a method named ShowInstructions. Once you press the Enter key, the IDE will update the primary *.vb code file with the following stub code:

```
Public Class ProcessUsernameWorkflow
  Inherits SequentialWorkflowActivity

  Private Sub ShowInstructions(ByVal sender As System.Object, _
    ByVal e As System.EventArgs)
  End Sub
End Class
```

Truth be told, ExecuteCode is an event of the CodeActivity class type. When the WF engine encounters this phase of the sequential workflow, the ExecuteCode event will fire and be handled by the ShowInstructions() method. Implement this method with a handful of Console.WriteLine() statements that display some basic instructions to the end user:

```
Private Sub ShowInstructions(ByVal sender As System.Object, _
 ByVal e As System.EventArgs)
  Dim previousColor As ConsoleColor = Console.ForegroundColor
  Console.ForegroundColor = ConsoleColor.Yellow
  Console.WriteLine("*****************************************")
  Console.WriteLine("***** Welcome to the first WF Example *****")
  Console.WriteLine("*****************************************" & vbLf)
  Console.WriteLine("I will now ask for your name and validate the data..." & vbLf)
  Console.ForegroundColor = previousColor
End Sub
```

Adding a While Activity

Recall that our business process will prompt the end user for his or her name until the input can be validated against a custom business rule (that is yet to be defined). Such looping behavior can be represented using the While activity. Specifically, a While activity allows us to define a set of related activities that will continuously execute while a specified condition is `True`.

To illustrate, switch back to the designer, and drag a While activity from the Windows Workflow Toolbox directly below the previous Code activity and rename this new activity AskForNameLoop-Activity. The next step is to define the condition that will be used to define the loop itself by setting the `Condition` value from the Properties window.

The `Condition` value (which is a common property of many activities) can be set in two key ways. First of all, you can establish a *code condition*. As the name implies, this option allows you to specify a method in your class that will be called by the activity in order to determine whether it should proceed. To inform the activity of this fact, the method specified will eventually need to return a `Boolean` value (`True` to repeat, `False` to exit) using the `Result` property of the incoming `ConditionalEventArgs` parameter.

The second way the `Condition` value can be set is by establishing a *declarative rule condition*. This option can be useful in that you are able to specify a single code statement that evaluates to `True` or `False`; however, this statement is not hard-coded in your assembly, but is instead offloaded to a `*.rules` file. One benefit of this approach is that it makes it possible to modify rules in a declarative manner.

Our condition will be based on some custom code that we have yet to author; however, the first step is to select the Code Condition option from the `Condition` value, and then specify the name of the method that will perform the test. Again using the Properties window, name this method `GetAndValidateUserName` (see Figure 26-7).

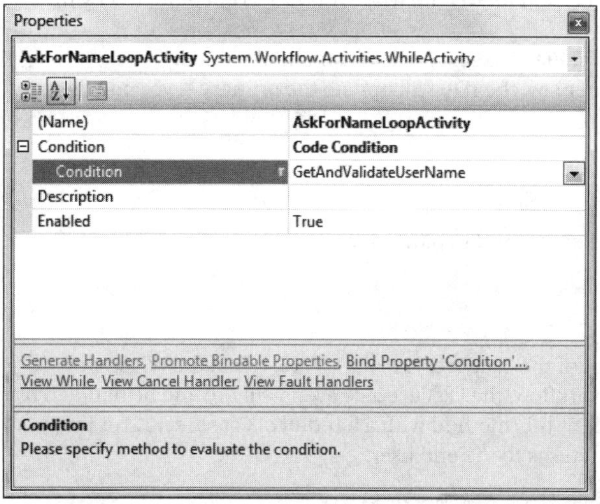

Figure 26-7. *The configured While activity*

As soon as you specify the name of the code condition used to test the While activity, the IDE will generate a method stub where the second parameter is of type `ConditionalEventArgs`. This type contains a property named `Result`, which can be set to `True` or `False` based on the success or failure of the condition you are modeling.

Add a new property of type `String` named `UserName` to your `ProcessUsernameWorkflow` class. Within the scope of the `GetAndValidateUserName()` method, ask the user to enter his or her name, and if the name consists of fewer than ten characters, set the `Result` property to `True` to keep on looping or `False` to stop looping. Here are the updates in question:

```
Public Class ProcessUsernameWorkflow
  Inherits SequentialWorkflowActivity

  ' To hold the name of the user.
  Private usrName As String
  Public Property UserName() As String
    Get
      Return usrName
    End Get
    Set(ByVal value As String)
      usrName = value
    End Set
  End Property

  Private Sub GetAndValidateUserName(ByVal sender As System.Object, _
  ByVal e As System.Workflow.Activities.ConditionalEventArgs)

    Console.Write("Please enter name, which must be less than 10 chars: ")
    UserName = Console.ReadLine()

    ' See if name is correct length, and set the result.
    e.Result = (UserName.Length >= 10)
  End Sub
...
End Class
```

The final task to complete the While activity involves adding at least a single activity within the scope of the While logic. Here we will add a new Code activity named NameNotValidActivity, which has been connected to a method named `NameNotValid` via the `ExecuteCode` value. Figure 26-8 shows the final workflow diagram.

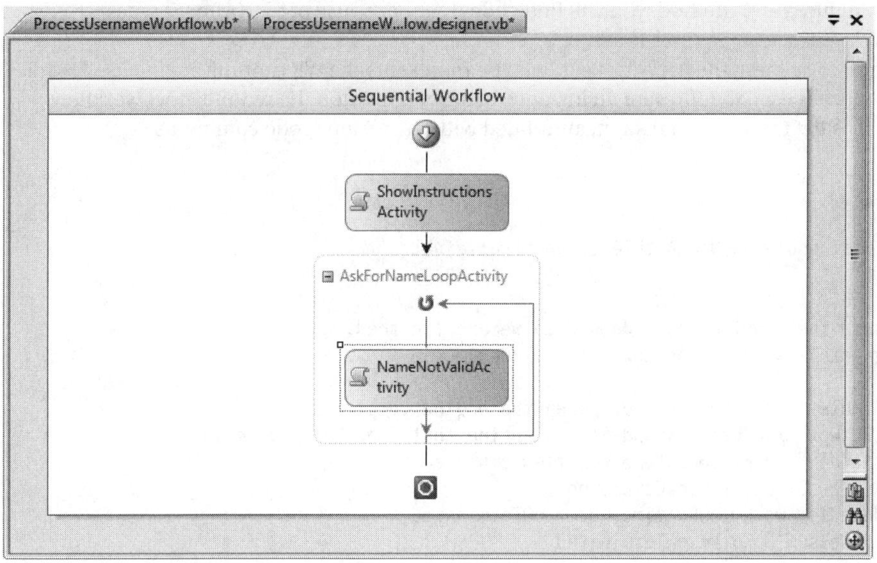

Figure 26-8. *The final workflow design*

The implementation of `NameNotValid()` is intentionally simple:

```
Private Sub NameNotValid(ByVal sender As System.Object, _
  ByVal e As System.EventArgs)
  Console.WriteLine("Sorry, try again...")
End Sub
```

At this point, you may compile and run this workflow-enabled application. When you execute the program, purposely enter more than ten characters a few times. You will notice that the runtime engine forces the user to reenter data until the business rule (a name of fewer than ten characters) is honored. Figure 26-9 shows one possible output.

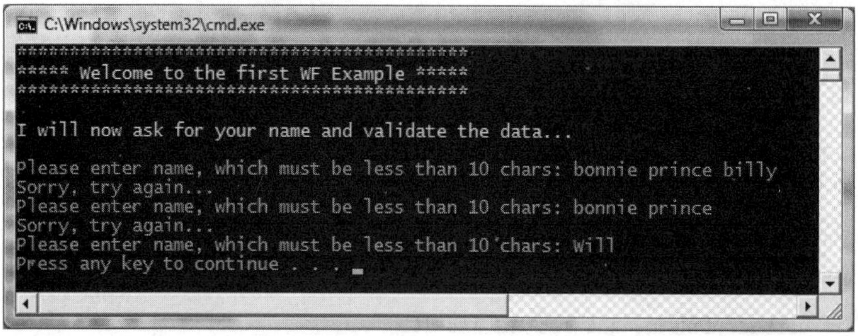

Figure 26-9. *The workflow-enabled application in action*

Examining the WF Engine Hosting Code

While our first example executes as expected, we have yet to examine the code that actually instructs the WF runtime engine to execute the tasks that represent the current workflow. To understand this aspect of WF, open the `Module1.vb` file that was created when you defined your initial project. Within the `Main()` method, you will find code that makes use of two primary types, `WorkflowRuntime` and `WorkflowInstance`.

As the names suggest, the `WorkflowRuntime` type represents the WF runtime engine itself, while `WorkflowInstance` is used to represent an instance of a given (pardon the redundancy) workflow instance. Here is the module in question, annotated with my various code comments:

```
Module Module1
  Class Program

    Shared WaitHandle As New AutoResetEvent(False)

    Shared Sub Main()
      ' Ensure the runtime shuts down when we are finished.
      Using workflowRuntime As New WorkflowRuntime()

        ' Handle events that capture when the engine completes
        ' the workflow process and if the engine shuts down with an error.
        AddHandler workflowRuntime.WorkflowCompleted, _
          AddressOf OnWorkflowCompleted
        AddHandler workflowRuntime.WorkflowTerminated, _
          AddressOf OnWorkflowTerminated
```

```
        ' Now, create a WF instance that represents our type.
        Dim workflowInstance As WorkflowInstance
        workflowInstance = workflowRuntime.CreateWorkflow _
          (GetType(ProcessUsernameWorkflow))
        workflowInstance.Start()
        WaitHandle.WaitOne()
      End Using
    End Sub

    Shared Sub OnWorkflowCompleted(ByVal sender As Object, _
    ByVal e As WorkflowCompletedEventArgs)
      WaitHandle.Set()
    End Sub

    Shared Sub OnWorkflowTerminated(ByVal sender As Object, _
    ByVal e As WorkflowTerminatedEventArgs)
      Console.WriteLine(e.Exception.Message)
      WaitHandle.Set()
    End Sub
  End Class
End Module
```

First of all, notice that the `WorkflowCompleted` and `WorkflowTerminated` events of `WorkflowRuntime` are handled. The `WorkflowCompleted` event fires when the WF engine has completed executing a workflow instance, while `WorkflowTerminated` fires if the engine terminates with an error.

Strictly speaking, you are not required to handle these events, although the IDE-generated code does so in order to inform the waiting thread these events have occurred using the `AutoResetEvent` type. This is especially important for a console-based application, as the WF engine is operating on a secondary thread of execution. If the workflow logic did not make use of some sort of wait handle, the main thread might terminate before the WF instance was able to perform its work.

The next point of interest regarding the code within `Main()` is the creation of the `WorkflowInstance` type. Notice that the `WorkflowRuntime` type exposes a method named `CreateWorkflow()`, which expects type information representing the workflow to be created. At this point, we simply call `Start()` from the returned object reference. This is all that is required to fire up the WF runtime engine and begin the processing of our custom workflow.

Adding Custom Startup Parameters

Before we move on to a more interesting workflow example, allow me to address how to define workflow-instance-wide parameters. If you examine the signature of the designer-generated methods used by our Code activities (`ShowInstructions()` and `NameNotValid()` specifically), you may have noticed that they are called via WF events that are making use of the `System.EventHandler` delegate (given the incoming parameters of type `Object` and `System.EventArgs`).

Because this .NET delegate demands the registered event handler and takes `System.Object` and `System.EventArgs` as arguments, you may wonder how to pass in *custom* parameters to be used by a Code activity. In fact, you may be wondering how to define custom arguments that can be used by any activity within the current workflow instance.

As it turns out, the WF engine supports the use of custom parameters using a generic `Dictionary(Of String, Object)` type. The name/value pairs added to the `Dictionary` object must then be associated to (identically named) properties on your workflow instance. Once you've done this, you can pass these arguments into the WF runtime engine when you start your workflow instance. Using this approach, you are able get and set custom parameters throughout a particular workflow instance.

■Note The names defined within a `Dictionary` object must map to public properties in your workflow class, *not* public member variables! If you attempt to do so, you will generate a runtime exception.

To try this out firsthand, begin by updating the code within `Main()` to define a `Dictionary(Of String, Object)` containing two data items. The first item is a `String` that represents the error message to display if the name is too long; the second item is a numeric value that will be used to specify the maximum length of the user name. To register these parameters with the WF runtime engine, pass in your `Dictionary` object as a second parameter to the `CreateWorkflow()` method. Here are the relevant updates:

```
Using workflowRuntime As New WorkflowRuntime()
...
  ' Define two parameters for use by our workflow.
  ' Remember! These must be mapped to identically named
  ' properties in our workflow class type.
  Dim parameters As New Dictionary(Of String, Object)()
  parameters.Add("ErrorMessage", "Ack!  Your name is too long!")
  parameters.Add("NameLength", 5)

  ' Pass parameters to WF instance.
  Dim workflowInstance As WorkflowInstance
  workflowInstance = workflowRuntime.CreateWorkflow _
    (GetType(ProcessUsernameWorkflow), parameters)
  workflowInstance.Start()
  WaitHandle.WaitOne()
End Using
```

■Note In the preceding code, the values assigned to the `ErrorMessage` and `NameLength` dictionary items are hard-coded. A more dynamic approach is to read these values from a related `*.config` file, or perhaps from incoming command-line arguments.

If you try running your program at this point, you will encounter a runtime exception, as you have yet to associate these incoming values to public properties on your workflow type. Once you have done so, however, the runtime will invoke them upon workflow creation. After this point, you can use these properties to get and set the underlying data values. Assume you have added the following properties (and member variables) to your `ProcessUsernameWorkflow` class type:

```
Private errMsg As String
Public Property ErrorMessage() As String
  Get
    Return errMsg
  End Get
  Set(ByVal value As String)
    errMsg = value
  End Set
End Property
```

```
Private nameLen As Integer
Public Property NameLength() As Integer
  Get
    Return nameLen
  End Get
  Set(ByVal value As Integer)
    nameLen = value
  End Set
End Property
```

With this, you can now update your existing methods as follows:

```
Private Sub GetAndValidateUserName(ByVal sender As System.Object, _
  ByVal e As System.Workflow.Activities.ConditionalEventArgs)
  Console.Write("Please enter name, which must be less than {0} chars:", _
    NameLength)
  UserName = Console.ReadLine()
  e.Result = (UserName.Length >= NameLength)
End Sub

Private Sub NameNotValid(ByVal sender As System.Object, _
    ByVal e As System.EventArgs)
  Console.WriteLine(ErrorMessage)
End Sub
```

Beyond the fact that you have added two new properties, notice that the `GetAndValidateUserName()` method is now checking for the length specified by the `NameLength` property, while the error message prints out the value found within the `ErrorMessage` property. In both cases, these values are determined via the `Dictionary` object passed in at the time the workflow instance was created.

■ Source Code The UserDataWFApp example is included under the Chapter 26 subdirectory.

Invoking Web Services Within Workflows

WF provides several activities that allow you to interact with traditional XML web services during the lifetime of your workflow-enabled application. When you wish to simply call an existing web service, you can make use of the InvokeWebService activity. The other web service–centric activities (such as WebServiceInputActivity and WebServiceOutputActivity) allow you to expose a workflow to external callers via a web service interface and will not be examined here.

■ Note Given that WCF is the preferred API to build services, this edition of the text does not cover the construction of XML web services in any great detail (Chapter 25 broached the topic in passing); therefore, the web service we will be calling here is intentionally simple.

Creating the MathWebService

The first task is to build an XML web service that can be utilized by a workflow-enabled application. To do so, create a brand-new XML web service project by accessing the File ➤ New Web Site menu option. Select the ASP.NET Web Service icon and be sure to select the HTTP location option in order to create this web service within a new IIS virtual directory mapped to `http://localhost/VbMathWebService` (see Figure 26-10).

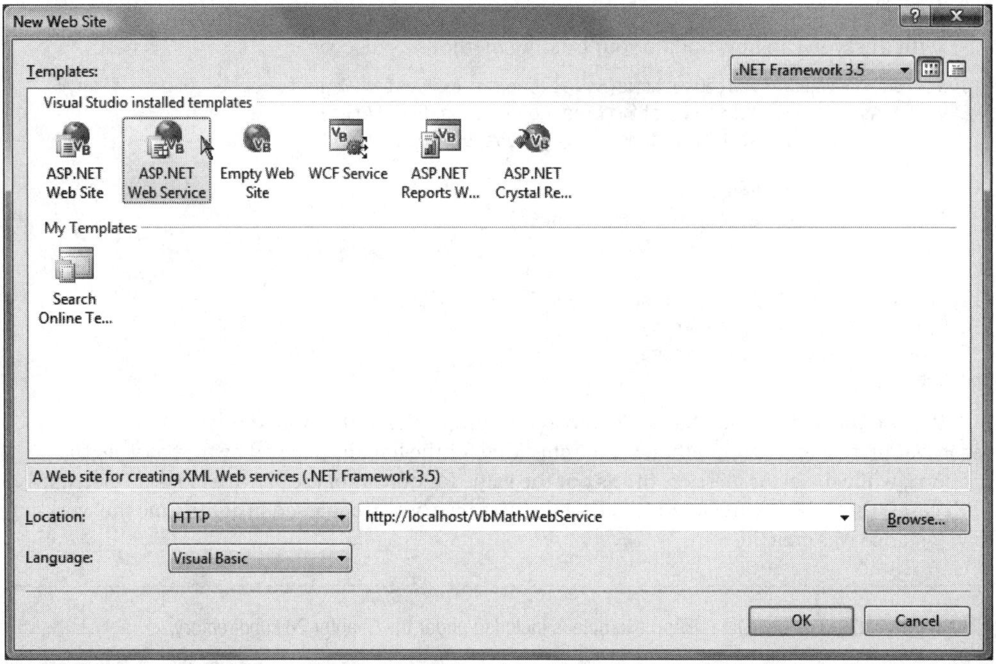

Figure 26-10. *Creating an XML web service project*

This XML web service will allow external callers to perform basic mathematical operations on two integers using the following `<WebMethod()>`-adorned public members:

```
<WebService(Namespace:="http://intertech.com/")> _
<WebServiceBinding(ConformsTo:=WsiProfiles.BasicProfile1_1)> _
Public Class MathService
  Inherits System.Web.Services.WebService

  <WebMethod()> _
  Public Function Add(ByVal x As Integer, ByVal y As Integer) As Integer
    Return x + y
  End Function

  <WebMethod()> _
  Public Function Subtract(ByVal x As Integer, ByVal y As Integer) As Integer
    Return x - y
  End Function
```

```
  <WebMethod()> _
  Public Function Multiply(ByVal x As Integer, ByVal y As Integer) As Integer
    Return x * y
  End Function

  <WebMethod()> _
  Public Function Divide(ByVal x As Integer, ByVal y As Integer) As Integer
    If y = 0 Then
      Return 0
    Else
      Return x / y
    End If
  End Function
End Class
```

Notice that we have accounted for a division by zero error by simply returning 0 if the y value is in fact zero. Also notice that we have renamed this service to MathService, and therefore we must also update the Class attribute in the *.asmx file as follows:

```
<%@ WebService Language="VB" CodeBehind="~/App_Code/Service.vb"
    Class="MathService" %>
```

At this point you can test your XML web service by running (Ctrl+F5) or debugging (F5) the project. When you do so, you will find a web-based testing front end that allows you to invoke each web method (see Figure 26-11).

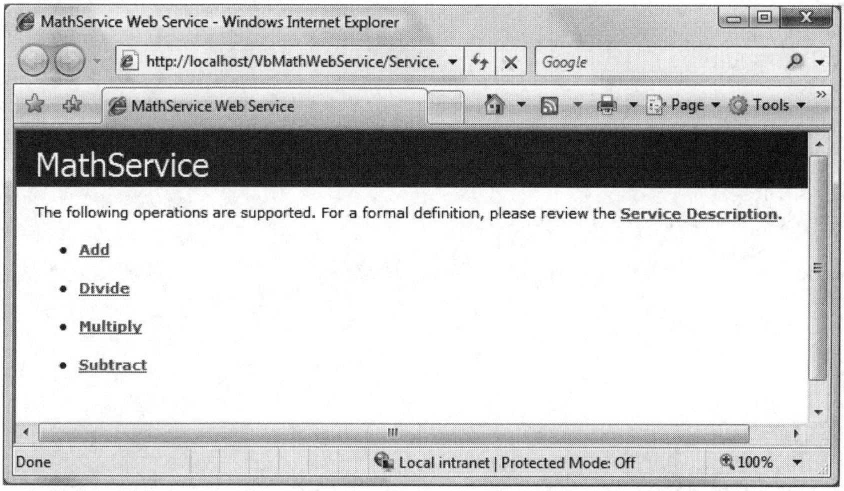

Figure 26-11. *Testing our XML web service*

At this point you can close down the web service project.

■ **Source Code** The MathWebService example is included under the Chapter 26 subdirectory.

Building the WF Web Service Consumer

Now create a new Sequential Workflow Console Application project named WFMathClient. Using Solution Explorer, rename your initial workflow file to `MathWF.vb`, and allow the IDE to change all occurrences of `Workflow1` to `MathWF` by selecting Yes from the resulting dialog box. This application will ask the user for data to process and which operation he or she wishes to perform (addition, subtraction, etc.). To begin, open your code file and define a new enum type named `MathOperation`:

```
Public Enum MathOperation
  Add
  Subtract
  Multiply
  Divide
End Enum
```

Next, define four properties in your class, two of which represent the numerical data to process, one of which represents the result of the operation, and one of which represents the mathematical operation itself (note the default constructor of `MathWF` sets the value of the `Operation` property to `MathOperation.Add`):

```
Public Class MathWF
  Inherits SequentialWorkflowActivity

  Private numb1 As Integer
  Public Property FirstNumber() As Integer
    Get
      Return numb1
    End Get
    Set(ByVal value As Integer)
      numb1 = value
    End Set
  End Property

  Private numb2 As Integer
  Public Property SecondNumber() As Integer
    Get
      Return numb2
    End Get
    Set(ByVal value As Integer)
      numb2 = value
    End Set
  End Property

  Private res As Integer
  Public Property Result() As Integer
    Get
      Return res
    End Get
    Set(ByVal value As Integer)
      res = value
    End Set
  End Property

  Private mathOp As MathOperation
  Public Property Operation() As MathOperation
    Get
      Return mathOp
    End Get
```

```
    Set(ByVal value As MathOperation)
      mathOp = value
    End Set
  End Property

  Sub New()

    ' This call is required by the Windows Form Designer.
    InitializeComponent()

    ' Add any initialization after the InitializeComponent() call.
    Operation = MathOperation.Add
  End Sub
End Class
```

Now, using the WF designer, add a new Code activity named GetNumericalInput that is mapped to a method named `GetNumbInput()`, by setting the `ExecuteCode` value via the Properties window. Within this method, prompt the user to enter two numerical values that are assigned to your `FirstNumber` and `SecondNumber` properties:

```
Private Sub GetNumbInput(ByVal sender As System.Object, _
  ByVal e As System.EventArgs)
  ' For simplicity, we are not bothering to verify that
  ' the input values are indeed numerical.
  Console.Write("Enter first number: ")
  FirstNumber = Integer.Parse(Console.ReadLine())

  Console.Write("Enter second number: ")
  SecondNumber = Integer.Parse(Console.ReadLine())
End Sub
```

Add a second Code activity named GetMathOpInput mapped to a method named `GetOpInput()` in order to ask the user how he or she wishes to process the numerical data. To do so, we will assume the user will specify the letters A, S, M, or D, and based on this character value, set the `MathOperation` property to the correct enumeration value. Here is one possible implementation:

```
Private Sub GetOpInput(ByVal sender As System.Object, _
  ByVal e As System.EventArgs)
  Console.WriteLine("Do you wish to A[dd], S[ubtract],")
  Console.Write("Do you wish to M[ultiply] or D[ivide]: ")
  Dim op As String = Console.ReadLine()

  Select Case op.ToUpper()
  Case "A"
    Operation = MathOperation.Add
    Exit Select
  Case "S"
    Operation = MathOperation.Subtract
    Exit Select
  Case "M"
    Operation = MathOperation.Multiply
    Exit Select
  Case "D"
    Operation = MathOperation.Divide
    Exit Select
  Case Else
    Operation = MathOperation.Add
    Exit Select
```

```
    End Select
End Sub
```

At this point we have the necessary data. Now let's check out how to pass it to our XML web service for processing.

Configuring an IfElse Activity

Given the fact that our numerical data can be processed in four unique manners, we will use an IfElse activity to determine which web method of the service to invoke. When you drag an IfElse activity onto your designer, you will automatically be given two branches. To add additional branches to an IfElse activity, right-click the IfElse activity icon and select the Add Branch menu option. Figure 26-12 shows the current view of the WF designer (note that each branch and the entire IfElse activity have been given proper names).

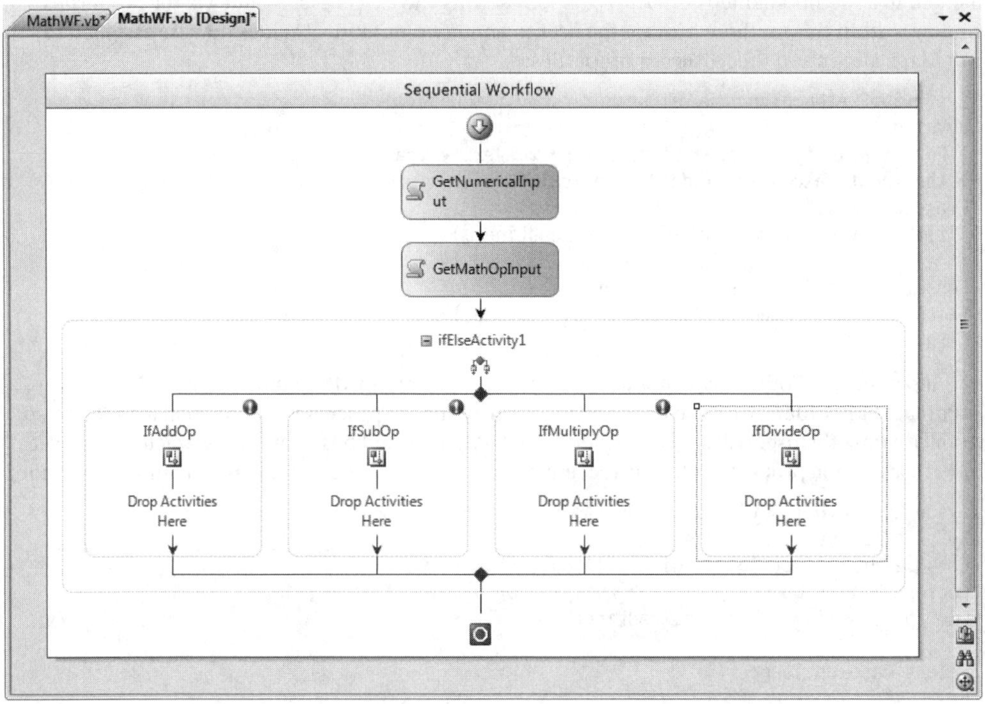

Figure 26-12. *A multibranching IfElse activity*

Each branch of an IfElse activity can contain any number of internal activities that represent what should take place if the decision logic results in moving the flow of the application down a given path. Before we add these subactivities, however, we first need to add the logic that allows the WF engine to determine which branch to take by setting the `Condition` value to each IfElseBranch activity.

Recall that the `Condition` property can be configured to establish a code condition or a declarative rule condition. The first example project in this chapter already illustrated how to create a code condition, so in this example we will opt for rule conditions. Starting with the addition branch, set the `Condition` value to Declarative Rule Condition using the Visual Studio Properties window. Next, click the ellipsis button for the ConditionName subnode, and click the New button from the resulting dialog box. Here, you are able to author a code expression that will determine the truth or falsity of the current branch. For this first branch, the expression is as follows:

```
Me.Operation = MathOperation.Add
```

You'll notice that this dialog box supports IntelliSense, which is always a welcome addition (see Figure 26-13).

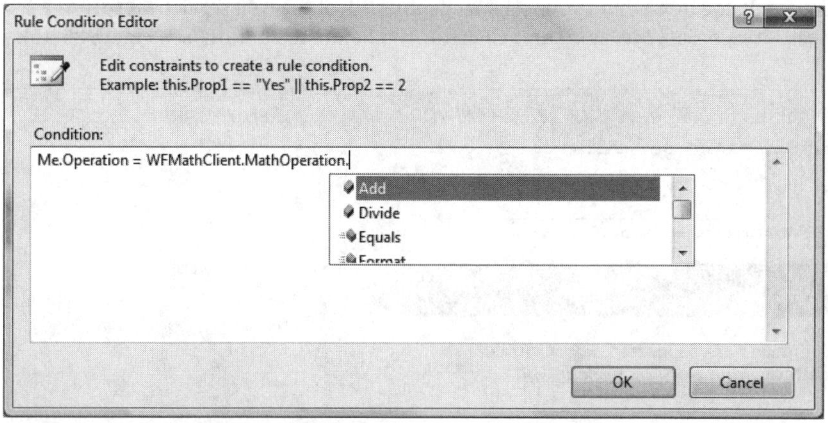

Figure 26-13. *Defining a declarative rule condition*

■Note Although you can author VB code when defining rule conditions, they are represented internally as C# code! Once you click the OK button of the Rule Condition Editor, your VB code will automatically be translated into C#. Thus, if you were to open an existing rule for editing, you will (surprisingly) find that VB code (`Me.Operation = WFMathClient.MathOperation.Add`) is now listed as `this.Operation == WFMathClient.MathOperation.Add`!

Once you have set the rule for each branch if the IfElse activity, you will now notice that a new file with a `*.rules` extension has been added to your project (see Figure 26-14, which assumes you have clicked the Show All Files option of Solution Explorer).

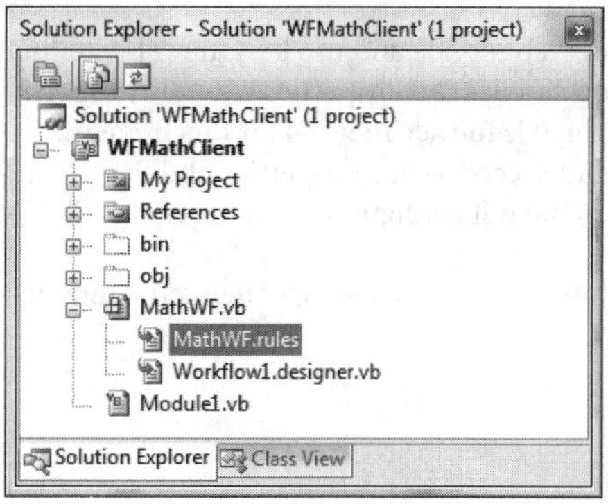

Figure 26-14. `*.rules` *files hold each declarative rule you have established for a workflow instance.*

If you were to open this file, you would find a number of `<RuleExpressionCondition>` elements that describe the conditions you have established.

Configuring the InvokeWebService Activities

The final tasks are to pass the incoming data to the correct web method and print out the result. Drag an InvokeWebService activity into the leftmost branch. Doing so will automatically open the Add Web Reference dialog box, where you can specify the URL of the web service (`http://localhost/VbMathWebService/Service.asmx`) and click the Add Reference button (see Figure 26-15).

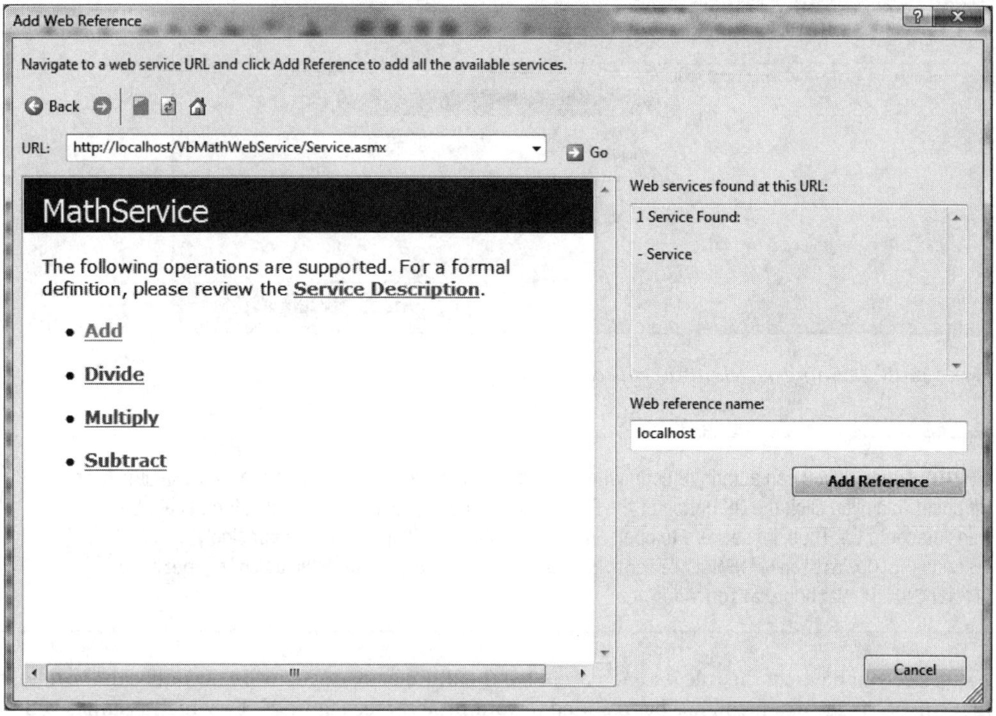

Figure 26-15. *Referencing our XML web service*

When you do so, the IDE will generate a proxy to your web service and use it as the value to the InvokeWebService's `ProxyClass` property. At this point, you can use the Properties window to specify the web method to invoke via the `MethodName` property (which is the `Add` method for this branch), and map the two input parameters to your `FirstNumber` and `SecondNumber` properties and the `(Return Value)` to the `Result` property. Figure 26-16 shows the full configuration of the first InvokeWebService activity.

You can now repeat this process for the remaining three IfElse branches, specifying the remaining web methods.

Note Be aware that even though the Add Web Reference dialog box will appear for each InvokeWebService activity, the IDE is smart enough to reuse the existing proxy, as each activity is communicating with the same endpoint.

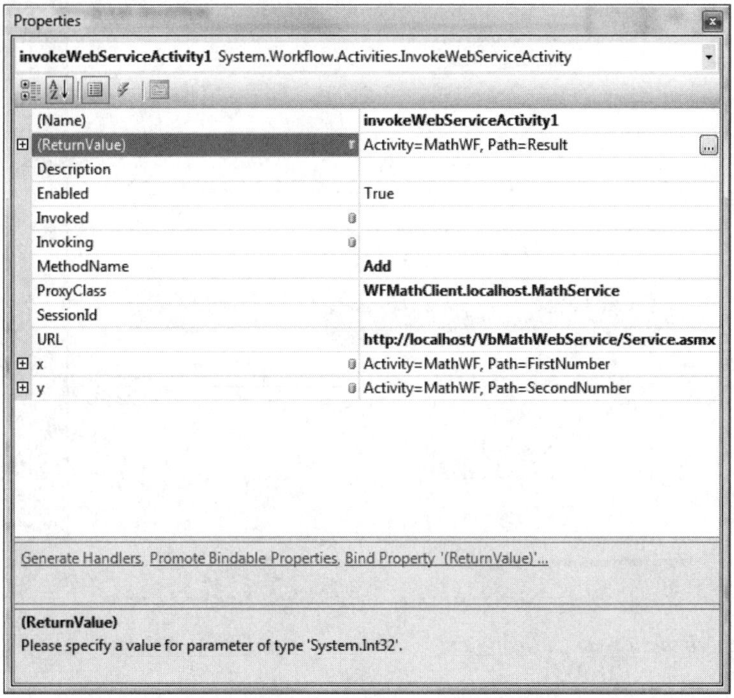

Figure 26-16. *A fully configured InvokeWebService activity*

Last but not least, we will add one final Code activity after the IfElse logic that will display the result of the user-selected operation. Name this activity DisplayResult, and set the ExecuteCode value to a method named ShowResult(), which is implemented as follows:

```
Private Sub ShowResult(ByVal sender As System.Object, _
  ByVal e As System.EventArgs)
  Console.WriteLine("{0} {1} {2} = {3}", _
    FirstNumber, Operation.ToString().ToUpper(), SecondNumber, Result)
End Sub
```

For simplicity, we are using the textual value of the Operation property to represent the selected mathematical operator, rather than adding additional code to map MathOperation.Add to a + sign and MathOperation.Subtract to a - sign, and so on. In any case, Figure 26-17 shows the final design of our workflow; Figure 26-18 shows one possible output.

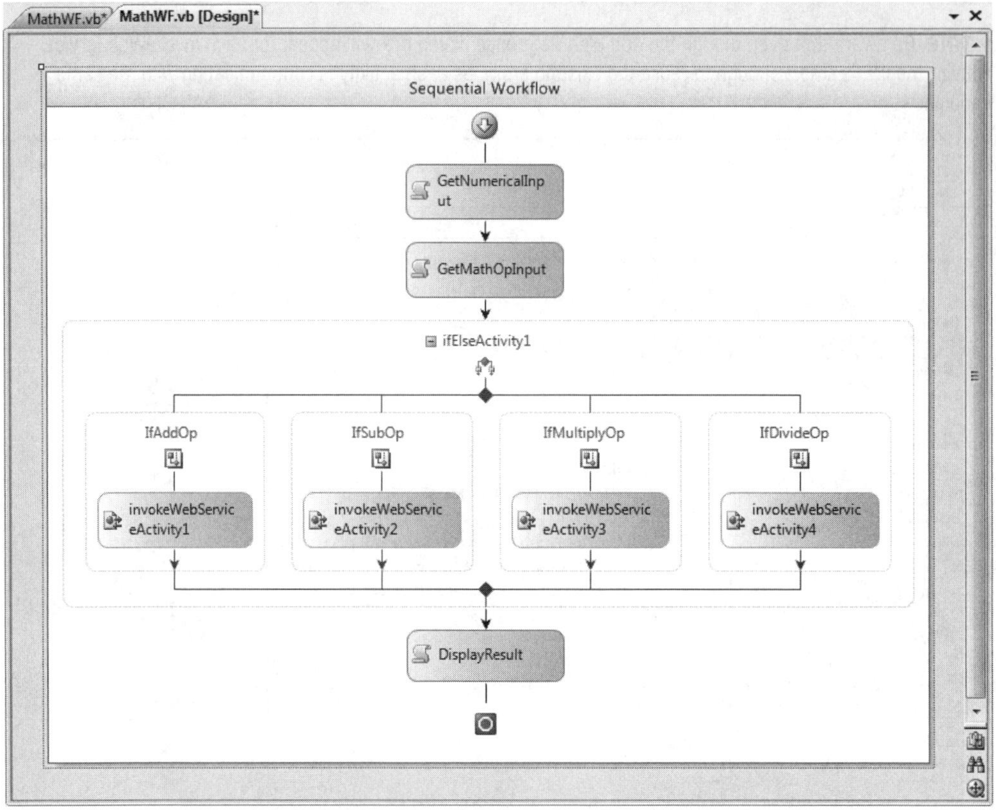

Figure 26-17. *The completed web service–centric workflow*

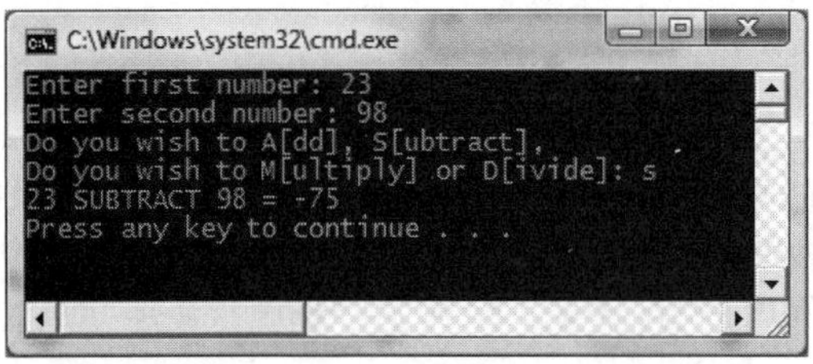

Figure 26-18. *Communicating with XML web services from a WF application*

Communicating with WCF Services

To complete this example, let's examine how a workflow-enabled application can communicate with WCF services. The .NET 3.5–centric `SendActivity` and `ReceiveActivity` types allow you to build workflow-enabled applications that communicate with WCF services. As the name implies, the `SendActivity` type can be used to make calls on WCF service operations, while `ReceiveActivity` provides a way for the WCF service to make calls back on the WF (in the case of a duplex calling contract).

Recall that in Chapter 25 we defined a WCF service contract that also manipulated two numbers via an addition operation, using the following service interface:

```
<ServiceContract(Namespace := "www.intertech.com")> _
Public Interface IBasicMath
  <OperationContract()> _
  Function Add(ByVal x As Integer, ByVal y As Integer) As Integer
End Interface
```

Also recall that this interface was implemented on a type named `MathService` and hosted by a Windows service named `MathWindowsServiceHost.exe`. The Windows service exposed said functionality from the following endpoint:

```
http://localhost:8080/MathService
```

Assuming you created and installed this service (see Chapter 25 for details), you can update your current WFMathClient project to communicate with it using the `SendActivity` type. The first step is to add a reference to the service in the expected manner, using the Add Service dialog box (see Figure 26-19). This will generate a client-side proxy and update your `App.config` file with WCF-specific settings.

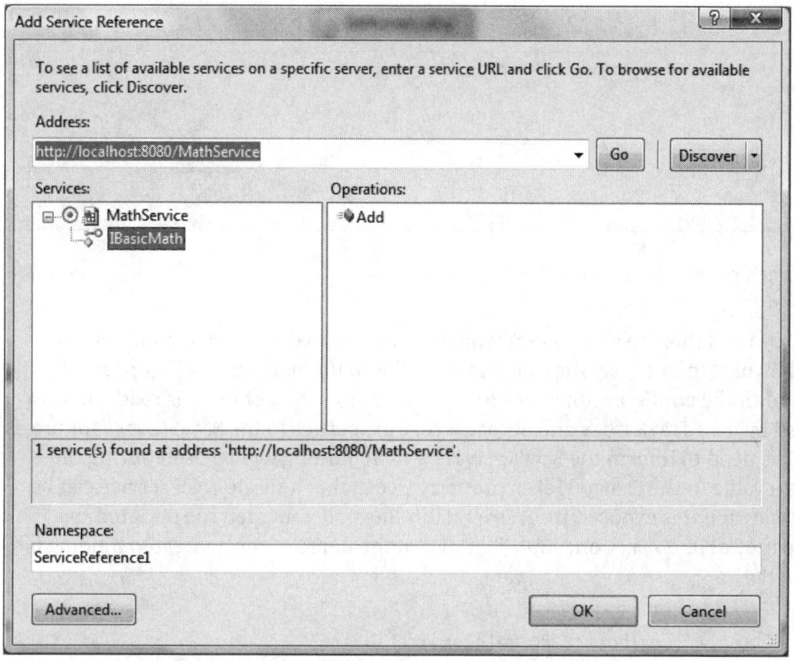

Figure 26-19. *Referencing the WCF Math Service*

Now, drag a `SendActivity` type (located under the Windows Workflow v3.5 tab of the Toolbox) onto your WF designer surface (named `WCFSendAddActivity`), directly after the final Code activity. Using the Properties window, click the ellipsis button of the `ServiceOperationInfo` property and from the resulting dialog box click Import. This will present you with a secondary dialog box where you are able to associate a `SendActivity` type with a metadata description for a given WCF service contract. Select the only contract available at this endpoint, `IBasicMath` (see Figure 26-20).

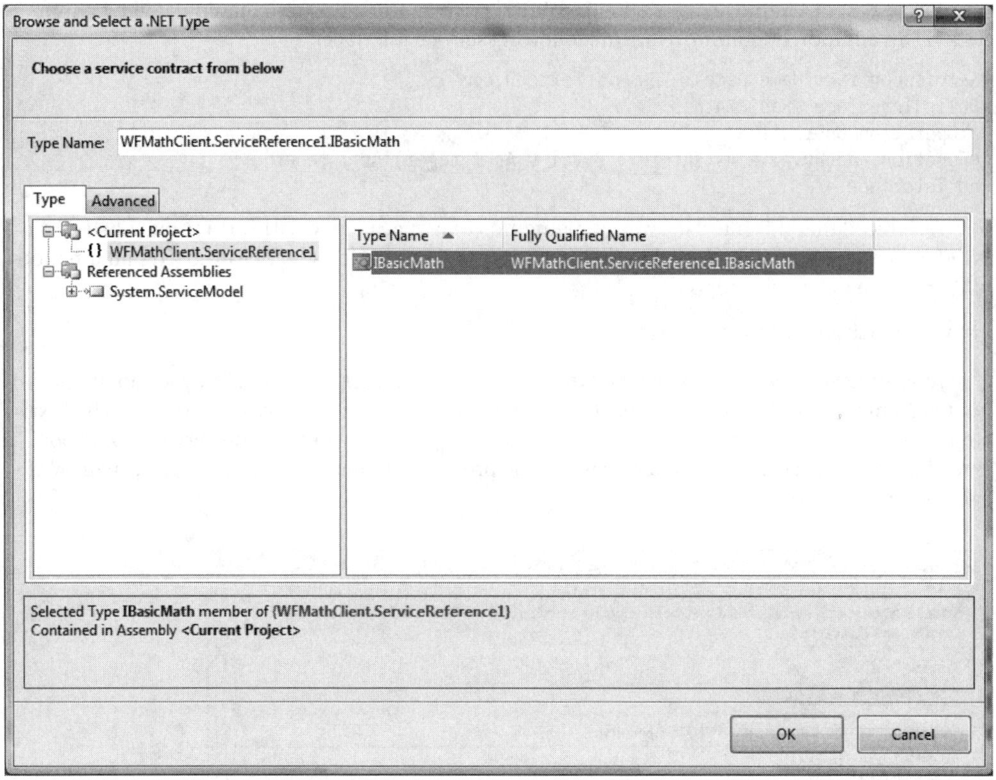

Figure 26-20. *Associating a service method to a* `SendActivity` *type*

Once you do so, you will then be able to pick which operation on the selected contract the `SendActivity` should invoke. In our case, the only option is the `Add()` method (see Figure 26-21).

We have a few additional configuration steps to take before the `SendActivity` is ready to pass the values maintained by the `FirstNumber` and `SecondNumber` properties to the `MathService` for processing. Specifically, we need to inform the `SendActivity` which binding will be used during the invocation by setting a value to the `ChannelToken` property (recall that a single WCF service can be configured in such a way that it is exposed from several bindings). If you open the updated `App.config` file and locate the `<client>` section, you will find that the name of the generated binding is `WSHttpBinding_IBasicMath`:

```
<client>
  <endpoint address="http://localhost:8080/MathServiceLibrary"
            binding="wsHttpBinding"
            bindingConfiguration="WSHttpBinding_IBasicMath"
            contract="WFMathClient.ServiceReference.IBasicMath"
            name="WSHttpBinding_IBasicMath"
    >
    <identity>
      <servicePrincipalName value="host/InterUber.intertech-inc.com" />
    </identity>
  </endpoint>
</client>
```

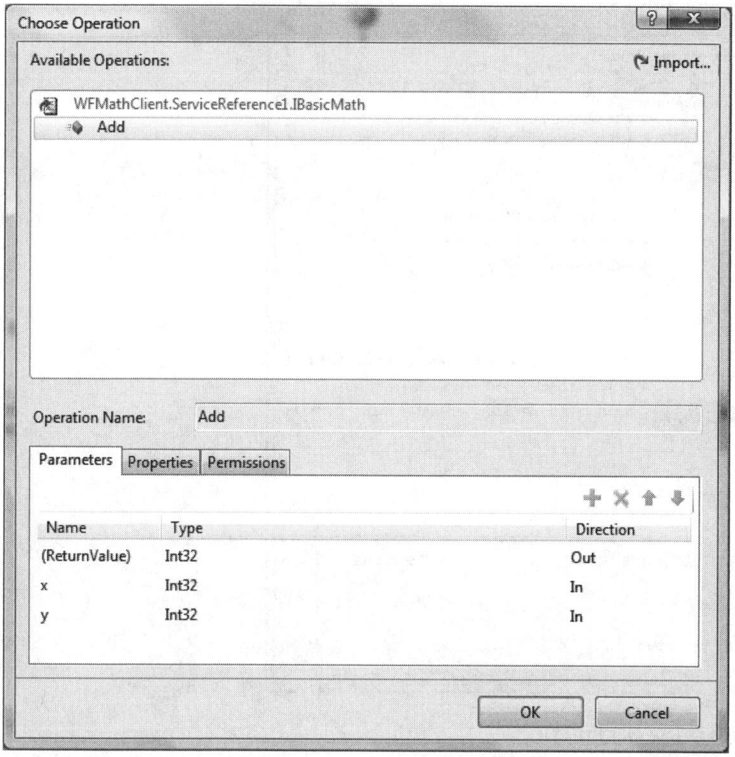

Figure 26-21. *Selecting the* `Add()` *operation*

Copy this value to your clipboard and paste it into the `ChannelToken` property using the IDE's Properties window. Once you have done so, you will notice that the `ChannelToken` property has two subnodes named `EndpointName` and `OwnerActivityName`. Because the MathService exposes only a single endpoint, copy the same value set to `ChannelToken` (`WSHttpBinding_IBasicMath`) to the `EndpointName`, and select the name of your workflow instance (`WCFSendAddActivity`) as the owner.

Last but not least, we need to connect the `x` and `y` parameters of the `Add()` method to our `FirstNumber` and `SecondNumber` properties, and the return value to our `Result` property. The process of doing so is identical to configuring the InvokeWebService activity (click the ellipsis buttons to pick the property name). Figure 26-22 shows the fully configured `SendActivity`.

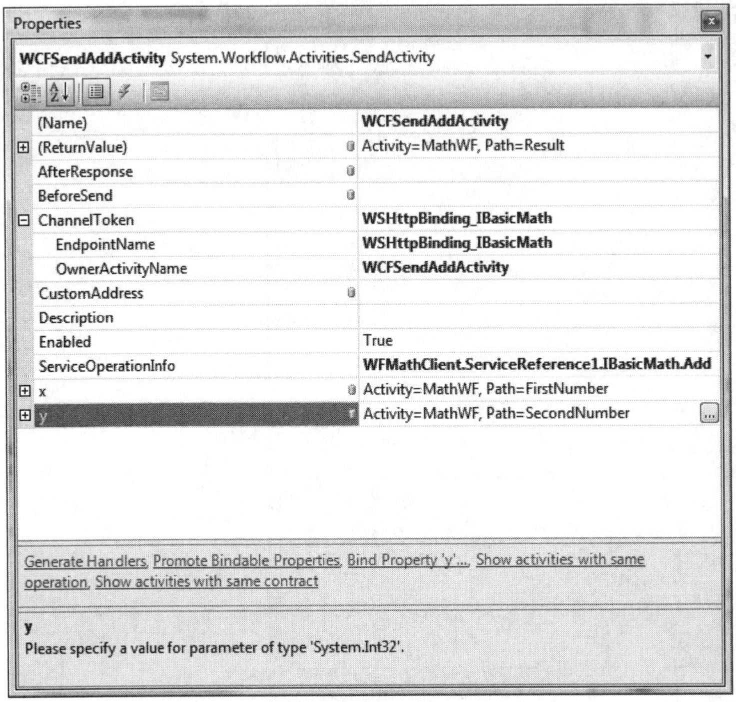

Figure 26-22. *The fully configured* `SendActivity`

To view the result, place a final Code activity on your workflow designer and assign the `ExecuteCode` value to a method named `WCFResult()`, which is implemented as follows:

```
Private Sub WCFResult(ByVal sender As System.Object, ByVal e As System.EventArgs)
  Console.WriteLine("***** WCF Service Addition *****")
  Console.WriteLine("{0} + {1} = {2}", _
    FirstNumber, SecondNumber, Result)
End Sub
```

Figure 26-23 shows the final output.

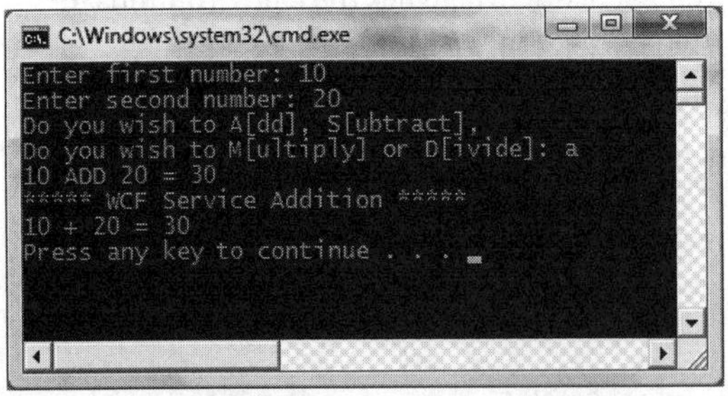

Figure 26-23. *Communicating with a WCF service*

Source Code The WFMathClient example is included under the Chapter 26 subdirectory.

Building a Reusable WF Code Library

These first examples allowed you to play around with various WF activities at design time, interact with the workflow runtime engine (by passing custom parameters), and get into the overall WF mind-set using a console-based WF host. While this is great from a learning point of view, I bet you can easily envision building workflow-enabled Windows Forms applications, WPF applications, or ASP.NET web applications. Furthermore, I am sure you can imagine the need to reuse a workflow across numerous applications by packaging the functionality within a reusable .NET code library.

The next WF example illustrates how to package workflows into `*.dll` assemblies and make use of them from a hosting Windows Forms application (which, by the way, is the same process as hosting an external workflow within any executable, such as a WPF application). We will design a workflow that models the basic process of checking credit to place an order to purchase an automobile from the AutoLot database created in Chapter 22.

Begin by creating a Sequential Workflow Library project named CreditCheckWFLib (see Figure 26-24) and rename your initial file to `CreditCheckWF.vb`.

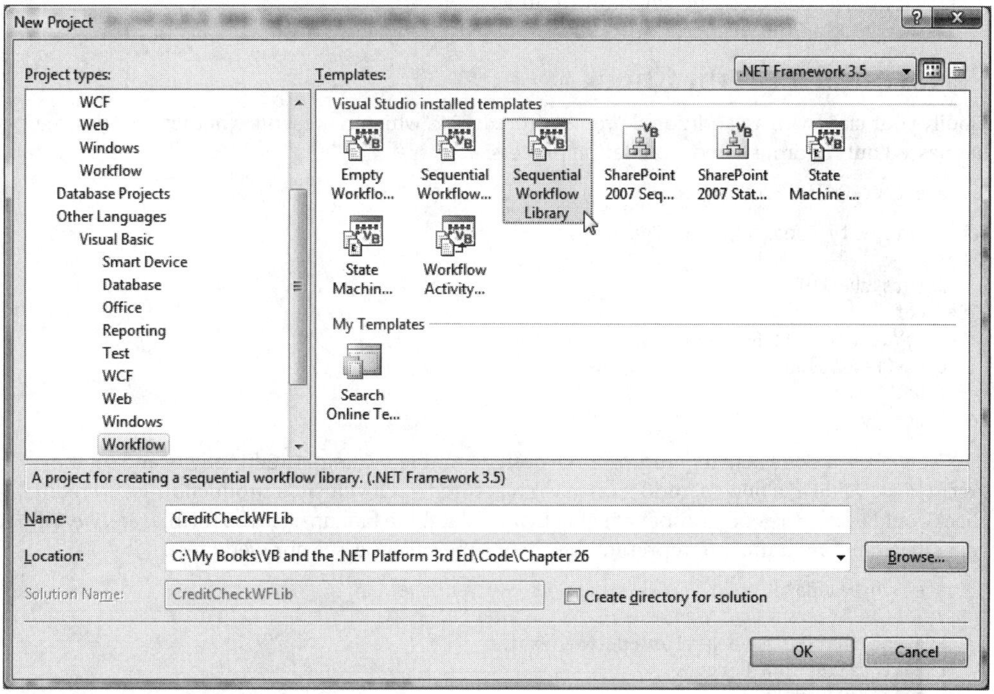

Figure 26-24. *Creating a Sequential Workflow Library project*

At this point, you will be provided with an initial workflow designer. Be aware that a single workflow code library can contain multiple workflows, each of which can be inserted using the Project ➤ Add New Item menu item. In any case, add a reference to your `AutoLotDAL.dll` assembly created in Chapter 22, and update your initial code file to import the `AutoLotConnectedLayer` namespace.

```
' Add the following import.
Imports AutoLotConnectedLayer
```

Next, add a property to represent the customer's ID:

```
Public Class CreditCheckWF
  Inherits SequentialWorkflowActivity

  ' ID of customer to check.
  Private custID As Integer
  Public Property ID() As Integer
    Get
      Return custID
    End Get
    Set(ByVal value As Integer)
      custID = value
    End Set
  End Property
End Class
```

When we build the client application at a later step, this property will be set using an incoming `Dictionary` object passed to the workflow runtime.

Performing a Credit Check

Modify your class with an additional property (`CreditOK`), which represents whether the customer has passed our "rigorous" credit validation process:

```
Private checkOK As Boolean

Public Property CreditOK() As Boolean
  Get
    Return checkOK
  End Get
  Set(ByVal value As Boolean)
    checkOK = value
  End Set
End Property
```

Now place a Code activity onto your WF designer named ValidateCreditActivity and set the `ExecuteCode` value to a new method named `ValidateCredit`. Obviously, a production-level credit check could involve a good number of subactivities, database lookups, and so forth. Here, we will generate a random number to represent the chance the caller passes our credit test:

```
Private Sub ValidateCredit(ByVal sender As System.Object, _
  ByVal e As System.EventArgs)
  ' Pretend that we have performed some exotic
  ' credit validation here...
  Dim r As New Random()
  Dim value As Integer = r.Next(500)
  If value > 300 Then
    CreditOK = True
  Else
    CreditOK = False
  End If
End Sub
```

Next, add an IfElse activity named CreditCheckPassedActivity with two branches named CreditCheckOK and CreditCheckFailed. Configure the left branch to be evaluated using a new declarative rule condition using the following conditional expression:

```
Me.CreditOK = True
```

If the user *fails* the credit check, our goal is to remove that user from the Customers table and add the user to the CreditRisks table. Given that Chapter 22 already accounted for this possibility using the `ProcessCreditRisk()` method of the `InventoryDAL` type, add a new Code activity within the CreditCheckFailed branch named ProcessCreditRiskActivity mapped to a method named `ProcessCreditRisk()`. Implement this method as follows:

```
Private Sub ProcessCreditRisk(ByVal sender As System.Object, _
  ByVal e As System.EventArgs)
  ' Ideally we would store the connection string externally.
  Dim dal As New InventoryDAL()
  dal.OpenConnection( _
   "Data Source=(local)\SQLEXPRESS;Integrated Security=SSPI;" & _
   "Initial Catalog=AutoLot")
  Try
    dal.ProcessCreditRisk(False, ID)
  Finally
    dal.CloseConnection()
  End Try
End Sub
```

■ **Note** Recall from Chapter 22 that we added a `Boolean` parameter to the `InventoryDAL.ProcessCreditRisk()` method to force the transaction to fail for testing purposes. Be sure to pass the value `False` as the first parameter.

If the credit check succeeds, we will simply display an informational message box to inform the caller that the credit check succeeded. In a real workflow, the next steps might involve placing an order, sending out an order verification e-mail, and so on. Assuming you have referenced the `System.Windows.Forms.dll` assembly, place a Code activity in the leftmost branch of your IfElse activity named PurchaseCarActivity, which is mapped to a method name `PurchaseCar()` implemented as follows:

```
Private Sub PurchaseCar(ByVal sender As System.Object, _
  ByVal e As System.EventArgs)
  ' Here, we will opt for simplicity. However, we could easily update
  ' AutoLotDAL.dll with a new method to place a new order within the Orders table.
  MessageBox.Show("Your credit has been approved!")
End Sub
```

To complete your workflow, add a final Code activity to the rightmost branch directly after the ProcessCreditRiskActitity. Name this new activity ShowDenyMessageActivity, which is mapped to the following method:

```
Private Sub CreditDenied(ByVal sender As System.Object, _
  ByVal e As System.EventArgs)
    MessageBox.Show("You are a CREDIT RISK!", _
    "Order Denied!")
End Sub
```

At this point, your workflow looks something like Figure 26-25.

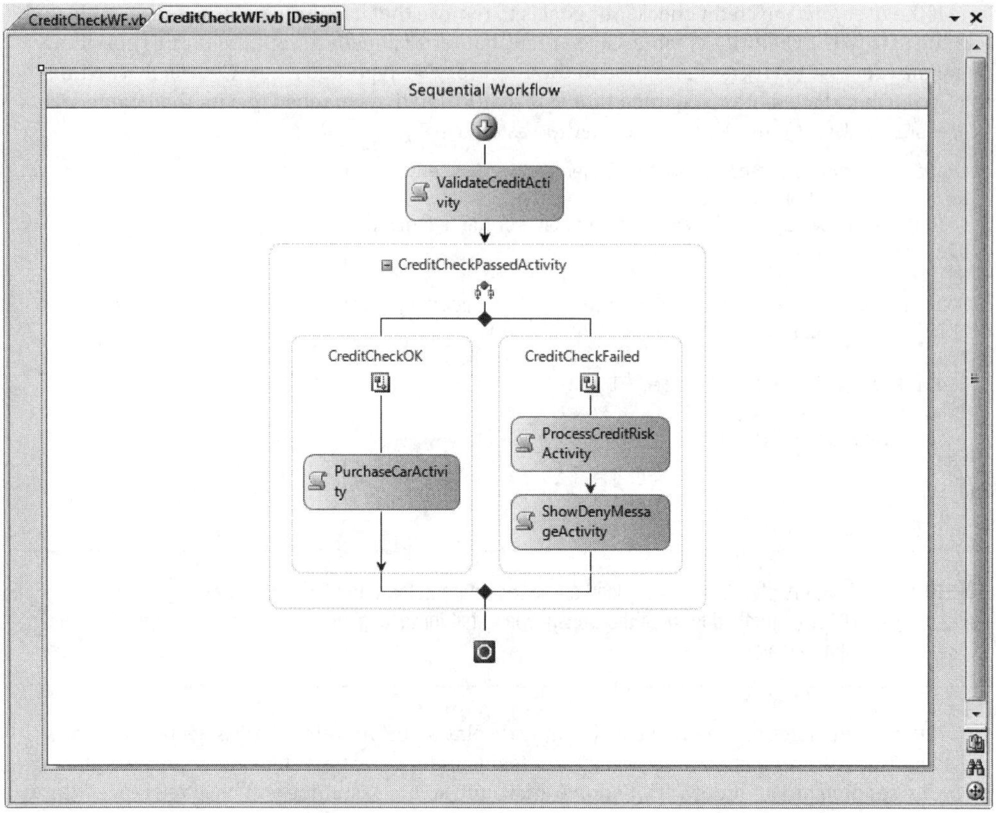

Figure 26-25. *The completed Sequential Workflow Library project*

Source Code The CreditCheckWFLib example is included under the Chapter 26 subdirectory.

Creating a Windows Forms Client Application

Now that you have authored a reusable .NET code library that contains a custom workflow, you are able to build any sort of .NET application to make use of it. Although we have not yet examined the details of building GUIs using the Windows Forms API, here we will build a very crude UI just to test our workflow logic (Chapter 27 will begin your investigation of GUI-based .NET applications). To begin, create a new Windows Forms Application project named CreditCheckApp (see Figure 26-26).

Once you have done so, rename your initial `Form1.vb` file to the more fitting `MainForm.vb` by right-clicking the `Form1.vb` icon in Solution Explorer and selecting the Rename option. Next, add a reference to each of the following .NET assemblies:

- `CreditCheckWFLib.dll`
- `System.Workflow.Runtime.dll`
- `System.Workflow.Activities.dll`
- `System.Workflow.ComponentModel.dll`

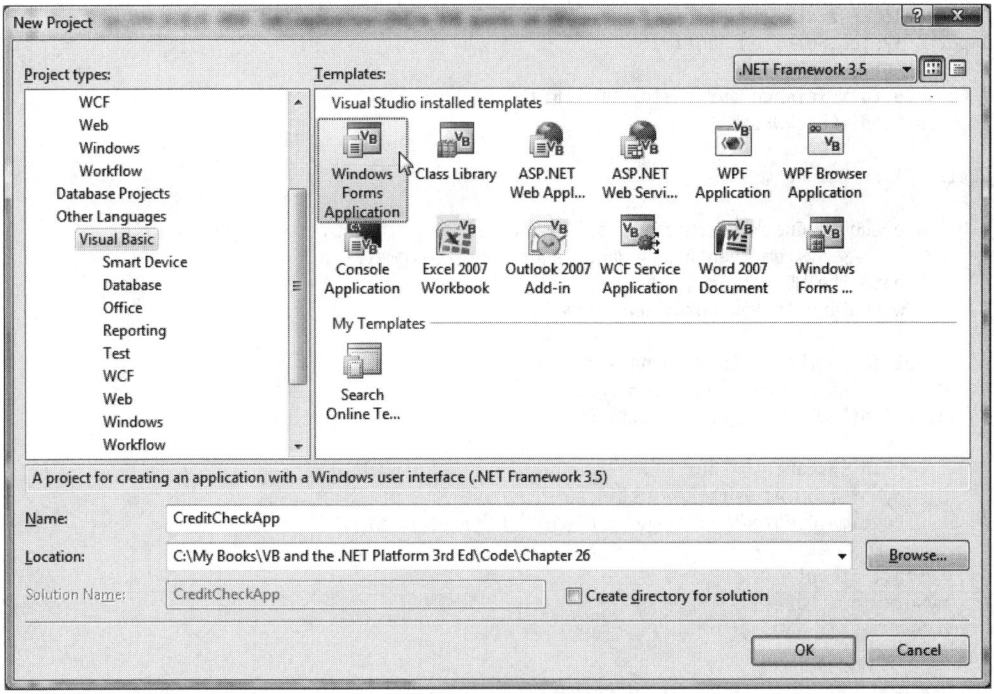

Figure 26-26. *Building a Windows Forms Application project to test our workflow library*

The user interface of our application will consist of a descriptive `Label`, a `TextBox` (named `txtCustomerID`), and a single `Button` type (named `btnExecuteWorkflow`) on the initial form. Figure 26-27 shows one possible design.

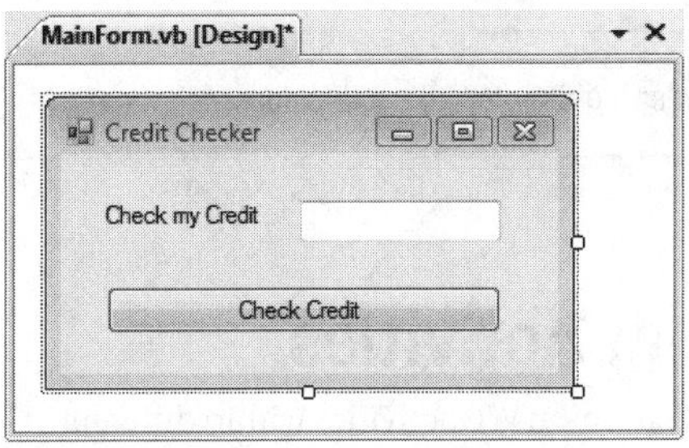

Figure 26-27. *A simple UI to test our workflow library*

Once you place these UI elements on the designer, handle the `Click` event of the `Button` type by double-clicking the button icon located on the designer surface.

Within your code file, implement the `Click` event handler to fire up the WF runtime engine and create an instance of your custom workflow. Notice that the following code is identical to that found within a console-based workflow application (minus the threading code required to keep the console program alive until the workflow completes):

```
' Need the WF runtime!
Imports System.Workflow.Runtime

' Be sure to reference our custom WF library.
Imports CreditCheckWFLib

Public Class MainForm

  Private Sub btnCheckCustomerCredit_Click(ByVal sender As System.Object, _
    ByVal e As System.EventArgs) Handles btnCheckCustomerCredit.Click
    ' Create the WF runtime.
    Dim wfRuntime As New WorkflowRuntime()

    ' Get ID in the TextBox to pass to the workflow.
    Dim args As New Dictionary(Of String, Object)()
    args.Add("ID", Integer.Parse(txtCustomerID.Text))

    ' Get an instance of our WF.
    Dim myWorkflow As WorkflowInstance = _
      wfRuntime.CreateWorkflow(GetType(CreditCheckWF), args)

    ' Start it up!
    myWorkflow.Start()
  End Sub
End Class
```

When you run your application, enter a customer ID value, ensuring that the customer ID you enter does not currently have a reference in the Orders table (to ensure that the item will be successfully deleted from the Customers table).

As you test credit ratings, you should eventually find that a risky customer has been deleted from the Customers table and placed into the CreditRisk table. In fact, for testing purposes, you may wish to add a dummy entry into the Customers table and attempt to verify credit for a fixed individual.

Source Code The WinFormsWFClient example is included under the Chapter 26 subdirectory.

A Brief Word Regarding Custom Activities

At this point, you have seen how to configure a handful of common WF activities within different types of projects. While these built-in activities certainly are a firm starting point for many WF applications, they do not account for every possible circumstance. Thankfully, the WF community has been creating new custom activities, many of which are freely downloadable, and others of which are offered through third parties at various price points.

Note If you are interested in examining some additional workflow activities, a good starting point is `http://netfx3.com/content/WFHome.aspx`. Here, you can download a good number of additional activities that extend those that ship with the product.

Despite the number of auxiliary activities that can be obtained from the online WF community, it is also entirely possible (and in some cases necessary) to build a custom activity from scratch. As you might guess, Visual Studio 2008 provides a Workflow Activity Library project template for this very purpose. If you select this project type, you will be given a designer surface to create your custom activity, using an identical approach to building a workflow itself (add new activities, connect them to code, etc.).

Much like the process of building a custom Windows Forms control, a custom activity can be adorned with numerous .NET attributes that control how the component should integrate within the IDE—for example, which bitmap image to display on the toolbar, which configuration dialog boxes (if any) to display when a property is configured within the Properties window, and so forth.

If you are interested in learning more about building custom activities, the .NET Framework 3.5 SDK documentation provides a number of interesting examples, including the construction of a "Send E-mail activity." For more details, simply browse the Custom Activities samples found under the WF Samples node of the provided documentation (see Figure 26-28).

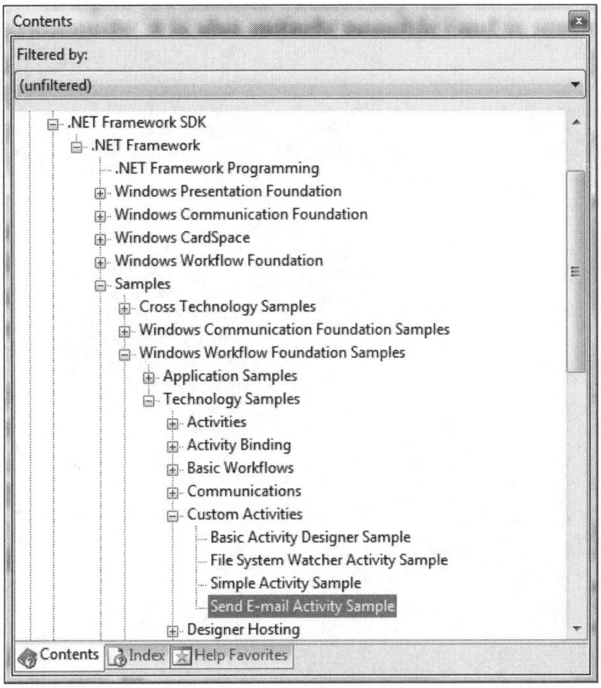

Figure 26-28. *The .NET Framework 3.5 SDK documentation provides numerous workflow examples.*

Summary

Windows Workflow Foundation is an API that was released with .NET 3.0. In essence, WF allows you to model an application's internal business processes directly within the application itself. Beyond simply modeling the overall workflow, however, WF provides a complete runtime engine and several services that round out this API's overall functionality (transaction services, persistence and tracking services, etc.). While this introductory chapter did not examine these services in any great detail, do remember that a production-level WF application will most certainly make use of these facilities.

When building a workflow-enabled application, Visual Studio 2008 provides several designer tools, including a workflow designer, configuration using the Properties window, and (most important) the Windows Workflow Toolbox. Here, you will find numerous built-in *activities* that constitute the overall composition of a particular workflow. Once you have modeled your workflow, you are then able to execute the workflow instance using the `WorkflowRuntime` type, using your application type of choice.

PART 6

Desktop Applications with Windows Forms

CHAPTER 27

Introducing Windows Forms

If you have read through the previous 26 chapters, you should have a solid handle on the VB 2008 programming language as well as the foundation of the .NET platform. While you could take your newfound knowledge and begin building the next generation of console applications (boring!), you are more likely to be interested in building an attractive graphical user interface (GUI) to allow users to interact with your system.

This chapter is the first of three aimed at introducing you to the process of building traditional form-based desktop applications using the Windows Forms API. Here, you'll learn how to build a highly stylized main window using the `Form` and `Application` classes. This chapter also illustrates how to capture and respond to user input (i.e., handle mouse and keyboard events) within the context of a GUI desktop environment. Finally, you will learn to construct menu systems, toolbars, status bars, and multiple document interface (MDI) applications, both by hand and using the designers incorporated into Visual Studio 2008.

Note Since the release of .NET 3.0, we have been provided with an alternative GUI toolkit named Windows Presentation Foundation (WPF), which is a supercharged toolkit used to build highly interactive and media-rich user interfaces. Chapters 30, 31, and 32 will expose you to WPF; however, this chapter and the following two chapters will focus on the original GUI toolkit of the .NET platform, Windows Forms.

Overview of the System.Windows.Forms Namespace

Like any namespace, `System.Windows.Forms` is composed of various classes, structures, delegates, interfaces, and enumerations. Although the difference in appearance between a console UI (CUI) and graphical UI (GUI) seems at first glance like night and day, in reality the process of building a Windows Forms application involves nothing more than learning how to manipulate a new set of types using the VB 2008 syntax you already know. From a high level, the many types within the `System.Windows.Forms` namespace can be grouped into the following broad categories:

- *Core infrastructure*: These are types that represent the core operations of a .NET Forms program (`Form`, `Application`, etc.) and various types to facilitate interoperability with legacy ActiveX controls.
- *Controls*: These are types used to create rich UIs (`Button`, `MenuStrip`, `ProgressBar`, `DataGridView`, etc.), all of which derive from the `Control` base class. Controls are configurable at design time and are visible (by default) at runtime.

- *Components*: These are types that do not derive from the `Control` base class but still provide visual features to a .NET Forms program (`ToolTip`, `ErrorProvider`, etc.). Many components (such as the `Timer`) are not visible at runtime but can be configured visually at design time.
- *Common dialog boxes*: Windows Forms provides a number of canned dialog boxes for common operations (`OpenFileDialog`, `PrintDialog`, etc.). As you would hope, you can certainly build your own custom dialog boxes if the standard dialog boxes do not suit your needs.

Given that the total number of types within `System.Windows.Forms` is well over 100 strong, it would be redundant (not to mention a terrible waste of paper) to list every member of the Windows Forms family. To set the stage for the next several chapters, however, Table 27-1 lists some of the core `System.Windows.Forms` types (consult the .NET Framework 3.5 SDK documentation for full details).

Table 27-1. *Core Types of the* `System.Windows.Forms` *Namespace*

Class	Meaning in Life
`Application`	This class encapsulates the runtime operation of a Windows Forms application.

`Button`
`CheckBox`
`ComboBox`
`DataGridView`
`DateTimePicker`
`ListBox`
`LinkLabel`
`MaskedTextBox`
`MonthCalendar`
`PictureBox`
`TreeView`
	These classes (in addition to many others) correspond to various GUI widgets. You'll examine many of these items in detail in Chapter 29.

`FlowLayoutPanel` `TableLayoutPanel`	Windows Forms supplies a handful of *layout managers* that automatically arrange a `Form`'s controls during resizing.
`Form`	This type represents a main window, dialog box, or MDI child window of a Windows Forms application.

`ColorDialog`
`OpenFileDialog`
`SaveFileDialog`
`FontDialog`
`PrintPreviewDialog`
`FolderBrowserDialog`
	These are various standard dialog boxes for common GUI operations.

`Menu`
`MainMenu`
`MenuItem`
`ContextMenu`
`MenuStrip`
`ContextMenuStrip`
	These types are used to build topmost and context-sensitive menu systems. These controls allow you to build menus that may contain traditional drop-down menu items as well as other controls (text boxes, combo boxes, and so forth).

`StatusBar`
`Splitter`
`ToolBar`
`ScrollBar`
`StatusStrip`
`ToolStrip`
	These types are used to adorn a `Form` with common child controls.

■Note Beyond `System.Windows.Forms`, the `System.Windows.Forms.dll` assembly defines additional GUI-centric namespaces. For the most part, these additional types are used internally by the Forms engine and/or the designer tools of Visual Studio 2008. Given this fact, we will keep focused on the core `System.Windows.Forms` namespace.

Working with the Windows Forms Types

When you build a Windows Forms application, you may choose to write all the relevant code by hand (using Notepad, perhaps) and feed the resulting `*.vb` files into the VB 2008 compiler using the `/target:winexe` flag. Taking time to build some Windows Forms applications by hand not only is a great learning experience, but also helps you understand the code generated by the various graphics designers found within various .NET IDEs.

To make sure you understand the basic process of building a Windows Forms application, the initial examples in this chapter will avoid the use of graphics designers. Once you feel comfortable with the process of building a Windows Forms application "wizard-free," you will then leverage the various designer tools provided by Visual Studio 2008.

Building a Main Window by Hand

To begin learning about Windows Forms programming, you'll build a minimal main window from scratch. Create a new folder on your hard drive (e.g., C:\MyFirstWindow) and create a new file within this directory named `MainWindow.vb` using your text editor of choice (again, Notepad would be perfect).

In the world of Windows Forms, the `Form` class is used to represent any window in your application. This includes a topmost main window in a single-document interface (SDI) application, modeless and modal dialog boxes, and the parent and child windows of an MDI application. When you are interested in creating and displaying the main window in your program, you have two mandatory steps:

1. Derive a new class from `System.Windows.Forms.Form`.
2. Configure your application's `Main()` method to invoke `Application.Run()`, passing an instance of your `Form`-derived type as an argument.

Given this, update your `MainWindow.vb` file with the following class definition (note that because our `Main()` subroutine is within a `Class` type, not a `Module`, we are required to define `Main()` using the `Shared` keyword):

```
Imports System.Windows.Forms

Namespace MyWindowsApp
  Public Class MainWindow
  Inherits Form
    ' Run this application and identify the main window.
    Shared Sub Main()
      Application.Run(New MainWindow())
    End Sub
  End Class
End Namespace
```

In addition to the always present `mscorlib.dll`, a Windows Forms application needs to reference the `System.dll` and `System.Windows.Forms.dll` assemblies. As you may recall from Chapter 2, the default VB 2008 response file (`vbc.rsp`) instructs `vbc.exe` to automatically include these assemblies during the compilation process, so you are good to go. Also recall that the `/target:winexe` option of `vbc.exe` instructs the compiler to generate a Windows executable.

Note Technically speaking, you can build a Windows application at the command line using the `/target:exe` option; however, if you do, you will find that a command window will be looming in the background (and it will stay there until you shut down the main window). When you specify `/target:winexe`, your executable runs as a native Windows Forms application (without the looming command window).

To compile your VB 2008 code file, open a Visual Studio 2008 command prompt, change to the directory containing your `*.vb` file, and issue the following command:

```
vbc /target:winexe *.vb
```

Figure 27-1 shows a test run.

Figure 27-1. *A simple main window à la Windows Forms*

Granted, the form is not altogether that interesting at this point. But simply by deriving from `Form`, you have a minimizable, maximizable, resizable, and closable main window (with a default system-supplied icon to boot!).

Honoring the Separation of Concerns

Currently, the `MainWindow` class defines the `Main()` method directly within its scope. If you prefer, you may create a dedicated module (I named mine `Program`) that is responsible for the task of launching the main window, leaving the `Form`-derived class responsible for representing the window itself:

```
Imports System.Windows.Forms

Namespace MyWindowsApp
  Public Class MainWindow
    Inherits Form
  End Class
```

```
  Public Module Program
    ' Run this application and identify the main window.
    Sub Main()
      Application.Run(New MainWindow())
    End Sub
  End Module
End Namespace
```

By doing so, you are abiding by an OO design principle termed *the separation of concerns*. Simply put, this rule of OO design states that a class should be in charge of doing the least amount of work possible. Given that you have refactored the initial class into two unique types, you have decoupled the `Form` from the class that creates it. The end result is a more portable window, as it can be dropped into any project without carrying the extra baggage of a project-specific `Main()` method.

Source Code The MyFirstWindow project can be found under the Chapter 27 subdirectory.

The Role of the Application Class

The `Application` class defines numerous shared members that allow you to control various low-level behaviors of a Windows Forms application. For example, the `Application` class defines a set of members that allow you to respond to events such as application shutdown and idle-time processing. In addition to the `Run()` method, here are some other methods to be aware of:

- `DoEvents()`: Provides the ability for an application to process messages currently in the message queue during a lengthy operation. This can be helpful when a single-threaded application enters a lengthy processing cycle (such as a looping construct) and periodically wants to process queued UI events.
- `Exit()`: Terminates the Windows application and unloads the hosting AppDomain.
- `EnableVisualStyles()`: Configures your application to support Windows XP visual styles. Do note that if you enable XP styles, this method must be called before loading your main window via `Application.Run()`.

The `Application` class also defines a number of properties, many of which are read-only in nature. As you examine Table 27-2, note that most of these properties represent an application-level trait such as company name, version number, and so forth. In fact, given what you already know about assembly-level attributes (see Chapter 14), many of these properties should look vaguely familiar.

Table 27-2. *Core Properties of the* `Application` *Type*

Property	Meaning in Life
`CompanyName`	Retrieves the value of the assembly-level `<AssemblyCompany()>` attribute
`ExecutablePath`	Gets the path for the executable file
`ProductName`	Retrieves the value of the assembly-level `<AssemblyProduct()>` attribute
`ProductVersion`	Retrieves the value of the assembly-level `<AssemblyVersion()>` attribute
`StartupPath`	Retrieves the path for the executable file that started the application

Finally, the Application class defines various shared events, some of which are as follows:

- ApplicationExit: Occurs when the application is just about to shut down.
- Idle: Occurs when the application's message loop has finished processing the current batch of messages and is about to enter an idle state (as there are no messages to process at the current time).
- ThreadExit: Occurs when a thread in the application is about to terminate. If the exiting thread is the main thread of the application, ThreadExit is fired before the ApplicationExit event.

Fun with the Application Class

To illustrate some of the functionality of the Application class, let's enhance your current MainWindow to perform the following:

- Reflect over select assembly-level attributes.
- Handle the shared ApplicationExit event.

The first task is to make use of select properties in the Application class to reflect over some assembly-level attributes. To begin, add the following attributes to your MainWindow.vb file (note you are now importing the System.Reflection namespace):

```
Imports System.Windows.Forms
Imports System.Reflection

' Assembly-level attributes.
<Assembly:AssemblyCompany("Intertech")>
<Assembly:AssemblyProduct("A Better Window")>
<Assembly:AssemblyVersion("1.1.0.0")>

Namespace MyWindowsApp
...
End Namespace
```

Rather than manually reflecting over the <AssemblyCompany()> and <AssemblyProduct()> attributes using the techniques illustrated in Chapter 16, the Application class will do so automatically using various shared properties. To illustrate, implement the default constructor of MainForm as follows:

```
Public Class MainWindow
  Inherits Form

  ' Reflect over attributes using Application type.
  Public Sub New()
    MessageBox.Show(String.Format("This app brought to you by {0}", _
      Application.CompanyName), Application.ProductName)
  End Sub
End Class
```

When you recompile and run this application, you'll see a message box that displays various bits of information (see Figure 27-2).

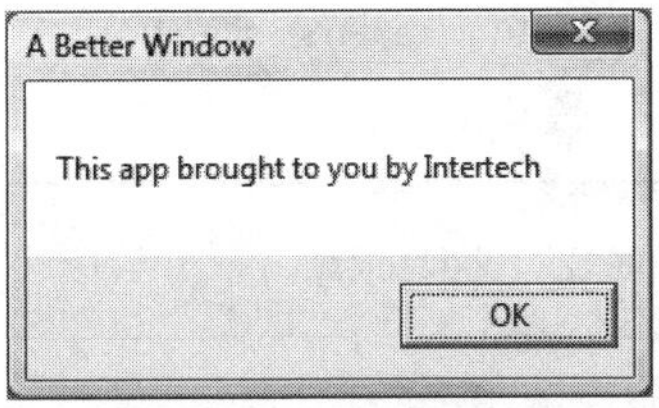

Figure 27-2. *Reading attributes via the* `Application` *type*

Now, let's equip this form to respond to the `ApplicationExit` event. When you wish to respond to events from within a Windows Forms application, you will be happy to find that the same event syntax detailed in Chapter 11 is used to handle GUI-based events. For example, if you wish to intercept the shared `ApplicationExit` event, simply register an event handler using the `AddHandler` statement:

```
Public Class MainWindow
  Inherits Form

  ' Reflect over attributes using Application type.
  Public Sub New()
...
    ' Handle Application.Exit event.
    AddHandler Application.ApplicationExit, AddressOf MainWindow_OnExit
  End Sub

  Public Sub MainWindow_OnExit(ByVal sender As Object, ByVal args As EventArgs)
    MessageBox.Show(String.Format("Form version {0} has terminated.", _
      Application.ProductVersion))
  End Sub
End Class
```

The System.EventHandler Delegate

The `ApplicationExit` event works in conjunction with the `System.EventHandler` delegate. This delegate must point to subroutines that conform to the following signature:

```
Sub MyEventHandler(ByVal sender As Object, ByVal args As EventArgs)
```

`System.EventHandler` is the most primitive delegate used to handle events within Windows Forms, but many variations do exist for other events. As far as `EventHandler` is concerned, the first parameter of the assigned method is of type `System.Object`, which represents the object sending the event (the form itself in this case). The second `EventArgs` parameter contains any relevant information regarding the current event.

■ **Note** `EventArgs` is the base class to numerous derived types that contain information for a family of related events. For example, mouse events work with the `MouseEventArgs` parameter, which contains details such as the (*x*, *y*) position of the cursor. Many keyboard events work with the `KeyEventArgs` type, which contains details regarding the current keypress, and so forth.

In any case, if you now recompile and run the application, you will find a final message box appears upon the termination of the application.

Source Code The AppClassExample project can be found under the Chapter 27 subdirectory.

The Anatomy of a Form

Now that you understand the role of the `Application` type, the next task is to examine the functionality of the `Form` class itself. Not surprisingly, the `Form` class inherits a great deal of functionality from its parent classes. Figure 27-3 shows the inheritance chain (including the set of implemented interfaces) of a `Form`-derived type using the Visual Studio 2008 Object Browser.

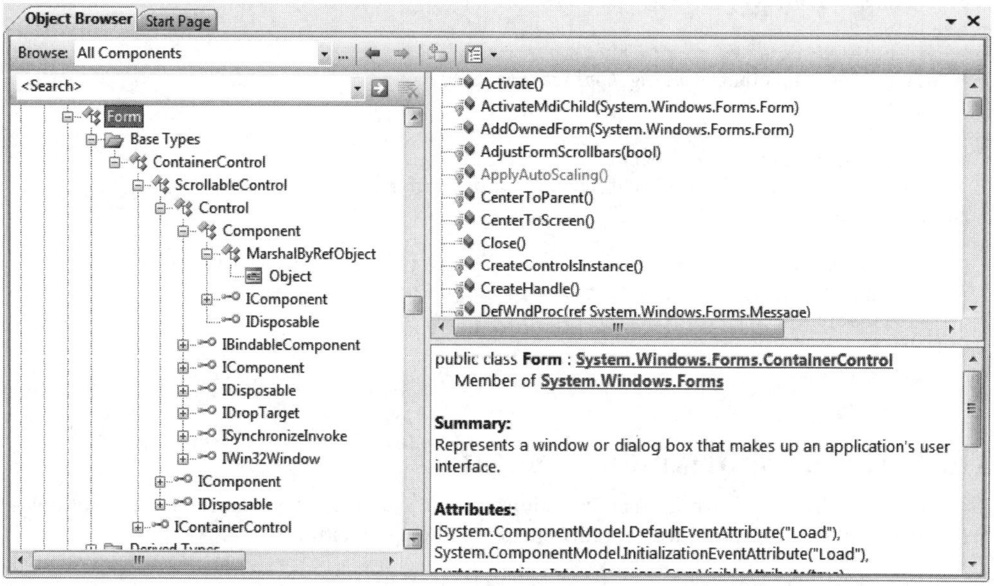

Figure 27-3. *The derivation of the* `Form` *type*

Although the complete derivation of a `Form` type involves numerous base classes and interfaces, do understand that you are *not* required to learn the role of each and every member from each and every parent class or implemented interface to be a proficient Windows Forms developer. In fact, the majority of the members (properties and events in particular) you will use on a daily basis are easily set using the Visual Studio 2008 IDE Properties window. Before we move on to examine some specific members inherited from these parent classes, take a look at Table 27-3, which outlines the basic role of each base class.

Table 27-3. *Base Classes in the Form Inheritance Chain*

Parent Class	Meaning in Life
`System.Object`	Like any class in .NET, a `Form` "is-a" object.
`System.MarshalByRefObject`	Types deriving from this class are accessed remotely via a *reference* (not a copy) of the remote type.
`System.ComponentModel.Component`	This class provides a default implementation of the `IComponent` interface. In the .NET universe, a component is a type that supports design-time editing, but is not necessarily visible at runtime.
`System.Windows.Forms.Control`	This class defines common UI members for all Windows Forms UI controls, including the `Form` type itself.
`System.Windows.Forms.ScrollableControl`	This class defines support for auto-scrolling behaviors.
`System.Windows.Forms.ContainerControl`	This class provides focus-management functionality for controls that can function as a container for other controls.
`System.Windows.Forms.Form`	This class represents any custom form, MDI child, or dialog box.

As you might guess, detailing each and every member of each class in the `Form`'s inheritance chain would require a large book in itself. However, it is important to understand the behavior supplied by the `Control` and `Form` types. I'll assume that you will spend time examining the full details behind each class at your leisure using the .NET Framework 3.5 SDK documentation.

The Functionality of the Control Class

The `System.Windows.Forms.Control` class establishes the common behaviors required by any GUI type. The core members of `Control` allow you to configure the size and position of a control, capture keyboard and mouse input, get or set the focus/visibility of a member, and so forth. Table 27-4 defines some (but not all) properties of interest, grouped by related functionality.

Table 27-4. *Core Properties of the* `Control` *Type*

Property	Meaning in Life

`BackColor`
`ForeColor`
`BackgroundImage`
`Font`
`Cursor`
	These properties define the core UI of the control (colors, font for text, mouse cursor to display when the mouse is over the widget, etc.).

`Anchor`
`Dock`
`AutoSize`
	These properties control how the control should be positioned within the container.

Continued

Table 27-4. *Continued*

Property	Meaning in Life

`Top`
`Left`
`Bottom`
`Right`
`Bounds`
`ClientRectangle`
`Height`
`Width`
	These properties specify the current dimensions of the control.

`Enabled`
`Focused`
`Visible`
	These properties each return a Boolean that specifies the state of the current control.

`ModifierKeys`	This shared property checks the current state of the modifier keys (Shift, Ctrl, and Alt) and returns the state in a `Keys` type.
`MouseButtons`	This shared property checks the current state of the mouse buttons (left, right, and middle mouse buttons) and returns this state in a `MouseButtons` type.
`TabIndex` `TabStop`	These properties are used to configure the tab order of the control.
`Text`	This property indicates the string data associated with this control.
`Controls`	This property allows you to access a strongly typed collection (`ControlCollection`) that contains any child controls within the current control.

As you would guess, the `Control` class also defines a number of events that allow you to intercept mouse, keyboard, painting, and drag-and-drop activities (among other things). Table 27-5 lists some (but not all) events of interest, grouped by related functionality.

Table 27-5. *Events of the* `Control` *Type*

Event	Meaning in Life

`Click`
`DoubleClick`
`MouseEnter`
`MouseLeave`
`MouseDown`
`MouseUp`
`MouseMove`
`MouseHover`
`MouseWheel`
	Various events that allow you to interact with the mouse

`KeyPress`
`KeyUp`
`KeyDown`
	Various events that allow you to interact with the keyboard

`DragDrop`
`DragEnter`
`DragLeave`
`DragOver`
	Various events used to monitor drag-and-drop activity

`Paint`	An event that allows you to interact with GDI+ in order to render graphical data on the `Control`-derived type (see Chapter 28)

Finally, the Control base class also defines a number of methods that allow you to interact with any Control-derived type. As you examine the methods of the Control type, you will notice that a good number of them have an On prefix followed by the name of a specific event (OnMouseMove, OnKeyUp, OnPaint, etc.). Each of these On-prefixed virtual methods is the default event handler for its respective event. If you override any of these virtual members, you gain the ability to perform any necessary pre- or postprocessing of the event before (or after) invoking your parent's default implementation:

```
Imports System.Windows.Forms

Public Class MainWindow
  Inherits Form
  Protected Overrides Sub OnMouseDown(ByVal e As MouseEventArgs)
    ' Add code for MouseDown event.

    ' Call parent implementation when finished.
    MyBase.OnMouseDown(e)
  End Sub
End Class
```

While this can be helpful in some circumstances (especially if you are building a custom control that derives from a standard control), you will often handle events using the VB 2008 Handles keyword (in fact, this is the default behavior of the Visual Studio 2008 designers). When you do so, the framework will call your custom event handler once the parent's implementation has completed:

```
Imports System.Windows.Forms

Public Class MainWindow
  Inherits Form
  Private Sub MainForm_MouseDown(ByVal sender As Object, _
    ByVal e As MouseEventArgs) Handles Me.MouseDown
    ' Add code for MouseDown event.
  End Sub
End Class
```

Beyond these OnXXX() methods, here are a few other methods provided by the Control class to be aware of:

- Hide(): Hides the control and sets the Visible property to False
- Show(): Shows the control and sets the Visible property to True
- Invalidate(): Forces the control to redraw itself by sending a Paint event

To be sure, the Control class does define additional properties, methods, and events beyond the subset you've just examined. You should, however, now have a solid understanding regarding the overall functionality of this base class. Let's see it in action.

Fun with the Control Class

To illustrate the usefulness of some members from the Control class, let's build a new Form that is capable of handling the following events:

- Respond to the MouseMove and MouseDown events.
- Capture and process keyboard input via the KeyUp event.

To begin, create a new class derived from `Form`. In the default constructor, you'll make use of various inherited properties to establish the initial look and feel. Note you're now importing the `System.Drawing` namespace to gain access to the `Color` structure (you'll examine this namespace in detail in the next chapter):

```
Imports System.Windows.Forms
Imports System.Drawing

Namespace MyWindowsApp
  Public Class MainWindow
    Inherits Form

    Public Sub New()
      ' Use inherited properties to set basic UI.
      Text = "My Fantastic Form"
      Height = 300
      Width = 500
      BackColor = Color.LemonChiffon
      Cursor = Cursors.Hand
    End Sub
  End Class

  Public Module Program
    ' Run this application and identify the main window.
    Sub Main()
      Application.Run(New MainWindow())
    End Sub
  End Module
End Namespace
```

Compile your application at this point, just to make sure you have not injected any typing errors:

```
vbc /target:winexe *.vb
```

Responding to the MouseMove Event

Next, you need to handle the `MouseMove` event. The goal is to display the current (*x*, *y*) location within the form's caption area. All mouse-centric events (`MouseMove`, `MouseUp`, etc.) work in conjunction with the `MouseEventHandler` delegate, which can call any subroutine matching the following signature:

```
Sub MyMouseHandler(ByVal sender As Object, ByVal e As MouseEventArgs)
```

The incoming `MouseEventArgs` structure extends the general `EventArgs` base class by adding a number of members particular to the processing of mouse activity (see Table 27-6).

Table 27-6. *Properties of the* `MouseEventArgs` *Type*

Property	Meaning in Life
`Button`	Gets which mouse button was pressed, as defined by the `MouseButtons` enumeration
`Clicks`	Gets the number of times the mouse button was pressed and released
`Delta`	Gets a signed count of the number of detents the mouse wheel has rotated (a *detent* being one notch of the mouse wheel)

Property	Meaning in Life
X	Gets the *x*-coordinate of a mouse click
Y	Gets the *y*-coordinate of a mouse click

Here, then, is the updated MainWindow class that handles the MouseMove event as intended:

```
Public Class MainWindow
  Inherits Form
...
  Public Sub MainWindow_MouseMove(ByVal sender As Object, _
    ByVal e As MouseEventArgs) Handles Me.MouseMove
    Text = string.Format("Current Pos: ({0} , {1})", e.X, e.Y)
  End Sub
End Class
```

If you now run your program and move the mouse over your form, you will find the current (*x*, *y*) value display on the caption area as shown in Figure 27-4.

Figure 27-4. *Monitoring mouse movement*

Determining Which Mouse Button Was Clicked

One thing to be aware of is that the MouseUp (or MouseDown) event is sent whenever any mouse button is clicked. If you wish to determine exactly which button was clicked (such as left, right, or middle), you need to examine the Button property of the MouseEventArgs class. The value of the Button property is constrained by the related MouseButtons enumeration defined in the System.Windows.Forms namespace. The following MouseUp event handler displays a message box indicating which mouse button was clicked:

```
Public Sub MainWindow_MouseUp(ByVal sender As Object, _
  ByVal e As MouseEventArgs) Handles Me.MouseUp
  If e.Button = System.Windows.Forms.MouseButtons.Left Then
    MessageBox.Show("Left click!")
  End If
  If e.Button = System.Windows.Forms.MouseButtons.Right Then
    MessageBox.Show("Right click!")
  End If
  If e.Button = System.Windows.Forms.MouseButtons.Middle Then
```

```
    MessageBox.Show("Middle click!")
  End If
End Sub
```

Responding to Keyboard Events

Processing keyboard input is almost identical to responding to mouse activity. The KeyUp and KeyDown events work in conjunction with the KeyEventHandler delegate, which can point to any subroutine taking an object as the first parameter and KeyEventArgs as the second:

```
Sub MyKeyboardHandler(ByVal sender As Object, ByVal e As KeyEventArgs)
```

KeyEventArgs has the members of interest shown in Table 27-7.

Table 27-7. *Properties of the* KeyEventArgs *Type*

Property	Meaning in Life
Alt	Gets a value indicating whether the Alt key was pressed
Control	Gets a value indicating whether the Ctrl key was pressed
Handled	Gets or sets a value indicating whether the event was fully handled in your handler
KeyCode	Gets the keyboard code for a KeyDown or KeyUp event
Modifiers	Indicates which modifier keys (Ctrl, Shift, and/or Alt) were pressed
Shift	Gets a value indicating whether the Shift key was pressed

Update your MainWindow to handle the KeyUp event. Once you do, display the name of the key that was pressed inside a message box using the KeyCode property.

```
Public Sub MainWindow_KeyUp(ByVal sender As Object, _
  ByVal e As KeyEventArgs) Handles Me.KeyUp
    MessageBox.Show(e.KeyCode.ToString(), "Key Pressed!")
End Sub
```

Now compile and run your program. You should be able to determine not only which mouse button was clicked, but also which keyboard key was pressed. That wraps up our look at the core functionality of the Control base class. Next up, let's check out the role of Form.

Source Code The ControlBehaviors project is included under the Chapter 27 subdirectory.

The Functionality of the Form Class

The Form class is typically (but not necessarily) the direct base class for your custom Form types. In addition to the large set of members inherited from the Control, ScrollableControl, and ContainerControl classes, the Form type adds additional functionality in particular to main windows, MDI child windows, and dialog boxes. Let's start with the core properties in Table 27-8.

Table 27-8. *Properties of the* `Form` *Type*

Property	Meaning in Life
`AcceptButton`	Gets or sets the button on the form that is clicked when the user presses the Enter key.
`ActiveMdiChild` `IsMdiChildIsMdiContainer`	Used within the context of an MDI application.
`CancelButton`	Gets or sets the button control that will be clicked when the user presses the Esc key.
`ControlBox`	Gets or sets a value indicating whether the form has a control box.
`FormBorderStyle`	Gets or sets the border style of the form. Used in conjunction with the `FormBorderStyle` enumeration.
`Menu`	Gets or sets the menu to dock on the form.
`MaximizeBox` `MinimizeBox`	Used to determine whether this form will enable the maximize and minimize boxes.
`ShowInTaskbar`	Determines whether this form will be seen on the Windows taskbar.
`StartPosition`	Gets or sets the starting position of the form at runtime, as specified by the `FormStartPosition` enumeration.
`WindowState`	Configures how the form is to be displayed on startup. Used in conjunction with the `FormWindowState` enumeration.

In addition to the expected `On`-prefixed default event handlers, the `Form` type defines several core methods, as listed in Table 27-9.

Table 27-9. *Key Methods of the* `Form` *Type*

Method	Meaning in Life
`Activate()`	Activates a given form and gives it focus.
`Close()`	Closes a form.
`CenterToScreen()`	Places the form in the dead-center of the screen.
`LayoutMdi()`	Arranges each child form (as specified by the `LayoutMdi` enumeration) within the parent form.
`ShowDialog()`	Displays a form as a modal dialog box. More on dialog box programming in Chapter 29.

Finally, the `Form` class defines a number of events, many of which fire during the form's lifetime. Table 27-10 hits the highlights.

Table 27-10. *Select Events of the* `Form` *Type*

Event	Meaning in Life
`Activated`	Occurs whenever the form is *activated*, meaning the form has been given the current focus on the desktop
`Closed` `Closing`	Used to determine when the form is about to close or has closed
`Deactivate`	Occurs whenever the form is *deactivated*, meaning the form has lost current focus on the desktop

Continued

Table 27-10. *Continued*

Event	Meaning in Life
Load	Occurs after the form has been allocated into memory, but is not yet visible on the screen
MdiChildActive	Sent when a child window is activated

The Life Cycle of a Form Type

Form-derived types have a number of events that fire during their lifetime. As you have seen, the life of a form begins when the type constructor is called prior to being passed into the Application.Run() method.

Once the object has been allocated on the managed heap, the framework fires the Load event. Within a Load event handler, you are free to configure the look and feel of the form, prepare any contained child controls (such as ListBoxes, TreeViews, and whatnot), or simply allocate resources used during the form's operation (database connections, proxies to remote objects, and whatnot).

Once the Load event has fired, the next event to fire is Activated. This event fires when the form receives focus as the active window on the desktop. The logical counterpart to the Activated event is Deactivate, which fires when the form loses focus as the active window. As you can guess, the Activated and Deactivate events can fire numerous times over the life of a given Form type as the user navigates between active applications.

When the user has chosen to close the form in question, two close-centric events fire: Closing and Closed. The Closing event is fired first and is an ideal place to prompt the end user with the much hated (but useful nonetheless) "Are you *sure* you wish to close this application?" message. This confirmational step is quite helpful to ensure the user has a chance to save any application-centric data before terminating the program.

The Closing event works in conjunction with the CancelEventHandler delegate defined in the System.ComponentModel namespace, which can call any subroutine taking Object as the first parameter and CancelEventArgs as the second. If you set the CancelEventArgs.Cancel property to True, you prevent the form from being destroyed and instruct it to return to normal operation. If you set CancelEventArgs.Cancel to False, the Closed event fires, and the Windows Forms application terminates, which unloads the AppDomain and terminates the process.

To solidify the sequence of events that take place during a form's lifetime, assume you have a new MainWindow.vb file that handles the Load, Activated, Deactivate, Closing, and Closed events (be sure to add a Imports directive for the System.ComponentModel namespace to obtain the definition of CancelEventArgs).

In the Load, Closed, Activated, and Deactivate event handlers, you are going to update the value of a new form-level System.String member variable (named lifeTimeInfo) with a simple message that displays the name of the event that has just been intercepted. As well, notice that within the Closed event handler, you will display the value of this string within a message box:

```
Public Class MainWindow
  Inherits Form

  Private lifeTimeInfo As String

  ' Handle the Load, Activated, Deactivate, and Closed events.
  Public Sub MainWindow_Load(ByVal sender As Object, _
    ByVal e as EventArgs) Handles Me.Load
    lifeTimeInfo = lifeTimeInfo & "Load event" & VbLf
  End Sub
```

```
  Public Sub MainWindow_Activated(ByVal sender As Object, _
    ByVal e as EventArgs) Handles Me.Activated
    lifeTimeInfo = lifeTimeInfo & "Activated event" & VbLf
  End Sub
  Public Sub MainWindow_Deactivate(ByVal sender As Object, _
    ByVal e as EventArgs) Handles Me.Deactivate
    lifeTimeInfo = lifeTimeInfo & "Deactivate event" & VbLf
  End Sub
  Public Sub MainWindow_Closed(ByVal sender As Object, _
    ByVal e as EventArgs) Handles Me.Closed
    lifeTimeInfo = lifeTimeInfo & "Closed event" & VbLf
    MessageBox.Show(lifeTimeInfo)
  End Sub
End Class
```

Within the `Closing` event handler, you will prompt the user to ensure he or she wishes to terminate the application using the incoming `CancelEventArgs`:

```
Private Sub MainWindow_Closing(ByVal sender As Object, _
  ByVal e As CancelEventArgs) Handles Me.Closing
  Dim dr As System.Windows.Forms.DialogResult = _
    MessageBox.Show("Do you REALLY want to close this app?", _
      "Closing event!", MessageBoxButtons.YesNo)
  If dr = System.Windows.Forms.DialogResult.No Then
    e.Cancel = True
  Else
    e.Cancel = False
  End If
End Sub
```

Notice that the `MessageBox.Show()` method returns a `DialogResult` type, which has been set to a value representing the button clicked by the end user (`Yes` or `No`). Now, compile your code at the command line:

```
vbc /target:winexe *.vb
```

Run your application and shift the form into and out of focus a few times (to trigger the `Activated` and `Deactivate` events). Once you shut down the form, you will see a message box that looks something like Figure 27-5.

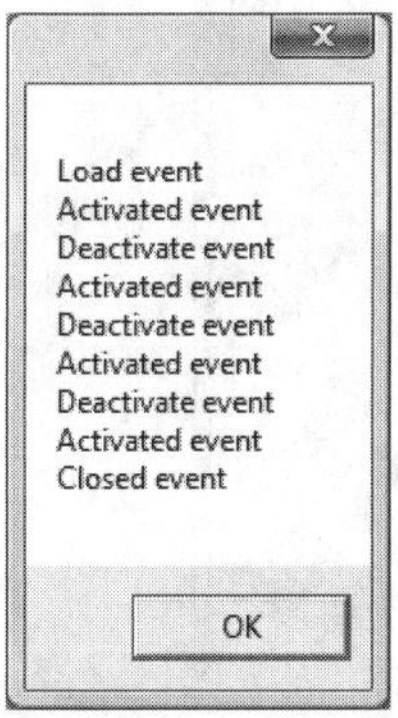

Figure 27-5. *The life and times of a* `Form`*-derived type*

Now, most of the really interesting aspects of the `Form` type have to do with its ability to create and host menu systems, toolbars, and status bars. While the code to do so is not complex, you will be happy to know that Visual Studio 2008 defines a number of graphical designers that take care of most of the mundane code on your behalf. Given this, let's say goodbye to the command-line compiler for the time being and turn our attention to the process of building Windows Forms applications using Visual Studio 2008.

Source Code The FormLifeTime project can be found under the Chapter 27 subdirectory.

Building Windows Applications with Visual Studio 2008

Visual Studio 2008 has specific project types dedicated to the creation of Windows Forms applications. When you select the Windows Forms Application project type, you not only receive an initial `Form`-derived type, but you also can make use of the VB 2008–specific *startup form*. As you may know, VB 2008 allows you to declaratively specify which form to show upon application startup, thereby removing the need to manually define a `Main()` method. However, if you do need to add additional startup logic, you are able to define a dedicated `Main()` method that will be called when your program launches.

Better yet, the IDE provides a number of graphical designers that make the process of building a UI very simple. Just to learn the lay of the land, create a new Windows Forms Application project workspace, as shown in Figure 27-6. You are not going to build a working example just yet, so name this project whatever you desire (for example, MyTesterWindowsApp).

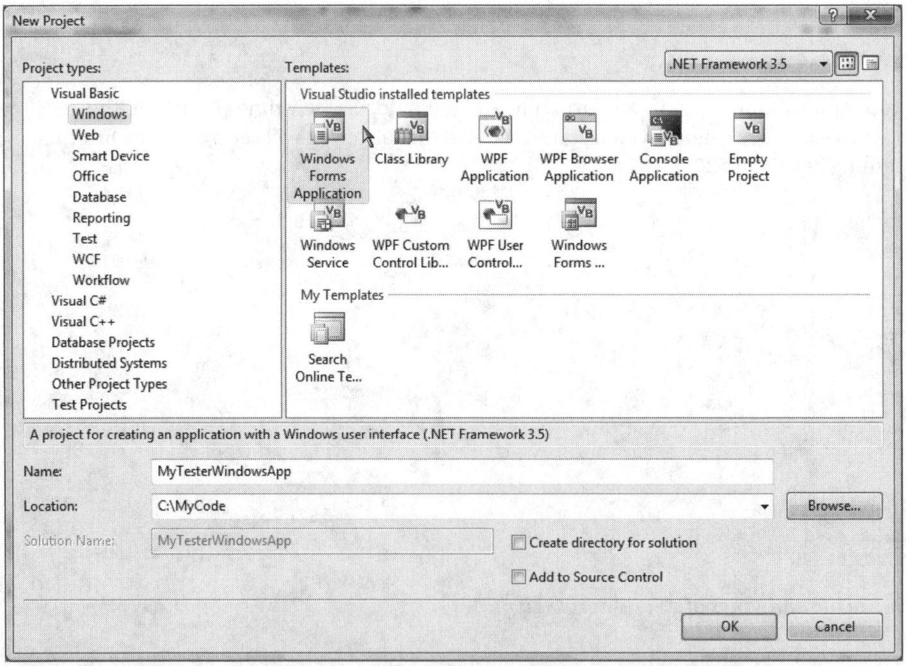

Figure 27-6. *The Visual Studio 2008 Windows Forms Application project*

Once the project has loaded, you will no doubt notice the Forms designer, which allows you to build a UI by dragging controls/components from the Toolbox (see Figure 27-7) and configuring their properties and events using the Properties window (see Figure 27-8).

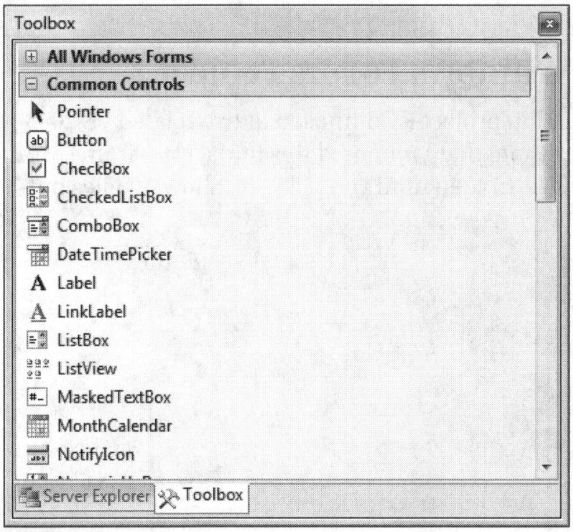

Figure 27-7. *The Visual Studio 2008 Toolbox*

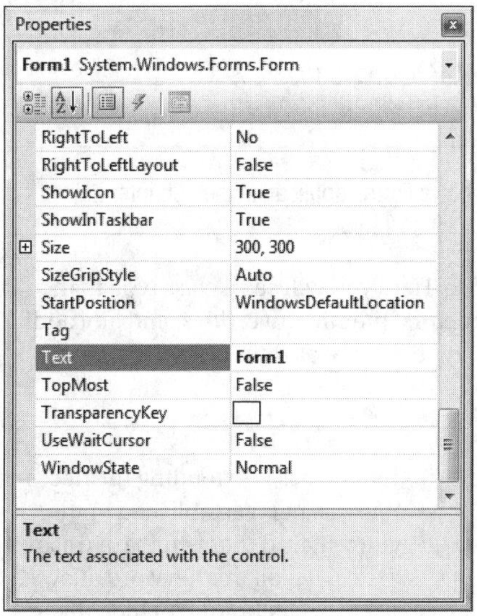

Figure 27-8. *The Visual Studio 2008 Properties window*

The Toolbox groups UI controls by various categories. While most are self-explanatory (e.g., Printing contains printing controls, Menus & Toolbars contains recommended menu/toolbar controls, etc.), a few categories deserve special mention:

- *Containers*: These items provide various ways to position controls within a form. You'll see some of these types at work in Chapter 29.
- *WPF Interoperability*: Here you will find components that allow a Windows Forms application to host WPF controls. Chapter 30 begins your study of the WPF API.

Dissecting a Visual Studio 2008 Windows Forms Project

Each `Form` in a Visual Studio 2008 Windows Application project is composed of two related VB 2008 files, which can be verified using Solution Explorer (note that I renamed this initial class from `Form1` to `MainWindow`). Be aware that the `*.Designer.vb` file is hidden until you click the Show All Files button in Solution Explorer, as shown in Figure 27-9.

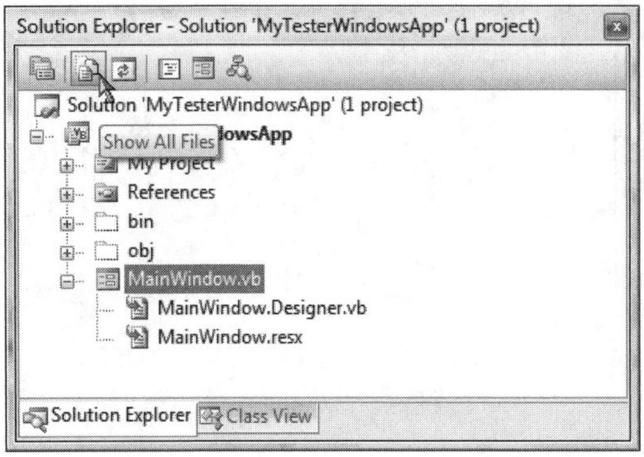

Figure 27-9. *Under Visual Studio 2008, each form is composed of two* `*.vb` *files.*

Note The `*.resx` file is used to manage resources within a Windows Forms application (see Chapter 28).

Right-click the `MainWindow.vb` icon and select View Code. Here you will see a class type that will contain all of the form's event handlers, custom constructors, member overrides, and any additional member you author yourself. Upon startup, the `Form` type is quite empty:

```
Public Class MainWindow
End Class
```

The first point of interest is it does not appear that the `MainWindow` class is extending the necessary `Form` base class. Rest assured this is the case; however, this detail has been established in the related `*.Designer.vb` file. If you open up the `*.Designer.vb` file, you will find that your `MainWindow` class is further defined via the `Partial` keyword examined in Chapter 5. Recall this keyword allows a single type to be defined across multiple files. Visual Studio 2008 uses this technique to hide the designer-generated code, allowing you to keep focused on the core logic of your `Form`-derived type. Here is the initial definition of this `Partial` class:

```
<Global.Microsoft.VisualBasic.CompilerServices.DesignerGenerated()> _
Partial Class MainWindow
  Inherits System.Windows.Forms.Form

  ' Form overrides dispose to clean up the component list.
  <System.Diagnostics.DebuggerNonUserCode()> _
  Protected Overrides Sub Dispose(ByVal disposing As Boolean)
```

```
    If disposing AndAlso components IsNot Nothing Then
      components.Dispose()
    End If
    MyBase.Dispose(disposing)
  End Sub

  ' Required by the Windows Forms designer
  Private components As System.ComponentModel.IContainer

  ' NOTE: The following procedure is required by the Windows Forms designer
  ' It can be modified using the Windows Forms designer.
  ' Do not modify it using the code editor.
  <System.Diagnostics.DebuggerStepThrough()> _
  Private Sub InitializeComponent()
    components = New System.ComponentModel.Container()
    Me.AutoScaleMode = System.Windows.Forms.AutoScaleMode.Font
    Me.Text = "Form1"
  End Sub
End Class
```

Notice the InitializeComponent() method. This method is maintained on your behalf by Visual Studio 2008, and it contains all of the code representing your design-time modifications. To illustrate, switch back to the Forms designer and locate the Text property in the Properties window. Change this value to something like My Test Window. Now open your MainWindow.Designer.vb file and notice that InitializeComponent() has been updated accordingly:

```
Private Sub InitializeComponent()
...
  Me.Text = "My Test Window"
  Me.ResumeLayout(False)
End Sub
```

In addition to maintaining InitializeComponent(), the *.Designer.vb file will define the member variables that represent each control placed on the designer. Again, to illustrate, drag a Button control onto the Forms designer. Now, using the Properties window, rename your member variable from Button1 to btnTestButton via the (Name) property.

■ **Note** It is always a good idea to rename the controls you place on the designer before handling events. If you fail to do so, you will most likely end up with a number of nondescript event handlers, such as Button27_Click, given that the default names simply suffix a numerical value to the variable name.

Once you do, you will find that the *.Designer.vb file now contains a new member variable definition of type Button (and the end of the class definition), which was defined using the WithEvents keyword:

```
Friend WithEvents btnTestButton As System.Windows.Forms.Button
```

■ **Note** In almost every case, you will not want to directly edit the *.Designer.vb files. If you were to author incorrect code, you could break the designer. Furthermore, Visual Studio 2008 will format and modify this file at design time, and therefore your custom code could be deleted! Given these points, you are safe to ignore these designer files and to allow Visual Studio to maintain them on your behalf.

Implementing Events at Design Time

Notice that the Properties window has a button depicting a lightning bolt. Although you are always free to handle UI events by authoring the necessary logic by hand (as done in the previous examples), this event button allows you to visually handle an event for a given item. Simply select the control you wish to interact with from the drop-down list box (mounted at the top of the Properties window), locate the event you are interested in handling, and type in the name to be used as an event handler (or simply double-click the event to generate a default name using the naming convention ControlName_EventName).

■ Note If you would rather make use of the drop-down list boxes supported by a *.vb code file to handle events, you are free to do so. Simply pick the item you wish to interact with in the left drop-down list box and the event you wish to handle from the right drop-down list box.

Assuming you have handled the Click event for the Button control, you will find that the MainWindow.vb file contains the following event handler:

```
Public Class MainWindow
  Private Sub btnTestButton_Click(ByVal sender As System.Object, _
    ByVal e As System.EventArgs) Handles btnTestButton.Click
    ' Add your code here!
  End Sub
End Class
```

■ Note Every control has a default event, which refers to the event that will be handled if you double-click the item on the control using the Forms designer. For example, a form's default event is Load, and if you double-click anywhere on a Form type, the IDE will automatically write code to handle this event.

The StartUp Object/Main() Sub Distinction

In the initial examples in this chapter, we were manually defining a Main() method that called Application.Run() in order to specify the main window of the program. However, when you create a new Windows Forms Application project using Visual Studio 2008, you will not find similar code. The reason is that VB 2008 uses the notion of a *startup form* that is automatically created upon application launch. By default, the startup form will always be the initial Form-derived type in your application, which can be viewed using the Application tab of the My Project dialog box, shown in Figure 27-10.

While this approach can simplify your project development, many times it is preferred to specify a custom Main() method in order to perform custom startup logic before the main form is shown (such as showing a splash screen while your program loads into memory). To do so, you must manually define a Class or Module that defines a proper Main() method. For example:

```
Module Program
  Sub Main()
    Application.Run(New MainWindow())
  End Sub
End Module
```

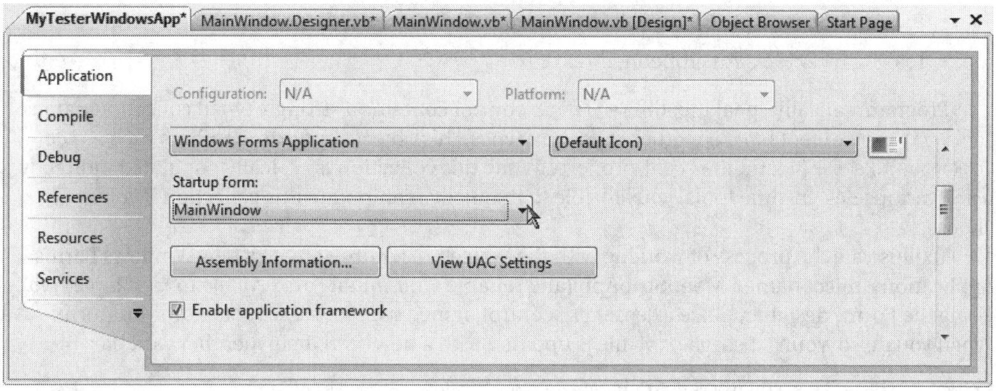

Figure 27-10. *Viewing the startup object*

To instruct the IDE to invoke your custom `Main()` method (rather than create an instance of the startup form automatically), uncheck the Enable application framework check box from the Application tab of the My Project dialog box, and select `Sub Main()` from the Startup object drop-down list, as shown in Figure 27-11.

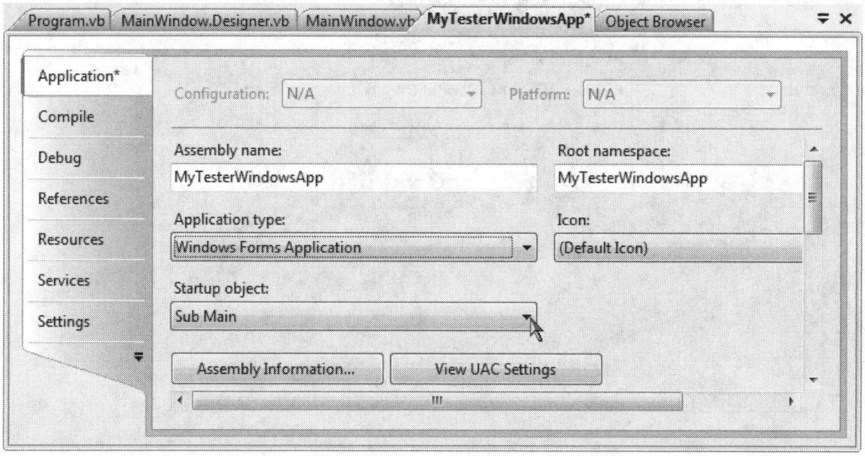

Figure 27-11. *Specifying a custom* `Main()` *method*

Working with MenuStrips and ContextMenuStrips

The recommended control for building a menu system is `MenuStrip`. This control allows you to create "normal" menu items such as File ➤ Exit, and you may also configure it to contain any number of relevant controls within the menu area. Here are some common UI elements that may be contained within a `MenuStrip`:

- `ToolStripMenuItem`: A traditional menu item
- `ToolStripComboBox`: An embedded `ComboBox`

- ToolStripSeparator: A simple line that separates content
- ToolStripTextBox: An embedded TextBox

Programmatically speaking, the MenuStrip control contains a strongly typed collection named ToolStripItemCollection. Like other collection types, this object supports members such as Add(), AddRange(), Remove(), and the Count property. While this collection is typically populated indirectly using various design-time tools, you are able to manually manipulate this collection if you so choose.

To illustrate the process of working with the MenuStrip control, create a new Windows Forms Application project named MenuStripApp (and rename your initial Form1.vb file to MainWindow.vb). Using the Forms designer, place a MenuStrip control named mainFormMenuStrip onto your form. When you do so, your *.Designer.vb file is updated with a new MenuStrip member variable:

```
Friend WithEvents mainFormMenuStrip As System.Windows.Forms.MenuStrip
```

MenuStrips can be highly customized using the Visual Studio 2008 Forms designer. For example, if you look at the extreme upper right of the control, you will notice a small arrow icon. After you select this icon, you are presented with a context-sensitive *inline editor*, as shown in Figure 27-12.

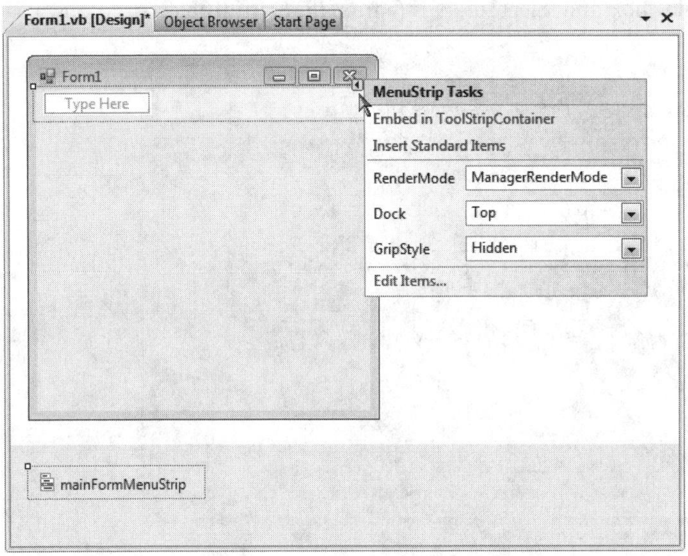

Figure 27-12. *The inline* MenuStrip *editor*

Many Windows Forms controls support such context-sensitive inline editors. As far as MenuStrip is concerned, the editor allows you to quickly do the following:

- Insert a "standard" menu system (File, Save, Tools, Help, etc.) using the Insert Standard Items link.
- Change the docking and gripping behaviors of the MenuStrip.
- Edit each item in the MenuStrip (this is simply a shortcut to selecting a specific item in the Properties window).

For this example, you'll ignore the options of the inline editor and stay focused on the design of the menu system. To begin, select the MenuStrip control on the designer and define a standard File ➤ Exit menu by typing in the names within the Type Here prompts, as shown in Figure 27-13.

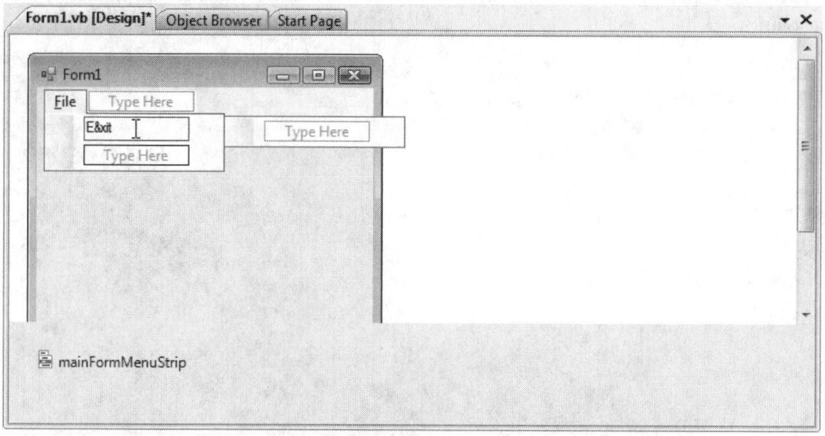

Figure 27-13. *Designing a menu system*

Note As you may know, when the ampersand character (&) is placed before a letter in a menu item, it denotes the item's shortcut key. In this example, you are creating &File ➤ E&xit; therefore, the user may activate the Exit menu by pressing Alt+F, and then X.

Each menu item you type into the designer is represented by the ToolStripMenuItem class type. If you open your *.Designer.vb file, you will find two new member variables for each item:

```
Partial Class MainWindow
  Inherits Form
...
  Friend WithEvents mainFormMenuStrip As System.Windows.Forms.MenuStrip
  Friend WithEvents FileToolStripMenuItem As System.Windows.Forms.ToolStripMenuItem
  Friend WithEvents ExitToolStripMenuItem As System.Windows.Forms.ToolStripMenuItem
End Class
```

To finish the initial code of this example, return to the designer and handle the Click event for the Exit menu item using the events button of the Properties window. Within the generated event handler, make a call to Application.Exit():

```
Public Class MainWindow
  Private Sub ExitToolStripMenuItem_Click(ByVal sender As System.Object, _
    ByVal e As System.EventArgs) Handles ExitToolStripMenuItem.Click
    Application.Exit()
  End Sub
End Class
```

At this point, you should be able to compile and run your program. Verify that you can terminate the application via File ➤ Exit as well as pressing Alt+F and then X on the keyboard.

Adding a TextBox to the MenuStrip

Now, let's create a new topmost menu item named Change Background Color. The subitem in this case will not be a traditional menu item (a static blob of text), but a ToolStripTextBox (see Figure 27-14). Once you have added the new control, rename this control to toolStripTextBoxColor using the Properties window.

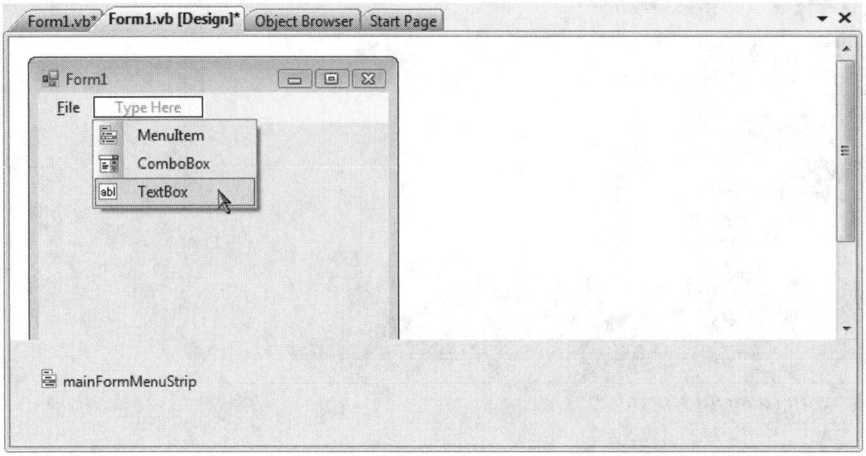

Figure 27-14. *Adding* TextBox*es to a* MenuStrip

The goal here is to allow the user to enter the name of a color (red, green, pink, etc.) that will be used to set the BackColor property of the window. First, handle the Leave event for the new ToolStripTextBox member variable using the Properties window (as you would guess, this event fires when the TextBox within the ToolStrip is no longer the active UI element).

Within the event handler, you will extract the string data entered within the ToolStripTextBox (via the Text property) and make use of the System.Drawing.Color.FromName() method. This shared method will return a Color type based on a known string value. To account for the possibility that the user enters an unknown color (or types bogus data), you will make use of some simple Try/Catch logic:

```
Public Class MainWindow
  Private Sub ExitToolStripMenuItem_Click(ByVal sender As System.Object, _
   ByVal e As System.EventArgs) Handles ExitToolStripMenuItem.Click
    Application.Exit()
  End Sub

  Private Sub toolStripTextBoxColor_Leave(ByVal sender As System.Object, _
   ByVal e As System.EventArgs) Handles toolStripTextBoxColor.Leave
    Try
      BackColor = Color.FromName(toolStripTextBoxColor.Text)
    Catch ' Just do nothing if the user provides bad data
    End Try
  End Sub
End Class
```

Go ahead and take your updated application out for another test drive and try entering in the names of various colors (red, green, blue, for example). Once you do, you should see your form's background color change as soon as you press the Tab key. If you are interested in checking out some valid color names, look up the System.Drawing.Color type using the Visual Studio 2008 Object Browser or the .NET Framework 3.5 SDK documentation.

Creating a Context Menu

Let's now examine the process of building a context-sensitive pop-up (i.e., right-click) menu using the ContextMenuStrip type. Similar to the MenuStrip type, ContextMenuStrip maintains a ToolStripItemCollection to represent the possible subitems (such as ToolStripMenuItem, ToolStripComboBox, ToolStripSeparator, ToolStripTextBox, etc.).

Drag a new ContextMenuStrip control from the Toolbox onto the Forms designer and rename the control to fontSizeContextStrip using the Properties window. Notice that you are able to populate the subitems graphically in much the same way you would edit the form's main MenuStrip. For this example, add three entries named Huge, Normal, and Tiny, as shown in Figure 27-15.

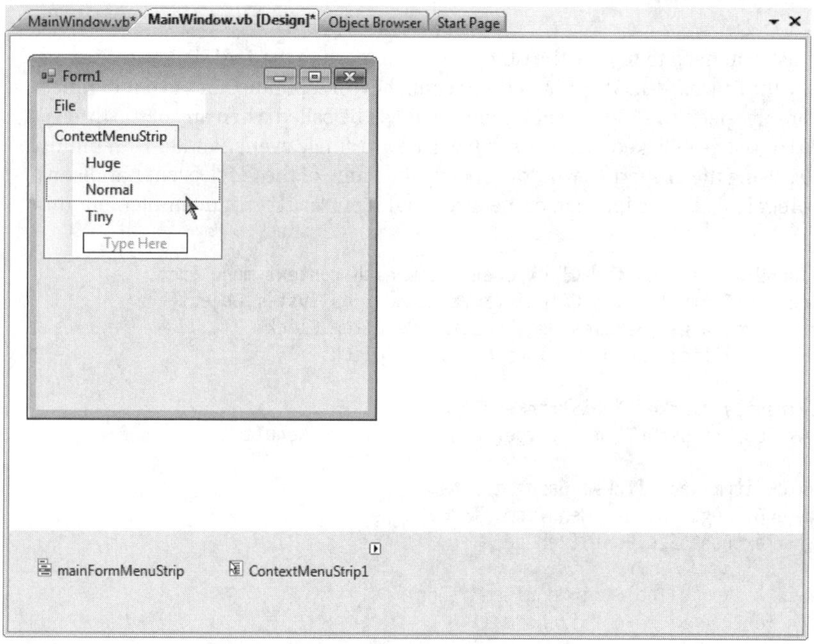

Figure 27-15. *Designing a* ContextMenuStrip

This context menu will be used to allow the user to select the size to render a message within the form's client area. To facilitate this endeavor, create an Enum type named TextFontSize and declare a new member variable of this type within your Form type (set to TextFontSize.FontSizeNormal):

```
Public Class MainWindow
  Private currFontSize As TextFontSize = TextFontSize.FontSizeNormal
...
End Class

' Helper enum for font size.
Public Enum TextFontSize
  FontSizeHuge = 30
```

```
  FontSizeNormal = 20
  FontSizeTiny = 8
End Enum
```

The next step is to handle the form's Paint event using the Properties window. As described in greater detail in the next chapter, the Paint event allows you to render graphical data (including stylized text) onto a form's client area. Here, you are going to draw a textual message using a font of user-specified size. Don't sweat the details at this point, but do implement your Paint event handler as follows:

```
Private Sub MainWindow_Paint(ByVal sender As System.Object, _
  ByVal e As System.Windows.Forms.PaintEventArgs) Handles MyBase.Paint
  Dim g As Graphics = e.Graphics
  g.DrawString("Right click on me...", _
    New Font("Times New Roman", currFontSize), _
    New SolidBrush(Color.Black), 50, 50)
End Sub
```

Last but not least, you need to handle the Click events for each of the ToolStripMenuItem types maintained by the ContextMenuStrip. While you could have a separate Click event handler for each, you will simply specify a single event handler that will be called when any of the three ToolStripMenuItems have been clicked, therefore you will have a single event handler with multiple Handles statements. Using the Properties window, specify the name of the Click event handler as ContextMenuItemSelection_Clicked for each of the three ToolStripMenuItems and implement this method like so:

```
' This one event handler handles the Click event from each context menu item.
Private Sub ContextMenuItemSelection_Clicked(ByVal sender As System.Object, _
  ByVal e As System.EventArgs) Handles HugeToolStripMenuItem.Click, _
  TinyToolStripMenuItem.Click, NormalToolStripMenuItem.Click

  ' Obtain the currently clicked ToolStripMenuItem.
  Dim miClicked As ToolStripMenuItem = CType(sender, ToolStripMenuItem)

  ' Figure out which item was clicked using its Name.
  If miClicked.Name = "HugeToolStripMenuItem" Then
    currFontSize = TextFontSize.FontSizeHuge
  End If
  If miClicked.Name = "NormalToolStripMenuItem" Then
    currFontSize = TextFontSize.FontSizeNormal
  End If
  If miClicked.Name = "TinyToolStripMenuItem" Then
    currFontSize = TextFontSize.FontSizeTiny
  End If

  ' Tell the Form to repaint itself.
  Invalidate()
End Sub
```

Notice that using the "sender" argument, you are able to determine the name of the ToolStripMenuItem member variable in order to set the current text size. Once you have done so, the call to Invalidate() fires the Paint event, which will cause your Paint event handler to execute.

The final step is to inform the form which ContextMenuStrip it should display when the right mouse button is clicked in its client area. To do so, simply use the Properties window to set the ContextMenuStrip property equal to the name of your context menu item. Once you have done so, you will find the following line within InitializeComponent():

```
Me.ContextMenuStrip = Me.fontSizeContextStrip
```

Note Be aware that any control can be assigned a context menu via the `ContextMenuStrip` property. For example, you could create a `Button` object on a dialog box that responds to a particular context menu. In this way, the menu would be displayed only if the mouse button were right-clicked within the bounding rectangle of the button.

If you now run the application, you should be able to change the size of the rendered text message via a right-click of your mouse.

Checking Menu Items

`ToolStripMenuItem` defines a number of members that allow you to check, enable, and hide a given item. Table 27-11 gives a rundown of some (but not all) of the interesting properties.

Table 27-11. *Members of the* `ToolStripMenuItem` *Type*

Member	Meaning in Life
`Checked`	Gets or sets a value indicating whether a check mark appears beside the text of the `ToolStripMenuItem`
`CheckOnClick`	Gets or sets a value indicating whether the `ToolStripMenuItem` should automatically appear checked/unchecked when clicked
`Enabled`	Gets or sets a value indicating whether the `ToolStripMenuItem` is enabled

Let's extend the previous pop-up menu to display a check mark next to the currently selected menu item. Setting a check mark on a given menu item is not at all difficult (just set the `Checked` property to `True`). However, tracking which menu item should be checked does require some additional logic. One possible approach is to define a distinct `ToolStripMenuItem` member variable that represents the currently checked item:

```
Public Class MainWindow
...
  ' Marks the item checked.
  Private WithEvents currentCheckedItem As ToolStripMenuItem
End Form
```

Recall that the default text size is `TextFontSize.FontSizeNormal`. Given this, the initial item to be checked is the `normalToolStripMenuItem` `ToolStripMenuItem` member variable. Add a default constructor to your `Form`-derived type, implemented like so:

```
Public Sub New()
  ' Call InitializeComponent() when defining your own constructor!
  InitializeComponent()

  ' Inherited method to center the form.
  CenterToScreen()

  ' Now check the "Normal" menu item.
  currentCheckedItem = normalToolStripMenuItem
  currentCheckedItem.Checked = True
End Sub
```

■Note When you redefine the default constructor for a `Form`-derived type, you must manually make a call to `InitializeComponent()` within its scope, as this will no longer automatically be done on your behalf. Thankfully, Visual Studio 2008 will automatically insert a call to `InitializeComponent()` when you press the Enter key after typing `Sub New()`.

Now that you have a way to programmatically identify the currently checked item, the last step is to update the `ContextMenuItemSelection_Clicked()` event handler to uncheck the previous item and check the new current `ToolStripMenuItem` object in response to the user selection:

```
' This one event handler handles the Click event from each context menu item.
Private Sub ContextMenuItemSelection_Clicked(ByVal sender As System.Object, _
  ByVal e As System.EventArgs) Handles HugeToolStripMenuItem.Click, _
  TinyToolStripMenuItem.Click, NormalToolStripMenuItem.Click

  ' Obtain the currently clicked ToolStripMenuItem.
  Dim miClicked As ToolStripMenuItem = CType(sender, ToolStripMenuItem)

  ' Uncheck the currently checked item.
  currentCheckedItem.Checked = False

  ' Figure out which item was clicked using its Name.
  If miClicked.Name = "HugeToolStripMenuItem" Then
    currFontSize = TextFontSize.FontSizeHuge
  End If
  If miClicked.Name = "NormalToolStripMenuItem" Then
    currFontSize = TextFontSize.FontSizeNormal
  End If
  If miClicked.Name = "TinyToolStripMenuItem" Then
    currFontSize = TextFontSize.FontSizeTiny
  End If

  ' Tell the form to repaint itself.
  Invalidate()

  ' Establish which item to check.
  If miClicked.Name = "HugeToolStripMenuItem" Then
    currFontSize = TextFontSize.FontSizeHuge
    currentCheckedItem = HugeToolStripMenuItem
  End If
  If miClicked.Name = "NormalToolStripMenuItem" Then
    currFontSize = TextFontSize.FontSizeNormal
    currentCheckedItem = NormalToolStripMenuItem
  End If
  If miClicked.Name = "TinyToolStripMenuItem" Then
    currFontSize = TextFontSize.FontSizeTiny
    currentCheckedItem = TinyToolStripMenuItem
  End If

  ' Check new item.
  currentCheckedItem.Checked = True
End Sub
```

Figure 27-16 shows the completed MenuStripApp project in action.

Figure 27-16. *Checking/unchecking* `ToolStripMenuItems`

Source Code The MenuStripApp application is located under the Chapter 27 subdirectory.

Working with StatusStrips

In addition to a menu system, many forms also maintain a *status bar* that is typically mounted at the bottom of the form. A status bar may be divided into any number of "panes" that hold some textual (or graphical) information such as menu help strings, the current time, or other application-specific information. In the Windows Forms API, the `StatusStrip` type is used to assemble such a UI element. Beyond using a `ToolStripStatusLabel` type to define panes to hold textual/graphical data, `StatusStrips` have the ability to contain additional items such as the following:

- `ToolStripProgressBar`: An embedded progress bar.
- `ToolStripDropDownButton`: An embedded button that displays a drop-down list of choices when clicked.
- `ToolStripSplitButton`: This is similar to the `ToolStripDropDownButton`, but the items of the drop-down list are displayed only if the user clicks directly on the drop-down area of the control. The `ToolStripSplitButton` also has normal buttonlike behavior and can thus support the `Click` event.

In this example, you will build a new `MainWindow` that supports a simple menu (File ➤ Exit and Help ➤ About) as well as a `StatusStrip`. The leftmost pane of the status strip will be used to display help string data regarding the currently selected menu subitem (e.g., if the user selects the Exit menu, the pane will display "Exits the app").

The far-right pane will display one of two dynamically created strings that will show either the current time or the current date. Finally, the middle pane will be a `ToolStripDropDownButton` type that allows the user to toggle the date/time display (with a happy face icon to boot!). Figure 27-17 shows the application in its completed form.

Figure 27-17. *The* `StatusStrip` *application*

Designing the Menu System

To begin, create a new Windows Forms application project named StatusStripApp. Place a `MenuStrip` control onto the Forms designer and build the two menu items (File ➤ Exit and Help ➤ About). Once you have done so, handle the `Click` and `MouseHover` events for each subitem (Exit and About) using the Properties window.

The implementation of the File ➤ Exit `Click` event handler will simply terminate the application, while the Help ➤ About `Click` event handler shows a friendly `MessageBox`.

```
Public Class MainForm
  Private Sub ExitToolStripMenuItem_Click(ByVal sender As System.Object, _
    ByVal e As System.EventArgs) Handles ExitToolStripMenuItem.Click
    Application.Exit()
  End Sub

  Private Sub AboutToolStripMenuItem_Click(ByVal sender As System.Object, _
    ByVal e As System.EventArgs) Handles AboutToolStripMenuItem.Click
    MessageBox.Show("My StatusStripApp!")
  End Sub

  Private Sub ExitToolStripMenuItem_MouseHover(ByVal sender As System.Object, _
    ByVal e As System.EventArgs) Handles ExitToolStripMenuItem.MouseHover
  End Sub

  Private Sub AboutToolStripMenuItem_MouseHover(ByVal sender As System.Object, _
    ByVal e As System.EventArgs) Handles AboutToolStripMenuItem.MouseHover
  End Sub
...
End Class
```

You will update the `MouseHover` event handlers to display the correct prompt in the leftmost pane of the `StatusStrip` in just a bit, so leave them empty for the time being.

Designing the StatusStrip

Next, place a `StatusStrip` control onto the designer and rename this control to `mainStatusStrip` (note this control automatically docks to the bottom of the designer window). Initially, a `StatusStrip` contains no panes whatsoever. To add panes, you may take various approaches:

- Author the code by hand without designer support (perhaps using a helper method named `CreateStatusStrip()` that is called in the form's constructor).
- Add the items via a dialog box activated through the Edit Items link using the `StatusStrip` context-sensitive inline editor (see Figure 27-18).

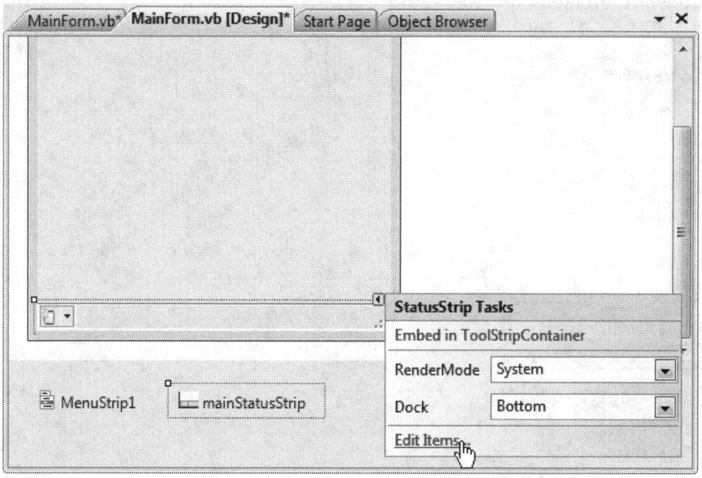

Figure 27-18. *The* `StatusStrip` *context editor*

- Add the items one by one via the new item drop-down editor mounted on the `StatusStrip` (see Figure 27-19).

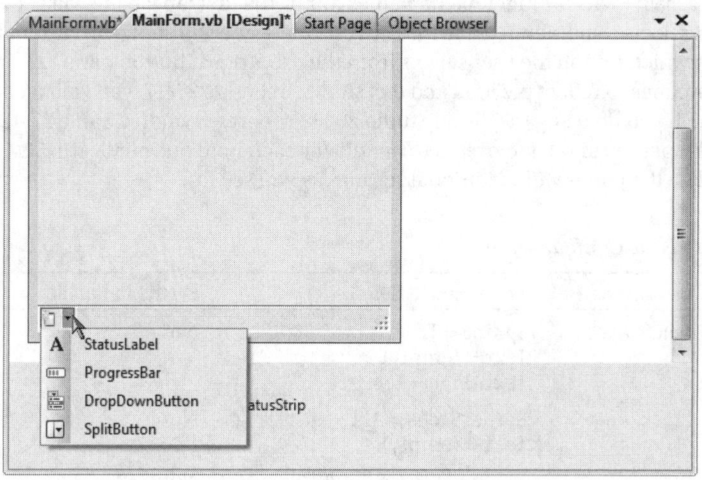

Figure 27-19. *Adding items via the* `StatusStrip` *new item drop-down editor*

For this example, you will leverage the new item drop-down editor as shown in Figure 27-19. Add two new `ToolStripStatusLabel` types named `toolStripStatusLabelMenuState` and `toolStripStatusLabelClock`, and a `ToolStripDropDownButton` named `toolStripDropDownButtonDateTime`. Now, select the `ToolStripDropDownButton` on the designer and add two new menu items named `currentTimeToolStripMenuItem` and `dayoftheWeekToolStripMenuItem` (see Figure 27-20).

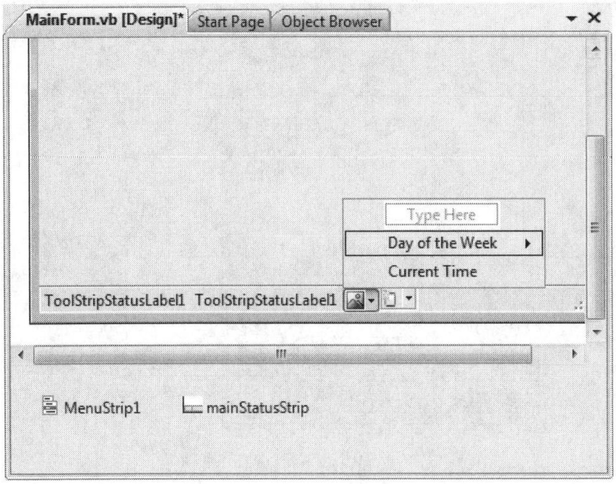

Figure 27-20. *Adding menu items to the* `ToolStripDropDownButton`

Once you have done so, the IDE will add new member variables in the `*.Designer.vb` file and update `InitializeComponent()` accordingly. As the names imply, the first label pane will show "help strings" when the user selects a submenu, while the second label pane will show the current time *or* current date, based on which option the user selects from the drop-down button pane.

To configure your panes to reflect the look and feel shown in Figure 27-17, you will need to set several properties, which you do using the Visual Studio 2008 Properties window. Table 27-12 documents the necessary properties to set and events to handle for each item on your `StatusStrip` (of course, feel free to stylize the panes with additional settings as you see fit).

Table 27-12. `StatusStrip` *Pane Configuration*

Pane Member Variable	Properties to Set	Events to Handle

`toolStripStatusLabelMenuState`	`Spring` = `True`
	`Text` = (empty)
	`TextAlign` = `TopLeft`
		None

`toolStripStatusLabelClock`	`BorderSides` = `All` `Text` = (empty)	None
`toolStripDropDownButtonDateTime`	`Image` = (see text that follows)	None
`dayoftheWeekToolStripMenuItem`	`Text` = `Day of the Week`	`MouseHover` `Click`
`currentTimeToolStripMenuItem`	`Text` = "Current Time"	`MouseHover` `Click`

The Image property of the toolStripDropDownButtonDateTime member can be set to any image file on your machine (of course, extremely large image files will be quite skewed). For this example, you may wish to use the HappyDude.jpg file included with this book's downloadable source code (please visit the Downloads section of the Apress website, http://www.apress.com).

So at this point, the GUI design is complete! However, before you implement the remaining event handlers, you need to get to know the role of the Timer component.

Working with the Timer Type

Recall that the second pane of the status bar should display the current time or current date based on user preference. The first step to take to achieve this design goal is to add a Timer member variable to the form. A Timer is a component that calls some method (specified using the Tick event) at a given interval (specified by the Interval property).

Drag a Timer component onto your Forms designer and rename it to timerDateTimeUpdate. Using the Properties window, set the Interval property to 1,000 (the value is in milliseconds) and set the Enabled property to True. Finally, handle the Tick event. Before implementing the Tick event handler, define a new enum type in your project named DateTimeFormat. This enum will be used to determine whether the second ToolStripStatusLabel should display the current time or the current day of the week:

```
Public Enum DateTimeFormat
  ShowClock
  ShowDay
End Enum
```

With this enum in place, update your MainWindow with the following code:

```
Public Class MainWindow
  ' Which format to display?
  Private dtFormat As DateTimeFormat = DateTimeFormat.ShowClock

  Private Sub timerDateTimeUpdate_Tick(ByVal sender As System.Object, _
  ByVal e As System.EventArgs) Handles timerDateTimeUpdate.Tick
    Dim panelInfo As String = String.Empty

    ' Create current format.
    If dtFormat = DateTimeFormat.ShowClock Then
      panelInfo = DateTime.Now.ToLongTimeString()
    Else
      panelInfo = DateTime.Now.ToLongDateString()
    End If

    ' Set text on pane.
    toolStripStatusLabelClock.Text = panelInfo
  End Sub
...
End Class
```

Notice that the Timer event handler makes use of the DateTime type. Here, you simply find the current system time or date using the Now property and use it to set the Text property of the toolStripStatusLabelClock member variable.

Toggling the Display

At this point, the Tick event handler should be displaying the current time within the toolStripStatusLabelClock pane, given that the initial value of your DateTimeFormat member variable has been set to DateTimeFormat.ShowClock. To allow the user to toggle between the date and time display, update your MainWindow as follows (note you are also toggling which of the two menu items in the ToolStripDropDownButton should be checked):

```
Public Class MainWindow
  ' Which format to display?
  Private dtFormat As DateTimeFormat = DateTimeFormat.ShowClock

  ' Marks the item checked.
  Private currentCheckedItem As ToolStripMenuItem

  Public Sub New()
    ' This call is required by the Windows Forms designer.
    InitializeComponent()

    ' These properties can also be set
    ' with the Properties window.
    Text = "Status Strip Example"
    CenterToScreen()
    currentCheckedItem = currentTimeToolStripMenuItem
    currentCheckedItem.Checked = True
  End Sub
...
  Private Sub currentTimeToolStripMenuItem_Click(ByVal sender As System.Object, _
  ByVal e As System.EventArgs) Handles currentTimeToolStripMenuItem.Click
    ' Toggle check mark and set pane format to time.
    currentCheckedItem.Checked = False
    dtFormat = DateTimeFormat.ShowClock
    currentCheckedItem = currentTimeToolStripMenuItem
    currentCheckedItem.Checked = True
  End Sub

  Private Sub dayoftheWeekToolStripMenuItem_Click(ByVal sender As System.Object, _
  ByVal e As System.EventArgs) Handles dayoftheWeekToolStripMenuItem.Click
    ' Toggle check mark and set pane format to date.
    currentCheckedItem.Checked = False
    dtFormat = DateTimeFormat.ShowDay
    currentCheckedItem = dayoftheWeekToolStripMenuItem
    currentCheckedItem.Checked = True
  End Sub
End Class
```

Displaying the Menu Selection Prompts

Finally, you need to configure the first pane to hold menu help strings. As you know, most applications send a small bit of text information to the first pane of a status bar whenever the end user selects a menu item (e.g., "This terminates the application"). Given that you have already handled the MouseHover events for each submenu on the MenuStrip and ToolStripDropDownButton, all you need to do is assign a proper value to the Text property for the toolStripStatusLabelMenuState member variable, for example:

```
Private Sub ExitToolStripMenuItem_MouseHover(ByVal sender As System.Object, _
  ByVal e As System.EventArgs) Handles ExitToolStripMenuItem.MouseHover
  toolStripStatusLabelMenuState.Text = "Exits the app."
End Sub
```

```
Private Sub AboutToolStripMenuItem_MouseHover(ByVal sender As System.Object, _
  ByVal e As System.EventArgs) Handles AboutToolStripMenuItem.MouseHover
  toolStripStatusLabelMenuState.Text = "Shows about box."
End Sub

Private Sub dayoftheWeekToolStripMenuItem_MouseHover( _
  ByVal sender As System.Object, _
  ByVal e As System.EventArgs) Handles dayoftheWeekToolStripMenuItem.MouseHover
  toolStripStatusLabelMenuState.Text = "Shows the day of the week."
End Sub

Private Sub currentTimeToolStripMenuItem_MouseHover(ByVal sender As System.Object, _
  ByVal e As System.EventArgs) Handles currentTimeToolStripMenuItem.MouseHover
  toolStripStatusLabelMenuState.Text = "Shows the current time."
End Sub
```

Take your updated project out for a test drive. You should now be able to find these informational help strings in the first pane of your `StatusStrip` as you select each menu item.

Establishing a "Ready" State

The final thing to do for this example is ensure that when the user deselects a menu item, the first text pane is set to a default message (e.g., "Ready"). With the current design, the previously selected menu prompt remains on the leftmost text pane, which is confusing at best. To rectify this issue, handle the `MouseLeave` event for the Exit, About, Day of the Week, and Current Time menu items. To simplify coding, we will make use of a single handler for each widget (note the multiple `Handles` statements):

```
Private Sub Handle_MouseLeave(ByVal sender As System.Object, _
  ByVal e As System.EventArgs) Handles currentTimeToolStripMenuItem.MouseLeave, _
  exitToolStripMenuItem.MouseLeave, _
  dayoftheWeekToolStripMenuItem.MouseLeave, _
  aboutToolStripMenuItem.MouseLeave
  toolStripStatusLabelMenuState.Text = "Ready."
End Sub
```

With this, you should find that the first pane resets to this default message as soon as the mouse cursor leaves any of your four menu items.

■ **Source Code** The StatusStripApp project is included under the Chapter 27 subdirectory.

Working with ToolStrips

The next form-level GUI item to examine in this chapter is the `ToolStrip` type. As you know, toolbars typically provide an alternative means to activate a given menu item. Thus, if the user clicks a Save button, this has the same effect as selecting File ➤ Save. Much like `MenuStrip` and `StatusStrip`, the `ToolStrip` type can contain numerous toolbar items, some of which you have already encountered in previous examples:

- `ToolStripButton`
- `ToolStripLabel`
- `ToolStripSplitButton`
- `ToolStripDropDownButton`
- `ToolStripSeparator`
- `ToolStripComboBox`
- `ToolStripTextBox`
- `ToolStripProgressBar`

Like other Windows Forms controls, the `ToolStrip` supports an inline editor (e.g., the small triangle on the upper right) that allows you to quickly add standard button types (File, Exit, Help, Copy, Paste, etc.) to a `ToolStrip`, change the docking position, and embed the `ToolStrip` in a `ToolStripContainer` (more details in just a bit).

To illustrate working with `ToolStrip`s, create a new Windows Forms application named ToolStripApp. Next, create a `ToolStrip` containing two `ToolStripButton` types (named `toolStripButtonGrowFont` and `toolStripButtonShrinkFont`), a `ToolStripSeparator`, and a `ToolStripTextBox` (named `toolStripTextBoxMessage`). The end user is able to enter a message to be rendered on the form via the `ToolStripTextBox`, and the two `ToolStripButton` types will be used to increase or decrease the font size. Figure 27-21 shows the end result of the project you will construct.

Figure 27-21. *ToolStripApp in action*

By now I'd guess you have a handle on working with the Visual Studio 2008 Forms designer, so I won't belabor the point of building the `ToolStrip`. Do note, however, that each `ToolStripButton` has a custom (albeit poorly drawn by yours truly) icon that was created using the Visual Studio 2008 image editor. If you wish to create image files for your project, simply select the Project ➤ Add New Item menu option, and from the resulting dialog box add a new icon file (see Figure 27-22).

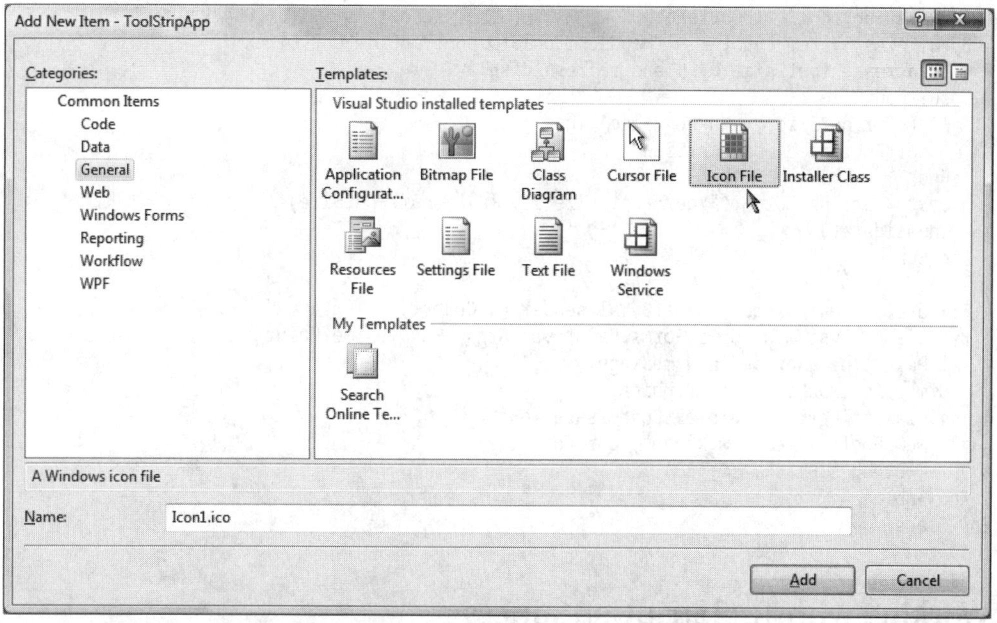

Figure 27-22. *Inserting new image files*

Once you have done so, you are able to edit your images using the Colors tab on the Toolbox and the Image Editor toolbox. In any case, once you have designed your icons, you are able to associate them with the `ToolStripButton` types via the `Image` property in the Properties window. Once you are happy with the `ToolStrip`'s look and feel, handle the `Click` event for each `ToolStripButton`.

The necessary code is extremely straightforward. In the following updated `MainWindow`, notice that the current font size is constrained between 12 and 70:

```
Public Class MainWindow
  ' The current, max, and min font sizes.
  Private currFontSize As Integer = 12
  Const MinFontSize As Integer = 12
  Const MaxFontSize As Integer = 70

  Public Sub New()
    InitializeComponent()
    CenterToScreen()
    Text = String.Format("Your Font size is: {0}", currFontSize)
  End Sub

  Private Sub toolStripButtonShrinkFont_Click(ByVal sender As System.Object, _
  ByVal e As System.EventArgs) Handles toolStripButtonShrinkFont.Click
    ' Reduce font size by 5 and refresh display.
    currFontSize -= 5
    If (currFontSize <= MinFontSize) Then
      currFontSize = MinFontSize
    End If
    Text = String.Format("Your Font size is: {0}", currFontSize)
    Invalidate()
  End Sub
```

```
  Private Sub toolStripButtonGrowFont_Click(ByVal sender As System.Object, _
  ByVal e As System.EventArgs) Handles toolStripButtonGrowFont.Click
    ' Increase font size by 5 and refresh display.
    currFontSize += 5
    If (currFontSize >= MaxFontSize) Then
      currFontSize = MaxFontSize
    End If
    Text = String.Format("Your Font size is: {0}", currFontSize)
    Invalidate()
  End Sub

  Private Sub MainWindow_Paint(ByVal sender As Object, _
  ByVal e As System.Windows.Forms.PaintEventArgs) Handles Me.Paint
    ' Paint the user-defined message.
    Dim g As Graphics = e.Graphics
    g.DrawString(toolStripTextBoxMessage.Text, _
      New Font("Times New Roman", currFontSize), _
        Brushes.Black, 10, 60)
  End Sub
End Class
```

Working with ToolStripContainers

A `ToolStrip`, if required, can be configured to be "dockable" against any or all sides of the form that contains it. To illustrate how you can accomplish this, right-click your current `ToolStrip` using the designer and select the Embed in ToolStripContainer menu option. Once you have done so, you will find that the `ToolStrip` has been contained within a `ToolStripContainer`. For this example, select the Dock Fill in Form option (see Figure 27-23).

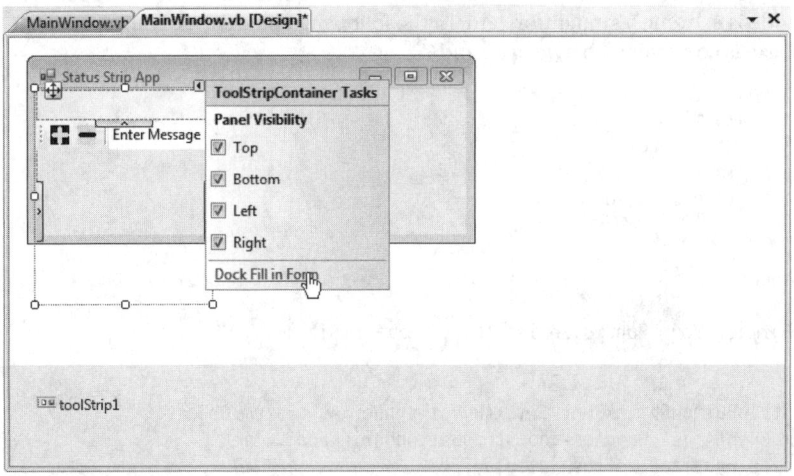

Figure 27-23. *Docking the* `ToolStripContainer` *within the entire form*

If you run your current update, you will find that the `ToolStrip` can be moved and docked to each side of the container. However, your custom message has now vanished. The reason for this is that `ToolStripContainers` are actually *child controls* of the form. Therefore, the graphical render is still taking place, but the output is being hidden by the container that now sits on top of the form's client area.

To fix this problem, you will need to handle the `Paint` event on the `ToolStripContainer` rather than on the form. First, handle the `Paint` event for the `ToolStripContainer` and move the rendering code from the existing form's `Paint` event handler into the container's `Paint` event handler (and delete the form's `Paint` handler when finished). Finally, you will need to replace each occurrence of the call to the form's `Invalidate()` method to the container's `Invalidate()` method. Here are the relevant code updates:

```
Public Class MainWindow
...
  Private Sub ContentPanel_Paint(ByVal sender As System.Object, _
  ByVal e As System.Windows.Forms.PaintEventArgs) _
  Handles toolStripContainer1.ContentPanel.Paint
    ' Paint the user-defined message.
    Dim g As Graphics = e.Graphics
    g.DrawString(toolStripTextBoxMessage.Text, _
      New Font("Times New Roman", currFontSize), _
      Brushes.Black, 10, 60)
  End Sub

  Private Sub toolStripButtonShrinkFont_Click(ByVal sender As System.Object, _
  ByVal e As System.EventArgs) Handles toolStripButtonShrinkFont.Click
...
    toolStripContainer1.Invalidate(True)
  End Sub

  Private Sub toolStripButtonGrowFont_Click(ByVal sender As System.Object, _
  ByVal e As System.EventArgs) Handles toolStripButtonGrowFont.Click
...
    toolStripContainer1.Invalidate(True)
  End Sub
End Class
```

Of course, the `ToolStripContainer` can be configured in various ways to tweak how it operates. I leave it to you to check out the .NET Framework 3.5 SDK documentation for complete details. Figure 27-24 shows the completed project.

Figure 27-24. *ToolStripApp, now with a dockable* `ToolStrip`

■ Source Code The ToolStripApp project is included under the Chapter 27 subdirectory.

Building an MDI Application

To wrap up our initial look at Windows Forms, I'll close this chapter by discussing how to configure a form to function as a parent to any number of child windows (i.e., an MDI container). MDI applications allow users to have multiple child windows open at the same time within the same topmost window. In the world of MDIs, each window represents a given "document" of the application. For example, Visual Studio 2008 is an MDI application in that you are able to have multiple documents open from within an instance of the application.

When you are building MDI applications using Windows Forms, your first task is to (of course) create a brand-new Windows Forms application, which we will name SimpleMdiApp. The initial form of the application typically hosts a menu system that allows you to create new documents (such as File ➤ New) as well as arrange existing open windows (cascade, vertical tile, and horizontal tile).

Creating the child windows is interesting, as you typically define a prototypical form that functions as a basis for each child window. Given that forms are class types, any private data defined in the child form will be unique to a particular instance. For example, if you were to create an MDI word processing application, you might create a child form that maintains a `StringBuilder` to represent the text. If a user created five new child windows, each form would maintain its own `StringBuilder` instance, which could be individually manipulated.

Additionally, MDI applications allow you to *merge menus*. As mentioned previously, parent windows typically have a menu system that allows the user to spawn and organize additional child windows. However, what if the child window also maintains a menuing system? If the user maximizes a particular child window, you need to merge the child's menu system within the parent form to allow the user to activate items from each menu system. The `System.Windows.Forms` namespace defines a number of properties, methods, and events that allow you to programmatically merge menu systems. In addition, there is a "default merge" system, which works in a good number of cases.

Building the Parent Form

To illustrate the basics of building an MDI application, begin by creating a brand-new Windows application named SimpleMdiApp. Almost all of the MDI infrastructure can be assigned to your initial `Form` using various design-time tools. To begin, locate the `IsMdiContainer` property for the form in the Properties window and set it to `True`. If you look at the design-time form, you'll see that the client area has been modified to visually represent a container of child windows.

Next, place a new `MenuStrip` control on your main form. Design this menu to specify three topmost items named File, Window, and Arrange Windows. The File menu contains two subitems named New and Exit. The Window menu does not contain any subitems, because you will programmatically add new items as the user creates additional child windows. Finally, the Arrange Window menu defines three subitems named Cascade, Vertical, and Horizontal.

Once you have created the menu UI, handle the `Click` event for the Exit, New, Cascade, Vertical, and Horizontal menu items (remember, the Window menu does not have any subitems just yet). You'll implement the File ➤ New handler in the next section, but for now here is the code behind the remaining menu selections:

```
' Handle File | Exit event and arrange all child windows.
Private Sub ExitToolStripMenuItem_Click(ByVal sender As System.Object, _
  ByVal e As System.EventArgs) Handles ExitToolStripMenuItem.Click
  Application.Exit()
End Sub
```

```
Private Sub CascadeToolStripMenuItem_Click(ByVal sender As System.Object, _
  ByVal e As System.EventArgs) Handles CascadeToolStripMenuItem.Click
  LayoutMdi(MdiLayout.Cascade)
End Sub

Private Sub VerticalToolStripMenuItem_Click(ByVal sender As System.Object, _
  ByVal e As System.EventArgs) Handles VerticalToolStripMenuItem.Click
  LayoutMdi(MdiLayout.TileVertical)
End Sub

Private Sub HorizontalToolStripMenuItem_Click(ByVal sender As System.Object, _
  ByVal e As System.EventArgs) Handles HorizontalToolStripMenuItem.Click
  LayoutMdi(MdiLayout.TileHorizontal)
End Sub
```

The main point of interest here is the use of the `LayoutMdi()` method and the corresponding `MdiLayout` enumeration. The code behind each menu select handler should be quite clear. When the user selects a given arrangement, you tell the parent form to automatically reposition any and all child windows.

Before you move on to the construction of the child form, you need to set one additional property of the `MenuStrip`. The `MdiWindowListItem` property is used to establish which topmost menu item should be used to automatically list the name of each child window as a possible menu selection. Set this property to the `WindowToolStripMenuItem` member variable. By default, this list is the value of the child's `Text` property followed by a numerical suffix (i.e., `Form1`, `Form2`, `Form3`, etc.).

Building the Child Form

Now that you have the shell of an MDI container, you need to create an additional form that functions as the prototype for a given child window. Begin by inserting a new `Form` type into your current project (using Project ➤ Add Windows Form) named `ChildPrototypeForm` and handle the `Click` event for this form. In the generated event handler, randomly set the background color of the client area. In addition, print out the "stringified" value of the new `Color` object into the child's caption bar. The following logic should do the trick:

```
Public Class ChildPrototypeForm
  Private Sub ChildPrototypeForm_Click(ByVal sender As System.Object, _
  ByVal e As System.EventArgs) Handles MyBase.Click
    ' Get three random numbers
    Dim r, g, b As Integer
    Dim ran As New Random()
    r = ran.Next(0, 255)
    g = ran.Next(0, 255)
    b = ran.Next(0, 255)

    ' Now create a color for the background.
    Dim currColor As Color = Color.FromArgb(r, g, b)
    Me.BackColor = currColor
    Me.Text = currColor.ToString()
  End Sub
End Class
```

Spawning Child Windows

Your final order of business is to flesh out the details behind the parent form's File ➤ New event handler. Now that you have defined a child form, the logic is simple: create and show a new instance of the ChildPrototypeForm type. As well, you need to set the value of the child form's MdiParent property to point to the containing form (in this case, your main window). Here is the update:

```
Private Sub NewToolStripMenuItem_Click(ByVal sender As System.Object, _
  ByVal e As System.EventArgs) Handles NewToolStripMenuItem.Click
  ' Make a new child window.
  Dim newChild As New ChildPrototypeForm()

  ' Set the parent form of the child window.
  newChild.MdiParent = Me

  ' Display the new form.
  newChild.Show()
End Sub
```

■ **Note** A child form may access the MdiParent property directly whenever it needs to manipulate (or communicate with) its parent window.

To take this application out for a test drive, begin by creating a set of new child windows and click each one to establish a unique background color. If you examine the subitems under the Windows menu, you should see each child form present and accounted for. As well, if you access the Arrange Windows menu items, you can instruct the parent form to vertically tile, horizontally tile, or cascade the child forms. Figure 27-25 shows the completed application.

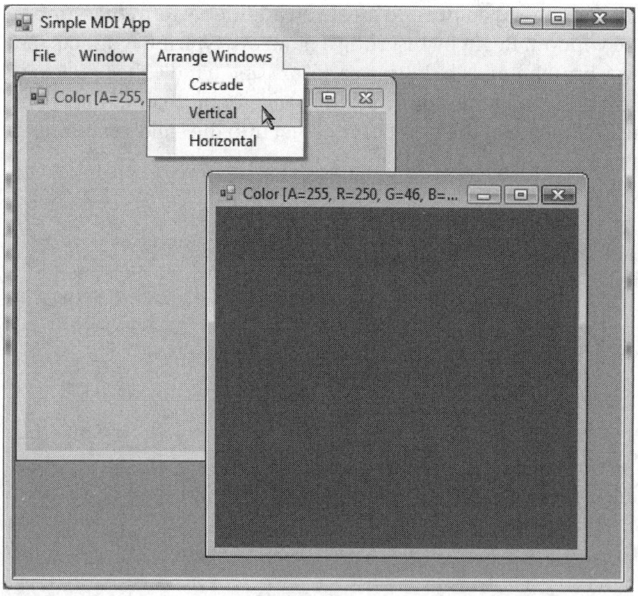

Figure 27-25. *An MDI application*

Source Code The SimpleMdiApp project can be found under the Chapter 27 subdirectory.

Summary

This chapter introduced the fine art of building a UI with the types contained in the `System.Windows.Forms` namespace. You began by building a number of applications by hand, and you learned along the way that at a minimum, a GUI application needs a class that derives from `Form` and a `Main()` method that invokes `Application.Run()`.

During the course of this chapter, you learned how to build topmost menus (and pop-up menus) and how to respond to a number of menu events. You also came to understand how to further enhance your `Form` types using toolbars and status bars. As you have seen, Windows Forms provides the `MenuStrips`, `ToolStrips`, and `StatusStrips` types to build such UI elements. Finally, this chapter wrapped up by illustrating how to construct MDI applications using Windows Forms.

CHAPTER 28

Rendering Graphical Data with GDI+

The previous chapter introduced you to the process of building a GUI-based desktop application using `System.Windows.Forms`. The point of this chapter is to examine the details of rendering graphics (including stylized text and image data) onto a Form's surface area. We'll begin by taking a high-level look at the numerous drawing-related namespaces, and we'll examine the role of the `Paint` event and the `Graphics` object.

The remainder of this chapter covers how to manipulate colors, fonts, geometric shapes, and graphical images. This chapter also explores a number of rendering-centric programming techniques, such as nonrectangular hit testing, drag-and-drop logic, and the .NET resource format. While *technically* not part of GDI+ proper, resources often involve the manipulation of graphical data (which, in my opinion, is "GDI+ enough" to be presented here).

Note GDI+ is the native graphical toolkit of the Windows Forms API. Understand that Windows Presentation Foundation (WPF) provides a completely different graphical rendering API, which you will examine in Chapter 32.

A Survey of the GDI+ Namespaces

The .NET platform provides a number of namespaces devoted to two-dimensional graphical rendering. In addition to the basic functionality you would expect to find in a graphics toolkit (colors, fonts, pens, brushes, etc.), you also find types that enable geometric transformations, antialiasing, palette blending, and document printing support. Collectively speaking, these namespaces make up the .NET facility we call *GDI+*, which is the native rendering toolkit of Windows Forms. Table 28-1 gives a high-level view of the core GDI+ namespaces.

Table 28-1. *Core GDI+ Namespaces*

Namespace	Meaning in Life
`System.Drawing`	This is the core GDI+ namespace that defines numerous types for basic rendering (fonts, pens, basic brushes, etc.) as well as the `Graphics` class.
`System.Drawing.Drawing2D`	This namespace provides types used for more advanced two-dimensional/vector graphics functionality (e.g., gradient brushes, pen caps, geometric transforms, etc.).

Continued

Table 28-1. *Continued*

Namespace	Meaning in Life
System.Drawing.Imaging	This namespace defines types that allow you to manipulate graphical images (e.g., change the palette, extract image metadata, manipulate metafiles, etc.).
System.Drawing.Printing	This namespace defines types that allow you to render images to the printed page, interact with the printer itself, and format the overall appearance of a given print job.
System.Drawing.Text	This namespace allows you to manipulate collections of fonts.

Note All of the GDI+ namespaces are defined within the `System.Drawing.dll` assembly. While Windows Forms project types automatically set a reference to this code library, you can manually reference `System.Drawing.dll` using the Add References dialog box if necessary.

An Overview of the System.Drawing Namespace

The vast majority of the types you'll use when programming GDI+ applications are found within the `System.Drawing` namespace. As you would expect, there are classes that represent images, brushes, pens, and fonts. Furthermore, `System.Drawing` defines a number of related utility types such as `Color`, `Point`, and `Rectangle`. Table 28-2 lists some of the core types to be aware of.

Table 28-2. *Core Types of the* `System.Drawing` *Namespace*

Type	Meaning in Life
Bitmap	This type encapsulates image data (*.bmp or otherwise).
Brush Brushes SolidBrush SystemBrushes TextureBrush	Brush objects are used to fill the interiors of graphical shapes such as rectangles, ellipses, and polygons.
BufferedGraphics	This type provides a graphics buffer for double buffering, which is used to reduce or eliminate flicker caused by redrawing a display surface.
Color SystemColors	The Color and SystemColors types define a number of shared read-only properties used to obtain specific colors for the construction of various pens/brushes.
Font FontFamily	The Font type encapsulates the characteristics of a given font (i.e., type name, bold, italic, point size, etc.). FontFamily provides an abstraction for a group of fonts having a similar design but with certain variations in style.
Graphics	This class represents a valid drawing surface, as well as a number of methods to render text, images, and geometric patterns.
Icon SystemIcons	These classes represent custom icons, as well as the set of standard system-supplied icons.
Pen Pens SystemPens	Pens are objects used to draw lines and curves. The Pens type defines a number of shared properties that return a new Pen of a given color.

Type	Meaning in Life
`Point` `PointF`	These structures represent an (*x*, *y*) coordinate mapping to an underlying integer or float, respectively.
`Rectangle` `RectangleF`	These structures represent a rectangular dimension (again mapping to an underlying integer or float).
`Size` `SizeF`	These structures represent a given height/width (again mapping to an underlying integer or float).
`StringFormat`	This type is used to encapsulate various features of textual layout (i.e., alignment, line spacing, etc.).
`Region`	This type describes the interior of a geometric image composed of rectangles and paths.

The System.Drawing Utility Types

Many of the drawing methods defined by the `System.Drawing.Graphics` object require you to specify the position or area in which you wish to render a given item. For example, the `DrawString()` method requires you to specify the location to render the text string on the `Control`-derived type. Given that `DrawString()` has been overloaded a number of times, this positional parameter may be specified using an (*x*, *y*) coordinate or the dimensions of a rectangle to draw within. Other GDI+ type methods may require you to specify the width and height of a given item, or the internal bounds of a geometric region.

To specify such information, the `System.Drawing` namespace defines the `Point`, `Rectangle`, `Region`, and `Size` types. Obviously, a `Point` represents an (*x*, *y*) coordinate. `Rectangle` types capture a pair of points representing the upper-left and bottom-right bounds of a rectangular region. `Size` types are similar to `Rectangles`, but this structure represents a particular dimension using a given length and width. Finally, `Regions` provide a way to represent and qualify nonrectangular surfaces.

The member variables used by the `Point`, `Rectangle`, and `Size` types are internally represented as an integer data type. If you need a finer level of granularity, you are free to make use of the corresponding `PointF`, `RectangleF`, and `SizeF` types, which (as you might guess) map to an underlying floating-point number. Regardless of the underlying data representation, each type has an identical set of members, including a number of overloaded operators.

The Point and PointF Types

The first utility types you should be aware of are `Point` and `PointF`, which define a number of helpful members, including

- `+`, `-`, `=`, `<>`: The `Point` type overloads various VB operators.
- `X`, `Y`: These members provide access to the underlying (*x*, *y*) values of the `Point`.
- `IsEmpty`: This member returns true if *x* and *y* are both set to 0.

To illustrate working with the GDI+ utility types, here is a Console Application (named DrawingUtilTypes) that makes use of the `System.Drawing.Point` type (be sure to set a reference to `System.Drawing.dll`, as this is not done automatically when building console projects).

```
Imports System.Drawing

Module Program
  Sub Main()
```

```
    Console.WriteLine("***** Working with Drawing utility types *****" & VbLf)
    UsePoint()
    Console.ReadLine()
  End Sub

  Sub UsePoint()
    Console.WriteLine("***** Exercise Point *****")

    ' Create and offset a point.
    Dim pt As New Point(100, 72)
    Console.WriteLine(pt)
    pt.Offset(20, 20)
    Console.WriteLine(pt)

    ' Overloaded Point operators.
    Dim pt2 As Point = pt
    If pt = pt2 Then
      Console.WriteLine("Points are the same")
    Else
      Console.WriteLine("Different points")
    End If

    ' Change pt2's X value.
    pt2.X = 4000

    ' Now show each point's value
    Console.WriteLine("First point: {0}", pt)
    Console.WriteLine("Second point: {0}", pt2)
  End Sub
End Module
```

The Rectangle and RectangleF Types

Rectangles, like Points, are useful in many applications (GUI based or otherwise). One of the more useful methods of the Rectangle type is Contains(). This method allows you to determine whether a given Point or Rectangle is within the current bounds of another object. Later in this chapter, you'll see how to make use of this method to perform hit testing of GDI+ images. Until then, here is a method making use of the Rectangle type (call this method from within Main() to test):

```
Sub UseRectangle()
  Console.WriteLine("***** Point in Rect? *****")
  Dim r1 As New Rectangle(0, 0, 100, 100)
  Dim pt3 As New Point(101, 101)
  If r1.Contains(pt3) Then
    Console.WriteLine("Point is within the rect!")
  Else
    Console.WriteLine("Point is not within the rect!")
  End If

  ' Now place point in rectangle's area.
  pt3.X = 50
  pt3.Y = 30
  If r1.Contains(pt3) Then
    Console.WriteLine("Point is within the rect!")
```

```
    Else
      Console.WriteLine("Point is not within the rect!")
    End If
  End Sub
```

The Region, Size, and SizeF Classes

The Region type represents the interior of a geometric shape. Given this last statement, it should make sense that the constructors of the Region class require you to send an instance of some existing geometric pattern. For example, assume you have created a 100×100-pixel rectangle. If you wish to gain access to the rectangle's interior region, you could write the following:

```
' Get the interior of this rectangle.
Dim r As New Rectangle(0, 0, 100, 100)
Dim rgn As New Region(r)
```

Once you have the interior dimensions of a given shape, you may manipulate it using various members such as the following:

- Complement(): Updates this Region to the portion of the specified graphics object that does not intersect with this Region
- Exclude(): Updates this Region to the portion of its interior that does not intersect with the specified graphics object
- GetBounds(): Returns a Rectangle that represents a rectangular region that bounds this Region
- Intersect(): Updates this Region to the intersection of itself with the specified graphics object
- Transform(): Transforms a Region by the specified Matrix object
- Union(): Updates this Region to the union of itself and the specified graphics object
- Translate(): Offsets the coordinates of this Region by a specified amount

The Size and SizeF types require little comment. These types each define Height and Width properties and a handful of overloaded operators. I'm sure you get the general idea behind these coordinate primitives; please consult the .NET Framework 3.5 SDK documentation if you require further details.

Source Code The DrawingUtilTypes project is included under the Chapter 28 subdirectory.

Understanding the Graphics Class

The System.Drawing.Graphics class is the gateway to GDI+ rendering functionality. This class not only represents the surface you wish to draw upon (such as a Form's surface, a control's surface, or even an allocated region of memory), but also defines dozens of members that allow you to render text, images (icons, bitmaps, etc.), and numerous geometric patterns. Table 28-3 gives a partial list of members.

Table 28-3. *Select Members of the* `Graphics` *Class*

Method	Meaning in Life
`FromHdc()`, `FromHwnd()`, `FromImage()`	These shared methods provide a way to obtain a valid `Graphics` object from a given image (e.g., icon, bitmap, etc.) or GUI widget.
`Clear()`	This method fills a `Graphics` object with a specified color, erasing the current drawing surface in the process.
`DrawArc()`, `DrawBezier()`, `DrawBeziers()`, `DrawCurve()`, `DrawEllipse()`, `DrawIcon()`, `DrawLine()`, `DrawLines()`, `DrawPie()`, `DrawPath()`, `DrawRectangle()`, `DrawRectangles()`, `DrawString()`	These methods are used to render a given image or geometric pattern. As you will see, `DrawXXX()` methods require the use of GDI+ `Pen` objects.
`FillEllipse()`, `FillPath()`, `FillPie()`, `FillPolygon()`, `FillRectangle()`	These methods are used to fill the interior of a given geometric shape. As you will see, `FillXXX()` methods require the use of GDI+ `Brush` objects.

As well as providing a number of rendering methods, the `Graphics` class defines additional members that allow you to configure the "state" of the `Graphics` object. By assigning values to the properties shown in Table 28-4, you are able to alter the current rendering operation.

Table 28-4. *Stateful Properties of the* `Graphics` *Class*

Property	Meaning in Life

`Clip`
`ClipBounds`
`VisibleClipBounds`
`IsClipEmpty`
`IsVisibleClipEmpty`
	These properties allow you to set the clipping options used with the current `Graphics` object.

`Transform`	This property allows you to transform "world coordinates" (more details on this later).

`PageUnit`
`PageScale`
`DpiX`
`DpiY`
	These properties allow you to configure the point of origin for your rendering operations, as well as the unit of measurement.

`SmoothingMode`
`PixelOffsetMode`
`TextRenderingHint`
	These properties allow you to configure the smoothness of geometric objects and text.

`CompositingMode`	This property determines whether drawing overwrites the background or is blended with the background.
`InterpolationMode`	This property specifies how data is interpolated between end points.

■ Note In addition to the standard `Graphics` class, the `System.Drawing` namespace provides a `BufferedGraphics` type that allows you to render graphics using a double-buffering system to minimize or eliminate the flickering that can occur during a rendering operation. Consult the .NET Framework 3.5 SDK documentation for full details.

Now, despite what you may be thinking, the Graphics class is not directly creatable via the New keyword, as there are no publicly defined constructors. How, then, do you obtain a valid Graphics object? Glad you asked!

Understanding Paint Sessions

The most common way to obtain a Graphics object is to interact with the Paint event. Recall from the previous chapter that the Control class defines a virtual method named OnPaint(). When you want a Form to render graphical data to its surface, you may override this method and extract a Graphics object from the incoming PaintEventArgs parameter. To illustrate, create a new Windows Forms project named BasicPaintForm, and update the Form-derived class as follows:

```
Public Class MainForm

  Protected Overrides Sub OnPaint(ByVal e As System.Windows.Forms.PaintEventArgs)
    ' If overriding OnPaint(), be sure to call base class implementation.
    MyBase.OnPaint(e)

    ' Obtain a Graphics object from the incoming
    ' PaintEventArgs.
    Dim g As Graphics = e.Graphics

   ' Render a textual message in a given font and color.
   g.DrawString("Hello GDI+", New Font("Times New Roman", 20), _
              Brushes.Green, 0, 0)
  End Sub

End Class
```

While overriding OnPaint() is permissible, it is more common to handle the Paint event using the associated PaintEventHandler delegate (in fact, this is the default behavior taken by Visual Studio 2008 when handling events with the Properties window). This delegate can point to any method taking a System.Object as the first parameter and a PaintEventArgs as the second. Assuming you have handled the Paint event, you are once again able to extract a Graphics object from the incoming PaintEventArgs. Here is the update:

```
Public Class MainForm

  Private Sub MainForm_Paint(ByVal sender As System.Object, _
    ByVal e As System.Windows.Forms.PaintEventArgs) Handles MyBase.Paint
    ' Obtain a Graphics object from the incoming
    ' PaintEventArgs.
    Dim g As Graphics = e.Graphics

   ' Render a textual message in a given font and color.
   g.DrawString("Hello GDI+", New Font("Times New Roman", 20), _
              Brushes.Green, 0, 0)
  End Sub

End Class
```

Regardless of how you respond to the Paint event, be aware that whenever a window becomes “dirty,” the Paint event will fire. As you may be aware, a window is considered “dirty” whenever it is resized, uncovered by another window (partially or completely), or minimized and then restored. In all these cases, the .NET platform ensures that when your Form needs to be redrawn, the Paint event handler (or overridden OnPaint() method) is called automatically.

Invalidating the Form's Client Area

During the flow of a GDI+ application, you may need to explicitly fire the `Paint` event, rather than waiting for the window to become "naturally dirty" due to user interaction. For example, you may be building a program that allows the user to select from a number of bitmap images using a custom dialog box. Once the dialog box is dismissed, you need to draw the newly selected image onto the Form's client area. Obviously, if you waited for the window to become "naturally dirty," the user would not see the change take place until the window was resized or uncovered by another window. To force a window to repaint itself programmatically, simply call the inherited `Invalidate()` method:

```
Public Class MainForm

  Private Sub MainForm_Paint(ByVal sender As System.Object, _
    ByVal e As System.Windows.Forms.PaintEventArgs) Handles MyBase.Paint
    Dim g As Graphics = e.Graphics
    ' Render a bitmap here...
  End Sub

  Private Sub RenderMyBitmap()
    ' Assume we have code here to load
    ' a bitmap from disk...
    Invalidate()  ' Fires Paint event!
  End Sub

End Class
```

The `Invalidate()` method has been overloaded a number of times to allow you to specify a specific rectangular region to repaint, rather than repainting the entire client area (which is the default). If you wish to only update the extreme upper-left rectangle of the client area, you could write the following:

```
' Repaint a given rectangular area of the Form.
Private Sub UpdateUpperArea()
  Dim myRect As New Rectangle(0, 0, 75, 150)
  Invalidate(myRect)
End Sub
```

Obtaining a Graphics Object Outside of a Paint Event Handler

In some cases, you may need to access a `Graphics` object *outside* the scope of a `Paint` event handler. For example, assume you wish to draw a small circle at the *(x, y)* position where the mouse has been clicked. To obtain a valid `Graphics` object from within the scope of a `MouseDown` event handler, one approach is to call the shared `Graphics.FromHwnd()` method. As you may know, an HWND is a data structure that represents a handle to a given window. Under the .NET platform, the inherited `Handle` property extracts the underlying `HWND`, which can be used as a parameter to `Graphics.FromHwnd()`:

```
Private Sub MainForm_MouseDown(ByVal sender As System.Object, _
  ByVal e As System.Windows.Forms.MouseEventArgs) Handles MyBase.MouseDown
  ' Grab a Graphics object via Hwnd.
  Dim g As Graphics = Graphics.FromHwnd(Me.Handle)

  ' Now draw a 10*10 circle at mouse click.
  g.FillEllipse(Brushes.Firebrick, e.X, e.Y, 10, 10)
```

```
  ' Dispose of all Graphics objects you create directly.
  g.Dispose()
End Sub
```

While this logic renders a circle outside an OnPaint() event handler, it is very important to understand that when the Form is invalidated (and thus redrawn), each of the circles is erased! This should make sense, given that this rendering happens only within the context of a MouseDown event. A far better approach is to have the MouseDown event handler create a new Point object, which is then added to an internal collection (such as a generic List(Of T)), followed by a call to Invalidate(). At this point, the Paint event handler can simply iterate over the collection and draw each Point:

```
Public Class MainForm
  ' Used to hold all the Points.
  Private myPts As New List(Of Point)()
...
  Private Sub MainForm_Paint(ByVal sender As System.Object, _
    ByVal e As System.Windows.Forms.PaintEventArgs) Handles MyBase.Paint
    Dim g As Graphics = e.Graphics
    g.DrawString("Hello GDI+", New Font("Times New Roman", 20), _
                 Brushes.Green, 0, 0)

    ' Now render all the Points.
    For Each p As Point In myPts
      g.FillEllipse(Brushes.DarkOrange, p.X, p.Y, 10, 10)
    Next
  End Sub

  Private Sub MainForm_MouseDown(ByVal sender As System.Object, _
  ByVal e As System.Windows.Forms.MouseEventArgs) Handles MyBase.MouseDown
    ' Add new point to list.
    myPts.Add(New Point(e.X, e.Y))
    Invalidate()
  End Sub
End Class
```

Using this approach, the rendered circles are always present and accounted for, as the graphical rendering has been handled within the Paint event. Figure 28-1 shows a test run of this initial GDI+ application.

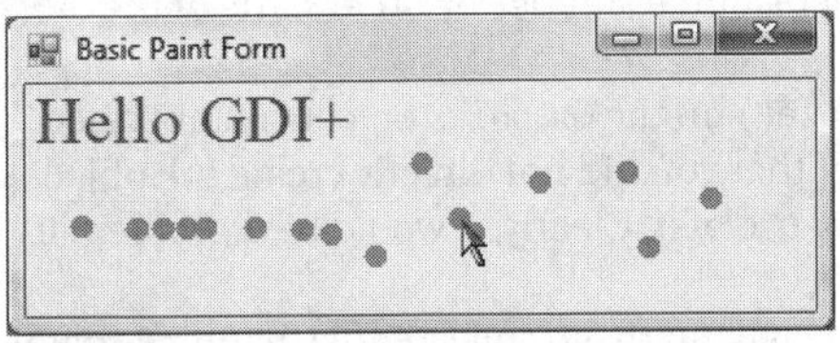

Figure 28-1. *A simple painting application*

Source Code The BasicPaintForm project is included under the Chapter 28 subdirectory.

Regarding the Disposal of a Graphics Object

If you were reading closely over the last several pages, you may have noticed that *some* of the sample code directly called the `Dispose()` method of the `Graphics` object, while other sample code did not. Given that a `Graphics` type is manipulating various underlying unmanaged resources, it should make sense that it would be advantageous to release said resources via `Dispose()` as soon as possible (rather than via the garbage collector in the finalization process). The same can be said for any type that supports the `IDisposable` interface. When working with GDI+ `Graphics` objects, remember the following rules of thumb:

- If you directly create a `Graphics` object, dispose of it when you are finished.
- If you reference an existing `Graphics` object, do *not* dispose of it.

To clarify, consider the following `Paint` event handler:

```
Private Sub MainForm_Paint(ByVal sender As System.Object, _
  ByVal e As System.Windows.Forms.PaintEventArgs) Handles MyBase.Paint
  ' Load a local *.jpg file.
  Dim myImageFile As Image = Image.FromFile("landscape.jpg")

  ' Create new Graphics object based on the image.
  Dim imgGraphics As Graphics = Graphics.FromImage(myImageFile)

  ' Render new data onto the image.
  imgGraphics.FillEllipse(Brushes.DarkOrange, 50, 50, 150, 150)

  ' Draw image to Form.
  Dim g As Graphics = e.Graphics
  g.DrawImage(myImageFile, New Point(0, 0))

  ' Release Graphics object we created.
  imgGraphics.Dispose()
End Sub
```

Now at this point in the chapter, don't become concerned if some of this GDI+ logic looks a bit foreign. However, notice that you are obtaining a `Graphics` object from a `*.jpg` file loaded from the local application directory (via the shared `Graphics.FromImage()` method). Because you have explicitly created this `Graphics` object, best practice states that you should `Dispose()` of the object when you have finished making use of it, to free up the internal resources for use by other parts of the system.

However, notice that you did not explicitly call `Dispose()` on the `Graphics` object you obtained from the incoming `PaintEventArgs`. This is due to the fact that you did not directly create the object and cannot ensure other parts of the program are making use of it. Clearly, it would be a problem if you released a `Graphics` object used elsewhere!

On a related note, recall from our examination of the .NET garbage collector in Chapter 8 that if you do forget to call `Dispose()` on a method implementing `IDisposable`, the internal resources will eventually be freed when the object is garbage collected at a later time. In this light, the manual disposal of the `imgGraphics` object is not technically necessary.

■ **Note** Although explicitly disposing of GDI+ objects you directly created is smart programming, in order to keep the code examples in this chapter crisp, I will not manually dispose of each GDI+ type and allow the garbage collector to reclaim the underlying memory.

The GDI+ Coordinate Systems

Our next task is to examine the underlying coordinate system. GDI+ defines three distinct coordinate systems, which are used by the runtime to determine the location and size of the content to be rendered. First we have what are known as *world coordinates*. World coordinates represent an abstraction of the size of a given GDI+ type, irrespective of the unit of measurement. For example, if you draw a rectangle using the dimensions (0, 0, 100, 100), you have specified a rectangle 100×100 "things" in size. As you may guess, the default "thing" is a pixel; however, it can be configured to be another unit of measure (inch, centimeter, etc.).

Next, we have *page coordinates*. Page coordinates represent an offset applied to the original world coordinates. This is helpful in that you are not the one in charge of manually applying offsets in your code (should you need them). For example, if you have a Form that needs to maintain a 100×100-pixel border, you can specify a (100*100) page coordinate to allow all rendering to begin at point (100*100). In your code base, however, you are able to specify simple world coordinates (thereby avoiding the need to manually calculate the offset).

Finally, we have *device coordinates*. Device coordinates represent the result of applying page coordinates to the original world coordinates. This coordinate system is used to determine exactly where the GDI+ type will be rendered. When you are programming with GDI+, you will typically think in terms of world coordinates, which are the baselines used to determine the size and location of a GDI+ type. To render in world coordinates requires no special coding actions—simply pass in the dimensions for the current rendering operation:

```
Private Sub MainForm_Paint(ByVal sender As System.Object, _
  ByVal e As System.Windows.Forms.PaintEventArgs) _
  Handles MyBase.Paint
  Dim g As Graphics = e.Graphics

  ' Render a rectangle in world coordinates.
  g.DrawRectangle(Pens.Black, 10, 10, 100, 100)
End Sub
```

Under the hood, your world coordinates are automatically mapped in terms of page coordinates, which are then mapped into device coordinates. In many cases, you will never directly make use of page or device coordinates unless you wish to apply some sort of graphical transformation. Given that the previous code did not specify any transformational logic, the world, page, and device coordinates are identical.

If you do wish to apply various transformations before rendering your GDI+ logic, you will make use of various members of the `Graphics` type (such as the `TranslateTransform()` method) to specify various "page coordinates" to your existing world coordinate system before the rendering operation. The result is the set of device coordinates that will be used to render the GDI+ type to the target device:

```
Private Sub MainForm_Paint(ByVal sender As System.Object, _
  ByVal e As System.Windows.Forms.PaintEventArgs) _
  Handles MyBase.Paint
  Dim g As Graphics = e.Graphics
  ' Specify page coordinate offsets (10 to the right, 10 pixels down).
  g.TranslateTransform(10, 10)
  g.DrawRectangle(Pens.Black, 10, 10, 100, 100)
End Sub
```

In this case, the rectangle is actually rendered with a top-left point of (20, 20), given that the world coordinates have been offset by the call to `TranslateTransform()`.

The Default Unit of Measure

Under GDI+, the default unit of measure is pixel based. The origin begins in the upper-left corner with the *x*-axis increasing to the right and the *y*-axis increasing downward (see Figure 28-2).

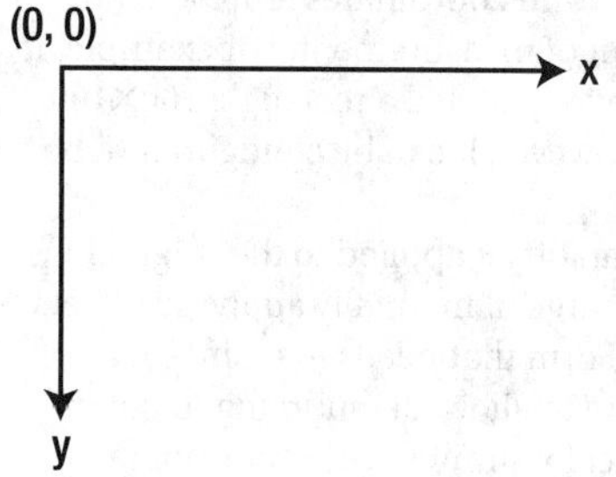

Figure 28-2. *The default coordinate system of GDI+*

Thus, if you render a Rectangle using a 5-pixel thick red pen as follows:

```
Private Sub MainForm_Paint(ByVal sender As System.Object, _
  ByVal e As System.Windows.Forms.PaintEventArgs) _
  Handles MyBase.Paint
  Dim g As Graphics = e.Graphics

  ' Set up world coordinates using the default unit of measure.
  g.DrawRectangle(New Pen(Color.Red, 5), 0, 0, 100, 100)
End Sub
```

you would see a square rendered starting on the top-left client edge of the Form, as shown in Figure 28-3.

Figure 28-3. *Rendering via pixel units*

Specifying an Alternative Unit of Measure

If you do not wish to render images using a pixel-based unit of measure, you are able to change this default setting by setting the PageUnit property of the Graphics object to alter the units used by the page coordinate system. The `PageUnit` property can be assigned any member of the `GraphicsUnit` enumeration:

```
Enum GraphicsUnit
  ' Specifies world coordinates.
  World
  ' Pixels for video displays and 1/100 inch for printers.
  Display
  ' Specifies a pixel.
  Pixel
  ' Specifies a printer's point (1/72 inch).
  Point
  ' Specifies an inch.
  Inch
  ' Specifies a document unit (1/300 inch).
  Document
  ' Specifies a millimeter.
  Millimeter
End Sub
```

To illustrate how to change the underlying `GraphicsUnit`, update the previous rendering code as follows:

```
Private Sub MainForm_Paint(ByVal sender As System.Object, _
  ByVal e As System.Windows.Forms.PaintEventArgs) _
  Handles MyBase.Paint

  ' Draw a rectangle in inches...not pixels.
  Dim g As Graphics = e.Graphics
  g.PageUnit = GraphicsUnit.Inch
  ' Set up world coordinates using the default unit of measure.
  g.DrawRectangle(New Pen(Color.Red, 5), 0, 0, 100, 100)
End Sub
```

You would find a *radically* different rectangle, as shown in Figure 28-4.

Figure 28-4. *Rendering using inch units*

The reason that 95 percent (or so) of the Form's client area is now filled with red is because you have configured a Pen with a 5-*inch* nib! The rectangle itself is 100×100 *inches* in size. In fact, the small gray box you see located in the lower-right corner is the upper-left interior of the rectangle.

Specifying an Alternative Point of Origin

Recall that when you make use of the default coordinate and measurement system, point (0, 0) is at the extreme upper left of the surface area. While this is often what you desire, what if you wish to alter the location where rendering begins? For example, let's assume that your application always needs to reserve a 100-pixel boundary around the Form's client area (for whatever reason). You need to ensure that all GDI+ operations take place somewhere within this internal region.

One approach you could take is to offset all your rendering code manually. This, of course, would be bothersome, as you would need to constantly apply some offset value to each and every rendering operation. It would be far better (and simpler) if you could set a property that says in effect, "Although my code might say render a rectangle with a point of origin at (0, 0), make sure to begin at point (100, 100)." This would simplify your life a great deal, as you could continue to specify your plotting points without modification.

In GDI+, you can adjust the point of origin by setting the transformation value using the TranslateTransform() method of the Graphics class, which allows you to specify a page coordinate system that will be applied to your original world coordinate specifications, for example:

```
Private Sub MainForm_Paint(ByVal sender As System.Object, _
  ByVal e As System.Windows.Forms.PaintEventArgs) _
  Handles MyBase.Paint

  Dim g As Graphics = e.Graphics
  ' Set page coordinate to (100, 100).
  g.TranslateTransform(100, 100)

  ' World origin is still (0, 0, 100, 100),
  ' however, device origin is now (100, 100, 200, 200).
  g.DrawRectangle(New Pen(Color.Red, 5), 0, 0, 100, 100)
End Sub
```

Here, you have set the world coordinate values (0, 0, 100, 100). However, the page coordinate values have specified an offset of (100, 100). Given this, the device coordinates map to (100, 100, 200, 200). Thus, although the call to DrawRectangle() looks as if you are rendering a rectangle on the upper left of the Form, the rendering shown in Figure 28-5 has taken place.

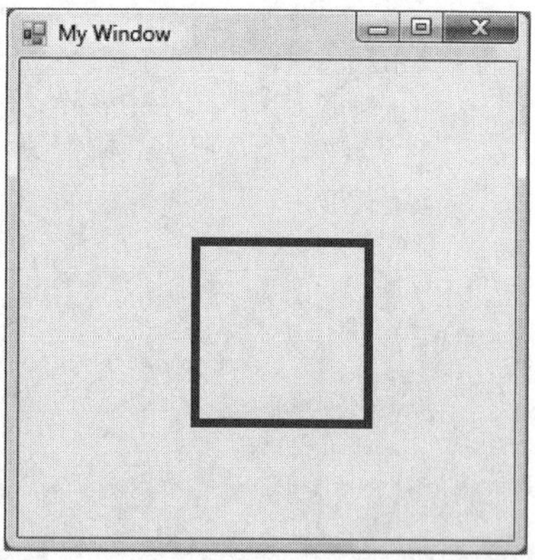

Figure 28-5. *The result of applying page offsets*

To help you experiment with some of the ways to alter the GDI+ coordinate system, this book's downloadable source code (visit the Source Code/Download section of the Apress website at `www.apress.com`) provides a sample application named CoorSystem. Using two menu items, you are able to alter the point of origin as well as the unit of measurement for a graphical rendering (see Figure 28-6).

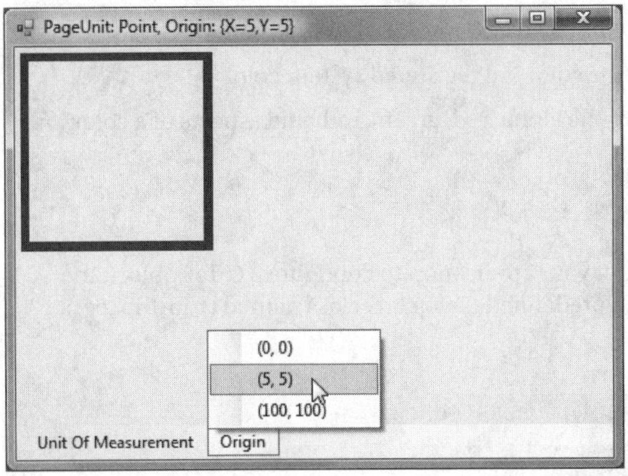

Figure 28-6. *Altering coordinate and measurement modes*

Now that you have a better understanding of the underlying transformations used to determine where to render a given GDI+ type onto a target device, the next order of business is to examine details of color manipulation.

Source Code The CoorSystem project is included under the Chapter 28 subdirectory.

Defining a Color Value

Many of the rendering methods defined by the `Graphics` class require you to specify the color that should be used during the drawing process. The `System.Drawing.Color` structure represents an alpha-red-green-blue (ARGB) color constant. Most of the `Color` type's functionality comes by way of a number of shared read-only properties, which return a specific `Color` type:

```
' One of many predefined colors...
Dim c As Color = Color.PapayaWhip
```

If the default color values do not fit the bill, you are also able to create a new `Color` object and specify the `A`, `R`, `G`, and `B` values using the `FromArgb()` method:

```
' Specify ARGB manually.
Dim myColor As Color = Color.FromArgb(0, 255, 128, 64)
```

As well, using the shared `FromName()` method, you are able to generate a `Color` object given a string value. The characters in the string parameter must match one of the members in the `KnownColor` enumeration (which includes values for various Windows color elements such as `KnownColor.WindowFrame` and `KnownColor.WindowText`):

```
' Get Color from a known name.
Dim myColor As Color = Color.FromName("Red")
```

Regardless of the method you use, the `Color` object can be interacted with using a variety of members:

- `GetBrightness()`: Returns the brightness of the color based on hue-saturation-brightness (HSB) measurements
- `GetSaturation()`: Returns the saturation of the color based on HSB measurements
- `GetHue()`: Returns the hue of the color object based on HSB measurements
- `IsSystemColor`: Determines whether the color is a registered system color
- `A`, `R`, `G`, `B`: Returns the value assigned to the alpha, red, green, and blue aspects of a color

The ColorDialog Class

If you wish to include a way for the end user of your application to configure a `Color` object, the `System.Windows.Forms` namespace provides a predefined dialog box class named `ColorDialog`, as shown in Figure 28-7.

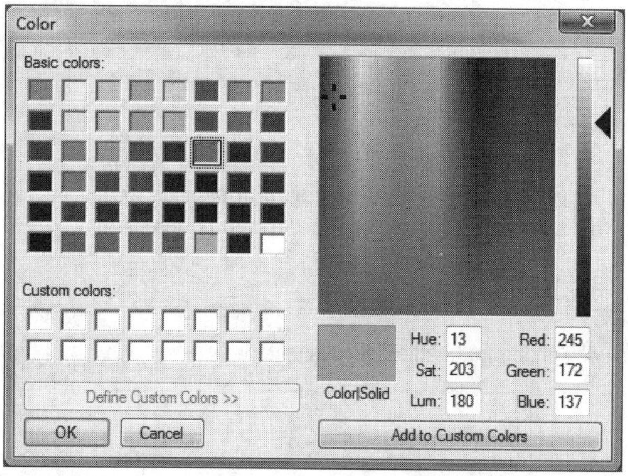

Figure 28-7. *The Windows Forms Color dialog box*

Working with this dialog box is quite simple. Using a valid instance of the `ColorDialog` type, call `ShowDialog()` to display the dialog box modally. Once the user has closed the dialog box, you can extract the corresponding `Color` object using the `ColorDialog.Color` property.

Assume you wish to allow the user to configure the background color of the Form's client area using the `ColorDialog`. To keep things simple, you will display the `ColorDialog` when the user clicks anywhere on the client area:

```
Public Class MainForm
  Private colorDlg As ColorDialog
  Private currColor As Color = Color.DimGray

  Sub New()
    ' This call is required by the Windows Forms designer.
    InitializeComponent()

    ' Add any initialization after the InitializeComponent() call.
    CenterToScreen()
```

```
    colorDlg = New ColorDialog()
    Text = "Click on me to change the color"
  End Sub

  Private Sub MainForm_MouseDown(ByVal sender As System.Object, _
  ByVal e As System.Windows.Forms.MouseEventArgs) _
  Handles MyBase.MouseDown
    If colorDlg.ShowDialog() <> Windows.Forms.DialogResult.Cancel Then
      currColor = colorDlg.Color
      Me.BackColor = currColor
      ' Show current color.
      Dim strARGB As String = colorDlg.Color.ToString()
      MessageBox.Show(strARGB, "Color is:")
    End If
  End Sub
End Class
```

Source Code The ColorDlg application is included under the Chapter 28 subdirectory.

Manipulating Fonts

Next, let's examine how to programmatically manipulate fonts. The `System.Drawing.Font` type represents a given font installed on the user's machine. Font types can be created using any number of overloaded constructors. Here are a few examples:

```
' Create a Font of a given type name and size.
Dim f As New Font("Times New Roman", 12)

' Create a Font with a given name, size, and style set.
Dim f2 As New Font("WingDings", 50, FontStyle.Bold Or FontStyle.Underline)
```

Here, `f2` has been created by OR-ing together a set of values from the `FontStyle` enumeration:

```
Enum FontStyle
  Regular
  Bold
  Italic
  Underline
  Strikeout
End Enum
```

Once you have configured the look and feel of your `Font` object, the next task is to pass it as a parameter to the `Graphics.DrawString()` method. Although `DrawString()` has also been overloaded a number of times, each variation typically requires the same basic information: the text to draw, the font to draw it in, a brush used for rendering, and a location in which to place it.

```
Private Sub MainForm_Paint(ByVal sender As System.Object, _
  ByVal e As System.Windows.Forms.PaintEventArgs) _
  Handles MyBase.Paint
  Dim g As Graphics = e.Graphics
```

```
  ' Specify (String, Font, Brush, Point) as args.
  g.DrawString("My string", New Font("WingDings", 25), _
    Brushes.Black, New Point(0, 0))

  ' Specify (String, Font, Brush, Integer, Integer)
  g.DrawString("Another string", New Font("Times New Roman", 16), _
    Brushes.Red, 40, 40)
End Sub
```

Working with Font Families

The System.Drawing namespace also defines the FontFamily type, which abstracts a group of typefaces having a similar basic design but with certain style variations. A family of fonts, such as Verdana, can include several fonts that differ in style and size. For example, Verdana 12-point bold and Verdana 24-point italic are different fonts within the Verdana font family.

The constructor of the FontFamily type takes a string representing the name of the font family you are attempting to capture. Once you create the "generic family," you are then able to create a more specific Font object:

```
Private Sub MainForm_Paint(ByVal sender As System.Object, _
  ByVal e As System.Windows.Forms.PaintEventArgs) _
  Handles MyBase.Paint
  Dim g As Graphics = e.Graphics

  ' Make a family of fonts.
  Dim myFamily As New FontFamily("Verdana")

  ' Pass family into ctor of Font.
  Dim myFont As New Font(myFamily, 12)
  g.DrawString("Hello!", myFont, Brushes.Blue, 10, 10)
End Sub
```

Of greater interest is the ability to gather statistics regarding a given family of fonts. For example, say you are building a text-processing application and wish to determine the average width of a character in a particular FontFamily. What if you wish to know the ascending and descending values for a given character? To answer such questions, the FontFamily type defines the key members shown in Table 28-5.

Table 28-5. *Members of the* FontFamily *Type*

Member	Meaning in Life
GetCellAscent()	Returns the ascender metric for the members in this family
GetCellDescent()	Returns the descender metric for members in this family
GetLineSpacing()	Returns the distance between two consecutive lines of text for this FontFamily with the specified FontStyle
GetName()	Returns the name of this FontFamily in the specified language
IsStyleAvailable()	Indicates whether the specified FontStyle is available

To illustrate, here is a Paint event handler that prints a number of characteristics of the Verdana font family:

```
Public Class MainForm

  Private Sub MainForm_Paint(ByVal sender As System.Object, _
  ByVal e As System.Windows.Forms.PaintEventArgs) _
  Handles MyBase.Paint
    Dim g As Graphics = e.Graphics
    Dim myFamily As New FontFamily("Verdana")
    Dim myFont As New Font(myFamily, 12)
    Dim y As Integer = 0
    Dim fontHeight As Integer = myFont.Height

    ' Show units of measurement for FontFamily members.
    Me.Text = "Measurements are in GraphicsUnit." & myFont.Unit.ToString()
    g.DrawString("The Verdana family.", myFont, Brushes.Blue, 10, y)
    y += 20
    ' Print our family ties...
    g.DrawString("Ascent for bold Verdana: " _
      & myFamily.GetCellAscent(FontStyle.Bold), _
      myFont, Brushes.Black, 10, y + fontHeight)
    y += 20
    g.DrawString("Descent for bold Verdana: " _
      & myFamily.GetCellDescent(FontStyle.Bold), _
      myFont, Brushes.Black, 10, y + fontHeight)
    y += 20
    g.DrawString("Line spacing for bold Verdana: " _
      & myFamily.GetLineSpacing(FontStyle.Bold), _
      myFont, Brushes.Black, 10, y + fontHeight)
    y += 20
    g.DrawString("Height for bold Verdana: " & _
      myFamily.GetEmHeight(FontStyle.Bold), _
      myFont, Brushes.Black, 10, y + fontHeight)
  End Sub

End Class
```

Figure 28-8 shows the result.

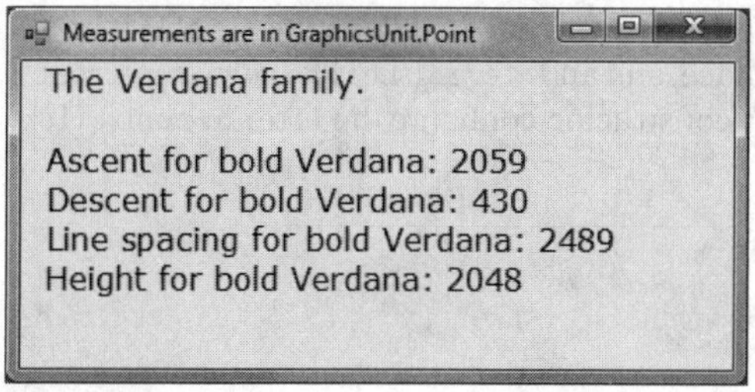

Figure 28-8. *Gathering statistics of the Verdana font family*

Note that these members of the `FontFamily` type return values using `GraphicsUnit.Point` (not `Pixel`) as the unit of measure, which corresponds to 1/72 inch. You are free to transform these values to other units of measure as you see fit.

Source Code The FontFamilyApp application is included under the Chapter 28 subdirectory.

Working with Font Faces and Font Sizes

Next, you'll build a more complex application that allows the user to manipulate a `Font` object maintained by a Form. The application will allow the user to select the current font face from a predefined set using the Configure ➤ Font Face menu selection. You'll also allow the user to indirectly control the size of the `Font` object using a Windows Forms `Timer` object. If the user activates the `Timer` using the Configure ➤ Swell? menu item, the size of the `Font` object increases at a regular interval (to a maximum upper limit). In this way, the text appears to swell and thus provides an animation of "breathing" text. Finally, you'll use a final menu item under the Configure menu named List Installed Fonts, which will be used to list all fonts installed on the end user's machine. Figure 28-9 shows the menu UI logic (notice that this Form maintains a `Timer` member variable that has been named `swellTimer`).

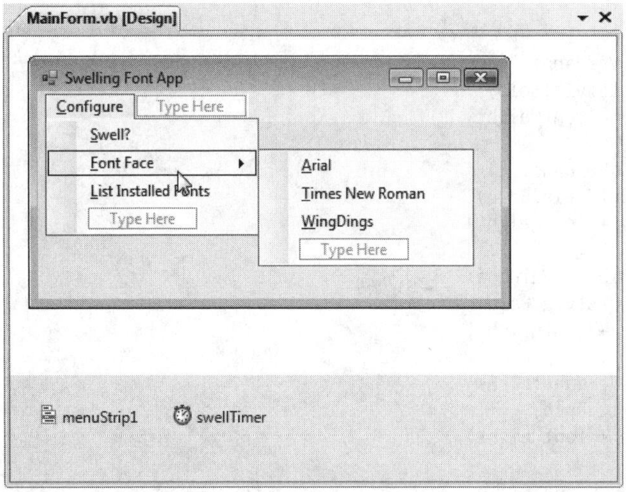

Figure 28-9. *Menu layout (and* `Timer`*) of the FontApp project*

To begin implementing the application, create a new Windows Forms Application (named SwellingFontApp) and update the initial Form with a `Timer` member variable (named `swellTimer`), a `String` (`strFontFace`) to represent the current font face, and an `Integer` (`swellValue`) to represent the amount to adjust the font size. Within the Form's constructor, configure the `Timer` to emit a `Tick` event every 100 milliseconds:

```
Public Class MainForm
  Private swellValue As Integer
  Private strFontFace As String = "WingDings"

  Sub New()
    ' This call is required by the Windows Forms designer.
    InitializeComponent()

    ' Add any initialization after the InitializeComponent() call.
    BackColor = Color.Honeydew
    CenterToScreen()
```

```
    ' Configure the Timer.
    swellTimer.Enabled = True
    swellTimer.Interval = 100
  End Sub

End Class
```

Now, handle the Tick event, and within the generated handler, increase the value of the swellValue data member by 5. Recall that the swellValue integer will be added to the current font size to provide a simple animation (assume swellValue has a maximum upper limit of 50). To help reduce the flicker that can occur when redrawing the entire client area, notice how the call to Invalidate() is only refreshing the upper rectangular area of the Form:

```
Private Sub swellTimer_Tick(ByVal sender As System.Object, _
  ByVal e As System.EventArgs) Handles swellTimer.Tick
  ' Increase current swellValue by 5.
  swellValue += 5
  ' If this value is greater than or equal to 50, reset to zero.
  If swellValue >= 50 Then
    swellValue = 0
  End If
  ' Just invalidate the "minimal dirty rectangle" to help reduce flicker.
  Invalidate(New Rectangle(0, 0, ClientRectangle.Width, 100))
End Sub
```

Now that the upper 100 pixels of your client area are refreshed with each tick of the Timer, you had better have something to render! In the Form's Paint handler, create a Font object based on the user-defined font face (as selected from the appropriate menu item) and current swellValue (as dictated by the Timer). Once you have your Font object fully configured, render a message into the center of the dirty rectangle:

```
Private Sub MainForm_Paint(ByVal sender As System.Object, _
 ByVal e As System.Windows.Forms.PaintEventArgs) _
 Handles MyBase.Paint
  Dim g As Graphics = e.Graphics
  Dim theFont As New Font(strFontFace, 12 + swellValue)
  Dim message As String = "Hello GDI+"

  ' Display message.
  Dim windowCenter As Single = CSng(Me.DisplayRectangle.Width / 2)
  Dim stringSize As SizeF = e.Graphics.MeasureString(message, theFont)
  Dim startPos As Single = windowCenter - (stringSize.Width / 2)
  g.DrawString(message, theFont, Brushes.Blue, startPos, 10)
End Sub
```

As you would guess, if a user selects a specific font face, the Clicked handler for each menu selection is in charge of updating the strFontFace string variable and invalidating the client area, for example:

```
Private Sub arialToolStripMenuItem_Click(ByVal sender As System.Object, _
  ByVal e As System.EventArgs) Handles arialToolStripMenuItem.Click
  strFontFace = "Arial"
  Invalidate()
End Sub
```

The Click menu handler for the Swell menu item will be used to allow the user to stop or start the swelling of the text (i.e., enable or disable the animation). To do so, toggle the Enabled property of the Timer as follows:

```
Private Sub swellToolStripMenuItem_Click(ByVal sender As System.Object, _
  ByVal e As System.EventArgs) Handles swellToolStripMenuItem.Click
  swellTimer.Enabled = Not swellTimer.Enabled
End Sub
```

Enumerating Installed Fonts

Next, let's expand this program to display the set of installed fonts on the target machine using types within `System.Drawing.Text`. This namespace contains a handful of types that can be used to discover and manipulate the set of fonts installed on the target machine. For our purposes, we are only concerned with the `InstalledFontCollection` class.

When the user selects the Configure ➤ List Installed Fonts menu item, the corresponding `Clicked` handler creates an instance of the `InstalledFontCollection` class. This class maintains an array named `FontFamily`, which represents the set of all fonts on the target machine and may be obtained using the `InstalledFontCollection.Families` property. Using the `FontFamily.Name` property, you are able to extract the font face (e.g., Times New Roman, Arial, etc.) for each font.

Add a private `String` data member to your Form named `installedFonts` to hold each font face. The logic in the List Installed Fonts menu handler creates an instance of the `InstalledFontCollection` type, reads the name of each string, and adds the new font face to the private `installedFonts` data member:

```
' Need this!
Imports System.Drawing.Text

Class MainForm
' Holds the list of fonts.
  Private installedFonts As String

  ' Menu handler to get the list of installed fonts.
  Private Sub listInstalledFontsToolStripMenuItem_Click( _
    ByVal sender As System.Object, _
    ByVal e As System.EventArgs) Handles listInstalledFontsToolStripMenuItem.Click
    Dim fonts As New InstalledFontCollection()
    For i As Integer = 0 To fonts.Families.Length - 1
      installedFonts &= fonts.Families(i).Name & " "
    Next

    ' This time, we need to invalidate the entire client area,
    ' as we will paint the installedFonts string on the lower half
    ' of the client rectangle.
    Invalidate()
  End Sub
...
End Class
```

The final task is to render the `installedFonts` string to the client area, directly below the screen real estate that is used for your swelling text:

```
Private Sub MainForm_Paint(ByVal sender As System.Object, _
  ByVal e As System.Windows.Forms.PaintEventArgs) Handles MyBase.Paint
  Dim g As Graphics = e.Graphics
  Dim theFont As New Font(strFontFace, 12 + swellValue)
  Dim message As String = "Hello GDI+"
```

```
    ' Display message in the center of the window!
    Dim windowCenter As Single = CSng(Me.DisplayRectangle.Width / 2)
    Dim stringSize As SizeF = e.Graphics.MeasureString(message, theFont)
    Dim startPos As Single = windowCenter - (stringSize.Width / 2)
    g.DrawString(message, theFont, Brushes.Blue, startPos, 10)

    ' Show installed fonts in the rectangle below the swell area.
    Dim myRect As _
      New Rectangle(0, 100, ClientRectangle.Width, ClientRectangle.Height)

    ' Paint this area of the Form black.
    g.FillRectangle(New SolidBrush(Color.Black), myRect)
    g.DrawString(installedFonts, New Font("Arial", 12), Brushes.White, myRect)
  End Sub
```

Recall that the size of the "dirty rectangle" has been mapped to the upper 100 pixels of the client rectangle. Because your `Tick` handler invalidates only a portion of the Form, the remaining area is not redrawn when the `Tick` event has been sent (to help optimize the rendering of the client area).

As a final touch to ensure proper redrawing, let's handle the Form's `Resize` event to ensure that if the user resizes the Form, the entire client area is redrawn correctly:

```
Private Sub MainForm_Resize(ByVal sender As System.Object, _
  ByVal e As System.EventArgs) Handles MyBase.Resize
  Invalidate()
End Sub
```

Figure 28-10 shows the result (with the text rendered in Wingdings!).

Figure 28-10. *The FontApp application in action*

Source Code The SwellingFontApp project is included under the Chapter 28 subdirectory.

The FontDialog Class

As you might assume, there is an existing font dialog box (`FontDialog`), as shown in Figure 28-11.

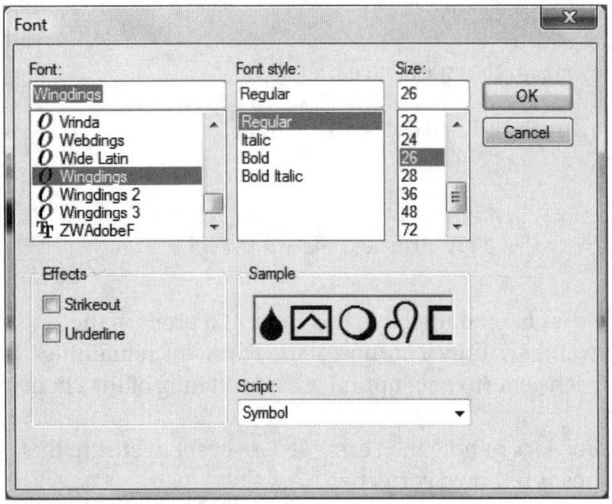

Figure 28-11. *The Windows Forms Font dialog box*

Like the `ColorDialog` type examined earlier in this chapter, when you wish to work with the `FontDialog`, simply call the `ShowDialog()` method. Using the `Font` property, you may extract the characteristics of the current selection for use in the application. To illustrate, here is a Form that mimics the logic of the previous `ColorDlg` project. When the user clicks anywhere on the Form, the Font dialog box displays and renders a message with the current selection:

```
Public Class MainForm
  Private fontDlg As New FontDialog()
  Private currFont As New Font("Times New Roman", 12)

  Private Sub MainForm_MouseDown(ByVal sender As System.Object, _
    ByVal e As System.Windows.Forms.MouseEventArgs) Handles MyBase.MouseDown
    If fontDlg.ShowDialog() <> Windows.Forms.DialogResult.Cancel Then
      currFont = fontDlg.Font
      Me.Text = String.Format("Selected Font: {0} ", currFont)
      Invalidate()
    End If
  End Sub

  Private Sub MainForm_Paint(ByVal sender As System.Object, _
  ByVal e As System.Windows.Forms.PaintEventArgs) Handles MyBase.Paint
    Dim g As Graphics = e.Graphics
    g.DrawString("Testing...", currFont, Brushes.Black, 0, 0)
  End Sub
End Class
```

Source Code The FontDlgForm application is included under the Chapter 28 subdirectory.

Survey of the System.Drawing.Drawing2D Namespace

Now that you have manipulated Font types, the next task is to examine how to manipulate Pen and Brush objects to render geometric patterns. While you could do so making use of nothing more than Brushes and Pens helper types to obtain preconfigured types in a solid color, you should be aware that many of the more "exotic" pens and brushes are found within the System.Drawing.Drawing2D namespace.

This additional GDI+ namespace provides a number of classes that allow you to modify the end cap (triangle, diamond, etc.) used for a given pen, build textured brushes, and work with vector graphic manipulations. Some core types to be aware of (grouped by related functionality) are shown in Table 28-6.

Table 28-6. *Classes of* System.Drawing.Drawing2D

Classes	Meaning in Life
AdjustableArrowCap CustomLineCap	Pen caps are used to paint the beginning and end points of a given line. These types represent an adjustable arrow-shaped and user-defined cap.
Blend ColorBlend	These classes are used to define a blend pattern (and colors) used in conjunction with a LinearGradientBrush.
GraphicsPath GraphicsPathIterator PathData	A GraphicsPath object represents a series of lines and curves. This class allows you to insert just about any type of geometrical pattern (arcs, rectangles, lines, strings, polygons, etc.) into the path. PathData holds the graphical data that makes up a path.
HatchBrush LinearGradientBrush PathGradientBrush	These are exotic brush types.

Also be aware that the System.Drawing.Drawing2D namespace defines another set of enumerations (DashStyle, FillMode, HatchStyle, LineCap, and so forth) that are used in conjunction with these core types.

Working with Pens

GDI+ Pen types are used to draw lines between two end points. However, a Pen in and of itself is of little value. When you need to render a geometric shape onto a Control-derived type, you send a valid Pen type to any number of render methods defined by the Graphics class. In general, the DrawXXX() methods are used to render some set of lines to a graphics surface and are typically used with Pen objects.

The Pen type defines a small set of constructors that allow you to determine the initial color and width of the pen nib. Most of a Pen's functionality comes by way of its supported properties. Table 28-7 gives a partial list.

Table 28-7. *Pen Properties*

Property	Meaning in Life
Brush	Determines the Brush used by this Pen.
Color	Determines the Color type used by this Pen.

Continued

Table 28-7. *Continued*

Property	Meaning in Life
`CustomStartCap` `CustomEndCap`	Get or set a custom cap style to use at the beginning or end of lines drawn with this `Pen`. *Cap style* is simply the term used to describe how the initial and final stroke of the `Pen` should look and feel. These properties allow you to build custom caps for your `Pen` types.
`DashCap`	Gets or sets the cap style used at the beginning or end of dashed lines drawn with this `Pen`.
`DashPattern`	Gets or sets an array of custom dashes and spaces. The dashes are made up of line segments.
`DashStyle`	Gets or sets the style used for dashed lines drawn with this `Pen`.
`StartCap` `EndCap`	Get or set the predefined cap style used at the beginning or end of lines drawn with this `Pen`. Set the cap of your `Pen` using the `LineCap` enumeration defined in the `System.Drawing.Drawing2D` namespace.
`Width`	Gets or sets the width of this `Pen`.
`DashOffset`	Gets or sets the distance from the start of a line to the beginning of a dash pattern.

Remember that in addition to the `Pen` type, GDI+ provides a `Pens` collection. Using a number of shared properties, you are able to retrieve a `Pen` (or a given color) on the fly, rather than creating a custom `Pen` by hand. Be aware, however, that the `Pen` objects returned will always have a width of 1. If you require a more exotic pen, you will need to create a `Pen` object by hand. This being said, let's render some geometric images using simple `Pen` objects. Assume you have a main Form object that is capable of responding to paint requests. The implementation is as follows:

```
Imports System.Drawing.Drawing2D

Public Class MainForm

  Private Sub MainForm_Paint(ByVal sender As System.Object, _
    ByVal e As System.Windows.Forms.PaintEventArgs) Handles MyBase.Paint
    Dim g As Graphics = e.Graphics
    ' Make a big blue pen.
    Dim bluePen As New Pen(Color.Blue, 20)

    ' Get a stock pen from the Pens type.
    Dim pen2 As Pen = Pens.Firebrick

    ' Render some shapes with the pens.
    g.DrawEllipse(bluePen, 10, 10, 100, 100)
    g.DrawLine(pen2, 10, 130, 110, 130)
    g.DrawPie(Pens.Black, 150, 10, 120, 150, 90, 80)

    ' Draw a purple dashed polygon as well...
    Dim pen3 As New Pen(Color.Purple, 5)
    pen3.DashStyle - DashStyle.DashDotDot
    g.DrawPolygon(pen3, New Point() {New Point(30, 140), _
     New Point(265, 200), New Point(100, 225), _
     New Point(190, 190), New Point(50, 330), _
     New Point(20, 180)})

    ' And a rectangle containing some text...
    Dim r As New Rectangle(150, 10, 130, 60)
```

```
    g.DrawRectangle(Pens.Blue, r)
    g.DrawString("Hello out there...How are ya?", _
     New Font("Arial", 12), Brushes.Black, r)
  End Sub

  Private Sub MainForm_Resize(ByVal sender As System.Object, _
    ByVal e As System.EventArgs) Handles MyBase.Resize
    Invalidate()
  End Sub
End Class
```

Notice that the Pen used to render your polygon makes use of the DashStyle enumeration (defined in System.Drawing.Drawing2D):

```
Enum DashStyle
  Solid
  Dash
  Dot
  DashDot
  DashDotDot
  Custom
End Enum
```

In addition to the preconfigured DashStyles, you are able to define custom patterns using the DashPattern property of the Pen type:

```
Private Sub MainForm_Paint(ByVal sender As System.Object, _
  ByVal e As System.Windows.Forms.PaintEventArgs) Handles MyBase.Paint
  Dim g As Graphics = e.Graphics
...
  ' Draw custom dash pattern all around the border of the Form.
  Dim customDashPen As New Pen(Color.BlueViolet, 10)
  Dim myDashes As Single() = {5.0F, 2.0F, 1.0F, 3.0F}
  customDashPen.DashPattern = myDashes
  g.DrawRectangle(customDashPen, ClientRectangle)
End Sub
```

Figure 28-12 shows the final output of this Paint event handler.

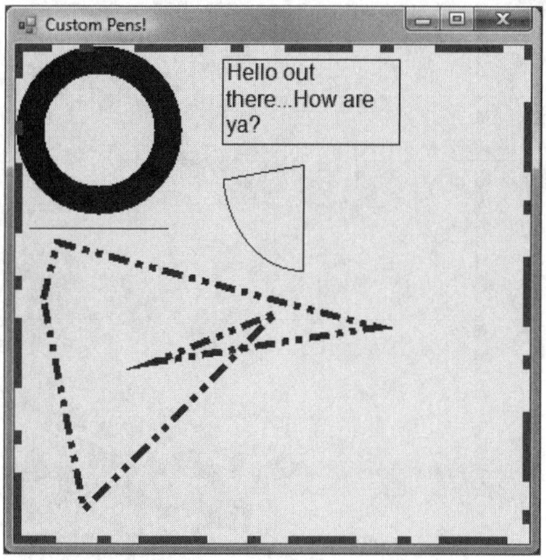

Figure 28-12. *Working with* Pen *types*

■ **Source Code** The CustomPenApp project is included under the Chapter 28 subdirectory.

Working with Pen Caps

If you examine the output of the previous pen example, you should notice that the beginning and end of each line was rendered using a standard pen protocol (an end cap composed of 90 degree angles). Using the `LineCap` enumeration, however, you are able to build `Pens` that exhibit a bit more flair:

```
Enum LineCap
  Flat
  Square
  Round
  Triangle
  NoAnchor
  SquareAnchor
  RoundAnchor
  DiamondAnchor
  ArrowAnchor
  AnchorMask
  Custom
End Enum
```

To illustrate, the following Pens application draws a series of lines using each of the `LineCap` styles. The end result can be seen in Figure 28-13.

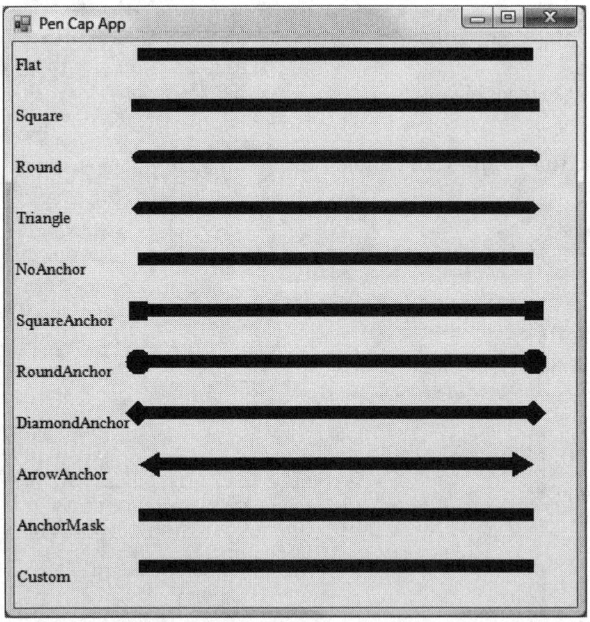

Figure 28-13. *Working with pen caps*

The code simply loops through each member of the LineCap enumeration and prints out the name of the item (e.g., ArrowAnchor). It then configures and draws a line with the current cap:

```
Imports System.Drawing.Drawing2D

Public Class MainForm
  Private Sub MainForm_Paint(ByVal sender As System.Object, _
    ByVal e As System.Windows.Forms.PaintEventArgs) Handles MyBase.Paint
    Dim g As Graphics = e.Graphics
    Dim thePen As New Pen(Color.Black, 10)
    Dim yOffSet As Integer = 10

    ' Get all members of the LineCap enum.
    Dim obj As Array = [Enum].GetValues(GetType(LineCap))

    For x As Integer = 0 To obj.Length - 1
      ' Draw a line with a LineCap member.
      ' Get next cap and configure pen.
      Dim temp As LineCap = CType(obj.GetValue(x), LineCap)
      thePen.StartCap = temp
      thePen.EndCap = temp
      ' Print name of LineCap enum.
      g.DrawString(temp.ToString(), New Font("Times New Roman", 10), _
       New SolidBrush(Color.Black), 0, yOffSet)
      ' Draw a line with the correct cap.
      g.DrawLine(thePen, 100, yOffSet, Width - 50, yOffSet)
      yOffSet += 40
    Next
  End Sub

  Private Sub MainForm_Resize(ByVal sender As System.Object, _
    ByVal e As System.EventArgs) Handles MyBase.Resize
    Invalidate()
  End Sub
End Class
```

Source Code The PenCapApp project is included under the Chapter 28 subdirectory.

Working with Brushes

System.Drawing.Brush-derived types are used to fill a region with a given color, pattern, or image. The Brush class itself is an abstract type and cannot be directly created. However, Brush serves as a base class to the other related brush types (e.g., SolidBrush, HatchBrush, LinearGradientBrush, and so forth). In addition to specific Brush-derived types, the System.Drawing namespace also defines two helper classes that return a configured brush using a number of shared properties: Brushes and SystemBrushes. In any case, once you obtain a brush, you are able to call any number of the FillXXX() methods of the Graphics type.

Interestingly enough, you are also able to build a custom Pen object based on a given brush. In this way, you are able to build some brush of interest (e.g., a brush that paints a bitmap image) and render geometric patterns with a configured Pen object. To illustrate, here is a small sample program that makes use of various Brush types:

```
Public Class MainForm
  Private Sub MainForm_Paint(ByVal sender As System.Object, _
  ByVal e As System.Windows.Forms.PaintEventArgs) Handles MyBase.Paint
    Dim g As Graphics = e.Graphics
    ' Make a blue SolidBrush.
    Dim blueBrush As New SolidBrush(Color.Blue)

    ' Get a stock brush from the Brushes type.
    Dim pen2 As SolidBrush = CType(Brushes.Firebrick, SolidBrush)

    ' Render some shapes with the brushes.
    g.FillEllipse(blueBrush, 10, 10, 100, 100)
    g.FillPie(Brushes.Black, 150, 10, 120, 150, 90, 80)

    ' Draw a purple polygon as well...
    Dim brush3 As New SolidBrush(Color.Purple)
    g.FillPolygon(brush3, New Point() {New Point(30, 140), _
      New Point(265, 200), New Point(100, 225), _
      New Point(190, 190), New Point(50, 330), _
      New Point(20, 180)})

    ' And a rectangle with some text...
    Dim r As New Rectangle(150, 10, 130, 60)
    g.FillRectangle(Brushes.Blue, r)
    g.DrawString("Hello out there...How are ya?", _
      New Font("Arial", 12), Brushes.White, r)
  End Sub
End Class
```

If you can't tell, this application is little more than the CustomPenApp program, this time making use of the `FillXXX()` methods and `SolidBrush` types, rather than pens and the related `DrawXXX()` methods. Figure 28-14 shows the output.

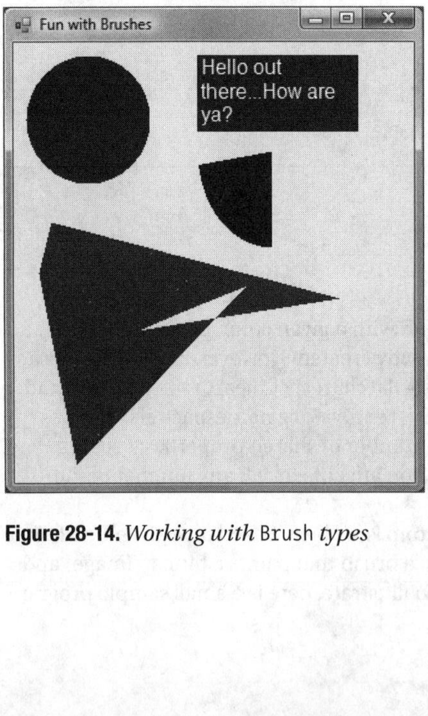

Figure 28-14. *Working with* Brush *types*

Source Code The SolidBrushApp project is included under the Chapter 28 subdirectory.

Working with HatchBrushes

The System.Drawing.Drawing2D namespace defines a Brush-derived type named HatchBrush. This type allows you to fill a region using a (very large) number of predefined patterns, represented by the HatchStyle enumeration. Here is a partial list of names:

```
Enum HatchStyle
  Horizontal
  Vertical
  ForwardDiagonal
  BackwardDiagonal
  Cross
  DiagonalCross
  LightUpwardDiagonal
...
End Enum
```

When constructing a HatchBrush, you need to specify the foreground and background colors to use during the fill operation. To illustrate, let's rework the logic seen previously in the PenCapApp example:

```
Imports System.Drawing.Drawing2D

Public Class MainForm
  Private Sub MainForm_Paint(ByVal sender As System.Object, _
  ByVal e As System.Windows.Forms.PaintEventArgs) Handles MyBase.Paint
    Dim g As Graphics = e.Graphics
    Dim yOffSet As Integer = 10

    ' Get all members of the HatchStyle enum.
    Dim obj As Array = [Enum].GetValues(GetType(HatchStyle))

    For x As Integer = 0 To 4
      ' Draw an oval with first 5 HatchStyle values.
      ' Configure Brush.
      Dim temp As HatchStyle = CType(obj.GetValue(x), HatchStyle)
      Dim theBrush As New HatchBrush(temp, Color.White, Color.Black)

      ' Print name of HatchStyle enum.
      g.DrawString(temp.ToString(), New Font("Times New Roman", 10), _
             Brushes.Black, 0, yOffSet)

      ' Fill a rectangle with the correct brush.
      g.FillEllipse(theBrush, 150, yOffSet, 200, 25)
      yOffSet += 40
    Next
  End Sub
End Class
```

The output renders a filled oval for the first five hatch values (see Figure 28-15).

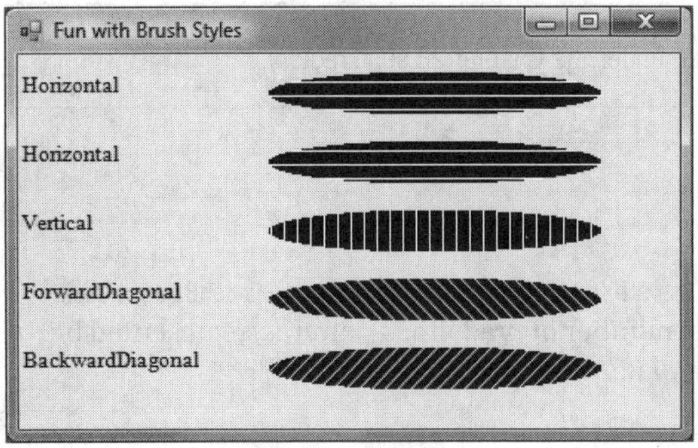

Figure 28-15. *Select hatch styles*

Source Code The BrushStyles application is included under the Chapter 28 subdirectory.

Working with TextureBrushes

The `TextureBrush` type allows you to attach a bitmap image to a brush, which can then be used in conjunction with a fill operation. In just a few pages, you will learn about the details of the GDI+ `Image` class. For the time being, understand that a `TextureBrush` is assigned an `Image` reference for use during its lifetime. The image itself is typically found stored in some local file (`*.bmp`, `*.gif`, `*.jpg`) or embedded into a .NET assembly.

Let's build a sample application that makes use of the `TextureBrush` type. One brush is used to paint the entire client area with the image found in a file named `clouds.bmp`, while the other brush is used to paint text with the image found within `soap bubbles.bmp`. The output is shown in Figure 28-16.

Figure 28-16. *Bitmaps as brushes*

To begin, your Form-derived class maintains two Brush member variables, which are assigned to a new TextureBrush in the constructor. Notice that the constructor of the TextureBrush type requires a type derived from Image. With these two TextureBrush types to use for rendering, the Paint event handler is quite straightforward:

```
Public Class MainForm
  Private texturedTextBrush As Brush
  Private texturedBGroundBrush As Brush

  Sub New()
    ' This call is required by the Windows Forms designer.
    InitializeComponent()

    ' Add any initialization after the InitializeComponent() call.
    CenterToScreen()

    ' Load images brushes.
    Try
      Dim bGroundBrushImage As Image = New Bitmap("Clouds.bmp")
      texturedBGroundBrush = New TextureBrush(bGroundBrushImage)
      Dim textBrushImage As Image = New Bitmap("Soap Bubbles.bmp")
      texturedTextBrush = New TextureBrush(textBrushImage)
    Catch
      MessageBox.Show("Can't find bitmap files!")
      Application.Exit()
    End Try
  End Sub

  Private Sub MainForm_Paint(ByVal sender As System.Object, _
    ByVal e As System.Windows.Forms.PaintEventArgs) Handles MyBase.Paint
    Dim g As Graphics = e.Graphics
    Dim r As Rectangle = ClientRectangle

    ' Paint the clouds on the client area.
    g.FillRectangle(texturedBGroundBrush, r)

    ' Some big bold text with a textured brush.
    g.DrawString("Bitmaps as brushes!  Way cool...", _
      New Font("Arial", 50, FontStyle.Bold Or FontStyle.Italic), _
      texturedTextBrush, r)
  End Sub

End Class
```

Note The *.bmp files used in this example must be in the same folder as the application (or specified using hard-coded paths). We'll address this limitation later in this chapter in the section "Understanding the .NET Resource Format."

Source Code The TexturedBrushes application is included under the Chapter 28 subdirectory.

Working with LinearGradientBrushes

Last but not least is the LinearGradientBrush type, which you can use whenever you want to blend two colors together in a gradient pattern. Working with this type is just as simple as working with the other brush types. The only point of interest is that when you build a LinearGradientBrush, you need to specify a pair of Color objects and the direction of the blend via the LinearGradientMode enumeration:

```
Enum LinearGradientMode
  Horizontal
  Vertical
  ForwardDiagonal
  BackwardDiagonal
End Enum
```

To test each value, let's render a series of rectangles using a LinearGradientBrush:

```
Imports System.Drawing.Drawing2D

Public Class MainForm

  Private Sub MainForm_Paint(ByVal sender As System.Object, _
  ByVal e As System.Windows.Forms.PaintEventArgs) Handles MyBase.Paint
    Dim g As Graphics = e.Graphics
    Dim r As New Rectangle(10, 10, 100, 100)

    ' A gradient brush.
    Dim theBrush As LinearGradientBrush = Nothing
    Dim yOffSet As Integer = 10

    ' Get all members of the LinearGradientMode enum.
    Dim obj As Array = [Enum].GetValues(GetType(LinearGradientMode))

    For x As Integer = 0 To obj.Length - 1
      ' Draw a rectangle with a LinearGradientMode member.
      ' Configure brush.
      Dim temp As LinearGradientMode = CType(obj.GetValue(x), LinearGradientMode)
      theBrush = New LinearGradientBrush(r, Color.GreenYellow, Color.Blue, temp)

      ' Print name of LinearGradientMode enum.
      g.DrawString(temp.ToString(), _
        New Font("Times New Roman", 10), _
        New SolidBrush(Color.Black), 0, yOffSet)

      ' Fill a rectangle with the correct brush.
      g.FillRectangle(theBrush, 150, yOffSet, 200, 50)
      yOffSet += 80
    Next
  End Sub
End Class
```

Figure 28-17 shows the end result.

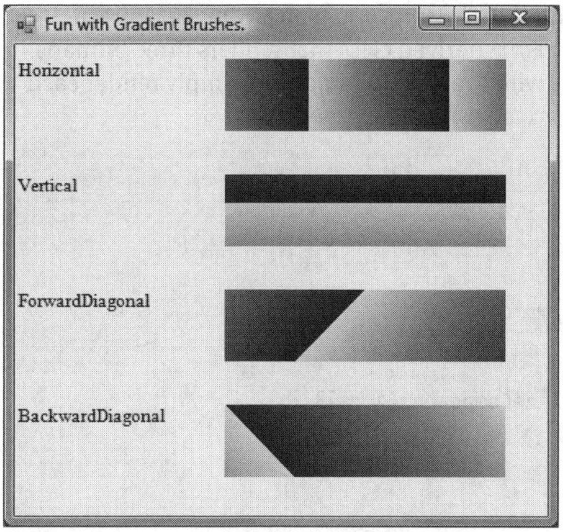

Figure 28-17. *Gradient brushes at work*

Source Code The GradientBrushes application is included under the Chapter 28 subdirectory.

Rendering Images

At this point, you have examined how to manipulate three of the four major GDI+ types: fonts, pens, and brushes. The final type you'll examine in this chapter is the `Image` class and related subtypes. The abstract `System.Drawing.Image` type defines a number of methods and properties that hold various bits of information regarding the underlying image data it represents. For example, the `Image` class supplies the `Width`, `Height`, and `Size` properties to retrieve the dimensions of the image. Other properties allow you to gain access to the underlying palette. The `Image` class defines the core members shown in Table 28-8.

Table 28-8. *Members of the* `Image` *Type*

Member	Meaning in Life
`FromFile()`	This shared method creates an `Image` from the specified file.
`FromStream()`	This shared method creates an `Image` from the specified data stream.

`Height`
`Width`
`Size`
`HorizontalResolution`
`VerticalResolution`
	These properties return information regarding the dimensions of this `Image`.

`Palette`	This property returns a `ColorPalette` data type that represents the underlying palette used for this `Image`.
`GetBounds()`	This method returns a `Rectangle` that represents the current size of this `Image`.
`Save()`	This method saves the data held in an `Image`-derived type to file.

Given that the abstract Image class cannot be directly created, you typically make a direct instance of the Bitmap type. Assume you have some Form-derived class that renders three bitmaps into the client area. Once you fill the Bitmap objects with the correct image file, simply render each one within your Paint event handler using the Graphics.DrawImage() method:

```
Public Class MainForm
  ' To hold the *.bmp data.
  Private myImages As Bitmap() = New Bitmap(2) {}

  Sub New()
    ' This call is required by the Windows Forms designer.
    InitializeComponent()

    ' Add any initialization after the InitializeComponent() call.
    myImages(0) = New Bitmap("imageA.bmp")
    myImages(1) = New Bitmap("imageB.bmp")
    myImages(2) = New Bitmap("imageC.bmp")
    CenterToScreen()
  End Sub

  Private Sub MainForm_Paint(ByVal sender As System.Object, _
      ByVal e As System.Windows.Forms.PaintEventArgs) Handles MyBase.Paint
    Dim g As Graphics = e.Graphics
    ' Render all three images.
    Dim yOffset As Integer = 10
    For Each b As Bitmap In myImages
      g.DrawImage(b, 10, yOffset, 90, 90)
      yOffset += 100
    Next
  End Sub
End Class
```

Figure 28-18 shows the output.

Figure 28-18. *Rendering images*

■ **Note** The *.bmp files used in this example must be in the same folder as the application (or specified using hard-coded paths). We'll resolve this limitation later in this chapter.

Finally, be aware that regardless of its name, the Bitmap class can contain image data stored in any number of file formats (*.tif, *.gif, *.bmp, etc.).

■ **Source Code** The BasicImages application is included under the Chapter 28 subdirectory.

Dragging and Hit Testing the PictureBox Control

While you are free to render Bitmap images directly onto any Control-derived class, you will find that you gain far greater control and functionality if you instead choose to make use of a PictureBox to contain your image. For example, because the PictureBox type "is-a" Control, you inherit a great deal of functionality, such as the ability to handle various events, assign a tool tip or context menu, and so forth. While you could achieve similar behaviors using a raw Bitmap, you would be required to author a fair amount of boilerplate code.

To showcase the usefulness of the PictureBox type, let's create a simple "game" that illustrates the ability to capture mouse activity over a graphical image. If the user clicks the mouse somewhere within the bounds of the image, he is in "dragging" mode and can move the image around the Form. To make things more interesting, let's monitor where the user releases the image. If it is within the bounds of a GDI+-rendered rectangle, you'll take some additional course of action (seen shortly). As you may know, the process of testing for mouse click events within a specific region is termed *hit testing*.

The PictureBox type gains most of its functionality from the Control base class. You've already explored a number of Control's members in the previous chapter, so let's quickly turn our attention to the process of assigning an image to the PictureBox member variable using the Image property (again, the happyDude.bmp file must be in the application directory):

```
Public Class MainForm
  Private happyBox As New PictureBox()
  Private oldX As Integer, oldY As Integer
  Private isDragging As Boolean
  Private dropRect As New Rectangle(100, 100, 140, 170)

  Sub New()
    ' This call is required by the Windows Forms designer.
    InitializeComponent()

    ' Add any initialization after the InitializeComponent() call.
    ' Configure the PictureBox and add to
    ' the Form's Controls collection.
    happyBox.SizeMode = PictureBoxSizeMode.StretchImage
    happyBox.Location = New System.Drawing.Point(64, 32)
    happyBox.Size = New System.Drawing.Size(50, 50)
    happyBox.Cursor = Cursors.Hand
    happyBox.Image = New Bitmap("happyDude.bmp")
```

```
    ' Add handlers for the following events.
    AddHandler happyBox.MouseDown, AddressOf happyBox_MouseDown
    AddHandler happyBox.MouseUp, AddressOf happyBox_MouseUp
    AddHandler happyBox.MouseMove, AddressOf happyBox_MouseMove
    Controls.Add(happyBox)
  End Sub
End Class
```

Beyond the Image property, the only other property of interest is SizeMode, which makes use of the PictureBoxSizeMode enumeration. This type is used to control how the associated image should be rendered within the bounding rectangle of the PictureBox. Here, you assigned PictureBoxSizeMode.StretchImage, indicating that you wish to skew the image over the entire area of the PictureBox type (which is set to 50×50 pixels).

The next task is to handle the MouseMove, MouseUp, and MouseDown events for the PictureBox member variable using the expected VB 2008 event syntax:

```
' Add handlers for the following events.
AddHandler happyBox.MouseDown, AddressOf happyBox_MouseDown
AddHandler happyBox.MouseUp, AddressOf happyBox_MouseUp
AddHandler happyBox.MouseMove, AddressOf happyBox_MouseMove
```

The MouseDown event handler is in charge of storing the incoming (*x*, *y*) location of the cursor within two Integer member variables (oldX and oldY) for later use, as well as setting a System.Boolean member variable (isDragging) to True, to indicate that a drag operation is in process. Implement the MouseDown event handler as follows:

```
Private Sub happyBox_MouseDown(ByVal sender As System.Object, _
  ByVal e As System.Windows.Forms.MouseEventArgs)
  isDragging = True
  ' Save the (x, y) of the mouse down click,
  ' because we need it as an offset when dragging the image.
  oldX = e.X
  oldY = e.Y
End Sub
```

The MouseMove event handler simply relocates the position of the PictureBox (using the Top and Left properties) by offsetting the current cursor location with the integer data captured during the MouseDown event:

```
Private Sub happyBox_MouseMove(ByVal sender As System.Object, _
  ByVal e As System.Windows.Forms.MouseEventArgs)
  If isDragging Then
    ' Need to figure new Y value based on where the mouse
    ' down click happened.
    happyBox.Top = happyBox.Top + (e.Y - oldY)

    ' Same deal for X (use oldX as a base line).
    happyBox.Left = happyBox.Left + (e.X - oldX)
  End If
End Sub
```

The MouseUp event handler sets the isDragging Boolean to False, to signal the end of the drag operation. As well, if the MouseUp event occurs when the PictureBox is contained within our GDI+-rendered Rectangle image, you can assume the user has won the (albeit rather simplistic) game. Given the Rectangle member variable (named dropRect) we added to the Form class, the MouseUp event handler can now be implemented like so:

```
Private Sub happyBox_MouseUp(ByVal sender As System.Object, _
  ByVal e As System.Windows.Forms.MouseEventArgs)
  isDragging = False
  ' Is the mouse within the area of the drop rect?
  If dropRect.Contains(happyBox.Bounds) Then
    MessageBox.Show("You win!", "What an amazing test of skill...")
  End If
End Sub
```

Finally, you need to render the rectangular area (maintained by the dropRect member variable) on the Form within a Paint event handler:

```
Private Sub MainForm_Paint(ByVal sender As System.Object, _
  ByVal e As System.Windows.Forms.PaintEventArgs) Handles MyBase.Paint
  ' Draw the drop box.
  Dim g As Graphics = e.Graphics
  g.FillRectangle(Brushes.BlueViolet, dropRect)
  ' Display instructions.
  g.DrawString("Drag the happy guy in here...", _
  New Font("Times New Roman", 25), Brushes.WhiteSmoke, dropRect)
End Sub
```

When you run the application, you are presented with what appears in Figure 28-19.

Figure 28-19. *The amazing happy-dude game*

If you have what it takes to win the game, you are rewarded with the kudos shown in Figure 28-20.

Source Code The DraggingImages application is included under the Chapter 28 subdirectory.

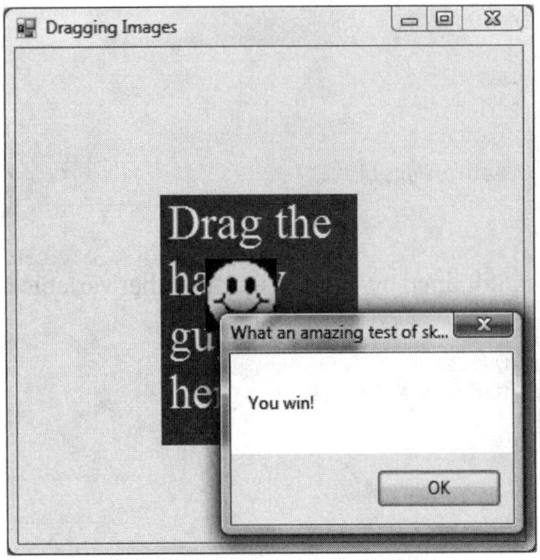

Figure 28-20. *You have nerves of steel!*

Hit Testing Rendered Images

Validating a hit test against a Control-derived type (such as the PictureBox) is very simple, as it can respond directly to mouse events. However, what if you wish to perform a hit test on a geometric shape rendered directly on the surface of a Form?

To illustrate the process, let's revisit the previous BasicImages application and add some new functionality. The goal is to determine when the user clicks one of the three images. Once you discover which image was clicked, you'll adjust the Text property of the Form and highlight the image with a 5-pixel outline.

The first step is to define a new set of member variables in the Form type that represents the Rectangles you will be testing against in the MouseDown event. When this event occurs, you need to programmatically figure out whether the incoming (*x*, *y*) coordinate is somewhere within the bounds of the Rectangles used to represent the dimension of each Image. If the user does click a given image, you set a private Boolean member variable (isImageClicked) to True and indicate which image was selected via another member variable of a custom enumeration named ClickedImage, defined as follows:

```
Enum ClickedImage
  ImageA
  ImageB
  ImageC
End Enum
```

With this, here is the initial update to the Form-derived class:

```
Public Class MainForm
...
  Private imageRects As Rectangle() = New Rectangle(2) {}
  Private isImageClicked As Boolean = False
  Private imageClicked As ClickedImage = ClickedImage.ImageA

  Sub New()
...
    ' Set up the rectangles.
    imageRects(0) = New Rectangle(10, 10, 90, 90)
```

```
    imageRects(1) = New Rectangle(10, 110, 90, 90)
    imageRects(2) = New Rectangle(10, 210, 90, 90)
    CenterToScreen()
  End Sub
...
  Private Sub MainForm_MouseDown(ByVal sender As System.Object, _
    ByVal e As System.Windows.Forms.MouseEventArgs) Handles MyBase.MouseDown
    ' Get (x, y) of mouse click.
    Dim mousePt As New Point(e.X, e.Y)

    ' See if the mouse is anywhere in the 3 Rectangles.
    If imageRects(0).Contains(mousePt) Then
      isImageClicked = True
      imageClicked = ClickedImage.ImageA
      Me.Text = "You clicked image A"
    ElseIf imageRects(1).Contains(mousePt) Then
      isImageClicked = True
      imageClicked = ClickedImage.ImageB
      Me.Text = "You clicked image B"
    ElseIf imageRects(2).Contains(mousePt) Then
      isImageClicked = True
      imageClicked = ClickedImage.ImageC
      Me.Text = "You clicked image C"
    Else
      ' Not in any shape, set defaults.
      isImageClicked = False
      Me.Text = "Hit Testing Images"
    End If
    ' Redraw the client area.
    Invalidate()
  End Sub
End Class
```

Notice that the final conditional check sets the `isImageClicked` member variable to `False`, indicating that the user did not click one of the three images. This is important, as you want to erase the outline of the previously selected image. Once all items have been checked, invalidate the client area. Here is the updated `Paint` handler:

```
Private Sub MainForm_Paint(ByVal sender As System.Object, _
  ByVal e As System.Windows.Forms.PaintEventArgs) Handles MyBase.Paint
  Dim g As Graphics = e.Graphics
...
  ' Draw outline (if clicked)
  If isImageClicked = True Then
    Dim outline As Pen = New Pen(Color.Red, 5)
    Select Case imageClicked
      Case ClickedImage.ImageA
        g.DrawRectangle(outline, imageRects(0))
        Exit Select
      Case ClickedImage.ImageB
        g.DrawRectangle(outline, imageRects(1))
        Exit Select
      Case ClickedImage.ImageC
        g.DrawRectangle(outline, imageRects(2))
        Exit Select
      Case Else
        Exit Select
```

```
    End Select
  End If
End Sub
```

At this point, you should be able to run your application and validate that an outline appears around each image that has been clicked (and that no outline is present when you click outside the bounds of said images).

Hit Testing Nonrectangular Images

Now, what if you wish to perform a hit test in a nonrectangular region, rather than a simple square? Assume you updated your application to render an oddball geometric shape that will also sport an outline when clicked (see Figure 28-21).

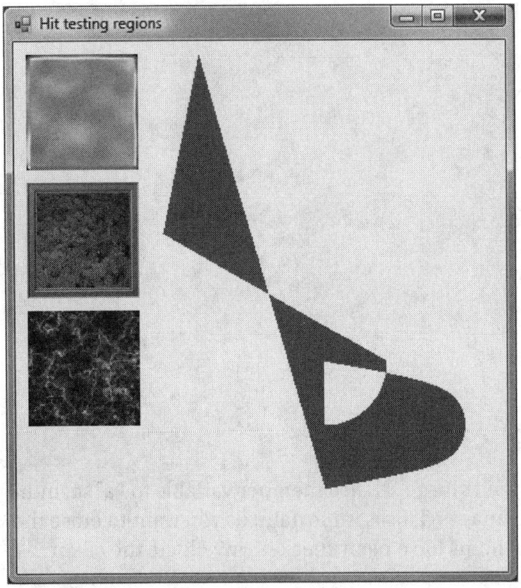

Figure 28-21. *Hit testing polygons*

This geometric image was rendered on the Form using the `FillPath()` method of the `Graphics` type. This method takes an instance of a `GraphicsPath` object, which encapsulates a series of connected lines, curves, and strings. Adding new items to a `GraphicsPath` instance is achieved using a number of related `Add` methods, as described in Table 28-9.

Table 28-9. `Add`-*Centric Methods of the* `GraphicsPath` *Class*

Method	Meaning in Life
`AddArc()`	Appends an elliptical arc to the current figure
`AddBezier()` `AddBeziers()`	Add a cubic Bezier curve or set of Bezier curves to the current figure
`AddClosedCurve()`	Adds a closed curve to the current figure
`AddCurve()`	Adds a curve to the current figure

Method	Meaning in Life
AddEllipse()	Adds an ellipse to the current figure
AddLine() AddLines()	Appends a line segment (or a set of lines) to the current figure
AddPath()	Appends the specified GraphicsPath to the current figure
AddPie()	Adds the outline of a pie shape to the current figure
AddPolygon()	Adds a polygon to the current figure
AddRectangle() AddRectangles()	Add one rectangle or more to the current figure
AddString()	Adds a text string to the current figure

Assuming you have imported the System.Drawing.Drawing2D namespace, add a new GraphicsPath member variable to your Form-derived class. In the Form's constructor, build the set of items that represent your path as follows:

```
Imports System.Drawing.Drawing2D

Public Class MainForm
...
  Private myPath As New GraphicsPath()

  Sub New()
...
    ' Create an interesting path.
    myPath.StartFigure()
    myPath.AddLine(New Point(150, 10), New Point(120, 150))
    myPath.AddArc(200, 200, 100, 100, 0, 90)
    Dim point1 As New Point(250, 250)
    Dim point2 As New Point(350, 275)
    Dim point3 As New Point(350, 325)
    Dim point4 As New Point(250, 350)
    Dim points As Point() = {point1, point2, point3, point4}
    myPath.AddCurve(points)
    myPath.CloseFigure()
  End Sub
...
End Class
```

Notice the calls to StartFigure() and CloseFigure(). When you call StartFigure(), you are able to insert a new item into the current path you are building. A call to CloseFigure() closes the current figure and begins a new figure (if you require one). Also know that if the figure contains a sequence of connected lines and curves (as in the case of the myPath instance), the loop is closed by connecting a line from the end point to the starting point. Add an additional name to the ImageClicked enumeration named StrangePath:

```
Enum ClickedImage
  ImageA
  ImageB
  ImageC
  StrangePath
End Enum
```

Next, update your existing MouseDown event handler to test for the presence of the cursor's (*x*, *y*) position within the bounds of the GraphicsPath. Like a Region type, this can be discovered using the IsVisible() member:

```
Private Sub MainForm_MouseDown(ByVal sender As System.Object, _
  ByVal e As System.Windows.Forms.MouseEventArgs) Handles MyBase.MouseDown
  ' Get (x, y) of mouse click.
  Dim mousePt As Point = New Point(e.X, e.Y)

  If imageRects(0).Contains(mousePt) Then
    isImageClicked = True
    imageClicked = ClickedImage.ImageA
    Me.Text = "You clicked image A"
  ElseIf imageRects(1).Contains(mousePt) Then
    isImageClicked = True
    imageClicked = ClickedImage.ImageB
    Me.Text = "You clicked image B"
  ElseIf imageRects(2).Contains(mousePt) Then
    isImageClicked = True
    imageClicked = ClickedImage.ImageC
    Me.Text = "You clicked image C"
  ElseIf myPath.IsVisible(mousePt) Then
    isImageClicked = True
    imageClicked = ClickedImage.StrangePath
    Me.Text = "You clicked the strange shape..."
  Else
    ' Not in any shape, set defaults.
    isImageClicked = False
    Me.Text = "Hit Testing Images"
  End If
  ' Redraw the client area.
  Invalidate()
End Sub
```

Finally, update the Paint handler as follows:

```
Private Sub MainForm_Paint(ByVal sender As System.Object, _
  ByVal e As System.Windows.Forms.PaintEventArgs) Handles MyBase.Paint
  Dim g As Graphics = e.Graphics
...
  ' Draw the graphics path.
  g.FillPath(Brushes.Sienna, myPath)

  ' Draw outline (if clicked)
  If isImageClicked = True Then
    Dim outline As New Pen(Color.Red, 5)
    Select Case imageClicked
    ...
      Case ClickedImage.StrangePath
        g.DrawPath(outline, myPath)
        Exit Select
      Case Else
        Exit Select
      End Select
  End If
End Sub
```

Source Code The HitTestingImages project is included under the Chapter 28 subdirectory.

Understanding the Windows Forms Resource Format

Up to this point in the chapter, each application that made use of external resources (such as bitmap files) demanded that the image files be within the client's application directory. Given this, you loaded your `*.bmp` files using an absolute name:

```
' Fill the images with bitmaps.
bMapImageA = New Bitmap("imageA.bmp")
bMapImageB = New Bitmap("imageB.bmp")
bMapImageC = New Bitmap("imageC.bmp")
```

This logic, of course, demands that the application directory does indeed contain three files named `imageA.bmp`, `imageB.bmp`, and `imageC.bmp`; otherwise, you will receive a runtime exception.

As you may recall from Chapter 15, an assembly is a collection of types and *optional resources*. Given this, your final task of the chapter is to learn how to bundle external resources (such as image files and strings) into the assembly itself. In this way, your .NET binary is truly self-contained. At the lowest level, bundling external resources into a .NET assembly involves the following steps:

1. Create a `*.resx` file that establishes name/value pairs for each resource in your application via XML data representation.
2. Use the `resgen.exe` command-line utility to convert your XML-based `*.resx` file into a binary equivalent (a `*.resources` file).
3. Using the `/resource` flag of the VB 2008 compiler, embed the binary `*.resources` file into your assembly.

As you might suspect, these steps are automated when using Visual Studio 2008. You'll examine how this IDE can assist you in just a moment. For the time being, let's check out how to generate and embed .NET resources at the command line.

The System.Resources Namespace

The key to understanding the .NET resource format is to know the types defined within the `System.Resources` namespace. This set of types provides the programmatic means to read and write `*.resx` (XML-based) and `*.resources` (binary) files, as well as obtain resources embedded in a given assembly. Table 28-10 provides a rundown of the core types.

Table 28-10. *Members of the* `System.Resources` *Namespace*

Member	Meaning in Life
`ResourceReader` `ResourceWriter`	These types allow you to read from and write to binary `*.resources` files.
`ResXResourceReader` `ResXResourceWriter`	These types allow you to read from and write to XML-based `*.resx` files.
`ResourceManager`	This type allows you to programmatically obtain embedded resources from a given assembly.

Programmatically Creating a *.resx File

As mentioned, a `*.resx` file is a block of XML data that assigns name/value pairs for each resource in your application. The `ResXResourceWriter` class provides a set of members that allow you to create the `*.resx` file, add binary and string-based resources, and commit them to storage. To illustrate, let's create a simple Windows Forms application (ResXWriter) that will generate a `*.resx` file containing an entry for the `happyDude.bmp` file (first seen in the DraggingImages example) and a single string resource. The GUI consists of a single `Button` type as shown in Figure 28-22.

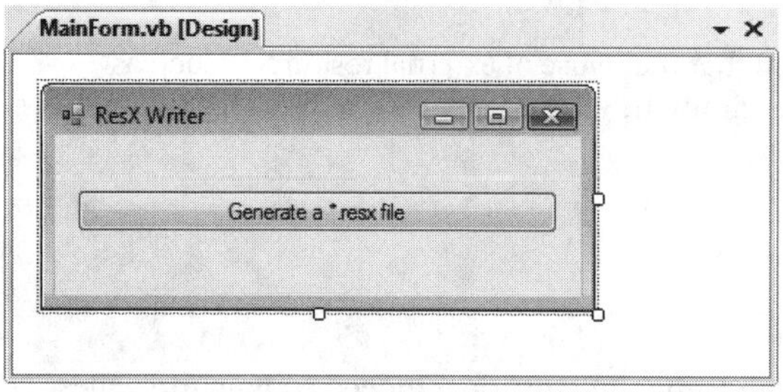

Figure 28-22. *The ResXWriter application*

The `Click` event handler for the `Button` adds the `happyDude.bmp` and string resource to the `*.resx` file, which is saved on the local C drive:

```
Imports System.Resources

Public Class MainForm
  Private Sub btnGenResX_Click(ByVal sender As System.Object, _
  ByVal e As System.EventArgs) Handles btnGenResX.Click
    ' Make a resx writer and specify the file to write to.
    Dim w As New ResXResourceWriter("C:\ResXForm.resx")
    ' Add happy dude and string.
    Dim bMap As New Bitmap("happyDude.bmp")
    w.AddResource("happyDude", bMap)
    w.AddResource("welcomeString", "Hello new resource format!")
    ' Commit it.
    w.Generate()
    w.Close()
  End Sub
End Class
```

The member of interest is `ResXResourceWriter.AddResource()`. This method has been overloaded a few times to allow you to insert binary data (as you did with the `happyDude.bmp` image), as well as textual data (as you have done for your test string). Notice that each version takes two parameters: the name of a given resource in the `*.resx` file and the data itself. The `Generate()` method commits the information to file. At this point, you have an XML description of the image and string resources. To verify, open the new `ResXForm.resx` file using a text editor (see Figure 28-23).

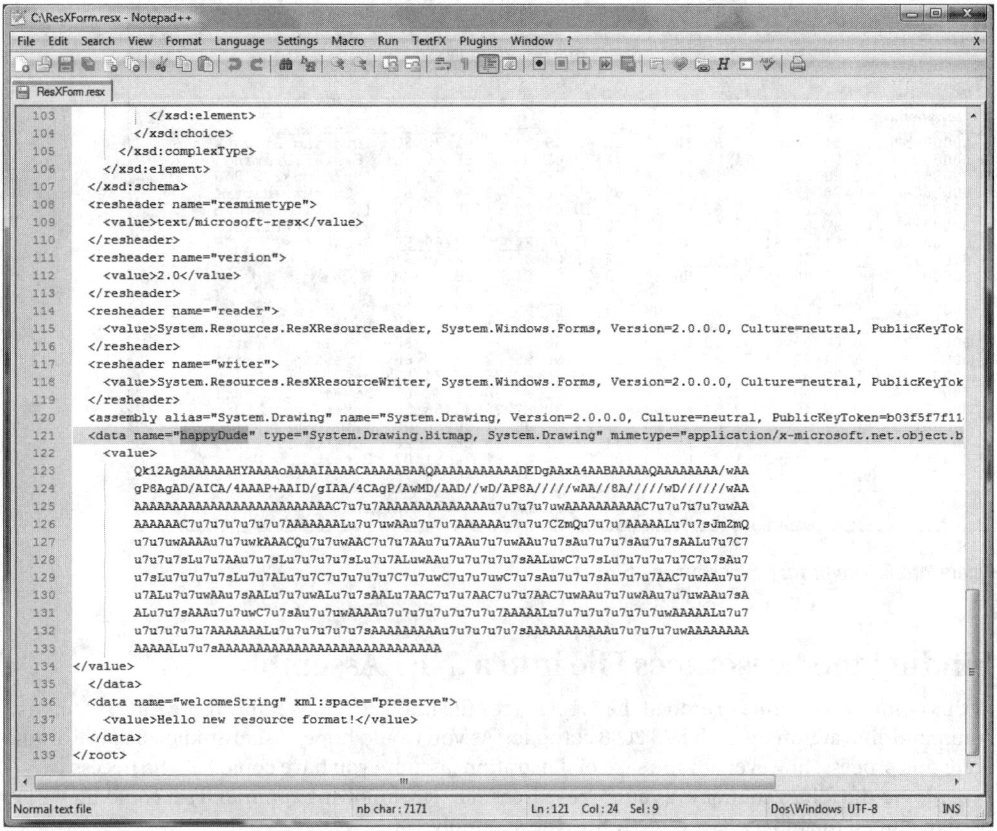

Figure 28-23. `*.resx` *expressed as XML*

Building the *.resources File

Now that you have a `*.resx` file, you can make use of the `resgen.exe` utility to produce the binary equivalent. To do so, open a Visual Studio 2008 command prompt, navigate to your C drive, and issue the following command:

```
resgen resxform.resx resxform.resources
```

You can now open the new `*.resources` file using Visual Studio 2008 and view the binary format, as shown in Figure 28-24.

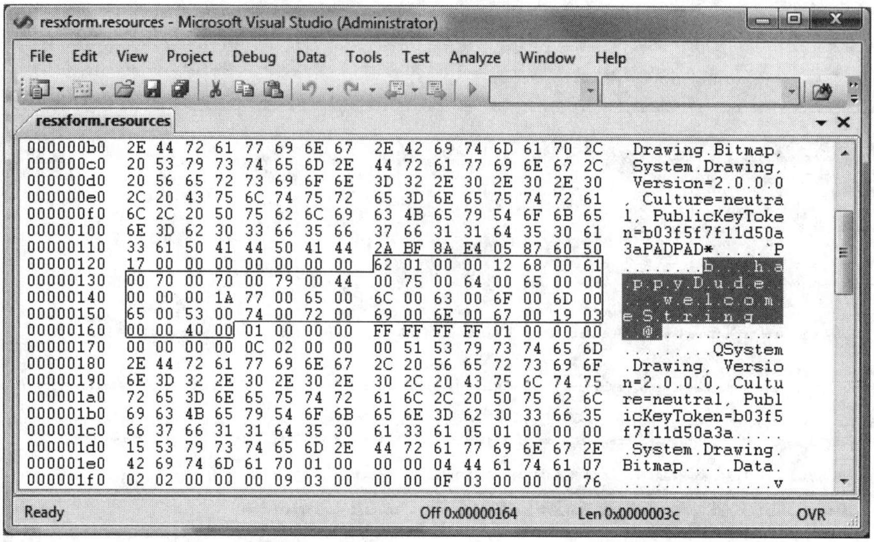

Figure 28-24. *The binary* `*.resources` *file*

Binding the *.resources File into a .NET Assembly

At this point, you are able to embed the `*.resources` file into a .NET assembly using the `/resources` command-line argument of the VB 2008 compiler. As you would hope, Visual Studio 2008 will automate this process; however, for the sake of illustration, assume you have copied all the necessary `*.vb` files to the folder containing your `*.resources` file. The following command set could then be used to embed the binary data directly into the assembly:

```
vbc /resource:resxform.resources *.vb
```

Working with ResourceWriters

The previous example made use of the `ResXResourceWriter` types to generate an XML file that contains name/value pairs for each application resource. The resulting `*.resx` file was then run through the `resgen.exe` utility. Finally, you saw how you could manually embed the `*.resources` file into the assembly using the `/resource` flag of the VB 2008 compiler. The truth of the matter is that you do not need to build a `*.resx` file (although having an XML representation of your resources can come in handy and is easily readable). If you do not require a `*.resx` file, you can make use of the `ResourceWriter` type to directly create a binary `*.resources` file:

```
Private Sub GenerateResourceFile()
  ' Make a new *.resources file.
  Dim rw As New ResourceWriter("C:\myResources.resources")
  ' Add 1 image and 1 string.
  rw.AddResource("happyDude", New Bitmap("happyDude.bmp"))
  rw.AddResource("welcomeString", "Hello new resource format!")
  rw.Generate()
  rw.Close()
End Sub
```

At this point, the `*.resources` file can be bundled into an assembly using the `/resources` option:

```
vbc /resource:myresources.resources *.vb
```

Source Code The ResXWriter project is included under the Chapter 28 subdirectory.

Generating Resources Using Visual Studio 2008

Although it is possible to work with `*.resx/*.resources` files manually at the command line, the good news is that Visual Studio 2008 automates the creation and embedding of your project's resources. To illustrate, create a new Windows Forms application named MyResourcesWinApp. Next, place a `PictureBox` component onto your main Form using the Toolbox, and assign its `Image` property to the `happyDude.bmp` image used earlier in this chapter. Now, if you open Solution Explorer (and select the Show All Files button), you will notice that each Form in your application has an associated `*.resx` file in place automatically, as shown in Figure 28-25 (you'll see the role of the Resources folder in just a moment).

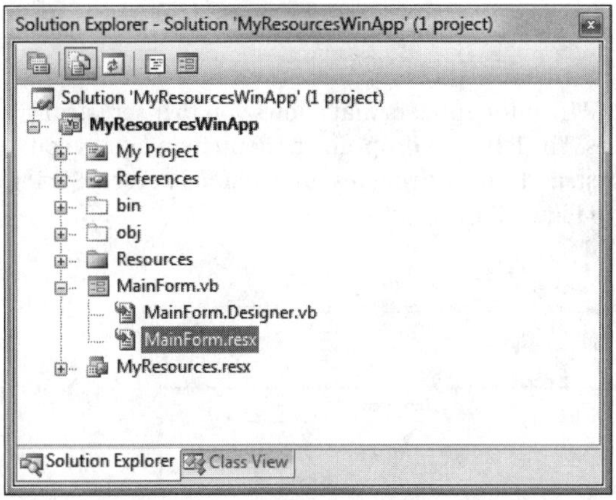

Figure 28-25. *The autogenerated* `*.resx` *files of Visual Studio 2008*

This `*.resx` file will be maintained automatically while you naturally add resources (such as an image in a `PictureBox` widget) using the visual designers. Now, despite what you may be thinking, you should *not* manually update this file to specify your custom resources, as Visual Studio 2008 regenerates this file with each compilation. To be sure, you will do well if you allow the IDE to manage a Form's `*.resx` file on your behalf.

When you want to maintain a custom set of resources that are not directly mapped to a given Form, simply insert a new `*.resx` file (named `MyResources.resx` in this example) using the Project ➤ Add New Item menu item (see Figure 28-26).

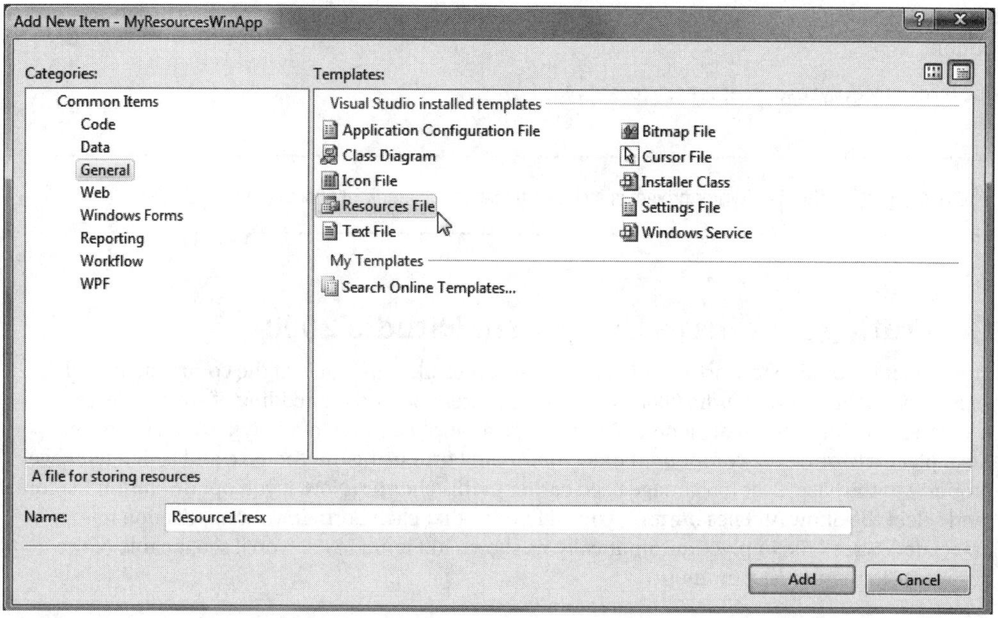

Figure 28-26. *Inserting a new* `*.resx` *file*

If you open your new `*.resx` file, a friendly GUI editor appears that allows you to insert string data, image files, sound clips, and other resources. The leftmost drop-down menu item allows you to select the type of resource you wish to add. First, add a new string resource named `WelcomeString` that is set to a message of your liking, as shown in Figure 28-27.

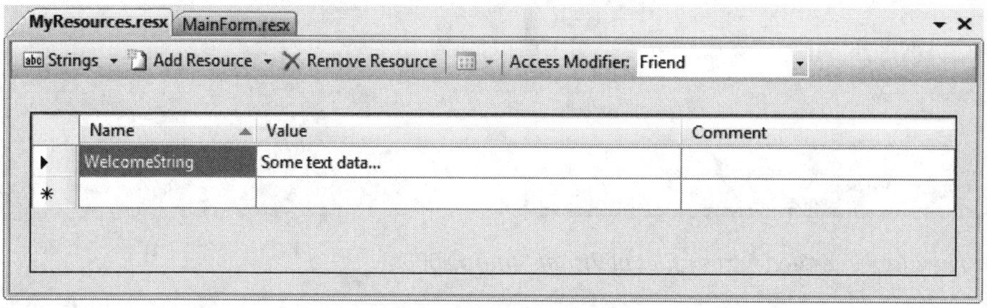

Figure 28-27. *Inserting new string resources with the* `*.resx` *editor*

Next, add the `happyDude.bmp` image file by selecting Images from the leftmost drop-down, choosing the Add Existing File option, as shown in Figure 28-28, and navigating to the `happyDude.bmp` file.

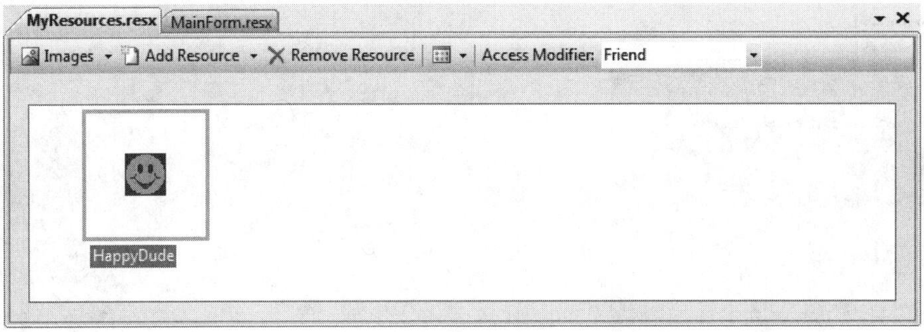

Figure 28-28. *Inserting new* `*.bmp` *resources with the* `*.resx` *editor*

At this point, you will find that the `*.bmp` file has been copied into your application directory. If you select the HappyDude icon from the `*.resx` editor, you can now specify that this image should be embedded directly into the assembly (rather than linked as an external stand-alone file) by adjusting the `Persistence` property, as you see in Figure 28-29.

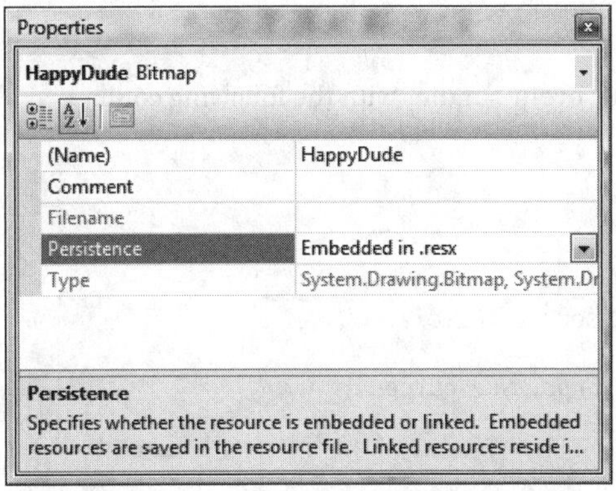

Figure 28-29. *Embedding specified resources*

Furthermore, Solution Explorer now has a new folder named Resources that contains each item to be embedded into the assembly. As you would guess, if you open a given resource, Visual Studio 2008 launches an associated editor. In any case, if you were to now compile your application, the string and image data would be embedded within your assembly.

Programmatically Reading Resources

Now that you understand the process of embedding resources into your assembly (using `vbc.exe` or Visual Studio 2008), you'll need to learn how to programmatically read them for use in your program using the `ResourceManager` type. To illustrate, add a new `Button` and an additional `PictureBox` widget on your Form type, as shown in Figure 28-30.

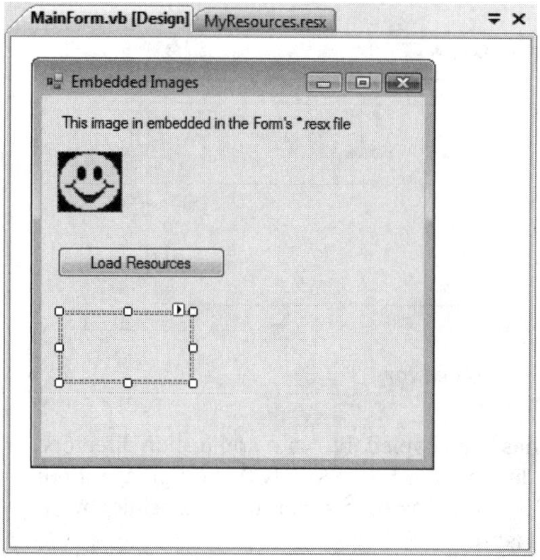

Figure 28-30. *The updated UI*

Next, handle the Button's Click event. Update the event handler with the following code:

```
Imports System.Resources
Imports System.Reflection

Public Class MainForm
  Private Sub btnLoadResources_Click(ByVal sender As System.Object, _
  ByVal e As System.EventArgs) Handles btnLoadResources.Click
    ' Make a resource manager.
    Dim rm As New ResourceManager("MyResourcesWinApp.MyResources", _
      Assembly.GetExecutingAssembly())

    ' Get the embedded string (case sensitive!)
    MessageBox.Show(rm.GetString("WelcomeString"))

    ' Get the embedded bitmap (case sensitive!)
    myPictureBox.Image = CType(rm.GetObject("HappyDude"), Bitmap)

    ' Clean up.
    rm.ReleaseAllResources()
  End Sub
End Class
```

Notice that the first constructor argument to the ResourceManager is the fully qualified name of your *.resx file (minus the file extension). The second parameter is a reference to the assembly that contains the embedded resource (which is the current assembly in this case). Once you have created the ResourceManager, you can call GetString() or GetObject() to extract the embedded data. If you were to run the application and click the button, you would find that the string data is displayed in the MessageBox and the image data has been extracted from the assembly and placed into the PictureBox.

■ **Source Code** The MyResourcesWinApp project is included under the Chapter 28 subdirectory.

Summary

GDI+ is the name given to a number of related .NET namespaces, each of which is used to render graphic images to a Control-derived type. The bulk of this chapter was spent examining how to work with core GDI+ object types such as colors, fonts, graphics images, pens, and brushes in conjunction with the almighty Graphics type. Along the way, you examined some GDI+-centric details such as hit testing and how to drag and drop images.

This chapter wrapped up by examining the Windows Forms resource format. As shown, a *.resx denotes resources using a set of name/value pairs describes as XML. This file can be fed into the resgen.exe utility, resulting in a binary format (*.resources) that can then be embedded into a related assembly. Finally, the ResourceManager type provides a simple way to programmatically retrieve embedded resources at runtime.

CHAPTER 29

Programming with Windows Forms Controls

This chapter is concerned with providing a road map of the controls defined in the System.Windows.Forms namespace. Chapter 27 already gave you a chance to work with some controls mounted onto a main Form such as MenuStrip, ToolStrip, and StatusStrip. In this chapter, however, you will examine various types that tend to exist within the boundaries of a Form's client area (e.g., Button, MaskedTextBox, WebBrowser, MonthCalendar, TreeView, and the like). Once you look at the core UI widgets, you will then cover the process of building custom Windows Forms controls that integrate into the Visual Studio 2008 IDE.

The chapter then investigates the process of building custom dialog boxes and the role of *form inheritance*, which allows you to build hierarchies of related Form types. The chapter wraps up with a discussion of how to establish the *docking* and *anchoring* behaviors for your family of GUI types, and the role of the FlowControlPanel and TableControlPanel types supplied by the Windows Forms API.

The World of Windows Forms Controls

The System.Windows.Forms namespace contains a number of types that represent common GUI widgets typically used to allow you to respond to user input in a Windows Forms application. Many of the controls you will work with on a day-to-day basis (such as Button, TextBox, and Label) are quite intuitive to work with. Other more exotic controls and components (such as TreeView, ErrorProvider, and TabControl) require a bit more explanation.

As you learned in Chapter 27, the System.Windows.Forms.Control type is the base class for all derived widgets. Recall that Control provides the ability to process mouse and keyboard events, establish the physical dimensions and position of the widget using various properties (Height, Width, Left, Right, Location, etc.), manipulate background and foreground colors, establish the active font/cursor, and so forth. As well, the Control base type defines members that control a widget's anchoring and docking behaviors (explained at the conclusion of this chapter).

As you read through this chapter, remember that the widgets you examine here gain a good deal of their functionality from the Control base class. Thus, we'll focus (more or less) on the unique members of a given widget. Do understand that this chapter does not attempt to fully describe each and every member of each and every control (that is a task for the .NET Framework 3.5 SDK documentation). Rest assured, though, that once you complete this chapter, you will have no problem understanding the widgets I have not directly described.

Adding Controls to Forms by Hand

Regardless of which type of control you choose to place on a Form, you will follow an identical set of steps to do so. First of all, you must define member variables that represent the controls themselves. Next, inside the Form's constructor (or within a helper method called by the constructor), you'll configure the look and feel of each control using the exposed properties, methods, and events. Finally (and most important), once you've set the control to its initial state, you must add it into the Form's internal controls collection using the inherited `Controls` property. If you forget this final step, your widgets will *not* be visible at runtime.

To illustrate the process of adding controls to a Form, let's begin by building a `Form` type "wizard-free" using your text editor of choice and the VB 2008 command-line compiler. Create a new VB 2008 file named `ControlsByHand.vb` and code a new `MainWindow` class as follows:

```
Imports System.Windows.Forms
Imports System.Drawing

Class MainWindow
  Inherits Form

  ' Form widget member variables.
  Private firstNameBox As New TextBox()
  Private WithEvents btnShowControls As New Button()

  Public Sub New()
    ' Configure Form.
    Me.Text = "Simple Controls"
    Me.Width = 300
    Me.Height = 200
    CenterToScreen()

    ' Add a new textbox to the Form.
    firstNameBox.Text = "Hello"
    firstNameBox.Size = New Size(150, 50)
    firstNameBox.Location = New Point(10, 10)
    Me.Controls.Add(firstNameBox)

    ' Add a new button to the Form.
    btnShowControls.Text = "Click Me"
    btnShowControls.Size = New Size(90, 30)
    btnShowControls.Location = New Point(10, 70)
    btnShowControls.BackColor = Color.DodgerBlue
    Me.Controls.Add(btnShowControls)
  End Sub

  ' Handle Button's Click event.
  Private Sub btnShowControls_Clicked(ByVal sender As Object, _
  ByVal e As EventArgs) Handles btnShowControls.Click
    ' Call ToString() on each control in the
    ' Form's Controls collection
    Dim ctrlInfo As String = ""
    For Each c As Control In Me.Controls
      ctrlInfo &= String.Format("Control: {0}" & Chr(10), c.ToString())
    Next
    MessageBox.Show(ctrlInfo, "Controls on Form")
  End Sub
End Class
```

Now, add a second class to the `ControlsByHand.vb` file that implements the program's `Main()` method:

```
Class Program
  Public Shared Sub Main()
    Application.Run(New MainWindow())
  End Sub
End Class
```

At this point, compile your VB 2008 file at the command line using the following command:

```
vbc/target:winexe *.vb
```

When you run your program and click the Form's button, you will find a message box that lists each item on the Form, as you see in Figure 29-1.

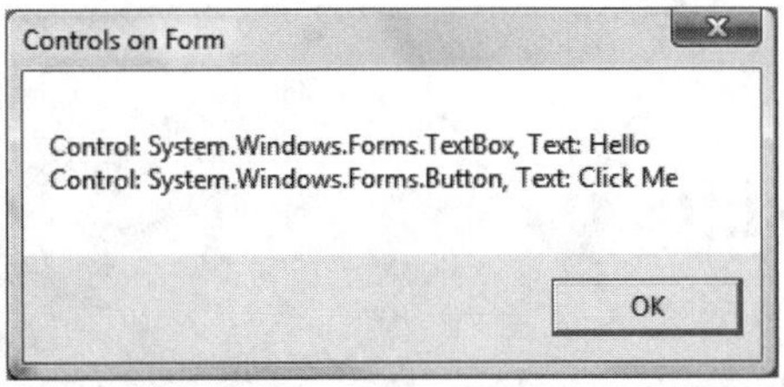

Figure 29-1. *Interacting with the Form's controls collection*

The Control.ControlCollection Type

While the process of adding a new widget to a Form is quite simple, I'd like to discuss the `Controls` property in a bit more detail. This property returns a reference to a nested class named `ControlCollection` defined within the `Control` class. The nested `ControlCollection` type maintains an entry for each widget placed on the Form. You can obtain a reference to this collection anytime you wish to "walk the list" of child widgets:

```
' Get access to the nested ControlCollection for this Form.
Dim coll As Control.ControlCollection = Me.Controls
```

Once you have a reference to this collection, you can manipulate its contents using the members shown in Table 29-1.

Table 29-1. `ControlCollection` *Members*

Member	Meaning in Life
`Add()` `AddRange()`	Insert a new `Control`-derived type (or array of types) in the collection
`Clear()`	Removes all entries in the collection
`Count`	Returns the number of items in the collection
`GetEnumerator()`	Returns the `IEnumerator` interface for this collection
`Remove()` `RemoveAt()`	Remove a control from the collection

Given that a Form maintains a collection of its controls, it is very simple under Windows Forms to dynamically create, remove, or otherwise manipulate visual elements. For example, assume you wish to disable all Button types on a given Form (or some such similar operation, such as change the background color of all TextBoxes). To do so, you can leverage the VB 2008 TypeOf/Is construct to determine who's who and change the state of the widgets accordingly:

```
Private Sub DisableAllButtons()
  For Each c As Control In Me.Controls
    If TypeOf c Is Button Then
      CType(c, Button).Enabled = False
    End If
    Next
End Sub
```

■ Source Code The ControlsByHand project is included under the Chapter 29 subdirectory.

Adding Controls to Forms Using Visual Studio 2008

Now that you understand the process of adding controls to a Form by hand, let's see how Visual Studio 2008 can automate the process. Create a new Windows Application project for testing purposes named whatever you choose. Similar to the process of designing with menu, toolbar, or status bar controls, when you drop a control from the Toolbox onto the Forms designer, the IDE responds by automatically adding the correct member variable to the *.Designer.vb file. As well, when you design the look and feel of the widget using the IDE's Properties window, the related code changes are added to the InitializeComponent() member function (also located within the *.Designer.vb file).

■ Note Recall that the Properties window also allows you to handle events for a given control when you click the lightning bolt icon. Simply select the widget from the drop-down list and type in the name of the method to be called for the events you are interested in responding to (or just double-click the event to generate a default event handler name, which always takes the form *NameOfControl_NameOfEvent()*).

Assume you have added a TextBox and Button type to the Forms designer. Notice that when you reposition a control on the designer, the Visual Studio 2008 IDE provides visual hints regarding the spacing and alignment of the current widget (see Figure 29-2).

Once you have placed the Button and TextBox on the designer, examine the code generated in the InitializeComponent() method. Here you will find that the control types have been allocated and inserted into the Form's ControlCollection automatically (in addition to any settings you may have made using the Properties window):

```
Private Sub InitializeComponent()
  Me.Button1 = New System.Windows.Forms.Button
  Me.TextBox1 = New System.Windows.Forms.TextBox
...
  Me.Controls.Add(Me.TextBox1)
  Me.Controls.Add(Me.Button1)
End Sub
```

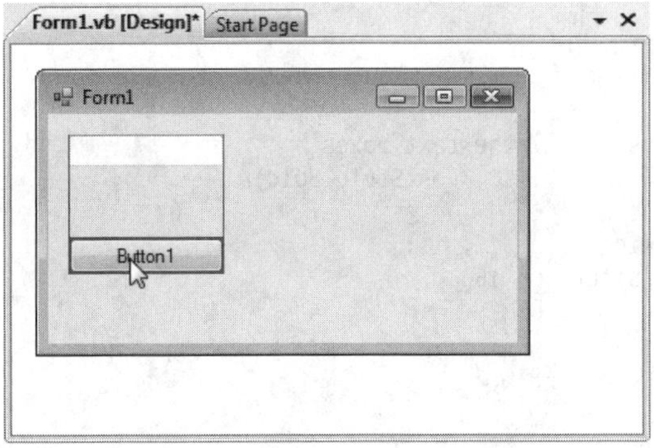

Figure 29-2. *Alignment and spacing hints*

As you can see, a tool such as Visual Studio 2008 simply saves you some typing time (and helps you avoid hand cramps). Although `InitializeComponent()` is maintained on your behalf, do understand that you are free to configure a given control directly in code anywhere you see necessary (constructors, event handlers, helper functions, etc.). The role of `InitializeComponent()` is simply to establish the initial state of your UI elements. If you want to keep your life simple, I suggest allowing Visual Studio 2008 to maintain `InitializeComponent()` on your behalf, given that the designers may ignore or overwrite edits you make within this method.

Working with the Basic Controls

The `System.Windows.Forms` namespace defines numerous "basic controls" that are commonplace to any windowing framework (buttons, labels, text boxes, check boxes, etc.). Although I would guess you are familiar with the basic operations of such types, let's examine some of the more interesting aspects of the following basic UI elements:

- `Label`, `TextBox`, and `MaskedTextBox`
- `Button`
- `CheckBox`, `RadioButton`, and `GroupBox`
- `CheckedListBox`, `ListBox`, and `ComboBox`

Once you have become comfortable with these basic `Control`-derived types, we will turn our attention to more exotic widgets such as `MonthCalendar`, `TabControl`, `TrackBar`, `WebBrowser`, and so forth.

Fun with Labels

The `Label` control is capable of holding read-only information (text or image based) that explains the role of the other controls to help the user along. Assume you have created a new Visual Studio 2008 Windows Forms project named LabelsAndTextBoxes. Define a method called `CreateLabelControl` in your `Form`-derived type that creates and configures a `Label` type, and then adds it to the Form's controls collection:

```
Private Sub CreateLabelControl()
  ' Create and configure a Label.
  Dim lblInstructions As New Label()
  lblInstructions.Name = "lblInstructions"
  lblInstructions.Text = "Please enter values in all the text boxes"
  lblInstructions.Font = New Font("Times New Roman", 10, FontStyle.Bold)
  lblInstructions.AutoSize = True
  lblInstructions.Location = New System.Drawing.Point(16, 13)
  lblInstructions.Size = New System.Drawing.Size(240, 16)

  ' Add to Form's controls collection.
  Me.Controls.Add(lblInstructions)
End Sub
```

If you were to call this helper function within your Form's constructor, you would find your prompt displayed in the upper portion of the main window:

```
Sub New()
  ' This call is required by the Windows Forms designer.
  InitializeComponent()

  ' Add any initialization after the InitializeComponent() call.
  CreateLabelControl()

  ' Inherited method to center Form on the screen.
  CenterToScreen()
End Sub
```

Unlike most other widgets, `Label` controls cannot receive focus via a Tab keypress. However, it is possible to create *mnemonic keys* for any `Label` by setting the `UseMnemonic` property to `True` (which happens to be the default setting). Once you have done so, a `Label`'s `Text` property can define a shortcut key (via the ampersand symbol, &), which is used to tab to the control that follows it in the tab order.

■ **Note** You'll learn more about configuring tab order later in this chapter, but for the time being, understand that a control's tab order is established via the `TabIndex` property. By default, a control's `TabIndex` is set based on the order in which it was added to the Forms designer. Thus, if you add a `Label` followed by a `TextBox`, the `Label` is set to `TabIndex 0` while the `TextBox` is set to `TabIndex 1`.

To illustrate, let's now leverage the Forms designer to build a UI containing a set of three `Labels` and three `TextBoxes` (be sure to leave room on the upper part of the Form to display the `Label` dynamically created in the `CreateLabelControl()` method). In Figure 29-3, note that each label has an underlined letter that was identified using the & character in the value assigned to the `Text` property (as you might know, &-specified characters allow the user to activate an item using the Alt+<*assigned key*> keystroke).

If you now run your project, you will be able to tab between each `TextBox` using the Alt+P, Alt+M, or Alt+U keystrokes.

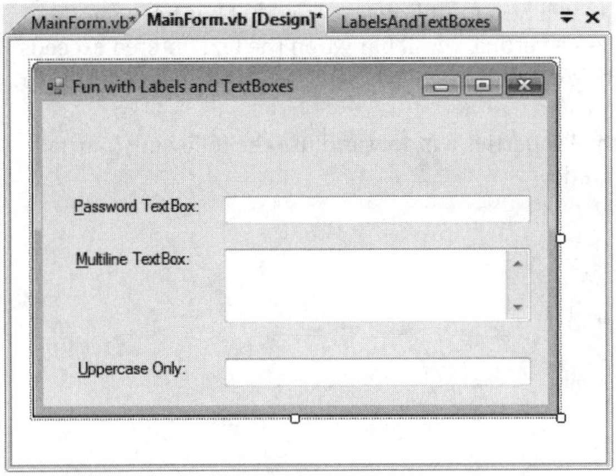

Figure 29-3. *Assigning mnemonics to* `Label` *controls*

Fun with TextBoxes

Unlike the `Label` control, the `TextBox` control is typically not read-only (although it could be if you set the `ReadOnly` property to `True`), and it is commonly used to allow the user to enter textual data for processing. The `TextBox` type can be configured to hold a single line or multiple lines of text, it can be configured with a *password character* (such as an asterisk, *), and it may support scroll bars in the case of multiline text boxes. In addition to the behavior inherited by its base classes, `TextBox` defines a few particular properties of interest (see Table 29-2).

Table 29-2. `TextBox` *Properties*

Property	Meaning in Life
`AcceptsReturn`	Gets or sets a value indicating whether pressing Enter in a multiline `TextBox` control creates a new line of text in the control or activates the "default button" for the Form
`CharacterCasing`	Gets or sets whether the `TextBox` control modifies the case of characters as they are typed
`PasswordChar`	Gets or sets the character used to mask characters in a single-line `TextBox` control used to enter passwords
`ScrollBars`	Gets or sets which scroll bars should appear in a multiline `TextBox` control
`TextAlign`	Gets or sets how text is aligned in a `TextBox` control, using the `HorizontalAlignment` enumeration

To illustrate some aspects of the `TextBox`, let's configure the three `TextBox` controls on the current Form. The first `TextBox` (named `txtPassword`) should be configured as a password text box, meaning the characters typed into the `TextBox` should not be directly visible, but are instead masked with a predefined password character via the `PasswordChar` property.

■ **Note** Be aware that the `PasswordChar` property does not encrypt the password data! It simply prevents the password data from being viewed within the `TextBox`.

The second TextBox (named txtMultiline) will be a multiline text area that has been configured to accept Enter key processing and displays a vertical scroll bar when the text entered exceeds the space of the TextBox area. Finally, the third TextBox (named txtUppercase) will be configured to translate the entered character data into uppercase.

Configure each TextBox accordingly via the Properties window and use the following (partial) InitializeComponent() implementation as a guide:

```
Private Sub InitializeComponent()
...
  ' txtPassword
  '
  Me.txtPassword.PasswordChar = '*'
...
  ' txtMultiline
  '
  Me.txtMultiline.Multiline = True
  Me.txtMultiline.ScrollBars = System.Windows.Forms.ScrollBars.Vertical
...
  ' txtUpperCase
  '
  Me.txtUpperCase.CharacterCasing = _
    System.Windows.Forms.CharacterCasing.Upper
...
End Sub
```

Notice that the ScrollBars property is assigned a value from the ScrollBars enumeration, which defines the following values:

```
Enum ScrollBars
  Auto
  Both
  Horizontal
  None
  Vertical
End Enum
```

The CharacterCasing property works in conjunction with the CharacterCasing enum, which is defined like so:

```
Enum CharacterCasing
  Normal
  Upper
  Lower
End Enum
```

Now assume you have placed a Button on the Form (named btnDisplayData) and added an event handler for the Button's Click event. The implementation of this method simply displays the value in each TextBox within a message box:

```
Private Sub btnDisplayData_Click(ByVal sender As System.Object, _
  ByVal e As System.EventArgs) Handles btnDisplayData.Click
  ' Get data from all the text boxes.
  Dim textBoxData As String = ""
  textBoxData &= String.Format("MultiLine: {0}" & Chr(10), txtMultiline.Text)
  textBoxData &= String.Format("Password: {0}" & Chr(10), _
   txtPassword.Text)
  textBoxData &= String.Format("Uppercase: {0}" & Chr(10), txtUpperCase.Text)
```

```
    ' Display all the data.
    MessageBox.Show(textBoxData, "Here is the data in your TextBoxes")
End Sub
```

Figure 29-4 shows one possible input session (note that you need to hold down the Alt key to see the label mnemonics).

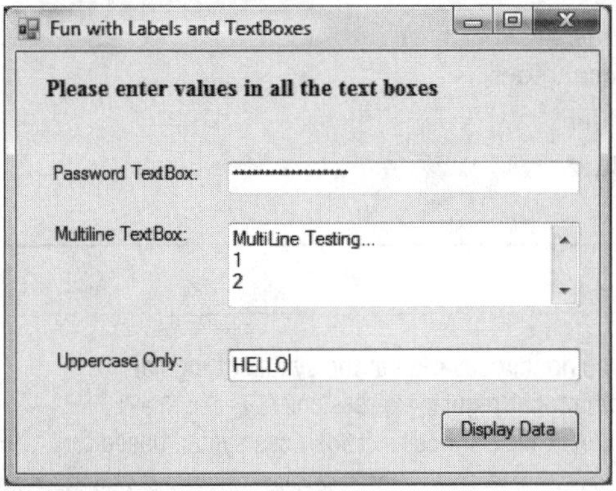

Figure 29-4. *The many faces of the* `TextBox` *type*

Figure 29-5 shows the result of clicking the `Button`.

Figure 29-5. *Extracting values from* `TextBox` *types*

Fun with MaskedTextBoxes

The `MaskedTextBox` allows you to specify a valid sequence of characters that will be accepted by the input area (Social Security number, phone number with area code, zip code, or whatnot). The mask to test against (termed a *mask expression*) is established using specific tokens embedded into a string literal. Once you have created a mask expression, this value is assigned to the `Mask` property. Table 29-3 documents some (but not all) valid masking tokens.

Table 29-3. *Mask Tokens of* `MaskedTextBox`

Mask Token	Meaning in Life
`0`	Represents a mandatory digit with the value 0–9
`9`	Represents an optional digit or a space
`L`	Required letter (in uppercase or lowercase), A–Z
`?`	Optional letter (in uppercase or lowercase), A–Z
`,`	Represents a thousands separator placeholder
`:`	Represents a time separator placeholder
`/`	Represents a date separator placeholder
`$`	Represents a currency symbol

■ **Note** The characters understood by the `MaskedTextBox` do not directly map to the syntax of regular expressions. Although .NET provides namespaces to work with proper regular expressions (`System.Text.RegularExpressions` and `System.Web.RegularExpressions`), the `MaskedTextBox` uses syntax based on the legacy `MaskedEdit` VB6 COM control.

In addition to the `Mask` property, the `MaskedTextBox` has additional members that determine how this control should respond if the user enters incorrect data. For example, `BeepOnError` will cause the control to (obviously) issue a beep when the mask is not honored, and it prevents the illegal character from being processed.

To illustrate the use of the `MaskedTextBox`, add an additional `Label` and `MaskedTextBox` to your current Form. Although you are free to build a mask pattern directly in code, the Properties window provides an ellipsis button for the `Mask` property that will launch a dialog box with a number of predefined masks, as shown in Figure 29-6.

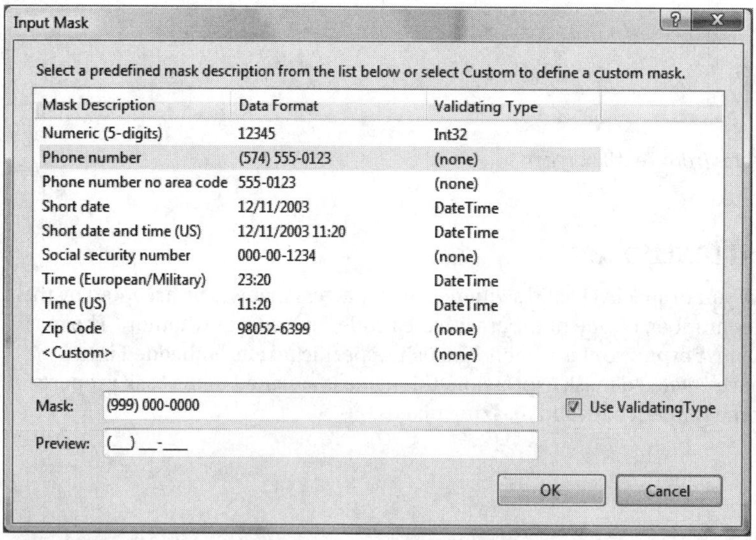

Figure 29-6. *Predefined mask values of the* `Mask` *property*

Find a masking pattern (such as Phone number), enable the BeepOnError property, and take your program out for another test run. You should find that you are unable to enter any alphabetic characters (in the case of the Phone number mask).

As you would expect, the MaskedTextBox will send out various events during its lifetime, one of which is MaskInputRejected, which is fired when the end user enters erroneous input. Handle this event using the Properties window and notice that the second incoming argument of the generated event handler is of type MaskInputRejectedEventArgs. This type has a property named RejectionHint that contains a brief description of the input error. For testing purposes, simply display the error on the Form's caption.

```
Private Sub txtMaskedTextBox_MaskInputRejected(ByVal sender As System.Object, _
  ByVal e As System.Windows.Forms.MaskInputRejectedEventArgs) _
  Handles txtMaskedTextBox.MaskInputRejected
  Me.Text = String.Format("Error: {0}", e.RejectionHint)
End Sub
```

Source Code The LabelsAndTextBoxes project is included under the Chapter 29 subdirectory.

Fun with Buttons

The role of the System.Windows.Forms.Button type is to provide a vehicle for user confirmation, typically in response to a mouse click or keypress. The Button class immediately derives from an abstract type named ButtonBase, which provides a number of key behaviors for all derived types (such as CheckBox, RadioButton, and Button). Table 29-4 describes some (but by no means all) of the core properties of ButtonBase.

Table 29-4. ButtonBase *Properties*

Property	Meaning in Life
FlatStyle	Gets or sets the flat style appearance of the Button control, using members of the FlatStyle enumeration.
Image	Configures which (optional) image is displayed somewhere within the bounds of a ButtonBase-derived type. Recall that the Control class also defines a BackgroundImage property, which is used to render an image over the entire surface area of a widget.
ImageAlign	Sets the alignment of the image on the Button control, using the ContentAlignment enumeration.
TextAlign	Gets or sets the alignment of the text on the Button control, using the ContentAlignment enumeration.

The TextAlign property of ButtonBase makes it extremely simple to position text at just about any location. To set the position of your Button's caption, use the ContentAlignment enumeration (defined in the System.Drawing namespace). As you will see, this same enumeration can be used to place an optional image on the Button type:

```
Enum ContentAlignment
  BottomCenter
  BottomLeft
  BottomRight
  MiddleCenter
```

```
    MiddleLeft
    MiddleRight
    TopCenter
    TopLeft
    TopRight
End Enum
```

FlatStyle is another property of interest. It is used to control the general look and feel of the Button control, and it can be assigned any value from the FlatStyle enumeration (defined in the System.Windows.Forms namespace):

```
Enum FlatStyle
    Flat
    Popup
    Standard
    System
End Enum
```

To illustrate working with the Button type, create a new Windows Forms application named Buttons. On the Forms designer, add three Button types (named btnFlat, btnPopup, and btnStandard) and set each Button's FlatStyle property value accordingly (e.g., FlatStyle.Flat, FlatStyle.Popup, or FlatStyle.Standard). As well, set the Text value of each Button to a fitting value and handle the Click event for the btnStandard Button. As you will see in just a moment, when the user clicks this button, you will reposition the button's text using the TextAlign property.

Now, add a final fourth Button (named btnImage) that supports a background image (set via the BackgroundImage property) and a small bull's-eye icon (set via the Image property), which will also be dynamically relocated when the btnStandard Button is clicked. Feel free to use any image files to assign to the BackgroundImage and Image properties, but do note that the downloadable source code contains the images used here.

Given that the designer has authored all the necessary UI prep code within InitializeComponent(), the remaining code makes use of the ContentAlignment enumeration to reposition the location of the text on btnStandard and the icon on btnImage. In the following code, notice that you are calling the shared Enum.GetValues() method to obtain the list of names from the ContentAlignment enumeration:

```
Public Class MainForm
  ' Hold the current text alignment
  Private currAlignment As ContentAlignment = ContentAlignment.MiddleCenter
  Private currEnumPos As Integer = 0

  Private Sub btnStandard_Click(ByVal sender As System.Object, _
  ByVal e As System.EventArgs) Handles btnStandard.Click
    ' Get all possible values
    ' of the ContentAlignment enum.
    Dim values As Array = [Enum].GetValues(currAlignment.GetType())

    ' Bump the current position in the enum.
    ' and check for wraparound.
    currEnumPos += 1
    If currEnumPos >= values.Length Then
      currEnumPos = 0
    End If

    ' Bump the current enum value.
    currAlignment = CType([Enum].Parse(currAlignment.GetType(), _
      values.GetValue(currEnumPos).ToString()), ContentAlignment)
    btnStandard.TextAlign = currAlignment
```

```
    ' Paint enum value name on button.
    btnStandard.Text = currAlignment.ToString()

    ' Now assign the location of the icon on
    ' btnImage...
    btnImage.ImageAlign = currAlignment
  End Sub
End Class
```

Now run your program. As you click the middle button, you will see its text is set to the current name and position of the `currAlignment` member variable. As well, the icon within the `btnImage` is repositioned based on the same value. Figure 29-7 shows the output.

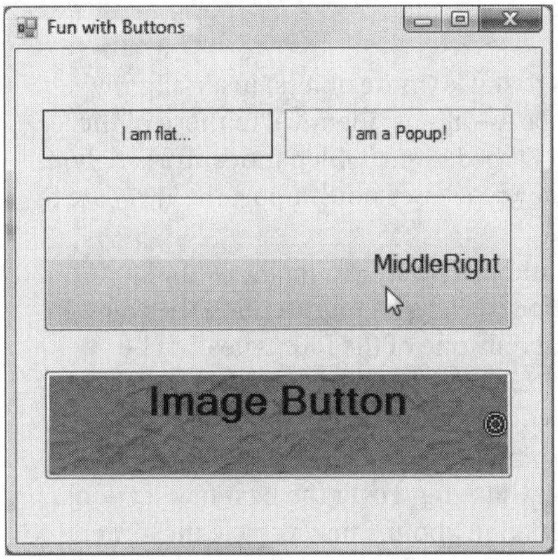

Figure 29-7. *The many faces of the* `Button` *type*

Source Code The Buttons project is included under the Chapter 29 directory.

Fun with CheckBoxes, RadioButtons, and GroupBoxes

The `System.Windows.Forms` namespace defines a number of other types that extend `ButtonBase`, specifically `CheckBox` (which can support up to three possible states) and `RadioButton` (which can be either selected or not selected). Like the `Button`, these types also receive most of their functionality from the `Control` base class. However, each class defines some additional functionality. First, consider the core properties of the `CheckBox` widget described in Table 29-5.

Table 29-5. `CheckBox` *Properties*

Property	Meaning in Life
`Appearance`	Configures the appearance of a `CheckBox` control, using the `Appearance` enumeration.
`AutoCheck`	Gets or sets a value indicating whether the `Checked` or `CheckState` value and the `CheckBox`'s appearance are automatically changed when it is clicked.

Continued

Table 29-5. *Continued*

Property	Meaning in Life
CheckAlign	Gets or sets the horizontal and vertical alignment of a CheckBox on a CheckBox control, using the ContentAlignment enumeration (much like the Button type).
Checked	Returns a Boolean value representing the state of the CheckBox (checked or unchecked). If the ThreeState property is set to True, the Checked property returns True for either checked or indeterminately checked values.
CheckState	Gets or sets a value indicating whether the CheckBox is checked, using a CheckState enumeration rather than a Boolean value.
ThreeState	Configures whether the CheckBox supports three states of selection (as specified by the CheckState enumeration) rather than two.

The RadioButton type requires little comment, given that it is (more or less) just a slightly redesigned CheckBox. In fact, the members of a RadioButton are almost identical to those of the CheckBox type. The only notable difference is the CheckedChanged event, which (not surprisingly) is fired when the Checked value changes. Also, the RadioButton type does not support the ThreeState property, as a RadioButton must be on or off.

Typically, multiple RadioButton objects are logically and physically grouped together to function as a whole. For example, if you have a set of four RadioButton types representing the color choice of a given automobile, you may wish to ensure that only one of the four types can be checked at a time. Rather than writing code programmatically to do so, simply use the GroupBox control to ensure all RadioButtons are mutually exclusive.

To illustrate working with the CheckBox, RadioButton, and GroupBox types, let's create a new Windows Forms application named CarConfig, which you will extend over the next few sections. The main Form allows users to enter (and confirm) information about a new vehicle they intend to purchase. The order summary is displayed in a Label type once the Confirm Order button has been clicked. Figure 29-8 shows the initial UI.

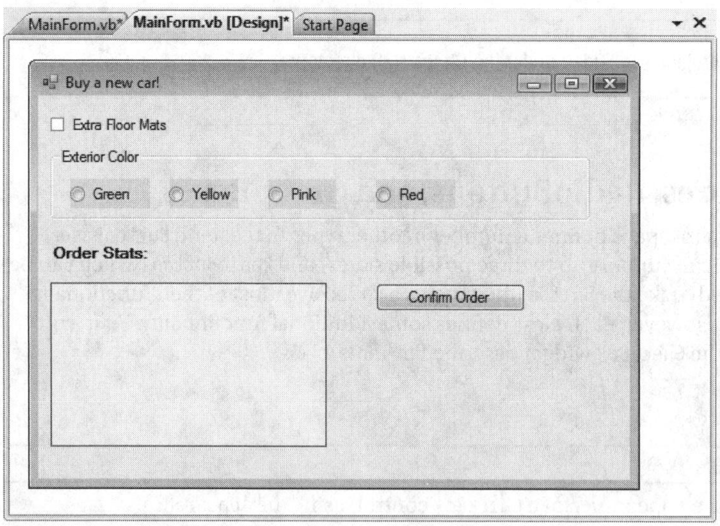

Figure 29-8. *The initial UI of the CarConfig Form*

Assuming you have leveraged the Forms designer to build your UI, you will now have numerous member variables representing each GUI widget. As well, the InitializeComponent() method will be updated accordingly. The first point of interest is the construction of the CheckBox control. As with any Control-derived type, once the look and feel has been established, it must be inserted into the Form's internal collection of controls:

```
Private Sub InitializeComponent()
...
  ' checkFloorMats
  '
  Me.checkFloorMats.Name = "checkFloorMats"
  Me.checkFloorMats.TabIndex = 0
  Me.checkFloorMats.Text = "Extra Floor Mats"
...
  Me.Controls.Add(Me.checkFloorMats)
End Sub
```

Next, you have the configuration of the GroupBox and its contained RadioButton types. When you wish to place a control under the ownership of a GroupBox, you want to add each item to the GroupBox's Controls collection (in the same way you add widgets to the Form's Controls collection).

```
Private Sub InitializeComponent()
...
  ' radioRed
  '
  Me.radioRed.Name = "radioRed"
  Me.radioRed.Size = new System.Drawing.Size(64, 23)
  Me.radioRed.Text = "Red"
  '
  ' groupBoxColor
  '
...
  Me.groupBoxColor.Controls.Add(Me.radioRed)
  Me.groupBoxColor.Text = "Exterior Color"
...
End Sub
```

To make things a bit more interesting, use the Properties window to handle the Enter and Leave events sent by the GroupBox object. Understand, of course, that you do not need to capture the Enter or Leave event for a GroupBox. However, to illustrate, the event handlers update the caption text of the GroupBox as shown here:

```
Public Class MainForm
  Private Sub groupBoxColor_Enter(ByVal sender As System.Object, _
  ByVal e As System.EventArgs) Handles groupBoxColor.Enter
    groupBoxColor.Text = "Exterior Color: You are in the group..."
  End Sub

  Private Sub groupBoxColor_Leave(ByVal sender As System.Object, _
  ByVal e As System.EventArgs) Handles groupBoxColor.Leave
    groupBoxColor.Text = "Exterior Color: Thanks for visiting the group..."
  End Sub
End Class
```

The final GUI widgets on this Form (the Label and Button types) will also be configured and inserted in the Form's Controls collection via InitializeComponent(). The Label is used to display the order confirmation, which is formatted in the Click event handler of the order Button, as shown here:

```
Private Sub btnOrder_Click(ByVal sender As Object, _
  ByVal e As System.EventArgs) Handles btnOrder.Click
  ' Build a string to display information.
  Dim orderInfo As String = ""
  If checkFloorMats.Checked Then
    orderInfo &= "You want floor mats." & Chr(10)
  End If
  If radioRed.Checked Then
    orderInfo &= "You want a red exterior." & Chr(10)
  End If
  If radioYellow.Checked Then
    orderInfo &= "You want a yellow exterior." & Chr(10)
  End If
  If radioGreen.Checked Then
    orderInfo &= "You want a green exterior." & Chr(10)
  End If
  If radioPink.Checked Then
    orderInfo &= "Why do you want a PINK exterior?" & Chr(10)
  End If
  ' Send this string to the Label.
  infoLabel.Text = orderInfo
End Sub
```

Notice that both the CheckBox and RadioButton support the Checked property, which allows you to investigate the state of the widget. Finally, recall that if you have configured a tri-state CheckBox, you will need to check the state of the widget using the CheckState property.

Fun with CheckedListBoxes

Now that you have explored the basic Button-centric widgets, let's move on to the set of list selection–centric types, specifically CheckedListBox, ListBox, and ComboBox. The CheckedListBox widget allows you to group related CheckBox options in a scrollable list control. Assume you have added such a control to your CarConfig Form that allows users to configure a number of options regarding an automobile's sound system (see Figure 29-9).

To insert new items in a CheckedListBox, call Add() for each item, or use the AddRange() method and send in an array of objects (strings, to be exact) that represent the full set of checkable items. Be aware that you can fill any of the list types at design time using the Items property located on the Properties window (just click the ellipsis button and type the string values). Here is the relevant code within InitializeComponent() that configures the CheckedListBox:

```
Private Sub InitializeComponent()
...
  ' checkedBoxRadioOptions
  '
  Me.checkedBoxRadioOptions.Items.AddRange(New Object() _
  {"Front Speakers", "8-Track Tape Player", _
  "CD Player", "Cassette Player", "Rear Speakers", "Ultra Base Thumper"})
...
  Me.Controls.Add (Me.checkedBoxRadioOptions)
End Sub
```

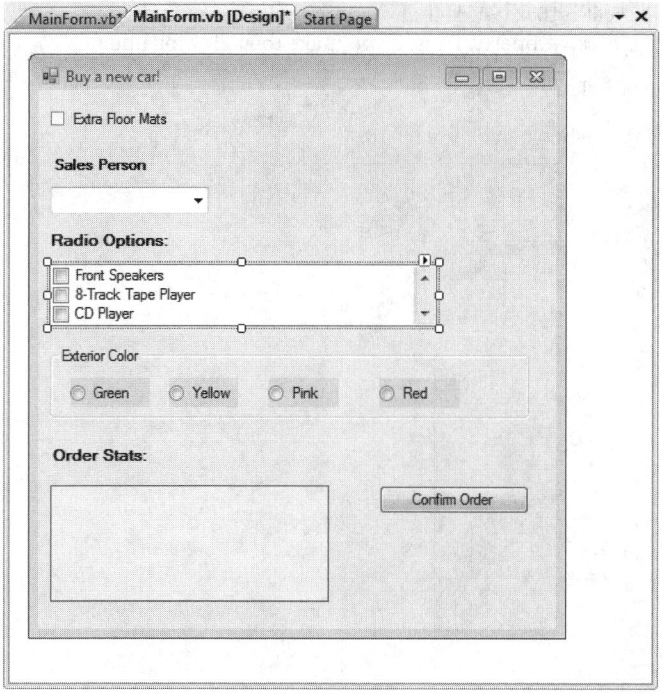

Figure 29-9. *The* `CheckedListBox` *type*

Now update the logic behind the `Click` event for the Confirm Order button. Ask the `CheckedListBox` which of its items are currently selected and add them to the `orderInfo` string. Here are the relevant code updates:

```
Private Sub btnOrder_Click(ByVal sender As Object, _
  ByVal e As EventArgs) Handles btnOrder.Click
  ' Build a string to display information.
  Dim orderInfo As String = ""
  ...
  orderInfo &= "--------------------------------" & Chr(10)
  For i As Integer = 0 To checkedBoxRadioOptions.Items.Count - 1
    ' For each item in the CheckedListBox:
    ' Is the current item checked?
    If checkedBoxRadioOptions.GetItemChecked(i) Then
      ' Get text of checked item and append to orderinfo string.
      orderInfo &= "Radio Item: "
      orderInfo &= checkedBoxRadioOptions.Items(i).ToString()
      orderInfo &= Chr(10)
   End If
  ...
  Next
End Sub
```

The final note regarding the CheckedListBox type is that it supports the use of multiple columns through the inherited MultiColumn property. Thus, if you make the following update:

```
checkedBoxRadioOptions.MultiColumn = True
```

you see the multicolumn CheckedListBox shown in Figure 29-10.

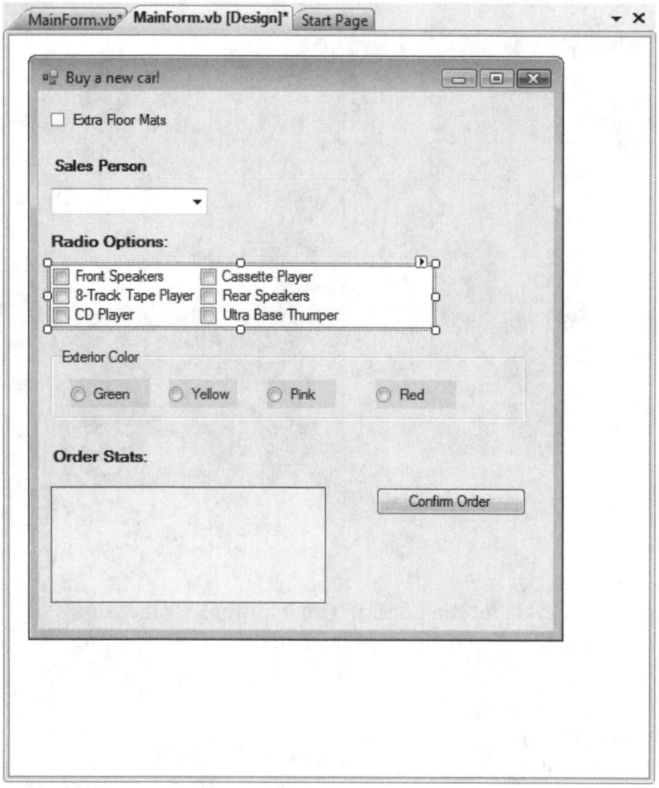

Figure 29-10. *Multicolumn* CheckedListBox *type*

Fun with ListBoxes

As mentioned earlier, the CheckedListBox type inherits most of its functionality from the ListBox type. To illustrate using the ListBox type, let's add another feature to the current CarConfig application: the ability to select the make (BMW, Yugo, etc.) of the automobile. Figure 29-11 shows the desired UI.

As always, begin by creating a member variable to manipulate your type (in this case, a ListBox type). Next, configure the look and feel using the following snapshot from InitializeComponent() as a guide:

```
Private Sub InitializeComponent()
...
  ' carMakeList
  '
  Me.carMakeList.Items.AddRange(New Object() {"BMW", "Caravan", "Ford", _
  "Grand Am", "Jeep", "Jetta", _
```

```
  "Saab", "Viper", "Yugo"})
...
  Me.Controls.Add (Me.carMakeList)
End Sub
```

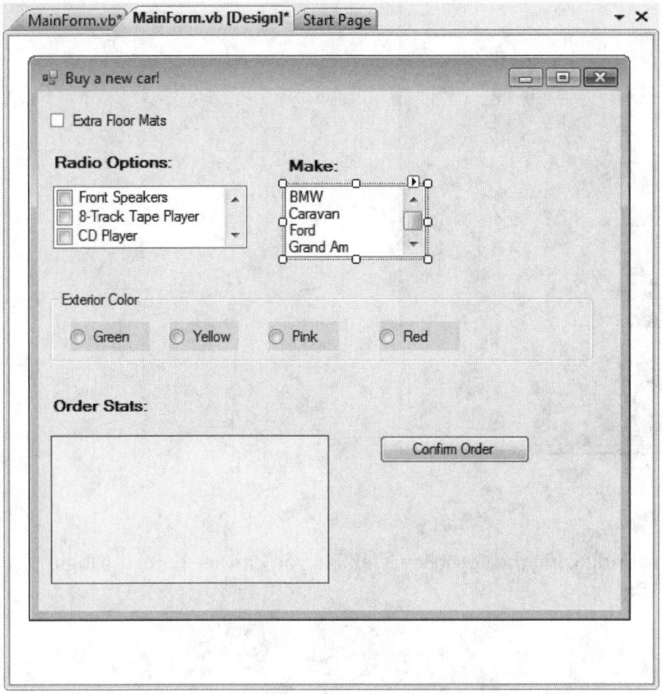

Figure 29-11. *The* `ListBox` *type*

The update to the `btnOrder_Click()` event handler is also simple:

```
Private Sub btnOrder_Click(ByVal sender As Object, _
  ByVal e As EventArgs) Handles btnOrder.Click
  ' Build a string to display information.
  Dim orderInfo As String = ""
...
  ' Get the currently selected item (not index of the item).
  If carMakeList.SelectedItem IsNot Nothing Then
    orderInfo &= "Make: " & carMakeList.SelectedItem & Chr(10)
...
  End If
End Sub
```

Fun with ComboBoxes

Like a `ListBox`, a `ComboBox` allows users to make a selection from a well-defined set of possibilities. However, the `ComboBox` type is unique in that users can also insert additional items. Recall that `ComboBox` derives from `ListBox` (which then derives from `Control`). To illustrate its use, add yet another GUI widget to the CarConfig Form that allows a user to enter the name of a preferred salesperson. If the salesperson in question is not on the list, the user can enter a custom name. One possible UI update is shown in Figure 29-12 (feel free to add your own salesperson monikers).

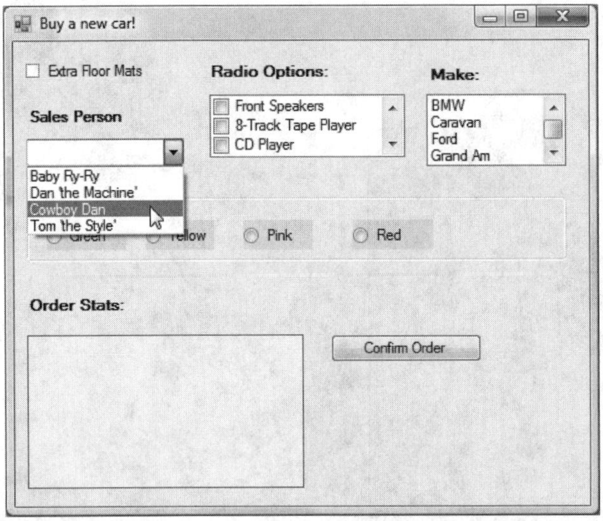

Figure 29-12. *The* ComboBox *type*

This modification begins with configuring the ComboBox itself. As you can see here, the logic looks identical to that for the ListBox:

```
Private Sub InitializeComponent()
...
  ' comboSalesPerson
  '
  Me.comboSalesPerson.Items.AddRange(New Object() _
  {"Baby Ry-Ry", "Dan 'the Machine'", _
  "Cowboy Dan", "Tom 'the Style' "})
...
  Me.Controls.Add (Me.comboSalesPerson)
End Sub
```

The update to the btnOrder_Click() event handler is again simple, as shown here:

```
Private Sub btnOrder_Click(ByVal sender As Object, _
ByVal e As EventArgs) Handles btnOrder.Click
  ' Build a string to display information.
  Dim orderInfo As String = ""
...
  ' Use the Text property to figure out the user's salesperson.
  If comboSalesPerson.Text <> "" Then
    orderInfo &= "Sales Person: " & comboSalesPerson.Text & Chr(10)
  Else
    orderInfo &= "You did not select a sales person!" & Chr(10)
...
  End If
End Sub
```

Configuring the Tab Order

Now that you have created a somewhat interesting Form, let's formalize the issue of tab order. As you may know, when a Form contains multiple GUI widgets, users expect to be able to shift focus using the Tab key. Configuring the tab order for your set of controls requires that you understand two key properties: TabStop and TabIndex.

The TabStop property can be set to True or False, based on whether or not you wish this GUI item to be reachable using the Tab key. Assuming the TabStop property has been set to True for a given widget, the TabOrder property is then set to establish its order of activation in the tabbing sequence (which is zero based). Consider this example:

```
' Configure tabbing properties.
radioRed.TabIndex = 2
radioRed.TabStop = True
```

The Tab Order Wizard

The Visual Studio 2008 IDE supplies a Tab Order Wizard, which you access by choosing View ➤ Tab Order (be aware that you will not find this menu option unless the Forms designer is active). Once activated, your design-time Form displays the current TabIndex value for each widget. To change these values, click each item in the order you choose (see Figure 29-13).

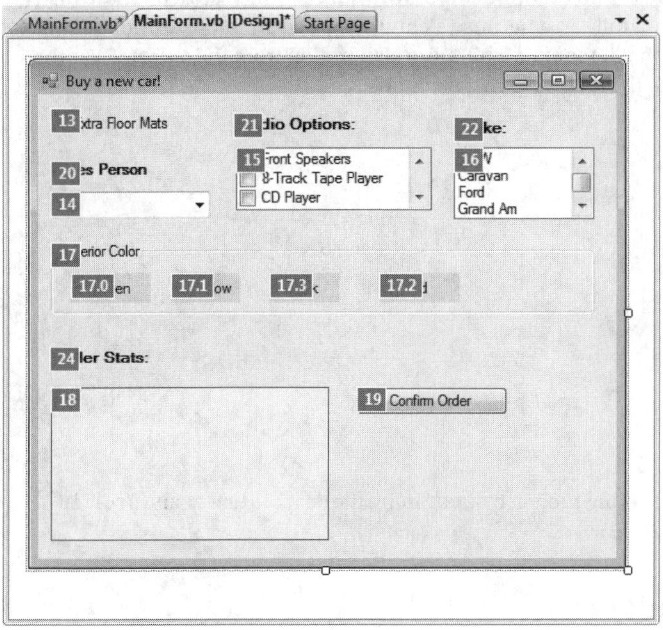

Figure 29-13. *The Tab Order Wizard*

To exit the Tab Order Wizard, simply press the Esc key.

Setting the Form's Default Input Button

Many user-input forms (especially dialog boxes) have a particular `Button` that will automatically respond to the user pressing the Enter key. For the current Form, if you wish to ensure that when the user presses the Enter key, the `Click` event handler for `btnOrder` is invoked, simply set the Form's `AcceptButton` property as follows:

```
' When the Enter key is pressed, it is as if
' the user clicked the btnOrder button.
Me.AcceptButton = btnOrder
```

■ **Note** Some Forms require the ability to simulate clicking the Form's Cancel button when the user presses the Esc key. This can be done by assigning the `CancelButton` property on the Form to the `Button` object representing the Cancel button.

Working with More Exotic Controls

At this point, you have seen how to work most of the basic Windows Forms controls (`Labels`, `TextBoxes`, and the like). The next task is to examine some GUI widgets, which are a bit more high-powered in their functionality. Thankfully, just because a control may seem "more exotic" does not mean it is hard to work with, only that it requires a bit more elaboration from the outset. Over the next several pages, we will examine the following GUI elements:

- `MonthCalendar`
- `ToolTip`
- `TabControl`
- `TrackBar`
- `Panel`
- The `UpDown` controls
- `ErrorProvider`
- `TreeView`
- `WebBrower`

To begin, let's wrap up the CarConfig project by examining the `MonthCalendar` and `ToolTip` controls.

Fun with MonthCalendars

The `System.Windows.Forms` namespace provides an extremely useful widget, the `MonthCalendar` control, that allows the user to select a date (or range of dates) using a friendly UI. To showcase this new control, update the existing CarConfig application to allow the user to enter in the new vehicle's delivery date. Figure 29-14 shows the updated (and slightly rearranged) Form running with its final design.

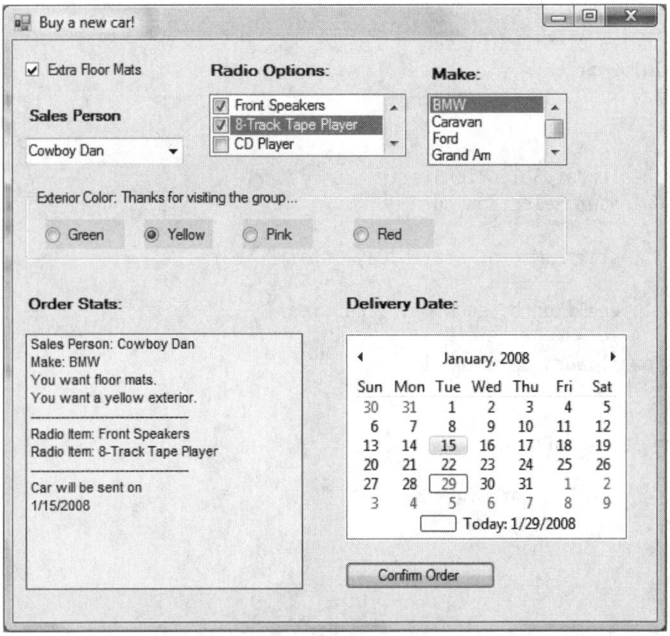

Figure 29-14. *The* `MonthCalendar` *type*

Although the `MonthCalendar` control offers a fair bit of functionality, it is very simple to programmatically capture the range of dates selected by the user. The default behavior of this type is to always select (and mark) today's date automatically. To obtain the currently selected date programmatically, you can update the `Click` event handler for the order `Button`, as shown here:

```
Private Sub btnOrder_Click(ByVal sender As System.Object, _
ByVal e As System.EventArgs) Handles btnOrder.Click
  ' Build a string to display information.
  Dim orderInfo As String = ""
...
  ' Get ship date.
  Dim d As DateTime = monthCalendar.SelectionStart
  Dim dateStr As String = _
    String.Format("{0}/{1}/{2} ", d.Month, d.Day, d.Year)
  orderInfo &= "Car will be sent: " & dateStr
...
End Sub
```

Notice that you can ask the `MonthCalendar` control for the currently selected date by using the `SelectionStart` property. This property returns a `DateTime` object, which you store in a local variable. Using a handful of properties of the `DateTime` type, you can extract the information you need in a custom format.

At this point, I assume the user will specify exactly one day on which to deliver the new automobile. However, what if you want to allow the user to select a range of possible shipping dates? In that case, all the user needs to do is drag the cursor across the range of possible shipping dates. You already have seen that you can obtain the start of the selection using the `SelectionStart` property. The end of the selection can be determined using the `SelectionEnd` property. Here is the code update:

```
Private Sub btnOrder_Click(ByVal sender As System.Object, _
ByVal e As System.EventArgs) Handles btnOrder.Click
  ' Build a string to display information.
  Dim orderInfo As String = ""
...
  ' Get ship date range....
  Dim startD As DateTime = monthCalendar.SelectionStart
  Dim endD As DateTime = monthCalendar.SelectionEnd
  Dim dateStartStr As String = _
    String.Format("{0}/{1}/{2} ", startD.Month, startD.Day, startD.Year)
  Dim dateEndStr As String = _
    String.Format("{0}/{1}/{2} ", endD.Month, endD.Day, endD.Year)

  ' The DateTime type supports overloaded operators!
  If dateStartStr <> dateEndStr Then
    orderInfo &= "Car will be sent between " & _
    dateStartStr & " and" & Chr(10) & dateEndStr
  Else
    orderInfo &= "Car will be sent on " & dateStartStr
    ' They picked a single date.
...
  End If
End Sub
```

■Note The Windows Forms toolkit also provides the `DateTimePicker` control, which exposes a `MonthCalendar` from a `DropDown` control.

Fun with ToolTips

As far as the CarConfig Form is concerned, we have one final point of interest. Most modern UIs support *tool tips*. In the `System.Windows.Forms` namespace, the `ToolTip` type represents this functionality. These widgets are simply small floating windows that display a helpful message when the cursor hovers over a given item.

To illustrate, add a tool tip to the CarConfig's `Calendar` type. Begin by dragging a new `ToolTip` control from the Toolbox onto your Forms designer, and rename it to `calendarTip`. Using the Properties window, you are able to establish the overall look and feel of the `ToolTip` widget, for example:

```
Private Sub InitializeComponent()
...
  ' calendarTip
  '
  Me.calendarTip.IsBalloon = True
  Me.calendarTip.ShowAlways = True
  Me.calendarTip.ToolTipIcon = System.Windows.Forms.ToolTipIcon.Info
...
End Sub
```

To associate a `ToolTip` with a given control, select the control that should activate the `ToolTip` and set the ToolTip on *controlName* property (see Figure 29-15).

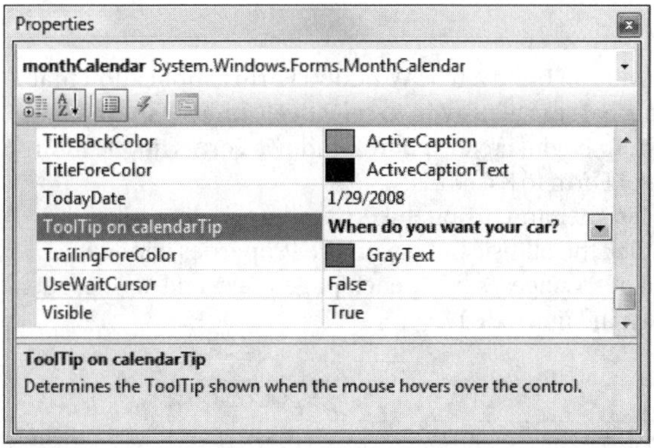

Figure 29-15. *Associating a* `ToolTip` *to a given widget*

At this point, the CarConfig project is complete. Figure 29-16 shows the `ToolTip` in action.

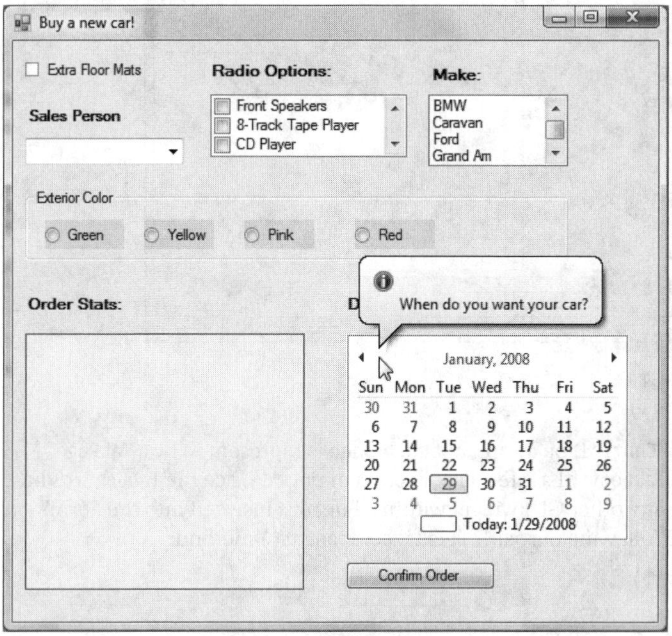

Figure 29-16. *The* `ToolTip` *in action*

Source Code The CarConfig project is included under the Chapter 29 directory.

Fun with TabControls

To illustrate the remaining "exotic" controls, you will build a new Windows Forms application that maintains a TabControl. As you may know, TabControls allow you to selectively hide or show pages of related GUI content via clicking a given tab. To begin, create a new Windows Forms application named ExoticControls and rename your initial Form to MainWindow.

Next, add a TabControl onto the Forms designer and, using the Properties window, open the page editor via the TabPages collection (just click the ellipsis button on the Properties window). A dialog configuration tool displays. Add a total of six pages, setting each page's Text and Name properties based on the completed TabControl shown in Figure 29-17.

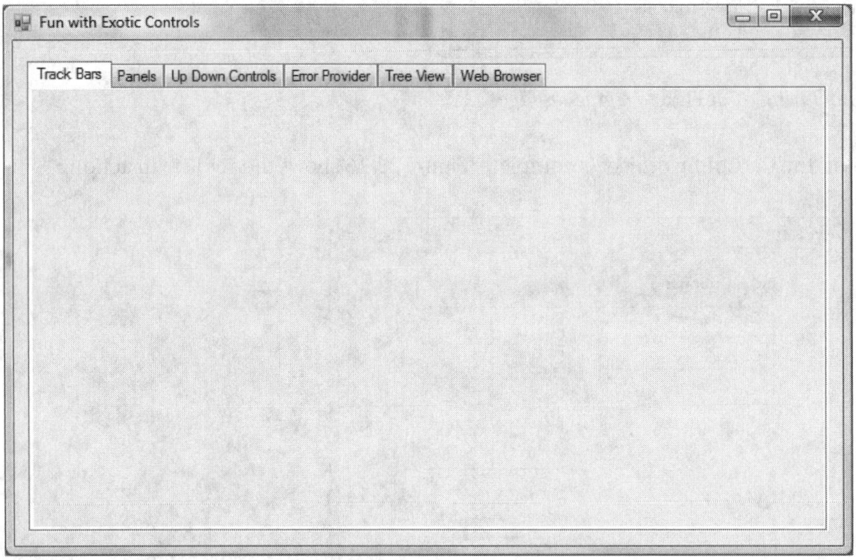

Figure 29-17. *A multipage* TabControl

As you are designing your TabControl, be aware that each page is represented by a TabPage object, which is inserted into the TabControl's internal collection of pages. Once the TabControl has been configured, this object (like any other GUI widget within a Form) is inserted into the Form's Controls collection. Consider the following partial InitializeComponent() method:

```
Private Sub InitializeComponent()
...
  '
  'tabControlExoticControls
  '
  Me.tabControlExoticControls.Controls.Add(Me.pageTrackBars)
  Me.tabControlExoticControls.Controls.Add(Me.pagePanels)
  Me.tabControlExoticControls.Controls.Add(Me.pageUpDown)
  Me.tabControlExoticControls.Controls.Add(Me.pageErrorProvider)
  Me.tabControlExoticControls.Controls.Add(Me.pageTreeView)
  Me.tabControlExoticControls.Controls.Add(Me.pageWebBrowser)
  Me.tabControlExoticControls.Location = New System.Drawing.Point(11, 16)
  Me.tabControlExoticControls.Name = "tabControlExoticControls"
  Me.tabControlExoticControls.SelectedIndex = 0
  Me.tabControlExoticControls.Size = New System.Drawing.Size(644, 367)
```

```
  Me.tabControlExoticControls.TabIndex = 1
...
  Me.Controls.Add(Me.tabControlExoticControls)
End Sub
```

Now that you have a basic Form supporting multiple tabs, you can build each page to illustrate the remaining exotic controls. First up, let's check out the role of the TrackBar.

■ **Note** The TabControl widget supports Selected, Selecting, Deselected, and Deselecting events. These can prove helpful when you need to dynamically generate the elements within a given page.

Fun with TrackBars

The TrackBar control allows users to select from a range of values, using a scroll bar–like input mechanism. When working with this type, you need to set the minimum and maximum range, the minimum and maximum change increments, and the starting location of the slider's thumb. Each of these aspects can be set using the properties described in Table 29-6.

Table 29-6. TrackBar *Properties*

Property	Meaning in Life
LargeChange	Defines the number of ticks by which the TrackBar changes when an event considered a large change occurs (e.g., clicking the mouse button while the cursor is on the sliding range and using the Page Up or Page Down key).
Maximum Minimum	Configure the upper and lower bounds of the TrackBar's range.
Orientation	Defines the orientation for this TrackBar. Valid values are from the Orientation enumeration (i.e., horizontally or vertically).
mallChange	Indicates the number of ticks by which the TrackBar changes when an event considered a small change occurs (e.g., using the arrow keys).
TickFrequency	Indicates how many ticks are drawn. For a TrackBar with an upper limit of 200, it is impractical to draw all 200 ticks on a control 2 inches long. If you set the TickFrequency property to 5, the TrackBar draws 40 total ticks (each tick represents 5 units).
TickStyle	Indicates how the TrackBar control draws itself. This affects both where the ticks are drawn in relation to the movable thumb and how the thumb itself is drawn (using the TickStyle enumeration).
Value	Gets or sets the current location of the TrackBar. Use this property to obtain the numeric value contained by the TrackBar for use in your application.

To illustrate, you'll update the first tab of your TabControl with three TrackBars, each of which has an upper range of 255 and a lower range of 0. As the user slides each thumb, the application intercepts the Scroll event and dynamically builds a new System.Drawing.Color object based on the value of each slider. This Color object will be used to display the color within a PictureBox widget (named colorBox) and the RGB values within a Label type (named lblCurrColor). Figure 29-18 shows the (completed) first page in action.

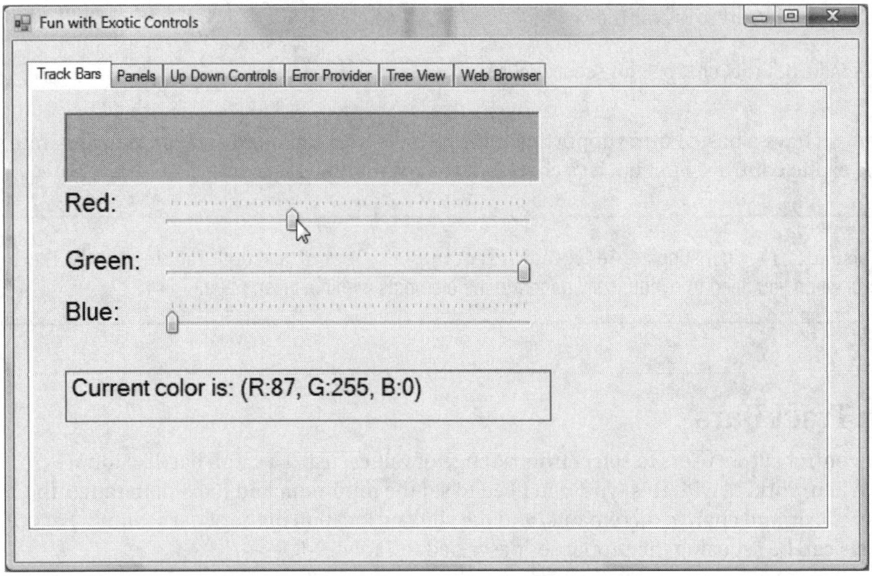

Figure 29-18. *The* TrackBar *page*

First, place three TrackBars onto the first tab using the Forms designer and rename your controls with an appropriate value (redTrackBar, greenTrackBar, and blueTrackBar). Here is the relevant code within InitializeComponent() for blueTrackBar (the remaining bars look almost identical):

```
Private Sub InitializeComponent()
...
  '
  'blueTrackBar
  '
  Me.blueTrackBar.Location = New System.Drawing.Point(132, 151)
  Me.blueTrackBar.Maximum = 255
  Me.blueTrackBar.Name = "blueTrackBar"
  Me.blueTrackBar.Size = New System.Drawing.Size(310, 45)
  Me.blueTrackBar.TabIndex = 18
  Me.blueTrackBar.TickFrequency = 5
  Me.blueTrackBar.TickStyle = System.Windows.Forms.TickStyle.TopLeft
...
End Sub
```

Next, handle the Scroll event for each of your TrackBar controls. Note that the default minimum value of the TrackBar is 0 and thus does not need to be explicitly set. Now, to handle the Scroll event handlers for each TrackBar, you make a call to a yet-to-be-written helper function named UpdateColor():

```
Private Sub blueTrackBar_Scroll(ByVal sender As System.Object, _
  ByVal e As System.EventArgs) Handles blueTrackBar.Scroll
  UpdateColor()
End Sub
```

UpdateColor() is responsible for two major tasks. First, you read the current value of each TrackBar and use this data to build a new Color variable using Color.FromArgb(). Once you have the newly configured color, update the PictureBox member variable (again, named colorBox) with the current background color you just created. Finally, UpdateColor() formats the thumb values in a string placed on the Label (lblCurrColor), as shown here:

```
Private Sub UpdateColor()
  ' Get the new color based on track bars.
  Dim c As Color = Color.FromArgb(redTrackBar.Value, _
    greenTrackBar.Value, blueTrackBar.Value)
  ' Change the color in the PictureBox.
  colorBox.BackColor = c
  ' Set color label.
  lblCurrColor.Text = _
  String.Format("Current color is: (R:{0}, G:{1}, B:{2})", _
  redTrackBar.Value, greenTrackBar.Value, blueTrackBar.Value)
End Sub
```

The final detail is to set the initial values of each slider when the Form comes to life and render the current color, within a custom default constructor:

```
Sub New()
  ' This call is required by the Windows Forms designer.
  InitializeComponent()

  CenterToScreen()
  ' Set initial position of each slider.
  redTrackBar.Value = 100
  greenTrackBar.Value = 255
  blueTrackBar.Value = 0
  UpdateColor()
End Sub
```

Fun with Panels

As you saw earlier in this chapter, the GroupBox control can be used to logically group a number of controls (such as RadioButtons) to function as a collective. Closely related to the GroupBox is the Panel control. Panels are also used to group related controls in a logical unit. One difference is that the Panel type derives from the ScrollableControl class, thus it can support scroll bars, which is not possible with a GroupBox.

Panels can also be used to conserve screen real estate. For example, if you have a group of controls that takes up the entire bottom half of a Form, you can contain the group in a Panel that is half the size and set the AutoScroll property to true. In this way, the user can use the scroll bar(s) to view the full set of items. Furthermore, if a Panel's BorderStyle property is set to None, you can use this type to simply group a set of elements that can be easily shown or hidden from view in a manner transparent to the end user.

To illustrate, let's update the second page of the TabControl with two Button types (btnShowPanel and btnHidePanel) and a single Panel (named panelTextBoxes) that contains a pair of text boxes (txtNormalText and txtUpperText) and an instructional Label. (Mind you, the widgets on the Panel are not terribly important for this example.) Figure 29-19 shows the final GUI.

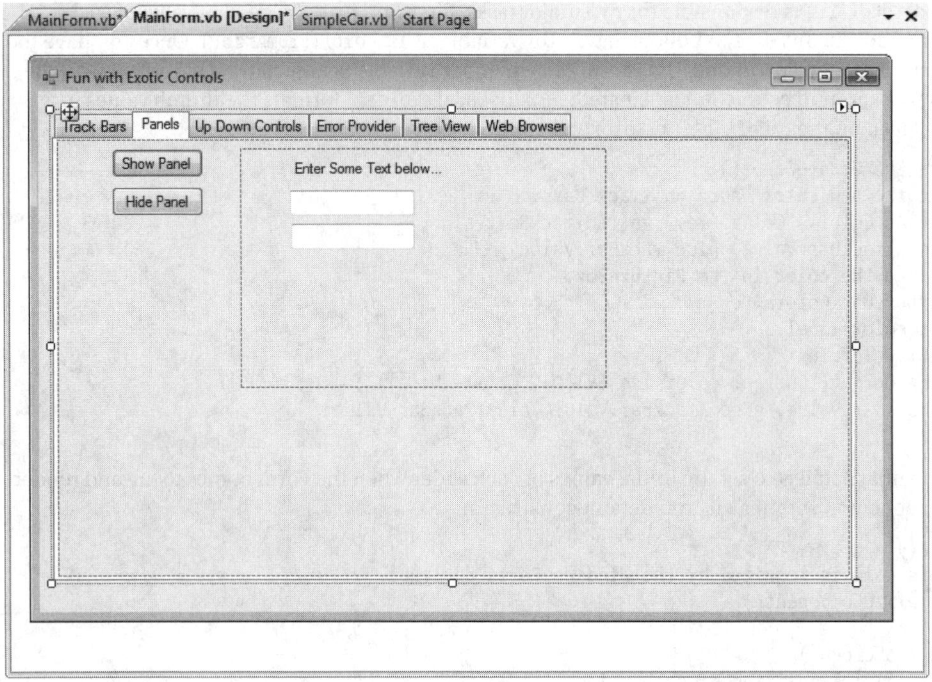

Figure 29-19. *The* `Panels` *page*

Using the Properties window, handle the `TextChanged` event for the first `TextBox`, and within the generated event handler, place an uppercase version of the text entered within `txtNormalText` into `txtUpperText`:

```
Private Sub txtNormalText_TextChanged(ByVal sender As System.Object, _
  ByVal e As System.EventArgs) Handles txtNormalText.TextChanged
  txtUpperText.Text = txtNormalText.Text.ToUpper()
End Sub
```

Now, handle the `Click` event for each button. As you might suspect, you will simply hide or show the `Panel` (and all of its contained UI elements):

```
Private Sub btnShowPanel_Click(ByVal sender As System.Object, _
  ByVal e As System.EventArgs) Handles btnShowPanel.Click
  panelTextBoxes.Visible = True
End Sub

Private Sub btnHidePanel_Click(ByVal sender As System.Object, _
  ByVal e As System.EventArgs) Handles btnHidePanel.Click
  panelTextBoxes.Visible = False
End Sub
```

If you now run your program and click either button, you will find that the `Panel`'s contents are shown and hidden accordingly. While this example is hardly fascinating, I am sure you can see the possibilities. For example, you may have a menu option (or security setting) that allows the user to see a "simple" or "complex" view. Rather than having to manually set the `Visible` property to `False` for multiple widgets, you can group them all within a `Panel` and set its `Visible` property accordingly.

Fun with the UpDown Controls

Windows Forms provide two widgets that function as *spin controls* (also known as *up/down controls*). Like the ComboBox and ListBox types, these new items also allow the user to choose an item from a range of possible selections. The difference is that when you're using a DomainUpDown or NumericUpDown control, the information is selected using a pair of small up and down arrows. For example, check out Figure 29-20.

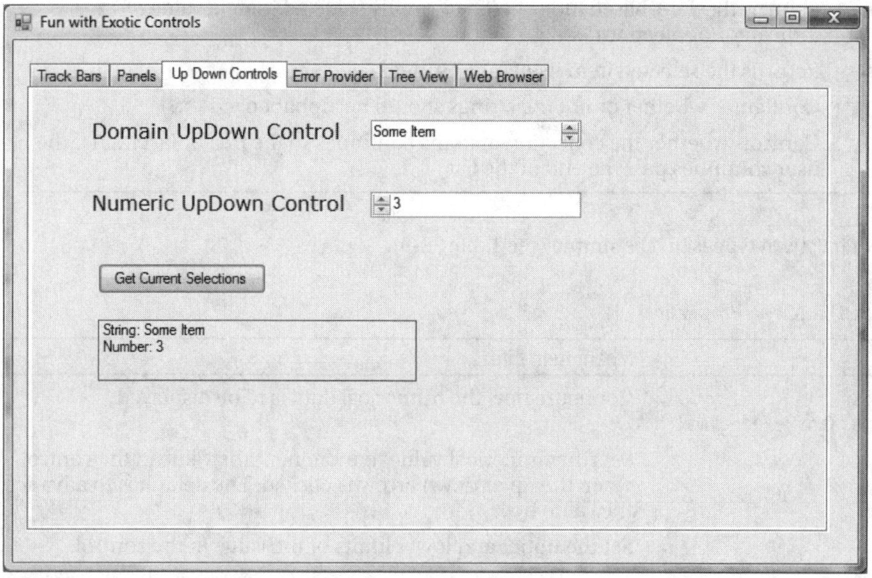

Figure 29-20. *Working with* UpDown *types*

Given your work with similar types, you should find working with the UpDown widgets painless. The DomainUpDown widget allows the user to select from a set of string data. NumericUpDown allows selections from a range of numeric data points. Each widget derives from a common direct base class, UpDownBase. Table 29-7 describes some important properties of this class.

Table 29-7. UpDownBase *Properties*

Property	Meaning in Life
InterceptArrowKeys	Gets or sets a value indicating whether the user can use the up arrow and down arrow keys to select values
ReadOnly	Gets or sets a value indicating whether the text can be changed only by the use of the up and down arrows and not by typing in the control to locate a given string
Text	Gets or sets the current text displayed in the spin control
TextAlign	Gets or sets the alignment of the text in the spin control
UpDownAlign	Gets or sets the alignment of the up and down arrows on the spin control, using the LeftRightAlignment enumeration

The DomainUpDown control adds a small set of properties (see Table 29-8) that allow you to configure and manipulate the textual data in the widget.

Table 29-8. DomainUpDown *Properties*

Property	Meaning in Life
Items	Allows you to gain access to the set of items stored in the widget
SelectedIndex	Returns the zero-based index of the currently selected item (a value of -1 indicates no selection)
SelectedItem	Returns the selected item itself (not its index)
Sorted	Configures whether or not the strings should be alphabetized
Wrap	Controls whether the collection of items continues to the first or last item if the user continues past the end of the list

The NumericUpDown type is just as simple (see Table 29-9).

Table 29-9. NumericUpDown *Properties*

Property	Meaning in Life
DecimalPlaces ThousandsSeparatorHexadecimal	Configure how the numerical data is to be displayed.
Increment	Sets the numerical value to increment the value in the control when the up or down arrow is clicked. The default is to advance the value by 1.
Minimum Maximum	Set the upper and lower limits of the value in the control.
Value	Returns the current value in the control.

The Click event handler for this page's Button simply asks each type for its current value and places it in the appropriate Label (lblCurrSel) as a formatted string, as shown here:

```
Private Sub btnGetSelections_Click(ByVal sender As System.Object, _
  ByVal e As System.EventArgs) Handles btnGetSelections.Click
  ' Get info from updowns...
  lblCurrSel.Text = _
    String.Format("String: {0}" & Chr(13) & "Number: {1}", _
    domainUpDown.Text, numericUpDown.Value)
End Sub
```

Fun with ErrorProviders

Most Windows Forms applications will need to validate user input in one way or another. This is especially true with dialog boxes, as you should inform users if they make a processing error before continuing forward. The ErrorProvider type can be used to provide a visual cue of user input error. For example, assume you have a Form containing a TextBox and Button widget. If the user enters more than five characters in the TextBox and the TextBox loses focus, the error information shown in Figure 29-21 could be displayed.

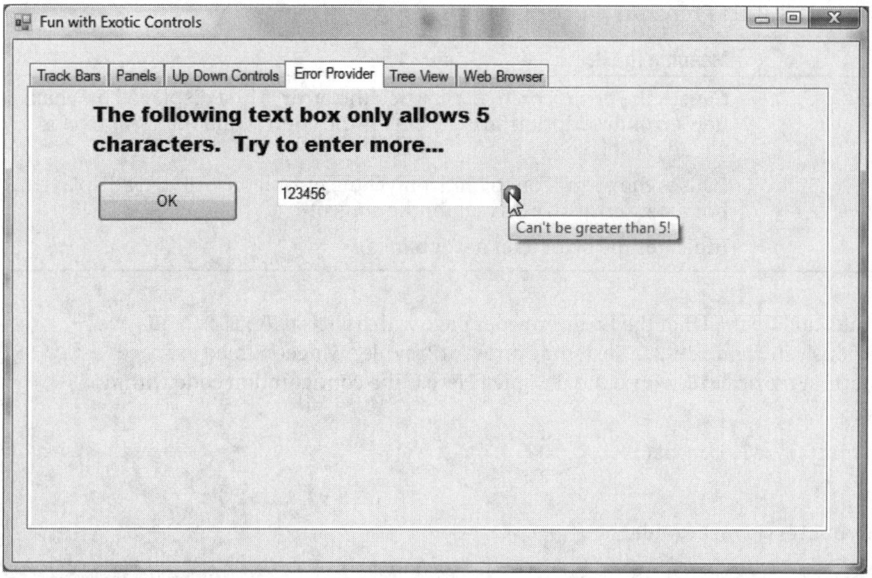

Figure 29-21. *The* `ErrorProvider` *in action*

Here, you have detected that the user entered more than five characters and responded by placing a small error icon (!) next to the `TextBox` object. When the user places his cursor over this icon, the descriptive error text appears as a pop-up. Also, this `ErrorProvider` is configured to cause the icon to blink a number of times to strengthen the visual cue (which, of course, you can't see without running the application).

If you wish to support this type of input validation, the first step is to understand the members of the `Control` class shown in Table 29-10.

Table 29-10. *Control Members Relating to the* `ErrorProvider` *Type*

Property	Meaning in Life
`CausesValidation`	Indicates whether selecting this control causes validation on the controls requiring validation
`Validated`	Occurs when the control is finished performing its validation logic
`Validating`	Occurs when the control is validating user input (e.g., when the control loses focus)

Every GUI widget can set the `CausesValidation` property to `True` or `False` (the default is `True`). If you set this bit of state data to `True`, the control forces the other controls on the Form to validate themselves when it receives focus. Once a validating control has received focus, the `Validating` and `Validated` events are fired for each control. In the scope of the `Validating` event handler, you configure a corresponding `ErrorProvider`. Optionally, the `Validated` event can be handled to determine when the control has finished its validation cycle.

The `ErrorProvider` type has a small set of members. The most important item for your purposes is the `BlinkStyle` property, which can be set to any of the values of the `ErrorBlinkStyle` enumeration described in Table 29-11.

Table 29-11. `ErrorBlinkStyle` *Properties*

Property	Meaning in Life
`AlwaysBlink`	Causes the error icon to blink when the error is first displayed or when a new error description string is set for the control and the error icon is already displayed
`BlinkIfDifferentError`	Causes the error icon to blink only if the error icon is already displayed, but a new error string is set for the control
`NeverBlink`	Indicates the error icon never blinks

To illustrate, update the UI of the Error Provider page with a `Button`, `TextBox`, and `Label` as shown previously in Figure 29-21. Next, drag an `ErrorProvider` widget named `tooManyCharactersErrorProvider` onto the designer. Here is the configuration code within `InitializeComponent()`:

```
Private Sub InitializeComponent()
...
  '
  ' tooManyCharactersErrorProvider
  '
  Me.tooManyCharactersErrorProvider.BlinkRate = 500
  Me.tooManyCharactersErrorProvider.BlinkStyle = _
    System.Windows.Forms.ErrorBlinkStyle.AlwaysBlink
  Me.tooManyCharactersErrorProvider.ContainerControl = Me
...
End Sub
```

Once you have configured how the `ErrorProvider` looks and feels, you handle the `Validating` event on the `TextBox` control and call `SetError` on the `ErrorProvider` control as follows:

```
Private Sub txtInput_Validating(ByVal sender As System.Object, _
  ByVal e As System.ComponentModel.CancelEventArgs) Handles txtInput.Validating
  ' Check whether the text length is greater than 5.
  If txtInput.Text.Length > 5 Then
    tooManyCharactersErrorProvider.SetError(txtInput, "Can't be greater than 5!")
  Else
    tooManyCharactersErrorProvider.SetError(txtInput, "")
    ' Things are OK, don't show anything.
  End If
End Sub
```

Fun with TreeViews

`TreeView` controls are very helpful types in that they allow you to visually display hierarchical data (such as a directory structure or any other type of parent/child relationship). As you would expect, the Window Forms `TreeView` control can be highly customized. If you wish, you can add custom images, node colors, node subcontrols, and other visual enhancements. (I'll assume interested readers will consult the .NET Framework 3.5 SDK documentation for full details of this widget.)

To illustrate the basic use of the `TreeView`, the next page of your `TabControl` will programmatically construct a `TreeView` defining a series of topmost nodes that represent a set of `Car` types. Each Car node has two subnodes that represent the selected car's current speed and favorite radio station. In Figure 29-22, notice that the selected item will be highlighted. Also note that if the selected node has a parent (and/or sibling), its name is presented in a `Label` widget.

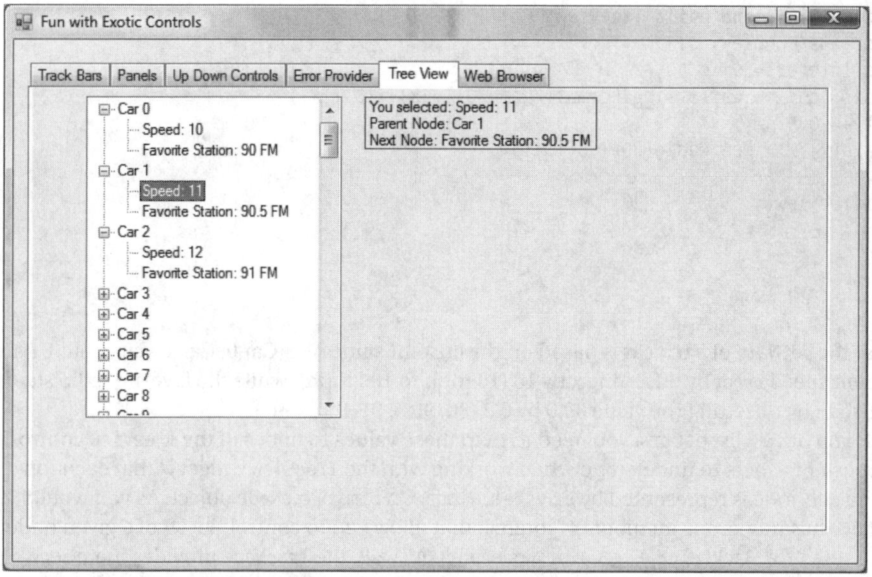

Figure 29-22. *The* `TreeView` *in action*

Assuming your Tree View UI is composed of a `TreeView` control (named `treeViewCars`) and a `Label` (named `lblNodeInfo`), insert a new VB 2008 file into your ExoticControls project that models a trivial `Car` that "has-a" `Radio`:

```
Class Car
  Public Sub New(ByVal pn As String, ByVal cs As Integer)
    petName = pn
    currSp = cs
  End Sub
  ' Public to keep the example simple.
  Public petName As String
  Public currSp As Integer
  Public r As Radio
End Class

Class Radio
  Public favoriteStation As Double
  Public Sub New(ByVal station As Double)
    favoriteStation = station
  End Sub
End Class
```

The `Form`-derived type will maintain a generic `List(Of T)` (named `listCars`) of 100 `Car` objects, which will be populated in the default constructor of the `MainForm` type. As well, the constructor will call a new subroutine named `BuildCarTreeView()` that takes no arguments. Here is the initial update:

```
Public Class MainForm
  ' Create a new generic List to hold the Car objects.
  Private listCars As New List(Of Car)()

  Sub New()
...
```

```
    ' Fill List(Of T) and build TreeView.
    Dim offset As Double = 0.5
    For x As Integer = 0 To 99
      listCars.Add(New Car(String.Format("Car {0}", x), 10 + x))
      offset += 0.5
      listCars(x).r = New Radio(89 + offset)
    Next
    BuildCarTreeView()
  End Sub

...
End Class
```

Note that the petName of each car is based on the current value of x (Car 0, Car 1, Car 2, etc.). As well, the current speed is set by offsetting x by 10 (10 mph to 109 mph), while the favorite radio station is established by offsetting the value 89.0 by 0.5 (90, 90.5, 91, 91.5, etc.).

Now that you have a list of Cars, you need to map these values to nodes of the TreeView control. The most important aspect to understand when working with the TreeView widget is that each topmost node and subnode is represented by a System.Windows.Forms.TreeNode object. As you would expect, TreeNode has numerous members of interest that allow you to control the UI of a given node (IsExpanded, IsVisible, BackColor, ForeColor, NodeFont). As well, the TreeNode provides members to navigate to the next (or previous) TreeNode. Given this, consider the initial implementation of BuildCarTreeView():

```
Sub BuildCarTreeView()
  ' Don't paint the TreeView until all the nodes have been created.
  treeViewCars.BeginUpdate()

  ' Clear the TreeView of any current nodes.
  treeViewCars.Nodes.Clear()

  ' Add a TreeNode for each Car object in the List(Of T).
  For Each c As Car In listCars
    ' Add the current Car as a topmost node.
    treeViewCars.Nodes.Add(New TreeNode(c.petName))

    ' Now, get the Car you just added to build
    ' two subnodes based on the speed and
    ' internal Radio object.
    treeViewCars.Nodes(listCars.IndexOf(c)).Nodes.Add(New _
      TreeNode(String.Format("Speed: {0}", c.currSp.ToString())))
    treeViewCars.Nodes(listCars.IndexOf(c)).Nodes.Add(New _
      TreeNode(String.Format("Favorite Station: {0} FM", _
      c.r.favoriteStation)))
  Next

  ' Now paint the TreeView.
  treeViewCars.EndUpdate()
End Sub
```

As you can see, the construction of the TreeView nodes are sandwiched between a call to BeginUpdate() and EndUpdate(). This can be helpful when you are populating a massive TreeView with a great many nodes, given that the widget will wait to display the items until you have finished filling the Nodes collection. In this way, the end user does not see the gradual rendering of the TreeView's elements.

The topmost nodes are added to the TreeView simply by iterating over the generic List(Of T) type and inserting a new TreeNode object into the TreeView's Nodes collection. Once a topmost node has been added, you pluck it from the Nodes collection (via the type indexer) to add its subnodes (which are also represented by TreeNode objects). As you might guess, if you wish to add subnodes to a current subnode, simply populate its internal collection of nodes via the Nodes property.

The next task for this page of the TabControl is to highlight the currently selected node (via the BackColor property) and display the selected item (as well as any parent or subnodes) within the Label widget. All of this can be accomplished by handling the TreeView control's AfterSelect event via the Properties window. This event fires after the user has selected a node via a mouse click or keyboard navigation. Here is the complete implementation of the AfterSelect event handler:

```
Private Sub treeViewCars_AfterSelect(ByVal sender As System.Object, _
  ByVal e As System.Windows.Forms.TreeViewEventArgs) _
  Handles treeViewCars.AfterSelect
  Dim nodeInfo As String = ""
  ' Build info about selected node.
  nodeInfo = String.Format("You selected: {0}" & Chr(10), e.Node.Text)
  If e.Node.Parent IsNot Nothing Then
    nodeInfo &= String.Format("Parent Node: {0}" & Chr(10), _
    e.Node.Parent.Text)
  End If
  If e.Node.NextNode IsNot Nothing Then
    nodeInfo &= String.Format("Next Node: {0}", e.Node.NextNode.Text)
  End If
  ' Show info and highlight node.
  lblNodeInfo.Text = nodeInfo
  e.Node.BackColor = Color.AliceBlue
End Sub
```

The incoming TreeViewEventArgs object contains a property named Node, which returns a TreeNode object representing the current selection. From here, you are able to extract the node's display name (via the Text property) as well as the parent and next node (via the Parent/NextNode properties). Note you are explicitly checking the TreeNode objects returned from Parent/NextNode for Nothing, in case the user has selected the topmost node or the very last subnode (if you did not do this, you might trigger a NullReferenceException).

Adding Node Images

To wrap up our examination of the TreeView type, let's spruce up the current example by defining three new *.bmp images that will be assigned to each node type. To do so, add a new ImageList component (named imageListTreeView) to the designer of the MainForm type. Next, add three new bitmap images to your project via the Project ➤ Add New Item menu selection (or make use of the supplied *.bmp files within this book's downloadable code) that represent (or at least closely approximate) a car, radio, and "speed" image. Do note that each of these *.bmp files is 16×16 pixels (set via the Properties window) so that they have a decent appearance within the TreeView.

Once you have created these image files, select the ImageList on your designer and populate the Images property with each of these three images, ordered as shown in Figure 29-23, to ensure you can assign the correct ImageIndex (0, 1, or 2) to each node.

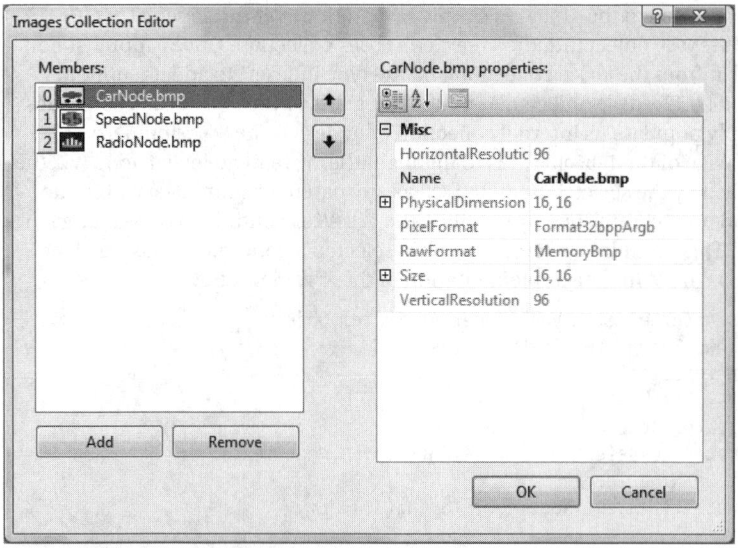

Figure 29-23. *Populating the* `ImageList`

As you recall from Chapter 28, when you incorporate resources (such as bitmaps) into your Visual Studio 2008 solutions, the underlying `*.resx` file is automatically updated. Therefore, these images will be embedded into your assembly with no extra work on your part. Now, using the Properties window, set the `TreeView` control's `ImageList` property to your `ImageList` member variable (see Figure 29-24).

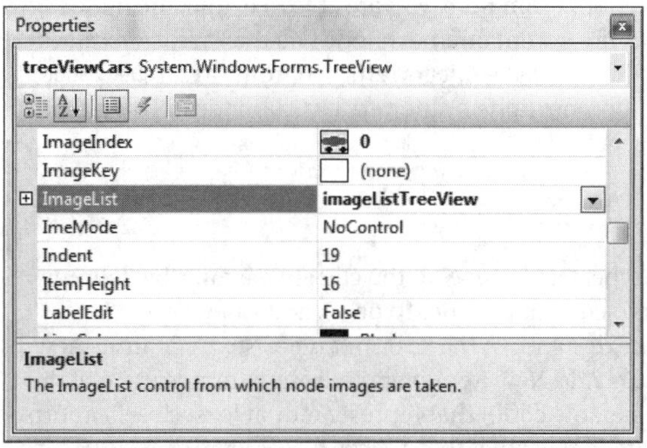

Figure 29-24. *Associating the* `ImageList` *to the* `TreeView`

Last but not least, update your `BuildCarTreeView()` method to specify the correct `ImageIndex` (via constructor arguments) when creating each `TreeNode`:

```
Sub BuildCarTreeView()
...
  ' Add a root TreeNode for each Car object in the List(Of T).
  For Each c As Car In listCars
    ' Add the current Car as a topmost node.
    treeViewCars.Nodes.Add(New TreeNode(c.petName, 0, 0))
```

```
    ' Now, get the Car you just added to build
    ' two subnodes based on the speed and
    ' internal Radio object.
    treeViewCars.Nodes(listCars.IndexOf(c)).Nodes.Add(New _
      TreeNode(String.Format("Speed: {0}", c.currSp.ToString()), 1, 1))
    treeViewCars.Nodes(listCars.IndexOf(c)).Nodes.Add(New _
    TreeNode(String.Format("Favorite Station: {0} FM", _
    c.r.favoriteStation), 2, 2))
  Next
...
End Sub
```

Notice that you are specifying each ImageIndex twice. The reason for this is that a given TreeNode can have two unique images assigned to it: one to display when unselected and another to display when selected. To keep things simple, you are specifying the same image for both possibilities. In any case, Figure 29-25 shows the updated TreeView type.

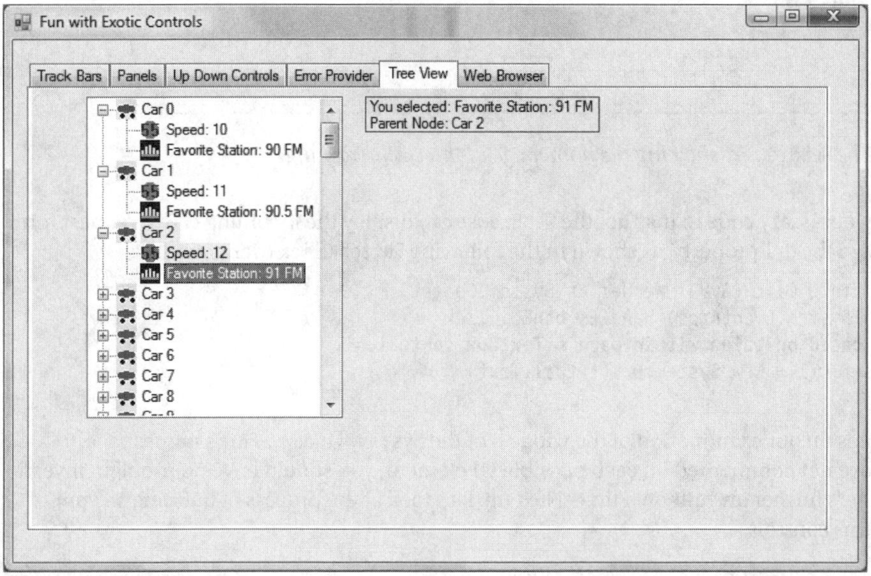

Figure 29-25. *The* TreeView *with images*

Fun with WebBrowsers

The final page of this example will make use of the System.Windows.Forms.WebBrowser control. This widget is a highly configurable mini web browser that may be embedded into any Form-derived type. As you would expect, this control defines a Url property that can be set to any valid URI, formally represented by the System.Uri type. On the Web Browser page, add a WebBrowser (configured to your liking), a TextBox (to enter the URL), and a Button (to perform the HTTP request). Figure 29-26 shows the runtime behavior of assigning the Url property to http://www.intertechtraining.com (yes, a shameless promotion for the company I am employed with).

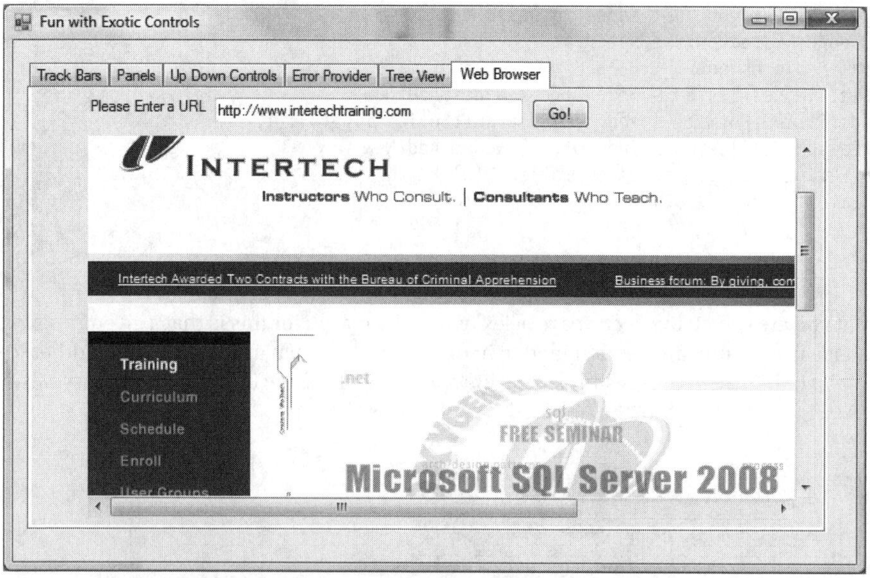

Figure 29-26. *The* `WebBrowser` *showing the homepage of Intertech Training*

The only necessary code to instruct the `WebBrowser` to display the incoming HTTP request form data is to assign the `Url` property, as shown in the following `Button Click` event handler:

```
Private Sub btnGO_Click(ByVal sender As System.Object, _
  ByVal e As System.EventArgs) Handles btnGO.Click
  ' Set URL based on value within page's TextBox control.
  myWebBrowser.Url = New System.Uri(txtUrl.Text)
End Sub
```

That wraps up our examination of the widgets of the `System.Windows.Forms` namespace. Although I have not commented on each possible UI element, you should have no problem investigating the others further on your own time. Next up, let's look at the process of building *custom* Windows Forms controls.

■ **Source Code** The ExoticControls project is included under the Chapter 29 directory.

Building Custom Windows Forms Controls

The .NET platform provides a very simple way for developers to build custom UI elements. Unlike (the now legacy) ActiveX controls, Windows Forms controls do not require vast amounts of COM infrastructure or complex memory management. Rather, .NET developers simply build a new class deriving from `UserControl` and populate the type with any number of properties, methods, and events. To demonstrate this process, during the next several pages you'll construct a custom control named `CarControl` using Visual Studio 2008.

■ **Note** As with any .NET application, you are always free to build a custom Windows Forms control using nothing more than the command-line compiler and a simple text editor. As you will see, custom controls reside in a `*.dll` assembly; therefore, you may specify the `/target:dll` option of `vbc.exe`.

To begin, fire up Visual Studio 2008 and select a new Windows Forms Control Library workspace named CarControlLibrary (see Figure 29-27).

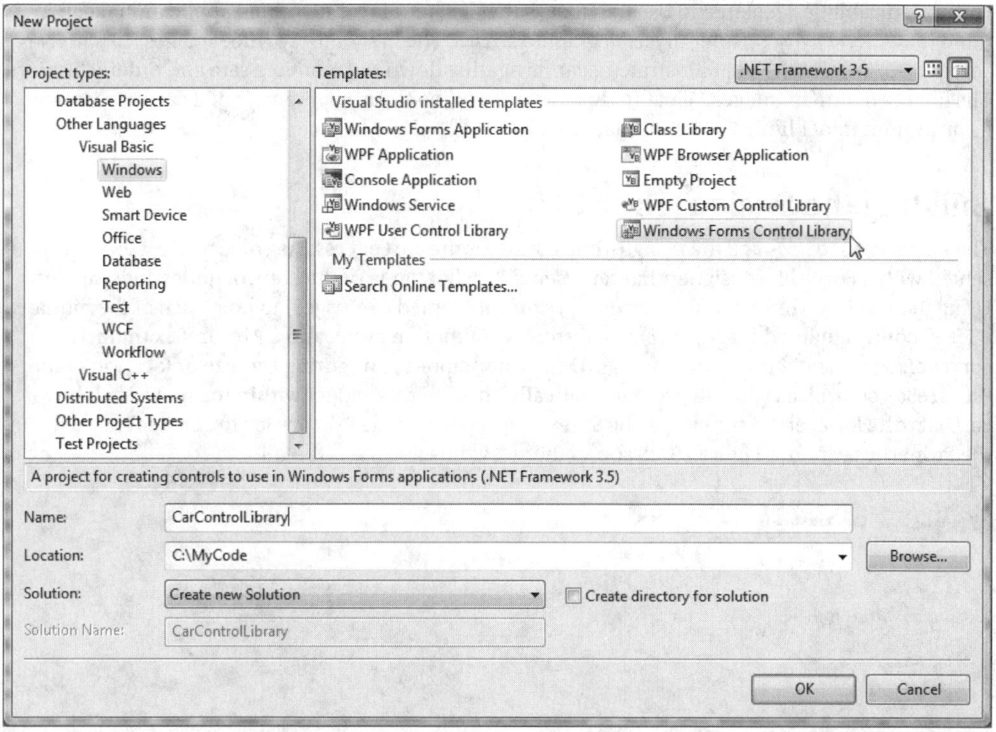

Figure 29-27. *Creating a new Windows Forms Control Library workspace*

When you are finished, rename the initial VB 2008 class to `CarControl`. Like a Windows Application project workspace, your custom control is composed of two partial classes. The `*.Designer.vb` file contains all of the designer-generated code and derives your type from `System.Windows.Forms.UserControl`:

```
Partial Class CarControl
  Inherits System.Windows.Forms.UserControl
  ...
End Class
```

Before we get too far along, let's establish the big picture of where you are going with this example. The `CarControl` type is responsible for animating through a series of bitmaps that will change based on the internal state of the automobile. If the car's current speed is safely under the car's maximum speed limit, the `CarControl` loops through three bitmap images that render an automobile driving safely along. If the current speed is 10 mph below the maximum speed, the `CarControl` loops through four images, with the fourth image showing the car slowly breaking down. Finally, if the car has surpassed its maximum speed, the CarControl loops over five images, where the fifth image represents a doomed automobile.

Creating the Images

Given the preceding design notes, the first order of business is to create a set of five *.bmp files for use by the animation loop. If you wish to create custom images, begin by activating the Project ➤ Add New Item menu selection and insert five new bitmap files. If you would rather not showcase your artistic abilities, feel free to use the images that accompany this sample application (keep in mind that I in *no way* consider myself a graphic artist!). The first of these three images (Lemon1.bmp, Lemon2.bmp, and Lemon3.bmp) illustrates a car navigating down the road in a safe and orderly fashion. The final two bitmap images (AboutToBlow.bmp and EngineBlown.bmp) represent a car approaching its maximum upper limit and its ultimate demise.

Building the Design-Time GUI

The next step is to leverage the design-time editor for the CarControl. As you can see, you are presented with a Form-like designer that represents the client area of the control under construction. Using the Toolbox window, add an ImageList control (named carImages) to hold each of the bitmaps, a Timer control (named imageTimer) to control the animation cycle, and a PictureBox (named currentImage) to hold the current image. Don't worry about configuring the size or location of the PictureBox control, as you will programmatically position this widget within the bounds of the CarControl. However, be sure to set the SizeMode property of the PictureBox to StretchImage via the Properties window. Figure 29-28 shows the story thus far.

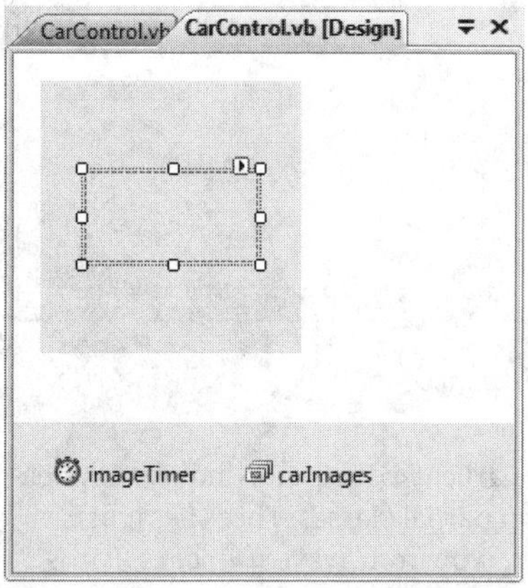

Figure 29-28. *Creating the design-time GUI*

Now, using the Properties window, configure the ImageList's Images collection by adding each bitmap to the list. Be aware that you will want to add these items sequentially (Lemon1.bmp, Lemon2.bmp, Lemon3.bmp, AboutToBlow.bmp, and EngineBlown.bmp) to ensure a linear animation cycle. Also be aware that the default width and height of *.bmp files inserted by Visual Studio 2008 is 47×47 pixels. Thus, the ImageSize of the ImageList should also be set to 47×47 (or else you will have some skewed rendering). Finally, configure the state of your Timer such that the Interval property is set to 200 and is initially disabled.

Implementing the Core CarControl

With this UI prep work out of the way, you can now turn to implementation of the type members. To begin, create a new public enumeration named AnimFrames, which has a member representing each item maintained by the ImageList. You will make use of this enumeration to determine the current frame to render into the PictureBox:

```
' Helper enum for images.
Public Enum AnimFrames
  Lemon1
  Lemon2
  Lemon3
  AboutToBlow
  EngineBlown
End Enum
```

The CarControl type maintains a good number of private data points to represent the animation logic. Here is the rundown of each member:

```
Public Class CarControl
  ' State data.
  Private currFrame As AnimFrames = AnimFrames.Lemon1
  Private currMaxFrame As AnimFrames = AnimFrames.Lemon3
  Private IsAnim As Boolean
  Private currSp As Integer = 50
  Private maxSp As Integer = 100
  Private carPetName As String = "Lemon"
  Private bottomRect As New Rectangle()
End Class
```

As you can see, you have data points that represent the current and maximum speed, the pet name of the automobile, and two members of type AnimFrames. The currFrame variable is used to specify which member of the ImageList is to be rendered. The currMaxFrame variable is used to mark the current upper limit in the ImageList (recall that the CarControl loops through three to five images based on the current speed). The IsAnim data point is used to determine whether the car is currently in animation mode. Finally, you have a Rectangle member (bottomRect), which is used to represent the bottom region of the CarControl type. Later, you render the pet name of the automobile into this piece of control real estate.

To divide the CarControl into two rectangular regions, create a private helper method named StretchBox(). The role of this member is to calculate the correct size of the bottomRect member and to ensure that the PictureBox widget is stretched out over the upper two-thirds (or so) of the CarControl type.

```
Private Sub StretchBox()
  ' Configure picture box.
  currentImage.Top = 0
  currentImage.Left = 0
  currentImage.Height = Me.Height - 50
  currentImage.Width = Me.Width
  currentImage.Image = carImages.Images(CType(AnimFrames.Lemon1, Integer))
  ' Figure out size of bottom rect.
  bottomRect.X = 0
  bottomRect.Y = Me.Height - 50
  bottomRect.Height = Me.Height - currentImage.Height
  bottomRect.Width = Me.Width
End Sub
```

Once you have carved out the dimensions of each rectangle, call StretchBox() from the default constructor:

```
Sub New()
  ' This call is required by the Windows Forms designer.
  InitializeComponent()
  StretchBox()
End Sub
```

Defining the Custom Events

The CarControl type supports two events that are fired back to the host Form based on the current speed of the automobile. The first event, AboutToBlow, is sent out when the CarControl's speed approaches the upper limit. BlewUp is sent to the container when the current speed is greater than the allowed maximum. Each of these events send out a single System.String as its parameter. You'll fire these events in just a moment, but for the time being, add the following members to the CarControl class:

```
' Car events.
Public Event AboutToBlow(ByVal msg As String)
Public Event BlewUp(ByVal msg As String)
```

Defining the Custom Properties

Like any class type, custom controls may define a set of properties to allow the outside world to interact with the state of the widget. For your current purposes, you are interested only in defining three properties. First, you have Animate. This property enables or disables the Timer type:

```
' Used to configure the internal Timer type.
Public Property Animate() As Boolean
  Get
    Return IsAnim
  End Get
  Set
    IsAnim = value
    imageTimer.Enabled = IsAnim
  End Set
End Property
```

The PetName property is what you would expect and requires little comment. Do notice, however, that when the user sets the pet name, you make a call to Invalidate() to render the name of the CarControl into the bottom rectangular area of the widget (you'll do this step in just a moment):

```
' Configure pet name.
Public Property PetName() As String
  Get
    Return carPetName
  End Get
  Set
    carPetName = value
    Invalidate()
  End Set
End Property
```

Next, you have the Speed property. In addition to simply modifying the currSp data member, Speed is the entity that fires the AboutToBlow and BlewUp events based on the current speed of the CarControl. Here is the complete logic:

```
' Adjust currSp and currMaxFrame, and fire our events.
Public Property Speed() As Integer
  Get
    Return currSp
  End Get
  Set(ByVal value As Integer)
    ' Within safe speed?
    If currSp <= maxSp Then
      currSp = value
      currMaxFrame = AnimFrames.Lemon3
    End If
    ' About to explode?
    If (maxSp - currSp) <= 10 Then
      RaiseEvent AboutToBlow("Slow down dude!")
      currMaxFrame = AnimFrames.AboutToBlow
    End If
    ' Maxed out?
    If currSp >= maxSp Then
      currSp = maxSp
      RaiseEvent BlewUp("Ug...you're toast...")
      currMaxFrame = AnimFrames.EngineBlown
    End If
    End Set
End Property
```

As you can see, if the current speed is 10 mph below the maximum upper speed, you fire the AboutToBlow event and adjust the upper frame limit to AnimFrames.AboutToBlow. If the user has pushed the limits of your automobile, you fire the BlewUp event and set the upper frame limit to AnimFrames.EngineBlown. If the speed is below the maximum speed, the upper frame limit remains as AnimFrames.Lemon3.

Controlling the Animation

The next detail to attend to is ensuring that the Timer type advances the current frame to render within the PictureBox. Again, recall that the number of frames to loop through depends on the current speed of the automobile. You only want to bother adjusting the image in the PictureBox if the Animate property has been set to True. Begin by handling the Tick event for the Timer object, and flesh out the details as follows:

```
Private Sub imageTimer_Tick(ByVal sender As System.Object, _
  ByVal e As System.EventArgs) Handles imageTimer.Tick
  If IsAnim Then
    currentImage.Image = carImages.Images(CType(currFrame, Integer))
  End If
  ' Bump frame.
  Dim nextFrame As Integer = (CType(currFrame, Integer)) + 1
  currFrame = CType(nextFrame, AnimFrames)
  If currFrame > currMaxFrame Then
    currFrame = AnimFrames.Lemon1
  End If
End Sub
```

Rendering the Pet Name

Before you can take your control out for a spin, you have one final detail to attend to: rendering the car's moniker. To do this, handle the Paint event for your CarControl, and within the handler, render the CarControl's pet name into the bottom rectangular region of the client area:

```
Private Sub CarControl_Paint(ByVal sender As System.Object, _
  ByVal e As System.Windows.Forms.PaintEventArgs) _
  Handles MyBase.Paint
  ' Render the pet name on the bottom of the control.
  Dim g As Graphics = e.Graphics
  g.FillRectangle(Brushes.GreenYellow, bottomRect)
  g.DrawString(PetName, _
    New Font("Times New Roman", 15), _
    Brushes.Black, bottomRect)
End Sub
```

At this point, your initial crack at the CarControl is complete. Go ahead and build your project.

Testing the CarControl Type

When you run or debug a Windows Forms Control Library project within Visual Studio 2008, the UserControl Test Container (a managed replacement for the now legacy ActiveX Control Test Container) automatically loads your control into its designer test bed. As you can see from Figure 29-29, this tool allows you to set each custom property (as well as all inherited properties) for testing purposes.

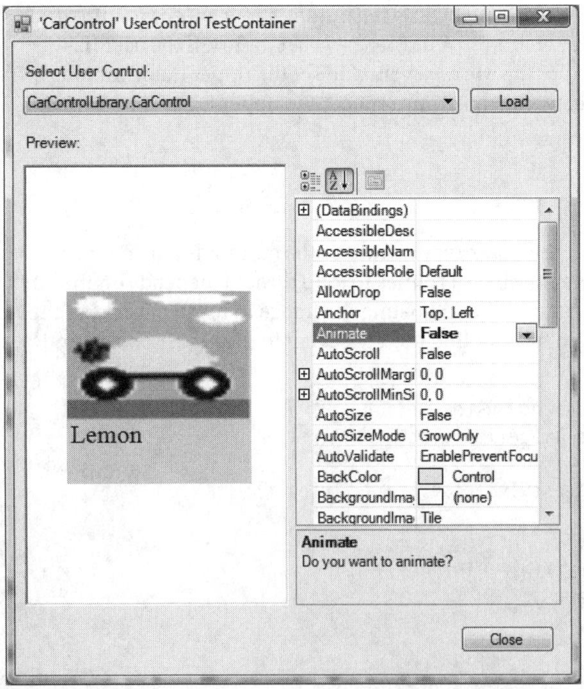

Figure 29-29. *Testing the* CarControl *with the UserControl Test Container*

If you set the Animate property to True, you should see the CarControl cycle through the first three *.bmp files. What you are unable to do with this testing utility, however, is handle events. To test this aspect of your UI widget, you need to build a custom Form.

Building a Custom CarControl Form Host

As with all .NET types, you are now able to make use of your custom control from any language targeting the CLR. Begin by closing down the current workspace and creating a new VB 2008 Windows Application project named CarControlTestForm. To reference your custom controls from within the Visual Studio 2008 IDE, right-click anywhere within the Toolbox window and select the Choose Items menu selection. Using the Browse button on the .NET Framework Components tab, navigate to your CarControlLibrary.dll library. Once you click OK, you will find a new icon on the Toolbox named, of course, CarControl.

Next, place a new CarControl widget (named myCarControl) onto the Forms designer. Notice that the Animate, PetName, and Speed properties are all exposed through the Properties window. Again, like the UserControl Test Container, the control is "alive" at design time. Thus, if you set the Animate property to True, you will find your car is animating on the Forms designer.

Once you have configured the initial state of your CarControl, add additional GUI widgets that allow the user to increase and decrease the speed of the automobile, and view the string data sent by the incoming events as well as the car's current speed (Label controls will do nicely for these purposes). One possible GUI design is shown in Figure 29-30.

Figure 29-30. *The client-side GUI*

Provided you have created a GUI identical to mine, the code within the Form-derived type is quite straightforward (here I am assuming you have handled each of the CarControl events using the Properties window):

```
Public Class MainForm

  Sub New()
    ' This call is required by the Windows Forms designer.
    InitializeComponent()
    lblCurrentSpeed.Text = String.Format("Current Speed: {0}", _
      Me.myCarControl.Speed.ToString())
    numericUpDownCarSpeed.Value = myCarControl.Speed
```

```
    ' Configure the car control.
    myCarControl.Animate = True
    myCarControl.PetName = "Zippy"
  End Sub

  Private Sub myCarControl_AboutToBlow(ByVal msg As System.String) _
    Handles myCarControl.AboutToBlow
    lblEventData.Text = String.Format("Event Data: {0}", msg)
  End Sub

  Private Sub myCarControl_BlewUp(ByVal msg As System.String) _
    Handles myCarControl.BlewUp
    lblEventData.Text = String.Format("Event Data: {0}", msg)
  End Sub

  Private Sub numericUpDownCarSpeed_ValueChanged(ByVal sender As System.Object, _
    ByVal e As System.EventArgs) Handles numericUpDownCarSpeed.ValueChanged
    ' Assume the min of this NumericUpDown is 0 and max is 300.
    Me.myCarControl.Speed = CType(numericUpDownCarSpeed.Value, Integer)

    lblCurrentSpeed.Text = String.Format("Current Speed: {0}", _
     Me.myCarControl.Speed.ToString())
    End Sub
End Class
```

At this point, you are able to run your client application and interact with the CarControl. As you can see, building and using custom controls is a fairly straightforward task, given what you already know about OOP, the .NET type system, GDI+ (aka System.Drawing.dll), and Windows Forms.

While you now have enough information to continue exploring the process of .NET Windows controls development, there is one additional programmatic aspect you have to contend with: design-time functionality. Before I describe exactly what this boils down to, you'll need to understand the role of the System.ComponentModel namespace.

The Role of the System.ComponentModel Namespace

The System.ComponentModel namespace defines a number of attributes (among other types) that allow you to describe how your custom controls should behave at design time. For example, you can opt to supply a textual description of each property, define a default event, or group related properties or events into a custom category for display purposes within the Visual Studio 2008 Properties window. When you are interested in making the sorts of modifications previously mentioned, you will want to make use of the core attributes shown in Table 29-12.

Table 29-12. *Select Members of* System.ComponentModel

Attribute	Applied To	Meaning in Life
Browsable	Properties and events	Specifies whether a property or an event should be displayed in the property browser. By default, all custom properties and events can be browsed.
Category	Properties and events	Specifies the name of the category in which to group a property or event.

Attribute	Applied To	Meaning in Life
`Description`	Properties and events	Defines a small block of text to be displayed at the bottom of the property browser when the user selects a property or event.
`DefaultProperty`	Properties	Specifies the default property for the component. This property is selected in the property browser when a user selects the control.
`DefaultValue`	Properties	Defines a default value for a property that will be applied when the control is "reset" within the IDE.
`DefaultEvent`	Events	Specifies the default event for the component. When a programmer double-clicks the control, stub code is automatically written for the default event.

Enhancing the Design-Time Appearance of CarControl

To illustrate the use of some of these new attributes, close down the CarControlTestForm project and reopen your CarControlLibrary project. Let's create a custom category called "Car Configuration" to which each property and event of the `CarControl` belongs. Also, let's supply a friendly description for each member and default value for each property. To do so, simply update each of the properties and events of the `CarControl` type to support the `<Category()>`, `<DefaultValue()>`, and `<Description()>` attributes as required (be sure to import the `System.ComponentModel` namespace):

```
Public Class CarControl
...
  ' Car events.
  <Category("Car Configuration"), _
   Description("Sent when the car is approaching terminal speed.")> _
  Public Event AboutToBlow(ByVal msg As String)
...
  ' Configure pet name.
  <Category("Car Configuration"), _
   Description("Name your car!"), _
   DefaultValue("Lemon")> _
  Public Property PetName() As String
...
    End Property
...
End Class
```

Now, let me make a comment on what it means to assign a *default value* to a property, because I can almost guarantee you it is not what you would (naturally) assume. Simply put, the `<DefaultValue()>` attribute does *not* ensure that the underlying value of the data point wrapped by a given property will be automatically initialized to the default value. Thus, although you specified a default value of "No Name" for the `PetName` property, the `carPetName` member variable will not be set to the value "Lemon" unless you do so via the type's constructor or via member initialization syntax (as you have already done):

```
Private carPetName As String = "Lemon"
```

Rather, the `<DefaultValue()>` attribute comes into play when the programmer "resets" the value of a given property using the Properties window. To reset a property using Visual Studio 2008, select the property of interest, right-click it, and select Reset. In Figure 29-31, notice that the `<Description>` value appears in the bottom pane of the Properties window.

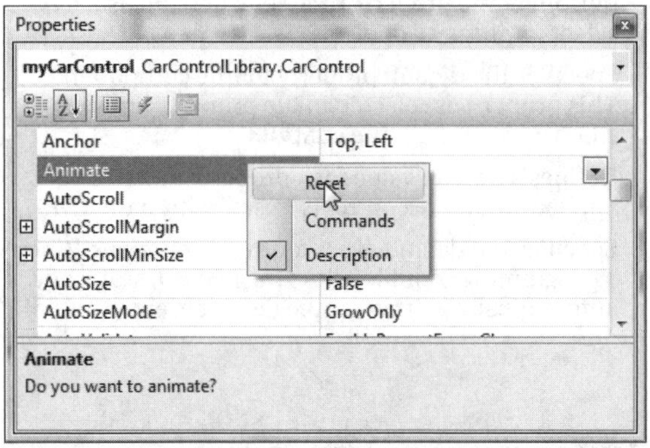

Figure 29-31. *Resetting a property to the default value*

The `<Category()>` attribute will be realized only if the programmer selects the categorized view of the Properties window (as opposed to the default alphabetical view) as shown in Figure 29-32.

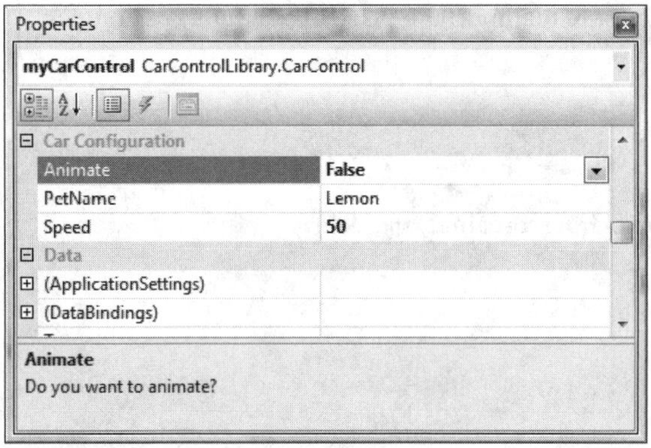

Figure 29-32. *The custom category*

Defining a Default Property and Default Event

In addition to describing and grouping like members into a common category, you may want to configure your controls to support default behaviors. A given control may support a default property. When you define the default property for a class using the `<DefaultProperty()>` attribute as follows:

```
' Mark the default property for this control.
<DefaultProperty("Animate")> _
Public Class CarControl
...
End Class
```

you ensure that when the user selects this control at design time, the Animate property is automatically highlighted in the Properties window. Likewise, if you configure your control to have a default event as follows:

```
' Mark the default event and property for this control.
<DefaultEvent("AboutToBlow"), _
DefaultProperty("Animate")> _
Public Class CarControl
...
End Class
```

you ensure that when the user double-clicks the widget at design time, stub code is automatically written for the default event (which explains why when you double-click a Button, the Click event is automatically handled; when you double-click a Form, the Load event is automatically handled; and so on).

Specifying a Custom Toolbox Bitmap

A final design-time bell-and-whistle any polished custom control should sport is a custom Toolbox bitmap image. Currently, when the user selects the CarControl, the IDE will show this type within the Toolbox using the default "gear" icon. If you wish to specify a custom image, your first step is to insert a new *.bmp file into your project (CarControl.bmp) that is configured to be 16×16 pixels in size (established via the Width and Height properties). Here, I simply reused the Car image used in the TreeView example.

Once you have created the image as you see fit, use the <ToolboxBitmap()> attribute (which is applied at the type level) to assign this image to your control. The first argument to the attribute's constructor is the type information for the control itself, while the second argument is the friendly name of the *.bmp file.

```
<DefaultEvent("AboutToBlow"), _
DefaultProperty("Animate"), _
ToolboxBitmap(GetType(CarControl), "CarControl")> _
Public Class CarControl
...
End Class
```

The final step is to make sure you set the Build Action value of the control's icon image to Embedded Resource (via the Properties window) to ensure the image data is embedded within your assembly, as shown in Figure 29-33.

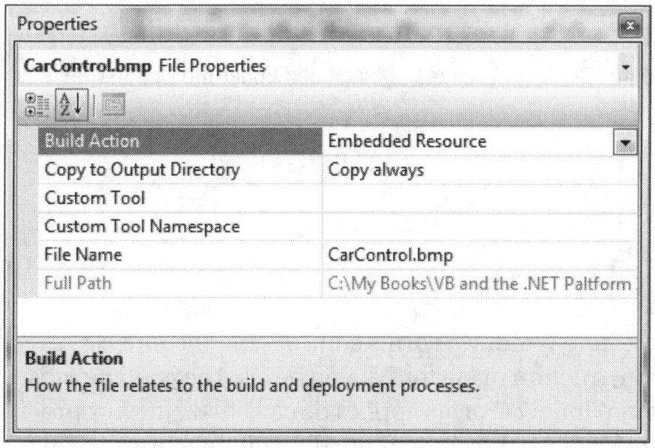

Figure 29-33. *Embedding the image resource*

■ **Note** The reason you are manually embedding the `*.bmp` file (in contrast to when you make use of the `ImageList` type) is that you are not assigning the `CarControl.bmp` file to a UI element at design time, therefore the underlying `*.resx` file will not automatically update.

Once you recompile your Windows Controls library, you can now load your previous CarControlTestForm project. Right-click the current `CarControl` icon within the Toolbox and select Delete. Next, read the `CarControl` widget to the Toolbox (by right-clicking and selecting Choose Items). This time, you should see your custom toolbox bitmap (see Figure 29-34).

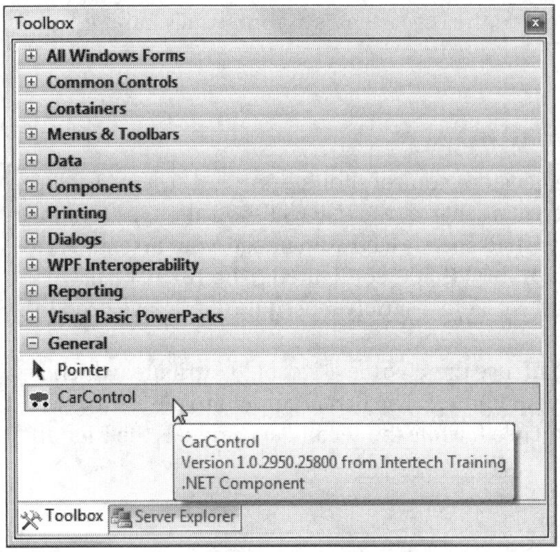

Figure 29-34. *The custom toolbox bitmap*

So, that wraps up our examination of the process of building custom Windows Forms controls. I hope this example sparked your interest in custom control development. Here, I stuck with the book's automobile theme. Imagine, though, the usefulness of a custom control that will render a pie chart based on the current inventory of a given table in a given database, or a control that extends the functionality of standard UI widgets.

■ **Source Code** The CarControlLibrary and CarControlTestForm projects are included under the Chapter 29 directory.

Building Custom Dialog Boxes

Now that you have a solid understanding of the core Windows Forms controls and the process of building custom controls, let's examine the construction of custom dialog boxes. The good news is that everything you have already learned about Windows Forms applies directly to dialog box programming. By and large, creating (and showing) a dialog box is no more difficult than inserting a new Form into your current project.

There is no “Dialog” base class in the System.Windows.Forms namespace. Rather, a dialog box is simply a stylized Form. For example, many dialog boxes are intended to be nonsizable, therefore you will typically want to set the FormBorderStyle property to FormBorderStyle.FixedDialog. As well, dialog boxes typically set the MinimizeBox and MaximizeBox properties to False. In this way, the dialog box is configured to be a fixed constant. Finally, if you set the ShowInTaskbar property to False, you will prevent the Form from being visible in the Windows task bar.

To illustrate the process of working with dialog boxes, create a new Windows application named SimpleModalDialog. The main Form type supports a MenuStrip that contains a File ➤ Exit menu item as well as Tools ➤ Configure. Build this UI now, and handle the Click event for the Exit and Configure menu items. As well, define a string member variable in your main Form type (named userMessage), and render this data within a Paint event handler of your main Form. Here is the current code within the MainForm.vb file:

```
Public Class MainForm
  Private userMessage As String = "Default Message"

  ' We will implement this method in just a bit...
  Private Sub configureToolStripMenuItem_Click(ByVal sender As System.Object, _
  ByVal e As System.EventArgs) Handles configureToolStripMenuItem.Click
  End Sub

  Private Sub exitToolStripMenuItem_Click(ByVal sender As System.Object, _
  ByVal e As System.EventArgs) Handles exitToolStripMenuItem.Click
    Application.Exit()
  End Sub

  Private Sub MainForm_Paint(ByVal sender As System.Object, _
  ByVal e As System.Windows.Forms.PaintEventArgs) Handles MyBase.Paint
  Dim g As Graphics = e.Graphics
  g.DrawString(userMessage, New Font("Times New Roman", 24), _
    Brushes.DarkBlue, 50, 50)
  End Sub
End Class
```

Now add a new Form to your current project using the Project ➤ Add Windows Form menu item named UserMessageDialog.vb. Set the ShowInTaskbar, MinimizeBox, and MaximizeBox properties to False. Next, build a UI that consists of two Buttons (for the OK and Cancel buttons), a single TextBox (named txtUserInput, to allow the user to enter her message), and an instructive Label. Figure 29-35 shows one possible UI.

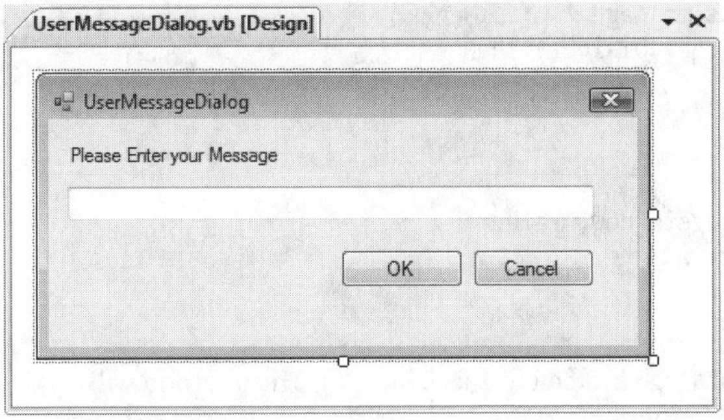

Figure 29-35. *A custom dialog box*

Finally, expose the Text value of the Form's TextBox using a custom property named Message:

```
Public Class UserMessageDialog
  Public Property Message() As String
    Get
      Return txtUserInput.Text
    End Get
    Set(ByVal value As String)
      txtUserInput.Text = value
    End Set
  End Property
End Class
```

The DialogResult Property

As a final UI task, select the OK button on the Forms designer and find the DialogResult property. Assign DialogResult.OK to your OK button and DialogResult.Cancel to your Cancel button. Formally, you can assign the DialogResult property to any value from the DialogResult enumeration:

```
Public Enum DialogResult
  Abort
  Cancel
  Ignore
  No
  None
  OK
  Retry
  Yes
End Enum
```

So, what exactly does it mean to assign a Button's DialogResult value? This property can be assigned to any Button instance (as well as the Form itself) and allows the parent Form to determine which button the end user selected. To illustrate, update the Tools ➤ Configure menu handler on the MainForm type as follows:

```
Private Sub configureToolStripMenuItem_Click(ByVal sender As System.Object, _
  ByVal e As System.EventArgs) Handles configureToolStripMenuItem.Click
  ' Create an instance of UserMessageDialog.
  Dim dlg As New UserMessageDialog()

  ' Place the current message in the TextBox.
  dlg.Message = userMessage

  ' If user clicked OK button, render his message.
  If Windows.Forms.DialogResult.OK = dlg.ShowDialog() Then
    userMessage = dlg.Message
    Invalidate()
  End If

  ' Have dialog box clean up internal widgets now, rather
  ' than when the GC destroys the object.
  dlg.Dispose()
End Sub
```

Here, you are showing the UserMessageDialog via a call to ShowDialog(). This method will launch the Form as a *modal* dialog box which, as you may know, means the user is unable to activate the main Form until he or she dismisses the dialog box. Once the user does dismiss the dialog box (by clicking the OK or Cancel button), the Form is no longer visible, but it is still in memory. Therefore, you are able to ask the `UserMessageDialog` instance (`dlg`) for its new `Message` value in the event the user has clicked the OK button. If so, you render the new message. If not, you do nothing.

■ **Note** If you wish to show a modeless dialog box (which allows the user to navigate between the parent and dialog Forms), call `Show()` rather than `ShowDialog()`.

Understanding Form Inheritance

One very appealing aspect of building dialog boxes under Windows Forms is *form inheritance*. As you are no doubt aware, inheritance is the pillar of OOP that allows one class to extend the functionality of another class. Typically, when you speak of inheritance, you envision one non-GUI type (e.g., `SportsCar`) deriving from another non-GUI type (e.g., `Car`). However, in the world of Windows Forms, it is possible for one Form to derive from another Form and in the process inherit the base class's widgets and implementation.

Form-level inheritance is a very powerful technique, as it allows you to build a base Form that provides core-level functionality for a family of related dialog boxes. If you were to bundle these base-level Forms into a .NET assembly, other members of your team could extend these types using the .NET language of their choice.

For the sake of illustration, assume you wish to subclass the `UserMessageDialog` to build a new dialog box that also allows the user to specify whether the message should be rendered in italics. To do so, choose the Project ➤ Add Windows Form menu item, but this time add a new Inherited Form named `ItalicUserMessageDialog.vb`, as shown in Figure 29-36.

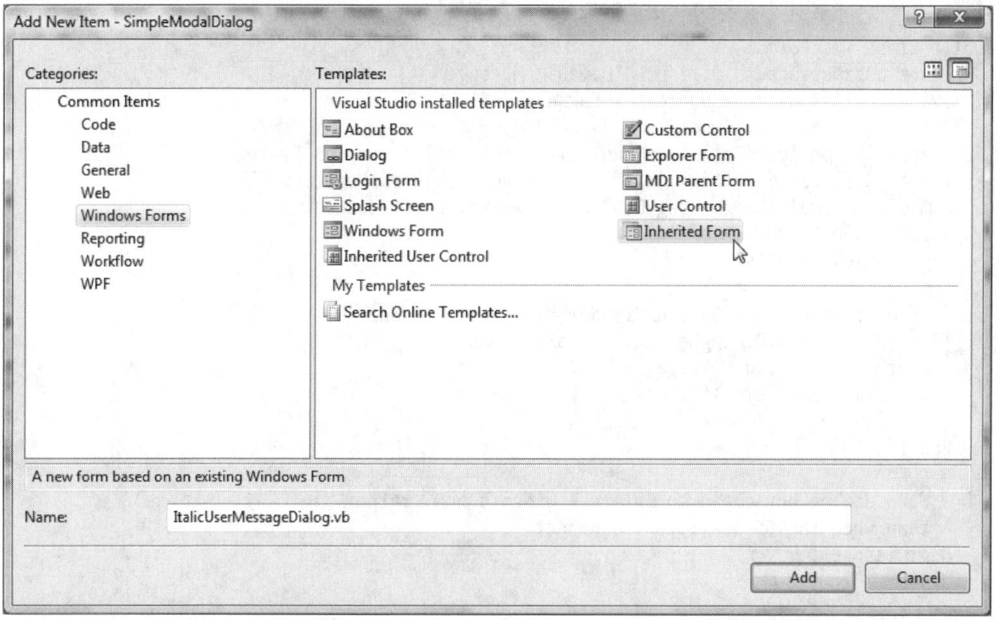

Figure 29-36. *A derived Form*

Once you select Add, you will be shown the *Inheritance Picker* utility, which allows you to choose from a Form in your current project or select a Form in an external assembly via the Browse button. For this example, select your existing UserMessageDialog type.

Note If you cannot find your Form listed in the Inheritance Picker, you have not yet built your project! This dialog box is using reflection to find all Form-derived types in your assembly, therefore if your build is out of date, the metadata has not been refreshed.

If you look in your *.Designer.vb file, you will find that your new class type extends the dialog class. At this point, you are free to extend this derived Form any way you choose. For test purposes, simply add a new CheckBox control (named checkBoxItalic) that is exposed through a property named Italic:

```
Public Class ItalicUserMessageDialog
  Public Property Italic() As Boolean
    Get
      Return checkBoxItalic.Checked
    End Get
    Set(ByVal value As Boolean)
      checkBoxItalic.Checked = value
    End Set
  End Property
End Class
```

Now that you have subclassed the basic UserMessageDialog type, update your MainForm to leverage the new Italic property. Simply add a new Boolean member variable that will be used to build an italic Font object, and update your Tools ➤ Configure Click menu handler to make use of ItalicUserMessageDialog. Here is the complete update:

```
Public Class MainForm
  Private userMessage As String = "Default Message"
  Private textIsItalic As Boolean = False

  Private Sub configureToolStripMenuItem_Click(ByVal sender As System.Object, _
  ByVal e As System.EventArgs) Handles configureToolStripMenuItem.Click
    Dim dlg As ItalicUserMessageDialog = New ItalicUserMessageDialog()
    dlg.Message = userMessage
    dlg.Italic = textIsItalic

    ' If user clicked OK button, render his or her message.
    If Windows.Forms.DialogResult.OK = dlg.ShowDialog() Then
      userMessage = dlg.Message
      textIsItalic = dlg.Italic
      Invalidate()
    End If

    ' Have dialog box clean up internal widgets now, rather
    ' than when the GC destroys the object.
    dlg.Dispose()
  End Sub
...
```

```
  Private Sub MainForm_Paint(ByVal sender As System.Object, _
  ByVal e As System.Windows.Forms.PaintEventArgs) Handles MyBase.Paint
    Dim g As Graphics = e.Graphics
    Dim f As Font = Nothing
    If textIsItalic Then
      f = New Font("Times New Roman", 24, FontStyle.Italic)
    Else
      f = New Font("Times New Roman", 24)
    End If
    g.DrawString(userMessage, f, Brushes.DarkBlue, 50, 50)
  End Sub
End Class
```

Source Code The SimpleModalDialog application is included under the Chapter 29 directory.

Dynamically Positioning Windows Forms Controls

To wrap up this chapter, let's examine a few techniques you can use to control the layout of widgets on a Form. By and large, when you build a `Form` type, the assumption is that the controls are rendered using *absolute position*, meaning that if you placed a `Button` on your Forms designer 10 pixels down and 10 pixels over from the upper-left portion of the Form, you expect the `Button` to stay put during its lifetime.

On a related note, when you are creating a Form that contains UI controls, you need to decide whether the Form should be resizable. Typically speaking, main windows are resizable, whereas dialog boxes are not. Recall that the resizability of a Form is controlled by the `FormBorderStyle` property, which can be set to any value of the `FormBorderStyle` enum.

```
Public Enum FormBorderStyle
  None
  FixedSingle
  Fixed3D
  FixedDialog
  Sizable
  FixedToolWindow
  SizableToolWindow
End Enum
```

Assume that you have allowed your Form to be resizable. This brings up some interesting questions regarding the contained controls. For example, if the user makes the Form smaller than the rectangle needed to display each control, should the controls adjust their size (and possibly location) to morph correctly with the Form?

The Anchor Property

In Windows Forms, the `Anchor` property is used to define a relative fixed position in which the control should always be rendered. Every `Control`-derived type has an `Anchor` property, which can be set to any of the values from the `AnchorStyles` enumeration described in Table 29-13.

Table 29-13. `AnchorStyles` *Values*

Value	Meaning in Life
`Bottom`	The control's bottom edge is anchored to the bottom edge of its container.
`Left`	The control's left edge is anchored to the left edge of its container.
`None`	The control is not anchored to any edges of its container.
`Right`	The control's right edge is anchored to the right edge of its container.
`Top`	The control's top edge is anchored to the top edge of its container.

To anchor a widget at the upper-left corner, you are free to OR styles together (e.g., `AnchorStyles.Top Or AnchorStyles.Left`). Again, the idea behind the `Anchor` property is to configure which edges of the control are anchored to the edges of its container. For example, if you configure a `Button` with the following `Anchor` value:

```
' Anchor this widget relative to the right position.
myButton.Anchor = AnchorStyles.Right
```

you are ensured that as the Form is resized, this `Button` maintains its position relative to the right side of the Form.

The Dock Property

Another aspect of Windows Forms programming is establishing the *docking behavior* of your controls. If you so choose, you can set a widget's `Dock` property to configure which side (or sides) of a Form the widget should be attached to. The value you assign to a control's `Dock` property is honored, regardless of the Form's current dimensions. Table 29-14 describes possible options.

Table 29-14. `DockStyle` *Values*

Value	Meaning in Life
`Bottom`	The control's bottom edge is docked to the bottom of its containing control.
`Fill`	All the control's edges are docked to all the edges of its containing control and sized appropriately.
`Left`	The control's left edge is docked to the left edge of its containing control.
`None`	The control is not docked.
`Right`	The control's right edge is docked to the right edge of its containing control.
`Top`	The control's top edge is docked to the top of its containing control.

So, for example, if you want to ensure that a given widget is always docked on the left side of a Form, you would write the following:

```
' This item is always located on the left of the Form, regardless
' of the Form's current size.
myButton.Dock = DockStyle.Left
```

To help you understand the implications of setting the `Anchor` and `Dock` properties, the downloadable code for this book contains a project named AnchoringControls. Once you build and run this application, you can make use of the Form's menu system to set various `AnchorStyles` and `DockStyle` values and observe the change in behavior of the `Button` type (see Figure 29-37).

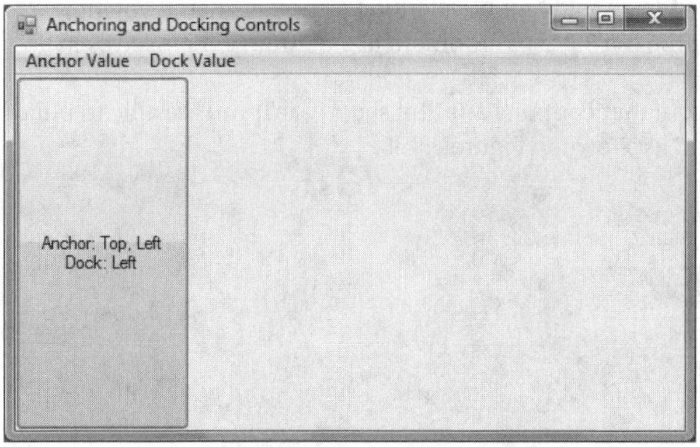

Figure 29-37. *The AnchoringControls application*

Be sure to resize the Form when changing the `Anchor` property to observe how the `Button` responds.

Source Code The AnchoringControls application is included under the Chapter 29 directory.

Table and Flow Layout

The Windows Forms API offers additional ways to control the layout of a Form's widgets using one of two layout managers. The `TableLayoutPanel` and `FlowLayoutPanel` types can be docked into a Form's client area to arrange the internal controls. For example, assume you place a new `FlowLayoutPanel` widget onto the Forms designer and configure it to dock fully within the parent Form, as you see in Figure 29-38.

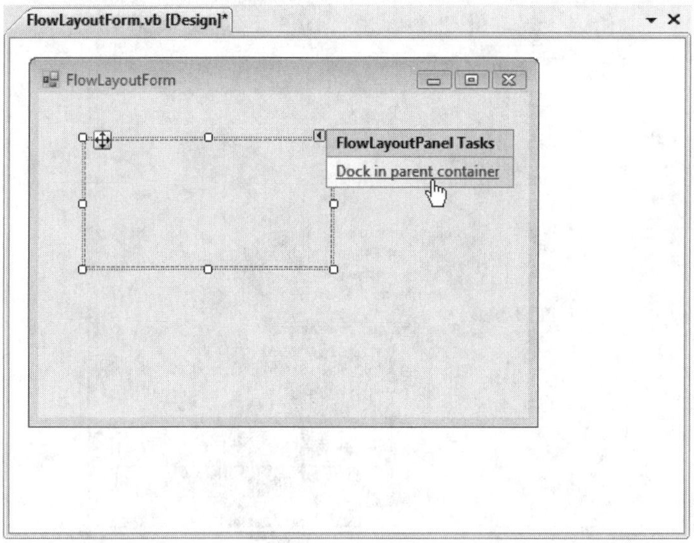

Figure 29-38. *Docking a* `FlowLayoutPanel` *into a Form*

Now, add ten new `Buttons` within the `FlowLayoutPanel` using the Forms designer. If you now run your application, you will notice that the ten `Buttons` automatically rearrange themselves in a manner very close to standard HTML.

On the other hand, if you create a Form that contains a `TableLayoutPanel`, you are able to build a UI that is partitioned into various "cells," as shown in Figure 29-39.

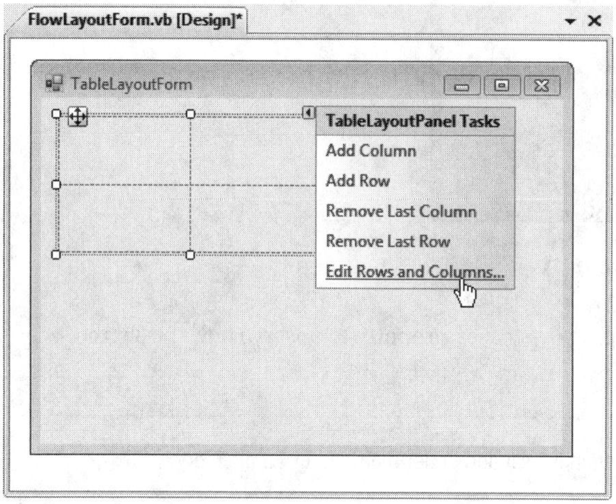

Figure 29-39. *The* `TableLayoutPanel` *type*

If you select the Edit Rows and Columns inline menu option using the Forms designer (as shown in Figure 29-39), you are able to control the overall format of the `TableLayoutPanel` on a cell-by-cell basis (see Figure 29-40).

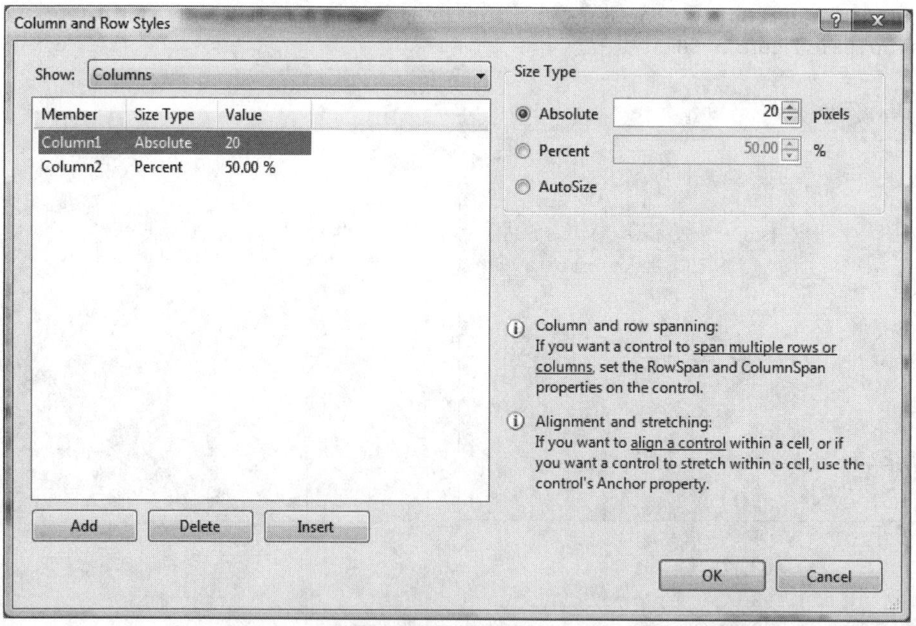

Figure 29-40. *Configuring the cells of the* `TableLayoutPanel` *type*

Truth be told, the only way to see the effects of the TableLayoutPanel type is to do so in a hands-on manner. I'll let interested readers handle that task.

Summary

This chapter rounded off your understanding of the Windows Forms namespace by examining the programming of numerous GUI widgets, from the simple (e.g., Label) to the more exotic (e.g., TreeView). After examining numerous control types, we moved on to cover the construction of custom controls, including the topic of design-time integration.

In the latter half of this chapter, you learned how to build custom dialog boxes and how to derive a new Form from an existing Form type using form inheritance. This chapter concluded by briefly exploring the various anchoring and docking behaviors you can use to enforce a specific layout of your GUI types, as well as the Windows Forms layout managers.

PART 7

Desktop Applications with WPF

CHAPTER 30

Introducing Windows Presentation Foundation and XAML

In the previous part, you were introduced to the functionality contained within the `System.Windows.Forms.dll` and `System.Drawing.dll` assemblies. As explained, the Windows Forms API is the original GUI toolkit of the .NET platform, which provides numerous types that can be used to build sophisticated desktop user interfaces. While it is true that Windows Forms/GDI+ is still entirely supported under .NET 3.5, Microsoft shipped a brand-new desktop API termed Windows Presentation Foundation (WPF) beginning with the release of .NET 3.0.

This initial WPF chapter begins by examining the motivation behind this new UI framework and provides a brief overview of the various types of WPF applications supported by the API. After this point, we will examine the core WPF programming model and come to know the role of the `Application` and `Window` types as well as the key WFP assemblies and namespaces.

The later part of this chapter will introduce you to a brand-new XML-based grammar: Extensible Application Markup Language (XAML). As you will see, XAML provides WPF developers with a way to partition UI definitions from the logic that drives them. Here, you will be exposed to several critical XAML topics, including attached property syntax, type converters, markup extensions, and understanding how to parse XAML at runtime. This chapter wraps up by examining the various WPF-specific tools that ship with the Visual Studio 2008 IDE and examines the role of Microsoft Expression Blend.

The Motivation Behind WPF

Over the years, Microsoft has developed numerous graphical user interface toolkits (raw C/C++/Win32 API development, VB6, MFC, etc.) to build desktop executables. Each of these APIs provided a code base to represent the basic aspects of a GUI application, including main windows, dialog boxes, controls, menu systems, and other necessities. With the initial release of the .NET platform, the Windows Forms API quickly became the preferred model for UI development, given its simple yet very powerful object model.

While many full-featured desktop applications have been successfully created using Windows Forms, the fact of the matter is that this programming model is rather *asymmetrical*. Simply put, `System.Windows.Forms.dll` and `System.Drawing.dll` do not provide direct support for many additional technologies required to build a full-fledged desktop application. To illustrate this point, consider the ad hoc nature of GUI development prior to the release of WPF (e.g., .NET 2.0; see Table 30-1).

Table 30-1. *.NET 2.0 Solutions to Desired Functionalities*

Desired Functionality	.NET 2.0 Solution
Building forms with controls	Windows Forms
2D graphics support	GDI+ (`System.Drawing.dll`)
3D graphics support	DirectX APIs
Support for streaming video	Windows Media Player APIs
Support for flow-style documents	Programmatic manipulation of PDF files

As you can see, a Windows Forms developer must pull in types from a number of different APIs and object models. While it is true that making use of these diverse APIs may look similar syntactically (it is just VB code, after all), you may also agree that each technology requires a radically different mind-set. For example, the skills required to create a 3D rendered animation using DirectX are completely different from those used to bind data to a grid. To be sure, it is very difficult for a Windows Forms programmer to master the diverse nature of each API.

Unifying Diverse APIs

WPF (introduced with .NET 3.0) was purposely created to merge these previously unrelated programming tasks into a single unified object model. Thus, if you need to author a 3D animation, you have no need to manually program against the DirectX API (although you could), as 3D functionality is baked directly into WPF. To see how well things have cleaned up, consider Table 30-2, which illustrates the desktop development model ushered in as of .NET 3.0 and higher.

Table 30-2. *.NET 3.0–3.5 Solutions to Desired Functionalities*

Desired Functionality	.NET 3.0 and Higher Solution
Building forms with controls	WPF
2D graphics support	WPF
3D graphics support	WPF
Support for streaming video	WPF
Support for flow-style documents	WPF

Providing a Separation of Concerns via XAML

Perhaps one of the most compelling benefits is that WPF provides a way to cleanly separate the look and feel of a Windows application from the programming logic that drives it. Using XAML, it is possible to define the UI of an application via *markup*. This markup (ideally created by those with an artistic mind-set using dedicated tools) can then be connected to a managed code base to provide the guts of the program's functionality.

■Note XAML is not limited to WPF applications! Any application can use XAML to describe a tree of .NET objects, even if they have nothing to do with a visible user interface. For example, it is possible to build custom activities for a Windows Workflow Foundation application using XAML.

As you dig into WPF, you may be surprised how much flexibility "desktop markup" provides. XAML allows you to define not only simple UI elements (buttons, grids, list boxes, etc.) in markup, but also graphical renderings, animations, data binding logic, and multimedia functionality (such as video playback). For example, defining a circular button control that animates a company logo requires just a few lines of markup. Even better, WPF elements can be modified through styles and templates, which allow you to change the overall look and feel of an application with minimum fuss and bother, independent of the core application processing code.

Given all these points, the need to build custom controls greatly diminishes under WPF. Unlike Windows Forms development, the only compelling reason to build a custom WPF control library is if you need to change the *behaviors* of a control (e.g., add custom methods, properties, or events; subclass an existing control to override virtual members; etc.). If you simply need to change the *look and feel* of a control (again, such as a circular animated button), you can do so entirely through markup.

■ **Note** Other valid reasons to build custom WPF controls include achieving binary reuse (via a WPF control library), as well as building controls that expose custom design-time functionality and integration with the Visual Studio 2008 IDE.

Providing an Optimized Rendering Model

Also be aware of the fact that WPF is optimized to take advantage of the new video driver model supported under the Windows Vista operating system. While WPF applications can be developed on and deployed to Windows XP machines (as well as Windows Server 2003 machines), the same application running on Vista will tend to perform much faster, especially when making use of animations/multimedia services. This is due to the fact that the display services of WPF are rendered via the DirectX engine, allowing for efficient hardware and software rendering.

■ **Note** Allow me to reiterate this key point: WPF is not limited to Windows Vista! Although the Vista operating system has the .NET 3.0 libraries (which include WPF) installed out of the box, you can build and execute WPF applications on XP and Windows Server 2003 once you install the .NET Framework 3.0 or higher SDK (for programmers) or .NET 3.0 or higher runtime (for end users).

WPF applications also tend to behave better under Vista. If one graphics-intensive application crashes, it will not take down the entire operating system (à la the blue screen of death); rather, the misbehaving application in question will simply terminate. As you may know, the most common cause of the infamous blue screen of death is misbehaving video drivers.

Additional WPF-Centric Bells and Whistles

To recap the story thus far, WPF is a new API to build desktop applications that integrates various desktop APIs into a single object model and provides a clean separation of concerns via XAML. In addition to these major points, WPF applications also benefit from various other bells and whistles, many of which are explained over the next several chapters. Here is a quick rundown of the core services:

- A number of layout managers (far more than Windows Forms) to provide extremely flexible control over placement and repositioning of content
- Use of an enhanced data-binding engine to bind content to UI elements in a variety of ways
- A built-in style engine, which allows you to define "themes" for a WPF application
- Use of vector graphics, which allows content to be automatically resized to fit the size and resolution of the screen hosting the application
- Support for 2D and 3D graphics, animations, and video and audio playback
- A rich typography API, such as support for XML Paper Specification (XPS) documents, fixed documents (WYSIWYG), flow documents, and document annotations (e.g., a "sticky notes" API)
- Support for interoperating with legacy GUI models (e.g., Windows Forms, ActiveX, and Win32 HWNDs)

The Various Flavors of WPF Applications

The WPF API can be used to build a variety of GUI-centric applications, which basically differ in their navigational structure and deployment models. The sections that follow present a high-level walk through each option.

Traditional Desktop Applications

The first (and most familiar) option is a traditional executable assembly that runs on a local machine. For example, you could use WPF to build a text editor, painting program, or multimedia program such as a digital music player, photo viewer, and so forth. Like any other desktop applications, these `*.exe` files can be installed using traditional means (setup programs, Windows Installer packages, etc.) or via ClickOnce technology to allow desktop applications to be distributed and installed via a remote web server.

In this light, WPF is simply a new API to build traditional desktop applications. Programmatically speaking, this type of WPF application will make use (at a minimum) of the `Window` and `Application` types, in addition to the expected set of dialog boxes, toolbars, status bars, menu systems, and other UI elements.

Navigation-Based WPF Applications

WPF applications can optionally choose to make use of a navigation-based structure, which makes a traditional desktop application take on the basic behavior of a web browser application. Using this model, you can build a desktop `*.exe` that provides a "forward" button and a "back" button that allow the end user to move back and forth between various UI displays called *pages*. The application itself maintains a list of each page and provides the necessary infrastructure to navigate between them, pass data across pages (similar to a web-based application variable), and maintain a history list. By way of a concrete example, consider Vista's Windows Explorer (see Figure 30-1), which makes use of such functionality. Notice the navigational buttons (and history list) mounted on the upper-left corner of the window.

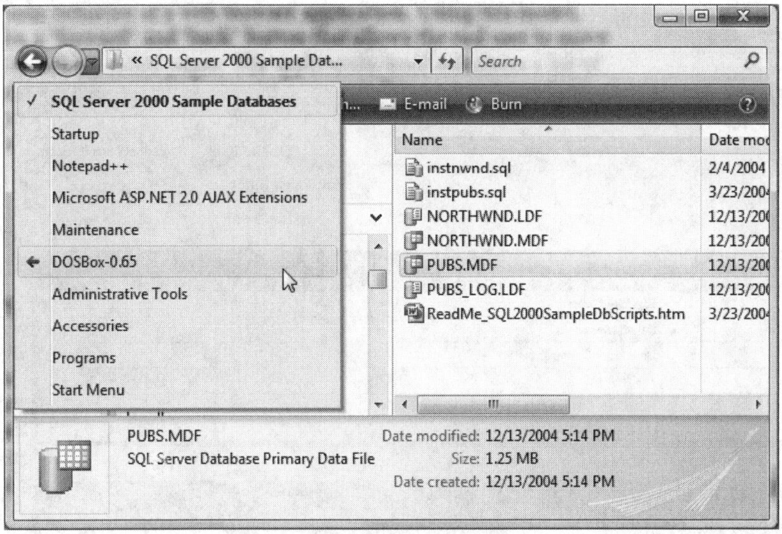

Figure 30-1. *A navigation-based desktop program*

Regardless of the fact that a WPF desktop application can take on a weblike navigational scheme, understand that this is simply a UI design issue. The application itself is still little more than a local executable assembly running on a desktop machine, and it has nothing to do with a web application beyond a slightly similar look and feel. Programmatically speaking, this navigational structure is represented using types such as `Page`, `NavigationWindow`, and `Frame`.

XBAP Applications

WPF also allows you to build applications that can be hosted *within* a web browser. This flavor of WPF application is termed a XAML browser application, or XBAP. Under this model, the end user navigates to a given URL, at which point the XBAP application (which takes an `*.xbap` file extension) is transparently downloaded and installed to the local machine. Unlike a traditional ClickOnce installation for an executable application, however, the XBAP program is hosted directly within the browser and adopts the browser's intrinsic navigational system. Figure 30-2 illustrates an XBAP program in action (specifically, the ExpenseIt WPF sample program that ships with the .NET Framework 3.5 SDK).

One possible downside to this flavor of WPF is that XBAPs must be hosted within Microsoft Internet Explorer 6.0 (or higher) or Firefox. If you are deploying such applications across a company intranet, browser compatibility should not be a problem, given that system administrators can play dictator regarding which browser should be installed on users' machines. However, if you want the outside world to make use of your XBAP, it is not possible to ensure each end user is making use of Internet Explorer/Firefox, and therefore some external users may not be able to view your WPF XBAP application.

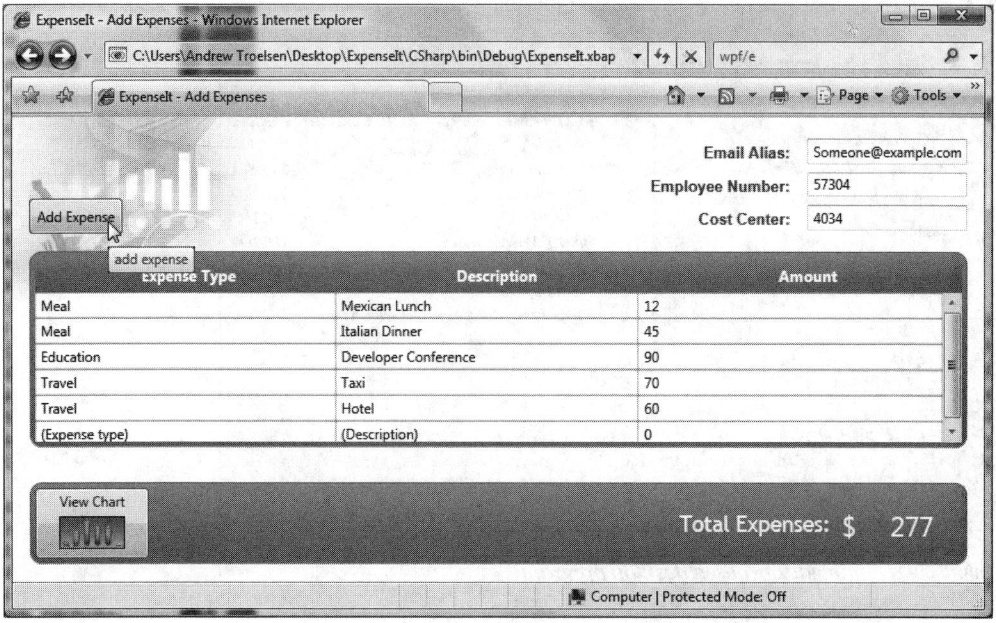

Figure 30-2. *XBAP programs are downloaded to a local machine and hosted within a web browser.*

Another issue to be aware of is that XBAP applications run within a security sandbox termed the *Internet zone*. .NET assemblies that are loaded into this sandbox have limited access to system resources (such as the local file system or system registry) and cannot freely use all aspects of specific .NET APIs that might pose a security threat. Specifically, XBAPs cannot perform the following tasks:

- Create and display stand-alone windows.
- Display application-defined dialog boxes.
- Display a Save dialog box launched by the XBAP itself.
- Access the file system (use of isolated storage is permitted).
- Make use of legacy UI models (Windows Forms, ActiveX) or call unmanaged code.

At first glance, the inability to create secondary windows (or dialog boxes) may seem very limiting. In reality, an XBAP can show users multiple user interfaces by using the page-navigation model mentioned previously.

Silverlight Applications

WPF and XAML also provide the foundation for a *cross-platform* WPF-centric plug-in termed *Silverlight*. Using the Silverlight SDK, it is possible to build browser-based applications that can be hosted by Mac OS X as well as Microsoft Windows (additional operating systems are supposedly also in the works).

With Silverlight, you are able to build extremely feature-rich (and interactive) web applications. For example, like WPF, Silverlight has a vector-based graphical system, animation support, a rich text document model, and multimedia support. Furthermore, as of Silverlight 1.1, you are able to incorporate a subset of the .NET base class library into your applications. This subset includes a number of WPF controls, LINQ support, generic collection types, web service support, and a healthy subset of `mscorlib.dll` (file I/O, XML manipulation, etc.).

Note This edition of the text does not address Silverlight. If you are interested in learning more about this API, check out `http://www.microsoft.com/silverlight`. Here you can download the free Silverlight SDK (including the Silverlight plug-in itself), view numerous sample projects, and discover more about this intriguing aspect of WPF-related development.

Investigating the WPF Assemblies

Regardless of which type of WPF application you wish to build, WPF is ultimately little more than a collection of types bundled within .NET assemblies. Table 30-3 describes the core assemblies used to build WPF applications, each of which must be referenced when creating a new project (as you would hope, Visual Studio 2008 WPF projects automatically reference the required assemblies).

Table 30-3. *Core WPF Assemblies*

Assembly	Meaning in Life
`PresentationCore.dll`	This assembly defines numerous types that constitute the foundation of the WPF GUI layer. For example, this assembly contains support for the WPF Ink API (for programming against stylus input for Pocket PCs and Tablet PCs), several animation primitives (via the `System.Windows.Media.Animation` namespace), and numerous graphical rendering types (via `System.Windows.Media`).
`PresentationFoundation.dll`	Here you will find the WPF control set, additional animation and multimedia types, data binding support, types that allow for programmatic access to XAML, and other WPF services.
`WindowsBase.dll`	This assembly defines the core (and in many cases lower-level) types that constitute the infrastructure of the WPF API. Here you will find types representing WPF threading types, security types, various type converters, and other basic programming primitives (`Point`, `Vector`, `Rect`, etc.).

Collectively, these three assemblies define a number of new namespaces and hundreds of new .NET classes, interfaces, structures, enumerations, and delegates. While you should consult the .NET Framework 3.5 SDK documentation for complete details, Table 30-4 documents the role of some (but certainly not all) of the core namespaces you should be aware of.

Table 30-4. *Core WPF Namespaces*

Namespace	Meaning in Life
`System.Windows`	This is the root namespace of WPF. Here you will find core types (such as `Application` and `Window`) that are required by any WPF desktop project.
`System.Windows.Controls`	Here you will find all of the expected WPF widgets, including types to build menu systems, tool tips, and numerous layout managers.

Continued

Table 30-4. *Continued*

Namespace	Meaning in Life
`System.Windows.Markup`	This namespace defines a number of types that allow XAML markup (and the equivalent binary format, BAML) to be parsed and processed programmatically.
`System.Windows.Media`	This is the root namespace to several media-centric namespaces. Within these namespaces you will find types to work with animations, 3D rendering, text rendering, and other multimedia primitives.
`System.Windows.Navigation`	This namespace provides types to account for the navigation logic employed by XAML browser applications (XBAPs) as well as standard desktop applications that require a navigational page model.
`System.Windows.Shapes`	This namespace defines various 2D graphic types (`Rectangle`, `Polygon`, etc.) used by various aspects of the WPF framework.

To begin our journey into the WPF programming model, we'll examine two members of the `System.Windows` namespace that are commonplace to any traditional desktop development effort: `Application` and `Window`.

The Role of the Application Class

The `System.Windows.Application` class type represents a global instance of a running WPF application. Like its Windows Forms counterpart, this type supplies a `Run()` method (to start the application), a series of events that you are able to handle in order to interact with the application's lifetime (such as `Startup` and `Exit`), and a number of members that are specific to XAML browser applications (such as events that fire as a user navigates between pages). Table 30-5 details some of the key members to be aware of.

Table 30-5. *Key Properties of the* `Application` *Type*

Property	Meaning in Life
`Current`	This shared property allows you to gain access to the running `Application` object from anywhere in your code. This can be very helpful when a window or dialog box needs to gain access to the `Application` object that created it.
`MainWindow`	This property allows you to programmatically get or set the main window of the application.
`Properties`	This property allows you to establish and obtain data that is accessible throughout all aspects of a WPF application (windows, dialog boxes, etc.). In many ways, this looks and feels very much like establishing application variables for an ASP.NET web application.
`StartupUri`	This property gets or sets a URI that specifies a window or page to open automatically when the application starts.
`Windows`	This property returns a `WindowCollection` object, which provides access to each window created from the thread that created the `Application` object. This can be very helpful when you wish to iterate over each open window of an application and alter its state (such as minimizing all windows).

Unlike its Windows Forms counterpart, however, the WPF `Application` type does not expose its functionality exclusively through shared members. Rather, WPF programs define a class that extends this type to represent the entry point to the executable. For example:

```
' Define the global application object
' for this WPF program.
Class MyApp
  Inherits Application

  <STAThread()> _
  Public Shared Sub Main()
    ' Handle events, run the application,
    ' launch the main window, etc.
  End Sub

End Class
```

You'll build a complete `Application`-derived type in an upcoming example. Until then, let's check out the core functionality of the `Window` type and learn about a number of key WPF base classes in the process.

Note Similar to Windows Forms, Visual Basic allows you to leverage the application framework option, which (among other things) will create an `Application`-derived type and `Main()` subroutine on your behalf.

The Role of the Window Class

The `System.Windows.Window` type represents a single window owned by the `Application`-derived type, including any dialog boxes displayed by the main window. As you might expect, the `Window` type has a series of parent classes, each of which brings more functionality to the table. Consider Figure 30-3, which shows the inheritance chain (and implemented interfaces) for the `System.Windows.Window` type as seen through the Visual Studio 2008 object browser.

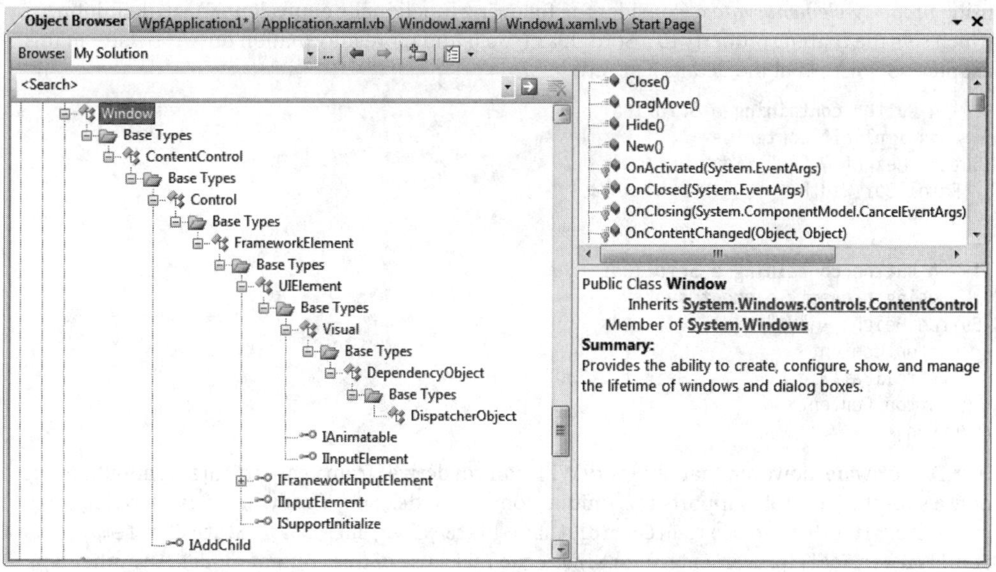

Figure 30-3. *The hierarchy of the* `Window` *type*

You'll come to understand the functionality provided by many of these base classes as you progress through this chapter and the chapters to come. However, to whet your appetite, the following sections present a breakdown of the functionality provided by each base class (consult the .NET Framework 3.5 SDK documentation for full details).

The Role of System.Windows.Controls.ContentControl

The direct parent of Window is ContentControl. This base class provides derived types with the ability to host *content*, which simply put refers to a collection of objects placed within the control's surface area. Under the WPF content model, a content control has the ability to contain a great number of UI elements beyond simple string data. For example, it is entirely possible to define a Button that contains an embedded ScrollBar as content. The ContentControl base class provides a key property named (not surprisingly) Content for this purpose.

If the value you wish to assign to the Content property can be represented as a simple string literal, you may set the Content property *explicitly* as an attribute within the element's opening definition:

```
<!-- Setting the Content value explicitly -->
<Button Height="80" Width="100" Content="ClickMe"/>
```

Alternatively, you are able to *implicitly* set the Content property by specifying a value within the scope of the content control's element definition. Consider the following functionally equivalent XAML description of the previous button:

```
<!-- Setting the Content value implicitly -->
<Button Height="80" Width="100">
  ClickMe
</Button>
```

However, if the value you wish to assign to the Content property cannot be represented as a simple array of characters, you are unable to assign the Content property using an attribute in the control's opening definition. For these cases, you must establish content either implicitly or by using *property-element syntax*. Consider the following functionally equivalent XAML definition, which sets the Content property to a ScrollBar (you'll find more information on XAML later in this chapter, so don't sweat the details just yet):

```
<!-- A Button containing a ScrollBar
     as implicit content -->
<Button Height = "80" Width = "100">
  <ScrollBar Width = "75" Height = "40"/>
</Button>

<!-- A Button containing a ScrollBar
     using property-element syntax -->
<Button Height = "80" Width = "100">
  <Button.Content>
    <ScrollBar Width = "75" Height = "40"/>
  </Button.Content>
</Button>
```

Do be aware, however, that not every WPF control derives from ContentControl, and therefore only a subset of controls supports this unique content model. Specifically, any class deriving from Frame, GroupItem, HeaderedContentControl, Label, ListBoxItem, ButtonBase, StatusBarItem, ScrollViewer, ToolTip, UserControl, or Window can make use of this content model. Any other type attempting to do so results in a markup/compile-time error. For example, consider this malformed ScrollBar type:

```
<!-- Error! ScrollBars don't derive from ContentControl! -->
<ScrollBar Height = "80" Width = "100">
  <Button Width = "75" Height = "40"/>
</ScrollBar >
```

Another important point regarding this new content model is that controls deriving from ContentControl (including the Window type itself) can assign only a *single* value to the Content property. Therefore, the following XAML Button definition is also illegal, as the Content property has been implicitly set twice:

```
<!-- Try to add a TextBox and an Ellipse to a Button? Error! -->
<Button Height = "200" Width = "200">
  <Ellipse Fill = "Green" Height = "80" Width = "80"/>
  <TextBox Width = "50" Height = "40"/>
</Button >
```

At first glance, this fact might appear to be extremely limiting (imagine how nonfunctional a dialog box would be with only a single button!). Thankfully, it is indeed possible to add numerous elements to a ContentControl-derived type using panels. To do so, each bit of content must first be arranged into one of the WPF panel types, after which point the panel becomes the single value assigned to the Content property. You will learn more about the WPF content model as well as the various panel types (and the controls they contain) in Chapter 31.

Note The System.Windows.ContentControl class also provides the HasContent property to determine whether the value of Content is currently Nothing.

The Role of System.Windows.Controls.Control

Unlike ContentControl, all WPF controls share the Control base class as a common parent. This base class provides numerous core members that account for basic UI functionality. For example, Control defines properties to establish the control's size, opacity, tab order logic, the display cursor, background color, and so forth. Furthermore, this parent class provides support for *templating services*. As explained in Chapter 32, WPF controls can dynamically change their appearance using templates, styles, and themes. Table 30-6 documents some key members of the Control type, grouped by related functionality.

Table 30-6. *Key Members of the* Control *Type*

Member	Meaning in Life
Background Foreground BorderBrush BorderThickness Padding HorizontalContentAlignment VerticalContentAlignment	These properties allow you to set basic settings regarding how the control will be rendered and positioned.
FontFamily FontSize FontStretch FontWeight	These properties control various font-centric settings.

Continued

Table 30-6. *Continued*

Member	Meaning in Life
`IsTabStop` `TabIndex`	These properties are used to establish tab order among controls on a window.
`MouseDoubleClick` `PreviewMouseDoubleClick`	These events handle the act of double-clicking a widget.
`Template`	This property allows you to get and set the control's template, which can be used to change the rendering output of the widget.

The Role of System.Windows.FrameworkElement

This base class provides a number of lower-level members that are used throughout the WPF framework, such as support for storyboarding (used within animations) and support for data binding, as well as the ability to name a member (via the `Name` property), obtain any resources defined by the derived type, and establish the overall dimensions of the derived type. Table 30-7 hits the highlights.

Table 30-7. *Key Members of the* `FrameworkElement` *Type*

Member	Meaning in Life

`ActualHeight`
`ActualWidth`
`MaxHeight`
`MaxWidth`
`MinHeight`
`MinWidth`
`Height`
`Width`
	Control the size of the derived type (not surprisingly)

`ContextMenu`	Gets or sets the pop-up menu associated with the derived type
`Cursor`	Gets or sets the mouse cursor associated with the derived type
`HorizontalAlignment` `VerticalAlignment`	Control how the type is positioned within a container (such as a panel or list box)
`Name`	Allows to you assign a name to the type, in order to access its functionality in a code file
`Resources`	Provides access to any resources defined by the type (see Chapter 32 for an examination of the WPF resource system)
`ToolTip`	Gets or sets the tool tip associated with the derived type

The Role of System.Windows.UIElement

Of all the types within a `Window`'s inheritance chain, the `UIElement` base class provides the greatest amount of functionality. The key task of `UIElement` is to provide the derived type with numerous events to allow the derived type to receive focus and process input requests. For example, this class provides numerous events to account for drag-and-drop operations, mouse movement, keyboard input, and stylus input (for Pocket PCs and Tablet PCs).

Chapter 31 digs into the WPF event model in detail; however, many of the core events will look quite familiar (`MouseMove`, `KeyUp`, `MouseDown`, `MouseEnter`, `MouseLeave`, etc.). In addition to defining dozens of events, this parent class provides a number of properties to account for control focus, enabled state, visibility, and hit testing logic, as shown in Table 30-8.

Table 30-8. *Key Members of the* `UIElement` *Type*

Member	Meaning in Life
`Focusable` `IsFocused`	Allow you to set focus on a given derived type
`IsEnabled`	Allows you to control whether a given derived type is enabled or disabled
`IsMouseDirectlyOver` `IsMouseOver`	Provide a simple way to perform hit-testing logic

`IsVisible`
`Visibility`
`Visible`
	Allow you to work with the visibility setting of a derived type

`RenderTransform`	Allows you to establish a transformation that will be used to render the derived type

The Role of System.Windows.Media.Visual

The `Visual` class type provides core rendering support in WPF, which includes hit testing of rendered data, coordinate transformation, and bounding box calculations. In fact, this type is the connection point between the managed WPF assembly stack and the unmanaged `milcore.dll` binary that communicates with the DirectX subsystem.

As examined in Chapter 32, WPF provides three possible manners in which you can render graphical data, each of which differs in terms of functionality and performance. Use of the `Visual` type (and its children, such as `DrawingVisual`) provides the most lightweight way to render graphical data, but it also entails the greatest amount of manual code to account for all the required services. Again, more details to come in Chapter 32.

The Role of System.Windows.DependencyObject

WPF supports a particular flavor of .NET properties termed *dependency properties*. Simply put, this approach allows a type to compute the value of a property based on the value of other properties (hence the term "dependency"). In order for a type to participate in this new property scheme, it will need to derive from the `DependencyObject` base class. In addition, `DependencyObject` allows derived types to support *attached properties*, which are a form of dependency property very useful when programming against the WPF data-binding model as well as when laying out UI elements within various WPF panel types.

The `DependencyObject` base class provides two key methods to all derived types: `GetValue()` and `SetValue()`. Using these members, you are able to establish the property itself. Other bits of infrastructure allow you to "register" who can use the dependent/attached property in question. While dependency properties are a key aspect of WPF development, much of the time their details are hidden from view. Chapter 31 dives further into the details of the "new" type of property.

The Role of System.Windows.Threading.DispatcherObject

The final base class of the `Window` type (beyond `System.Object`, which I assume needs no further explanation at this point in the text) is `DispatcherObject`. This type provides one property of interest, `Dispatcher`, which returns the associated `System.Windows.Threading.Dispatcher` object. The `Dispatcher` type is the entry point to the event queue of the WPF application, and it provides the basic constructs for dealing with concurrency and threading. By and large, this is a lower-level class that can be ignored by the majority of your WPF applications.

Building a (XAML-Free) WPF Application

Given all of the functionality provided by the parent classes of the `Window` type, it is possible to represent a window in your application by either directly creating a `Window` type or using this class as the parent to a strongly typed descendent. Let's examine both approaches in the following code example. Although most WPF applications will make use of XAML, doing so is entirely optional. Anything that can be expressed in XAML can be expressed in code and (for the most part) vice versa. If you wish, it is possible to build a complete WPF application using the underlying object model and procedural code.

To illustrate, let's create a minimal but complete application *without* the use of Visual Studio or XAML, using the `Application` and `Window` types directly within your text editor of choice (Notepad will be perfect for this first example). Consider the following VB code file (`SimpleWPFApp.vb`), which creates a main window of modest functionality:

```
' A simple WPF application, written without XAML or Visual Studio.
Imports System
Imports System.Windows
Imports System.Windows.Controls

' In this first example, we are defining a single class type to
' represent the application itself and the main window.
Class MyWPFApp
  Inherits Application

  <STAThread()> _
  Shared Sub Main()
    ' Handle the Startup and Exit events, and then run the application.
    Dim app As New MyWPFApp()
    AddHandler app.Startup, AddressOf AppStartUp
    AddHandler app.Exit, AddressOf AppExit

    ' Fire the Startup event.
    app.Run()
  End Sub

  Shared Sub AppExit(ByVal sender As Object, ByVal e As ExitEventArgs)
    MessageBox.Show("App has exited")
  End Sub

  Shared Sub AppStartUp(ByVal sender As Object, ByVal e As StartupEventArgs)
    ' Create a Window object and set some basic properties.
    Dim mainWindow As New Window()
    mainWindow.Title = "My First WPF App!"
    mainWindow.Height = 200
    mainWindow.Width = 300
    mainWindow.WindowStartupLocation = _
      WindowStartupLocation.CenterScreen
    mainWindow.Show()
  End Sub
End Class
```

■ **Note** The `Main()` method of a WPF application must be attributed with the `<STAThread()>` attribute, which ensures any legacy COM objects used by your application are thread safe. If you do not annotate `Main()` in this way, you will trigger a runtime exception!

Note that the MyWPFApp class extends the System.Windows.Application type. Within this type's Main() method, we create an instance of our application object and handle the Startup and Exit events using the AddHandler statement. Recall from Chapter 11 that this notation allows us to handle events from objects not declared with the WithEvents keyword.

Under the hood, the Startup event works in conjunction with the StartupEventHandler delegate, which can only point to methods taking an Object as the first parameter and a StartupEventArgs as the second. The Exit event, on the other hand, works with the ExitEventHandler delegate, which demands that the method pointed to take an Object as the first parameter and an ExitEventArgs type as the second parameter.

The AppStartUp() method has been configured to create a Window object, establish some very basic property settings, and call Show() to display the window on the screen in a modeless fashion (like Windows Forms, the inherited ShowDialog() method can be used to launch a modal dialog box). The AppExit() method simply makes use of the WPF MessageBox type to display a diagnostic message when the application is being terminated.

To compile this VB code at the command line into an executable WPF application, assume that you have created a VB response file named build.rsp that references each of the WPF assemblies. Note that the path to each assembly should be defined on a single line (see Chapter 2 for more information on response files and working with the command-line compiler):

```
# build.rsp
#
/target:winexe
/out:SimpleWPFApp.exe
/r:"C:\Program Files\Reference Assemblies\Microsoft\Framework\v3.0\WindowsBase.dll"
/r:"C:\Program Files\Reference Assemblies\Microsoft\Framework
    \v3.0\PresentationCore.dll"
/r:"C:\Program Files\Reference Assemblies\Microsoft\Framework
    \v3.0\PresentationFramework.dll"
*.vb
```

You can now compile this WPF program at a Visual Studio 2008 command prompt as follows:

```
vbc @build.rsp
```

Once you run the program, you will find a very simple main window that can be minimized, maximized, and closed. To spice things up a bit, we need to add some user interface elements. Before we do, however, let's refactor our code base to account for a strongly typed and well-encapsulated Window-derived class.

Extending the Window Class Type

Currently, our Application-derived class directly creates an instance of the Window type upon application startup. Ideally, we would create a class deriving from Window in order to encapsulate its functionality. Assume we have created the following class definition within our current VB file:

```
Class MainWindow
  Inherits Window

  ' Let the constructor tend to the window's configuration.
  Public Sub New(ByVal windowTitle As String, _
    ByVal height As Integer, ByVal width As Integer)
    Me.Title = windowTitle
    Me.WindowStartupLocation = WindowStartupLocation.CenterScreen
    Me.Height = height
    Me.Width = width
```

```
    Me.Show()
  End Sub

End Class
```

We can now update our Startup event handler to simply directly create an instance of MainWindow:

```
Shared Sub AppStartUp(ByVal sender As Object, ByVal e As StartupEventArgs)
  ' Create a MainWindow object.
  Dim wnd As new MainWindow("My better WPF App!", 200, 300)
End Sub
```

Once the program is recompiled and executed, the output is identical. The obvious benefit is that we now have a strongly typed class to build upon.

■ Note When you create a Window (or Window-derived) object, it will automatically be added to the internal windows collection of the Application type (via some constructor logic found in the Window class itself). Given this fact, a window will be alive in memory until it is terminated or is explicitly removed from the collection via the Application.Windows property.

Creating a Simple User Interface

Adding UI elements into a Window-derived type is similar (but not identical) to adding UI elements into a System.Windows.Forms.Form-derived type:

1. Define a member variable to represent the required control.
2. Configure the control's look and feel upon the creation of your Window type.
3. Add the control to the Window's client area via a call to AddChild().

Although the process might feel familiar to Windows Forms development, one obvious difference is that the UI controls used by WPF are defined within the System.Windows.Controls namespace rather than System.Windows.Forms (thankfully, in many cases, they are identically named and feel quite similar to their Windows Forms counterparts).

A more drastic change from Windows Forms is the fact that a Window-derived type can contain only a *single child element* (due to the WPF content model). When a window needs to contain multiple UI elements (which will be the case for practically any window), you will need to make use of a layout manager such as DockPanel, Grid, Canvas, or StackPanel to control their positioning.

For this example, we will add a single button to the Window-derived type. When we click this button, we terminate the application by gaining access to the global application object (via the Application.Current property) in order to call the Shutdown() method. Ponder the following update to the MainWindow class:

```
Class MainWindow
  Inherits Window
  ' Our UI element.
  Private btnExitApp As New Button()

  Public Sub New(ByVal windowTitle As String, ByVal height As Integer, _
    ByVal width As Integer)
    ' Configure button and set the child control.
    AddHandler btnExitApp.Click, AddressOf btnExitApp_Clicked
```

```
    btnExitApp.Content = "Exit Application"
    btnExitApp.Height = 25
    btnExitApp.Width = 100

    ' Set the content of this window to a single button.
    Me.AddChild(btnExitApp)

    ' Configure the window.
    Me.Title = windowTitle
    Me.WindowStartupLocation = WindowStartupLocation.CenterScreen
    Me.Height = height
    Me.Width = width
    Me.Show()
  End Sub

  Sub btnExitApp_Clicked(ByVal sender As Object, ByVal e As RoutedEventArgs)
    ' Get a handle to the current application and shut it down.
    Application.Current.Shutdown()
  End Sub
End Class
```

Given your work with Windows Forms earlier in this text, the code within the window's constructor should not look too threatening. Be aware, however, that the `Click` event of the WPF button works in conjunction with a delegate named `RoutedEventHandler`, which obviously begs the question, what is a routed event? You'll examine the details of the WPF event model in the next chapter; for the time being, simply understand that targets of the `RoutedEventHandler` delegate must supply an `Object` as the first parameter and a `RoutedEventArgs` as the second.

In any case, once you recompile and run this application, you will find the customized window shown in Figure 30-4. Notice that our button is automatically placed in the dead center of the window's client area, which is the default behavior when content is not placed within a WPF panel type.

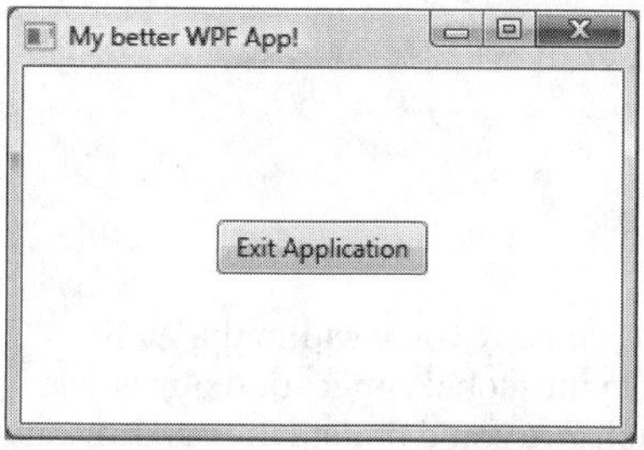

Figure 30-4. *A somewhat interesting WPF application*

Source Code The SimpleWPFApp project is included under the Chapter 30 subdirectory.

Additional Details of the Application Type

Now that you have created a simple WPF program using a 100-percent pure code approach, let's explore some additional details of the `Application` type, beginning with the construction of application-wide data. To do so, we will extend the previous SimpleWPFApp application with new functionality.

Application-Wide Data and Processing Command-Line Arguments

Recall that the `Application` type defines a property named `Properties`, which allows you to define a collection of name/value pairs via a type indexer. Because this indexer has been defined to operate on type `System.Object`, you are able to store any sort of item within this collection (including instances of your custom classes), to be retrieved at a later time using a friendly moniker. Using this approach, it is simple to share data across all windows in a WPF application.

To illustrate, we will update the current `Startup` event handler to check the incoming command-line arguments for a value named `/GODMODE` (a common cheat code for many PC video games). If we find such a token, we will establish a `Boolean` value set to `True` within the properties collection of the same name (otherwise, we will set the value to `False`).

Sounds simple enough, but one question you may have is, how are we going to pass the incoming command-line arguments (typically obtained from the `Main()` method) to our `Startup` event handler? One approach is to call the shared `Environment.GetCommandLineArgs()` method. However, these same arguments are automatically added to the incoming `StartupEventArgs` parameter and can be accessed via the `Args` property. This being said, here is our first update of the `Startup` event handler:

```
Shared Sub AppStartUp(ByVal sender As Object, ByVal e As StartupEventArgs)
  ' Check the incoming command-line arguments and see if they
  ' specified a flag for /GODMODE.
  Application.Current.Properties("GodMode") = False
  For Each arg As String In e.Args
    If arg.ToLower() = "/godmode" Then
      Application.Current.Properties("GodMode") = True
      Exit For
    End If
  Next

  ' Create a MainWindow object.
  Dim wnd As New MainWindow("My better WPF App!", 200, 300)
End Sub
```

Now recall that this new name/value pair can be accessed from anywhere within the WPF application. All we are required to do is obtain an access point to the global application object (via `Application.Current`) and investigate the collection. For example, we could update the `Click` event handler of the `Button` type of the main window like so:

```
Sub btnExitApp_Clicked(ByVal sender As Object, ByVal e As RoutedEventArgs)
  ' Did user enable /godmode?
  If CBool(Application.Current.Properties("GodMode")) Then
    MessageBox.Show("Cheater!")
  End If

  ' Get a handle to the current application and shut it down.
  Application.Current.Shutdown()
End Sub
```

Now, recompile your application using the same response file used previously. With this, if the end user launches our program as follows:

```
SimpleWPFApp.exe /godmode
```

he or she will see our shameful message box displayed when terminating the application.

Iterating over the Application's Windows Collection

Another interesting property exposed by Application is Windows, which provides access to a collection representing each window loaded into memory for the current WPF application. Recall that as you create new Window objects, they are automatically added into the global application object's Windows collection. We have no need to update our current example to illustrate this; however, here is an example method that will minimize each window of the application (perhaps in response to a given keyboard gesture or menu option triggered by the end user):

```
Sub MinimizeAllWindows()
  For Each wnd As Window In Application.Current.Windows
    wnd.WindowState = WindowState.Minimized
  Next
End Sub
```

Additional Events of the Application Type

Like many types within the .NET base class libraries, Application also defines a set of events that you can intercept. You have already seen the Startup and Exit events in action. You should also be aware of Activated and Deactivated. At first glance these events can seem a bit confusing, given that the Window type supplies identically named methods. Unlike their UI counterparts, however, the Activated and Deactivated events fire whenever *any* window maintained by the application object receives or loses focus (in contrast to the same events of the Window type, which are unique to that Window object).

Our current example has no need to handle these two events, but if you need to do so, be aware that each event works in conjunction with the System.EventHandler delegate, and therefore the event handler will take an Object as the first parameter and System.EventArgs as the second.

■ **Note** A majority of the remaining events of the Application type are specific to a navigation-based WPF application. Using these events, you are able to intercept the process of moving between Page objects of your program.

Additional Details of the Window Type

The Window type, as you saw earlier in this chapter, gains a ton of functionality from its set of parent classes and implemented interfaces. Over the chapters to come, you'll glean more and more information about what these base classes bring to the table; however, it is important to revisit the Window type itself and come to understand some core services you'll need to use on a day-to-day basis, beginning with the set of events that are fired over its lifetime.

The Lifetime of a Window Object

Like the System.Windows.Forms.Form type, System.Windows.Window has a set of events that will fire over the course of its lifetime. When you handle some (or all) of these events, you will have a convenient manner in which you can perform custom logic as your Window goes about its business. First of all, because a window is a class type, the very first step in its initialization entails a call to a specified constructor. After that point, the first WPF-centric event that fires is SourceInitialized, which is only useful if your Window is making use of various interoperability services (e.g., using legacy ActiveX controls in a WPF application). Even then, the need to intercept this event is limited, so consult the .NET Framework 3.5 documentation if you require more information.

The first immediately useful event that fires after the Window's constructor is Activate, which works in conjunction with the System.EventHandler delegate. This event is fired when a window receives focus and thus becomes the foreground window. The counterpart to this event is Deactivate (which also works with the System.EventHandler delegate), which fires when a window loses focus.

Here is an update to our existing Window-derived type that adds an informative message to a private String variable (you'll see the usefulness of this string variable in just a bit) when the Activate and Deactivate events occur:

```
Class MainWindow
  Inherits Window
  Private btnExitApp As New Button()

  ' This string will document which events fire, and when.
  Private lifeTimeData As String = String.Empty

  Protected Sub MainWindow_Activated(ByVal sender As Object, ByVal e As EventArgs)
    lifeTimeData &= "Activate Event Fired!" & vbLf
  End Sub
  Protected Sub MainWindow_Deactivated(ByVal sender As Object, ByVal e As EventArgs)
    lifeTimeData &= "Deactivated Event Fired!" & vbLf
  End Sub

  Public Sub New(ByVal windowTitle As String, ByVal height As Integer, _
    ByVal width As Integer)
    ' Rig up events.
    AddHandler Me.Activated, AddressOf MainWindow_Activated
    AddHandler Me.Deactivated, AddressOf MainWindow_Deactivated
    ...
  End Sub
End Class
```

■ **Note** Recall that you can handle application-level activation/deactivation for all windows with the Application.Activated and Application.Deactivated events.

Once the Activated event fires, the next event to do so is Loaded (which works with the RoutedEventHandler delegate), which signifies that the window has been for all practical purposes fully laid out and rendered, and is ready to respond to user input.

■ **Note** While the Activated event can fire many times as a window gains or loses focus, the Loaded event will fire only one time during the window's lifetime.

Assume that our MainWindow class has handled the Loaded event (via an AddHandler statement) and defines the following event handler:

```
Protected Sub MainWindow_Loaded(ByVal sender As Object, ByVal e As EventArgs)
  lifeTimeData &= "Loaded Event Fired!" & vbLf
End Sub
```

Note Should the need arise (which can be the case with custom WPF controls), you can capture the exact moment when a window's content has been loaded by handling the `ContentRendered` event.

Handling the Closing of a Window Object

End users can shut down a window using numerous built-in system-level techniques (e.g., clicking the "X" close button on the window's frame) or by indirectly calling the `Close()` method in response to some user interaction element (e.g., a File ➤ Exit menu item). In either case, WPF provides two events that you can intercept to determine whether the user is truly ready to shut down the window and remove it from memory. The first event to fire is `Closing`, which works in conjunction with the `CancelEventHandler` delegate.

This delegate expects target methods to take `System.ComponentModel.CancelEventArgs` as the second parameter. `CancelEventArgs` provides the `Cancel` property, which when set to `False` will prevent the window from actually closing (this is handy when you have asked the user where he or she really wants to close the window or perhaps needs to save his or her work).

If the user did indeed wish to close the window, `CancelEventArgs.Cancel` can be set to `True`, which will then cause the `Closed` event to fire (which works with the `System.EventHandler` delegate), which is the point at which the window is about to be closed for good. Assuming the `MainWindow` type has handled these two events (via `AddHandler` statements), consider the final event handlers:

```
Sub MainWindow_Closing(ByVal sender As Object, _
  ByVal e As System.ComponentModel.CancelEventArgs)
  lifeTimeData &= "Closing Event Fired!" & vbLf

  ' See if the user really wants to shut down this window.
  Dim msg As String = "Do you want to close without saving?"
  Dim result As MessageBoxResult = MessageBox.Show(msg, _
    "My App", MessageBoxButton.YesNo, MessageBoxImage.Warning)
  If result = MessageBoxResult.No Then
    ' If user doesn't want to close, cancel closure.
    e.Cancel = True
  End If
End Sub

Sub MainWindow_Closed(ByVal sender As Object, ByVal e As EventArgs)
  lifeTimeData &= "Closed Event Fired!" & vbLf
  MessageBox.Show(lifeTimeData)
End Sub
```

Given the way we constructed our application, the `Closing` event handler will prevent the application from terminating only when the user clicks the X button of the window, not when the user clicks the `Button` control within the window's client area. This is because our `Button Click` event handler forces the application to terminate completely (via a call to `Application.Current.Shutdown()`). If you wish to ensure that the user can opt out of terminating the application when clicking the button, modify your event handler as follows:

```
Sub btnExitApp_Clicked(ByVal sender As Object, ByVal e As RoutedEventArgs)
...
  ' Comment out the current call to Shutdown().
  ' Application.Current.Shutdown()

  ' This will only close this window, not force the
  ' entire application to shut down.
  Me.Close()
End Sub
```

When you compile and run your application, shift the window into and out of focus a few times. Also attempt to close the window once or twice. When you do indeed close the window for good, you will see a message box pop up that displays the events that fired during the window's lifetime (Figure 30-5 shows one possible test run).

Figure 30-5. *The life and times of a* `System.Windows.Window`

Handling Window-Level Mouse Events

Much like Windows Forms, the WPF API provides a number of events you can capture in order to interact with the mouse. Specifically, the `UIElement` base class defines a number of mouse-centric events such as `MouseMove`, `MouseUp`, `MouseDown`, `MouseEnter`, `MouseLeave`, and so forth.

Consider, for example, the act of handling the `MouseMove` event. This event works in conjunction with the `System.Windows.Input.MouseEventHandler` delegate, which expects its target to take a `System.Windows.Input.MouseEventArgs` type as the second parameter. Using `MouseEventArgs` (like a Windows Forms application), you are able to extract out the (*x*, *y*) position of the mouse and other relevant details. Consider the following partial definition:

```
Public Class MouseEventArgs
  Inherits InputEventArgs
  ...
  Public Function GetPosition(ByVal relativeTo As IInputElement) As Point
  Public ReadOnly Property LeftButton() As MouseButtonState
  Public ReadOnly Property MiddleButton() As MouseButtonState
  Public ReadOnly Property MouseDevice() As MouseDevice
  Public ReadOnly Property RightButton() As MouseButtonState
  Public ReadOnly Property StylusDevice() As StylusDevice
  Public ReadOnly Property XButton1() As MouseButtonState
  Public ReadOnly Property XButton2() As MouseButtonState
End Class
```

The GetPosition() method allows you to get the (*x*, *y*) value relative to a UI element on the window. If you are interested in capturing the position relative to the activated window, simply pass in Me. Assuming you have added an AddHandler statement to capture the MouseMove event, here is an event handler for MouseMove that will display the location of the mouse in the window's title area (notice we are translating the returned Point type into a string value via ToString()):

```
' You will need to update your window's constructor with
' the following code statement to handle the MouseMove event:
' AddHandler Me.MouseMove, AddressOf MainWindow_MouseMove
Protected Sub MainWindow_MouseMove(ByVal sender As Object, _
  ByVal e As System.Windows.Input.MouseEventArgs)

  ' Set the title of the window to the current X,Y of the mouse.
  Me.Title = e.GetPosition(Me).ToString()
End Sub
```

Handling Window-Level Keyboard Events

Processing keyboard input is also very straightforward. UIElement defines a number of events that you can capture to intercept keypresses from the keyboard on the active element (e.g., KeyUp, KeyDown, etc.). The KeyUp and KeyDown events both work with the System.Windows.Input.KeyEventHandler delegate, which expects the target's second event handler to be of type KeyEventArgs, which defines several public properties of interest:

```
Public Class KeyEventArgs
  Inherits KeyboardEventArgs
  ...
  Public ReadOnly Property IsDown() As Boolean
  Public ReadOnly Property IsRepeat() As Boolean
  Public ReadOnly Property IsToggled() As Boolean
  Public ReadOnly Property IsUp() As Boolean
  Public ReadOnly Property Key() As Key
  Public ReadOnly Property KeyStates() As KeyStates
  Public ReadOnly Property SystemKey() As Key
End Class
```

To illustrate handling the KeyUp event, the following event handler will display the previously pressed key on the window's title (be sure to update your window's constructor with an appropriate AddHandler statement):

```
' You will need to update your window's constructor with
' the following code statement to handle the KeyUp event:
' AddHandler Me.KeyUp, AddressOf MainWindow_KeyUp
Protected Sub MainWindow_KeyUp(ByVal sender As Object, _
  ByVal e As System.Windows.Input. KeyEventArgs)

  ' Display keypress.
  Me.Title = e.Key.ToString()
End Sub
```

At this point in the chapter, WPF might look like nothing more than a new GUI model that is providing (more or less) the same services as Windows Forms. If this were in fact the case, you might question the usefulness of yet another UI toolkit. To truly see what makes WPF so unique requires an understanding of a new XML-based grammar, XAML.

■ **Source Code** The SimpleWPFAppRevisited project is included under the Chapter 30 subdirectory.

Building a (XAML-Centric) WPF Application

Extensible Application Markup Language, or XAML, is an XML-based grammar that allows you to define the state (and, to some extent, the functionality) of a tree of .NET objects through markup. While XAML is frequently used when building UIs with WPF, in reality it can be used to describe any tree of *nonabstract* .NET types (including your own custom types defined in a custom .NET assembly), provided each supports a default constructor. As you will see, the markup found within a `*.xaml` file is transformed into a full-blown object model that maps directly to the types within a related .NET namespace.

Because XAML is an XML-based grammar, we gain all the benefits and drawbacks XML affords us. On the plus side, XAML files are very self-describing (as any XML document should be). By and large, each element in a XAML file represents a type name (such as `Button`, `Window`, or `Application`) within a given .NET namespace. Attributes within the scope of an opening element map to properties (`Height`, `Width`, etc.) and events (`Startup`, `Click`, etc.) of the specified type.

Given the fact that XAML is simply a declarative way to define the state of an object, it is possible to define a WPF widget via markup or procedural code. For example, the following XAML:

```
<!-- Defining a WPF Button in XAML -->
<Button Name = "btnClickMe" Height = "40" Width = "100" Content = "Click Me" />
```

can be represented programmatically as follows:

```
' Defining the same WPF Button in VB code.
Dim btnClickMe As New Button()
btnClickMe.Height = 40
btnClickMe.Width = 100
btnClickMe.Content = "Click Me"
```

On the downside, XAML can be verbose and is (like any XML document) case sensitive, thus complex XAML definitions can result in a good deal of markup. Most developers will not need to manually author a complete XAML description of their WPF applications. Rather, the majority of this task will (thankfully) be relegated to development tools such as Visual Studio 2008, Microsoft Expression Blend, or any number of third-party products. Once the tools generate the basic markup, you can go in and fine-tune the XAML definitions by hand if necessary.

While tools can generate a good deal of XAML on your behalf, it is important for you to understand the basic workings of XAML syntax and how this markup is eventually transformed into a valid .NET assembly. To illustrate XAML in action, in our next example we'll build a WPF application using nothing more than a pair of `*.xaml` files.

Defining MainWindow in XAML

Our first `Window`-derived class (`MainWindow`) was defined in VB as a class type that extends the `System.Windows.Window` base class. This class contains a single `Button` type that calls a registered event handler when clicked. Defining this same `Window` type in the grammar of XAML can be achieved as follows (assume this markup has been defined in a file named `MainWindow.xaml` using your text editor of choice—remember, we are not using Visual Studio yet!):

```
<!-- Here is our Window definition -->
<Window x:Class="SimpleXamlApp.MainWindow"
  xmlns="http://schemas.microsoft.com/winfx/2006/xaml/presentation"
  xmlns:x="http://schemas.microsoft.com/winfx/2006/xaml"
  Title="My Xaml App" Height="200" Width="300"
  WindowStartupLocation ="CenterScreen">

  <!--Set the content of this window -->
  <Button Width="133" Height="24" Name="btnExitApp" Click ="btnExitApp_Clicked">
    Exit Application
  </Button>

  <!--The implementation of our button's Click event handler! -->
  <x:Code>
  <![CDATA[
  Sub btnExitApp_Clicked(ByVal sender As Object, ByVal e As RoutedEventArgs)
    ' Get a handle to the current app and shut it down.
    Application.Current.Shutdown()
  End Sub
  ]]>
  </x:Code>
</Window>
```

First of all, notice that the root element, <Window>, defines the name of the derived type via the Class attribute. Unlike the first two examples, this time our class (MainWindow) has been wrapped in a custom namespace (SimpleXamlApp). This is not mandatory; however, doing so will better approximate how Visual Studio WPF applications behave, as you'll see later in this chapter.

The x prefix is used to denote that this attribute is defined within the XAML-centric XML namespace, http://schemas.microsoft.com/winfx/2006/xaml (more details on these XML namespaces later in this chapter). Within the scope of the opening <Window> element we have specified values for the Title, Height, Width, and WindowsStartupLocation attributes, which as you can see are a direct mapping to properties of the same name supported by the System.Windows.Window type.

Next up, notice that within the scope of the window's definition, we have authored markup to describe the look and feel of the Button instance, which will be used to implicitly set the Content property of the window. Beyond setting up the variable name and its overall dimensions, we have also handled the Click event of the Button type by assigning the method to delegate to when the Click event occurs.

The final aspect of this XAML file is the <Code> element, which allows us to author event handlers and other methods of this class directly within a *.xaml file. As a safety measure, the code itself is wrapped within a CDATA scope, to prevent XML parsers from attempting to directly interpret the data (although this is not strictly required for the current example).

It is important to point out that authoring functionality within a <Code> element is not recommended. Although this "single-file approach" isolates all the action to one location, inline code does not provide us with a clear separation of concerns between UI markup and programming logic. In most WPF applications, "real code" will be found within an associated VB code file (which we will do eventually).

Defining the Application Object in XAML

Remember that XAML can be used to define in markup any nonabstract .NET class that supports a default constructor. Given this, we could most certainly define our application object in markup as well. Consider the following content within a new file, MyApp.xaml:

```
<!-- The Main() method seems to be missing!
     However, the StartupUri attribute is the
     functional equivalent -->
<Application x:Class="SimpleXamlApp.MyApp"
  xmlns="http://schemas.microsoft.com/winfx/2006/xaml/presentation"
  xmlns:x="http://schemas.microsoft.com/winfx/2006/xaml"
  StartupUri="MainWindow.xaml">
</Application>
```

Here, you might agree, the mapping between the Application-derived VB class type and its XAML description is not as clear-cut as was the case for our MainWindow's XAML definition. Specifically, there does not seem to be any trace of a Main() method. Given that any .NET executable must have a program entry point, you are correct to assume it is generated at compile time, based in part on the StartupUri property. The assigned *.xaml file will be used to determine which Window-derived class to create when this application starts up.

Although the Main() method is automatically created at compile time, we are free to use the <Code> element to establish our Exit event handler if we so choose, as follows (notice this method is no longer shared, as it will be translated into an instance-level member in the MyApp class):

```
<Application x:Class="SimpleXamlApp.MyApp"
  xmlns="http://schemas.microsoft.com/winfx/2006/xaml/presentation"
  xmlns:x="http://schemas.microsoft.com/winfx/2006/xaml"
  StartupUri="MainWindow.xaml" Exit = "AppExit">
  <x:Code>
    <![CDATA[
    Sub AppExit(ByVal Sender As Object, ByVal e As ExitEventArgs)
      MessageBox.Show("App has exited")
    End Sub
    ]]>
  </x:Code>
</Application>
```

Processing the XAML Files via msbuild.exe

At this point, we are ready to transform our markup into a valid .NET assembly. When doing so, we cannot make direct use of the VB compiler and a response file. To date, the VB compiler does not have a direct understanding of XAML markup. However, the msbuild.exe command-line utility does understand how to transform XAML into VB code and compile this code on the fly when it is informed of the correct *.targets files.

msbuild.exe is a tool that allows you to define complex build scripts via (surprise, surprise) an XML grammar. One interesting aspect of these XML definitions is that they are the same format as Visual Studio *.vbproj files. Given this, we are able to define a single file for automated command-line builds as well as a Visual Studio 2008 project. Consider the following minimalist build file, SimpleXamlApp.vbproj:

```
<Project DefaultTargets="Build"
  xmlns="http://schemas.microsoft.com/developer/msbuild/2003">
  <PropertyGroup>
    <RootNamespace>SimpleXamlApp</RootNamespace>
    <AssemblyName>SimpleXamlApp</AssemblyName>
    <OutputType>winexe</OutputType>
  </PropertyGroup>
  <ItemGroup>
```

```
    <Reference Include="System" />
    <Reference Include="WindowsBase" />
    <Reference Include="PresentationCore" />
    <Reference Include="PresentationFramework" />
  </ItemGroup>
  <ItemGroup>
    <ApplicationDefinition Include="MyApp.xaml" />
    <Page Include="MainWindow.xaml" />
  </ItemGroup>
  <Import Project="$(MSBuildBinPath)\Microsoft.VisualBasic.targets" />
  <Import Project="$(MSBuildBinPath)\Microsoft.WinFX.targets" />
</Project>
```

Here, the `<PropertyGroup>` element is used to specify some basic aspects of the build, such as the root namespace, the name of the resulting assembly, and the output type (the equivalent of the `/target:winexe` option of `vbc.exe`).

The first `<ItemGroup>` specifies the set of external assemblies to reference with the current build, which as you can see are the core WPF assemblies examined earlier in this chapter. The second `<ItemGroup>` is much more interesting. Notice that the `<ApplicationDefinition>` element's `Include` attribute is assigned to the `*.xaml` file that defines our application object. The `<Page>`'s `Include` attribute can be used to list each of the remaining `*.xaml` files that define the windows (and pages, which are often used when building XAML browser applications) processed by the application object.

However, the "magic" of this `*.vbproj` file is the final `<Import>` subelements. Notice that our build script is referencing two `*.targets` files, each of which contains numerous other instructions used during the build process. The `Microsoft.WinFX.targets` file contains the necessary build settings to transform the XAML definitions into equivalent VB code files, while `Microsoft.VisualBasic.Targets` contains data to interact with the VB compiler itself.

■ Note A full examination of the `msbuild.exe` utility is beyond the scope of this text. If you'd like to learn more, perform a search for the topic "MSBuild" in the .NET Framework 3.5 SDK documentation.

At this point, we can pass our `SimpleXamlApp.vbproj` file into `msbuild.exe` for processing:

```
msbuild SimpleXamlApp.vbproj
```

Once the build has completed, you should be able to find your assembly within the generated \bin\Debug folder. At this point, you can launch your WPF application as expected. As you may agree, it is quite bizarre to generate valid .NET assemblies by authoring a few lines of markup. However, to be sure, if you open `SimpleXamlApp.exe` in `ildasm.exe`, you can see that (somehow) your XAML has been transmogrified into an executable application (see Figure 30-6).

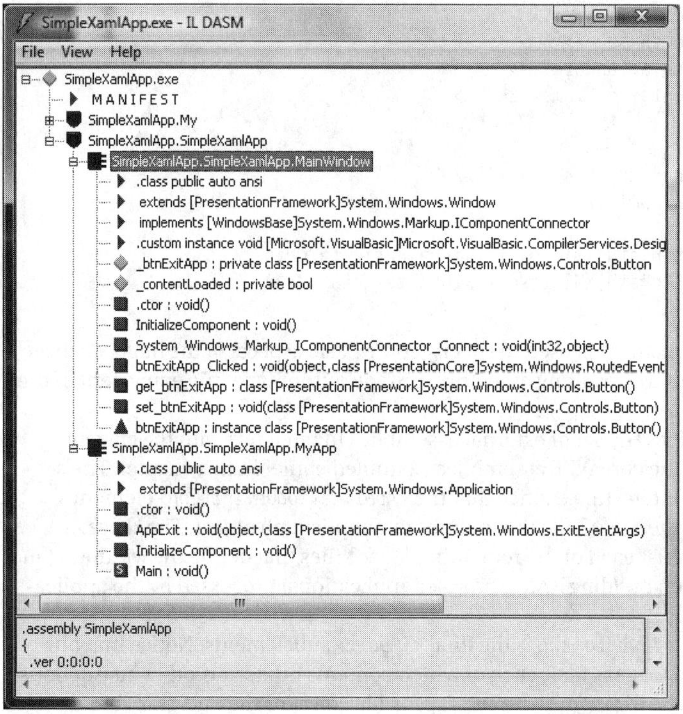

Figure 30-6. *Transforming markup into a .NET assembly? Interesting . . .*

Transforming Markup into a .NET Assembly

To understand exactly how our markup was transformed into a .NET assembly, we need to dig a bit deeper into the msbuild.exe process and examine a number of compiler-generated files, including a particular binary resource embedded within the assembly at compile time.

Mapping XAML to VB Code

As mentioned, the *.targets files specified in an MSBuild script define numerous instructions to translate XAML elements into VB code for compilation. When msbuild.exe processed our *.vbproj file, it produced two files with the form *.g.vb (where g denotes auto*generated*), which were saved into the \obj\Debug directory. Based on the names of our *.xaml file names, the VB files in question are MainWindow.g.vb and MyApp.g.vb.

If you open the MainWindow.g.vb file, you will find your class extends the Window base class and contains the btnExitApp_Clicked() method as expected. Also, this class defines a member variable of type System.Windows.Controls.Button. Strangely enough, there does *not* appear to be any code that establishes the property settings for the Button or Window type (Height, Width, Title, etc.). This part of the mystery will become clear in just a moment.

Finally, note that this class defines a private member variable of type Boolean (named _contentLoaded), which was not directly accounted for in the XAML markup. Here is a partial definition of the generated MainWindow type:

```
Partial Public Class MainWindow
  Inherits System.Windows.Window
  Implements System.Windows.Markup.IComponentConnector

  Friend WithEvents btnExitApp As System.Windows.Controls.Button
  Private _contentLoaded As Boolean

  Sub btnExitApp_Clicked(ByVal sender As Object, ByVal e As RoutedEventArgs)
    ' Get a handle to the current app and shut it down.
    Application.Current.Shutdown()
  End Sub
...
End Class
```

This Windows-derived class also explicitly implements the WPF IComponentConnector interface defined in the System.Windows.Markup namespace. This interface defines a single method, Connect(), which has been implemented to rig up the event logic as specified within the original MainWindow.xaml file. Note the use of AddHandler to capture our button's Click event:

```
Sub System_Windows_Markup_IComponentConnector_Connect(ByVal _
  connectionId As Integer, ByVal target As Object) Implements _
  System.Windows.Markup.IComponentConnector.Connect
  If (connectionId = 1) Then
    Me.btnExitApp = CType(target,System.Windows.Controls.Button)
    AddHandler Me.btnExitApp.Click, _
      New System.Windows.RoutedEventHandler(AddressOf Me.btnExitApp_Clicked)
    Return
  End If
  Me._contentLoaded = true
End Sub
```

Finally, the MainWindow class also implements a method named InitializeComponent(). This method ultimately resolves the location of an embedded resource within the assembly, given the name of the original *.xaml file. Once the resource is located, it is loaded into the current application object via a call to Application.LoadComponent(). Finally, the private Boolean member variable (mentioned previously) is set to True, to ensure the requested resource is loaded exactly once during the lifetime of this application:

```
Public Sub InitializeComponent() Implements _
  System.Windows.Markup.IComponentConnector.InitializeComponent
  If _contentLoaded Then
    Return
  End If
  _contentLoaded = true
  Dim resourceLocater As System.Uri = New System.Uri _
    ("/SimpleXamlApp;component/mainwindow.xaml", _
      System.UriKind.Relative)

  System.Windows.Application.LoadComponent(Me, resourceLocater)
End Sub
```

At this point, the question becomes, *what exactly is this embedded resource?*

The Role of BAML

When msbuild.exe processed our *.vbproj file, it generated a file with a *.baml file extension, which is named based on the initial MainWindow.xaml file (located under obj\debug). As you might have guessed from the name, Binary Application Markup Language (BAML) is a binary representation of XAML. This `*.baml` file is embedded as a resource (via a generated `*.g.resources` file) into the compiled assembly. Using BAML, WPF assemblies contain within them their complete XAML definition (in a much more compact format). You can verify this for yourself by opening your assembly using `reflector.exe`, as shown in Figure 30-7.

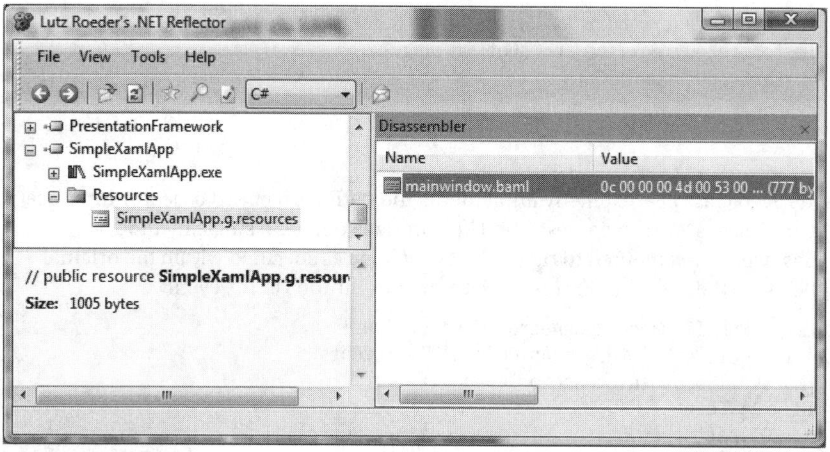

Figure 30-7. *Viewing the embedded* `*.baml` *resource via Lutz Roeder's .NET Reflector*

The call to `Application.LoadComponent()` reads the embedded BAML resource and populates the tree of defined objects with their correct state (such as the window's `Height` and `Width` properties). In fact, if you open the `*.baml` or `*.g.resources` file via Visual Studio, you can see traces of the initial XAML attributes. As an example, Figure 30-8 highlights the `StartupLocation.CenterScreen` property.

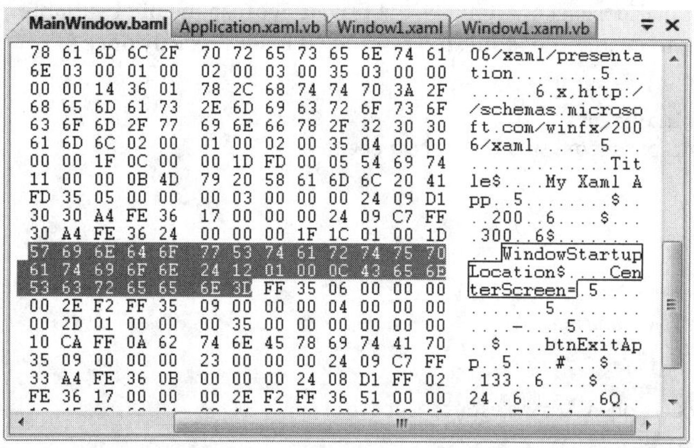

Figure 30-8. *Behold the BAML!*

The final piece of the autogenerated code puzzle occurs in the `MyApp.g.vb` file. Here we see our `Application`-derived class with a proper `Main()` entry point method. The implementation of this method calls `InitializeComponent()` on the `Application`-derived type, which in turn sets the

StartupUri property, allowing each of the objects to establish its correct property settings based on the binary XAML definition. Here is the relevant code:

```
Partial Public Class MyApp
  Inherits System.Windows.Application

  Sub AppExit(ByVal Sender As Object, ByVal e As ExitEventArgs)
    MessageBox.Show("App has exited")
  End Sub

  Public Sub InitializeComponent()
    AddHandler [Exit], New System.Windows.ExitEventHandler(AddressOf Me.AppExit)
    Me.StartupUri = New System.Uri("MainWindow.xaml", System.UriKind.Relative)
  End Sub

  Public Shared Sub Main()
    Dim app As SimpleXamlApp.MyApp = New SimpleXamlApp.MyApp
    app.InitializeComponent()
    app.Run()
  End Sub
End Class
```

XAML-to-Assembly Process Summary

Whew! So, at this point we have created a full-blown .NET assembly using nothing but three XML documents (one of which was used by the msbuild.exe utility). As you have seen, msbuild.exe leverages auxiliary settings defined within the *.targets file to process the XAML files (and generate the *.baml) for the build process. While these gory details happen behind the scenes, Figure 30-9 illustrates the overall picture regarding the compile-time processing of *.xaml files.

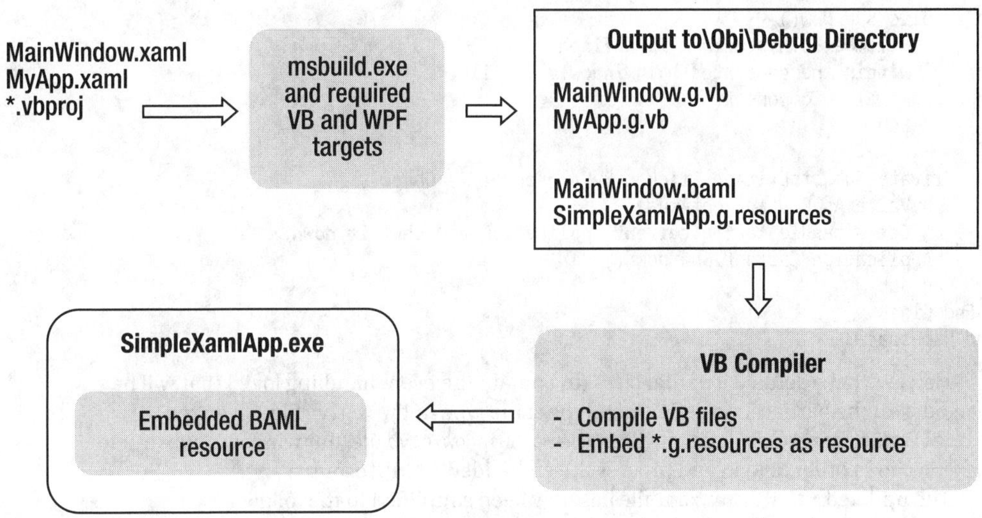

Figure 30-9. *The XAML-to-assembly compile-time process*

It is also important to point out that once the compiler has processed all of your *.xaml files in order to build the related VB code and binary resource, they are technically no longer required (and would never need to be shipped along with your executable). However, as shown at the end of this chapter, it is possible to dynamically create a `Window` object by reading a `*.xaml` file programmatically. In this case, the physical `*.xaml` file would indeed need to be shipped with the application itself.

■ **Source Code** The SimpleXamlApp project can be found under the Chapter 30 subdirectory.

Separation of Concerns Using Code-Behind Files

Before we truly begin digging into the details of XAML, we have one final aspect of the basic programming WPF model to address: the separation of concerns. Recall that one of the major motivations for WPF was to separate UI content from programming logic, which our current examples have not done.

Rather than directly embedding our event handlers (and other custom methods) within the scope of the XAML `<Code>` element, it is preferable to create a separate VB file to hold the implementation logic, leaving the `*.xaml` files to contain nothing but UI markup content. Assume the following code-behind file, `MainWindow.xaml.vb` (by convention, the name of a VB code-behind file takes the form `*.xaml.vb`):

```
' MainWindow.xaml.vb
Imports System
Imports System.Windows
Imports System.Windows.Controls

Namespace SimpleXamlApp
  Public Partial Class MainWindow
    Inherits Window
    Public Sub New()
      ' Remember! This method is defined
      ' within the generated MainWindow.g.vb file.
      InitializeComponent()
    End Sub

    Private Sub btnExitApp_Clicked(ByVal sender As Object, _
      ByVal e As RoutedEventArgs)
      ' Get a handle to the current application and shut it down.
      Application.Current.Shutdown()
    End Sub
  End Class
End Namespace
```

Here, we have defined a partial class (to contain the event handling logic) that will be merged with the partial class definition of the same type in the `*.g.vb` file. Given that `InitializeComponent()` is defined within the `MainWindow.g.vb` file, our window's constructor makes a call in order to load and process the embedded BAML resource.

The updated `MainWindow.xaml` file has now been simplified to the following:

```
<!-- Here is our Window definition -->
<Window x:Class="SimpleXamlApp.MainWindow"
  xmlns="http://schemas.microsoft.com/winfx/2006/xaml/presentation"
  xmlns:x="http://schemas.microsoft.com/winfx/2006/xaml"
  Title="My Xaml App" Height="200" Width="300"
  WindowStartupLocation ="CenterScreen">
```

```
  <!-- Define our button type -->
  <Button Width="133" Height="24" Name="btnExitApp" Click ="btnExitApp_Clicked">
    Exit Application
  </Button>
</Window>
```

If desired, we could also build a code-behind file for our Application-derived type. Because most of the action takes place in the MyApp.g.vb file, the code within MyApp.xaml.vb is little more than the following:

```
' MyApp.xaml.vb
Imports System
Imports System.Windows
Imports System.Windows.Controls

Namespace SimpleXamlApp
  Public Partial Class MyApp
    Inherits Application
    Private Sub AppExit(ByVal sender As Object, ByVal e As ExitEventArgs)
      MessageBox.Show("App has exited")
    End Sub
  End Class
End Namespace
```

The related MyApp.xaml file would now look like so:

```
<!-- The main method seems to be missing!
   However, the StartupUri attribute is the
   functional equivalent -->
<Application x:Class="SimpleXamlApp.MyApp"
    xmlns="http://schemas.microsoft.com/winfx/2006/xaml/presentation"
    xmlns:x="http://schemas.microsoft.com/winfx/2006/xaml"
    StartupUri="MainWindow.xaml" Exit="AppExit">
</Application>
```

Before we recompile our files using msbuild.exe, we need to update our *.vbproj file to account for the new VB files to include in the compilation process, via the <Compile> elements (shown in bold):

```
<Project DefaultTargets="Build"
  xmlns="http://schemas.microsoft.com/developer/msbuild/2003">
  <PropertyGroup>
    <RootNamespace>SimpleXamlApp</RootNamespace>
    <AssemblyName>SimpleXamlApp</AssemblyName>
    <OutputType>winexe</OutputType>
  </PropertyGroup>
  <ItemGroup>
    <Reference Include="System" />
    <Reference Include="WindowsBase" />
    <Reference Include="PresentationCore" />
    <Reference Include="PresentationFramework" />
  </ItemGroup>
  <ItemGroup>
    <ApplicationDefinition Include="MyApp.xaml" />
    <Compile Include = "MainWindow.xaml.vb" />
    <Compile Include = "MyApp.xaml.vb" />
    <Page Include="MainWindow.xaml" />
  </ItemGroup>
  <Import Project="$(MSBuildBinPath)\Microsoft.VisualBasic.targets" />
```

```
  <Import Project="$(MSBuildBinPath)\Microsoft.WinFX.targets" />
</Project>
```

Once we pass our build script into msbuild.exe, we find once again the same executable assembly. However, as far as development is concerned, we now have a clean partition of presentation (XAML) from programming logic (VB). Given that this is the preferred method for WPF development, you'll be happy to know that WPF applications created using Visual Studio 2008 always make use of the code-behind model just presented.

■ **Source Code** The CodeBehindXamlApp project can be found under the Chapter 30 subdirectory.

The Syntax of XAML

As mentioned earlier in this chapter, the chances of your needing to manually author reams of XAML markup in your WPF applications will be slim to none, as this task will be done on your behalf using dedicated tools (Visual Studio 2008, Microsoft Expression Blend, etc.). Nevertheless, the more you understand about the syntax of a well-formed *.xaml file, the better equipped you will be to tweak and modify autogenerated markup, and the deeper your understanding of WPF itself.

This being said, let's dig into the core syntax of XAML (subsequent chapters will provide additional XAML syntax examples where required). Be aware that at the conclusion of this chapter, you will build a custom XAML editor (SimpleXamlPad.exe) using Visual Studio, which will allow you to test the markup shown over the next several pages. However, before you are able to actually build the SimpleXamlPad application, you must be familiar with the grammar of the XAML.

XAML Namespaces and XAML Keywords

As you have already seen in this chapter's earlier examples, the root element of a WPF-centric XAML file (such as a <Window>, <Page>, or <Application> definition) is typically defined to make reference to two XML namespaces:

```
<Window
  xmlns="http://schemas.microsoft.com/winfx/2006/xaml/presentation"
  xmlns:x="http://schemas.microsoft.com/winfx/2006/xaml">
  <Grid>

  </Grid>
</Window>
```

The first namespace, http://schemas.microsoft.com/winfx/2006/xaml/presentation, maps a slew of WPF-centric namespaces for use by the current *.xaml file (System.Windows, System.Windows.Controls, System.Windows.Data, System.Windows.Ink, System.Windows.Media, System.Windows.Navigation, etc.). This one-to-many mapping is actually hard-coded within the WPF assemblies (WindowsBase.dll, PresentationCore.dll, and PresentationFramework.dll) using the assembly-level [XmlnsDefinition] attribute (if you load these WPF assemblies into reflector.exe, you can view these mappings firsthand).

The second XML namespace, http://schemas.microsoft.com/winfx/2006/xaml, is used to include XAML-specific keywords as well as a subset of types within the System.Windows.Markup namespace. A well-formed XML document must define a root element that designates a single XML namespace as the primary namespace, which typically is the namespace that contains the most commonly used items. If a root element requires the inclusion of additional secondary namespaces (as seen here), they must be defined using a unique prefix (to resolve any possible name clashes). As a convention in XAML, the prefix is simply x; however, this can be any unique token you require, such as XamlSpecificStuff:

```
<Window
  xmlns="http://schemas.microsoft.com/winfx/2006/xaml/presentation"
  xmlns:XamlSpecificStuff="http://schemas.microsoft.com/winfx/2006/xaml">
  <Grid>

  </Grid>
</Window>
```

The obvious downside of defining wordy XML namespace prefixes is you would be required to type XamlSpecificStuff each time your XAML file needs to refer to one of the types defined in the namespace in question. For example, one of the items within http://schemas.microsoft.com/winfx/2006/xaml is the XAML keyword Code, which as you have seen allows you to embed VB code within a XAML document. Another XAML keyword is Class, which allows you to define the name of the generated VB class type.

If we were to change the definition of the SimpleXamlApp.MyApp XAML definition created earlier in this chapter to make use of this more verbose XML namespace prefix, we would now be required to author the following:

```
<Application XamlSpecificStuff:Class="SimpleXamlApp.MyApp"
  xmlns="http://schemas.microsoft.com/winfx/2006/xaml/presentation"
  xmlns:XamlSpecificStuff ="http://schemas.microsoft.com/winfx/2006/xaml"
  StartupUri="MainWindow.xaml" Exit="AppExit">

  <XamlSpecificStuff:Code>
    <![CDATA[
    Private Sub AppExit(ByVal sender As Object, ByVal e As ExitEventArgs)
      MessageBox.Show("App has exited")
    End Sub
    ]]>
  </XamlSpecificStuff:Code>

</Application>
```

Given that XamlSpecificStuff requires many additional keystrokes, let's just stick with x (this is also helpful, as this is how XAML tends to be documented in the .NET Framework 3.5 SDK documentation). In any case, beyond the Class and Code keywords, including the http://schemas.microsoft.com/winfx/2006/xaml XML namespace also provides access to additional XAML keywords (and members of the System.Windows.Markup namespace), the core of which are shown in Table 30-9.

Table 30-9. *XAML Keywords*

XAML Keyword	Meaning in Life
Array	Represents a .NET array type in XAML.
ClassModifier	Allows you to define the visibility of the class type (internal or public) denoted by the Class keyword.
DynamicResource	Allows you to make reference to a WPF resource that should be monitored for changes.

Continued

Table 30-9. *Continued*

XAML Keyword	Meaning in Life
`FieldModifier`	Allows you to define the visibility of a type member (internal, public, private, or protected) for any named subelement of the root (e.g., a `<Button>` within a `<Window>` element). A "named element" is defined using the `Name` XAML keyword.
`Key`	Allows you to establish a key value for a XAML item that will be placed into a dictionary element.
`Name`	Allows you to specify the generated VB name of a given XAML element.
`Null`	Represents a `Nothing` reference.
`Static`	Allows you to make reference to a shared member of a type.
`StaticResource`	Allows you to make reference to a WPF resource that should not be monitored for changes.
`Type`	Extracts a `System.Type` based on the supplied name (the XAML equivalent of the VB `GetType` operator).
`TypeArguments`	Allows you to establish an element as a generic type with a specific type parameter (e.g., `List(Of Integer)` vs. `List(Of Boolean)`).

You will see many of these keywords in action where required; however, by way of a simple example, consider the following XAML `<Window>` definition that makes use of the `ClassModifier` and `FieldModifier` keywords, as well as `Name` and `Class`:

```
<!-- This class will now be internal.
     If using a code file, the partial class must
     also be defined as internal! -->
<Window x:Class="MyWPFApp.MainWindow" x:ClassModifier ="internal"
    xmlns="http://schemas.microsoft.com/winfx/2006/xaml/presentation"
    xmlns:x="http://schemas.microsoft.com/winfx/2006/xaml">

  <!-- This button will be public in the *.g.vb file -->
  <Button x:Name ="myButton" x:FieldModifier ="public">
    OK
  </Button>
</Window>
```

By default, all VB/XAML type definitions are public, while members default to `internal`, which is represented in terms of Visual Basic using the `Friend` keyword. However, based on our XAML definition, the resulting autogenerated file contains an internal class type with a public `Button` type.

XAML Elements and XAML Attributes

Once you have established your root element and any required XML namespaces, your next task is to populate the root with a *child element*. As mentioned, in a real-world WPF application, the child will be one of the panel types, which contains in turn any number of additional UI elements that describe the user interface. The next chapter examines these panel types in detail, so for the time being assume that our `<Window>` type will contain a single `Button` element.

As you have already seen over the course of this chapter, XAML elements map to a class or structure type within a given .NET namespace, while the attributes within the opening element tag map to properties or events of the type (you cannot reference the methods of a type via a XAML attribute). Thus, when you author code such as the following:

```
<Window x:Class="MyWPFApp.MainWindow" x:ClassModifier ="internal"
  xmlns="http://schemas.microsoft.com/winfx/2006/xaml/presentation"
  xmlns:x="http://schemas.microsoft.com/winfx/2006/xaml">

  <!-- This assumes you have a method named myButton_Click in
       your code file! -->
  <Button x:Name ="myButton" x:FieldModifier ="public"
   Height ="50" Width ="100" Click ="myButton_Click">
    OK
  </Button>
</Window>
```

you have effectively authored a Button that could be expressed in code as follows:

```
Dim myButton As New Button()
myButton.Height = 50
myButton.Width = 100
myButton.Content = "OK"
AddHandler myButton.Click, New RoutedEventHandler(myButton_Click)
```

Given your work thus far in the chapter, this mapping may seem straightforward; however, consider the assignment of the button's content. Recall that many WPF controls derive from ContentControl. By doing so, they are able to contain any number of internal items. Here, the Content property was implicitly set due to the fact that we placed the text "OK" within the opening and closing element. If we wish, we could explicitly set the Content property as follows:

```
<Button x:Name ="myButton"
  Height ="50" Width ="100" Content = "OK">
</Button>
```

At this point, the act of setting the Content property implicitly or explicitly may seem to be nothing more than a personal preference. The story becomes more interesting when you consider how you would use XAML to assign a Button's content to be an object other than a simple string (a graphical rendering, a ScrollBar or TextBox, etc.). As mentioned earlier in this chapter, the solution is to use property-element syntax.

Understanding XAML Property-Element Syntax

Property-element syntax allows you to assign complex objects to a property. Here is a XAML description for the "scrollbar in a button" scenario that sets the Content property using property-element syntax:

```
<Button x:Name ="myButton" Height ="100" Width ="100">
  <Button.Content>
    <ScrollBar Height = "50" Width = "20"/>
  </Button.Content>
</Button>
```

Notice that in this case, we have made use of a nested element named <Button.Content> to define the ScrollBar type. Property-element syntax always breaks down to the pattern <TypeName.PropertyName>; obviously the type in this case is <Button> while the property is Content. Figure 30-10 shows the rendered XAML.

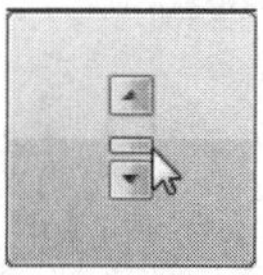

Figure 30-10. *Property-element syntax allows you to assign complex objects to properties.*

Also recall that the child element of a ContentControl-derived type will automatically be used to set the Content property, therefore the following definition is also legal:

```
<Button x:Name ="myButton" Height ="100" Width ="100">
  <ScrollBar Height = "50" Width = "20"/>
</Button>
```

Property-element syntax is not limited to setting the Content property. Rather, this XAML syntax can be used whenever you need to set a complex object to a type property. Consider, for example, the Background property of the Button type. This property can be set on any Brush type found within the WPF APIs. If you need a solid color brush type, the following markup is all that is required, as the string value assigned to properties requiring a Brush-derived type (such as Background) is converted into a brush type automatically:

```
<!-- Here, "Green" maps to Brushes.Green -->
<Button x:Name ="myButton" Height ="100" Width ="100" Background ="Green">
  <Button.Content>
    <ScrollBar Height = "50" Width = "20"/>
  </Button.Content>
</Button>
```

However, if you need a more elaborate brush (such as a LinearGradientBrush), name/value syntax will not suffice. Considering that LinearGradientBrush is a full-blown class type, we must make use of property-element syntax to pass in startup values to the type:

```
<Button x:Name ="myButton" Height ="100" Width ="100">
  <Button.Content>
    <ScrollBar Height = "50" Width = "20"/>
  </Button.Content>
  <Button.Background>
    <LinearGradientBrush StartPoint="0,0" EndPoint="1,1">
      <GradientStop Color="Blue" Offset="0" />
      <GradientStop Color="Yellow" Offset="0.25" />
      <GradientStop Color="Green" Offset="0.75" />
      <GradientStop Color ="Red" Offset="0.50" />
    </LinearGradientBrush>
  </Button.Background>
</Button>
```

Don't concern yourself with the configuration of the LinearGradientBrush type for the time being (Chapter 32 addresses WPF's graphical rendering services). Simply notice that we have used property-element syntax to establish the Content and Background property of the Button type. Figure 30-11 shows the rendering of this rather fancy button.

Figure 30-11. *A very fancy button*

While property-element syntax is most often used to assign complex objects (such as `LinearGradientBrush`) to property values, it is permissible to make use of simple string values as well:

```
<Button x:Name ="myButton" Height ="100" Width ="100">
  <Button.Content>
    <ScrollBar Height = "50" Width = "20"/>
  </Button.Content>
  <Button.Background>
    Pink
  </Button.Background>
</Button>
```

In this case, you have really gained nothing. Rather, you have just complicated the process, as you could simply have typed the following:

```
<Button x:Name ="myButton" Height ="100" Width ="100" Background = "Pink">
  <Button.Content>
    <ScrollBar Height = "50" Width = "20"/>
  </Button.Content>
</Button>
```

Understanding XAML Attached Properties

In addition to property-element syntax, XAML defines syntax used to define an *attached property*. While attached properties have many uses, one purpose of an attached property is to allow different child elements to specify unique values for a property that is actually defined in a parent element. The most common use of attached property syntax is to position UI elements within one of the WPF panel types (`Grid`, `DockPanel`, etc.). The next chapter dives into these panels in some detail. For the time being, here is an example of attached-property syntax:

```
<Window
  xmlns="http://schemas.microsoft.com/winfx/2006/xaml/presentation"
  xmlns:x="http://schemas.microsoft.com/winfx/2006/xaml">

  <DockPanel LastChildFill ="True">
    <!-- Dock items to the panel using attached properties -->
    <Label DockPanel.Dock ="Top" Name="lblInstruction"
           FontSize="15">Enter Car Information</Label>
    <Label DockPanel.Dock ="Left" Name="lblMake">Make</Label>
    <Label DockPanel.Dock ="Right" Name="lblColor">Color</Label>
    <Label DockPanel.Dock ="Bottom" Name="lblPetName">Pet Name</Label>
    <Button Name="btnOK">OK</Button>
  </DockPanel>

</Window>
```

Here, we have defined a DockPanel that contains four Label objects docked within the container. Notice the format of this particular attached property syntax is <ParentType.ParentProperty> (e.g., DockPanel.Dock). Note that the Button does not specify a docking area; however, it will take over the remaining area in the DockPanel, giving the assignment of the LastChildFill property in the opening <DockPanel> definition.

There are a few items to be aware of regarding attached properties. First and foremost, this is not an all-purpose syntax that can be applied to *any* element of *any* parent. For example, the following XAML cannot be parsed without error:

```
<!-- Set Height property on Button via attached property? -->
<Button x:Name ="myButton" Width ="100">
  <Button.Content>
    <ScrollBar Button.Height = "100" Height = "50" Width = "20"/>
  </Button.Content>
  <Button.Background>
    Pink
  </Button.Background>
</Button>
```

In reality, attached properties are a specialized form of a WPF-specific concept termed a *dependency property*. In a nutshell, dependency properties allow the value of a field to be computed based on multiple inputs. Dependency properties, and therefore attached properties, need to "register" which properties can be set by which objects (which has not been done for the ScrollBar/Button scenario just shown).

WPF uses the dependency property mechanism under the hood for several technologies such as data binding, styles and themes, and animation services. As well, a dependency property can be implemented to provide self-contained validation, default values, and a callback mechanism, and it provides a way to establish property values based on runtime information.

The odd thing about dependency properties is the fact that *setting* a dependency property value looks no different from setting a "normal" .NET property. Therefore, in most cases, you will be blissfully unaware that you have set a dependency property value.

However, the manner in which dependency properties are implemented behind the scenes is quite different indeed. For the vast majority of your WPF applications, you will *not* need to author custom dependency properties. The only time this may become a common task is when you are in the position of building custom WPF controls, which again is not a common activity in the first place given the advent of XAML. You will explore dependency properties in a bit more detail in Chapter 31.

Understanding XAML Type Converters

For all practical purposes, when you are assigning values to attributes (e.g., Background = "Pink") or implicitly setting content within the scope of an opening and closing element (e.g., <Button>OK</Button>), you can simply assume the values to be string data. However, if you think this through, it clearly could not be the case. Consider, for example, the definition of the Background property of the Button type (which we inherited from the Control base class):

```
' The System.Windows.Controls.Control.Background property.
Public Property Background() As Brush
  ...
End Property
```

As you can see, this property is wrapping a Brush type, not a System.String! This begs the question, what is transforming "Pink" into (in this case) a SolidColorBrush object with RGB values that equal the color pink? Here's another example. Consider the following XAML definition of a purple ellipse of a given size:

```
<Ellipse Fill = "Purple" Width = "100.5" Height = "87.4">
</Ellipse>
```

If you were to look at the definition of the Width and Height properties of the Ellipse type, you would find they are prototyped to operate on Doubles, not Strings.

Behind the scenes, XAML parsers make use of various *type converters* to transform this string data into the correct underlying object. For example, the value "Pink", when assigned to a property prototyped to operate on brush types, makes use of the ColorConverter and BrushConverter types. Numerous other converters exist as well: SizeConverter (used to set the Width and Height properties of the previous Ellipse), RectConverter, VectorConverter, and so on.

Regardless of their names, all type converters derive from the System.ComponentModel.TypeConverter base class. This type defines a number of virtual methods such as CanConvertTo(), ConvertTo(), CanConvertFrom(), and ConvertFrom(), which can be overridden by a derived type to account for the underlying translation.

For the most part, you do not need to know *which* type converter is mapping your XAML string data to the correct underlying object. At the very least, simply understand that they are used transparently in the background to simplify XAML definitions.

■ **Note** Although XAML itself is a relativity new technology, the concept of type converters has existed since the release of the .NET platform. Windows Forms and GDI+ make use of various converters behind the scenes. For example, the GDI+ System.Drawing namespace defines a type converter named FontConverter, which can map the string "Wingdings" into a Font object using the Wingdings font face.

Understanding XAML Markup Extensions

Type converters are interesting constructs in that there is no physical evidence that you are interacting with them at the level of XAML. Rather, type converters are used internally behind the scenes when a *.xaml file is processed. In contrast, XAML also supports *markup extensions.* Like a type converter, markup extensions allow you to transform a simple markup value into a runtime object. The difference, however, is that markup extensions have a very specific XAML syntax.

Given that type converters and markup extensions appear to serve an identical purpose, you might wonder why we have two approaches to generate type definitions. Simply put, markup extensions allow for a greater level of flexibility than type converters and provide a way to cleanly extend the grammar of XAML with new functionality.

Using markup extensions, you could assign the value of a property to the return value of a shared property on another type, declare an array of data via markup, or obtain type information. In fact, a subset of XAML keywords (such as Array, Null, Static, and Type) are markup extensions in disguise. Like type converters, a markup extension is represented internally as a class that derives from MarkupExtension (as a naming convention, all types that subclass MarkupExtension take an Extension suffix).

To see a markup extension in action, assume you wish to set the Content property for a set of Labels to display information regarding the machine your application is executing on using shared members of System.Environment. Here is the complete markup, with a discussion to follow:

```
<Window
  xmlns="http://schemas.microsoft.com/winfx/2006/xaml/presentation"
  xmlns:x="http://schemas.microsoft.com/winfx/2006/xaml"
  xmlns:CorLib="clr-namespace:System;assembly=mscorlib">
```

```
  <StackPanel>
    <Label Content ="{x:Static CorLib:Environment.MachineName}"/>
    <Label Content ="{x:Static CorLib:Environment.OSVersion}"/>
    <Label Content ="{x:Static CorLib:Environment.ProcessorCount}"/>
  </StackPanel>
</Window>
```

■ **Note** As you know, class-level members are called shared members in the vernacular of VB. In terms of XAML, however, shared members are called *static*, and therefore we must use the `{x:Static}` token, rather than the expected `{x:Shared}` token.

First of all, notice that the `<Window>` definition has a new XML namespace declaration, which we have given the namespace prefix of `CorLib` (the name of this prefix, like any XML namespace prefix, is arbitrary). The value assigned to this XML namespace is unique, however, as we are making use of a registered token named `clr-namespace` (which allows us to point to a .NET namespace that contains the type definition) and another token named `assembly` (which represents the friendly name of the assembly containing the namespace).

With this XML namespace established, notice how each of the `Label` types can invoke a shared member of the `Environment` type via the `Static` markup extension. As you can see, markup extensions are always sandwiched between curly brackets. In its simplest form, the markup extension takes two values: the name of the markup extension (`Static` in this case) followed by the value to assign it (such as `CorLib:System.Environment.OSVersion`).

```
<!-- Using the "Static" markup extension to set the Content property to
  the value of a shared property. -->
<Label Content ="{x:Static CorLib:Environment.OSVersion}"/>
```

Here is another example. Assume you wish to obtain the fully qualified name of various types to assign the `Content` property to another set of `Label` types. In this case, you can make use of the baked-in `Type` markup extension:

```
<Window
  xmlns="http://schemas.microsoft.com/winfx/2006/xaml/presentation"
  xmlns:x="http://schemas.microsoft.com/winfx/2006/xaml"
  xmlns:CorLib="clr-namespace:System;assembly=mscorlib">

  <StackPanel>
    <Label Content ="{x:Static CorLib:Environment.MachineName}"/>
    <Label Content ="{x:Static CorLib:Environment.OSVersion}"/>
    <Label Content ="{x:Static CorLib:Environment.ProcessorCount}"/>

    <Label Content ="{x:Type Label}" />
    <Label Content ="{x:Type Page}" />
    <Label Content ="{x:Type CorLib:Boolean}" />
    <Label Content ="{x:Type x:TypeExtension}" />
  </StackPanel>
</Window>
```

Here you are obtaining the fully qualified names of the WPF `Label` type, the `Page` type, as well as the `Boolean` data type within `mscorlib.dll` and, just for good measure, the fully qualified name of the `Type` markup extension itself. If you were to view this page within the `SimpleXamlPad.exe` application (which you will build next), you would find something like Figure 30-12.

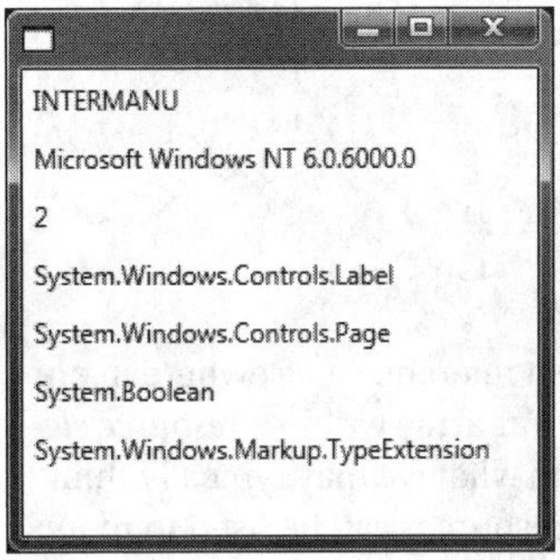

Figure 30-12. *Using markup extensions to set properties to values of static members and obtain type information*

A Preview of Resources and Data Binding

To wrap up our introductory look at the syntax of XAML, this final example will not only illustrate using the Array markup extension (represented by the ArrayExtension class type), but also show some simple declarative data binding and preview the concept of WPF resources. The Array markup extension allows you to assign an array of data to a given property. When using XAML to define such an array, we do so by making use of the Type markup extension to establish what kind of array we are creating (array of strings, array of bitmaps, etc.). Consider the following <Window> definition:

```
<Window
  xmlns="http://schemas.microsoft.com/winfx/2006/xaml/presentation"
  xmlns:x="http://schemas.microsoft.com/winfx/2006/xaml"
  xmlns:CorLib="clr-namespace:System;assembly=mscorlib">

  <StackPanel>
    <Label Content ="{x:Array Type = CorLib:String}"/>
  </StackPanel>
</Window>
```

If you view the rendered markup, you will see the value System.String[] print out in the view pane. Using the expected curly bracket syntax, we have no way to populate the array with data. To do so, we must create our array using subelements that match the specified type of the array. Consider the following partial XAML definition:

```
<x:Array Type="CorLib:String">
  <CorLib:String>Sun Kil Moon</CorLib:String>
  <CorLib:String>Red House Painters</CorLib:String>
  <CorLib:String>Besnard Lakes</CorLib:String>
</x:Array>
```

Here, we have created an array of strings. Within the scope of the <x:Array> element, we add in three textual values and close the definition. While this is valid XAML markup, the next question is, where we can place our array declaration? If we were to place it directly within the scope of a <Window> element, we have just set the Content property of the <Window> implicitly and we would (once again) see System.String[] display in the view port of xamlpad.exe (which is not quite what we are aiming for).

```
<Window
  xmlns="http://schemas.microsoft.com/winfx/2006/xaml/presentation"
  xmlns:x="http://schemas.microsoft.com/winfx/2006/xaml"
  xmlns:CorLib="clr-namespace:System;assembly=mscorlib">
```

```
  <!-- Hmmm, we just set the Content property here! -->
    <x:Array Type="CorLib:String">
      <CorLib:String>Sun Kil Moon</CorLib:String>
      <CorLib:String>Red House Painters</CorLib:String>
      <CorLib:String>Besnard Lakes</CorLib:String>
    </x:Array>
</Window>
```

What we really would like to do is give this array a name and then reference it elsewhere in our markup (e.g., to fill a ListBox). We can do this very thing *if* we define our array within a *resource element.* Now, let me be clear that WPF "resources" do not always map to what we may typically think (string tables, icons, bitmaps, etc.). While they certainly could, WPF resources can be used to represent any custom blob of markup, such as our array of strings (more information on WPF resources can be found in Chapter 32).

Consider the final <Window> definition that adds a string array resource named "GoodMusic" to a <StackPanel> via the Key markup extension. Once we have added this resource, we then set the ItemsSource property of the ListBox to our array using the StaticResource markup extension (notice we are referencing the same key at this time):

```
<Window
  xmlns="http://schemas.microsoft.com/winfx/2006/xaml/presentation"
  xmlns:x="http://schemas.microsoft.com/winfx/2006/xaml"
  xmlns:CorLib="clr-namespace:System;assembly=mscorlib">

  <StackPanel>
    <StackPanel.Resources>
      <x:Array Type="CorLib:String" x:Key = "GoodMusic">
        <CorLib:String>Sun Kil Moon</CorLib:String>
        <CorLib:String>Red House Painters</CorLib:String>
        <CorLib:String>Besnard Lakes</CorLib:String>
      </x:Array>
    </StackPanel.Resources>

    <Label Content ="Really good music"/>
    <ListBox Width = "200" ItemsSource ="{StaticResource GoodMusic}"/>
  </StackPanel>
</Window>
```

As you can see, we are nesting within the scope of the <StackPanel> a nested <StackPanel.Resources> element as the home for our array of strings. The StaticResource markup extensions represent any resource that is not expected to change after the initial binding (hence the notion of "static"). If you are working with a resource that may change after the first bind (such as a given system color), you can use the alternative markup extension, DynamicResource. In any case, Figure 30-13 shows some possible output.

Figure 30-13. *Markup extensions, static resources, and simple data binding*

■ **Note** The reason that the `Key` and `StaticResource` markup extensions have not been qualified with an `x` prefix (unlike the other markup extensions examined here) is because they are defined within the root `http://schemas.microsoft.com/winfx/2006/xaml/presentation` XML namespace (as they are WPF-centric).

So! At this point you have seen numerous examples that showcase each of the core aspects of XAML syntax. As you might agree, XAML is very interesting in that it allows us to describe a tree of .NET objects in a declarative manner. While this is extremely helpful when configuring graphical user interfaces, do remember that XAML can describe *any* type from *any* assembly provided it is a nonabstract type containing a default constructor.

Building WPF Applications Using Visual Studio 2008

Over the course of this chapter, you created examples using no-frills text editors and various command-line tools (specifically, `vbc.exe` and `msbuild.exe`). The reason for doing so, of course, was to focus on the core syntax of WPF applications without getting distracted by the bells and whistles of a graphical designer. However, now that you have seen how to build WPF applications in the raw, let's examine how Visual Studio 2008 can simplify the construction of WPF applications.

The WPF Project Templates

The New Project dialog box of Visual Studio 2008 defines a set of WPF-centric project workspaces, all of which are contained under the Window node of the Visual Basic root. As you can see in Figure 30-14, you can choose from a WPF Application, WPF User Control Library, WPF Custom Control Library, and WPF Browser Application (e.g., XBAP).

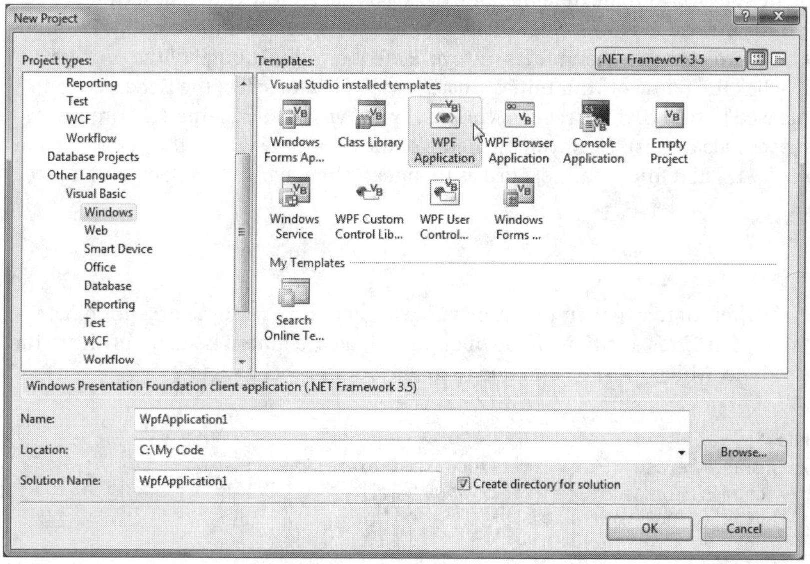

Figure 30-14. *The WPF project templates of Visual Studio 2008*

When you wish to build a WPF desktop application, you'll want to select the WPF Application project workspace type. Beyond automatically setting references to each of the WPF assemblies (`PresentationCore.dll`, `PresentationFoundation.dll`, and `WindowsBase.dll`), you will also be provided with initial `Window`- and `Application`-derived types, making use of code files and a XAML definition (see Figure 30-15).

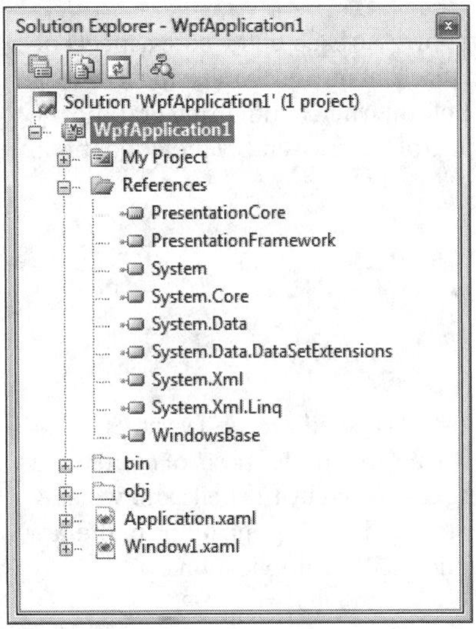

Figure 30-15. *The initial files of a WPF Application project type*

Changing the Name of the Initial Window

For a production-level project, you will most certainly wish to rename your initial `Window`-derived type (and the file that defines it) from the default name of `Window1` to a more fitting description (such as `MainWindow`, `MainForm`, etc.). However, given all of the moving parts required by a WPF application, doing so is a bit more complex than meets the eye. Here is a walk-through of the process.

First, if you right-click the name of your initial `Window1.xaml` file and select the Rename menu option, you will be pleased to find that the related `Windows1.xaml.vb` is also renamed according to your selection (e.g., `MainWindow.xaml`). However, the name of the class type within the `*.xaml.vb` file will still be named `Window1`. Therefore, your next task is to indeed change the class declaration like so:

```
Class MainWindow
End Class
```

At this point, if you attempt to run your program, you will generate a runtime exception! The first reason for this is that the `Class` attribute of the opening `<Window>` element is still referring to the original `Window1` class name, which must be updated to match your new class name:

```
<Window x:
    Class="MainWindow"
    xmlns="http://schemas.microsoft.com/winfx/2006/xaml/presentation"
    xmlns:x="http://schemas.microsoft.com/winfx/2006/xaml"
    Title="Window1" Height="300" Width="300">
    <Grid>

    </Grid>
</Window>
```

Last but not least, the `StartupUri` property in the `<Application>` declaration must also be updated to specify the name of the renamed XAML file containing the initial `Window` type (`MainWindow.xaml`):

```
<Application x:Class="Application"
    xmlns="http://schemas.microsoft.com/winfx/2006/xaml/presentation"
    xmlns:x="http://schemas.microsoft.com/winfx/2006/xaml"
    StartupUri="MainWindow.xaml"
  >
    <Application.Resources>

    </Application.Resources>
</Application>
```

At this point, you should be able to compile and run your application without error.

Note When you insert new `Window` types into a WPF project (via the Project ➤ Add Window menu option), the name of your initial file will be used to correctly name the files and type definitions, so no additional configuration is required.

The WPF Designer

Similar to a Windows Forms application, the Visual Studio 2008 Toolbox contains numerous WPF controls, a visual designer that can be used to assemble your UI, and a Properties window to set the properties of a selected control. The designer for a `*.xaml` file is divided into two panes. By default, the upper pane displays the look and feel of the window you are creating, while the bottom pane displays the XAML definition (see Figure 30-16).

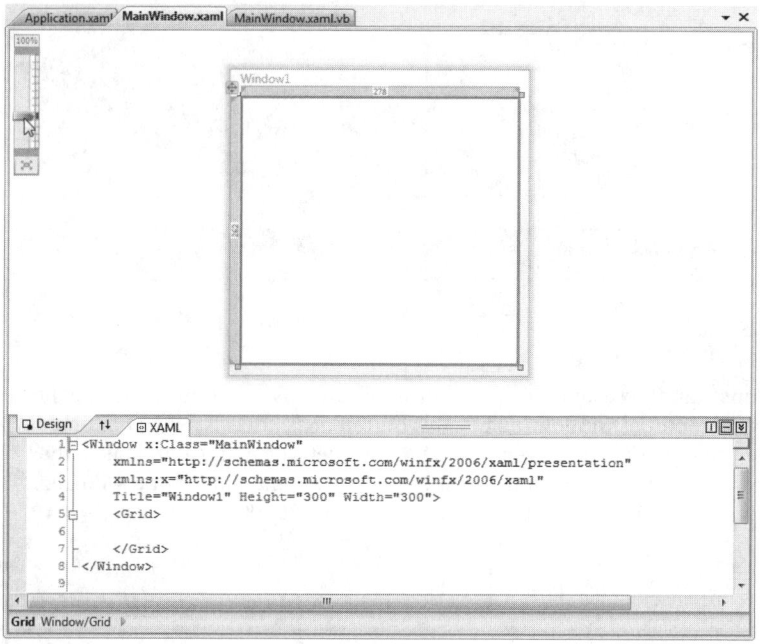

Figure 30-16. *The WPF designer*

■ **Note** You can reposition the display panes of the visual designer using the buttons embedded within the splitter window—for example, the Swap Panes button (indicated by the up/down arrows), the Horizontal and Vertical split buttons, and so on. Take a moment to find a configuration you are comfortable with.

When you author XAML markup in the XAML pane, you will find the expected IntelliSense. For example, if you type a `Button` declaration in the scope of the initial `<Grid>` type, you will see a list of the properties and events supported by the type. Furthermore, when you select a property member, you will see a list of possible values, as shown in Figure 30-17.

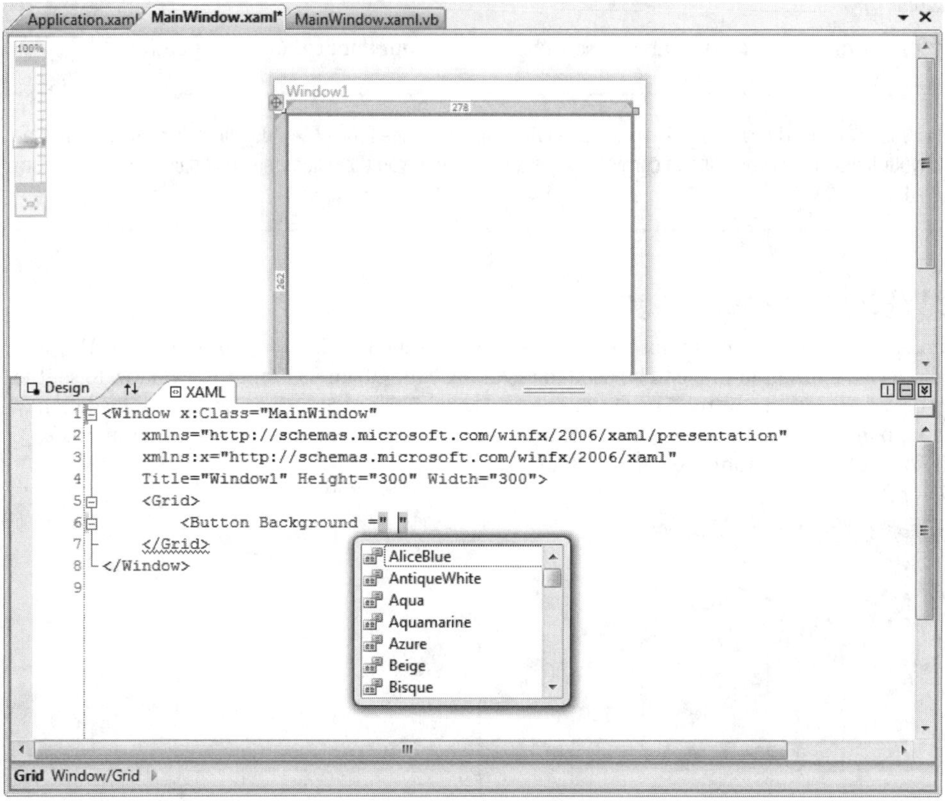

Figure 30-17. *XAML IntelliSense*

Unlike Windows Forms, handling events within a WPF application is *not* done by clicking the lightning bolt button of the Properties window (in fact, this button does not exist when building WPF applications). When you wish to handle events for a WPF widget, you could author all of the code manually using the expected VB syntax; however, if you type an event name in the XAML editor, you will activate the New Event Handler pop-up menu (see Figure 30-18).

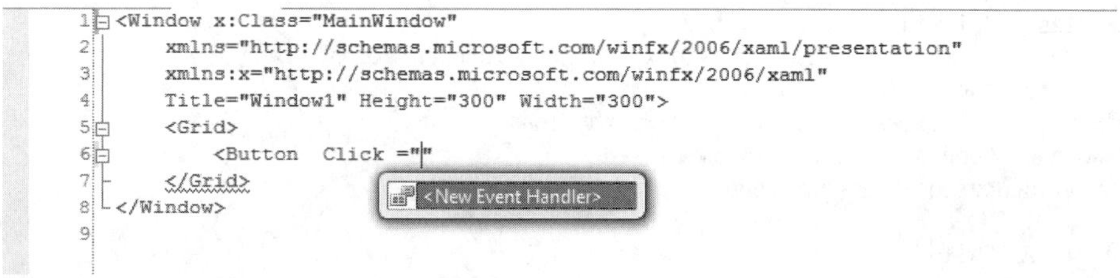

Figure 30-18. *Handling events using the visual designer*

If you manually enter an event name (encased in quotation marks, as required by XAML), you can specify any method name you wish. If you would rather simply have the IDE generate a default name (which takes the form *NameOfControl_NameOfEvent*), you can double-click the <New Event Handler> pop-up menu item. In either case, the IDE responds by adding the correct event handler in your code file:

```
Class MainWindow

  Private Sub Button_Click(ByVal sender As System.Object, _
    ByVal e As System.Windows.RoutedEventArgs)

  End Sub
End Class
```

■ **Note** Recall that if you wish the IDE to define a member variable of a control type, you will need to assign a value to the `Name` property. If you handle events for unnamed controls, the event handler name is simply *TypeOfControl_NameOfEvent[_Number]* (e.g., `Button_Click`, `Button_Click_1`, `Button_Click_2`, etc.).

Now that you have seen the basic tools used within Visual Studio 2008 to manipulate WPF applications, let's leverage this IDE to build an example program that illustrates the process of parsing XAML at runtime.

Processing XAML at Runtime: SimpleXamlPad.exe

The WPF API supports the ability to load, parse, and save XAML descriptions programmatically. Doing so can be quite useful in a variety of situations. For example, assume you have five different XAML files that describe the look and feel of a `Window` type. As long as the names of each control (and any necessary event handlers) are identical within each file, it would be possible to dynamically apply "skins" to the window (perhaps based on a startup argument passed into the application).

Interacting with XAML at runtime revolves around the `XamlReader` and `XamlWriter` types, both of which are defined within the `System.Windows.Markup` namespace. To illustrate how to programmatically hydrate a `Window` object from an external `*.xaml` file, we will create a WPF Application project (named SimpleXamlPad).

This application will allow you to enter XAML definitions, view the results, and save the XAML to an external file. Once you have created the SimpleXamlPad project using Visual Studio 2008, rename your initial window to `MainWindow` (using the process described previously) and update the initial XAML definition as follows:

```
<Window x:Class="MainWindow"
  xmlns="http://schemas.microsoft.com/winfx/2006/xaml/presentation"
  xmlns:x="http://schemas.microsoft.com/winfx/2006/xaml"
  Title="Simple XAMl Viewer" Height="338" Width="1041"
  Loaded="Window_Loaded" Closed="Window_Closed"
  WindowStartupLocation="CenterScreen">

  <DockPanel LastChildFill="True" >
    <!-- This button will launch a window with defined XAML -->
    <Button DockPanel.Dock="Top" Name = "btnViewXaml" Width="100" Height="40"
      Content ="View Xaml" Click="btnViewXaml_Click" />

    <!-- This will be the area to type within -->
    <TextBox AcceptsReturn ="True" Name ="txtXamlData"
      FontSize ="14" Background="Black" Foreground="Yellow"
      BorderBrush ="Blue" VerticalScrollBarVisibility="Auto"
      AcceptsTab="True">
    </TextBox>
  </DockPanel>

</Window>
```

■ **Note** The next chapter will dive into the details of working with controls and panels, so don't fret over the details of the control declarations.

First of all, notice that we have replaced the initial `<Grid>` with a `<DockPanel>` type that contains a `Button` (named `btnViewXaml`) and a `TextBox` (named `txtXamlData`), and that the `Click` event of the `Button` has been handled. Also notice that the `Loaded` and `Closed` events of the `Window` itself have been handled within the opening `<Window>` element. If you have used the designer to handle your events (as described previously), you should find the following code in your `MainWindow.xaml.vb` file:

```
Class MainWindow
  Private Sub btnViewXaml_Click(ByVal sender As System.Object, _
    ByVal e As System.Windows.RoutedEventArgs)
  End Sub

  Private Sub Window_Closed(ByVal sender As System.Object, _
    ByVal e As System.EventArgs)
  End Sub

  Private Sub Window_Loaded(ByVal sender As System.Object, _
    ByVal e As System.Windows.RoutedEventArgs)
  End Sub
End Class
```

Before continuing, be sure to import the following namespaces into your `MainWindow.xaml.vb` file:

```
Imports System.IO
Imports System.Windows.Markup
```

Implementing the Loaded Event

The Loaded event of our main window is in charge of determining whether there is currently a file named YourXaml.xaml in the folder containing the application. If this file does exist, you will read in the data and place it into the TextBox on the main window. If not, you will fill the TextBox with an initial default XAML description of an empty window (this description is the exact same markup as an initial window definition, except that we are using a <StackPanel>, rather than a <Grid>, to set the Window's Content property [implicitly]).

Note Recall from Chapter 24 that Visual Basic 2008 allows you to build XML literals directly within your VB source code. At runtime this will be represented as an XElement type, the inner XML of which can be obtained by calling ToString().

```
Private Sub Window_Loaded(ByVal sender As System.Object, _
  ByVal e As System.Windows.RoutedEventArgs)
  ' When the main window of the app loads,
  ' place some basic XAML text into the text block.
  If File.Exists(System.Environment.CurrentDirectory & "\YourXaml.xaml") Then
    txtXamlData.Text = File.ReadAllText("YourXaml.xaml")
  Else
    txtXamlData.Text = _
  <Window
    xmlns="http://schemas.microsoft.com/winfx/2006/xaml/presentation"
    xmlns:x="http://schemas.microsoft.com/winfx/2006/xaml">
    <StackPanel>

    </StackPanel>
  </Window>.ToString()

  End If
End Sub
```

Using this approach, the SimpleXamlPad.exe application will be able to load the XAML entered in a previous session, or supply a default block of markup if necessary. At this point, you should be able to run your program and find the display shown in Figure 30-19 within the TextBox type.

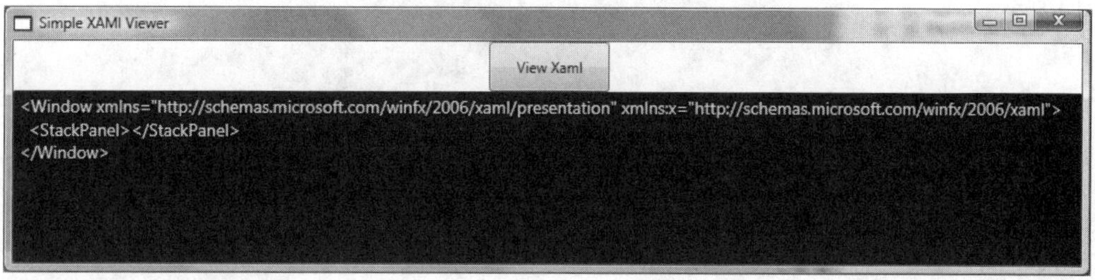

Figure 30-19. *The first run of* SimpleXamlPad.exe

Implementing the Button's Click Event

When you click the Button, you will first save the current data in the TextBox into the YourXaml.xaml file. At this point, you will read in the persisted data via File.Open() to obtain a Stream-derived type.

This is necessary, as the XamlReader.Load() method requires a Stream-derived type (rather than a simple System.String) to represent the XAML to be parsed.

Once you have loaded the XAML description of the <Window> you wish to construct, create an instance of System.Windows.Window based on the in-memory XAML, and display the Window as a modal dialog box:

```
Private Sub btnViewXaml_Click(ByVal sender As System.Object, _
  ByVal e As System.Windows.RoutedEventArgs)
  ' Write out the data in the text block to a local *.xaml file.
  File.WriteAllText("YourXaml.xaml", txtXamlData.Text)

  ' This is the window that will be dynamically XAML-ed.
  Dim myWindow As Window = Nothing

  ' Open local *.xaml file.
  Try
    Using sr As Stream = File.Open("YourXaml.xaml", FileMode.Open)
      ' Connect the XAML to the Window object.
      myWindow = DirectCast(XamlReader.Load(sr), Window)
      myWindow.ShowDialog()
    End Using
  Catch ex As Exception
    MessageBox.Show(ex.Message)
  End Try
End Sub
```

Note that we are wrapping much of our logic within a Try/Catch block. In this way, if the YourXaml.xaml file contains ill-formed markup, we can see the error of our ways within the resulting message box.

Implementing the Closed Event

Finally, the Closed event of our Window type will ensure that the latest and greatest data in the TextBox is persisted to the YourXaml.xaml file:

```
Private Sub Window_Closed(ByVal sender As System.Object, _
  ByVal e As System.EventArgs)
  ' Write out the data in the text block to a local *.xaml file.
  File.WriteAllText("YourXaml.xaml", txtXamlData.Text)
End Sub
```

Testing the Application

Now fire up your program and enter some XAML into your text area. Do be aware that this program does not allow you to specify any code generation–centric XAML attributes (such as Class or any event handlers). As a test, update the <StackPanel> scope as follows:

```
<StackPanel>
  <Rectangle Fill = "Green" Height = "40" Width = "200" />
  <Button Content = "OK!" Height = "40" Width = "100" />
  <Label Content ="{x:Type Label}" />
</StackPanel>
```

Once you click the button, you will see a window appear that renders your XAML definitions (or possibly you'll see a parsing error in the message box—watch your typing!). Figure 30-20 shows possible output.

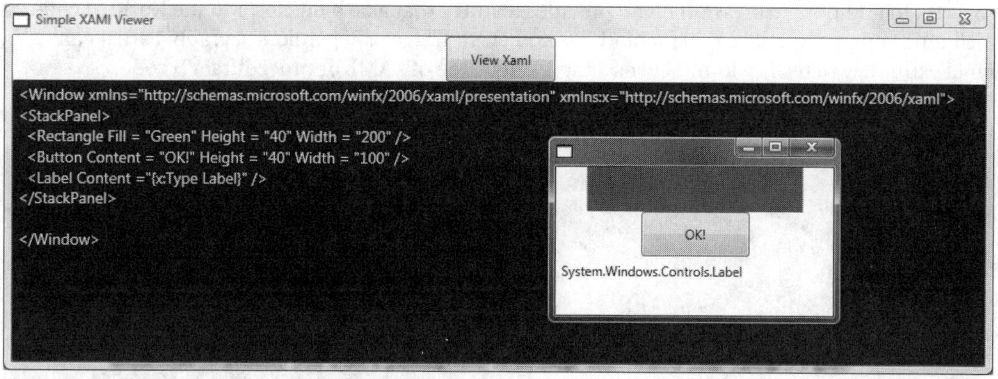

Figure 30-20. `SimpleXamlPad.exe` *in action*

Great! I am sure you can think of many possible enhancements to this application, but to do so you need to be aware of how to work with WPF controls and the panels that contain them. Before examining the WPF control model in the next chapter, we will close this chapter by quickly examining the Microsoft Expression Blend application.

Source Code The SimpleXamlPad project can be found under the Chapter 30 subdirectory.

The Role of Microsoft Expression Blend

While learning new technologies such as XAML and WPF is exciting to most developers, few of us are thrilled by the thought of authoring thousands of lines of markup to describe windows, 3D images, animations, and other such things. Even with the assistance of Visual Studio 2008, generating a feature-rich XAML description of complex entities is tedious and error-prone. Truth be told, Visual Studio 2008 is much better equipped to author procedural code and *tweak* XAML definitions generated by a tool that is dedicated to the automation of XAML descriptions.

Recall that one of the biggest benefits of WPF is the separation of concerns. However, WPF does not simply use separation of concerns at the file level (e.g., VB code files and XAML files). In fact, a WPF application honors the separation of concerns at the level of the tools we use to build our applications. This is important, as a professional WPF application will typically require you to make use of the services of a talented graphic artist to give the application the proper look and feel. As you can imagine, nontechnical individuals would rather *not* use Visual Studio 2008 to author XAML.

To address these problems, Microsoft has created a new family of products that fall under the Expression umbrella. Full details of each member of the Expression family can be found at `http://www.microsoft.com/expression`, but in a nutshell, Expression Blend is a tool geared toward building feature-rich WPF front ends.

Benefits of Expression Blend

The first major benefit of Expression Blend is that the manner in which a graphic artist would author the UI feels similar (but certainly not identical) to other multimedia applications such as Adobe Photoshop or Macromedia Director. For example, Expression Blend supports tools to build story frames for animations, color blending utilities, layout and graphical transformation tools, and so forth. In addition, Expression Blend provides features that lean a bit closer to the world of code, including support to establish data bindings and event triggers. Regardless, a graphic artist can build extremely rich UIs without ever seeing a single line of XAML or procedural VB code. Figure 30-21 shows a screen shot of Expression Blend in action.

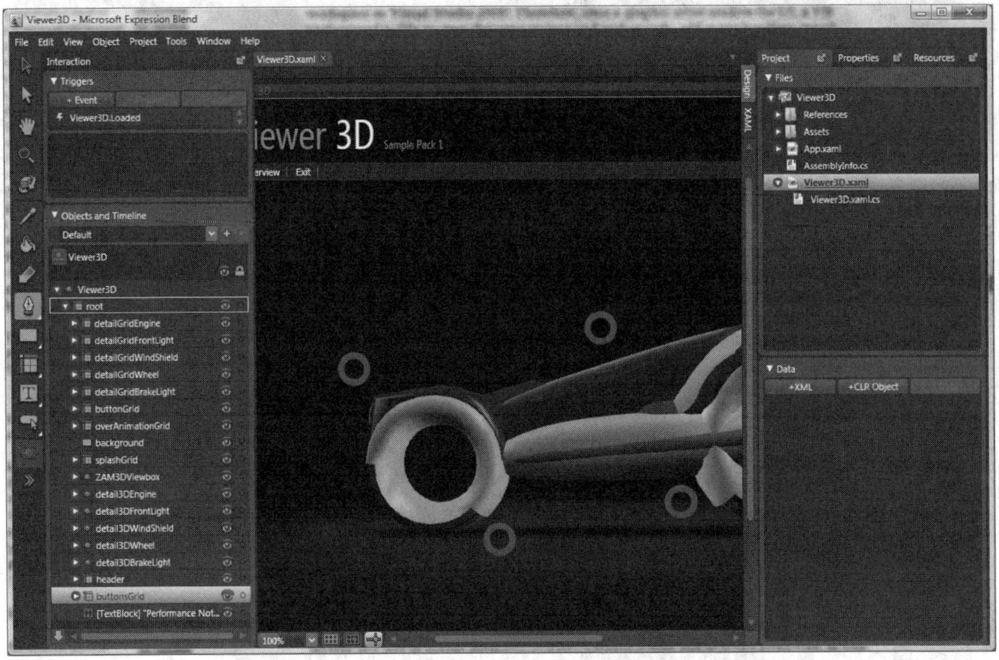

Figure 30-21. *Expression Blend generates XAML transparently in the background.*

The next major benefit of Expression Blend is that it makes use of the *same* exact project workspace as Visual Studio 2008! Therefore, once a graphic artist renders the UI, a VB professional is able to open the same project and author code, add event handlers, tweak XAML, and so forth. Likewise, graphic artists can open existing Visual Studio 2008 WPF projects in Expression Blend to spruce up a lackluster front end. The short answer is, WPF is a highly collaborative endeavor between related code files *and* development tools.

While it is true that use of a tool like Expression Blend is more or less mandatory when using WPF to generate bleeding-edge media-rich applications, this edition of the text will not cover the details of doing so. To be sure, the purpose of this book is to examine the underlying programming model of WPF, not to dive into the details of art theory. However, if you are interested in learning more, you are able to download evaluation copies of the members of the Microsoft Expression family from the supporting website. At the very least I suggest downloading a trial copy of Expression Blend just to see what this tool is capable of.

■ **Note** If you are interested in learning how to use Expression Blend, I'd recommend picking up a copy of *Foundation Expression Blend 2: Building Applications in WPF and Silverlight* by Victor Gaudioso (friends of ED, 2008).

Summary

Windows Presentation Foundation is a user interface toolkit introduced since the release of .NET 3.0. The major goal of WPF is to integrate and unify a number of previously unrelated desktop technologies (2D graphics, 3D graphics, window and control development, etc.) into a single unified programming model. Beyond this point, WPF programs typically make use of Extendable Application Markup Language, which allows you to declare the look and feel of your WPF elements via markup.

As you have seen in this chapter, XAML allows you to describe trees of .NET objects using a declarative syntax. During this chapter's investigation of XAML, you were exposed to several new bits of syntax, including property-element syntax and attached properties, as well as the role of type converters and XAML markup extensions. The chapter wrapped up with an examination of how you can programmatically interact with XAML definitions using the `XamlReader` and `XamlWriter` types, you took a tour of the WPF-specific features of Visual Studio 2008, and you briefly looked at the role of Microsoft Expression Blend.

CHAPTER 31

Programming with WPF Controls

The previous chapter provided a foundation on the WPF programming model, including an examination of the `Window` and `Application` types as well as several details regarding the Extensible Application Markup Language (XAML). Here, you will build upon your current understanding by digging into the WPF control set. We begin this chapter with a survey of the intrinsic WPF controls, followed by an examination of two important WPF control-related topics: dependency properties and routed events.

Once you have been exposed to the core control programming model, the remainder of this chapter will illustrate several interesting ways to use WPF controls within your applications. For example, you will learn how to organize controls within various WPF containers (`Canvas`, `Grid`, `StackPanel`, `WrapPanel`, etc.) and how to construct a main window complete with a menu system, status bar, and toolbar. This chapter concludes by examining how to make use of *control commands* (which can be used to tack on built-in behaviors to UI elements and input commands) and introduces you to the WPF *data binding* model.

Note Many of the control XAML definitions have been included in the code download as "loose XAML files." To view the rendered output, you can copy and paste the markup within a given `*.xaml` file into your `SimpleXamlPad.exe` application you created in Chapter 30. As an alternative, you can change the `<Window>` and `</Window>` elements to `<Page>` and `</Page>` and double-click the file to view them within Internet Explorer.

A Survey of the WPF Control Library

Unless you are very new to the concept of building graphical user interfaces, the intrinsic set of WPF controls should not raise any eyebrows, regardless of which GUI toolkit you have used in the past (MFC, Java AWT/Swing, Windows Forms, VB6, Mac OS X [Cocoa], GTK+/GTK#, etc.). Table 31-1 provides a road map of the core WPF controls, grouped by related functionality.

Table 31-1. *The Core WPF Controls*

WPF Control Category	Example Members	Meaning in Life
Core user input controls	`Button`, `RadioButton`, `ComboBox`, `CheckBox`, `Expander`, `ListBox` `Slider`, `ToggleButton`, `TreeView`, `ContextMenu`, `ScrollBar`, `Slider`, `TabControl`, `TextBox`, `RepeatButton`, `RichTextBox`, `Label`	As expected, WPF provides a whole family of controls that can be used to build the crux of a user interface.

Continued

Table 31-1. *Continued*

WPF Control Category	Example Members	Meaning in Life
Window frame adornment controls	Menu, ToolBar, StatusBar, ToolTip, ProgressBar	These UI elements are used to decorate the frame of a Window object with input devices (such as the Menu) and user informational elements (StatusBar, ToolTip, etc.).
Media controls	Image, MediaElement, SoundPlayerAction	These provide support for audio/video playback and image display.
Layout controls	Border, Canvas, DockPanel, Grid, GridView, GroupBox, Panel, StackPanel, Viewbox, WrapPanel	WPF provides numerous controls that allow you to group and organize other controls for the purpose of layout management.

Beyond the GUI types in Table 31-1, WPF defines additional controls for advanced document processing (DocumentViewer, FlowDocumentReader, etc.) as well as types to support the Ink API (useful for Tablet PC development) and various dialog boxes (PasswordBox, PrintDialog, FileDialog, OpenFileDialog, and SaveFileDialog).

■ Note The FileDialog, OpenFileDialog, and SaveFileDialog types are defined within the Microsoft.Win32 namespace of the PresentationFramework.dll assembly.

If you are coming to WPF from a Windows Forms background, you may notice that the current offering of intrinsic controls is somewhat less than that of Windows Forms (for example, WPF does not have "spin button" controls). The good news is that many of these missing controls can be expressed in XAML quite quickly and can even be modeled as a user control or custom control for reuse between projects.

■ Note This edition of the text does not cover the construction of custom WPF user controls or WPF control libraries. If you are interested in learning how to do so, consult the .NET Framework 3.5 SDK documentation.

WPF Controls and Visual Studio 2008

When you create a new WPF Application project using Visual Studio 2008 (see the previous chapter), you will see a majority of controls exposed from the Toolbox, as shown in Figure 31-1.

Like a Windows Forms project, these controls can be dragged onto the visual designer and configured with the Properties window. Furthermore, recall from Chapter 30 that if you handle events using the XAML editor, the IDE will autogenerate an appropriate event handler in your code file.

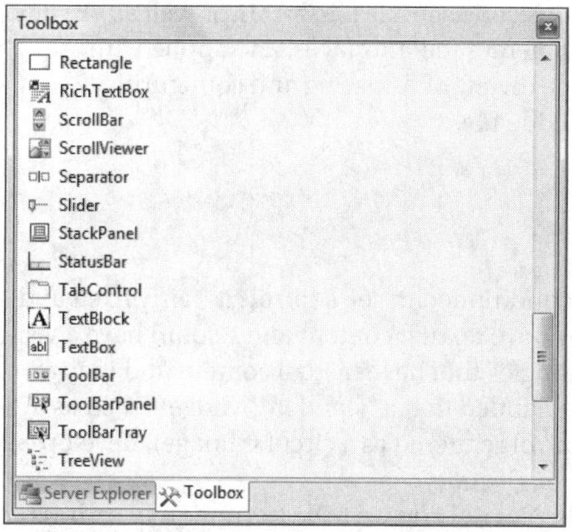

Figure 31-1. *The Visual Studio 2008 Toolbox exposes the intrinsic WPF controls.*

The Details Are in the Documentation

Now, despite what you may be thinking, the intent of this chapter is *not* to walk through each and every member of each and every WPF control. Rather, you will receive an overview of the core controls with emphasis on the underlying programming model (dependency properties, routed events, commands, etc.) and key services common to most WPF controls.

To round out your understanding of the particular functionality of a given control, be sure to consult the .NET Framework 3.5 SDK documentation—specifically, the "Control Library" section of the help system, located under .NET Framework ➤ Windows Presentation Foundation ➤ Controls (see Figure 31-2).

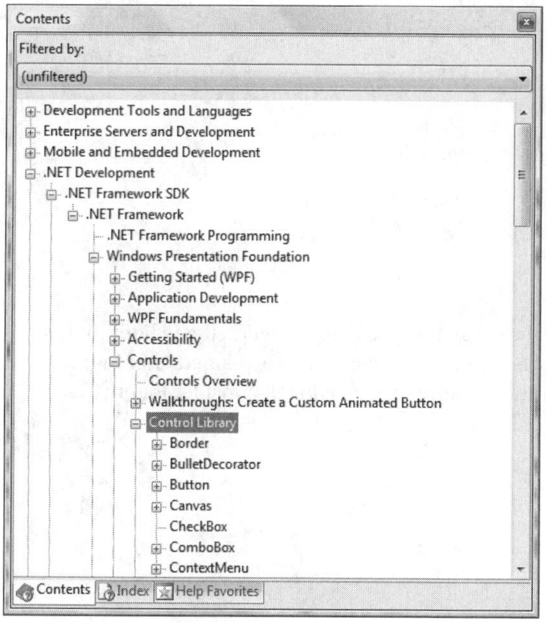

Figure 31-2. *Full details of each WPF control is just a keypress away (F1).*

Here you will find full details of each control, various code samples (in XAML as well as VB) and information regarding a control's inheritance chain, implemented interfaces, and applied attributes. With this disclaimer aside, let's begin with a quick review of declaring and configuring controls in XAML, and using them within a related VB code file.

Declaring Controls in XAML

Over the course of many years, developers have been conditioned to see controls as fairly fixed and predictable entities. For example, `Label` widgets always have textual content and seldom have a visible border (although they could). `Button`s are gray rectangles that have textual content and may on occasion have an embedded image. When a project demanded that a "standard" widget (such as a `Button`) needed to be customized (such as a `Button` control rendered as a circular image), developers were often forced to build a customized control through code.

WPF radically changes the way we look at controls. Not only do we have the option to express a control's look and feel through markup, but also many WPF controls (specifically, any descendant of `ContentControl`) have been designed to contain any sort of *content* you desire. Recall from Chapter 30 that the `Content` property may be set explicitly (as an attribute within an element's opening tag) or implicitly by specifying nested content as the child element of the root.

Create a new Visual Studio 2008 WPF Application project named ControlReview. Rather than assume that "all `Button`s are gray rectangles that have text and maybe an image," we can describe via XAML the following implicit content for a `Button` type (this should be declared within the `<Grid>` element of your initial `<Window>`):

```
<!-- A custom button with built-in selections! -->
<Button Name="btnPurchaseOptions" Height="100" Width = "300">
  <StackPanel>
    <Label Name="lblInstructions" Foreground = "DarkGreen"
           Content = "Select Your Options and Press to Commit"/>
    <StackPanel Orientation = "Horizontal">
      <Expander Name="colorExpander" Header = "Color">
        <!-- Assume items are placed here... -->
      </Expander>
      <Expander Name="MakeExpander" Header = "Make">
        <!-- Assume items are placed here... -->
      </Expander>
      <Expander Name="paymentExpander" Header = "Payment Plan">
        <!-- Assume items are placed here... -->
      </Expander>
   </StackPanel>
  </StackPanel>
</Button>
```

Notice that this `<Button>` type contains three `Expander` types (explained in detail later in this chapter), which are arranged within a set of `<StackPanel>` elements (also explained later in this chapter). Without getting too hung up on the functionality of each widget, consider Figure 31-3, which shows the rendered output.

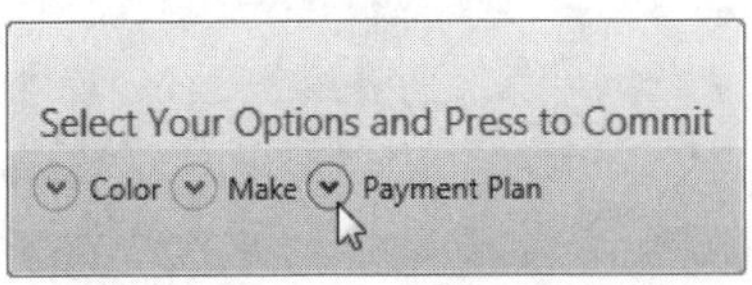

Figure 31-3. *A customized* `Button` *declared via XAML*

By way of a simple compare and contrast, consider how this same control would be built using Windows Forms. Under this API, you could achieve this control only by building a custom Button-derived type that manually handled the rendering of the graphical content, updated the internal controls collection, overrode various event handlers, and so forth.

Given the birth of desktop markup, the only compelling reasons to build custom WPF controls are if you need a widget that supports custom behaviors (events, overriding of virtual methods, support for additional interface types, etc.) or must support customized design-time configuration utilities. If you are only concerned with generating a customized rendering, XAML fits the bill.

Interacting with Controls in Code Files

Recall from the previous chapter that the properties of a WPF type can be set using attributes within an element's opening tag (or alternatively using property-element syntax). In the majority of cases, attributes of a XAML element directly map to the properties and events of the control's class representation within the System.Windows.Controls namespace. As such, you always have the option to define a control completely in markup or completely in code, or to use a mix of the two.

■ **Note** You can only gain direct access to a control within a related code file if it has been declared using the Name attribute in the opening element of the XAML definition.

Given that the previous XAML markup contains elements that have been assigned a Name attribute, you can directly access these elements in your code file as well as handle any declared events. For example, we could change the value of the Label's FontSize property as follows:

```
Class MainWindow
  Sub New()
    InitializeComponent()
    ' Change FontSize of Label.
    lblInstructions.FontSize = 14
  End Sub
End Class
```

This is possible because controls that are given a Name attribute in the XAML definition result in a member variable in the autogenerated *.g.vb file (see Chapter 30):

```
Partial Public Class MainWindow
  Inherits System.Windows.Window
  Implements System.Windows.Markup.IComponentConnector

  ' Member variables defined based on the XAML markup.
  Friend WithEvents btnPurchaseOptions As System.Windows.Controls.Button
  Friend WithEvents lblInstructions As System.Windows.Controls.Label
  Friend WithEvents colorExpander As System.Windows.Controls.Expander
  Friend WithEvents MakeExpander As System.Windows.Controls.Expander
  Friend WithEvents paymentExpander As System.Windows.Controls.Expander
...
End Class
```

When you wish to handle events for a given control, you are able to assign a method name to a given event in your XAML definition as follows:

```
<Button Name="btnPurchaseOptions"
  Click="btnPurchaseOptions_Click"
  Height="100" Width = "300">
```

```
...
</Button>
```

The related code file would contain a definition of this method, whose format will be based on the underlying delegate (recall again that the Visual Studio 2008 IDE will update your code file automatically):

```
Private Sub btnPurchaseOptions_Click(ByVal sender As System.Object, _
  ByVal e As System.Windows.RoutedEventArgs)
  MessageBox.Show("Button has been clicked")
End Sub
```

On a related note, you are free to handle your events entirely in code. For example, if the previous `Click` event XAML definition were deleted, you could update the current event handler as follows:

```
Private Sub btnPurchaseOptions_Click(ByVal sender As System.Object, _
  ByVal e As System.Windows.RoutedEventArgs) _
  Handles btnPurchaseOptions.Click
    MessageBox.Show("Button has been clicked")
End Sub
```

Now that the basic control model is fresh in your mind, the next task is to examine the details of two important (but somewhat challenging) aspects of the WPF control model: dependency properties and routed events. While the details of these concepts are typically hidden from view during your day-to-day WPF programming tasks, the more you understand these lower-level details, the better prepared you will be to dive into more advanced WPF programming tasks in the future.

■ **Source Code** The ControlReview project is included under the Chapter 31 subdirectory.

Understanding the Role of Dependency Properties

As you would assume, the Windows Presentation Foundation APIs make use of each member of the .NET type system (classes, structures, interfaces, delegates, enumerations) and each possible type member (properties, methods, events, constant data/read-only fields, etc.) within its implementation. However, WPF introduces a new programming mechanism termed a *dependency property*.

■ **Note** Dependency properties are a WPF-specific programming construct. To date, no .NET programming language has a native syntax to define this particular flavor of a property.

Like a "normal" .NET property (often termed a *CLR property* in the WPF literature), dependency properties can be set declaratively using XAML or programmatically within a code file. Furthermore, dependency properties (like CLR properties) exist to encapsulate data fields and can be configured as read-only, write-only, or read-write, and so forth.

To make matters more interesting, in most cases you will be blissfully unaware that you have actually set a dependency property as opposed to a CLR property! For example, the `Height` and `Width` properties inherited from `FrameworkElement`, as well as the `Content` member inherited from `ControlContent`, are all dependency properties:

```
<!-- You just set three dependency properties! -->
<Button Name = "btnMyButton" Height = "50" Width = "100" Content = "OK"/>
```

Given all of these similarities, you may wonder exactly why WPF has introduced a new term for a familiar concept. The answer lies in how a dependency property is implemented under the hood. Once implemented, dependency properties provide a number of powerful features that are used by various WPF technologies including data binding, animation services, themes and styles, and so forth. In a nutshell, dependency properties provide the following benefits above and beyond the simple data encapsulation found with a CLR property:

- Dependency properties can inherit their values from a parent element's XAML definition.
- Dependency properties support the ability to have values set by external types (recall from Chapter 30 that attached properties do this very thing, as attached properties are based on dependency properties).
- Dependency properties allow WPF to compute a value based on multiple external values.
- Dependency properties provide the infrastructure for callback notifications and triggers (used quite often when building animations, styles, and themes).
- Dependency properties allow for shared storage of their data (which helps conserve memory consumption).

One key difference of a dependency property is that it allows WPF to compute a value based on values from multiple property inputs. The other properties in question could include OS system properties (including systemwide user preferences), values based on data binding and animation/storyboard logic, resources and styles, or values known through parent/child relationships with other XAML elements.

Another major difference is that dependency properties can be configured to monitor changes of the property value to force external actions to occur. For example, changing the value of a dependency property might cause WPF to change the layout of controls on a `Window`, rebind to external data sources, or move through the steps of a custom animation.

Examining an Existing Dependency Property

To be completely honest, the chances that you will need to manually build a dependency property for your WPF projects are quite slim. In reality, the only time you will typically need to do so is if you are building a custom WPF control library, where you have subclassed an existing control to modify its behaviors. In this case, if you are creating a property that needs to work with the WPF data binding engine, theme engine, or animation engine, or if the property must broadcast when it has changed, a dependency property is the correct course of action. In all other cases, a normal CLR property will do.

While this is true, it is helpful to understand the basic composition of a dependency property, as it will make some of the more "mysterious" features of WPF less so and deepen your understanding of the underlying WPF programming model. To illustrate the internal composition of a dependency property, consider the following VB code, which approximates the implementation of the `Height` property of the `FrameworkElement` class type:

```
Public Class FrameworkElement
  Inherits UIElement
  Implements IFrameworkInputElement
  Implements IInputElement
  Implements ISupportInitialize
  Implements IHaveResources
  ...
```

```
  ' Notice this is a shared field of type DependencyProperty.
  Public Shared ReadOnly HeightProperty As DependencyProperty

  ' The shared DependencyProperty field is created and "registered"
  ' in the shared constructor.
  Shared Sub New()
    HeightProperty = DependencyProperty.Register("Height", GetType(Double), _
      GetType(FrameworkElement), _
      New FrameworkPropertyMetadata(CDbl(1) / CDbl(0), _
        FrameworkPropertyMetadataOptions.AffectsMeasure, _
        New PropertyChangedCallback(FrameworkElement.OnTransformDirty)), _
      New ValidateValueCallback(FrameworkElement.IsWidthHeightValid))
  End Sub

  ' Note that the Height property still has get/set blocks.
  ' However, the implemention is using the inherited
  ' GetValue()/SetValue() methods.
  Public Property Height() As Double
    Get
      Return CDbl(MyBase.GetValue(HeightProperty))
    End Get
    Set(ByVal value As Double)
      MyBase.SetValue(HeightProperty, value)
    End Set
  End Property
End Class
```

As you can see, dependency properties require quite a bit of additional logic from a typical CLR property! Here is a breakdown of what is happening: first and foremost, dependency properties are represented using the `System.Windows.DependencyProperty` class type and are almost always declared as public, shared read-only fields. Recall that one benefit of dependency properties is that they are not directly tied to an object instance (which helps memory consumption), hence the use of shared data.

Registering a Dependency Property

Given that dependency properties are declared as shared, they are assigned an initial value within the shared constructor of the type. However, unlike a simple numerical field, the `DependencyProperty` object is created indirectly by capturing the return value of the shared `DependencyProperty.Register()` method. This method has been overloaded a number of times; however, in this example, `Register()` is invoked as follows:

```
HeightProperty = DependencyProperty.Register("Height", GetType(Double), _
  GetType(FrameworkElement), _
  New FrameworkPropertyMetadata(CDbl(1) / CDbl(0), _
    FrameworkPropertyMetadataOptions.AffectsMeasure, _
    New PropertyChangedCallback(FrameworkElement.OnTransformDirty)), _
  New ValidateValueCallback(FrameworkElement.IsWidthHeightValid))
```

The first argument to `Register()` is the name of the "normal" CLR property on the class that makes use of the `DependencyProperty` field (`Height` in this case), while the second argument is the type information of the underlying data type it is bound to (a `Double`).

The third argument specifies the type information of the class that this property belongs to (`FrameworkElement` in this case). While this might seem redundant (after all, the `HeightProperty` field is already defined within the `FrameworkElement` class), this is a very clever aspect of WPF in that it allows one type to "attach" properties to another type (even if the class definition has been sealed!).

■Note Recall that VB 2008 extension methods (see Chapter 13) also allow you to add new members to sealed types. Extension methods would be the most direct way of adding new functionality to types that do not need to participate in WPF-centric services (e.g., animation).

The final arguments passed to Register() are what really give dependency properties their own flavor. Here we are able to provide a FrameworkPropertyMetadata object that describes all of the details regarding how WPF should handle this property with respect to callback notifications (if the property needs to notify others when the value changes), how the value will be validated, and various options (represented by the FrameworkPropertyMetadataOptions enum) that control what is effected by the property in question (does it work with data binding, can it be inherited, etc.).

Defining a Wrapper Property for a DependencyProperty Field

Once the details of configuring the DependencyProperty object have been established within a shared constructor, the final task is to wrap the field within a typical CLR property (Height in this case). Notice, however, that the Get and Set scopes do not simply return or set a class-level double-member variable, but do so indirectly using the GetValue() and SetValue() methods from the System.Windows.DependencyObject base class:

```
Public Property Height() As Double
  Get
    Return CDbl(MyBase.GetValue(HeightProperty))
  End Get
  Set(ByVal value As Double)
    MyBase.SetValue(HeightProperty, value)
  End Set
End Property
```

■Note Strictly speaking, you do not need to build a wrapper property for a DependencyProperty field, if the field is public, as you can access it as a shared member when calling the inherited GetValue()/SetValue() public methods. In practice, most dependency properties do have a friendly wrapper, as it is very XAML-friendly.

Now that you have seen the details of how a dependency property is assembled under the hood, be aware that it would be entirely possible to use a normal CLR property that supported the same services as a WPF dependency property (notifications, shared memory allocation, etc.). However, to do so would require a good deal of boilerplate code that you would need to author by hand and replicate in numerous places. Using the intrinsic DependencyProperty type (and additional bits of infrastructure), we are provided with an out-of-the-box implementation of the same services.

Because a dependency property is built using various WPF-centric types, it would certainly be possible for you to build your own dependency properties, which will not be necessary for the examples in this text. However, the following code summarizes the core pieces of a dependency property declaration (note here we are registering the property at the time we declare the shared read-only DependencyProperty type):

```
Public Class MyOwnerClass
  Inherits DependencyObject
  ' Using a DependencyProperty as the backing store for MyProperty.
  ' This enables animation, styling, binding, etc...
  Public Shared ReadOnly MyPropertyProperty As DependencyProperty = _
```

```
    DependencyProperty.Register("MyProperty", GetType(Integer), _
    GetType(OwnerClass), New UIPropertyMetadata(0))

  ' XAML-friendly wrapper for the
  ' shared read-only field. This is necessary,
  ' as we can't call methods (GetValue/SetValue)
  ' in XAML.
  Public Property MyProperty() As Integer
    ' GetValue/SetValue come from the
    ' DependencyObject base class.
    Get
      Return CInt(GetValue(MyPropertyProperty))
    End Get
    Set (ByVal value As Integer)
      SetValue(MyPropertyProperty, value)
    End Set
  End Property
End Class
```

If you are interested in learning further details regarding this WPF programming construct, check out the topic “Custom Dependency Properties” within the .NET Framework 3.5 SDK documentation.

Understanding Routed Events

Properties are not the only .NET programming construct to be given a facelift to work well within the WPF API. The standard CLR event model has also been refined just a bit to ensure that events can be processed in a manner that is fitting for XAML's description of a tree of objects.

Create a new WPF Application project named WPFControlEvents. Now, update the initial XAML description of the initial window by adding the following `<Button>` type within the initial `<Grid>`:

```
<Button Name="btnClickMe" Height="75" Width = "250" Click ="btnClickMe_Clicked">
  <StackPanel Orientation ="Horizontal">
    <Label Height="50" FontSize ="20">Fancy Button!</Label>
    <Canvas Height ="50" Width ="100" >
    <Ellipse Name = "outerEllipse" Fill ="Green" Height ="25"
             Width ="50" Cursor="Hand" Canvas.Left="25" Canvas.Top="12"/>
    <Ellipse Name = "innerEllipse" Fill ="Yellow" Height = "15" Width ="36"
             Canvas.Top="17" Canvas.Left="32"/>
    </Canvas>
  </StackPanel>
</Button>
```

Notice in the `<Button>`'s opening definition we have handled the `Click` event by specifying the name of a method to be called when the event is raised. The `Click` event works with the `RoutedEventHandler` delegate, which expects an event handler that takes an `Object` as the first parameter and a `System.Windows.RoutedEventArgs` as the second:

```
Private Sub btnClickMe_Clicked(ByVal sender As System.Object, _
  ByVal e As System.Windows.RoutedEventArgs)
  ' Do something when button is clicked.
  MessageBox.Show("Clicked the button")
End Sub
```

Figure 31-4 shows the expected output when clicking the current control (for display purposes, I changed the initial <Grid> type to a <StackPanel>, which explains why the Button is mounted on the top center of this Window, rather than positioned in the center).

Figure 31-4. *Handling events for a composite* Button *type*

Now, consider the current composition of our Button. It contains numerous nested elements to fully represent its user interface (Canvas, Ellipse, Label, etc.). Imagine how tedious WPF event handling would be if we were forced to handle a Click event for each and every one of these subelements. After all, the end user could click anywhere within the scope of the button's boundaries (on the Label, on the green area of the oval, on the surface of the button, etc.). Not only would the creation of separate event handlers for each aspect of the Button be labor intensive, we would end up with some mighty nasty code to maintain down the road.

Under the Windows Forms event model, a custom control such as this would require us to handle the Click event for each item on the button. Thankfully, WPF *routed events* take care of this automatically. Simply put, the routed events model automatically propagates an event up (or down) a tree of objects, looking for an appropriate handler.

Specifically speaking, a routed event can make use of three "routing strategies." If an event is moving from the point of origin up to other defining scopes within the object tree, the event is said to be a *bubbling event*. Conversely, if an event is moving from its point of origin down into related subelements, the event is said to be a *tunneling event*. Finally, if an event is raised and handled only by the originating element (which is what could be described as a normal CLR event), it is said to be a *direct event*.

■ **Note** Like dependency properties, routed events are a WPF-specific construct implemented using WPF-specific helper types. Thus, there is no special VB syntax you need to learn to handle routed events.

The Role of Routed Bubbling Events

In the current example, if the user clicks the inner yellow oval, the Click event bubbles out to the next level of scope (the Canvas), and then to the StackPanel, and finally to the Button where the Click event handler is handled. In a similar way, if the user clicks the Label, the event is bubbled to the StackPanel and then finally to the Button type.

Given this routed bubbling event pattern, we have no need to worry about registering specific Click event handlers for all members of a composite control. However, if you wished to perform custom clicking logic for multiple elements within the same object tree, you can do so. By way of illustration, assume you need to handle the clicking of the outerEllipse control in a unique manner. First, handle the MouseDown event for this subelement (graphically rendered types such as the Ellipse do not support a "click" event; however, they can monitor mouse button activity via MouseDown, MouseUp, etc.):

```
<Button Name="btnClickMe" Height="75" Width = "250" Click ="btnClickMe_Clicked">
  <StackPanel Orientation ="Horizontal">
    <Label Height="50" FontSize ="20">Fancy Button!</Label>
    <Canvas Height ="50" Width ="100" >
    <Ellipse Name = "outerEllipse" Fill ="Green"
             Height ="25" MouseDown ="outerEllipse_MouseDown"
             Width ="50" Cursor="Hand" Canvas.Left="25" Canvas.Top="12"/>
    <Ellipse Name = "innerEllipse" Fill ="Yellow" Height = "15" Width ="36"
             Canvas.Top="17" Canvas.Left="32"/>
    </Canvas>
  </StackPanel>
</Button>
```

Then implement an appropriate event handler, which for illustrative purposes will simply change the Title property of the main window:

```
Private Sub outerEllipse_MouseDown(ByVal sender As System.Object, _
  ByVal e As System.Windows.Input.MouseButtonEventArgs)
  ' Change title of window.
  Me.Title = "You clicked the outer ellipse!"
End Sub
```

With this, we now can take different courses of action depending on where the end user has clicked (which boils down to the outer ellipse and everywhere else within the button's scope).

■ **Note** Routed bubbling events always move from the point of origin to the *next defining scope*. Thus, in this example, if we were to click the innerEllipse object, the event would be bubbled to the Canvas, *not* to the outerEllipse, as they are both Ellipse types within the scope of Canvas.

Continuing or Halting Bubbling

Currently, if the user clicks the outerEllipse object, it will trigger the registered MouseDown event handler for this Ellipse type and bubble to the Button's Click event handler. If you wish to inform WPF to stop bubbling up the object tree, you can set the Handled property of the RountedEventArgs type to True:

```
Private Sub outerEllipse_MouseDown(ByVal sender As System.Object, _
  ByVal e As System.Windows.Input.MouseButtonEventArgs)
  ' Change title of window.
  Me.Title = "You clicked the outer ellipse!"

  ' Stop bubbling!
  e.Handled = True
End Sub
```

In this case, we would find that the title of the window is changed; however, the `MessageBox` displayed within the `Click` event handler of the `Button` type will not execute.

In a nutshell, routed bubbling events make it possible to allow a complex group of content to act either as a single logical element (e.g., a `Button`) or as discrete items (e.g., an `Ellipse` within the `Button`).

The Role of Routed Tunneling Events

Strictly speaking, routed events can be *bubbling* (as just described) or *tunneling* in nature. Tunneling events (which all begin with the `Preview` suffix—e.g., `PreviewMouseDown`) drill down from the originating element into the inner scopes of the object tree. By and large, each bubbling event in the WPF base class libraries is paired with a related tunneling event that fires *before* the bubbling counterpart. For example, before the bubbling `MouseDown` event fires, the tunneling `PreviewMouseDown` event fires first.

Handling a tunneling event looks just like the process of handling any other event; simply assign the event handler name in XAML (or, if needed, using the corresponding VB event handling syntax in your code file) and implement the handler in the code file. Just to illustrate the interplay of tunneling and bubbling events, begin by handling the `PreviewMouseDown` event for the `outerEllipse` object:

```
<Ellipse Name = "outerEllipse" Fill ="Green" Height ="25"
  MouseDown ="outerEllipse_MouseDown"
  PreviewMouseDown ="outerEllipse_PreviewMouseDown"
  Width ="50" Cursor="Hand" Canvas.Left="25" Canvas.Top="12"/>
```

Next, retrofit the current VB class definition by updating each event handler (for all types) to append data to and eventually display the value within a new `String` member variable. This will allow us to observe the flow of events firing in the background:

```
Class MainWindow
  ' This is used to hold data on the mouse-related
  ' activity.
  Private mouseActivityOuterEllipse As String = String.Empty

  Public Sub New()
    InitializeComponent()
  End Sub

  Public Sub btnClickMe_Clicked(ByVal sender As Object, ByVal e As RoutedEventArgs)
    ' Show the final string.
    mouseActivityOuterEllipse &= "Button Click event fired!" & vbLf
    MessageBox.Show(mouseActivityOuterEllipse)

    ' Clear string for next test.
    mouseActivityOuterEllipse = String.Empty
  End Sub

  Public Sub outerEllipse_MouseDown(ByVal sender As Object, _
    ByVal e As RoutedEventArgs)
    ' Add data to string.
    mouseActivityOuterEllipse &= "MouseDown event fired!" & vbLf
  End Sub

  Public Sub outerEllipse_PreviewMouseDown(ByVal sender As Object, _
    ByVal e As RoutedEventArgs)
    ' Add data to string.
```

```
    mouseActivityOuterEllipse = "PreviewMouseDown event fired!" & vbLf
  End Sub
End Class
```

When you run the program and do not click within the bounds of the outer ellipse, you will simply see the message "Button Click event fired!" displayed within the message box. However, if you do click within the outer ellipse image, the message box shown in Figure 31-5 will display.

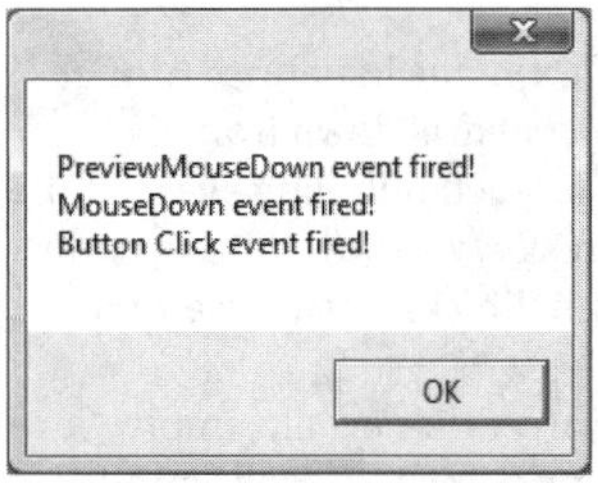

Figure 31-5. *Tunneling first, bubbling second*

So you may be wondering why in the world WPF events typically tend to come in pairs (one tunneling and one bubbling)? The answer is that by previewing events, you have the power to perform any special logic (data validation, disable bubbling action, etc.) before the bubbling counterpart fires. In a vast majority of cases, you will *not need* to handle the `Preview` prefixed tunneling events and simply have to worry about the (non–`Preview`-prefixed) bubbling events.

Much like the task of manually authoring a dependency property, the need to handle tunneling events is typically only necessary when subclassing an existing WPF control. On a related note, if you are building a custom WPF control, be aware that you can create custom routed events (which may be bubbling or tunneling) using a mechanism similar to that of building a custom dependency property. If you are interested, check out the topic "How to: Create a Custom Routed Event" within the .NET Framework 3.5 SDK documentation.

Source Code The WPFControlEvents project is included under the Chapter 31 subdirectory.

Working with Button Types

Now that you have examined the details of dependency properties and routed events, you are in a good position to better understand the WPF controls themselves, beginning with button types. Instinctively, we all know the role of button types. They are UI elements that can be pressed via the mouse or via the keyboard (with the Enter key or spacebar) if they have the current focus. In WPF, the `ButtonBase` class serves as a parent for three core derived types: `Button`, `RepeatButton`, and `ToggleButton`.

The ButtonBase Type

Like any parent class, `ButtonBase` provides a polymorphic interface for derived types (in addition to the members inherited from its base class `ContentControl`). For example, it is `ButtonBase` that defines the `Click` event. As well, this parent class defines the `IsPressed` property, which allows you to take a course of action when the derived type has been pressed, but not yet released. In addition, Table 31-2 describes some other members of interest for the ButtonBase abstract base class.

Table 31-2. *Members of the* ButtonBase *Type*

ButtonBase Member	Meaning in Life
ClickMode	This property allows you to establish when the Click event should fire, based on values from the ClickMode enumeration.
Command	As explained later in this chapter in the section "Understanding WPF Control Commands," many UI elements can have an associated "command" that can be attached to a UI element by assigning the Command property.
CommandParameter	This property allows you to pass parameters to the item specified by the Command property.
CommandTarget	This property allows you to establish the recipient of the command set by the Command property.

Beyond the command-centric members (examined at the conclusion of this chapter), the most interesting member would be ClickMode, which allows you to specify three different modes of clicking a button. This property can be assigned any value from the related System.Windows.Controls.ClickMode enumeration:

```
Public Enum ClickMode
  Release
  Press
  Hover
End Enum
```

For example, assume you have the following XAML description for a Button type using the ClickMode.Hover value for the ClickMode property:

```
<Button Name = "bntHoverClick" ClickMode = "Hover" Click ="btnHoverClick_Click"/>
```

With this, the Click event will fire as soon as the mouse cursor is anywhere within the bounds of the Button. While this may not be the most helpful course of action for a typical push button, hover mode can be useful when building custom styles, templates, or animations.

The Button Type

The first derived type, Button, provides two properties of immediate interest, IsCancel and IsDefault, which are very helpful when building dialog boxes containing OK and Cancel buttons. When IsCancel is set to True, the button will be artificially clicked when the user presses the Esc key. If IsDefault is set to True, the button will be artificially clicked when the user presses the Enter key. Consider the following XAML description of two Button instances:

```
<!-- Assume these are defined within a <StackPanel> of a Window type -->
<Button Name ="btnOK" IsDefault = "true" Click ="btnOK_Click" Content = "OK"/>
<Button Name ="btnCancel" IsCancel= "true"
  Click ="btnCancel_Click" Content = "Cancel"/>
```

If you were to implement each of the declared event handlers in a related code file, you would be able to run the application and verify the correct handler is invoked when the Enter key or Esc key is pressed. This would be the case even if another UI element of the window (such as a text entry area) has the current focus.

The ToggleButton Type

The ToggleButton type (defined in the System.Windows.Controls.Primitives namespace) has by default a UI identical to the Button type; however, it has the unique ability to hold its pressed state when clicked. To account for this, ToggleButton provides an IsChecked property, which toggles between True and False when the end user clicks the UI element. Furthermore, ToggleButton provides two events (Checked and Unchecked) that can be handled to intercept this state change. Here is a XAML description of a simple toggle that handles each event on two unique event handlers:

```
<!-- A Yes/No toggle button -->
<ToggleButton Name ="toggleOnOffButton"
  Checked ="toggleOnOffButton_Checked"
  Unchecked ="toggleOnOffButton_Unchecked">
  Off!
</ToggleButton >
```

The event handlers simply update the Content property with a fitting textual message:

```
Private Sub toggleOnOffButton_Checked(ByVal sender As Object, _
  ByVal e As RoutedEventArgs)
  toggleOnOffButton.Content = "On!"
End Sub

Private Sub toggleOnOffButton_Unchecked(ByVal sender As Object, _
  ByVal e As RoutedEventArgs)
  toggleOnOffButton.Content = "Off!"
End Sub
```

If you wish to consolidate your code-behind file to use a single handler for each event, you could update your XAML definition so that the Checked and Unchecked events both point to a single handler (say, toggleOnOffButtonPressed), and then use the IsChecked property to flip between the messages:

```
Private Sub toggleOnOffButtonPressed(ByVal sender As Object, _
  ByVal e As RoutedEventArgs)
  If toggleOnOffButton.IsChecked = False
    toggleOnOffButton.Content = "Off!"
  Else
    toggleOnOffButton.Content = "On!"
  End If
End Sub
```

Finally, be aware that ToggleButton also supports tri-state functionality (via the IsThreeState property and Indeterminate event), allowing you to test whether the widget is checked, unchecked, or neither. While it might seem odd for a button to monitor itself in this manner, it makes perfect sense for types that derive from ToggleButton, such as the CheckBox type examined in just a moment.

■ **Note** As a general rule, types defined in the System.Windows.Controls.Primitives namespace (including the ToggleButton) are not assumed to be very useful out of the box without additional customizations.

The RepeatButton Type

The final ButtonBase-derived type to discuss is the RepeatButton type, also defined within System.Windows.Controls.Primitives. This type also has a default look and feel to a standard Button; however, it supports the ability to continuously fire its Click event when the end user has the widget in a pressed state. The frequency in which it will fire the Click event is dependent upon the values you assign to the Delay and Interval properties (both of which are recorded in milliseconds).

In reality, the RepeatButton type (like the ToggleButton type) is not that useful on its own. However, the exposed behavior is useful when constructing customized user interfaces. To illustrate, consider the fact that unlike Windows Forms, the initial release of WPF does not supply a spin button control, which allows the user to adjust a numerical value using up and down arrows. Composing a spin button widget can be done quite simply in XAML given the functionality of RepeatButton.

To illustrate, create a new Visual Studio WPF Application project named CustomSpinButtonApp. Replace the initial <Grid> definition with a <StackPanel> containing the following markup:

```
<Window x:Class="MainWindow"
  xmlns="http://schemas.microsoft.com/winfx/2006/xaml/presentation"
  xmlns:x="http://schemas.microsoft.com/winfx/2006/xaml"
  Title="CustomSpinButtonApp" Height="300" Width="300">
  <StackPanel>
    <!-- The "Up" button -->
    <RepeatButton Height ="25" Width = "25" Name ="repeatAddValueButton"
      Delay ="200" Interval ="1" Click ="repeatAddValueButton_Click"
      Content = "+"/>

    <!-- Displays the current value -->
    <Label Name ="lblCurrentValue" Background ="LightGray"
           Height ="30" Width = "25" VerticalContentAlignment="Center"
           HorizontalContentAlignment="Center" FontSize="15"/>

    <!-- The "Down" button -->
    <RepeatButton Height ="25" Width = "25" Name ="repeatRemoveValueButton"
      Delay ="200" Interval ="1"
      Click ="repeatRemoveValueButton_Click" Content = "-"/>
  </StackPanel>
</Window>
```

Notice how each RepeatButton type handles the Click event with a unique event handler. With this, we can author the following VB logic to increase or decrease the value displayed within the <Label> (feel free to add extra logic to trap maximum and minimum values if you so choose):

```
Class MainWindow
  Private currValue As Integer = 0

  Public Sub New()
    InitializeComponent()
    lblCurrentValue.Content = currValue
  End Sub

  Protected Sub repeatAddValueButton_Click(ByVal sender As Object, _
    ByVal e As RoutedEventArgs)
    ' Add 1 to the current value and show in label.
    currValue += 1
    lblCurrentValue.Content = currValue
  End Sub
```

```
  Protected Sub repeatRemoveValueButton_Click(ByVal sender As Object, _
    ByVal e As RoutedEventArgs)
    ' Subtract 1 from the current value and show in label.
    currValue -= 1
    lblCurrentValue.Content = currValue
  End Sub
End Class
```

As you can see, when the user clicks either RepeatButton, we increment or decrement the private currValue accordingly, and set the Content property of the Label type. Figure 31-6 shows our custom spin button UI in action.

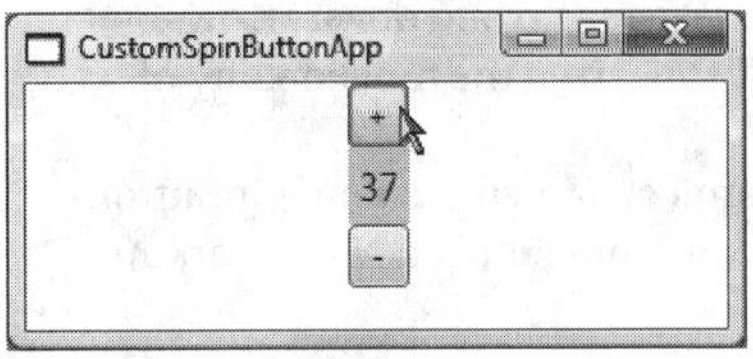

Figure 31-6. *Building a spin button using* RepeatButton *as a starting point*

■ **Source Code** The CustomSpinButtonApp project is included under the Chapter 31 subdirectory.

Working with CheckBoxes and RadioButtons

As mentioned previously, CheckBox "is-a" ToggleButton, which "is-a" ButtonBase, which may seem very odd given that the UI of a button looks very different from that of a check box. However, a CheckBox type, like a Button, can be clicked, responds to mouse and keyboard input, and follows the WPF content model. Given all of these similarities, it turns out that the CheckBox type simply overrides various virtual members of ToggleButton to establish a check box look and feel (recall that a major motivator of WPF is to decouple the display of a control from its functionality). Consider the following <CheckBox> declarations, which yield the output shown in Figure 31-7:

```
<StackPanel>
  <!-- CheckBox types -->
  <CheckBox Name ="checkInfo" >Send me more information</CheckBox>
  <CheckBox Name ="checkPhoneContact" >Contact me over the phone</CheckBox>
</StackPanel>
```

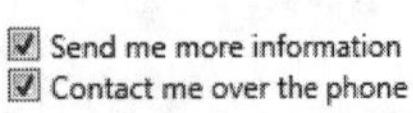

Figure 31-7. *Simple* CheckBox *types*

RadioButton is another type that "is-a" ToggleButton. Unlike the CheckBox type, however, it has the innate ability to ensure all RadioButtons in the same container (such as a StackPanel, Grid, or whatnot) are mutually exclusive without any additional work on your part. Consider the following:

```
<StackPanel>
  <!-- RadioButton types for music selection -->
  <Label FontSize = "15" Content = "Select Your Music Media"/>
  <RadioButton>CD Player</RadioButton>
  <RadioButton>MP3 Player</RadioButton>
  <RadioButton>8-Track</RadioButton>

  <!-- RadioButton types for color selection -->
  <Label FontSize = "15" Content = "Select Your Color Choice"/>
  <RadioButton>Red</RadioButton>
  <RadioButton>Green</RadioButton>
  <RadioButton>Blue</RadioButton>
</StackPanel>
```

If you were to test this XAML, you would find that you can select only one of the six options, which is probably not what is intended, as there seem to be two separate groups within the mix (radio options and color options).

Establishing Logical Groupings

When you wish to have a single container with multiple RadioButton instances, which behave as distinct physical groupings, you can do so by setting the GroupName property in the <RadioButton> start tag:

```
<StackPanel>
  <!-- The Music group  -->
  <Label FontSize = "15" Content = "Select Your Music Media"/>
  <RadioButton GroupName = "Music" >CD Player</RadioButton>
  <RadioButton GroupName = "Music" >MP3 Player</RadioButton>
  <RadioButton GroupName = "Music" >8-Track</RadioButton>

  <!-- The Color group (optional for this example, see Note that follows) -->
  <Label FontSize = "15" Content = "Select Your Color Choice"/>
  <RadioButton GroupName = "Color">Red</RadioButton>
  <RadioButton GroupName = "Color">Green</RadioButton>
  <RadioButton GroupName = "Color">Blue</RadioButton>
</StackPanel>
```

With this, we will now be able to set each logical grouping independently, even though they are in the same physical container.

■ **Note** By default, all RadioButton instances in a container that do not have a GroupName value work as a single physical group. Therefore, in the previous example, the color-centric buttons would have been mutually exclusive, even with the GroupName omitted, given the presence of the Music group.

Framing Related Elements in GroupBoxes

When you design a collection of radio buttons or check boxes, it is common to surround them with a visual container to denote that they behave as a group. The most common way to do so is using a GroupBox control. As the Header property of a GroupBox is prototyped to operate on a System.Object, you are able to assign any object to function as the header (a simple string, a colored rectangle, a button, etc.). Consider the following two GroupBox declarations, which frame the previous RadioButtons in various manners:

```
<StackPanel>
  <GroupBox Header = "Select Your Music Media" BorderBrush ="Black">
    <StackPanel>
      <RadioButton GroupName = "Music" >CD Player</RadioButton>
      <RadioButton GroupName = "Music" >MP3 Player</RadioButton>
      <RadioButton GroupName = "Music" >8-Track</RadioButton>
    </StackPanel>
  </GroupBox>

  <GroupBox BorderBrush ="Black">
    <GroupBox.Header>
      <Label Background = "Blue" Foreground = "White"
             FontSize = "15" Content = "Select your color choice"/>
    </GroupBox.Header>
    <StackPanel>
      <RadioButton>Red</RadioButton>
      <RadioButton>Green</RadioButton>
      <RadioButton>Blue</RadioButton>
    </StackPanel>
  </GroupBox>
</StackPanel>
```

The output can be seen in Figure 31-8.

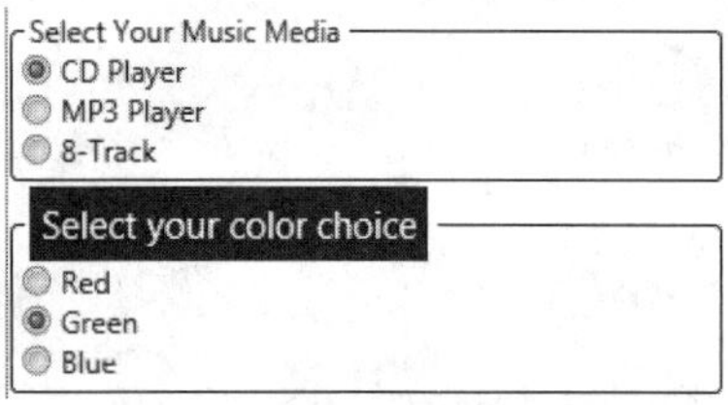

Figure 31-8. GroupBox *types framing* RadioButton *types*

Framing Related Elements in Expanders

In addition to the customary group box, WPF ships with a new UI element that can group a collection of UI elements that can be hidden or shown via a toggle. This element, the Expander type, allows you to define the direction elements will be displayed (up, down, left, or right) using the ExpandDirection property. Consider the following XAML (which basically just changes <GroupBox> to <Expander>):

```
<StackPanel>
  <Expander Header = "Select Your Music Media" BorderBrush ="Black">
    <StackPanel>
      <RadioButton GroupName = "Music" >CD Player</RadioButton>
      <RadioButton GroupName = "Music" >MP3 Player</RadioButton>
      <RadioButton GroupName = "Music" >8-Track</RadioButton>
    </StackPanel>
  </Expander>

  <Expander BorderBrush ="Black">
    <Expander.Header>
      <Label Background = "Blue" Foreground = "White"
             FontSize = "15" Content = "Select your color choice"/>
```

```
      </Expander.Header>
      <StackPanel>
        <RadioButton>Red</RadioButton>
        <RadioButton>Green</RadioButton>
        <RadioButton>Blue</RadioButton>
      </StackPanel>
    </Expander>
  </StackPanel>
```

Figure 31-9 shows each Expander in the collapsed state.

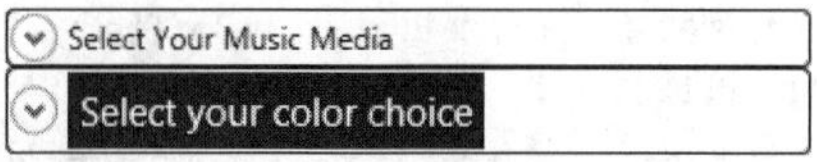

Figure 31-9. *Collapsed* Expanders

Figure 31-10 shows each Expander (pardon the redundancy) expanded.

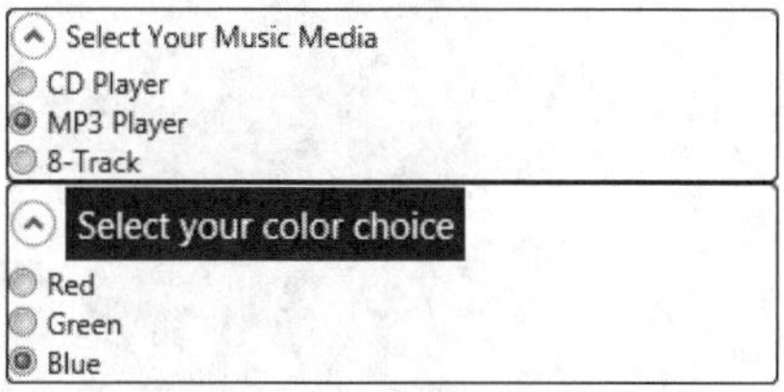

Figure 31-10. *Expanded* Expanders

■ **Source Code** The CheckRadioGroup.xaml file is included under the Chapter 31 subdirectory.

Working with the ListBox and ComboBox Types

As you would hope, WPF provides types that contain a group of selectable items, such as ListBox and ComboBox, both of which derive from the ItemsControl abstract base class. Most importantly, this parent class defines a property named Items, which returns a strongly typed ItemCollection object that holds onto the subitems. As it turns out, the ItemCollection type has been constructed to operate on System.Object types, and therefore it can contain anything whatsoever. If you wish to fill an ItemsControl-derived type with simply textual data via markup, you can do so using a set of <ListBoxItem> types. For example, consider the following XAML:

```
<!-- Simple list box -->
<ListBox Name = "lstVideoGameConsoles">
  <ListBoxItem>Microsoft XBox 360</ListBoxItem>
  <ListBoxItem>Sony Playstation 3</ListBoxItem>
  <ListBoxItem>Nintendo Wii</ListBoxItem>
  <ListBoxItem>Sony PSP</ListBoxItem>
  <ListBoxItem>Nintendo DS</ListBoxItem>
</ListBox>
```

```
<!-- Simple combo box -->
<ComboBox Name = "comboVideoGameConsoles">
  <ListBoxItem>Microsoft XBox 360</ListBoxItem>
  <ListBoxItem>Sony Playstation 3</ListBoxItem>
  <ListBoxItem>Nintendo Wii</ListBoxItem>
  <ListBoxItem>Sony PSP</ListBoxItem>
  <ListBoxItem>Nintendo DS</ListBoxItem>
</ComboBox>
```

Note ComboBox types can also be populated using <ComboBoxItem> elements, rather than <ListBoxItem>. By doing so, you gain access to the IsHighlighted property, which is not used by the ListBoxItem type.

Not surprisingly, we find the rendering shown in Figure 31-11.

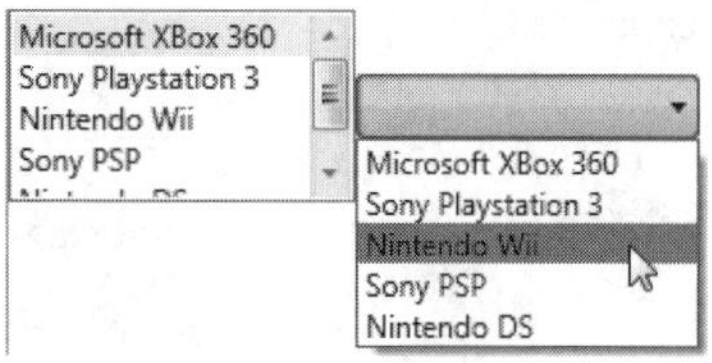

Figure 31-11. *A simple* ListBox *and* ComboBox

Filling List Controls Programmatically

Oftentimes, the data contained within a list control is not known until runtime; for example, you may need to fill items in a list box based on values returned from a database read, invoking a WCF service or reading an external file. When you need to populate a ListBox or ComboBox control programmatically, simply use the members of the ItemCollection type to do so (Add(), Remove(), etc.). Assume you have a new Visual Studio 2008 WPF Application project named ListControls. The previous XAML declaration of the lstVideoGameConsole type could be defined in XAML as follows:

```
<Window x:Class="MainWindow"
  xmlns="http://schemas.microsoft.com/winfx/2006/xaml/presentation"
  xmlns:x="http://schemas.microsoft.com/winfx/2006/xaml"
  Title="ListControls" Height="300" Width="300" >
  <StackPanel>
    <!-- This is filled via code -->
    <ListBox Name = "lstVideoGameConsoles">
    </ListBox>
  </StackPanel>
</Window>
```

and populated in a related code file as follows:

```
Class MainWindow

  Public Sub New()
    InitializeComponent()
    FillListBox()
  End Sub
```

```
  Private Sub FillListBox()
    ' Add items to the list box.
    lstVideoGameConsoles.Items.Add("Microsoft XBox 360")
    lstVideoGameConsoles.Items.Add("Sony Playstation 3")
    lstVideoGameConsoles.Items.Add("Nintendo Wii")
    lstVideoGameConsoles.Items.Add("Sony PSP")
    lstVideoGameConsoles.Items.Add("Nintendo DS")
  End Sub
End Class
```

One thing that might strike you as odd is that in the XAML description of the `ListBox`, we made use of `<ListBoxItem>` types to populate the items; however, here we have made use of `String` objects when calling the `Add()` method. The short explanation is that when using XAML, `<ListBoxItem>` types are more convenient in that they are defined within the `http://schemas.microsoft.com/winfx/2006/xaml/presentation` XML namespace, and therefore we have a direct reference to them.

Under the hood, `ToString()` is called on each `<ListBoxItem>` type, so the end result is identical. If you truly wanted to use a `System.String` to fill the `ListBox` (or `ComboBox`) type in XAML, you would need to define a new XML namespace to bring in `mscorlib.dll` (see Chapter 30 for more details):

```
<StackPanel xmlns:CorLib = "clr-namespace:System;assembly=mscorlib">
  <ListBox Name = "lstVideoGameConsoles">
    <CorLib:String>Microsoft XBox 360</CorLib:String>
    <CorLib:String>Sony Playstation 3</CorLib:String>
    <CorLib:String>Nintendo Wii</CorLib:String>
    <CorLib:String>Sony PSP</CorLib:String>
    <CorLib:String>Nintendo DS</CorLib:String>
  </ListBox>
</StackPanel>
```

Conversely, if you really wanted to, you could programmatically populate an `ItemsControl`-derived type using strongly typed `ListBoxItem` objects; however, you really gain nothing for the current example and have in fact created additional work for yourself (as the `ListBoxItem` does not have a constructor to set the `Content` property!).

Adding Arbitrary Content

Because `ListBox` and `ComboBox` both have `ContentControl` in their inheritance chain, they can contain data well beyond a simple string. Consider the following `ListBox`, which contains various `<StackPanel>` elements containing 2D graphical objects and a descriptive label:

```
<StackPanel>
  <!-- A ListBox with content! -->
  <ListBox Name = "lstColors">
    <StackPanel Orientation ="Horizontal">
      <Ellipse Fill ="Yellow" Height ="50" Width ="50"/>
      <Label FontSize ="20" HorizontalAlignment="Center"
             VerticalAlignment="Center">Yellow</Label>
    </StackPanel>
    <StackPanel Orientation ="Horizontal">
      <Ellipse Fill ="Blue" Height ="50" Width ="50"/>
      <Label FontSize ="20" HorizontalAlignment="Center"
             VerticalAlignment="Center">Blue</Label>
    </StackPanel>
    <StackPanel Orientation ="Horizontal">
      <Ellipse Fill ="Green" Height ="50" Width ="50"/>
      <Label FontSize ="20" HorizontalAlignment="Center"
             VerticalAlignment="Center">Green</Label>
```

```
    </StackPanel>
  </ListBox>
</StackPanel>
```

Figure 31-12 shows the output of our current list elements.

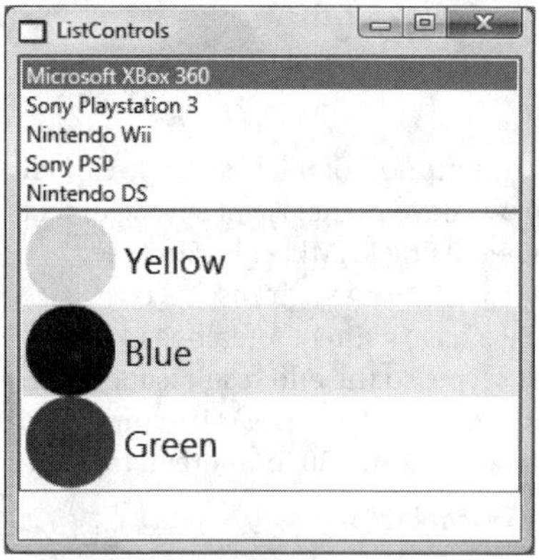

Figure 31-12. `ItemsControl`*-derived types can contain any sort of content you desire.*

Determining the Current Selection

Once you have populated a `ListBox` or `ComboBox` instance, the next obvious issue is how to determine at runtime which item the user has selected. As it turns out, you have three ways to do so. If you are interested in finding the numerical index of the item selected, you can use the `SelectedIndex` property (which is zero based; a value of `-1` represents no selection). If you wish to obtain the object within the list that has been selected, the `SelectedItem` property fits the bill. Finally, the `SelectedValue` allows you to obtain the value of the selected object (typically obtained via a call to `ToString()`).

Sounds simple enough, right? Well, to test how each property behaves, assume you have defined two new `Button` types for the current window, both of which handle the `Click` event:

```
<!-- Buttons to get the selected items -->
<Button Name ="btnGetGameSystem" Click ="btnGetGameSystem_Click">
  Get Video Game System
</Button>
<Button Name ="btnGetColor" Click ="btnGetColor_Click">
  Get Color
</Button>
```

The `Click` handler for `btnGetGameSystem` will obtain the values of the `SelectedIndex`, `SelectedItem`, and `SelectedValue` properties of the `lstVideoGameConsoles` object and display them in a message box:

```
Private Sub btnGetGameSystem_Click(ByVal sender As System.Object, _
  ByVal e As System.Windows.RoutedEventArgs)
    Dim data As String = String.Empty

    data &= String.Format("SelectedIndex = {0}" & vbLf, _
      lstVideoGameConsoles.SelectedIndex)
```

```
    data &= String.Format("SelectedItem = {0}" & vbLf, _
      lstVideoGameConsoles.SelectedItem)

    data &= String.Format("SelectedValue = {0}" & vbLf, _
      lstVideoGameConsoles.SelectedValue)

    MessageBox.Show(data, "Your Game Info")
  End Sub
```

If you were to select Nintendo Wii from the list of game consoles by clicking the related button, you would find the message box shown in Figure 31-13, which is self-explanatory.

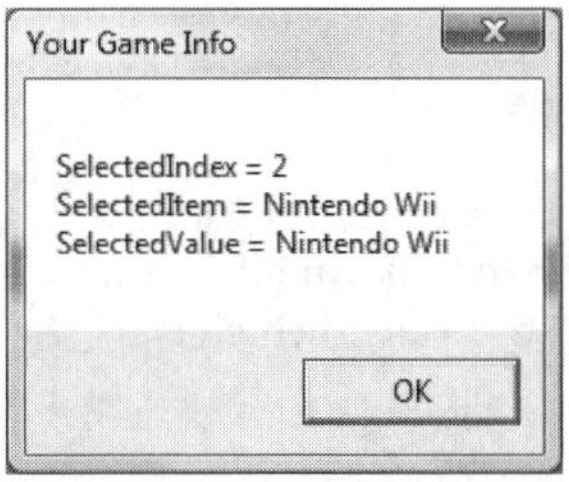

Figure 31-13. *Finding a selected string*

However, what about obtaining the selected color?

Determining the Current Selection for Nested Content

Assume the `Click` event handler for the `btnGetColor` `Button` has implemented `btnGetColor_Click()` to print out the current selection, index, and value of the `lstColors` `ListBox` object. Now, if you were to select the first item in the `lstColors` list box (and click the related button), you may be surprised to find the output shown in Figure 31-14.

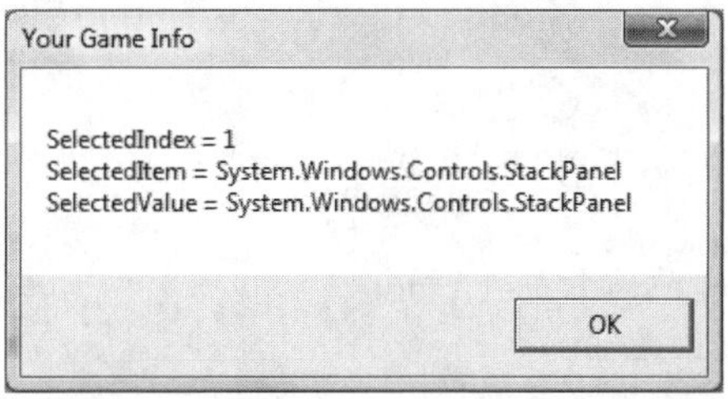

Figure 31-14. *Finding a selected . . .* `StackPanel`*?*

The reason for this output is the fact that the `lstColors` object is maintaining three `StackPanel` objects, each of which contains nested content. Therefore, `SelectedItem` and `SelectedValue` are simply calling `ToString()` on the `StackPanel` instance, which returns its fully qualified name.

While you would be able to simply figure out which item was selected using the numerical value returned from `SelectedIndex`, another approach is to drill into the `StackPanel`'s child collection to grab the `Content` value of the `Label` using the `StackPanel`'s internally maintained `Children` collection as follows:

```
Private Sub btnGetColor_Click(ByVal sender As System.Object, _
  ByVal e As System.Windows.RoutedEventArgs)

  ' Get the Content value in the selected Label in the StackPanel.
  Dim selectedStack As StackPanel = _
    DirectCast(lstColors.Items(lstColors.SelectedIndex), StackPanel)
  Dim color As String = DirectCast((selectedStack.Children(1)), _
    Label).Content.ToString()

  Dim data As String = String.Empty
  data &= String.Format("SelectedIndex = {0}" & vbLf, lstColors.SelectedIndex)
  data &= String.Format("Color = {0}", color)

  MessageBox.Show(data, "Your Game Info")
End Sub
```

While this does the trick, this solution is very fragile in that we have hard-coded positions within the StackPanel (the second child, being the Label) and are required to perform numerous casting operations. Another alternative is to set the Tag property of each StackPanel, which is defined in the FrameworkElement base class:

```
<ListBox Name = "lstColors">
  <StackPanel Orientation ="Horizontal" Tag ="Yellow">
...
  </StackPanel>
  <StackPanel Orientation ="Horizontal" Tag ="Blue">
...
  </StackPanel>
  <StackPanel Orientation ="Horizontal" Tag ="Green">
...
  </StackPanel>
</ListBox>
```

Using this approach, our code cleans up considerably, as we can pluck out the value assigned to Tag programmatically as follows:

```
Protected Sub btnGetColor_Click(ByVal sender As Object, _
  ByVal args As RoutedEventArgs)
  Dim data As String = String.Empty
  data &= String.Format("SelectedIndex = {0}" & vbLf, lstColors.SelectedIndex)
  data &= String.Format("SelectedItem = {0}" & vbLf, lstColors.SelectedItem)
  data &= String.Format("SelectedValue = {0}", _
    TryCast(lstColors.Items(lstColors.SelectedIndex), StackPanel).Tag)
  MessageBox.Show(data, "Your Color Info")
End Sub
```

While this approach is a bit cleaner than our first attempt, there are other manners in which you can capture values from a complex control using *data templates*. To do so requires an understanding of the WPF data binding engine, which you will examine at the conclusion of this chapter in the section "Understanding the WPF Data Binding Model."

Source Code The ListControls project is included under the Chapter 31 subdirectory.

Working with Text Areas

WPF ships with a number of UI elements that allow you to gather textual-based user input. The most primitive types would be TextBox and PasswordBox, which we will examine here using a new Visual Studio 2008 WPF Application project named TextControls.

Working with the TextBox Type

Like other TextBox types you have used in the past, the WPF TextBox type can be configured to hold a single line of text (the default setting) or multiple lines of text if the AcceptReturn property is set to True. Information within a TextBox will always be treated as character data, and therefore the "content" is always a String type that can be set and retrieved using the Text property:

```
<TextBox Name ="txtData" Text = "Hello!" BorderBrush ="Blue" Width ="100"/>
```

One aspect of the WPF TextBox type that is very unique is that it has the built-in ability to check the spelling of the data entered within it by setting the SpellCheck.IsEnabled property to True. When you do so, you will notice that like Microsoft Office, misspelled words are underlined in a red squiggle. Even better, there is an underlying programming model that gives you access to the spell checker engine, which allows you to get a list of suggestions for misspelled words.

Update your current window XAML definition to make use of a Label, TextBox, and Button as follows (notice this TextBox supports multiple lines of text and has enabled spell checking):

```
<Window x:Class="MainWindow"
    xmlns="http://schemas.microsoft.com/winfx/2006/xaml/presentation"
    xmlns:x="http://schemas.microsoft.com/winfx/2006/xaml"
    Title="TextControls" Height="204" Width="292" >

  <StackPanel>
    <Label FontSize ="15">Is this word spelled correctly?</Label>
    <TextBox SpellCheck.IsEnabled ="True" AcceptsReturn ="True"
      Name ="txtData"  FontSize ="12"
      BorderBrush ="Blue" Height ="100">
    </TextBox>
    <Button Name ="btnOK" Content ="Get Selections"
            Width = "100" Click ="btnOK_Click"/>
  </StackPanel>

</Window>
```

With just this much functionality, you will already notice that when you type misspelled words into your TextBox, errors are marked as such. To complete our simple spell checker, implement the Click event handler for the Button as follows:

```
Private Sub btnOK_Click(ByVal sender As System.Object, _
  ByVal e As System.Windows.RoutedEventArgs)
  Dim spellingHints As String = String.Empty

  ' Try to get a spelling error at the current caret location.
  Dim err As SpellingError = txtData.GetSpellingError(txtData.CaretIndex)
  If err IsNot Nothing Then
    ' Build a string of spelling suggestions.
    For Each s As String In err.Suggestions
      spellingHints &= s & vbLf
    Next
```

```
    ' Show suggestions.
    MessageBox.Show(spellingHints, "Try these instead")
  End If
End Sub
```

The code is quite simple. We simply figure the current location of the caret in the text box using the CaretIndex property in order to extract a SpellingError object. If there is an error at said location (meaning the value is not Nothing), we loop over the list of suggestions via the aptly named Suggestions property. Finally, we display the possibilities using a simple MessageBox.Show() request. Figure 31-15 shows a possible test run when the caret is within the misspelled word "auromatically."

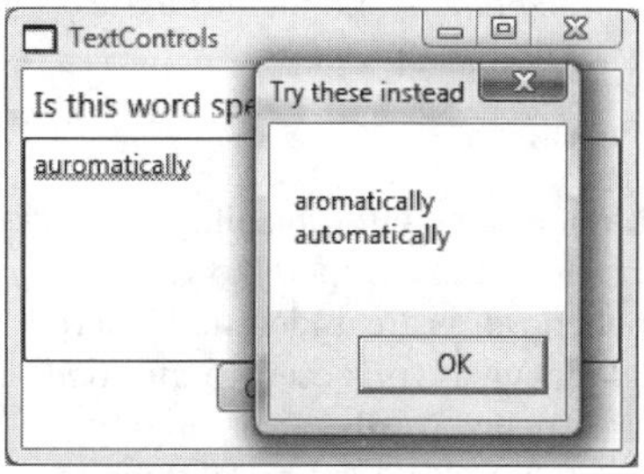

Figure 31-15. *A custom spell checker!*

Working with the PasswordBox Type

The PasswordBox type, not surprisingly, allows you to define a safe place to enter sensitive text data. By default, the password character is a circle type; however, this can be changed using the PasswordChar property. To obtain the value entered by the end user, simply check the Password property. Let's update our current spell checking application by requiring the correct password to see the list of spelling suggestions. First, update your existing <StackPanel> with a nested <StackPanel> that places the PasswordBox horizontally alongside the existing <Button>:

```
<StackPanel>
  <Label FontSize ="15">Is this word spelled correctly?</Label>
  <TextBox SpellCheck.IsEnabled ="True" AcceptsReturn ="True"
           Name ="txtData"  FontSize ="14"
           BorderBrush ="Blue" Height ="100">
  </TextBox>
  <StackPanel Orientation ="Horizontal">
    <PasswordBox Name ="pwdText" BorderBrush ="Black" Width ="100"></PasswordBox>
    <Button Name ="btnOK" Content ="Get Selections"
            Width = "100" Click ="btnOK_Click"/>
  </StackPanel>
</StackPanel>
```

Now update your current Button Click event handler to make a call to a helper function named CheckPassword(), which tests against a hard-coded string. Be sure to only allow the suggestions to be presented if the check is successful. Here are the relevant updates:

```
Class MainWindow

  Private Sub btnOK_Click(ByVal sender As System.Object, _
    ByVal e As System.Windows.RoutedEventArgs)
```

```
    If CheckPassword() Then
      ' Same spell checking logic as before...
      ...
    Else
      MessageBox.Show("Security error!!")
    End If
  End Sub

  Private Function CheckPassword() As Boolean
    If pwdText.Password = "Chucky" Then
      Return True
    Else
      Return False
    End If
  End Function
End Class
```

Beyond TextBox and PasswordBox, do be aware that if you are building an application that has a text area that can contain any type of content (graphical renderings, text, etc.), WPF also provides the RichTextBox. Furthermore, if you require the horsepower to build an extremely text-intensive application, WPF provides an entire document presentation API represented primarily within the System.Windows.Documents namespace.

Here you will find types that allow you to build *flow documents,* which allow you to programmatically represent (in XAML or VB code) paragraphs, sections of related text blocks, sticky notes, annotations, tables, and other rich document-centric types. This edition of the text does not cover the RichTextBox or the flow document API, however; be sure to consult the .NET Framework 3.5 SDK documentation for further details if you are so inclined.

■ **Source Code** The TextControls project is included under the Chapter 31 subdirectory.

That wraps up our initial look at the WPF control set. You'll see how to build menu systems, status bars, and toolbars throughout this chapter. The next task, however, is to learn how to arrange UI elements within a Window type using any number of panel types.

Controlling Content Layout Using Panels

A real-world WPF application invariability contains a good number of UI elements (user input controls, graphical content, menu systems, status bars, etc.) that need to be well organized within the containing window. As well, once the UI widgets have been placed in their new home, you will want to make sure they behave as intended when the end user resizes the window or possibly a portion of the window (as in the case of a splitter window). To ensure your WPF controls retain their position within the hosting window, we are provided with a good number of *panel* types.

As you may recall from the previous chapter, when you place content within a window that does not make use of panels, it is positioned dead center within the container. Consider the following simple window declaration containing a single Button. Regardless of how you resize the window, the UI widget is always equidistant on all four sides of the client area.

```
<!-- This button is in the center of the window at all times -->
<Window x:Class="MainWindow"
  xmlns="http://schemas.microsoft.com/winfx/2006/xaml/presentation"
  xmlns:x="http://schemas.microsoft.com/winfx/2006/xaml"
```

```
  Title="Fun with Panels!" Height="285" Width="325">
  <Button Name="btnOK" Height = "100" Width="80">OK</Button>
</Window>
```

Also recall that if you attempt to place multiple elements directly within the scope of a `<Window>`, you will receive markup and/or compile-time errors. The reason for these errors is that a window (or any descendant of `ContentControl` for that matter) can assign only a single object to its `Content` property:

```
<!-- Error! Content property is implicitly set more than once! -->
<Window x:Class="MainWindow"
  xmlns="http://schemas.microsoft.com/winfx/2006/xaml/presentation"
  xmlns:x="http://schemas.microsoft.com/winfx/2006/xaml"
  Title="Fun with Panels!" Height="285" Width="325">

  <!-- Ack! Two direct child elements of the <Window>! -->
  <Label Name="lblInstructions"
    Width="328" Height="27" FontSize="15">Enter Car Information</Label>
  <Button Name="btnOK" Height = "100" Width="80">OK</Button>
</Window>
```

Obviously a window that can contain only a single item is of little use. When a window needs to contain multiple elements, they must be arranged within any number of panels. The panel will contain all of the UI elements that represent the window, after which the panel itself is used as the object assigned to the `Content` property.

The Core Panel Types of WPF

The `System.Windows.Controls` namespace provides numerous panel types, each of which controls how subelements are positioned. Using panels, you can establish how the widgets behave when the end user resizes the window, whether they remain exactly where placed at design time, whether they reflow horizontally left to right or vertically top to bottom, and so forth.

To build complex user interfaces, panel controls can be intermixed (e.g., a `DockPanel` that contains a `StackPanel`) to provide for a great deal of flexibility and control. Furthermore, the panel types can work in conjunction with other document-centric controls (such as the `ViewBox`, `TextBlock`, `TextFlow`, and `Paragraph` types) to further customize how content is arranged within a given panel. Table 31-3 documents the role of some commonly used WPF panel controls.

Table 31-3. *Core WPF Panel Controls*

Panel Control	Meaning in Life
`Canvas`	Provides a "classic" mode of content placement. Items stay exactly where you put them at design time.
`DockPanel`	Locks content to a specified side of the panel (`Top`, `Bottom`, `Left`, or `Right`).
`Grid`	Arranges content within a series of cells, maintained within a tabular grid.
`StackPanel`	Stacks content in a vertical or horizontal manner, as dictated by the `Orientation` property.
`WrapPanel`	Positions content from left to right, breaking the content to the next line at the edge of the containing box. Subsequent ordering happens sequentially from top to bottom or from right to left, depending on the value of the `Orientation` property.

To illustrate the use of these commonly used panel types, in the next sections we'll build the UI shown in Figure 31-16 within various panels and observe how the positioning changes when the window is resized.

Figure 31-16. *Our target UI layout*

Positioning Content Within Canvas Panels

Far and away, the simplest panel is Canvas. Most likely, Canvas is the panel you will feel most at home with, as it emulates the default layout of a Windows Forms application. Simply put, a Canvas panel allows for absolute positioning of UI content. If the end user resizes the window to an area that is smaller than the layout maintained by the Canvas panel, the internal content will not be visible until the container is stretched to a size equal to or larger than the Canvas area.

To add content to a Canvas, define the required subelements within the scope of the opening <Canvas> and closing </Canvas> tags and specify the location where rendering should occur (note that the content position can be relative to the left/right or top/bottom of the Canvas, but not both). If you wish to have the Canvas stretch over the entire surface of the container, simply omit the Height and Width properties. Consider the following XAML markup, which defines the layout shown in Figure 31-16:

```
<Window
  xmlns="http://schemas.microsoft.com/winfx/2006/xaml/presentation"
  xmlns:x="http://schemas.microsoft.com/winfx/2006/xaml"
  Title="Fun with Panels!" Height="285" Width="325">

  <Canvas Background="LightSteelBlue">
    <Button Canvas.Left="212" Canvas.Top="203" Name="btnOK" Width="80">OK</Button>
    <Label Canvas.Left="17" Canvas.Top="14" Name="lblInstructions"
           Width="328" Height="27" FontSize="15">Enter Car Information</Label>
    <Label Canvas.Left="17" Canvas.Top="60" Name="lblMake">Make</Label>
    <TextBox Canvas.Left="94" Canvas.Top="60" Name="txtMake"
             Width="193" Height="25"/>
    <Label Canvas.Left="17" Canvas.Top="109" Name="lblColor">Color</Label>
    <TextBox Canvas.Left="94" Canvas.Top="107" Name="txtColor"
             Width="193" Height="25"/>
    <Label Canvas.Left="17" Canvas.Top="155" Name="lblPetName">Pet Name</Label>
    <TextBox Canvas.Left="94" Canvas.Top="153" Name="txtPetName"
             Width="193" Height="25"/>
  </Canvas>

</Window>
```

In this example, each item within the <Canvas> scope is qualified by a Canvas.Left and Canvas.Top value, which control the content's top-left positioning within the panel, using attached property syntax (see Chapter 30). As you may have gathered, vertical positioning is controlled using the Top or Bottom property, while horizontal positioning is established using Left or Right.

Given that each widget has been placed within the <Canvas> element, we find that as the window is resized, widgets are covered up if the container's surface area is smaller than the content (see Figure 31-17).

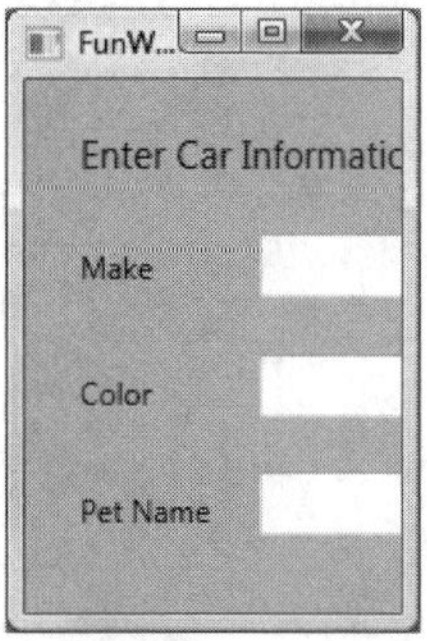

Figure 31-17. *Content in a* Canvas *panel allows for absolute positioning.*

The order you declare content within a Canvas is not used to calculate placement, as this is based on the control's size and the Canvas.Top, Canvas.Bottom, Canvas.Left, and Canvas.Right properties. Given this, the following markup (which groups together like-minded controls) results in an identical rendering:

```
<Canvas Background="LightSteelBlue">
  <TextBox Canvas.Left="94" Canvas.Top="153" Name="txtColor"
           Width="193" Height="25"/>
  <TextBox Canvas.Left="94" Canvas.Top="60" Name="txtPetName"
           Width="193" Height="25"/>
  <TextBox Canvas.Left="94" Canvas.Top="107" Name="txtMake"
           Width="193" Height="25"/>

  <Label Canvas.Left="17" Canvas.Top="14" Name="lblInstructions"
   Width="328" Height="27" FontSize="15">Enter Car Information</Label>
  <Label Canvas.Left="17" Canvas.Top="109" Name="lblColor">Color</Label>
  <Label Canvas.Left="17" Canvas.Top="155" Name="lblMake">Pet Name</Label>
  <Label Canvas.Left="17" Canvas.Top="60" Name="lblPetName">Make</Label>

  <Button Canvas.Left="212" Canvas.Top="203" Name="btnOK" Width="80">OK</Button>
</Canvas>
```

■ **Note** If subelements within a Canvas do not define a specific location using attached property syntax, they automatically attach to the extreme upper-left corner of the Canvas.

Although using the Canvas type may seem like a preferable way to arrange content (because it feels so familiar), it does suffer from some limitations. First of all, items within a Canvas do not dynamically resize themselves when applying styles or templates (e.g., their font sizes are unaffected). The other obvious limitation is that the Canvas will not attempt to keep elements visible when the end user resizes the window to a smaller surface.

Perhaps the best use of the Canvas type is to position graphical content. For example, if you were building a custom image using XAML, you certainly would want the lines, shapes, and text to remain in the same location, rather than having them dynamically repositioned as the user resizes the window! You'll revisit the Canvas in the next chapter when we examine WPF's graphical rendering services.

Source Code The SimpleCanvas.xaml file can be found under the Chapter 31 subdirectory.

Positioning Content Within WrapPanel Panels

A WrapPanel allows you to define content that will flow across the panel as the window is resized. When positioning elements in a WrapPanel, you do not specify top, bottom, left, and right docking values as you typically do with the Canvas. However, each subelement is free to define a Height and Width value (among other property values) to control its overall size in the container.

Because content within a WrapPanel does not "dock" to a given side of the panel, the order in which you declare the elements is critical (content is rendered sequentially from the first element to the last). Consider the following XAML snippet:

```
<WrapPanel Background="LightSteelBlue">
  <Label Name="lblInstruction" Width="328"
        Height="27" FontSize="15">Enter Car Information</Label>
  <Label Name="lblMake">Make</Label>
  <TextBox Name="txtMake" Width="193" Height="25"/>
  <Label Name="lblColor">Color</Label>
  <TextBox Name="txtColor" Width="193" Height="25"/>
  <Label Name="lblPetName">Pet Name</Label>
  <TextBox Name="txtPetName" Width="193" Height="25"/>
  <Button Name="btnOK" Width="80">OK</Button>
</WrapPanel>
```

When you view this markup, the content will look out of sorts as you resize the width, as it is flowing left to right across the window (see Figure 31-18).

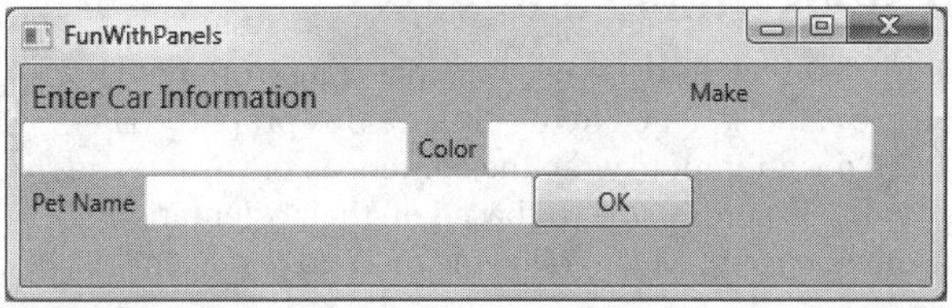

Figure 31-18. *Content in a* WrapPanel *behaves much like a vanilla-flavored HTML page.*

By default, content within a WrapPanel flows left to right. However, if you change the value of the Orientation property to Vertical, you can have content wrap in a top-to-bottom manner:

```
<WrapPanel Background="LightSteelBlue" Orientation ="Vertical">
```

A WrapPanel (as well as some other panel types) may be declared by specifying ItemWidth and ItemHeight values, which control the default size of each item. If a subelement does provide its own Height and/or Width value, it will be positioned relative to the size established by the panel. Consider the following markup:

```
<WrapPanel Background="LightSteelBlue" ItemWidth ="200" ItemHeight ="30">
  <Label Name="lblInstruction"
        FontSize="15">Enter Car Information</Label>
  <Label Name="lblMake">Make</Label>
  <TextBox Name="txtMake"/>
  <Label Name="lblColor">Color</Label>
  <TextBox Name="txtColor"/>
  <Label Name="lblPetName">Pet Name</Label>
  <TextBox Name="txtPetName"/>
  <Button Name="btnOK" Width ="80">OK</Button>
</WrapPanel>
```

When rendered, we find the output shown in Figure 31-19 (notice the size and position of the Button widget).

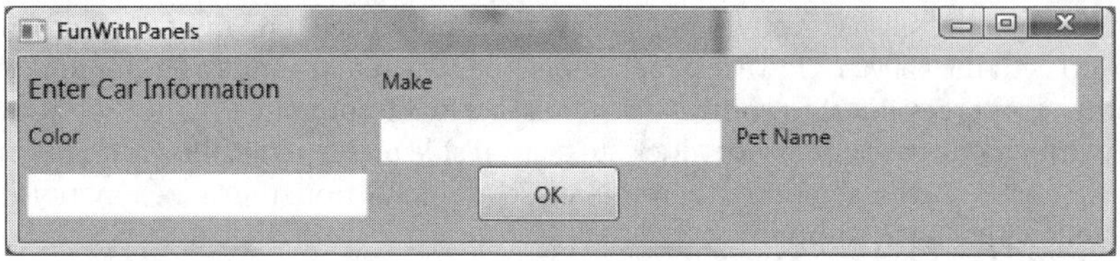

Figure 31-19. *A* WrapPanel *can establish the width and height of a given item.*

As you might agree after looking at Figure 31-19, a WrapPanel is not typically the best choice for arranging content directly in a window, as the elements can become scrambled as the user resizes the window. In most cases, a WrapPanel will be a subelement to another panel type, to allow a small area of the window to wrap its content when resized.

Source Code The SimpleWrapPanel.xaml file can be found under the Chapter 31 subdirectory.

Positioning Content Within StackPanel Panels

Like a WrapPanel, a StackPanel control arranges content into a single line that can be oriented horizontally or vertically (the default), based on the value assigned to the Orientation property. The difference, however, is that the StackPanel will *not* attempt to wrap the content as the user resizes the window. Rather, the items in the StackPanel will simply stretch (based on their orientation) to accommodate the size of the StackPanel itself. For example, the following markup results in the output shown in Figure 31-20:

```
<StackPanel Background="LightSteelBlue">
  <Label Name="lblInstruction"
        FontSize="15">Enter Car Information</Label>
  <Label Name="lblMake">Make</Label>
  <TextBox Name="txtMake"/>
  <Label Name="lblColor">Color</Label>
  <TextBox Name="txtColor"/>
  <Label Name="lblPetName">Pet Name</Label>
  <TextBox Name="txtPetName"/>
  <Button Name="btnOK">OK</Button>
</StackPanel>
```

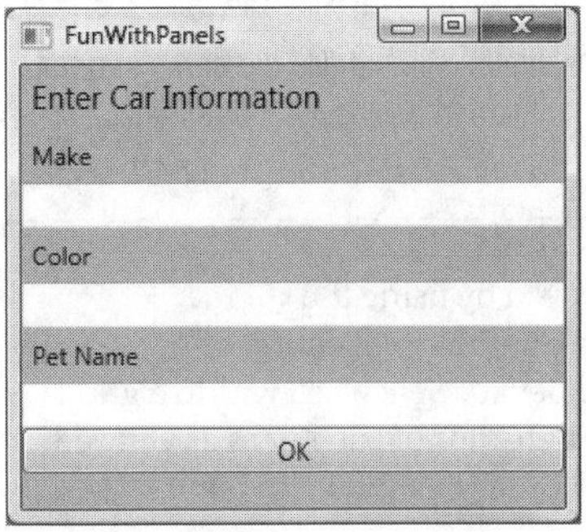

Figure 31-20. *Vertical stacking of content*

If we assign the `Orientation` property to `Horizontal` as follows, the rendered output will match that of Figure 31-21:

```
<StackPanel Background="LightSteelBlue" Orientation ="Horizontal">
```

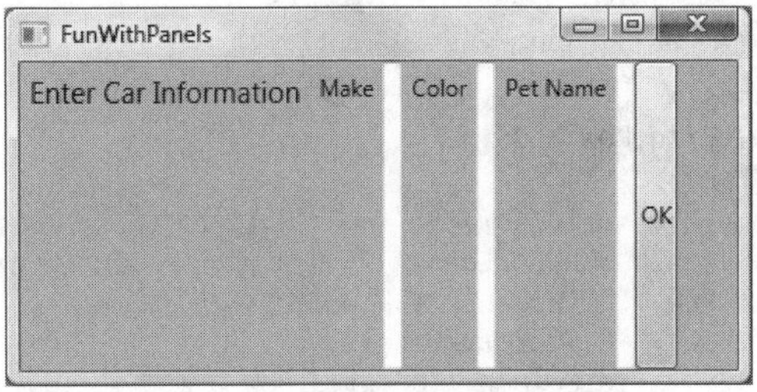

Figure 31-21. *Horizontal stacking of content*

Again, like the `WrapPanel`, you will seldom want to use a `StackPanel` to directly arrange content within a window. Rather, a `StackPanel` is better suited as a subpanel to a master panel.

Source Code The `SimpleStackPanel.xaml` file can be found under the Chapter 31 subdirectory.

Positioning Content Within Grid Panels

Of all the panels provided with the WPF APIs, `Grid` is far and away the most flexible. Like an HTML table, the `Grid` can be carved up into a set of cells, each one of which provides content. When defining a `Grid`, you perform three steps:

1. Define and configure each column.
2. Define and configure each row.
3. Assign content to each cell of the grid using attached property syntax.

■ **Note** If you do not define any rows or columns, the `<Grid>` defaults to a single cell that fills the entire surface of the window. Furthermore, if you do not assign a cell value for a subelement within a `<Grid>`, it automatically attaches to column 0, row 0.

The first two steps (defining the columns and rows) are achieved by using the `<Grid.ColumnDefinitions>` and `<Grid.RowDefinitions>` elements, which contain a collection of `<ColumnDefinition>` and `<RowDefinition>` elements, respectively. Because each cell within a grid is indeed a true .NET type, you can configure the look and feel and behavior of each item as you see fit. Here is a rather simple `<Grid>` definition that arranges our UI content as shown in Figure 31-22:

```
<Grid ShowGridLines ="True" Background ="AliceBlue">
  <!-- Define the rows/columns -->
  <Grid.ColumnDefinitions>
    <ColumnDefinition/>
    <ColumnDefinition/>
  </Grid.ColumnDefinitions>
  <Grid.RowDefinitions>
    <RowDefinition/>
    <RowDefinition/>
  </Grid.RowDefinitions>

  <!-- Now add the elements to the grid's cells -->
  <Label Name="lblInstruction" Grid.Column ="0" Grid.Row ="0"
         FontSize="15">Enter Car Information</Label>
  <Button Name="btnOK"  Height ="30" Grid.Column ="0" Grid.Row ="0" >OK</Button>
  <Label Name="lblMake" Grid.Column ="1" Grid.Row ="0">Make</Label>
  <TextBox Name="txtMake" Grid.Column ="1" Grid.Row ="0" Width="193" Height="25"/>
  <Label Name="lblColor" Grid.Column ="0" Grid.Row ="1" >Color</Label>
  <TextBox Name="txtColor" Width="193" Height="25" Grid.Column ="0" Grid.Row ="1" />

  <!-- Just to keep things interesting, add some color to the pet name cell -->
  <Rectangle Fill ="LightGreen" Grid.Column ="1" Grid.Row ="1" />
  <Label Name="lblPetName" Grid.Column ="1" Grid.Row ="1" >Pet Name</Label>
  <TextBox Name="txtPetName" Grid.Column ="1" Grid.Row ="1"
           Width="193" Height="25"/>
</Grid>
```

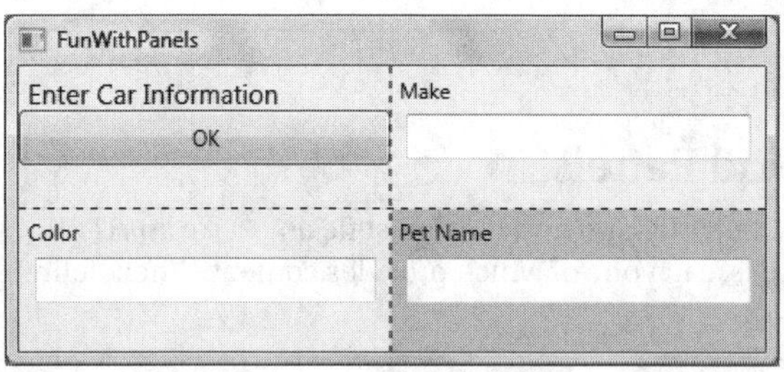

Figure 31-22. *The* `Grid` *panel in action*

Notice that each element (including a light green `Rectangle` element, thrown in for good measure) connects itself to a cell in the grid using the `Grid.Row` and `Grid.Column` attached properties. By default, the ordering of cells in a grid begins at the upper left, which is specified via `Grid.Column="0"`

`Grid.Row="0"`. Given that our grid defines a total of four cells, the bottom-right cell can be identified via `Grid.Column="1" Grid.Row="1"`.

Source Code The `SimpleGrid.xaml` file can be found under the Chapter 31 subdirectory.

Grids with GridSplitter Types

`Grid` types can also support splitters. As you most likely know, splitters allow the end user to resize rows or columns of a grid. As this is done, the content within each resizable cell will reshape itself based on how the items have been contained. Adding splitters to a `Grid` is very easy to do; simply define the `<GridSplitter>` element, using attached property syntax to establish which row or column it affects. Do be aware that you must assign a `Width` or `Height` value (depending on vertical or horizontal splitting) in order to be visible on the screen. Consider the following simple `Grid` type with a splitter on the first column (`Grid.Column = "0"`):

```
<Window
  xmlns="http://schemas.microsoft.com/winfx/2006/xaml/presentation"
  xmlns:x="http://schemas.microsoft.com/winfx/2006/xaml"
  Title="FunWithPanels" Height="191" Width="436">
  <Grid Background ="AliceBlue">
    <!-- Define columns -->
    <Grid.ColumnDefinitions>
      <ColumnDefinition Width ="Auto"/>
      <ColumnDefinition/>
    </Grid.ColumnDefinitions>

    <!-- Add this label to cell 0 -->
    <Label Name="lblLeft" Background ="GreenYellow"
     Grid.Column="0" Content ="Left!"/>

    <!-- Define the splitter -->
    <GridSplitter Grid.Column ="0" Width ="5"/>

    <!-- Add this label to cell 1 -->
    <Label Name="lblRight" Grid.Column ="1" Content ="Right!"/>
  </Grid>
</Window>
```

First and foremost, notice that the column that will support the splitter has a `Width` property of `Auto`. Next, notice that the `<GridSplitter>` makes use of attached property syntax to establish which column it is working with. If you were to view this output, you would find a 5-pixel splitter that allows you to resize each `Label` (because we have not specified `Height` or `Width` properties for either `Label`, they fill up the entire cell), as shown in Figure 31-23.

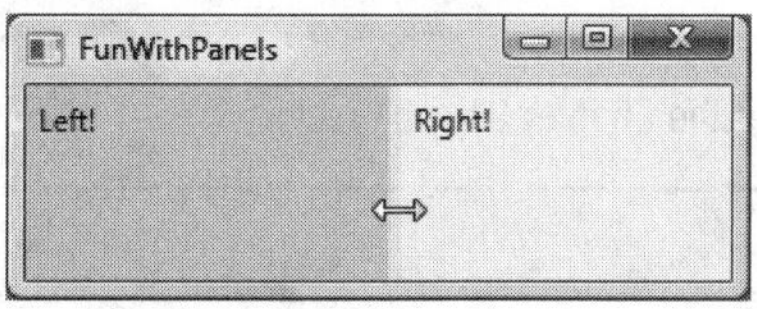

Figure 31-23. `Grid` *types containing splitters*

■ **Source Code** The `GridWithSplitter.xaml` file can be found under the Chapter 31 subdirectory.

Positioning Content Within DockPanel Panels

`DockPanel` is typically used as a master panel that contains any number of additional panels for grouping related content. `DockPanels` make use of attached property syntax as seen with the `Canvas` type, to control where their upper-left corner (the default) will attach itself within the panel. Here is a very simple `DockPanel` definition, which results in the output shown in Figure 31-24:

```
<DockPanel LastChildFill ="True">
  <!-- Dock items to the panel -->
  <Label DockPanel.Dock ="Top" Name="lblInstruction"
         FontSize="15">Enter Car Information</Label>
  <Label DockPanel.Dock ="Left" Name="lblMake">Make</Label>
  <Label DockPanel.Dock ="Right" Name="lblColor">Color</Label>
  <Label DockPanel.Dock ="Bottom" Name="lblPetName">Pet Name</Label>
  <Button Name="btnOK">OK</Button>
</DockPanel>
```

Figure 31-24. *A simple* `DockPanel`

■ **Note** If you add multiple elements to the same side of a `DockPanel`, they will be stacked along the specified edge in the order that they are declared.

The benefit of using `DockPanel` is that as the user resizes the window, each element remains "connected" to the specified side of the panel (via `DockPanel.Dock`). Also notice that the opening `<DockPanel>` element sets the `LastChildFill` attribute to `True`. Given that the `Button` has not specified any `DockPanel.Dock` value, it will therefore be stretched within the remaining space.

■ **Source Code** The `SimpleDockPanel.xaml` file can be found under the Chapter 31 subdirectory.

Enabling Scrolling for Panel Types

It is worth pointing out that WPF supplies a `<ScrollViewer>` type, which provides automatic scrolling behaviors for nested panel types:

```
<ScrollViewer>
  <StackPanel>
    <Button Content ="First" Background = "Green" Height ="40"/>
    <Button Content ="Second" Background = "Red" Height ="40"/>
    <Button Content ="Third" Background = "Pink" Height ="40"/>
    <Button Content ="Fourth" Background = "Yellow" Height ="40"/>
    <Button Content ="Fifth" Background = "Blue" Height ="40"/>
  </StackPanel>
</ScrollViewer>
```

The result of the previous XAML definition is shown in Figure 31-25.

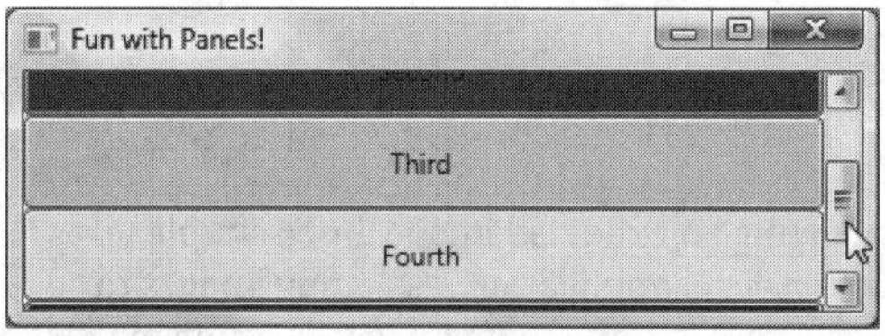

Figure 31-25. *Working with the* ScrollViewer *type*

Source Code The ScrollViewer.xaml file can be found under the Chapter 31 subdirectory.

As you would expect, each panel provides numerous members that allow you to fine-tune content placement. On a related note, WPF controls all support two properties of interest (Padding and Margin) that allow the control itself to inform the panel how it wishes to be treated. Specifically, the Padding property controls how much extra space should surround the interior control, while Margin controls the extra space around the exterior of a control.

This wraps up our look at the major panel types of WPF and the various ways they position their content. Next, we will see an example using nested panels to create a layout system for a main window. To do so, we will enhance the functionality of the TextControls project (e.g., the spell checker app) to support a main menu, a status bar, and a toolbar.

Building a Window's Frame Using Nested Panels

This updated version of the application (which we will assume is a new Visual Studio 2008 WPF Application project named MySpellChecker) will be extended and finalized over the pages to come, so for the time being, you will construct the core layout and base functionality.

Our goal is to construct a layout where the main window has a topmost menu system, a toolbar, and a status bar mounted on the bottom of the window. The status bar will contain a pane to hold text prompts that are displayed when the user selects a menu item (or toolbar button), while the menu system and toolbar will offer UI triggers to close the application and display spelling suggestions in an Expander widget. Figure 31-26 shows the initial layout we are shooting for, displaying spelling suggestions for "XAML."

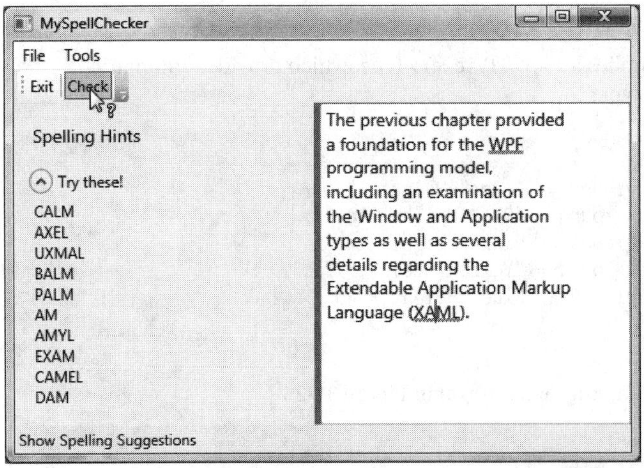

Figure 31-26. *Using nested panels to establish a window's UI*

Notice that our two toolbar buttons are not supporting an expected image, but a simple text value. While this would not be sufficient for a production-level application, assigning images to toolbar buttons typically involves using embedded resources, a topic that you will examine in Chapter 32 (so text data will do for now). Also note that as the mouse button is placed over the Check button, the mouse cursor changes, and the single pane of the status bar displays a useful UI message.

To begin building this UI, update the initial XAML definition for your `Window` type to make use of a `<DockPanel>` child element, rather than the default `<Grid>`:

```
<Window x:Class-"MainWindow"
  xmlns="http://schemas.microsoft.com/winfx/2006/xaml/presentation"
  xmlns:x="http://schemas.microsoft.com/winfx/2006/xaml"
  Title="MySpellChecker" Height="331" Width="508"
  WindowStartupLocation ="CenterScreen" >

  <!-- This panel establishes the content for the window -->
  <DockPanel>
  </DockPanel>

</Window>
```

Building the Menu System

Menu systems in WPF are represented by the `Menu` type, which maintains a collection of `MenuItem` objects. When building a menu system in XAML, each `MenuItem` may handle various events, most notably `Click`, which occurs when the end user selects a subitem. In our example, we will build two topmost menu items (File and Tools), which expose Exit and Spelling Hints subitems (respectively). In addition to handling the `Click` event for each subitem, we will also handle the `MouseEnter` and `MouseExit` events, which will be used to set the status bar text in a later step. Add the following markup within your `<DockPanel>` scope:

```
<!-- Doc menu system on the top -->
<Menu DockPanel.Dock ="Top"
      HorizontalAlignment="Left" Background="White" BorderBrush ="Black">
```

```
  <MenuItem Header="_File" Click ="FileExit_Click" >
    <Separator/>
    <MenuItem Header ="_Exit" MouseEnter ="MouseEnterExitArea"
     MouseLeave ="MouseLeaveArea" Click ="FileExit_Click"/>
    </MenuItem>
    <MenuItem Header="_Tools">
      <MenuItem Header ="_Spelling Hints" MouseEnter ="MouseEnterToolsHintsArea"
       MouseLeave ="MouseLeaveArea" Click ="ToolsSpellingHints_Click"/>
  </MenuItem>
</Menu>
```

Notice that we have docked the menu system to the top of the DockPanel. As well, the <Separator> element has been used to insert a thin horizontal line in the menu system, directly before the Exit option. Also notice that the Header values for each MenuItem contain an embedded underbar token (for example, _Exit). This is used to establish which letter will be underlined when the end user presses the Alt key (for keyboard shortcuts).

To complete the menu system definition, we now need to implement the various event handlers. First, we have the File ➤ Exit handler, FileExit_Click(), which will simply terminate the application via Application.Current.Shutdown(). The MouseEnter and MouseExit event handlers for each subitem will eventually update our status bar; however, for now, we will simply provide shells. Finally, the ToolsSpellingHints_Click() handler for the Tools ➤ Spelling Hints menu item will also be a shell for the time being. Here are the current updates to your code-behind file:

```
Class MainWindow

  Private Sub FileExit_Click(ByVal sender As System.Object, _
    ByVal e As System.Windows.RoutedEventArgs)
    ' Terminate the application.
    Application.Current.Shutdown()
  End Sub

  Private Sub ToolsSpellingHints_Click(ByVal sender As System.Object, _
    ByVal e As System.Windows.RoutedEventArgs)
  End Sub

  Private Sub MouseLeaveArea(ByVal sender As System.Object, _
    ByVal e As System.Windows.Input.MouseEventArgs)
  End Sub

  Private Sub MouseEnterToolsHintsArea(ByVal sender As System.Object, _
    ByVal e As System.Windows.Input.MouseEventArgs)
  End Sub

  Private Sub MouseEnterExitArea(ByVal sender As System.Object, _
    ByVal e As System.Windows.Input.MouseEventArgs)
  End Sub
End Class
```

Building the ToolBar

Toolbars (represented by the ToolBar type in WPF) typically provide an alternative manner to activate a menu option. Add the following markup directly after the closing scope of your <Menu> definition:

```
<!-- Put Toolbar under the Menu -->
<ToolBar DockPanel.Dock ="Top" >
  <Button Content ="Exit" MouseEnter ="MouseEnterExitArea"
          MouseLeave ="MouseLeaveArea" Click ="FileExit_Click"/>
  <Separator/>
  <Button Content ="Check" MouseEnter ="MouseEnterToolsHintsArea"
          MouseLeave ="MouseLeaveArea" Click ="ToolsSpellingHints_Click"
          Cursor="Help" />
</ToolBar>
```

Our <ToolBar> consists of two Button instances, which just so happen to handle the same events and are handled by the same methods in our code file. Using this technique, we are able to double-up our handlers to serve both menu items and toolbar buttons. Although this toolbar is making use of the typical push buttons, do know that the ToolBar type "is-a" ContentControl, and therefore you are free to embed any types into its surface (drop-down lists, images, graphics, etc.). The only other point of interest is that the Check button supports a custom mouse cursor via the Cursor property.

■ **Note** The ToolBar type may optionally be wrapped within a <ToolBarTray> element, which controls layout, docking, and drag-and-drop operations for a set of ToolBar objects. Consult the .NET Framework 3.5 SDK documentation for details.

Building the StatusBar

The StatusBar will be docked to the lower portion of the <DockPanel> and contain a single <TextBlock> type, which up until this point in the chapter we have not made use of. Like a TextBox, a TextBlock can be used to hold text. In addition, TextBlock instances honor the use of numerous textual annotations such as bold text, underlined text, line breaks, and so forth. While our StatusBar does not technically need this support, another benefit of a TextBlock type is that it is optimized for small blurbs of text, such as UI prompts in a status bar pane. Add the following markup directly after the previous ToolBar definition:

```
<!-- Put a StatusBar at the bottom -->
<StatusBar DockPanel.Dock ="Bottom" Background="Beige" >
  <StatusBarItem>
    <TextBlock Name="statBarText">Ready</TextBlock>
  </StatusBarItem>
</StatusBar>
```

At this point, your Visual Studio designer should look something like Figure 31-27.

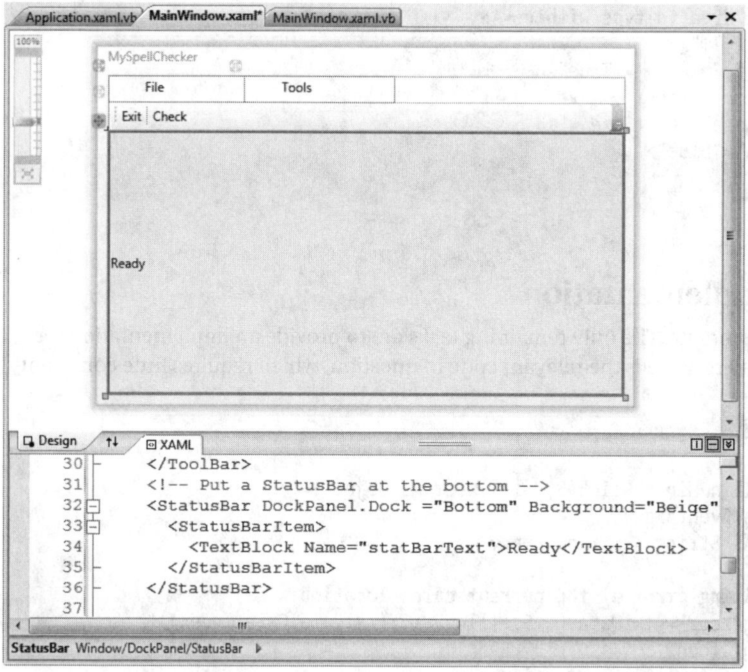

Figure 31-27. *The current user interface of our spell checker application*

Finalizing the UI Design

The final aspect of our UI design is to define a splittable Grid that defines two columns. On the left will be the Expander that will display a list of spelling suggestions, wrapped within a <StackPanel>. On the right will be a TextBox that supports multiple lines and has enabled spell checking. The entire <Grid> will be mounted to the left of the parent <DockPanel>. Add the following XAML markup to complete the definition of our Window's UI:

```
<Grid DockPanel.Dock ="Left" Background ="AliceBlue">
  <!-- Define the rows and columns -->
  <Grid.ColumnDefinitions>
    <ColumnDefinition />
    <ColumnDefinition />
  </Grid.ColumnDefinitions>
  <GridSplitter Grid.Column ="0" Width ="5" Background ="Gray" />
  <StackPanel Grid.Column="0" VerticalAlignment ="Stretch" >
    <Label Name="lblSpellingInstructions" FontSize="14" Margin="10,10,0,0">
     Spelling Hints
    </Label>

    <Expander Name="expanderSpelling" Header ="Try these!" Margin="10,10,10,10">
      <!-- This will be filled programmatically -->
      <Label Name ="lblSpellingHints" FontSize ="12"/>
    </Expander>
  </StackPanel>
```

```
  <!-- This will be the area to type within -->
  <TextBox  Grid.Column ="1"
            SpellCheck.IsEnabled ="True"
            AcceptsReturn ="True"
            Name ="txtData"  FontSize ="14"
            BorderBrush ="Blue">
  </TextBox>
</Grid>
```

Finalizing the Implementation

At this point, your UI is complete. The only remaining tasks are to provide an implementation for the remaining event handlers. Here is the relevant code in question, which requires little comment by this point in the chapter:

```
Class MainWindow
...
  Private Sub ToolsSpellingHints_Click(ByVal sender As Object, _
    ByVal args As RoutedEventArgs)
    Dim spellingHints As String = String.Empty

    ' Try to get a spelling error at the current caret location.
    Dim err As SpellingError = txtData.GetSpellingError(txtData.CaretIndex)
    If err IsNot Nothing Then
      ' Build a string of spelling suggestions.
      For Each s As String In err.Suggestions
        spellingHints &= s & vbLf
      Next

      ' Show suggestions on Label within Expander.
      lblSpellingHints.Content = spellingHints

      ' Expand the expander.
      expanderSpelling.IsExpanded = True
    End If
  End Sub

  Private Sub MouseEnterExitArea(ByVal sender As Object, _
    ByVal args As RoutedEventArgs)
    statBarText.Text = "Exit the Application"
  End Sub

  Private Sub MouseEnterToolsHintsArea(ByVal sender As Object, _
    ByVal args As RoutedEventArgs)
    statBarText.Text = "Show Spelling Suggestions"
  End Sub

  Private Sub MouseLeaveArea(ByVal sender As Object, _
    ByVal args As RoutedEventArgs)
    statBarText.Text = "Ready"
  End Sub
End Class
```

So there you have it! With just a few lines of procedural code (and a healthy dose of XAML), we have the beginnings of a functional word processor. To add just a bit more pizzazz requires an understanding of *control commands*.

Understanding WPF Control Commands

The next major discussion of this chapter is to examine the topic of *control commands*. Windows Presentation Foundation provides support for what might be considered "control-agnostic events" via control commands. As you know, a typical .NET event is defined within a specific base class and can be used only by that class or a derivative thereof. Furthermore, normal .NET events are tightly coupled to the class in which they are defined.

In contrast, WPF control commands are eventlike entities that are independent from a specific control and in many cases can be successfully applied to numerous (and seemingly unrelated) control types. By way of a few examples, WPF supports Copy, Paste, and Cut commands, which can be applied to a wide variety of UI elements (menu items, toolbar buttons, custom buttons) as well as keyboard shortcuts (Ctrl+C, Ctrl+V, etc.).

While other UI toolkits (such as Windows Forms) provided standard events for such purposes, the end result was typically redundant and hard-to-maintain code. Under the WPF model, commands can be used as an alternative. The end result typically yields a smaller and more flexible code base.

The Intrinsic Control Command Objects

WPF ships with numerous built-in control commands, all of which can be configured with associated keyboard shortcuts (or other input gestures). Programmatically speaking, a WPF control command is any object that supports a property (often called `Command`) that returns an object implementing the `ICommand` interface, shown here:

```
Public Interface ICommand
  ' Occurs when changes occur that affect whether
  ' or not the command should execute.
  Event CanExecuteChanged As EventHandler

  ' Defines the method that determines whether the command
  ' can execute in its current state.
  Function CanExecute(ByVal parameter As Object) As Boolean

  ' Defines the method to be called when the command is invoked.
  Sub Execute(ByVal parameter As Object)
End Interface
```

While you could provide your own implementation of this interface to account for a control command, the chances that you will need to are slim, given functionality provided by the five WPF command objects out of the box. These shared classes define numerous properties that expose objects that implement `ICommand`, most commonly the `RoutedUICommand` type, which adds support for the WPF routed event model.

Table 31-4 documents some core properties exposed by each of the intrinsic command objects (be sure to consult the .NET Framework 3.5 SDK documentation for complete details).

Table 31-4. *The Intrinsic WPF Control Command Objects*

WPF Control Command Object	Example Control Command Properties	Meaning in Life
`ApplicationCommands`	`Close`, `Copy`, `Cut`, `Delete`, `Find`, `Open`, `Paste`, `Save`, `SaveAs`, `Redo`, `Undo`	Defines properties that represent application-level commands
`ComponentCommands`	`MoveDown`, `MoveFocusBack`, `MoveLeft`, `MoveRight`, `ScrollToEnd`, `ScrollToHome`	Defines properties that map to common commands performed by UI elements
`MediaCommands`	`BoostBase`, `ChannelUp`, `ChannelDown`, `FastForward`, `NextTrack`, `Play`, `Rewind`, `Select`, `Stop`	Defines properties that allow various media-centric controls to issue common commands
`NavigationCommands`	`BrowseBack`, `BrowseForward`, `Favorites`, `LastPage`, `NextPage`, `Zoom`	Defines numerous properties that are used for the applications that utilize the WPF navigation model
`EditingCommands`	`AlignCenter`, `CorrectSpellingError`, `DecreaseFontSize`, `EnterLineBreak`, `EnterParagraphBreak`, `MoveDownByLine`, `MoveRightByWord`	Defines numerous properties typically used when programming with objects exposed by the WPF document API

Connecting Commands to the Command Property

If you wish to connect any of these command properties to a UI element that supports the `Command` property (such as a `Button` or `MenuItem`), you have very little work to do. To see how to do so, update the current menu system to support a new topmost menu item named Edit and three subitems to account for copying, pasting, and cutting of textual data:

```
<Menu DockPanel.Dock ="Top"
  HorizontalAlignment="Left" Background="White" BorderBrush ="Black">
  <MenuItem Header="_File" Click ="FileExit_Click" >
    <Separator/>
    <MenuItem Header ="_Exit" MouseEnter ="MouseEnterExitArea"
     MouseLeave ="MouseLeaveArea" Click ="FileExit_Click"/>
  </MenuItem>

  <!-- New menu item with commands! -->
  <MenuItem Header="_Edit">
    <MenuItem Command ="ApplicationCommands.Copy"/>
    <MenuItem Command ="ApplicationCommands.Cut"/>
    <MenuItem Command ="ApplicationCommands.Paste"/>
  </MenuItem>

  <MenuItem Header="_Tools">
  <MenuItem Header ="_Spelling Hints" MouseEnter ="MouseEnterToolsHintsArea"
    MouseLeave ="MouseLeaveArea" Click ="ToolsSpellingHints_Click"/>
  </MenuItem>
</Menu>
```

Notice that each subitem has a value assigned to the `Command` property. By doing so, the menu items automatically receive the correct name and shortcut key (for example, Ctrl+C for a cut operation) in the menu item UI, and the application is now "copy, cut, and paste" aware with no procedural code. Thus, if you were to run the application and select some of your text, you would be able to use your new menu items out of the box as shown in Figure 31-28.

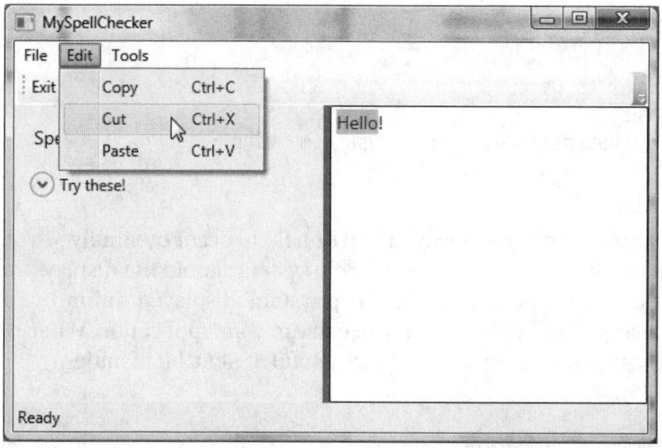

Figure 31-28. *Command objects provide a good deal of canned functionality for free.*

Connection Commands to Arbitrary UI Elements

If you wish to connect a command to a UI element that does not support the Command property, doing so requires you to drop down to procedural code. Doing so is certainly not complex, but it does involve a bit more logic than you see in XAML. For example, what if you wished to have the entire window respond to the F1 key, so that when the end user presses this key, he or she would activate an associated help system?

First, add a custom constructor to your existing Window-derived class. Next, update your main window to define a new method named SetF1CommandBinding(), which is called within the window's constructor after the call to InitializeComponent().

```
Public Sub New()
  InitializeComponent()
  SetF1CommandBinding()
End Sub
```

This new method will programmatically create a new CommandBinding object, which is configured to operate with the ApplicationCommands.Help option, which is automatically F1-aware:

```
Private Sub SetF1CommandBinding()
  Dim helpBinding As New CommandBinding(ApplicationCommands.Help)
  AddHandler helpBinding.CanExecute, AddressOf CanHelpExecute
  AddHandler helpBinding.Executed, AddressOf HelpExecuted
  CommandBindings.Add(helpBinding)
End Sub
```

Most CommandBinding objects will want to handle the CanExecute event (which allows you to specify whether the command occurs or not based on the operation of your program) and the Executed event (which is where you can author the content that should occur once the command occurs). Add the following event handlers to your Window-derived type (take note of the signature of each method as required by the associated delegates):

```
Private Sub CanHelpExecute(ByVal sender As Object, _
  ByVal e As CanExecuteRoutedEventArgs)
  ' Here, you can set CanExecute to False if you wish to prevent the
  ' command from executing.
  e.CanExecute = True
End Sub

Private Sub HelpExecuted(ByVal sender As Object, _
  ByVal e As ExecutedRoutedEventArgs)
  MessageBox.Show("Dude, it is not that difficult. Just type something!", _
                "Help!")
End Sub
```

Here, we have implemented `CanHelpExecute()` to always allow F1 help to occur by simply returning `True`. However, if you have certain situations where the help system should not display, you can account for this and return `False` when necessary. Our "help system" displayed within `HelpExecute()` is little more than a message box. At this point, you can run your application. When you press the F1 key on your keyboard, you will see your (less than helpful, if not a bit insulting) user guidance system (see Figure 31-29).

Figure 31-29. *Our custom help system*

Source Code The MySpellChecker project can be found under the Chapter 31 subdirectory.

Understanding the WPF Data Binding Model

Controls are often the target of various data binding operations. Simply put, *data binding* is the act of connecting control properties to data values that may change over the course of your application's lifetime. By doing so, a user interface element can display the state of a variable in your code; for example:

- Checking a CheckBox control based on a Boolean property of a given object
- Displaying data in TextBox types from a relational database table
- Connecting an integer to a Label to represent the number of files in a folder

When using the intrinsic WPF data binding engine, you must be aware of the distinction between the *source* and the *destination* of the binding operation. As you might expect, the source of a data binding operation is the data itself (a Boolean property, relational data, etc.), while the destination (or target) is the UI control property that will use the data content (a CheckBox, TextBox, and so on).

■ **Note** The target property of a data binding operation must be a dependency property of the UI control.

Truth be told, using the WPF data binding infrastructure is always optional. If a developer were to roll his or her own data binding logic, the connection between a source and destination typically would involve handling various events and authoring procedural code to connect the source and destination. For example, if you had a ScrollBar on a window that needed to display its value on a Label type, you might handle the ScrollBar's ValueChanged event and update the Label's content accordingly.

However, using WPF data binding, you can connect the source and destination directly in XAML (or using VB code in your code file) without the need to handle various events or hard-code the connections between the source/destination. As well, based on how you set up your data binding logic, you can ensure that the source and destination stay in sync if either of their values change.

A First Look at Data Binding

To begin examining WPF's data binding capabilities, assume you have a new WPF Application project (named SimpleDataBinding) that defines the following markup for a Window type:

```
<Window x:Class="MainWindow"
  xmlns="http://schemas.microsoft.com/winfx/2006/xaml/presentation"
  xmlns:x="http://schemas.microsoft.com/winfx/2006/xaml"
  Title="Simple Data Binding" Height="152" Width="300"
  WindowStartupLocation="CenterScreen">

  <StackPanel Width="250">
    <Label Content="Move the scroll bar to see the current value"/>

    <!-- The scrollbar's value is the source of this data bind -->
    <ScrollBar Orientation="Horizontal" Height="30" Name="mySB"
             Minimum = "1" Maximum = "100" LargeChange="1" SmallChange="1"/>

    <!-- The label's content value is the target of the data bind -->
    <Label Height="30" BorderBrush="Blue" BorderThickness="2"
         Content = "{Binding ElementName=mySB, Path=Value}"
    />
  </StackPanel>
</Window>
```

Notice that the <ScrollBar> element (which we have named mySB) has been configured with a range between 1 and 100. As you reposition the thumb of the scrollbar (or click the left or right arrows), the Label will be automatically updated with the current value. The "glue" that makes this happen is the {Binding} markup extension that has been assigned to the Label's Content property.

Here, the `ElementName` value represents the source of the data binding operation (the `ScrollBar` object), while the `Path` value represents (in this case) the property of the element to obtain.

■ **Note** `ElementName` and `Path` may seem oddly named, as you might expect to find more intuitive names such as "Source" and "Destination." However, as you will see later in this chapter, XML documents can be the source of a data binding operation (typically using XPath). In this case, the names `ElementName` and `Path` fit the bill.

As an alternative format, it is possible to break out the values specified by the `{Binding}` markup extension by explicitly setting the `DataContext` property to the source of the binding operation as follows:

```
<!-- Breaking object/value apart via DataContext -->
<Label Height="30" BorderBrush="Blue" BorderThickness="2"
  DataContext = "{Binding ElementName=mySB}"
  Content = "{Binding Path=Value}"
/>
```

In either case, if you were to run this application, you would be pleased to find this `Label` updating without the need to write any procedural VB code (see Figure 31-30).

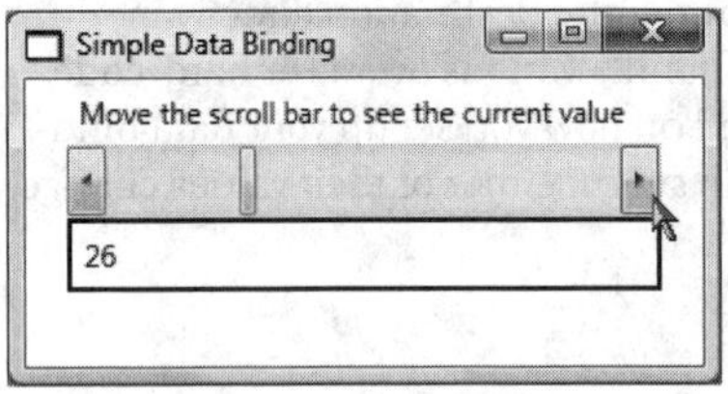

Figure 31-30. *Binding the* `ScrollBar` *value to a* `Label`

The DataContext Property

In the current example, you have seen two approaches to establish the source and destination of a data binding operation, both of which resulted in the same output. Given this point, you might wonder when you would want to explicitly set the `DataContext` property. This property can be very helpful in that it is a dependency property, and therefore its value can be inherited by subelements. In this way, you can easily set the same data source to a family of controls, rather than having to repeat a bunch of redundant `"{Binding ElementName=X, Path=Y}"` XAML values to multiple controls. Consider the following updated XAML definition for our current `<StackPanel>`:

```
<!-- Note the StackPanel sets the DataContext property -->
<StackPanel Width="250" DataContext = "{Binding ElementName=mySB}">
  <Label Content="Move the scroll bar to see the current value"/>

  <ScrollBar Orientation="Horizontal" Height="30" Name="mySB"
             Maximum = "100" LargeChange="1" SmallChange="1"/>

  <!-- Now both UI elements use the scrollbar's value in unique ways. -->
  <Label Height="30" BorderBrush="Blue" BorderThickness="2"
         Content = "{Binding Path=Value}"/>
```

```
  <Button Content="Click" Height="200"
          FontSize = "{Binding Path=Value}"/>
</StackPanel>
```

Here, the DataContext property has been set on the <StackPanel> directly. Therefore, as we move the thumb, not only will we see the current value on the Label, but we will also find the font size of the Button grow and shrink accordingly based on the same value.

The Mode Property

When establishing a data binding operation, you are able to choose among various modes of operation by setting a value to the Mode property at the time you establish the Path value. By default, the Mode property is set to the value OneWay, which specifies that changes in the target do not affect the source. In our example, changing the Content property of the Label does not set the position of the ScrollBar's thumb.

If you wish to keep changes between the source and the target in sync, you can set the Mode property to TwoWay. Thus, changing the value of the Label's content changes the value of the scrollbar's thumb position. Of course, the end user would be unable to change the content of the Label, as the content is presented in a read-only manner (we could of course change the value programmatically).

To illustrate the use of the TwoWay mode, assume we have replaced the Label displaying the current scrollbar value with the following TextBox (note the value of the Text property). In this case, when you type a new value into the text area, the thumb position (and font of the Button type) automatically update when you tab off the TextBox object:

```
<TextBox Height="30" BorderBrush="Blue"
         BorderThickness="2" Text = "{Binding Path=Value}"/>
```

Note You may also set the Mode property to OneTime. This option sets the target when initialized but does not track further changes.

Data Conversion Using IValueConverter

The ScrollBar type uses a Double to represent the value of the thumb, rather than an expected whole number (e.g., an integer). Therefore, as you drag the thumb, you will find various floating-point numbers displayed within the TextBox (such as 61.0576923076923), which would be rather unintuitive to the end user, who is most likely expecting to see whole numbers (such as 61, 62, 63, and so on).

When you wish to convert the value of a data binding operation into an alternative format, one way to do so is to create a custom class type that implements the IValueConverter interface of the System.Windows.Data namespace. This interface defines two members that allow you to perform the conversion to and from the target and destination. Once you define this class, you can use it to further qualify the processing of your data binding operation.

Note While any data binding operation can be achieved entirely using procedural code, the following examples will make use of XAML to convert between data types. Doing so involves the use of custom resources, which will be fully examined in Chapter 32. Therefore, don't fret if some of the markup appears unfamiliar.

Assuming that you wish to display whole numbers within the TextBox control, you could build the following class type (defined within a new *.vb file):

```
Class MyDoubleConverter
  Implements IValueConverter

  Public Function Convert(ByVal value As Object, ByVal targetType As Type, _
    ByVal parameter As Object, _
    ByVal culture As System.Globalization.CultureInfo) As Object _
    Implements IValueConverter.Convert

    ' Convert the Double to an Integer.
    Dim v As Double = CDbl(value)
    Return CInt(v)
  End Function

  Public Function ConvertBack(ByVal value As Object, _
    ByVal targetType As Type, _
    ByVal parameter As Object, _
    ByVal culture As System.Globalization.CultureInfo) As Object _
    Implements IValueConverter.ConvertBack
    ' Return the incoming value directly.
    ' This will be used for 2-way bindings.
    ' In our example, when the user tabs out
    ' of the TextBox.
    Return value
  End Function
End Class
```

The Convert() method will be called when the value is transferred from the source (the ScrollBar) to the destination (the Text property of the TextBox). While we receive a number of incoming arguments, for this conversion we only need to manipulate the incoming Object, which is the value of the current Double. Using this type, we simply cast the type into an integer and return the new number.

The ConvertBack() method will be called when the value is passed from the destination to the source (if you have enabled a two-way binding mode). Here, we simply return the value straightaway. By doing so, we are able to type a floating-point value into the TextBox (such as 99.9) and have it automatically convert to a whole number value (99) when the user tabs off the control. This "free" conversion happens due to the fact that the Convert() method is called once again after a call to ConvertBack(). If you were to simply return Nothing from ConvertBack(), your binding would appear to be out of sync, as the text box would still be displaying a floating-point number!

With this class in place, consider the following XAML updates, which will leverage our custom converter class to display data in the TextBox:

```
<Window x:Class="MainWindow"
  xmlns="http://schemas.microsoft.com/winfx/2006/xaml/presentation"
  xmlns:x="http://schemas.microsoft.com/winfx/2006/xaml"
  xmlns:myConverters ="clr-namespace:SimpleDataBinding"
  Title="Simple Data Binding" Height="334" Width="288"
  WindowStartupLocation="CenterScreen">

  <!-- Resource dictionaries allow us to define objects that can
       be obtained by their key. More details in Chapter 32 -->
  <Window.Resources>
    <myConverters:MyDoubleConverter x:Key="DoubleConverter"/>
  </Window.Resources>
```

```
  <!-- The panel is setting the data context to the scrollbar object -->
  <StackPanel Width="250" DataContext = "{Binding ElementName=mySB}">

    <Label Content="Move the scroll bar to see the current value"/>

    <ScrollBar Orientation="Horizontal" Height="30" Name="mySB"
      Maximum = "100" LargeChange="1" SmallChange="1"/>

    <!-- Notice that the {Binding} extension now
     sets the Converter property. -->
    <TextBox Height="30" BorderBrush="Blue" BorderThickness="2" Name="txtThumbValue"
     Text = "{Binding Path=Value, Converter={StaticResource DoubleConverter}}"/>

    <Button Content="Click" Height="200"
     FontSize = "{Binding Path=Value}"/>

  </StackPanel>
</Window>
```

Once we define a custom XML namespace that maps to our project's root namespace (see Chapter 30), we add to the Window's resource dictionary an instance of our MyDoubleConverter type, which we can obtain later in the XAML file by the key name DoubleConverter. The Text property of the TextBox has been modified to make use of our MyDoubleConverter type, assigning the Converter property to yet another markup extension named SharedResource. Again, full details of the WPF resource system can be found in Chapter 32. In any case, if you were to run your application, you would find that only whole numbers will be displayed in the TextBox.

Converting Between Diverse Data Types

An implementation of the IValueConverter interface can be used to convert between any data types, even if they do not seem related on the surface. In reality, you are able to use the current value of the ScrollBar's thumb to return any object type to connect to a dependency property. Consider the following ColorConverter type, which uses the value of the thumb to return a new green SolidColorBrush (with a green value between 155 and 255):

```
Class MyColorConverter
  Implements IValueConverter

  Public Function Convert(ByVal value As Object, _
    ByVal targetType As Type, _
    ByVal parameter As Object, _
    ByVal culture As System.Globalization.CultureInfo) As Object _
    Implements IValueConverter.Convert

    ' Use value of thumb to build a varied green brush.
    Dim d As Double = CDbl(value)
    Dim v As Byte = CByte(d)

    Dim color As New Color()
    color.A = 255
    color.G = CByte((155 + v))
    Return New SolidColorBrush(color)
  End Function

  Public Function ConvertBack(ByVal value As Object, _
    ByVal targetType As Type, _
```

```
    ByVal parameter As Object, _
    ByVal culture As System.Globalization.CultureInfo) As Object _
    Implements IValueConverter.ConvertBack

    Return value
  End Function
End Class
```

If we were to add a new member to our resource dictionary as follows:

```
<Window.Resources>
  <myConverters:MyDoubleConverter x:Key="DoubleConverter"/>
  <myConverters:MyColorConverter x:Key="ColorConverter"/>
</Window.Resources>
```

we could then use the key name to set the Background property of our Button type as follows:

```
<Button Content="Click" Height="200"
  FontSize = "{Binding Path=Value}"
  Background= "{Binding Path=Value, Converter={StaticResource ColorConverter}}"/>
```

Sure enough, if you run your application once again, you'll find the color of the Button change based on the scrollbar's position. To wrap up our look at WPF data binding, let's check out how to map custom objects and XML document data to our UI layer.

Source Code The SimpleDataBinding project can be found under the Chapter 31 subdirectory.

Binding to Custom Objects

The next flavor of data binding we will examine is how to connect the properties of custom objects to your UI layer. Begin by creating a new WPF Application project named CarViewerApp. Next, handle the Loaded event of MainWindow (recall the IDE will autogenerate an empty event handler, which we will implement later) and update the <Grid> definition to contain two rows and two columns:

```
<Window x:Class="MainWindow"
  xmlns="http://schemas.microsoft.com/winfx/2006/xaml/presentation"
  xmlns:x="http://schemas.microsoft.com/winfx/2006/xaml"
  Title="Car Viewer Application" Height="294" Width="502"
  ResizeMode="NoResize" WindowStartupLocation="CenterScreen"
  Loaded="Window_Loaded"
  >
<Grid>
  <Grid.ColumnDefinitions>
    <ColumnDefinition Width="200"/>
    <ColumnDefinition Width="*"/>
  </Grid.ColumnDefinitions>
  <Grid.RowDefinitions>
    <RowDefinition Height="Auto"/>
    <RowDefinition Height="*"/>
  </Grid.RowDefinitions>
</Grid>
</Window>
```

The first row of the <Grid> will consist of a <DockPanel> representing a menu system containing a File menu with two submenus (Add New Car and Exit). Notice that we are handling the Click event of each submenu (we will implement the handlers in just a bit), and that we are assigning an "input gesture" to the Exit menu to allow the item to be activated when the user presses the Alt+F4 keystroke. Finally, notice the value of Grid.ColumnSpan has been set to 2, allowing the menu system to be positioned within each cell of the first row.

```
<!-- Menu Bar -->
<DockPanel
  Grid.Column="0"
  Grid.ColumnSpan="2"
  Grid.Row="0">
  <Menu DockPanel.Dock ="Top" HorizontalAlignment="Left" Background="White">
    <MenuItem Header="File">
      <MenuItem Header="New Car" Click="AddNewCarWizard"/>
      <Separator />
      <MenuItem Header="Exit" InputGestureText="Alt-F4"
      Click="ExitApplication"/>
    </MenuItem>
  </Menu>
</DockPanel>
```

The left portion of the <Grid> consists of a ListBox, while the right portion of the <Grid> contains a single TextBlock. The ListBox type will eventually become the destination for a data binding operation involving a collection of custom objects, so set the ItemsSource property to the {Binding} markup extension (the source of the binding will be specified in code in just a bit). As the user selects one of the items in the ListBox, we will capture the SelectionChanged event in order to update the content within the TextBlock. Here is the definition of these remaining types:

```
<!-- Left pane of grid -->
<ListBox Grid.Column="0"
  Grid.Row="2" Name="allCars" SelectionChanged="ListItemSelected"
  Background="LightBlue" ItemsSource="{Binding}">
</ListBox>

<!-- Right pane of grid -->
<TextBlock Name="txtCarStats" Background="LightYellow"
  Grid.Column="1" Grid.Row="2"/>
```

At this point, the UI of your window should look like what you see in Figure 31-31.

Before we implement the data binding logic, finalize the File ➤ Exit menu handler as follows:

```
Private Sub ExitApplication(ByVal sender As System.Object, _
  ByVal e As System.Windows.RoutedEventArgs)
  Application.Current.Shutdown()
End Sub
```

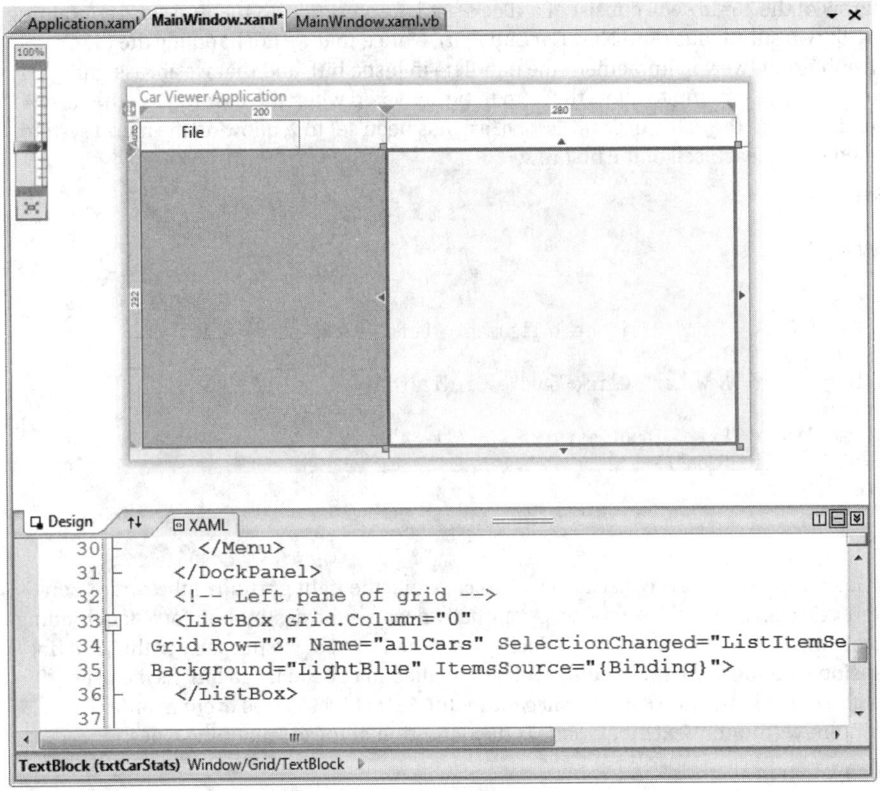

Figure 31-31. *The UI of our main window*

Working with the ObservableCollection(Of T) Type

.NET 3.0 introduced a new collection type within the `System.Collections.ObjectModel` namespace named `ObservableCollection(Of T)`. The benefit of working with this type is that when its contents are updated, it will send notifications to interested listeners, such as the destination of a data binding operation. Insert a new VB file into your application that defines a class named `CarList` that extends `ObservableCollection(Of T)`, where `T` is of type `Car`. This iteration of the `Car` type makes use of public properties (omitted for readability) to establish some basic state data (which can be set using a custom constructor), and provides a fitting implementation of `ToString()`:

```
Imports System.Collections.ObjectModel

Public Class CarList
  Inherits ObservableCollection(Of Car)

  Public Sub New()
    ' Add a few entries to the list.
    Add(New Car(40, "BMW", "Black", "Sidd"))
    Add(New Car(55, "VW", "Black", "Mary"))
    Add(New Car(100, "Ford", "Tan", "Mel"))
    Add(New Car(0, "Yugo", "Green", "Clunker"))
  End Sub
End Class
```

```
Public Class Car
  ' Assume four public properties are in the Car
  ' class named Speed, Make, Color and PetName.

  Public Sub New(ByVal CarSpeed As Integer, ByVal CarMake As String, _
    ByVal CarColor As String, ByVal CarName As String)
    Speed = CarSpeed
    Make = CarMake
    Color = CarColor
    PetName = CarName
  End Sub
  Public Sub New()
  End Sub

  Public Overrides Function ToString() As String
    Return String.Format("{0} the {1} {2} is going {3} MPH", _
      PetName, Color, Make, Speed)
  End Function
End Class
```

Now, open the code file for your `MainWindow` class and define and create a member variable of type `CarList` named `myCars`:

```
Class MainWindow
  Private myCars As New CarList()
...
End Class
```

Within the `Loaded` event handler of your `Window` type, set the `DataContext` property of the `allCars` `ListBox` to the `myCars` object (recall we did not set this value via XAML with the `{Binding}` extension, therefore for a change of pace, we will do so using procedural code):

```
Private Sub Window_Loaded(ByVal sender As System.Object, _
  ByVal e As System.Windows.RoutedEventArgs)
    ' Set the data context.
    allCars.DataContext = myCars
End Sub
```

At this point, you should be able to run your application and see the `ListBox` containing the `ToString()` values for each `Car` in the custom `ObservableCollection(Of T)`, as shown in Figure 31-32.

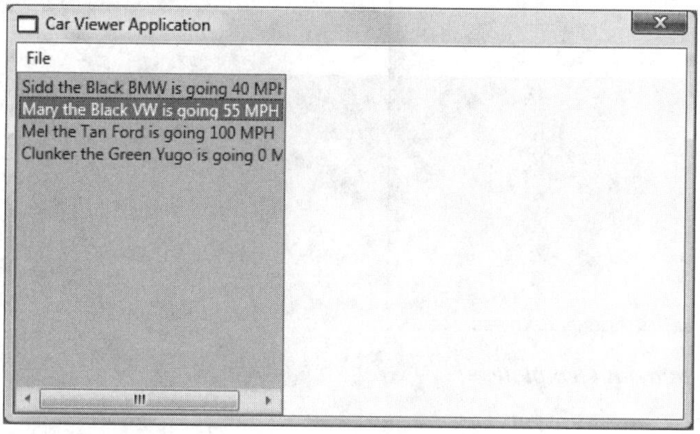

Figure 31-32. *The initial data binding operation*

Creating a Custom Data Template

Currently, ListBox is displaying each item in the CarList object; however, because we have not specified a binding path, each list entry is simply the result of calling ToString() on the subobjects. As we have already examined how to establish simple binding paths, this time we will construct a custom *data template*. Simply put, a data template can be used to inform the destination of a data binding operation how to display the data connected to it. Our template will fill each item in the ListBox with a <StackPanel> that consists of an Ellipse object and a TextBlock that has been bound to the PetName property of each item in the CarList type. Here is the modified markup of the ListBox type:

```
<ListBox Grid.Column="0"
  Grid.Row="2" Name="allCars" SelectionChanged="ListItemSelected"
   Background="LightBlue" ItemsSource="{Binding}">
  <ListBox.ItemTemplate>
    <DataTemplate>
      <StackPanel Orientation="Horizontal">
        <Ellipse Height="10" Width="10" Fill="Blue"/>
        <TextBlock FontStyle="Italic" FontSize="14" Text="{Binding Path=PetName}"/>
      </StackPanel>
    </DataTemplate>
  </ListBox.ItemTemplate>
</ListBox>
```

Here we connect our <DataTemplate> to the ListBox using the <ListBox.ItemTemplate> element. Before we see the result of this data template, implement the SelectionChanged handler of your ListBox to display the ToString() of the current selection within the rightmost TextBlock:

```
Private Sub ListItemSelected(ByVal sender As System.Object, _
  ByVal e As System.Windows.Controls.SelectionChangedEventArgs)
  ' Get correct car from the ObservableCollection based
  ' on the selected item in the list box. Then call toString().
  txtCarStats.Text = myCars(allCars.SelectedIndex).ToString()
End Sub
```

With this update, you should now see a more stylized display of our data, as shown Figure 31-33.

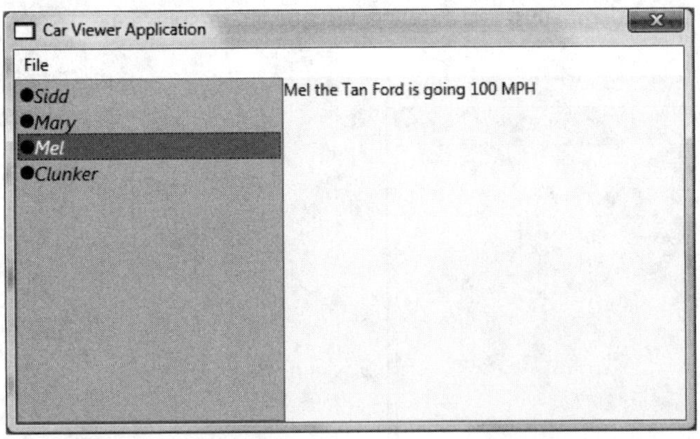

Figure 31-33. *Data binding with a custom data template*

Binding UI Elements to XML Documents

The next task is to build a custom dialog box that will use data binding to display the content of an external XML file within a stylized `ListView` object. First, insert the `Inventory.xml` file you created in Chapter 24 during the NavigationWithLinqToXmlObjectModel project using the Project ➤ Add Existing Item menu option. As you may recall, this XML file contains a set of `<Car>` elements within the root `<Inventory>`, for example:

```
<?xml version="1.0" encoding="utf-8"?>
<Inventory>
  <Car carID ="0">
    <Make>Ford</Make>
    <Color>Blue</Color>
    <PetName>Chuck</PetName>
  </Car>
...
</Inventory>
```

Select this file icon within Solution Explorer, and using the Properties window, set the Copy to Output Directory option to Copy Always. This will ensure that when you compile your application, the `Inventory.xml` file will be copied to your \bin\Debug folder.

Building a Custom Dialog Box

Insert a new WPF `Window` type into your project (named `AddNewCarDialog`) using the Project ➤ Add Window menu option of Visual Studio 2008. This new `Window` will display the content of the `Inventory.xml` file within a customized `ListView` type (named `lstCars`), via data binding. The first step is to author the XAML to define the look and feel of this new window. Here is the full markup, with analysis to follow:

```
<Window x:Class="AddNewCarDialog"
    xmlns="http://schemas.microsoft.com/winfx/2006/xaml/presentation"
    xmlns:x="http://schemas.microsoft.com/winfx/2006/xaml"
    Title="AddNewCarDialog" Height="234" Width="529"
    ResizeMode="NoResize" WindowStartupLocation="CenterScreen" >
  <Grid>
    <Grid.RowDefinitions>
      <RowDefinition Height="144" />
      <RowDefinition Height="51" />
    </Grid.RowDefinitions>

    <!-- Use the XmlDataProvider -->
    <Grid.Resources>
      <XmlDataProvider x:Key="CarsXmlDoc"
       Source="Inventory.xml"/>
    </Grid.Resources>

    <!-- Now, build a grid of data, mapping attributes/elements to columns
         using XPath expressions -->
    <ListView Name="lstCars" Grid.Row="0" ItemsSource=
     "{Binding Source={StaticResource CarsXmlDoc}, XPath=/Inventory/Car}"
    >
      <ListView.View>
        <GridView>
          <GridViewColumn Width="100" Header="ID"
                          DisplayMemberBinding="{Binding XPath=@carID}"/>
```

```
            <GridViewColumn Width="100" Header="Make"
                            DisplayMemberBinding="{Binding XPath=Make}"/>
            <GridViewColumn Width="100" Header="Color"
                            DisplayMemberBinding="{Binding XPath=Color}"/>
            <GridViewColumn Width="150" Header="Pet Name"
                            DisplayMemberBinding="{Binding XPath=PetName}"/>
          </GridView>
        </ListView.View>
      </ListView>

      <WrapPanel Grid.Row="1">
        <Label Content="Select a Row to Add to your car collection" Margin="10" />
        <Button Name="btnOK" Content="OK" Width="80" Height="25"
                Margin="10" IsDefault="True" TabIndex="1" Click="btnOK_Click"/>
        <Button Name="btnCancel" Content="Cancel" Width="80" Height="25"
                Margin="10" IsCancel="True" TabIndex="2"/>
      </WrapPanel>
    </Grid>
  </Window>
```

Starting at the top, notice that the opening `<Window>` element has been defined by specifying a value of `NoResize` to the `ResizeMode` attribute, given that most dialog boxes do not allow the user to alter the size of the window's dimensions.

Beyond carving up our `<Grid>` into two rows of a given size, the next point of interest is that we are placing into the grid's resource dictionary a new object of type `XmlDataProvider`. This type can be connected to an external `*.xml` file via the `Source` attribute. As we have configured the `Inventory.xml` file to be located within the application directory of our current project, we have no need to worry about hard-coding a fixed path.

The real bulk of this markup takes place within the definition of the `ListView` element. First of all, notice that the `ItemsSource` attribute has been assigned to the `CarsXmlDoc` resource, which is qualified using the `XPath` attribute. Based on your experience, you may know that XPath is an XML technology that allows you to navigate within an XML document using a querylike syntax. Here we are saying that our initial data binding path begins with the `<Car>` element of the `<Inventory>` root.

To inform the `ListView` type to display a gridlike front end, we next make use of the `<ListView.View>` element to define a `<GridView>` consisting of four `<GridViewColumn>` elements. Each of these types specifies a `Header` value (for display purposes) and most importantly a `DisplayMemberBinding` data binding value. Given that the `<ListView>` element has already specified the initial path within the XML document to be the `<Car>` subelement of `<Inventory>`, each of the `XPath` bindings for the column types use this as a starting point.

The first `<GridViewColumn>` is displaying the `ID` attribute of the `<Car>` element using an `XPath`-specific syntax for plucking our attribute values (`@carID`). The remaining columns simply further qualify the path within the XML document by appending the next subelement using the `XPath` qualifier of the `{Binding}` markup extension.

Last but not least, the final row of the `<Grid>` contains a `<WrapPanel>` that contains two `Buttons` (and a descriptive `Label`) to complete the UI. The only points of interest here would be that we are handling the `Click` event of the OK button and the use of the `IsDefault` and `IsCancel` properties. These establish which button on a window should respond to the `Click` event when the Enter key or Esc key is pressed.

Finally, note that these `Button` elements specify a `TabIndex` value and a `Margin` value, the latter of which allows you to define spacing around each item in the `<WrapPanel>`.

Assigning the DialogResult Value

Before we display this new dialog box, we need to implement the `Click` handler for the OK button. Similar to Windows Forms (see Chapter 27), WPF dialog boxes can inform the caller which button has been clicked via the `DialogResult` property. However, *unlike* the `DialogResult` property found in Windows Forms, in the WPF model, this property operates on a nullable Boolean value, rather than a strongly typed enumeration. Thus, if you wish to inform the caller the user wants to employ the data in the dialog box for use within the program (typically indicated by clicking an OK, Yes, or Accept button), set the inherited `DialogResult` property to `True` in the `Click` handler of said button:

```
Partial Public Class AddNewCarDialog

  Private Sub btnOK_Click(ByVal sender As System.Object, _
  ByVal e As System.Windows.RoutedEventArgs)
    DialogResult = True
  End Sub
End Class
```

As the default value of `DialogResult` is `False`, we have no need to do anything if the user clicks the Cancel button.

Obtaining the Current Selection

Finally, add a custom read-only property to your `AddNewCarDialog` class named `SelectedCar`, which returns a new `Car` object to the caller based on the values of the selected row of the grid:

```
Public ReadOnly Property SelectedCar() As Car
  Get
    ' Cast selected item on grid to an XmlElement.
    Dim carRow As System.Xml.XmlElement = _
        DirectCast(lstCars.SelectedItem, System.Xml.XmlElement)

    ' Make sure the user selected something!
    If carRow Is Nothing Then
      Return Nothing
    Else
      ' Generate a random speed.
      Dim r As New Random()
      Dim speed As Integer = r.Next(100)

      ' Return new Car based on the data in selected XmlElement/speed.
      Return New Car(speed, carRow("Make").InnerText, _
        carRow("Color").InnerText, _
        carRow("PetName").InnerText)
    End If
  End Get
End Property
```

Notice we cast the return value of the `SelectedItem` property (which is of type `System.Object`) into an `XmlElement` type. This is possible because our `ListView` is indeed connected to the `Inventory.xml` file via our data binding operation. Once we nab the current `XmlElement`, we are able to access the `Make`, `Color`, and `PetName` elements (using the type indexer) and extract out the values by calling `InnerText`.

■Note If you have never worked with the types of the `System.Xml` namespace, simply know that the `InnerText` property obtains the value between the opening and closing elements of an XML node. For example, the inner text of `<Make>Ford</Make>` would be `Ford`.

Displaying a Custom Dialog Box

Now that our dialog box is complete, we are able to launch it from the `Click` handler of the File ➤ Add New Car menu option:

```
Private Sub AddNewCarWizard(ByVal sender As System.Object, _
  ByVal e As System.Windows.RoutedEventArgs)
  Dim dlg As New AddNewCarDialog()
  If True = dlg.ShowDialog() Then
    If dlg.SelectedCar IsNot Nothing Then
      myCars.Add(dlg.SelectedCar)
    End If
  End If
End Sub
```

Like Windows Forms, a WPF dialog box may be shown as a modal dialog box (by calling `ShowDialog()`) or as a modeless dialog (by calling `Show()`). If the return value of `ShowDialog()` is `True`, we ask the dialog box for the new `Car` object and add it to our `ObservableCollection(Of T)`. Because this collection type sends out notifications when its contents are altered, you will find your `ListBox` will automatically refresh itself as you insert new items. Figure 31-34 shows the UI of our custom dialog box.

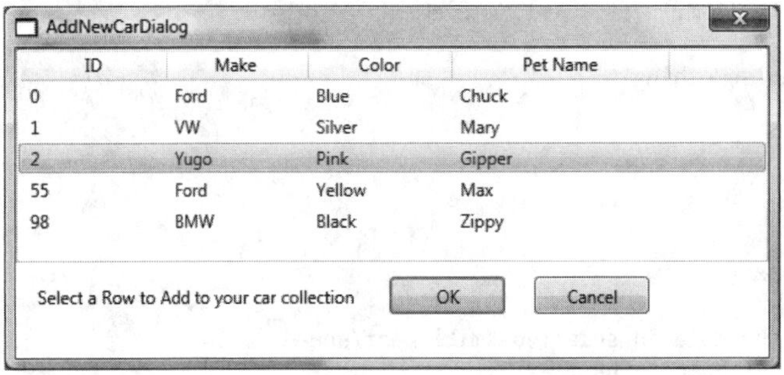

Figure 31-34. *A custom grid of data, bound to an XML document*

■Source Code The CarViewerApp project can be found under the Chapter 31 subdirectory.

That wraps up our look at the WPF data binding engine and the core controls found within this UI API. In the next chapter, you will complete your investigation of Windows Presentation Foundation by examining the role of graphical rendering, resource management, and the construction of custom themes.

Summary

This chapter examined several aspects of WPF controls, beginning with a discussion of dependency properties and routed events. These WPF mechanisms are very important for several aspects of WPF programming, including data binding, animation services, and a slew of other features. Over the course of this chapter, you have had a chance to configure and tweak several controls and learned to arrange your UI content in various panel types.

More importantly, you examined the use of WPF commands. Recall that these control-agnostic events can be attached to a UI element or an input gesture to automatically inherit out-of-the-box services (such as clipboard operations). You also dove into the mechanics of the WPF data binding engine and learned how to bind property values, custom objects, and XML documents to your UI layer. At this time, you also learned how to build WPF dialog boxes and discovered the role of the `IValueConverter` and `ObservableCollection(Of T)` types.

CHAPTER 32

WPF 2D Graphical Rendering, Resources, and Themes

The purpose of this chapter is to examine three ultimately independent, yet interrelated topics, which will enable you to build more sophisticated Windows Presentation Foundation applications than shown in the previous two chapters. The first order of business is to investigate the WPF 2D graphical programming APIs. Here you will examine numerous ways to render 2D geometric images (via shapes, drawings, and visuals) and work with graphical primitives such as brushes and pens. Along the way, you will also be introduced to the topic of WPF animation services and the types of the `System.Windows.Media.Animation` namespace.

Once you understand the basic 2D graphical rendering/animation primitives of WPF, we will then move on to an examination of how WPF allows you to define, embed, and reference application resources. Generally speaking, the term "application resources" refers to string tables, image files, icons, and other non-code-based entities used by an application. While this is still true under WPF, a "resource" can also represent custom graphical and UI objects you wish to embed into an assembly for later use.

The final topic of this chapter closes the gap between these two seemingly unrelated topics by examining how to define styles and templates for your control types. As you will see, creating styles and templates almost always involves making extensive use of WPF's graphical rendering/animation services and packaging them into your assembly as application resources.

Note You may recall from Chapter 30 that WPF provides comprehensive support for 3D graphics programming, which is beyond the scope of this text. If you require details regarding this aspect of WPF, check out *Pro WPF with VB 2008: Windows Presentation Foundation with .NET 3.5, Second Edition* by Matthew MacDonald (Apress, 2008).

The Philosophy of WPF Graphical Rendering Services

WPF makes use of a particular flavor of graphical rendering that goes by the term *retained mode graphics.* Simply put, this means that as you are using XAML or procedural code to generate graphical renderings, it is the responsibility of the WPF runtime to persist these visual items and ensure they are correctly redrawn and refreshed in an optimal manner. Thus, when you render graphical data, it is always present regardless of whether the end user hides the image by resizing the window, minimizing the window, covering the window with another, and so forth.

In stark contrast, previous Microsoft graphical rendering APIs (including GDI+) were *immediate mode* graphics systems. Under this model, it is up to the programmer to ensure that rendered visuals are correctly "remembered" and updated during the life of the application. For example, recall from Chapter 28 that under GDI+, rendering a rectangle involves handling the `Paint` event (or overriding the virtual `OnPaint()` method), obtaining a `Graphics` object to draw the rectangle and, most important, adding the infrastructure to ensure that the image is persisted when the user resizes the window (e.g., create member variables to represent the position of the rectangle, call `Invalidate()` throughout your program, etc.). This conceptual shift from immediate mode to retained mode graphics is indeed a good thing, as programmers have much less grungy graphics code to author and maintain.

However, this point is not to suggest that the WPF graphics API is *completely* different from earlier rendering toolkits. For example, like GDI+, WPF supports various brush types and pen types, the ability to render graphics at runtime through code, techniques for hit-testing support, and so forth. So to this end, if you currently have a background in GDI+, you already know a good deal about how to perform basic renderings under WPF.

WPF Graphical Rendering Options

Like other aspects of WPF development, you have a number of choices regarding *how* you will perform your graphical rendering, above and beyond the decision to do so via XAML or procedural VB code. Specifically, WPF provides three distinct ways to render graphical data:

- `System.Windows.Shapes`: This namespace defines a number of types used to render 2D geometric objects (rectangles, ellipses, polygons, etc.). While these types are very simple to use, they do come with a good deal of overhead.
- `System.Windows.Media.Drawing`: This abstract base class defines a more lightweight set of services for a number of derived types (`GeometryDrawing`, `ImageDrawing`, etc.).
- `System.Windows.Media.Visual`: This abstract base class provides the most lightweight approach to render graphical data; however, it also requires authoring a fair amount of procedural code.

The motivation behind offering a number of different ways to do the exact same thing (e.g., render graphical data) has to do with memory usage and ultimately application performance. Given that WPF is such a graphically intensive system, it is not unreasonable for an application to render hundreds of different images upon a window's surface, and your choice of implementation (shapes, drawings, or visuals) could have a huge impact.

To set the stage for the sections to come, let's begin with a brief overview of each option, from the "heaviest" to the "lightest." If you wish to try out each option firsthand, create a new WPF Windows Application project named WPFGraphicsOptions, change the name of your initial `Window` type to `MainWindow`, and replace the window's initial XAML `<Grid>` definition with a `<StackPanel>`:

```
<Window x:Class="MainWindow"
  xmlns="http://schemas.microsoft.com/winfx/2006/xaml/presentation"
  xmlns:x="http://schemas.microsoft.com/winfx/2006/xaml"
  Title="WPFGraphicsOptions" Height="300" Width="300" >
  <StackPanel>

  </StackPanel>
</Window>
```

Use of the Shape-Derived Types

The members of the System.Windows.Shapes namespace (Ellipse, Line, Path, Polygon, Polyline, and Rectangle) are the absolute simplest way to render a 2D image and are appropriate when you need to render infrequently used images (such as a region of a stylized button) or you need a graphical image that can support user interaction. Using these types typically entails selecting a "brush" for the interior fill and a "pen" for the border outline (you'll examine WPF's brush and pen options later in this chapter). To illustrate the basic use of shape types, if you add the following to your <StackPanel>, you will find a simple light blue rectangle with a blue outline:

```
<!-- Draw a rectangle using Shape types -->
<Rectangle Height="55" Width="105" Stroke="Blue"
  StrokeThickness="5" Fill="LightBlue"/>
```

While these types are ridiculously simple to use, they are a bit on the bloated side due to the fact that their parent class, Sysem.Windows.Shapes.Shape, attempts to be all things to all people (if you will). Shape inherits a ton of services from its long list of parents in the inheritance chain: Shape "is-a" FrameworkElement, which "is-a" UIElement, which "is-a" Visual, which "is-a" DependencyObject, DispatcherObject, and Object!

Collectively, these base classes provide the derived types with support for styles and templates, data binding support, resource management, the ability to send numerous events, the ability to monitor keyboard and mouse input, complex layout management, and animation services. Figure 32-1 illustrates the inheritance of the Shape type, as seen through the eyes of the Visual Studio object browser.

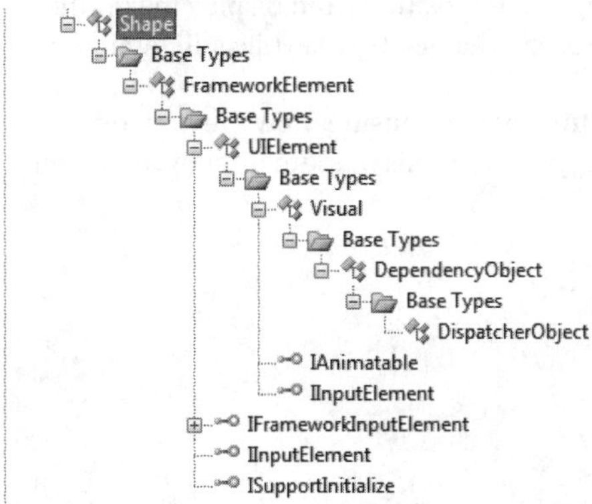

Figure 32-1. Shape*-derived types gain a ton of functionality from their parent types.*

While each parent adds various bits of functionality, UIElement is a key culprit. For example, UIElement defines over *80 events* to handle numerous forms of input (mouse, keyboard, and stylus for Tablet PCs). FrameworkElement is the other suspect, in that this type provides members for changing the mouse cursor, various events representing object lifetime, context menus support, and so on. Given this, the Shape-derived types can be as interactive as other UI elements such as Buttons, ProgressBars, and other widgets.

The bottom line is that while the Shape-derived types are very simple to use and quite powerful, this very fact makes them the heaviest option for rendering 2D graphics. Again, using these types is just fine for "occasional rendering" (the definition of which can be more of a gut feel than a hard science) or when you honestly do need a graphical rendering that is responsive to user interaction. However, if you are designing a more graphically intensive application, you will likely find some performance gains by using the Drawing-derived types.

Use of the Drawing-Derived Types

The `System.Windows.Media.Drawing` abstract base class represents the bare bones of a two-dimensional surface. The derived types (such as `GeometryDrawing`, `ImageDrawing`, and `VideoDrawing`) are more lightweight than the `Shape`-derived types in that neither `UIElement` nor `FrameworkElement` is in the inheritance chain. Given this, `Drawing`-derived types do not have intrinsic support for handling input events (although it is possible to programmatically perform hit-testing logic); however, they can be animated due to the fact that `Animatable` is in the family (see Figure 32-2).

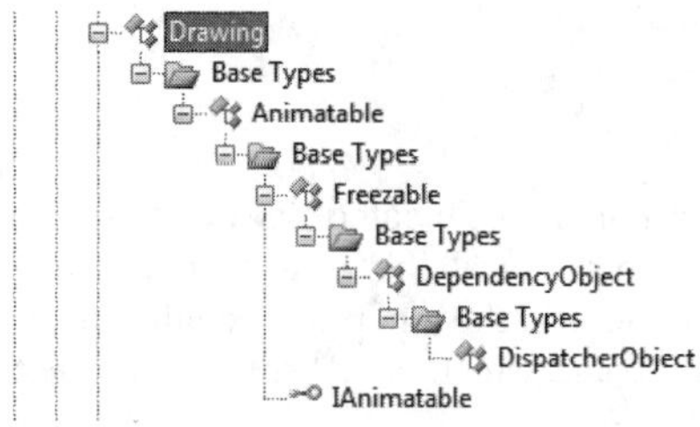

Figure 32-2. `Drawing`*-derived types are significantly more lightweight than* `Shape`*-derived types.*

Another key difference between `Drawing`-derived types and `Shape`-derived types is that `Drawing`-derived types have no ability to render themselves, as they do not derive from `UIElement`! Rather, derived types must be placed within a hosting object (such as `DrawingImage`, `DrawingBrush`, or `DrawingVisual`) to display their content. This decoupling of composition from display makes the `Drawing`-derived types much more lightweight than the `Shape`-derived types, while still retaining key services.

Without getting too hung up on the details for the time being, consider how the previous `Rectangle` could be rendered using the drawing-centric types (add this markup directly after your previous `<Rectangle>` if you are following along):

```
<!-- Draw a rectangle using Drawing types -->
<Image Height="55" Width="105">
  <Image.Source>
    <DrawingImage>
      <DrawingImage.Drawing>
        <GeometryDrawing Brush="LightBlue">
          <GeometryDrawing.Pen>
            <Pen Brush="Blue" Thickness="5"/>
          </GeometryDrawing.Pen>
          <GeometryDrawing.Geometry>
            <RectangleGeometry Rect="0,0,100,50"/>
          </GeometryDrawing.Geometry>
        </GeometryDrawing>
      </DrawingImage.Drawing>
    </DrawingImage>
  </Image.Source>
</Image>
```

While the output is identical to the previous `<Rectangle>`, it is clearly more verbose. What we have here is the classic "more code for better performance" dilemma. Thankfully, when you make use of XAML graphical design tools (such as Microsoft Expression Blend or Microsoft Expression Design), the underlying markup is rendered behind the scenes (see Chapter 30 for information regarding the Microsoft Expression product family).

Use of the Visual-Derived Types

The abstract `System.Windows.Media.Visual` class type provides a minimal and complete set of services to render a derived type (rendering, hit testing, transformation), but it does not provide support for addition nonvisual services, which can lead to code bloat (input events, layout services, styles, and data binding). Given this, the `Visual`-derived types (`DrawingVisual`, `Viewport3DVisual`, and `ContainerVisual`) are the most lightweight of all graphical rendering options and offer the best performance. Notice the simple inheritance chain of the `Visual` type, as shown in Figure 32-3.

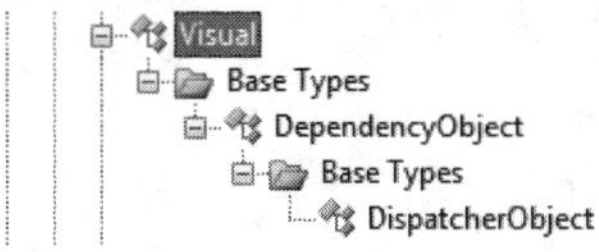

Figure 32-3. *The* `Visual` *type provides basic hit testing, coordinate transformation, and bounding box calculations.*

Because the `Visual` type exposes the lowest level of functionality, it has limited support for direct XAML definitions (unless you use a `Visual` within a type that *can* be expressed in XAML). Using these types feels a bit closer to making use of GDI/GDI+ rendering APIs, in that they are often manipulated through procedural code. When doing so, you are manually populating the object graph representing your window with custom `Visual`-derived types. Furthermore, you are required to override various virtual methods that will be called by the WPF graphics system to figure out how many items you are rendering, and the `Visual` item itself to be rendered.

To illustrate how you can use the `Visual`-derived types to render 2D data, open the code file for your main window type and comment out the entire definition (so you can restore it shortly, with minimal effort):

```
' Class MainWindow
' End Class
```

Now create the following `Window`-derived type that renders a rectangle directly on the surface of the window, bypassing any content defined in the XAML markup (your previous XAML descriptions will be ignored and not displayed):

```
Class MainWindow
  Inherits System.Windows.Window
  ' Our single drawing visual.
  Private rectVisual As New DrawingVisual()
  Private Const NumberOfVisualItems As Integer = 1

  Public Sub New()
    InitializeComponent()

    ' Helper function to create the rectangle.
    CreateRectVisual()
  End Sub

  Private Sub CreateRectVisual()
    Using drawCtx As DrawingContext = rectVisual.RenderOpen()
      ' The top, left, bottom, and right position of the rectangle.
      Dim rect As New Rect(50, 50, 105, 55)
      drawCtx.DrawRectangle(Brushes.AliceBlue, New Pen(Brushes.Blue, 5), rect)
    End Using
```

```
    ' Register our visual with the object tree,
    ' to ensure it supports routed events, hit testing, etc.
    AddVisualChild(rectVisual)
    AddLogicalChild(rectVisual)
  End Sub

  ' Necessary overrides. The WPF graphics system
  ' will call these to figure out how many items to
  ' render and what to render.
  Protected Overrides ReadOnly Property VisualChildrenCount() As Integer
    Get
      Return NumberOfVisualItems
    End Get
  End Property

  Protected Overrides Function GetVisualChild(ByVal index As Integer) As Visual
    ' Collection is zero based, so subtract 1.
    If index <> (NumberOfVisualItems - 1) Then
      Throw New ArgumentOutOfRangeException("index", "Don't have that visual!")
    End If
    Return rectVisual
  End Function
End Class
```

Notice that the DrawingVisual instance (rectVisual) provides the RenderOpen() method, which will return a DrawingContext object. Similar to GDI+'s Graphics object, DrawingContext has numerous methods that can be used to render a variety of items (DrawRectangle(), DrawEllipse(), etc.). Once you have constructed your rectangle, you make calls to two inherited methods (AddVisualChild() and AddLogicalChild()), which, while technically optional, ensure your custom Visual-derived item integrates into the window's tree of objects.

Last but not least, you are required to override the virtual VisualChildrenCount read-only property and GetVisualChild() method. These members are called by the WPF graphics engine to determine exactly what to render (a single DrawingVisual in this example).

As you can see, as soon as you move into the realm of working with Visual-derived types, you are knee-deep in procedural code and therefore have a great deal of control and power (and the associated complexity that follows).

Building a Custom Visual Rendering Agent

Your current custom Visual rendering operation was set up in such a way that the window's content (e.g., the <StackPanel>) was blown away and therefore not rendered, in favor of the hard-coded DrawingVisual. Just to dig a bit deeper into the Visual programming layer, what if you wished to use XAML descriptions for a majority of your window's rendering and dip into the Visual layer for just a small portion of the overall UI?

One approach to do so is to define a custom class deriving from FrameworkElement and override the virtual OnRender() method. This method (which is in fact what the Shape-derived types use to render their output) can contain the same sort of code found in our previous CreateRectVisual() helper method. Once you have defined this custom class, you can then refer to your custom class type from within a window's XAML description.

To illustrate, to your current project add a new class named MyCustomRenderer, which extends the FrameworkElement base class. Now, implement your type as follows:

```
Public Class MyCustomRenderer
  Inherits FrameworkElement
  ' Default size for our rectangle.
  Private m_rectWidth As Double = 105, m_rectHeight As Double = 55

  ' Allow user to override the defaults.
  Public Property RectHeight() As Double
    Get
      Return m_rectHeight
    End Get
    Set(ByVal value As Double)
      m_rectHeight = value
    End Set
  End Property
  Public Property RectWidth() As Double
    Get
      Return m_rectWidth
    End Get
    Set(ByVal value As Double)
      m_rectWidth = value
    End Set
  End Property

  Protected Overloads Overrides Sub OnRender(ByVal drawCtx As DrawingContext)
    ' Do parent rendering first.
    MyBase.OnRender(drawCtx)

    ' Add our custom rendering.
    Dim rect As New Rect()
    rect.Width = m_rectWidth
    rect.Height = m_rectHeight
    drawCtx.DrawRectangle(Brushes.LightBlue, New Pen(Brushes.Blue, 5), rect)
  End Sub
End Class
```

Most of the action of our custom type takes place in the OnRender() implementation. Notice that we have set the size of the local Rect variable based on our rectHeight and rectWidth members which, while not necessary, allow the creator to define the overall size of the image.

Gaining access to this type in XAML is simply a matter of defining a custom XML namespace that maps to the name of our type and using this prefix to create our type. Here are the relevant updates to the <StackPanel> type (recall from Chapter 30 that XML namespaces that map to your own .NET namespaces must be defined using the clr-namespace token):

```
<StackPanel xmlns:custom = "clr-namespace:WPFGraphicsOptions">
  ...
  <custom:MyCustomRenderer RectHeight ="100" RectWidth ="100"/>
</StackPanel>
```

Before you run your application, be sure to *uncomment* your original main window definition and *comment* out your custom window definition. Once you do, you can run your application and see three rectangular renderings, using each of the WPF 2D graphics programming techniques (see Figure 32-4).

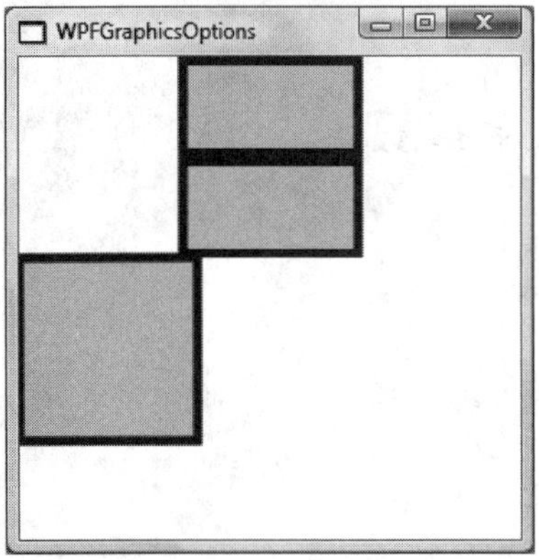

Figure 32-4. *Three rectangles, three approaches*

Source Code The WPFGraphicsOptions project can be found under the Chapter 32 subdirectory.

Picking Your Poison

At this point, you have seen three different approaches to interacting with the WPF 2D graphical rendering services (shapes, drawings, and visuals). By and large, the need to render graphics using the `Visual`-derived types is only necessary if you are building custom controls, or you need a great deal of control over the rendering process. This is a good thing, as working with `Visual` and friends entails a healthy amount of effort compared to simple XAML descriptions. Given this, I will not dive into the `Visual` rending APIs beyond this point in the chapter (do feel free to consult the .NET Framework 3.5 SDK documentation for further details if you are interested).

Using the `Drawing`-derived types is a perfect middle-of-the-road approach, as these types still support core non-UI services (such as hit testing, etc.) at a lower cost than the `Shape` types. While this approach does entail more markup than required by the `Shape` types, you end up with an application using less overhead. We will examine more details of the `Drawing`-derived types a bit later in this chapter.

That being said, however, the `Shape` types are still a perfectly valid approach when you need to render a handful of 2D images within a given window. Recall that if you truly do need 2D shapes that are just about as capable as traditional UI elements, the `Shape` types are a perfect choice, given that the required infrastructure is already in place.

Note Always remember that your choice of rendering services can affect your application's performance. Thankfully, you are provided with a collection of various WPF profiling utilities to monitor your current application. Look up the topic "Performance Profiling Tools for WPF" within the .NET Framework 3.5 SDK documentation for further details.

Exploring the Shape-Derived Types

To continue exploring 2D graphical rendering, let's start by digging into the details of the members of the System.Windows.Shapes namespace. Recall these types provide the most straightforward, yet most bloated, way to render a two-dimensional image. This namespace (defined in the PresentationFramework.dll assembly) is quite small and consists of only six sealed types that extend the abstract Shape base class: Ellipse, Line, Path, Polygon, Polyline, and Rectangle.

Because the Shape base class "is-a" FrameworkElement, you are able to assign derived types as content using XAML or procedural VB code without the additional complexities of working with drawing geometries:

```
<Window x:Class="MainWindow"
  xmlns="http://schemas.microsoft.com/winfx/2006/xaml/presentation"
  xmlns:x="http://schemas.microsoft.com/winfx/2006/xaml"
  Height="300" Width="300" >

  <!-- A window with a circle as content -->
  <Ellipse Height = "100" Width = "100" Fill = "Black" />
</Window>
```

Like any other UI element, if you are building a window that requires multiple contained widgets, you will need to define your 2D types within a panel type, as described in Chapter 31.

The Functionality of the Shape Base Class

While most of Shape's functionality comes from its long list of parent classes, this type does define some specific properties (most of which are dependency properties) that are common to the child types, some of the more interesting of which are shown in Table 32-1.

Table 32-1. *Key Properties of the* Shape *Base Class*

Property	Meaning in Life
Fill	Allows you to specify a brush type to render the interior part of a derived type.
GeometryTransform	Allows you to apply a transformation to the rendering of the derived type.
Stretch	Describes how to fill a shape within its allocated space. This is controlled using the corresponding System.Windows.Media.Stretch enumeration.
Stroke StrokeDashArray StrokeEndLineCap StrokeThickness	Control how lines are configured when drawing the border of a shape.

Also recall that Shape-derived types have support for hit testing, themes and styles, tool tips, and numerous services.

Working with Rectangles, Ellipses, and Lines

To check out some of the derived types firsthand, create a new Visual Studio 2008 WPF Windows Application named FunWithSystemWindowsShapes. Declaring Rectangle, Ellipse, and Line types in XAML is quite straightforward and requires little comment. One interesting feature of the Rectangle type is that it defines RadiusX and RadiusY properties to allow you to render curved corners if you require. Line represents its starting and ending points using the X1, X2, Y1, and Y2 properties (given that "height" and "width" make little sense when describing a line). Without belaboring the point, consider the following <StackPanel>:

```
<StackPanel>
  <!-- A line that monitors the mouse entering its area -->
  <Line Name ="SimpleLine" X1 ="0" X2 ="50" Y1 ="0" Y2 ="50"
    Stroke ="DarkOliveGreen" StrokeThickness ="5"
    ToolTip ="This is a line!" MouseEnter ="SimpleLine_MouseEnter"/>

  <!-- A rectangle with curved corners -->
  <Rectangle RadiusX ="20" RadiusY ="50"
             Fill ="DarkBlue" Width ="150" Height ="50"/>
</StackPanel>
```

The MouseEnter event of the SimpleLine object simply updates the Title property of the window with the location of the mouse cursor at the time it entered the Line object:

```
Class MainWindow
  Private Sub SimpleLine_MouseEnter(ByVal sender As System.Object, _
    ByVal e As System.Windows.Input.MouseEventArgs)
    Me.Title = String.Format("Mouse entered at: {0}", _
    e.GetPosition(SimpleLine))
  End Sub
End Class
```

Working with Polylines, Polygons, and Paths

The Polyline type allows you to define a collection of (*x*, *y*) coordinates (via the Points property) to draw a series of connected line segments that do not require connecting ends. The Polygon type is similar; however, it is programmed in such a way that it will always close the starting and ending points. Consider the following additions to the current <StackPanel>:

```
<!-- Polyline types do not have connecting ends -->
<Polyline Stroke ="Red" StrokeThickness ="20" StrokeLineJoin ="Round"
  Points ="10,10  40,40  10,90  300,50"/>

<!-- A Polygon always closes the end points-->
<Polygon Fill ="AliceBlue" StrokeThickness ="5" Stroke ="Green"
  Points ="40,10 70,80 10,50" />
```

Figure 32-5 shows the rendered output for each of these Shape-derived items.

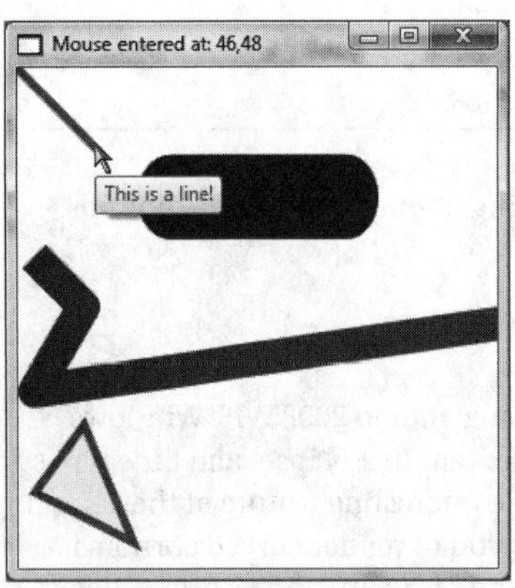

Figure 32-5. *Rendered* Shape-*derived types*

The final type, Path (not examined here), can be considered the superset of Rectangle, Ellipse, Polyline, and Polygon in that Path can render any of these types. In fact, all 2D types could be rendered using nothing but Path (however, doing so would require additional work).

■ **Source Code** The FunWithSystemWindowsShapes project can be found under the Chapter 32 subdirectory.

Working with WPF Brushes

Each of the WPF graphical rendering options (shape types, drawing types, and visual types) makes extensive use of *brushes*, which allow you to control how the interior of a 2D surface is filled. WPF provides six different brush types, all of which extend System.Windows.Media.Brush. While Brush is abstract, the descendents described in Table 32-2 can be used to fill a region with just about any conceivable option.

Table 32-2. *WPF* Brush-*Derived Types*

Brush Type	Meaning in Life
DrawingBrush	Paints an area with a Drawing-derived object (GeometryDrawing, ImageDrawing, or VideoDrawing)
ImageBrush	Paints an area with an image (represented by an ImageSource object)
LinearGradientBrush	Paints an area with a linear gradient
RadialGradientBrush	Paints an area with a radial gradient
SolidColorBrush	Represents a brush consisting of a single color, set with the Color property
VisualBrush	Paints an area with a Visual-derived object (DrawingVisual, Viewport3DVisual, and ContainerVisual)

The DrawingBrush and VisualBrush types allow you to build a brush based on the Drawing- or Visual-derived types examined at the beginning of this chapter. The remaining brush types are quite straightforward to make use of and are very close in functionality to similar types found within GDI+. The following sections present a quick overview of SolidColorBrush, LinearGradientBrush, RadialGradientBrush, and ImageBrush.

■ **Note** Given that these examples will not respond to any events, you can enter each of the following examples directly into the custom XAML viewer you created in Chapter 30, rather than creating new Visual Studio 2008 WPF Application project workspaces.

Building Brushes with Solid Colors

The SolidColorBrush type provides the Color property to establish a solid-colored brush type. The Color property takes a System.Windows.Media.Color type, which contains various properties (such as A, R, G, and B) to establish the color itself. While the capability to have solid colors is useful, ironically you typically will not need to directly create a SolidColorBrush explicitly, given that XAML supports a type converter that maps known color names (e.g., "Blue") to a SolidColorBrush object behind the scenes. Consider the following approaches to fill an Ellipse with a solid color:

```
<StackPanel>
  <!-- Solid brush using type converter -->
  <Ellipse Fill ="DarkRed" Height ="50" Width ="50"/>

  <!-- Using the SolidColorBrush type -->
  <Ellipse Height ="50" Width ="50">
    <Ellipse.Fill>
      <SolidColorBrush Color ="DarkGoldenrod"/>
    </Ellipse.Fill>
  </Ellipse>

  <!-- Using the SolidColorBrush and Color type -->
  <Ellipse Height ="50" Width ="50">
    <Ellipse.Fill>
      <SolidColorBrush>
        <SolidColorBrush.Color>
          <Color A ="40" R ="100" G ="87" B ="98"/>
        </SolidColorBrush.Color>
      </SolidColorBrush>
    </Ellipse.Fill>
  </Ellipse>
</StackPanel>
```

The output is what you would expect (three circles of various solid colors); however, the approach you take to define the color scheme will be based on the level of flexibility you require. For example, if you do need to change the value of the Opacity property (to control transparency), you will need to declare a <SolidColorBrush> element to gain direct access to its members. In all other cases, you are able to make use of a simple string value assigned to the Fill property.

■ **Note** The WPF graphics API provides a helper class named Brushes, which defines properties for dozens of predefined colors. This is very useful when you need a solid-colored brush in procedural code.

Working with Gradient Brushes

The two gradient brush types (LinearGradientBrush and RadialGradientBrush) allow you to fill an area by transitioning between two (or more) colors. The distinction is that while a LinearGradientBrush always transitions between colors using a straight line (which could, of course, be rotated into any position using a graphical transformation or by setting the starting and ending points), a RadialGradientBrush transitions from a specified starting point outward within an elliptical boundary. Consider the following:

```
<!-- A rectangle with a linear fill -->
<Rectangle RadiusX ="15" RadiusY ="15" Height ="40" Width ="100">
  <Rectangle.Fill>
    <LinearGradientBrush StartPoint="0,0.5" EndPoint="1,0.5">
      <GradientStop Color="LimeGreen" Offset="0.0" />
      <GradientStop Color="Orange" Offset="0.25" />
      <GradientStop Color="Yellow" Offset="0.75" />
      <GradientStop Color="Blue" Offset="1.0" />
    </LinearGradientBrush>
```

```
  </Rectangle.Fill>
</Rectangle>

<!-- An ellipse with a radial fill -->
<Ellipse  Height ="75" Width ="75">
  <Ellipse.Fill>
    <RadialGradientBrush GradientOrigin="0.5,0.5"
      Center="0.5,0.5" RadiusX="0.5" RadiusY="0.5">
      <GradientStop Color="Yellow" Offset="0" />
      <GradientStop Color="Red" Offset="0.25" />
      <GradientStop Color="Blue" Offset="0.75" />
      <GradientStop Color="LimeGreen" Offset="1" />
    </RadialGradientBrush>
  </Ellipse.Fill>
</Ellipse>
```

Notice how both brush types maintain a list of <GradientStop> types (which can be of any number) that specify a color and offset value, which specifies where in the image the next color will peak to blend with the previous color.

The ImageBrush Type

The final brush type we will examine here is ImageBrush, which as the name suggests allows you to load an external image file (or better yet, to load an embedded image resource) as the basis of a brush type. To assign an external file to an ImageBrush, one approach requires you to set the ImageSource property to a valid BitmapImage object. Consider the following simple definition, which assumes you have a *.jpg file, Gooseberry0007.JPG, located in the same location as this *.xaml file:

```
<!-- A large rectangle built using an image brush -->
<Rectangle Height ="100" Width ="300">
  <Rectangle.Fill>
    <ImageBrush>
      <ImageBrush.ImageSource>
        <BitmapImage UriSource ="Gooseberry0007.JPG"/>
      </ImageBrush.ImageSource>
    </ImageBrush>
  </Rectangle.Fill>
</Rectangle>
```

Figure 32-6 shows each of our brush types in action.

Source Code The FunWithBrushes.xaml file can be found under the Chapter 32 subdirectory.

Figure 32-6. *Numerous brushes at work*

Working with WPF Pens

In comparison to brushes, the topic of pens is trivial, as the Pen type is really nothing more than a Brush in disguise. Specifically, Pen represents a brush type that has a specified thickness, represented by a Double value. Given this point, you could create a Pen that has a Thickness property value so large that it appears to be, in fact, a brush! However, in most cases you will build a Pen of more modest thickness to represent how to render the outline of a 2D image.

In many cases, you will not directly need to create a Pen type, as this will be done indirectly when you assign a value to properties such as StrokeThickness. However, building a custom Pen type is very handy when working with Drawing-derived types (described next). Before we see a customized pen doing something useful, consider the following example:

```
<Pen Thickness="10" LineJoin="Round" EndLineCap="Triangle" StartLineCap="Round" />
```

This particular Pen instance has set the LineJoin property, which controls how to render the connection point between two lines (e.g., the corners). EndLineCap, as the name suggests, controls how to render the endpoint of a line stroke (a triangle in this case), while StartLineCap controls the same setting at the line's point of origin.

A Pen can also be configured to make use of a *dash style*, which affects how the pen draws the line itself. The default setting is to use a solid color (as dictated by a given brush); however, the DashStyle property may be assigned to any custom DashStyle object. While creating a custom DashStyle object gives you complete control over how a Pen should render its data, the DashStyles helper class defines a number of shared members that provide common default styles. Because these are shared *members of a class* rather than values from an enumeration, we must make use of the XAML {x:Static} markup extension:

```
<Pen Thickness="10" LineJoin="Round" EndLineCap="Triangle"
  StartLineCap="Round" DashStyle = "{x:Static DashStyles.DashDotDot}" />
```

Now that you have a better idea of the Pen type, let's make use of some of them within various Drawing-derived types.

Exploring the Drawing-Derived Types

Recall that while the Shape types allow you to generate any sort of interactive two-dimensional surface, they entail quite a bit of overhead due to their rich inheritance chain. As an alternative, WPF provides a sophisticated drawing and geometry programming interface, which renders more lightweight 2D images. The entry point into this API is the abstract `System.Windows.Media.Drawing` class, which on its own does little more than define a bounding rectangle to hold the rendering. WPF provides five types that extend `Drawing`, each of which represents a particular flavor of drawing content, as described in Table 32-3.

Table 32-3. *WPF* `Drawing`*-Derived Types*

Type	Meaning in Life
`DrawingGroup`	Used to combine a collection of separate `Drawing`-derived types into a single composite rendering.
`GeometryDrawing`	Used to render 2D shapes.
`GlyphRunDrawing`	Used to render textual data using WPF graphical rendering services.
`ImageDrawing`	Used to render an image file into a bounding rectangle.
`VideoDrawing`	Used to play (not "draw") an audio file or video file. This type can only be fully exploited using procedural code. If you wish to play videos via XAML, the `MediaPlayer` type is a better choice.

While each of these types is useful in its own right, `GeometryDrawing` is the type of interest when you wish to render 2D images, and it is the one we will focus on during this section. In a nutshell, the `GeometryDrawing` type represents a *geometric type* detailing the structure of the 2D image, a `Brush`-derived type to fill its interior, and a `Pen` to draw its border.

The Role of Geometry Types

The geometric structure described by a `GeometryDrawing` type is actually one of the WPF geometry-centric class types, or possibly a collection of geometry-centric types that work together as a single unit. Each of these geometries can be expressed in XAML or via VB code. All of the geometries derive from the `System.Windows.Media.Geometry` base class, which defines a number of useful members common to all derived types, some of which appear in Table 32-4.

Table 32-4. *Select Members of the* `System.Windows.Media.Geometry` *Type*

Member	Meaning in Life
`Bounds`	A property used to establish the current bounding rectangle.
`FillContains()`	Allows you to determine whether a given `Point` (or other `Geometry` type) is within the bounds of a particular `Geometry`-derived type. Obviously, this is useful for hit-testing calculations.
`GetArea()`	Returns a `Double` that represents the entire area a `Geometry`-derived type occupies.
`GetRenderBounds()`	Returns a `Rect` that contains the smallest possible rectangle that could be used to render the `Geometry`-derived type.
`Transform`	Allows you to assign a `Transform` object to the geometry to alter the rendering.

WPF provides a good number of Geometry-derived types out of the box, and these can be grouped into two simple categories: basic shapes and paths. The first batch of geometric types, RectangleGeometry, EllipseGeometry, LineGeometry, and PathGeometry, are used to render basic shapes. As luck would have it, these four types mimic the functionality of the System.Windows.Media.Shapes types you have already examined (and in many cases they have identical members).

For many of your rendering operations, the basic shape types will do just fine. Do be aware, however, that if you require more exotic geometries, WPF supplies numerous auxiliary types that work in conjunction with the PathGeometry type. In a nutshell, PathGeometry maintains a collection of "path segments," which can be any of the following: BezierSegment, LineSegment, PolyBezierSegment, PolyLineSegment, PolyQuadraticBezierSegment, and QuadraticBezierSegment.

Dissecting a Simple Drawing Geometry

Let's take a closer look at the <GeometryDrawing> instance created at the beginning of this chapter:

```
<GeometryDrawing Brush ="LightBlue">
  <GeometryDrawing.Pen>
    <Pen Brush ="Blue" Thickness ="5"/>
  </GeometryDrawing.Pen>
  <GeometryDrawing.Geometry>
    <RectangleGeometry Rect="0,0,100,50"/>
  </GeometryDrawing.Geometry>
</GeometryDrawing>
```

Recall that a <GeometryDrawing> consists of a brush, pen, and any of the WPF geometry types. Here, we have indirectly defined a light blue SolidColorBrush using the Brush property in the <GeometryDrawing> start tag. The Pen is declared using property-element syntax, to define a blue brush with a specific thickness. Here, we are making use of a <RectangleGeometry> as the value assigned to the Geometry property of <GeometryDrawing>.

If you attempt to author this XAML directly within a <Page> scope (or within any ContentControl-derived type), you will generate a markup error that essentially tells you that <GeometryDrawing> does not extend the UIElement base class and therefore cannot be used as a value to the Content property.

This brings up an interesting aspect of working with the Drawing-derived types: they do not have any user interface in and of themselves! Types such as <GeometryDrawing> simply describe how a 2D element *would* look if placed into a suitable container. WPF provides three different hosting objects for Drawing objects: DrawingImage, DrawingBrush, and DrawingVisual.

Containing Drawing Types in a DrawingImage

The DrawingImage type allows you to plug your drawing geometry into a WPF <Image> control. Thus, if you wish to render the previous <GeometryDrawing>, you would need to wrap it as follows:

```
<Image Height="55" Width="105">
  <Image.Source>
    <DrawingImage>
      <DrawingImage.Drawing>
        <GeometryDrawing Brush ="LightBlue">
          ...
        </GeometryDrawing>
      </DrawingImage.Drawing>
    </DrawingImage>
  </Image.Source>
</Image>
```

Notice how the Source property of the Image type is assigned a Drawing-derived type (DrawingImage) that contains the previous GeometryDrawing.

Containing Drawing Types in a DrawingBrush

If you instead wrap a <GeometryDrawing> using a DrawingBrush type, you have essentially created a complex custom brush, given that DrawingBrush is actually one of the Brush-derived types (more information on brushes in the next section). You could then use it anywhere a Brush type is required, such as the Background property of the <Window> element:

```
<Window x:Class="MainWindow"
  xmlns="http://schemas.microsoft.com/winfx/2006/xaml/presentation"
  xmlns:x="http://schemas.microsoft.com/winfx/2006/xaml"
  Title="FunWithDrawingAndGeometries" Height="190" Width="224">

  <!-- Set the background of this window to a custom DrawingBrush -->
  <Window.Background>
    <DrawingBrush>
      <DrawingBrush.Drawing>
        <GeometryDrawing Brush ="LightBlue">
          <GeometryDrawing.Pen>
            <Pen Brush ="Blue" Thickness ="5"/>
          </GeometryDrawing.Pen>
          <GeometryDrawing.Geometry>
            <RectangleGeometry Rect="0,0,100,50"/>
          </GeometryDrawing.Geometry>
        </GeometryDrawing>
      </DrawingBrush.Drawing>
    </DrawingBrush>
  </Window.Background>
</Window>
```

A More Complex Drawing Geometry

A DrawingImage object can be composed of multiple individual Drawing objects, placed in a <DrawingGroup> in order to build much more elaborate 2D images. Consider the following Image, which uses a <DrawingImage> as its source:

```
<Image>
  <Image.Source>
    <DrawingImage>
      <DrawingImage.Drawing>
        <!-- A group of various geometries -->
        <DrawingGroup>
          <GeometryDrawing>
            <GeometryDrawing.Geometry>
              <GeometryGroup>
                <RectangleGeometry Rect="0,0,20,20" />
                <RectangleGeometry Rect="160,120,20,20" />
                <EllipseGeometry Center="75,75" RadiusX="50" RadiusY="50" />
                <LineGeometry StartPoint="75,75" EndPoint="180,0" />
              </GeometryGroup>
            </GeometryDrawing.Geometry>
            <!-- A custom pen to draw the borders -->
            <GeometryDrawing.Pen>
             <Pen Thickness="10" LineJoin="Round"
```

```
                  EndLineCap="Triangle" StartLineCap="Round">
              <Pen.Brush>
                <LinearGradientBrush>
                  <GradientStop Offset="0.0" Color="Red" />
                  <GradientStop Offset="1.0" Color="Green" />
                </LinearGradientBrush>
              </Pen.Brush>
            </Pen>
          </GeometryDrawing.Pen>
        </GeometryDrawing>
      </DrawingGroup>
    </DrawingImage.Drawing>
  </DrawingImage>
</Image.Source>
</Image>
```

The <DrawingImage> is composed of a <DrawingGroup> that contains a <GeometryGroup> to build an image consisting of two rectangles, an ellipse, and a line. The borders of our images are rendered using a custom pen type, which is in turn composed of a custom LinearGradientBrush. The end result can be seen in Figure 32-7.

Figure 32-7. *An image consisting of a* DrawingGroup

If we were to update our Pen type to make use of a DashStyle such as DashStyles.DashDotDot (seen previously):

```
<Pen Thickness="10" LineJoin="Round"
  EndLineCap="Triangle" StartLineCap="Round"
  DashStyle = "{x:Static DashStyles.DashDotDot}"
>
  <Pen.Brush>
    <LinearGradientBrush>
      <GradientStop Offset="0.0" Color="Red" />
      <GradientStop Offset="1.0" Color="Green" />
    </LinearGradientBrush>
  </Pen.Brush>
</Pen>
```

we would now find the rendering shown in Figure 32-8.

Figure 32-8. *A* `Pen` *with a* `DashStyle` *setting of dash-dot-dot*

■ Source Code The `FunWithDrawingGeometries.xaml` file can be found under the Chapter 32 subdirectory.

The Role of UI Transformations

Before moving on to the topic of animation services, allow me to wrap up our look at 2D graphic rendering by examining the topic of *transformations*. WPF ships with numerous types that extend the `Transform` abstract base class, which can be applied to any `FrameworkElement` (e.g., descendents of `Shape` as well as UI elements such as `Button`, `TextBox`, etc.). Using these types, you are able to render a `FrameworkElement` at a given angle, skew the image across a surface, and expand or shrink the image in a variety of ways.

Transform-Derived Types

Table 32-5 documents many of the key out-of-the-box `Transform` types.

Table 32-5. *Key Descendents of the* `System.Windows.Media.Transform` *Type*

Type	Meaning in Life
`MatrixTransform`	Creates an arbitrary matrix transformation that is used to manipulate objects or coordinate systems in a 2D plane
`RotateTransform`	Rotates an object clockwise about a specified point in a 2D (*x*, *y*) coordinate system
`ScaleTransform`	Scales an object in the 2D (*x*, *y*) coordinate system
`SkewTransform`	Skews an object in the 2D (*x*, *y*) coordinate system
`TransformGroup`	Represents a composite `Transform` composed of other `Transform` objects

Once you create a Transform-derived object, you can apply it to two properties provided by the FrameworkElement base class. The LayoutTransform property of FrameworkElement is helpful in that the transformation occurs before elements are rendered into a panel. The RenderTransform property, on the other hand, occurs after the items are in their container, and therefore it is quite possible that elements can be transformed in such a way that they overlap each other. As well, types that extend UIElement can also assign a value to the RenderTransformOrigin property, which simply specifies an (*x*, *y*) position to begin the transformation.

Applying Transformations

Assume we have a <Grid> containing a single row with four columns. Within each cell, we will rotate, skew, and scale various UIElements, for example:

```
<!-- A Rectangle with a rotate transformation -->
<Rectangle Height ="100" Width ="40" Fill ="Red" Grid.Row="0" Grid.Column="0">
  <Rectangle.LayoutTransform>
    <RotateTransform Angle ="45"/>
  </Rectangle.LayoutTransform>
</Rectangle>

<!-- A Button with a skew transformation -->
<Button Content ="Click Me!" Grid.Row="0" Grid.Column="1" Width="95" Height="40">
  <Button.RenderTransform>
    <SkewTransform AngleX ="20" AngleY ="20"/>
  </Button.RenderTransform>
</Button>

<!-- An Ellipse that has been scaled by 20% -->
<Ellipse Fill ="Blue" Grid.Row="0" Grid.Column="2" Width="5" Height="5">
  <Ellipse.RenderTransform>
    <ScaleTransform ScaleX ="20" ScaleY ="20"/>
  </Ellipse.RenderTransform>
</Ellipse>

<!-- A Button that has been skewed, rotated, and skewed again -->
<Button Content ="Me Too!" Grid.Row="0" Grid.Column="3" Width="50" Height="40">
  <Button.RenderTransform>
    <TransformGroup>
    <SkewTransform AngleX ="20" AngleY ="20"/>
    <RotateTransform Angle ="45"/>
    <SkewTransform AngleX ="5" AngleY ="20"/>
    </TransformGroup>
  </Button.RenderTransform>
</Button>
```

Our first UI element, the <Rectangle>, makes use of a RotateTransform object that renders the UI item at a 45-degree angle via the Angle property. The first <Button> uses a SkewTransform object, which slants the rendering of the widget based on (at minimum) the AngleX and AngleY properties. The ScaleTransform object used by the <Ellipse> grows the height and width of the circle quite a bit. Notice, for example, that the Height and Width properties of the <Ellipse> are set to 5, while the rendered output is much larger. Last but not least, the final <Button> makes use of a TransformGroup to apply a skew and a rotation. Figure 32-9 shows the rendered output.

Figure 32-9. *Applying transformations*

■ **Source Code** The `FunWithTransformations.xaml` file can be found under the Chapter 32 subdirectory.

Understanding WPF's Animation Services

In addition to providing a full-fledged API to support 2D (and 3D) graphical rendering, WPF supplies a programming interface to support animation services. The term "animation" may bring to mind visions of spinning company logos, a sequence of rotating image resources (to provide the illusion of movement), text bouncing across the screen, or specific types of programs such as video games or multimedia applications.

While WPF's animation APIs could certainly be used for such purposes, animation can be used anytime you wish to give an application additional flair. For example, you could build an animation for a button on a screen that magnifies slightly in size when the mouse cursor hovers within its boundaries (and shrinks back once the mouse cursor moves beyond the boundaries). Perhaps you wish to animate a window so that it closes using a particular visual appearance (such as slowly fading into transparency). The short answer is that WPF's animation support can be used within any sort of application (business application, multimedia programs, etc.) whenever you wish to provide a more engaging user experience.

Like many other aspects of WPF, the notion of building animations is nothing new in and of itself. However, unlike other APIs you may have used in the past (including GDI+), developers are not required to author the necessary infrastructure by hand. Under WPF, we have no need to create the background threads (or timers) used to advance the animation sequence, define custom types to represent the animation, or bother with numerous mathematical calculations.

Like other aspects of WPF, we are able to build an animation entirely using XAML, entirely using VB code, or a combination of the two. Furthermore, Microsoft Expression Blend (mentioned a few times within these WPF-centric chapters) can be used to design an animation using integrated tools and wizards without seeing a bit of VB or XAML in the foreground. This approach is ideal for graphic artists, who may not feel comfortable viewing such details.

The Role of Animation-Suffixed Types

To understand WPF's animation support, we must begin by examining the core animation types within the `System.Windows.Media.Animation` namespace of `PresentationCore.dll`. Here you will find a number of class types that all take the `Animation` suffix (`ByteAnimation`, `ColorAnimation`, `DoubleAnimation`, `Int32Animation`, etc.). Obviously, these types are *not* used to somehow provide an animation sequence directly to a variable to a particular data type (after all, how exactly could we animate the value 9 using an `Int32Animation`?). Rather, these `Animation`-suffixed types can be connected to any *dependency property* of a given type that matches the underlying types.

■ **Note** Allow me to repeat this key point: `Animation`-suffixed types can work in conjunction only with dependency properties (see Chapter 30), not normal CLR properties. If you attempt to apply animation objects to CLR properties, you will receive a compile-time error.

For example, consider the `Label` type's `Height` and `Width` properties, both of which are dependency properties wrapping a `Double`. If you wish to define an animation that would increase the height of a label over a time span, you could connect a `DoubleAnimation` object to the `Height` property and allow WPF to take care of the details of performing the actual animation itself. By way of another example, if you wish to transition the color of a brush type from green to yellow, you could do so using the `ColorAnimation` type.

Regardless of which `Animation`-suffixed type you wish to make use of, they all define a handful of key properties that control the starting and ending values used to perform the animation:

- `To`: This property represents the animation's ending value.
- `From`: This property represents the animation's starting value.
- `By`: This property represents the total amount by which the animation changes its starting value.

Despite the fact that all `Animation`-suffixed types support the `To`, `From`, and `By` properties, they do not receive them via virtual members of a base class. The reason for this is that the underlying types wrapped by these properties vary greatly (integers, colors, `Thickness` objects, etc.), and representing all possibilities using a `System.Object` would cause numerous boxing/unboxing penalties for stack-based data.

You might also wonder why .NET generics were not used to define a single animation class with a single type parameter (e.g., `Animate<T>`). Again, given that there are so many underlying data types (colors, vectors, integers, strings, etc.) used by animated dependency properties, it would not be as clean a solution as you might expect (not to mention XAML has only limited support for generic types).

The Role of the Timeline Base Class

Although a single base class was not used to define virtual `To`, `From`, and `By` properties, the `Animation`-suffixed types do share a common base class: `System.Windows.Media.Timeline`. This type provides a number of additional properties that control the pacing of the animation, as described in Table 32-6.

Table 32-6. *Key Members of the* `Timeline` *Base Class*

Property	Meaning in Life

`AccelerationRatio`
`DecelerationRatio`
`SpeedRatio`
	These properties can be used to control the overall pacing of the animation sequence.

`AutoReverse`	This property gets or sets a value that indicates whether the timeline plays in reverse after it completes a forward iteration.
`BeginTime`	This property gets or sets the time at which this timeline should begin. The default value is 0, which begins the animation immediately.

Property	Meaning in Life
Duration	This property allows you to set a duration of time to play the timeline.
FillBehavior RepeatBehavior	These properties are used to control what should happen once the timeline has completed (e.g., repeat the animation, do nothing, etc.).

Authoring an Animation in VB Code

Our first look at WPF's animation services will make use of the DoubleAnimation type to control various properties of various Label types on a main window. Create a new WPF Windows Application project named AnimatedLabel, and design a <Grid> consisting of two rows and two columns. Into the first column place a Button type in each cell and handle the Click event for each widget. In the second column, place a Label type into each cell (named lblHeight and lblTransparency). Figure 32-10 shows one possible UI.

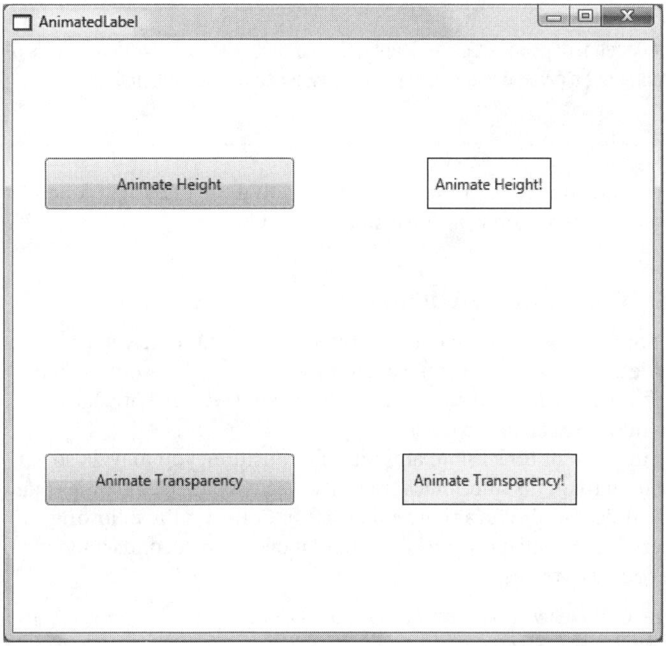

Figure 32-10. *The initial UI of the AnimatedLabel application*

Now, within each Click event handler, author the following code:

```
Imports System.Windows.Media.Animation

Class MainWindow

  Private Sub btnAnimatelblMessage_Click(ByVal sender As System.Object, _
     ByVal e As System.Windows.RoutedEventArgs)
    ' This will grow the height of the label.
    Dim dblAnim As New DoubleAnimation()
    dblAnim.From = 40
    dblAnim.To = 60
```

```
    lblHeight.BeginAnimation(Label.HeightProperty, dblAnim)
  End Sub

  Private Sub btnAnimatelblTransparency_Click(ByVal sender As System.Object, _
     ByVal e As System.Windows.RoutedEventArgs)
    ' This will change the opacity of the label.
    Dim dblAnim As New DoubleAnimation()
    dblAnim.From = 1
    dblAnim.To = 0
    lblTransparency.BeginAnimation(Label.OpacityProperty, dblAnim)
  End Sub
End Class
```

Notice in each Click event handler we set the From and To values of the DoubleAnimation type to represent the beginning and ending value. After this point, we call BeginAnimation() on the correct Label object, passing in the correct dependency property field of the related widget (again, the Label) followed by the Animation-suffixed object used to perform the animation.

■ **Note** Recall from our examination of dependency properties in Chapter 31 that public read-only shared fields of type DependencyObject are used to represent a given dependency property exposed by the (optional) CLR property wrapper.

If you now run your application and click each button, you will find that the lblHeight label will grow in size, while the lblTransparency button will slowly fade from view.

Controlling the Pacing of an Animation

By default, an animation will take approximately one second to transition between the values assigned to the From and To properties. For example, if you were to modify the Click event handler that grows the Height of the Label from 40 to 200 (a larger increase than what we currently have in place), it would still take approximately one second to do so.

If you wish to define a custom amount of time for an animation's transition, you may do so via the Duration property, which can be set to an instance of a Duration object. Typically, the time span is established by passing a TimeSpan object to the Duration's constructor. Consider the following update to the current Click handlers, which will grow the label's height over four seconds and fade the other label from view over the course of ten seconds:

```
Private Sub btnAnimatelblMessage_Click(ByVal sender As System.Object, _
  ByVal e As System.Windows.RoutedEventArgs)
  ' Take four seconds to complete the animation.
  Dim dblAnim As New DoubleAnimation()
  dblAnim.From = 40
  dblAnim.To = 200

  dblAnim.Duration = New Duration(TimeSpan.FromSeconds(4))
  lblHeight.BeginAnimation(Label.HeightProperty, dblAnim)
End Sub

Private Sub btnAnimatelblTransparency_Click(ByVal sender As System.Object, _
  ByVal e As System.Windows.RoutedEventArgs)
  ' This will change the opacity of the label
  Dim dblAnim As New DoubleAnimation()
  dblAnim.From = 1
```

```
    dblAnim.To = 0
    dblAnim.Duration = New Duration(TimeSpan.FromSeconds(10))
    lblTransparency.BeginAnimation(Label.OpacityProperty, dblAnim)
End Sub
```

Note The BeginTime property of an Animation-suffixed type also takes a TimeSpan object. Recall this property can be set to establish a wait time before starting an animation sequence.

Reversing and Looping an Animation

You can also tell Animation-suffixed types to play an animation in reverse at the completion of the animation sequence by setting the AutoReverse property to True. For example, the following update to our Click event handler will cause the Label to grow from 40 to 200 pixels in height, after which it will "shrink" from 100 back to 40 (over the course of eight seconds, four seconds each "direction"):

```
' Reverse when done.
dblAnim.AutoReverse = True
```

If you wish to have an animation repeat some number of times (or to never stop once activated), you can do so using the RepeatBehavior property, which is common to all Animation-suffixed types. The RepeatBehavior property is set to an object of the same name. If you pass in a simple numerical value to the constructor, you can specify a hard-coded number of times to repeat. On the other hand, if you pass in a TimeSpan object to the constructor, you can establish an amount of time the animation should repeat. Finally, if you wish an animation to loop ad infinitum, you can simply specify RepeatBehavior.Forever. Consider the following ways we could change the height of our Label object:

```
' Loop forever.
dblAnim.RepeatBehavior = RepeatBehavior.Forever

' Loop three times.
dblAnim.RepeatBehavior = New RepeatBehavior(3)

' Loop for 30 seconds.
dblAnim.RepeatBehavior = New RepeatBehavior(TimeSpan.FromSeconds(30))
```

Source Code The AnimatedLabel project can be found under the Chapter 32 subdirectory.

Authoring an Animation in XAML

When you need to dynamically interact with the state of an animation, your best approach is to do so in procedural code, as we have just done. However, if you have a "fixed" animation that is predefined and will not require runtime interaction, you can author your entire animation sequence in XAML. For the most part, this process is identical to what you have already seen; however, the various Animation-suffixed types are wrapped within *storyboard* types. The storyboard types in turn are associated to an *event trigger*.

Let's walk through a complete example of an animation defined in terms of XAML, followed by a detailed breakdown. Our goal is to represent the eternally growing and shrinking Label of the previous example using XAML. Consider the following markup, which will be examined in the next several sections:

```
<Label Content = "Interesting...">
  <Label.Triggers>
    <EventTrigger RoutedEvent = "Label.Loaded">
      <EventTrigger.Actions>
        <BeginStoryboard>
          <Storyboard TargetProperty = "Height">
            <DoubleAnimation From ="40" To = "200" Duration = "0:0:4"
                             RepeatBehavior = "Forever"/>
          </Storyboard>
        </BeginStoryboard>
      </EventTrigger.Actions>
    </EventTrigger>
  </Label.Triggers>
</Label>
```

The Role of Storyboards

Working from the innermost element outward, we first encounter the `<DoubleAnimation>` element, which is making use of the same properties we set in procedural code (`From`, `To`, `Duration`, and `RepeatBehavior`). As mentioned, `Animation`-suffixed types are placed within a `<Storyboard>` element, which is used to map the animation to a given property on the parent element via the `TargetProperty` property (which again in this case is `Height`).

The reason for this level of indirection is that XAML does not support a syntax to invoke methods on objects, such as the necessary `BeginAnimation()` method of the `Label`. Essentially a `<Storyboard>` and the `<BeginStoryboard>` parent are the XAML-centric version of specifying the following procedural code:

```
' This necessary animation logic is represented with storyboards in XAML.
lblHeight.BeginAnimation(Label.HeightProperty, dblAnim)
```

The Use of <EventTrigger>

Once the `<Storyboard>` has been defined, we next need to define an event trigger to contain it. WPF supports three different types of triggers that allow you to define a set of actions that will occur when a given routed event is raised.

The first type of trigger observes conditions for dependency properties on a type. When defining triggers for dependency properties, you will do so by defining the trigger using `<Trigger>` elements. The second type of trigger accounts for "normal" .NET property types and is defined within a `<DataTrigger>` element. This flavor of trigger can be helpful for data binding operations. We will look at the `<Trigger>` element later in this chapter during our examination of styles and themes.

The final type of trigger relevant for the current example is an *event trigger* (defined within an `<EventTrigger>` element), which is used when building WPF animations. Here, our `<EventTrigger>` is connected to the `Loaded` event of the `Label`. When this event fires, the action to take is to execute the `<DoubleAnimation>` sequence on the `Label`'s `Height` property.

Source Code The `AnimationInXaml.xaml` file can be found under the Chapter 32 subdirectory.

The Role of Animation Key Frames

The final aspect of the WPF animation system we will examine is the use of *key frames*. The System.Windows.Media.Animation namespace also contains a number of types that end with the AnimationUsingKeyFrames suffix (ByteAnimationUsingKeyFrames, ColorAnimationUsingKeyFrames, DoubleAnimationUsingKeyFrames, Int32AnimationUsingKeyFrames, etc.). Each of these types provides a Duration property, which controls how long the entire animation sequence should take. However, it is up to the key frames themselves to inform the animation system when they are up for duty.

Unlike the Animation-suffixed types, which can only move between a starting point and an ending point, the *key frame* counterparts allow us to create a collection of specific values for an animation that should take place at specific times. For example, the AnimationUsingKeyFrames-suffixed types could allow us to create an animation that bounces a circle around a window, causes a custom image to move around the outline of a geometric shape, or cycles the colors within a text box over a time slice.

Within the scope of an AnimationUsingKeyFrames-suffixed element, you may add a collection of three different key frame types, each of which controls that frame of movement of the animated item:

- LinearXXXKeyFrame: The linear key frame types are used to move an item between points on a straight line.
- SplineXXXKeyFrame: The spline key frame types are used to move an item along a Bezier curve, using the KeySpline property.
- DiscreteXXXKeyFrame: The discrete key frame types do not provide a transition between key frames. For example, this can be useful when "animating" string data that grows in size or a border that "animates" between various colors.

Following a similar pattern, the exact name of the subelements will be based on the type of item you are animating (doubles, colors, Booleans, etc.). Here, XXX is obviously being used as a placeholder. The real names of any of these three key frame types would be along the lines of LinearDoubleKeyFrame, SplineDoubleKeyFrame, and DiscreteDoubleKeyFrame.

Animation Using Discrete Key Frames

To illustrate the use of a discrete key frame type, assume you wish to build a Button that animates its content in such a way that over the course of three seconds, the value "OK!" appears one character at a time. Also assume that this behavior should happen as soon as the button has loaded into memory, and it should repeat continuously. To see this behavior firsthand, author the following XAML within the SimpleXamlApp.exe program you created in Chapter 30:

```
<Window xmlns="http://schemas.microsoft.com/winfx/2006/xaml/presentation"
  xmlns:x="http://schemas.microsoft.com/winfx/2006/xaml">
  <Grid>
    <Button Name="myButton" Height="40"
     FontSize="16pt" FontFamily="Verdana" Width = "100">
     <Button.Triggers>
       <EventTrigger RoutedEvent="Button.Loaded">
         <BeginStoryboard>
           <Storyboard>
             <StringAnimationUsingKeyFrames RepeatBehavior = "Forever"
               Storyboard.TargetName="myButton" Storyboard.TargetProperty="Content"
               Duration="0:0:3" FillBehavior="HoldEnd">
               <DiscreteStringKeyFrame Value="" KeyTime="0:0:0" />
               <DiscreteStringKeyFrame Value="O" KeyTime="0:0:1" />
               <DiscreteStringKeyFrame Value="OK" KeyTime="0:0:1.5" />
```

```
            <DiscreteStringKeyFrame Value="OK!" KeyTime="0:0:2" />
          </StringAnimationUsingKeyFrames>
        </Storyboard>
      </BeginStoryboard>
    </EventTrigger>
  </Button.Triggers>
  </Button>
 </Grid>
</Window>
```

Notice first of all that we have defined an event trigger for our button to ensure that our storyboard executes when the button has loaded. The `StringAnimationUsingKeyFrames` element is in charge of changing the content of our button, via the `Storyboard.TargetName` and `Storyboard.TargetProperty` values. Within the scope of our `<StringAnimationUsingKeyFrames>` element, we have defined three `DiscreteStringKeyFrame` elements, which change the button's content over the course of two seconds (note that the duration established by `StringAnimationUsingKeyFrames` is a total of three seconds, so we will see a slight pause between the final "!" and looping "O").

■ **Source Code** The `AnimatedButtonWithDiscreteKeyFrames.xaml` file can be found under the Chapter 32 subdirectory.

Animation Using Linear Key Frames

To see the use of a linear key frame at work, consider the following XAML, which spins a `Button` in a complete circle using the center of the button as the point of origin. Once the 360-degree rotation has completed, the button will then flip itself upside down (and then right side up again). Assume this XAML markup is defined within a `<Grid>`:

```
<!-- This button will rotate in a circle, then flip, when clicked -->
<Button Name="myAnimatedButton" Width="120" Height = "40"
  RenderTransformOrigin="0.5,0.5" Content = "OK">

  <Button.RenderTransform>
    <RotateTransform Angle="0"/>
  </Button.RenderTransform>

  <!-- The animation is triggered when the button is clicked -->
  <Button.Triggers>
    <EventTrigger RoutedEvent="Button.Click">
      <BeginStoryboard>
        <Storyboard>
          <DoubleAnimationUsingKeyFrames
           Storyboard.TargetName="myAnimatedButton"
           Storyboard.TargetProperty=
           "(Button.RenderTransform).(RotateTransform.Angle)"
           Duration="0:0:2" FillBehavior="Stop">
             <DoubleAnimationUsingKeyFrames.KeyFrames>
              <LinearDoubleKeyFrame Value="360" KeyTime="0:0:1" />
              <DiscreteDoubleKeyFrame Value="180" KeyTime="0:0:1.5" />
            </DoubleAnimationUsingKeyFrames.KeyFrames>
          </DoubleAnimationUsingKeyFrames>
        </Storyboard>
      </BeginStoryboard>
```

```
    </EventTrigger>
  </Button.Triggers>
</Button>
```

This Button's definition begins by specifying a value to the RenderTransformOrigin property, which ensures the rotation occurs using the dead center of the button as the turning point. Next, we establish the initial starting value for the rendering transformation, using the nested <Button.RenderTransform> scope (note the starting angle is zero). Finally, we define an event trigger to ensure our storyboard will execute when the user clicks the button.

With these initial settings complete, we create a <Storyboard> scope that makes use of the DoubleAnimationUsingKeyFrames type. Notice that the target of this storyboard is our Button instance (myAnimatedButton) and the property we are targeting on this object is ultimately the Angle property. However, notice the new bit of XAML syntax that we must use when assigning a dependency property to a property value:

```
<DoubleAnimationUsingKeyFrames
  Storyboard.TargetName="myAnimatedButton"
  Storyboard.TargetProperty="(Button.RenderTransform).(RotateTransform.Angle)"
  Duration="0:0:2" FillBehavior="Stop">
```

As you can see, we must wrap dependency properties within parentheses; therefore, the single bold line of code allows us to say in effect, "I am animating the Angle property of the RotateTransform object exposed by the button." This point aside, the total time allowed for this animation is set to two seconds.

Within the scope of our DoubleAnimationUsingKeyFrames element, we add two key frames. The first (LinearDoubleKeyFrame) will rotate the button 360 degrees over a one-second time period. Approximately half a second later, the DiscreteDoubleKeyFrame flips the button 180 degrees (turning the button upside down). Finally, once the animation expires (again, half a second later, given our Duration property of the DoubleAnimationUsingKeyFrames type), the button flips right side up again, as the DoubleAnimationUsingKeyFrames type has a FillBehavior value of Stop (which returns the item to the initial state).

■ **Source Code** The SpinButtonWithLinearKeyFrames.xaml file can be found under the Chapter 32 subdirectory.

That wraps up our look at the basic animation services (and 2D rendering techniques) that are baked into WPF. Both of these topics could easily require a book of their own to cover all of the bells and whistles. Nevertheless, at this time you should be in a solid position for further exploration. Next up, we will turn our attention to how to package application resources.

Understanding the WPF Resource System

Our next task is to examine the seemingly unrelated topic of embedding and accessing application resources. WPF supports two flavors of resources, the first of which is *binary resources*, which represents what most programmers consider a "resource" in the traditional sense of the word (bitmap files, icons, string tables, etc.).

The second flavor of resources, termed *object resources* or *logical resources*, represents any type of .NET object that is named and embedded within an assembly. As you will see, logical resources are extremely helpful when working with graphical data of any sort, given that you can define commonly used graphic primitives (brushes, pens, animations, etc.) within a resources dictionary.

Working with Binary Resources

As mentioned, binary resources are the auxiliary bits used by a .NET application, such as string tables, icons, and image files (e.g., company logos, images for an animation, etc.). If you are creating a WPF application using Visual Studio, you are able to instruct the compiler to embed an external resource into the assembly simply by specifying the Resource build option. To illustrate, create a new WPF Windows Application project named FunWithResources. Update your initial XAML definition for the main window with a three-column `<Grid>`, where the first cell contains an `Image` widget:

```
<Window x:Class="MainWindow"
  xmlns="http://schemas.microsoft.com/winfx/2006/xaml/presentation"
  xmlns:x="http://schemas.microsoft.com/winfx/2006/xaml"
  Title="FunWithResources" Height="207" Width="612"
  WindowStartupLocation="CenterScreen">
  <Grid>
    <Grid.ColumnDefinitions>
      <ColumnDefinition/>
      <ColumnDefinition/>
      <ColumnDefinition/>
    </Grid.ColumnDefinitions>
    <Image Grid.Column ="0" Name ="companyLogo"/>
  </Grid>
</Window>
```

The first goal is to embed an image file into our application as a binary resource, which will be used to set the `Source` property of the `companyLogo` `Image` control. Using your image file of choice, add it into your current project using the Project ➤ Add Existing Item menu option of Visual Studio (here, I am assuming a file named `IntertechBlue.gif`).

The Resource Build Action

Once you have added an external image file to your application, you should now see it listed within Solution Explorer. When selected, the Properties window can now be used to instruct the compiler how to process these external files using the Build Action option (see Figure 32-11).

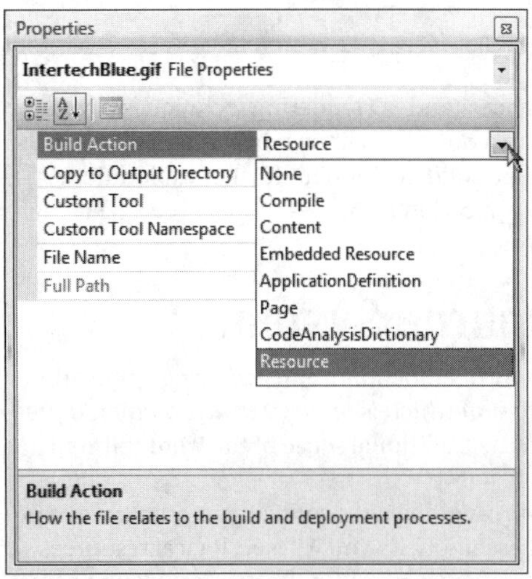

Figure 32-11. *Options for packaging binary resources*

If you select the default setting, Resource, the compiler will embed the data into the .NET assembly, and therefore these external files do not need to be shipped with the completed application. Assuming you have set the Build Action of your image file to Resource, you can update the XAML definition of the `Image` control as follows (notice you refer to the name of the binary resource by name):

```
<Image Grid.Column ="0" Name ="companyLogo" Source ="IntertechBlue.gif"/>
```

When you now compile and run your program, you should see your image file stretched within the first cell of your `<Grid>`.

Note Be careful that your WPF applications use the Resource option to embed resources, which is a WPF-aware option. The tempting-sounding Embedded Resource option is used for Windows Forms applications.

If you load your compiled application into `reflector.exe` (see Chapter 2), you can view the embedded resource directly, as shown in Figure 32-12.

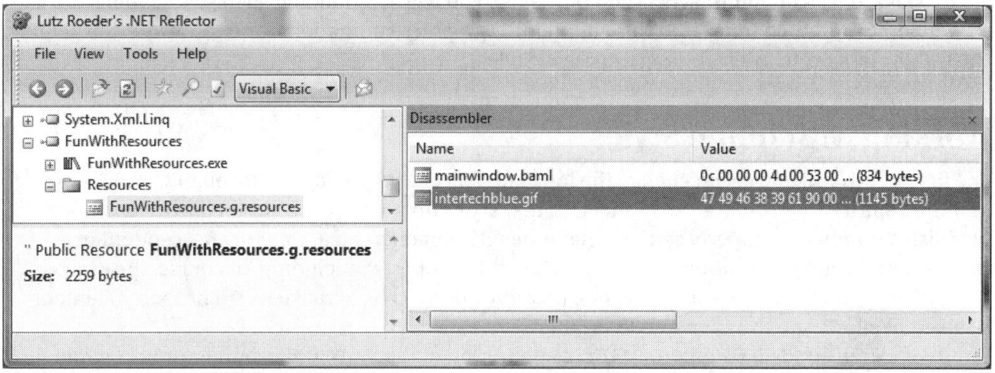

Figure 32-12. *An embedded binary resource*

The Content Build Action

It is also possible to set the Build Action of a related external file to Content, rather than Resource. When you do so, your assembly is compiled in such a way that it is aware of the relative location of the external file, but does not actually contain the binary data. This setting can be helpful when you deploy an application that contains a subfolder (or two) containing external resources that need to be replaced from time to time, or when the location of external resources is on a network share point.

In these cases, the WPF resource management system defines a number of additional URI formats (including a syntax to load resources embedded in an external assembly) beyond a simple file name. If you are interested in examining the various URI formats that can be used with local resources not compiled into the current assembly, look up the topic "Pack URIs in Windows Presentation Foundation" within the .NET Framework 3.5 SDK documentation.

The Role of Object (aka Logical) Resources

WPF resources really come into their own when you embed custom .NET objects into an assembly for use within your application. At first glance, this may seem like a very odd thing to do. However, by doing so you can define commonly used graphical elements (brushes, pens, etc.) for use by multiple areas of your program. This technique is often used when creating custom themes and styles for your WPF applications, which we will examine next.

Defining and Applying Styles for WPF Controls

When you are building the UI of a WPF application, it is not uncommon for a family of widgets to all have a shared look and feel. For example, you may wish to ensure that all button types have the same height, width, background color, and font size for their string content. While you could do so by setting each button's individual properties to identical values, this approach certainly makes it difficult to implement changes down the road, as you would need to reset the same set of properties on multiple objects for every change.

Thankfully, WPF offers numerous ways to change the look and feel of UI elements (styles, templates, skins, etc.) with minimal fuss and bother. As you will see, building such styles entails the use of each topic presented thus far in this chapter (2D graphics, animations, and resources). To get the ball rolling, let's begin by examining the use of styles.

Working with Inline Styles

The first way in which you can change the look and feel of a WPF widget is through *styles*. A style is a kindred spirit to a web-based style sheet, in that styles do not have a UI of their own, but simply establish a number of property settings that other UI elements can adopt. Any descendent of `Control` has the ability to support styles (via the `Style` property), including, of course, the `Window` itself. When you wish to author a style, one possible approach is to make use of property-element syntax that allows you to assign a style "inline."

To illustrate, update your current `<Grid>` definition of the FunWithResources project to define a `Button` within the remaining two cells. Now, consider the following markup, which establishes a custom style for a button named `btnClickMe` (but not the second button, `btnClickMeToo`):

```
<Window x:Class="MainWindow"
  xmlns="http://schemas.microsoft.com/winfx/2006/xaml/presentation"
  xmlns:x="http://schemas.microsoft.com/winfx/2006/xaml"
  Title="FunWithResources" Height="207" Width="612"
  WindowStartupLocation="CenterScreen">
  <Grid>
  <Grid.ColumnDefinitions>
    <ColumnDefinition/>
    <ColumnDefinition/>
    <ColumnDefinition/>
  </Grid.ColumnDefinitions>
  <Image Grid.Column ="0" Name ="companyLogo" Source ="IntertechBlue.gif"/>

  <!-- This button has an inline style! -->
  <Button Grid.Column ="1" Name="btnClickMe" Height="80"
   Width = "100" Content ="Click Me">
    <Button.Style>
      <Style>
        <Setter Property ="Button.FontSize" Value ="20"/>
        <Setter Property ="Button.Background">
```

```
          <Setter.Value>
            <LinearGradientBrush StartPoint="0,0" EndPoint="1,1">
              <GradientStop Color="Green" Offset="0" />
              <GradientStop Color="Yellow" Offset="0.25" />
              <GradientStop Color="Pink" Offset="0.75" />
              <GradientStop Color ="Red" Offset="1" />
            </LinearGradientBrush>
          </Setter.Value>
        </Setter>
      </Style>
    </Button.Style>
  </Button>

  <!-- No style for this button! -->
  <Button Grid.Column ="2" Name="btnClickMeToo"
   Height="80" Width = "100" Content ="Me Too"/>
  </Grid>
</Window>
```

As you can see, a WPF style is defined using the <Style> element. Within this scope, we define any number of <Setter> elements, which are used to establish the name/value pairs of the properties we wish to set. Here we have established a FontSize property of the Button to be 20, and the Background property of the Button via a LinearGradientBrush that is composed of four interconnected colors.

■ **Note** If necessary, you can programmatically establish a style in your code file. Simply set the Style property on the control-derived type.

While this approach to building a style is syntactically correct, one obvious limitation is that inline styles are bound to a specific instance of a UI type (btnClickMe in our example), not each button within the scope. In Figure 32-13, notice that the second Button type, btnClickMeToo, is unaffected by the style assigned to btnClickMe.

Figure 32-13. *Inline styles are bound to the control that defined them.*

Working with Named Styles

To define a style that can be used by multiple UI elements of the same type (e.g., all Buttons, all ListBoxes, etc.), you may define the style within a container's *resource dictionary*, thereby defining an object (aka logical) resource. For example, you could add a named style to the <Window>'s resource dictionary and identify it by name through the Key property. That way, the same theme can be referenced everywhere in your XAML document. Consider the following update:

```
<Window x:Class="MainWindow"
  xmlns="http://schemas.microsoft.com/winfx/2006/xaml/presentation"
  xmlns:x="http://schemas.microsoft.com/winfx/2006/xaml"
  Title="FunWithResources" Height="207"
  Width="612" WindowStartupLocation="CenterScreen">

  <!-- Add a logical resource to the window's resource dictionary -->
  <Window.Resources>
    <Style x:Key ="MyFunkyStyle">
      <Setter Property ="Button.FontSize" Value ="20"/>
      <Setter Property ="Button.Background">
        <Setter.Value>
          <LinearGradientBrush StartPoint="0,0" EndPoint="1,1">
            <GradientStop Color="Green" Offset="0" />
            <GradientStop Color="Yellow" Offset="0.25" />
            <GradientStop Color="Pink" Offset="0.75" />
            <GradientStop Color ="Red" Offset="1" />
          </LinearGradientBrush>
        </Setter.Value>
      </Setter>
    </Style>
  </Window.Resources>
  <Grid>
  <Grid.ColumnDefinitions>
    <ColumnDefinition/>
    <ColumnDefinition/>
    <ColumnDefinition/>
  </Grid.ColumnDefinitions>
  <Image Grid.Column ="0" Name ="companyLogo" Source ="IntertechBlue.gif"/>

  <!-- Both buttons now use the same style -->
  <Button Grid.Column ="1" Name="btnClickMe" Height="80" Width = "100"
          Style ="{StaticResource MyFunkyStyle}" Content = "Click Me"/>
  <Button Grid.Column ="2" Name="btnClickMeToo" Height="80" Width = "100"
          Style ="{StaticResource MyFunkyStyle}" Content = "Me Too"/>
  </Grid>
</Window>
```

This time, note that the style has been defined within the scope of a <Window.Resources> element and has been assigned the name MyFunkyStyle via the Key attribute. Beyond these points, the style declaration itself is identical to the previous style we created inline. Also notice that when we want to apply a style (as we do within the <Button> definitions), we do so using the StaticResource markup extension (see Chapter 30). With this update, each button takes on the same look and feel, as shown in Figure 32-14.

Figure 32-14. *Named styles can be used by multiple UI elements in the same scope.*

Overriding Style Settings

It is important to point out that when a UI element adopts a particular style (either an inline style or a named style) it has the freedom to "override" a property setting. For example, assume you want the second `Button` to make use of the `Background` setting established by `MyFunkyStyle`, but you prefer a smaller font. To do so, simply assign a new value to the property you wish to change within the XAML start tag:

```
<Button Grid.Column ="2" Name="btnClickMeToo" Height="80" Width = "100"
  Style ="{StaticResource MyFunkyStyle}" FontSize = "10" Content = "Me Too"/>
```

Subclassing Existing Styles

It is also possible to build new styles using an existing style, via the `BasedOn` property, provided the style you are extending has been given a specific name via the `Key` property. For example, the following `NewFunkyStyle` style (which is added as a new child element of the `<Window.Resources>` scope) gathers the font size and background color of `MyFunkyStyle`, but rotates the UI element 20 degrees:

```
<Style x:Key ="NewFunkyStyle" BasedOn = "{StaticResource MyFunkyStyle}">
  <Setter Property = "Button.Foreground" Value = "Blue"/>
  <Setter Property = "Button.RenderTransform">
    <Setter.Value>
      <RotateTransform Angle = "20"/>
    </Setter.Value>
  </Setter>
</Style>
```

Figure 32-15 shows the new style in action when applied to each button.

Figure 32-15. *Using a derived style*

Widening Styles

Moving a style into a resource dictionary is a step in the right direction to be sure. However, what if you want to use the same style for multiple UI elements? Currently, MyFunkyStyle can only be applied to button widgets, given that the style explicitly references the Button type using property-element syntax.

One of the very interesting aspects of WPF styles is that the values assigned within a <Setter> scope honor the concept of inheritance. Thus, if we set properties on the common parent of all UI elements (System.Windows.Controls.Control) within our style, we can effectively define a style that is common to all WPF controls. For example, the following style update:

```
<Window.Resources>
  <Style x:Key ="MyFunkyStyle">
    <Setter Property ="Control.FontSize" Value ="20"/>
    <Setter Property ="Control.Background">
      <Setter.Value>
        <LinearGradientBrush StartPoint="0,0" EndPoint="1,1">
          <GradientStop Color="Green" Offset="0" />
          <GradientStop Color="Yellow" Offset="0.25" />
          <GradientStop Color="Pink" Offset="0.75" />
          <GradientStop Color ="Red" Offset="1" />
        </LinearGradientBrush>
      </Setter.Value>
    </Setter>
  </Style>
...
</Window.Resources>
```

allows us to apply MyFunkyStyle to TextBox items as well as Button items (or to any item extending Control, for that matter). Assume the following new UI element added within a new column of the current <Grid>:

```
<TextBox Grid.Column ="3" Name="txtAndMe" Height="40" Width = "100"
                  Style ="{StaticResource MyFunkyStyle}" Text = "And me!"/>
```

■ **Note** When you are building a style that is making use of a base class type, you needn't be concerned if you assign a value to a dependency property not supported by derived types. If the derived type does not support a given dependency property, it is ignored.

Narrowing Styles

If you wish to define a style that can be applied *only* to certain types of UI elements (e.g., only Buttons and nothing else), you can do so by setting the TargetType property on the style's start tag. This property expects a metadata description of the target widget, so you will make use of the x:Type markup extension (see Chapter 30). By way of illustration, we could update MyFunkyStyle as follows. With this update, it would now be a markup error for the previous TextBox to attempt to apply this style.

```
<Style x:Key ="MyFunkyStyle" TargetType = "{x:Type Button}">
...
</Style>
```

Assigning Styles Implicitly

WPF styles also support the ability to be implicitly set to all UI widgets within a given XAML scope. When you build a named style, assigning a Key property is technically optional, *if* you have narrowed the application of your style using the TargetType property:

```
<Style TargetType = "{x:Type Button}">
...
</Style>
```

By doing so, all Button items within scope will implicitly take on the MyFunkyStyle style, even though they are not making use of the StaticResource markup extension:

```
<Button Grid.Column ="1" Name="btnClickMe"
  Height="80" Width = "100" Content = "Click Me"/>

<Button Grid.Column ="2" Name="btnClickMeToo"
  Height="80" Width = "100" Content = "Me Too"/>
```

Be aware that when you define a style using the TargetType property that does *not* have a Key value established, the style is applied only to identically named types. Therefore, if we were to update the current style to the following:

```
<Style TargetType = "{x:Type Control}">
  ...
</Style>
```

neither the Button nor the TextBox type would adopt the style! Again, the reason is that this iteration of our style is targeting the Control base class. Always remember that the notion of a style representing a class or a derivative thereof works only for named styles.

Source Code The FunWithResources project can be found under the Chapter 32 subdirectory.

Defining Styles with Triggers

The next aspect of WPF styles to examine here is the notion of *triggers*, which allow you to define certain <Setter> elements in such a way that they will only be applied if a given condition is true. For example, perhaps you want to increase the size of a font when the mouse is over a button. Or maybe you want to make sure that the text box with the current focus is highlighted with a given color. Triggers are very useful for these sorts of situations, in that they allow you to take specific actions when a property changes without the need to author explicit VB code in a code-behind file.

The following XAML markup defines three TextBox items, all of which have their Style property set to the TextBoxStyle style. While all text boxes will have a shared look and feel (height, width, etc.), only the text box that has the current focus will receive a yellow background.

```
<Window
    xmlns="http://schemas.microsoft.com/winfx/2006/xaml/presentation"
    xmlns:x="http://schemas.microsoft.com/winfx/2006/xaml">

  <Window.Resources>
    <Style x:Key ="TextBoxStyle" TargetType = "{x:Type TextBox}">
      <Setter Property = "Foreground" Value = "Black"/>
      <Setter Property = "Background" Value = "LightGray"/>
      <Setter Property = "Height" Value = "30"/>
      <Setter Property = "Width" Value = "100"/>
```

```
      <!-- The following setter will only be applied when the text box is
           in focus. -->
       <Style.Triggers>
         <Trigger Property = "IsFocused" Value = "True">
           <Setter Property = "Background" Value = "Yellow"/>
         </Trigger>
       </Style.Triggers>
     </Style>
  </Window.Resources>

  <StackPanel>
    <TextBox Name = "txtOne" Style = "{StaticResource TextBoxStyle}" />
    <TextBox Name = "txtTwo" Style = "{StaticResource TextBoxStyle}" />
    <TextBox Name = "txtThree" Style = "{StaticResource TextBoxStyle}" />
   </StackPanel>
</Window>
```

If you author the previous XAML into the SimpleXamlPad.exe application you created in Chapter 30, you will now find that as you tab between your TextBox objects, the currently selected widget has a bright yellow background, while the others receive the default assigned background color of gray. Triggers are also very smart, in that when the trigger's condition is *not true*, the widget automatically receives the default value assignment. Therefore, as soon as a TextBox loses focus, it also automatically becomes the default assigned color without any work on your part.

Triggers can also be designed in such a way that the defined <Setter> elements will be applied when *multiple conditions* are true (similar to building an If statement for multiple conditions). Let's say that we want to set the background of a text box to yellow only if it has the active focus and the mouse is hovering within its boundaries. To do so, we can make use of the <MultiTrigger> element to define each condition:

```
<Window.Resources>
  <Style x:Key ="TextBoxStyle" TargetType = "{x:Type TextBox}">
    <Setter Property = "Foreground" Value = "Black"/>
    <Setter Property = "Background" Value = "LightGray"/>
    <Setter Property = "Height" Value = "30"/>
    <Setter Property = "Width" Value = "100"/>
    <!-- The following setter will only be applied when the text box is
             in focus and the mouse is over the text box. -->
      <Style.Triggers>
        <MultiTrigger>
        <MultiTrigger.Conditions>
          <Condition Property = "IsFocused" Value = "True"/>
          <Condition Property = "IsMouseOver" Value = "True"/>
        </MultiTrigger.Conditions>
        <Setter Property = "Background" Value = "Yellow"/>
      </MultiTrigger>
    </Style.Triggers>
  </Style>
</Window.Resources>
```

Source Code The StyleWithTriggers.xaml file can be found under the Chapter 32 subdirectory.

Assigning Styles Programmatically

To conclude our examination of styles, let's now build a simple application that illustrates how you can assign styles to UI elements in code using a new Visual Studio 2008 WPF Windows Application project named StylesAtRuntime.

Our goal is to define three different styles for a `Button` item within the resource dictionary of the `<Window>` element. The first style, `TiltStyle`, rotates the button 10 degrees. The second style, `GreenStyle`, simply sets the `Background`, `Foreground`, and `FontSize` properties to preset values. The final style, `MouseOverStyle`, is based on `GreenStyle`, but adds a trigger condition that will increase the font size of the button widget. Here are the XAML descriptions for each style:

```
<Window.Resources>
  <!-- This style tilts buttons at a 10-degree angle -->
  <Style x:Key ="TiltStyle" TargetType = "{x:Type Button}">
    <Setter Property = "RenderTransform">
      <Setter.Value>
        <RotateTransform Angle = "10"/>
      </Setter.Value>
    </Setter>
  </Style>

  <!-- This style gives buttons a springtime feel -->
  <Style x:Key ="GreenStyle" TargetType = "{x:Type Button}">
    <Setter Property = "Background" Value ="Green"/>
    <Setter Property = "Foreground" Value ="Yellow"/>
    <Setter Property ="FontSize" Value ="15" />
  </Style>

  <!-- This style increases the font size of a button when
       the mouse is over it -->
  <Style x:Key ="MouseOverStyle"  BasedOn ="{StaticResource GreenStyle}"
         TargetType = "{x:Type Button}">
    <Style.Triggers>
      <Trigger Property ="IsMouseOver" Value ="True">
        <Setter Property ="FontSize" Value ="20" />
        <Setter Property ="Foreground" Value ="Black" />
      </Trigger>
    </Style.Triggers>
  </Style>
</Window.Resources>
```

The `Window` object will maintain a `Grid` that maps out locations for a `TextBlock`, `ListBox`, and `Button`. This `ListBox` will contain the names of each style and will handle the `SelectionChanged` event. Here is the relevant XAML for the UI:

```
<Grid>
  <Grid.ColumnDefinitions>
    <ColumnDefinition />
    <ColumnDefinition />
  </Grid.ColumnDefinitions>
  <StackPanel Grid.Column="0">
    <TextBlock TextWrapping ="Wrap" FontSize ="20"
      Padding="5,5,5,5">
        Please select a style for the button on the right.
    </TextBlock>
    <ListBox Name ="lstStyles" Height ="60" Background = "Yellow"
      SelectionChanged ="lstStyles_Changed" />
```

```
    </StackPanel>
  <Button Name="btnMouseOverStyle" Grid.Column="1"
    Height="40" Width="100">My Button</Button>
</Grid>
```

The final task it to fill the `ListBox` and handle the `SelectionChanged` event in the related code file. Notice in the following code how we are able to extract the current resource by name, using the inherited `FindResource()` method:

```
Class MainWindow

  Public Sub New()
    InitializeComponent()

    ' Add items to our list box.
    lstStyles.Items.Add("TiltStyle")
    lstStyles.Items.Add("GreenStyle")
    lstStyles.Items.Add("MouseOverStyle")
  End Sub

  Private Sub lstStyles_Changed(ByVal sender As System.Object, _
    ByVal e As System.Windows.Controls.SelectionChangedEventArgs)
    ' Get the selected style name from the list box.
    Dim currStyle As System.Windows.Style = _
      DirectCast(FindResource(lstStyles.SelectedValue), _
      System.Windows.Style)

    ' Set the style of the button type.
    Me.btnMouseOverStyle.Style = currStyle
  End Sub
End Class
```

Once we have done so, we can compile the application. As you click each list item, you can watch the button take on a new identity (see Figure 32-16).

Figure 32-16. *Setting styles programmatically*

Source Code The StylesAtRuntime project can be found under the Chapter 32 subdirectory.

Altering a Control's UI Using Templates

Styles are a great (and simple) way to change the basic look of a WPF control, by establishing a default set of values for a widget's property set. However, even though styles allow us to change various UI settings, the overall look and feel of the widget remains intact. Regardless of how we style a Button using various properties, it is basically still the same rectangular widget we have come to know over the years.

However, what if you wish to completely replace the look and feel of the Button type (such as a hexagonal 3D image) while still having it behave as a Button? What if you wish to use the functionality of the WPF progress bar, but you would rather have it render its UI as a pie chart to show the completion percentage? Rather than building a custom control by hand (as we would have to do with many other GUI toolkits), WPF provides *control templates.*

Templates provide a clear separation between the *UI* of a control (i.e., the look and feel) and the *behavior* of the control (i.e., its set of events and methods). Using templates, you are free to completely change the rendered output of a WPF widget. Programmatically speaking, control templates are represented by the ControlTemplate base class, which can be expressed in XAML using the identically named <ControlTemplate> element. Once you have established your template, you can then attach it to WPF pages, windows, or controls using the Template property.

One interesting aspect of building a control template is that you have full control over how the widget's content is positioned within the template using the <ContentPresenter> element. Using this element, you are able to specify the location and UI of the content for a given control template. More important, if you do not define a <ContentPresenter> element within a template, the control that adopts it will not render *any* content, even if it defines it:

```
<!-- If the applied template does not have a <ContentPresenter>,
     it will not display "Click!" -->
<Button Name ="myButton" Template ="{StaticResource roundButtonTemplate}">
  Click!
</Button>
```

Beyond this point, when you are defining a control template, you may not be too surprised by the fact that it feels similar to the process of building a style. For example, templates are typically stored within a resource dictionary, can support triggers, and so on. Given this, you are already quite well equipped to build templates. Let's see some in action using a new WPF Windows Application project named ControlTemplates.

Building a Custom Template

Here is a simple template that defines a round button using two <Ellipse> elements contained within a <Grid>. The content will be in the dead center of the control, as we have set the HorizontalAlignment and VerticalAlignment properties to Center. Notice that our template has been given the name of roundButtonTemplate (via a resource key), which is made reference to when assigning the Template property of the Button:

```
<Window x:Class="MainWindow"
  xmlns="http://schemas.microsoft.com/winfx/2006/xaml/presentation"
  xmlns:x="http://schemas.microsoft.com/winfx/2006/xaml"
  Title="Fun with Control Templates" Height="162" Width="281" >
  <Grid>
    <Grid.Resources>
      <!-- A simple template for a round button for items in this grid -->
        <ControlTemplate x:Key ="roundButtonTemplate" TargetType ="{x:Type Button}">
        <Grid>
          <Ellipse Name ="OuterRing" Width ="75" Height ="75" Fill ="DarkGreen"/>
          <Ellipse Name ="InnerRing" Width ="60" Height ="60" Fill ="MintCream"/>
```

```
        <ContentPresenter HorizontalAlignment="Center"
                          VerticalAlignment="Center"/>
      </Grid>
    </ControlTemplate>
  </Grid.Resources>

  <!-- Applying our template to a Button -->
  <Button Name ="myButton" Foreground ="Black" FontSize ="20" FontWeight ="Bold"
        Template ="{StaticResource roundButtonTemplate}"
         Click ="myButton_Click"> Click!
  </Button>
 </Grid>
</Window>
```

Also notice that our `Button` is handling the `Click` event (assume the `Click` event handler simply displays an informative message via the `MessageBox.Show()` method). This is significant, as the `Button`—despite the fact that it no longer looks anything like a traditional "gray rectangle"—is still a `System.Windows.Controls.Button` type and has all of the same properties, methods, and events as the canned UI look and feel. Figure 32-17 shows our custom button type in action.

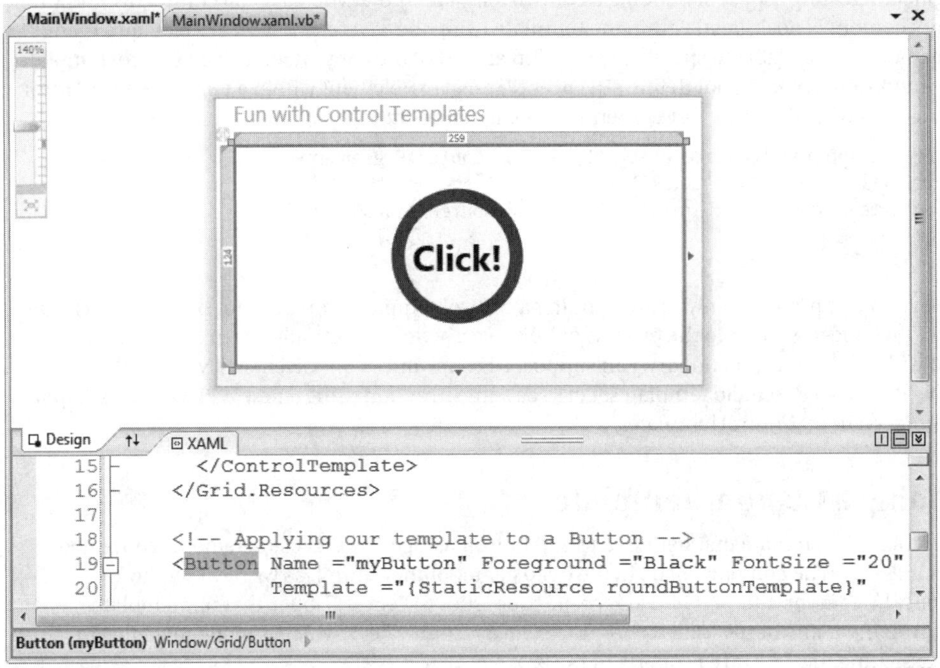

Figure 32-17. *A simple template for the* `Button` *type*

Adding Triggers to Templates

Currently, our control template allows a `Button` to render itself in a circular fashion. However, if you actually click the button, you will notice that the `Click` event does fire (as the `MessageBox.Show()` method will display your string data); however, there is no visual sign of the button being pressed. The reason is that the default push-button animation has been gutted and replaced by our custom

UI! If you wish to put back (or replace) this notion of push-button animation, you will need to add your own custom triggers.

Here is an update to our current template that handles two triggers. The first trigger will monitor whether the mouse is over the button. If so, we will change the background color of the outer ellipse (a simple visual effect). The second trigger will monitor whether the mouse is clicked over the surface of the button. If this is the case, we will increase the `Height` and `Width` values of the outer ellipse to provide visual feedback to the user:

```
<Grid.Resources>
  <!-- A simple template for a round button-->
  <ControlTemplate x:Key ="roundButtonTemplate" TargetType ="{x:Type Button}">
    <Grid>
      <Ellipse Name ="OuterRing" Width ="75" Height ="75" Fill ="DarkGreen"/>
      <Ellipse Name ="InnerRing" Width ="60" Height ="60" Fill ="MintCream"/>
      <ContentPresenter HorizontalAlignment="Center"
                        VerticalAlignment="Center"/>
    </Grid>
    <!-- Triggers to give the "push" effect -->
    <ControlTemplate.Triggers>
      <Trigger Property ="IsMouseOver" Value ="True">
        <Setter TargetName ="OuterRing" Property ="Fill" Value ="MediumSeaGreen"/>
      </Trigger>
      <Trigger Property ="IsPressed" Value ="True">
        <Setter TargetName ="OuterRing" Property ="Height" Value ="90"/>
        <Setter TargetName ="OuterRing" Property ="Width" Value ="90"/>
      </Trigger>
    </ControlTemplate.Triggers>
  </ControlTemplate>
</Grid.Resources>
```

Figure 32-18 shows the effect of the `IsMouseOver` trigger, and Figure 32-19 shows the result of the `IsPressed` trigger.

Figure 32-18. *The* `IsMouseOver` *trigger in action*

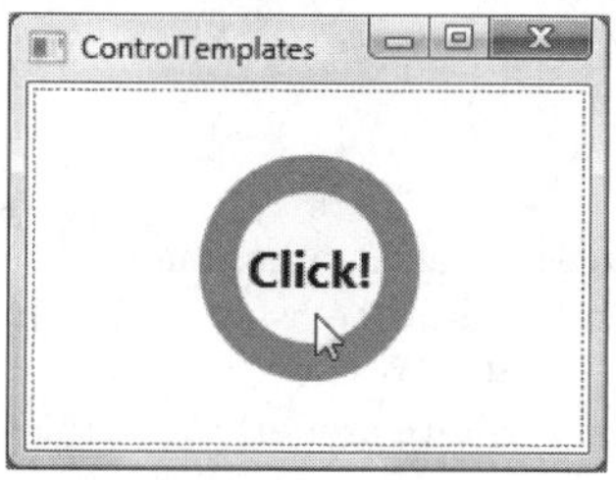

Figure 32-19. *The* `IsPressed` *trigger in action*

Incorporating Templates into Styles

Currently, our template simply defines the look and feel of the Button type. The process of establishing the basic properties of the widget (content, font size, font weight, etc.) is the responsibility of the Button itself:

```
<!-- Currently the Button must set basic property values, not the template -->
<Button Name ="myButton" Foreground ="Black" FontSize ="20" FontWeight ="Bold"
  Template ="{StaticResource roundButtonTemplate}" Click ="myButton_Click">
```

It would be ideal to establish these values *in the template*. By doing so, we can effectively create a default look and feel. As you may have already realized, this is a job for WPF styles. When you build a style (to account for basic property settings), you can define a template *within the style*! Here is our updated grid resource, with analysis to follow:

```
<Grid.Resources>
  <!-- Our style defines basic settings for the Button here -->
  <Style x:Key ="roundButtonTemplate" TargetType ="{x:Type Button}">
    <Setter Property ="Foreground" Value ="Black"/>
    <Setter Property ="FontSize" Value ="20"/>
    <Setter Property ="FontWeight" Value ="Bold"/>

    <!-- Here is our template! -->
    <Setter Property ="Template">
      <Setter.Value>
        <!-- A simple template for a round button-->
        <ControlTemplate TargetType ="{x:Type Button}">
          <Grid>
           <Ellipse Name ="OuterRing" Width ="75" Height ="75" Fill ="DarkGreen"/>
           <Ellipse Name ="InnerRing" Width ="60" Height ="60" Fill ="MintCream"/>
           <ContentPresenter HorizontalAlignment="Center"
                             VerticalAlignment="Center"/>
          </Grid>

          <!-- A trigger to give the "push" effect -->
          <ControlTemplate.Triggers>
            <Trigger Property ="IsMouseOver" Value ="True">
              <Setter TargetName ="OuterRing"
               Property ="Fill" Value ="MediumSeaGreen"/>
            </Trigger>
            <Trigger Property ="IsPressed" Value ="True">
              <Setter TargetName ="OuterRing" Property ="Height" Value ="90"/>
              <Setter TargetName ="OuterRing" Property ="Width" Value ="90"/>
            </Trigger>
          </ControlTemplate.Triggers>
        </ControlTemplate>
      </Setter.Value>
    </Setter>
  </Style>
</Grid.Resources>
```

First of all, notice that the <Style> has now been given the resource key value, rather than the <ControlTemplate>. Next, notice that the style is setting the same basic properties we were setting in the Button item's declaration (Foreground, FontSize, and FontWeight). The <ControlTemplate> element is defined using a normal style <Setter> element by tweaking the Template property. With this update, we can now create our custom buttons by setting the Style property as follows:

```
<!-- Applying our style/template to a Button -->
<Button Name ="myButton"
  Style ="{StaticResource roundButtonTemplate}"
  Click ="myButton_Click">
  Click!
</Button>
```

While the rendering and behavior of the button is identical, the benefit of nesting templates within styles is that you are able to provide a canned set of values for common properties. Recall, of course, that you are free to change these defaults on a widget-by-widget value:

```
<!-- Get style, but change foreground color -->
<Button Name ="myButton"
  Style ="{StaticResource roundButtonTemplate}"
  Click ="myButton_Click" Foreground ="Red">
  Click!
</Button>
```

Source Code The ControlTemplates project can be found under the Chapter 32 subdirectory.

That wraps up our look at the styling and template mechanism of WPF. As you have seen, templates are typically composed on numerous graphical types and are ultimately bundled into your application as binary resources.

For that matter, this concludes our examination of WPF itself for this edition of the text. Over the last three chapters, you have learned quite a bit about the underlying WPF programming model, the syntax of XAML, control manipulation, and the generation of graphical content. While there is certainly much more to WPF than examined here, you should be in a solid position for further exploration as you see fit.

Summary

Given the fact that Windows Presentation Foundation is such a graphically intensive GUI API, it comes as no surprise that we are provided with a number of ways to render graphical output. This chapter began by examining each of three ways a WPF application can do so (shapes, drawings, and visuals), and along the way discussed various rendering primitives such as brushes, pens, and transformations.

Next, we covered the role of WPF animation services, from the perspective of procedural VB code as well as XAML declarations. Here you learned various details regarding timelines, storyboards, and key frames. You were exposed to the WPF resource management APIs and came to see that WPF resources can entail items other than the expected set of string tables, icons, and bitmap types, but can also represent custom objects that can be held in a resource dictionary.

The chapter wrapped up by pulling together all of these topics into a cohesive unit and exploring the role of WPF styles and templates. As shown, WPF makes it very simple to stylize the look and feel of a control using graphical primitives, animation services, and a collection of embedded resources.

PART 8

Building Web Applications with ASP.NET

CHAPTER 33

Building ASP.NET Web Pages

Until now, all of the example applications in this text have focused on console-based and desktop GUI-based front ends. In the final three chapters of this text, you'll explore how the .NET platform facilitates the construction of browser-based presentation layers using a technology named ASP.NET. To begin, you'll quickly review a number of key web-centric concepts (HTTP, HTML, client-side scripting, and server-side scripting) and examine the role of Microsoft's commercial web server (IIS) as well as the ASP.NET development web server, `WebDev.WebServer.exe`.

With this web primer out of the way, the remainder of this chapter concentrates on the structure of ASP.NET web pages (including the single-file page and code-behind models) and examines the composition of a `Page`-derived type. This chapter also introduces the role of the `web.config` file, which will be used in the chapters to come.

Note If you have downloaded the sample code for this book, you may open any of the ASP.NET web projects in Visual Studio 2008 by selecting the File ➤ Open ➤ Web Site menu option. From there, simply select the folder containing the web content you wish to examine.

The Role of HTTP

Web applications are very different animals from traditional desktop applications (to say the least). The first obvious difference is that a production-level web application will always involve at least two networked machines (of course, during development it is entirely possible to have a single machine play the role of both the browser-based client and the web server itself). Given the nature of web applications, the networked machines in question must agree upon a particular wire protocol to determine how to send and receive data. The wire protocol that connects the computers in question is the Hypertext Transfer Protocol (HTTP).

The HTTP Request/Response Cycle

When a client machine launches a web browser (such as Opera, Mozilla Firefox, or Microsoft Internet Explorer) and submits a URL, an HTTP request is made to access a particular resource (typically a web page) on the remote server machine. HTTP is a text-based protocol that is built upon a standard request/response paradigm. For example, if you navigate to `http://www.intertech.com`, the browser software leverages a web technology termed *Domain Name Service* (DNS) that converts the registered URL into a four-part, 32-bit numerical value, termed an *IP address*. At this point, the browser opens a socket connection (typically via port 80 for a nonsecure connection) and sends the HTTP request for processing to the target site.

The web server receives the incoming HTTP request and may choose to process out any client-supplied input values (such as values within a text box, check box selections, etc.) in order to format a proper HTTP response. Web programmers may leverage any number of technologies (CGI, ASP, ASP.NET, JSP, etc.) to dynamically generate the content to be emitted into the HTTP response. At this point, the client-side browser renders the HTML sent from the web server. Figure 33-1 illustrates the basic HTTP request/response cycle.

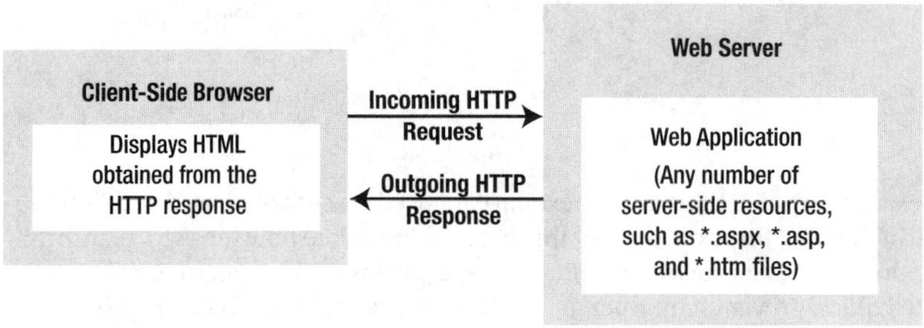

Figure 33-1. *The HTTP request/response cycle*

HTTP Is a Stateless Protocol

Another aspect of web development that is markedly different from traditional desktop programming is the fact that HTTP is essentially a *stateless* wire protocol. As soon as the web server emits a response to the client, everything about the previous interaction is forgotten. This is certainly not the case for a traditional desktop application, where the state of the executable is most often alive and kicking until the user shuts down the application in question.

Given this point, as a web developer, it is up to you take specific steps to "remember" information (such as items in a shopping cart, credit card numbers, home and work addresses, etc.) about the users who are currently logged on to your site. As you will see in Chapter 35, ASP.NET provides numerous ways to handle state, many of which are commonplace to any web platform (session variables, cookies, and application variables) as well as some .NET-particular techniques such as the ASP.NET profile management API.

Understanding Web Applications and Web Servers

A *web application* can be understood as a collection of files (`*.htm`, `*.asp`, `*.aspx`, image files, XML-based file data, etc.) and related components (such as a .NET code library or legacy COM server) stored within a particular set of directories on a given web server. As shown in Chapter 35, ASP.NET web applications have a specific life cycle and provide numerous events (such as initial startup or final shutdown) that you can hook into to perform specialized processing during your website's operation.

A *web server* is a software product in charge of hosting your web applications, and it typically provides a number of related services such as integrated security, File Transfer Protocol (FTP) support, mail exchange services, and so forth. Internet Information Services (IIS) is Microsoft's enterprise-level web server product, and as you would guess, it has intrinsic support for classic ASP as well as ASP.NET web applications.

When you build production-ready ASP.NET web applications, you will often need to interact with IIS. Be aware, however, that IIS is *not* automatically selected as an installation option when you install the Windows operating system (also be aware that not all versions of Windows can support IIS, such as Windows XP Home). Thus, depending on the configuration of your development machine, you may wish to install IIS before proceeding through this chapter. To do so, simply access the Add/Remove Program applet from the Control Panel folder and select Add/Remove Windows Components. Consult the Windows help system if you require further details.

■ **Note** Ideally, your development machine will have IIS installed *before* you install Visual Studio 2008. If you install IIS *after* you install Visual Studio 2008, none of your ASP.NET web applications will execute correctly (you will simply get back a blank page). Luckily, you can reconfigure IIS to host .NET applications by running the `aspnet_regiis.exe` command-line tool within a Visual Studio 2008 command prompt and specifying the `/i` option.

Assuming you have IIS properly installed on your workstation, you can interact with IIS from the Administrative Tools folder (located in the Control Panel folder) by double-clicking the Internet Information Services applet. For the purposes of this chapter, you are concerned only with the Default Web Site node (see Figure 33-2).

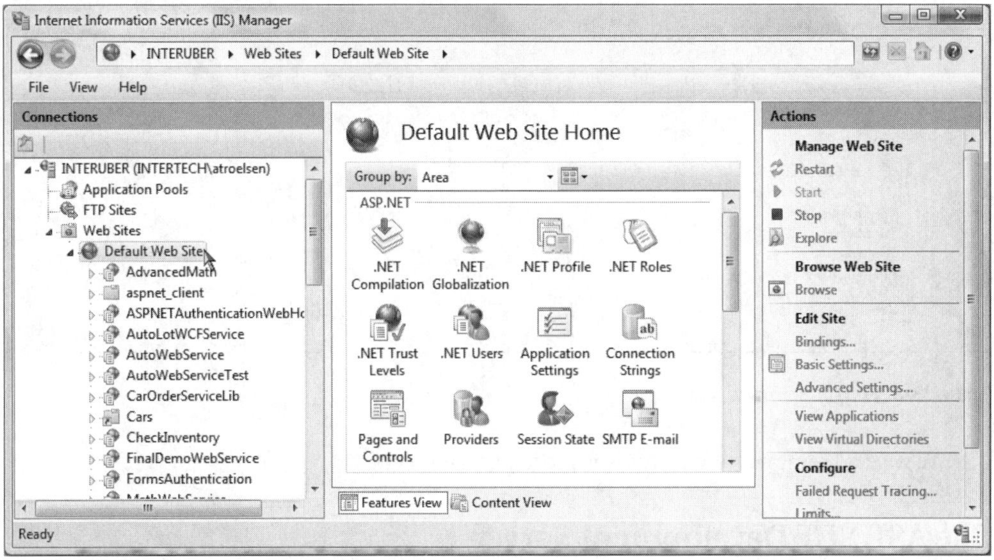

Figure 33-2. *The IIS applet*

The Role of IIS Virtual Directories

A single IIS installation is able to host numerous web applications, each of which resides in a *virtual directory*. Each virtual directory is mapped to a physical directory on the hard drive. Therefore, if you create a new virtual directory named CarsRUs, the outside world can navigate to this site using a URL such as `http://www.SomeDomain.com/CarsRUs` (assuming your site's IP address has been registered with the world at large). Under the hood, this virtual directory maps to a physical root directory on the web server, such as C:\inetpub\wwwroot\AspNetCarsSite, which contains the content of the CarsRUs web application.

As you will see later in this chapter, when you create ASP.NET web applications using Visual Studio 2008, you have the option of having the IDE generate a new virtual directory for the current website automatically. If required, you are certainly able to manually create a virtual directory by hand by right-clicking the Default Web Site node of IIS and selecting New ➤ Virtual Directory (or on Vista, simply Add Virtual Directory) from the context menu.

When you select the option to create a new virtual directory, you will be prompted for the alias (i.e., name) and physical folder that will contain the web content. To illustrate working with IIS (and to set us up for our first web example), create a new directory on your hard drive that will hold yet-to-be-generated web content. For this discussion I'll assume this directory to be C:\CodeTests\CarsWebSite. Now, right-click the Default Web Site node of IIS to create a new virtual directory named Cars that maps to this new directory. Figure 33-3 shows the end result (note that here I clicked the Content View tab at the bottom of the window).

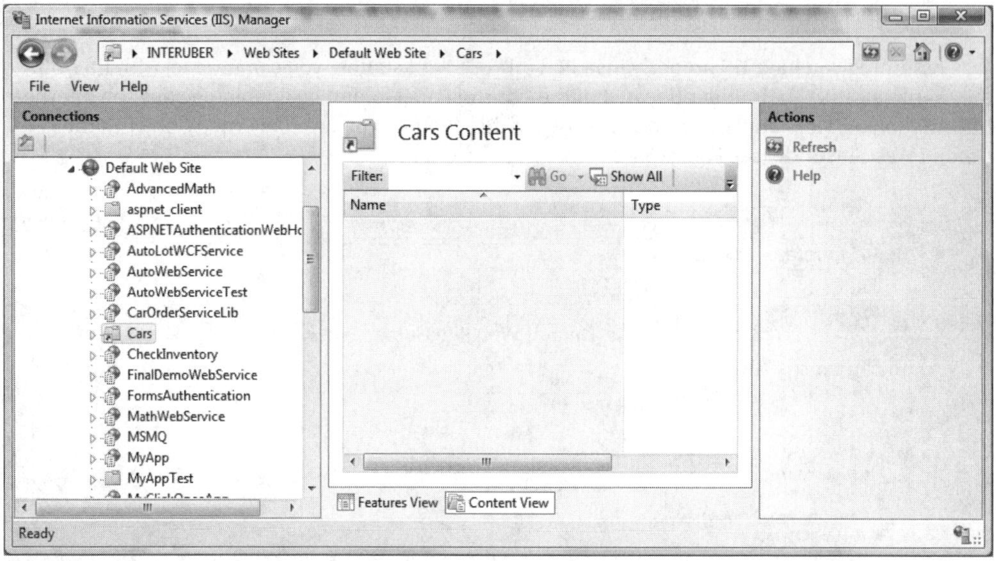

Figure 33-3. *The Cars virtual directory*

We will add some content to this website in just a moment.

The ASP.NET Development Server

Prior to .NET 2.0, ASP.NET developers were required to make use of IIS virtual directories during the development and testing of their web content. In many cases, this tight dependency on IIS made team development more complex than necessary (not to mention that many network administrators frowned upon installing IIS on every developer's machine). Thankfully, we now have the option to use a lightweight web server named `WebDev.WebServer.exe`. This utility allows developers to host an ASP.NET web application outside the bounds of IIS. Using this tool, you can build and test your web pages from any directory on your machine. This is quite helpful for team development scenarios and for building ASP.NET web programs on versions of Windows that do not support IIS installations (such as Windows XP Home).

Note `WebDev.WebServer.exe` cannot be used to test or host classic (COM-based) ASP web applications. This web server can host only ASP.NET web applications and/or .NET-based XML web services.

When building a website with Visual Studio 2008, you have the option of using WebDev.WebServer.exe to host your pages (as you will see a bit later in this chapter). However, you are also able to manually interact with this tool from a Visual Studio 2008 command prompt. If you change to the following directory (using the cd command):

```
C:\Program Files\Common Files\microsoft shared\DevServer\9.0\
```

and enter the following command:

```
WebDev.WebServer.exe
```

you will be presented with a message box that describes the valid command-line options. In a nutshell, you will need to specify an unused port via the /port: option, the root directory of the web application via the /path: option, and an optional virtual path using the /vpath: option (if you do not supply a /vpath: option, the default is simply /). Consider the following usage, which opens an arbitrary port to view content in the C:\CodeTests\CarsWebSite directory created previously:

```
WebDev.WebServer.exe /port:12345 /path:"C:\CodeTests\CarsWebSite"
```

Once you have entered this command, you can launch your web browser of choice to request pages. Thus, if the CarsWebSite folder had a file named Default.aspx (which it currently does not), you could enter the following URL:

```
http://localhost:12345/Default.aspx
```

Many of the examples in this chapter and the next will make use of WebDev.WebServer.exe indirectly via Visual Studio 2008, rather than hosting web content under an IIS virtual directory. While this approach can simplify the development of your web application, do be aware that WebDev.WebServer.exe is *not* intended to host production-level web applications. It is intended purely for development and testing purposes. Once a web application is ready for prime time, your site will need to be copied to an IIS virtual directory.

The Role of HTML

Now that you have configured a directory to host your web application, and you have chosen a web server to serve as the host, you need to create the content itself. Recall that "web application" is simply the term given to the set of files that constitute the functionality of the site. To be sure, a vast number of these files will contain tokens defined by Hypertext Markup Language (HTML). HTML is a standard markup language used to describe how literal text, images, external links, and various HTML-based UI widgets are to be rendered within the client-side browser.

This particular aspect of web development is one of the major reasons why many programmers dislike building web-based programs. While it is true that modern IDEs (including Visual Studio 2008) and web development platforms (such as ASP.NET) generate much of the HTML automatically, having a working knowledge of HTML as you work with ASP.NET is certainly a good idea.

■ **Note** Recall from Chapter 2 that Microsoft has released a number of free IDEs under the Express family of products (such as Visual Basic 2008 Express). If you are interested in web development, you may wish to also download Visual Web Developer 2008 Express. This free IDE is geared exclusively at the construction of ASP.NET web applications.

While this section will most certainly not cover all aspects of HTML (by any means), let's check out some basics and build a simple web application using HTML, classic (COM-based) ASP, and IIS.

This will serve as a foundation for those of you coming to ASP.NET from a traditional desktop application development background.

Note If you are already comfortable with the overall process of web page development, feel free to skip ahead to the section "Problems with Classic ASP."

HTML Document Structure

An HTML file consists of a set of tags that describe the look and feel of a given web page. As you would expect, the basic structure of an HTML document tends to remain the same. For example, `*.htm` files (or, equivalently, `*.html` files) open and close with `<html>` and `</html>` tags, typically define a `<body>` section, and so forth. Keep in mind that traditional HTML is *not* case sensitive. Therefore, in the eyes of the hosting browser, `<HTML>`, `<html>`, and `<HtmL>` are identical.

To illustrate some HTML basics, open Visual Studio 2008, create an empty HTML file using the File ➤ New ➤ File menu selection, and save this file under your C:\CodeTests\CarsWebSite directory as `default.htm`. As you can see, the initial markup is rather uneventful:

```
<!DOCTYPE html PUBLIC "-//W3C//DTD XHTML 1.0 Transitional//EN"
"http://www.w3.org/TR/xhtml1/DTD/xhtml1-transitional.dtd">
<html xmlns="http://www.w3.org/1999/xhtml" >
<head>
  <title>Untitled Page</title>
</head>
<body>

</body>
</html>
```

First of all, notice that this HTML file opens with a `DOCTYPE` processing instruction. This informs the IDE that the contained HTML tags should be validated against the XHTML Transitional standard. As suggested, traditional HTML was very "loose" in its syntax. For example, it was permissible to define an opening element (such as `<br>`, for a line break) that did not have a corresponding closing break (`</br>` in this case), was not case sensitive, and so forth. The XHTML standard is a W3C specification that adds some much needed rigor to HTML.

Note By default, Visual Studio 2008 validates all HTML documents against the XHTML 1.0 Transitional validation scheme. Simply put, HTML *validation schemes* are used to ensure the markup is in sync with specific standards. If you wish to specify an alternative validation scheme, activate the Tools ➤ Options dialog box, and then select the Validation node under Text Editor ➤ HTML. If you would rather not see validation errors, simply uncheck the Show Errors check box.

The `<html>` and `</html>` tags are used to mark the beginning and end of your document. Notice that the opening `<html>` tag is further qualified with an `xmlns` (XML namespace) attribute that qualifies the various tags that may appear within this document (again, by default these tags are based on the XHTML standard). Web browsers use these particular tags to understand where to begin applying the rendering formats specified in the body of the document. The `<body>` scope is where the vast majority of the actual content is defined. To spruce things up just a bit, update the title of your page as follows:

```
<head>
  <title>This Is the Cars Web site</title>
</head>
```

Not surprisingly, the <title> tags are used to specify the text string that should be placed in the title bar of the calling web browser.

HTML Form Development

The real meat of most *.htm files occurs within the scope of the <form> elements. An *HTML form* is simply a named group of related UI elements used to gather user input, which is then transmitted to the web application via an HTTP request. Do not confuse an HTML form with the entire display area shown by a given browser. In reality, an HTML form is more of a *logical grouping* of widgets placed in the <form> and </form> tag set:

```
<html xmlns="http://www.w3.org/1999/xhtml" >
<head>
  <title>This Is the Cars Web site</title>
</head>
<body>
  <form id="defaultPage">
    <!-- Insert web UI content here ->
  </form>
</body>
</html>
```

This form has been assigned the id value of "defaultPage". Typically, the opening <form> tag also supplies an action attribute that specifies the URL to which to submit the form data, as well as the method of transmitting that data itself (POST or GET). You will examine this aspect of the <form> tag in just a bit. For the time being, let's look at the sorts of items that can be placed in an HTML form (beyond simple literal text). Visual Studio 2008 provides an HTML tab on the Toolbox that allows you to select each HTML-based UI widget, as shown in Figure 33-4.

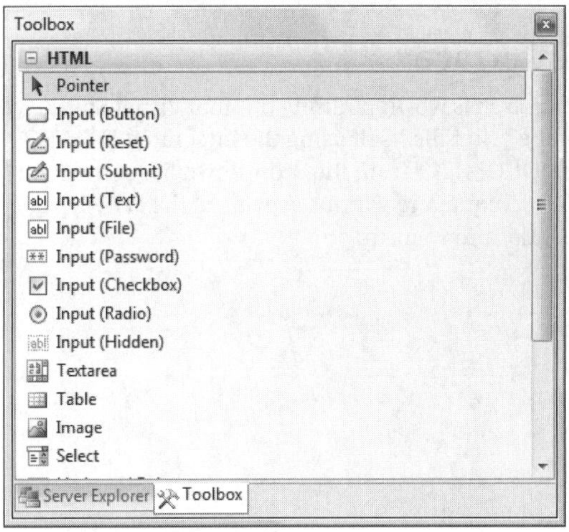

Figure 33-4. *The HTML tab of the Toolbox*

Similar to the process of building a Windows Forms or WPF application, these HTML controls can be dragged onto the HTML designer surface. If you click the Split tab of your HTML designer, the bottom pane of the HTML editor will display the HTML visual layout, while the upper pane will show the related markup. Another benefit of this editor is that as you select markup or an HTML UI element, the corresponding representation is highlighted. This makes it very simple to see the scope of your changes (see Figure 33-5).

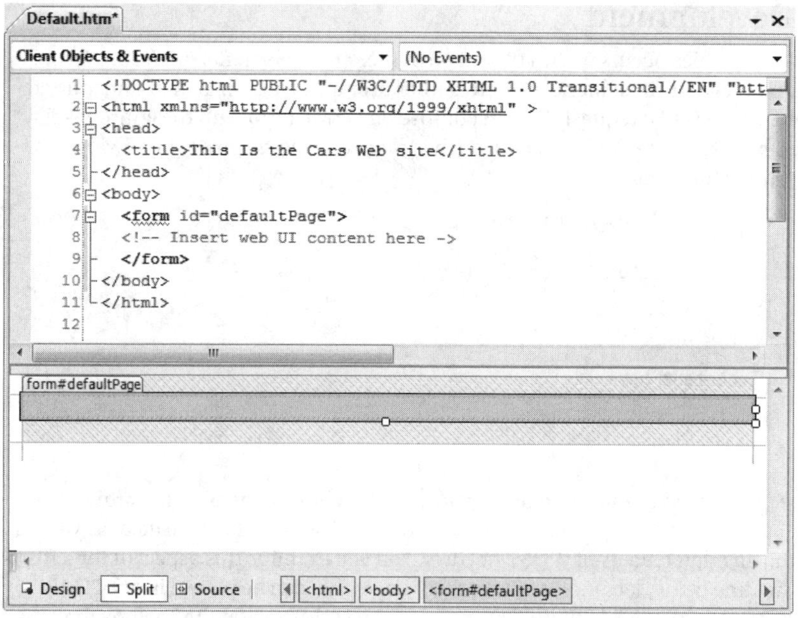

Figure 33-5. *The Visual Studio 2008 HTML editor displays markup and UI layout.*

Building an HTML-Based User Interface

Before you add the HTML widgets to the HTML `<form>`, it is worth pointing out that Visual Studio 2008 allows you to edit the overall look and feel of the `*.htm` file itself using the integrated HTML designer and the Properties window. If you select DOCUMENT from the drop-down list of the Properties window, as shown in Figure 33-6, you are able to configure various aspects of the HTML page, such as the background color, background image, title, and so forth.

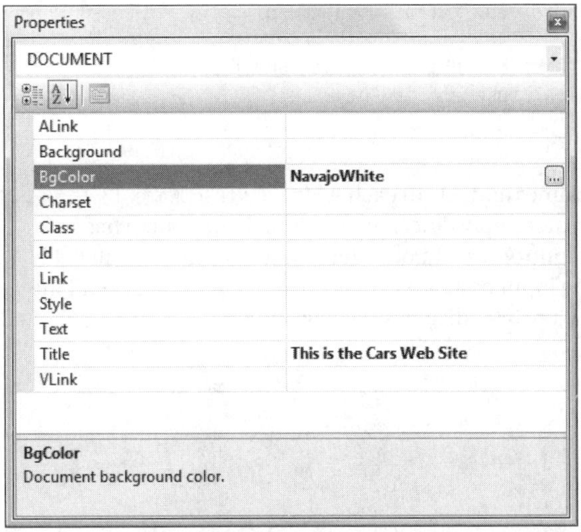

Figure 33-6. *Editing an HTML document via the Visual Studio 2008 Properties window*

Now, update the <body> of the default.htm file to display some literal text that prompts the user to enter a username and password, and choose a background color of your liking (be aware that you can enter and format literal textual content by typing directly in the HTML designer):

```
<html xmlns="http://www.w3.org/1999/xhtml" >
<head>
  <title>This is the Cars Web Site</title>
</head>
<body bgcolor="NavajoWhite">
  <!-- Prompt for user input-->
  <h1 align="center">The Cars Login Page</h1>
  <p align="center"> <br/>
    Please enter your <i>user name</i> and <i>password</i>.
  </p>
  <form id="defaultPage">
  </form>
</body>
</html>
```

Now let's build the HTML form itself. In general, each type of HTML widget is described using an id attribute (used to identify the item programmatically) and a type attribute (used to specify which UI element you are interested in placing in the <form> declaration). Depending on which UI widget you manipulate, you will find additional attributes specific to that particular item that can be modified using the Properties window.

The UI you will build here will contain two text fields (one of which is a Password input widget) and two button types (one to submit the form data and the other to reset the form data to the default values):

```
<!-- Build a form to get user info -->
<form id="defaultPage">
  <p align="center">
    User Name:
    <input  type="text" name="txtUserName" id="txtUserName"/></p>
  <p align="center">
    Password:
```

```
    <input type="password" name="txtPassword" id="txtPassword"/></p>
  <p align="center">
    <input type="submit" value="Submit" name="btnSubmit" id="btnSubmit"/>
    <input type="reset" value="Reset" name="btnReset" id="btnReset"/>
  </p>
</form>
```

Notice that you have assigned relevant names and IDs to each widget (`txtUserName`, `txtPassword`, `btnSubmit`, and `btnReset`). Of greater importance, note that each input item has an extra attribute named `type` that marks these controls as UI items that automatically clear all fields to their initial values (`type="reset"`), mask the input as a password (`type="password"`), or send the form data to the recipient (`type="submit"`). Figure 33-7 displays the page thus far.

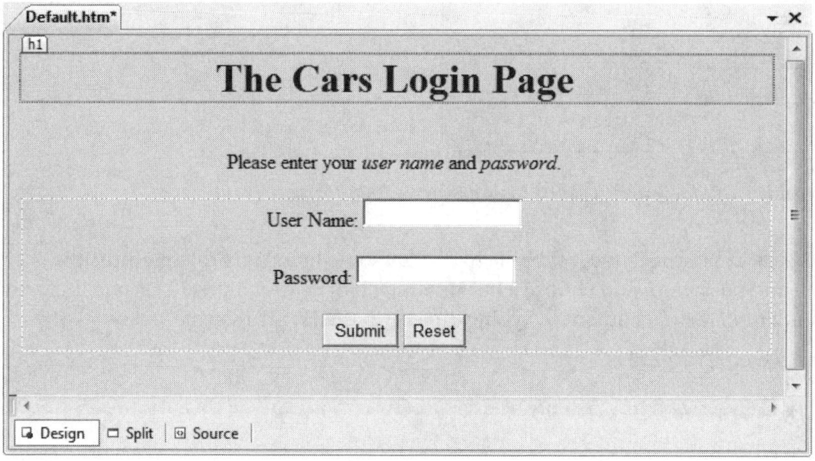

Figure 33-7. *Our initial crack at the* `default.htm` *page*

The Role of Client-Side Scripting

In addition to HTML UI elements, a given `*.htm` file may contain blocks of script code that will be emitted into the response stream and processed by the requesting browser. There are two major reasons why client-side scripting is used:

- To validate user input in the browser before posting back to the web server
- To interact with the Document Object Model (DOM) of the target browser

Regarding the first point, understand that the inherent evil of a web application is the need to make frequent round-trips (termed *postbacks*) to the server machine to update the HTML rendered into the browser. While postbacks are unavoidable, you should always be mindful of ways to minimize travel across the wire. One technique that saves round-trips is to use client-side scripting to validate user input before submitting thc form data to the web server. If an error is found (such as not supplying data within a required field), you can alert the user to the error without incurring the cost of posting back to the web server (after all, nothing is more annoying to users than posting back on a slow connection, only to receive instructions to address input errors!).

■ Note Do be aware that even when performing client-side validation (for improved response time), validation should *also* occur on the web server itself. This will help ensure that the data has not been tampered with as it was sent across the wire. As explained in the following chapter, the ASP.NET validation controls will automatically perform client- and server-side validation.

In addition to validating user input, client-side scripts can also be used to interact with the underlying object model (the DOM) of the web browser itself. Most commercial browsers expose a set of objects that can be leveraged to control how the browser should behave. One major annoyance is the fact that different browsers tend to expose similar, but not identical, object models. Thus, if you emit a block of client-side script code that interacts with the DOM, it may not work identically on all browsers.

■ Note ASP.NET provides the `HttpRequest.Browser` property, which allows you to determine at runtime the capacities of the browser that sent the current request. This makes it easier for you to write server-side (ASP.NET) code that generates the correct variant of client-side script for the current browser.

There are many scripting languages that can be used to author client-side script code. Two of the more popular ones are VBScript and JavaScript. VBScript is a subset of the Visual Basic 6.0 programming language. Be aware that Microsoft Internet Explorer is the only web browser that has built-in support for client-side VBScript support (other browsers may or may not provide optional plug-ins). Thus, if you wish your HTML pages to work correctly in any commercial web browser, do *not* use VBScript for your client-side scripting logic.

The other popular scripting language is JavaScript. Be very aware that JavaScript is in no way, shape, or form a subset of the Java language. While JavaScript and Java have a somewhat similar syntax, JavaScript is not a full-fledged OOP language, and thus it is far less powerful than Java. The good news is that all modern-day web browsers support JavaScript, which makes it a natural candidate for client-side scripting logic.

■ Note To further confuse the issue, recall that JScript .NET is a managed language that can be used to build valid .NET assemblies using a scriptlike syntax.

A Client-Side Scripting Example

To illustrate the role of client-side scripting, let's first examine how to intercept events sent from client-side HTML GUI widgets. Assume you have added an additional HTML button (`btnHelp`) to your `default.htm` page that allows the user to view help information. To capture the `Click` event for this button, select `btnHelp` from the upper-left drop-down list of the HTML form designer and select the `onclick` event from the right drop-down list. This will add an `onclick` attribute to the definition of the new `Button` type:

```
<input type="button" value="Help" name="btnHelp" id="btnHelp"
       onclick="return btnHelp_onclick()" />
```

Visual Studio 2008 will also create an empty JavaScript function that will be called when the user clicks the button. Within this stub, simply make use of the `alert()` method to display a client-side message box:

```
<script language="javascript" type="text/javascript">
// <!CDATA[
function btnHelp_onclick() {
  alert("Dude, it is not that hard. Click the Submit button!");
}
// ]]>
</script>
```

Note that the scripting block has been wrapped within a CDATA section. The reason for this is simple. If your page ends up on a browser that does not support JavaScript, the code will be treated as a comment block and ignored. Of course, your page may be less functional, but the upside is that your page will not blow up when rendered by the browser.

Validating the default.htm Form Data

Now, let's update the default.htm page to support some client-side validation logic. The goal is to ensure that when the user clicks the Submit button, you call a JavaScript function that checks each text box for empty values. If a text box is left empty, you pop up an alert that instructs the user to enter the required data. First, handle an onclick event for the Submit button:

```
<input type="submit" value="Submit" name="btnSubmit" id="btnSubmit"
 onclick="return btnSubmit_onclick()">
```

Implement this handler like so:

```
function btnSubmit_onclick(){
  // If they forget either item, pop up a message box.
  if((defaultPage.txtUserName.value == "") ||
    (defaultPage.txtPassword.value == ""))
  {
    alert("You must supply a user name and password!");
    return false;
  }
  return true;
}
```

At this point, save your work. You can open your browser of choice, navigate to the default.htm page hosted by your Cars virtual directory (remember, this first example is not using WebDev.WebServer.exe), and test out your client-side script logic:

```
http://localhost/Cars/default.htm
```

If you click the Help or Submit button, you should find the correct message box launched by your browser of choice. Do notice that if you enter some random data into your text boxes, you will not see the validation error displayed when you do click the Submit button.

Submitting the Form Data (GET and POST)

Now that you have a simple HTML page, you need to examine how to transmit the form data back to the web server for processing. When you build an HTML form, you typically supply an action attribute on the opening <form> tag to specify the recipient of the incoming form data. Possible receivers include mail servers, other HTML files, an Active Server Pages (ASP) file, and so forth. For this example, you'll use a classic ASP file named ClassicAspPage.asp. Update your default.htm file by specifying the following attribute in the opening <form> tag:

```
<form id="defaultPage"
 action="http://localhost/Cars/ClassicAspPage.asp" method="get">
...
</form>
```

These extra attributes ensure that when the Submit button for this form is clicked, the form data is sent to `ClassicAspPage.asp` at the specified URL. When you specify `method="get"` as the mode of transmission, the form data is appended to the query string as a set of name/value pairs separated by ampersands:

```
http://localhost/Cars/ClassicAspPage.asp?txtUserName=
Andrew&txtPassword=Foo$&btnSubmit=Submit
```

The other method of transmitting form data to the web server is to specify `method="post"`:

```
<form id="defaultPage"
  action="http://localhost/Cars/ClassicAspPage.asp" method="post">
...
</form>
```

In this case, the form data is not appended to the query string, but instead is written to a separate line within the HTTP header. Using POST, the form data is not directly visible to the outside world. More important, POST data does not have a character-length limitation (many browsers have a limit for GET queries). For the time being, make use of HTTP GET to send the form data to the receiving `*.asp` page.

Building a Classic ASP Page

A classic ASP page is a hodgepodge of HTML and *server-side script code*. If you have never worked with classic ASP, understand that the goal of ASP is to dynamically build HTML on the fly using a server-side script using a small set of COM objects and a bit of elbow grease. For example, you may have a server-side VBScript (or JavaScript) block that reads a table from a data source using classic ADO and returns the rows as a generic HTML table.

For this example, the ASP page uses the intrinsic ASP `Request` COM object to read the values of the incoming form data (appended to the query string) and echo them back to the caller (not terribly exciting, but it illustrates the basic operation of the request/response cycle). The server-side script logic will make use of VBScript (as denoted by the `language` directive).

To do so, create a new HTML file using Visual Studio 2008 and save this file under the name `ClassicAspPage.asp` into the folder to which your virtual directory has been mapped (e.g., C:\CodeTests\CarsWebSite). Implement this page as follows:

```
<%@ language="VBScript" %>
<html>
<head>
  <title>The Cars Page</title>
</head>
  <body>
    <h1 align="center">Here is what you sent me:</h1>
    <P align="center"> <b>User Name: </b>
    <%= Request.QueryString("txtUserName") %> <br>
    <b>Password: </b>
    <%= Request.QueryString("txtPassword") %> <br>
    </P>
  </body>
</html>
```

Here, you use the classic ASP `Request` COM object to call the `QueryString()` method to examine the values contained in each HTML widget submitted via `method="get"`. The `<%= ...%>` notation is a shorthand way of saying, "Insert the following directly into the outbound HTTP response." To gain a finer level of flexibility, you could interact with the ASP `Response` COM object within a full server-side script block (denoted by the `<%, %>` notation). You have no need to do so here; however, the following is a simple example:

```
<%
  Dim pwd
  pwd = Request.QueryString("txtPassword")
  Response.Write(pwd)
%>
```

Obviously, the `Request` and `Response` objects of classic ASP provide a number of additional members beyond those shown here. Furthermore, classic ASP also defines a small number of additional COM objects (`Session`, `Server`, `Application`, etc.) that you can use while constructing your web application.

■ **Note** Under ASP.NET, these COM objects are officially dead. However, you will see that the `System.Web.UI.Page` base class defines identically named properties that expose objects with similar functionality.

At this point be sure to save each of your web files. To test the ASP logic, simply load the `default.htm` page from a browser and submit the form data. Once the script is processed on the web server, you are returned a brand-new (dynamically generated) HTML display, as you see in Figure 33-8.

Figure 33-8. *The dynamically generated HTML*

Currently, your `default.htm` file specifies HTTP GET as the method of sending the form data to the target `*.asp` file. Using this approach, the values contained in the various GUI widgets are appended to the end of the query string. It is important to note that the ASP `Request.QueryString()` method is *only* able to extract data submitted via the GET method.

If you would rather submit form data to the web resource using HTTP POST, you can use the `Request.Form` collection to read the values on the server, for example:

```
<body>
  <h1 align="center">Here is what you sent me:</h1>
  <P align="center">
    <b>User Name: </b>
```

```
    <%= Request.Form("txtUserName") %> <br>
    <b>Password: </b>
    <%= Request.Form("txtPassword") %> <br>
  </P>
</body>
```

That wraps up our basic web primer. Hopefully, if you're new to web development you now have a better understanding of the building blocks of a web-based application. Before we check out how the ASP.NET web platform improves upon the current state of affairs, let's take a brief moment to critique classic ASP and understand its core limitations.

Source Code The CarsWebSite project is included under the Chapter 33 subdirectory.

Problems with Classic ASP

While many successful websites have been created using classic ASP, this architecture is not without its downsides. Perhaps the biggest downside of classic ASP is the same thing that makes it a powerful platform: server-side scripting languages. Scripting languages such as VBScript and JavaScript are interpreted, typeless entities that do not lend themselves to robust OO programming techniques.

Another problem with classic ASP is the fact that an `*.asp` page does not yield very modularized code. Given that ASP is a blend of HTML and script in a *single* page, most ASP web applications are a confused mix of two different programming techniques. While it is true that classic ASP allows you to partition reusable code into distinct include files, the underlying object model does not support true separation of concerns. In an ideal world, a web framework would allow the presentation logic (i.e., HTML tags) to exist independently from the business logic (i.e., functional code).

A final issue to consider here is the fact that classic ASP demands a good deal of boilerplate, redundant script code that tends to repeat between projects. Almost all web applications need to validate user input, repopulate the state of HTML widgets before emitting the HTTP response, generate an HTML table of data, and so forth.

Major Benefits of ASP.NET 1.x

The first releases of ASP.NET (versions 1.0–1.1) did a fantastic job of addressing each of the limitations found with classic ASP. In a nutshell, the .NET platform brought about the following techniques to the Microsoft web development paradigm:

- ASP.NET provides a model termed *code-behind*, which allows you to separate presentation logic from business logic.
- ASP.NET pages are coded using .NET programming languages, rather than interpreted scripting languages. The code files are compiled into valid .NET assemblies (which translates into much faster execution).
- Web controls allow programmers to build the GUI of a web application in a manner similar to building a Windows Forms/WPF application.
- ASP.NET web controls automatically maintain their state during postbacks using a hidden form field named `__VIEWSTATE`.

- ASP.NET web applications are completely object-oriented and make use of the Common Type System (CTS).
- ASP.NET web applications can be easily configured using standard IIS settings *or* using a web application configuration file (`web.config`).

Major Enhancements of ASP.NET 2.0

While ASP.NET 1.x was a major step in the right direction, ASP.NET 2.0 provided additional bells and whistles. Consider this partial list:

- Introduction of the `WebDev.WebServer.exe` testing web server
- A large number of additional web controls (navigation controls, security controls, new data controls, new UI controls, etc.)
- The introduction of *master pages*, which allow you to attach a common UI frame to a set of related pages
- Support for *themes*, which offer a declarative manner to change the look and feel of the entire web application
- Support for *Web Parts*, which can be used to allow end users to customize the look and feel of a web page
- Introduction of a web-based configuration and management utility that maintains your `web.config` files

Major ASP.NET 3.5 Web Enhancements

As you would expect, .NET 3.5 further increases the scope of the ASP.NET programming model. Perhaps most important, we now have

- New controls to support Silverlight development (recall that this is a WPF-based API for designing rich media content for a website)
- Integrated support for Ajax-style development, which essentially allows for "micro-postbacks" to refresh part of a web page as quickly as possible

Given that this book is not focused exclusively on web development, be sure to consult the .NET Framework 3.5 SDK documentation for details of topics not covered in the remainder of this text. The truth of the matter is that if I were to truly do justice to every aspect of ASP.NET, this book would easily double in size. Rest assured that by the time you complete this section of the text, you will have a solid ASP.NET foundation to build upon as you see fit.

■ **Note** If you require a comprehensive examination of ASP.NET, I suggest picking up a copy of *Beginning ASP.NET 3.5 in VB 2008: From Novice to Professional, Second Edition* by Matthew MacDonald (Apress, 2007).

The ASP.NET Namespaces

As of .NET 3.5, there are well over 30 web-centric namespaces in the base class libraries. From a high level, these namespaces can be grouped into several major categories:

- Core functionality (e.g., types that allow you to interact with the HTTP request and response, Web Form infrastructure, theme and profiling support, Web Parts, security, etc.)
- Web Form and HTML controls
- Mobile web development
- Silverlight development
- Ajax development

Table 33-1 describes several (but certainly not all) of the core ASP.NET namespaces.

Table 33-1. *The Core ASP.NET Web-Centric Namespaces*

Namespaces	Meaning in Life
`System.Web`	Defines types that enable browser/web server communication (such as request and response capabilities, cookie manipulation, and file transfer)
`System.Web.Caching`	Defines types that facilitate caching support for a web application
`System.Web.Hosting`	Defines types that allow you to build custom hosts for the ASP.NET runtime
`System.Web.Management`	Defines types for managing and monitoring the health of an ASP.NET web application
`System.Web.Profile`	Defines types that are used to implement ASP.NET user profiles
`System.Web.Security`	Defines types that allow you to programmatically secure your site
`System.Web.SessionState`	Defines types that allow you to maintain stateful information on a per-user basis (e.g., session state variables)
`System.Web.UI`, `System.Web.UI.WebControls`, `System.Web.UI.HtmlControls`	Define a number of types that allow you to build a GUI front end for your web application

The ASP.NET Web Page Code Model

ASP.NET web pages can be constructed using one of two approaches. You are free to create a single `*.aspx` file that contains a blend of server-side code and HTML (much like classic ASP). Using the single-file page model, server-side code is placed within a `<script>` scope, but the code itself is *not* script code proper (e.g., VBScript/JavaScript). Rather, the code statements within a `<script>` block are written in your .NET language of choice (VB, C#, etc.).

If you are building a page that contains very little code (but a good deal of HTML), a single-file page model may be easier to work with, as you can see the code and the markup in one unified `*.aspx` file. In addition, placing your procedural code and HTML markup into a single `*.aspx` file provides a few other advantages:

- Pages written using the single-file page model are slightly easier to deploy or to send to another developer.
- Because there is no dependency between files, a single-file page is easier to rename.
- Managing files in a source code control system is slightly easier, as all the action is taking place in a single file.

The default approach taken by Visual Studio 2008 (when creating a new website solution, described in just a moment) is to make use of a technique known as code-behind, which allows you to separate your programming code from your HTML presentation logic using two distinct files. This model works quite well when your pages contain a significant amount of code or when multiple developers are working on the same website. The code-behind model offers several benefits as well:

- Because code-behind pages offer a clean separation of HTML markup and code, it is possible to have designers working on the markup while programmers author the VB code.
- Code is not exposed to page designers or others who are working only with the page markup (as you might guess, HTML folks are not always interested in viewing reams of VB code).
- Code files can be used across multiple `*.aspx` files.

Regardless of which approach you take, do know that there is *no* difference in terms of performance. Also be aware that the single-file `*.aspx` model is no longer frowned upon as it was under .NET 1.x. In fact, many ASP.NET web applications will benefit by building sites that make use of both approaches.

Building a Data-Centric Single-File Test Page

First up, let's examine the single-file page model. Our goal is to build an `*.aspx` file that displays the Inventory table of the AutoLot database (created in Chapter 22). While you could build this page using nothing but Notepad, Visual Studio 2008 can simplify matters via IntelliSense, code completion, and a visual page designer.

To begin, open Visual Studio 2008 and create a new Web Form using the File ➤ New ➤ File menu option (see Figure 33-9). Once you have done so, save this file (with the name `Default.aspx`) under a new directory on your hard drive named C:\CodeTests\SinglePageModel.

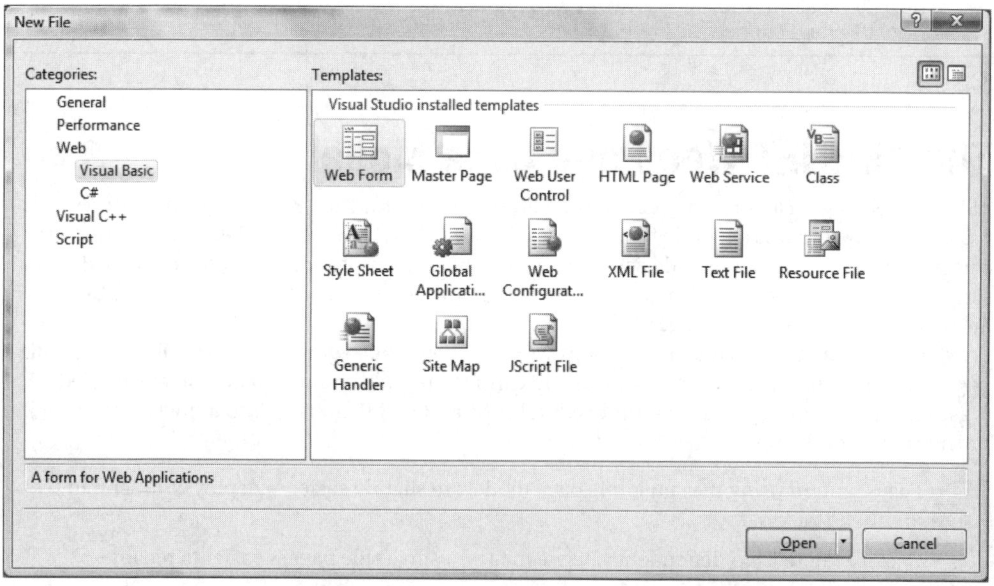

Figure 33-9. *Creating a new* `*.aspx` *file*

Manually Referencing AutoLotDAL.dll

Next, use Windows Explorer to create a subdirectory under the SinglePageModel folder named "bin". The specially named \bin subdirectory is a registered name with the ASP.NET runtime engine. Into the \bin folder of a website's root, you are able to deploy any private assemblies used by the web application. For this example, place a copy of `AutoLotDAL.dll` (see Chapter 22) into the C:\CodeTests\SinglePageModel\bin folder.

Note As shown later in this chapter, when you use Visual Studio 2008 to create a full-blown ASP.NET web application, the IDE will maintain the \bin folder on your behalf.

Designing the UI

Now, using the Visual Studio 2008 Toolbox, select the Standard tab and drag and drop a `Button`, `Label`, and `GridView` control onto the page designer (the `GridView` widget can be found under the Data tab of the Toolbox). Feel free to make use of the Properties window (or the HTML IntelliSense) to set various UI properties and give each web widget a proper name via the `ID` property. Figure 33-10 shows one possible design. (I kept the example's look and feel intentionally bland to minimize the amount of generated control markup, but feel free to spruce things up to your liking.)

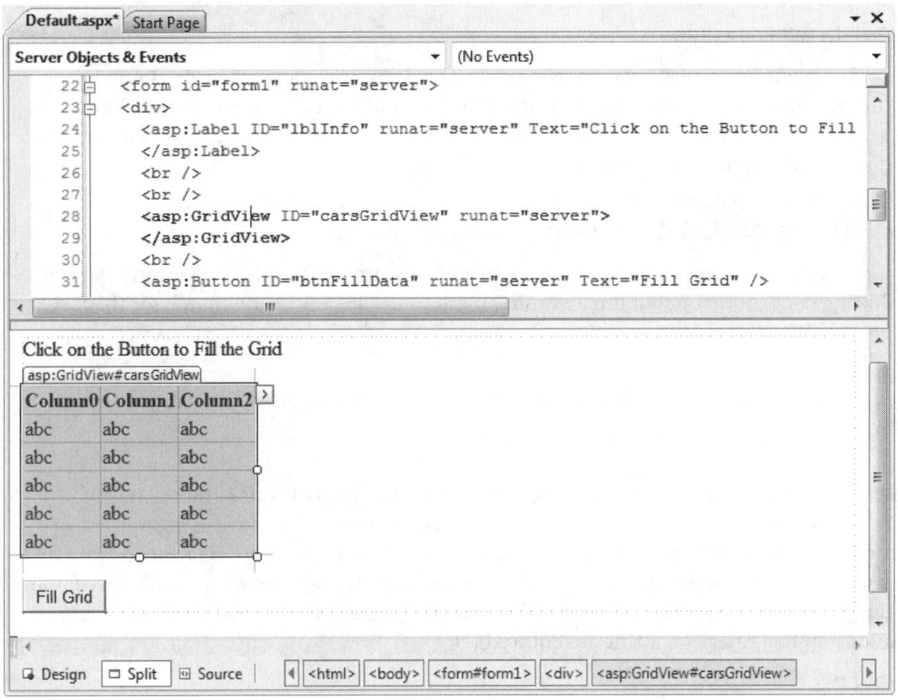

Figure 33-10. *The* `Default.aspx` *UI*

Now, locate the `<form>` section of your page. Notice how each web control has been defined using an `<asp:>` tag. Before the closing `</form>` tag, you will find a series of name/value pairs that correspond to the settings you made in the Properties window:

```
<form id="form1" runat="server">
<div>
  <asp:Label ID="lblInfo" runat="server"
    Text="Click on the Button to Fill the Grid">
  </asp:Label>
  <br />
  <br />
  <asp:GridView ID="carsGridView" runat="server">
  </asp:GridView>
  <br />
  <asp:Button ID="btnFillData" runat="server" Text="Fill Grid" />
</div>
</form>
```

You will dig into the full details of ASP.NET web controls later in Chapter 34. Until then, understand that web controls are objects processed on the web server that emit back their HTML representation into the outgoing HTTP response automatically (that's right—you don't author the HTML!). Beyond this major benefit, ASP.NET web controls mimic a desktoplike programming model, given that the names of the properties, methods, and events typically echo a Windows Forms/WPF equivalent.

Adding the Data Access Logic

Handle the `Click` event for the `Button` type using either the Visual Studio 2008 Properties window (via the lightning bolt icon) or using the drop-down boxes mounted at the top of the designer window. Once you do, you will find your `Button`'s definition has been updated with an `OnClick` attribute that is assigned to the name of your `Click` event handler:

```
<asp:Button ID="btnFillData" runat="server"
     Text="Fill Grid" OnClick="btnFillData_Click"/>
```

As well, you receive an empty `<script>` block to author your server-side `Click` event handler. Add the following code, noticing that the incoming parameters are a dead-on match for the target of the `System.EventHandler` delegate:

```
<script runat="server">
  Protected Sub btnFillData_Click(ByVal sender As Object, ByVal e As EventArgs)
  End Sub
</script>
```

The next step is to populate the `GridView` using the functionality of your `AutoLotDAL.dll` assembly. To do so, you must use the `<%@ Import %>` directive to specify you are using the `AutoLotConnectedLayer` namespace. In addition, you need to inform the ASP.NET runtime that this single-file page is referencing the `AutoLotDAL.dll` assembly, via the `<%@ Assembly %>` directive (more details on directives in just a moment). Here is the remaining relevant page logic of the `Default.aspx` file (modify your connection string as required):

```
<%@ Page Language="VB" %>
<%@ Import Namespace="AutoLotConnectedLayer" %>
<%@ Assembly Name="AutoLotDAL" %>

<!DOCTYPE html PUBLIC "-//W3C//DTD XHTML 1.0 Transitional//EN"
  "http://www.w3.org/TR/xhtml1/DTD/xhtml1-transitional.dtd">
```

```
<script runat="server">
  Protected Sub btnFillData_Click(ByVal sender As Object, ByVal e As EventArgs)
    Dim dal As New InventoryDAL()
    dal.OpenConnection("Data Source=(local)\SQLEXPRESS;" & _
      "Initial Catalog=AutoLot;Integrated Security=True")
    carsGridView.DataSource = dal.GetAllInventory()
    carsGridView.DataBind()
    dal.CloseConnection()
  End Sub
</script>
<html xmlns="http://www.w3.org/1999/xhtml" >
...
</html>
```

Before we dive into the details behind the format of this `*.aspx` file, let's try a test run. First, save your `*.aspx` file. If you wish to make use of `WebDev.WebServer.exe` manually, open a .NET command prompt and run the `WebDev.WebServer.exe` utility, making sure you specify the path where you saved your `Default.aspx` file, for example (here I specified an arbitrary port of 12345):

```
webdev.webserver.exe /port:12345 /path:"C:\CodeTests\SinglePageModel"
```

Now, using your browser of choice, enter the following URL (technically, you do not need to specify `Default.aspx`, because, well, it is the default!):

```
http://localhost:12345/Default.aspx
```

When the page is served, you will initially see your `Label` and `Button` types. However, when you click the button, a postback occurs to the web server, at which point the web controls render back their corresponding HTML tags.

As a shortcut, you can indirectly launch `WebDev.WebServer.exe` from Visual Studio 2008. Simply right-click the page you wish to browse and select the View In Browser menu option. In either case, Figure 33-11 shows the output once you click the Fill Grid button.

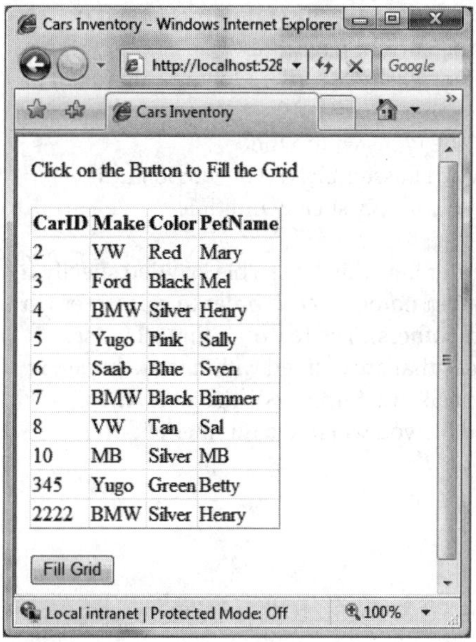

Figure 33-11. *Web-based data access*

That was simple, yes? Of course, as they say, the devil is in the details, so let's dig a bit deeper into the composition of this `*.aspx` file, beginning by examining the role of the *page directive*.

Understanding the Role of ASP.NET Directives

The first thing to be aware of is that a given `*.aspx` file will typically open with a set of *directives*. ASP.NET directives are always denoted with `<%@ XXX %>` markers and may be qualified with various attributes to inform the ASP.NET runtime how to process the attribute in question.

Every `*.aspx` file must have at minimum a `<%@Page%>` directive that is used to define the managed language used within the page (via the `Language` attribute). Also, the `<%@Page%>` directive may define the name of the related code-behind file (if any), enable tracing support, and so forth. Table 33-2 documents some of the more interesting `<%@Page%>`-centric attributes.

Table 33-2. *Select Attributes of the* `<%@Page%>` *Directive*

Attribute	Meaning in Life
`CodePage`	Specifies the name of the related code-behind file
`CompilerOptions`	Allows you to define any command-line flags (represented as a single string) passed into the compiler when this page is processed
`EnableTheming`	Establishes whether the controls on the `*.aspx` page support ASP.NET themes (see Chapter 34)
`EnableViewState`	Indicates whether view state is maintained across page requests (more details on this property in Chapter 35)
`Inherits`	Defines a class in the code-behind page the `*.aspx` file derives from, which can be any class derived from `System.Web.UI.Page`
`MasterPageFile`	Sets the master page used in conjunction with the current `*.aspx` page
`Trace`	Indicates whether tracing is enabled

In addition to the `<%@Page%>` directive, a given `*.aspx` file may specify various `<%@Import%>` directives to explicitly state the namespaces required by the current page and `<%@Assembly%>` directives to specify the external code libraries used by the site (typically placed under the \bin folder of the website).

In this example, we specified we were making use of the types within the `AutoLotConnectedLayer` namespace within the `AutoLotDAL.dll` assembly. As you would guess, if you need to make use of additional .NET namespaces, you simply specify multiple `<%@Import%>`/`<%@Assembly%>` directives.

Given your current knowledge of .NET, you may wonder how this `*.aspx` file avoided specifying additional `<%@Import%>` directives to gain access to the `System` namespace in order to gain access to the `System.Object` and `System.EventHandler` types (among others). The reason is that all `*.aspx` pages automatically have access to a set of key namespaces that are defined within the `web.config` file under your installation path of the .NET platform (typically C:\Windows\Microsoft.NET\Framework\v2.0.50727\CONFIG). Within this XML-based file you will find a number of autoimported namespaces:

```
<pages>
  <namespaces>
    <add namespace="System"/>
    <add namespace="System.Collections"/>
    <add namespace="System.Collections.Specialized"/>
    <add namespace="System.Configuration"/>
    <add namespace="System.Text"/>
```

```
    <add namespace="System.Text.RegularExpressions"/>
    <add namespace="System.Web"/>
    <add namespace="System.Web.Caching"/>
    <add namespace="System.Web.SessionState"/>
    <add namespace="System.Web.Security"/>
    <add namespace="System.Web.Profile"/>
    <add namespace="System.Web.UI"/>
    <add namespace="System.Web.UI.WebControls"/>
    <add namespace="System.Web.UI.WebControls.WebParts"/>
    <add namespace="System.Web.UI.HtmlControls"/>
...
  </namespaces>
</pages>
```

To be sure, ASP.NET does define a number of other directives that may appear in an `*.aspx` file above and beyond `<%@Page%>`, `<%@Import%>`, and `<%@Assembly%>`; however, I'll reserve commenting on those for the time being.

Analyzing the Script Block

Under the single-file page model, an `*.aspx` file may contain server-side scripting logic that executes on the web server. Given this, it is *critical* that all of your server-side code blocks are defined to execute at the server, using the `runat="server"` attribute. If the `runat="server"` attribute is not supplied, the runtime assumes you have authored a block of *client-side* script to be emitted into the outgoing HTTP response:

```
<script runat="server">
  Protected Sub btnFillData_Click(ByVal sender As Object, ByVal e As EventArgs)
    Dim dal As New InventoryDAL()
    dal.OpenConnection("Data Source=(local)\SQLEXPRESS;" & _
      "Initial Catalog=AutoLot;Integrated Security=True")
    carsGridView.DataSource = dal.GetAllInventory()
    carsGridView.DataBind()
    dal.CloseConnection()
  End Sub
</script>
```

The signature of this helper method should look strangely familiar. Recall from our examination of Windows Forms (or WPF for that matter) that a given control event handler must match the pattern defined by a related .NET delegate. And, just like Windows Forms, when you wish to handle a server-side button click, the delegate in question is `System.EventHandler`, which, as you recall, can only call methods that take `System.Object` as the first parameter and `System.EventArgs` as the second.

Looking at the ASP.NET Control Declarations

The final point of interest for this first example is the declaration of the `Button`, `Label`, and `GridView` Web Form controls. Like classic ASP and raw HTML, ASP.NET web widgets are scoped within `<form>` elements. This time, however, the opening `<form>` element is marked with the `runat="server"` attribute. This again is critical, as this tag informs the ASP.NET runtime that before the HTML is emitted into the response stream, the contained ASP.NET widgets have a chance to render their HTML appearance:

```
<form id="form1" runat="server">
<div>
  <asp:Label ID="lblInfo" runat="server"
```

```
    Text="Click on the Button to Fill the Grid">
  </asp:Label>
  <br />
  <br />
  <asp:GridView ID="carsGridView" runat="server">
  </asp:GridView>
  <br />
  <asp:Button ID="btnFillData" runat="server" Text="Fill Grid" />
</div>
</form>
```

Note that the ASP.NET web controls are declared with `<asp>` and `</asp>` tags, and they are also marked with the `runat="server"` attribute. Within the opening tag, you will specify the name of the Web Form control and any number of name/value pairs that will be used at runtime to render the correct HTML.

Source Code The SinglePageModel example is included under the Chapter 33 subdirectory.

Working with the Code-Behind Page Model

To illustrate the code-behind page model, let's re-create the previous example using the Visual Studio 2008 ASP.NET Web Site template. (Do know that Visual Studio 2008 is not required to build pages using code-behind; however, this is the out-of-the-box behavior for new websites.) Activate the File ➤ New ➤ Web Site menu option, and select the ASP.NET Web Site template, as shown in Figure 33-12.

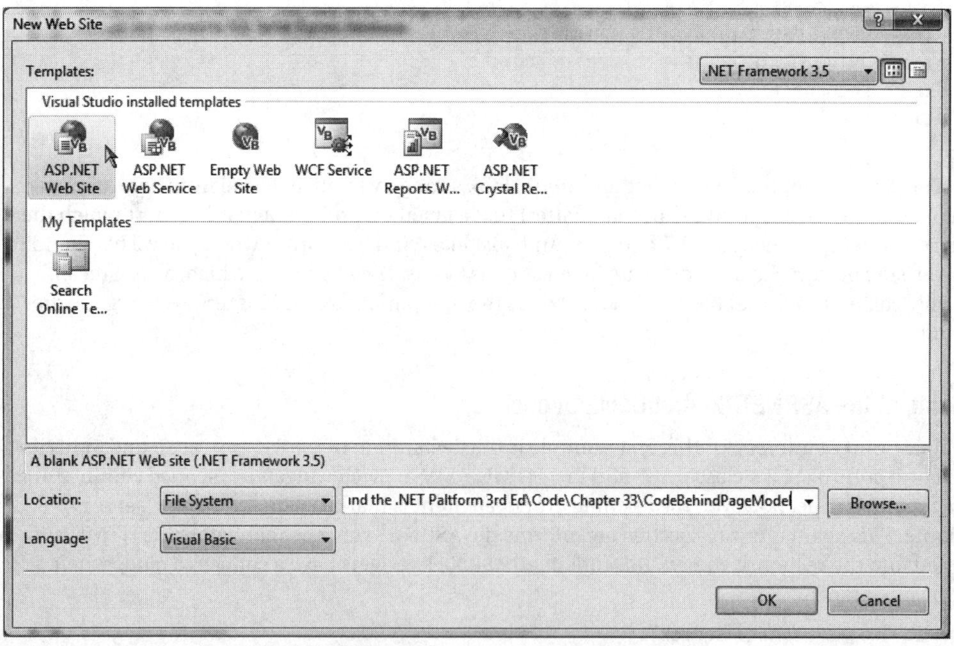

Figure 33-12. *The Visual Studio 2008 ASP.NET Web Site template*

Notice in Figure 33-12 that you are able to select the location of your new site. If you select File System, your content files will be placed within a local directory and pages will be served via WebDev.WebServer.exe. If you select FTP or HTTP, your site will be hosted within a new virtual directory maintained by IIS. For this example, it makes no difference which option you select, but for simplicity I suggest selecting the File System option and specifying a new folder on your C drive (e.g., C:\CodeBehindPageModel).

Once again, make use of the designer to build a UI consisting of a Label, Button, and GridView, and make use of the Properties window to build a UI of your liking.

■ **Note** When you wish to open an existing website into Visual Studio 2008, select the File ➤ Open ➤ Web Site menu option and select the folder (or IIS virtual directory) containing the web content.

Note that the <%@Page%> directive has been updated with a few new attributes:

```
<%@ Page Language="VB" AutoEventWireup="false"
    CodeFile="Default.aspx.vb" Inherits="_Default" %>
```

The CodeFile attribute is used to specify the related external file that contains this page's coding logic. By default, these code-behind files are named by adding the suffix .vb to the name of the *.aspx file (Default.aspx.vb in this example). If you examine Solution Explorer, you will see this code-behind file is visible via a subnode on the Web Form icon (see Figure 33-13).

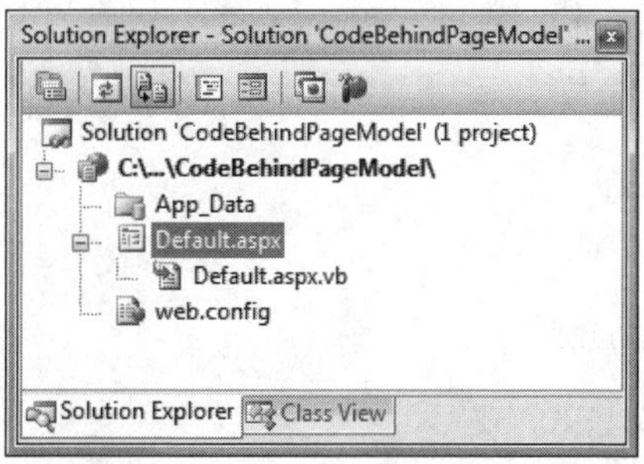

Figure 33-13. *The associated code-behind file for a given* *.aspx *file*

If you were to open your code-behind file, you would find a partial class. Notice that the name of this class (_Default) is identical to the Inherits attribute within the <%@Page%> directive:

```
Partial Class _Default
  Inherits System.Web.UI.Page
End Class
```

Referencing the AutoLotDAL.dll Assembly

As previously mentioned, when creating web application projects using Visual Studio 2008, you do not need to manually build a \bin subdirectory and copy private assemblies by hand. For this example, activate the Add Reference dialog box using the Website menu option and reference AutoLotDAL.dll. When you do so, you will see the new \bin folder within Solution Explorer, as shown in Figure 33-14.

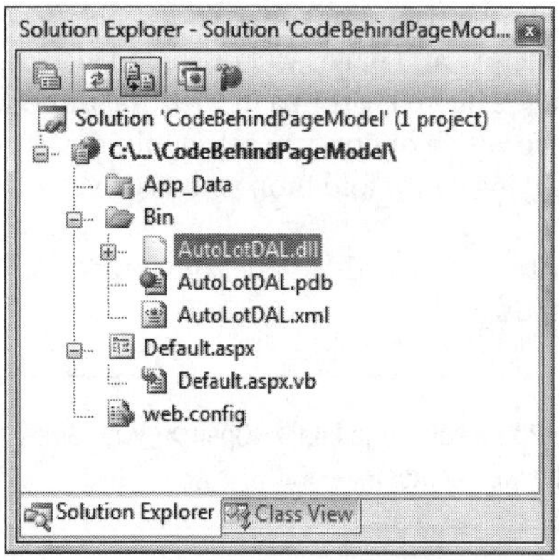

Figure 33-14. *Visual Studio typically maintains "special" ASP.NET folders*

Updating the Code File

Handle the `Click` event for the `Button` type by double-clicking the `Button` placed on the designer. This time, the server-side event handler is no longer placed within a `<script>` scope of the `*.aspx` file, but as a method of the `_Default` class type.

To complete this example, add an `Imports` statement for `AutoLotConnectedLayer` inside your code-behind file and implement the handler using the previous logic:

```
Imports AutoLotConnectedLayer

Partial Class _Default
  Inherits System.Web.UI.Page

  Protected Sub btnFillGrid_Click(ByVal sender As Object, _
   ByVal e As System.EventArgs) Handles btnFillGrid.Click
    Dim dal As New InventoryDAL()
    dal.OpenConnection("Data Source=(local)\SQLEXPRESS;" & _
      "Initial Catalog=AutoLot;Integrated Security=True")

    carsGridView.DataSource = dal.GetAllInventory()
    carsGridView.DataBind()
    dal.CloseConnection()
  End Sub
End Class
```

If you selected the File System option when you created the website project, `WebDev.WebServer.exe` starts up automatically when you run your web application (if you selected IIS, this obviously does not occur). In either case, the default browser should now display the page's content.

Debugging and Tracing ASP.NET Pages

By and large, when you are building ASP.NET web projects, you can use the same debugging techniques as you would with any other sort of Visual Studio 2008 project type. Thus, you can set breakpoints in your code-behind file (as well as embedded "script" blocks in an `*.aspx` file), start a debug session (via the F5 key, by default), and step through your code.

However, to debug your ASP.NET web applications, your site must contain a properly configured web.config file. The conclusion of this chapter will introduce you to web.config files, but in a nutshell these XML files have the same general purpose as an executable assembly's App.config file. By default, all Visual Studio 2008 web projects will automatically have a web.config file. However, debugging support is initially disabled (as this will degrade performance). When you start a debugging session, the IDE will prompt you for permissions to enable debugging. Once you have opted to do so, the opening <compilation> element of the web.config file is updated like so:

```
<compilation debug="true" strict="false" explicit="true">
```

On a related note, you are also able to enable *tracing support* for an *.aspx file by setting the Trace attribute to true within the <%@Page%> directive (it is also possible to enable tracing for your entire site by modifying the web.config file):

```
<%@ Page Language="VB" AutoEventWireup="false"
      CodeFile="Default.aspx.vb" Inherits="_Default" Trace="true" %>
```

Once you do, the emitted HTML contains numerous details regarding the previous HTTP request/response (server variables, session and application variables, request/response, etc.). To insert your own trace messages into the mix, you can use the Trace property of the System.Web.UI.Page type. Anytime you wish to log a custom message (from a script block or VB source code file), simply call the Write() method:

```
Protected Sub btnFillGrid_Click(ByVal sender As Object, _
  ByVal e As System.EventArgs) Handles btnFillGrid.Click
  Trace.Write("My Category", "Filling the grid!")
...
End Sub
```

If you run your project once again and post back to the web server, you will find your custom category and custom message are present and accounted for. In Figure 33-15, take note of the highlighted message that displays the trace information.

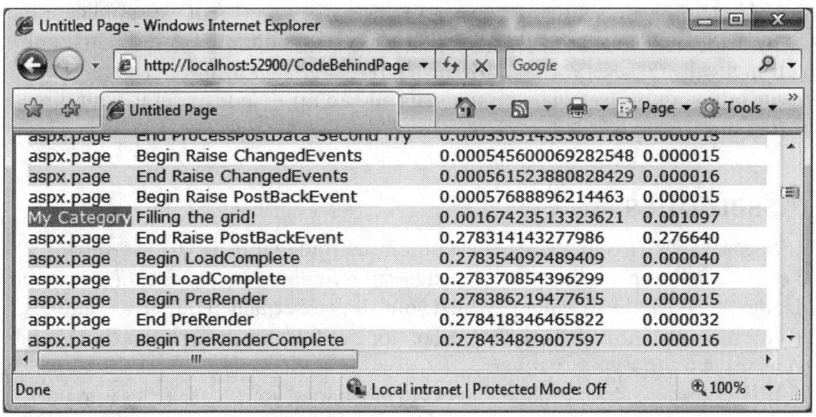

Figure 33-15. *Logging custom trace messages*

Source Code The CodeBehindPageModel example is included under the Chapter 33 subdirectory.

Details of an ASP.NET Website Directory Structure

By default, new Visual Studio 2008 web applications will be provided with an initial web page, a `web.config` file, and a particular folder named App_Data (which is empty by default). ASP.NET websites may contain any number of specifically named subdirectories, each of which has a special meaning to the ASP.NET runtime. Table 33-3 documents these "special subdirectories."

Table 33-3. *Special ASP.NET Subdirectories*

Subfolder	Meaning in Life
App_Browsers	Folder for browser definition files that are used to identify individual browsers and determine their capabilities.
App_Code	Folder for source code for components or classes that you want to compile as part of your application. ASP.NET compiles the code in this folder when pages are requested. Code in the App_Code folder is automatically accessible by your application.
App_Data	Folder for storing Access `*.mdb` files, SQL Express `*.mdf` files, XML files, or other data stores.
App_GlobalResources	Folder for `*.resx` files that are accessed programmatically from application code.
App_LocalResources	Folder for `*.resx` files that are bound to a specific page.
App_Themes	Folder that contains a collection of files that define the appearance of ASP.NET web pages and controls.
App_WebReferences	Folder for proxy classes, schemas, and other files associated with using a web service in your application.
Bin	Folder for compiled private assemblies (`*.dll` files). Assemblies in the Bin folder are automatically referenced by your application.

If you are interested in adding any of these known subfolders to your current web application, you may do so explicitly using the Website ➤ Add ASP.NET Folder menu option. However, in many cases, the IDE will automatically do so as you "naturally" insert related files into your site (e.g., inserting a new class file into your project will automatically add an App_Code folder to your directory structure if one does not currently exist).

Referencing Assemblies

As described in a few pages, ASP.NET web pages are eventually compiled into a .NET assembly. Given this, it should come as no surprise that your websites can reference any number of private or shared assemblies. Under ASP.NET, the manner in which your site's externally required assemblies are recorded is quite different from ASP.NET 1.x. The reason for this fundamental shift is that Visual Studio 2008 treats websites in a *projectless manner*.

Although the Web Site template does generate an `*.sln` file to load your `*.aspx` files into the IDE, there is no longer a related `*.vbproj` file. As you may know, ASP.NET 1.x Web Application projects recorded all external assemblies within `*.vbproj`. This fact brings up the obvious question, where are the external assemblies recorded under ASP.NET?

As you have seen, when you reference a private assembly, Visual Studio 2008 will automatically create a \bin directory within your directory structure to store a local copy of the binary. When your code base makes use of types within these code libraries, they are automatically loaded on demand.

If you reference a shared assembly, Visual Studio 2008 will update the `web.config` file in your current web solution by recording the external reference within the `<assemblies>` element. For example, if you again activate the Website ➤ Add Reference menu option and this time select a shared assembly (such as System.Data.OracleClient.dll), you will find that your web.config file has been updated as follows:

```
<assemblies>
...
  <add assembly="System.Data.OracleClient, Version=2.0.0.0,
     Culture=neutral, PublicKeyToken=B77A5C561934E089"/>
</assemblies>
```

As you can see, each assembly is described using the same information required for a dynamic load via the Assembly.Load() method (see Chapter 16).

The Role of the App_Code Folder

The App_Code folder is used to store source code files that are not directly tied to a specific web page (such as a code-behind file) but are to be compiled for use by your website. Code within the App_Code folder will be automatically compiled on the fly on an as-needed basis. After this point, the assembly is accessible to any other code in the website. To this end, the App_Code folder is much like the \bin folder, except that you can store source code in it instead of compiled code. The major benefit of this approach is that it is possible to define custom types for your web application without having to compile them independently.

A single App_Code folder can contain code files from multiple languages. At runtime, the appropriate compiler kicks in to generate the assembly in question. If you would rather partition your code, however, you can define multiple subdirectories that are used to hold any number of managed code files (*.vb, *.cs, etc.).

For example, assume you have added an App_Code folder to the root directory of a website application that has two subfolders (MyCSharpCode and MyVbCode) that contain language-specific files. Once you do, you are able to update your web.config file to specify these subdirectories using a <codeSubDirectories> element nested within the <compilation> element:

```
<compilation debug="true" strict="false" explicit="true">
  <codeSubDirectories>
    <add directoryName="MyCSharpCode" />
    <add directoryName="MyVbCode" />
  </codeSubDirectories>
</compilation>
```

■ **Note** The App_Code directory will also be used to contain files that are not language files, but are useful nonetheless (*.xsd files, *.wsdl files, etc.).

Beyond \bin and App_Code, the App_Data and App_Themes folders are two additional "special subdirectories" that you should be familiar with, both of which will be detailed in the next couple of chapters. As always, consult the .NET Framework 3.5 SDK documentation for full details of the remaining ASP.NET subdirectories if you require further information.

The ASP.NET Page Compilation Cycle

Regardless of which page model you make use of (single-file page or code-behind), your *.aspx files (and any related code-behind file) are compiled on the fly into a valid .NET assembly. This assembly is then hosted by the ASP.NET worker process within its own application domain boundary (see

Chapter 17 for details on AppDomains). The manner in which your website's assembly is compiled under ASP.NET, however, is quite different.

Compilation Cycle for Single-File Pages

If you are making use of the single-file page model, the HTML markup, `<script>` blocks, and web control definitions are dynamically compiled into a class type deriving from `System.Web.UI.Page`. The name of this class is based on the name of the `*.aspx` file and takes an `_aspx` suffix (e.g., a page named `MyPage.aspx` becomes a class type named `MyPage_aspx`). Figure 33-16 illustrates the basic process.

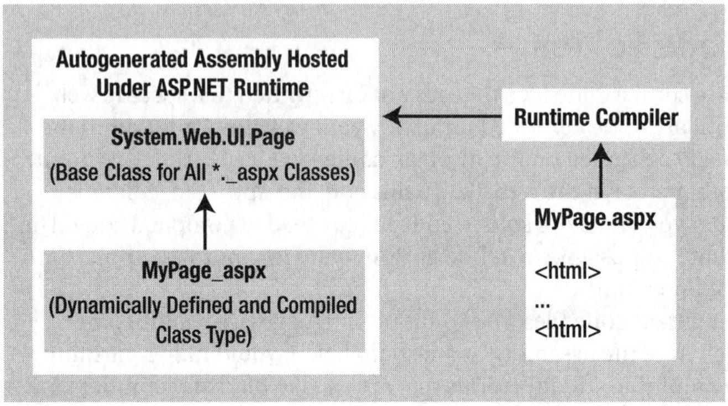

Figure 33-16. *The compilation model for single-file pages*

This dynamically compiled assembly is deployed to a runtime-defined subdirectory under the C:\WINDOWS\Microsoft.NET\Framework\v2.0.50727\Temporary ASP.NET Files root directory. The path beneath this root will differ based on a number of factors (hash codes, etc.), but if you are determined, eventually you will find the `*.dll` (and supporting files) in question. Figure 33-17 shows the generated assembly for the SinglePageModel example shown earlier in this chapter.

■ **Note** Because these autogenerated assemblies are true-blue .NET binaries, if you were to open your web applications–related `*.dll` using `ildasm.exe` or `reflector.exe` you would indeed find CIL code, metadata, and an assembly-level manifest.

Compilation Cycle for Multifile Pages

The compilation process of a page making use of the code-behind model is similar to that of the single-file page model. However, the type deriving from `System.Web.UI.Page` is composed of three (yes, *three*) files rather than the expected two.

Looking back at the previous CodeBehindPageModel example, recall that the `Default.aspx` file was connected to a partial class named `_Default` within the code-behind file. If you have a background in ASP.NET 1.x, you may wonder what happened to the member variable declarations for the various web controls as well as the code within `InitializeComponent()`, such as event handling logic. Under ASP.NET, these details are accounted for by a third "file" generated in memory. In reality, this is not a literal file, but an in-memory representation of the partial class. Consider Figure 33-18.

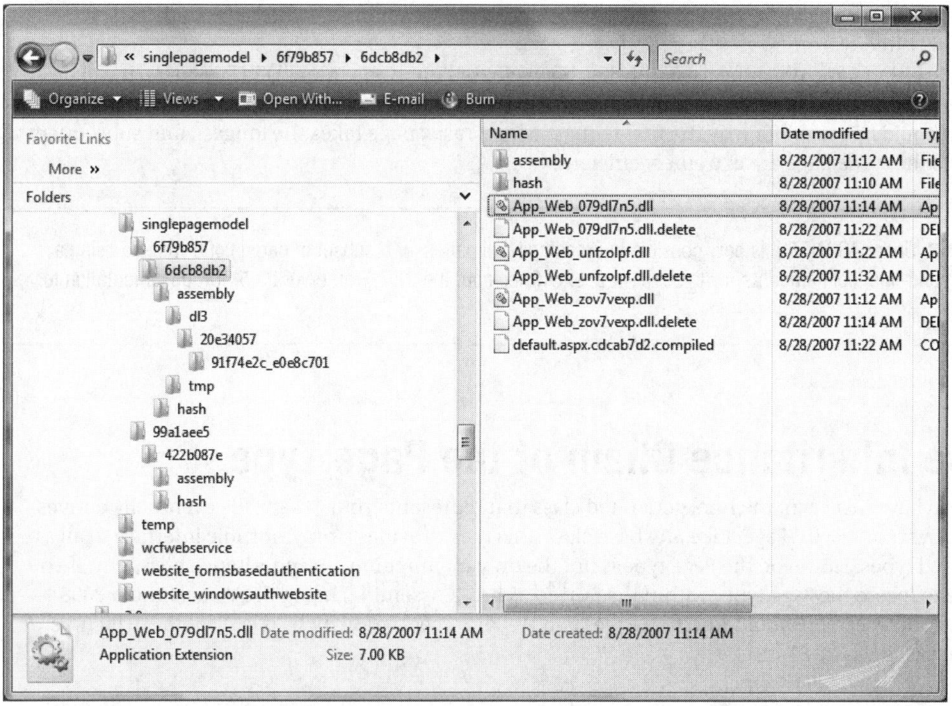

Figure 33-17. *The ASP.NET autogenerated assembly*

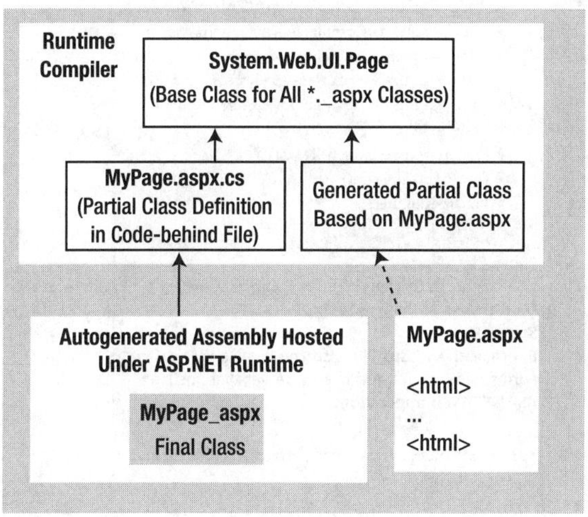

Figure 33-18. *The compilation model for multifile pages*

In this model, the web controls declared in the `*.aspx` file are used to build the additional partial class that defines each UI member variable and the configuration logic that used to be found within the `InitializeComponent()` method of ASP.NET 1.x (we just never directly see it). This partial class is combined at compile time with the code-behind file to result in the *base class* of the generated `_aspx` class type (in the single-file page compilation model, the generated `_aspx` file derived directly from `System.Web.UI.Page`).

In either case, once the assembly has been created upon the initial HTTP request, it will be reused for all subsequent requests, and thus will not have to be recompiled. Understanding this factoid should help explain why the first request of an `*.aspx` page takes the longest, and subsequent hits to the same page are extremely efficient.

■ **Note** Under ASP.NET, it is now possible to precompile all pages (or a subset of pages) of a website using a command-line tool named `aspnet_compiler.exe`. Check out the .NET Framework 3.5 SDK documentation for details.

The Inheritance Chain of the Page Type

As you have just seen, the final generated class that represents your `*.aspx` file eventually derives from `System.Web.UI.Page`. Like any base class, this type provides a polymorphic interface to all derived types. However, the `Page` type is not the only member in your inheritance hierarchy. If you were to locate the `Page` type (within the `System.Web.dll` assembly) using the Visual Studio 2008 object browser, you would find that `Page` "is-a" `TemplateControl`, which "is-a" `Control`, which "is-a" `Object` (see Figure 33-19).

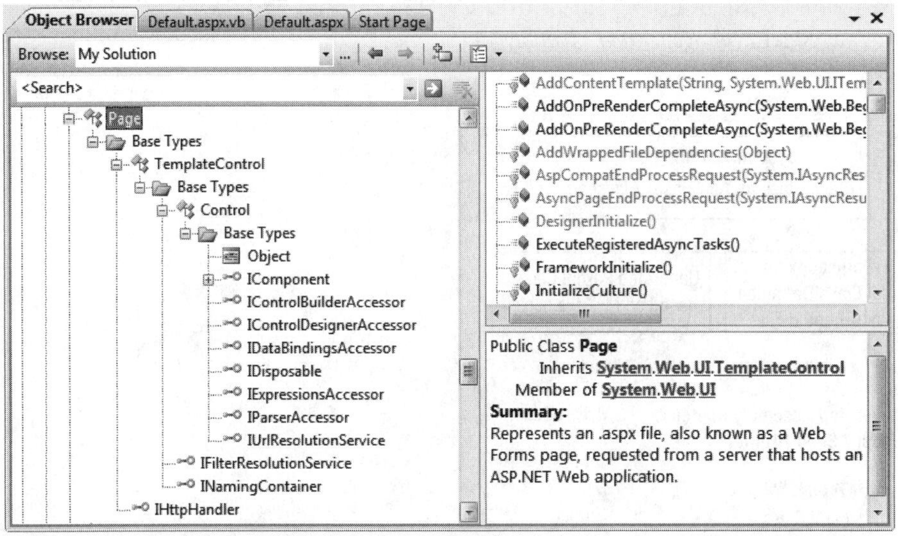

Figure 33-19. *The derivation of an ASP.NET page*

As you would guess, each of these base classes brings a good deal of functionality to each and every `*.aspx` file. For the majority of your projects, you will make use of the members defined within the `Page` and `Control` parent classes. By and large, the functionality gained from the `System.Web.UI.TemplateControl` class is only of interest if you are building custom Web Form controls or interacting with the rendering process. This being said, let's get to know the overall role of the `Page` type.

The first parent class of interest is Page itself. Here you will find numerous properties that enable you to interact with various web primitives such as application and session variables, the HTTP request/response, theme support, and so forth. Table 33-4 describes some (but by no means all) of the core properties.

Table 33-4. *Properties of the* Page *Type*

Property	Meaning in Life
Application	Allows you to interact with application variables (see Chapter 35) for the current website
Cache	Allows you to interact with the cache object for the current website
ClientTarget	Allows you to specify how this page should render itself based on the requesting browser
IsPostBack	Gets a value indicating whether the page is being loaded in response to a client postback or whether it is being loaded and accessed for the first time
MasterPageFile	Establishes the master page for the current page
Request	Provides access to the current HTTP request
Response	Allows you to interact with the outgoing HTTP response
Server	Provides access to the HttpServerUtility object, which contains various server-side helper functions
Session	Allows you to interact with the session data (see Chapter 35) for the current caller
Theme	Gets or sets the name of the theme used for the current page
Trace	Provides access to a TraceContext object, which allows you to log custom messages during debugging sessions

Interacting with the Incoming HTTP Request

As you saw earlier in this chapter, the basic flow of a web session begins with a client logging on to a site, filling in user information, and clicking a Submit button to post back the HTML form data to a given web page for processing. In most cases, the opening tag of the form statement specifies an action attribute and a method attribute that indicates the file on the web server that will be sent the data in the various HTML widgets, as well as the method of sending this data (GET or POST):

```
<form name="defaultPage" id="defaultPage"
 action="http://localhost/Cars/ClassicAspPage.asp" method="get">
...
</form>
```

Unlike classic ASP, ASP.NET does not support an object named Request. However, all ASP.NET pages do inherit the System.Web.UI.Page.Request *property*, which provides access to an instance of the HttpRequest class type. Table 33-5 lists some core members that, not surprisingly, mimic the same members found within the legacy classic ASP Request object.

Table 33-5. *Members of the* `HttpRequest` *Type*

Member	Meaning in Life
`ApplicationPath`	Gets the ASP.NET application's virtual application root path on the server
`Browser`	Provides information about the capabilities of the client browser
`Cookies`	Gets a collection of cookies sent by the client browser
`FilePath`	Indicates the virtual path of the current request
`Form`	Gets a collection of HTTP form variables
`Headers`	Gets a collection of HTTP headers
`HttpMethod`	Indicates the HTTP data transfer method used by the client (GET, POST)
`IsSecureConnection`	Indicates whether the HTTP connection is secure (i.e., HTTPS)
`QueryString`	Gets the collection of HTTP query string variables
`RawUrl`	Gets the current request's raw URL
`RequestType`	Indicates the HTTP data transfer method used by the client (GET, POST)
`ServerVariables`	Gets a collection of web server variables
`UserHostAddress`	Gets the IP host address of the remote client
`UserHostName`	Gets the DNS name of the remote client

In addition to these properties, the `HttpRequest` type has a number of useful methods, including the following:

- `MapPath()`: Maps the virtual path in the requested URL to a physical path on the server for the current request. This is useful if you need to write some code in your web page that requires you to access a file on the web server's file system.
- `SaveAs()`: Saves details of the current HTTP request to a file on the web server (which can prove helpful for debugging purposes).
- `ValidateInput()`: If the validation feature is enabled via the `Validate` attribute of the page directive, this method can be called to check all user input data (including cookie data) against a predefined list of potentially dangerous input data.

Obtaining Brower Statistics

The first interesting aspect of the `HttpRequest` type is the `Browser` property, which provides access to an underlying `HttpBrowserCapabilities` object. `HttpBrowserCapabilities` in turn exposes numerous members that allow you to programmatically investigate statistics regarding the browser that sent the incoming HTTP request.

Create a new ASP.NET website named `FunWithPageMembers` (again, elect to use the File System option). Your first task is to build a UI that allows users to click a `Button` web control (named `btnGetBrowserStats`) to view various statistics about the calling browser. These statistics will be generated dynamically and attached to a `Label` type (named `lblOutput`). The `Click` event handler is as follows:

```
Protected Sub btnGetBrowserStats_Click(ByVal sender As Object, _
  ByVal e As System.EventArgs) Handles btnGetBrowserStats.Click
  Dim theInfo As String = ""

  theInfo &= String.Format("<li>Is the client AOL? {0}</li>", _
  Request.Browser.AOL)
```

```
  theInfo &= _
  String.Format("<li>Does the client support ActiveX? {0}</li>", _
  Request.Browser.ActiveXControls)

  theInfo &= String.Format("<li>Is the client a Beta? {0}</li>", _
  Request.Browser.Beta)

  theInfo &= _
  String.Format("<li>Does the client support Java Applets? {0}</li>", _
  Request.Browser.JavaApplets)

  theInfo &= _
  String.Format("<li>Does the client support Cookies? {0}</li>", _
  Request.Browser.Cookies)

  theInfo &= _
  String.Format("<li>Does the client support VBScript? {0}</li>", _
  Request.Browser.VBScript)

  lblOutput.Text = theInfo
End Sub
```

Here you are testing for a number of browser capabilities. As you would guess, it is (very) helpful to discover a browser's support for ActiveX controls, Java applets, and client-side VBScript code. If the calling browser does not support a given web technology, your *.aspx page would be able to take an alternative course of action.

Access to Incoming Form Data

Other aspects of the HttpResponse type are the Form and QueryString properties. These two properties allow you to examine the incoming form data using name/value pairs, and they function identically to classic ASP. Recall from our earlier discussion of classic ASP that if the data is submitted using HTTP GET, the form data is accessed using the QueryString property, whereas data submitted via HTTP POST is obtained using the Form property.

While you could most certainly make use of the HttpRequest.Form and HttpRequest.QueryString properties to access client-supplied form data on the web server, these old-school techniques are (for the most part) unnecessary. Given that ASP.NET supplies you with server-side web controls, you are able to treat HTML UI elements as true objects. Therefore, rather than obtaining the value within a text box as follows:

```
Protected Sub btnGetFormData_Click(ByVal sender As Object, _
  ByVal e As System.EventArgs) Handles btnGetFormData.Click
  ' Get value for a widget with ID txtFirstName.
  Dim firstName As String = Request.Form("txtFirstName")

  ' Use this value in your page...
End Sub
```

you can simply ask the server-side widget directly via the Text property for use in your program:

```
Protected Sub btnGetFormData_Click(ByVal sender As Object, _
  ByVal e As System.EventArgs) Handles btnGetFormData.Click
  ' Get value for a widget with ID txtFirstName.
  Dim firstName As String = txtFirstName.Text

  ' Use this value in your page...
End Sub
```

Not only does this approach lend itself to solid OO principles, but also you do not need to concern yourself with how the form data was submitted (GET or POST) before obtaining the values. Furthermore, working with the widget directly is much more type-safe, given that typing errors are discovered at compile time rather than runtime. Of course, this is not to say that you will *never* need to make use of the `Form` or `QueryString` property in ASP.NET; rather, the need to do so has greatly diminished and is usually optional.

The IsPostBack Property

Another very important member of `Page` is the `IsPostBack` property. Recall that "postback" refers to the act of returning to a particular web page while still in session with the server. Given this definition, understand that the `IsPostBack` property will return `True` if the current HTTP request has been sent by a currently logged-on user and `False` if this is the user's first interaction with the page.

Typically, the need to determine whether the current HTTP request is indeed a postback is most helpful when you wish to execute a block of code only the first time the user accesses a given page. For example, you may wish to populate an ADO.NET `DataSet` when the user first accesses an `*.aspx` file and cache the object for later use. When the caller returns to the page, you can avoid the need to hit the database unnecessarily (of course, some pages may require that the `DataSet` always be updated upon each request, but that is another issue). Assuming your `*.aspx` file has handled the page's `Load` event (described in detail later in this chapter), you could programmatically test for postback conditions as follows:

```
Protected Sub Page_Load(ByVal sender As Object, _
  ByVal e As System.EventArgs) Handles Me.Load
  ' Only fill DataSet the very first time
  ' the user comes to this page.
  If Not IsPostBack Then
    ' Populate DataSet and cache it!
  End If
  ' Use cached DataSet.
End Sub
```

Interacting with the Outgoing HTTP Response

Now that you have a better understanding of how the `Page` type allows you to interact with the incoming HTTP request, the next step is to see how to interact with the outgoing HTTP response. In ASP.NET, the `Response` property of the `Page` class provides access to an instance of the `HttpResponse` type. This type defines a number of properties that allow you to format the HTTP response sent back to the client browser. Table 33-6 lists some core properties.

Table 33-6. *Properties of the* `HttpResponse` *Type*

Property	Meaning in Life
`Cache`	Returns the caching semantics of the web page (e.g., expiration time, privacy, vary clauses)
`ContentEncoding`	Gets or sets the HTTP character set of the output stream
`ContentType`	Gets or sets the HTTP MIME type of the output stream
`Cookies`	Gets the `HttpCookie` collection sent by the current request
`IsClientConnected`	Gets a value indicating whether the client is still connected to the server
`Output`	Enables custom output to the outgoing HTTP content body

Property	Meaning in Life
OutputStream	Enables binary output to the outgoing HTTP content body
StatusCode	Gets or sets the HTTP status code of output returned to the client
StatusDescription	Gets or sets the HTTP status string of output returned to the client
SuppressContent	Gets or sets a value indicating that HTTP content will not be sent to the client

Also, consider the partial list of methods supported by the HttpResponse type described in Table 33-7.

Table 33-7. *Methods of the* HttpResponse *Type*

Method	Meaning in Life
AddCacheDependency()	Adds an object to the application cache (see Chapter 35)
Clear()	Clears all headers and content output from the buffer stream
End()	Sends all currently buffered output to the client, and then closes the socket connection
Flush()	Sends all currently buffered output to the client
Redirect()	Redirects a client to a new URL
Write()	Writes values to an HTTP output content stream
WriteFile()	Writes a file directly to an HTTP content output stream

Emitting HTML Content

Perhaps the most well-known aspect of the HttpResponse type is the ability to write content directly to the HTTP output stream. The HttpResponse.Write() method allows you to pass in any HTML tags and/or text literals. The HttpResponse.WriteFile() method takes this functionality one step further, in that you can specify the name of a physical file on the web server whose contents should be rendered to the output stream (this is quite helpful to quickly emit the contents of an existing *.htm file).

To illustrate, assume you have added another Button type to your current *.aspx file that implements the server-side Click event handler like so:

```
Protected Sub btnHttpResponse_Click(ByVal sender As Object, _
  ByVal e As System.EventArgs) Handles btnHttpResponse.Click

  Response.Write("<b>My name is:</b><br>")
  Response.Write(Me.ToString())
  Response.Write("<br><br><b>Here was your last request:</b><br>")

  ' This assumes that you have a file of this name
  ' in your virtual directory!
  Response.WriteFile("MyHTMLPage.htm")
End Sub
```

The role of this event handler is quite simple. The only point of interest is the fact that the HttpResponse.WriteFile() method is now emitting the contents of a server-side *.htm file within the root directory of the website.

Again, while you can always take this old-school approach and render HTML tags and content using the Write() method, this approach is far less common under ASP.NET than with classic ASP. The reason is (once again) due to the advent of server-side web controls. Thus, if you wish to render a block of textual data to the browser, your task is as simple as assigning a string to the Text property of a Label widget.

Redirecting Users

Another aspect of the HttpResponse type is the ability to redirect the user to a new URL:

```
Protected Sub btnSomeTraining_Click(ByVal sender As Object, _
  ByVal e As System.EventArgs) Handles btnSomeTraining.Click
  Response.Redirect("http://www.IntertechTraining.com")
End Sub
```

If this event handler is invoked via a client-side postback, the user will automatically be redirected to the specified URL.

■ **Note** The HttpResponse.Redirect() method will always entail a trip back to the client browser. If you simply wish to transfer control to an *.aspx file in the same virtual directory, Server.Transfer() is more efficient.

So much for investigating the functionality of System.Web.UI.Page. We will examine the role of the System.Web.UI.Control base class in the next chapter. Next up, let's examine the life and times of a Page-derived object.

■ **Source Code** The FunWithPageMembers files are included under the Chapter 33 subdirectory.

The Life Cycle of an ASP.NET Web Page

Every ASP.NET web page has a fixed life cycle. When the ASP.NET runtime receives an incoming request for a given *.aspx file, the associated System.Web.UI.Page-derived type is allocated into memory using the type's default constructor. After this point, the framework will automatically fire a series of events. By default, the Load event is automatically accounted for, where you can add your custom code:

```
Partial Class _Default
  Inherits System.Web.UI.Page

  Protected Sub Page_Load(ByVal sender As Object, _
  ByVal e As System.EventArgs) Handles Me.Load
    ' Perform load logic here...
  End Sub
End Class
```

Beyond the Load event, a given Page is able to intercept any of the core events in Table 33-8, which are listed in the order in which they are encountered (consult the .NET Framework 3.5 SDK documentation for details on all possible events that may fire during a page's lifetime).

Table 33-8. *Select Events of the* `Page` *Type*

Event	Meaning in Life
`PreInit`	The framework uses this event to allocate any web controls, apply themes, establish the master page, and set user profiles. You may intercept this event to customize the process.
`Init`	The framework uses this event to set the properties of web controls to their previous values via postback or view state data.
`Load`	When this event fires, the page and its controls are fully initialized, and their previous values are restored. At this point, it is safe to interact with each web widget.
"Event that triggered the postback"	There is, of course, no event of this name. This "event" simply refers to whichever event caused the browser to perform the postback to the web server (such as a `Button` click).
`PreRender`	All control data binding and UI configuration has occurred and the controls are ready to render their data into the outbound HTTP response.
`Unload`	The page and its controls have finished the rendering process, and the page object is about to be destroyed. At this point, it is a runtime error to interact with the outgoing HTTP response. You may, however, capture this event to perform any page-level cleanup (close file or database connections, perform any form of logging activity, dispose of objects, etc.).

When you need to handle page-level events, you can do so using the drop-down list boxes of a page's code file. In the left list box, select (Page Events). In the right list box, select the event you wish to handle (see Figure 33-20).

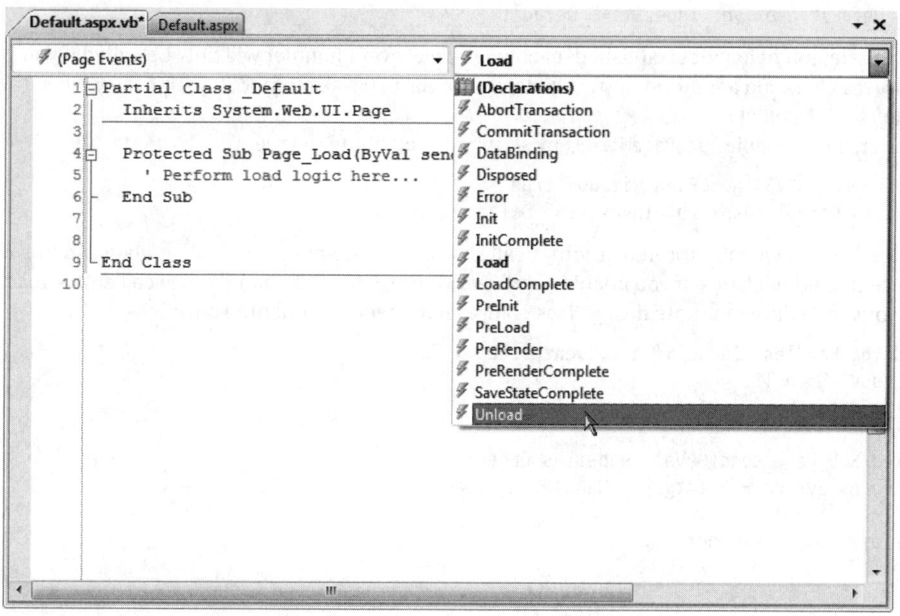

Figure 33-20. *Handling page-level events*

For example, if you were to select the Unload event, the IDE would author the following stub code:

```
Protected Sub Page_Unload(ByVal sender As Object, _
  ByVal e As System.EventArgs) Handles Me.Unload

End Sub
```

By default, each of the page-level event handlers follows a specific naming convention and always takes the same incoming arguments:

```
Protected Sub Page_NameOfEvent(ByVal sender As Object, _
  ByVal e As System.EventArgs) Handles Me.NameOfEvent
```

Notice that the event name specified by the Handles clause will be identical to the name of the event specified after the Page_ prefix.

■ **Note** Each event of the Page type works in conjunction with the System.EventHandler delegate; therefore, the subroutines that handle these events always take an Object as the first parameter and an EventArgs as the second parameter.

The Role of the AutoEventWireup Attribute

When you wish to handle events for your page, you will need to update your <script> block or code-behind file with an appropriate event handler. On a related note, if you examine the <%@Page%> directive, you will notice a specific attribute named AutoEventWireUp, which by default is set to false:

```
<%@ Page Language="VB" AutoEventWireup="false"
CodeFile="Default.aspx.vb" Inherits="_Default" %>
```

With this default behavior established, each page-level event handler will only be called if you use the Handles clause on a method in your code file (or via an OnXXX method in your *.aspx file's server-side <script> block).

However, if you enable AutoPageWireUp by setting this attribute to true

```
<%@ Page Language="VB" AutoEventWireup="true"
    CodeFile="Default.aspx.vb" Inherits="_Default" %>
```

the page-level events will be captured automatically, even if you do *not* use a Handles clause in the code file event handlers. Thus, if you enable AutoEventWireup, you could handle the Load and Unload events in your code file as so (note the Handles clauses have been commented out):

```
' No need for Handles clause if AutoEventWireup = True!
Partial Class _Default
  Inherits System.Web.UI.Page

  Protected Sub Page_Load(ByVal sender As Object, _
    ByVal e As System.EventArgs) ' Handles Me.Load

    ' Perform load logic here...
  End Sub

  Protected Sub Page_Unload(ByVal sender As Object, _
  ByVal e As System.EventArgs) ' Handles Me.Unload
```

```
        ' Perform unload logic here...
    End Sub
End Class
```

As its name suggests, this attribute (when enabled) will generate the necessary event riggings within the autogenerated partial class described earlier in this chapter (via an AddHandler statement). By and large you will simply leave AutoEventWireup disabled and allow the IDE to generate the event infrastructure for your page-level events.

The Error Event

Another event that may occur during your page's life cycle is Error. This event will be fired if a method on the Page-derived type triggered an exception that was not explicitly handled. Assume that you have handled the Click event for a given Button on your page, and within the event handler (which I named btnGetFile_Click), you attempt to write out the contents of a local file to the HTTP response.

Also assume you have *failed* to test for the presence of this file via standard structured exception handling. If you have rigged up the page's Error event, you have one final chance to deal with the problem on this page before the end user finds an ugly error. Consider the following code:

```
Partial Class _Default
  Inherits System.Web.UI.Page

  Protected Sub Page_Load(ByVal sender As Object, _
  ByVal e As System.EventArgs) Handles Me.Load
    Response.Write("Load event fired!")
  End Sub

  Protected Sub Page_Unload(ByVal sender As Object, _
  ByVal e As System.EventArgs) Handles Me.Unload
    ' No longer possible to emit data to the HTTP
    ' response at this point, so we will write to a local file.
    System.IO.File.WriteAllText("C:\MyLog.txt", "Page unloading!")
  End Sub

  Protected Sub Page_Error(ByVal sender As Object, _
  ByVal e As System.EventArgs) Handles Me.Error
    Response.Clear()
    Response.Write("I am sorry...I can't find a required file.<br>")
    Response.Write(String.Format("The error was: <b>{0}</b>", _
        Server.GetLastError().Message))
    Server.ClearError()
  End Sub

  Protected Sub btnPostback_Click(ByVal sender As Object, _
  ByVal e As System.EventArgs) Handles btnPostback.Click
    ' This is just here to allow a postback.
  End Sub

  Protected Sub btnTriggerError_Click(ByVal sender As Object, _
  ByVal e As System.EventArgs) Handles btnTriggerError.Click
    ' Try to open a nonexistent file on the web server.
    ' This will fire the Error event for this page.
    System.IO.File.ReadAllText("C:\IDontExist.txt")
  End Sub
End Class
```

Notice that your `Error` event handler begins by clearing out any content currently within the HTTP response and emits a generic error message. If you wish to gain access to the specific `System.Exception` object, you may do so using the `Server.GetLastError()` method exposed by the inherited `Server` property.

Finally, note that before exiting this generic error handler, you are explicitly calling the `HttpServerUtility.ClearError()` method via the `Server` property. This is required, as it informs the runtime that you have dealt with the issue at hand and require no further processing. If you forget to do so, the end user will be presented with the runtime's error page. Figure 33-21 shows the result of this error-trapping logic.

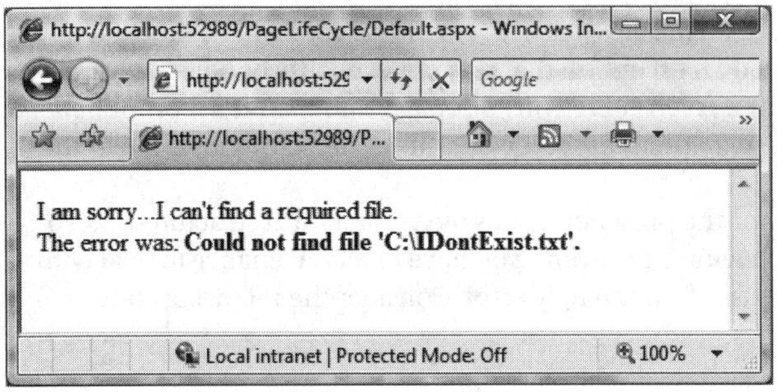

Figure 33-21. *Page-level error handling*

At this point, you should feel confident with the composition of an ASP.NET `Page` type. Now that you have such a foundation, you can turn your attention to the role of ASP.NET web controls, themes, and master pages, all of which are the subject of the next chapter. To wrap up this chapter, however, let's examine the role of the `web.config` file.

Source Code The PageLifeCycle files are included under the Chapter 33 subdirectory.

The Role of the web.config File

By default, all VB ASP.NET web applications created with Visual Studio 2008 are automatically provided with a `web.config` file. However, if you ever need to manually insert a `web.config` file into your site (e.g., when you are working with the single-file page model and have not created a web solution), you may do so using the using the Website ➤ Add New Item menu option. In either case, within this scope of a `web.config` file you are able to add settings that control how your web application will function at runtime.

Note It is not mandatory for your web applications to include a `web.config` file. If you do not have such a file, your website will be granted the default web-centric settings recorded in the `web.config` file for your .NET installation folder.

Recall during your examination of .NET assemblies (in Chapter 15) that you learned client applications can leverage an XML-based configuration file to instruct the CLR how it should handle binding requests, assembly probing, and other runtime details. The same holds true for ASP.NET web applications, with the notable exception that web-centric configuration files are always named `web.config` (unlike `*.exe` configuration files, which are named based on the related client executable).

The default structure of a `web.config` file is rather verbose with the release of .NET 3.5, but the essentials settings break down as follows. Table 33-9 outlines some of the more interesting subelements that can be found within a `web.config` file.

Table 33-9. *Select Elements of a* `web.config` *File*

Element	Meaning in Life
`<appSettings>`	This element is used to establish custom name/value pairs that can be programmatically read in memory for use by your pages using the `ConfigurationManager` type.
`<authentication>`	This security-related element is used to define the authentication mode for this web application.
`<authorization>`	This is another security-centric element used to define which users can access which resources on the web server.
`<connectionStrings>`	This element is used to hold external connection strings used within this website.
`<customErrors>`	This element is used to tell the runtime exactly how to display errors that occur during the functioning of the web application.
`<globalization>`	This element is used to configure the globalization settings for this web application.
`<namespaces>`	This element documents all of the namespaces to include if your web application has been precompiled using the new `aspnet_compiler.exe` command-line tool.
`<sessionState>`	This element is used to control how and where session state data will be stored by the .NET runtime.
`<trace>`	This element is used to enable (or disable) tracing support for this web application.

A `web.config` file may contain additional subelements above and beyond the set presented in Table 33-9. The vast majority of these items are security related, while the remaining items are useful only during advanced ASP.NET scenarios such as creating custom HTTP headers or custom HTTP modules (topics that are not covered here).

If you wish to see the complete set of elements (and the related attributes) that can appear in a `web.config` file, you may do so using the .NET Framework 3.5 SDK documentation. Simply search for the topic "ASP.NET Configuration Settings" as shown in Figure 33-22, and dive in.

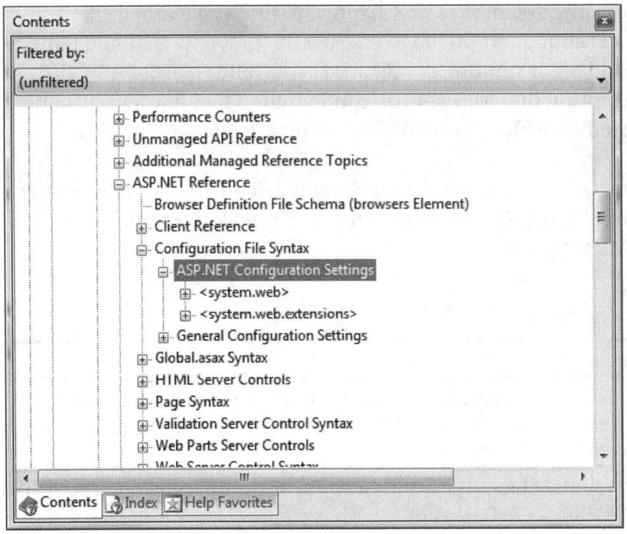

Figure 33-22. *Documentation details of a* `web.config` *file*

You will come to know various aspects of the `web.config` file over the remainder of this text.

The ASP.NET Web Site Administration Tool

Although you are always free to modify the content of a `web.config` file directly using Visual Studio 2008, ASP.NET web projects can make use of handy web-based editor that will allow you to graphically edit numerous elements and attributes of your project's `web.config` file. To launch this tool, shown in Figure 33-23, simply activate the Website ➤ ASP.NET Configuration menu option.

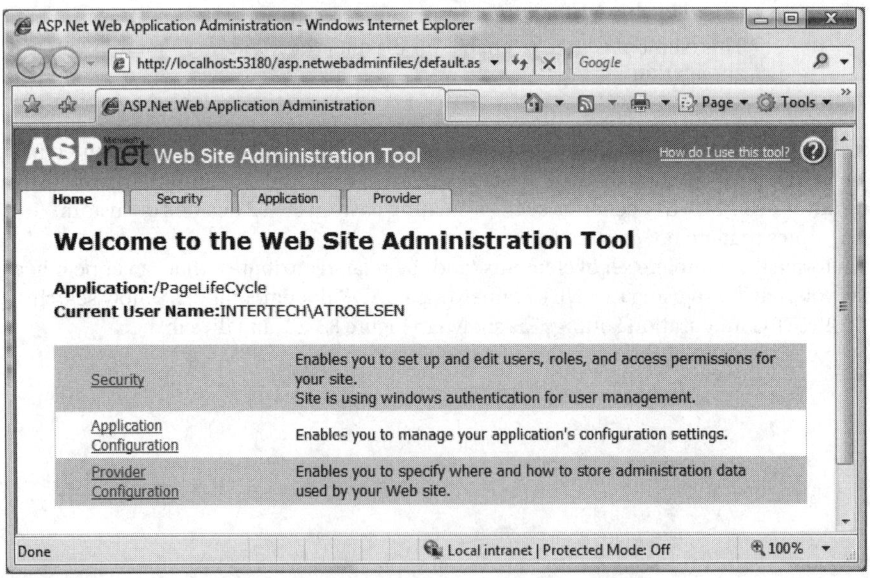

Figure 33-23. *The ASP.NET Web Site Administration Tool*

If you were to click the tabs located at the top of the page, you would quickly notice that most of this tool's functionality is used to establish security settings for your website. However, this tool also makes it possible to add settings to your `<appSettings>` element, define debugging and tracing settings, and establish a default error page.

You'll see more of this tool in action where necessary; however, do be aware that this utility will *not* allow you to add all possible settings to a `web.config` file. There will most certainly be times when you will need to manually update this file using your text editor of choice.

Summary

Building web applications requires a different frame of mind than is used to assemble traditional desktop applications. In this chapter, you began with a quick and painless review of some core web topics, including HTML, HTTP, the role of client-side scripting, and server-side scripts using classic ASP. The bulk of this chapter was spent examining the architecture of an ASP.NET page. As you have seen, each `*.aspx` file in your project has an associated `System.Web.UI.Page`-derived class. Using this OO approach, ASP.NET allows you to build more reusable and OO-aware systems.

After examining some of the core functionality of a page's inheritance chain, this chapter then discussed how your pages are ultimately compiled into a valid .NET assembly. We wrapped up by exploring the role of the `web.config` file and overviewed the ASP.NET Web Site Administration Tool.

CHAPTER 34

ASP.NET Web Controls, Themes, and Master Pages

The previous chapter concentrated on the composition and behavior of ASP.NET page objects. This chapter will dive into the details of the "web controls" that make up a page's user interface. After examining the overall nature of an ASP.NET web control, you will come to understand how to make use of several UI elements including the validation controls and data-centric controls.

The latter half of this chapter will examine the role of "master pages" and demonstrate how they provide a simplified manner to define a common UI skeleton that will be replicated across the pages in your website. I wrap up by showing you how to apply *themes* to your pages, in order to define a consistent look and feel for your page's controls. As you will see, the ASP.NET theme engine provides a server-side alternative to client-side style sheets.

Understanding the Nature of Web Controls

Perhaps the major benefit of ASP.NET is the ability to assemble the UI of your pages using the types defined in the `System.Web.UI.WebControls` namespace. As you have seen, these controls (which go by the names *server controls, web controls,* or *Web Form controls*) are *extremely* helpful in that they automatically generate the necessary HTML for the requesting browser and expose a set of events that may be processed on the web server. Furthermore, because each ASP.NET control has a corresponding class in the `System.Web.UI.WebControls` namespace, it can be manipulated in an OO manner from your `*.aspx` file (within a `<script>` block) as well as within the associated class defined in the code-behind file.

As you have seen, when you configure the properties of a web control using the Visual Studio 2008 Properties window, your edits are recorded in the open declaration of a given widget in the `*.aspx` file as a series of name/value pairs. Thus, if you add a new `TextBox` to the designer of a given `*.aspx` file and change the ID, `BorderStyle`, `BorderWidth`, `BackColor`, `Text`, and `BorderColor` properties using the IDE, the opening `<asp:TextBox>` tag is modified as follows:

```
<asp:TextBox ID="txtNameTextBox" runat="server"
     BackColor="#C0FFC0" BorderStyle="Dotted" BorderWidth="5px"
     Text = "Enter Your Name">
</asp:TextBox>
```

Given that the HTML declaration of a web control eventually becomes a member variable from the `System.Web.UI.WebControls` namespace (via the dynamic compilation cycle), you are able to interact with the members of this type within a server-side `<script>` block or the page's code-behind file. For example, if you handled the `Click` event for a given `Button` type, you could change the background color of the `TextBox` as follows:

```
Partial Class _Default
  Inherits System.Web.UI.Page

  Protected Sub btnChangeTextBoxColor_Click(ByVal sender As Object, _
    ByVal e As System.EventArgs) Handles btnChangeTextBoxColor.Click
    Me.txtNameTextBox.BackColor = Drawing.Color.DarkBlue
  End Sub
End Class
```

All ASP.NET web controls ultimately derive from a common base class named `System.Web.UI.WebControls.WebControl`. `WebControl` in turn derives from `System.Web.UI.Control` (which derives from `System.Object`). `Control` and `WebControl` each define a number of properties common to all server-side controls. Before we examine the inherited functionality, let's formalize what it means to handle a server-side event.

Qualifying Server-Side Event Handling

Given the current state of the World Wide Web, it is impossible to avoid the fundamental nature of browser/web server interaction. Whenever these two entities communicate, there is always an underlying, stateless, HTTP request-and-response cycle. While ASP.NET server controls do a great deal to shield you from the details of the raw HTTP, always remember that treating the Web as an event-driven entity is just a magnificent smoke-and-mirrors show provided by the CLR, and it is not identical to the event-driven model of a Windows-based UI.

Thus, although the `System.Windows.Forms` and `System.Web.UI.WebControls` namespaces define types with the same simple names (`Button`, `TextBox`, `Calendar`, `Label`, and so on), they do not expose an identical set of events. For example, there is no way to handle a server-side `MouseMove` event when the user moves the cursor over a Web Form `Button` type. Obviously, this is a good thing. (Who wants to post back to the server each time the mouse moves?)

The bottom line is that a given ASP.NET web control will expose a limited set of events, all of which ultimately result in a postback to the web server. Any necessary client-side event processing will require you to author blurbs of *client-side* JavaScript/VBScript script code to be processed by the requesting browser's scripting engine. Given that ASP.NET is primarily a server-side technology, I will not be addressing the topic of authoring client-side scripts in this text.

■ **Note** Handling an event for a given web control using Visual Studio 2008 can be done in an identical manner to a Windows Forms control. Simply select the widget from the designer and click the lightning bolt icon on the Properties window.

The AutoPostBack Property

It is also worth pointing out that many of the ASP.NET web controls support a property named `AutoPostBack` (most notably, the `CheckBox`, `RadioButton`, and `TextBox` controls, as well as any widget that derives from the abstract `ListControl` type). By default, this property is set to `False`, which disables the automatic processing of server-side events (even if you have indeed rigged up the event in the code-behind file). In many cases, this is the exact behavior you require, given that UI elements such as check boxes typically don't require immediate postback functionality (as the page object can obtain the state of the widget within a more natural `Button Click` event handler).

However, if you wish to cause any of these widgets to post back to a server-side event handler, simply set the value of `AutoPostBack` to `True`. This technique can be helpful if you wish to have the state of one widget automatically populate another value within another widget on the same page.

To illustrate, create a tester website that contains a single TextBox (named txtAutoPostback) and a single ListBox control (named lstTextBoxData). Here is the relevant markup generated by the designer:

```
<form id="form1" runat="server">
  <asp:TextBox ID="txtAutoPostback" runat="server"></asp:TextBox>
  <br/>
  <asp:ListBox ID="lstTextBoxData" runat="server"></asp:ListBox>
</form>
```

Now, handle the TextChanged event of the TextBox, and within the server-side event handler, populate the ListBox with the current value in the TextBox:

```
Partial Class _Default
  Inherits System.Web.UI.Page

  Protected Sub txtAutoPostback_TextChanged(ByVal sender As Object, _
  ByVal e As System.EventArgs) Handles txtAutoPostback.TextChanged
    lstTextBoxData.Items.Add(txtAutoPostback.Text)
  End Sub
End Class
```

If you run the application as is, you will find that as you type in the TextBox, nothing happens. Furthermore, if you type in the TextBox and tab to the next control, nothing happens. The reason is that the AutoPostBack property of the TextBox is set to False by default. However, if you set this property to True:

```
<asp:TextBox ID="txtAutoPostback"
runat="server" AutoPostBack="True">
</asp:TextBox>
```

you will find that when you tab off the TextBox (or press the Enter key), the ListBox is automatically populated with the current value in the TextBox. To be sure, beyond the need to populate the items of one widget based on the value of another widget, you will typically not need to alter the state of a widget's AutoPostBack property.

The System.Web.UI.Control Type

The System.Web.UI.Control base class defines various properties, methods, and events that allow the ability to interact with core (typically non-GUI) aspects of a web control. Table 34-1 documents some, but not all, members of interest.

Table 34-1. *Select Members of* System.Web.UI.Control

Member	Meaning in Life
Controls	This property gets a ControlCollection object that represents the child controls within the current control.
DataBind()	This method binds a data source to the invoked server control and all its child controls.
EnableThemeing	This property establishes whether the control supports theme functionality.
HasControls()	This method determines whether the server control contains any child controls.

Continued

Table 34-1. *Continued*

Member	Meaning in Life
ID	This property gets or sets the programmatic identifier assigned to the server control.
Page	This property gets a reference to the Page instance that contains the server control.
Parent	This property gets a reference to the server control's parent control in the page control hierarchy.
SkinID	This property gets or sets the "skin" to apply to the control. Since ASP.NET 2.0, it is possible to establish a control's overall look and feel on the fly via skins.
Visible	This property gets or sets a value that indicates whether a server control is rendered as a UI element on the page.

Enumerating Contained Controls

The first aspect of System.Web.UI.Control we will examine is the fact that all web controls (including Page itself) inherit a custom controls collection (accessed via the Controls property). Much like in a Windows Forms application, the Controls property provides access to a strongly typed collection of WebControl-derived types. Like any .NET collection, you have the ability to add, insert, and remove items dynamically at runtime.

While it is technically possible to directly add web controls to a Page-derived type, it is easier (and a wee bit safer) to make use of a Panel widget. The System.Web.UI.WebControls.Panel class represents a container of widgets that may or may not be visible to the end user (based on the value of its Visible and BorderStyle properties).

To illustrate, create a new website named DynamicCtrls. Using the Visual Studio 2008 page designer, add a Panel type (named myPanel) that contains a TextBox, Button, and a HyperLink widget named whatever you choose (be aware that the designer requires that you drag internal items within the UI of the Panel type). Once you have done so, the <form> element of your *.aspx file will have been updated as follows:

```
<asp:Panel ID="myPanel" runat="server" Height="50px" Width="125px">
  <asp:TextBox ID="TextBox1" runat="server"></asp:TextBox><br/>
  <asp:Button ID="Button1" runat="server" Text="Button"/><br/>
  <asp:HyperLink ID="HyperLink1" runat="server">HyperLink
  </asp:HyperLink>
</asp:Panel>
```

Next, place a Label widget (named lblControlInfo) outside the scope of the Panel to hold the rendered output. Assume in the Page_Load() event you wish to obtain a list of all the controls contained within the Panel and assign the results to the Label type (named lblControlInfo):

```
Partial Class _Default
  Inherits System.Web.UI.Page

  Private Sub ListControlsInPanel()
    Dim theInfo As String
    theInfo = String.Format("Has controls? {0} <br/>", myPanel.HasControls())
    For Each c As Control In myPanel.Controls
      If c.GetType() IsNot GetType(System.Web.UI.LiteralControl) Then
        theInfo &= "***************************<br/>"
        theInfo &= String.Format("Control Name? {0} <br/>", c.ToString())
        theInfo &= String.Format("ID? {0} <br>", c.ID)
        theInfo &= String.Format("Control Visible? {0} <br/>", c.Visible)
```

```
        theInfo &= String.Format("ViewState? {0} <br/>", c.EnableViewState)
      End If
    Next
    lblControlInfo.Text = theInfo
  End Sub

  Protected Sub Page_Load(ByVal sender As Object, _
  ByVal e As System.EventArgs) Handles Me.Load
    ListControlsInPanel()
  End Sub
End Class
```

Here, you iterate over each `WebControl` maintained on the `Panel` and perform a check to see whether the current type is of type `System.Web.UI.LiteralControl`. This type is used to represent literal HTML tags and content (such as `<br>`, text literals, etc.). If you do not do this sanity check, you might be surprised to find a total of seven types in the scope of the `Panel` (given the `*.aspx` declaration seen previously). Assuming the type is not literal HTML content, you then print out some various statistics about the widget. Figure 34-1 shows the output.

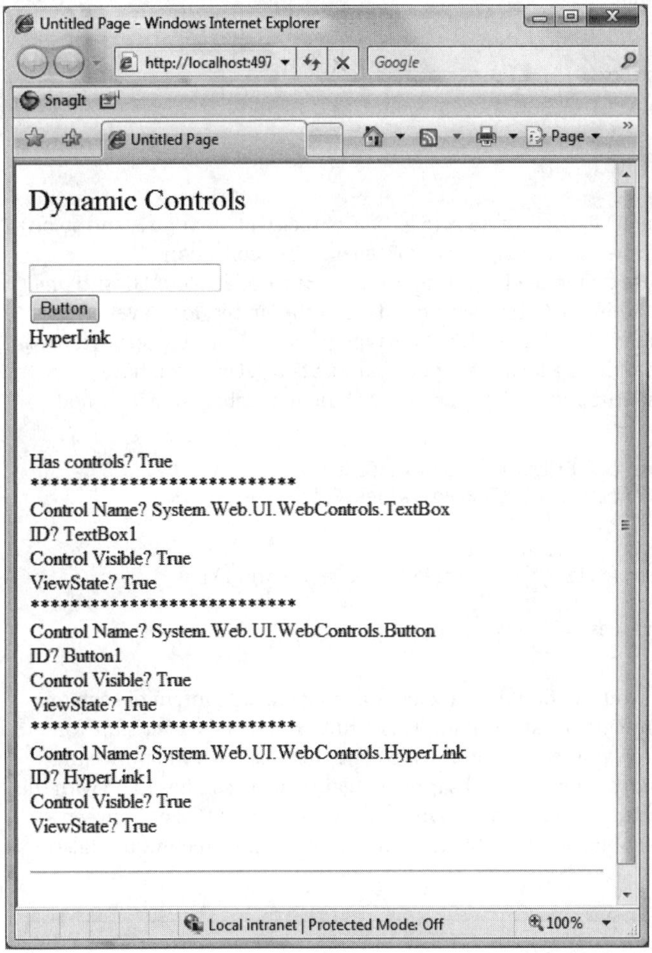

Figure 34-1. *Enumerating contained widgets*

Dynamically Adding (and Removing) Controls

Now, what if you wish to modify the contents of a Panel at runtime? The process should look very familiar to you, given your work with Windows Forms earlier in this text. Let's update the current page to support an additional Button (named btnAddWidgets) that dynamically adds five new TextBox types to the Panel, and another Button (named btnRemovePanelItems) that clears the Panel widget of all controls. The Click event handlers for each are shown here:

```
Protected Sub btnRemovePanelItems_Click(ByVal sender As Object, _
  ByVal e As System.EventArgs) Handles btnRemovePanelItems.Click
    myPanel.Controls.Clear()
    ListControlsInPanel()
End Sub

Protected Sub btnAddWidgets_Click(ByVal sender As Object, _
  ByVal e As System.EventArgs) Handles btnAddWidgets.Click
  For i As Integer = 0 To 4
    ' Assign a name so we can get
    ' the text value out later
    ' using the HttpRequest.Form()
    ' method.
    Dim t As New TextBox()
    t.ID = String.Format("newTextBox{0}", i)
    myPanel.Controls.Add(t)
    ListControlsInPanel()
  Next
End Sub
```

Notice that you assign a unique ID to each TextBox (e.g., newTextBox1, newTextBox2, and so on) to obtain its contained text programmatically using the HttpRequest.Form collection.

To obtain the values within these dynamically generated TextBoxes, update your UI with one additional Button and Label type. Within the Click event handler for the Button, loop over each item contained within the HttpRequest.NameValueCollection type (accessed via HttpRequest.Form) and concatenate the textual information to a locally scoped System.String. Once you have exhausted the collection, assign this string to the Text property of the new Label widget named lblTextBoxText:

```
Protected Sub btnGetTextBoxValues_Click(ByVal sender As Object, _
  ByVal e As System.EventArgs) Handles btnGetTextBoxValues.Click
  Dim textBoxValues As String = ""
  For i As Integer = 0 To Request.Form.Count - 1
    textBoxValues &= String.Format("<li>{0}</li><br/>", Request.Form(i))
  Next
  lblTextBoxText.Text = textBoxValues
End Sub
```

When you run the application, you will find that you are able to view the content of each text box, including some rather long (unreadable) string data. This string contains the *view state* for each widget on the page and will be examined later in the next chapter. Also, you will notice that once the request has been processed, the text boxes disappear. Again, the reason has to do with the stateless nature of HTTP. If you wish to maintain these dynamically created TextBoxes between postbacks, you need to persist these objects using ASP.NET state programming techniques (also examined in the next chapter).

Source Code The DynamicCtrls files are included under the Chapter 34 subdirectory.

Key Members of the System.Web.UI.WebControls.WebControl Type

As you can tell, the `Control` type provides a number of non-GUI-related behaviors (the controls collection, autopostback support, etc.). On the other hand, the `WebControl` base class provides a graphical polymorphic interface to all web widgets, as suggested in Table 34-2.

Table 34-2. *Properties of the* `WebControl` *Base Class*

Property	Meaning in Life
`BackColor`	Gets or sets the background color of the web control
`BorderColor`	Gets or sets the border color of the web control
`BorderStyle`	Gets or sets the border style of the web control
`BorderWidth`	Gets or sets the border width of the web control
`Enabled`	Gets or sets a value indicating whether the web control is enabled
`CssClass`	Allows you to assign a class defined within a Cascading Style Sheet to a web widget
`Font`	Gets font information for the web control
`ForeColor`	Gets or sets the foreground color (typically the color of the text) of the web control
`Height` `Width`	Get or set the height and width of the web control
`TabIndex`	Gets or sets the tab index of the web control
`ToolTip`	Gets or sets the tool tip for the web control to be displayed when the cursor is over the control

I'd bet that almost all of these properties are self-explanatory, so rather than drill through the use of all these properties, let's shift gears a bit and check out a number of ASP.NET Web Form controls in action.

Categories of ASP.NET Web Controls

The types in `System.Web.UI.WebControls` can be broken down into several broad categories:

- Simple controls
- (Feature) Rich controls
- Data-centric controls
- Input validation controls
- Web part controls
- Login controls

The *simple controls* are so named because they are ASP.NET web controls that map to standard HTML widgets (buttons, lists, hyperlinks, image holders, tables, etc.). Next, we have a small set of controls named the *rich controls* for which there is no direct HTML equivalent (such as the `Calendar`, `TreeView`, `Menu`, `Wizard`, etc.). The *data-centric controls* are widgets that are typically populated via a given data connection. The best (and most exotic) example of such a control would be the ASP.NET `GridView`. Other members of this category include "repeater" controls and the lightweight `DataList`.

The *validation controls* are server-side widgets that automatically emit client-side JavaScript, for the purpose of form field validation. Finally, the base class libraries ship with a number of security-centric controls. These UI elements completely encapsulate the details of logging into a site, providing password-retrieval services and managing user roles. The full set of ASP.NET web controls can be seen using the Visual Studio 2008 Toolbox. Notice in Figure 34-2 that related controls are grouped together under a specific tab.

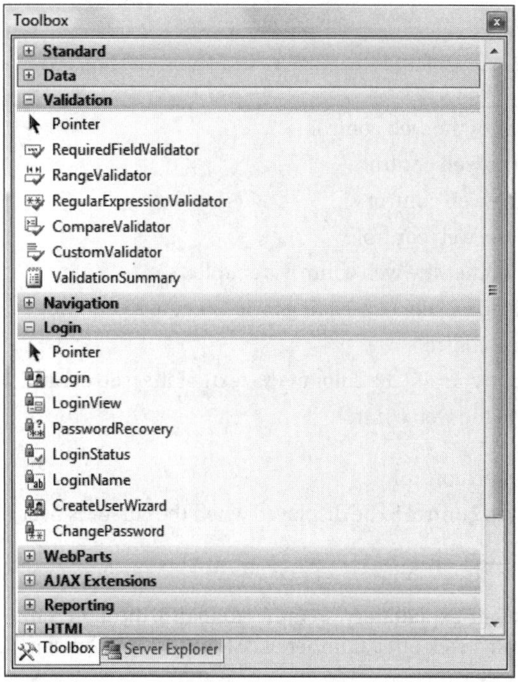

Figure 34-2. *The ASP.NET web controls*

■Note This text will not address the topic of web parts or the ASP.NET security controls. If you are interested in learning about these technologies, I'd recommend obtaining a copy of *Beginning ASP.NET 3.5 in VB 2008: From Novice to Professional, Second Edition* by Matthew MacDonald (Apress, 2007) to complete your understanding of ASP.NET.

A Brief Word Regarding System.Web.UI.HtmlControls

Truth be told, there are two distinct web control toolkits that ship with ASP.NET. In addition to the ASP.NET web controls (within the `System.Web.UI.WebControls` namespace), the base class libraries also provide the `System.Web.UI.HtmlControls` widgets.

The HTML controls are a collection of types that allow you to make use of traditional HTML controls on a Web Forms page. However, unlike raw HTML tags, HTML controls are OO entities that can be configured to run on the server and thus support server-side event handling. Unlike ASP.NET web controls, HTML controls are quite simplistic in nature and offer little functionality beyond standard HTML tags (`HtmlButton`, `HtmlInputControl`, `HtmlTable`, etc.). As you would expect, Visual

Studio 2008 provides a specific section of the Toolbox to contain the HTML control types (see Figure 34-3).

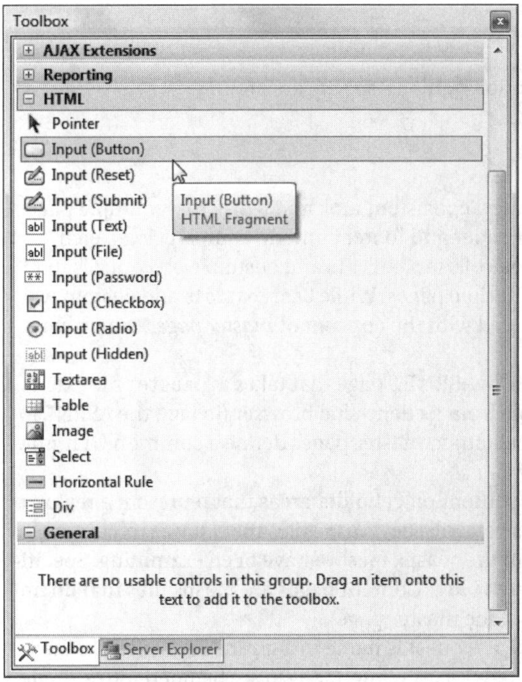

Figure 34-3. *The HTML controls*

The HTML controls provide a public interface that mimics standard HTML attributes. For example, to obtain the information within an input area, you make use of the `Value` property, rather than the web control–centric `Text` property. Given that the HTML controls are not as feature-rich as the ASP.NET web controls, I won't make further mention of them in this text. If you wish to investigate these types, consult the .NET Framework 3.5 SDK documentation for further details.

■ **Note** The HTML controls can be useful if your team has a clear division between those who build HTML UIs and .NET developers. HTML folks can make use of their web editor of choice using familiar markup tags and pass the HTML files to the development team. At this point, developers can configure these HTML controls to run as server controls (by right-clicking an HTML widget within Visual Studio 2008). This will allow developers to handle server-side events and work with the HTML widget programmatically.

Building an ASP.NET Website

Given that many of the "simple" controls look and feel so close to their Windows Forms counterparts, I won't bother to enumerate the details of the basic widgets (`Buttons`, `Labels`, `TextBoxes`, etc.). Rather, let's build a new website that illustrates working with several of the more exotic controls as well as the master page model and enhanced data binding engine. Specifically, this next example will illustrate the following techniques:

- Working with master pages
- Working with the `Menu` control
- Working with the `GridView` control
- Working with the `Wizard` control

To begin, create a new ASP.NET web application named AspNetCarsSite.

Working with Master Pages

As I am sure you are aware, many websites provide a consistent look and feel across multiple pages (a common menu navigation system, common header and footer content, company logo, etc.). Under ASP.NET 1.*x*, developers made extensive use of `UserControls` and custom web controls to define web content that was to be used across multiple pages. While `UserControls` and custom web controls are still a valid option, we are now provided with the concept of *master pages*, which complements these existing technologies.

Simply put, a master page is little more than an ASP.NET page that takes a `*.master` file extension. On their own, master pages are not viewable from a client-side browser (in fact, the ASP.NET runtime will not serve this flavor of web content). Rather, master pages define a common UI frame shared by all pages (or a subset of pages) in your site.

As well, a `*.master` page will define various content placeholder areas that represent a region of UI real estate other `*.aspx` files may plug into. As you will see, `*.aspx` files that plug their content into a master file look and feel a bit different from the `*.aspx` files we have been examining. Specifically, this flavor of an `*.aspx` file is termed a *content page*. Content pages are `*.aspx` files that do not define an HTML `<form>` element (that is the job of the master page).

However, as far as the end user is concerned, a request is made to a given `*.aspx` file. On the web server, the related `*.master` file and any related `*.aspx` content pages are blended into a single unified page. To illustrate the use of master pages and content pages, begin by inserting a new master page into your website via the Website ➤ Add New Item menu selection (Figure 34-4 shows the resulting dialog box).

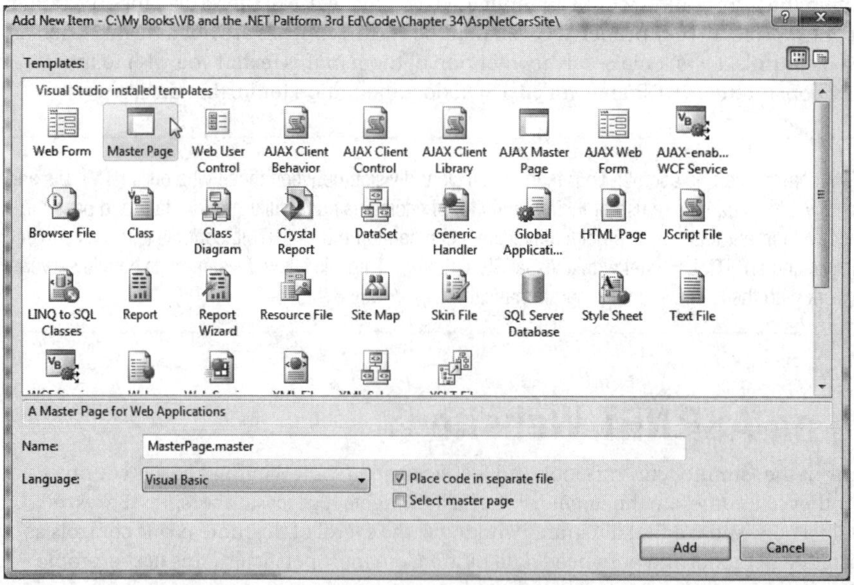

Figure 34-4. *Inserting a new* `*.master` *file*

The initial markup of the `MasterPage.master` file looks like the following:

```
<%@ Master Language="VB" CodeFile="MasterPage.master.vb"
Inherits="MasterPage" %>

<!DOCTYPE html PUBLIC "-//W3C//DTD XHTML 1.0 Transitional//EN"
  "http://www.w3.org/TR/xhtml1/DTD/xhtml1-transitional.dtd">

<html xmlns="http://www.w3.org/1999/xhtml" >
<head runat="server">
    <title>Untitled Page</title>
</head>
<body>
    <form id="form1" runat="server">
    <div>
        <asp:ContentPlaceHolder id="ContentPlaceHolder1" runat="server">
        </asp:ContentPlaceHolder>
    </div>
    </form>
</body>
</html>
```

The first point of interest is the new `<%@Master%>` directive. For the most part, this directive supports the same attributes as the `<%@Page%>` directive described in the previous chapter. For example, notice how by default a master page makes use of a code-behind file (which is technically optional). Like `Page` types, a master page derives from a specific base class, which in this case is `MasterPage`. If you were to open up your related code file, you would find the following class definition:

```
Partial Class MasterPage
  Inherits System.Web.UI.MasterPage
End Class
```

The other point of interest within the markup of the master is the `<asp:ContentPlaceHolder>` type. This region of a master page represents the area of the master that the UI widgets of the related `*.aspx` content file may plug into, not the content defined by the master page itself. If you flip to the designer surface of the `*.master` page, you will find that each `<asp:ContentPlaceHolder>` element is accounted for, as shown in Figure 34-5.

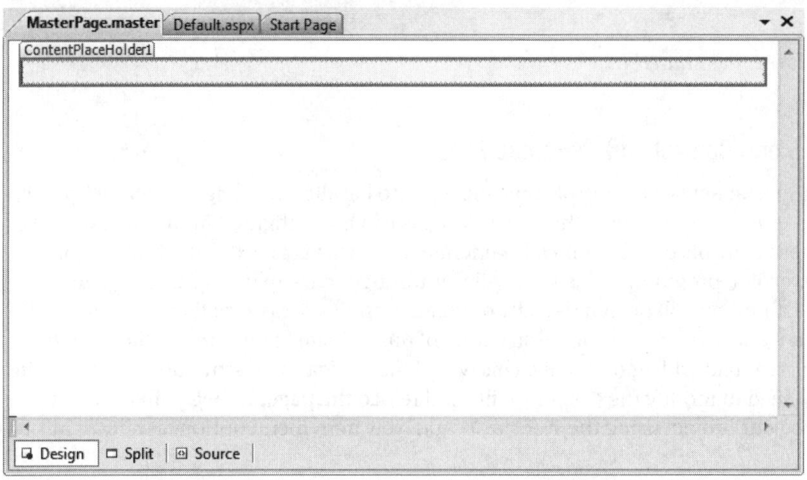

Figure 34-5. *The design-time view of a* `*.master` *file's* `<asp:ContentPlaceHolder>` *tags*

If you do intend to blend an *.aspx file within this region, the scope within the <asp:ContentPlaceHolder> and </asp:ContentPlaceHolder> tags will be empty. However, if you so choose, you are able to populate this area with various web controls that function as a default UI to use in the event that a given *.aspx file in the site does not supply specific content. For this example, assume that each *.aspx page in your site will indeed supply custom content, and therefore our <asp:ContentPlaceHolder> elements will be empty.

Note A *.master page may define as many content placeholders as necessary. As well, a single *.master page may nest additional *.master pages.

As you would hope, you are able to build a common UI of a *.master file using the same Visual Studio 2008 designers used to build *.aspx files. For your site, you will add a descriptive Label (to serve as a common welcome message), an AdRotator control (which will randomly display one of two images), and a Menu control (to allow the user to navigate to other areas of the site). Figure 34-6 shows one possible UI of the master page that we will be constructing (again notice that the content placeholder is empty). Also notice that the AdRotator widget is not yet displaying content, as we have not specified an image file (we will remedy this situation in just a few pages).

Figure 34-6. *The* *.master *file's shared UI*

Working with the Menu Control and *.sitemap Files

ASP.NET ships with several new web controls that allow you to handle site navigation: SiteMapPath, TreeView, and Menu. As you would expect, these web widgets can be configured in multiple ways. For example, each of these controls can dynamically generate its nodes via an external XML file (or an XML-based *.sitemap file), programmatically in code, or through markup using the designers of Visual Studio 2008. Our menu will be dynamically populated using a *.sitemap file. The benefit of this approach is that we can define the overall structure of our website in an external file, and then bind it to a Menu (or TreeView) widget on the fly. This way, if the navigational structure of our website changes, we simply need to modify the *.sitemap file and reload the page. To begin, insert a new Web.sitemap file into your project using the Website ➤ Add New Item menu option, as shown in Figure 34-7.

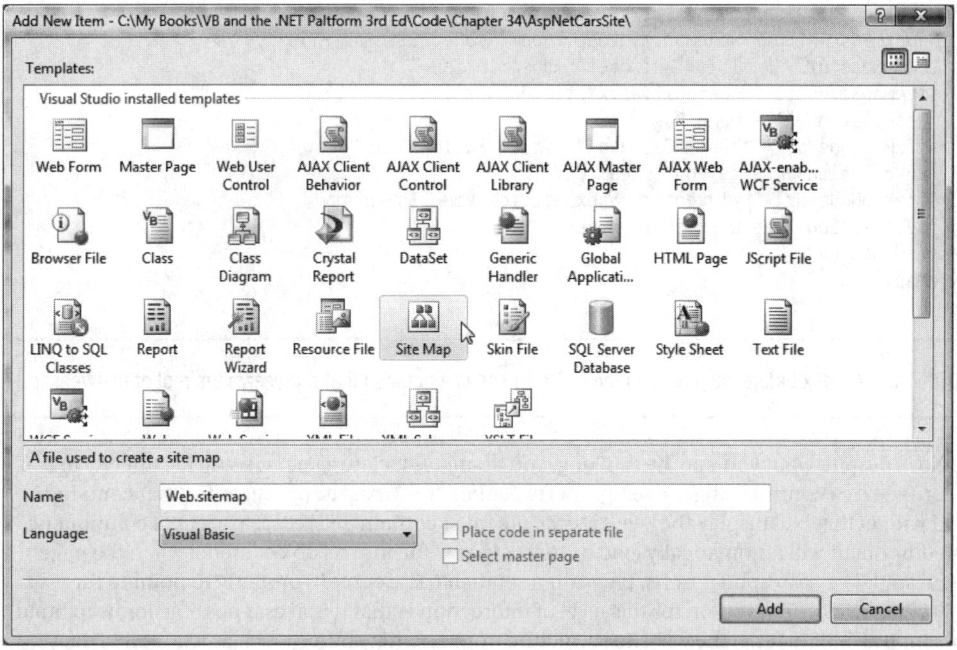

Figure 34-7. *Inserting a new* `Web.sitemap` *file*

As you can see, the initial `Web.sitemap` file defines a topmost item with two subnodes:

```
<?xml version="1.0" encoding="utf-8" ?>
<siteMap xmlns="http://schemas.microsoft.com/AspNet/SiteMap-File-1.0" >
  <siteMapNode url="" title=""  description="">
    <siteMapNode url="" title=""  description="" />
    <siteMapNode url="" title=""  description="" />
  </siteMapNode>
</siteMap>
```

If we were to bind this structure to a `Menu` control (using a `SiteMapDataProvider`, described in just a moment), we would find a topmost menu item with two submenus. Therefore, when you wish to define subitems, simply define new `<siteMapNode>` elements within the scope of an existing `<siteMapNode>`. In any case, the goal is to define the overall structure of your website within a `Web.sitemap` file using various `<siteMapNode>` elements. Each one of these elements can define a description, title, and URL attribute. The URL attribute represents which `*.aspx` file to navigate to when the user clicks a given menu item (or node of a `TreeView`). Our site will contain three subelements, which are set up as follows:

- *Home*: `Default.aspx`
- *Build a Car*: `BuildCar.aspx`
- *View Inventory*: `Inventory.aspx`

Our menu system will have a single topmost "Welcome" item with three subelements. Therefore, we can update the `Web.sitemap` file as follows. (Be aware that each `url` value must be unique! If not, you receive a runtime error.)

```
<?xml version="1.0" encoding="utf-8" ?>
<siteMap xmlns="http://schemas.microsoft.com/AspNet/SiteMap-File-1.0" >
  <siteMapNode url="" title="Welcome!"  description="">
    <siteMapNode url="~/Default.aspx" title="Home"
      description="The Home Page" />
    <siteMapNode url="~/BuildCar.aspx" title="Build a car"
      description="Create your dream car" />
    <siteMapNode url="~/Inventory.aspx" title="View Inventory"
      description="See what is in stock" />
  </siteMapNode>
</siteMap>
```

Note The ~/ prefix before each page in the url attribute is a notation that represents the root of the website.

Now, despite what you may be thinking, you do not associate a Web.sitemap file directly to a Menu or TreeView control using a given property. Rather, the *.master or *.aspx file that contains the UI widget that will display the Web.sitemap file must contain a SiteMapDataSource component. This component will automatically load the Web.sitemap file into its object model when the page is requested. The Menu and TreeView types then set their DataSourceID property to point to the SiteMapDataSource. The reason for this level of indirection is that it makes it possible for us to build a custom provider to fetch the website's structure from another source (such as a table in a database). Figure 34-8 illustrates the interplay between a Web.sitemap, SiteMapDataSource, and various UI elements.

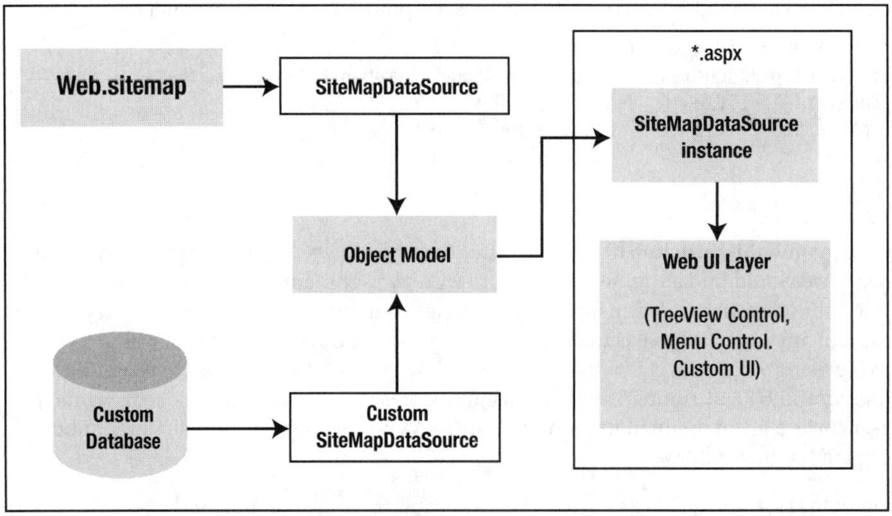

Figure 34-8. *The ASP.NET sitemap navigation model*

To add a new SiteMapDataSource to your *.master file and automatically set the DataSourceID property, you can make use of the Visual Studio 2008 designer. Activate the inline editor of the Menu widget and choose New Data Source, as shown in Figure 34-9.

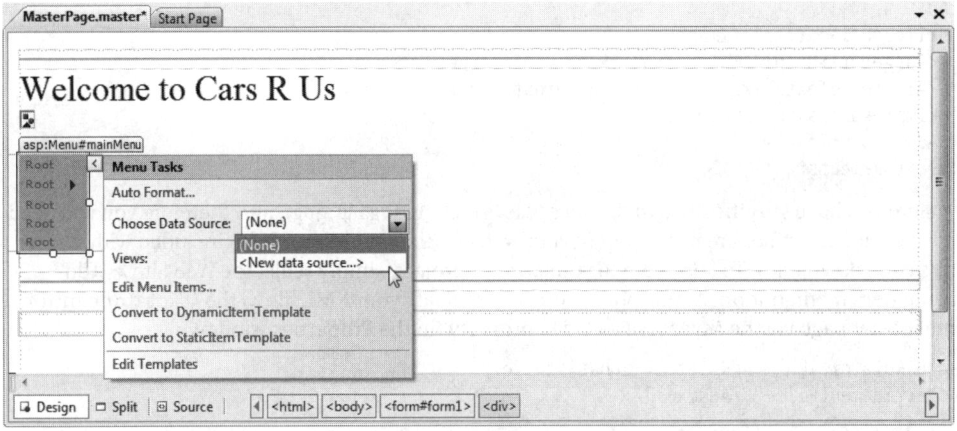

Figure 34-9. *Adding a new* `SiteMapProvider`

From the resulting dialog box, select the SiteMap icon. This will set the `DataSourceID` property of the `Menu` item as well as add a new `SiteMapDataSource` component to your page. This is all you need to do to configure your `Menu` widget to navigate to the additional pages on your site. If you wish to perform additional processing when the user selects a given menu item, you may do so by handling the `MenuItemClick` event. There is no need to do so for this example, but be aware that you are able to determine which menu item was selected using the incoming `MenuEventArgs` parameter.

Establishing Bread Crumbs with the SiteMapPath Type

Before moving on to the `AdRotator` control, add a `SiteMapPath` type onto your `*.master` file, beneath the content placeholder element. This widget will automatically adjust its content based on the current selection of the menu system. As you may know, this can provide a helpful visual cue for the end user (formally, this UI technique is termed *bread crumbs*). Once you complete this example, you will notice that when you select the Welcome ➤ Build a Car menu item, the `SiteMapPath` widget updates accordingly automatically.

Working with the AdRotator

The role of the ASP.NET `AdRotator` widget is to randomly display a given image at some position in the browser. When you first place an `AdRotator` widget on the designer, it is displayed as an empty placeholder. Functionally, this control cannot do its magic until you assign the `AdvertisementFile` property to point to the source file that describes each image. For this example, the data source will be a simple XML file named `Ads.xml`.

Once you have inserted this new XML file to your site, specify a unique `<Ad>` element for each image you wish to display (note that the root element is `<Advertisements>`). At minimum, each `<Ad>` element specifies the image to display (`ImageUrl`), the URL to navigate to if the image is selected (`TargetUrl`), mouseover text (`AlternateText`), and the weight of the ad (`Impressions`):

```
<Advertisements>
  <Ad>
    <ImageUrl>SlugBug.jpg</ImageUrl>
    <TargetUrl>http://www.Cars.com</TargetUrl>
    <AlternateText>Your new Car?</AlternateText>
    <Impressions>80</Impressions>
  </Ad>
```

```
  <Ad>
    <ImageUrl>car.gif</ImageUrl>
    <TargetUrl>http://www.CarSuperSite.com</TargetUrl>
    <AlternateText>Like this Car?</AlternateText>
    <Impressions>80</Impressions>
  </Ad>
</Advertisements>
```

Here you have specified two image files (car.gif and slugbug.jpg), and therefore you will need to ensure that these files are in the root of your website (these files have been included with this book's code download). To add them to your current project, simply select the Web Site ➤ Add Existing Item menu option. At this point, you can associate your XML file to the AdRotator control in the master page via the AdvertisementFile property (in the Properties window):

```
<asp:AdRotator ID="myAdRotator" runat="server"
  AdvertisementFile="~/Ads.xml"/>
```

Later when you run this application and post back to the page, you will be randomly presented with one of two image files. Figure 34-10 illustrates the initial UI of the master page.

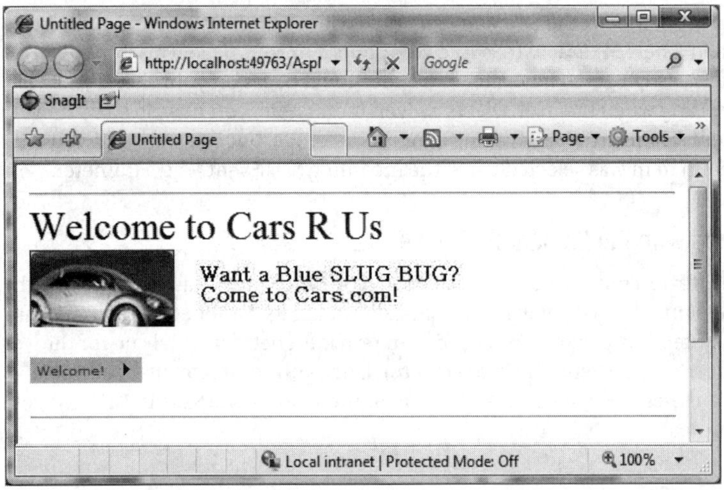

Figure 34-10. *The* AdRotator *control at work*

Defining the Default.aspx Content Page

Now that you have a master page established, you can begin designing the individual *.aspx pages that will define the UI content to merge within the <asp:ContentPlaceHolder> tag of the master page. When you created this website originally, Visual Studio 2008 automatically provided you with an initial *.aspx file, but as the file now stands, it cannot be merged within the master page (unless you modify the initial code quite a bit).

The reason is that it is the *.master file that defines the <form> section of the final HTML page. Therefore, the existing <form> area within the *.aspx file will need to be replaced with an <asp:Content> scope. While you could update the markup of your initial *.aspx file by hand, go ahead and delete Default.aspx from your project. When you wish to automatically insert a new content page to your project, simply right-click the content placeholder region of the *.master file in the designer and select the Add Content Page menu option. This will generate a new *.aspx file with the following initial markup:

```
<%@ Page Language="VB" MasterPageFile="~/MasterPage.master"
  AutoEventWireup="false" CodeFile="Default.aspx.vb"
  Inherits="_Default" title="Untitled Page" %>
<asp:Content ID="Content1"
 ContentPlaceHolderID="ContentPlaceHolder1" Runat="Server">
</asp:Content>
```

First, notice that the `<%@Page%>` directive has been updated with a new `MasterPageFile` attribute that is assigned to your `*.master` file. Also note that rather than having a `<form>` element, we have an `<asp:Content>` scope (currently empty) that has set the `ContentPlaceHolderID` value identically to the `<asp:ContentPlaceHolder>` widget in the master file.

Given these associations, you will now find that when you switch back to the design view, the master's UI is now visible, yet it is grayed out, indicating that it cannot be edited from the content page. The content area is visible as well, although it is currently empty. There is no need to build a complex UI for your `Default.aspx` content area, so for this example, simply add some literal text that provides some basic site instructions, as you see in Figure 34-11.

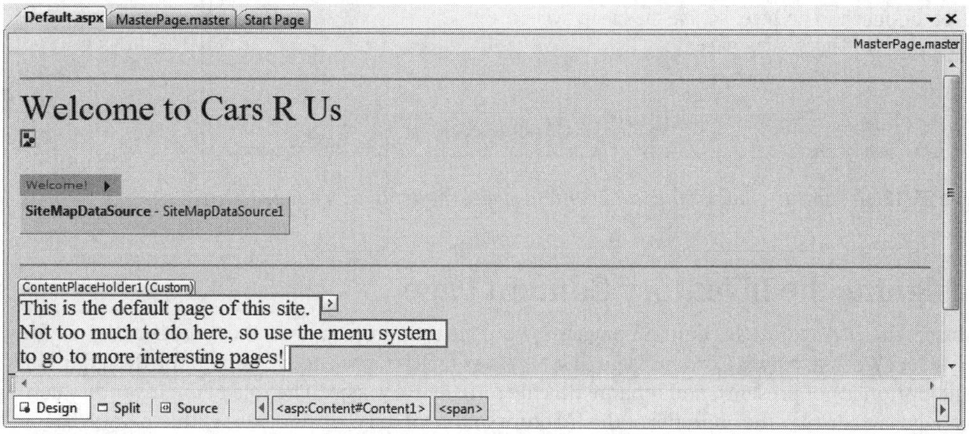

Figure 34-11. *Content pages merge with their master page at design time.*

Now, if you run your project, you will find that the UI content of the `*.master` and `Default.aspx` files have been merged into a single stream of HTML. As you can see from Figure 34-12, the end user is unaware that the master page even exists.

Note Master pages can be assigned programmatically within the `PreInit` event using the `Master` property. Furthermore, it is possible for a content page to communicate with its master via the `Master` property.

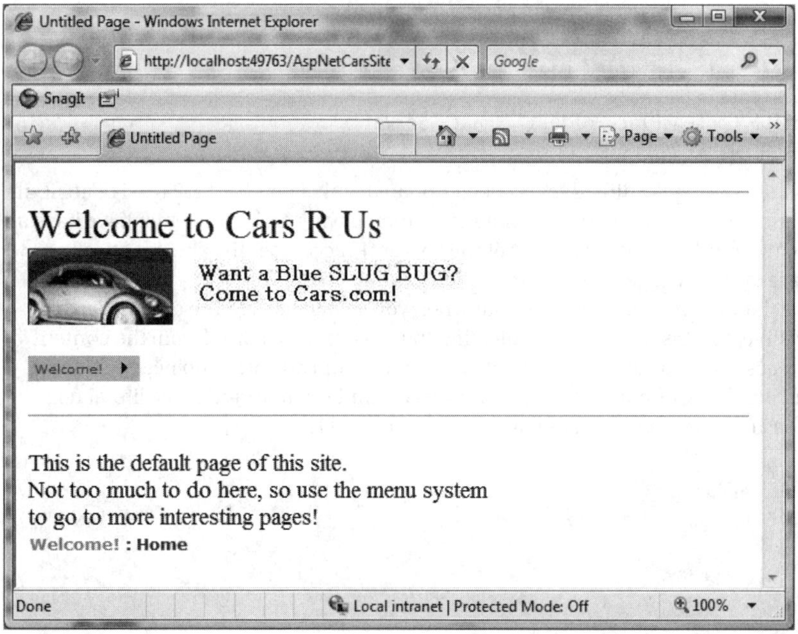

Figure 34-12. *At runtime, master files and content pages render back a single* `<form>`.

Designing the Inventory Content Page

To insert the `Inventory.aspx` content page into your current project, open the `*.master` page in the IDE, select Website ➤ Add Content Page (if a `*.master` file is not the active item in the designer, this menu option is not present), and rename this file to `Inventory.aspx`. The role of the Inventory content page is to display the contents of the Inventory table of the Cars database within a `GridView` control.

Using this control (and the enhanced ASP.NET data binding engine), it is now possible to represent connection string data and SQL `Select`, `Insert`, `Update`, and `Delete` statements (or alternatively stored procedures) *in markup*. Therefore, rather than authoring all of the necessary ADO.NET code by hand, you can make use of the `SqlDataSource` type. Using the visual designers, you are able to declaratively create the necessary markup, and then assign the `DataSourceID` property of the `GridView` to the `SqlDataSource` component.

■ **Note** Despite the name, the `SqlDataSource` provider can be configured to communicate with any ADO.NET data provider (ODBC, Oracle, etc.) that ships with the Microsoft .NET platform; it is not limited to Microsoft SQL Server. You may set the underlying DBMS via the `Provider` property.

With a few simple mouse clicks, you can configure the `GridView` to automatically select, update, and delete records of the underlying data store. While this zero-code mindset greatly simplifies the amount of boilerplate code, understand that this simplicity comes with a loss of control and may not be the best approach for an enterprise-level application. This model can be wonderful for low-trafficked pages, prototyping a website, or smaller in-house applications.

To illustrate how to work with the `GridView` (and the new data binding engine) in a declarative manner, update the `Inventory.aspx` content page with a descriptive label. Next, open the Server

Explorer tool (via the View menu) and make sure you have added a data connection to the AutoLot database created during our examination of ADO.NET (see Chapter 23 for a walkthrough of the process of adding a data connection). Now, select the Inventory table icon of Server Explorer and drag it onto the content area of the `Inventory.aspx` file. Once you have done so, the IDE responds by performing the following steps:

1. Your `web.config` file is updated with a new `<connectionStrings>` element.
2. A `SqlDataSource` component is configured with the necessary `Select`, `Insert`, `Update`, and `Delete` logic.
3. The `DataSourceID` property of the `GridView` is set to the new `SqlDataSource` component.

Note As an alternative, you can configure a `GridView` using the inline editor. Click the smart tag for the `GridView`, and then select New Data Source from the Choose Data Source drop-down box. This will activate a wizard that walks you through a series of steps to connect this component to the required data source.

If you examine the opening declaration of the `GridView` control, you will see that the `DataSourceID` property has been set to the `SqlDataSource` you just defined:

```
<asp:GridView ID="GridView1" runat="server" AutoGenerateColumns="False"
    DataKeyNames="CarID" DataSourceID="CarsDataSource"...>
...
</asp:GridView>
```

The `SqlDataSource` type is where a majority of the action is taking place. In the markup that follows, notice that this type has recorded the necessary SQL statements (with parameterized queries no less) to interact with the Inventory table of the Cars database. As well, using the new "$" syntax of the `ConnectionString` property, this component will automatically read the `<connectionString>` value from `web.config`:

```
<asp:SqlDataSource ID="SqlDataSource1" runat="server"
 ConnectionString="<%$ ConnectionStrings:CarsConnectionString1%>"
  DeleteCommand="DELETE FROM [Inventory] WHERE [CarID] = @CarID"
  InsertCommand="INSERT INTO [Inventory] ([CarID], [Make], [Color], [PetName])
    VALUES (@CarID, @Make, @Color, @PetName)"
  ProviderName="<%$ ConnectionStrings:CarsConnectionString1.ProviderName %>"
  SelectCommand="SELECT [CarID], [Make], [Color], [PetName] FROM [Inventory]"
  UpdateCommand="UPDATE [Inventory] SET [Make] = @Make,
    [Color] = @Color, [PetName] = @PetName WHERE [CarID] = @CarID">
  <DeleteParameters>
    <asp:Parameter Name="CarID" Type="Int32" />
  </DeleteParameters>
  <UpdateParameters>
    <asp:Parameter Name="Make" Type="String" />
    <asp:Parameter Name="Color" Type="String" />
    <asp:Parameter Name="PetName" Type="String" />
    <asp:Parameter Name="CarID" Type="Int32" />
  </UpdateParameters>
  <InsertParameters>
    <asp:Parameter Name="CarID" Type="Int32" />
    <asp:Parameter Name="Make" Type="String" />
    <asp:Parameter Name="Color" Type="String" />
    <asp:Parameter Name="PetName" Type="String" />
  </InsertParameters>
</asp:SqlDataSource>
```

At this point, you are able to run your web program, click the View Inventory menu item, and view your data, as shown in Figure 34-13. Also notice that the "bread crumbs" provided by the `SiteMapPath` widget have updated automatically.

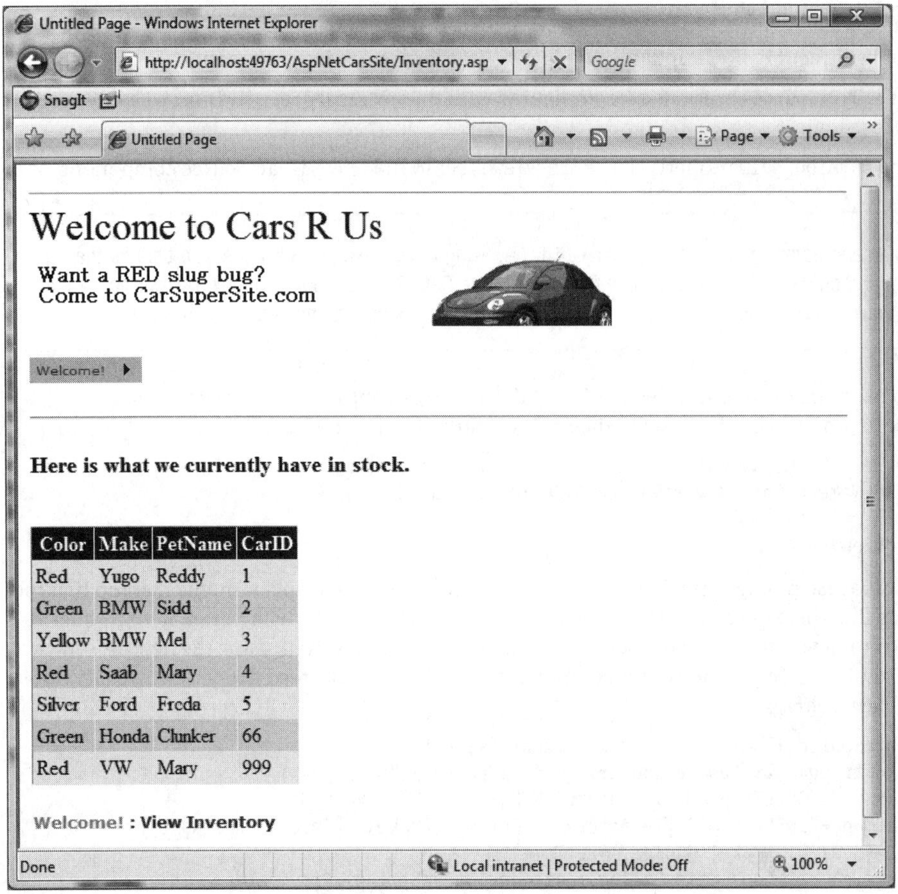

Figure 34-13. *The "zero-code" model of the* `SqlDataSource` *component*

Enabling Sorting and Paging

The `GridView` control can easily be configured for sorting (via column name hyperlinks) and paging (via numeric or next/previous hyperlinks). To do so, click the smart tag for the `GridView` to activate the inline editor and check the appropriate options, as shown in Figure 34-14.

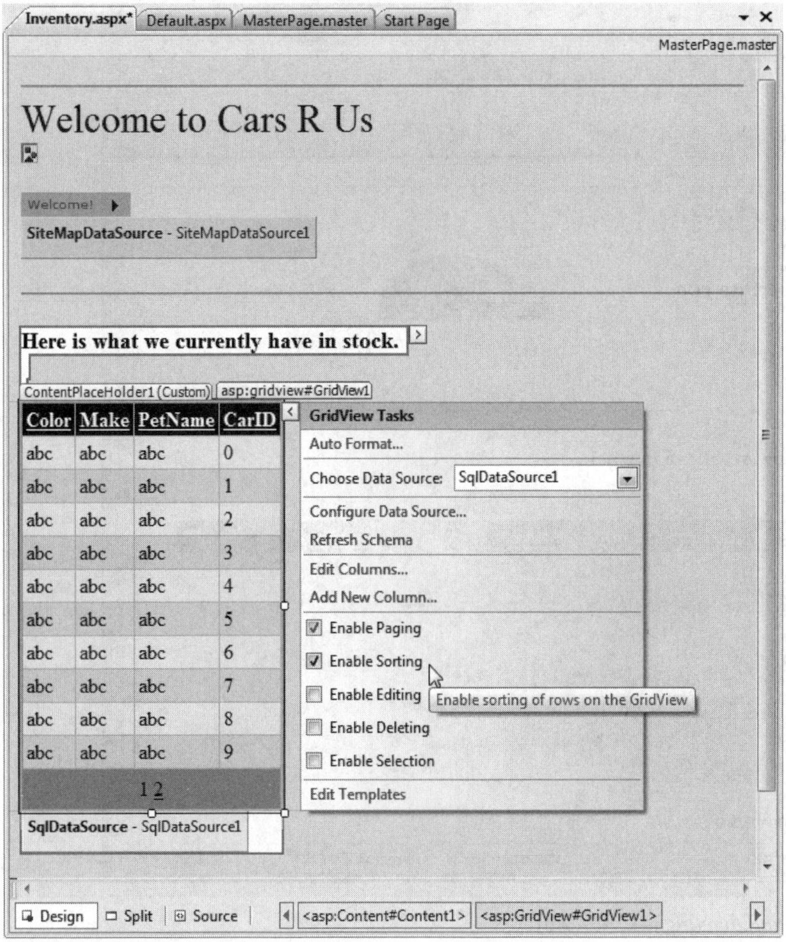

Figure 34-14. *Enabling sorting and paging*

When you run your page again, you will be able to sort your data by clicking the column names and scrolling through your data via the paging links (provided you have enough records in the Inventory table!).

Enabling In-Place Editing

The final detail of this page is to enable the `GridView` control's support for in-place editing. Given that your `SqlDataSource` already has the necessary `Delete` and `Update` logic, all you need to do is check the Enable Deleting and Enable Editing check boxes of the `GridView` (refer back to Figure 34-14). Sure enough, when you navigate back to the `Inventory.aspx` page, you are able to edit and delete records, as shown in Figure 34-15, and update the underlying Inventory table of the AutoLot database.

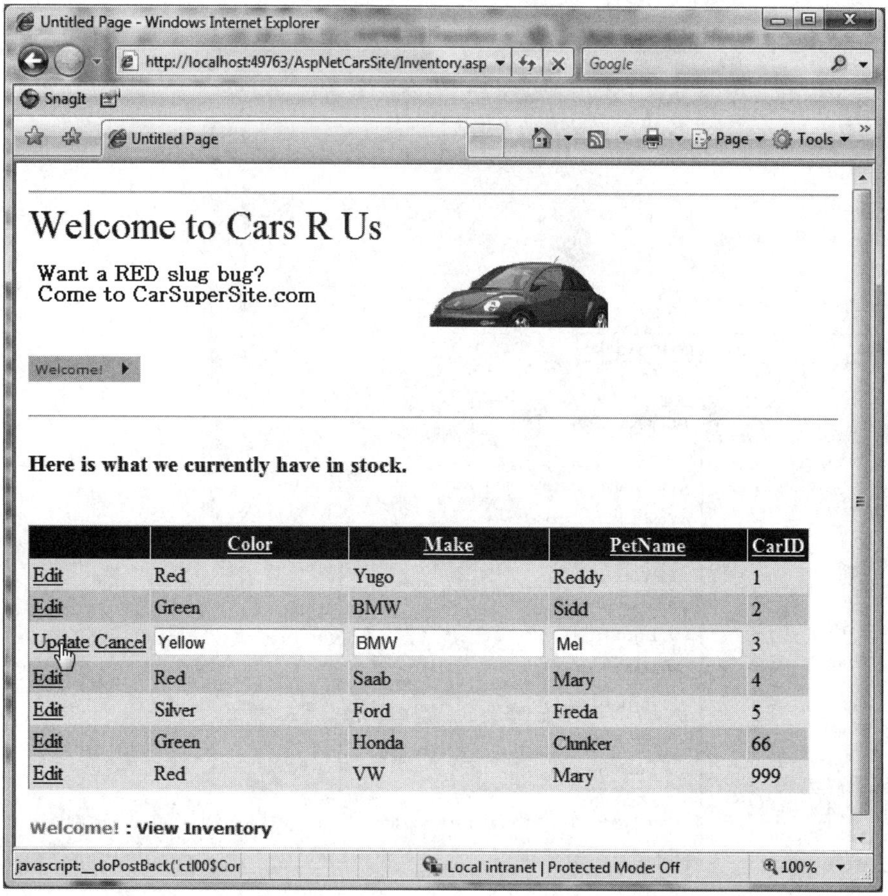

Figure 34-15. *Editing and deleting functionality*

Designing the Build-a-Car Content Page

The final task for this example is to design the `BuildCar.aspx` content page. Insert this file into the current project (via the Website ➤ Add Content Page menu option). This new page will make use of the `Wizard` web control, which provides a simple way to walk the end user through a series of related steps. Here, the steps in question will simulate the act of building an automobile for purchase.

Place a descriptive `Label` and `Wizard` control onto the content area. Next, click the smart tag for the `Wizard` control to activate the inline editor for the `Wizard` and click the Add/Remove WizardSteps link. Add a total of four steps, as shown in Figure 34-16.

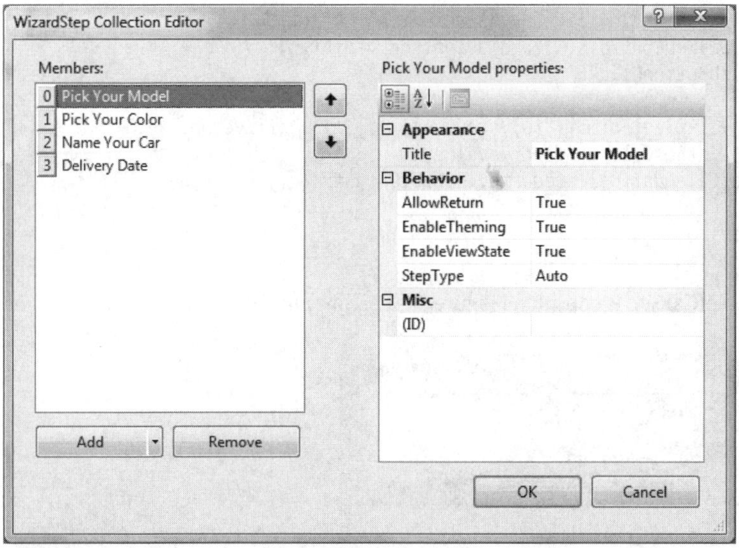

Figure 34-16. *Configuring our wizard*

Once you have defined these steps, you will notice that the `Wizard` defines an empty content area where you can now drag and drop controls for the currently selected step. For this example, update each step with the following UI elements (be sure to provide a decent ID value for each item using the Properties window):

- *Pick Your Model*: A single `TextBox` control
- *Pick Your Color*: A single `ListBox` control
- *Name Your Car*: A single `TextBox` control
- *Delivery Date*: A `Calendar` control

The `ListBox` control is the only UI element of the `Wizard` that requires additional steps. Select this item on the designer (making sure you first select the Pick Your Color link) and fill this widget with a set of colors using the `Items` property of the Properties window. Once you do, you will find markup much like the following within the scope of the `Wizard` definition:

```
<asp:ListBox ID="ListBoxColors" runat="server" Width="237px">
  <asp:ListItem>Purple</asp:ListItem>
  <asp:ListItem>Green</asp:ListItem>
  <asp:ListItem>Red</asp:ListItem>
  <asp:ListItem>Yellow</asp:ListItem>
  <asp:ListItem>Pea Soup Green</asp:ListItem>
  <asp:ListItem>Black</asp:ListItem>
  <asp:ListItem>Lime Green</asp:ListItem>
</asp:ListBox>
```

Now that you have defined each of the steps, you can handle the `FinishButtonClick` event for the autogenerated Finish button. Within the server-side event handler, obtain the selections from each UI element and build a description string that is assigned to the `Text` property of an additional `Label` type named `lblOrder`:

```
Protected Sub carWizard_FinishButtonClick(ByVal sender As Object, _
  ByVal e As System.Web.UI.WebControls.WizardNavigationEventArgs) _
  Handles carWizard.FinishButtonClick
    ' Get each value.
    Dim order As String = String.Format("{0}, your {1} {2} will arrive on {3}.", _
    txtCarPetName.Text, ListBoxColors.SelectedValue, _
    txtCarModel.Text, carCalendar.SelectedDate.ToShortDateString())
    ' Assign to label
    lblOrder.Text = order
End Sub
```

At this point your AspNetCarSite is complete! Figure 34-17 shows the Wizard in action.

Figure 34-17. *The* `Wizard` *widget in action*

That wraps up our examination of various core UI web controls. To be sure, there are many other widgets we haven't covered here. You should feel comfortable, though, with the basic programming model and be able to dig into the other widgets on your own terms. Next up, let's look at the validation controls.

Source Code The AspNetCarsSite files are included under the Chapter 34 subdirectory.

The Role of the Validation Controls

The next Web Form controls we will examine are known collectively as *validation controls*. Unlike the other Web Form controls we've examined, validation controls are not used to emit HTML, but are used to emit client-side JavaScript (and possibly server-side operations) for the purpose of form validation. As illustrated at the beginning of this chapter, client-side form validation is quite useful in that you can ensure that various constraints are in place before posting back to the web server, thereby avoiding expensive round-trips. Table 34-3 gives a rundown of the ASP.NET validation controls.

Table 34-3. *ASP.NET Validation Controls*

Control	Meaning in Life
`CompareValidator`	Validates that the value of an input control is equal to a given value of another input control or a fixed constant.
`CustomValidator`	Allows you to build a custom validation function that validates a given control.
`RangeValidator`	Determines that a given value is in a predetermined range.
`RegularExpressionValidator`	Checks whether the value of the associated input control matches the pattern of a regular expression.
`RequiredFieldValidator`	Ensures that a given input control contains a value (i.e., is not empty).
`ValidationSummary`	Displays a summary of all validation errors of a page in a list, bulleted list, or single-paragraph format. The errors can be displayed inline and/or in a pop-up message box.

All of the validation controls (except `ValidationSummary`) ultimately derive from a common base class named `System.Web.UI.WebControls.BaseValidator`, and therefore they have a set of common features. Table 34-4 documents the key members.

Table 34-4. *Common Properties of the ASP.NET Validators*

Member	Meaning in Life
`ControlToValidate`	Gets or sets the input control to validate
`Display`	Gets or sets the display behavior of the error message in a validation control
`EnableClientScript`	Gets or sets a value indicating whether client-side validation is enabled
`ErrorMessage`	Gets or sets the text for the error message
`ForeColor`	Gets or sets the color of the message displayed when validation fails

While we could update the previous example with several validation controls (within the wizard steps, for example), let's create a new Web Site project named ValidatorCtrls. To begin, place four `TextBox` objects (with four corresponding and descriptive `Labels`) onto your page. Next, add a single `Button` and final `Label`. Finally, place a `RequiredFieldValidator`, `RangeValidator`,

RegularExpressionValidator, and CompareValidator type adjacent to each respective field, and set the ErrorMessage property of each validation control (see Figure 34-18).

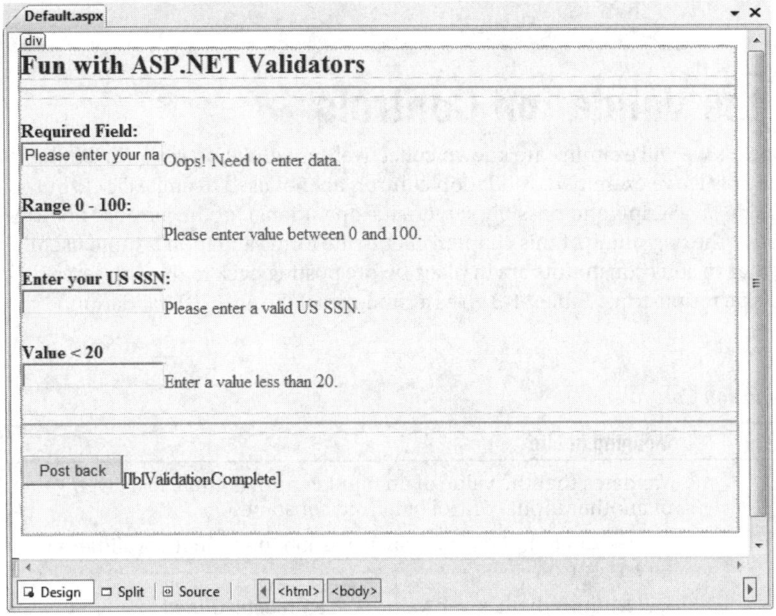

Figure 34-18. *Various validators*

Now that you have a UI, let's walk through the process of configuring each member.

The RequiredFieldValidator

Configuring the RequiredFieldValidator is straightforward. Simply set the ErrorMessage and ControlToValidate properties accordingly using the Visual Studio 2008 Properties window. The resulting *.aspx definition is as follows:

```
<asp:RequiredFieldValidator ID="RequiredFieldValidator1"
  runat="server" ControlToValidate="txtRequiredField"
  ErrorMessage="Oops!  Need to enter data.">
</asp:RequiredFieldValidator>
```

One nice thing about the RequiredFieldValidator is that it supports an InitialValue property. You can use this property to ensure that the user enters any value other than the initial value in the related TextBox. For example, when the user first posts to a page, you may wish to configure a TextBox to contain the value "Please enter your name". Now, if you did not set the InitialValue property of the RequiredFieldValidator, the runtime would assume that the string "Please enter your name" is valid. Thus, to ensure a required TextBox is valid only when the user enters anything other than "Please enter your name", configure your widgets as follows:

```
<asp:RequiredFieldValidator ID="RequiredFieldValidator1"
  runat="server" ControlToValidate="txtRequiredField"
  ErrorMessage="Oops!  Need to enter data."
  InitialValue="Please enter your name">
</asp:RequiredFieldValidator>
```

The RegularExpressionValidator

The RegularExpressionValidator can be used when you wish to apply a pattern against the characters entered within a given input field. To ensure that a given TextBox contains a valid US Social Security number, you could define the widget as follows:

```
<asp:RegularExpressionValidator ID="RegularExpressionValidator1"
  runat="server" ControlToValidate="txtRegExp"
  ErrorMessage="Please enter a valid US SSN."
  ValidationExpression="\d{3}-\d{2}-\d{4}">
</asp:RegularExpressionValidator>
```

Notice how the RegularExpressionValidator defines a ValidationExpression property. If you have never worked with regular expressions before, all you need to be aware of for this example is that they are used to match a given string pattern. Here, the expression "\d{3}-\d{2}\d{4}" is capturing a standard US Social Security number of the form xxx-xx-xxxx (where x is any digit).

This particular regular expression is fairly self-explanatory; however, assume you wish to test for a valid Japanese phone number. The correct expression now becomes much more complex: "(0\d{1,4}-|\(0\d{1,4}\)?)?\d{1,4}-\d{4}". The good news is that when you select the ValidationExpression property using the Properties window, you can pick from a predefined set of common regular expressions by clicking the Ellipse button.

Note If you are interested in regular expressions, you will be happy to know that the .NET platform supplies two namespaces (System.Text.RegularExpressions and System.Web.RegularExpressions) devoted to the programmatic manipulation of such patterns.

The RangeValidator

In addition to a MinimumValue and MaximumValue property, RangeValidators have a property named Type. Because you are interested in testing the user-supplied input against a range of whole numbers, you need to specify Integer (which is *not* the default!):

```
<asp:RangeValidator ID="RangeValidator1"
  runat="server" ControlToValidate="txtRange"
  ErrorMessage="Please enter value between 0 and 100."
  MaximumValue="100" MinimumValue="0" Type="Integer">
</asp:RangeValidator>
```

The RangeValidator can also be used to test whether a given value is between a currency value, date, floating-point number, or string data (the default setting).

The CompareValidator

Finally, notice that the CompareValidator supports an Operator property:

```
<asp:CompareValidator ID="CompareValidator1" runat="server"
  ControlToValidate="txtComparison"
  ErrorMessage="Enter a value less than 20." Operator="LessThan"
  ValueToCompare="20">
</asp:CompareValidator>
```

Given that the role of this validator is to compare the value in the text box against another value using a binary operator, it should be no surprise that the Operator property may be set to values such as LessThan, GreaterThan, Equal, and NotEqual. Also note that the ValueToCompare is used to establish a value to compare against.

■ **Note** The CompareValidator can also be configured to compare a value within another Web Form control (rather than a hard-coded value) using the ControlToValidate property.

To finish up the code for this page, handle the Click event for the Button type and inform the user he or she has succeeded in the validation logic:

```
Partial Class _Default
  Inherits System.Web.UI.Page

  Protected Sub btnPostback_Click(ByVal sender As Object, _
  ByVal e As System.EventArgs) Handles btnPostback.Click
    lblValidationComplete.Text = "You passed validation!"
  End Sub
End Class
```

Now, navigate to this page using your browser of choice. At this point, you should not see any noticeable changes. However, when you attempt to click the Submit button after entering bogus data, your error message is suddenly visible. Once you enter valid data, the error messages are removed and postback occurs.

If you look at the HTML rendered by the browser, you see that the validation controls generate a client-side JavaScript function that makes use of a specific library of JavaScript functions that is automatically downloaded to the user's machine. Once the validation has occurred, the form data is posted back to the server, where the ASP.NET runtime will perform the *same* validation tests on the web server (just to ensure that no along-the-wire tampering has taken place).

On a related note, if the HTTP request was sent by a browser that does not support client-side JavaScript, all validation will occur on the server. In this way, you can program against the validation controls without being concerned with the target browser; the returned HTML page redirects the error processing back to the web server.

Creating Validation Summaries

The final validation-centric topic we will examine here is the use of the ValidationSummary widget. Currently, each of your validators displays its error message at the exact place in which it was positioned at design time. In many cases, this may be exactly what you are looking for. However, on a complex form with numerous input widgets, you may not want to have random blobs of red text pop up. Using the ValidationSummary type, you can instruct all of your validation types to display their error messages at a specific location on the page.

The first step is to simply place a ValidationSummary on your *.aspx file. You may optionally set the HeaderText property of this type as well as the DisplayMode, which by default will list all error messages as a bulleted list.

```
<asp:ValidationSummary id="ValidationSummary1"
  runat="server" Width="353px"
  HeaderText="Here are the things you must correct.">
</asp:ValidationSummary>
```

Next, you need to set the Display property to None for each of the individual validators (e.g., RequiredFieldValidator, RangeValidator, etc.) on the page. This will ensure that you do not see duplicate error messages for a given validation failure (one in the summary pane and another at the validator's location).

Last but not least, if you would rather have the error messages displayed using a client-side `MessageBox`, set the `ShowMessageBox` property (on the `ValidationSummary` control) to `True` and the `ShowSummary` property to `False`.

Source Code The ValidatorCtrls files are included under the Chapter 34 subdirectory.

Working with Themes

At this point, you have had the chance to work with numerous ASP.NET web controls. As you have seen, each control exposes a set of properties (many of which are inherited by `System.Web.UI.WebControls.WebControl`) that allow you to establish a given UI look and feel (background color, font size, border style, and whatnot). Of course, on a multipaged website it is quite common for the site as a whole to define a common look and feel for various types of widgets. For example, all `TextBoxes` might be configured to support a given font, all `Buttons` have a custom image, and all `Calendars` are light blue.

Obviously, it would be very labor intensive (and error prone) to establish the *same* property settings for every widget on *every* page within your website. Even if you were able to manually update the properties of each UI widget on each page, imagine how painful it would be when you now need to change the background color for each `TextBox` yet again. Clearly there must be a better way to apply sitewide UI settings.

One approach that can be taken to simplify applying a common UI look and feel is to define *Cascading Style Sheets* (CSS). If you have a background in web development, you are aware that style sheets define a common set of UI-centric settings that are applied on the browser. As you would hope, ASP.NET web controls can be assigned a given style by assigning the `CssStyle` property.

However, ASP.NET ships with an alternative technology to define a common UI termed *themes*. Unlike a style sheet, themes are applied on the web server (rather than the browser), and can be done so programmatically or declaratively. Given that a theme is applied on the web server, it has access to all the server-side resources on the website. Furthermore, themes are defined by authoring the same markup you would find within any `*.aspx` file (as you may agree, the syntax of a style sheet is a bit on the terse side).

Recall from Chapter 25 that ASP.NET web applications may define any number of "special" subdirectories, one of which is App_Themes. This single subdirectory may be further partitioned with additional subdirectories, each of which represents a possible theme on your site. For example, consider Figure 34-19, which illustrates a single App_Themes folder containing three subdirectories, each of which has a set of files that make up the theme itself.

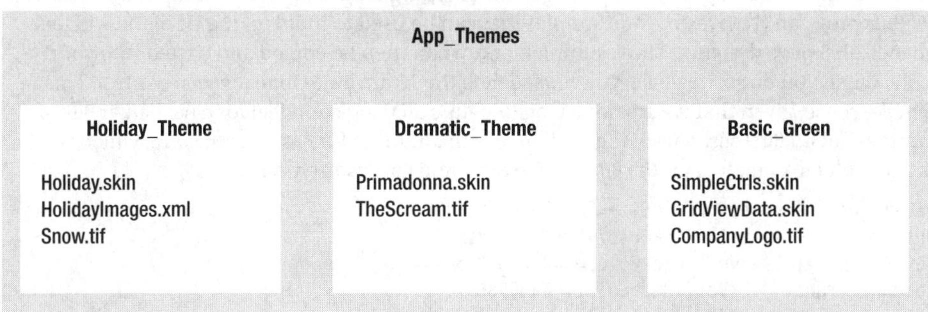

Figure 34-19. *A single App_Themes folder may define numerous themes.*

Understanding *.skin Files

The one file that every theme subdirectory is sure to have is a `*.skin` file. These files define the look and feel for various web controls. To illustrate, create a new website named FunWithThemes. Next, insert a new `*.skin` file (using the Website ➤ Add New Item menu option) named `BasicGreen.skin`, as shown in Figure 34-20.

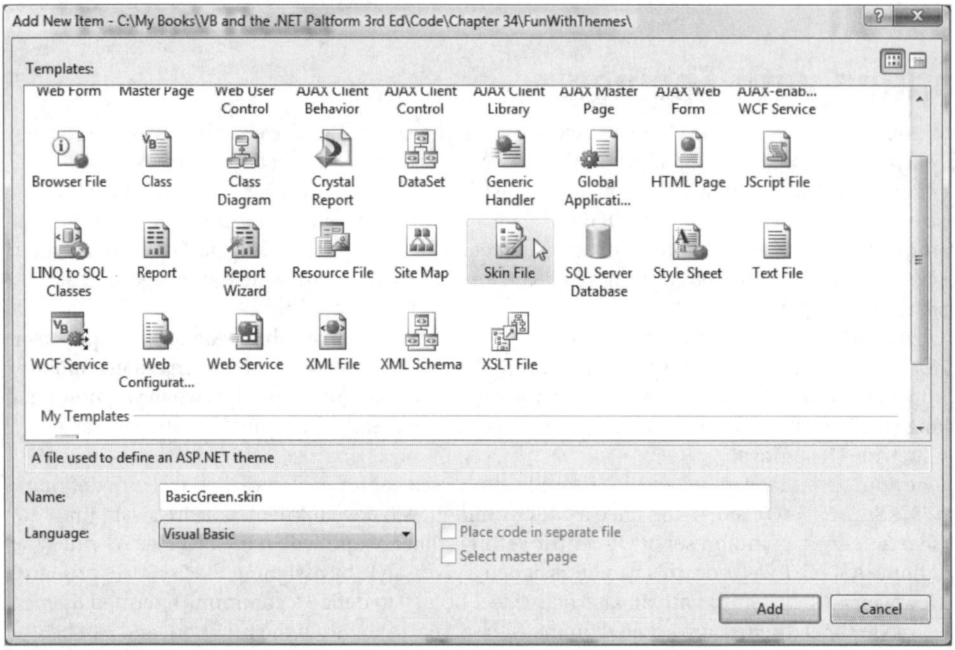

Figure 34-20. *Inserting* `*.skin` *files*

Visual Studio 2008 will prompt you to confirm this file can be added into an App_Themes folder (which is exactly what we want). If you were now to look in your Solution Explorer, you would indeed find your App_Themes folder has a subfolder named BasicGreen containing your new `BasicGreen.skin` file.

Recall that a `*.skin` file is where you are able to define the look and feel for various widgets using ASP.NET control declaration syntax. Sadly, the IDE does not currently provide designer support for `*.skin` files. One way to reduce the amount of typing time is to insert a temporary `*.aspx` file into your program (`temp.aspx`, for example) that can be used to build up the UI of the widgets using the VS 2008 page designer. The resulting markup can then be copied and pasted into your `*.skin` file. When you do so, however, you *must* delete the `ID` attribute for each web control! This should make sense, given that we are not trying to define a UI look and feel for a particular `Button` (for example) but *all* `Button`s. This being said, here is the markup for `BasicGreen.skin`, which defines a default look and feel for the `Button`, `TextBox`, and `Calendar` types:

```
<asp:Label runat="server" Font-Size="XX-Large"/>
<asp:Button runat="server" BackColor="#80FF80"/>
<asp:TextBox runat="server" BackColor="#80FF80"/>
<asp:Calendar runat="server" BackColor="#80FF80"/>
```

Notice that each widget still has the `runat="server"` attribute (which is mandatory) and none of the widgets have been assigned an `ID` attribute.

Now, let's define a second theme named CrazyOrange. Using Solution Explorer, right-click your App_Themes folder and add a new theme named CrazyOrange. This will create a new subdirectory under your site's App_Themes folder. Next, right-click the new CrazyOrange folder within Solution Explorer and select Add New Item. From the resulting dialog box, add a new `*.skin` file. Update the `CrazyOrange.skin` file to define a very obnoxious UI look and feel for the same four web controls. For example:

```
<asp:Button runat="server" BackColor="#FF8000"/>
<asp:TextBox runat="server" BackColor="#FF8000"/>
<asp:Calendar BackColor="White" BorderColor="Black"
  BorderStyle="Solid" CellSpacing="1"
  Font-Names="Verdana" Font-Size="9pt" ForeColor="Black" Height="250px"
  NextPrevFormat="ShortMonth" Width="330px" runat="server">
  <SelectedDayStyle BackColor="#333399" ForeColor="White" />
  <OtherMonthDayStyle ForeColor="#999999" />
  <TodayDayStyle BackColor="#999999" ForeColor="White" />
  <DayStyle BackColor="#CCCCCC" />
  <NextPrevStyle Font-Bold="True" Font-Size="8pt" ForeColor="White" />
  <DayHeaderStyle Font-Bold="True" Font-Size="8pt"
    ForeColor="#333333" Height="8pt" />
  <TitleStyle BackColor="#333399" BorderStyle="Solid"
    Font-Bold="True" Font-Size="12pt"
    ForeColor="White" Height="12pt" />
</asp:Calendar>
```

So now that your site has a few themes defined, the next logical question is how to apply them to your pages. As you might guess, there are many ways to do so.

Applying Sitewide Themes

If you wish to make sure that every page in your site adheres to the same theme, the simplest way to do so is to update your `web.config` file. Open your current `web.config` file and locate the `<pages>` element within the scope of your `<system.web>` root element. If you add a theme attribute to the `<pages>` element, this will ensure that every page in your website is assigned the selected theme (which is, of course, the name of one of the subdirectories under App_Themes). Here is the core update:

```
<configuration>
  <system.web>
...
    <pages theme="BasicGreen">
...
    </pages>
  </system.web>
</configuration>
```

If you were to now place various `Buttons`, `Calendars`, and `TextBoxes` onto your `Default.aspx` file and run the application, you would find each widget has the UI of BasicGreen. If you were to update the theme attribute to CrazyOrange and run the page again, you would find the UI defined by this theme is used instead.

Applying Themes at the Page Level

It is also possible to assign themes on a page-by-page level. This can be helpful in a variety of circumstances. For example, perhaps your `web.config` file defines a sitewide theme (as described in the previous section); however, you wish to assign a different theme to a specific page. To do so, you can simply update the <%@Page%> directive by setting the Theme attribute. If you are using Visual Studio 2008 to do so, you will be happy to find that IntelliSense will display each defined theme within your App_Themes folder (see Figure 34-21).

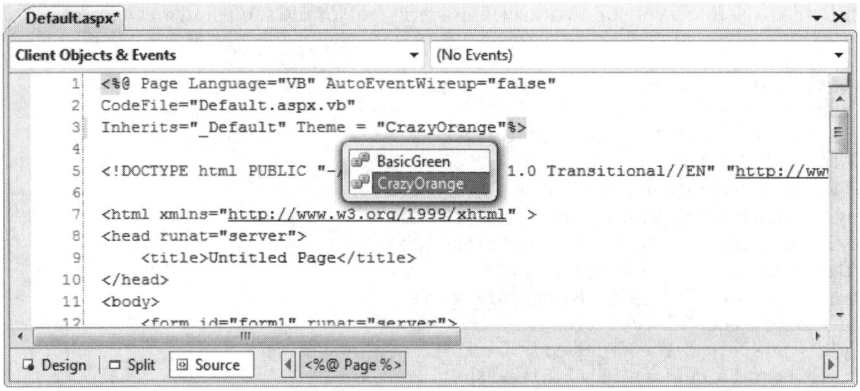

Figure 34-21. *Assigning themes on the page level*

If we were to assign the CrazyOrange theme to this page, but the web.config file specified the BasicGreen theme, then all pages *but this page* would be rendered using BasicGreen.

The SkinID Property

Sometimes you wish to define a set of possible UI look and feels for a single widget. For example, assume you want to define two possible UIs for the Button type within the CrazyOrange theme. When you wish to do so, you may differentiate each look and feel using the SkinID property:

```
<asp:Button runat="server" BackColor="#FF8000"/>
<asp:Button runat="server" SkinID = "BigFontButton"
Font-Size="30pt" BackColor="#FF8000"/>
```

Now, if you have a page that makes use of the CrazyOrange theme, each Button will by default be assigned the unnamed Button skin. If you wish to have various buttons within the *.aspx file make use of the BigFontButton skin, simply specify the SkinID property within the markup:

```
<asp:Button ID="Button2" runat="server"
SkinID="BigFontButton"
Text="Button" />
```

As an example, Figure 34-22 shows a page that is making use of the CrazyOrange theme. The topmost Button is assigned the unnamed Button skin, while the Button on the bottom of the page has been assigned the SkinID of BigFontButton.

Figure 34-22. *Fun with* `SkinIDs`

Assigning Themes Programmatically

Last but not least, it is possible to assign a theme in code. This can be helpful when you wish to provide a way for end users to select a theme for their current session. Of course, we have not yet examined how to build stateful web applications, so the current theme selection will be forgotten between postbacks. In a production-level site, you may wish to store the user's current theme selection within a session variable or persist the theme selection to a database.

Although we really have not examined the use of session variables at this point in the text, to illustrate how to assign a theme programmatically, update the UI of your `Default.aspx` file with three new `Buttons` as shown in Figure 34-23. Once you have done so, handle the `Click` event for each `Button`.

Figure 34-23. *The updated UI*

Now be aware that you can only assign a theme programmatically during specific phases of your page's life cycle. Typically, this will be done within the `Page_PreInit` event. This being said, update your code file as follows:

```
Partial Class _Default
  Inherits System.Web.UI.Page

  Protected Sub btnNoTheme_Click(ByVal sender As Object, _
  ByVal e As System.EventArgs) Handles btnNoTheme.Click
    ' Empty strings result in no theme being applied.
    Session("UserTheme") = ""
    ' Trigger the PreInit event again.
    Server.Transfer(Request.FilePath)
  End Sub

  Protected Sub btnGreenTheme_Click(ByVal sender As Object, _
  ByVal e As System.EventArgs) Handles btnGreenTheme.Click
    Session("UserTheme") = "BasicGreen"
    ' Trigger the PreInit event again.
    Server.Transfer(Request.FilePath)
  End Sub

  Protected Sub btnOrangeTheme_Click(ByVal sender As Object, _
  ByVal e As System.EventArgs) Handles btnOrangeTheme.Click
    Session("UserTheme") = "CrazyOrange"
    ' Trigger the PreInit event again.
    Server.Transfer(Request.FilePath)
  End Sub

  Protected Sub Page_PreInit(ByVal sender As Object, _
  ByVal e As System.EventArgs) Handles Me.PreInit
    Try
      Theme = Session("UserTheme").ToString()
    Catch
```

```
      ' Empty strings result in no theme being applied.
        Theme = ""
      End Try
    End Sub
End Class
```

Without getting too hung up on the notion of a "session variable" (see Chapter 35 for details), simply notice that we are storing a given theme within a session variable named UserTheme, which is formally assigned within the Page_PreInit() event handler. Also note that when the user clicks a given Button, we programmatically force the PreInit event to fire by calling Server.Transfer() and requesting the current page once again. If you were to run this page, you would now find that you can establish your theme via various Button clicks.

Source Code The FunWithThemes files are included under the Chapter 34 subdirectory.

Summary

This chapter examined how to make use of various ASP.NET web controls. We began by examining the role of the Control and WebControl base classes, and you came to learn how to dynamically interact with a panel's internal controls collection. Along the way, you were exposed to the new site navigation model (*.sitemap files and the SiteMapDataSource component), the new data binding engine (via the SqlDataSource component and the GridView type), and various validation controls.

The latter half of this chapter examined the role of master pages and themes. Recall that master pages can be used to define a common frame for a set of pages on your site. Also recall that the *.master file defines any number of "content placeholders" to which content pages plug in their custom UI content. Finally, as you were shown, the ASP.NET theme engine allows you to declaratively or programmatically apply a common UI look and feel to your widgets on the web server.

CHAPTER 35

ASP.NET State Management Techniques

The previous two chapters concentrated on the composition and behavior of ASP.NET pages and the web controls they contain. This chapter builds on that information by examining the role of the Global.asax file and the underlying HttpApplication type. As you will see, the functionality of HttpApplication allows you to intercept numerous events that enable you to treat your web applications as a cohesive unit, rather than a set of stand-alone *.aspx files.

In addition to investigating the HttpApplication type, this chapter also addresses the all-important topic of state management. Here you will learn the role of view state, session and application variables (including the *application cache*), as well as the ASP.NET profile API. As you will see, the profile API provides an out-of-the-box approach to persisting user data to a relational database.

The Issue of State

At the beginning of the Chapter 33, I pointed out that HTTP on the Web results in a *stateless* wire protocol. This very fact makes web development extremely different from the process of building an executable assembly. For example, when you are building a Windows Forms application, you can rest assured that any member variables defined in the Form-derived class will typically exist in memory until the user explicitly shuts down the form:

```
Public Class MainWindow
  ' State data!
  Private userFavoriteCar As String
End Class
```

In the world of the World Wide Web, however, you are not afforded the same luxurious assumption. To prove the point, create a new ASP.NET website named SimpleStateExample. Within the code-behind file of your initial *.aspx file, define a page-level string variable named userFavoriteCar:

```
Partial Class _Default
  Inherits System.Web.UI.Page
  ' Hmmm...State data?
  Private userFavoriteCar As String
End Class
```

Next, construct the web UI as shown in Figure 35-1.

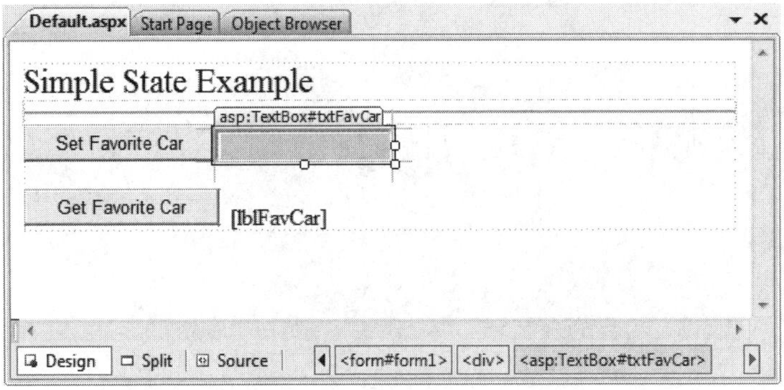

Figure 35-1. *The UI for the simple state page*

The server-side `Click` event handler for the Set button (named `btnSetCar`) will allow the user to assign the string member variable to the value within the `TextBox` (named `txtFavCar`):

```
Protected Sub btnSetCar_Click(ByVal sender As Object, _
  ByVal e As System.EventArgs) Handles btnSetCar.Click
  ' Store favorite car in member variable.
  userFavoriteCar = txtFavCar.Text
End Sub
```

while the `Click` event handler for the Get button (`btnGetCar`) will display the current value of the member variable within the page's `Label` widget (`lblFavCar`):

```
Protected Sub btnGetCar_Click(ByVal sender As Object, _
  ByVal e As System.EventArgs) Handles btnGetCar.Click
  ' Set label text to value of member variable.
  lblFavCar.Text = userFavoriteCar
End Sub
```

Now, if you were building a Windows Forms application, you would be right to assume that once the user sets the initial value, it would be remembered throughout the life of the window's application. Sadly, when you run this web application, you will find that each time you post back to the web server, the value of the `userFavoriteCar` string variable is set back to the initial empty value; therefore, the `Label`'s text is continuously empty.

Again, given that HTTP has no clue how to automatically remember data once the HTTP response has been sent, it stands to reason that the `Page` object is destroyed almost instantly. Therefore, when the client posts back to the `*.aspx` file, a new `Page` object is constructed that will reset any page-level member variables. This is clearly a major dilemma. Imagine how painful online shopping would be if every time you posted back to the web server, any and all information you previously entered (such as the items you wish to purchase) were discarded. When you wish to remember information regarding the users who are logged on to your site, you need to make use of various state management techniques.

■ Note This issue is in no way limited to ASP.NET. Java servlets, CGI applications, classic ASP, and PHP applications all must contend with the thorny issue of state management.

To remember the value of the userFavoriteCar string type between postbacks, one way to do so is to store data values within a *session variable*. You will examine the exact details of session state in the pages that follow. For the sake of completion, however, here are the necessary updates for the current page (note that you are no longer using the private String member variable, therefore feel free to comment out or remove the definition altogether):

```
Partial Class _Default
  Inherits System.Web.UI.Page
  Protected Sub btnSetCar_Click(ByVal sender As Object, _
    ByVal e As System.EventArgs) Handles btnSetCar.Click
    ' Store favorite car in session variable.
    Session("UserFavCar") = txtFavCar.Text
  End Sub

  Protected Sub btnGetCar_Click(ByVal sender As Object, _
    ByVal e As System.EventArgs) Handles btnGetCar.Click
    ' Set label text to value of session variable.
    lblFavCar.Text = CType(Session("UserFavCar"), String)
  End Sub
End Class
```

If you now run the application, the value of your favorite automobile will be preserved across postbacks, thanks to the HttpSessionState object manipulated indirectly by the inherited Session property. Of course, once the user terminates his or her session (by closing the web browser window) with your web application, session data is discarded. If you wish to persist user information beyond the current session, you can roll your own infrastructure to do so or make use of the ASP.NET profile API (explained at the conclusion of this chapter).

Source Code The SimpleStateExample project is included under the Chapter 35 subdirectory.

ASP.NET State Management Techniques

ASP.NET provides several mechanisms that you can use to maintain stateful information in your web applications. Specifically, you have the following options:

- Make use of ASP.NET view state.
- Make use of ASP.NET control state.
- Define application-level variables.
- Make use of the cache object.
- Define session-level variables.
- Define cookie data.

The one thing each of these approaches has in common is that they each demand that a given user is in session and that the web application is loaded into memory. As soon as a user logs off your site (or your website is shut down), your site is once again stateless. If you wish to persist user data in a permanent manner, ASP.NET provides an out-of-the-box profile API. We'll examine the details of each approach in turn, beginning with the topic of ASP.NET view state.

Understanding the Role of ASP.NET View State

The term *view state* has been thrown out numerous times here and in the previous two chapters without a formal definition, so let's demystify this term once and for all. Under classic (COM-based) ASP, web developers were required to manually repopulate the values of the incoming form widgets during the process of constructing the outgoing HTTP response. For example, if the incoming HTTP request contained five text boxes with specific values, the `*.asp` file required script code to extract the current values (via the `Form` or `QueryString` collections of the `Request` object) and manually place them back into the HTTP response stream (needless to say, this was a drag). If the developer failed to do so, the caller was presented with a set of five empty text boxes!

Under ASP.NET, we are no longer required to manually scrape out and repopulate the values contained within the HTML widgets because the ASP.NET runtime will automatically embed a hidden form field (named `__VIEWSTATE`), which will flow between the browser and a specific page. The data assigned to this field is a Base64-encoded string that contains a set of name/value pairs that represent the values of each GUI widget on the page at hand.

The `System.Web.UI.Page` base class's `Init` event handler is the entity in charge of reading the incoming values found within the `__VIEWSTATE` field to populate the appropriate member variables in the derived class (which is why it is risky at best to access the state of a web widget within the scope of a page's `Init` event handler).

Also, just before the outgoing response is emitted back to the requesting browser, the `__VIEWSTATE` data is used to repopulate the form's widgets, to ensure that the current values of the HTML widgets appear as they did prior to the previous postback.

Clearly, the best thing about this aspect of ASP.NET is that it just happens without any work on your part. Of course, you are always able to interact with, alter, or disable this default functionality if you so choose. To understand how to do this, let's see a concrete view state example.

Demonstrating View State

First, create a new ASP.NET web application called ViewStateApp. On your initial `*.aspx` page, add a single ASP.NET `ListBox` web control (named `myListBox`) and a single `Button` type (named `btnPostback`) to provide a way for the user to post back to the web server (there is no need to handle the `Click` event to do so).

Now, using the Visual Studio Properties window, access the `Items` property of the `ListBox` and add four `ListItems` to the `ListBox`. The resulting markup looks like this:

```
<asp:ListBox ID="myListBox" runat="server">
  <asp:ListItem>Item One</asp:ListItem>
  <asp:ListItem>Item Two</asp:ListItem>
  <asp:ListItem>Item Three</asp:ListItem>
  <asp:ListItem>Item Four</asp:ListItem>
</asp:ListBox>
```

Note that you are hard-coding the items in the `ListBox` directly within the `*.aspx` file. As you already know, all `<asp:>` definitions found within an HTML form will automatically render back their HTML representation before the final HTTP response (provided they have the `runat="server"` attribute).

The `<%@Page%>` directive at the top of the `*.aspx` file has an optional attribute called `EnableViewState` that by default is set to `true`. To disable this behavior, simply update the `<%@Page%>` directive as follows:

```
<%@ Page Language="VB" AutoEventWireup="false"
  CodeFile="Default.aspx.vb" Inherits="_Default"
  EnableViewState ="false"
%>
```

So, what exactly does it mean to disable view state? The answer is, it depends. Given the previous definition of the term, you would think that if you disable view state for an `*.aspx` file, the values within your `ListBox` would not be remembered between postbacks to the web server. However, if you were to run this application as is, you might be surprised to find that the information in the `ListBox` is retained regardless of how many times you post back to the page. In fact, if you examine the source HTML returned to the browser, you may be further surprised to see that the hidden `__VIEWSTATE` field is *still present*:

```
<input type="hidden" name="__VIEWSTATE" id="__VIEWSTATE"
 value="/wEPDwUKLTM4MTM2MDM4NGRkqGC6gjEV25JnddkJiRmoIc1OSIA=" />
```

The reason why the view state string is still visible is the fact that the `*.aspx` file has explicitly defined the `ListBox` items within the scope of the HTML `<form>` tags. Thus, the `ListBox` items will be autogenerated each time the web server responds to the client.

However, assume that your `ListBox` is dynamically populated within the code-behind file rather than within the HTML `<form>` definition. First, remove the `<asp:ListItem>` declarations from the current `*.aspx` file:

```
<asp:ListBox ID="myListBox" runat="server">
</asp:ListBox>
```

Next, fill the list items within the `Load` event handler within your code-behind file:

```
Protected Sub Page_Load(ByVal sender As Object, _
  ByVal e As System.EventArgs) Handles Me.Load
  If Not IsPostBack Then
    ' Fill ListBox dynamically!
    myListBox.Items.Add("Item One")
    myListBox.Items.Add("Item Two")
    myListBox.Items.Add("Item Three")
    myListBox.Items.Add("Item Four")
  End If
End Sub
```

If you post to this updated page, you will find that the first time the browser requests the page, the values in the `ListBox` are present and accounted for. However, on postback, the `ListBox` is suddenly empty. The first rule of ASP.NET view state is that its effect is only realized when you have widgets whose values are dynamically generated through code. If you hard-code values within the `*.aspx` file's `<form>` tags, the state of these items is retrieved from the markup across postbacks (even when you set `EnableViewState` to `false` for a given page).

Furthermore, view state is most useful when you have a dynamically populated web widget that always needs to be repopulated for each and every postback (such as an ASP.NET `GridView`, which is always filled using a database hit). If you did not disable view state for pages that contain such widgets, the entire state of the grid is represented within the hidden `__VIEWSTATE` field. Given that complex pages may contain numerous ASP.NET web controls, you can imagine how large this string would become. As the payload of the HTTP request/response cycle could become quite heavy, this may become a problem for the dial-up web surfers of the world. In cases such as these, you may find faster throughput if you disable view state for the page.

If the idea of disabling view state for the entire `*.aspx` file seems a bit too aggressive, do know that every descendent of the `System.Web.UI.Control` base class inherits the `EnableViewState` property, which makes it very simple to disable view state on a control-by-control basis:

```
<asp:GridView id="myHugeDynamicallyFilledDataGrid" runat="server"
 EnableViewState="false">
</asp:GridView>
```

Note ASP.NET pages reserve a small part of the __VIEWSTATE string for internal use. Given this, you will find that the __VIEWSTATE field will still appear in the client-side source even when the entire page (and all the controls) have disabled view state.

Adding Custom View State Data

In addition to the EnableViewState property, the System.Web.UI.Control base class also provides an inherited property named ViewState. Under the hood, this property provides access to a System.Web.UI.StateBag type, which represents all the data contained within the __VIEWSTATE field. Using the indexer of the StateBag type, you can embed custom information within the hidden __VIEWSTATE form field using a set of name/value pairs. Here's a simple example:

```
Protected Sub btnAddToVS_Click(ByVal sender As Object, _
  ByVal e As System.EventArgs) Handles btnAddToVS.Click
  ViewState("CustomViewStateItem") = "Some user data"
  lblVSValue.Text = CType(ViewState("CustomViewStateItem"), String)
End Sub
```

Because the System.Web.UI.StateBag type has been designed to operate on any System.Object, when you wish to access the value of a given key, you should explicitly cast it into the correct underlying data type (in this case, a System.String). Be aware, however, that values placed within the __VIEWSTATE field cannot literally be any object. Specifically, the only valid types are Strings, Integers, Booleans, ArrayLists, Hashtables, or an array of these types.

So, given that *.aspx pages may insert custom bits of information into the __VIEWSTATE string, the next logical question is when you would want to do so. Most of the time, custom view state data is best suited for user-specific preferences. For example, you may establish a point of view state data that specifies how a user wishes to view the UI of a GridView (such as a sort order).

View state data is not well suited for full-blown user data, such as items in a shopping cart, cached DataSets, or whatnot. When you need to store this sort of complex information, you are required to work with session or application data. Before we get to that point, you need to understand the role of the Global.asax file.

Source Code The ViewStateApp project is included under the Chapter 35 subdirectory.

A Brief Word Regarding Control State

Since the release of ASP.NET 2.0, a control's state data can now be persisted via *control state* rather than view state. This technique is most helpful if you have written a custom ASP.NET web control that must remember data between round-trips. While the ViewState property can be used for this purpose, if view state is disabled at a page level, the custom control is effectively broken. For this very reason, web controls now support a ControlState property.

Control state works identically to view state; however, it will not be disabled if view state is disabled at the page level. As mentioned, this feature is most useful for those who are developing custom web controls (a topic not covered in this text). Consult the .NET Framework 3.5 SDK documentation for further details.

The Role of the Global.asax File

At this point, an ASP.NET application may seem to be little more than a set of `*.aspx` files and their respective web controls. While you could build a web application by simply linking a set of related web pages, you will most likely need a way to interact with the web application as a whole. To this end, your ASP.NET web applications may choose to include an optional `Global.asax` file via the Web Site ➤ Add New Item menu option, as shown in Figure 35-2.

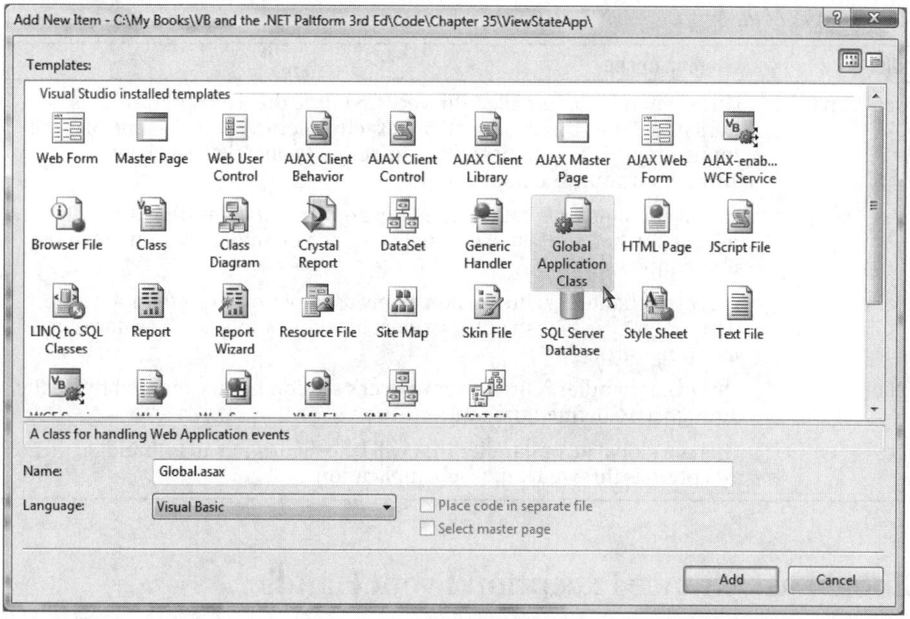

Figure 35-2. *The* `Global.asax` *file*

Simply put, `Global.asax` is just about as close to a traditional double-clickable `*.exe` as we can get in the world of ASP.NET; meaning this type represents the runtime behavior of the website itself. Once you insert a `Global.asax` file into a web project, you will notice it is little more than a `<script>` block containing a set of event handlers:

```
<%@ Application Language="VB" %>
<script runat="server">
Sub Application_Start(ByVal sender As Object, ByVal e As EventArgs)
End Sub

Sub Application_End(ByVal sender As Object, ByVal e As EventArgs)
End Sub

Sub Application_Error(ByVal sender As Object, ByVal e As EventArgs)
End Sub

Sub Session_Start(ByVal sender As Object, ByVal e As EventArgs)
End Sub

Sub Session_End(ByVal sender As Object, ByVal e As EventArgs)
End Sub
</script>
```

Looks can be deceiving, however. At runtime, the code within this <script> block is assembled into a class type deriving from System.Web.HttpApplication. If you have a background in ASP.NET 1.*x*, you may recall that the Global.asax code-behind file literally did define a class deriving from HttpApplication.

As mentioned, the members defined inside Global.asax are event handlers that allow you to interact with application-level (and session-level) events. Table 35-1 documents the role of each member.

Table 35-1. *Core Types of the* System.Web *Namespace*

Event Handler	Meaning in Life
Application_Start()	This event handler is called the very first time the web application is launched. Thus, this event will fire exactly once over the lifetime of a web application. This is an ideal place to define application-level data used throughout your web application.
Application_End()	This event handler is called when the application is shutting down. This will occur when the last user times out or if you manually shut down the application via IIS.
Session_Start()	This event handler is fired when a new user logs on to your application. Here you may establish any user-specific data points (such as items in a shopping cart).
Session_End()	This event handler is fired when a user's session has terminated (typically through a predefined timeout).
Application_Error()	This is a global error handler that will be called when an unhandled exception is thrown by the web application.

The Global Last Chance Exception Event Handler

First, let me point out the role of the Application_Error() event handler. Recall that a specific page may handle the Error event to process any unhandled exception that occurred within the scope of the page itself. In a similar light, the Application_Error() event handler is the final place to handle an exception that was not handled by a given page. As with the page-level Error event, you are able to access the specific System.Exception using the inherited Server property:

```
Sub Application_Error(ByVal sender As Object, ByVal e As EventArgs)
  ' Obtain the unhandled error.
  Dim ex As Exception = Server.GetLastError()

  ' Process error here...

  ' Clear error when finished.
  Server.ClearError()
End Sub
```

Given that the Application_Error() event handler is the last-chance exception handler for your web application, it is quite common to implement this method in such a way that the user is transferred to a predefined error page on the server. Other common duties may include sending an e-mail to the web administrator (via the types within the System.Web.Mail namespace), writing to an external error log, or what have you.

The HttpApplication Base Class

As mentioned, the `Global.asax` script is dynamically generated into a class deriving from the `System.Web.HttpApplication` base class, which supplies the same sort of functionality as the `System.Web.UI.Page` type. Table 35-2 documents the key members of interest.

Table 35-2. *Key Members Defined by the* `System.Web.HttpApplication` *Type*

Property	Meaning in Life
`Application`	This property allows you to interact with application-level variables (via the underlying `HttpApplicationState` object).
`Request`	This property allows you to interact with the incoming HTTP request (via the underlying `HttpRequest` object).
`Response`	This property allows you to interact with the incoming HTTP response (via the underlying `HttpResponse` object).
`Server`	This property gets the intrinsic server object for the current request (via the underlying `HttpServerUtility` object).
`Session`	This property allows you to interact with session-level variables (via the underlying `HttpSessionState` object).

Again, given that the `Global.asax` file does not explicitly document that `HttpApplication` is the underlying base class, it is important to remember that all of the rules of the "is-a" relationship do indeed apply. For example, if you were to apply the dot operator to the `MyBase` keyword within any of the members within `Global.asax`, you would find you have immediate access to all members of the chain of inheritance, as you see in Figure 35-3.

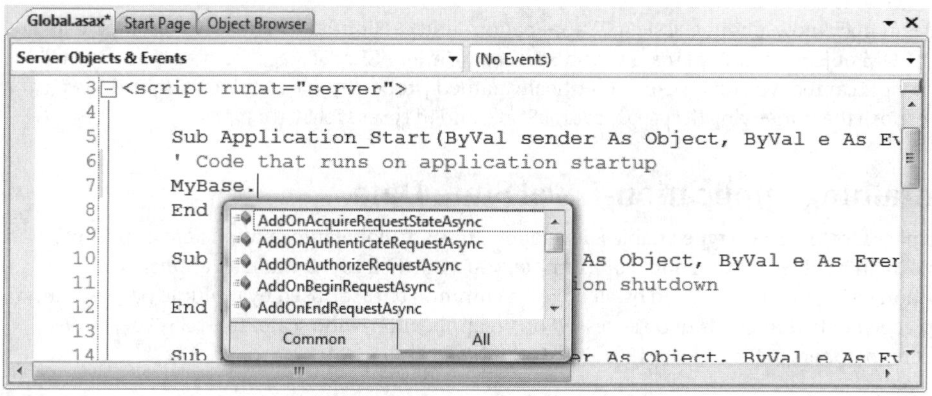

Figure 35-3. *Remember that* `HttpApplication` *is the parent of the type lurking within* `Global.asax`.

Understanding the Application/Session Distinction

Under ASP.NET, application state is maintained by an instance of the `HttpApplicationState` type. This class enables you to share global information across all users (and all pages) who are logged on to your ASP.NET application. Not only can application data be shared by all users on your site, but also if the value of an application-level data point changes, the new value is seen by all users on their next postback.

On the other hand, session state is used to remember information for a specific user (again, such as items in a shopping cart). Physically, a user's session state is represented by the `HttpSessionState` class type. When a new user logs on to an ASP.NET web application, the runtime will automatically assign that user a new session ID, which by default will expire after 20 minutes of inactivity. Thus, if 20,000 users are logged on to your site, you have 20,000 distinct `HttpSessionState` objects, each of which is automatically assigned a unique session ID. The relationship between a web application and web sessions is shown in Figure 35-4.

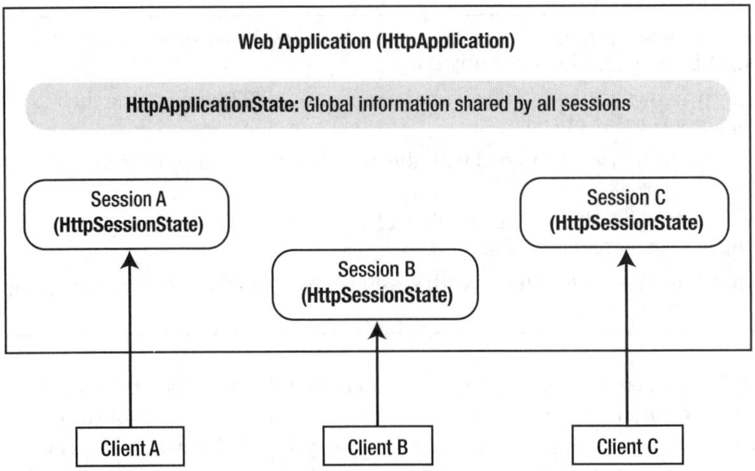

Figure 35-4. *The application/session state distinction*

As you may know, under classic ASP, application- and session-state data is represented using distinct COM objects (e.g., `Application` and `Session`). Under ASP.NET, `Page`-derived types as well as the `HttpApplication` type make use of identically named properties (i.e., `Application` and `Session`), which expose the underlying `HttpApplicationState` and `HttpSessionState` types.

Maintaining Application-Level State Data

The `HttpApplicationState` type enables developers to share global information across multiple sessions in an ASP.NET application. For example, you may wish to maintain an application-wide connection string that can be used by all pages, a common `DataSet` used by multiple pages, or any other piece of data that needs to be accessed on an application-wide scale. Table 35-3 describes some core members of the `HttpApplicationState` object.

Table 35-3. *Members of the* `HttpApplicationState` *Type*

Member	Meaning in Life
`AllKeys`	This property returns an array of `System.String` objects that represent all the names in the `HttpApplicationState` type.
`Count`	This property gets the number of item objects in the `HttpApplicationState` object.
`Add()`	This method allows you to add a new name/value pair into the `HttpApplicationState` object . Do note that this method is typically *not* used in favor of the indexer of the `HttpApplicationState` class.
`Clear()`	This method deletes all items in the `HttpApplicationState` object. This is functionally equivalent to the `RemoveAll()` method.

Member	Meaning in Life
Lock() Unlock()	These two methods are used when you wish to alter a set of application variables in a thread-safe manner.
RemoveAll() Remove() RemoveAt()	The RemoveAll() and Remove() methods remove a specific item (by string name) within the HttpApplicationState object. RemoveAt() removes the item via a numerical indexer.

To illustrate working with application state, create a new ASP.NET web application named AppState and insert a new Global.asax file. When you create data members that can be shared among all active sessions, you need to establish a set of name/value pairs. In most cases, the most natural place to do so is within the Application_Start() event handler of the HttpApplication-derived type, for example:

```
Sub Application_Start(ByVal sender As Object, ByVal e As EventArgs)
  ' Set up some application variables.
  Application("SalesPersonOfTheMonth") = "Chucky"
  Application("CurrentCarOnSale") = "Colt"
  Application("MostPopularColorOnLot") = "Black"
End Sub
```

During the lifetime of your web application (which is to say, until the web application is manually shut down or until the final user times out), any user (on any page) may access these values as necessary. Assume you have a page that will display the current discount car within a Label via a button's Click event handler:

```
Protected Sub btnShowCarOnSale_Click(ByVal sender As Object, _
  ByVal e As System.EventArgs) Handles btnShowCarOnSale.Click
    ' Get current sales item.
    lblCurrCarOnSale.Text = String.Format("Sale on {0}'s today!", _
    CType(Application("CurrentCarOnSale"), String))
End Sub
```

Like the ViewState property, notice how you should cast the value returned from the HttpApplicationState object into the correct underlying type as the Application property operates on general System.Object types.

Now, given that the HttpApplicationState type can hold any type, it should stand to reason that you can place custom types (or any .NET type) within your site's application state. Assume you would rather maintain the three current application variables within a strongly typed class named CarLotInfo, which is defined in a new VB class file named CarLotInfo.vb.

```
Public Class CarLotInfo
  Public Sub New(ByVal sPerson As String, _
    ByVal saleCar As String, ByVal popularColor As String)
    salesPersonOfTheMonth = sPerson
    currentCarOnSale = saleCar
    mostPopularColorOnLot = popularColor
  End Sub

  ' Public for easy access.
  Public salesPersonOfTheMonth As String
  Public currentCarOnSale As String
  Public mostPopularColorOnLot As String
End Class
```

With this helper class in place, you could modify the Application_Start() event handler as follows:

```
Sub Application_Start(ByVal sender As Object, ByVal e As EventArgs)
  ' Place a custom object in the application data sector.
  Application("CarSiteInfo") = _
    New CarLotInfo("Chucky", "Colt", "Black")
End Sub
```

and then access the information using the public field data within a server-side `Click` event handler for a `Button` type named `btnShowAppVariables`:

```
Protected Sub btnShowAppVariables_Click(ByVal sender As Object, _
  ByVal e As System.EventArgs) Handles btnShowAppVariables.Click
  ' Get object from application variable.
  Dim appVars As CarLotInfo = _
  CType(Application("CarSiteInfo"), CarLotInfo)

  Dim appState As String = _
  String.Format("<li>Car on sale: {0}</li>", _
  appVars.currentCarOnSale)

  appState &= _
    String.Format("<li>Most popular color: {0}</li>", _
    appVars.mostPopularColorOnLot)

  appState &= _
    String.Format("<li>Big shot SalesPerson: {0}</li>", _
    appVars.salesPersonOfTheMonth)
  lblAppVariables.Text = appState
End Sub
```

Given that the current car-on-sale data is now exposed from a custom class type, your `btnShowCarOnSale` `Click` event handler would also need to be updated like so:

```
Protected Sub btnShowCarOnSale_Click(ByVal sender As Object, _
ByVal e As System.EventArgs) Handles btnShowCarOnSale.Click
  lblCurrCarOnSale.Text = String.Format("Sale on {0}'s today!", _
  CType(Application("CarSiteInfo"), CarLotInfo).currentCarOnSale)
End Sub
```

If you were now to run this page, you would find that a list of each application variable is displayed on the page's `Label` types, as displayed in Figure 35-5.

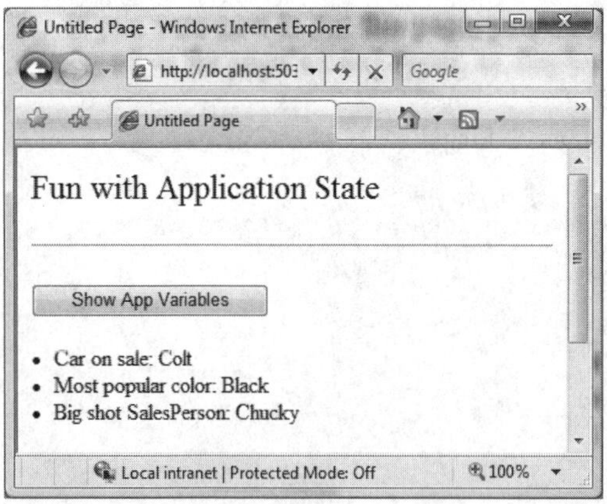

Figure 35-5. *Displaying application data*

Modifying Application Data

You may programmatically update or delete any or all members using members of the HttpApplicationState object during the execution of your web application. For example, to delete a specific item, simply call the Remove() method. If you wish to destroy all application-level data, call RemoveAll():

```
Private Sub CleanAppData()
  ' Remove a single item via string name.
  Application.Remove("SomeItemIDontNeed")

  ' Destroy all application data!
  Application.RemoveAll()
End Sub
```

If you wish to simply change the value of an existing application-level variable, you only need to make a new assignment to the data item in question. Assume your page now supports a new Button that allows your user to change the current hotshot salesperson by reading in a value from a TextBox named txtNewSP. The Click event handler is as you would expect:

```
Protected Sub btnSetNewSP_Click(ByVal sender As Object, _
  ByVal e As System.EventArgs) Handles btnSetNewSP.Click
  ' Set the new Salesperson.
  CType(Application("CarSiteInfo"), CarLotInfo).salesPersonOfTheMonth _
    = txtNewSP.Text
End Sub
```

If you run the web application, you will find that the application-level variable has been updated. Furthermore, given that application variables are accessible from all user sessions, if you were to launch three or four instances of your web browser, you would find that if one instance changes the current hotshot salesperson, each of the other browsers displays the new value on postback.

Understand that if you have a situation where a set of application-level variables must be updated as a unit, you risk the possibility of data corruption (given that it is technically possible that an application-level data point may be changed while another user is attempting to access it!). While you could take the long road and manually lock down the logic using threading primitives of the System.Threading namespace, the HttpApplicationState type has two methods, Lock() and Unlock(), that automatically ensure thread safety:

```
' Safely access related application data.
Application.Lock()
Application("SalesPersonOfTheMonth") = "Maxine"
Application("CurrentBonusedEmployee") = Application("SalesPersonOfTheMonth")
Application.Unlock()
```

■ **Note** Much like the VB SyncLock statement, if an exception occurs after the call to Lock() but before the call to Unlock(), the lock will automatically be released.

Handling Web Application Shutdown

The HttpApplicationState type is designed to maintain the values of the items it contains until one of two situations occurs: the last user on your site times out (or manually logs out) or someone manually shuts down the website via IIS. In each case, the Application_End() method of the

HttpApplication-derived type will automatically be called. Within this event handler, you are able to perform whatever sort of cleanup code is necessary:

```
Sub Application_End(ByVal sender As Object, ByVal e As EventArgs)
  ' Write current application variables
  ' to a database or whatever else you need to do...
End Sub
```

■ **Source Code** The AppState project is included under the Chapter 35 subdirectory.

Working with the Application Cache

ASP.NET provides a second and more flexible manner to handle application-wide data. As you recall, the values within the HttpApplicationState object remain in memory as long as your web application is alive and kicking. Sometimes, however, you may wish to maintain a piece of application data only for a specific period of time. For example, you may wish to obtain an ADO.NET DataSet that is valid for only five minutes. After that time, you may want to obtain a fresh DataSet to account for possible database updates. While it is technically possible to build this infrastructure using HttpApplicationState and some sort of handcrafted monitor, your task is greatly simplified using the ASP.NET application cache.

As suggested by its name, the ASP.NET System.Web.Caching.Cache object (which is accessible via the Context.Cache property) allows you to define an object that is accessible by all users (from all pages) for a fixed amount of time. In its simplest form, interacting with the cache looks identical to interacting with the HttpApplicationState object:

```
' Add an item to the cache.
' This item will *not* expire.
Context.Cache("SomeStringItem") = "This is the string item"

' Get item from the cache.
Dim s As String = CType(Context.Cache("SomeStringItem"), String)
```

■ **Note** If you wish to access the Cache from within Global.asax, you are required to use the Context property. However, if you are within the scope of a System.Web.UI.Page-derived type, you can make use of the Cache object directly.

Now, understand that if you have no interest in automatically updating (or removing) an application-level data point (as seen here), the Cache object is of little benefit, as you can directly use the HttpApplicationState type. However, when you do wish to have a data point destroyed after a fixed point of time—and optionally be informed when this occurs—the Cache type is extremely helpful.

The System.Web.Caching.Cache class defines only a small number of members beyond the type's indexer. For example, the Add() method can be used to insert a new item into the cache that is not currently defined (if the specified item is already present, Add() does nothing). The Insert() method will also place a member into the cache. If, however, the item is currently defined, Insert() will replace the current item with the new object. Given that this is most often the behavior you will desire, I'll focus on the Insert() method exclusively.

Fun with Data Caching

Let's see an example. To begin, create a new ASP.NET web application named CacheState, insert a Global.asax file, and add a reference to the AutoLotDAL.dll assembly you created in Chapter 22. Like an application-level variable maintained by the HttpApplicationState type, the Cache may hold any System.Object-derived type and is often populated within the Application_Start() event handler.

For this example, the goal is to automatically update the contents of a DataTable every 15 seconds. The DataTable in question will contain the current set of records from the Inventory table of the AutoLot database created in Chapter 22. Given these stats, update your Global class type like so (code analysis to follow):

```
<%@ Application Language="VB" %>
<%@ Import Namespace = "System.Data" %>
<%@ Import Namespace = "AutoLotConnectedLayer" %>

<script runat="server">
  ' Define a shared Cache member variable.
  Shared theCache As Cache
  Shared cnStr As String

  Sub Application_Start(ByVal sender As Object, ByVal e As EventArgs)
    ' First assign the shared "theCache" variable.
    theCache = Context.Cache

    ' Connection string.
    cnStr = "Data Source=(local)\SQLEXPRESS;" & _
            "Initial Catalog=AutoLot;Integrated Security=True"

    ' Add a DataTable to the cache via a helper function.
    AddDataTableToCache()
  End Sub

  Shared Sub AddDataTableToCache()
    ' When the application starts up,
    ' read the current records in the
    ' Inventory table of the AutoLot DB.
    Dim dal As New InventoryDAL()
    dal.OpenConnection(cnStr)
    Dim theCars As DataTable = dal.GetAllInventory()
    dal.CloseConnection()

    ' Now store DataTable in the cache.
    theCache.Insert("AppDataTable", _
      theCars, _
      Nothing, _
      DateTime.Now.AddSeconds(15), _
      Cache.NoSlidingExpiration, _
      CacheItemPriority.Default, _
      New CacheItemRemovedCallback(AddressOf UpdateCarInventory))
  End Sub

  ' The target for the CacheItemRemovedCallback delegate.
  Shared Sub UpdateCarInventory(ByVal key As String, ByVal item As Object, _
    ByVal reason As CacheItemRemovedReason)
```

```
    Dim dal As New InventoryDAL()
    dal.OpenConnection(cnStr)
    Dim theCars As DataTable = dal.GetAllInventory()
    dal.CloseConnection()

    ' Now store DataTable in the cache.
    theCache.Insert("AppDataTable", _
      theCars, _
      Nothing, _
      DateTime.Now.AddSeconds(15), _
      Cache.NoSlidingExpiration, _
      CacheItemPriority.Default, _
      New CacheItemRemovedCallback(AddressOf UpdateCarInventory))
  End Sub
...
</script>
```

First, notice that the Global script section has defined a shared Cache member variable. The reason is that you have defined two shared methods (AddDataTableToCache() and UpdateCarInventory()) and each method needs access to the Cache (recall that shared members do not have access to inherited members, therefore you can't use the Context property!).

Inside the Application_Start() event handler, you fill a DataTable and place the object within the application cache via a call to AddDataTableToCache(). As you would guess, the Context.Cache.Insert() method has been overloaded a number of times. Here, you supply a value for each possible parameter. Consider the following commented call to Insert():

```
' Note! It is a syntax error to have comments after a line
' continuation character, but this is the cleanest way to show each param!
theCache.Insert("AppDataTable", _ ' Name used to identify item in the cache.
  theCars, _                      ' Object to put in the cache.
  Nothing, _                      ' Any dependencies for this object?
  DateTime.Now.AddSeconds(15), _  ' How long item will be in cache.
  Cache.NoSlidingExpiration, _    ' Fixed or sliding time?
  CacheItemPriority.Default, _    ' Priority level of cache item.
  ' Delegate for CacheItemRemoved event
  New CacheItemRemovedCallback(UpdateCarInventory))
```

The first two parameters simply make up the name/value pair of the item. The third parameter allows you to define a CacheDependency object (which is Nothing in this case).

■ Note The ability to define a CacheDependency type is quite interesting. For example, you could establish a dependency between a member and an external file. If the contents of the file were to change, the type can be automatically updated. Check out the .NET Framework 3.5 SDK documentation for further details.

The next two parameters are used to define the amount of time the item will be allowed to remain in the application cache and its level of priority. Here, you specify the read-only Cache.NoSlidingExpiration field, which informs the cache that the specified time limit (15 seconds) is absolute.

Finally, and most important for this example, you create a new CacheItemRemovedCallback delegate type, and pass in the address of the method to call when the item is purged from the cache. As you can see from the signature of the UpdateCarInventory() method, the CacheItemRemovedCallback delegate can only call methods that match the following signature:

```
Shared Sub UpdateCarInventory(ByVal key As String, ByVal item As Object, _
  ByVal reason As CacheItemRemovedReason)
...
End Sub
```

So, at this point, when the application starts up, the DataTable is populated and cached. Every 15 seconds, the DataTable is purged, updated, and reinserted into the cache. To see the effects of doing this, you need to create a Page that allows for some degree of user interaction.

Modifying the *.aspx File

Update the UI of your initial *.aspx file as shown in Figure 35-6.

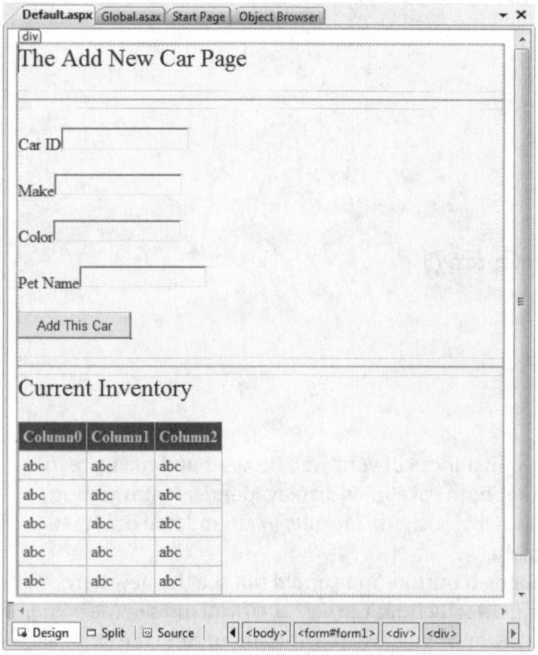

Figure 35-6. *The cache application GUI*

In the page's Load event handler, configure your GridView to display the current contents of the cached DataSet the first time the user posts to the page (be sure to import the System.Data and System.Data.SqlClient namespaces within your *.vb code file):

```
Protected Sub Page_Load(ByVal sender As Object, _
  ByVal e As System.EventArgs) Handles Me.Load
  If Not IsPostBack Then
    carsGridView.DataSource = CType(Cache("AppDataTable"), DataTable)
    carsGridView.DataBind()
  End If
End Sub
```

In the Click event handler of the Add This Car button, insert the new record into the Cars database using an ADO.NET SqlCommand object. Once the record has been inserted, call a helper function named RefreshGrid(), which will update the UI (don't forget to import the System.Data and AutoLotConnectedLayer namespaces). Here are the methods in question:

```
Partial Class _Default
  Inherits System.Web.UI.Page

  Private cnStr As String = "Data Source=(local)\SQLEXPRESS;" & _
    "Initial Catalog=AutoLot;Integrated Security=True"

  Protected Sub btnAddCar_Click(ByVal sender As Object, _
                               ByVal e As EventArgs) Handles btnAddCar.Click
    ' Update the Inventory table
    ' and call RefreshGrid().
    Dim dal As New InventoryDAL()
    dal.OpenConnection(cnStr)

    dal.InsertAuto(Integer.Parse(txtCarID.Text), txtCarColor.Text, _
                   txtCarMake.Text, txtCarPetName.Text)
    dal.CloseConnection()
    RefreshGrid()
  End Sub

  Private Sub RefreshGrid()
    ' Populate grid.
    Dim dal As New InventoryDAL()
    dal.OpenConnection(cnStr)
    Dim theCars As DataTable = dal.GetAllInventory()
    carsGridView.DataSource = theCars
    carsGridView.DataBind()
    dal.CloseConnection()
  End Sub
...
End Class
```

Now, to test the use of the cache, launch two instances of your web browser and navigate to this *.aspx page. At this point, you should see that both DataGrids display identical information. From one instance of the browser, add a new Car. Obviously, this results in an updated GridView viewable from the browser that initiated the postback.

In the second browser instance, click the Refresh button. You should not see the new item, given that the Page_Load event handler is reading directly from the cache. (If you did see the value, the 15 seconds had already expired. Either type faster or increase the amount of time the DataTable will remain in the cache.) Wait a few seconds and click the Refresh button from the second browser instance one more time. Now you should see the new item, given that the DataTable in the cache has expired and the CacheItemRemovedCallback delegate target method has automatically updated the cached DataSet.

As you can see, the major benefit of the Cache type is that you can ensure that when a member is removed, you have a chance to respond. In this example, you certainly could avoid using the Cache and simply have the Page_Load() event handler always read directly from the AutoLot database. Nevertheless, the point should be clear: the cache allows you to automatically refresh data using the cache mechanism.

■ **Note** Unlike the HttpApplicationState type, the Cache class does not support the Lock() and Unlock() methods. If you need to update interrelated items, you will need to directly make use of the types within the System.Threading namespace or the VB SyncLock keyword.

Source Code The CacheState project is included under the Chapter 35 subdirectory.

Maintaining Session Data

So much for our examination of application-level and cached data. Next, let's check out the role of per-user data stores. As mentioned earlier, a *session* is little more than a given user's interaction with a web application, which is represented via a unique HttpSessionState object. To maintain stateful information for a particular user, the HttpApplication-derived type and any System.Web.UI.Page-derived types may access the Session property. The classic example of the need to maintain per-user data would be an online shopping cart. Again, if ten people all log on to an online store, each individual will maintain a unique set of items that she (may) intend to purchase.

When a new user logs on to your web application, the .NET runtime will automatically assign the user a unique session ID, which is used to identify the user in question. Each session ID is assigned a custom instance of the HttpSessionState type to hold on to user-specific data. Inserting or retrieving session data is syntactically identical to manipulating application data, for example:

```
' Add/retrieve a session variable for current user.
Session("DesiredCarColor") = "Green"
Dim color As String = CType(Session("DesiredCarColor"), String)
```

The HttpApplication-derived type allows you to intercept the beginning and end of a session via the Session_Start() and Session_End() event handlers. Within Session_Start(), you can freely create any per-user data items, while Session_End() allows you to perform any work you may need to do when the user's session has terminated:

```
<%@ Application Language="VB" %>
<script runat="server">
...
  Sub Session_Start(ByVal sender As Object, ByVal e As EventArgs)
    ' Code that runs when a new session is started
  End Sub

  Sub Session_End(ByVal sender As Object, ByVal e As EventArgs)
    ' Code that runs when a session ends.

    ' Note: The Session_End event is raised
    ' only when the sessionstate mode
    ' is set to InProc in the web.config file.

    ' If session mode is set to StateServer
    ' or SQLServer, the event is not raised.
  End Sub
</script>
```

Note The code comments that are placed within the Session_End() event handler will make much more sense when we examine the role of the ASP.NET session state server later in this chapter.

Like the HttpApplicationState type, the HttpSessionState may hold any System.Object-derived type, including your custom classes. For example, assume you have a new web application

(SessionState) that defines a new class named `UserShoppingCart` within a file named `UserShoppingCart.vb`:

```
Public Class UserShoppingCart
  Public desiredCar As String
  Public desiredCarColor As String
  Public downPayment As Single
  Public isLeasing As Boolean
  Public dateOfPickUp As DateTime

  Public Overrides Function ToString() As String
    Return String.Format("Car: {0}<br>Color: {1}<br>" & _
      "$ Down: {2}<br>Lease: {3} <br>Pick-up Date: {4}", _
      desiredCar, desiredCarColor, downPayment, _
      isLeasing, dateOfPickUp.ToShortDateString())
  End Function
End Class
```

Next, add a `Global.asax` file into your current web application. Within the `Session_Start()` event handler, you can now assign each user a new instance of the `UserShoppingCart` class:

```
Sub Session_Start(ByVal sender As Object, ByVal e As EventArgs)
  Session("UserShoppingCartInfo") = New UserShoppingCart()
End Sub
```

As the user traverses your web pages, you are able to pluck out the `UserShoppingCart` instance and fill the fields with user-specific data. For example, assume you have a simple `*.aspx` page that defines a set of input widgets (specifically, three `TextBox` controls named `txtCarColor`, `txtCarMake`, and `txtDownPayment` as well as a `CheckBox` control named `chkIsLeasing`) that correspond to each field of the `UserShoppingCart` type. Also add a `Button` (named `btnSubmit`) to set the values and two `Labels` (named `lblUserID` and `lblUserInfo`) to display the user's session ID and session information (see Figure 35-7).

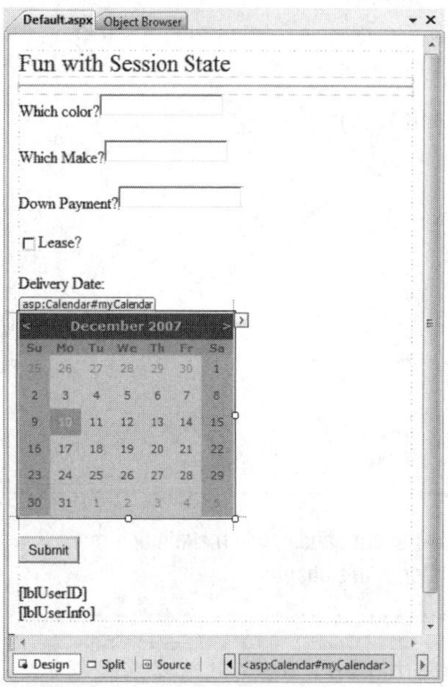

Figure 35-7. *The session application GUI*

The server-side Click event handler is straightforward (scrape out values from TextBoxes and display the shopping cart data on a Label type):

```
Partial Class _Default
  Inherits System.Web.UI.Page

  Protected Sub btnSubmit_Click(ByVal sender As Object, _
    ByVal e As System.EventArgs) Handles btnSubmit.Click
    ' Set current user prefs.
    Try
      Dim u As UserShoppingCart = _
        CType(Session("UserShoppingCartInfo"), UserShoppingCart)
      u.dateOfPickUp = myCalendar.SelectedDate
      u.desiredCar = txtCarMake.Text
      u.desiredCarColor = txtCarColor.Text
      u.downPayment = Single.Parse(txtDownPayment.Text)
      u.isLeasing = chkIsLeasing.Checked
      lblUserInfo.Text = u.ToString()
      Session("UserShoppingCartInfo") = u
    Catch ex As Exception
      lblUserInfo.Text = ex.Message
    End Try
  End Sub
End Class
```

Within Session_End(), you may wish to persist the fields of the UserShoppingCart to a database or whatnot (however, as you will see in the section "Understanding the ASP.NET Profile API" later in this chapter, the ASP.NET profile API will do so automatically).

In any case, if you were to launch two or three instances of your browser of choice, you would find that each user is able to build a custom shopping cart that maps to his or her unique instance of HttpSessionState.

Additional Members of HttpSessionState

The HttpSessionState class defines a number of other members of interest beyond the type indexer. First, the SessionID property will return the current user's unique ID. If you wish to view the automatically assigned session ID for this example, handle your Load event of your page as follows:

```
Protected Sub Page_Load(ByVal sender As Object, _
  ByVal e As System.EventArgs) Handles Me.Load
  If Not IsPostBack Then
    lblUserID.Text = String.Format("Here is your ID: {0}", _
      Session.SessionID)
  End If
End Sub
```

The Remove() and RemoveAll() methods may be used to clear items out of the user's instance of HttpSessionState:

```
Session.Remove("SomeItemWeDontNeedAnymore")
```

The HttpSessionState type also defines a set of members that control the expiration policy of the current session. Again, by default each user has 20 minutes of inactivity before the HttpSessionState object is destroyed. Thus, if a user enters your web application (and therefore obtains a unique session ID), but does not return to the site within 20 minutes, the runtime assumes the user is no longer interested and destroys all session data for that user. You are free to change this default 20-minute expiration value on a user-by-user basis using the `Timeout` property. The most common place to do so is within the scope of your `Global.Session_Start()` method:

```
Sub Session_Start(ByVal sender As Object, ByVal e As EventArgs)
  ' Each user has 5 minutes of inactivity.
  Session.Timeout = 5
  Session("UserShoppingCartInfo") = New UserShoppingCart()
End Sub
```

■Note If you do not need to tweak each user's `Timeout` value, you are able to alter the 20-minute default for all users via the `timeout` attribute of the `<sessionState>` element within the `web.config` file (examined at the end of this chapter).

The benefit of the `Session.Timeout` property is that you have the ability to assign specific timeout values discretely for each user. For example, imagine you have created a web application that allows users to pay cash for a given membership level. You may say that Gold members should time out within one hour, while Wood members should get only 30 seconds. This possibility begs the question, how can you remember user-specific information (such as the current membership level) across web visits? One possible answer is through the use of the `HttpCookie` type. (And speaking of cookies . . .)

■Source Code The SessionState project is included under the Chapter 35 subdirectory.

Understanding Cookies

The next state management technique examined here is the act of persisting data within a *cookie*, which is often realized as a text file (or set of files) on the user's machine. When a user logs on to a given site, the browser checks to see whether the user's machine has a cookie file for the URL in question and, if so, appends this data to the HTTP request.

The receiving server-side web page could then read the cookie data to create a GUI that may be based on the current user preferences. I am sure you've noticed that when you visit one of your favorite websites, it somehow "just knows" the sort of content you wish to see. The reason (in part) may have to do with a cookie stored on your computer that contains information relevant to a given website.

The exact location of your cookie files will depend on which browser you happen to be using. For those using Microsoft Internet Explorer on Windows XP, cookies are stored by default under C:\Documents and Settings*<loggedOnUser>*\Cookies. Vista users will find cookies stored under C:\Users*<loggedOnUser>*\AppData\Local\Microsoft\Windows\Temporary Internet Files, as shown in Figure 35-8.

The contents of a given cookie file will obviously vary among URLs, but keep in mind that they are ultimately text files. Thus, cookies are a horrible choice when you wish to maintain sensitive information about the current user (such as a credit card number, password, or whatnot). Even if you take the time to encrypt the data, a crafty hacker could possibly decrypt the value and use it for purely evil pursuits. In any case, cookies do play a role in the development of web applications, so let's check out how ASP.NET handles this particular state management technique.

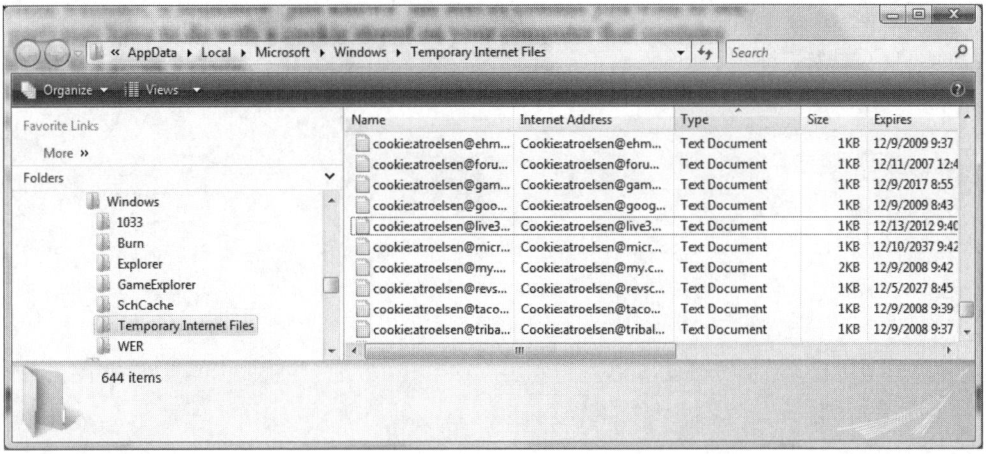

Figure 35-8. *Cookie data as persisted under Vista*

Creating Cookies

First of all, understand that ASP.NET cookies can be configured to be either persistent or temporary. A *persistent* cookie is typically regarded as the classic definition of cookie data, in that the set of name/value pairs is physically saved to the user's hard drive. *Temporary* cookies (also termed *session cookies*) contain the same data as a persistent cookie, but the name/value pairs are never saved to the user's machine; rather, they exist *only* within the HTTP header. Once the user logs off your site, all data contained within the session cookie is destroyed.

■ **Note** Most browsers support cookies of up to 4,096 bytes. Because of this size limit, cookies are best used to store small amounts of data, such as a user ID that can be used to identify the user and pull details from a database.

The `System.Web.HttpCookie` type is the class that represents the server side of the cookie data (persistent or temporary). When you wish to create a new cookie, you access the `Response.Cookies` property. Once the new `HttpCookie` object is inserted into the internal collection, the name/value pairs flow back to the browser within the HTTP header.

To check out cookie behavior firsthand, create a new ASP.NET web application (CookieStateApp) and create the UI displayed in Figure 35-9 (assume we have named the `Buttons` `btnNewCookie` and `btnShowCookie`, while the `TextBox` controls have been named `txtCookieName` and `txtCookieValue`).

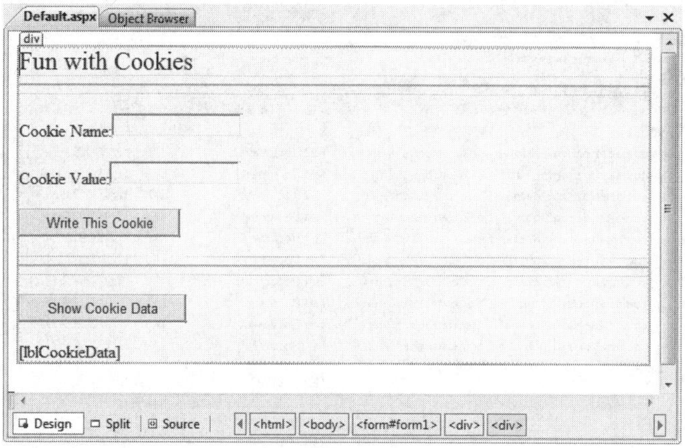

Figure 35-9. *The UI of CookieStateApp*

Within the `Button`'s `Click` event handler, build a new `HttpCookie` and insert it into the `Cookie` collection exposed from the `HttpRequest.Cookies` property. Be very aware that the data will not persist itself to the user's hard drive unless you explicitly set an expiration date using the `HttpCookie.Expires` property. Thus, the following implementation will create a temporary cookie that is destroyed when the user shuts down the browser:

```
Protected Sub btnNewCookie_Click(ByVal sender As Object, _
  ByVal e As System.EventArgs) Handles btnNewCookie.Click
  ' Make a new (temp) cookie.
  Dim theCookie As New HttpCookie(txtCookieName.Text, _
    txtCookieValue.Text)
  Response.Cookies.Add(theCookie)
End Sub
```

However, the following generates a persistent cookie that will expire on March 26, 2009:

```
Protected Sub btnNewCookie_Click(ByVal sender As Object, _
  ByVal e As System.EventArgs) Handles btnNewCookie.Click
  ' Make a new (persistent) cookie.
  Dim theCookie As New HttpCookie(txtCookieName.Text, _
    txtCookieValue.Text)
  theCookie.Expires = DateTime.Parse("03/26/2009")
  Response.Cookies.Add(theCookie)
End Sub
```

If you were to run this application and insert some cookie data, the browser would automatically persist this data to disk. When you open this text file saved under your cookie folder, you will see something similar to Figure 35-10.

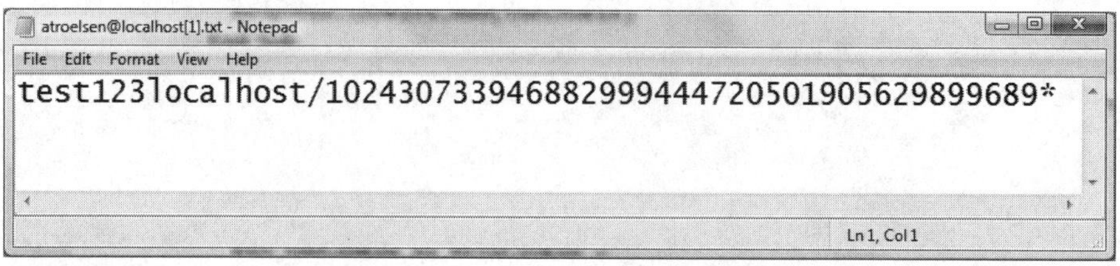

Figure 35-10. *The persistent cookie data*

Reading Incoming Cookie Data

Recall that the browser is the entity in charge of accessing persisted cookies when navigating to a previously visited page. To interact with the incoming cookie data under ASP.NET, access the `Request.Cookies` property. To illustrate, if you were to update your current UI with the means to obtain current cookie data via a `Button` widget, you could iterate over each name/value pair and present the information within a `Label` widget:

```
Protected Sub btnShowCookie_Click(ByVal sender As Object, _
  ByVal e As System.EventArgs) Handles btnShowCookie.Click
  Dim cookieData As String = ""
  For Each s As String In Request.Cookies
    cookieData &= String.Format _
      ("<li><b>Name</b>: {0}, <b>Value</b>: {1}</li>", _
      s, Request.Cookies(s).Value)
  Next
  lblCookieData.Text = cookieData
End Sub
```

If you now run the application and click your new button, you will find that the cookie data has indeed been sent by your browser (see Figure 35-11).

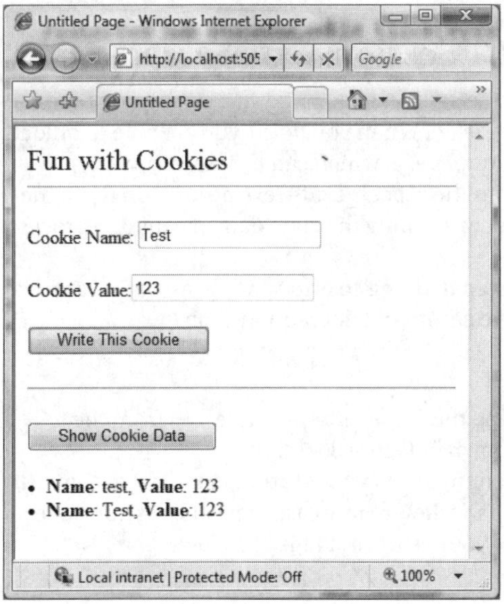

Figure 35-11. *Viewing cookie data*

Source Code The CookieStateApp project is included under the Chapter 35 subdirectory.

The Role of the <sessionState> Element

At this point in the chapter, you have examined numerous ways to remember information about your users. As you have seen, view state and application, cache, session, and cookie data are manipulated in more or less the same way (via a class indexer). As you have also seen, the HttpApplication type is often used to intercept and respond to events that occur during your web application's lifetime.

By default, ASP.NET will store session state using an in-process *.dll hosted by the ASP.NET worker process. Like any *.dll, the plus side is that access to the information is as fast as possible. However, the downside is that if this AppDomain crashes (for whatever reason), all of the user's state data is destroyed. Furthermore, when you store state data as an in-process *.dll, you cannot interact with a networked web farm. This default behavior is recorded in the <sessionState> element (nested within <system.web>) of your web.config file like so:

```
<sessionState
  mode="InProc"
  stateConnectionString="tcpip=127.0.0.1:42626"
  sqlConnectionString="data source=127.0.0.1;Trusted_Connection=yes"
  cookieless="false"
  timeout="20"
/>
```

This default mode of storage works just fine if your web application is hosted by a single web server. As you might guess, however, this model is not ideal for a farm of web servers, given that session state is "trapped" within a given AppDomain.

Storing Session Data in the ASP.NET Session State Server

Under ASP.NET, you can instruct the runtime to host the session state *.dll in a surrogate process named the ASP.NET session state server (aspnet_state.exe). When you do so, you are able to offload the *.dll from the ASP.NET worker process into a unique *.exe, which can be located on any machine within the web farm. Even if you intend to run the aspnet_state.exe process on the same machine as the web server, you do gain the benefit of partitioning the state data in a unique process (as it is more durable).

To make use of the session state server, the first step in doing so is to start the aspnet_state.exe Windows service on the target machine. To do so at the command line, simply type

```
net start aspnet_state
```

Alternatively, you can start aspnet_state.exe using the Services applet accessed from the Administrative Tools folder of the Control Panel, as shown in Figure 35-12.

The key benefit of this approach is that you can configure aspnet_state.exe to start automatically when the machine boots up using the Properties window. In any case, once the session state server is running, alter the <sessionState> element of your web.config file as follows:

```
<sessionState
  mode="StateServer"
  stateConnectionString="tcpip=127.0.0.1:42626"
  sqlConnectionString="data source=127.0.0.1;Trusted_Connection=yes"
  cookieless="false"
  timeout="20"
/>
```

Here, the mode attribute has been set to StateServer. That's it! At this point, the CLR will host session-centric data within aspnet_state.exe. In this way, if the AppDomain hosting the web application crashes, the session data is preserved. Notice as well that the <sessionState> element can also support a stateConnectionString attribute. The default TCP/IP address value (127.0.0.1) points to the local machine. If you would rather have the .NET runtime use the aspnet_state.exe service located on another networked machine (again, think web farms), you are free to update this value.

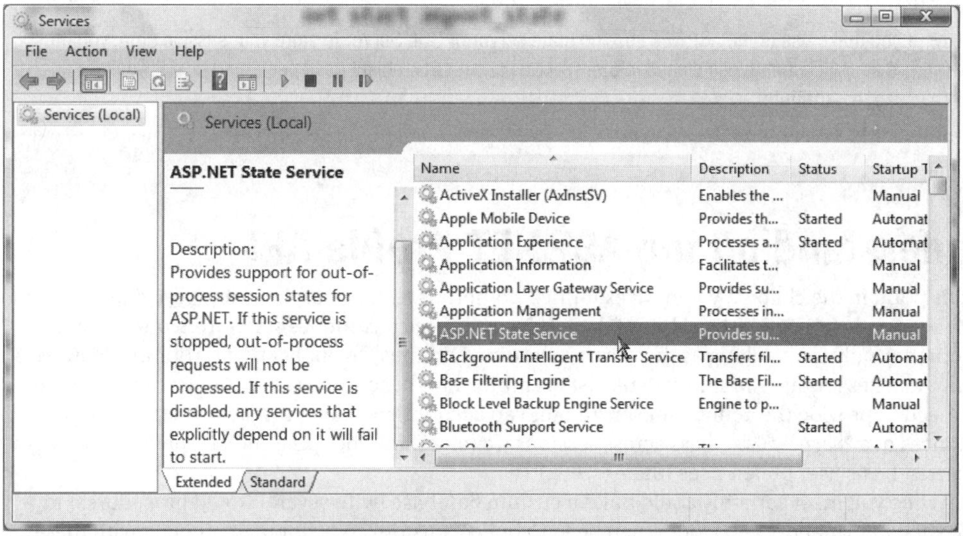

Figure 35-12. *The Services applet*

Storing Session Data in a Dedicated Database

Finally, if you require the highest degree of isolation and durability for your web application, you may choose to have the runtime store all your session state data within Microsoft SQL Server. The appropriate update to the `web.config` file is simple:

```
<sessionState
  mode="SQLServer"
  stateConnectionString="tcpip=127.0.0.1:42626"
  sqlConnectionString="data source=127.0.0.1;Trusted_Connection=yes"
  cookieless="false"
  timeout="20"
/>
```

However, before you attempt to run the associated web application, you need to ensure that the target machine (specified by the `sqlConnectionString` attribute) has been properly configured. When you install the .NET Framework 3.5 SDK (or Visual Studio), you will be provided with two files named `InstallSqlState.sql` and `UninstallSqlState.sql`, located by default under C:\Windows\Microsoft.NET\Framework\v2.0.50727 (this is true, regardless of whether you have installed .NET 3.0 or .NET 3.5). On the target machine, you must run the `InstallSqlState.sql` file using a tool such as the SQL Server Management Studio (which ships with Microsoft SQL Server).

Once this SQL script has executed, you will find a new SQL Server database has been created (ASPState) that contains a number of stored procedures called by the ASP.NET runtime and a set of tables used to store the session data itself (also, the tempdb database has been updated with a set of tables for swapping purposes). As you would guess, configuring your web application to store session data within SQL Server is the slowest of all possible options. The benefit is that user data is as durable as possible (even if the web server is rebooted).

■Note If you make use of the ASP.NET session state server or SQL Server to store your session data, you must make sure that any custom types placed in the `HttpSessionState` object have been marked with the `<Serializable>` attribute.

Understanding the ASP.NET Profile API

At this point in the chapter, you have examined numerous techniques that allow you to remember user-level and application-level bits of data. However, these techniques suffer from one major limitation: they only exist as long as the user is in session and the web application is running! However, many websites require the ability to persist user information across sessions. For example, perhaps you need to provide the ability for users to build an account on your site. Maybe you need to persist instances of a `ShoppingCart` class across sessions (for an online shopping site). Or perhaps you wish to persist basic user preferences (themes, etc.).

While you most certainly could build a custom database (with several stored procedures) to hold such information, you would then need to build a custom code library to interact with these database atoms. This is not necessarily a complex task, but the bottom line is that *you* are the individual in charge of building this sort of infrastructure. To help simplify matters, ASP.NET ships with an out-of-the box user profile management API and database system for this very purpose. In addition to providing the necessary infrastructure, the profile API also allows you to define the data to be persisted directly within your `web.config` file (for purposes of simplification); however, you are also able to persist any `<Serializable>` type. Before we get too far ahead of ourselves, let's check out where the profile API will be storing the specified data.

The ASPNETDB Database

Recall that every ASP.NET website built with Visual Studio automatically provides an App_Data subdirectory. By default, the profile API (as well as other services, such as the ASP.NET role membership provider) is configured to make use of a local SQL Server 2005 Express database named `ASPNETDB.mdf`, located within the App_Data folder. This default behavior is due to settings within the `machine.config` file for the .NET installation on your machine. In fact, when your code base makes use of any ASP.NET service requiring the App_Data folder, the `ASPNETDB.mdf` data file will be automatically created on the fly if a copy does not currently exist.

If you would rather have the ASP.NET runtime communicate with an `ASPNETDB.mdf` file located on another networked machine, or you would rather install this database on an instance of MS SQL Server 7.0 (or higher), you will need to manually build `ASPNETDB.mdf` using the `aspnet_regsql.exe` command-line utility. Like any good command-line tool, `aspnet_regsql.exe` provides numerous options; however, if you run the tool with no arguments using a Visual Studio 2008 command prompt:

```
aspnet_regsql
```

you will launch a GUI-based wizard to help walk you through the process of creating and installing `ASPNETDB.mdf` on your machine (and version of SQL Server) of choice.

Now, assuming your site is not making use of a local copy of the database under the App_Data folder, the final step is to update your `web.config` file to point to the unique location of your `ASPNETDB.mdf`. Assume you have installed `ASPNETDB.mdf` on a machine named ProductionServer. The following (partial) `web.config` file (for a website named ShoppingCart) could be used to instruct the profile API where to find the necessary database items:

```
<configuration>
  <connectionStrings>
    <add name="SqlServices"
         connectionString ="Data Source=ProductionServer;Integrated
         Security=SSPI;Initial Catalog=aspnetdb;"
         providerName="System.Data.SqlClient"/>
  </connectionStrings>
  <system.web>
    <profile defaultProvider ="SqlProvider">
      <providers>
        <clear/>
        <add name="AspNetSqlProfileProvider"
             connectionStringName="SqlServices"
             applicationName="ShoppingCart"
             type="System.Web.Profile.SqlProfileProvider, System.Web,
              Version=.0.0,
              Culture=neutral, PublicKeyToken=b03f5f7f11d50a3a" />
      </providers>
    </profile>
  </system.web>
</configuration>
```

Like most *.config files, it looks worse than it is. Basically we are defining a <connectionString> element with the necessary data, followed by a named instance of the SqlProfileProvider (this is the default provider used regardless of physical location of the ASPNETDB.mdf). If you require further information regarding this configuration syntax, be sure to check out the .NET Framework 3.5 SDK documentation.

Note For simplicity, I will be assuming that you will simply make use of the autogenerated ASPNETDB.mdf database located under your web application's App_Data subdirectory.

Defining a User Profile Within web.config

As mentioned, a user profile is defined within a web.config file. The really nifty aspect of this approach is that you can interact with this profile in a strongly typed manner in your VB code files using the Profile property. To illustrate this, create a new website named FunWithProfiles and open your web.config file for editing. Our goal is to make a profile that models the home address for a user as well as the total number of times they have posted to this site. Not surprisingly, profile data is defined within a <profile> element using a set of name/data type pairs. Consider the following profile, which is created within the scope of the <system.web> element:

```
<profile>
  <properties>
   <add name="StreetAddress" type="System.String" />
   <add name="City" type="System.String" />
   <add name="State" type="System.String" />
  </properties>
</profile>
```

Here, we have specified a name and CLR data type for each item in the profile (of course, we could add additional items for ZIP code, name, and so forth, but I am sure you get the idea). Strictly speaking, the type attribute is optional; however, the default is a System.String. As you would guess, there are many other attributes that can be specified in a profile entry to further qualify how this information should be persisted in ASPNETDB.mdf. Table 35-4 illustrates some of the core attributes.

Table 35-4. *Select Attributes of Profile Data*

Attribute	Example Values	Meaning in Life
name	String	A unique identifier for this property.
type	*Primitive* | *User-defined type*	A .NET primitive type or class. Class names must be fully qualified (e.g., MyApp.UserData.ColorPrefs).
serializeAs	String | Xml | Binary	Format of value when persisting in data store.
allowAnonymous	true | false	Restricts or allows anonymous access to this value. If set to false, anonymous users won't have access to this profile value.
provider	String	The provider used to manage this value. Overrides the defaultProvider setting in web.config or machine.config.
defaultValue	String	Value to return if property has not been explicitly set.
readOnly	true | false	Restricts or allows write access.

We will see some of these attributes in action as we modify the current profile. For now, let's see how to access this data programmatically from within our pages.

Accessing Profile Data Programmatically

Recall that the whole purpose of the ASP.NET profile API is to automate the process of writing data to (and reading data from) a dedicated database. To test this out for yourself, update the UI of your default.aspx file with a set of TextBoxes (and descriptive Labels) to gather the street address, city, and state of the user. As well, add a Button type (named btnSubmit) and a final Label (named lblUserData) that will be used to display the persisted data, as shown in Figure 35-13.

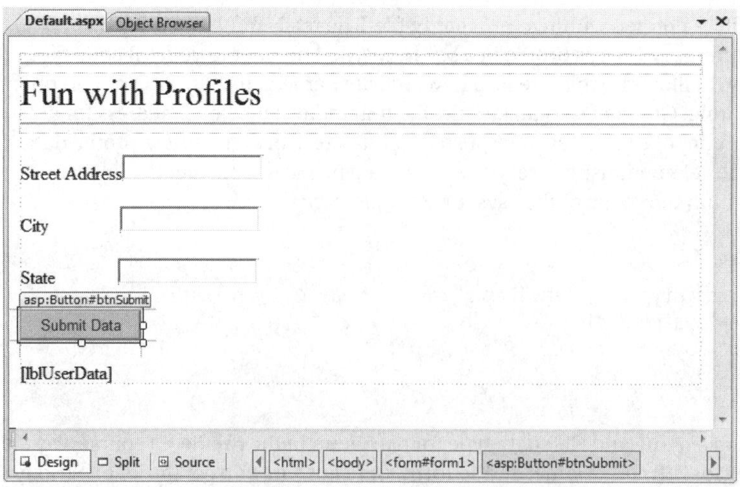

Figure 35-13. *The UI of the FunWithProfiles* default.aspx *page*

Now, within the `Click` event handler of the button, make use of the inherited `Profile` property to persist each point of profile data based on what the user has entered in the related `TextBox`. As you can see from Figure 35-14, Visual Studio 2008 will expose each bit of profile data as a strongly typed property. In effect, the `web.config` file has been used to define a custom structure!

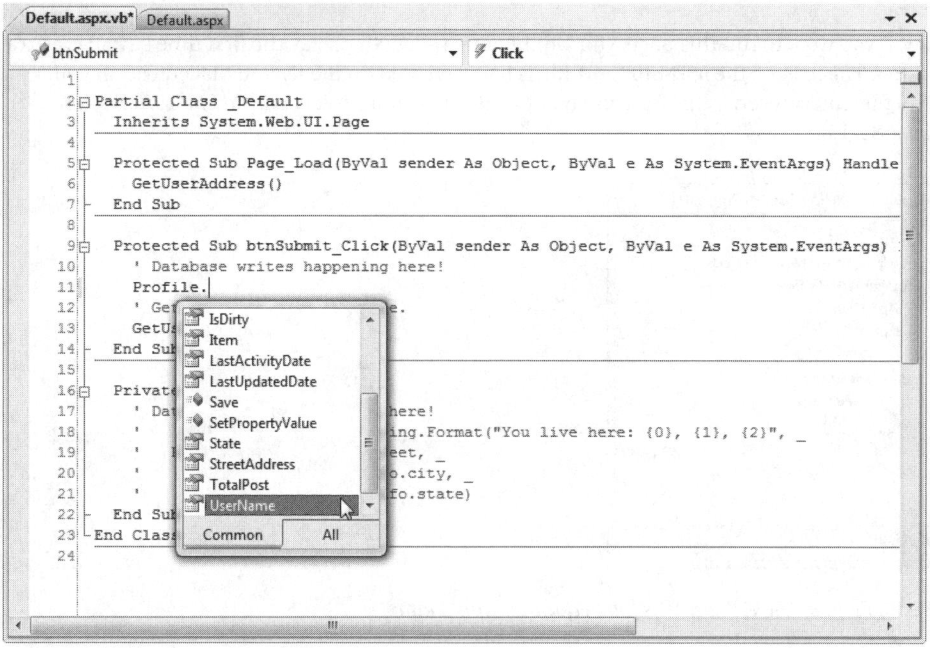

Figure 35-14. *Profile data is strongly typed*

Once you have persisted each piece of data within `ASPNETDB.mdf`, read each piece of data out of the database, and format it into a `String` that is displayed on the `lblUserData Label` type. Finally, handle the page's `Load` event, and display the same information on the `Label` type. In this way, when users come to the page, they can see their current settings. Here is the complete code file:

```
Partial Class _Default
  Inherits System.Web.UI.Page

  Protected Sub Page_Load(ByVal sender As Object, _
  ByVal e As System.EventArgs) Handles Me.Load
    GetUserAddress()
  End Sub

  Protected Sub btnSubmit_Click(ByVal sender As Object, _
  ByVal e As System.EventArgs) Handles btnSubmit.Click
    ' Database writes happening here!
    Profile.City = txtCity.Text
    Profile.StreetAddress = txtStreetAddress.Text
    Profile.State = txtState.Text

    ' Get settings from database.
    GetUserAddress()
  End Sub
```

```
  Private Sub GetUserAddress()
    ' Database reads happening here!
    lblUserData.Text = String.Format("You live here: {0}, {1}, {2}", _
      Profile.StreetAddress, Profile.City, Profile.State)
  End Sub
End Class
```

Now, if you were to run this page, you would notice a lengthy delay the first time Default.aspx is requested. The reason: the ASPNETDB.mdf file is being created on the fly and placed within your App_Data file. You can verify this for yourself by refreshing your project within Solution Explorer (see Figure 35-15).

Figure 35-15. *Behold!* ASPNETDB.mdf *is located under App_Data.*

You will also find that the first time you come to this page, the lblUserData Label does not display any profile data, as you have not yet entered your data into the correct table of ASPNETDB.mdf. Once you enter values in the TextBox controls and post back to the server, you will find this Label is formatted with the persisted data.

Now, for the really interesting aspect of this technology. If you were to shut down your browser and rerun your website, you would find that your previously entered profile data has indeed been persisted, as the Label displays the correct information. This begs the following obvious question: how were you remembered?

For this example, the profile API made use of your Windows network identity, which was obtained by your current login credentials. However, when you are building public websites (where the users are not part of a given domain), rest assured that the profile API integrates with the Forms-based authentication model of ASP.NET and also supports the notion of "anonymous profiles," which allow you to persist profile data for users who do not currently have an active identity on your site.

Note This text does not cover the details of ASP.NET security, so consult the .NET Framework 3.5 SDK documentation for further details.

Grouping Profile Data and Persisting Custom Objects

To wrap up this chapter, allow me to make a few additional comments on how profile data may be defined within a `web.config` file. The current profile simply defined four pieces of data that were exposed directly from the profile type. When you build more complex profiles, it can be helpful to group related pieces of data under a unique name. Consider the following update:

```
<profile>
  <properties>
    <group name ="Address">
      <add name="StreetAddress" type="String" />
      <add name="City" type="String" />
      <add name="State" type="String" />
    </group>
  </properties>
</profile>
```

This time we have defined a custom group named `Address` to expose the street address, city, and state of our user. To access this data in our pages would now require us to update our code base by specifying `Profile.Address` to get each subitem. For example, here is the updated `GetUserAddress()` method (the `Click` event handler for the `Button` type would need to be updated in a similar manner):

```
Private Sub GetUserAddress()
  ' Database reads happening here!
  lblUserData.Text = String.Format("You live here: {0}, {1}, {2}", _
    Profile.Address.StreetAddress, Profile.Address.City, Profile.Address.State)
End Sub
```

■ Note A profile can contain as many groups as you feel are necessary. Simply define multiple `<group>` elements within your `<properties>` scope.

Finally, it is worth pointing out that a profile may also persist (and obtain) custom objects to and from `ASPNETDB.mdf`. To illustrate, assume that you wanted to build a custom class (or structure) that will represent the user's address data. The only requirement expected by the profile API is that the type be marked with the `<Serializable()>` attribute. For example:

```
<Serializable()> _
Public Class UserAddress
  Public street As String
  Public city As String
  Public state As String
End Class
```

With this class in place, our profile definition can now be updated as follows (notice I removed the custom group, although this is not mandatory):

```
<profile>
  <properties>
    <add name="AddressInfo" type="UserAddress"  serializeAs ="Binary"/>
  </properties>
</profile>
```

Notice that when you are adding `<Serializable()>` types to a profile, the `type` attribute is the fully qualified name of the type being persisted. Thus, if you were adding an `ArrayList` to a profile, `type` would be set to `System.Collections.ArrayList`. As well, you can control how this state data should be persisted into `ASPNETDB.mdf` using the `serializeAs` attribute. As you will see from the Visual Studio IntelliSense, your core choices are binary, XML, or string data.

Now that we are capturing street address information as a custom class type, we would (once again) need to update our code base. For example:

```
Private Sub GetUserAddress()
  ' Database reads happening here!
  lblUserData.Text = String.Format("You live here: {0}, {1}, {2}", _
    Profile.AddressInfo.street, Profile.AddressInfo.city, _
    Profile.AddressInfo.state)
End Sub
```

To wrap things up for this chapter, it is worth pointing out that there is much more to the profile API than I have had space to cover here. For example, the `Profile` property actually encapsulates a type named `ProfileCommon`. Using this type, you are able to programmatically obtain all information for a given user, delete (or add) profiles to `ASPNETDB.mdf`, update aspects of a profile, and so forth.

As well, the profile API has numerous points of extensibility that can allow you to optimize how the profile manager accesses the tables of the `ASPNETDB.mdf` database. As you would expect, there are numerous ways to decrease the number of "hits" this database takes. I'll assume interested readers will consult the .NET Framework 3.5 SDK documentation for further details.

Summary

In this chapter, you rounded out your knowledge of ASP.NET by examining how to leverage the `HttpApplication` type. As you have seen, this type provides a number of default event handlers that allow you to intercept various application- and session-level events. The bulk of this chapter was spent examining a number of state management techniques. Recall that view state is used to automatically repopulate the values of HTML widgets between postbacks to a specific page. Next, you checked out the distinction of application- and session-level data, cookie management, and the ASP.NET application cache.

The remainder of this chapter exposed you to the ASP.NET profile API. As you have seen, this technology provides an out-of-the-box solution to the issue of persisting user data across sessions. Using your website's `web.config` file, you are able to define any number of profile items (including groups of items and `<Serializable()>` types) that will automatically be persisted into `ASPNETDB.mdf`.

Index

B

G

I

J

N

O

P

Q

S

T

W